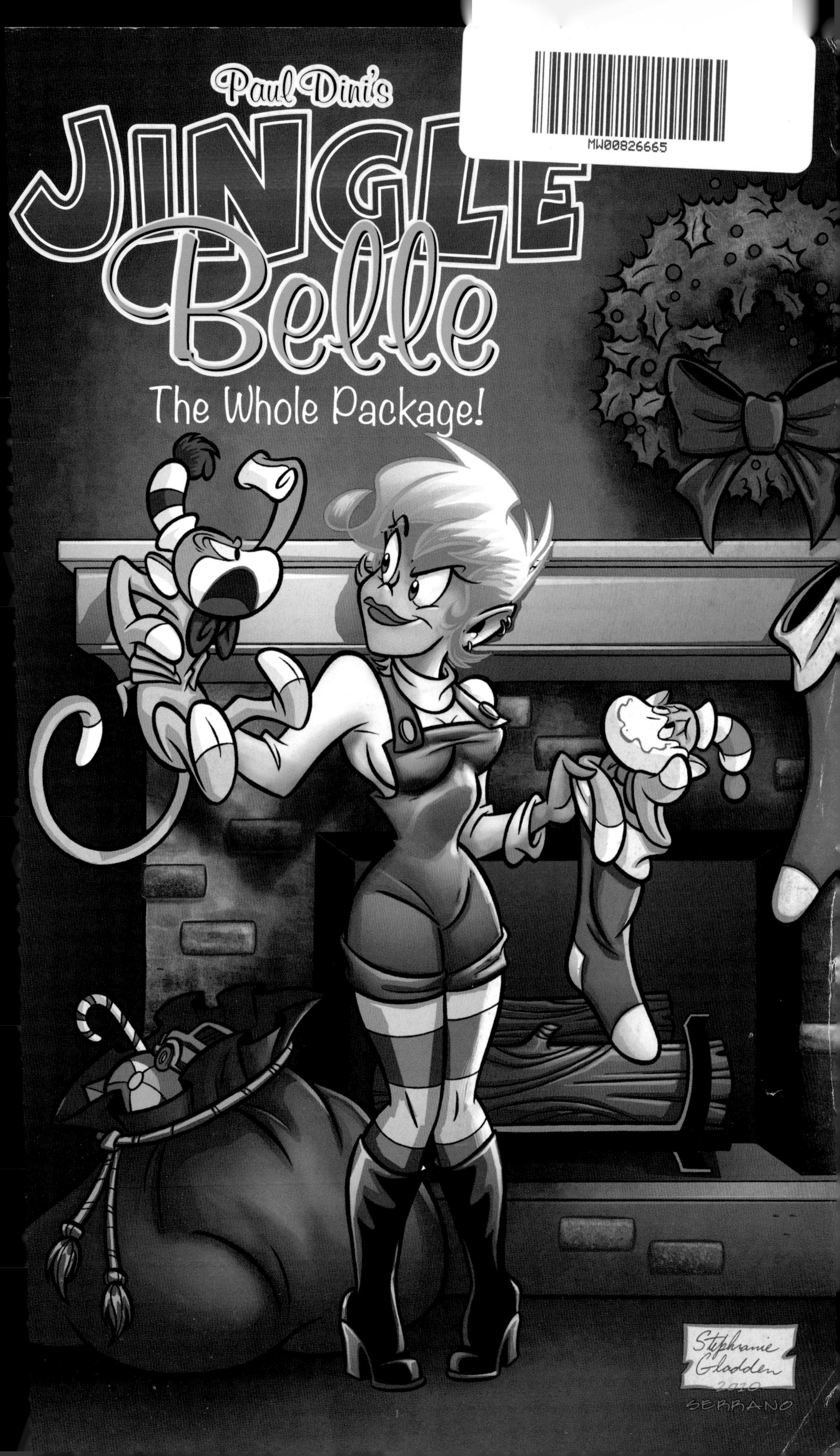
Paul Dini's
JINGLE
Belle
The Whole Package!
Stephanie Gladden 2010
SERRANO

Become our fan on Facebook facebook.com/idwpublishing
Follow us on Twitter @idwpublishing
Subscribe to us on YouTube youtube.com/idwpublishing
See what's new on Tumblr tumblr.idwpublishing.com
Check us out on Instagram instagram.com/idwpublsing

ISBN: 978-1-63140-703-1   19 18 17 16 1 2 3 4

Originally published by Oni Press as "Sanity Clauses" from
DINI DOUBLE FEATURE #13, JINGLE BELLE issues #1–2,
"Belle of the Brawl" in ONI PRESS SUMMER VACATION
SUPERCOLOR FUN SPECIAL, JINGLE BELLE'S ALL-STAR
HOLIDAY HULLABALOO, THE MIGHTY ELVES, JUBILEE,
WINTER WINGDING, by Dark Horse Comics as JINGLE BELLE
issues #1–4, THE BAKERS MEET JINGLE BELLE, THE FIGHT
BEFORE CHRISTMAS, and by Top Cow as SANTA CLAUS VS
FRANKENSTEIN, and GROUNDED.

Ted Adams, CEO & Publisher
Greg Goldstein, President & COO
Robbie Robbins, EVP/Sr. Graphic Artist
Chris Ryall, Chief Creative Officer/Editor-in-Chief
Laurie Windrow, Senior Vice President of Sales & Marketing
Matthew Ruzicka, CPA, Chief Financial Officer
Dirk Wood, VP of Marketing
Lorelei Bunjes, VP of Digital Services
Jeff Webber, VP of Licensing, Digital and Subsidiary Rights
Jerry Bennington, VP of New Product Development

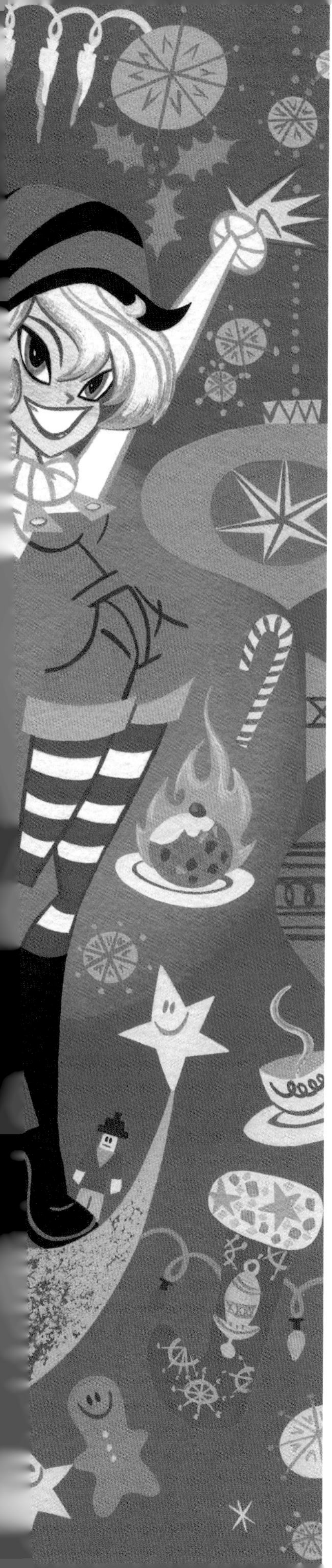

Jingle Belle

created by *Paul Dini*

Cover Art by

Stephanie Buscema

Collection Edits by

Justin Eisinger and

Alonzo Simon

Collection Design by

Ron Estevez

Publisher

Ted Adams

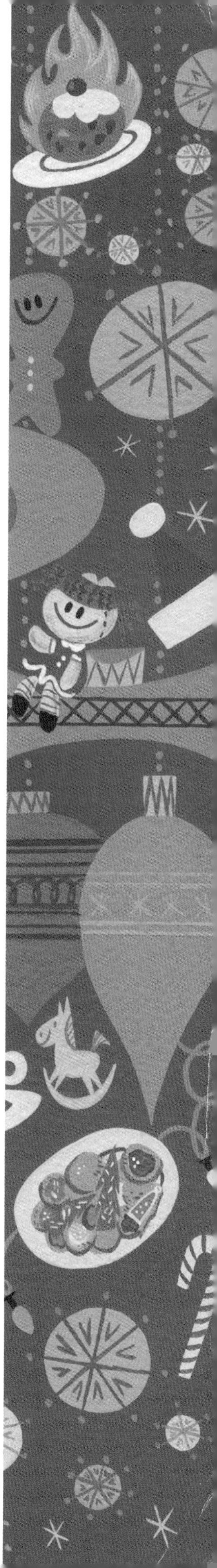

Written by **Paul Dini**

Sanity Clauses
Art and Letters by Stephen DeStefano

Miserable on 34th Street
Art by Stephen DeStefano
Inking Assist by David Mazzucchelli
Letters by Sean Konot

Santa's Little Hellion
Art by Stephen DeStefano
Letters by Sean Konot

Jingle Belle Conquers the Martians
Painted by Lawrence Marvit

Belle of the Brawl
Art by Stephen DeStefano
Colors by Laura Allred
Letters by Sean Konot

Little Matchstick Girl
Art and Letters by Barry Caldwell
Colors by Laura Allred

A Carol's Christmas
Story by Bill Morrison and Paul Dini
Pencils by Bill Morrison
Inks by Mike DeCarlo
Letters by John Dranski

Visions of Sugar Plums
Script by Paul Dini & Shane Glines
Layouts by Stephen DeStefano
Finishes by Shane Glines
Letters by James Lucas Jones

That Olde Christmas Spirit
Art and Letters by J. Bone

Blue Belles
Story, Art, and Letters by Chynna Clugston-Major

Coal Comfort
Art by Jeff Smith
Tones by Steve Hamaker

Belle's Belles
Story by Sergio Aragones & Mark Evenier
Art by Sergio Aragones
Letters by Stan Sakai

The Mighty Elves
Art and Letters by J. Bone

Jubilee
Art by Steve Rolston, Dan DeCarlo, Bill Morrison, and J. Bone

Treats
By Jill Thompson

Winter Wingding
Art by Spike Brandt & Tony Cervone
Letters by John Dranski

Santa: Rusty: Jing
Written by Robbie Busch & Stephen DeStefano
Art and Letters by Stephen DeStefano

Nibble, Nibble
Art by Stephanie Gladden
Colors by Lucas Marangon
Letters by Chris Eliopoulos

A Very Special Jingle Belle Special
Art by Jose Garibaldi
Letters by Chris Eliopoulos

Belle's Beaus
Art by Jose Garibaldi
Letters by Chris Eliopoulos

Kiyotes' Christmas Party
Art by J. Bone
Letters by Chris Eliopoulos

Ring-a-Ding Jing
Art by Jose Garibaldi
Letters by Chris Eliopoulos

Jingle Belle Meets The Bakers
Art by Kyle Baker

The Fight Before Christmas
Art by Stephanie Gladden
Colors by Dan Jackson
Letters by Michael David Thomas

Hot Rod Lemming
Art by Jose Garibaldi
Letters by Michael David Thomas

Oh, Christmas Tree
Art and Letters by J. Bone

Santa Claus vs. Frankenstein
Art by Stephanie Gladden
Colors by Felix Serrano
Letters by Troy Peteri

Grounded
Art by Stephanie Gladden
Colors by Felix Serrano
Letters by Troy Peteri

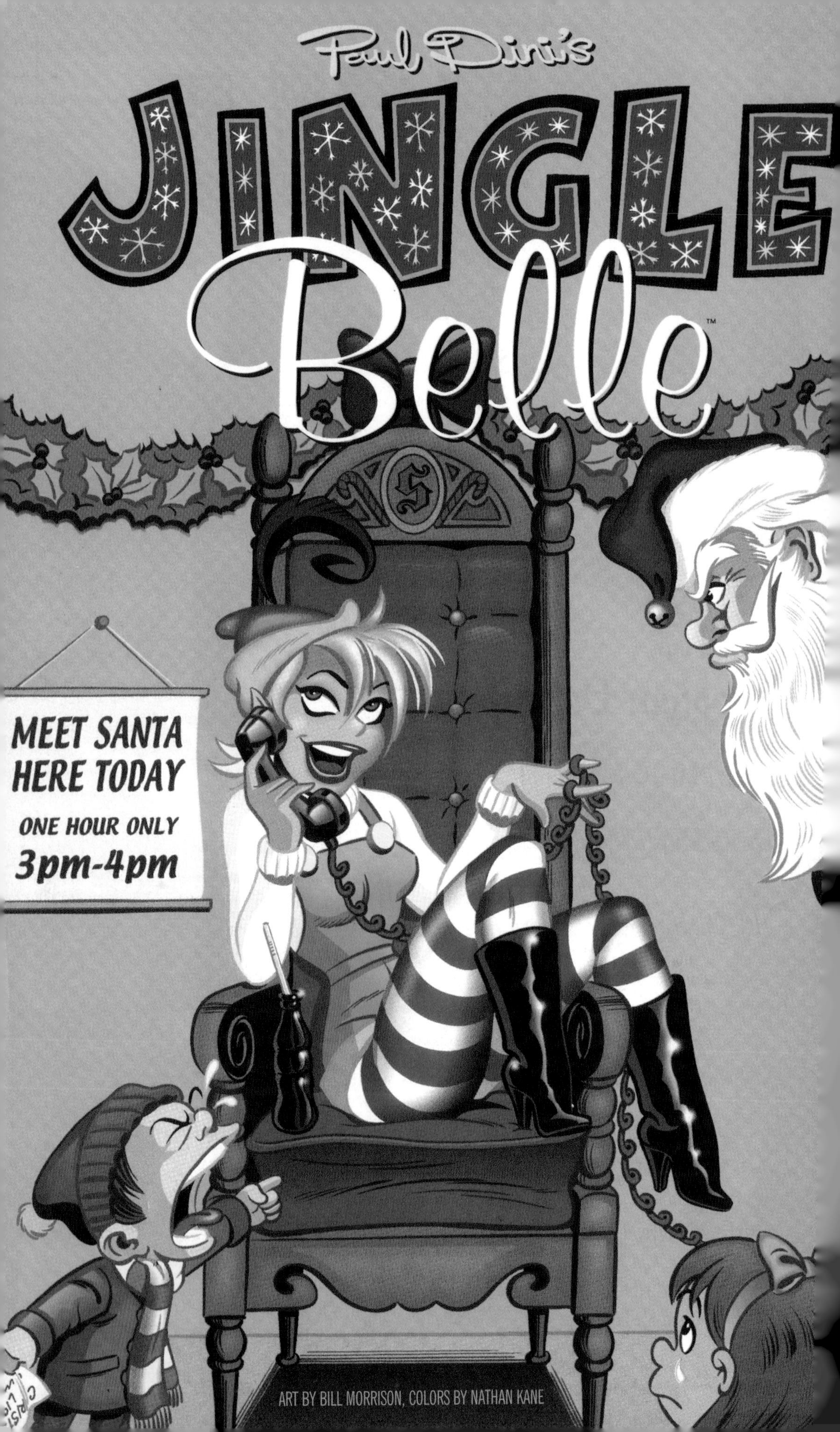
Paul Dini's
JINGLE
Belle™
MEET SANTA
HERE TODAY
ONE HOUR ONLY
3pm-4pm
ART BY BILL MORRISON, COLORS BY NATHAN KANE

Sanity Clauses

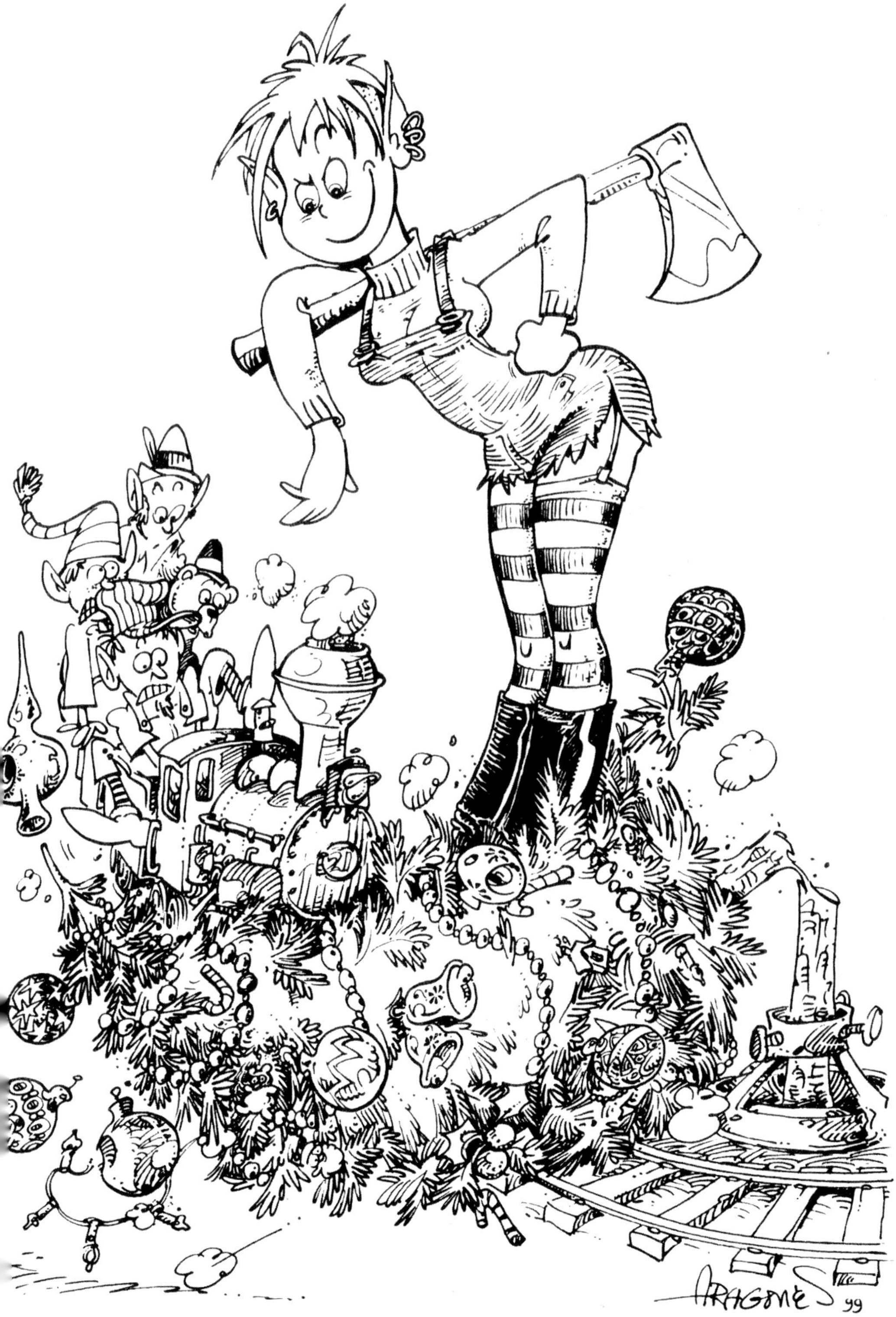

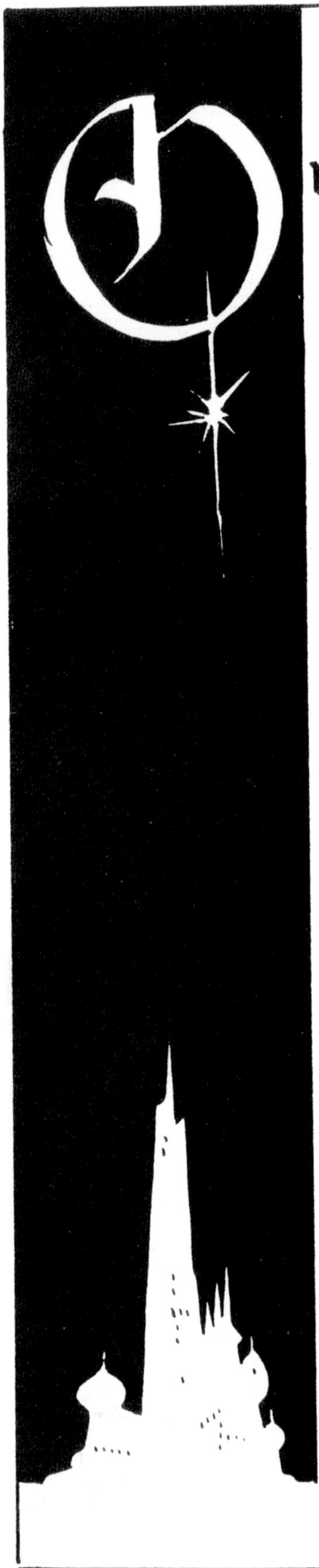

Once long ago...

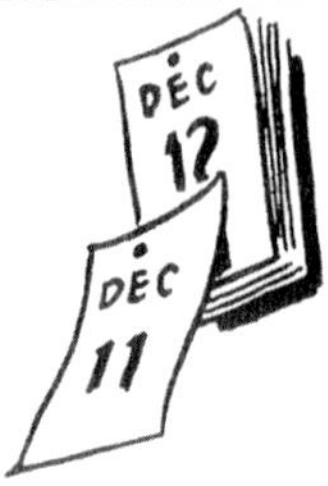
DEC
12
DEC
11

at the cold north pole,
a birth took place, or so it was told.

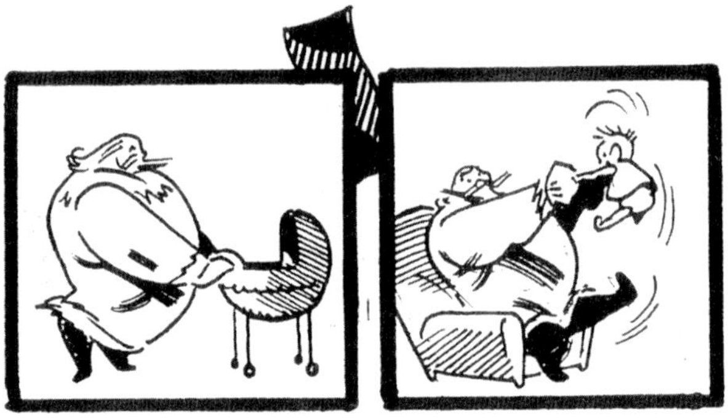

Santa, that friend to kids 'round the world, and his wife were blessed with a sweet baby girl.

. . . .

Her laughter was a silvery, twinkling knell, so the Kringles named their daughter Jingle Belle.

Baby Jing was the joy of her loving Mom & Pop. She fed the reindeer...

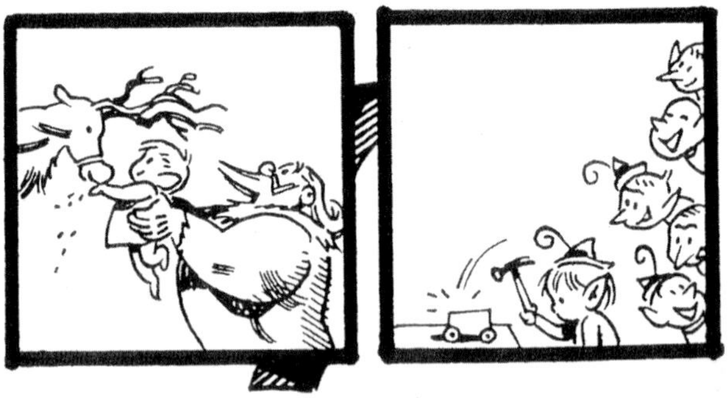

And helped make toys in the shop.

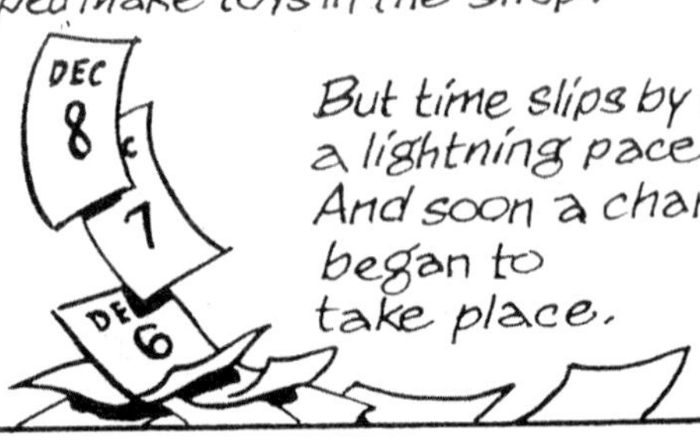
DEC
8
7
DE
6

But time slips by at a lightning pace. And soon a change began to take place.

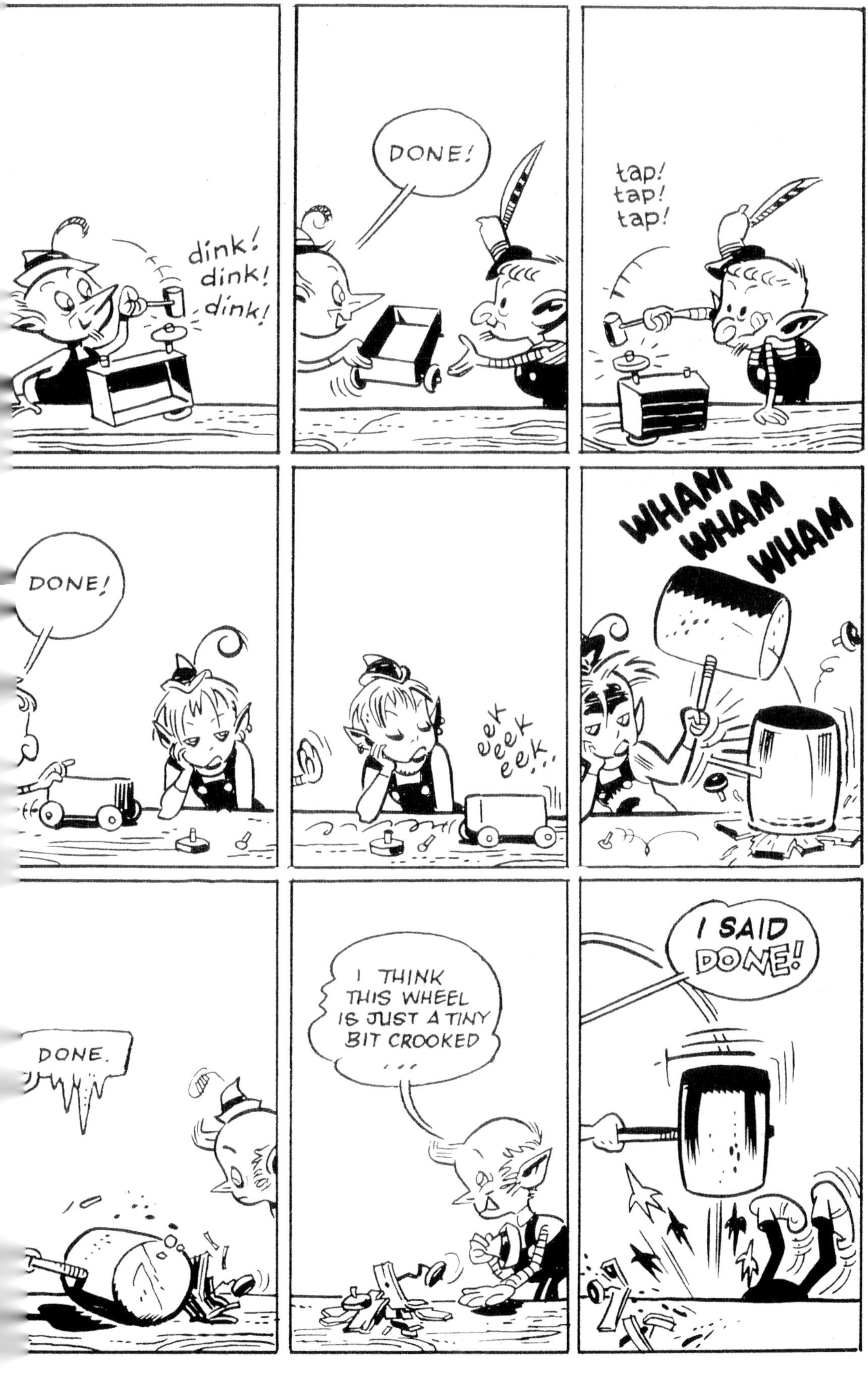
dink! dink! dink!
DONE!
tap! tap! tap!
DONE!
eek eek eek
WHAM WHAM WHAM
DONE.
I THINK THIS WHEEL IS JUST A TINY BIT CROOKED ...
I SAID DONE!

Santa's baby girl is now a teen brat, from her big black boots to her little elf hat.

No longer content to sit making toys, she'd rather be cruising for Eskimo boys.

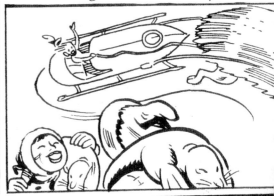

COFF!

PWING?

HONEST! THE IGLOO JUMPED OUT RIGHT IN FRONT OF ME!

Naturally, as one might start to guess, Jing's antics cause her folks no end of stress. Which is the reason now, you see ...

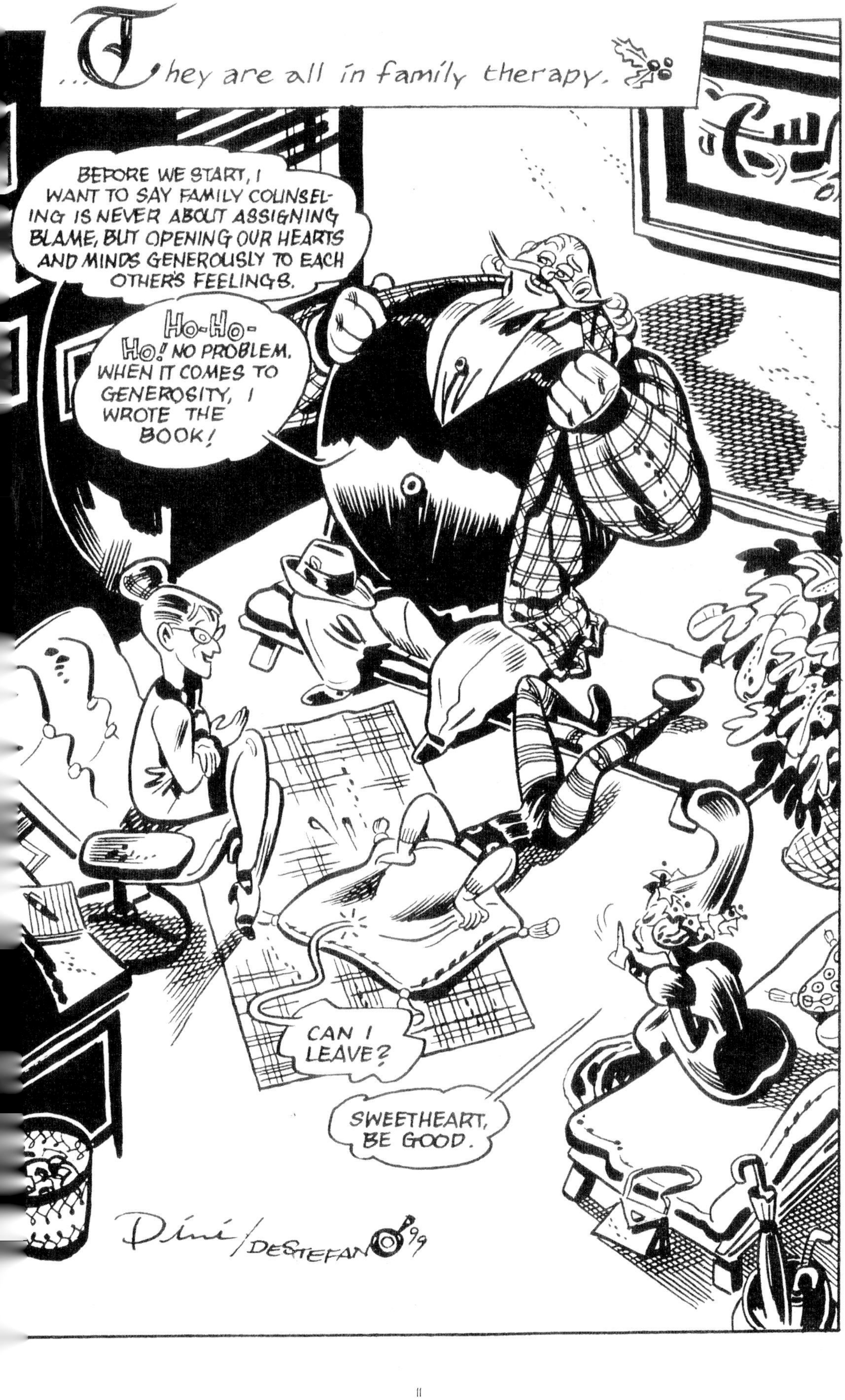
...They are all in family therapy.
BEFORE WE START, I WANT TO SAY FAMILY COUNSELING IS NEVER ABOUT ASSIGNING BLAME, BUT OPENING OUR HEARTS AND MINDS GENEROUSLY TO EACH OTHER'S FEELINGS.
HO-HO-HO! NO PROBLEM. WHEN IT COMES TO GENEROSITY, I WROTE THE BOOK!
CAN I LEAVE?
SWEETHEART, BE GOOD.
Dini / DeStefano '99

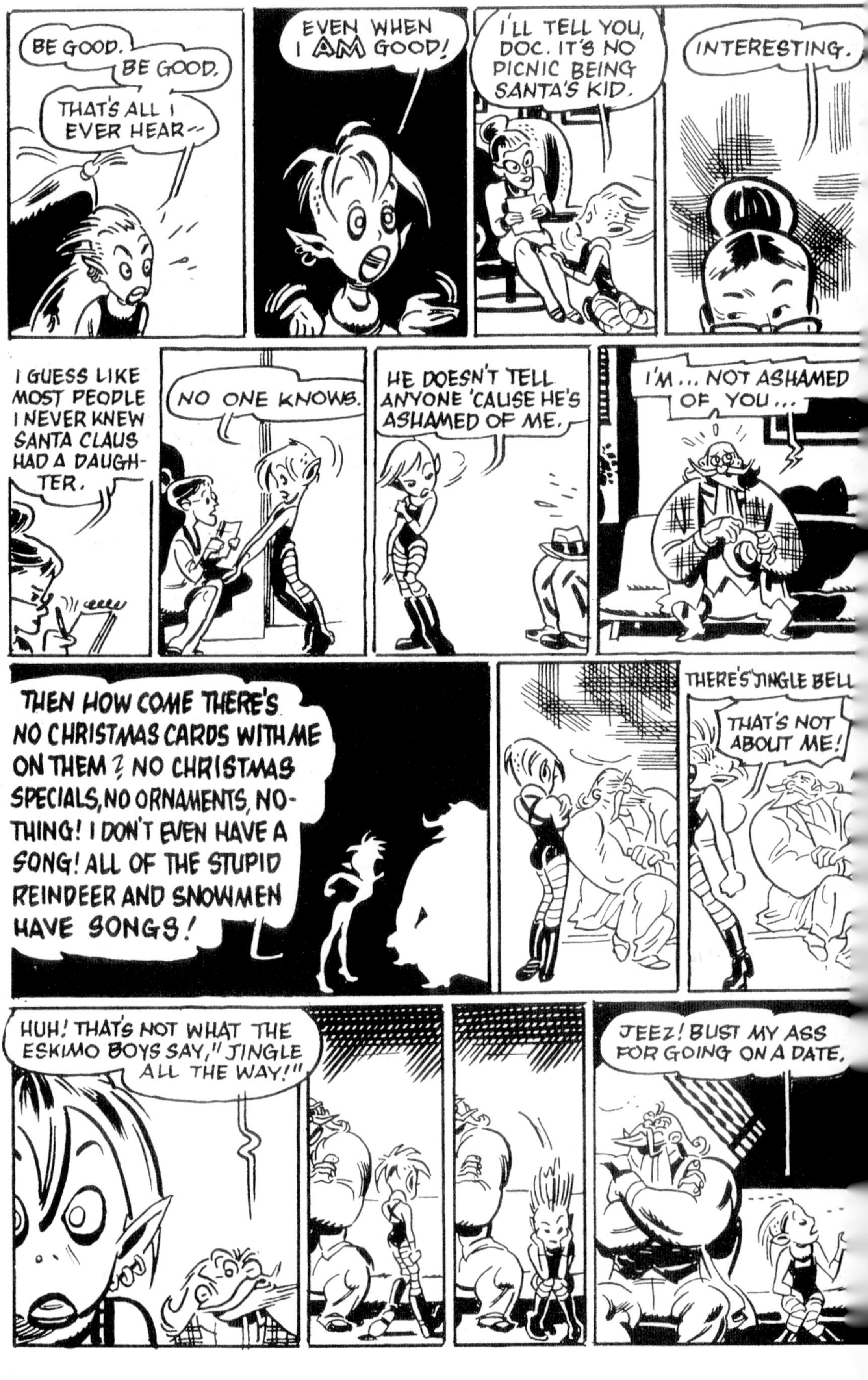
BE GOOD.
BE GOOD.
THAT'S ALL I EVER HEAR--
EVEN WHEN I AM GOOD!
I'LL TELL YOU, DOC. IT'S NO PICNIC BEING SANTA'S KID.
INTERESTING.
I GUESS LIKE MOST PEOPLE I NEVER KNEW SANTA CLAUS HAD A DAUGHTER.
NO ONE KNOWS.
HE DOESN'T TELL ANYONE 'CAUSE HE'S ASHAMED OF ME.
I'M... NOT ASHAMED OF YOU...
THEN HOW COME THERE'S NO CHRISTMAS CARDS WITH ME ON THEM? NO CHRISTMAS SPECIALS, NO ORNAMENTS, NOTHING! I DON'T EVEN HAVE A SONG! ALL OF THE STUPID REINDEER AND SNOWMEN HAVE SONGS!
THERE'S JINGLE BELL
THAT'S NOT ABOUT ME!
HUH! THAT'S NOT WHAT THE ESKIMO BOYS SAY," JINGLE ALL THE WAY!"
JEEZ! BUST MY ASS FOR GOING ON A DATE.

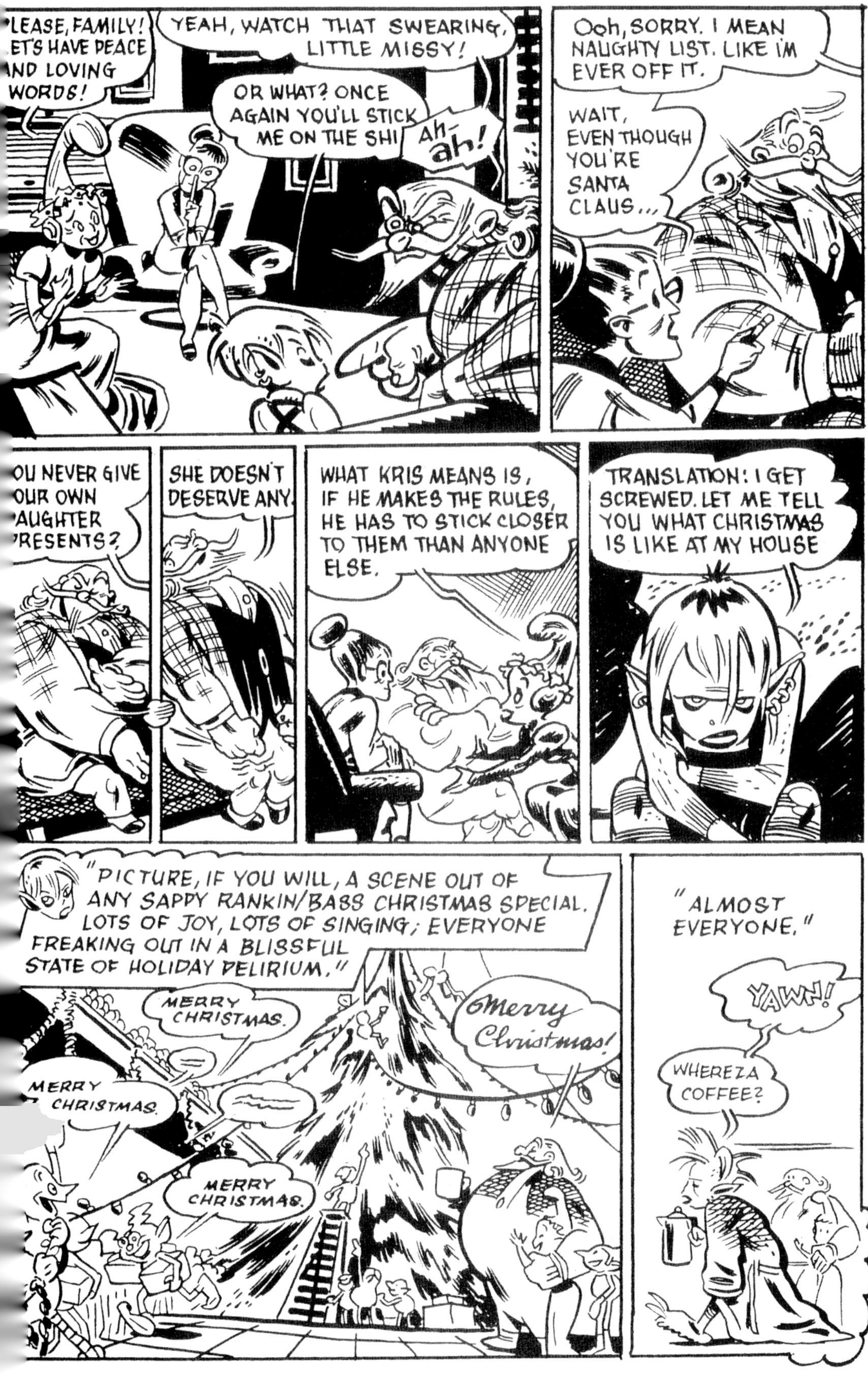
LEASE, FAMILY! ET'S HAVE PEACE ND LOVING WORDS!
YEAH, WATCH THAT SWEARING, LITTLE MISSY!
OR WHAT? ONCE AGAIN YOU'LL STICK ME ON THE SHI
Ah-ah!
Ooh, SORRY. I MEAN NAUGHTY LIST. LIKE I'M EVER OFF IT.
WAIT, EVEN THOUGH YOU'RE SANTA CLAUS...
OU NEVER GIVE OUR OWN AUGHTER RESENTS?
SHE DOESN'T DESERVE ANY.
WHAT KRIS MEANS IS, IF HE MAKES THE RULES, HE HAS TO STICK CLOSER TO THEM THAN ANYONE ELSE.
TRANSLATION: I GET SCREWED. LET ME TELL YOU WHAT CHRISTMAS IS LIKE AT MY HOUSE
"PICTURE, IF YOU WILL, A SCENE OUT OF ANY SAPPY RANKIN/BASS CHRISTMAS SPECIAL. LOTS OF JOY, LOTS OF SINGING; EVERYONE FREAKING OUT IN A BLISSFUL STATE OF HOLIDAY DELIRIUM."
MERRY CHRISTMAS.
Merry Christmas!
MERRY CHRISTMAS.
MERRY CHRISTMAS.
"ALMOST EVERYONE."
YAWN!
WHEREZA COFFEE?

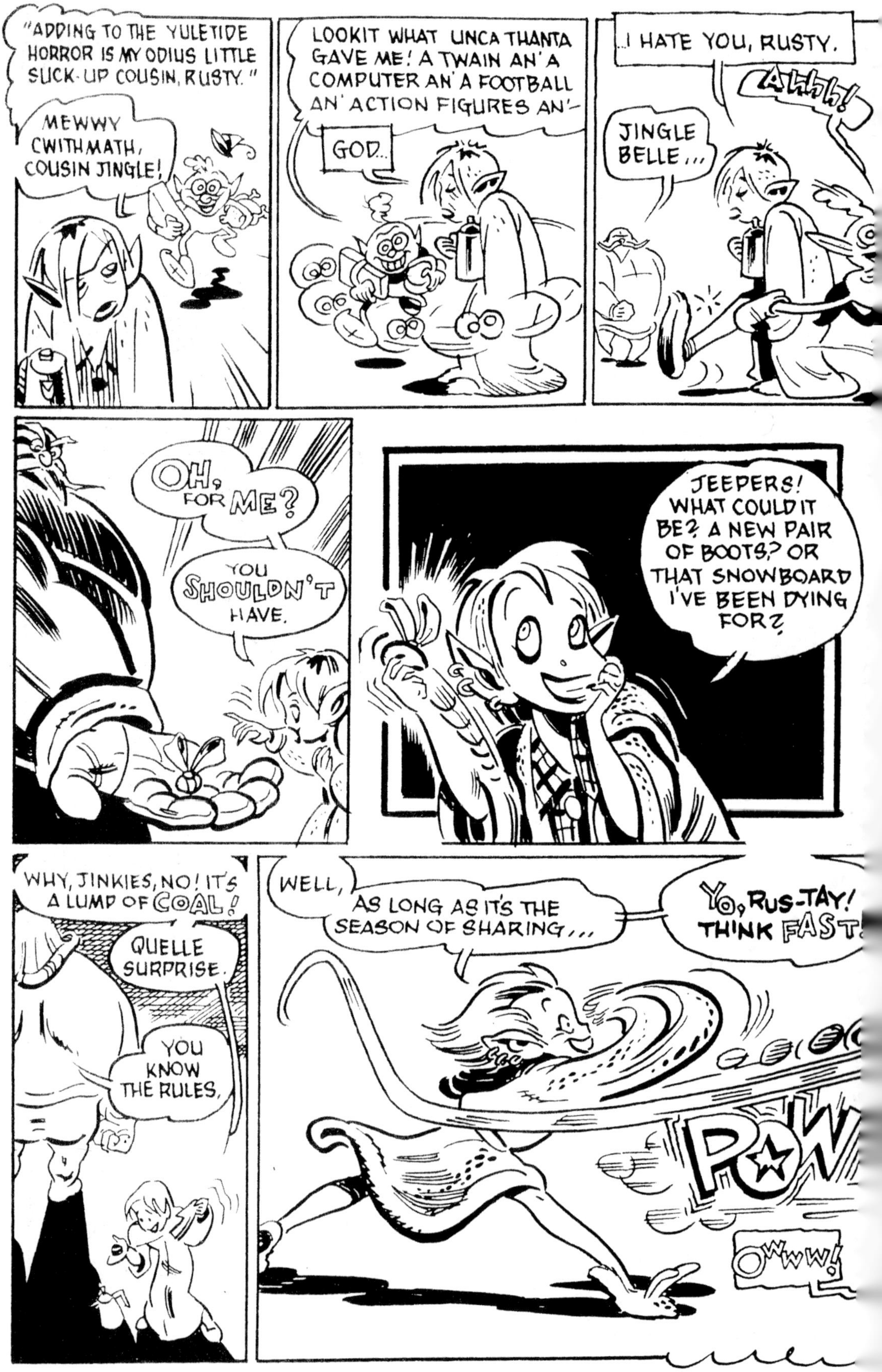
"ADDING TO THE YULETIDE HORROR IS MY ODIUS LITTLE SUCK-UP COUSIN, RUSTY."
MEWWY CWITHMATH, COUSIN JINGLE!
LOOKIT WHAT UNCA THANTA GAVE ME! A TWAIN AN' A COMPUTER AN' A FOOTBALL AN' ACTION FIGURES AN'-
GOD...
...I HATE YOU, RUSTY.
JINGLE BELLE...
Ahhh!
OH, FOR ME?
YOU SHOULDN'T HAVE.
JEEPERS! WHAT COULD IT BE? A NEW PAIR OF BOOTS? OR THAT SNOWBOARD I'VE BEEN DYING FOR?
WHY, JINKIES, NO! IT'S A LUMP OF COAL!
QUELLE SURPRISE.
YOU KNOW THE RULES.
WELL,
AS LONG AS IT'S THE SEASON OF SHARING...
YO, RUS-TAY! THINK FAST!
POW
OWWW!

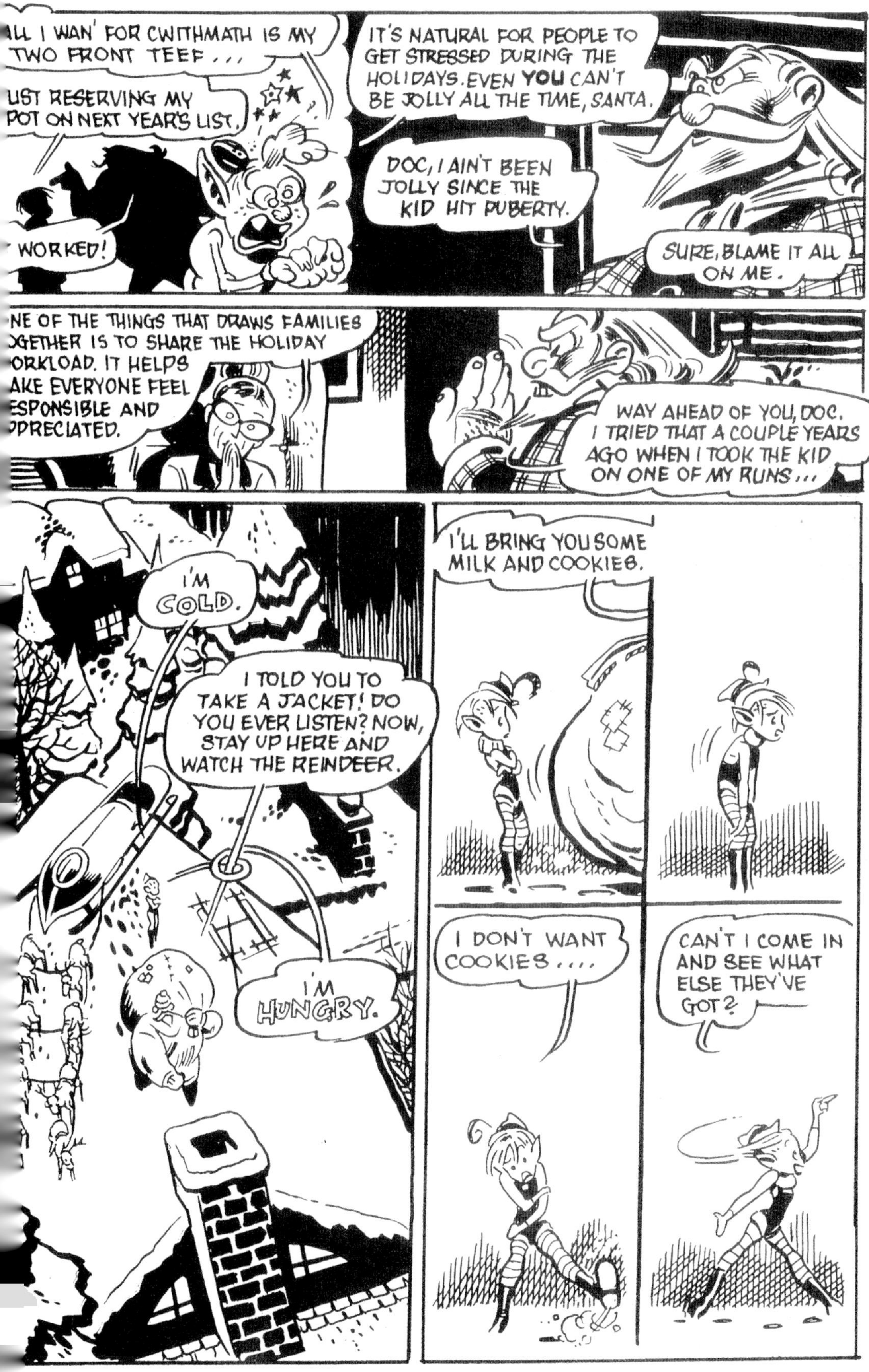

ALL I WAN' FOR CWITHMATH IS MY TWO FRONT TEEF...
UST RESERVING MY POT ON NEXT YEAR'S LIST.
WORKED!
IT'S NATURAL FOR PEOPLE TO GET STRESSED DURING THE HOLIDAYS. EVEN YOU CAN'T BE JOLLY ALL THE TIME, SANTA.
DOC, I AIN'T BEEN JOLLY SINCE THE KID HIT PUBERTY.
SURE, BLAME IT ALL ON ME.
NE OF THE THINGS THAT DRAWS FAMILIES OGETHER IS TO SHARE THE HOLIDAY ORKLOAD. IT HELPS AKE EVERYONE FEEL ESPONSIBLE AND PPRECIATED.
WAY AHEAD OF YOU, DOC. I TRIED THAT A COUPLE YEARS AGO WHEN I TOOK THE KID ON ONE OF MY RUNS...
I'M COLD.
I TOLD YOU TO TAKE A JACKET! DO YOU EVER LISTEN? NOW, STAY UP HERE AND WATCH THE REINDEER.
I'M HUNGRY.
I'LL BRING YOU SOME MILK AND COOKIES.
I DON'T WANT COOKIES....
CAN'T I COME IN AND SEE WHAT ELSE THEY'VE GOT?

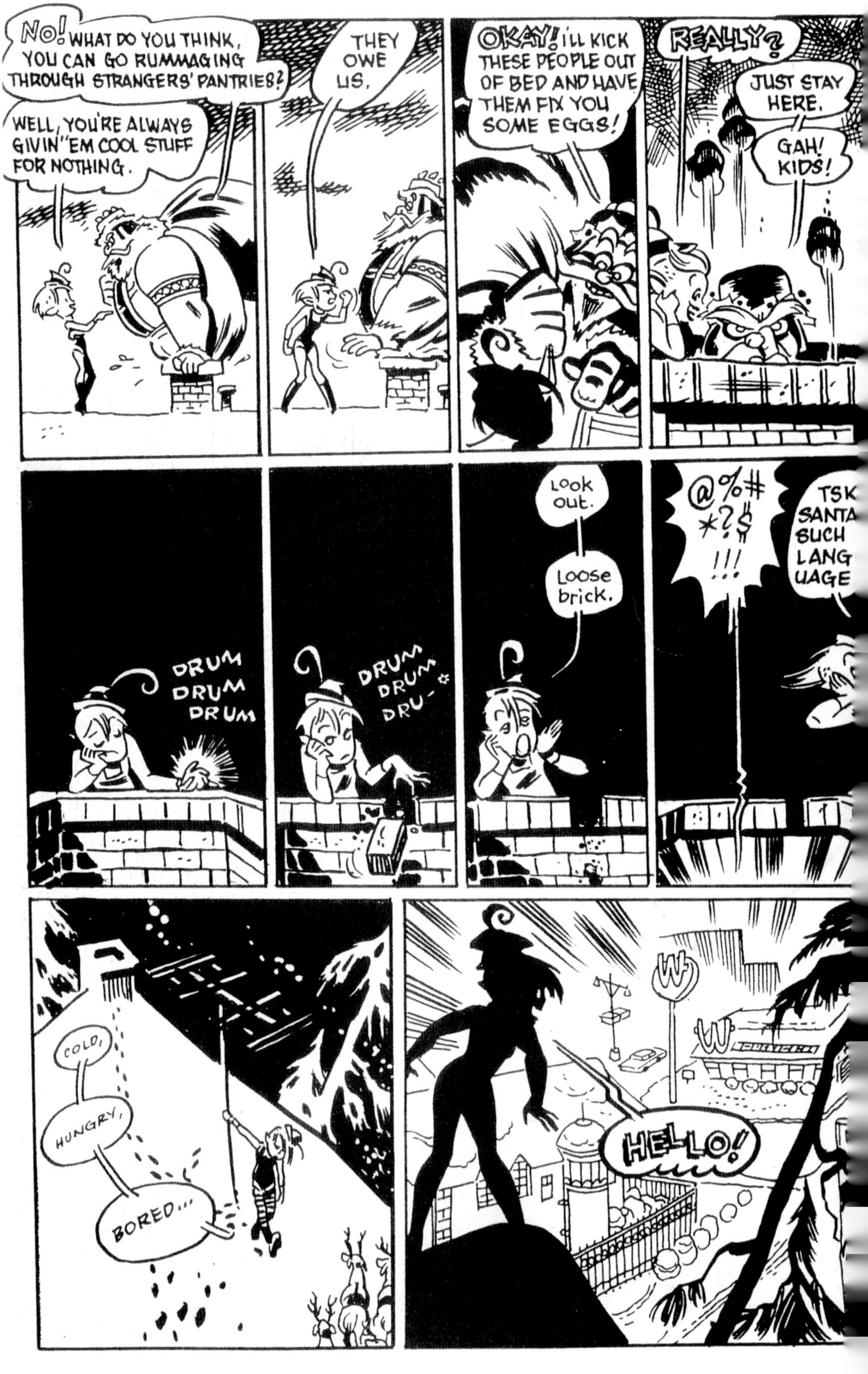
No! WHAT DO YOU THINK, YOU CAN GO RUMMAGING THROUGH STRANGERS' PANTRIES?
WELL, YOU'RE ALWAYS GIVIN' 'EM COOL STUFF FOR NOTHING.
THEY OWE US.
OKAY! I'LL KICK THESE PEOPLE OUT OF BED AND HAVE THEM FIX YOU SOME EGGS!
REALLY?
JUST STAY HERE.
GAH! KIDS!
DRUM DRUM DRUM
DRUM DRUM DRU-
Look out.
Loose brick.
@%# *?$!!!
TSK SANTA SUCH LANG UAGE
COLD,
HUNGRY,
BORED...
HELLO!

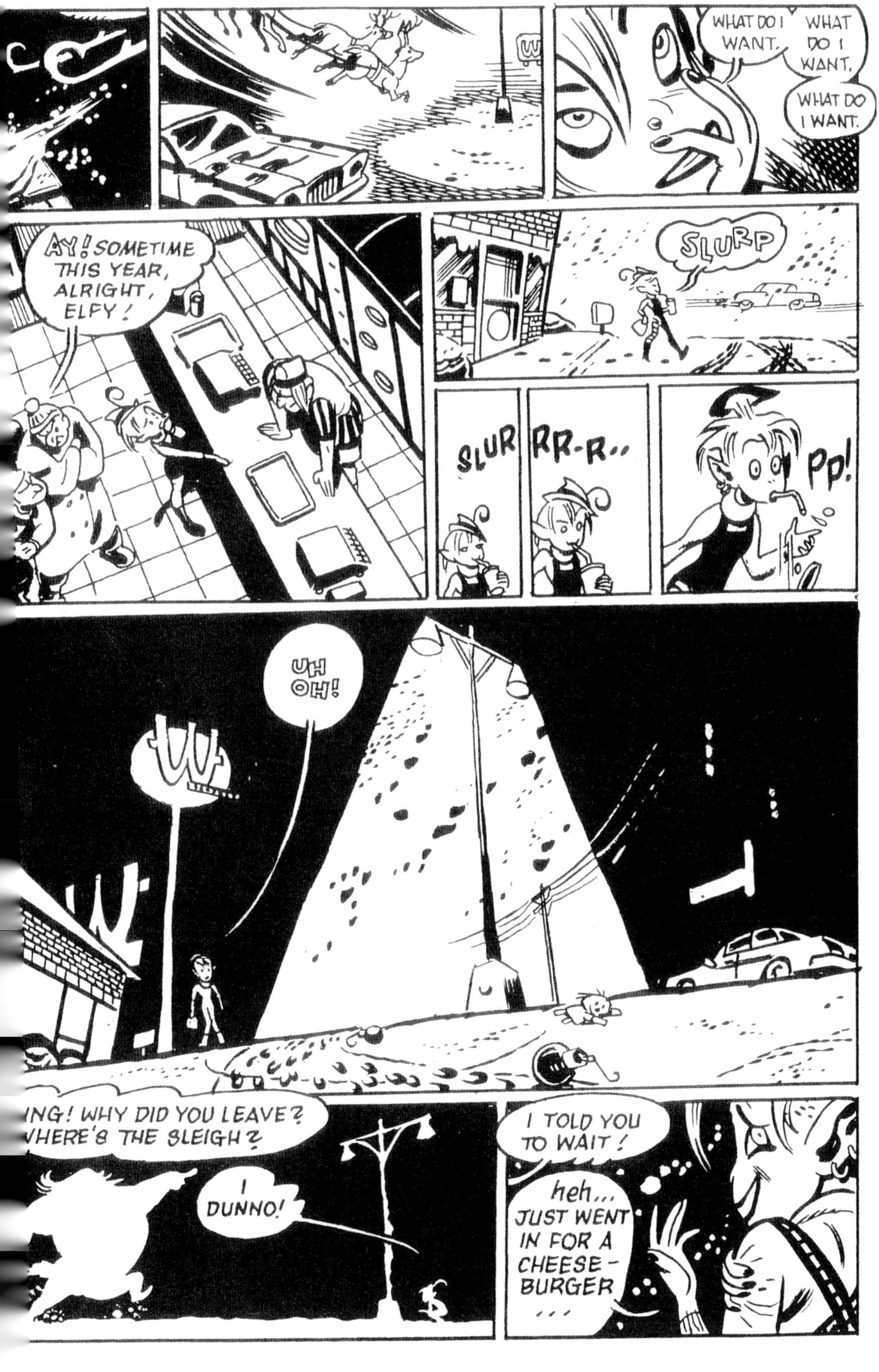
WHAT DO I WANT.
WHAT DO I WANT.
WHAT DO I WANT.
AY! SOMETIME THIS YEAR, ALRIGHT, ELFY!
SLURP
SLURRR-R..
PP!
UH OH!
ING! WHY DID YOU LEAVE? WHERE'S THE SLEIGH?
I DUNNO!
I TOLD YOU TO WAIT!
heh... JUST WENT IN FOR A CHEESE-BURGER ...

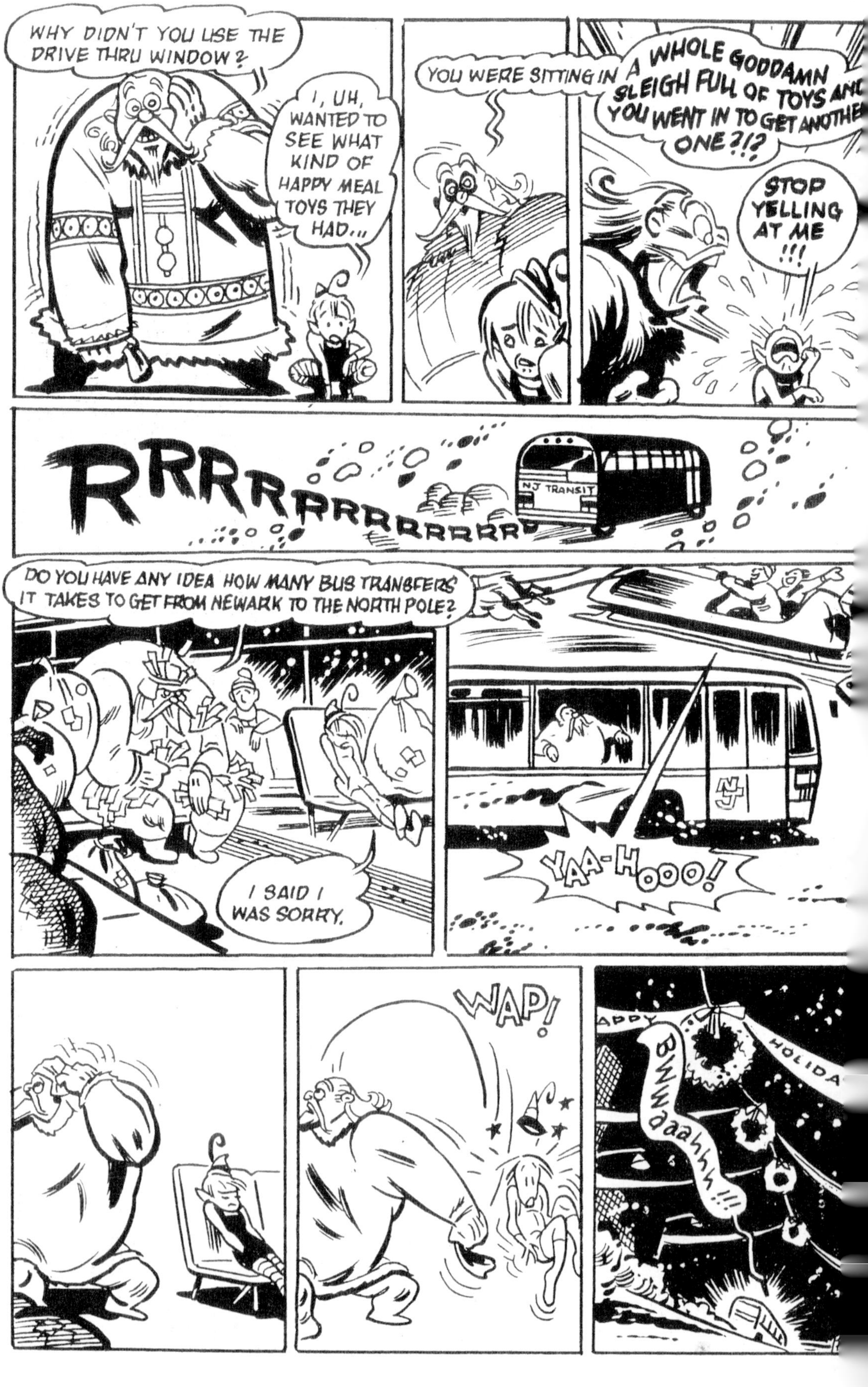
WHY DIDN'T YOU USE THE DRIVE THRU WINDOW?
I, UH, WANTED TO SEE WHAT KIND OF HAPPY MEAL TOYS THEY HAD...
YOU WERE SITTING IN A WHOLE GODDAMN SLEIGH FULL OF TOYS AND YOU WENT IN TO GET ANOTHER ONE?!?
STOP YELLING AT ME !!!
RRRRRRRRRRRRRR
NJ TRANSIT
DO YOU HAVE ANY IDEA HOW MANY BUS TRANSFERS IT TAKES TO GET FROM NEWARK TO THE NORTH POLE?
I SAID I WAS SORRY.
YAA-HOOOO!
WAP!
APPY
HOLIDA
BWWaaahhh!!

OKAY, THAT WAS MY BAD.

BUT, JEEZ, CAN YOU IMAGINE THE PRESSURE ON ME ALL THE TIME?

BEING SANTA'S KID, I GET NO SLACK AT ALL.

I MAY BE PART ELF, BUT I'M STILL HUMAN. I SCREW UP, I LOSE MY TEMPER, AND YOU KNOW WHAT?

THAT MAKES ME JUST LIKE ANY OTHER GIRL. SORRY, FOLKS, I'LL NEVER BE PERFECT, SO YOU'LL JUST HAVE TO SETTLE FOR NORMAL.

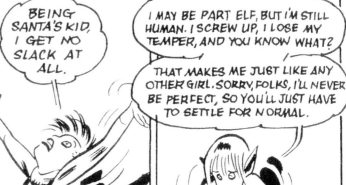

DAD, YOU ASK EVERY KID IN THE WORLD TO BELIEVE IN YOU...

....

WELL, CAN'T YOU BELIEVE IN ME, TOO?

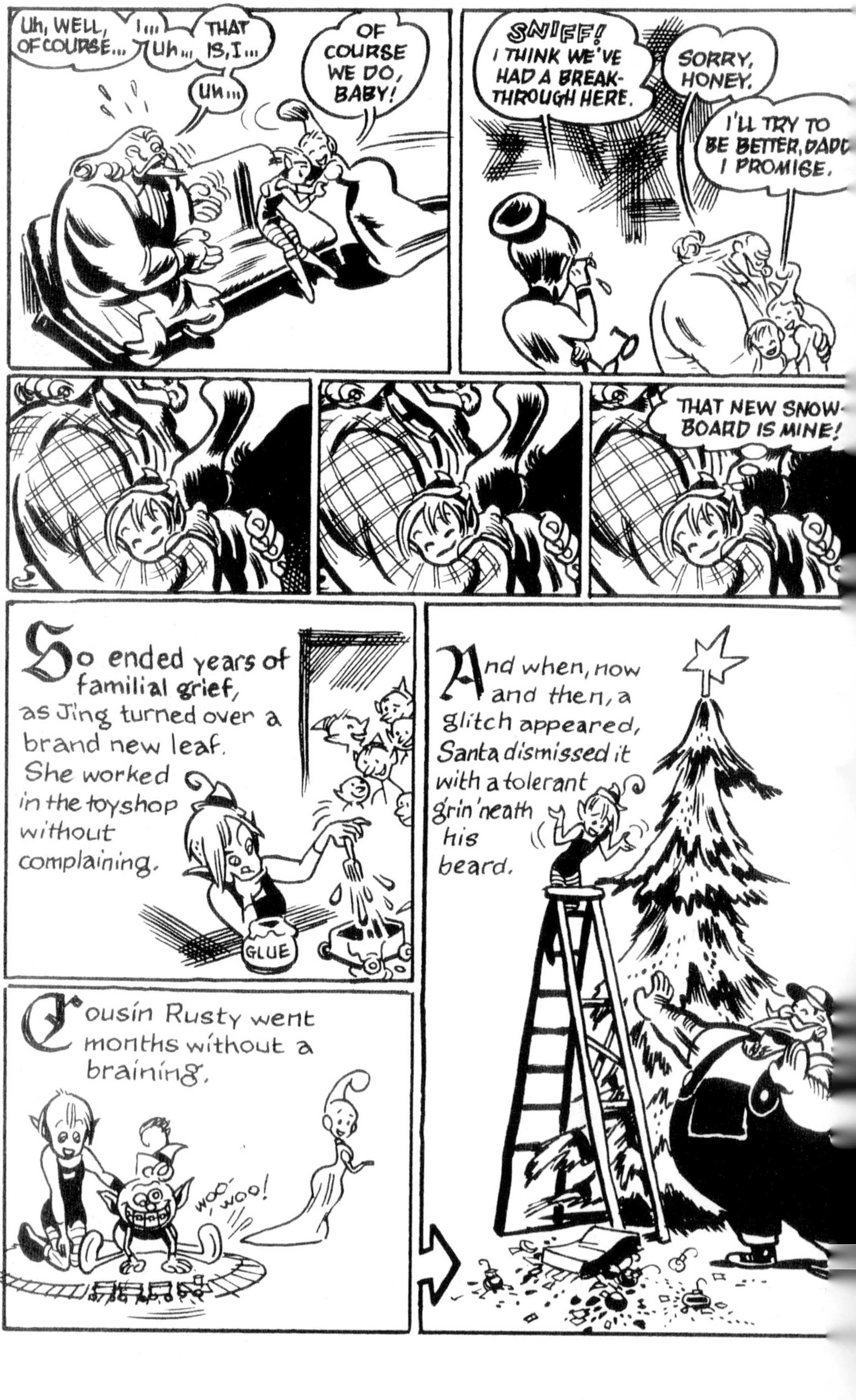

Uh, WELL, OF COURSE...
I...
Uh...
THAT IS, I...
Uh...
OF COURSE WE DO, BABY!
SNIFF! I THINK WE'VE HAD A BREAK-THROUGH HERE.
SORRY, HONEY.
I'LL TRY TO BE BETTER, DADD
I PROMISE.
THAT NEW SNOW-BOARD IS MINE!
So ended years of familial grief, as Jing turned over a brand new leaf. She worked in the toyshop without complaining.
GLUE
And when, now and then, a glitch appeared, Santa dismissed it with a tolerant grin 'neath his beard.
Cousin Rusty went months without a braining.
WOO, WOO!

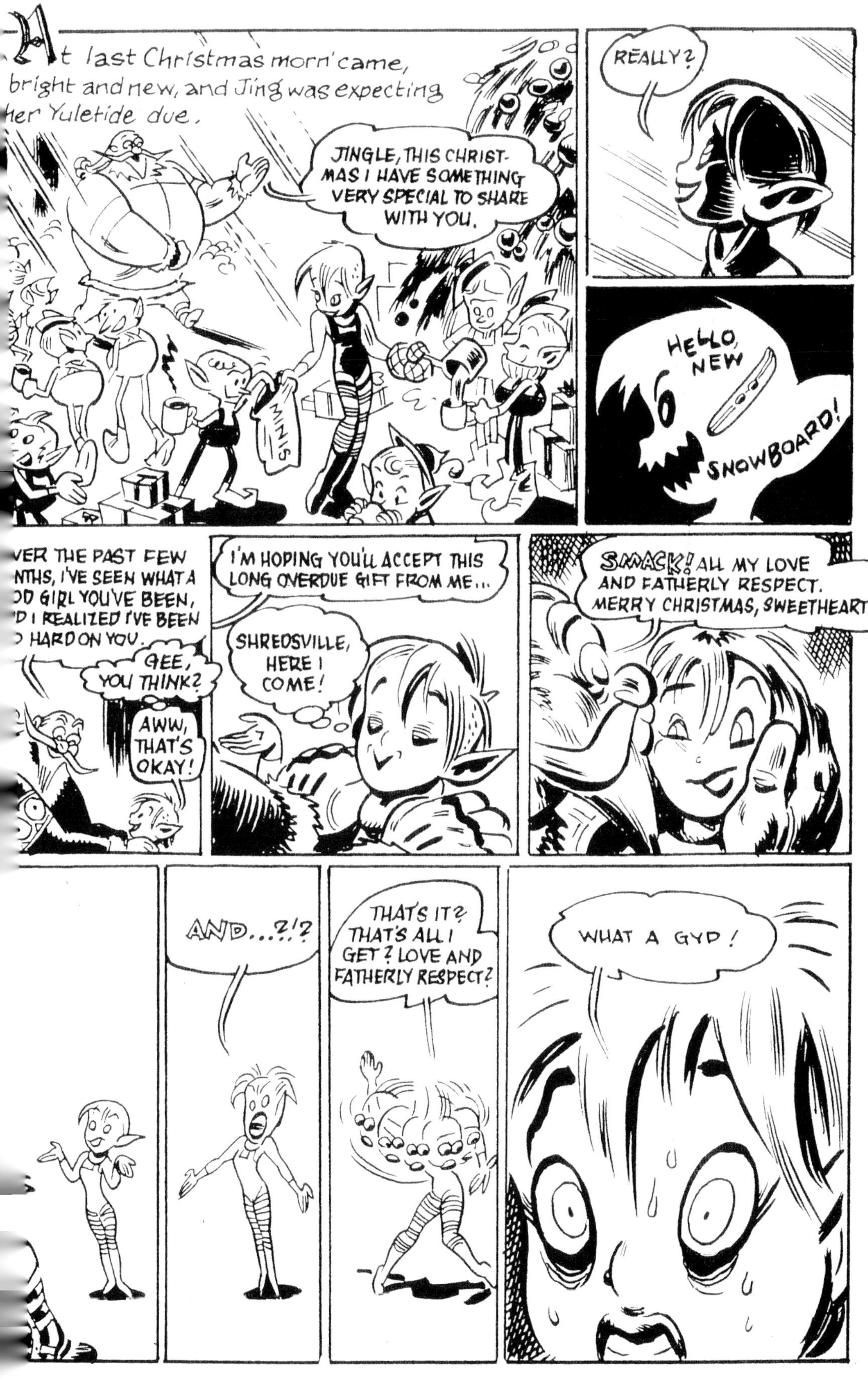
At last Christmas morn came, bright and new, and Jing was expecting her Yuletide due.
JINGLE, THIS CHRISTMAS I HAVE SOMETHING VERY SPECIAL TO SHARE WITH YOU.
MINIS
REALLY?
HELLO, NEW SNOWBOARD!
VER THE PAST FEW NTHS, I'VE SEEN WHAT A OD GIRL YOU'VE BEEN, D I REALIZED I'VE BEEN O HARD ON YOU.
GEE, YOU THINK?
AWW, THAT'S OKAY!
I'M HOPING YOU'LL ACCEPT THIS LONG OVERDUE GIFT FROM ME...
SHREDSVILLE, HERE I COME!
SMACK! ALL MY LOVE AND FATHERLY RESPECT. MERRY CHRISTMAS, SWEETHEART.
AND...?!?
THAT'S IT? THAT'S ALL I GET? LOVE AND FATHERLY RESPECT?
WHAT A GYP!

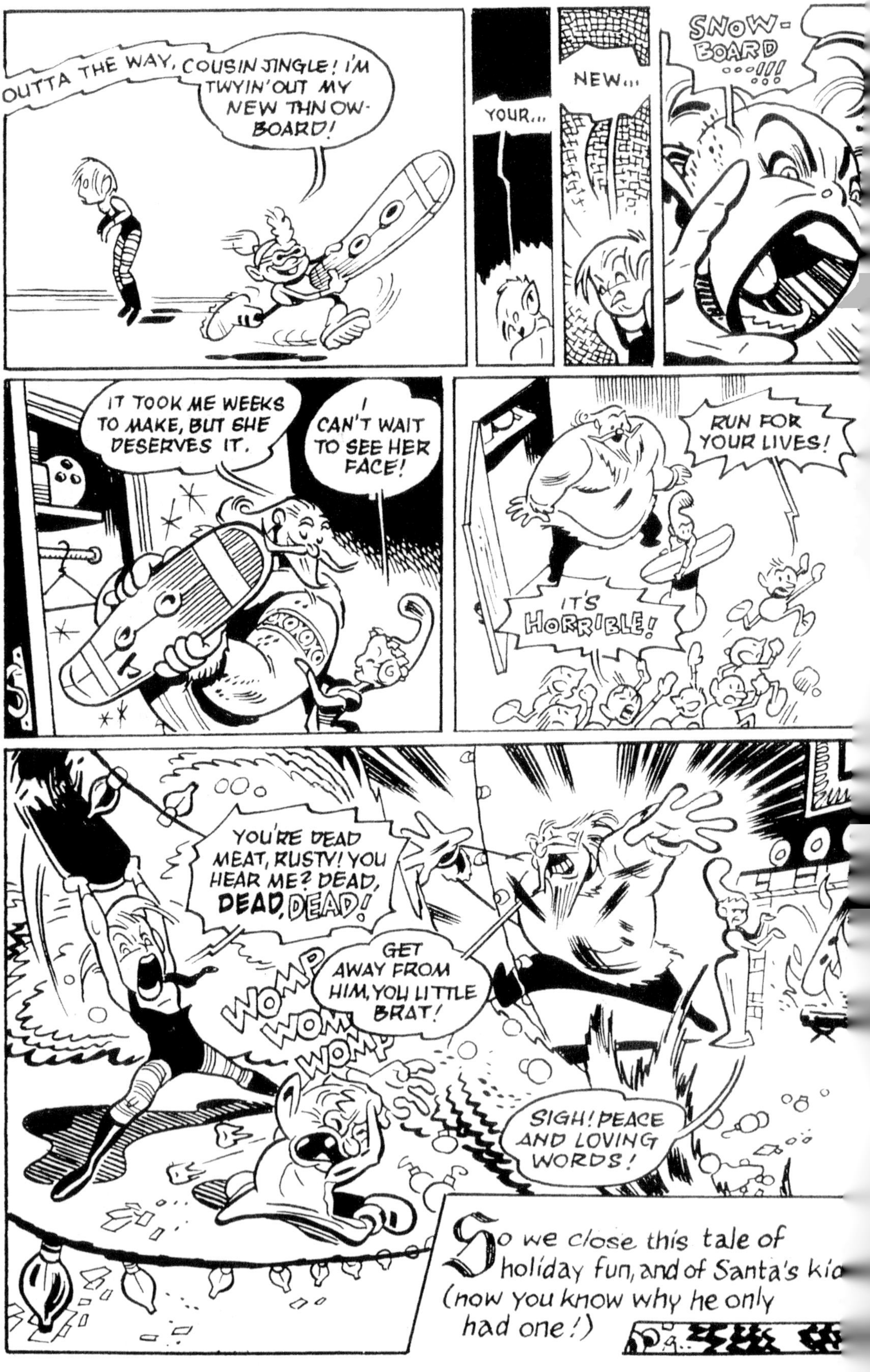
OUTTA THE WAY, COUSIN JINGLE! I'M TWYIN' OUT MY NEW THNOW-BOARD!
YOUR...
NEW...
SNOW-BOARD!!!
IT TOOK ME WEEKS TO MAKE, BUT SHE DESERVES IT.
I CAN'T WAIT TO SEE HER FACE!
RUN FOR YOUR LIVES!
IT'S HORRIBLE!
YOU'RE DEAD MEAT, RUSTY! YOU HEAR ME? DEAD, DEAD, DEAD!
GET AWAY FROM HIM, YOU LITTLE BRAT!
WOMP WOMP WOMP
SIGH! PEACE AND LOVING WORDS!
So we close this tale of holiday fun, and of Santa's kid (now you know why he only had one!)

Miserable on 34th Street

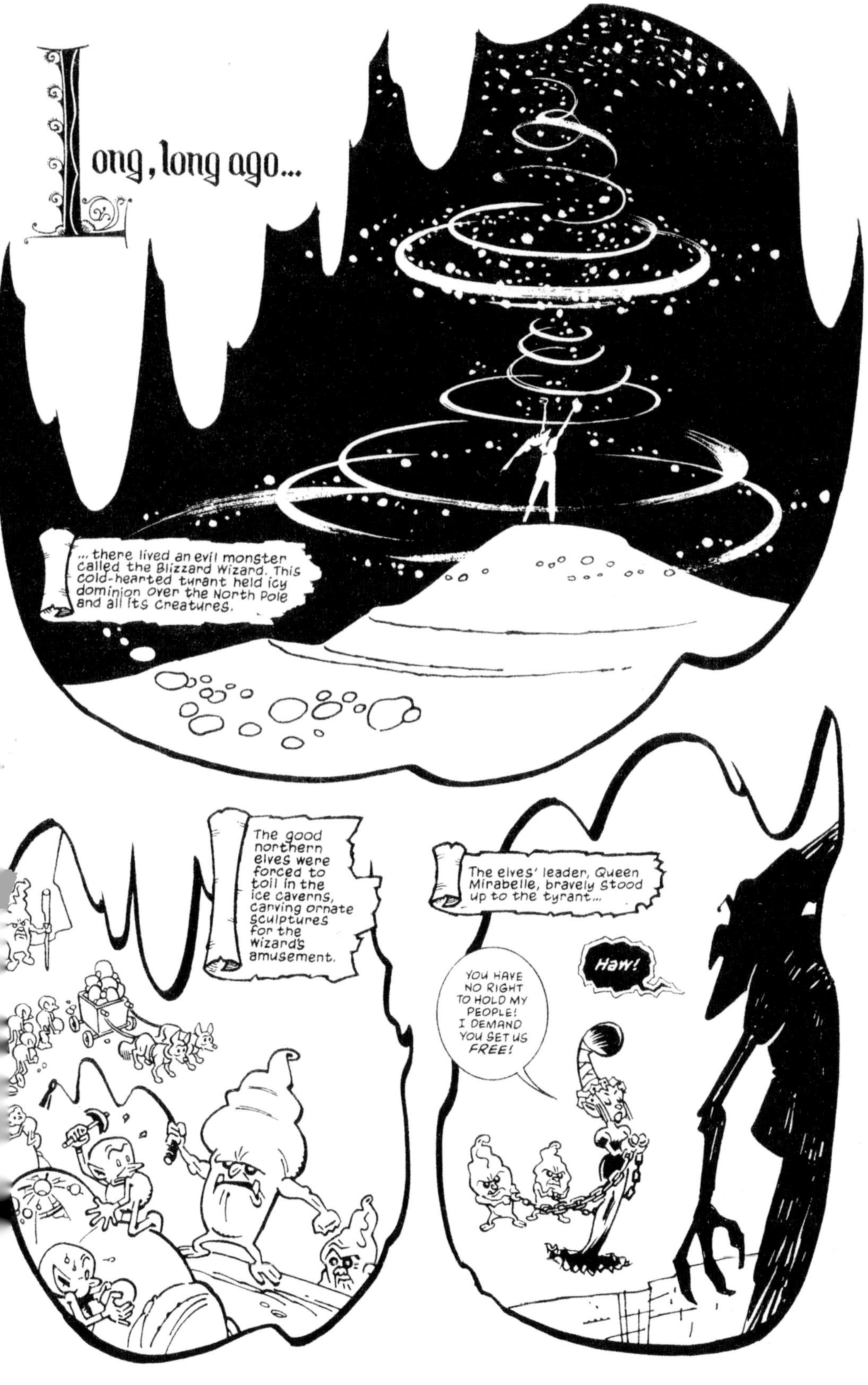
Long, long ago...
...there lived an evil monster called the Blizzard Wizard. This cold-hearted tyrant held icy dominion over the North Pole and all its creatures.
The good northern elves were forced to toil in the ice caverns, carving ornate sculptures for the Wizard's amusement.
The elves' leader, Queen Mirabelle, bravely stood up to the tyrant...
YOU HAVE NO RIGHT TO HOLD MY PEOPLE! I DEMAND YOU SET US FREE!
Haw!

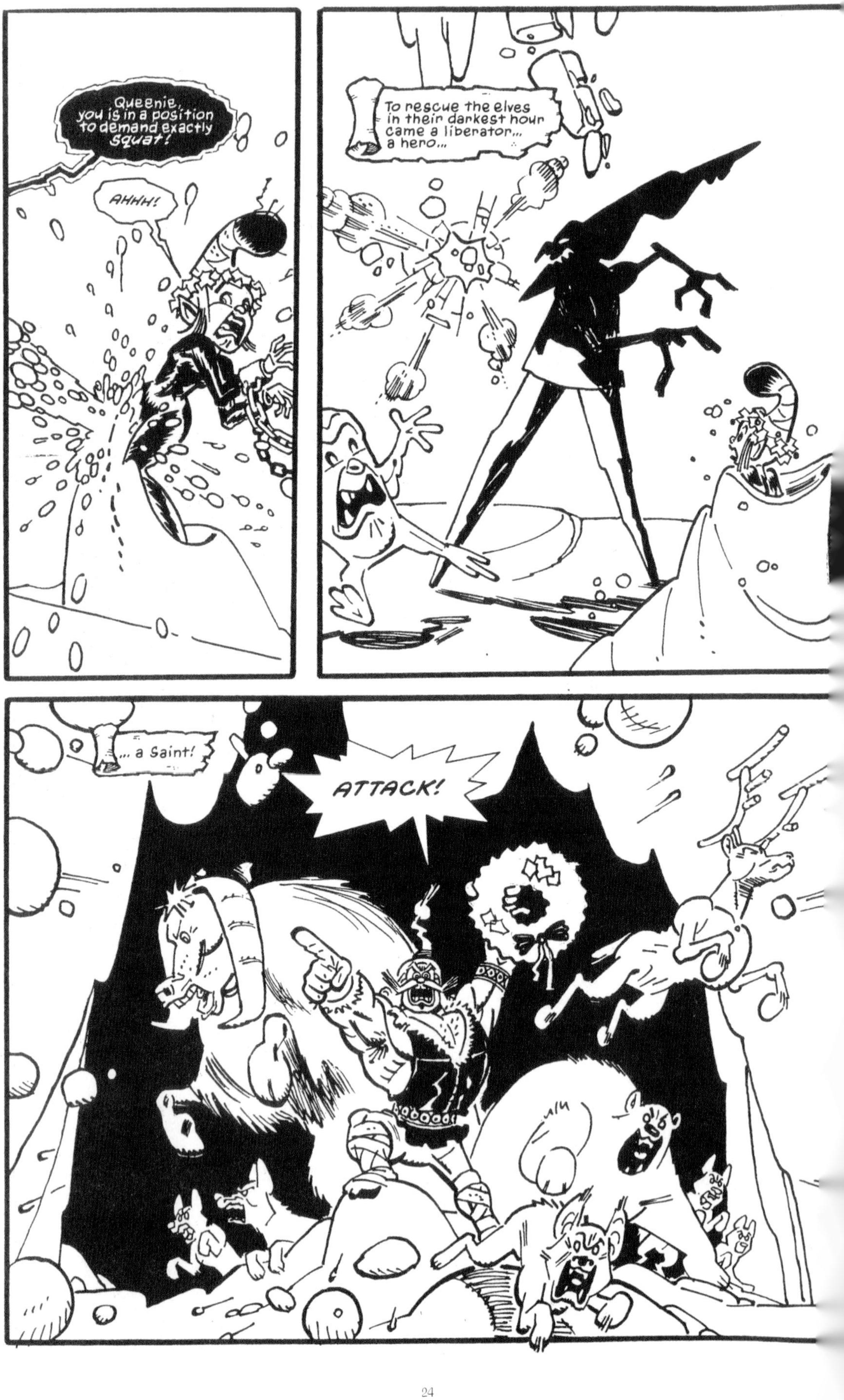
Queenie, you is in a position to demand exactly squat!
AHHH!
To rescue the elves in their darkest hour came a liberator... a hero...
... a Saint!
ATTACK!

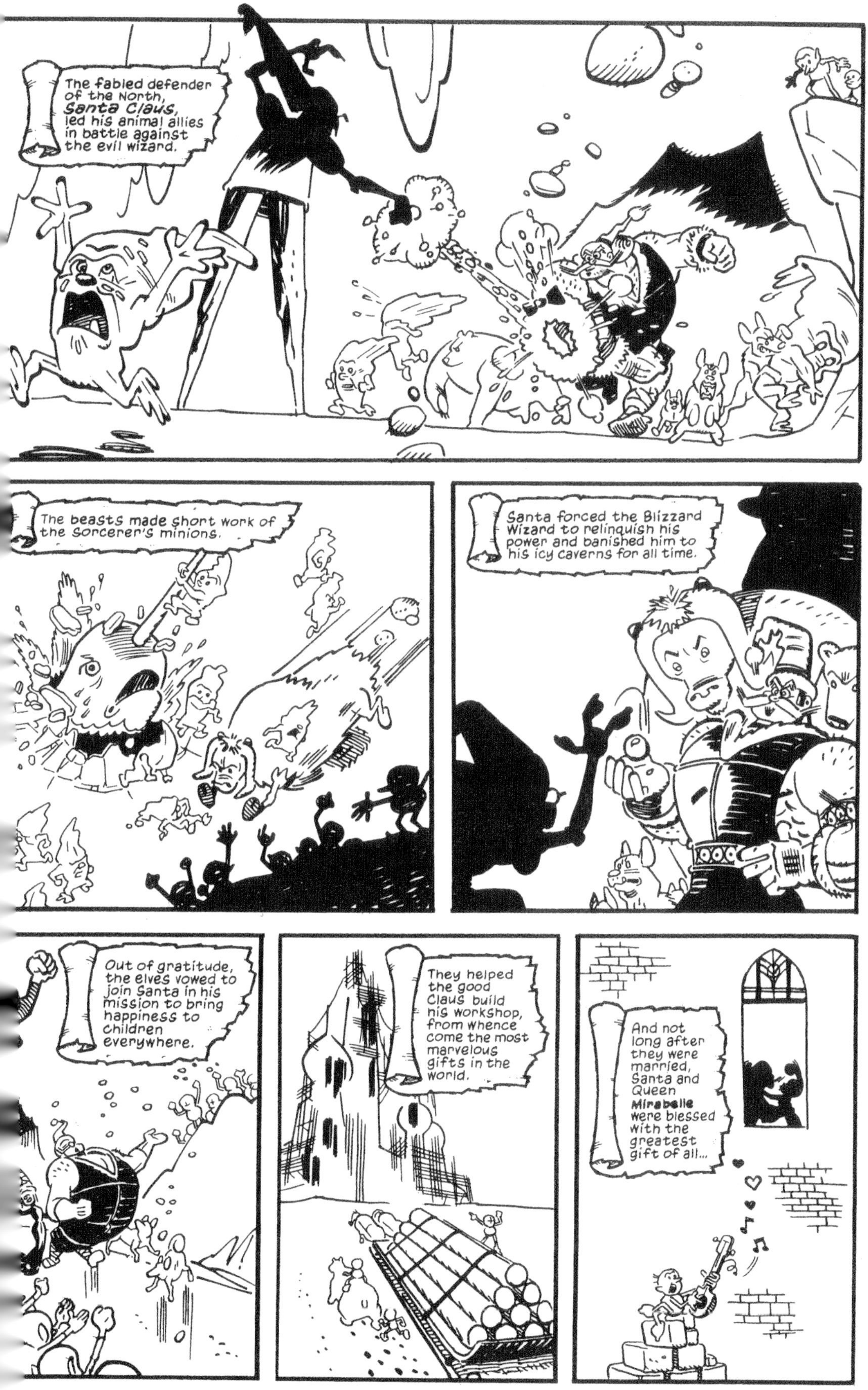
The fabled defender of the North, Santa Claus, led his animal allies in battle against the evil wizard.
The beasts made short work of the sorcerer's minions.
Santa forced the Blizzard Wizard to relinquish his power and banished him to his icy caverns for all time.
Out of gratitude, the elves vowed to join Santa in his mission to bring happiness to children everywhere.
They helped the good Claus build his workshop, from whence come the most marvelous gifts in the world.
And not long after they were married, Santa and Queen Mirabelle were blessed with the greatest gift of all...

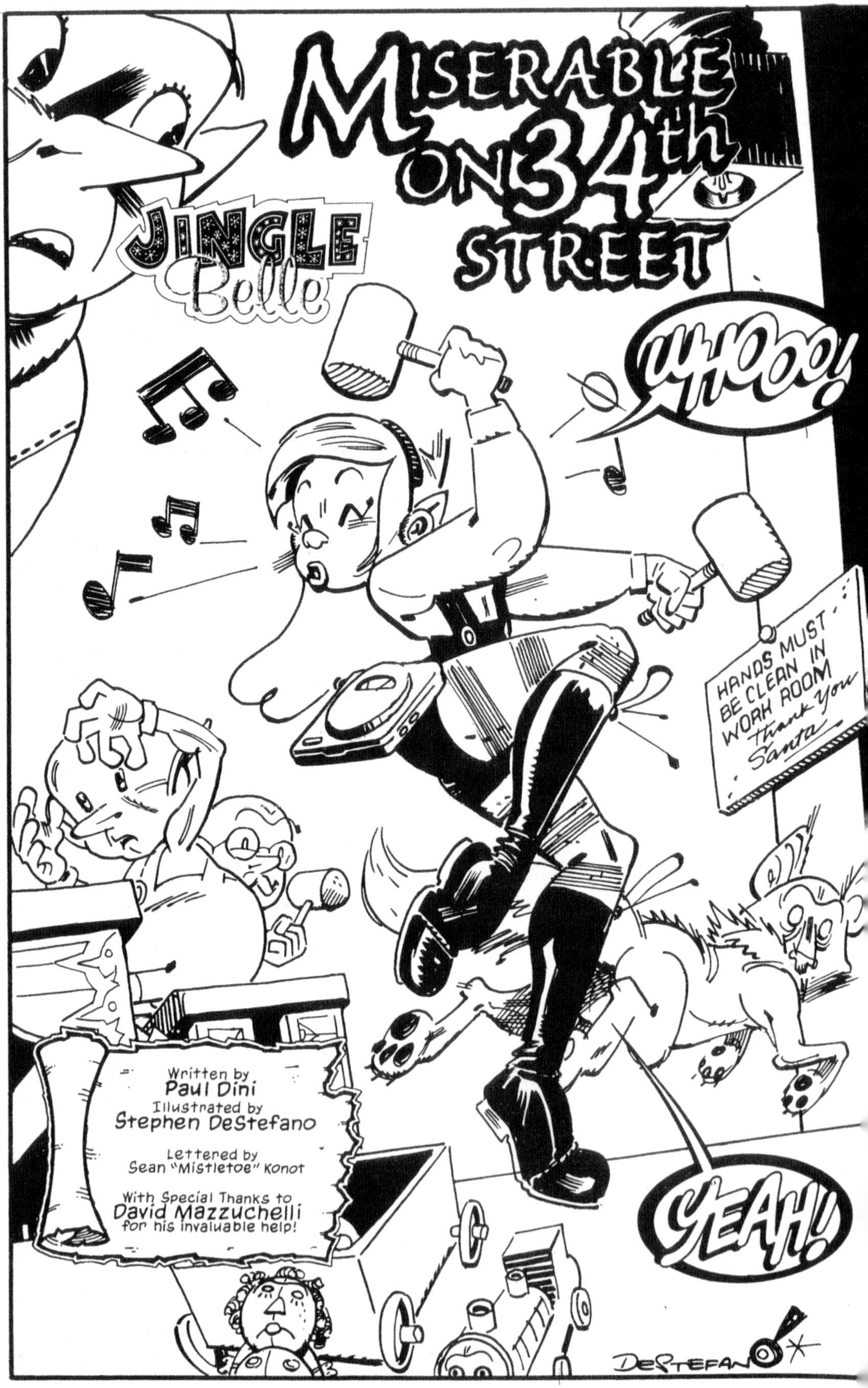

Jingle Belle
Miserable on 34th Street
WHOOO!
HANDS MUST BE CLEAN IN WORK ROOM thank you Santa
Written by Paul Dini
Illustrated by Stephen DeStefano
Lettered by Sean "Mistletoe" Konot
With Special Thanks to David Mazzuchelli for his invaluable help!
YEAH!
DESTEFANO

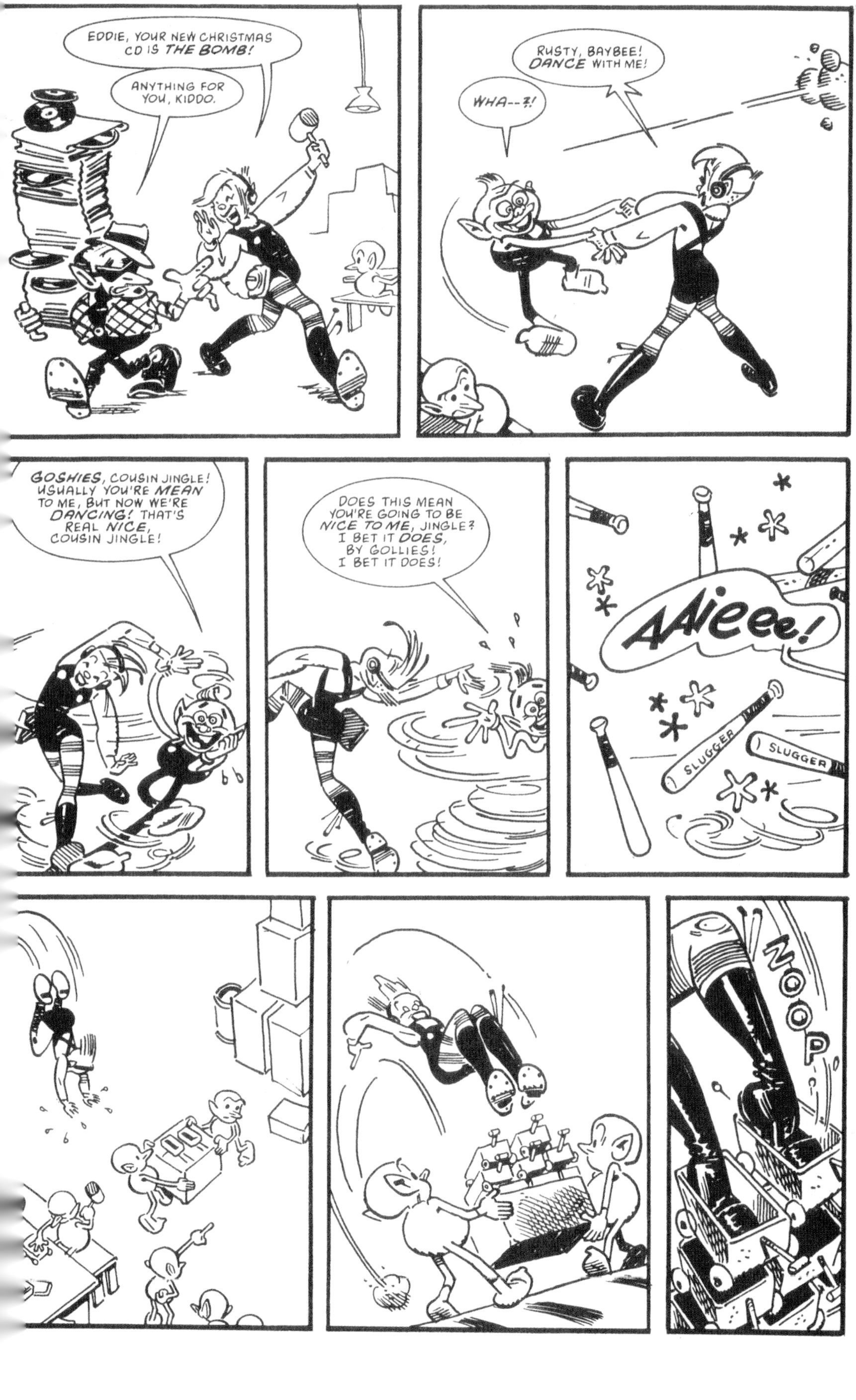
EDDIE, YOUR NEW CHRISTMAS CD IS THE BOMB!
ANYTHING FOR YOU, KIDDO.
RUSTY, BAYBEE! DANCE WITH ME!
WHA--?!
GOSHIES, COUSIN JINGLE! USUALLY YOU'RE MEAN TO ME, BUT NOW WE'RE DANCING! THAT'S REAL NICE, COUSIN JINGLE!
DOES THIS MEAN YOU'RE GOING TO BE NICE TO ME, JINGLE? I BET IT DOES, BY GOLLIES! I BET IT DOES!
AAIeee!
SLUGGER
SLUGGER
NOOP

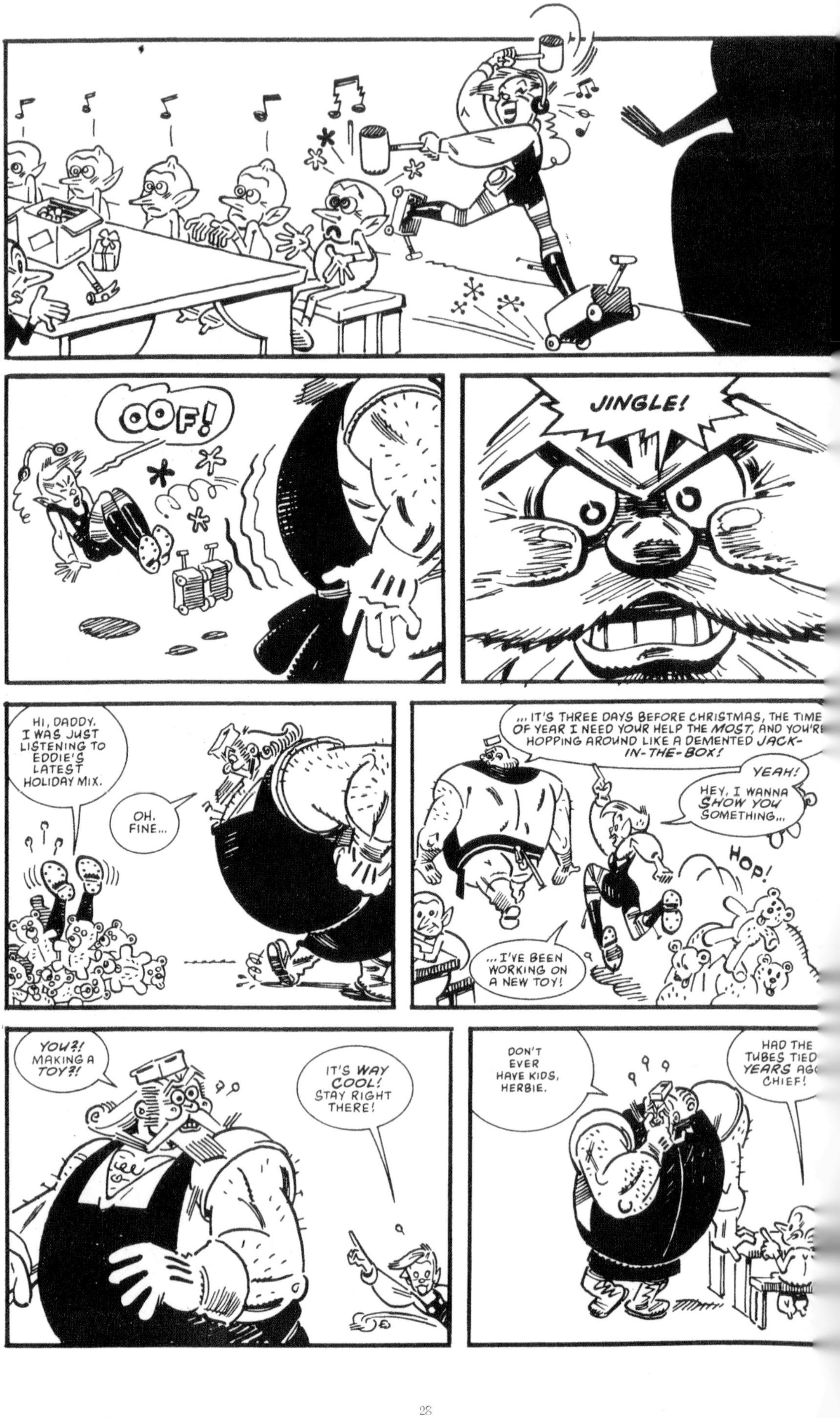
OOF!
JINGLE!
HI, DADDY. I WAS JUST LISTENING TO EDDIE'S LATEST HOLIDAY MIX.
OH. FINE...
...IT'S THREE DAYS BEFORE CHRISTMAS, THE TIME OF YEAR I NEED YOUR HELP THE MOST, AND YOU'RE HOPPING AROUND LIKE A DEMENTED JACK-IN-THE-BOX!
YEAH!
HEY, I WANNA SHOW YOU SOMETHING...
HOP!
...I'VE BEEN WORKING ON A NEW TOY!
YOU?! MAKING A TOY?!
IT'S WAY COOL! STAY RIGHT THERE!
DON'T EVER HAVE KIDS, HERBIE.
HAD THE TUBES TIED YEARS AGO CHIEF!

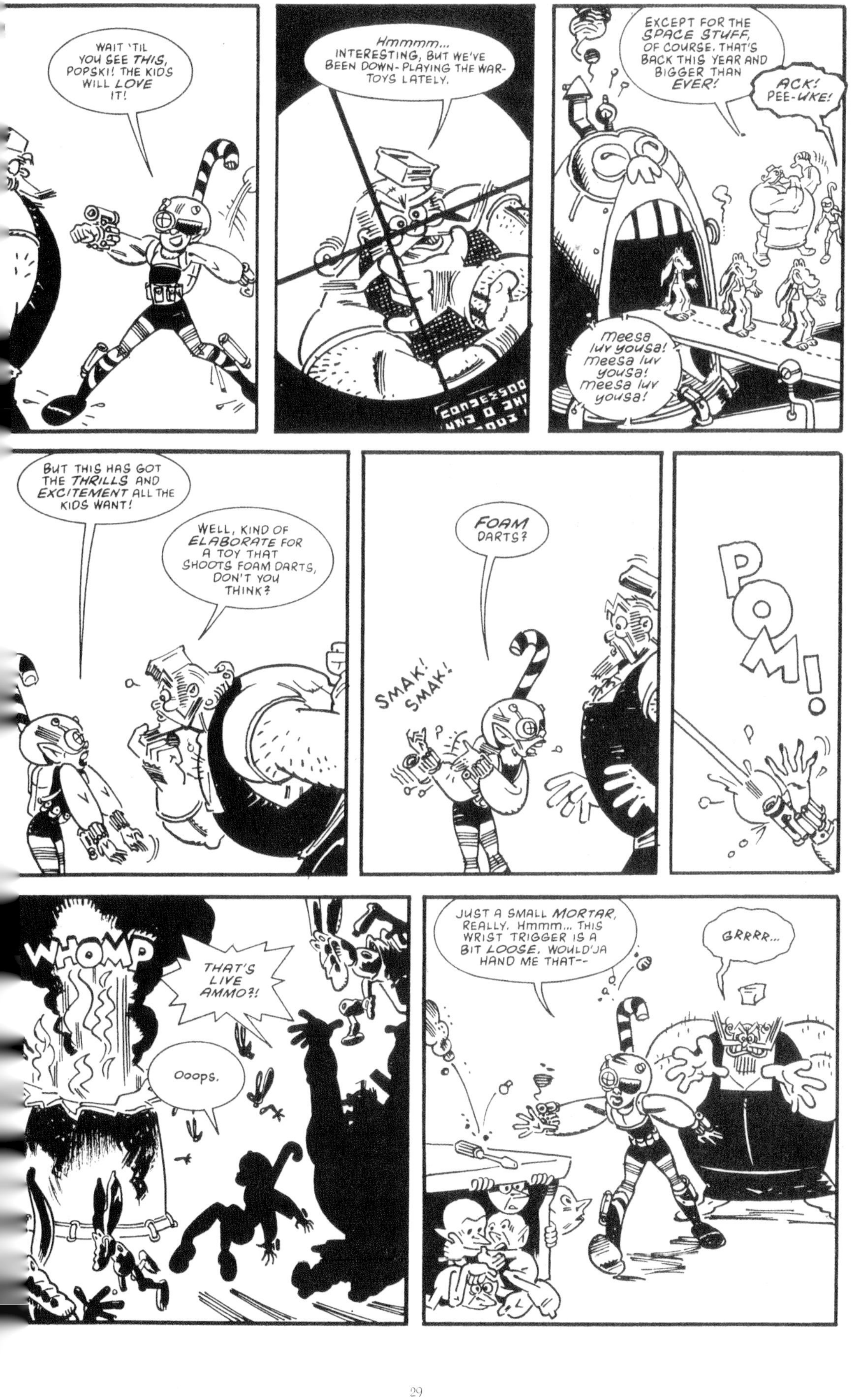
WAIT 'TIL YOU SEE *THIS*, POPSKI! THE KIDS WILL *LOVE* IT!
Hmmmm... INTERESTING, BUT WE'VE BEEN DOWN-PLAYING THE WAR-TOYS LATELY.
EXCEPT FOR THE *SPACE STUFF*, OF COURSE. THAT'S BACK THIS YEAR AND BIGGER THAN *EVER!*
ACK! PEE-UKE!
meesa luv yousa! meesa luv yousa! meesa luv yousa!
BUT THIS HAS GOT THE *THRILLS* AND *EXCITEMENT* ALL THE KIDS WANT!
WELL, KIND OF *ELABORATE* FOR A TOY THAT SHOOTS FOAM DARTS, DON'T YOU THINK?
FOAM DARTS?
SMAK! SMAK!
POM!
WHOMP
THAT'S LIVE AMMO?!
Ooops.
JUST A SMALL *MORTAR*, REALLY. Hmmm... THIS WRIST TRIGGER IS A BIT *LOOSE*. WOULD'JA HAND ME THAT--
GRRRR...

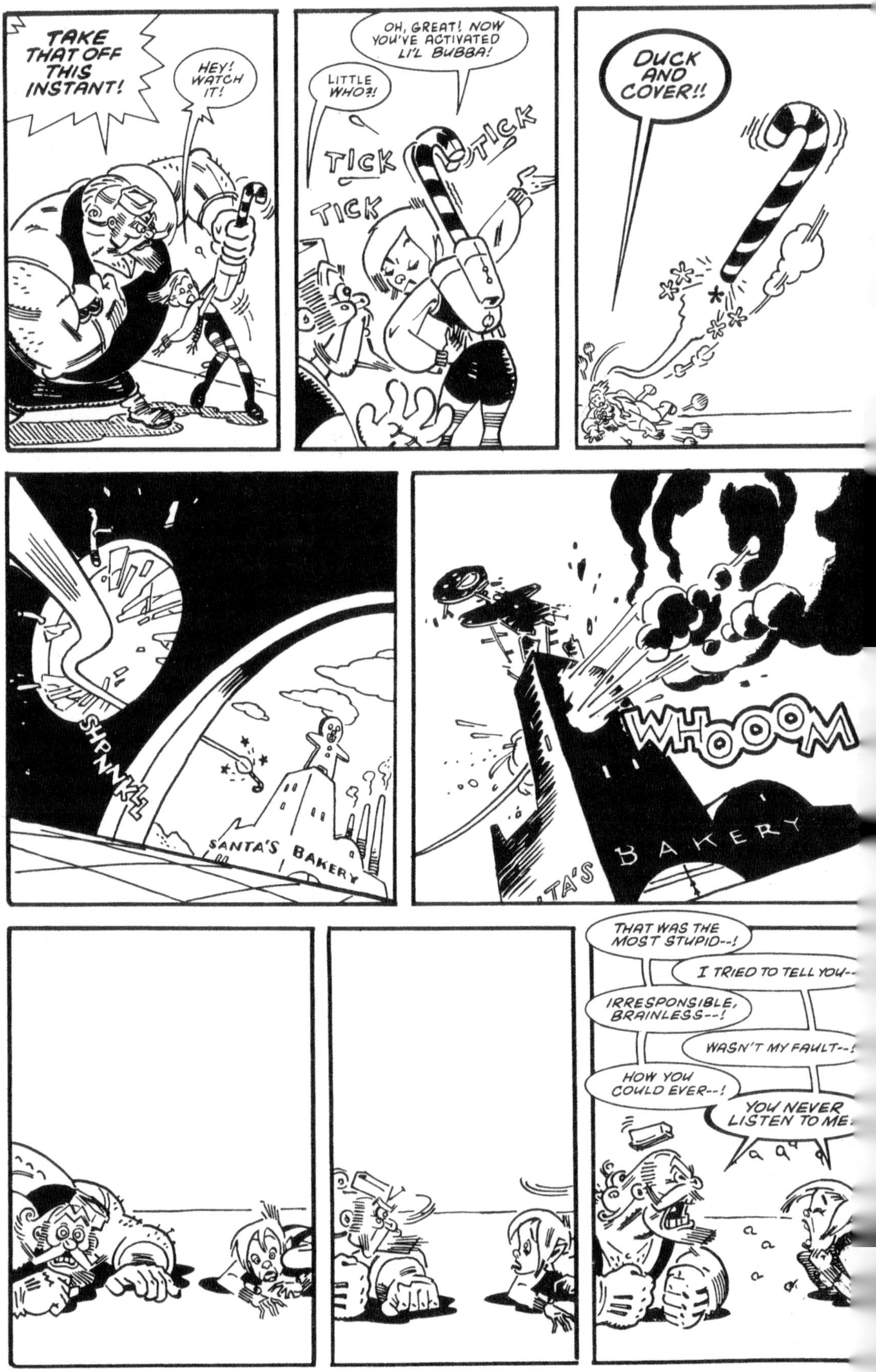
TAKE THAT OFF THIS INSTANT!
HEY! WATCH IT!
OH, GREAT! NOW YOU'VE ACTIVATED LI'L BUBBA!
LITTLE WHO?!
TICK
TICK
TICK
DUCK AND COVER!!
SHPNNKL
SANTA'S BAKERY
WHOOOM
BAKERY
THAT WAS THE MOST STUPID--!
I TRIED TO TELL YOU--
IRRESPONSIBLE, BRAINLESS--!
WASN'T MY FAULT--!
HOW YOU COULD EVER--!
YOU NEVER LISTEN TO ME!

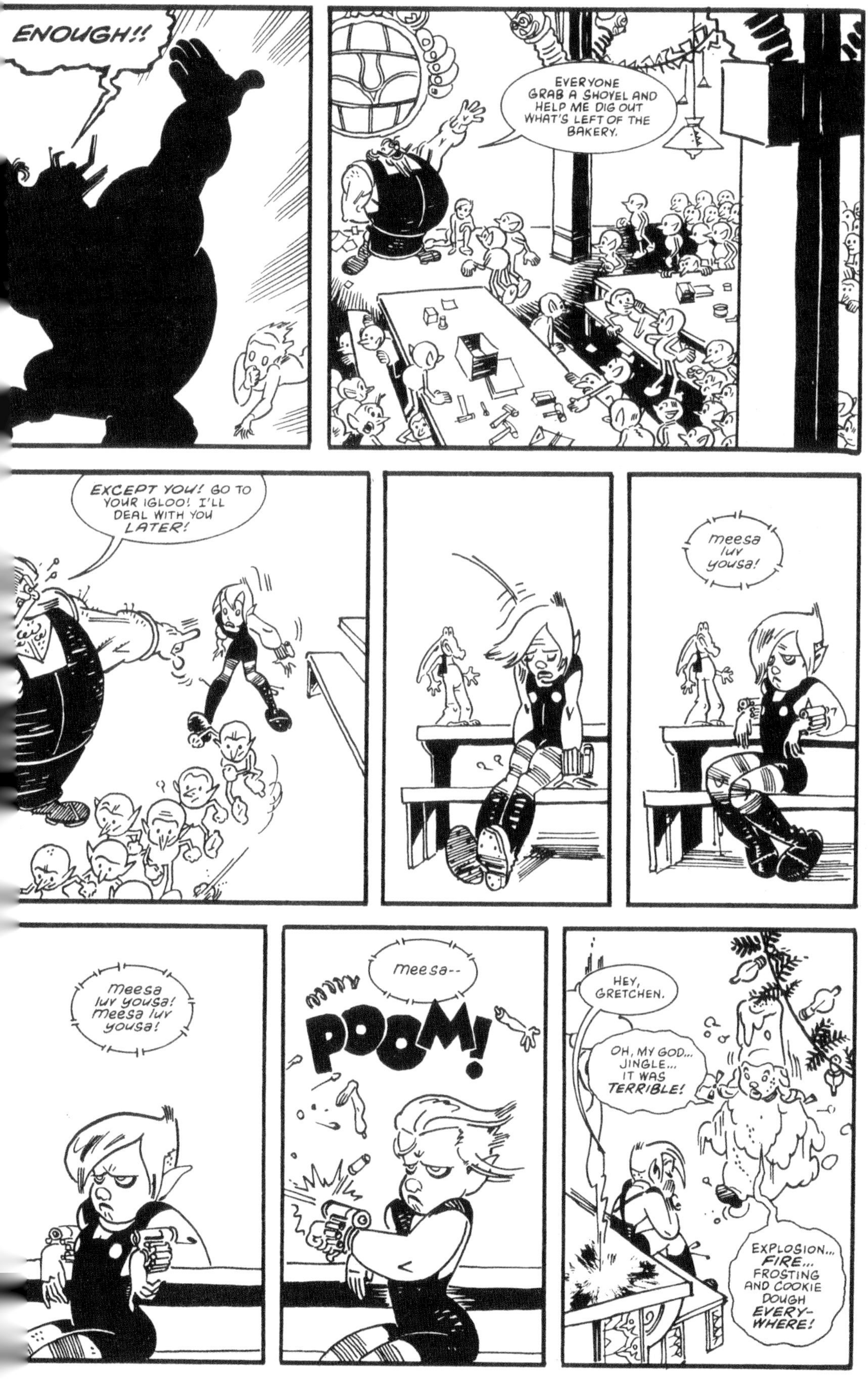

ENOUGH!!
EVERYONE GRAB A SHOVEL AND HELP ME DIG OUT WHAT'S LEFT OF THE BAKERY.
EXCEPT YOU! GO TO YOUR IGLOO! I'LL DEAL WITH YOU LATER!
meesa luv yousa!
meesa luv yousa! Meesa luv yousa!
meesa--
POOM!
HEY, GRETCHEN.
OH, MY GOD... JINGLE... IT WAS TERRIBLE!
EXPLOSION... FIRE... FROSTING AND COOKIE DOUGH EVERY-WHERE!

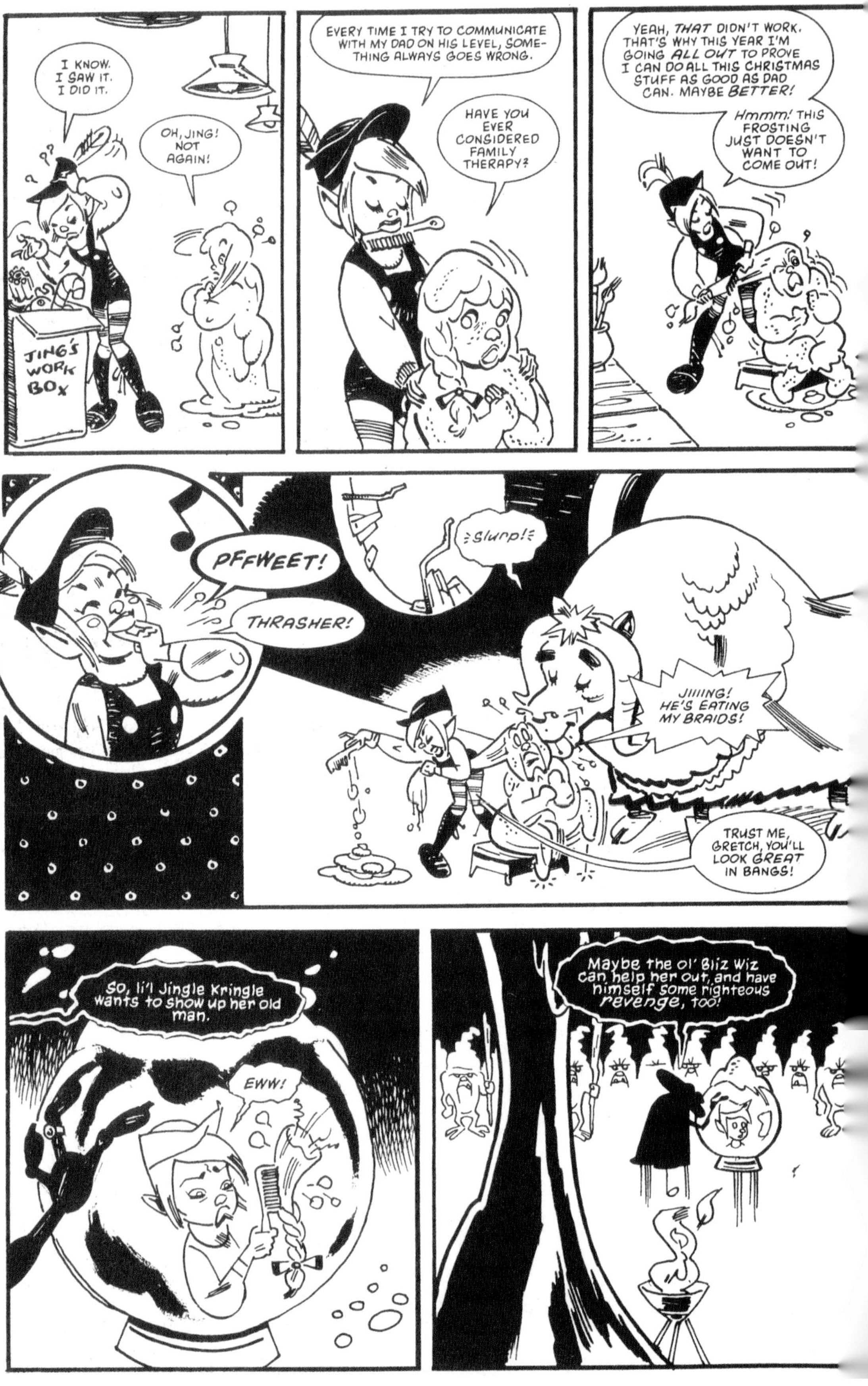
I KNOW. I SAW IT. I DID IT.
OH, JING! NOT AGAIN!
JING'S WORK BOX
EVERY TIME I TRY TO COMMUNICATE WITH MY DAD ON HIS LEVEL, SOMETHING ALWAYS GOES WRONG.
HAVE YOU EVER CONSIDERED FAMILY THERAPY?
YEAH, THAT DIDN'T WORK. THAT'S WHY THIS YEAR I'M GOING ALL OUT TO PROVE I CAN DO ALL THIS CHRISTMAS STUFF AS GOOD AS DAD CAN. MAYBE BETTER!
Hmmm! THIS FROSTING JUST DOESN'T WANT TO COME OUT!
PFFWEET!
THRASHER!
Slurp!
JIIIING! HE'S EATING MY BRAIDS!
TRUST ME, GRETCH, YOU'LL LOOK GREAT IN BANGS!
So, li'l Jingle Kringle wants to show up her old man.
EWW!
Maybe the ol' Bliz Wiz can help her out, and have himself some righteous revenge, too!

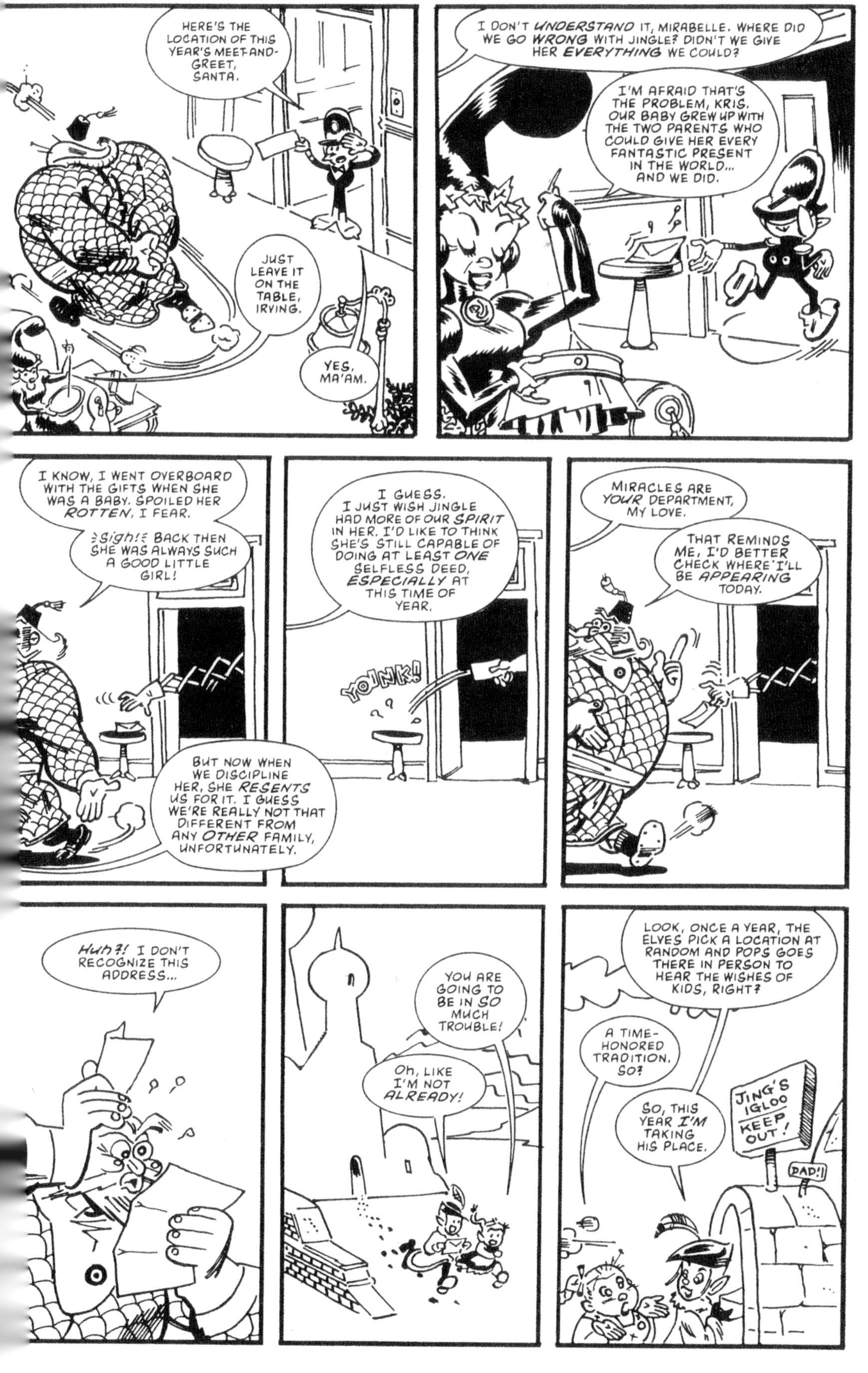
HERE'S THE LOCATION OF THIS YEAR'S MEET-AND-GREET, SANTA.
JUST LEAVE IT ON THE TABLE, IRVING.
YES, MA'AM.
I DON'T UNDERSTAND IT, MIRABELLE. WHERE DID WE GO WRONG WITH JINGLE? DIDN'T WE GIVE HER EVERYTHING WE COULD?
I'M AFRAID THAT'S THE PROBLEM, KRIS. OUR BABY GREW UP WITH THE TWO PARENTS WHO COULD GIVE HER EVERY FANTASTIC PRESENT IN THE WORLD... AND WE DID.
I KNOW, I WENT OVERBOARD WITH THE GIFTS WHEN SHE WAS A BABY. SPOILED HER ROTTEN, I FEAR.
Sigh! BACK THEN SHE WAS ALWAYS SUCH A GOOD LITTLE GIRL!
BUT NOW WHEN WE DISCIPLINE HER, SHE RESENTS US FOR IT. I GUESS WE'RE REALLY NOT THAT DIFFERENT FROM ANY OTHER FAMILY, UNFORTUNATELY.
I GUESS. I JUST WISH JINGLE HAD MORE OF OUR SPIRIT IN HER. I'D LIKE TO THINK SHE'S STILL CAPABLE OF DOING AT LEAST ONE SELFLESS DEED, ESPECIALLY AT THIS TIME OF YEAR.
YOINK!
MIRACLES ARE YOUR DEPARTMENT, MY LOVE.
THAT REMINDS ME, I'D BETTER CHECK WHERE I'LL BE APPEARING TODAY.
Huh?! I DON'T RECOGNIZE THIS ADDRESS...
YOU ARE GOING TO BE IN SO MUCH TROUBLE!
Oh, LIKE I'M NOT ALREADY!
LOOK, ONCE A YEAR, THE ELVES PICK A LOCATION AT RANDOM AND POPS GOES THERE IN PERSON TO HEAR THE WISHES OF KIDS, RIGHT?
A TIME-HONORED TRADITION. SO?
SO, THIS YEAR I'M TAKING HIS PLACE.
JING'S IGLOO KEEP OUT!
DAD!!

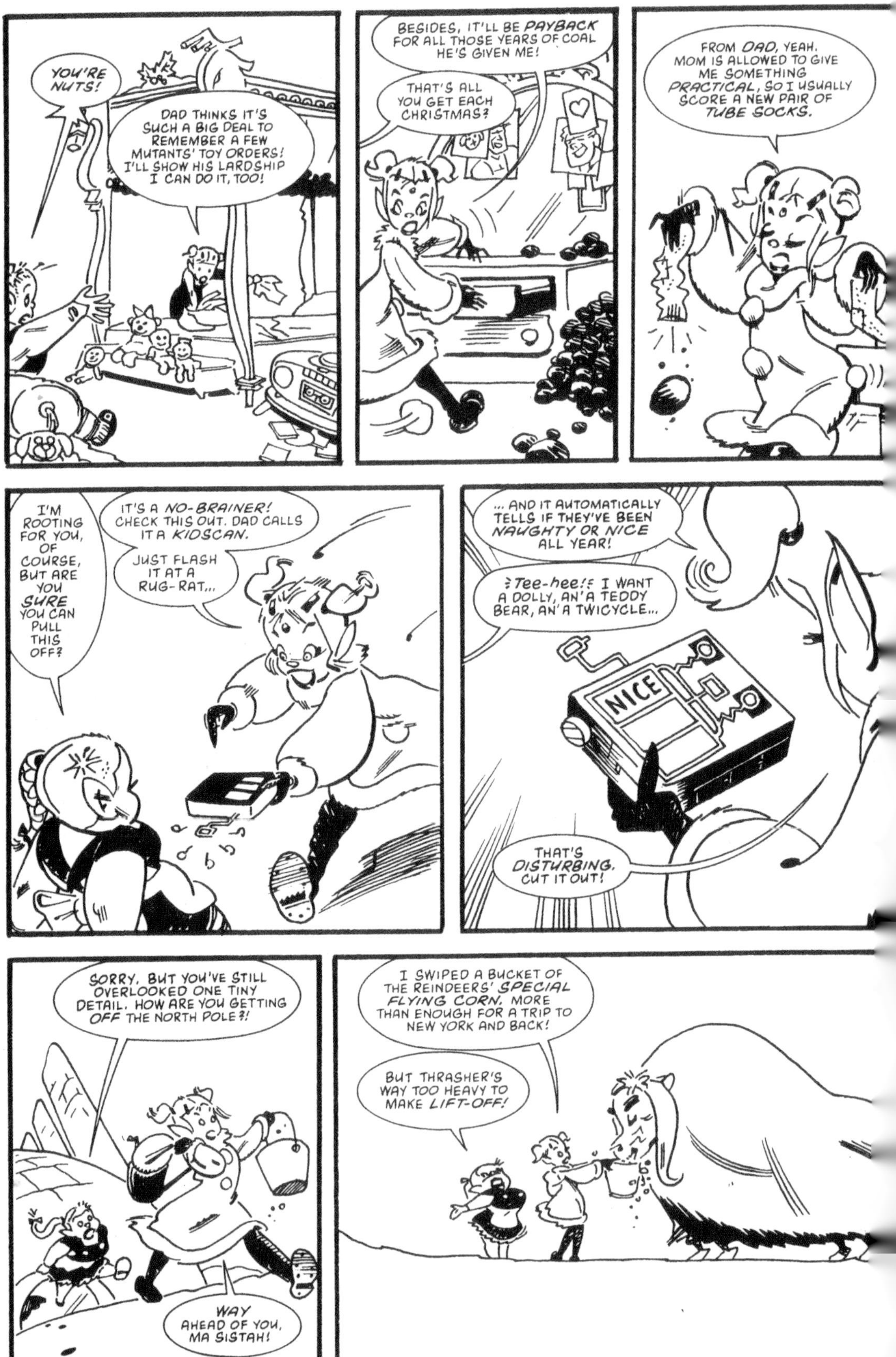
YOU'RE NUTS!
DAD THINKS IT'S SUCH A BIG DEAL TO REMEMBER A FEW MUTANTS' TOY ORDERS! I'LL SHOW HIS LARDSHIP I CAN DO IT, TOO!
BESIDES, IT'LL BE PAYBACK FOR ALL THOSE YEARS OF COAL HE'S GIVEN ME!
THAT'S ALL YOU GET EACH CHRISTMAS?
FROM DAD, YEAH. MOM IS ALLOWED TO GIVE ME SOMETHING PRACTICAL, SO I USUALLY SCORE A NEW PAIR OF TUBE SOCKS.
I'M ROOTING FOR YOU, OF COURSE, BUT ARE YOU SURE YOU CAN PULL THIS OFF?
IT'S A NO-BRAINER! CHECK THIS OUT. DAD CALLS IT A KIDSCAN.
JUST FLASH IT AT A RUG-RAT...
... AND IT AUTOMATICALLY TELLS IF THEY'VE BEEN NAUGHTY OR NICE ALL YEAR!
Tee-hee! I WANT A DOLLY, AN'A TEDDY BEAR, AN'A TWICYCLE...
NICE
THAT'S DISTURBING. CUT IT OUT!
SORRY, BUT YOU'VE STILL OVERLOOKED ONE TINY DETAIL. HOW ARE YOU GETTING OFF THE NORTH POLE?!
WAY AHEAD OF YOU, MA SISTAH!
I SWIPED A BUCKET OF THE REINDEERS' SPECIAL FLYING CORN. MORE THAN ENOUGH FOR A TRIP TO NEW YORK AND BACK!
BUT THRASHER'S WAY TOO HEAVY TO MAKE LIFT-OFF!

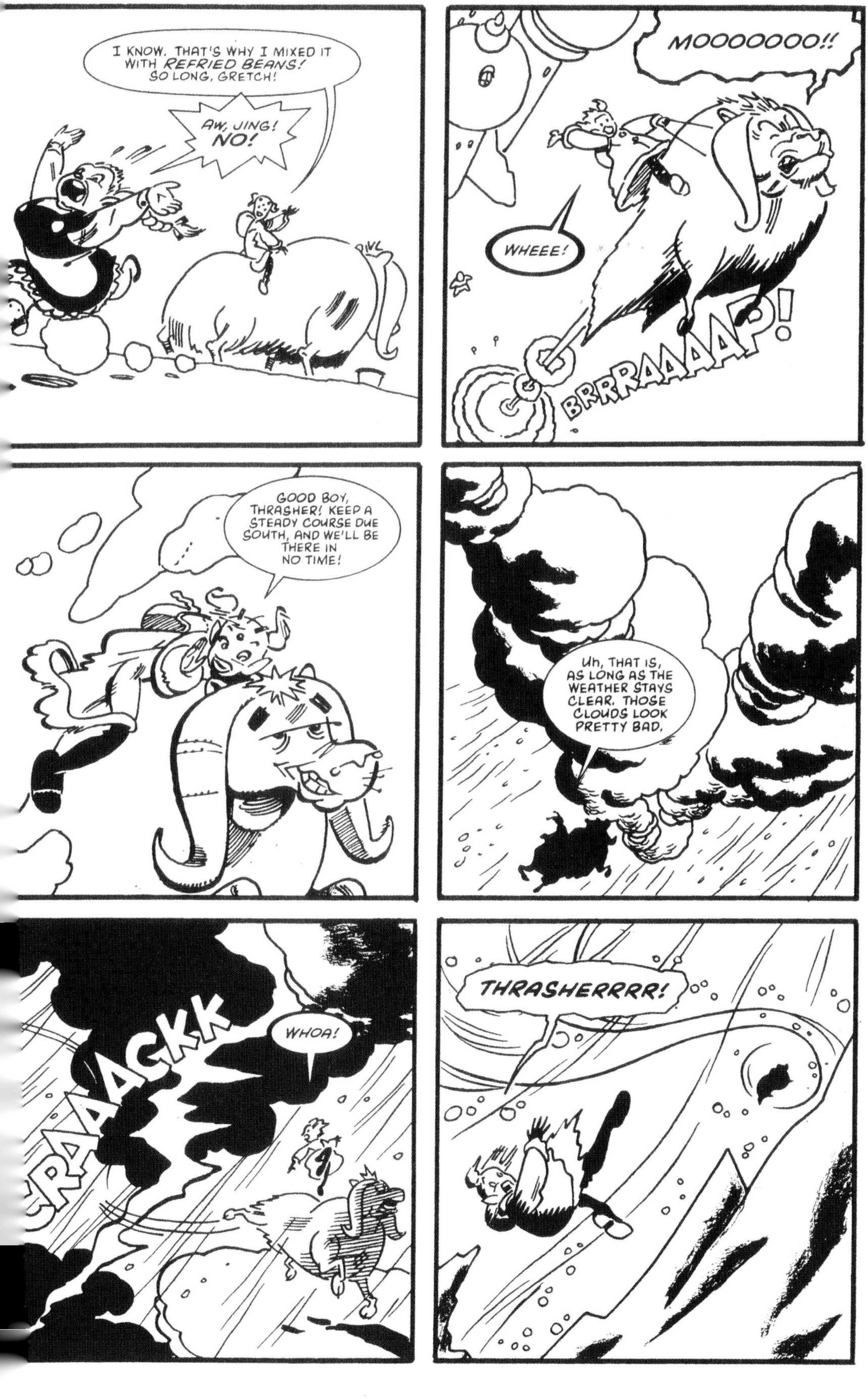
I KNOW. THAT'S WHY I MIXED IT WITH REFRIED BEANS! SO LONG, GRETCH!
AW, JING! NO!
MOOOOOOO!!
WHEEE!
BRRRAAAAAP!
GOOD BOY, THRASHER! KEEP A STEADY COURSE DUE SOUTH, AND WE'LL BE THERE IN NO TIME!
Uh, THAT IS, AS LONG AS THE WEATHER STAYS CLEAR. THOSE CLOUDS LOOK PRETTY BAD.
CRAAACKK
WHOA!
THRASHERRRR!

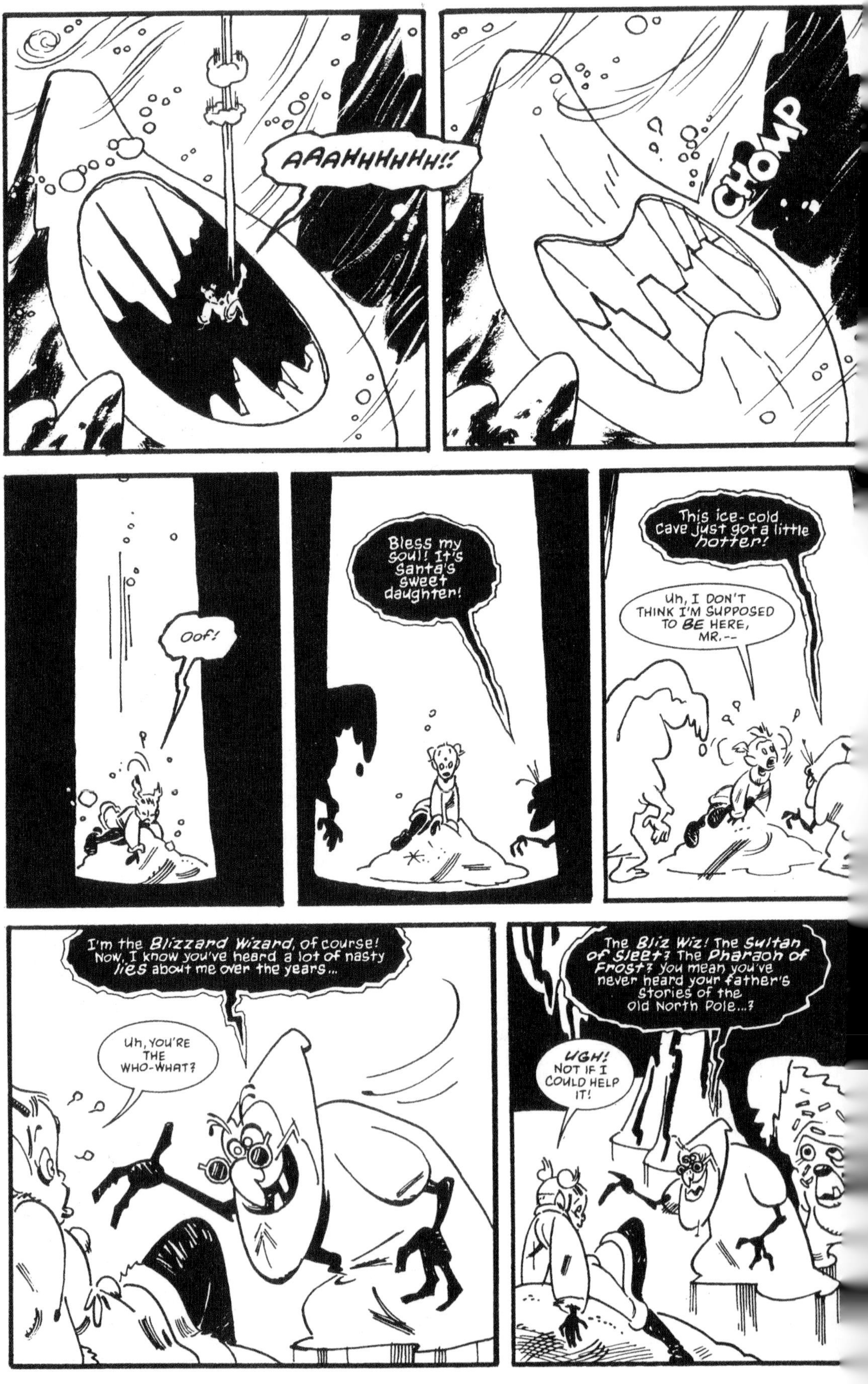

AAAHHHHHH!!
CHOMP
Oof!
Bless my soul!! It's Santa's sweet daughter!
This ice-cold Cave just got a little hotter!
Uh, I DON'T THINK I'M SUPPOSED TO BE HERE, MR.--
I'm the Blizzard Wizard, of course! Now, I know you've heard a lot of nasty lies about me over the years...
Uh, YOU'RE THE WHO-WHAT?
The Bliz Wiz! The Sultan of Sleet? The Pharaoh of Frost? You mean you've never heard your father's stories of the old North Pole...?
UGH! NOT IF I COULD HELP IT!

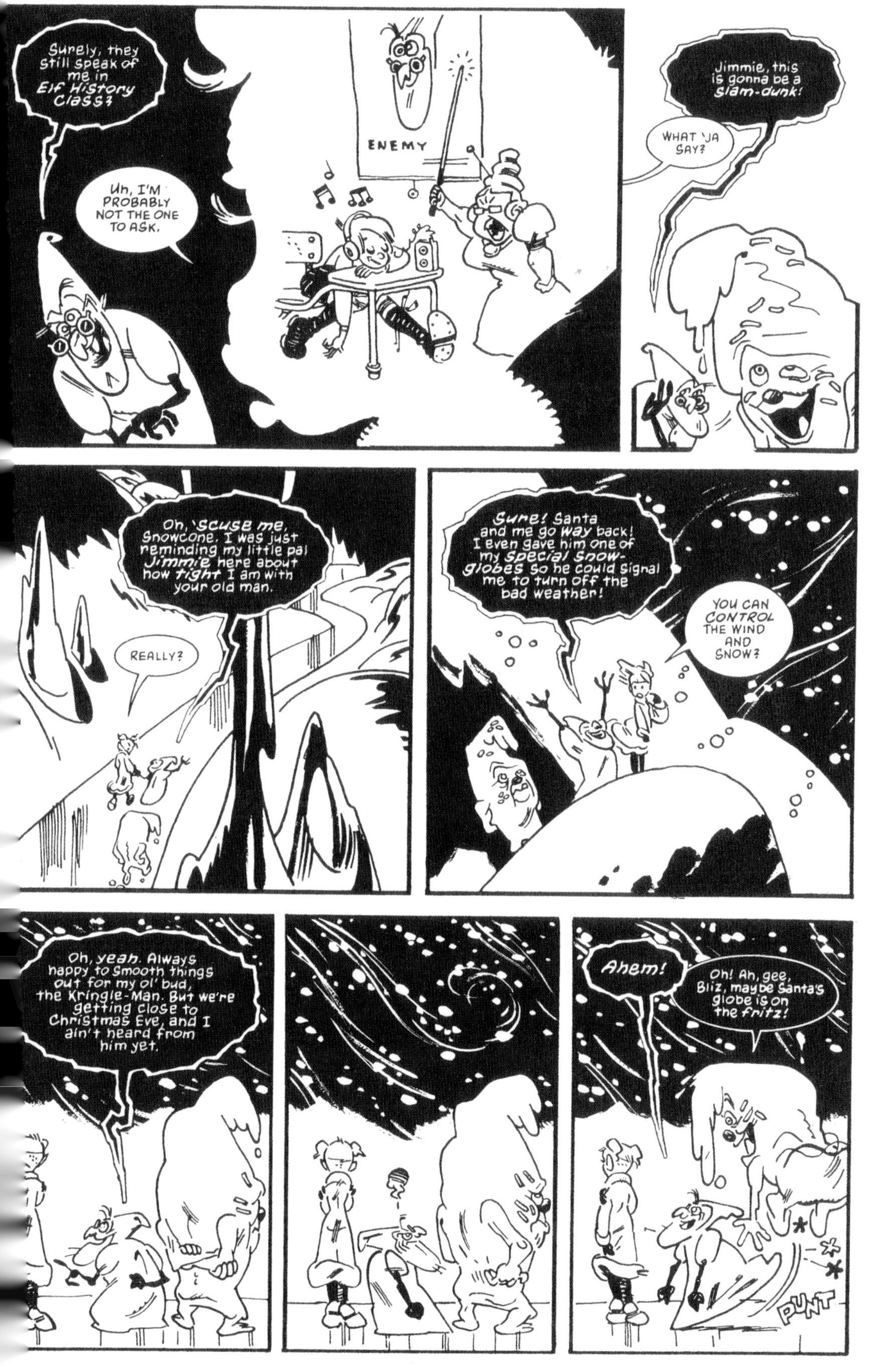
Surely, they still speak of me in Elf History Class?
Uh, I'M PROBABLY NOT THE ONE TO ASK.
ENEMY
Jimmie, this is gonna be a slam-dunk!
WHAT 'JA SAY?
Oh, 'scuse me, Snowcone. I was just reminding my little pal Jimmie here about how tight I am with your old man.
REALLY?
Sure! Santa and me go way back! I even gave him one of my special Snow-globes so he could signal me to turn off the bad weather!
YOU CAN CONTROL THE WIND AND SNOW?
Oh, yeah. Always happy to smooth things out for my ol' bud, the Kringle-Man. But we're getting close to Christmas Eve, and I ain't heard from him yet.
Ahem!
Oh! Ah, gee, Bliz, maybe Santa's globe is on the fritz!
PUNT

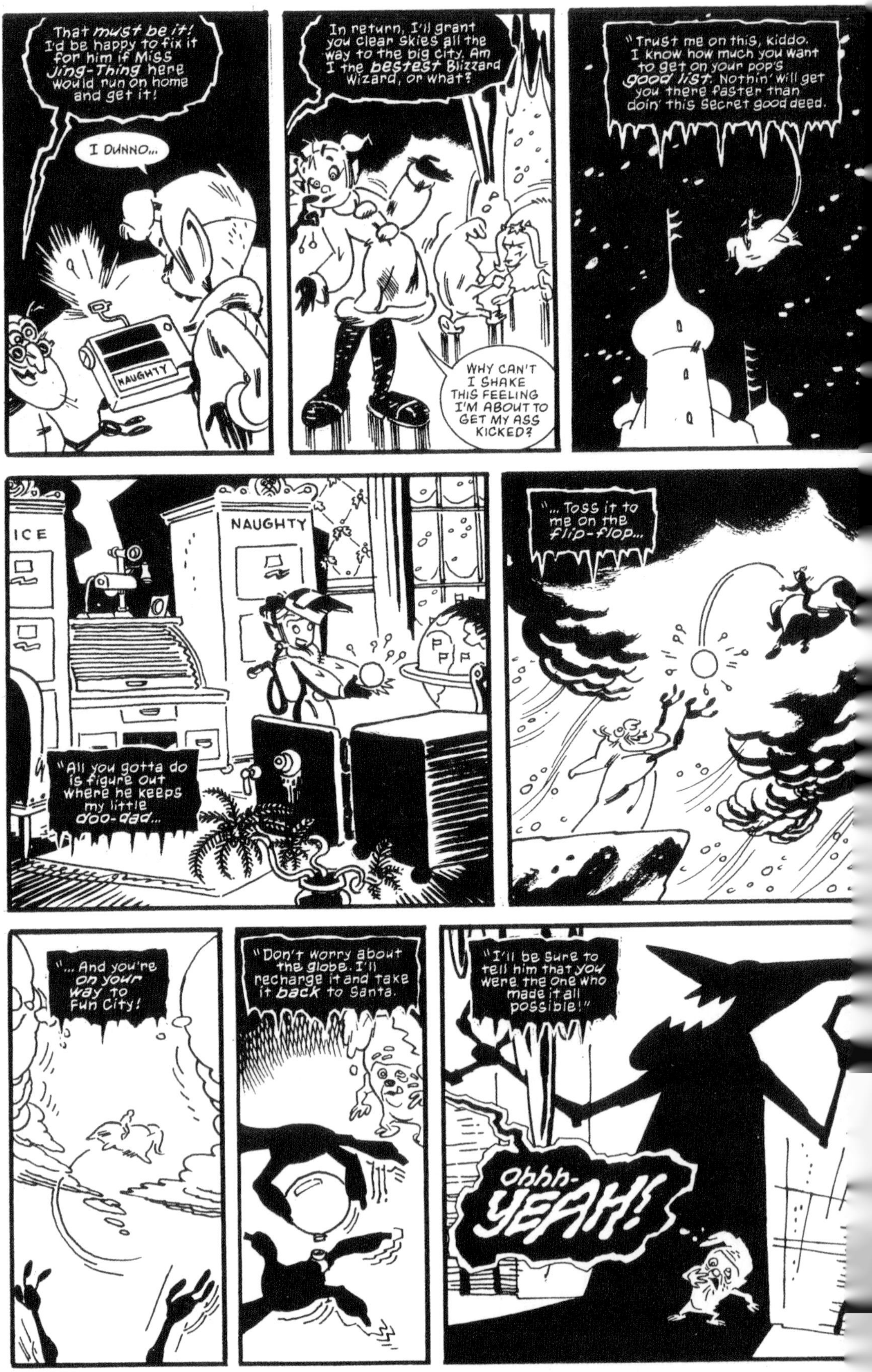
That must be it! I'd be happy to fix it for him if Miss Jing-Thing here would run on home and get it!
I DUNNO...
NAUGHTY
In return, I'll grant you clear skies all the way to the big city. Am I the bestest Blizzard Wizard, or what?
WHY CAN'T I SHAKE THIS FEELING I'M ABOUT TO GET MY ASS KICKED?
"Trust me on this, kiddo. I know how much you want to get on your pop's good list. Nothin' will get you there faster than doin' this secret good deed.
ICE
NAUGHTY
"All you gotta do is figure out where he keeps my little doo-dad...
"... Toss it to me on the flip-flop...
"... And you're on your way to Fun City!
"Don't worry about the globe. I'll recharge it and take it back to Santa.
"I'll be sure to tell him that you were the one who made it all possible!"
Ohhh-YEAH!

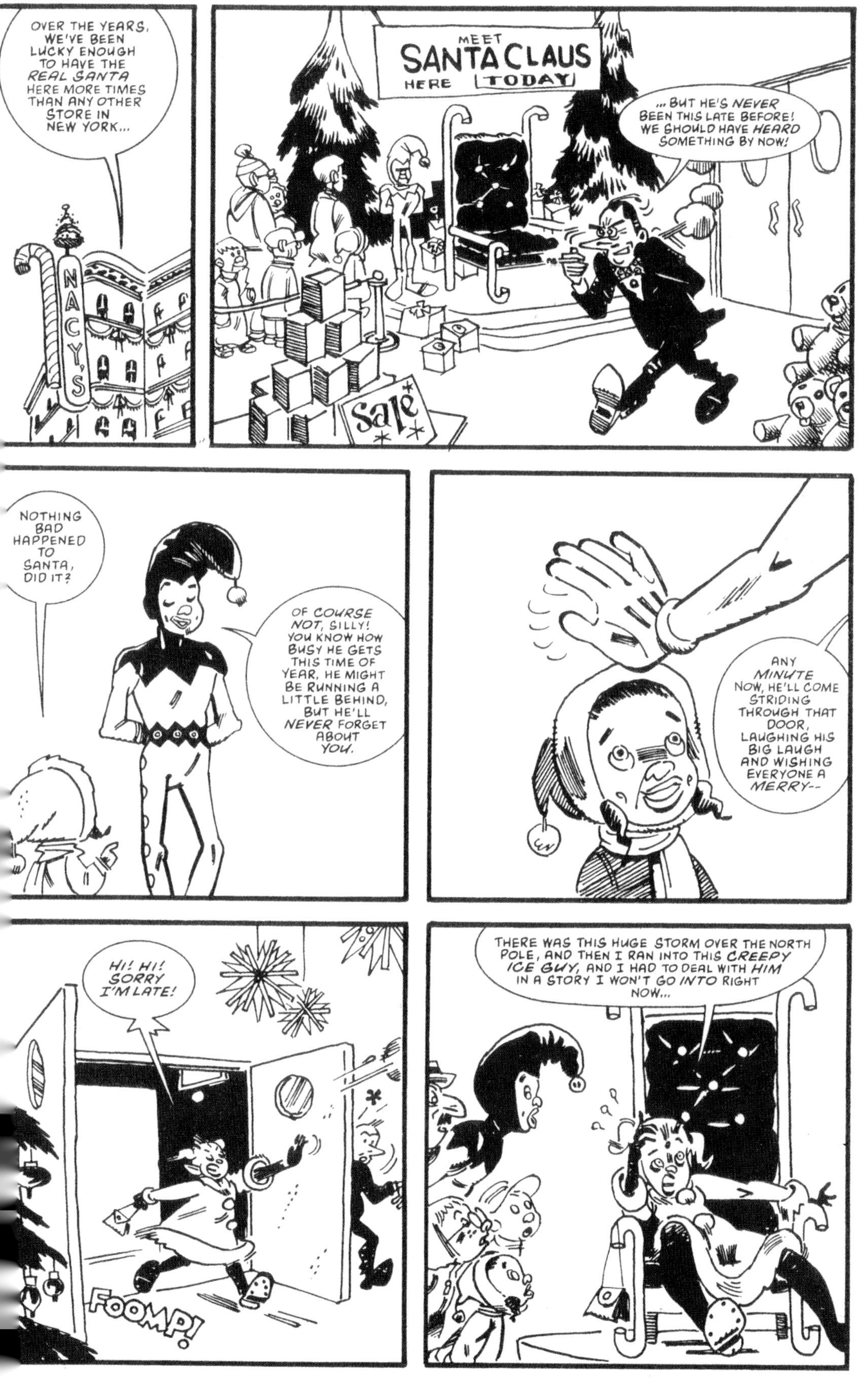
OVER THE YEARS, WE'VE BEEN LUCKY ENOUGH TO HAVE THE REAL SANTA HERE MORE TIMES THAN ANY OTHER STORE IN NEW YORK...
NACY'S
MEET SANTA CLAUS HERE TODAY
...BUT HE'S NEVER BEEN THIS LATE BEFORE! WE SHOULD HAVE HEARD SOMETHING BY NOW!
SALE
NOTHING BAD HAPPENED TO SANTA, DID IT?
OF COURSE NOT, SILLY! YOU KNOW HOW BUSY HE GETS THIS TIME OF YEAR. HE MIGHT BE RUNNING A LITTLE BEHIND, BUT HE'LL NEVER FORGET ABOUT YOU.
ANY MINUTE NOW, HE'LL COME STRIDING THROUGH THAT DOOR, LAUGHING HIS BIG LAUGH AND WISHING EVERYONE A MERRY--
HI! HI! SORRY I'M LATE!
FOOMP!
THERE WAS THIS HUGE STORM OVER THE NORTH POLE, AND THEN I RAN INTO THIS CREEPY ICE GUY, AND I HAD TO DEAL WITH HIM IN A STORY I WON'T GO INTO RIGHT NOW...

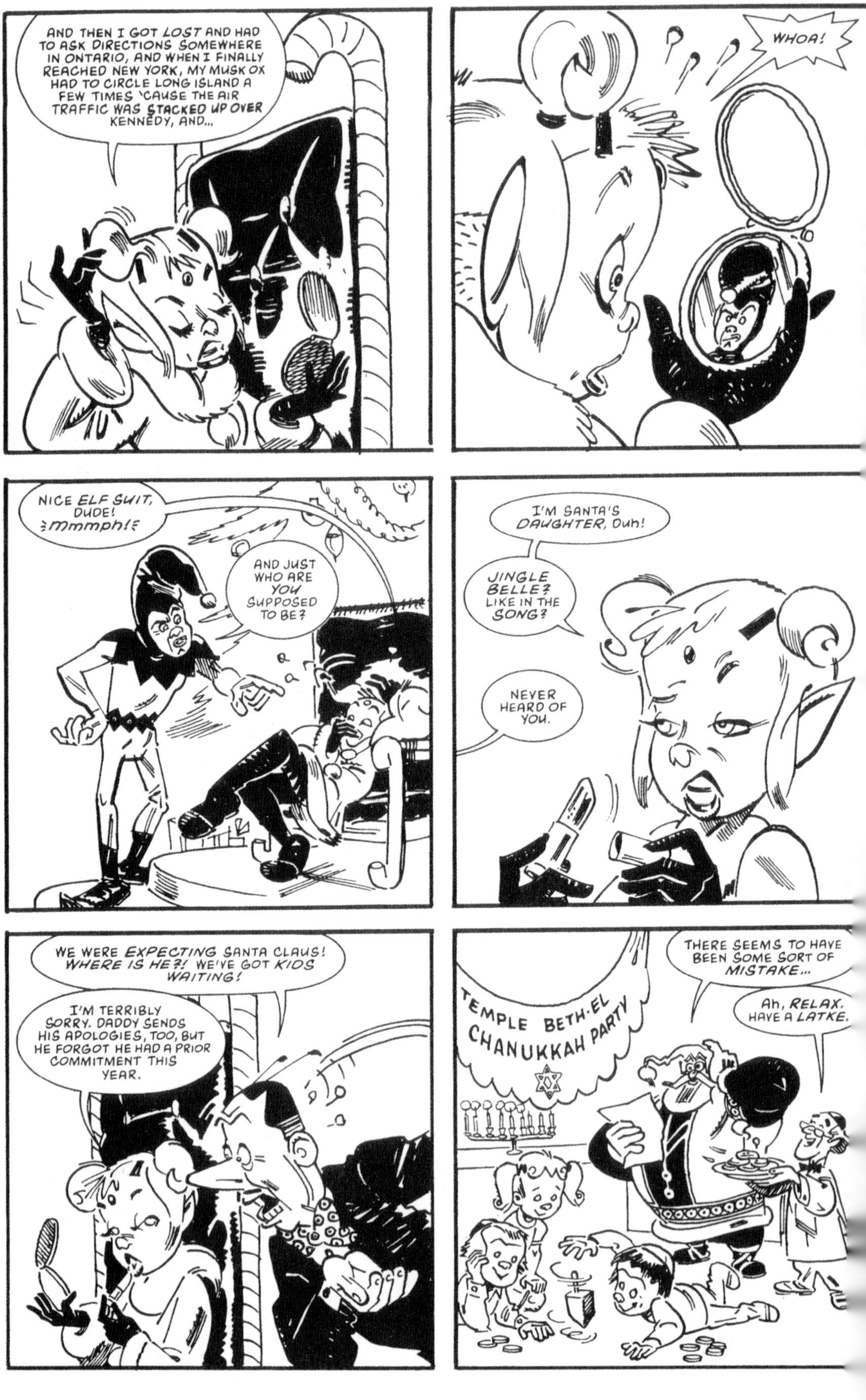
AND THEN I GOT LOST AND HAD TO ASK DIRECTIONS SOMEWHERE IN ONTARIO, AND WHEN I FINALLY REACHED NEW YORK, MY MUSK OX HAD TO CIRCLE LONG ISLAND A FEW TIMES 'CAUSE THE AIR TRAFFIC WAS STACKED UP OVER KENNEDY, AND...
WHOA!
NICE ELF SUIT, DUDE! Mmmph!
AND JUST WHO ARE YOU SUPPOSED TO BE?
I'M SANTA'S DAUGHTER, Duh!
JINGLE BELLE? LIKE IN THE SONG?
NEVER HEARD OF YOU.
WE WERE EXPECTING SANTA CLAUS! WHERE IS HE?! WE'VE GOT KIDS WAITING!
I'M TERRIBLY SORRY. DADDY SENDS HIS APOLOGIES, TOO, BUT HE FORGOT HE HAD A PRIOR COMMITMENT THIS YEAR.
TEMPLE BETH-EL CHANUKKAH PARTY
THERE SEEMS TO HAVE BEEN SOME SORT OF MISTAKE...
Ah, RELAX. HAVE A LATKE.

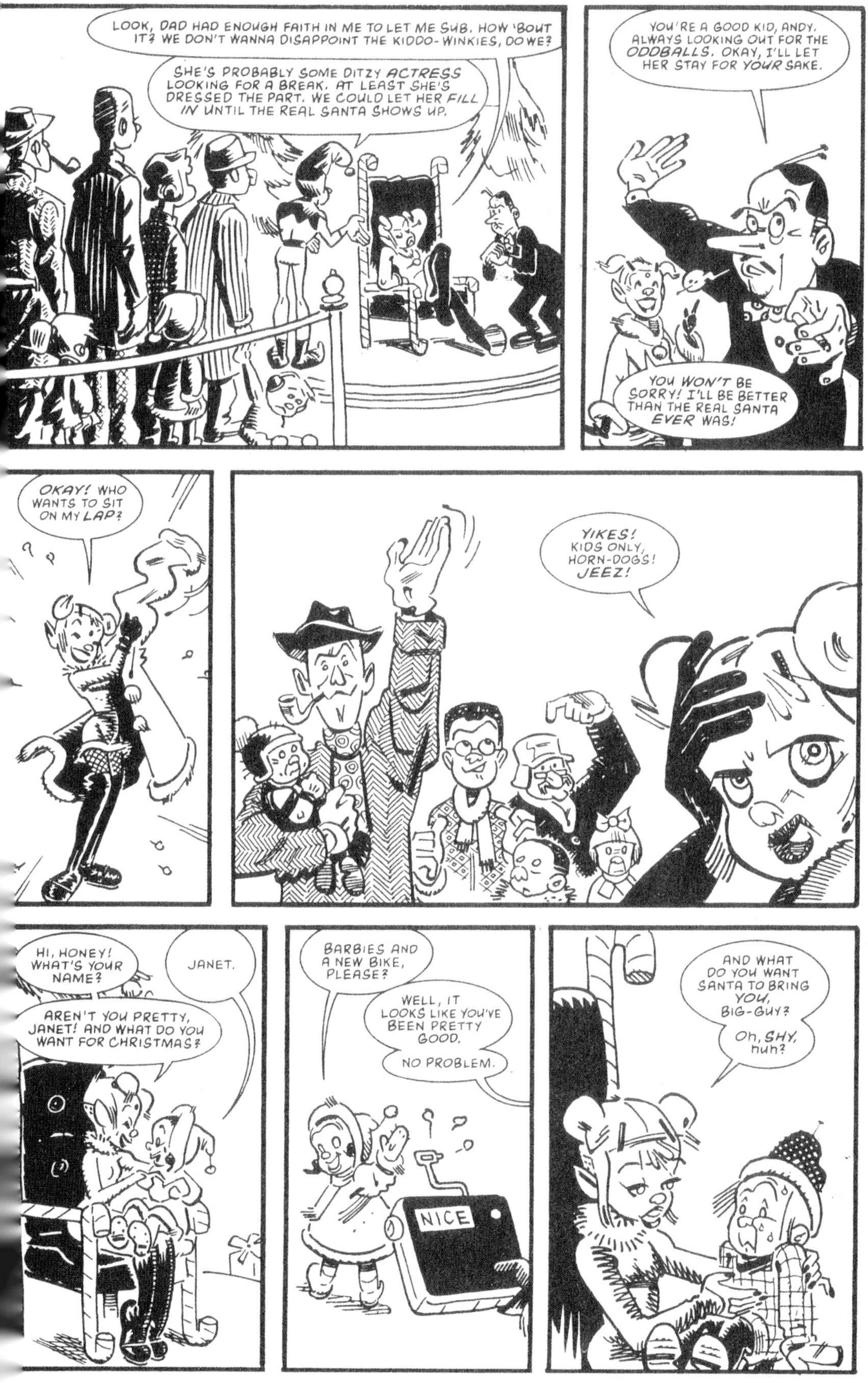
LOOK, DAD HAD ENOUGH FAITH IN ME TO LET ME SUB. HOW 'BOUT IT? WE DON'T WANNA DISAPPOINT THE KIDDO-WINKIES, DO WE?
SHE'S PROBABLY SOME DITZY ACTRESS LOOKING FOR A BREAK. AT LEAST SHE'S DRESSED THE PART. WE COULD LET HER FILL IN UNTIL THE REAL SANTA SHOWS UP.
YOU'RE A GOOD KID, ANDY. ALWAYS LOOKING OUT FOR THE ODDBALLS. OKAY, I'LL LET HER STAY FOR YOUR SAKE.
YOU WON'T BE SORRY! I'LL BE BETTER THAN THE REAL SANTA EVER WAS!
OKAY! WHO WANTS TO SIT ON MY LAP?
YIKES! KIDS ONLY, HORN-DOGS! JEEZ!
HI, HONEY! WHAT'S YOUR NAME?
JANET.
AREN'T YOU PRETTY, JANET! AND WHAT DO YOU WANT FOR CHRISTMAS?
BARBIES AND A NEW BIKE, PLEASE?
WELL, IT LOOKS LIKE YOU'VE BEEN PRETTY GOOD.
NO PROBLEM.
NICE
AND WHAT DO YOU WANT SANTA TO BRING YOU, BIG-GUY?
Oh, SHY, huh?

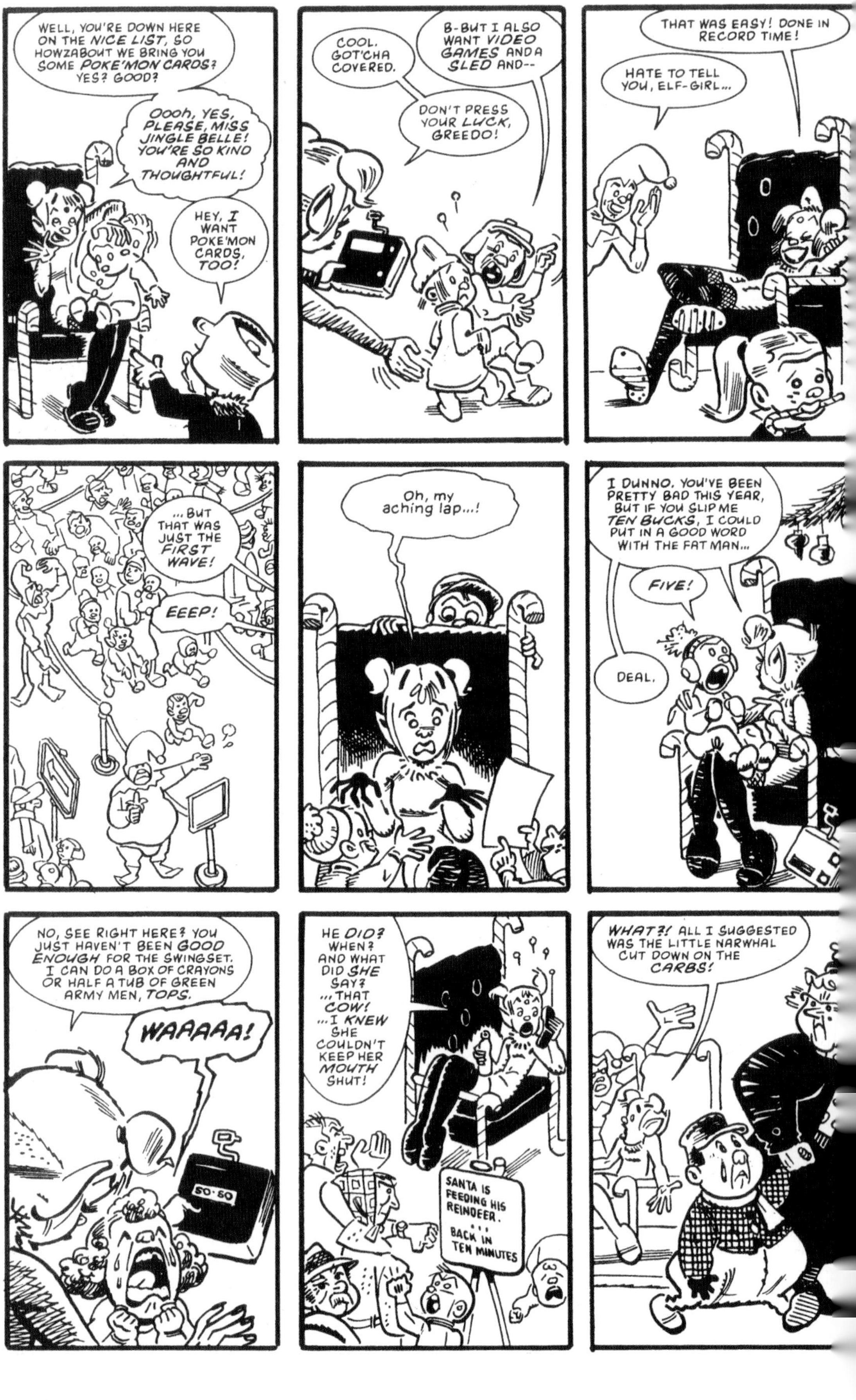
WELL, YOU'RE DOWN HERE ON THE NICE LIST, SO HOWZABOUT WE BRING YOU SOME POKE'MON CARDS? YES? GOOD?
Oooh, YES, PLEASE, MISS JINGLE BELLE! YOU'RE SO KIND AND THOUGHTFUL!
HEY, I WANT POKE'MON CARDS, TOO!
COOL. GOT'CHA COVERED.
B-BUT I ALSO WANT VIDEO GAMES AND A SLED AND--
DON'T PRESS YOUR LUCK, GREEDO!
THAT WAS EASY! DONE IN RECORD TIME!
HATE TO TELL YOU, ELF-GIRL...
...BUT THAT WAS JUST THE FIRST WAVE!
EEEP!
Oh, my aching lap...!
I DUNNO. YOU'VE BEEN PRETTY BAD THIS YEAR, BUT IF YOU SLIP ME TEN BUCKS, I COULD PUT IN A GOOD WORD WITH THE FAT MAN...
FIVE!
DEAL.
NO, SEE RIGHT HERE? YOU JUST HAVEN'T BEEN GOOD ENOUGH FOR THE SWINGSET. I CAN DO A BOX OF CRAYONS OR HALF A TUB OF GREEN ARMY MEN, TOPS.
WAAAAA!
50·50
HE DID? WHEN? AND WHAT DID SHE SAY? ...THAT COW! ...I KNEW SHE COULDN'T KEEP HER MOUTH SHUT!
SANTA IS FEEDING HIS REINDEER. ... BACK IN TEN MINUTES
WHAT?! ALL I SUGGESTED WAS THE LITTLE NARWHAL CUT DOWN ON THE CARBS!

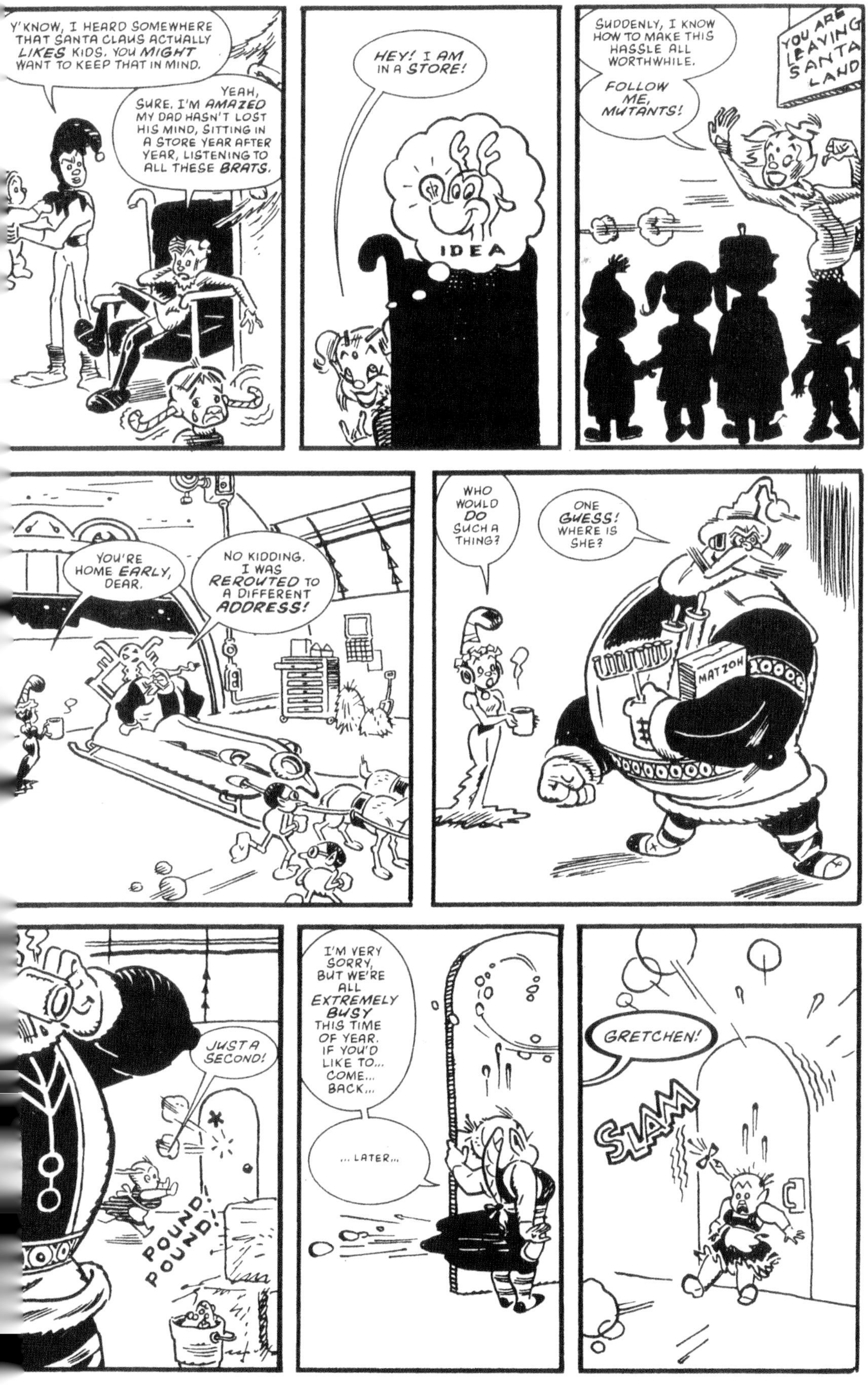
Y'KNOW, I HEARD SOMEWHERE THAT SANTA CLAUS ACTUALLY LIKES KIDS. YOU MIGHT WANT TO KEEP THAT IN MIND.
YEAH, SURE. I'M AMAZED MY DAD HASN'T LOST HIS MIND, SITTING IN A STORE YEAR AFTER YEAR, LISTENING TO ALL THESE BRATS.
HEY! I AM IN A STORE!
IDEA
SUDDENLY, I KNOW HOW TO MAKE THIS HASSLE ALL WORTHWHILE.
FOLLOW ME, MUTANTS!
YOU ARE LEAVING SANTA LAND
YOU'RE HOME EARLY, DEAR.
NO KIDDING. I WAS REROUTED TO A DIFFERENT ADDRESS!
WHO WOULD DO SUCH A THING?
ONE GUESS! WHERE IS SHE?
MATZOH
JUST A SECOND!
POUND! POUND!
I'M VERY SORRY, BUT WE'RE ALL EXTREMELY BUSY THIS TIME OF YEAR. IF YOU'D LIKE TO... COME... BACK...
...LATER...
GRETCHEN!
SLAM

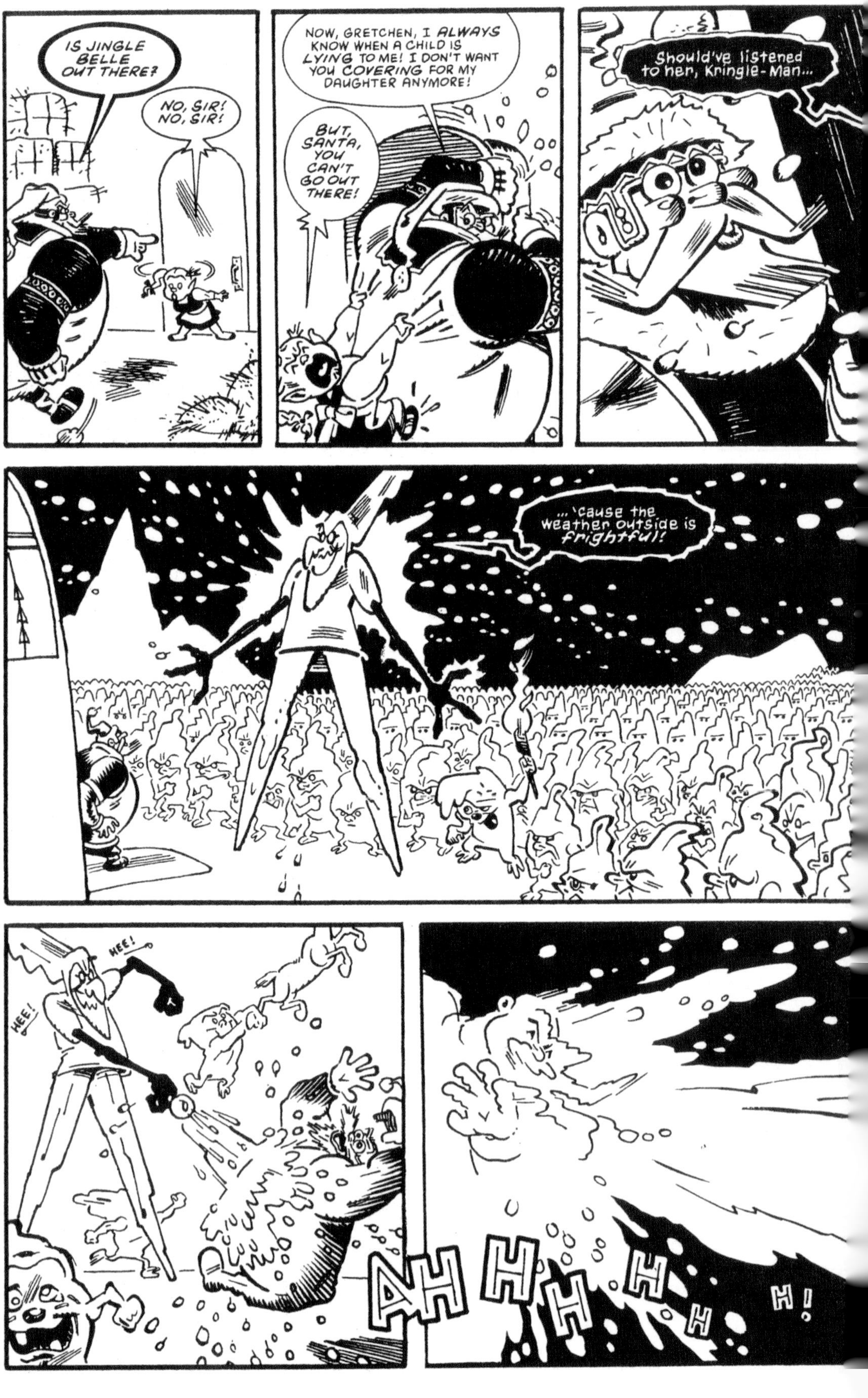
IS JINGLE BELLE OUT THERE?
NO, SIR! NO, SIR!
NOW, GRETCHEN, I ALWAYS KNOW WHEN A CHILD IS LYING TO ME! I DON'T WANT YOU COVERING FOR MY DAUGHTER ANYMORE!
BUT, SANTA, YOU CAN'T GO OUT THERE!
Should've listened to her, Kringle-Man...
...'cause the weather outside is frightful!
HEE!
HEE!
AHHHHHHH!

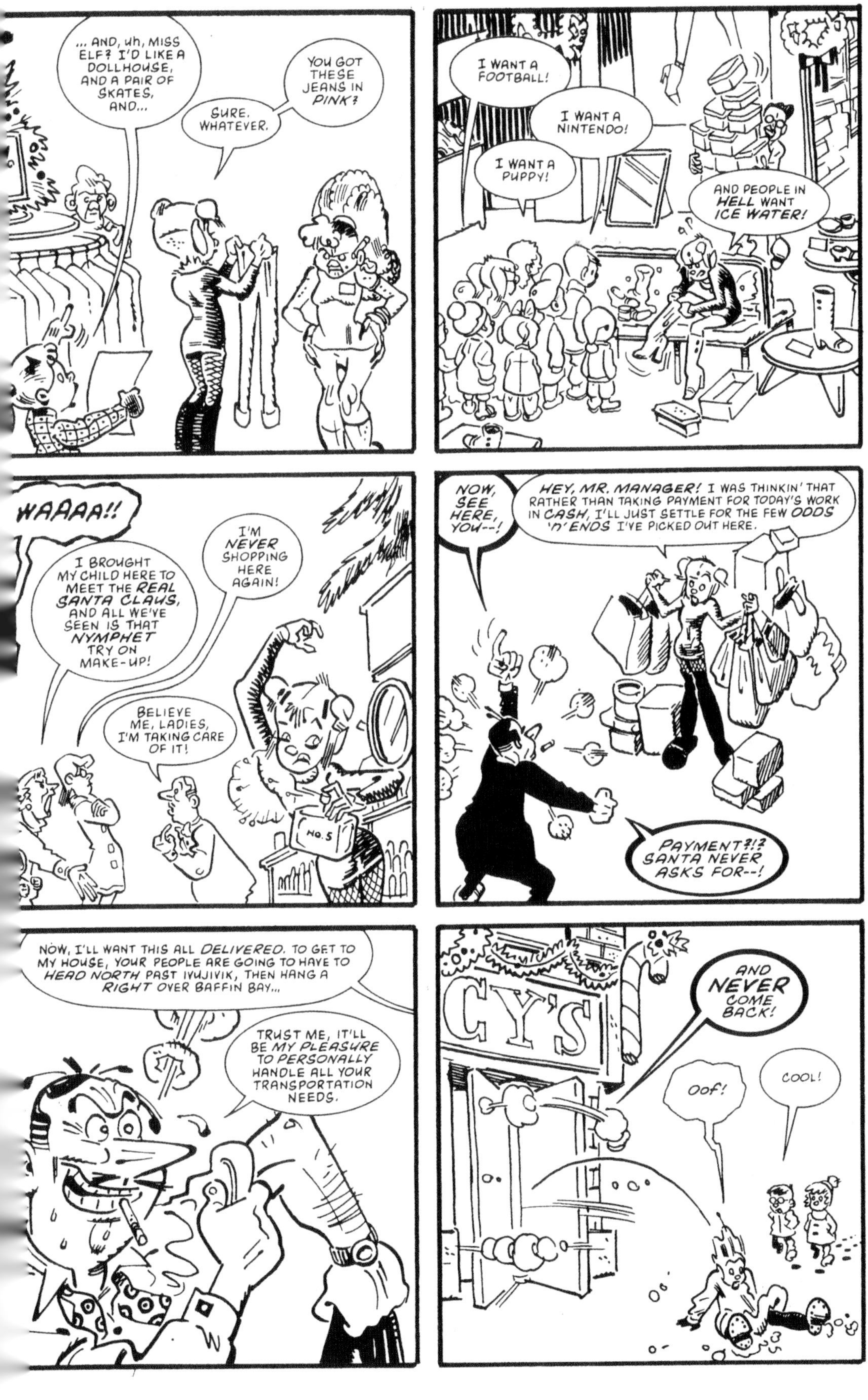
... AND, uh, MISS ELF? I'D LIKE A DOLLHOUSE, AND A PAIR OF SKATES, AND...
SURE. WHATEVER.
YOU GOT THESE JEANS IN PINK?
I WANT A FOOTBALL!
I WANT A NINTENDO!
I WANT A PUPPY!
AND PEOPLE IN HELL WANT ICE WATER!
WAAAAA!!
I BROUGHT MY CHILD HERE TO MEET THE REAL SANTA CLAUS, AND ALL WE'VE SEEN IS THAT NYMPHET TRY ON MAKE-UP!
I'M NEVER SHOPPING HERE AGAIN!
BELIEVE ME, LADIES, I'M TAKING CARE OF IT!
NO. 5
NOW, SEE HERE, YOU--!
HEY, MR. MANAGER! I WAS THINKIN' THAT RATHER THAN TAKING PAYMENT FOR TODAY'S WORK IN CASH, I'LL JUST SETTLE FOR THE FEW ODDS 'N' ENDS I'VE PICKED OUT HERE.
PAYMENT?!? SANTA NEVER ASKS FOR--!
NOW, I'LL WANT THIS ALL DELIVERED. TO GET TO MY HOUSE, YOUR PEOPLE ARE GOING TO HAVE TO HEAD NORTH PAST IVUJIVIK, THEN HANG A RIGHT OVER BAFFIN BAY...
TRUST ME, IT'LL BE MY PLEASURE TO PERSONALLY HANDLE ALL YOUR TRANSPORTATION NEEDS.
CY'S
AND NEVER COME BACK!
Oof!
COOL!

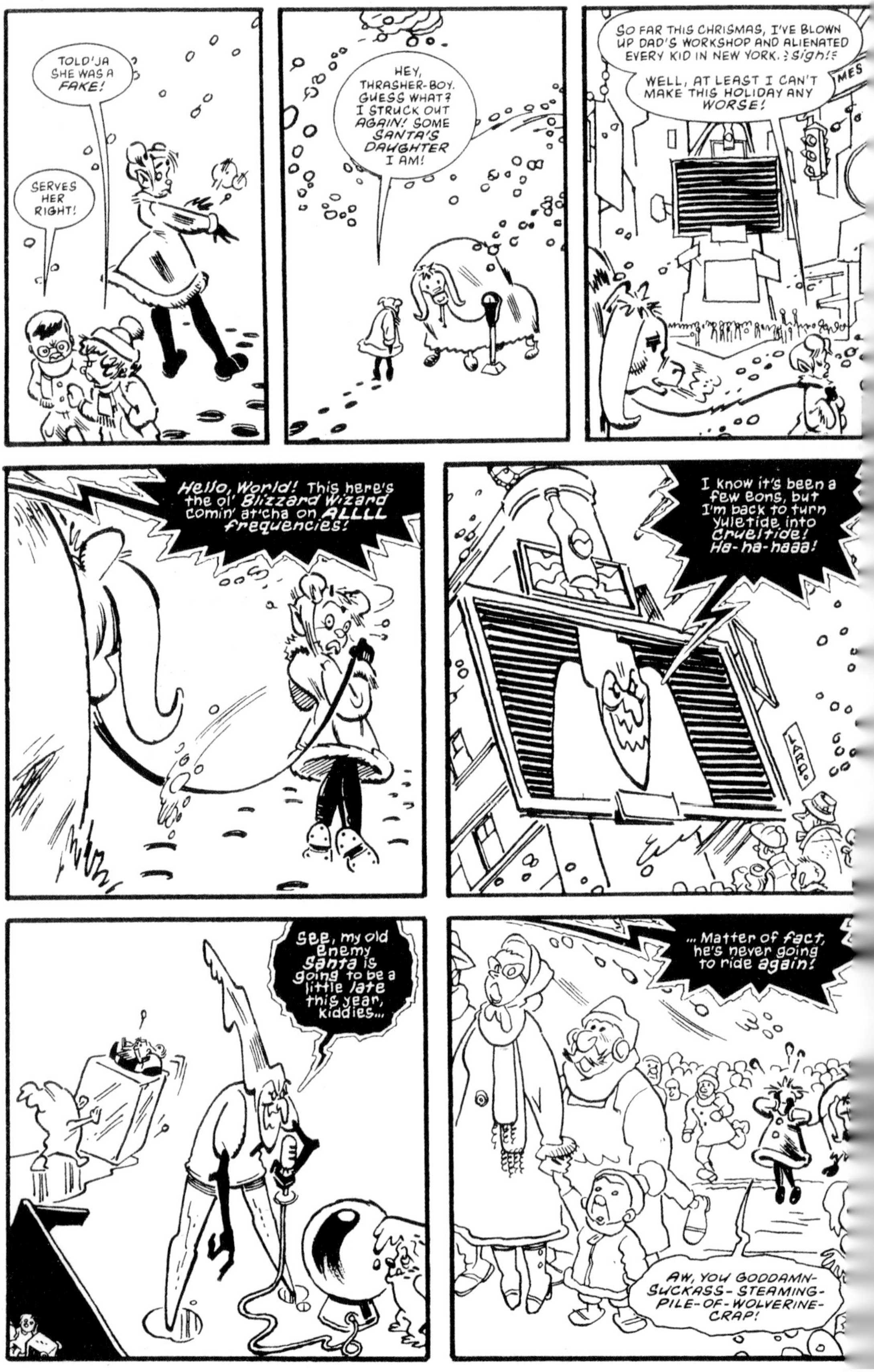
TOLD'JA SHE WAS A FAKE!
SERVES HER RIGHT!
HEY, THRASHER-BOY. GUESS WHAT? I STRUCK OUT AGAIN! SOME SANTA'S DAUGHTER I AM!
SO FAR THIS CHRISMAS, I'VE BLOWN UP DAD'S WORKSHOP AND ALIENATED EVERY KID IN NEW YORK. *SIGH!*
WELL, AT LEAST I CAN'T MAKE THIS HOLIDAY ANY WORSE!
Hello, World! This here's the ol' Blizzard Wizard comin' at'cha on ALLLL frequencies!
I know it's been a few eons, but I'm back to turn yuletide into Crueltide! Ha-ha-haaa!
See, my old enemy Santa is going to be a little late this year, kiddies...
... Matter of fact, he's never going to ride again!
AW, YOU GODDAMN-SUCKASS-STEAMING-PILE-OF-WOLVERINE-CRAP!

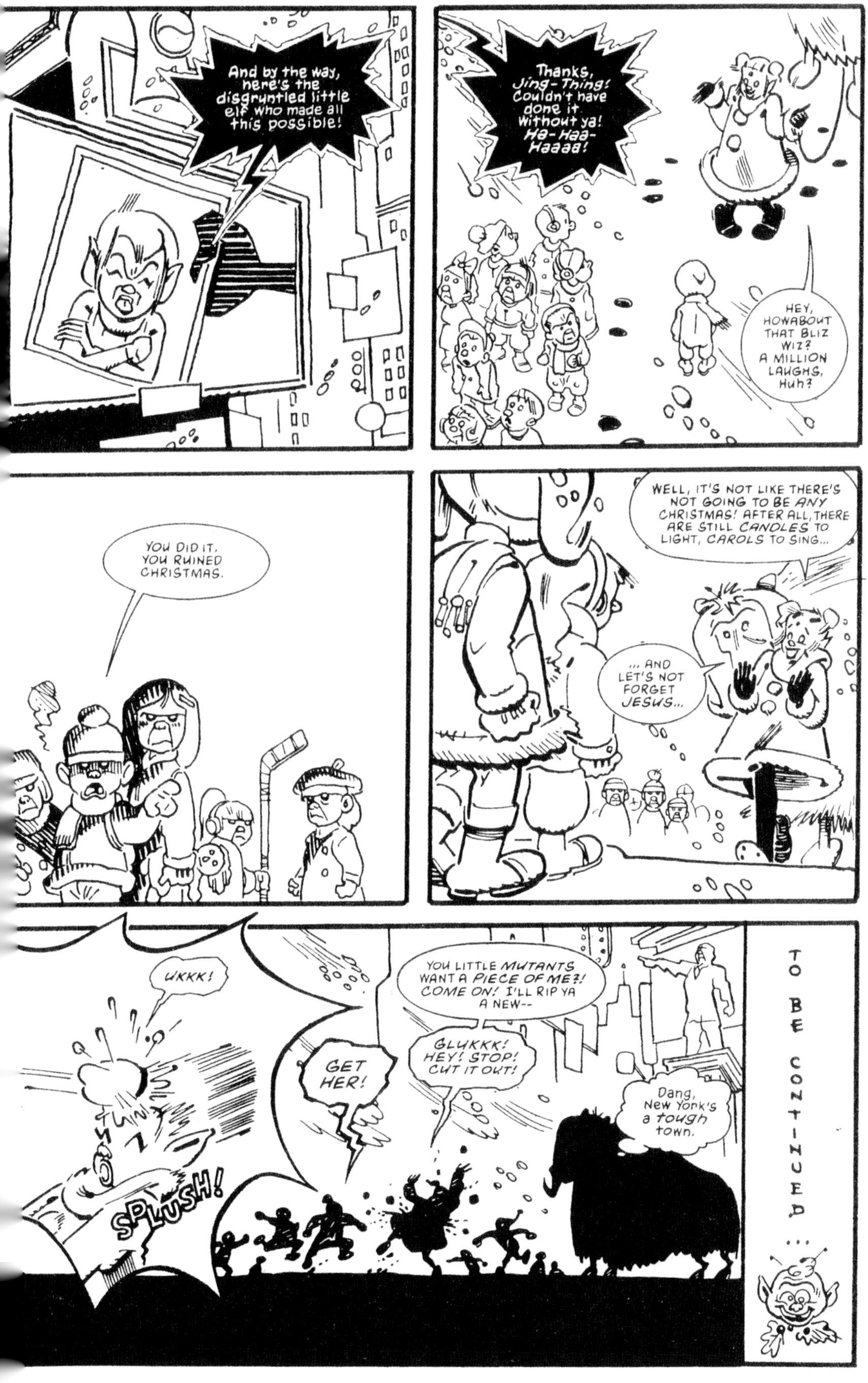

And by the way, here's the disgruntled little elf who made all this possible!
Thanks, Jing-Thing! Couldn't have done it without ya! Ha-Haa-Haaaa!
HEY, HOWABOUT THAT BLIZ WIZ? A MILLION LAUGHS, Huh?
YOU DID IT. YOU RUINED CHRISTMAS.
WELL, IT'S NOT LIKE THERE'S NOT GOING TO BE ANY CHRISTMAS! AFTER ALL, THERE ARE STILL CANDLES TO LIGHT, CAROLS TO SING...
... AND LET'S NOT FORGET JESUS...
UKKK!
THWOK
SPLUSH!
GET HER!
YOU LITTLE MUTANTS WANT A PIECE OF ME?! COME ON! I'LL RIP YA A NEW--
GLUKKK! HEY! STOP! CUT IT OUT!
Dang, New York's a tough town.
TO BE CONTINUED...

Santa's Little Hellion

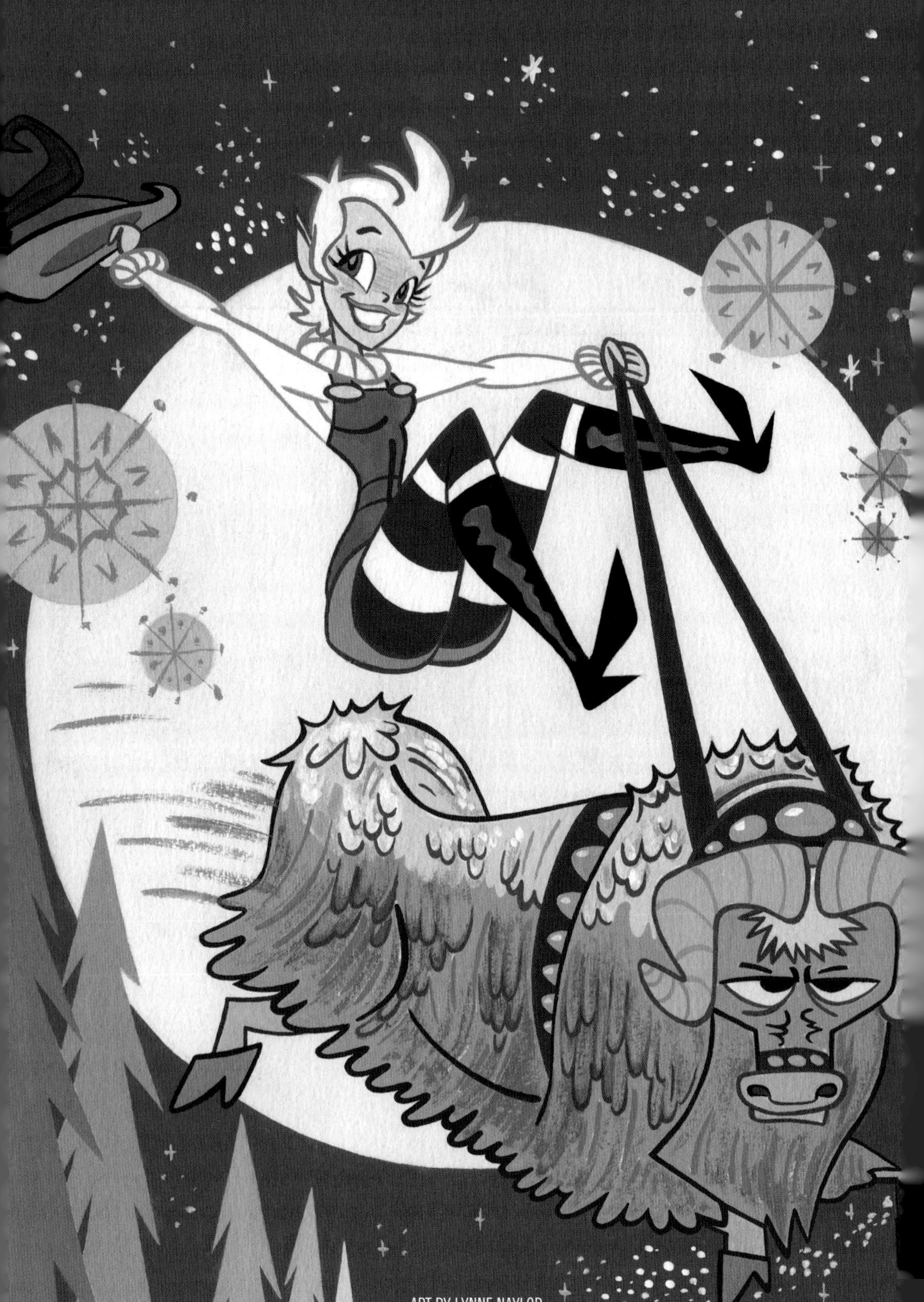

ART BY LYNNE NAYLOR

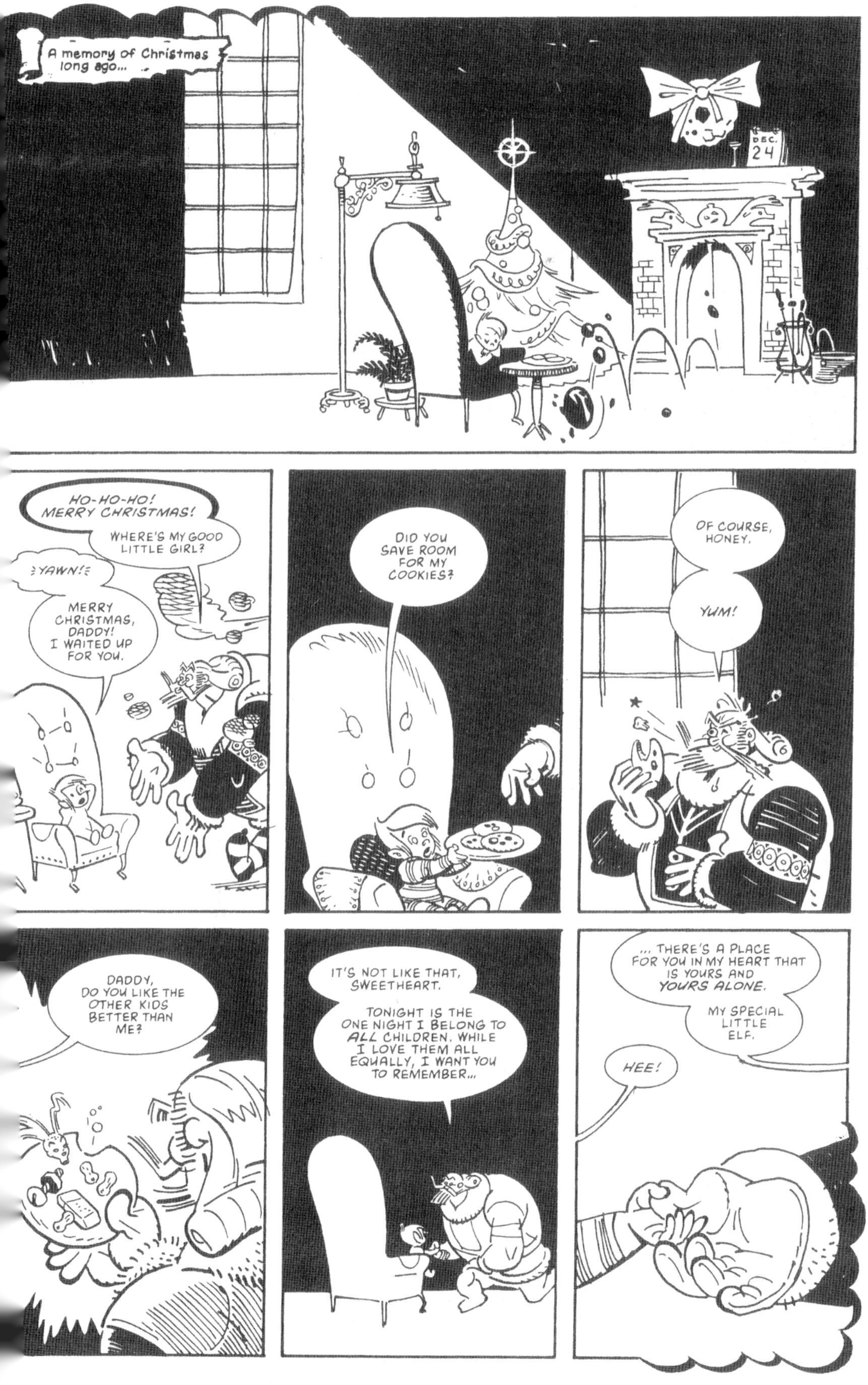
A memory of Christmas long ago...
DEC. 24
HO-HO-HO! MERRY CHRISTMAS!
WHERE'S MY GOOD LITTLE GIRL?
YAWN!
MERRY CHRISTMAS, DADDY! I WAITED UP FOR YOU.
DID YOU SAVE ROOM FOR MY COOKIES?
OF COURSE, HONEY.
YUM!
DADDY, DO YOU LIKE THE OTHER KIDS BETTER THAN ME?
IT'S NOT LIKE THAT, SWEETHEART.
TONIGHT IS THE ONE NIGHT I BELONG TO ALL CHILDREN. WHILE I LOVE THEM ALL EQUALLY, I WANT YOU TO REMEMBER...
... THERE'S A PLACE FOR YOU IN MY HEART THAT IS YOURS AND YOURS ALONE.
MY SPECIAL LITTLE ELF.
HEE!

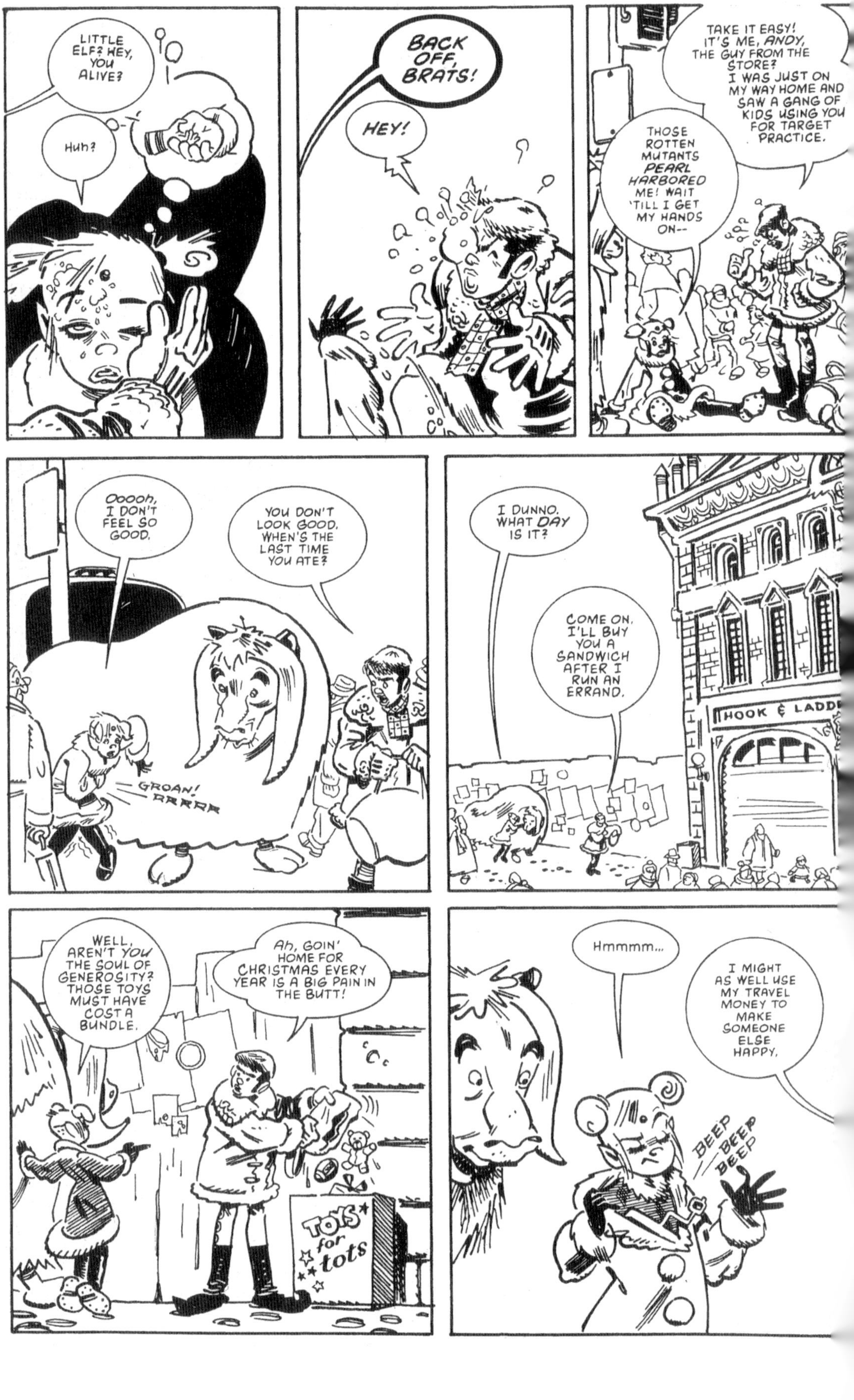
LITTLE ELF? HEY, YOU ALIVE?
Huh?
BACK OFF, BRATS!
HEY!
TAKE IT EASY! IT'S ME, ANDY, THE GUY FROM THE STORE? I WAS JUST ON MY WAY HOME AND SAW A GANG OF KIDS USING YOU FOR TARGET PRACTICE.
THOSE ROTTEN MUTANTS PEARL HARBORED ME! WAIT 'TILL I GET MY HANDS ON--
Ooooh, I DON'T FEEL SO GOOD.
YOU DON'T LOOK GOOD. WHEN'S THE LAST TIME YOU ATE?
GROAN! RRRRR
I DUNNO. WHAT DAY IS IT?
COME ON. I'LL BUY YOU A SANDWICH AFTER I RUN AN ERRAND.
HOOK & LADD
WELL, AREN'T YOU THE SOUL OF GENEROSITY? THOSE TOYS MUST HAVE COST A BUNDLE.
Ah, GOIN' HOME FOR CHRISTMAS EVERY YEAR IS A BIG PAIN IN THE BUTT!
TOYS for tots
Hmmmm...
I MIGHT AS WELL USE MY TRAVEL MONEY TO MAKE SOMEONE ELSE HAPPY.
BEEP BEEP BEEP

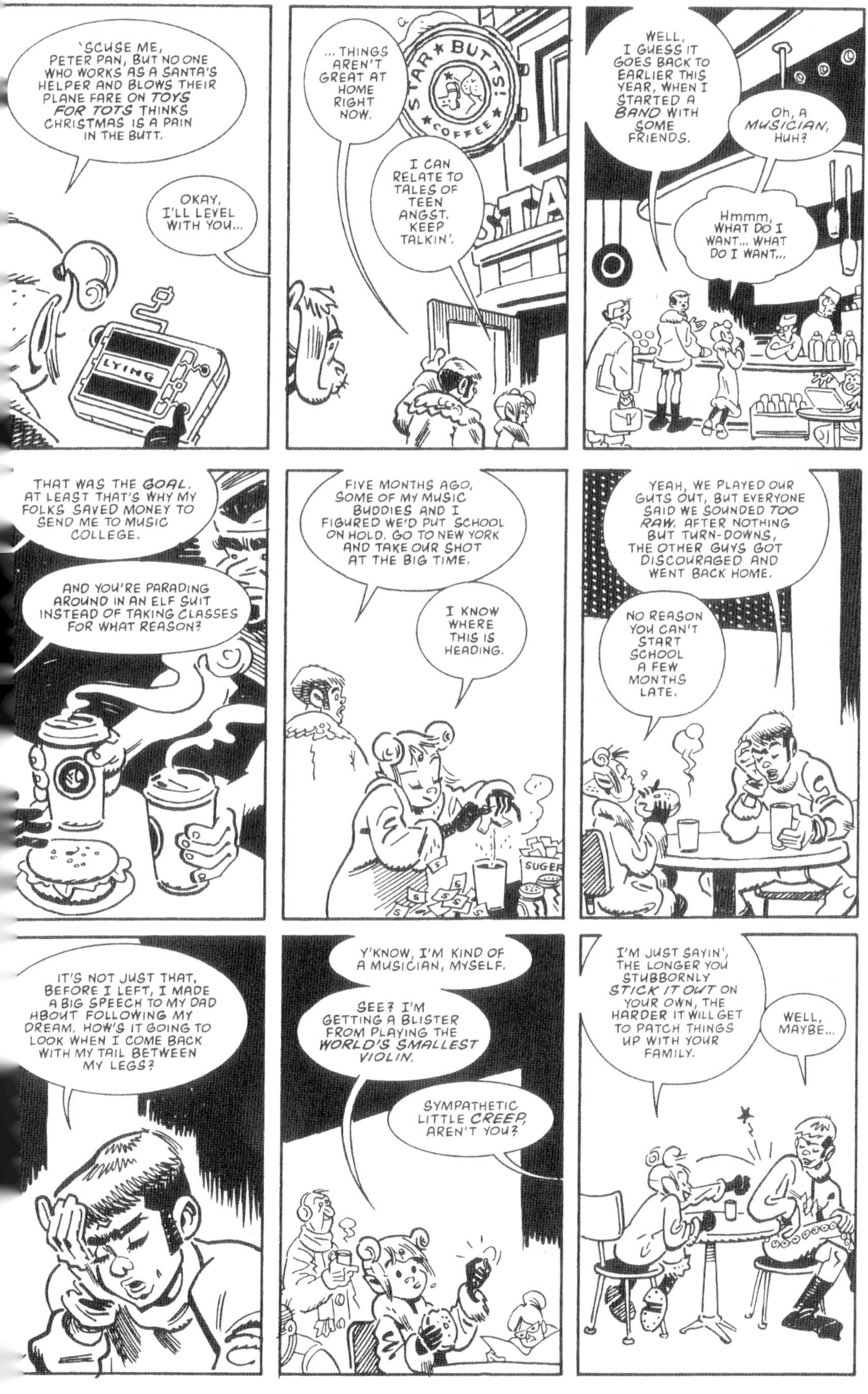
'SCUSE ME, PETER PAN, BUT NO ONE WHO WORKS AS A SANTA'S HELPER AND BLOWS THEIR PLANE FARE ON TOYS FOR TOTS THINKS CHRISTMAS IS A PAIN IN THE BUTT.
OKAY, I'LL LEVEL WITH YOU...
LYING
...THINGS AREN'T GREAT AT HOME RIGHT NOW.
STAR★BUTTS! COFFEE
I CAN RELATE TO TALES OF TEEN ANGST. KEEP TALKIN'.
WELL, I GUESS IT GOES BACK TO EARLIER THIS YEAR, WHEN I STARTED A BAND WITH SOME FRIENDS.
Oh, A MUSICIAN, HUH?
Hmmm, WHAT DO I WANT... WHAT DO I WANT...
THAT WAS THE GOAL. AT LEAST THAT'S WHY MY FOLKS SAVED MONEY TO SEND ME TO MUSIC COLLEGE.
AND YOU'RE PARADING AROUND IN AN ELF SUIT INSTEAD OF TAKING CLASSES FOR WHAT REASON?
FIVE MONTHS AGO, SOME OF MY MUSIC BUDDIES AND I FIGURED WE'D PUT SCHOOL ON HOLD, GO TO NEW YORK AND TAKE OUR SHOT AT THE BIG TIME.
I KNOW WHERE THIS IS HEADING.
SUGER
YEAH, WE PLAYED OUR GUTS OUT, BUT EVERYONE SAID WE SOUNDED TOO RAW. AFTER NOTHING BUT TURN-DOWNS, THE OTHER GUYS GOT DISCOURAGED AND WENT BACK HOME.
NO REASON YOU CAN'T START SCHOOL A FEW MONTHS LATE.
IT'S NOT JUST THAT. BEFORE I LEFT, I MADE A BIG SPEECH TO MY DAD ABOUT FOLLOWING MY DREAM. HOW'S IT GOING TO LOOK WHEN I COME BACK WITH MY TAIL BETWEEN MY LEGS?
Y'KNOW, I'M KIND OF A MUSICIAN, MYSELF.
SEE? I'M GETTING A BLISTER FROM PLAYING THE WORLD'S SMALLEST VIOLIN.
SYMPATHETIC LITTLE CREEP, AREN'T YOU?
I'M JUST SAYIN', THE LONGER YOU STUBBORNLY STICK IT OUT ON YOUR OWN, THE HARDER IT WILL GET TO PATCH THINGS UP WITH YOUR FAMILY.
WELL, MAYBE...

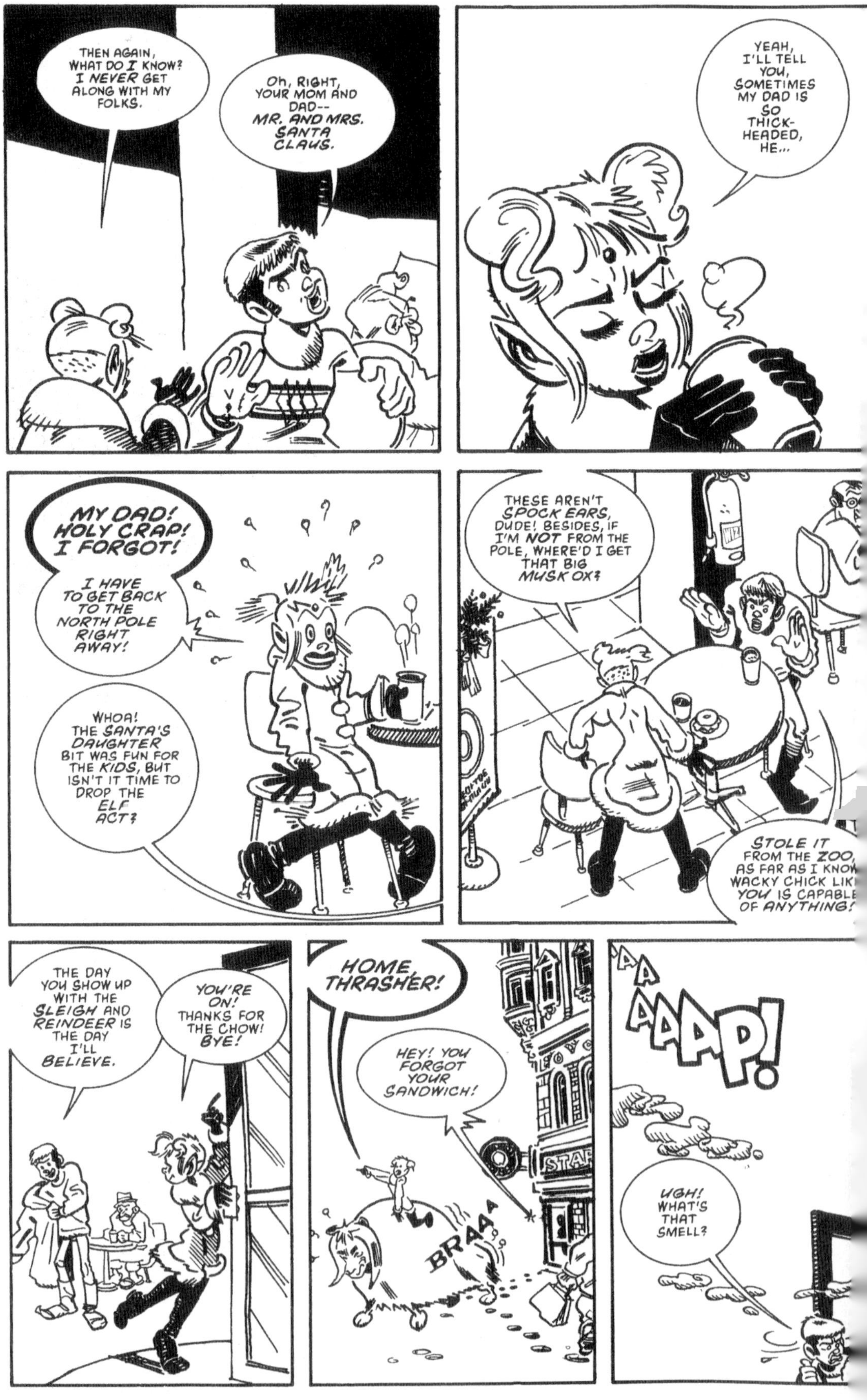
THEN AGAIN, WHAT DO I KNOW? I NEVER GET ALONG WITH MY FOLKS.
Oh, RIGHT, YOUR MOM AND DAD-- MR. AND MRS. SANTA CLAUS.
YEAH, I'LL TELL YOU, SOMETIMES MY DAD IS SO THICK-HEADED, HE...
MY DAD! HOLY CRAP! I FORGOT!
I HAVE TO GET BACK TO THE NORTH POLE RIGHT AWAY!
WHOA! THE SANTA'S DAUGHTER BIT WAS FUN FOR THE KIDS, BUT ISN'T IT TIME TO DROP THE ELF ACT?
THESE AREN'T SPOCK EARS, DUDE! BESIDES, IF I'M NOT FROM THE POLE, WHERE'D I GET THAT BIG MUSK OX?
STOLE IT FROM THE ZOO, AS FAR AS I KNOW WACKY CHICK LIKE YOU IS CAPABLE OF ANYTHING!
THE DAY YOU SHOW UP WITH THE SLEIGH AND REINDEER IS THE DAY I'LL BELIEVE.
YOU'RE ON! THANKS FOR THE CHOW! BYE!
HOME THRASHER!
HEY! YOU FORGOT YOUR SANDWICH!
BRAAA
AAAAP!
UGH! WHAT'S THAT SMELL?

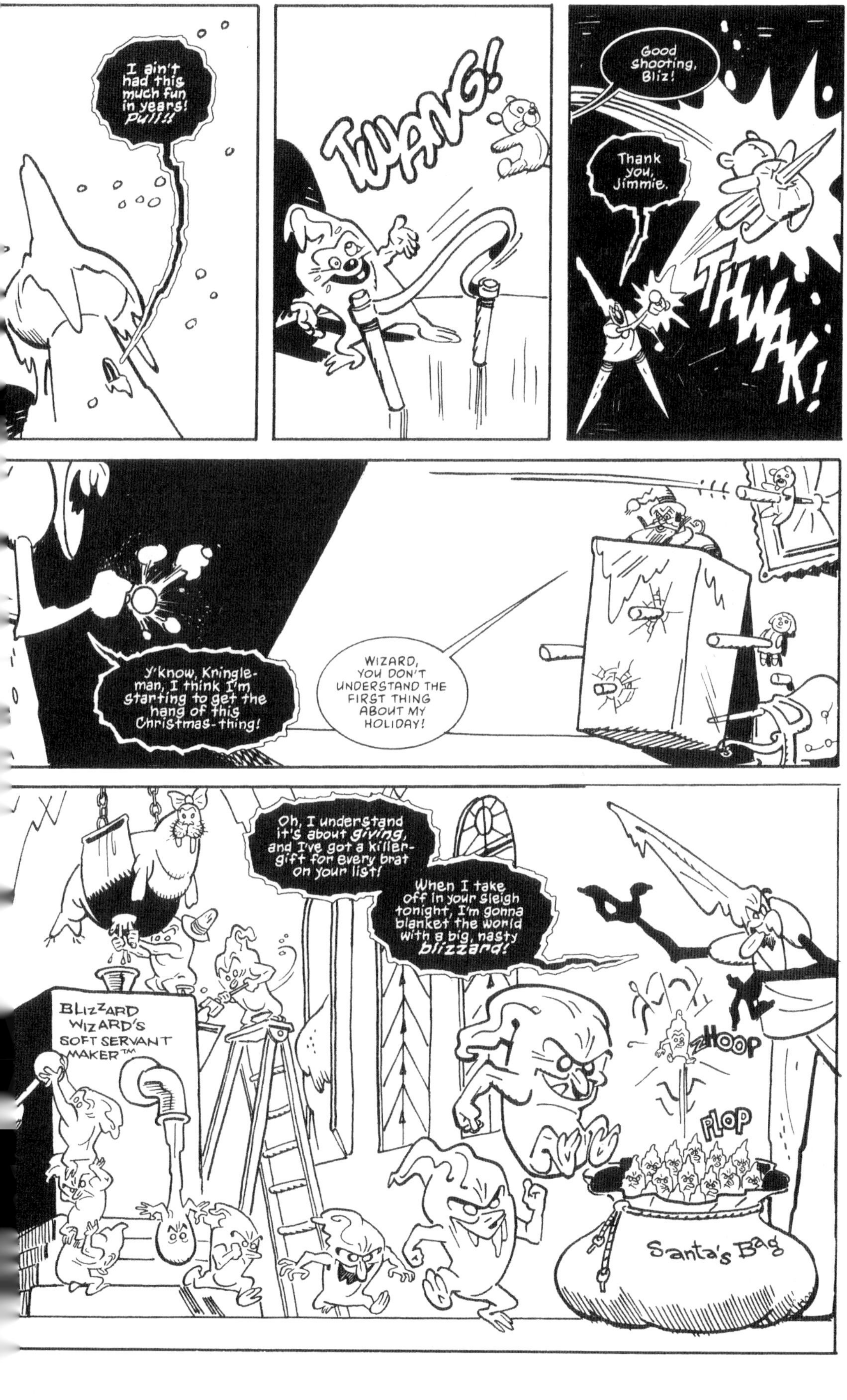
I ain't had this much fun in years! Pull!!
TWANG!
Good shooting, Bliz!
Thank you, Jimmie.
THWAK!
Y'know, Kringle-man, I think I'm starting to get the hang of this Christmas-thing!
WIZARD, YOU DON'T UNDERSTAND THE FIRST THING ABOUT MY HOLIDAY!
Oh, I understand it's about giving, and I've got a killer-gift for every brat on your list!
When I take off in your sleigh tonight, I'm gonna blanket the world with a big, nasty blizzard!
BLIZZARD WIZARD'S SOFT SERVANT MAKER™
ZHOOP
PLOP
Santa's Bag

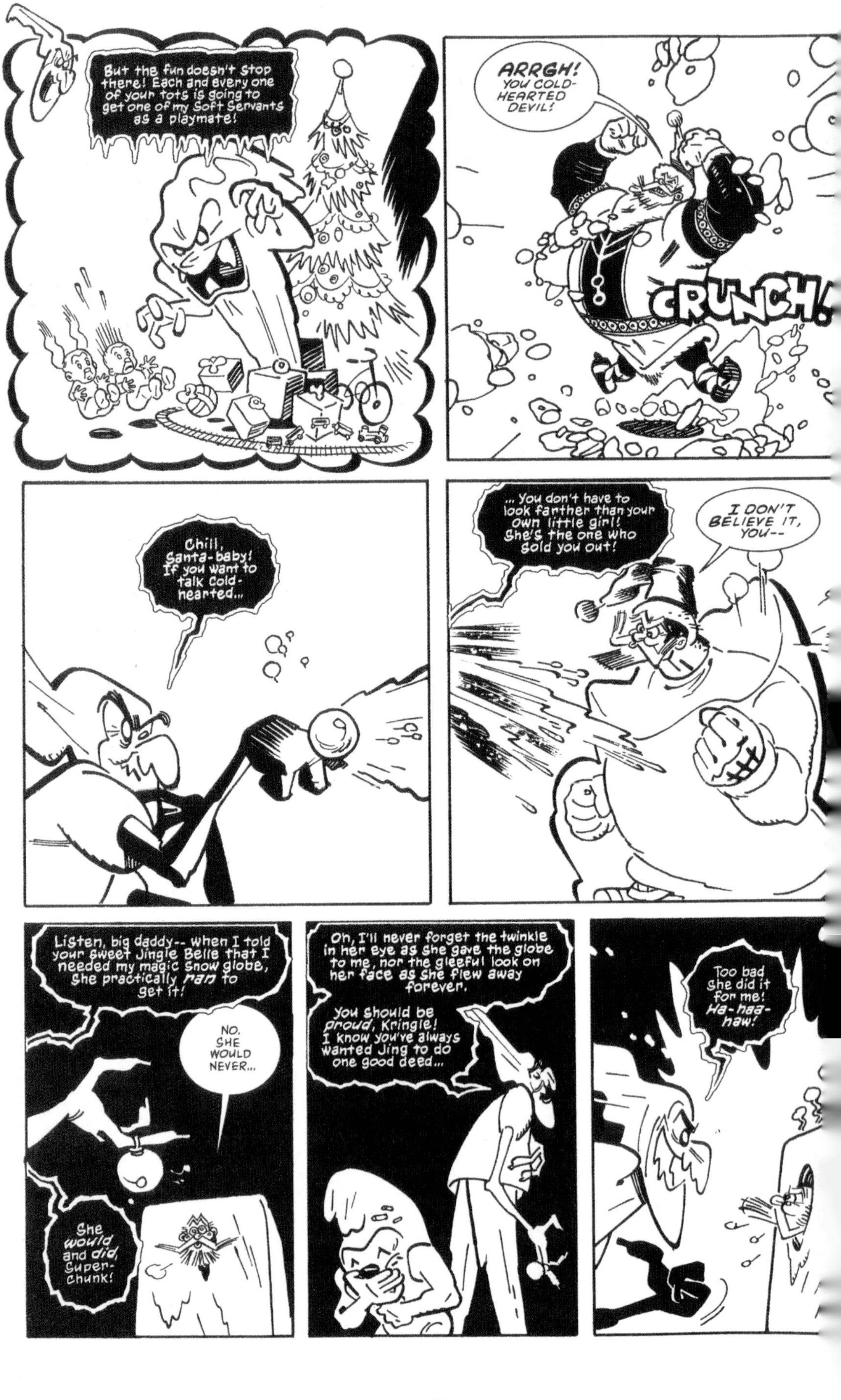
But the fun doesn't stop there! Each and every one of your tots is going to get one of my Soft Servants as a playmate!
ARRGH! YOU COLD-HEARTED DEVIL!
CRUNCH!
Chill, Santa-baby! If you want to talk cold-hearted...
...You don't have to look farther than your own little girl! She's the one who sold you out!
I DON'T BELIEVE IT, YOU--
Listen, big daddy-- when I told your sweet Jingle Belle that I needed my magic snow globe, she practically *ran* to get it!
NO. SHE WOULD NEVER...
She *would* and *did*, Super-chunk!
Oh, I'll never forget the twinkle in her eye as she gave the globe to me, nor the gleeful look on her face as she flew away forever.
You should be *proud*, Kringle! I know you've always wanted Jing to do one good deed...
Too bad she did it for me! *Ha-haa-haw!*

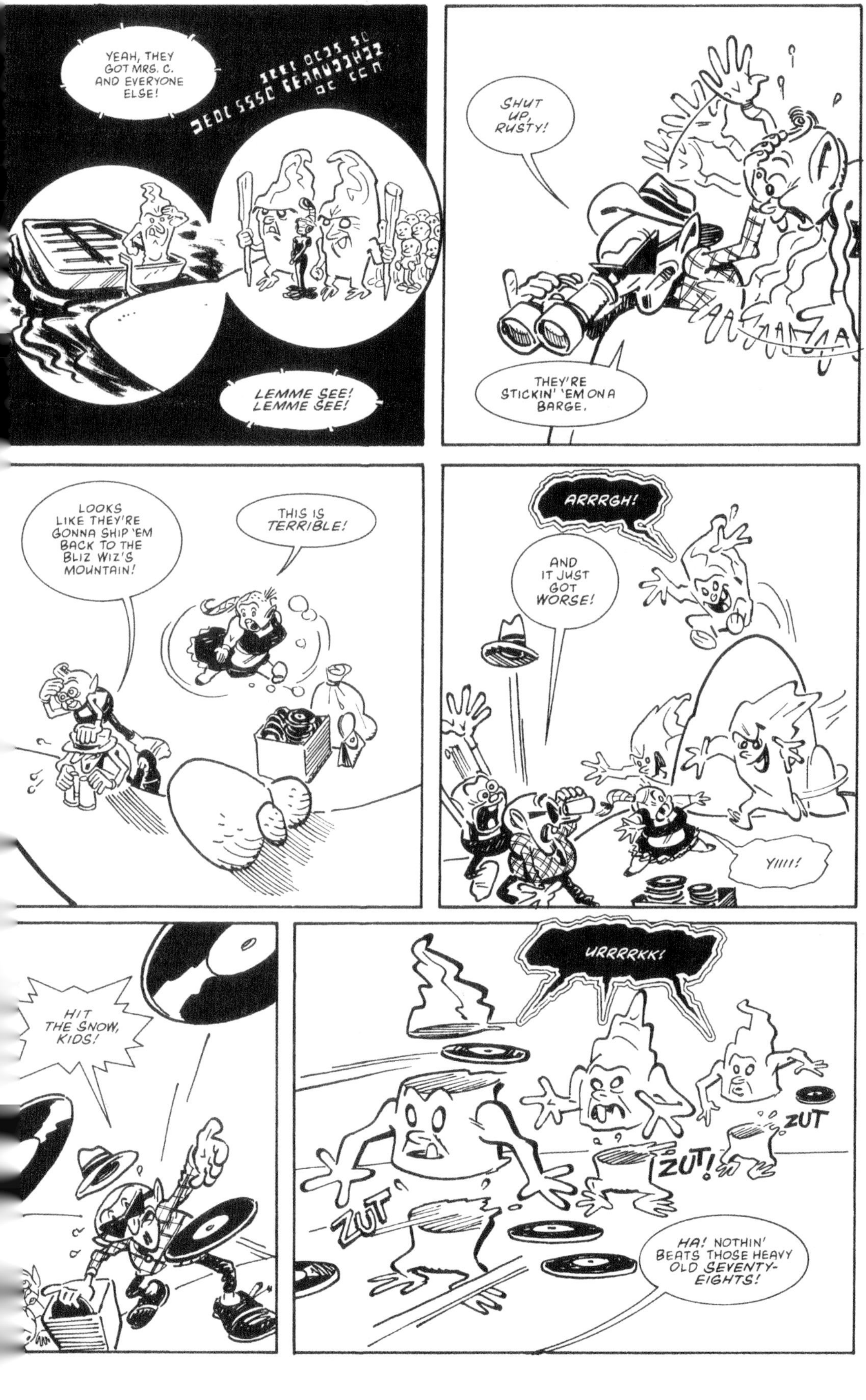
YEAH, THEY GOT MRS. C. AND EVERYONE ELSE!
LEMME SEE! LEMME SEE!
SHUT UP, RUSTY!
THEY'RE STICKIN' 'EM ON A BARGE.
LOOKS LIKE THEY'RE GONNA SHIP 'EM BACK TO THE BLIZ WIZ'S MOUNTAIN!
THIS IS TERRIBLE!
ARRRGH!
AND IT JUST GOT WORSE!
YIII!
HIT THE SNOW, KIDS!
URRRRKK!
ZUT
ZUT!
ZUT
HA! NOTHIN' BEATS THOSE HEAVY OLD SEVENTY-EIGHTS!

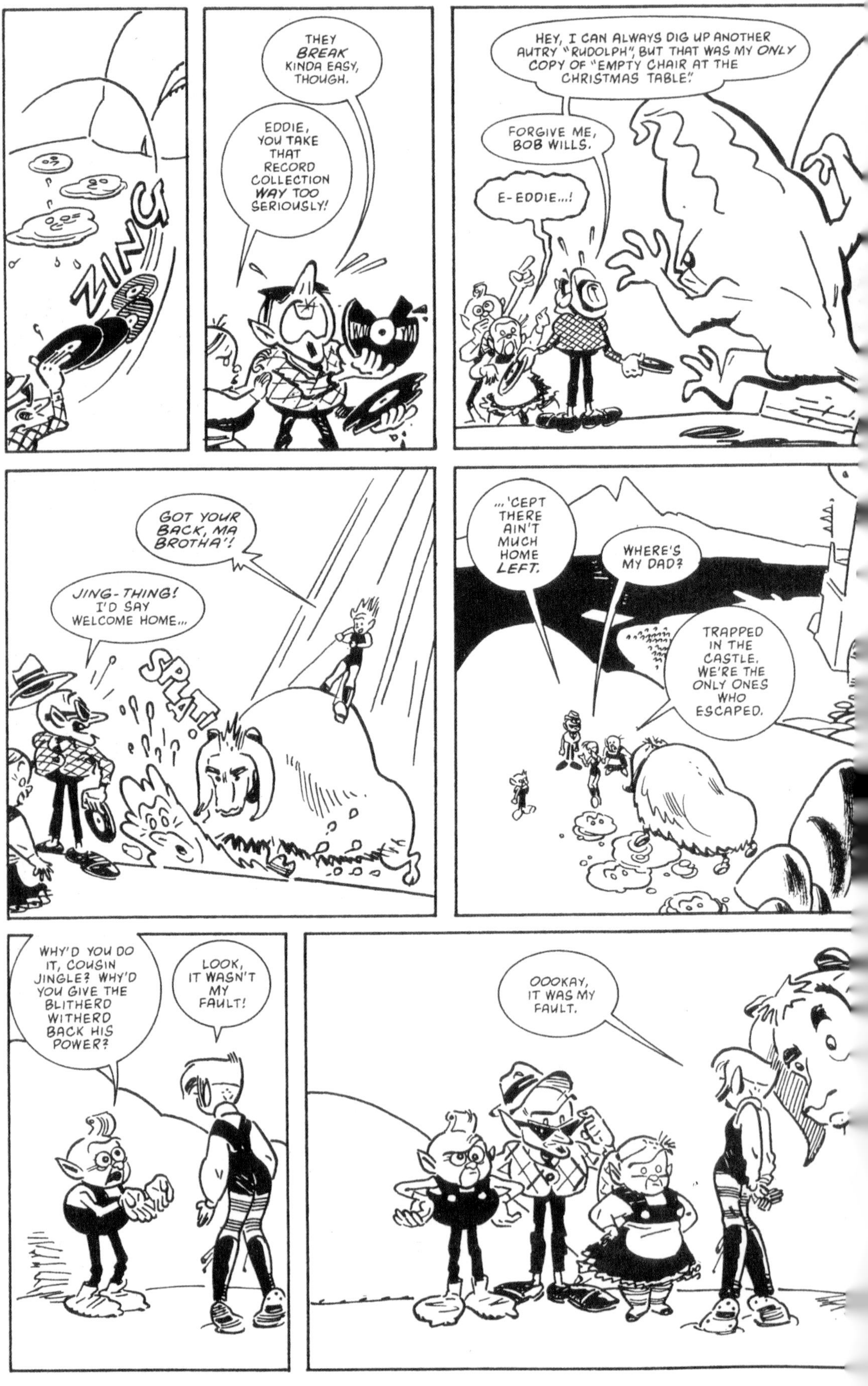
ZING
THEY BREAK KINDA EASY, THOUGH.
EDDIE, YOU TAKE THAT RECORD COLLECTION WAY TOO SERIOUSLY!
HEY, I CAN ALWAYS DIG UP ANOTHER AUTRY "RUDOLPH", BUT THAT WAS MY ONLY COPY OF "EMPTY CHAIR AT THE CHRISTMAS TABLE."
FORGIVE ME, BOB WILLS.
E-EDDIE...!
GOT YOUR BACK, MA BROTHA'!
JING-THING! I'D SAY WELCOME HOME...
SPLAT
...'CEPT THERE AIN'T MUCH HOME LEFT.
WHERE'S MY DAD?
TRAPPED IN THE CASTLE. WE'RE THE ONLY ONES WHO ESCAPED.
WHY'D YOU DO IT, COUSIN JINGLE? WHY'D YOU GIVE THE BLITHERD WITHERD BACK HIS POWER?
LOOK, IT WASN'T MY FAULT!
OOOKAY, IT WAS MY FAULT.

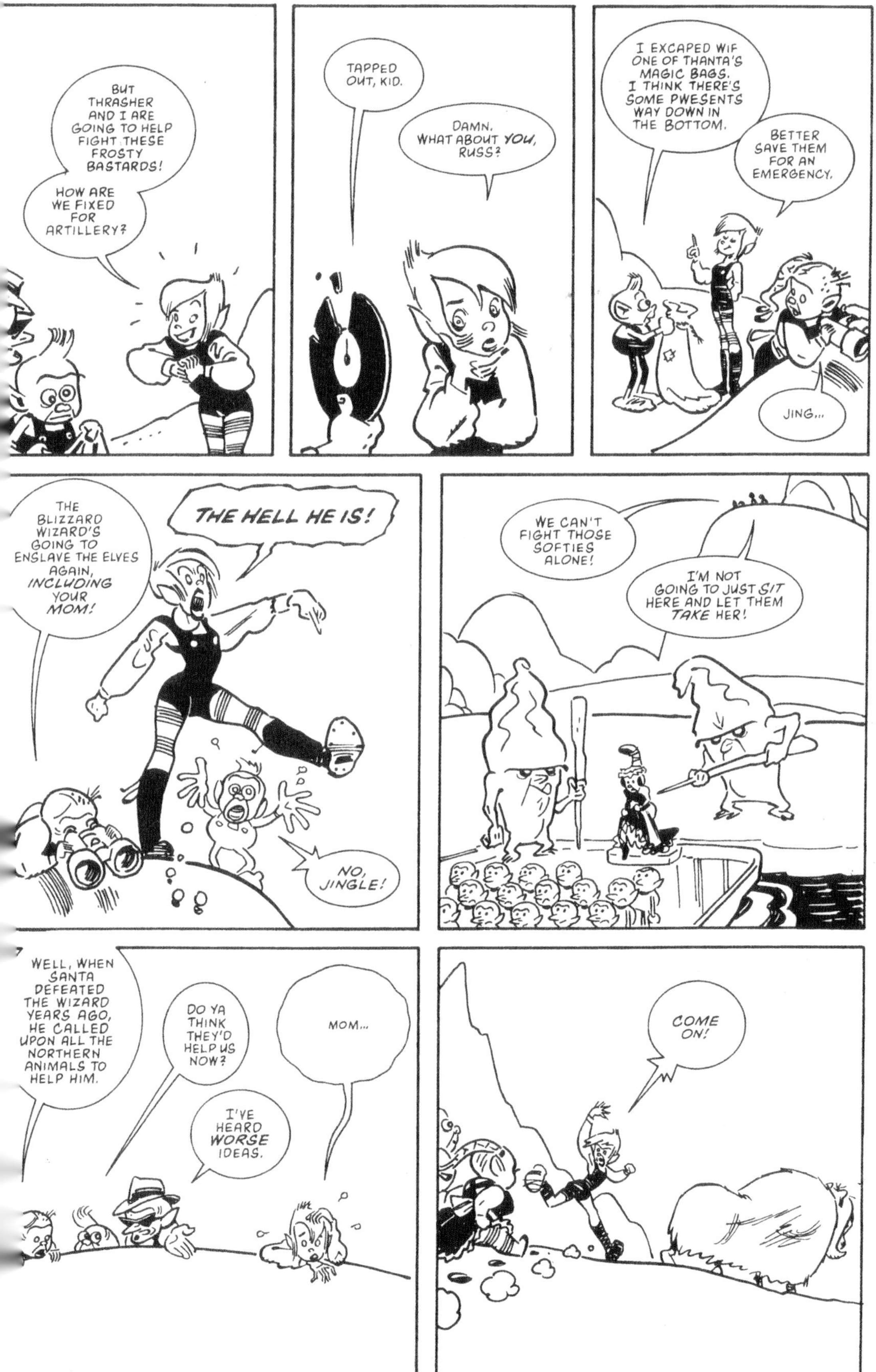
BUT THRASHER AND I ARE GOING TO HELP FIGHT THESE FROSTY BASTARDS!
HOW ARE WE FIXED FOR ARTILLERY?
TAPPED OUT, KID.
DAMN. WHAT ABOUT YOU, RUSS?
I EXCAPED WIF ONE OF THANTA'S MAGIC BAGS. I THINK THERE'S SOME PWESENTS WAY DOWN IN THE BOTTOM.
BETTER SAVE THEM FOR AN EMERGENCY.
JING...
THE BLIZZARD WIZARD'S GOING TO ENSLAVE THE ELVES AGAIN, INCLUDING YOUR MOM!
THE HELL HE IS!
NO, JINGLE!
WE CAN'T FIGHT THOSE SOFTIES ALONE!
I'M NOT GOING TO JUST SIT HERE AND LET THEM TAKE HER!
WELL, WHEN SANTA DEFEATED THE WIZARD YEARS AGO, HE CALLED UPON ALL THE NORTHERN ANIMALS TO HELP HIM.
DO YA THINK THEY'D HELP US NOW?
MOM...
I'VE HEARD WORSE IDEAS.
COME ON!

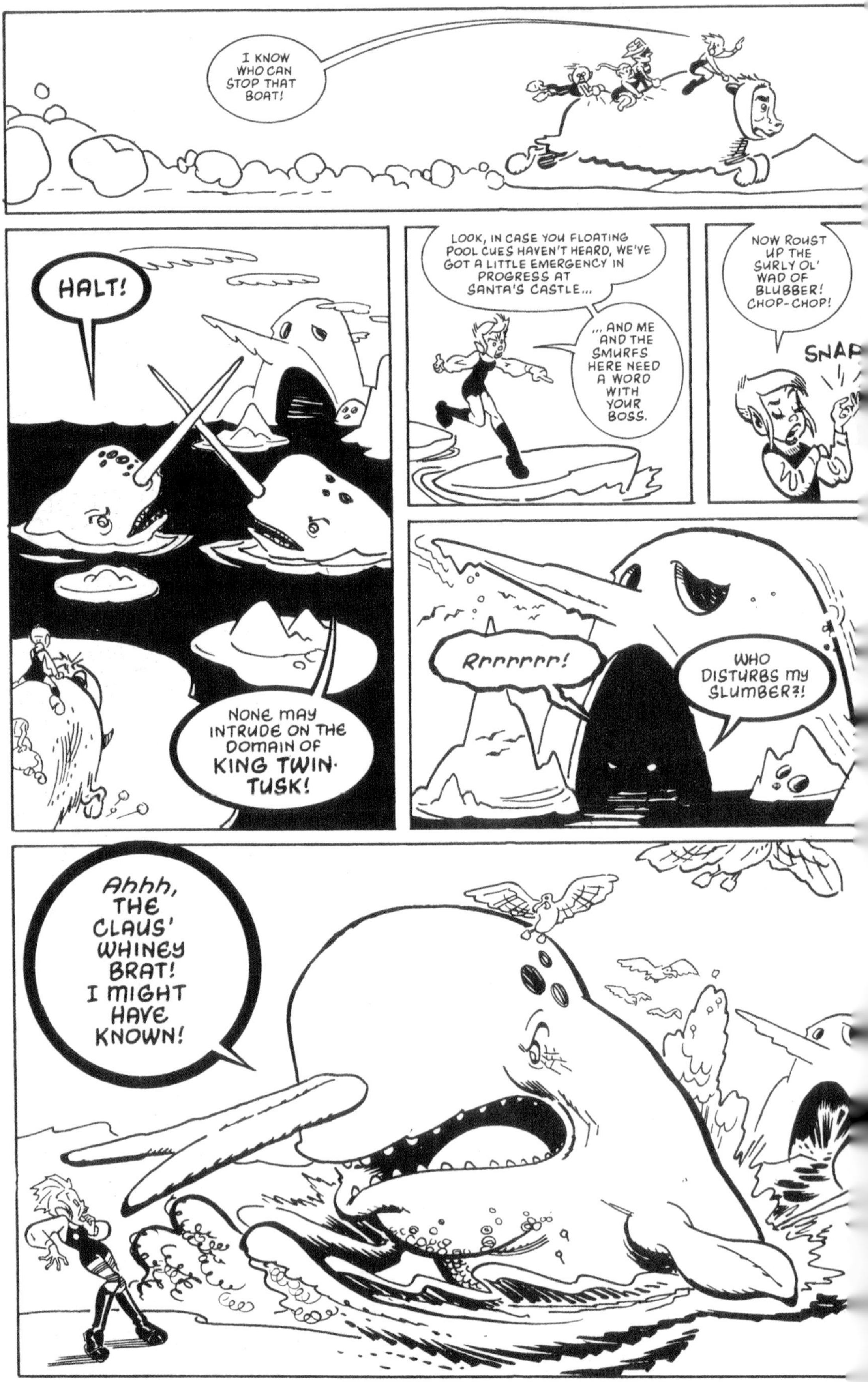

I KNOW WHO CAN STOP THAT BOAT!
HALT!
NONE MAY INTRUDE ON THE DOMAIN OF KING TWIN-TUSK!
LOOK, IN CASE YOU FLOATING POOL CUES HAVEN'T HEARD, WE'VE GOT A LITTLE EMERGENCY IN PROGRESS AT SANTA'S CASTLE...
...AND ME AND THE SMURFS HERE NEED A WORD WITH YOUR BOSS.
NOW ROUST UP THE SURLY OL' WAD OF BLUBBER! CHOP-CHOP!
SNAP
Rrrrrrr!
WHO DISTURBS MY SLUMBER?!
Ahhh, THE CLAUS' WHINEY BRAT! I MIGHT HAVE KNOWN!

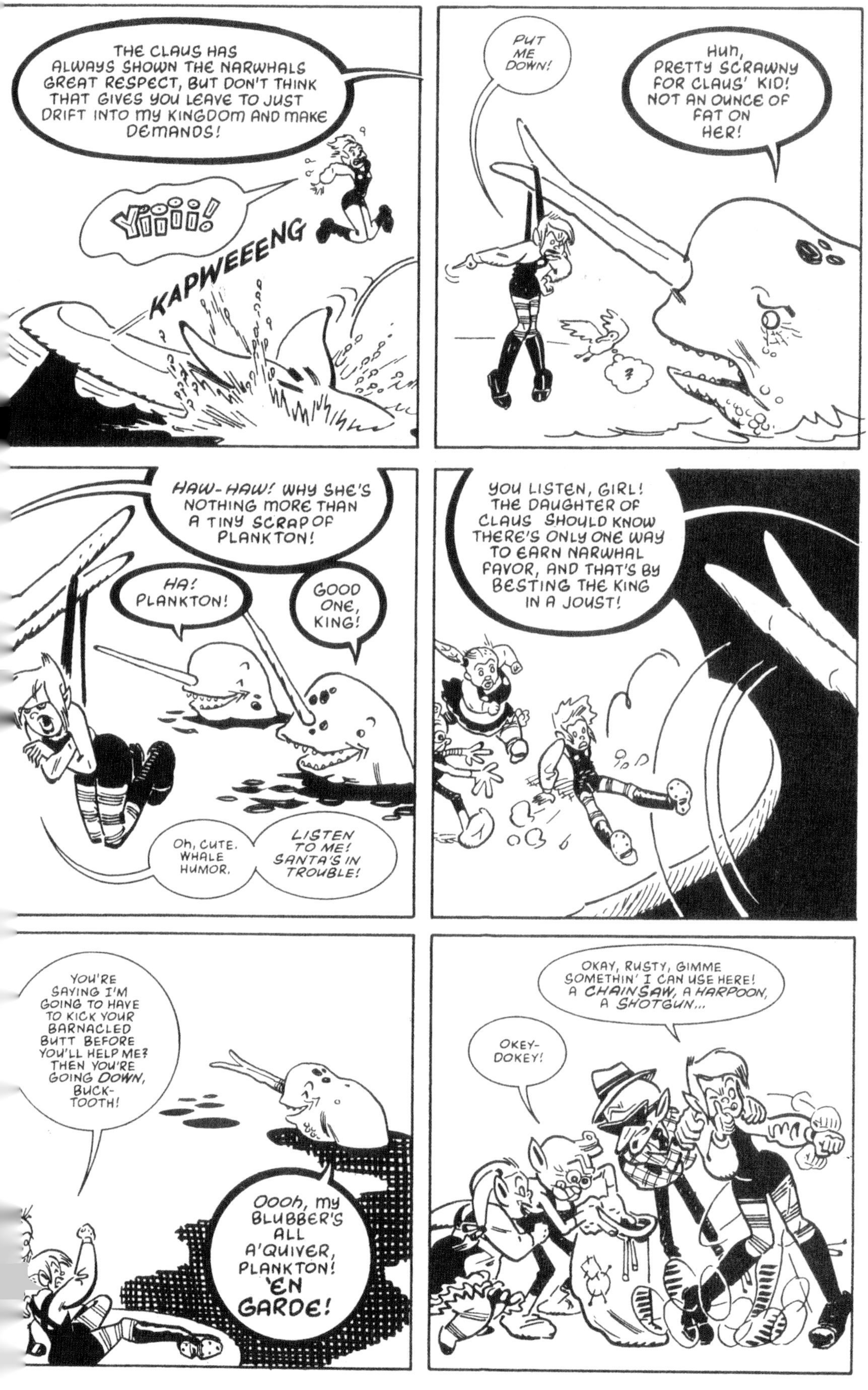
THE CLAUS HAS ALWAYS SHOWN THE NARWHALS GREAT RESPECT, BUT DON'T THINK THAT GIVES YOU LEAVE TO JUST DRIFT INTO MY KINGDOM AND MAKE DEMANDS!
YIIIII!
KAPWEEENG
PUT ME DOWN!
HUH, PRETTY SCRAWNY FOR CLAUS' KID! NOT AN OUNCE OF FAT ON HER!
HAW-HAW! WHY SHE'S NOTHING MORE THAN A TINY SCRAP OF PLANKTON!
HA! PLANKTON!
GOOD ONE, KING!
Oh, CUTE. WHALE HUMOR.
LISTEN TO ME! SANTA'S IN TROUBLE!
YOU LISTEN, GIRL! THE DAUGHTER OF CLAUS SHOULD KNOW THERE'S ONLY ONE WAY TO EARN NARWHAL FAVOR, AND THAT'S BY BESTING THE KING IN A JOUST!
YOU'RE SAYING I'M GOING TO HAVE TO KICK YOUR BARNACLED BUTT BEFORE YOU'LL HELP ME? THEN YOU'RE GOING DOWN, BUCK-TOOTH!
Oooh, MY BLUBBER'S ALL A'QUIVER, PLANKTON! 'EN GARDE!
OKAY, RUSTY, GIMME SOMETHIN' I CAN USE HERE! A CHAINSAW, A HARPOON, A SHOTGUN...
OKEY-DOKEY!

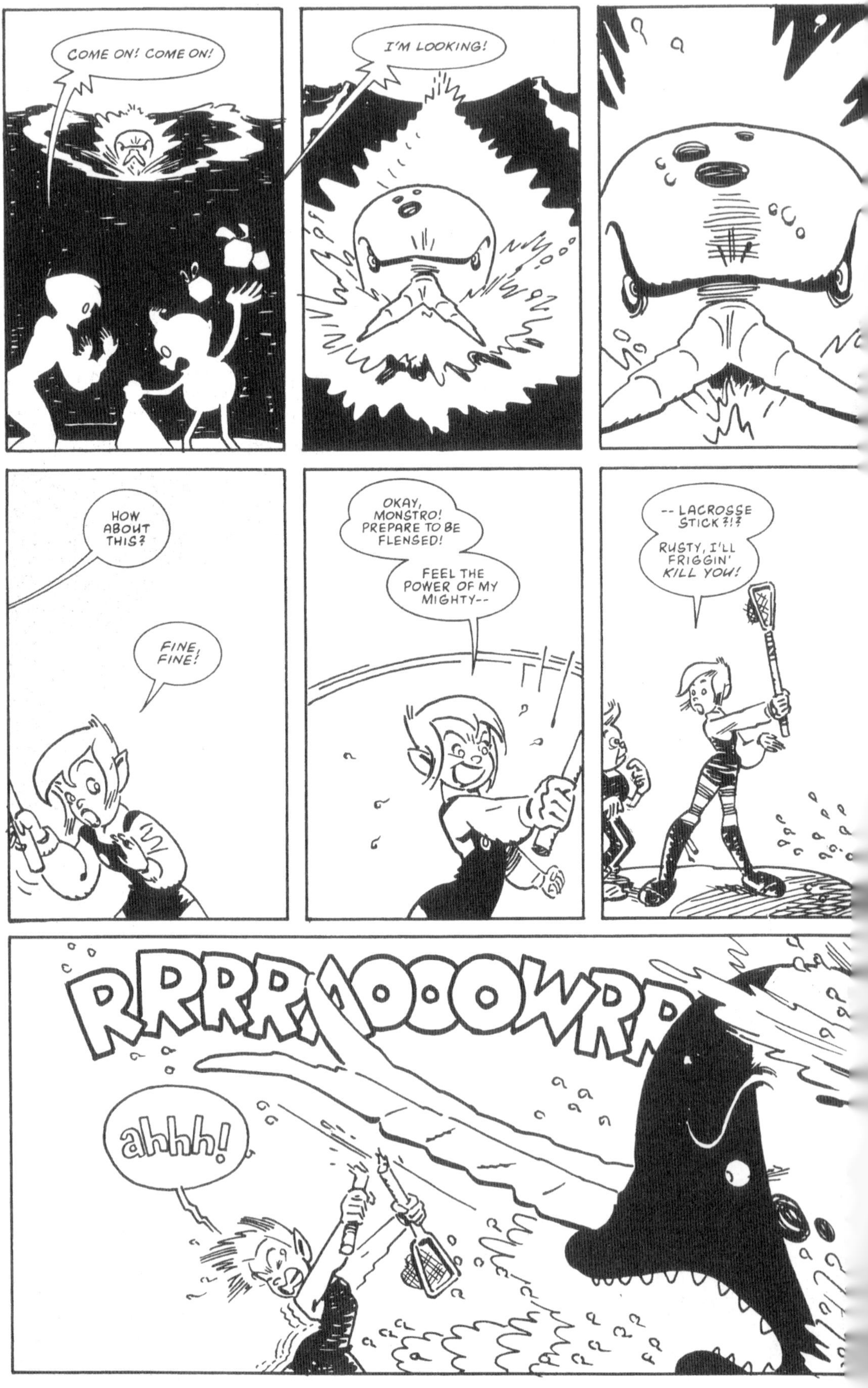
COME ON! COME ON!
I'M LOOKING!
HOW ABOUT THIS?
FINE, FINE!
OKAY, MONSTRO! PREPARE TO BE FLENSED!
FEEL THE POWER OF MY MIGHTY--
-- LACROSSE STICK?!?
RUSTY, I'LL FRIGGIN' KILL YOU!
ahhh!

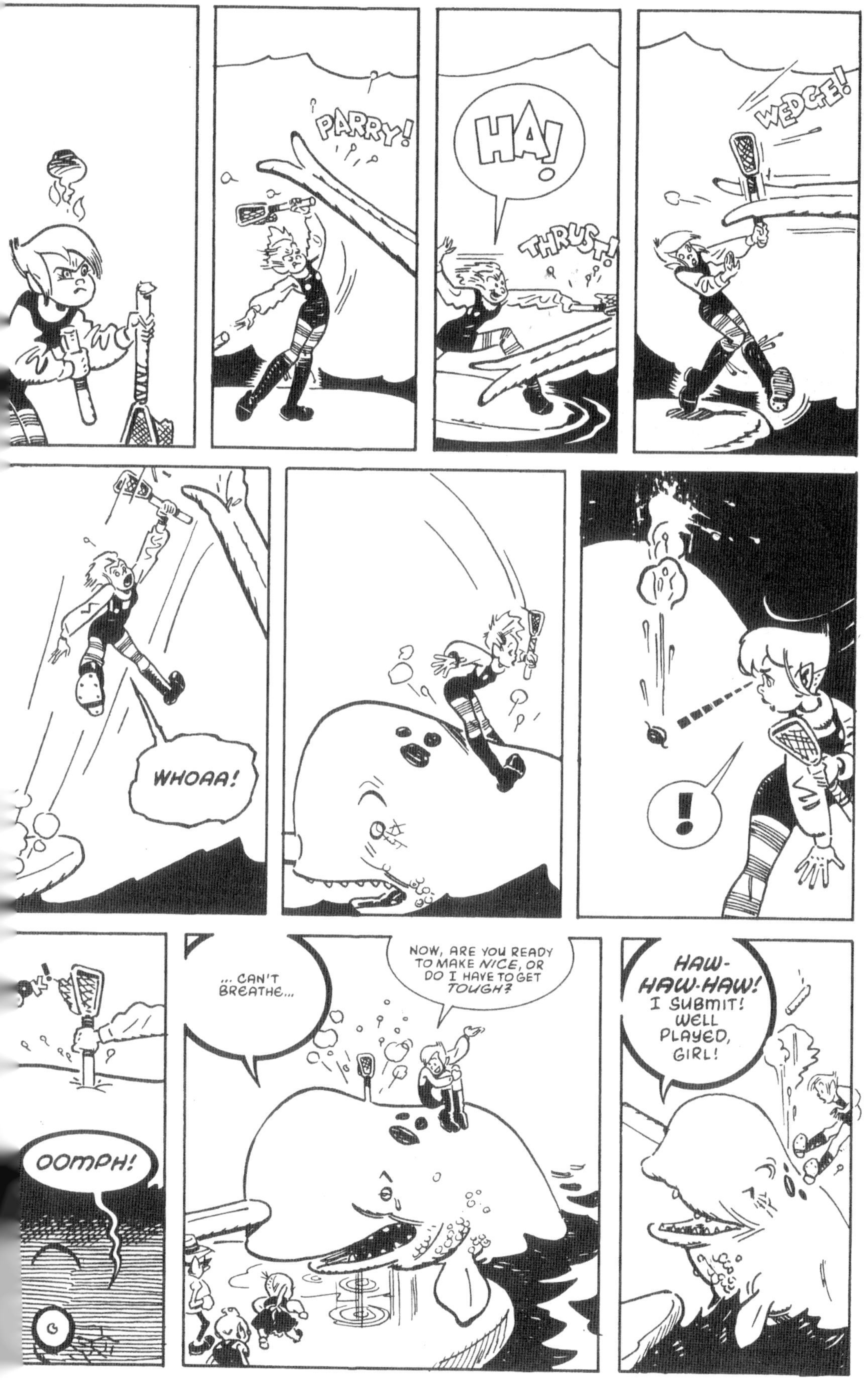
PARRY!
HA!
THRUST!
WEDGE!
WHOAA!
!
OOMPH!
... CAN'T BREATHE...
NOW, ARE YOU READY TO MAKE NICE, OR DO I HAVE TO GET TOUGH?
HAW-HAW-HAW! I SUBMIT! WELL PLAYED, GIRL!

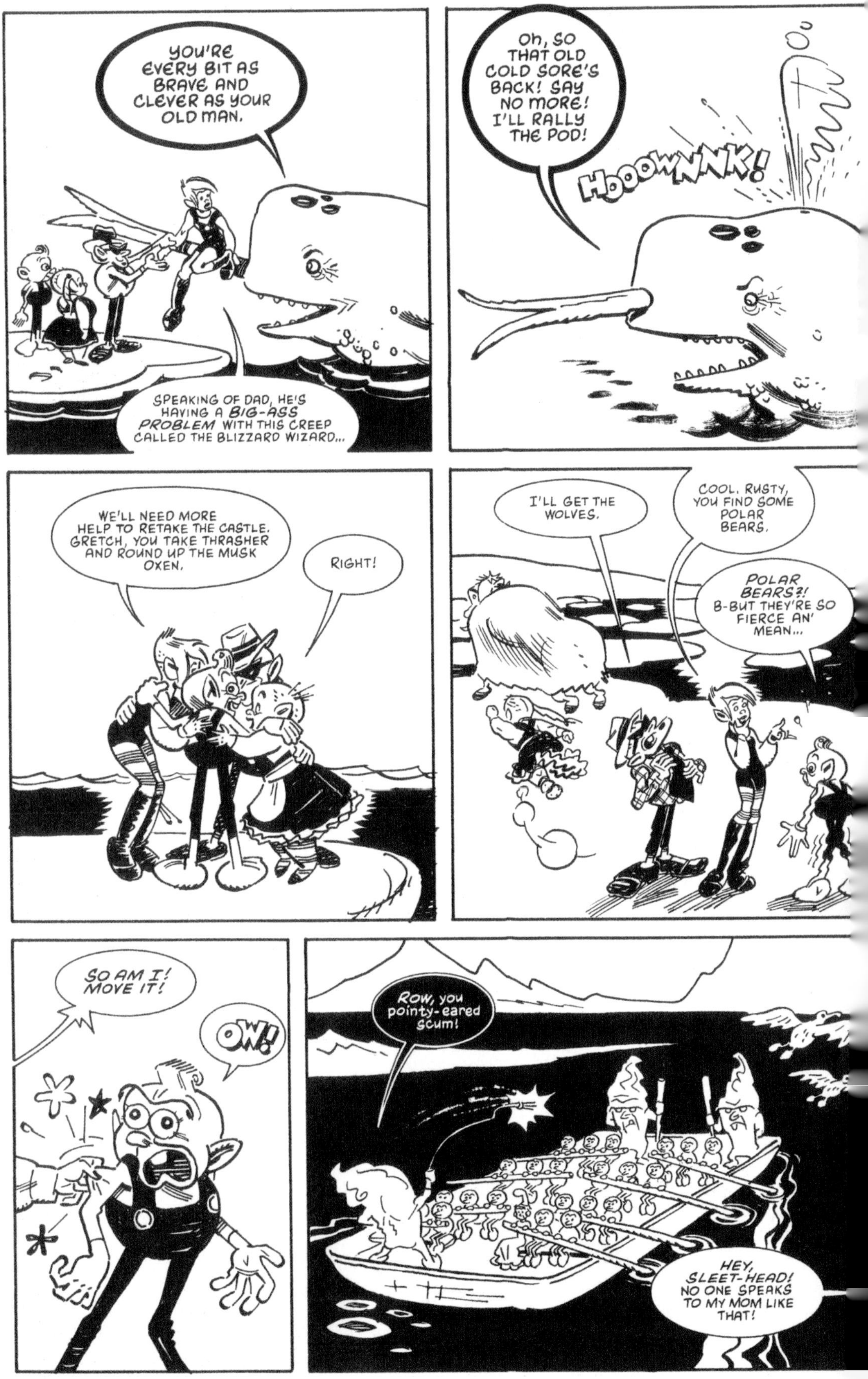
YOU'RE EVERY BIT AS BRAVE AND CLEVER AS YOUR OLD MAN.
SPEAKING OF DAD, HE'S HAVING A BIG-ASS PROBLEM WITH THIS CREEP CALLED THE BLIZZARD WIZARD...
Oh, SO THAT OLD COLD SORE'S BACK! SAY NO MORE! I'LL RALLY THE POD!
HOOOWNNK!
WE'LL NEED MORE HELP TO RETAKE THE CASTLE. GRETCH, YOU TAKE THRASHER AND ROUND UP THE MUSK OXEN.
RIGHT!
I'LL GET THE WOLVES.
COOL. RUSTY, YOU FIND SOME POLAR BEARS.
POLAR BEARS?! B-BUT THEY'RE SO FIERCE AN' MEAN...
SO AM I! MOVE IT!
OW!
Row, you pointy-eared scum!
HEY, SLEET-HEAD! NO ONE SPEAKS TO MY MOM LIKE THAT!

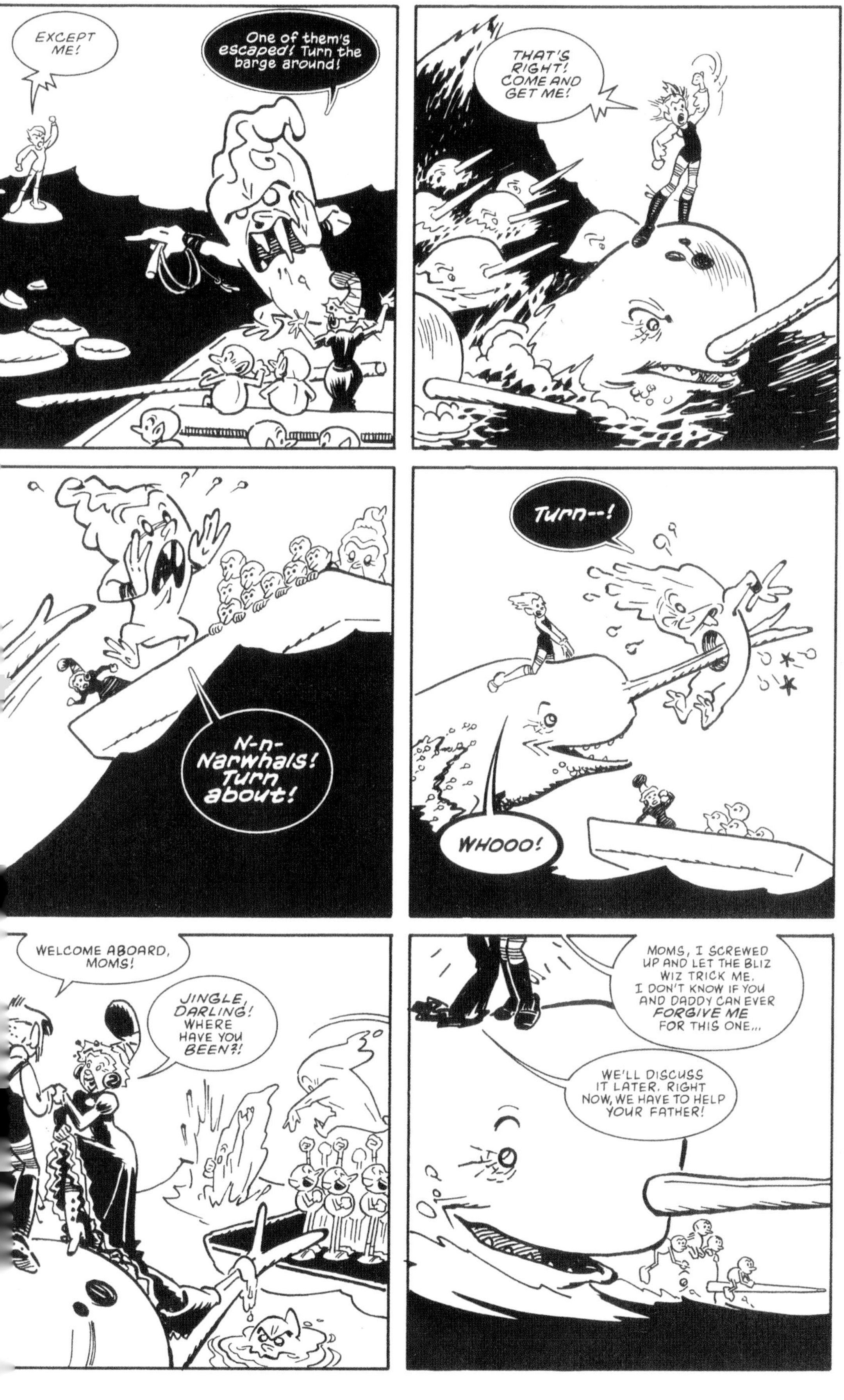
EXCEPT ME!
One of them's escaped! Turn the barge around!
THAT'S RIGHT! COME AND GET ME!
N-n-Narwhals! Turn about!
Turn--!
WHOOO!
WELCOME ABOARD, MOMS!
JINGLE, DARLING! WHERE HAVE YOU BEEN?!
MOMS, I SCREWED UP AND LET THE BLIZ WIZ TRICK ME. I DON'T KNOW IF YOU AND DADDY CAN EVER FORGIVE ME FOR THIS ONE...
WE'LL DISCUSS IT LATER. RIGHT NOW, WE HAVE TO HELP YOUR FATHER!

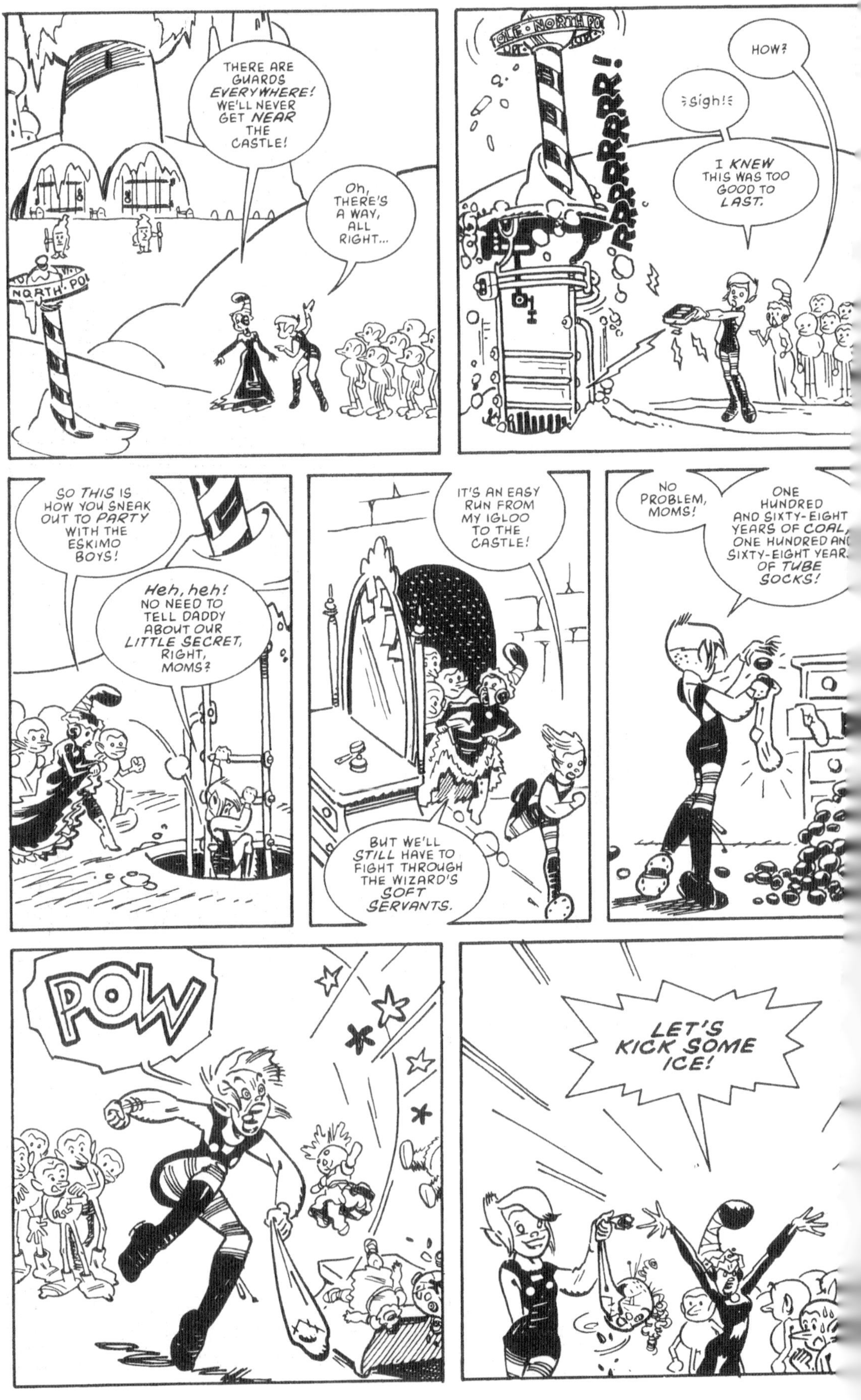

THERE ARE GUARDS EVERYWHERE! WE'LL NEVER GET NEAR THE CASTLE!
Oh, THERE'S A WAY, ALL RIGHT...
NORTH POL
OLE NORTH PO
RRRRRRRRRR!
HOW?
sigh!
I KNEW THIS WAS TOO GOOD TO LAST.
SO THIS IS HOW YOU SNEAK OUT TO PARTY WITH THE ESKIMO BOYS!
Heh, heh! NO NEED TO TELL DADDY ABOUT OUR LITTLE SECRET, RIGHT, MOMS?
IT'S AN EASY RUN FROM MY IGLOO TO THE CASTLE!
BUT WE'LL STILL HAVE TO FIGHT THROUGH THE WIZARD'S SOFT SERVANTS.
NO PROBLEM, MOMS!
ONE HUNDRED AND SIXTY-EIGHT YEARS OF COAL, ONE HUNDRED AND SIXTY-EIGHT YEARS OF TUBE SOCKS!
POW
LET'S KICK SOME ICE!

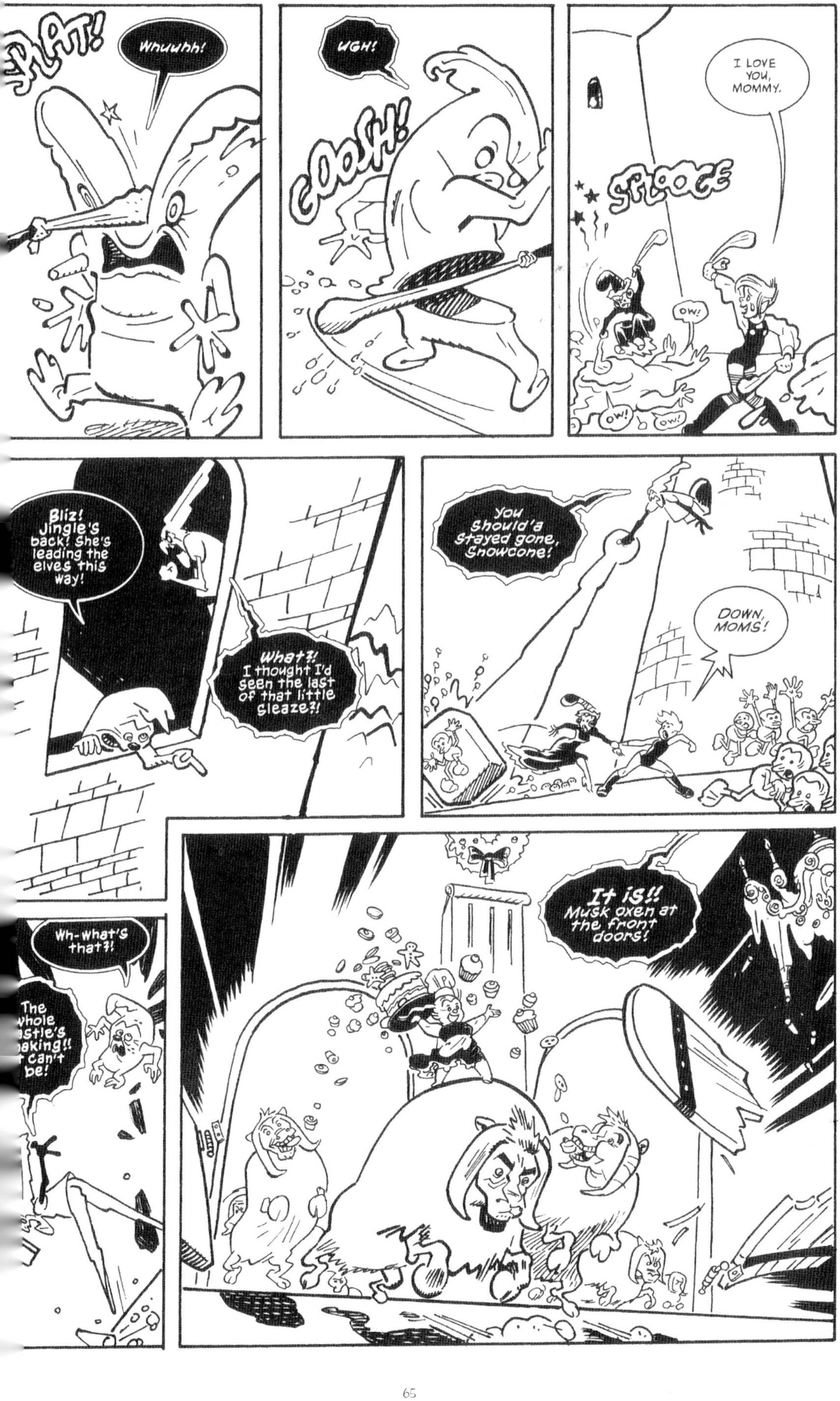
Whuuhh!
UGH!
GOOSH!
I LOVE YOU, MOMMY.
SPLOOGE
OW!
OW!
OW!
Bliz! Jingle's back! She's leading the elves this way!
What?! I thought I'd seen the last of that little gleaze?!
You should'a stayed gone, Snowcone!
DOWN, MOMS!
Wh-what's that?!
The whole astle's aking!! t can't be!
It is!! Musk oxen at the front doors!

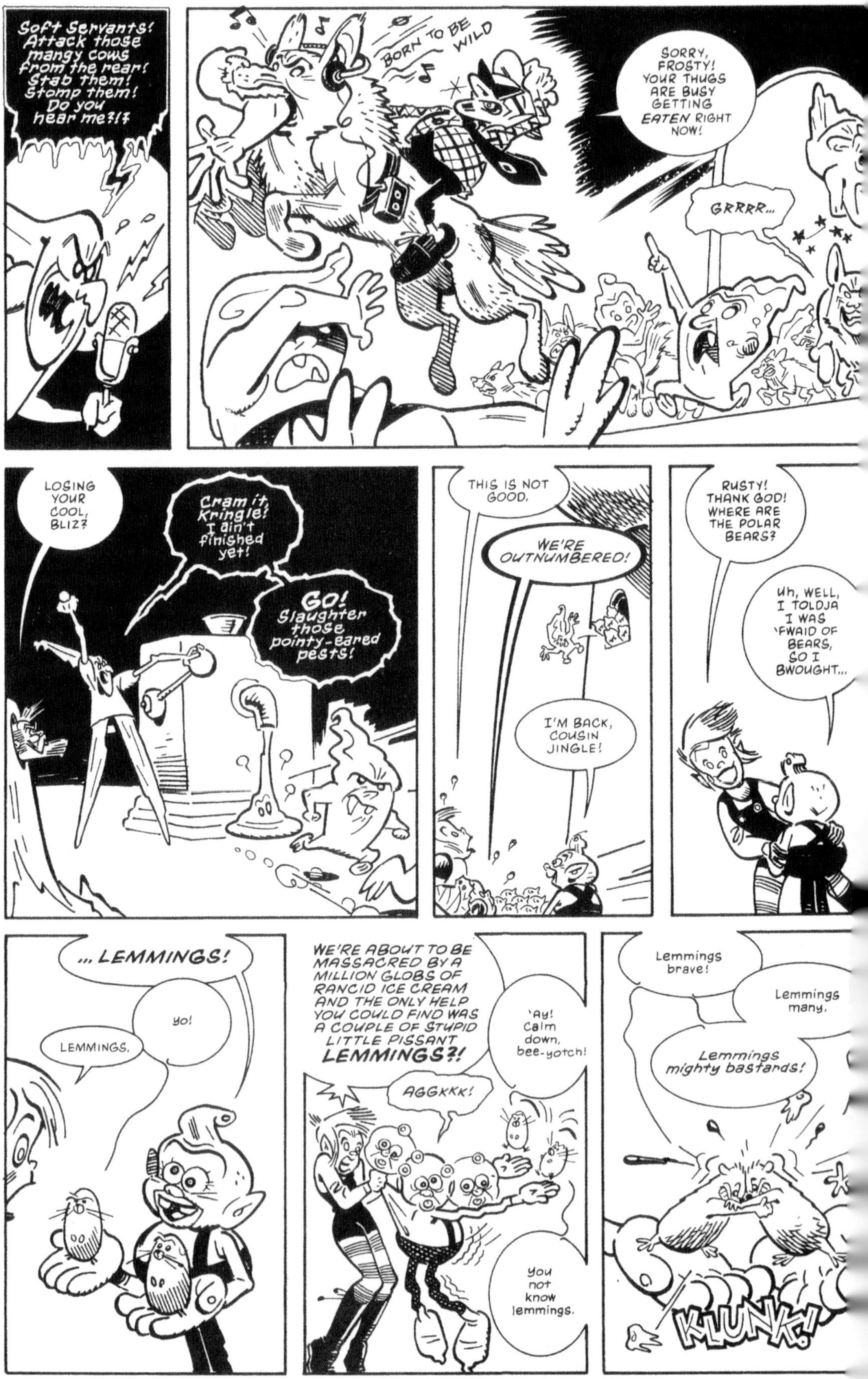
Soft Servants! Attack those mangy cows from the rear! Stab them! Stomp them! Do you hear me?!?
BORN TO BE WILD
SORRY, FROSTY! YOUR THUGS ARE BUSY GETTING EATEN RIGHT NOW!
GRRRR...
LOSING YOUR COOL, BLIZ?
Cram it, Kringle! I ain't finished yet!
GO! Slaughter those pointy-eared pests!
THIS IS NOT GOOD.
WE'RE OUTNUMBERED!
I'M BACK, COUSIN JINGLE!
RUSTY! THANK GOD! WHERE ARE THE POLAR BEARS?
Uh, WELL, I TOLDJA I WAS 'FWAID OF BEARS, SO I BWOUGHT...
...LEMMINGS!
LEMMINGS.
yo!
WE'RE ABOUT TO BE MASSACRED BY A MILLION GLOBS OF RANCID ICE CREAM AND THE ONLY HELP YOU COULD FIND WAS A COUPLE OF STUPID LITTLE PISSANT LEMMINGS?!
'Ay! Calm down, bee-yotch!
AGGKKK!
You not know lemmings.
Lemmings brave!
Lemmings many.
Lemmings mighty bastards!
KLUNK!

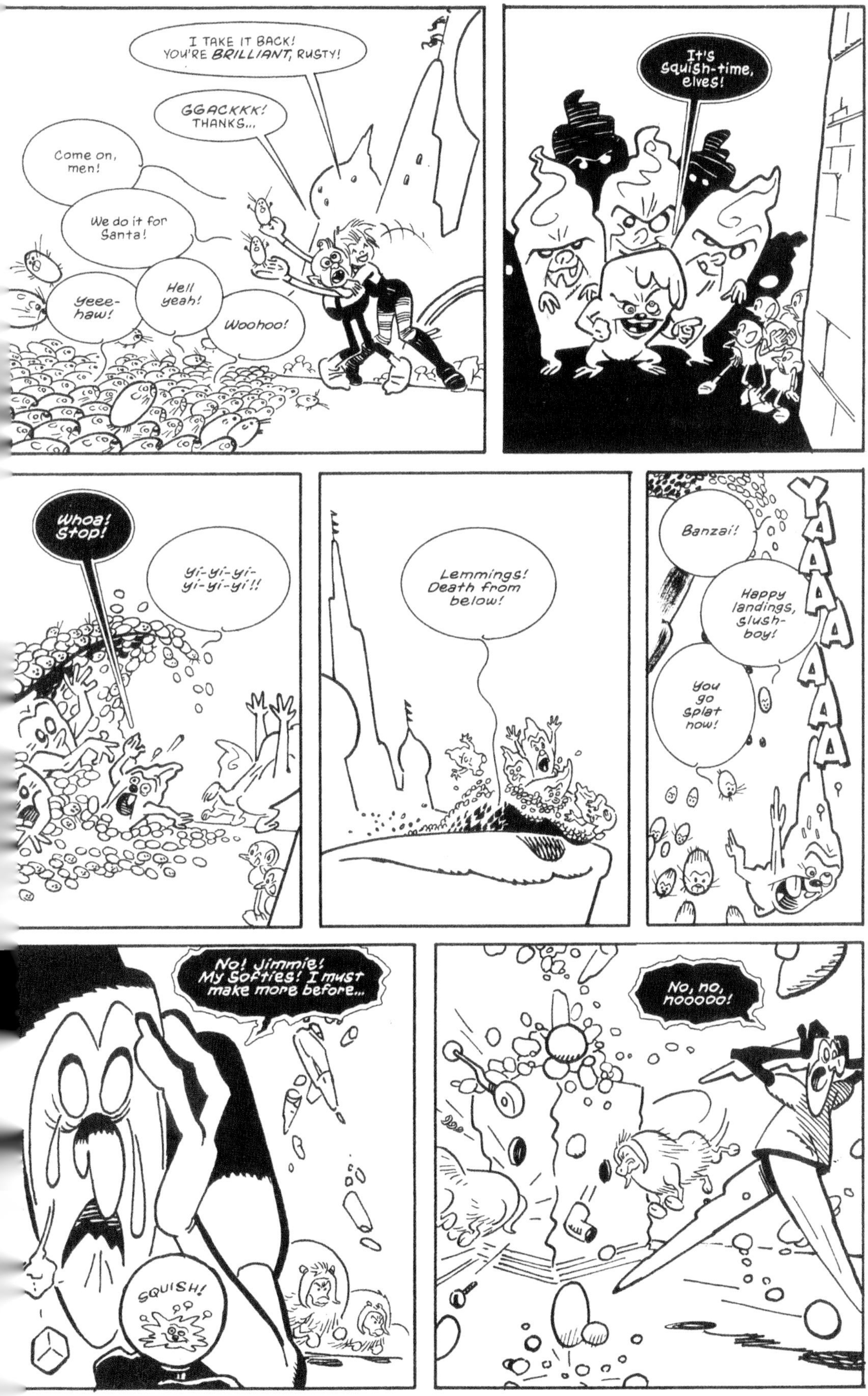
I TAKE IT BACK! YOU'RE BRILLIANT, RUSTY!
GGACKKK! THANKS...
Come on, men!
We do it for Santa!
Yeee-haw!
Hell yeah!
Woohoo!
It's squish-time, elves!
Whoa! Stop!
yi-yi-yi-yi-yi-yi!!
Lemmings! Death from below!
Banzai!
Happy landings, slush-boy!
You go splat now!
YAAAAAAAA
No! Jimmie! My Softies! I must make more before...
SQUISH!
No, no, nooooo!

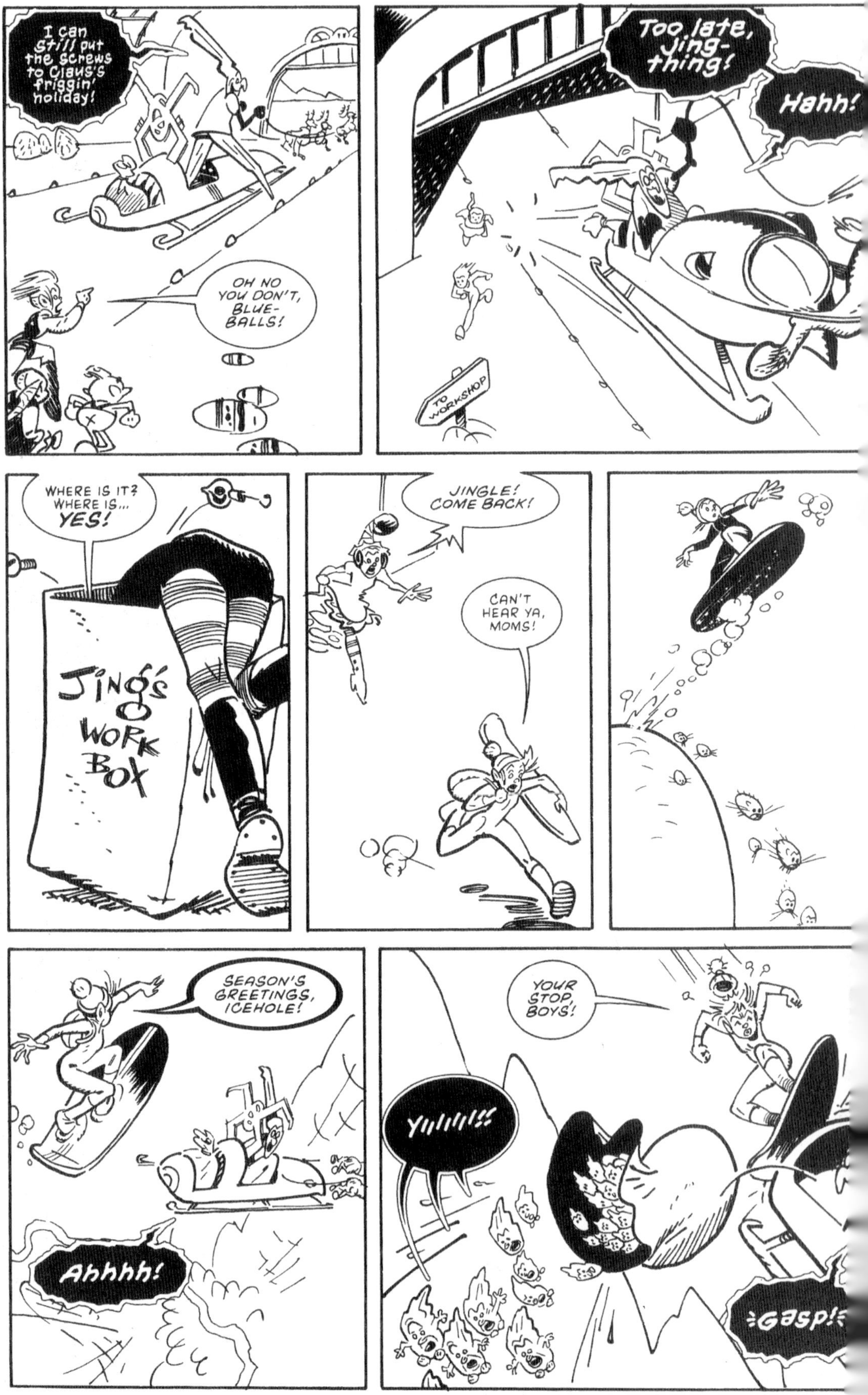
I can still put the screws to Claus's friggin' holiday!
OH NO YOU DON'T, BLUE-BALLS!
Too late, Jing-thing!
Hahh!
TO WORKSHOP
WHERE IS IT? WHERE IS... YES!
JING'S WORK BOX
JINGLE! COME BACK!
CAN'T HEAR YA, MOMS!
SEASON'S GREETINGS, ICEHOLE!
Ahhhh!
YOUR STOP, BOYS!
Yiiiii!!
!Gasp!

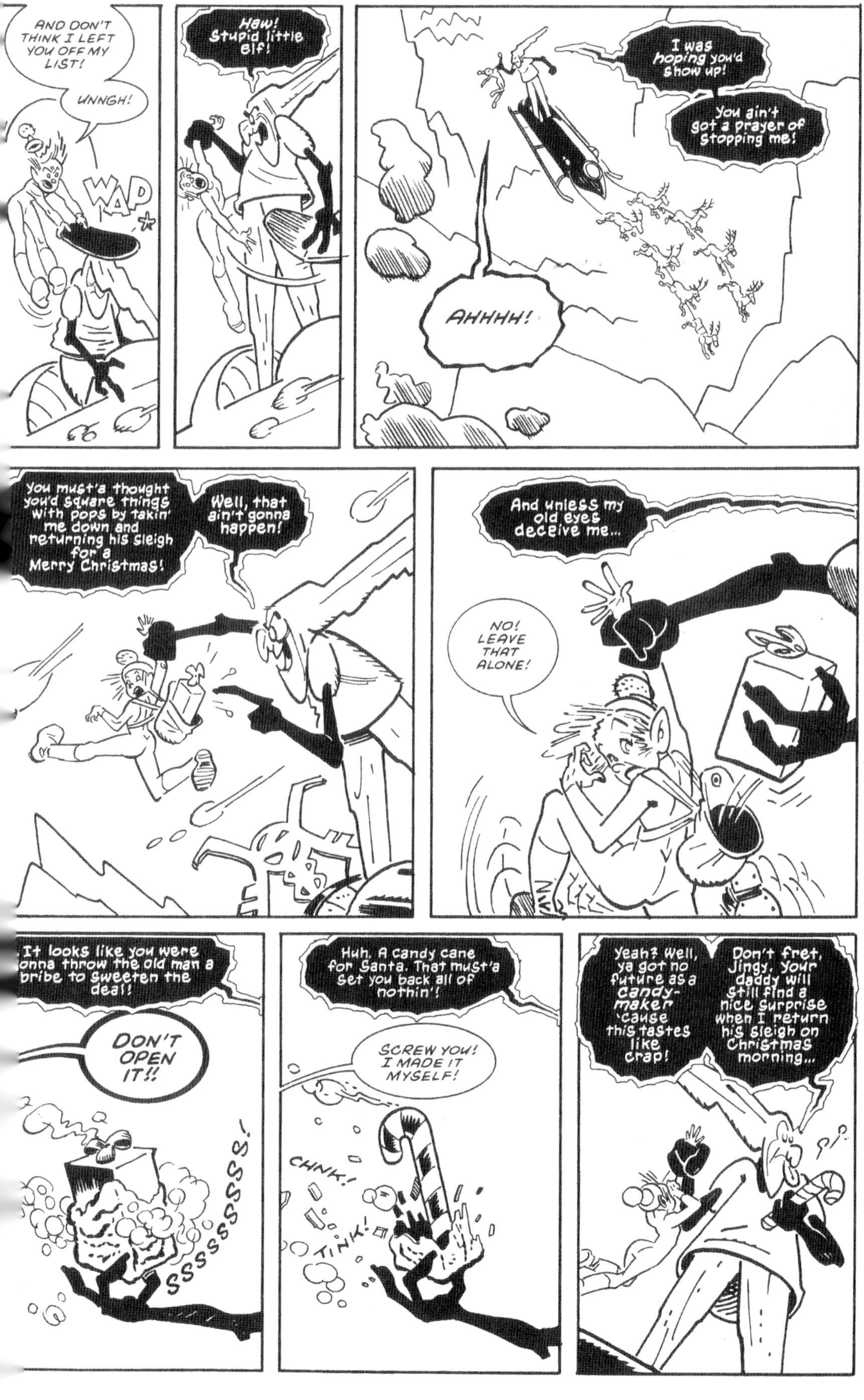
AND DON'T THINK I LEFT YOU OFF MY LIST!
UNNGH!
WAP
Haw! Stupid little Elf!
I was hoping you'd show up!
You ain't got a prayer of stopping me!
AHHHH!
You must'a thought you'd square things with pops by takin' me down and returning his sleigh for a Merry Christmas!
Well, that ain't gonna happen!
And unless my old eyes deceive me...
NO! LEAVE THAT ALONE!
It looks like you were gonna throw the old man a bribe to sweeten the deal!
DON'T OPEN IT!!
SSSSSSSSS!
Huh. A candy cane for Santa. That must'a set you back all of nothin'!
SCREW YOU! I MADE IT MYSELF!
CHNK!
TINK!
Yeah? Well, ya got no future as a candy-maker 'cause this tastes like crap!
Don't fret, Jingy. Your daddy will still find a nice surprise when I return his sleigh on Christmas morning...

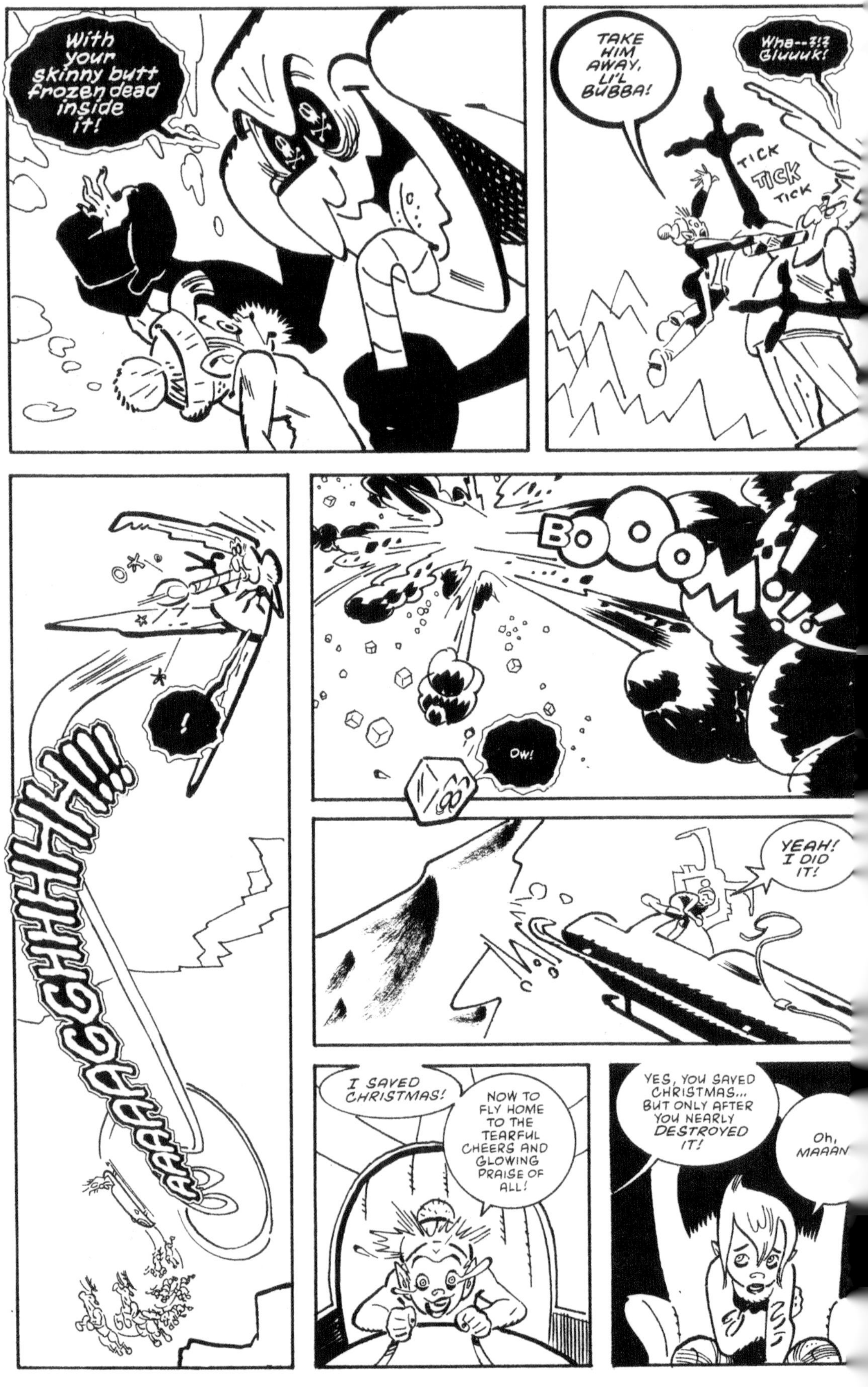
With your skinny butt frozen dead inside it!
TAKE HIM AWAY, LI'L BUBBA!
Wha--?!? Gluuuk!
TICK
TICK
TICK
AAAAAGGHHHHH!!!
!
BOOOOM!!!
OW!
YEAH! I DID IT!
I SAVED CHRISTMAS!
NOW TO FLY HOME TO THE TEARFUL CHEERS AND GLOWING PRAISE OF ALL!
YES, YOU SAVED CHRISTMAS... BUT ONLY AFTER YOU NEARLY DESTROYED IT!
Oh, MAAAN

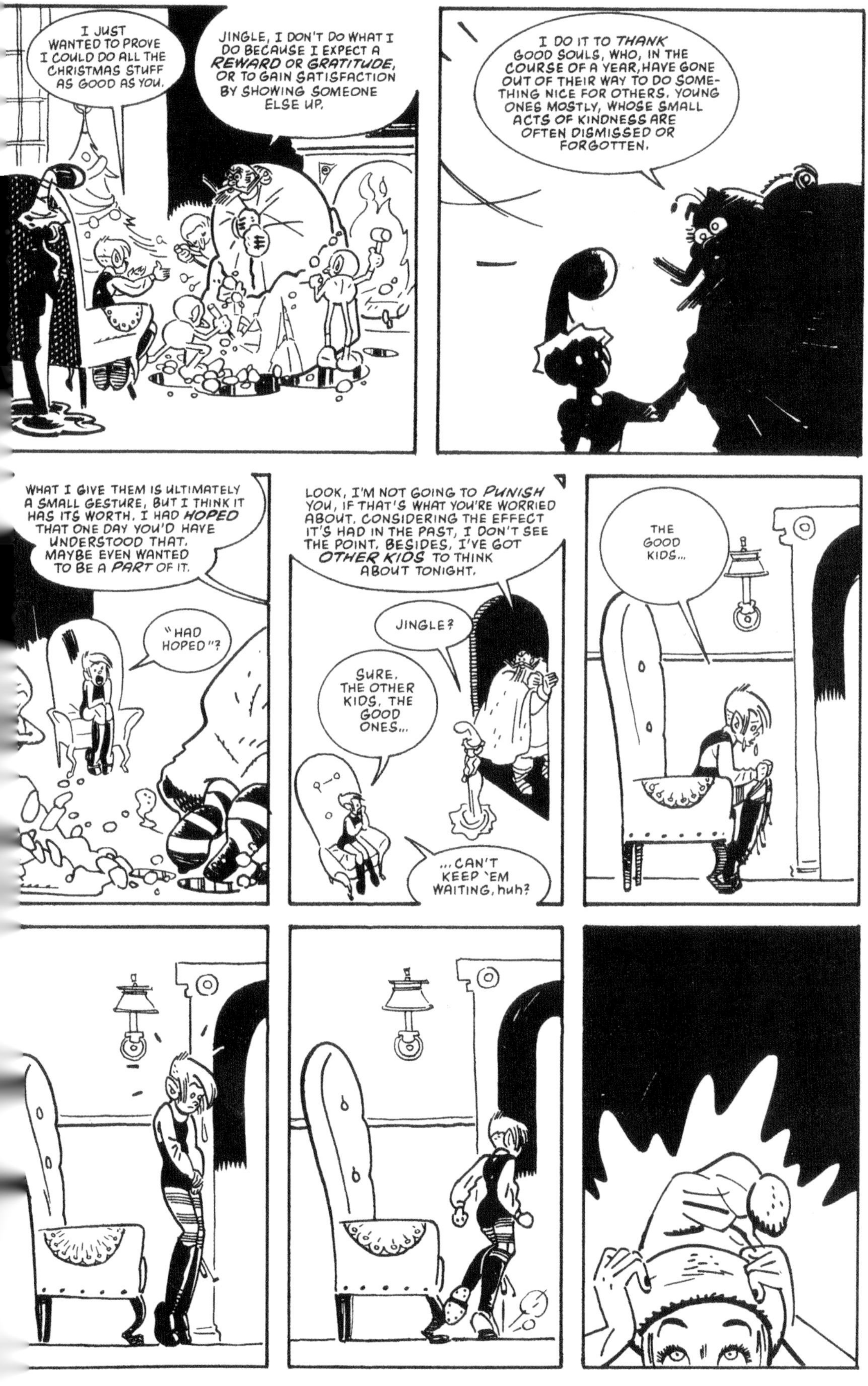
I JUST WANTED TO PROVE I COULD DO ALL THE CHRISTMAS STUFF AS GOOD AS YOU.
JINGLE, I DON'T DO WHAT I DO BECAUSE I EXPECT A REWARD OR GRATITUDE, OR TO GAIN SATISFACTION BY SHOWING SOMEONE ELSE UP.
I DO IT TO THANK GOOD SOULS, WHO, IN THE COURSE OF A YEAR, HAVE GONE OUT OF THEIR WAY TO DO SOMETHING NICE FOR OTHERS. YOUNG ONES MOSTLY, WHOSE SMALL ACTS OF KINDNESS ARE OFTEN DISMISSED OR FORGOTTEN.
WHAT I GIVE THEM IS ULTIMATELY A SMALL GESTURE, BUT I THINK IT HAS ITS WORTH. I HAD HOPED THAT ONE DAY YOU'D HAVE UNDERSTOOD THAT. MAYBE EVEN WANTED TO BE A PART OF IT.
"HAD HOPED"?
LOOK, I'M NOT GOING TO PUNISH YOU, IF THAT'S WHAT YOU'RE WORRIED ABOUT. CONSIDERING THE EFFECT IT'S HAD IN THE PAST, I DON'T SEE THE POINT. BESIDES, I'VE GOT OTHER KIDS TO THINK ABOUT TONIGHT.
JINGLE?
SURE. THE OTHER KIDS. THE GOOD ONES...
...CAN'T KEEP 'EM WAITING, huh?
THE GOOD KIDS...

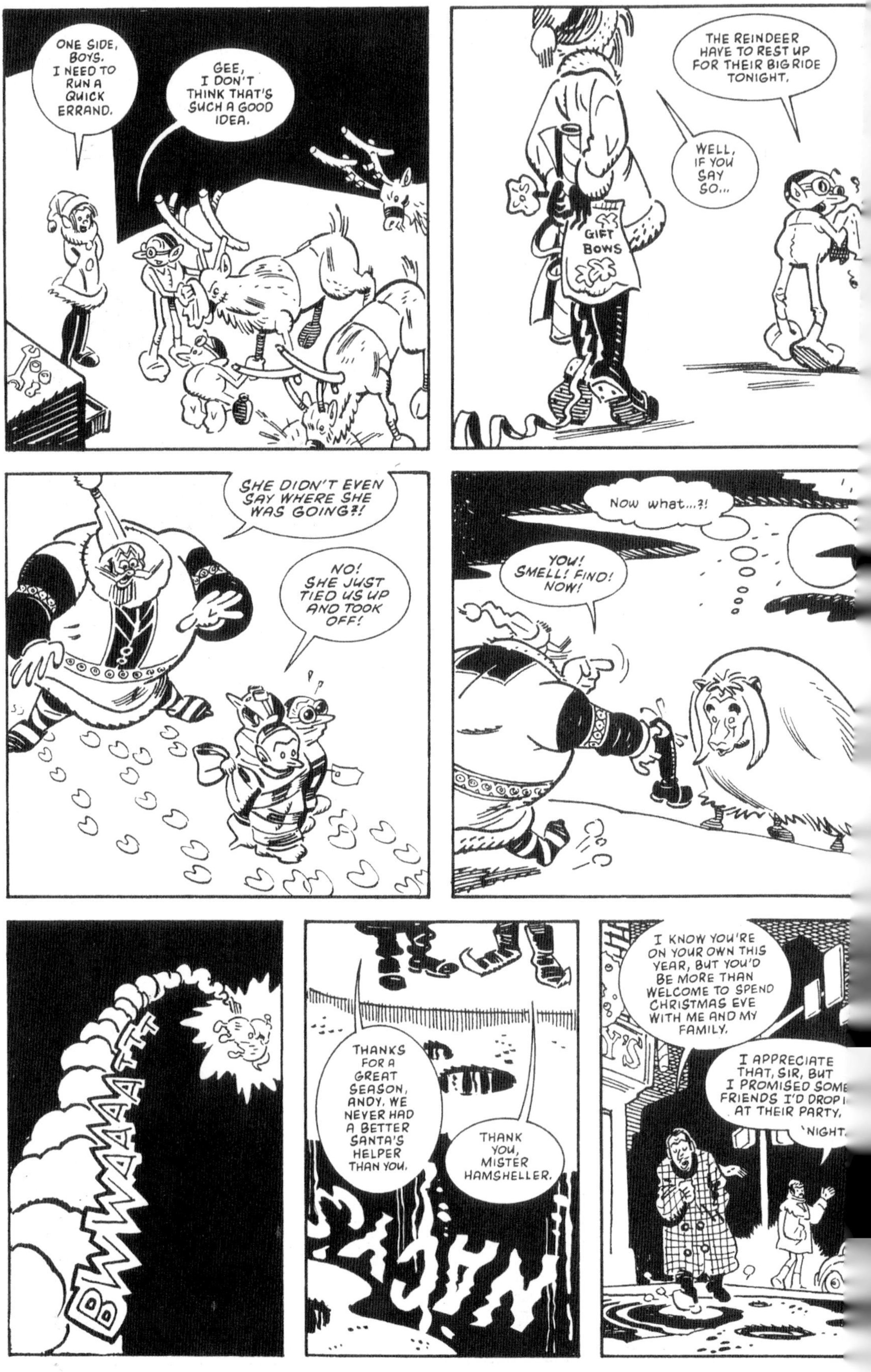
ONE SIDE, BOYS. I NEED TO RUN A QUICK ERRAND.
GEE, I DON'T THINK THAT'S SUCH A GOOD IDEA.
THE REINDEER HAVE TO REST UP FOR THEIR BIG RIDE TONIGHT.
WELL, IF YOU SAY SO...
GIFT BOWS
SHE DIDN'T EVEN SAY WHERE SHE WAS GOING?!
NO! SHE JUST TIED US UP AND TOOK OFF!
Now what...?!
YOU! SMELL! FIND! NOW!
BWWAAAATTT
THANKS FOR A GREAT SEASON, ANDY. WE NEVER HAD A BETTER SANTA'S HELPER THAN YOU.
THANK YOU, MISTER HAMSHELLER.
I KNOW YOU'RE ON YOUR OWN THIS YEAR, BUT YOU'D BE MORE THAN WELCOME TO SPEND CHRISTMAS EVE WITH ME AND MY FAMILY.
I APPRECIATE THAT, SIR, BUT I PROMISED SOME FRIENDS I'D DROP I AT THEIR PARTY.
'NIGHT.

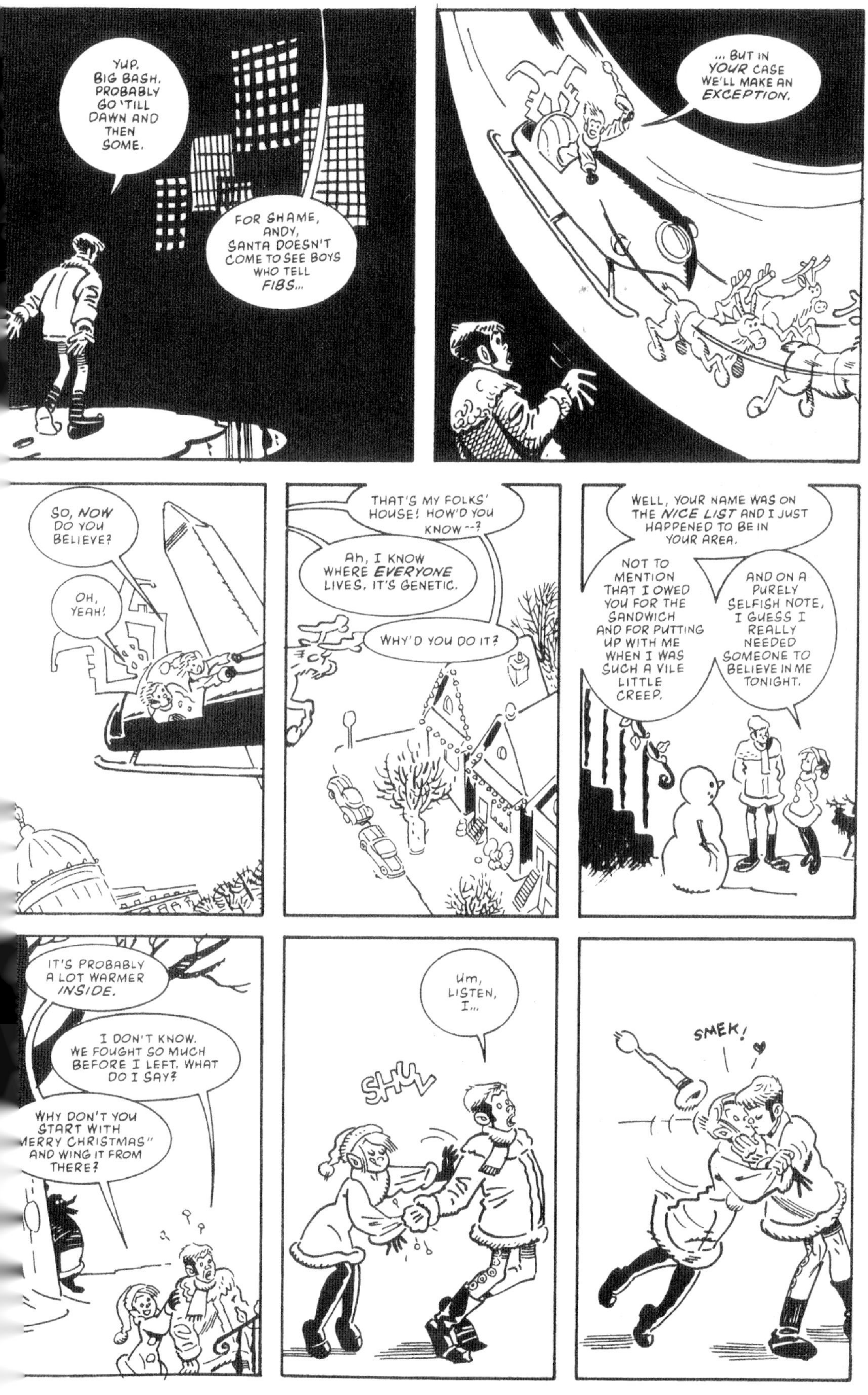
YUP. BIG BASH. PROBABLY GO 'TILL DAWN AND THEN SOME.
FOR SHAME, ANDY, SANTA DOESN'T COME TO SEE BOYS WHO TELL FIBS...
... BUT IN YOUR CASE WE'LL MAKE AN EXCEPTION.
SO, NOW DO YOU BELIEVE?
OH, YEAH!
THAT'S MY FOLKS' HOUSE! HOW'D YOU KNOW --?
Ah, I KNOW WHERE EVERYONE LIVES. IT'S GENETIC.
WHY'D YOU DO IT?
WELL, YOUR NAME WAS ON THE NICE LIST AND I JUST HAPPENED TO BE IN YOUR AREA.
NOT TO MENTION THAT I OWED YOU FOR THE SANDWICH AND FOR PUTTING UP WITH ME WHEN I WAS SUCH A VILE LITTLE CREEP.
AND ON A PURELY SELFISH NOTE, I GUESS I REALLY NEEDED SOMEONE TO BELIEVE IN ME TONIGHT.
IT'S PROBABLY A LOT WARMER INSIDE.
I DON'T KNOW. WE FOUGHT SO MUCH BEFORE I LEFT. WHAT DO I SAY?
WHY DON'T YOU START WITH "MERRY CHRISTMAS" AND WING IT FROM THERE?
Um, LISTEN, I...
SHUV
SMEK!

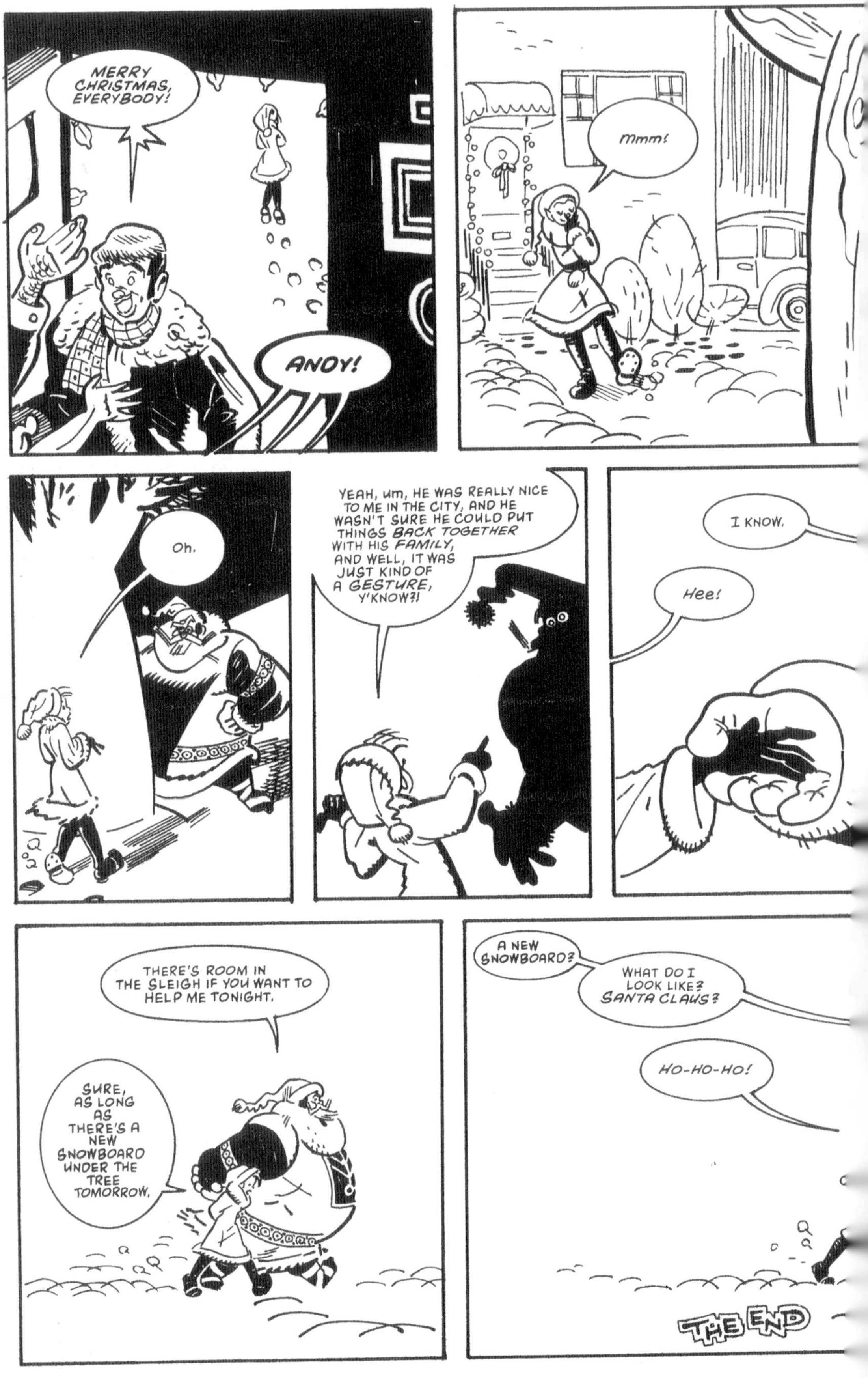
MERRY CHRISTMAS, EVERYBODY!
ANDY!
Mmm!
Oh.
YEAH, um, HE WAS REALLY NICE TO ME IN THE CITY, AND HE WASN'T SURE HE COULD PUT THINGS BACK TOGETHER WITH HIS FAMILY, AND WELL, IT WAS JUST KIND OF A GESTURE, Y'KNOW?!
I KNOW.
Hee!
THERE'S ROOM IN THE SLEIGH IF YOU WANT TO HELP ME TONIGHT.
SURE, AS LONG AS THERE'S A NEW SNOWBOARD UNDER THE TREE TOMORROW.
A NEW SNOWBOARD?
WHAT DO I LOOK LIKE? SANTA CLAUS?
HO-HO-HO!
THE END

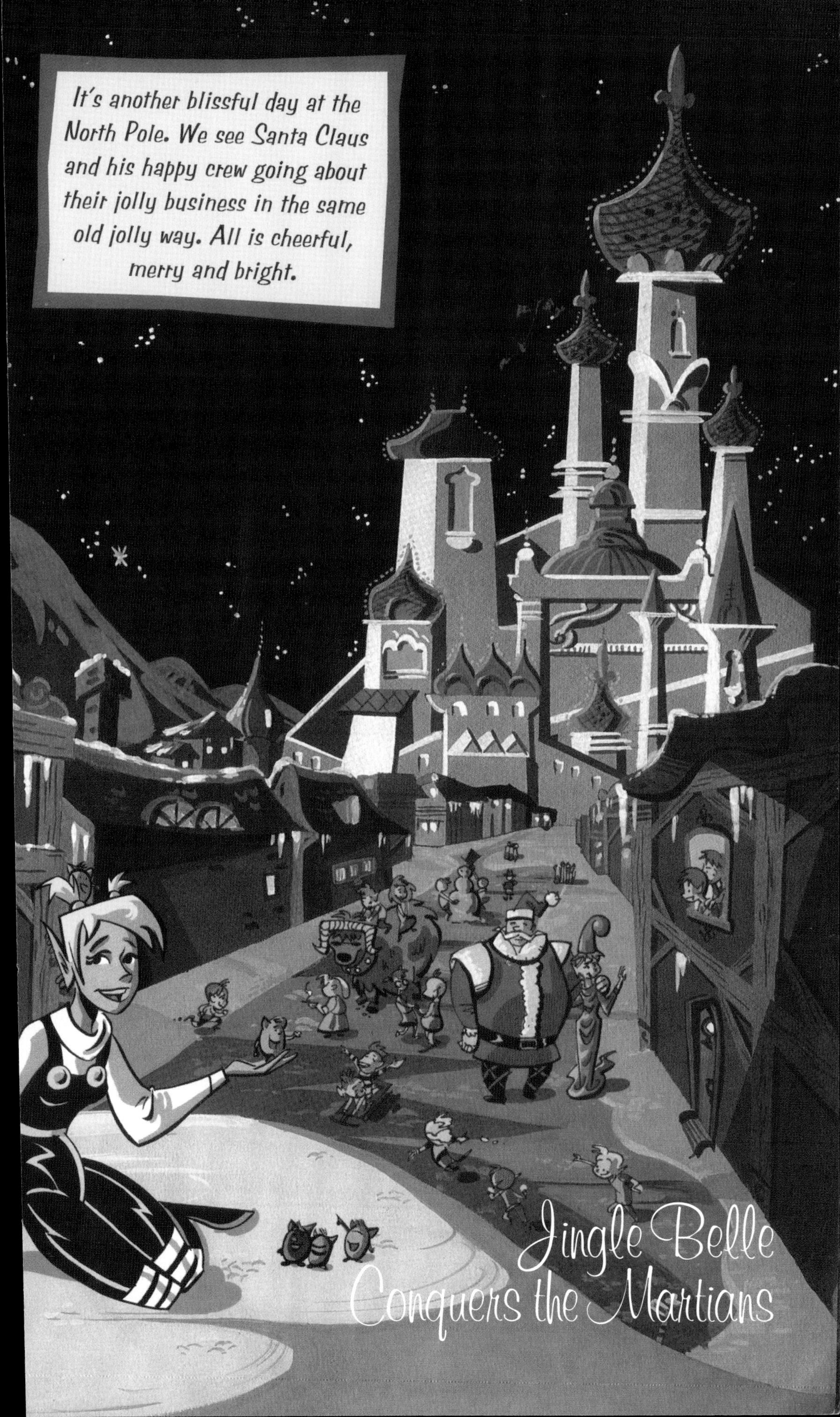
It's another blissful day at the North Pole. We see Santa Claus and his happy crew going about their jolly business in the same old jolly way. All is cheerful, merry and bright.
Jingle Belle Conquers the Martians

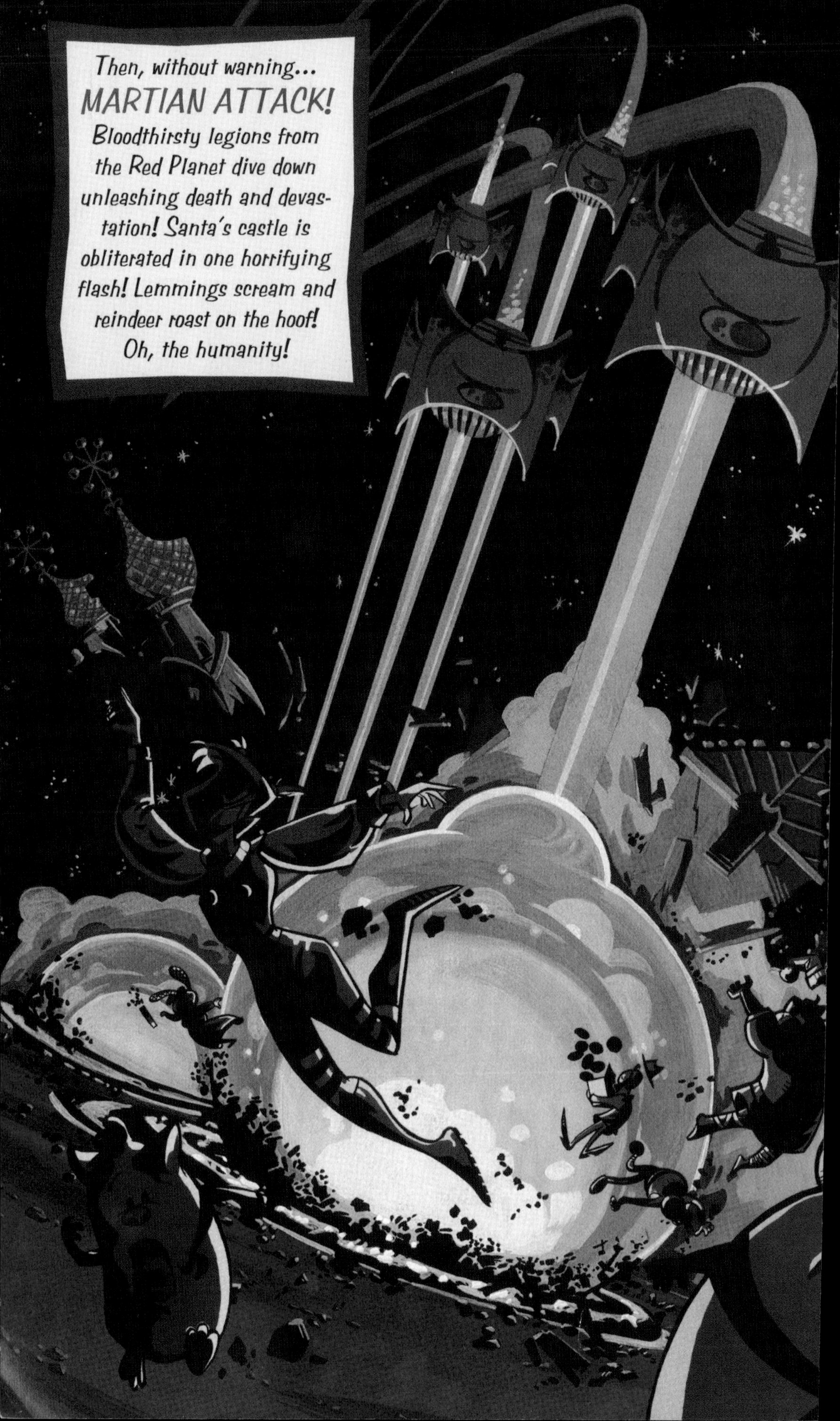
Then, without warning...
MARTIAN ATTACK!
Bloodthirsty legions from the Red Planet dive down unleashing death and devastation! Santa's castle is obliterated in one horrifying flash! Lemmings scream and reindeer roast on the hoof! Oh, the humanity!

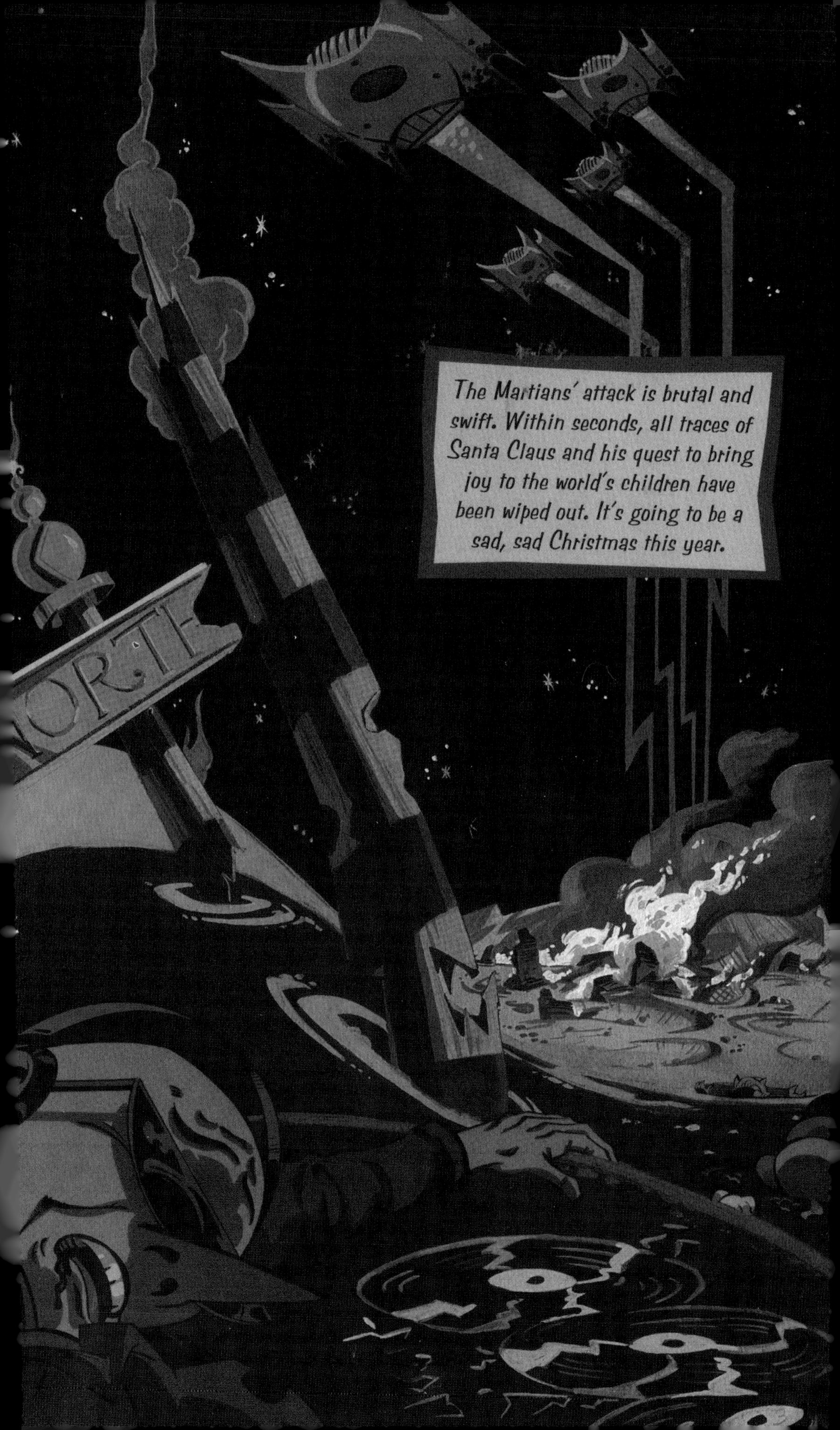
The Martians' attack is brutal and swift. Within seconds, all traces of Santa Claus and his quest to bring joy to the world's children have been wiped out. It's going to be a sad, sad Christmas this year.

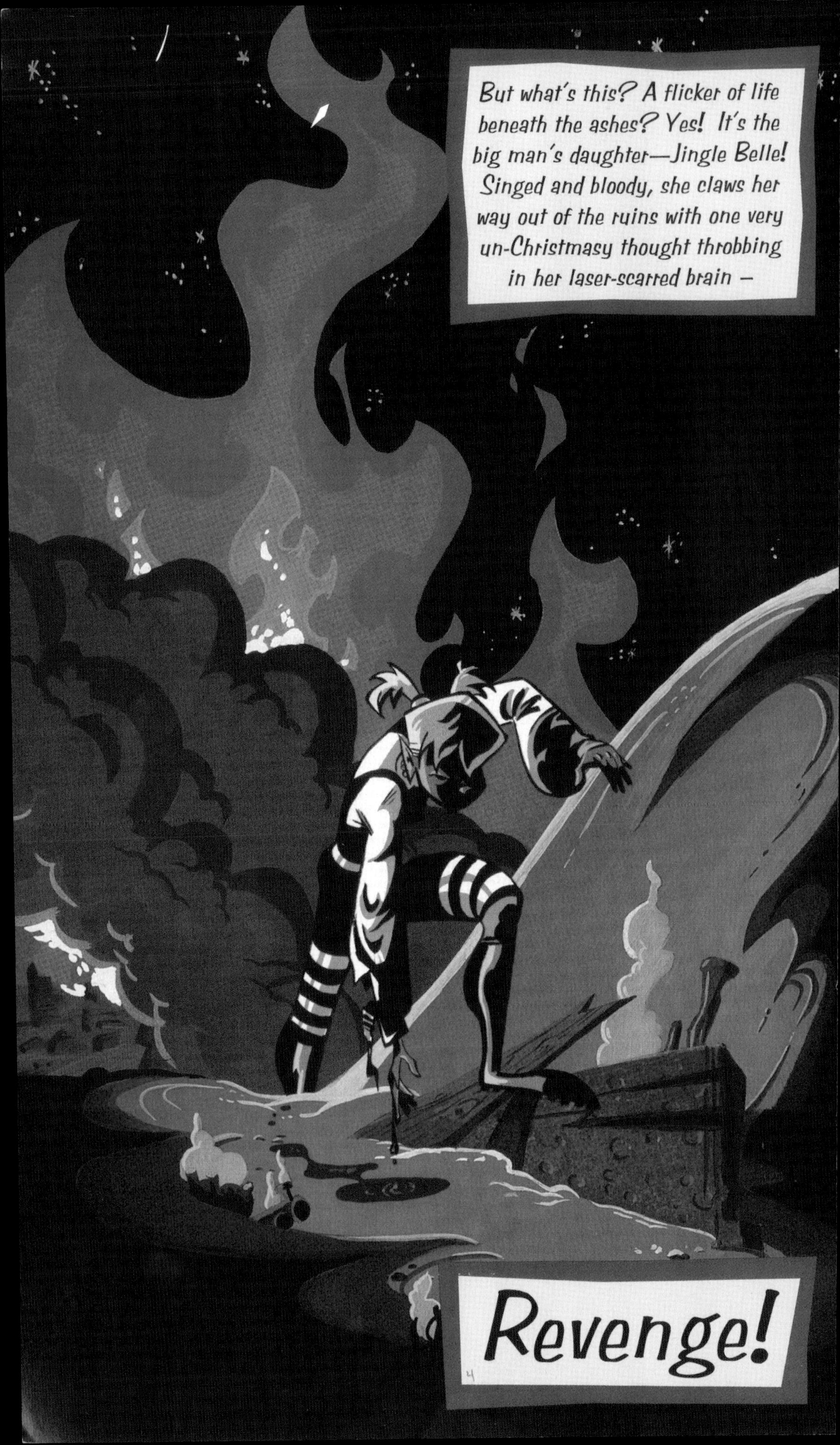
But what's this? A flicker of life beneath the ashes? Yes! It's the big man's daughter—Jingle Belle! Singed and bloody, she claws her way out of the ruins with one very un-Christmasy thought throbbing in her laser-scarred brain –
Revenge!

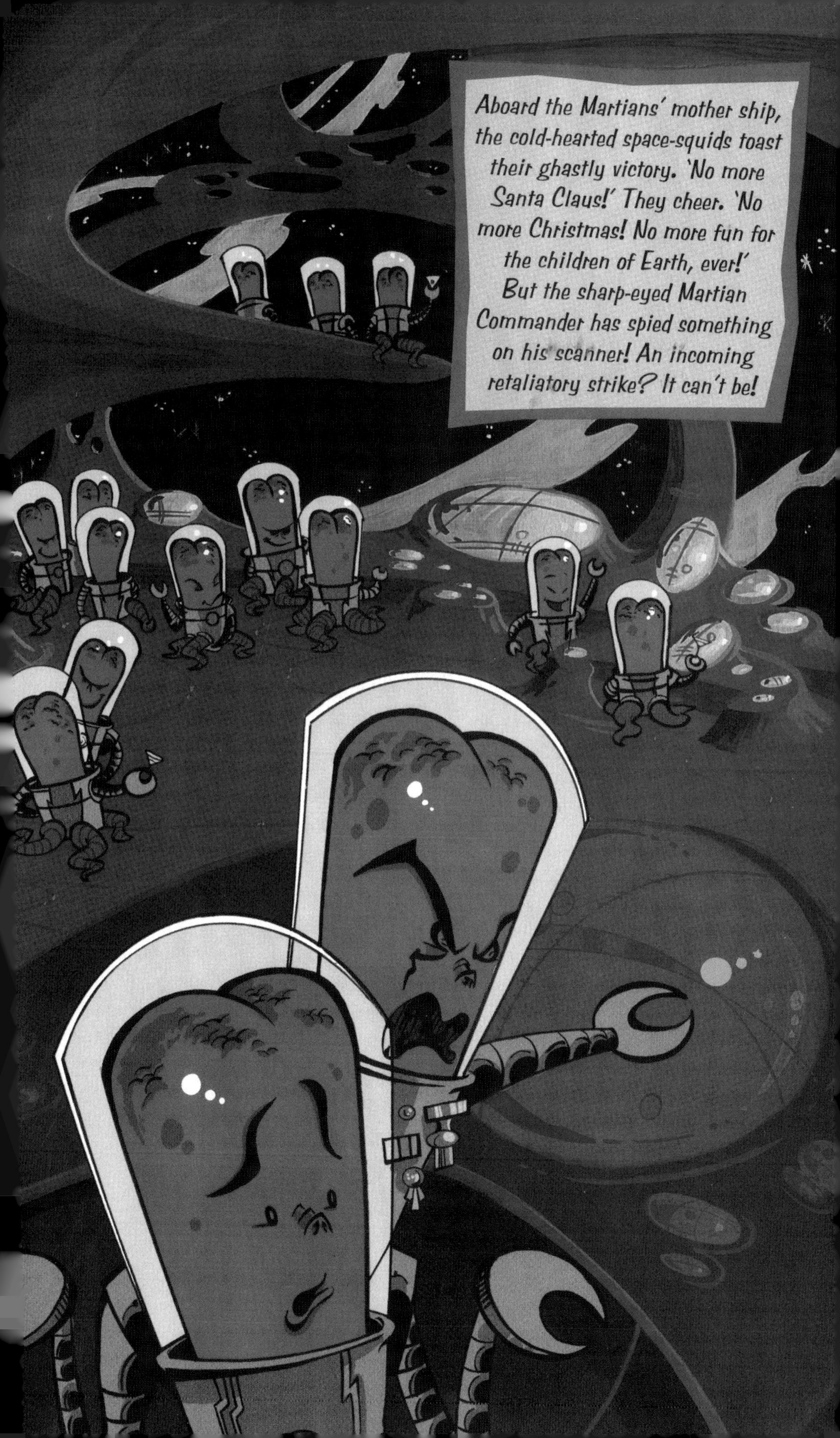
Aboard the Martians' mother ship, the cold-hearted space-squids toast their ghastly victory. 'No more Santa Claus!' They cheer. 'No more Christmas! No more fun for the children of Earth, ever!' But the sharp-eyed Martian Commander has spied something on his scanner! An incoming retaliatory strike? It can't be!

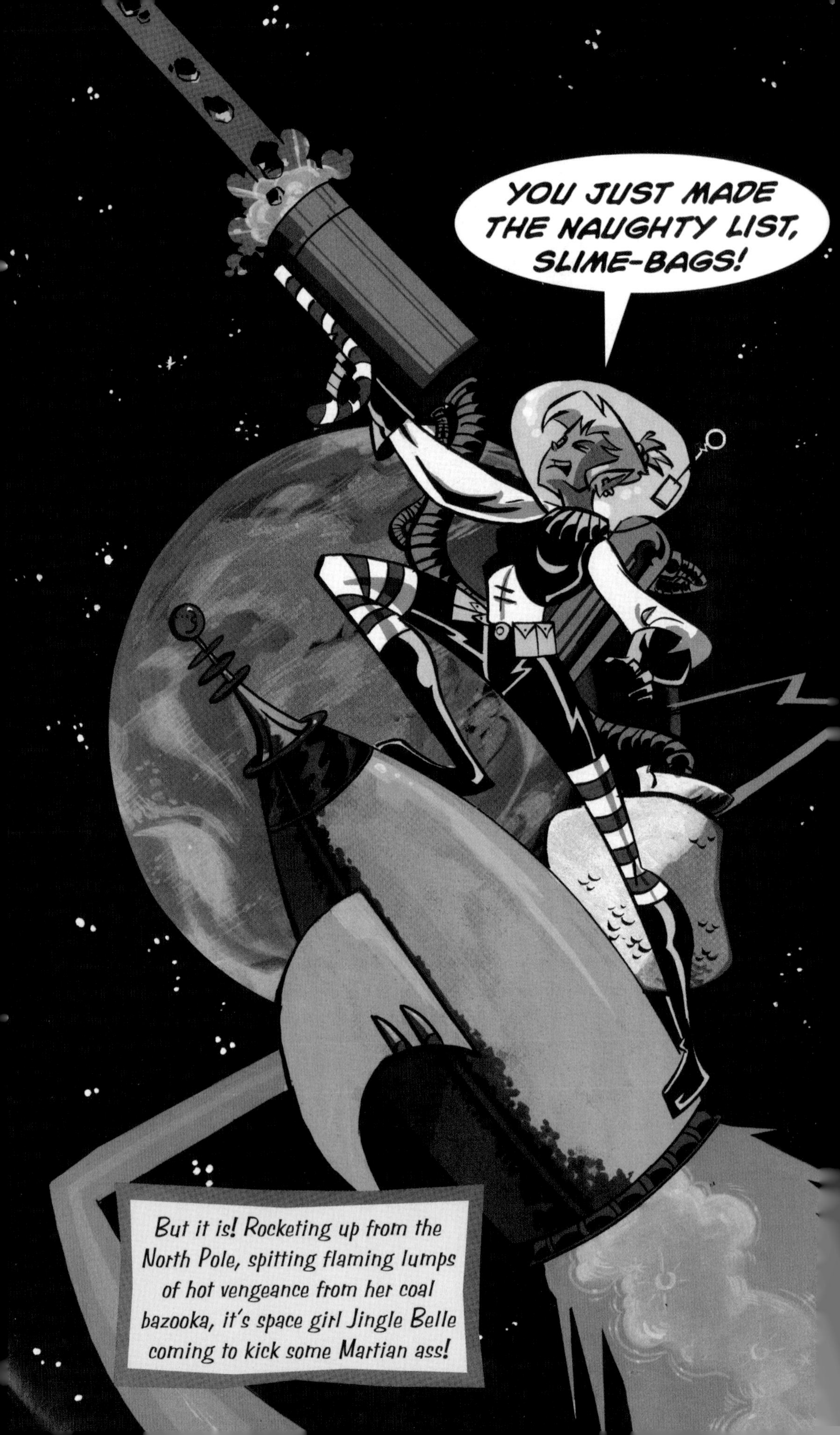
YOU JUST MADE THE NAUGHTY LIST, SLIME-BAGS!
But it is! Rocketing up from the North Pole, spitting flaming lumps of hot vengeance from her coal bazooka, it's space girl Jingle Belle coming to kick some Martian ass!

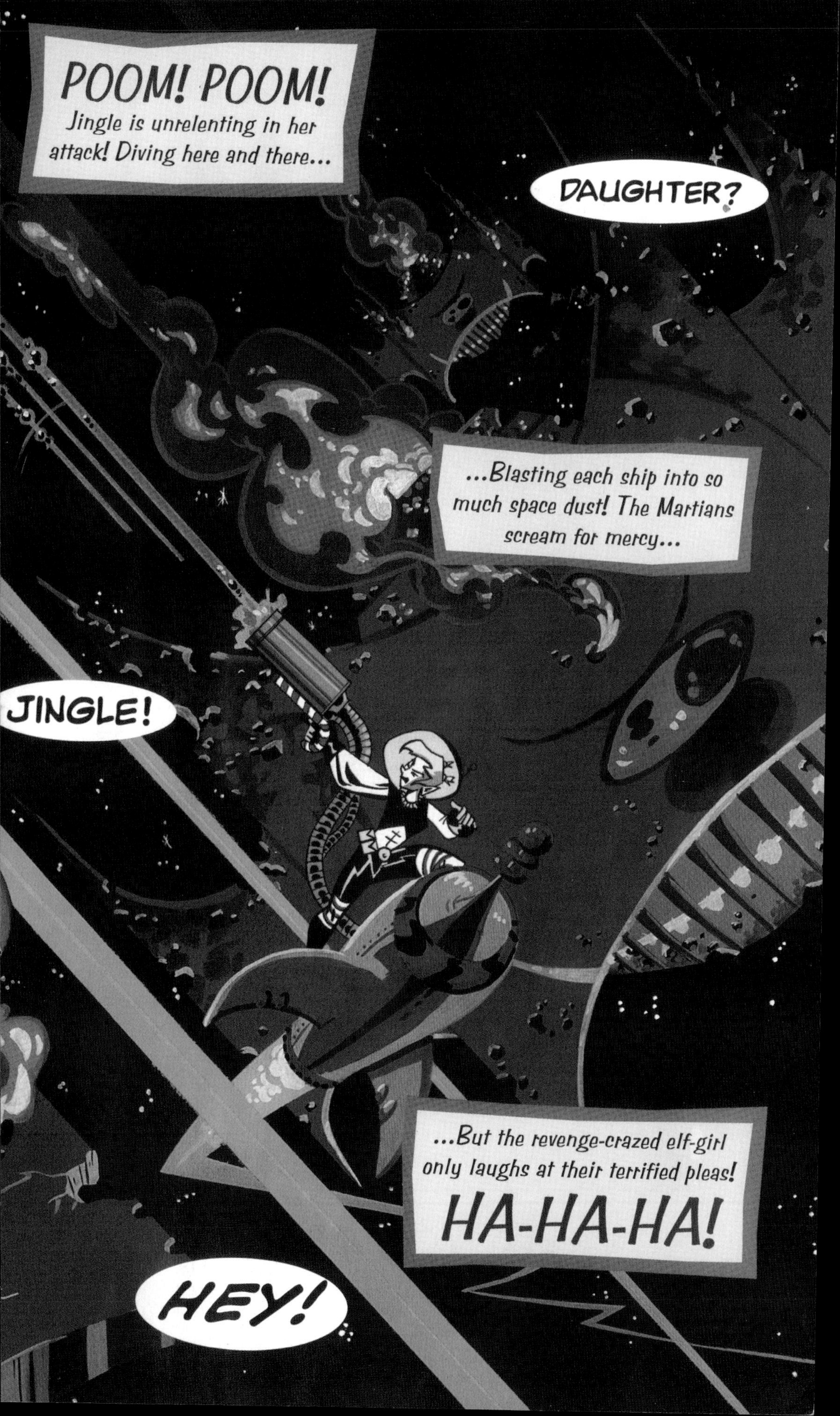
POOM! POOM!
Jingle is unrelenting in her attack! Diving here and there...
DAUGHTER?
...Blasting each ship into so much space dust! The Martians scream for mercy...
JINGLE!
...But the revenge-crazed elf-girl only laughs at their terrified pleas!
HA-HA-HA!
HEY!

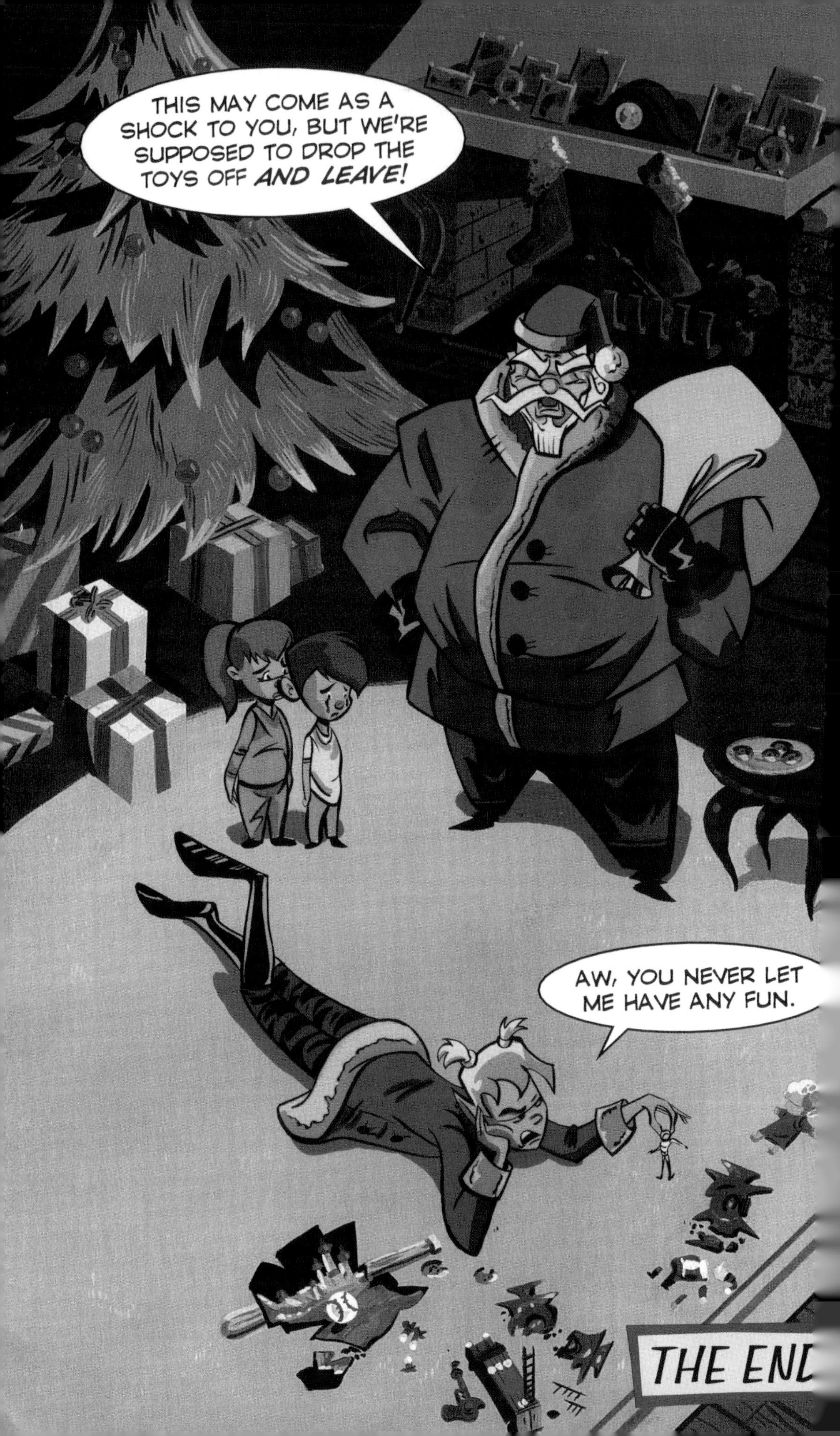
THIS MAY COME AS A SHOCK TO YOU, BUT WE'RE SUPPOSED TO DROP THE TOYS OFF AND LEAVE!
AW, YOU NEVER LET ME HAVE ANY FUN.
THE END

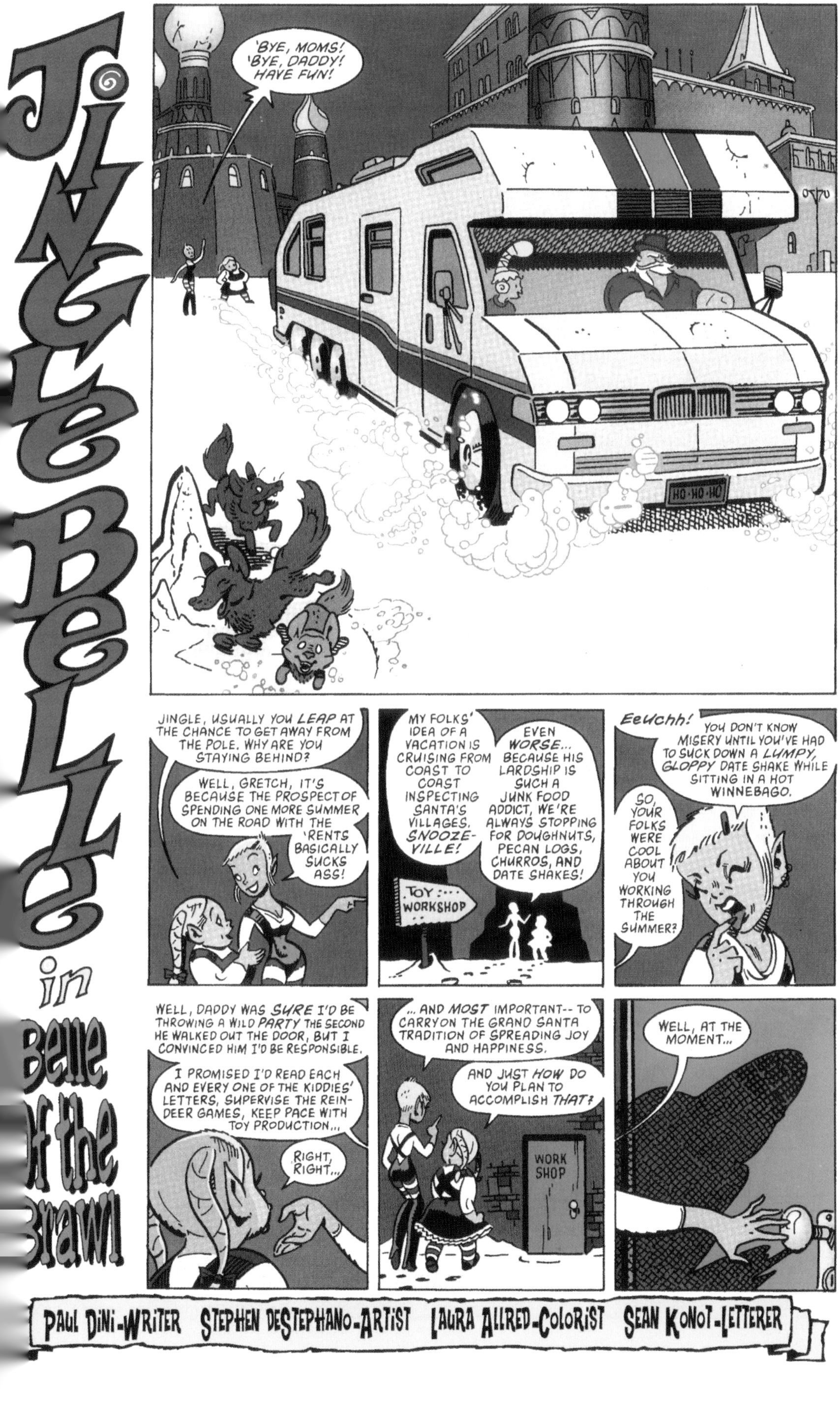
Jingle Belle in Belle of the Brawl
'BYE, MOMS! 'BYE, DADDY! HAVE FUN!
HO-HO-HO
JINGLE, USUALLY YOU LEAP AT THE CHANCE TO GET AWAY FROM THE POLE. WHY ARE YOU STAYING BEHIND?
WELL, GRETCH, IT'S BECAUSE THE PROSPECT OF SPENDING ONE MORE SUMMER ON THE ROAD WITH THE 'RENTS BASICALLY SUCKS ASS!
MY FOLKS' IDEA OF A VACATION IS CRUISING FROM COAST TO COAST INSPECTING SANTA'S VILLAGES. SNOOZE-VILLE!
EVEN WORSE... BECAUSE HIS LARDSHIP IS SUCH A JUNK FOOD ADDICT, WE'RE ALWAYS STOPPING FOR DOUGHNUTS, PECAN LOGS, CHURROS, AND DATE SHAKES!
TOY WORKSHOP
Eeuchh! YOU DON'T KNOW MISERY UNTIL YOU'VE HAD TO SUCK DOWN A LUMPY, GLOPPY DATE SHAKE WHILE SITTING IN A HOT WINNEBAGO.
SO, YOUR FOLKS WERE COOL ABOUT YOU WORKING THROUGH THE SUMMER?
WELL, DADDY WAS SURE I'D BE THROWING A WILD PARTY THE SECOND HE WALKED OUT THE DOOR, BUT I CONVINCED HIM I'D BE RESPONSIBLE.
I PROMISED I'D READ EACH AND EVERY ONE OF THE KIDDIES' LETTERS, SUPERVISE THE REINDEER GAMES, KEEP PACE WITH TOY PRODUCTION...
RIGHT, RIGHT...
... AND MOST IMPORTANT-- TO CARRY ON THE GRAND SANTA TRADITION OF SPREADING JOY AND HAPPINESS.
AND JUST HOW DO YOU PLAN TO ACCOMPLISH THAT?
WORK SHOP
WELL, AT THE MOMENT...
PAUL DINI-WRITER STEPHEN DESTEPHANO-ARTIST LAURA ALLRED-COLORIST SEAN KONOT-LETTERER

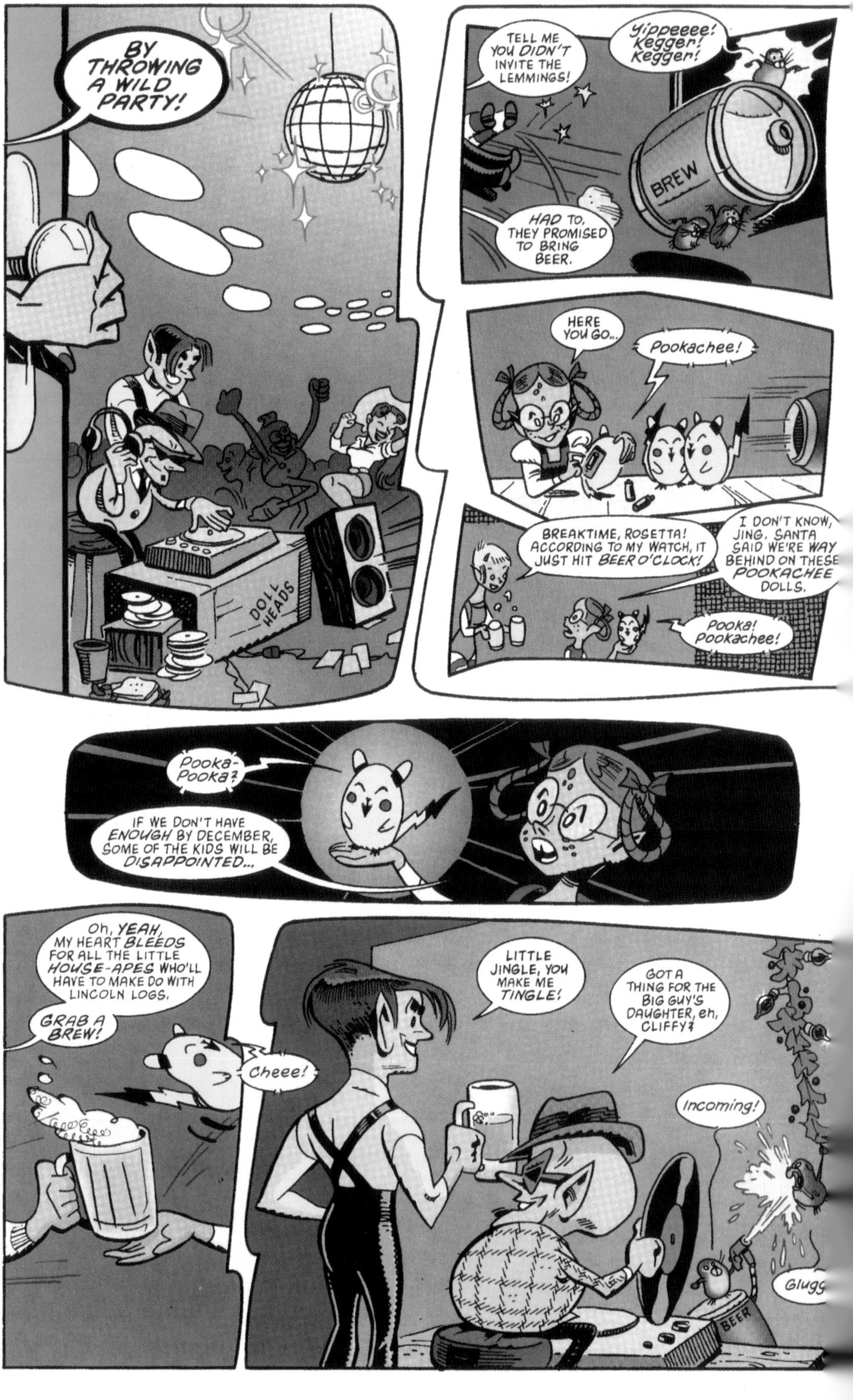
BY THROWING A WILD PARTY!
TELL ME YOU DIDN'T INVITE THE LEMMINGS!
Yippeeee! Kegger! Kegger!
HAD TO. THEY PROMISED TO BRING BEER.
BREW
HERE YOU GO...
Pookachee!
BREAKTIME, ROSETTA! ACCORDING TO MY WATCH, IT JUST HIT BEER O'CLOCK!
I DON'T KNOW, JING. SANTA SAID WE'RE WAY BEHIND ON THESE POOKACHEE DOLLS.
Pooka! Pookachee!
Pooka-Pooka?
IF WE DON'T HAVE ENOUGH BY DECEMBER, SOME OF THE KIDS WILL BE DISAPPOINTED...
Oh, YEAH, MY HEART BLEEDS FOR ALL THE LITTLE HOUSE-APES WHO'LL HAVE TO MAKE DO WITH LINCOLN LOGS.
GRAB A BREW!
Cheee!
LITTLE JINGLE, YOU MAKE ME TINGLE!
GOT A THING FOR THE BIG GUY'S DAUGHTER, eh, CLIFFY?
Incoming!
Glugg
BEER

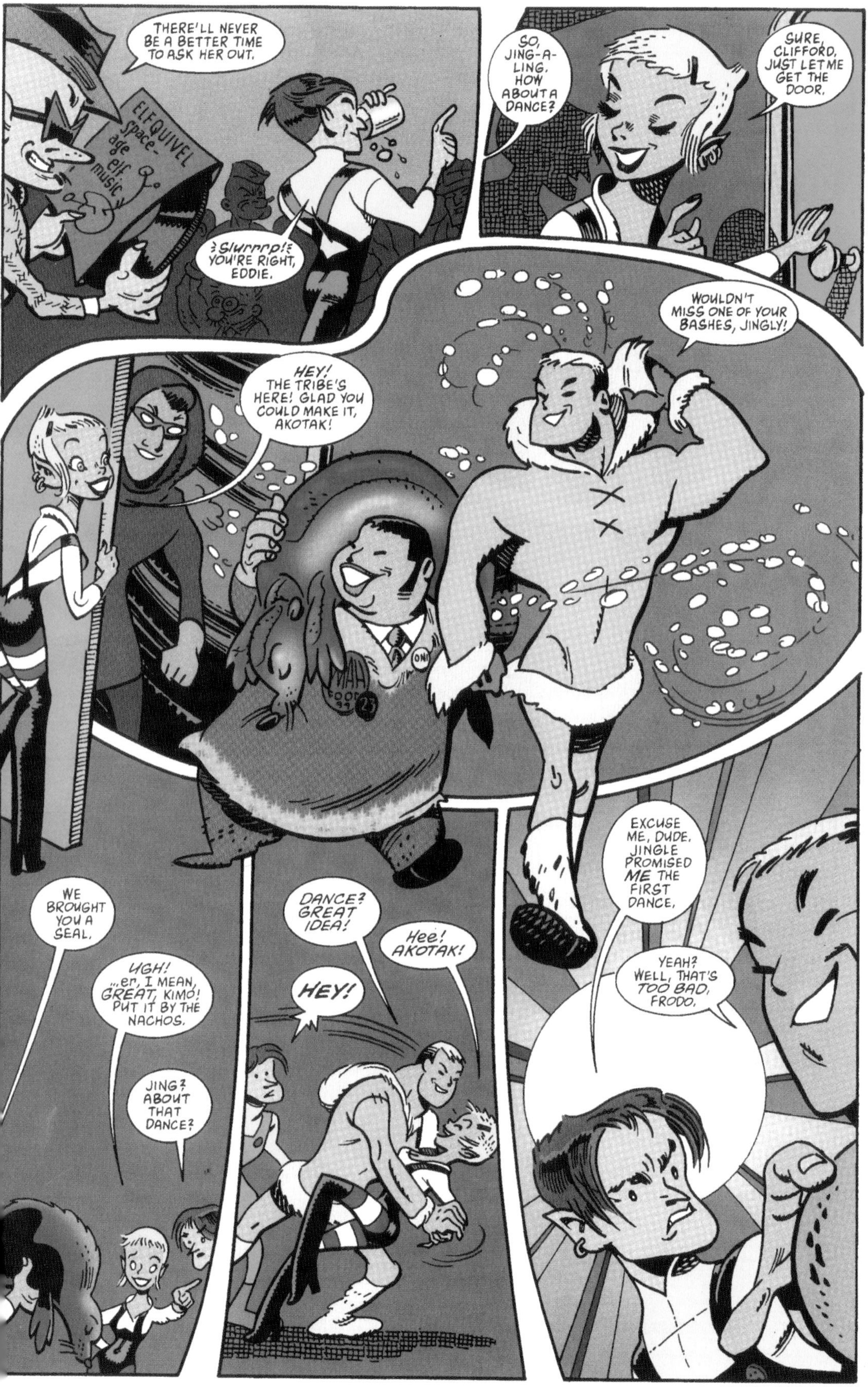
THERE'LL NEVER BE A BETTER TIME TO ASK HER OUT.
ELFQUIVEL space-age elf music
≷Slurrrp!≶ YOU'RE RIGHT, EDDIE.
SO, JING-A-LING, HOW ABOUT A DANCE?
SURE, CLIFFORD, JUST LET ME GET THE DOOR.
WOULDN'T MISS ONE OF YOUR BASHES, JINGLY!
HEY! THE TRIBE'S HERE! GLAD YOU COULD MAKE IT, AKOTAK!
WE BROUGHT YOU A SEAL.
UGH! ...er, I MEAN, GREAT, KIMO! PUT IT BY THE NACHOS.
JING? ABOUT THAT DANCE?
DANCE? GREAT IDEA!
Hee! AKOTAK!
HEY!
EXCUSE ME, DUDE. JINGLE PROMISED ME THE FIRST DANCE.
YEAH? WELL, THAT'S TOO BAD, FRODO.

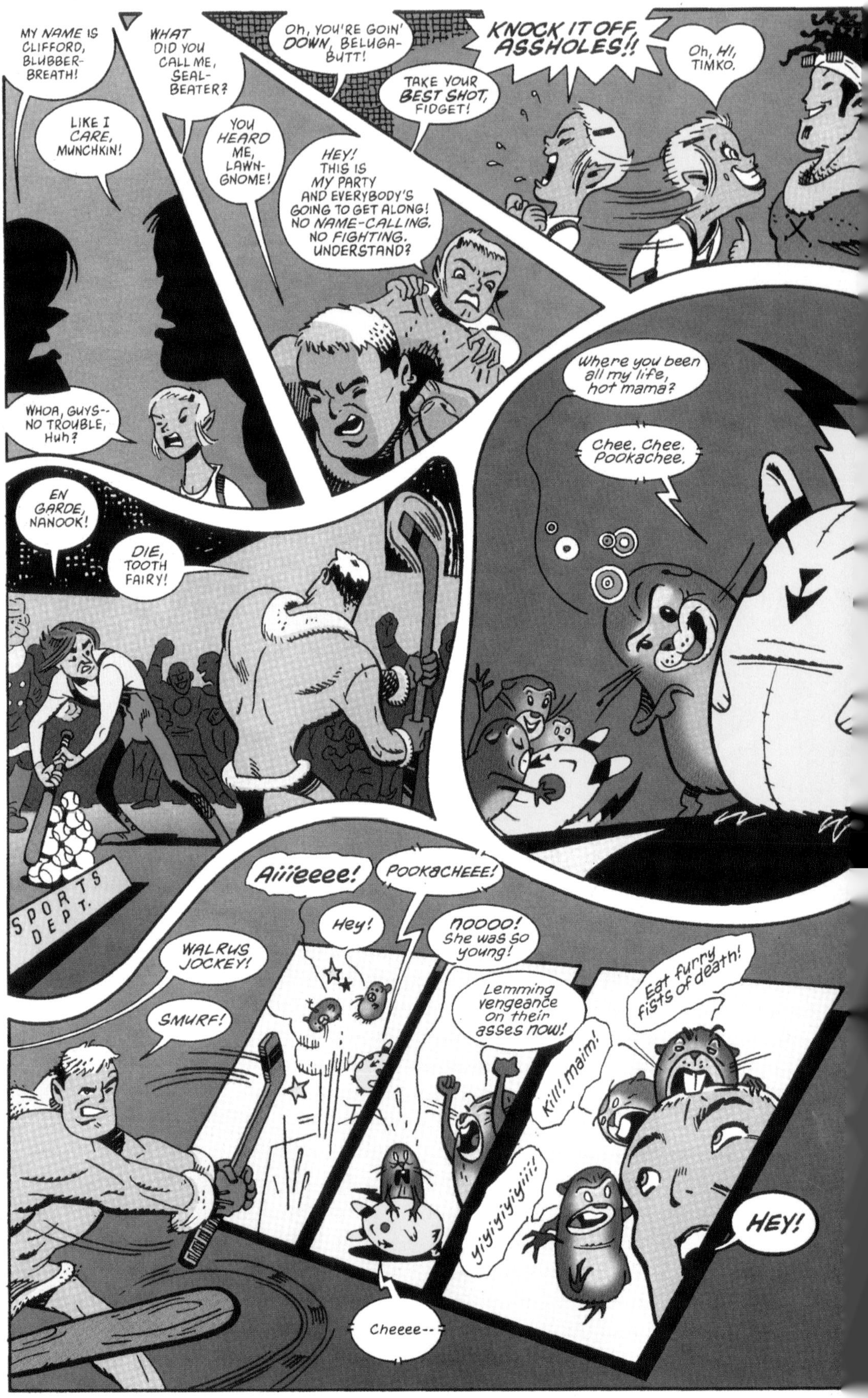
MY NAME IS CLIFFORD, BLUBBER-BREATH!
WHAT DID YOU CALL ME, SEAL-BEATER?
Oh, YOU'RE GOIN' DOWN, BELUGA-BUTT!
KNOCK IT OFF, ASSHOLES!!
Oh, HI, TIMKO.
LIKE I CARE, MUNCHKIN!
YOU HEARD ME, LAWN-GNOME!
TAKE YOUR BEST SHOT, FIDGET!
HEY! THIS IS MY PARTY AND EVERYBODY'S GOING TO GET ALONG! NO NAME-CALLING. NO FIGHTING. UNDERSTAND?
WHOA, GUYS-- NO TROUBLE, Huh?
Where you been all my life, hot mama?
Chee. Chee. Pookachee.
EN GARDE, NANOOK!
DIE, TOOTH FAIRY!
SPORTS DEPT.
Aiiieeee!
POOKACHEEE!
Hey!
WALRUS JOCKEY!
SMURF!
nOOOO! She was so young!
Lemming vengeance on their asses now!
Eat furry fists of death!
Kill! maim!
yiyiyiyiyiii!
HEY!
Cheeee--

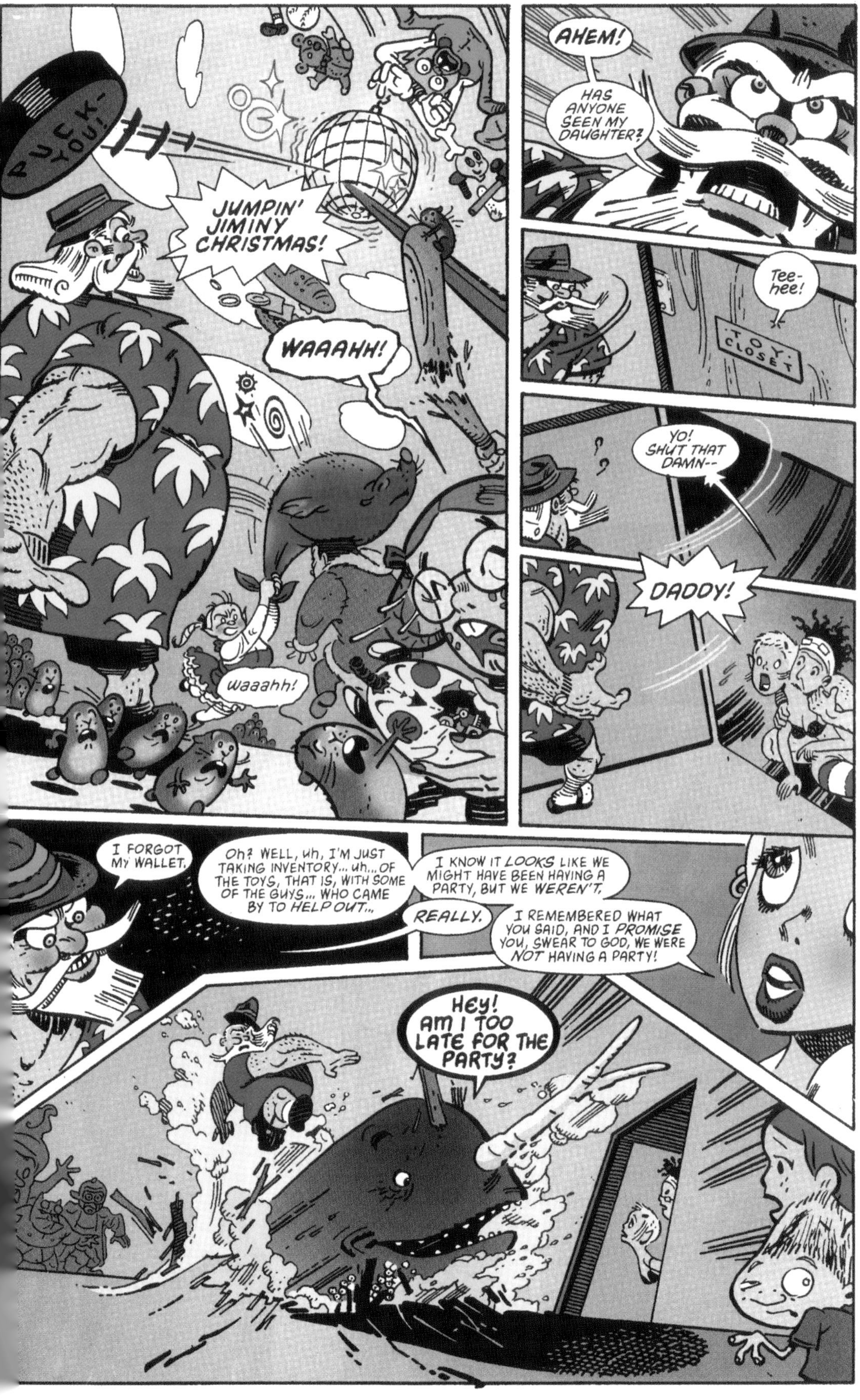
PUCK-YOU!
JUMPIN' JIMINY CHRISTMAS!
WAAAHH!
waaahh!
AHEM!
HAS ANYONE SEEN MY DAUGHTER?
Tee-hee!
TOY CLOSET
YO! SHUT THAT DAMN--
DADDY!
I FORGOT MY WALLET.
Oh? WELL, uh, I'M JUST TAKING INVENTORY... uh... OF THE TOYS, THAT IS, WITH SOME OF THE GUYS... WHO CAME BY TO HELP OUT...
I KNOW IT LOOKS LIKE WE MIGHT HAVE BEEN HAVING A PARTY, BUT WE WEREN'T.
REALLY.
I REMEMBERED WHAT YOU SAID, AND I PROMISE YOU, SWEAR TO GOD, WE WERE NOT HAVING A PARTY!
HEY! AM I TOO LATE FOR THE PARTY?

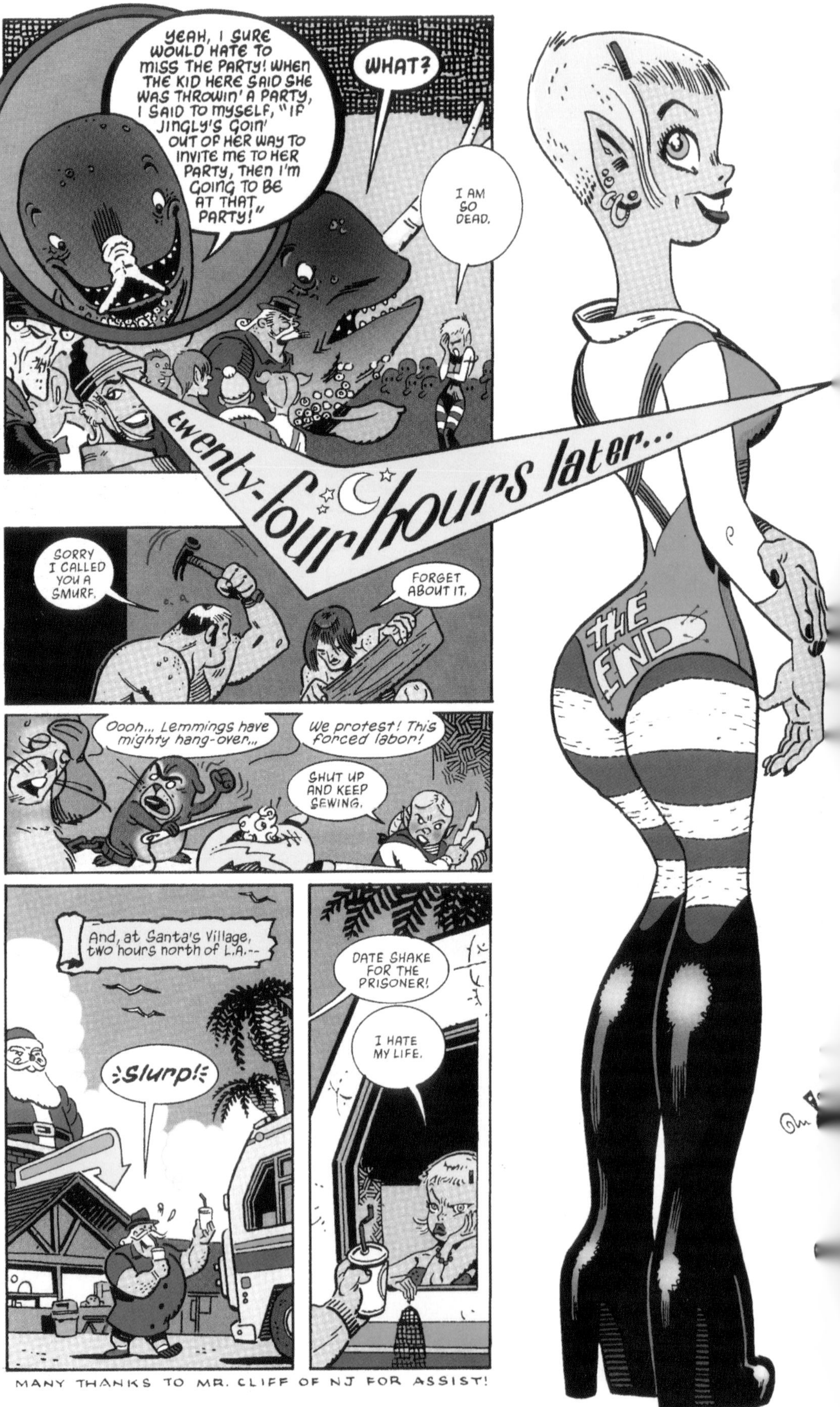
YEAH, I SURE WOULD HATE TO MISS THE PARTY! WHEN THE KID HERE SAID SHE WAS THROWIN' A PARTY, I SAID TO MYSELF, "IF JINGLY'S GOIN' OUT OF HER WAY TO INVITE ME TO HER PARTY, THEN I'M GOING TO BE AT THAT PARTY!"
WHAT?
I AM SO DEAD.
twenty-four hours later...
SORRY I CALLED YOU A SMURF.
FORGET ABOUT IT.
Oooh... Lemmings have mighty hang-over...
We protest! This forced labor!
SHUT UP AND KEEP SEWING.
And, at Santa's Village, two hours north of L.A.--
Slurp!
DATE SHAKE FOR THE PRISONER!
I HATE MY LIFE.
THE END
MANY THANKS TO MR. CLIFF OF NJ FOR ASSIST!

Little Matchstick Girl

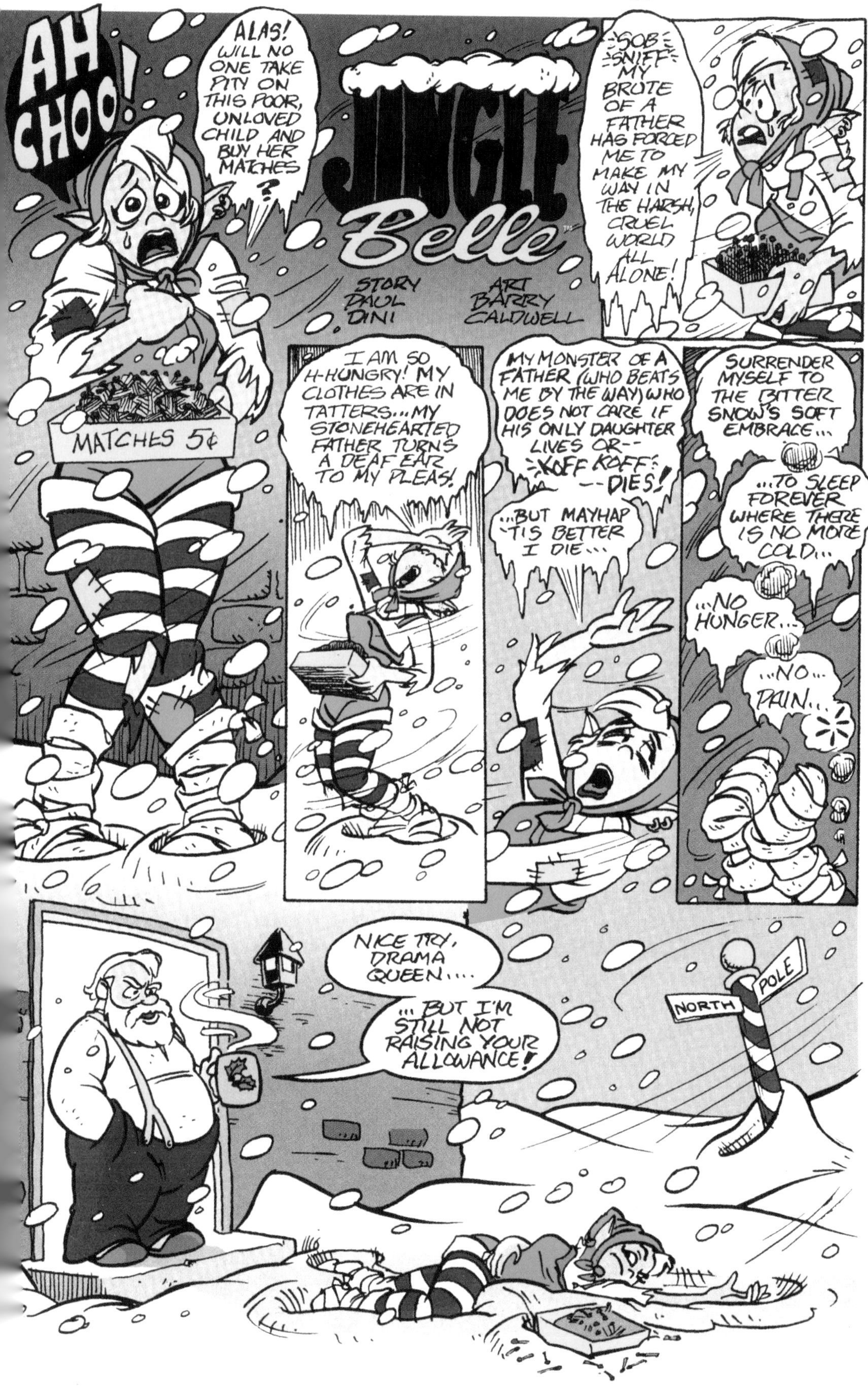
AH CHOO!
ALAS! WILL NO ONE TAKE PITY ON THIS POOR, UNLOVED CHILD AND BUY HER MATCHES?
JINGLE Belle
STORY PAUL DINI
ART BARRY CALDWELL
MATCHES 5¢
SOB SNIFF MY BRUTE OF A FATHER HAS FORCED ME TO MAKE MY WAY IN THE HARSH, CRUEL WORLD ALL ALONE!
I AM SO H-HUNGRY! MY CLOTHES ARE IN TATTERS... MY STONEHEARTED FATHER TURNS A DEAF EAR TO MY PLEAS!
MY MONSTER OF A FATHER (WHO BEATS ME BY THE WAY) WHO DOES NOT CARE IF HIS ONLY DAUGHTER LIVES OR-- KOFF KOFF --DIES!
...BUT MAYHAP 'TIS BETTER I DIE...
SURRENDER MYSELF TO THE BITTER SNOW'S SOFT EMBRACE...
...TO SLEEP FOREVER WHERE THERE IS NO MORE COLD...
...NO HUNGER...
...NO PAIN...
NICE TRY, DRAMA QUEEN....
...BUT I'M STILL NOT RAISING YOUR ALLOWANCE!
NORTH
POLE

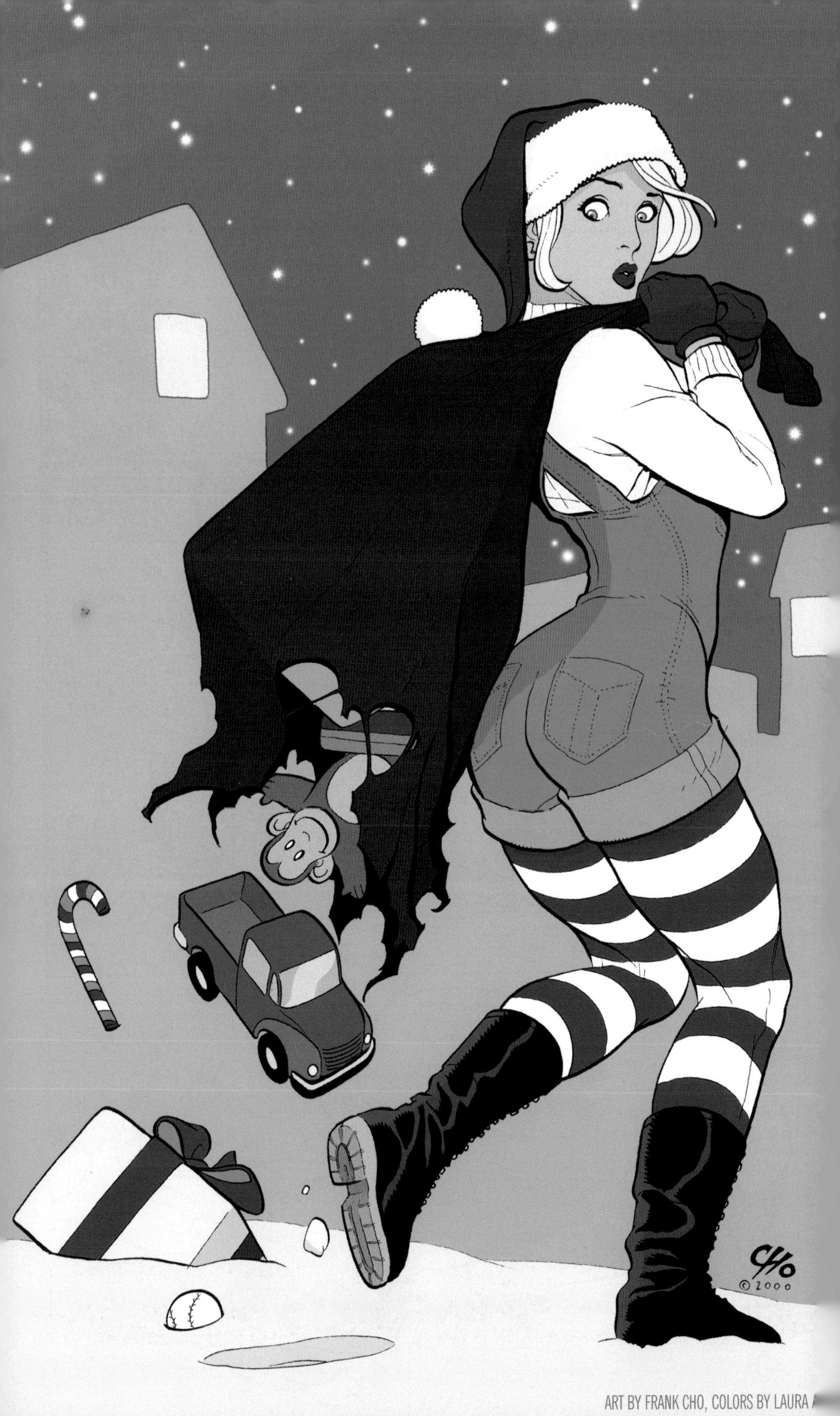
CHO
©2000

ART BY FRANK CHO, COLORS BY LAURA

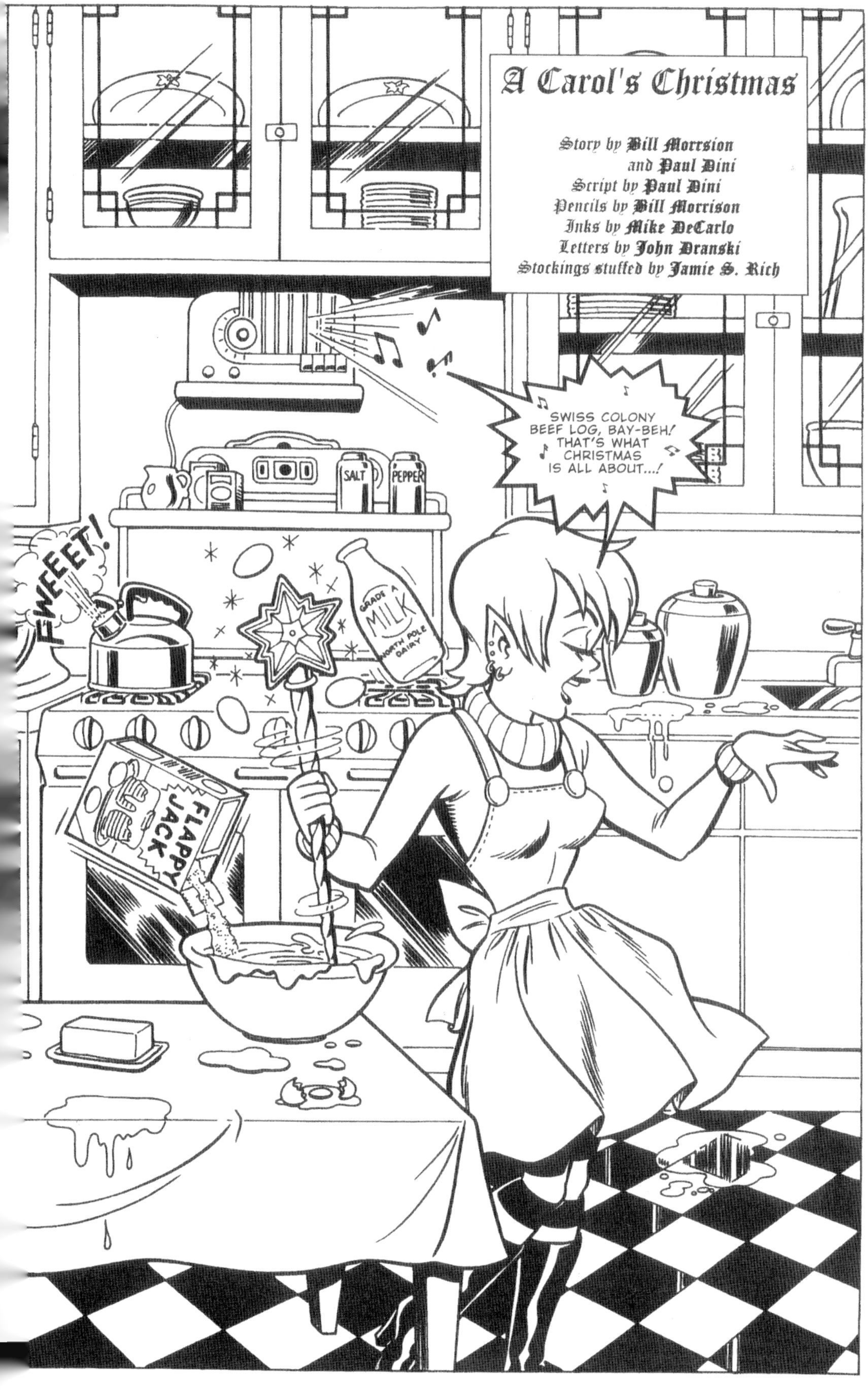
A Carol's Christmas
Story by Bill Morrsion and Paul Dini
Script by Paul Dini
Pencils by Bill Morrison
Inks by Mike DeCarlo
Letters by John Dranski
Stockings stuffed by Jamie S. Rich
SWISS COLONY BEEF LOG, BAY-BEH! THAT'S WHAT CHRISTMAS IS ALL ABOUT...!
FWEEEET!
SALT
PEPPER
GRADE A MILK NORTH POLE DAIRY
FLAPPY JACK

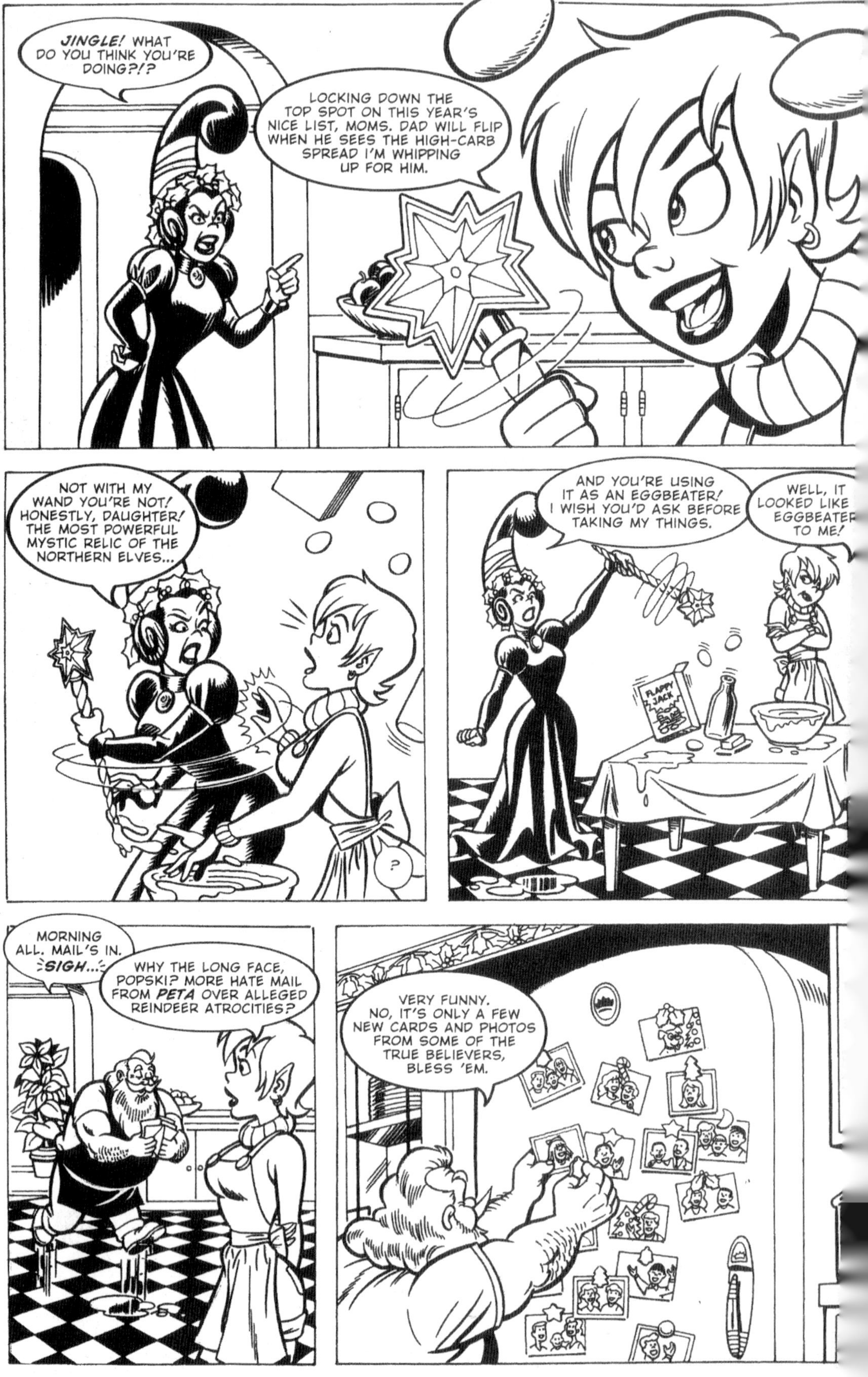
JINGLE! WHAT DO YOU THINK YOU'RE DOING?!?
LOCKING DOWN THE TOP SPOT ON THIS YEAR'S NICE LIST, MOMS. DAD WILL FLIP WHEN HE SEES THE HIGH-CARB SPREAD I'M WHIPPING UP FOR HIM.
NOT WITH MY WAND YOU'RE NOT! HONESTLY, DAUGHTER! THE MOST POWERFUL MYSTIC RELIC OF THE NORTHERN ELVES...
?
AND YOU'RE USING IT AS AN EGGBEATER! I WISH YOU'D ASK BEFORE TAKING MY THINGS.
WELL, IT LOOKED LIKE EGGBEATER TO ME!
FLAPPY JACK
MORNING ALL. MAIL'S IN. SIGH...
WHY THE LONG FACE, POPSKI? MORE HATE MAIL FROM PETA OVER ALLEGED REINDEER ATROCITIES?
VERY FUNNY. NO, IT'S ONLY A FEW NEW CARDS AND PHOTOS FROM SOME OF THE TRUE BELIEVERS, BLESS 'EM.

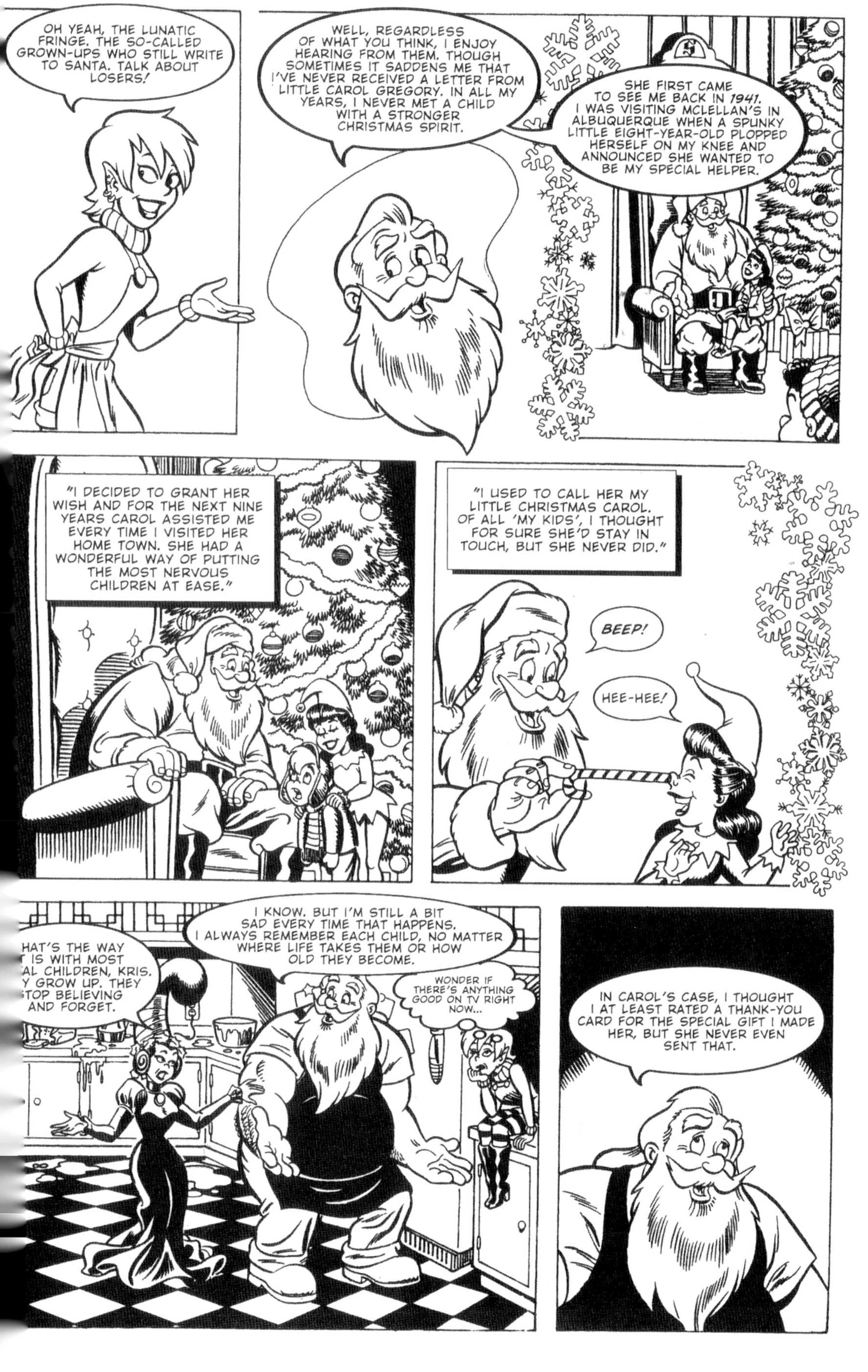
OH YEAH, THE LUNATIC FRINGE. THE SO-CALLED GROWN-UPS WHO STILL WRITE TO SANTA. TALK ABOUT LOSERS!
WELL, REGARDLESS OF WHAT YOU THINK, I ENJOY HEARING FROM THEM. THOUGH SOMETIMES IT SADDENS ME THAT I'VE NEVER RECEIVED A LETTER FROM LITTLE CAROL GREGORY. IN ALL MY YEARS, I NEVER MET A CHILD WITH A STRONGER CHRISTMAS SPIRIT.
SHE FIRST CAME TO SEE ME BACK IN 1941. I WAS VISITING MCLELLAN'S IN ALBUQUERQUE WHEN A SPUNKY LITTLE EIGHT-YEAR-OLD PLOPPED HERSELF ON MY KNEE AND ANNOUNCED SHE WANTED TO BE MY SPECIAL HELPER.
"I DECIDED TO GRANT HER WISH AND FOR THE NEXT NINE YEARS CAROL ASSISTED ME EVERY TIME I VISITED HER HOME TOWN. SHE HAD A WONDERFUL WAY OF PUTTING THE MOST NERVOUS CHILDREN AT EASE."
"I USED TO CALL HER MY LITTLE CHRISTMAS CAROL. OF ALL 'MY KIDS', I THOUGHT FOR SURE SHE'D STAY IN TOUCH, BUT SHE NEVER DID."
BEEP!
HEE-HEE!
HAT'S THE WAY T IS WITH MOST AL CHILDREN, KRIS. Y GROW UP. THEY STOP BELIEVING AND FORGET.
I KNOW. BUT I'M STILL A BIT SAD EVERY TIME THAT HAPPENS. I ALWAYS REMEMBER EACH CHILD, NO MATTER WHERE LIFE TAKES THEM OR HOW OLD THEY BECOME.
WONDER IF THERE'S ANYTHING GOOD ON TV RIGHT NOW...
IN CAROL'S CASE, I THOUGHT I AT LEAST RATED A THANK-YOU CARD FOR THE SPECIAL GIFT I MADE HER, BUT SHE NEVER EVEN SENT THAT.

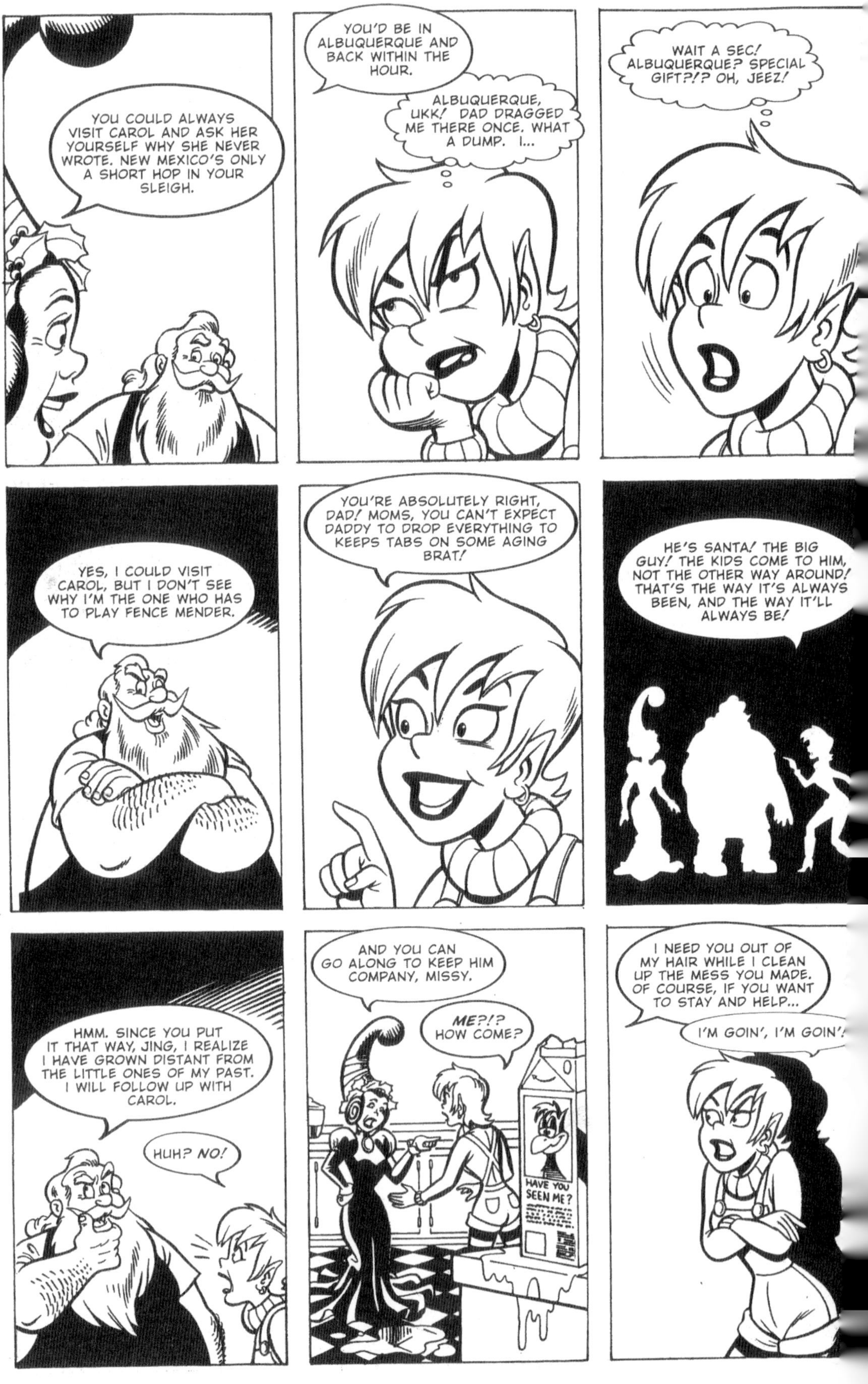

YOU COULD ALWAYS VISIT CAROL AND ASK HER YOURSELF WHY SHE NEVER WROTE. NEW MEXICO'S ONLY A SHORT HOP IN YOUR SLEIGH.
YOU'D BE IN ALBUQUERQUE AND BACK WITHIN THE HOUR.
ALBUQUERQUE, UKK! DAD DRAGGED ME THERE ONCE. WHAT A DUMP. I...
WAIT A SEC! ALBUQUERQUE? SPECIAL GIFT?!? OH, JEEZ!
YES, I COULD VISIT CAROL, BUT I DON'T SEE WHY I'M THE ONE WHO HAS TO PLAY FENCE MENDER.
YOU'RE ABSOLUTELY RIGHT, DAD! MOMS, YOU CAN'T EXPECT DADDY TO DROP EVERYTHING TO KEEPS TABS ON SOME AGING BRAT!
HE'S SANTA! THE BIG GUY! THE KIDS COME TO HIM, NOT THE OTHER WAY AROUND! THAT'S THE WAY IT'S ALWAYS BEEN, AND THE WAY IT'LL ALWAYS BE!
HMM. SINCE YOU PUT IT THAT WAY, JING, I REALIZE I HAVE GROWN DISTANT FROM THE LITTLE ONES OF MY PAST. I WILL FOLLOW UP WITH CAROL.
HUH? NO!
AND YOU CAN GO ALONG TO KEEP HIM COMPANY, MISSY.
ME?!? HOW COME?
HAVE YOU SEEN ME?
I NEED YOU OUT OF MY HAIR WHILE I CLEAN UP THE MESS YOU MADE. OF COURSE, IF YOU WANT TO STAY AND HELP...
I'M GOIN', I'M GOIN'!

SO MAYBE THIS CHICK IS LIKE, DEAD OR SOMETHING. DIDJA EVER THINK OF THAT?

NO, MY SNOW GLOBE TOLD ME SHE'S STILL ALIVE AND WORKING AS A TEACHER.

NOW, WE DON'T WANT TO STARTLE HER, SO LET'S JUST OBSERVE THINGS FROM A DISTANCE FIRST.

HEY, I DIDN'T EVEN WANT TO COME, REMEMBER?

AH! I SEE SHE STILL HAS THAT SPECIAL WAY WITH KIDS.

MISS GREGORY, DO YOU THINK MY DRAWING LOOKS LIKE SANTA CLAUS?

DIVIS
$4\sqrt{48}$

HOW SHOULD I KNOW?!? GIVE ME THAT! YOU'RE TOO OLD FOR THIS NONSENSE!

IT'S HIGH TIME YOU ALL LEARNED THERE IS NO SANTA CLAUS...

MULTIPLICATION
$5 \times 5 = 25$
$6 \times 6 = 36$
$7 \times 9 = 6?$
$4 \times 7 = ?$

...AND THERE NEVER WAS!

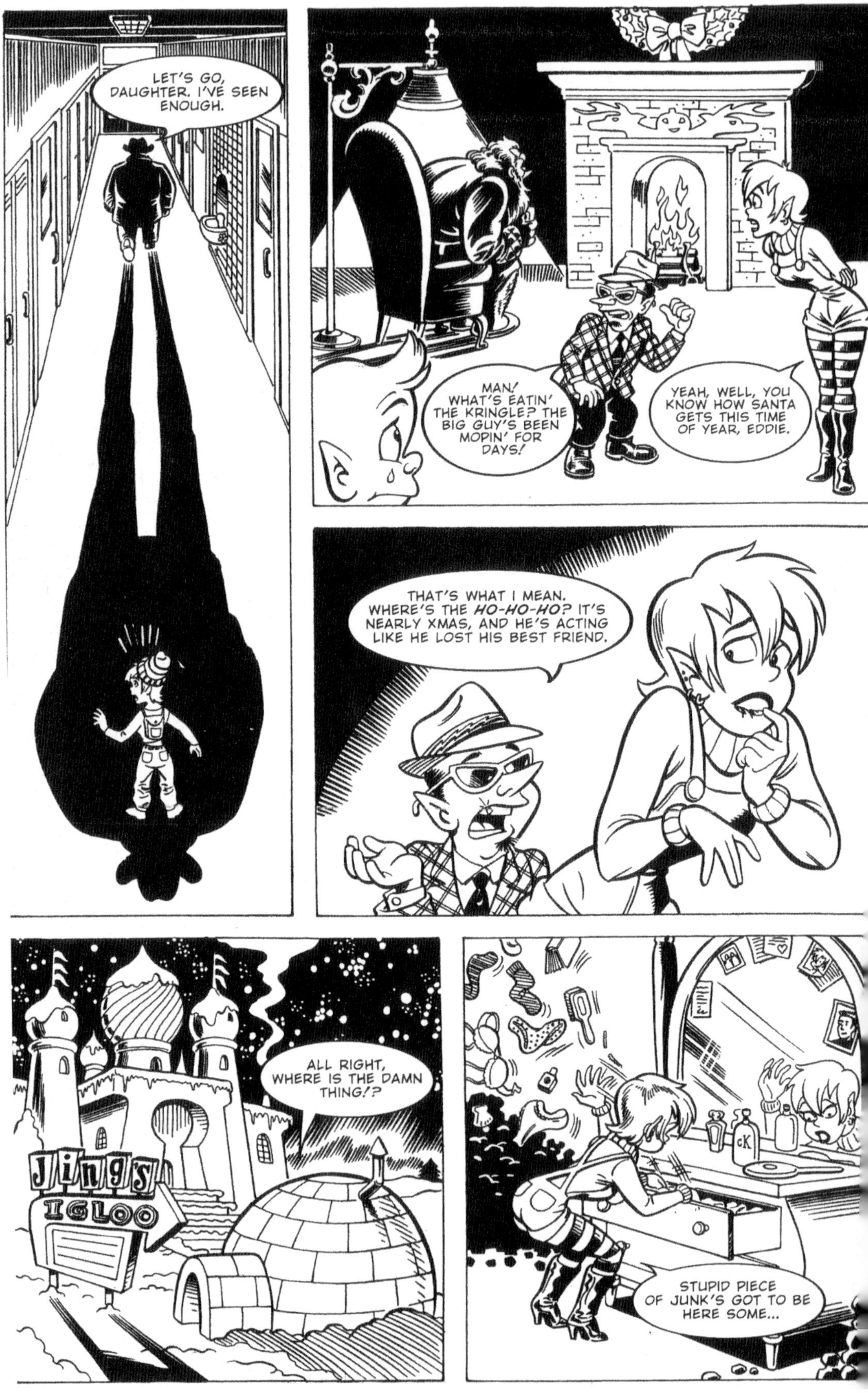
LET'S GO, DAUGHTER. I'VE SEEN ENOUGH.
MAN! WHAT'S EATIN' THE KRINGLE? THE BIG GUY'S BEEN MOPIN' FOR DAYS!
YEAH, WELL, YOU KNOW HOW SANTA GETS THIS TIME OF YEAR, EDDIE.
THAT'S WHAT I MEAN. WHERE'S THE HO-HO-HO? IT'S NEARLY XMAS, AND HE'S ACTING LIKE HE LOST HIS BEST FRIEND.
JING'S IGLOO
ALL RIGHT, WHERE IS THE DAMN THING!?
STUPID PIECE OF JUNK'S GOT TO BE HERE SOME...

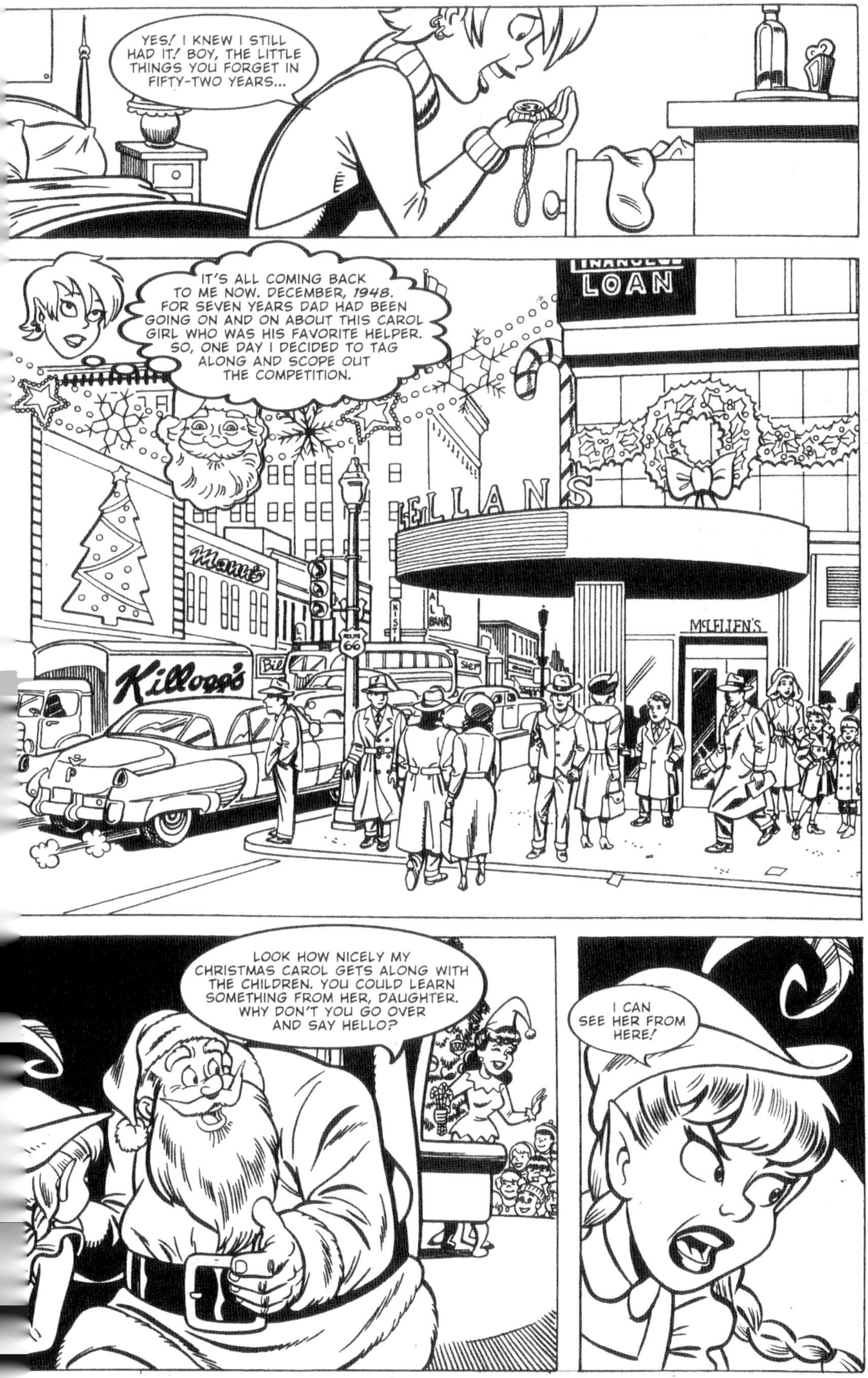
YES! I KNEW I STILL HAD IT! BOY, THE LITTLE THINGS YOU FORGET IN FIFTY-TWO YEARS...
IT'S ALL COMING BACK TO ME NOW. DECEMBER, 1948. FOR SEVEN YEARS DAD HAD BEEN GOING ON AND ON ABOUT THIS CAROL GIRL WHO WAS HIS FAVORITE HELPER. SO, ONE DAY I DECIDED TO TAG ALONG AND SCOPE OUT THE COMPETITION.
LOAN
ELLANS
Mann's
Killogg's
ROUTE 66
BANK
McELLEN'S
LOOK HOW NICELY MY CHRISTMAS CAROL GETS ALONG WITH THE CHILDREN. YOU COULD LEARN SOMETHING FROM HER, DAUGHTER. WHY DON'T YOU GO OVER AND SAY HELLO?
I CAN SEE HER FROM HERE!

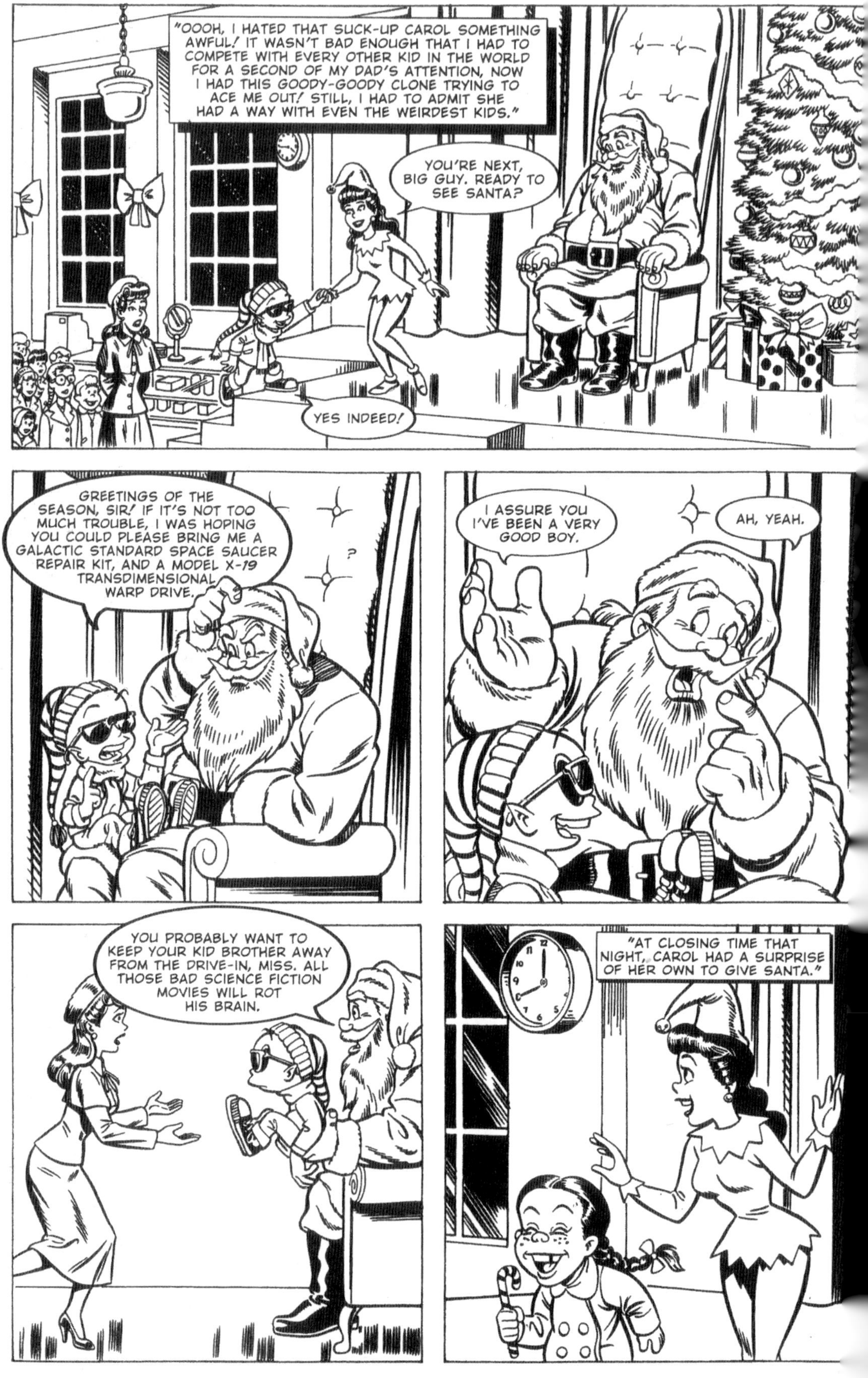
"OOOH, I HATED THAT SUCK-UP CAROL SOMETHING AWFUL! IT WASN'T BAD ENOUGH THAT I HAD TO COMPETE WITH EVERY OTHER KID IN THE WORLD FOR A SECOND OF MY DAD'S ATTENTION, NOW I HAD THIS GOODY-GOODY CLONE TRYING TO ACE ME OUT! STILL, I HAD TO ADMIT SHE HAD A WAY WITH EVEN THE WEIRDEST KIDS."
YOU'RE NEXT, BIG GUY. READY TO SEE SANTA?
YES INDEED!
GREETINGS OF THE SEASON, SIR! IF IT'S NOT TOO MUCH TROUBLE, I WAS HOPING YOU COULD PLEASE BRING ME A GALACTIC STANDARD SPACE SAUCER REPAIR KIT, AND A MODEL X-19 TRANSDIMENSIONAL WARP DRIVE.
?
I ASSURE YOU I'VE BEEN A VERY GOOD BOY.
AH, YEAH.
YOU PROBABLY WANT TO KEEP YOUR KID BROTHER AWAY FROM THE DRIVE-IN, MISS. ALL THOSE BAD SCIENCE FICTION MOVIES WILL ROT HIS BRAIN.
"AT CLOSING TIME THAT NIGHT, CAROL HAD A SURPRISE OF HER OWN TO GIVE SANTA."

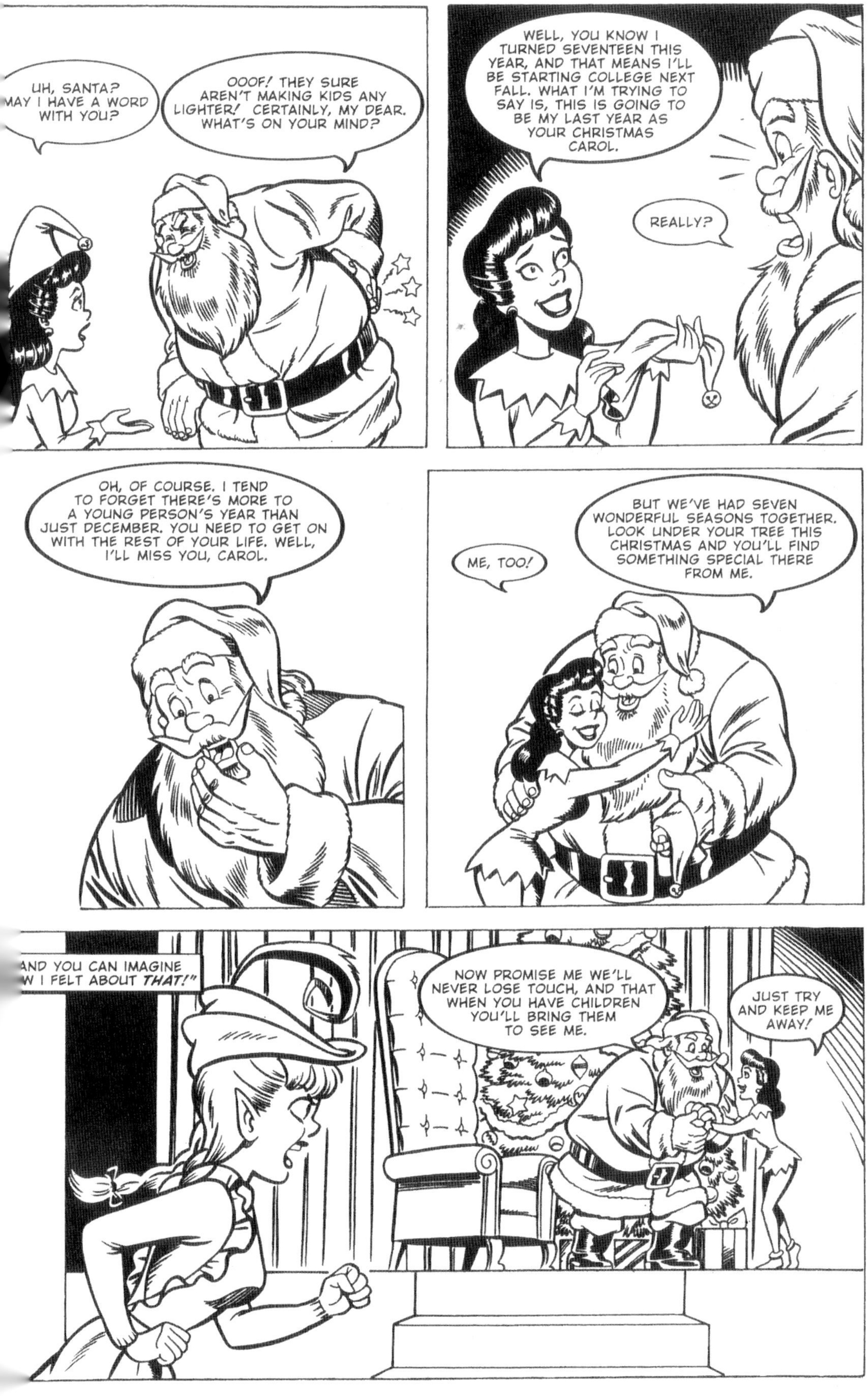
UH, SANTA? MAY I HAVE A WORD WITH YOU?
OOOF! THEY SURE AREN'T MAKING KIDS ANY LIGHTER! CERTAINLY, MY DEAR. WHAT'S ON YOUR MIND?
WELL, YOU KNOW I TURNED SEVENTEEN THIS YEAR, AND THAT MEANS I'LL BE STARTING COLLEGE NEXT FALL. WHAT I'M TRYING TO SAY IS, THIS IS GOING TO BE MY LAST YEAR AS YOUR CHRISTMAS CAROL.
REALLY?
OH, OF COURSE. I TEND TO FORGET THERE'S MORE TO A YOUNG PERSON'S YEAR THAN JUST DECEMBER. YOU NEED TO GET ON WITH THE REST OF YOUR LIFE. WELL, I'LL MISS YOU, CAROL.
ME, TOO!
BUT WE'VE HAD SEVEN WONDERFUL SEASONS TOGETHER. LOOK UNDER YOUR TREE THIS CHRISTMAS AND YOU'LL FIND SOMETHING SPECIAL THERE FROM ME.
AND YOU CAN IMAGINE
W I FELT ABOUT *THAT!*"
NOW PROMISE ME WE'LL NEVER LOSE TOUCH, AND THAT WHEN YOU HAVE CHILDREN YOU'LL BRING THEM TO SEE ME.
JUST TRY AND KEEP ME AWAY!

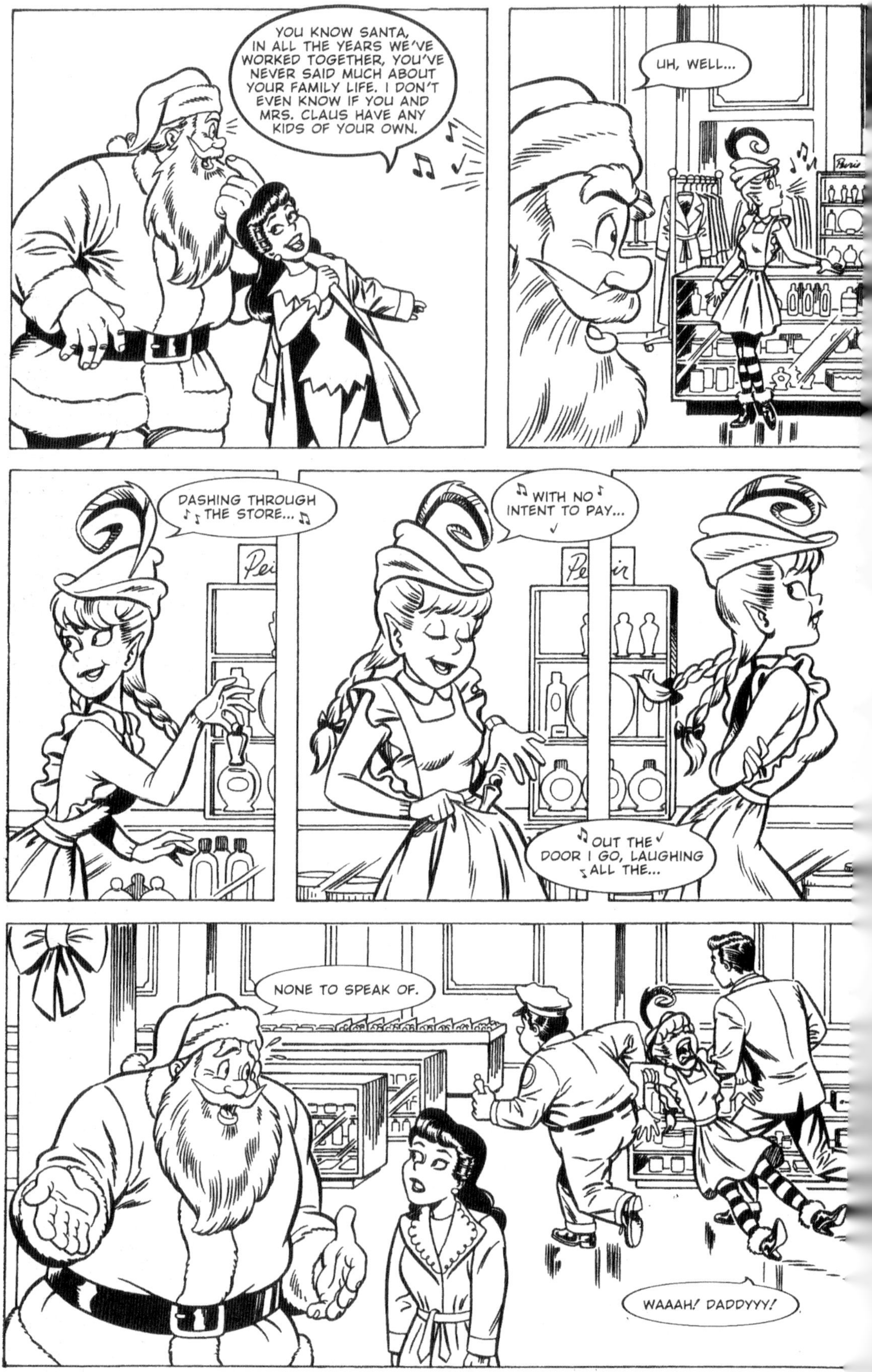
YOU KNOW SANTA, IN ALL THE YEARS WE'VE WORKED TOGETHER, YOU'VE NEVER SAID MUCH ABOUT YOUR FAMILY LIFE. I DON'T EVEN KNOW IF YOU AND MRS. CLAUS HAVE ANY KIDS OF YOUR OWN.
UH, WELL...
DASHING THROUGH THE STORE...
WITH NO INTENT TO PAY...
OUT THE DOOR I GO, LAUGHING ALL THE...
NONE TO SPEAK OF.
WAAAH! DADDYYY!

"LATER, AFTER CLEARING UP THE, UH, MISUNDERSTANDING WITH THE STORE GUARDS, DAD SET TO WORK MAKING CAROL'S PRESENT."

"BY MORNING HE HAD FASHIONED A BEAUTIFUL GOLDEN LOCKET."

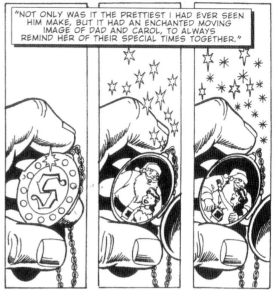

"NOT ONLY WAS IT THE PRETTIEST I HAD EVER SEEN HIM MAKE, BUT IT HAD AN ENCHANTED MOVING IMAGE OF DAD AND CAROL, TO ALWAYS REMIND HER OF THEIR SPECIAL TIMES TOGETHER."

"NO WAY WAS I GOING TO LET THAT LITTLE KISS-ASS KEEP IT! STILL, SANTA HAD PROMISED CAROL A SPECIAL PRESENT..."

NORTH POLE

"SO I SUBSTITUTED ONE OF MY OWN!"

"I IMAGINED OVER AND OVER WHAT IT MUST HAVE BEEN LIKE, LITTLE MISS PERFECT BEAMING WITH DELIGHT WHEN SHE FOUND THE BOX ON CHRISTMAS MORNING..."

"AND THEN THE LOOK ON HER FACE WHEN SHE FOUND THE LUMP OF COAL AND LETTER I PUT INSIDE!"

Carol,
how could you break my heart this way? I thought we'd be together forever. You're a very bad girl. Here's what you deserve for leaving me.
Santa

"I FIGURED THAT CAROL MIGHT WRITE A LETTER OF HER OWN, APOLOGIZING FOR ANY UNWITTING OFFENSE AND BEGGING SANTA'S FORGIVENESS."

"BUT I MADE IT A POINT TO GO THROUGH THE MAIL *FIRST* THAT MONTH AFTER CHRISTMAS."

NORTH POLE POSTAL DELIVERY

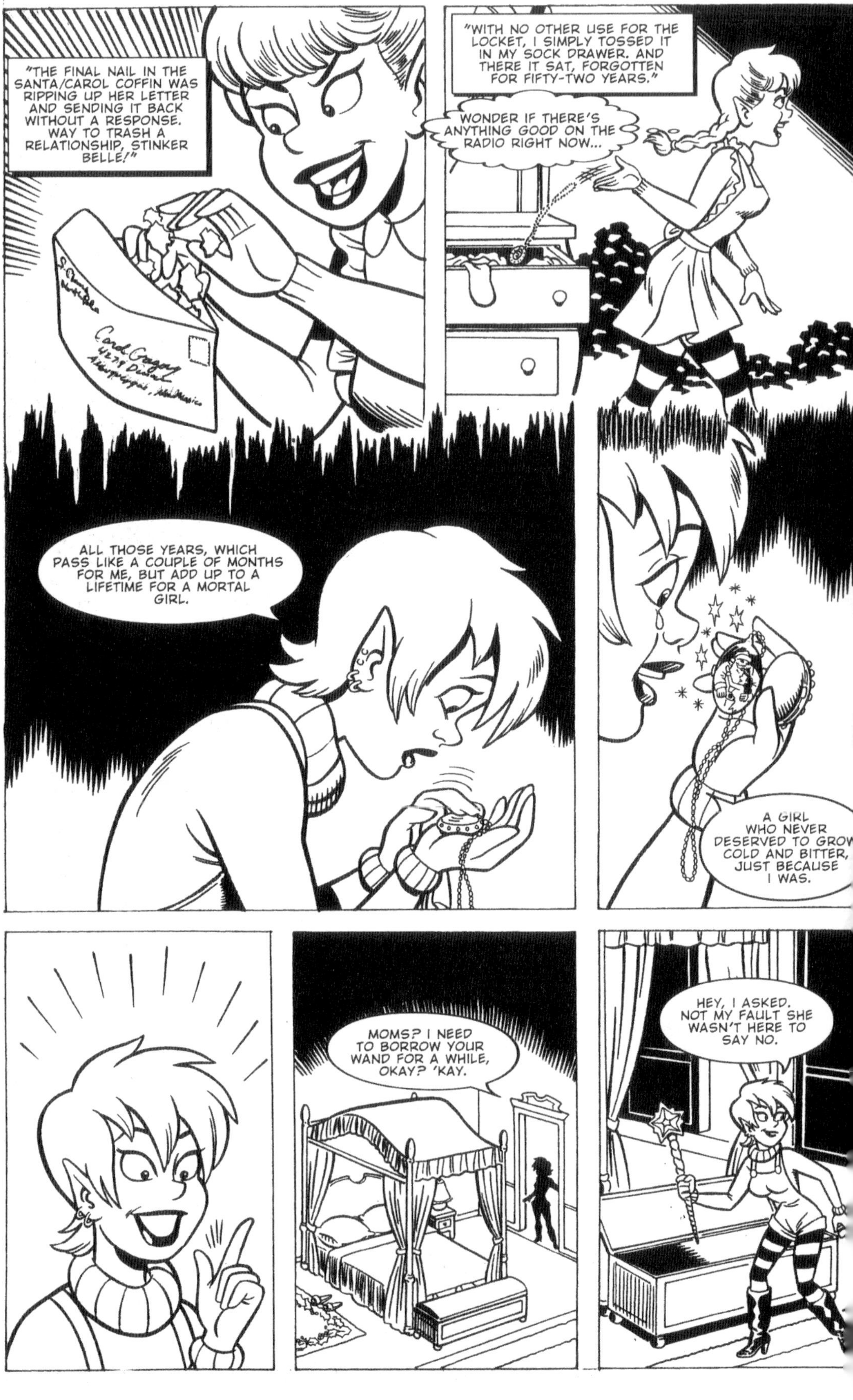
"THE FINAL NAIL IN THE SANTA/CAROL COFFIN WAS RIPPING UP HER LETTER AND SENDING IT BACK WITHOUT A RESPONSE. WAY TO TRASH A RELATIONSHIP, STINKER BELLE!"
"WITH NO OTHER USE FOR THE LOCKET, I SIMPLY TOSSED IT IN MY SOCK DRAWER. AND THERE IT SAT, FORGOTTEN FOR FIFTY-TWO YEARS."
WONDER IF THERE'S ANYTHING GOOD ON THE RADIO RIGHT NOW...
ALL THOSE YEARS, WHICH PASS LIKE A COUPLE OF MONTHS FOR ME, BUT ADD UP TO A LIFETIME FOR A MORTAL GIRL.
A GIRL WHO NEVER DESERVED TO GROW COLD AND BITTER, JUST BECAUSE I WAS.
MOMS? I NEED TO BORROW YOUR WAND FOR A WHILE, OKAY? 'KAY.
HEY, I ASKED. NOT MY FAULT SHE WASN'T HERE TO SAY NO.

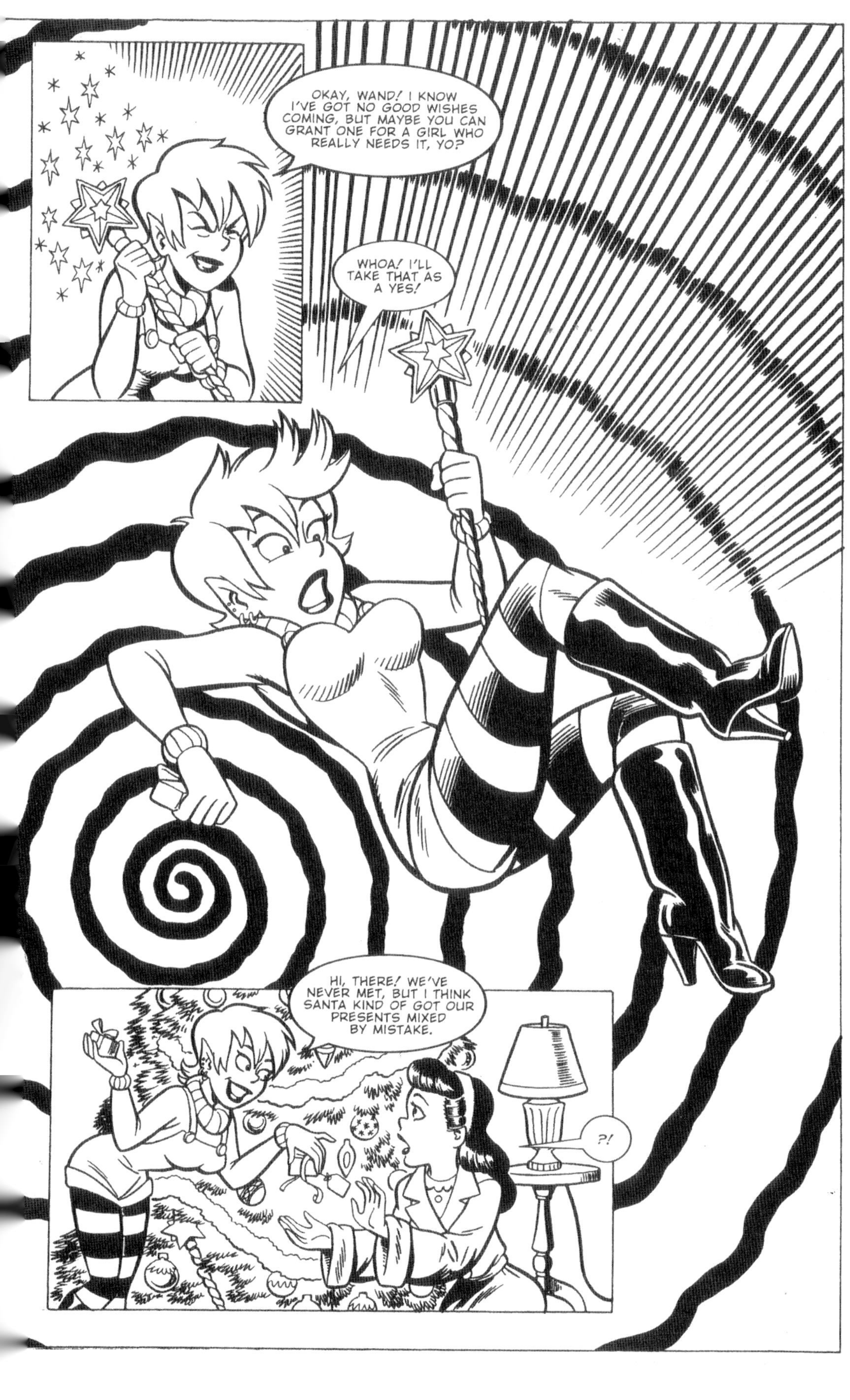
OKAY, WAND! I KNOW I'VE GOT NO GOOD WISHES COMING, BUT MAYBE YOU CAN GRANT ONE FOR A GIRL WHO REALLY NEEDS IT, YO?
WHOA! I'LL TAKE THAT AS A YES!
HI, THERE! WE'VE NEVER MET, BUT I THINK SANTA KIND OF GOT OUR PRESENTS MIXED BY MISTAKE.
?!

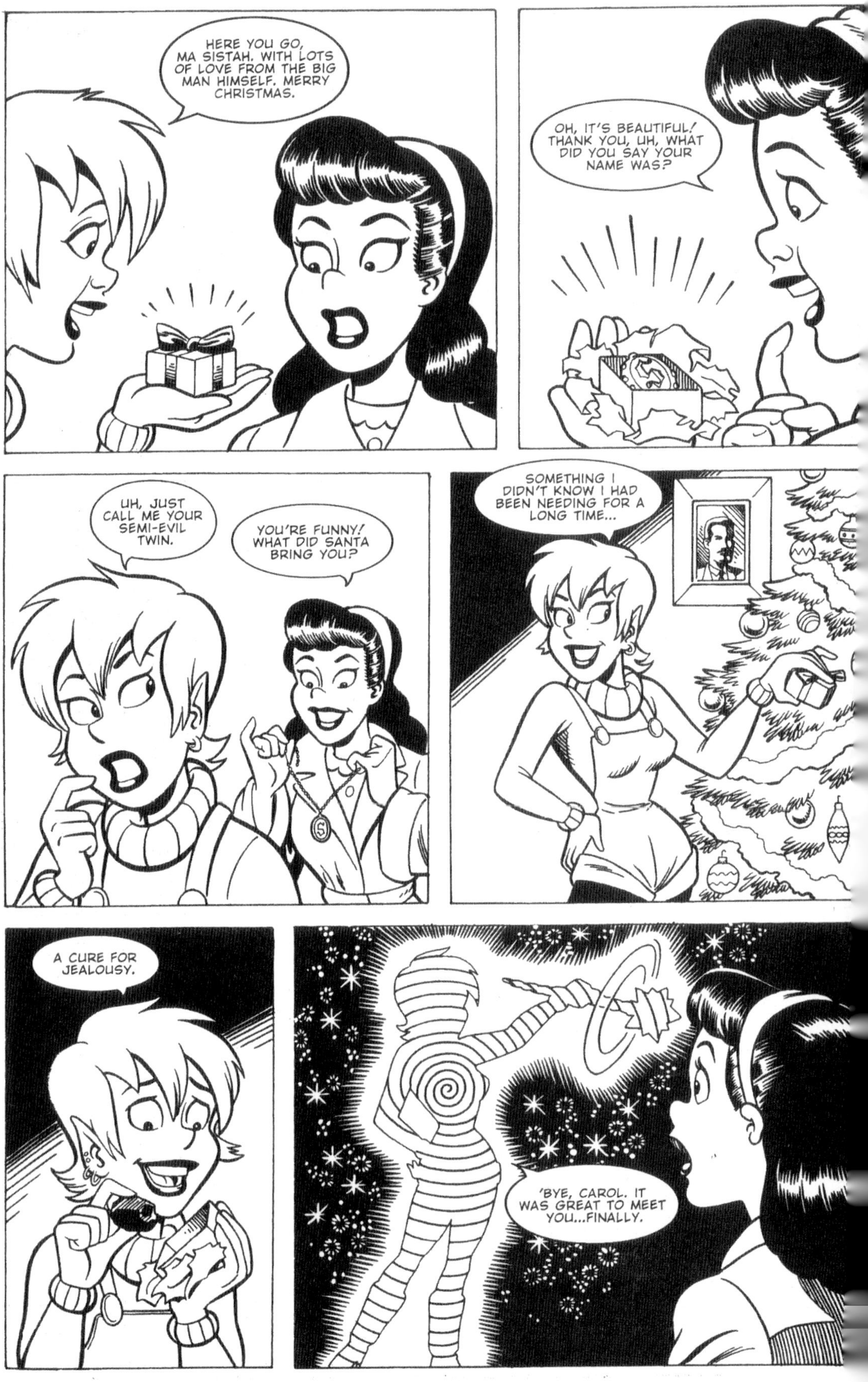
HERE YOU GO, MA SISTAH. WITH LOTS OF LOVE FROM THE BIG MAN HIMSELF. MERRY CHRISTMAS.
OH, IT'S BEAUTIFUL! THANK YOU, UH, WHAT DID YOU SAY YOUR NAME WAS?
UH, JUST CALL ME YOUR SEMI-EVIL TWIN.
YOU'RE FUNNY! WHAT DID SANTA BRING YOU?
SOMETHING I DIDN'T KNOW I HAD BEEN NEEDING FOR A LONG TIME...
A CURE FOR JEALOUSY.
'BYE, CAROL. IT WAS GREAT TO MEET YOU...FINALLY.

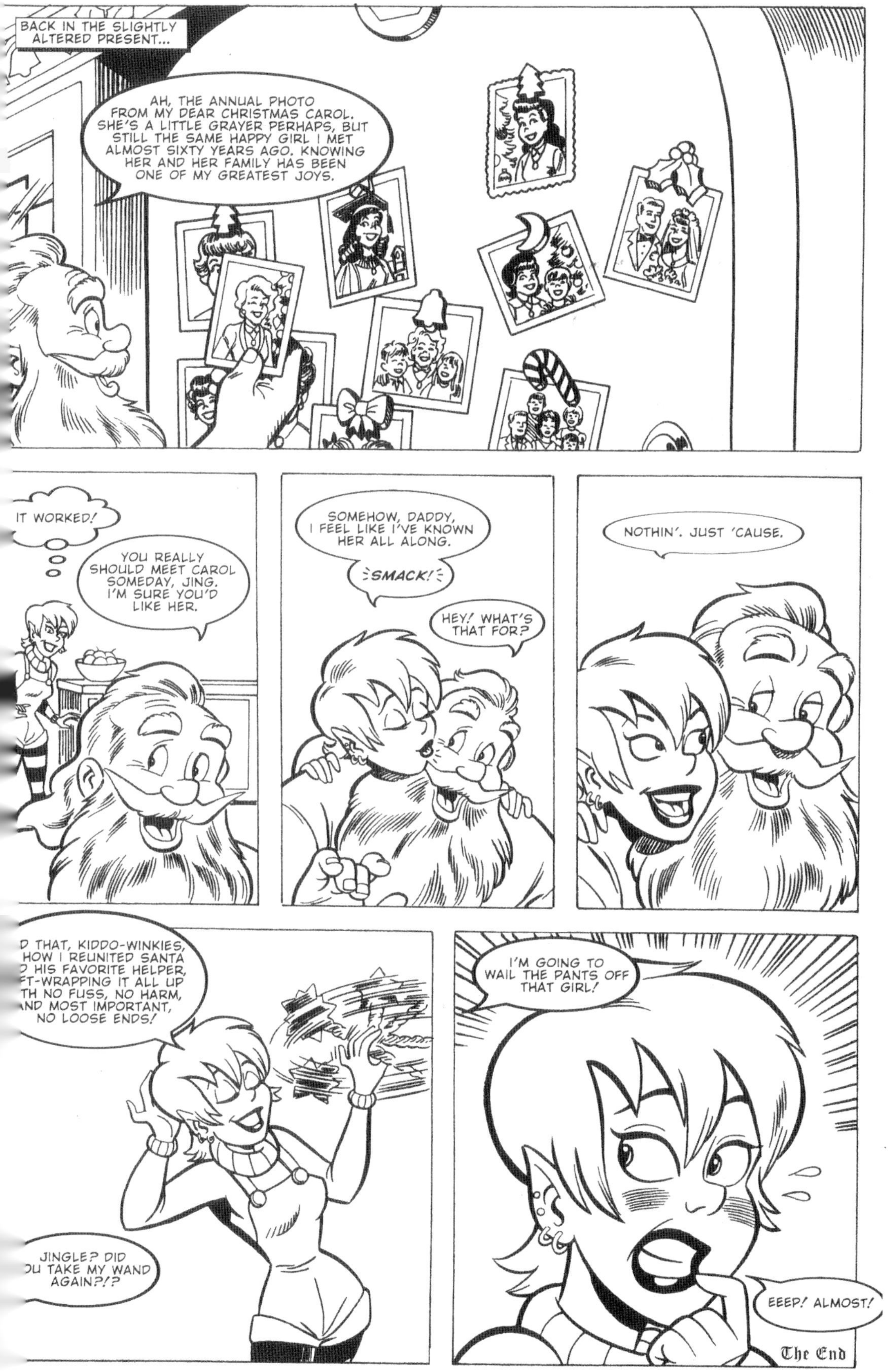
BACK IN THE SLIGHTLY ALTERED PRESENT...
AH, THE ANNUAL PHOTO FROM MY DEAR CHRISTMAS CAROL. SHE'S A LITTLE GRAYER PERHAPS, BUT STILL THE SAME HAPPY GIRL I MET ALMOST SIXTY YEARS AGO. KNOWING HER AND HER FAMILY HAS BEEN ONE OF MY GREATEST JOYS.
IT WORKED!
YOU REALLY SHOULD MEET CAROL SOMEDAY, JING. I'M SURE YOU'D LIKE HER.
SOMEHOW, DADDY, I FEEL LIKE I'VE KNOWN HER ALL ALONG.
SMACK!
HEY! WHAT'S THAT FOR?
NOTHIN'. JUST 'CAUSE.
D THAT, KIDDO-WINKIES, HOW I REUNITED SANTA D HIS FAVORITE HELPER, FT-WRAPPING IT ALL UP TH NO FUSS, NO HARM, AND MOST IMPORTANT, NO LOOSE ENDS!
JINGLE? DID OU TAKE MY WAND AGAIN?!?
I'M GOING TO WAIL THE PANTS OFF THAT GIRL!
EEEP! ALMOST!
The End

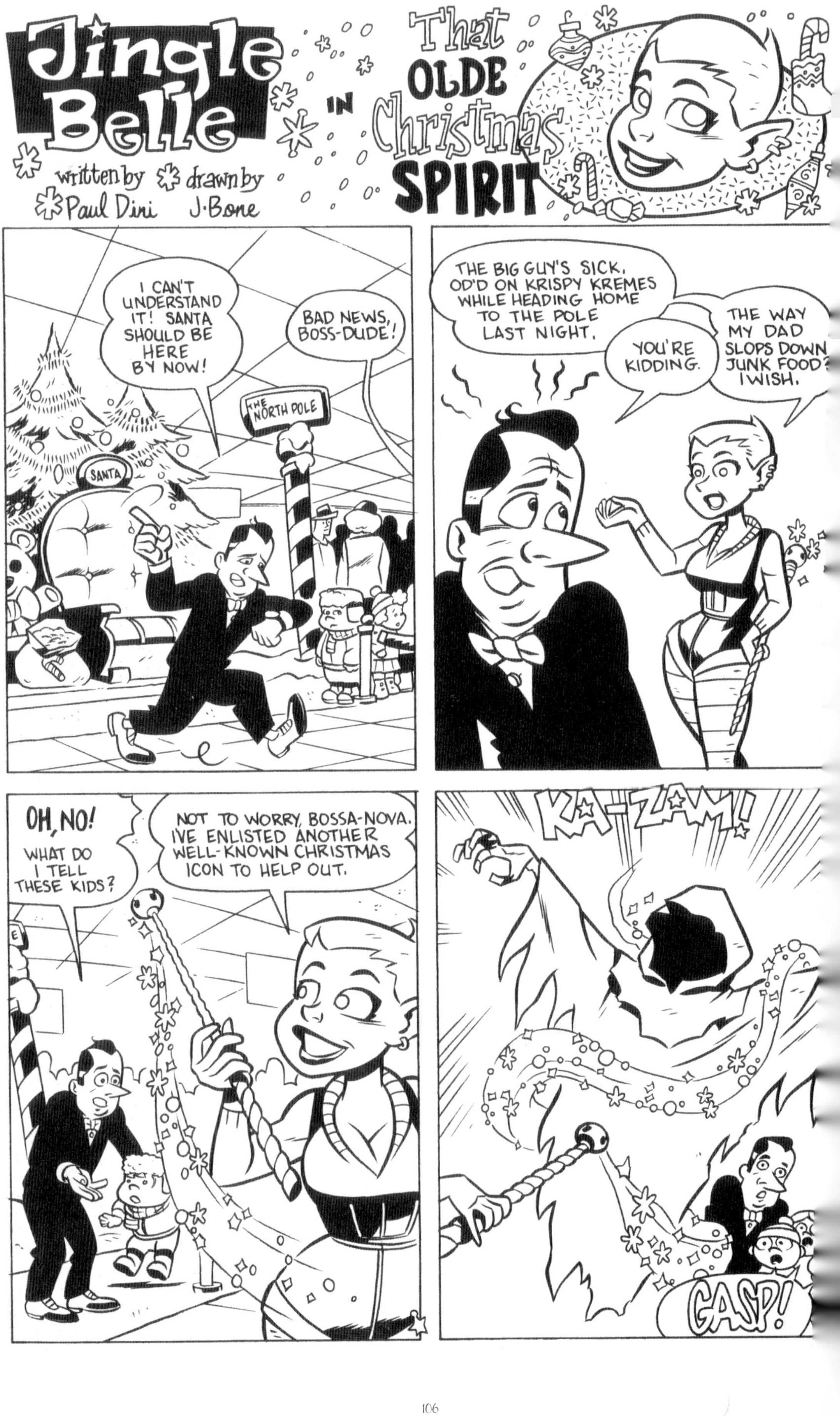
Jingle Belle
IN
That OLDE Christmas SPIRIT
written by Paul Dini
drawn by J. Bone
I CAN'T UNDERSTAND IT! SANTA SHOULD BE HERE BY NOW!
BAD NEWS, BOSS-DUDE!
THE NORTH POLE
SANTA
THE BIG GUY'S SICK. OD'D ON KRISPY KREMES WHILE HEADING HOME TO THE POLE LAST NIGHT.
YOU'RE KIDDING.
THE WAY MY DAD SLOPS DOWN JUNK FOOD? I WISH.
OH, NO!
WHAT DO I TELL THESE KIDS?
NOT TO WORRY, BOSSA-NOVA. I'VE ENLISTED ANOTHER WELL-KNOWN CHRISTMAS ICON TO HELP OUT.
KA-ZAM!
GASP!

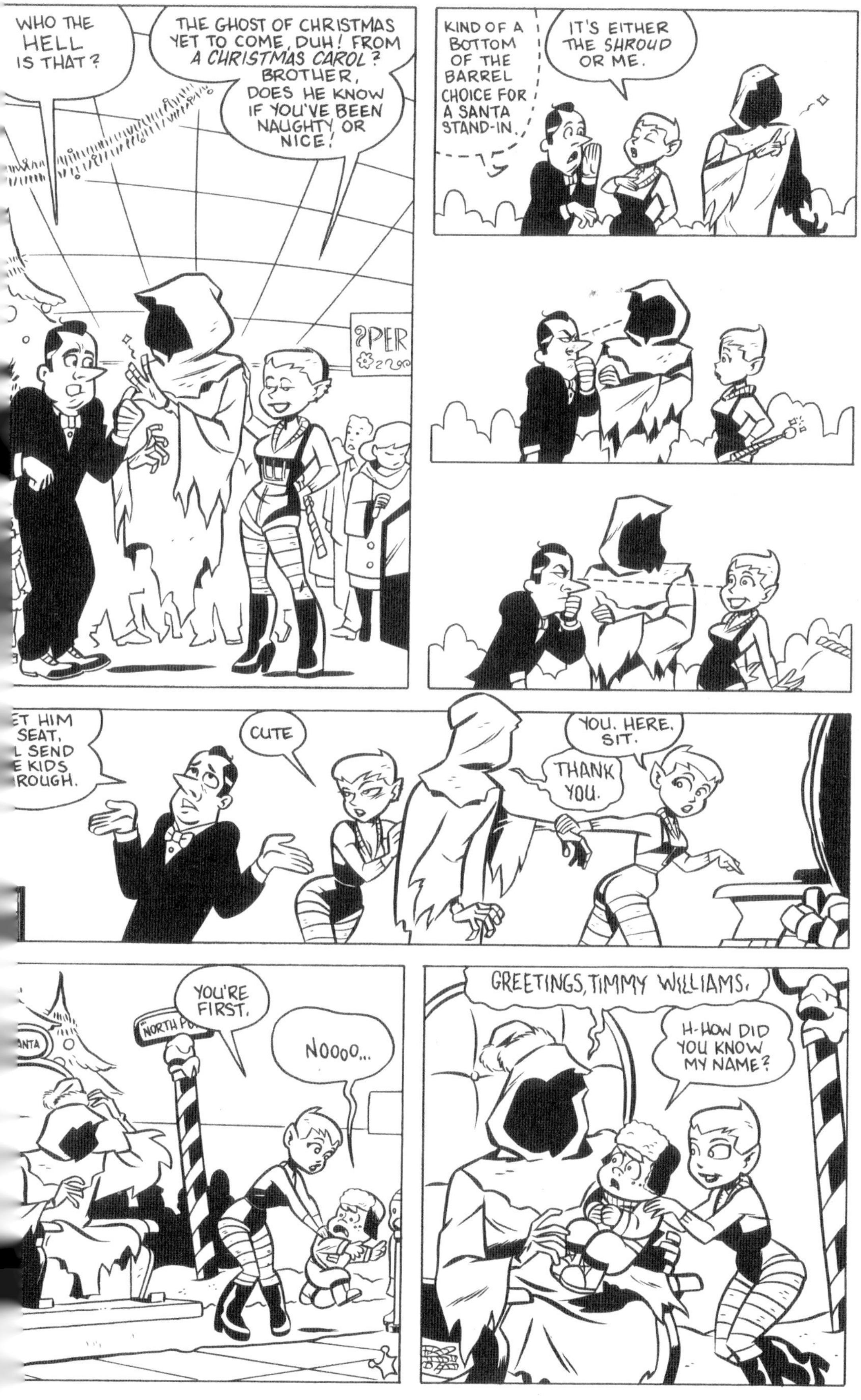
WHO THE HELL IS THAT?
THE GHOST OF CHRISTMAS YET TO COME, DUH! FROM *A CHRISTMAS CAROL*? BROTHER, DOES HE KNOW IF YOU'VE BEEN NAUGHTY OR NICE!
KIND OF A BOTTOM OF THE BARREL CHOICE FOR A SANTA STAND-IN.
IT'S EITHER THE *SHROUD* OR ME.
ET HIM SEAT, L SEND E KIDS ROUGH.
CUTE
YOU. HERE. SIT.
THANK YOU.
YOU'RE FIRST.
NOOOO...
GREETINGS, TIMMY WILLIAMS.
H-HOW DID YOU KNOW MY NAME?

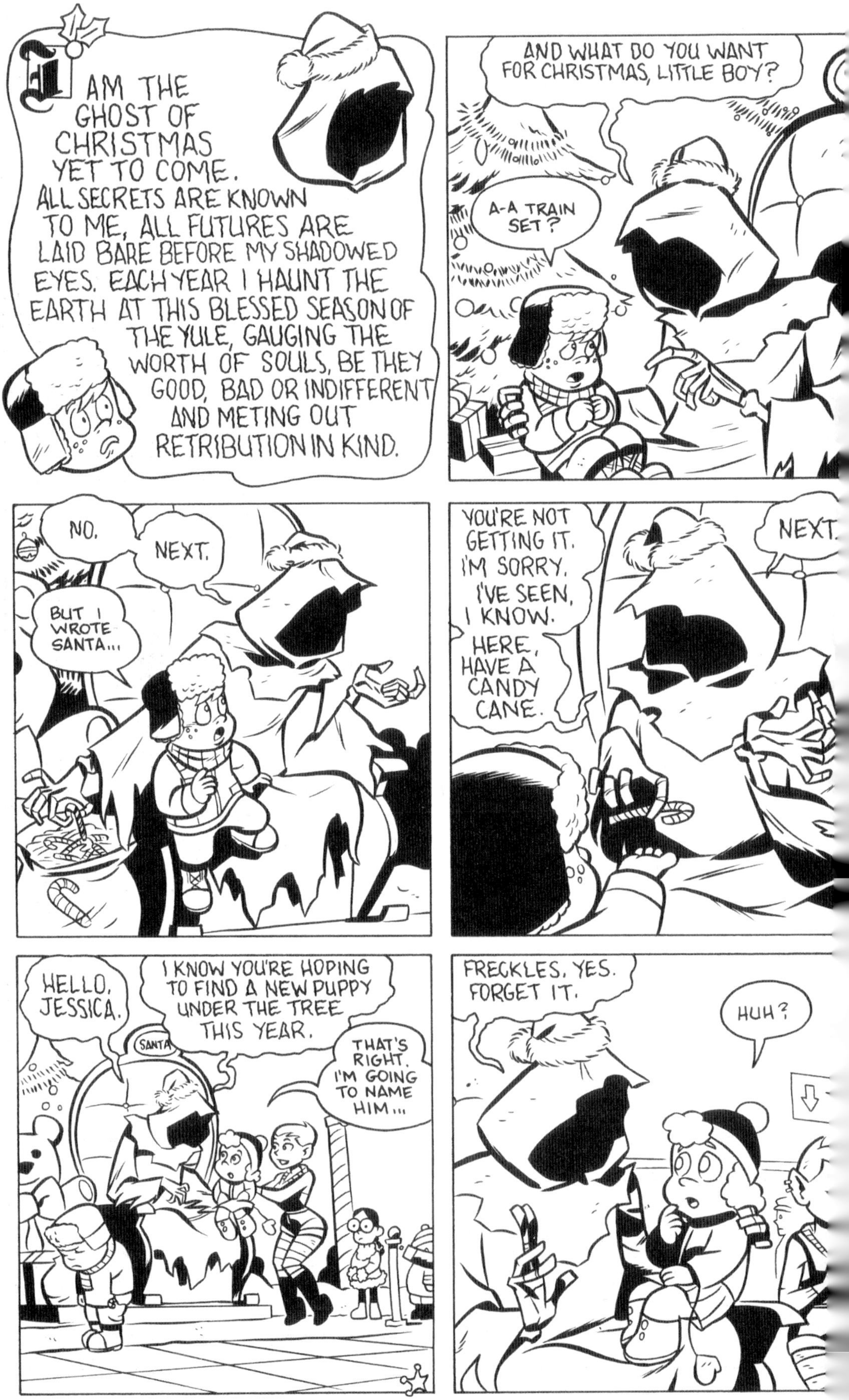
I AM THE GHOST OF CHRISTMAS YET TO COME. ALL SECRETS ARE KNOWN TO ME, ALL FUTURES ARE LAID BARE BEFORE MY SHADOWED EYES. EACH YEAR I HAUNT THE EARTH AT THIS BLESSED SEASON OF THE YULE, GAUGING THE WORTH OF SOULS, BE THEY GOOD, BAD OR INDIFFERENT AND METING OUT RETRIBUTION IN KIND.
AND WHAT DO YOU WANT FOR CHRISTMAS, LITTLE BOY?
A-A TRAIN SET?
NO.
NEXT.
BUT I WROTE SANTA...
YOU'RE NOT GETTING IT. I'M SORRY. I'VE SEEN, I KNOW.
HERE, HAVE A CANDY CANE.
NEXT.
HELLO, JESSICA.
I KNOW YOU'RE HOPING TO FIND A NEW PUPPY UNDER THE TREE THIS YEAR.
SANTA
THAT'S RIGHT. I'M GOING TO NAME HIM...
FRECKLES. YES. FORGET IT.
HUH?

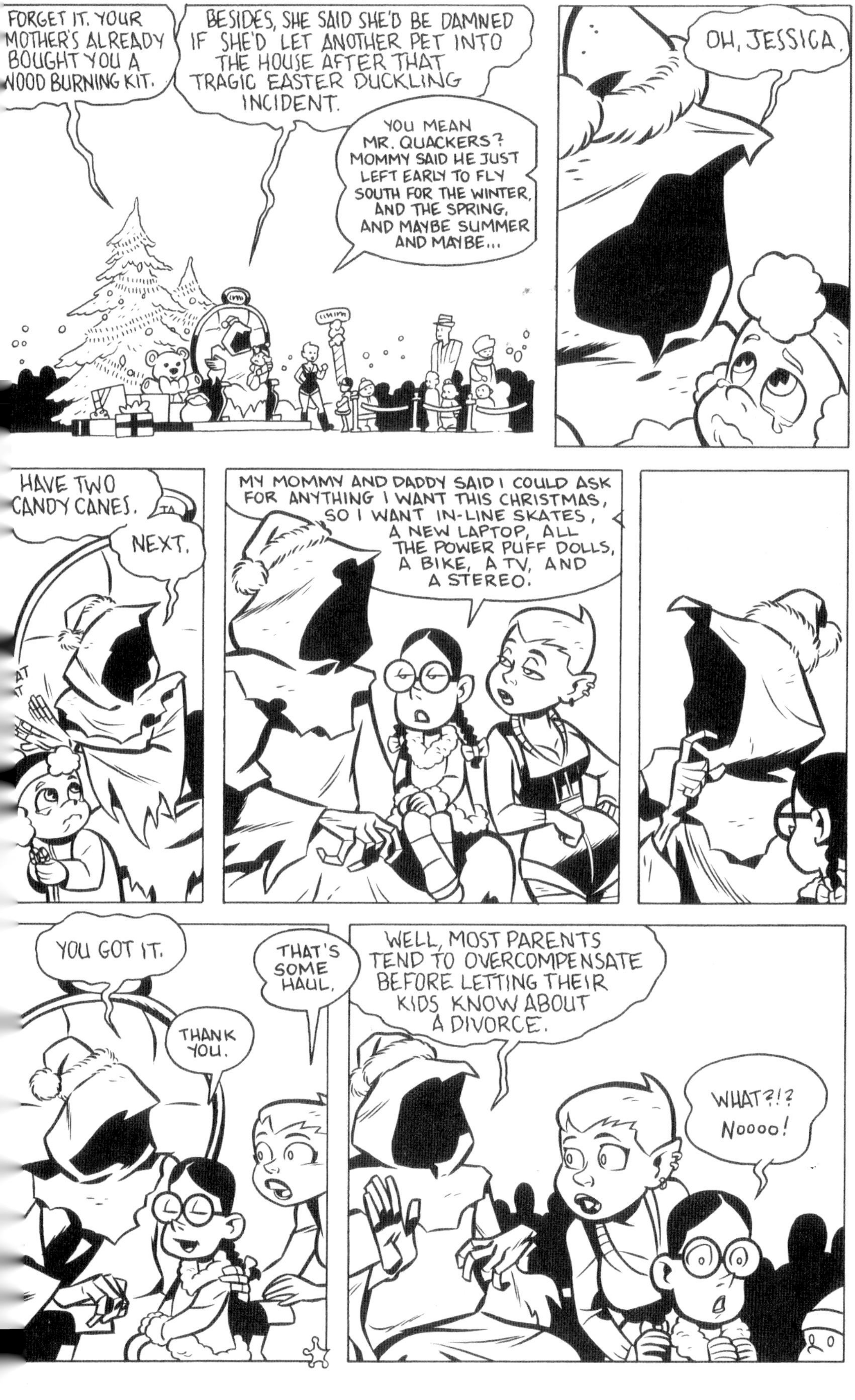
FORGET IT. YOUR MOTHER'S ALREADY BOUGHT YOU A WOOD BURNING KIT.
BESIDES, SHE SAID SHE'D BE DAMNED IF SHE'D LET ANOTHER PET INTO THE HOUSE AFTER THAT TRAGIC EASTER DUCKLING INCIDENT.
YOU MEAN MR. QUACKERS? MOMMY SAID HE JUST LEFT EARLY TO FLY SOUTH FOR THE WINTER, AND THE SPRING, AND MAYBE SUMMER AND MAYBE...
OH, JESSICA.
HAVE TWO CANDY CANES.
NEXT.
MY MOMMY AND DADDY SAID I COULD ASK FOR ANYTHING I WANT THIS CHRISTMAS, SO I WANT IN-LINE SKATES, A NEW LAPTOP, ALL THE POWER PUFF DOLLS, A BIKE, A TV, AND A STEREO.
YOU GOT IT.
THANK YOU.
THAT'S SOME HAUL.
WELL, MOST PARENTS TEND TO OVERCOMPENSATE BEFORE LETTING THEIR KIDS KNOW ABOUT A DIVORCE.
WHAT?!?
Noooo!

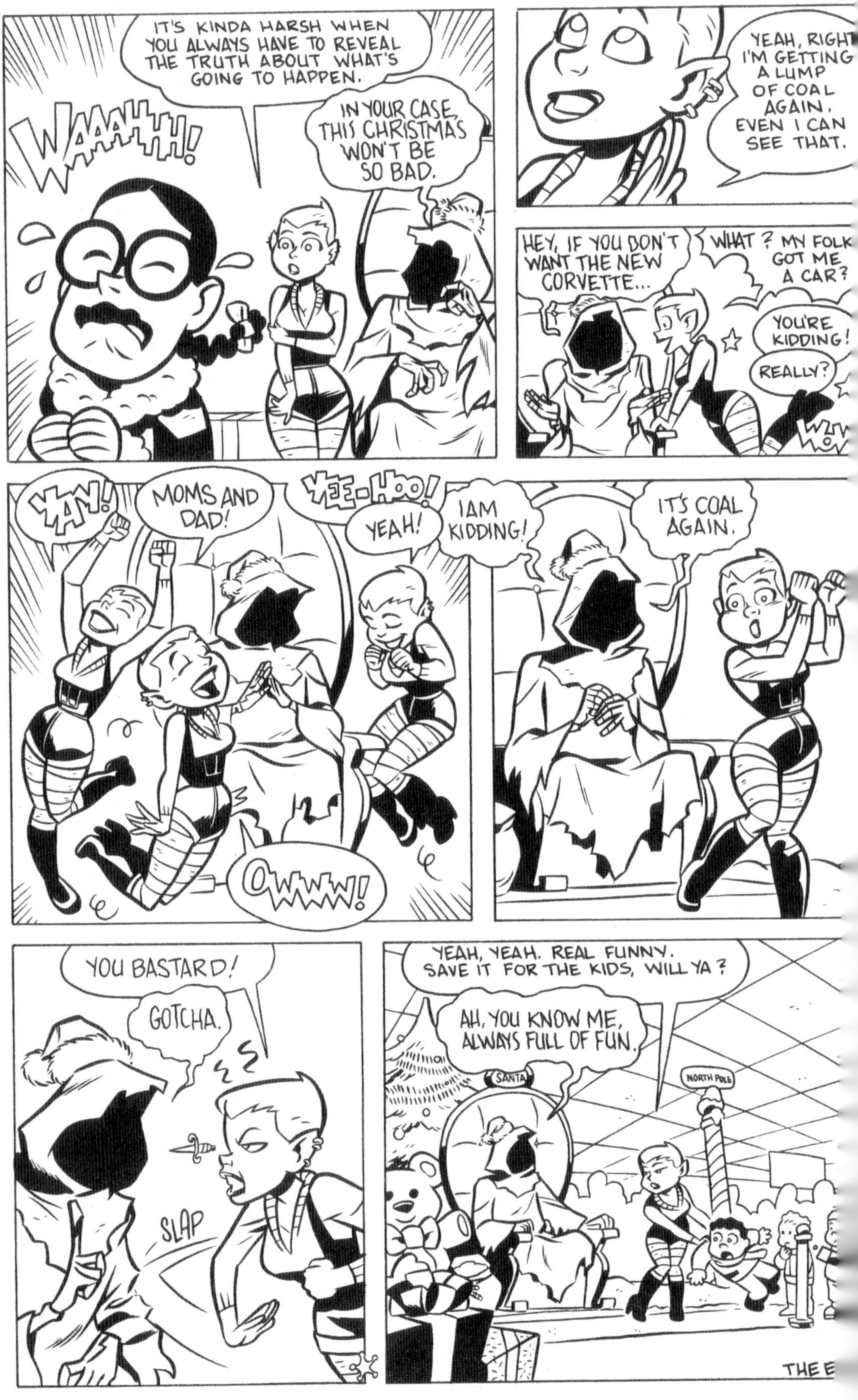
IT'S KINDA HARSH WHEN YOU ALWAYS HAVE TO REVEAL THE TRUTH ABOUT WHAT'S GOING TO HAPPEN.
WAAAHHH!
IN YOUR CASE, THIS CHRISTMAS WON'T BE SO BAD.
YEAH, RIGHT I'M GETTING A LUMP OF COAL AGAIN. EVEN I CAN SEE THAT.
HEY, IF YOU DON'T WANT THE NEW CORVETTE...
WHAT? MY FOLK GOT ME A CAR?
YOU'RE KIDDING!
REALLY?
YAY!
MOMS AND DAD!
YEE-HOO!
YEAH!
OWWW!
I AM KIDDING!
IT'S COAL AGAIN.
YOU BASTARD!
GOTCHA.
SLAP
YEAH, YEAH. REAL FUNNY. SAVE IT FOR THE KIDS, WILL YA?
AH, YOU KNOW ME, ALWAYS FULL OF FUN.
SANTA
NORTH POLE
THE E

JingleBelle

STORY & SCRIPT BY
PAUL DINI & SHANE GLINES
LAYOUTS BY
STEPHEN DESTEFANO
FINISHED ART BY
SHANE GLINES
LETTERS BY
JARED & JAMES JONES

!

Sugarizer

POPPI, MOMS WANTS YOU FOR DINNER RIGHT NOW.

WHEW! AS SOON AS I WASH UP.

MMM! MAKIN' A NEW TREAT, HUH? COOL! I'LL JUST HELP MYSELF.

1

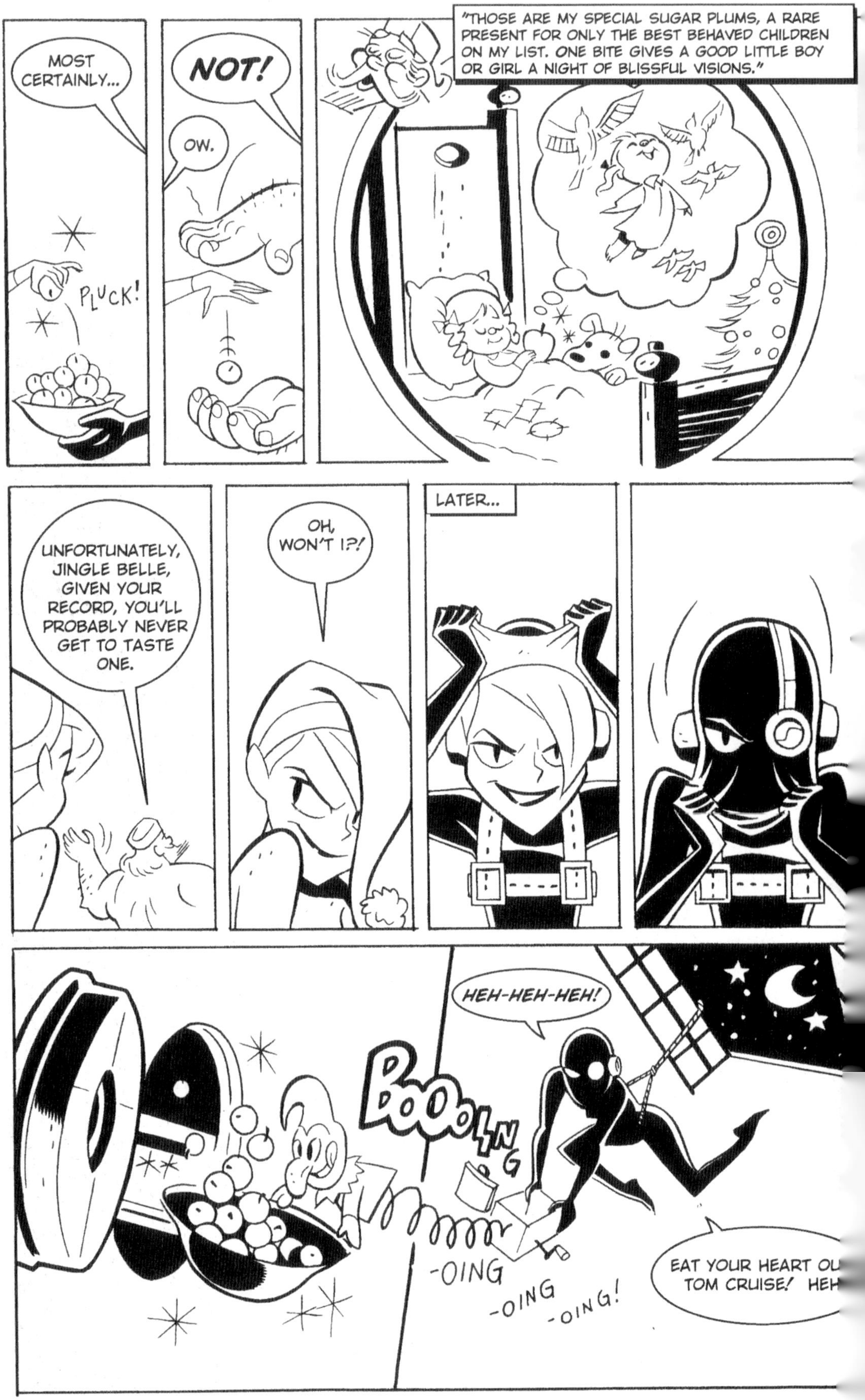
MOST CERTAINLY...
PLUCK!
NOT!
OW.
"THOSE ARE MY SPECIAL SUGAR PLUMS, A RARE PRESENT FOR ONLY THE BEST BEHAVED CHILDREN ON MY LIST. ONE BITE GIVES A GOOD LITTLE BOY OR GIRL A NIGHT OF BLISSFUL VISIONS."
UNFORTUNATELY, JINGLE BELLE, GIVEN YOUR RECORD, YOU'LL PROBABLY NEVER GET TO TASTE ONE.
OH, WON'T I?!
LATER...
HEH-HEH-HEH!
BOOOOING
-OING
-OING
-OING!
EAT YOUR HEART OU
TOM CRUISE! HEH

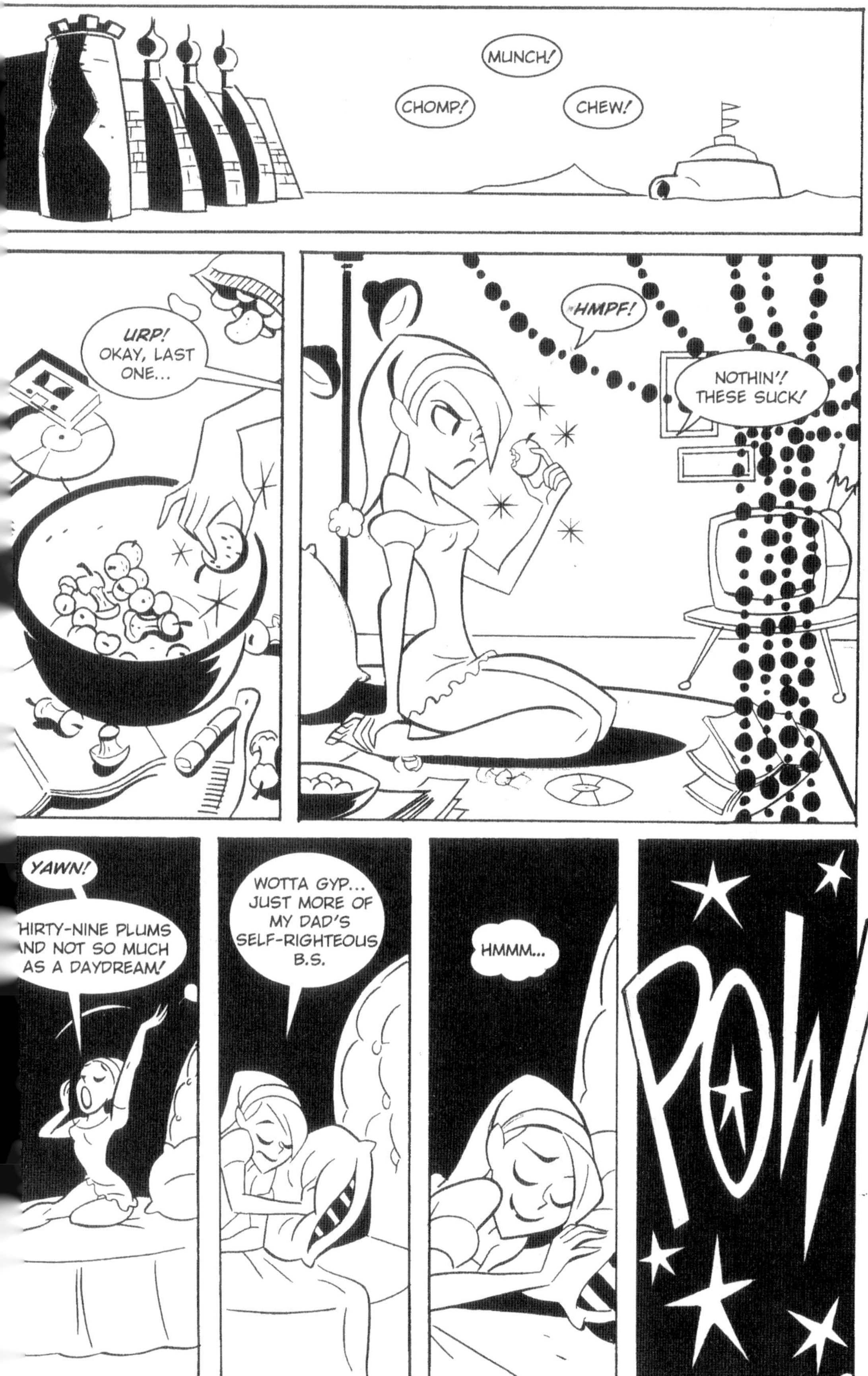
MUNCH!
CHOMP!
CHEW!
URP!
OKAY, LAST ONE...
HMPF!
NOTHIN'! THESE SUCK!
YAWN!
HIRTY-NINE PLUMS
ND NOT SO MUCH AS A DAYDREAM!
WOTTA GYP... JUST MORE OF MY DAD'S SELF-RIGHTEOUS B.S.
HMMM...
POW
3

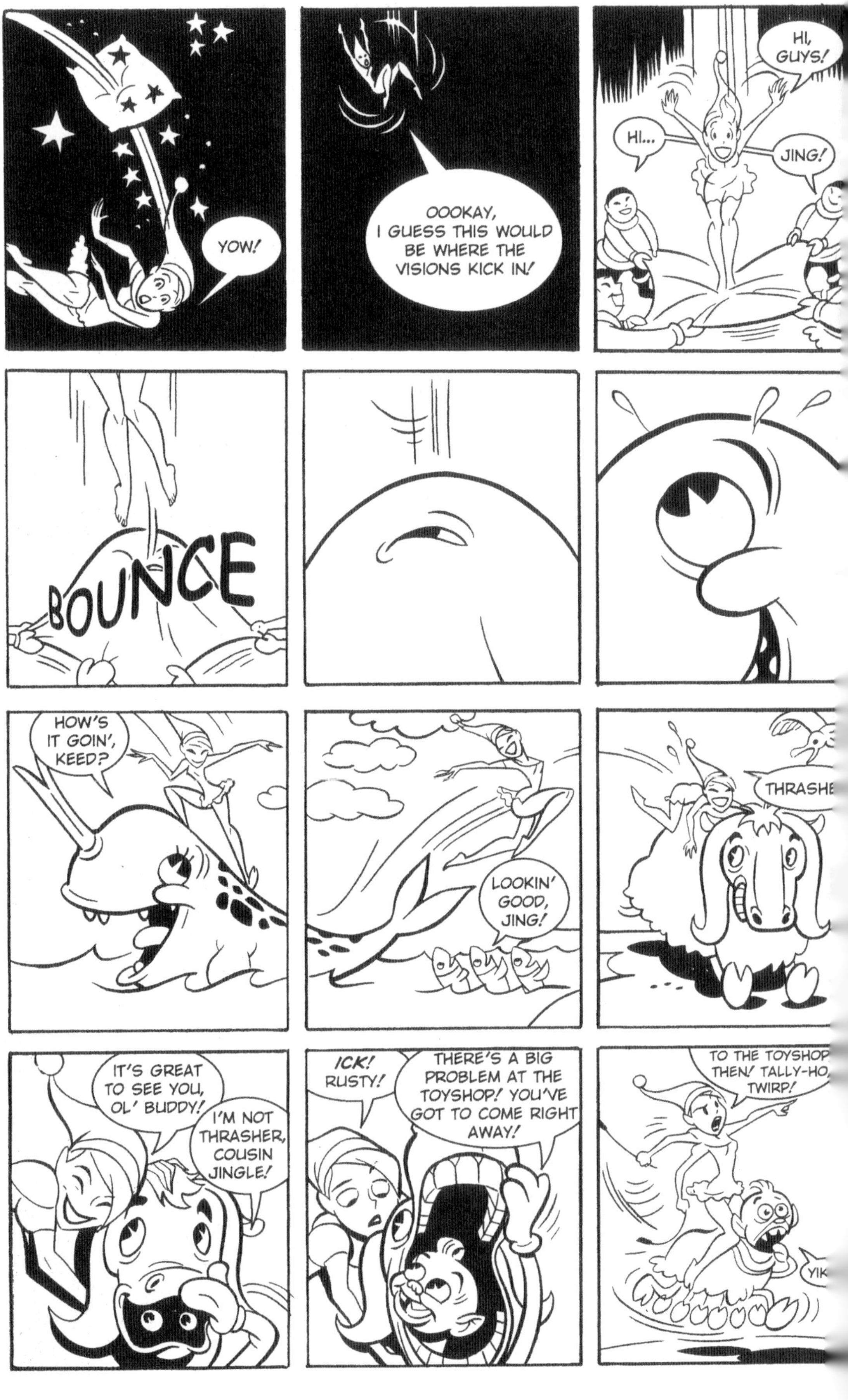
YOW!
OOOKAY, I GUESS THIS WOULD BE WHERE THE VISIONS KICK IN!
HI, GUYS!
HI...
JING!
BOUNCE
HOW'S IT GOIN', KEED?
LOOKIN' GOOD, JING!
THRASHE
IT'S GREAT TO SEE YOU, OL' BUDDY!
I'M NOT THRASHER, COUSIN JINGLE!
ICK! RUSTY!
THERE'S A BIG PROBLEM AT THE TOYSHOP! YOU'VE GOT TO COME RIGHT AWAY!
TO THE TOYSHOP THEN! TALLY-HO, TWIRP!
YIK

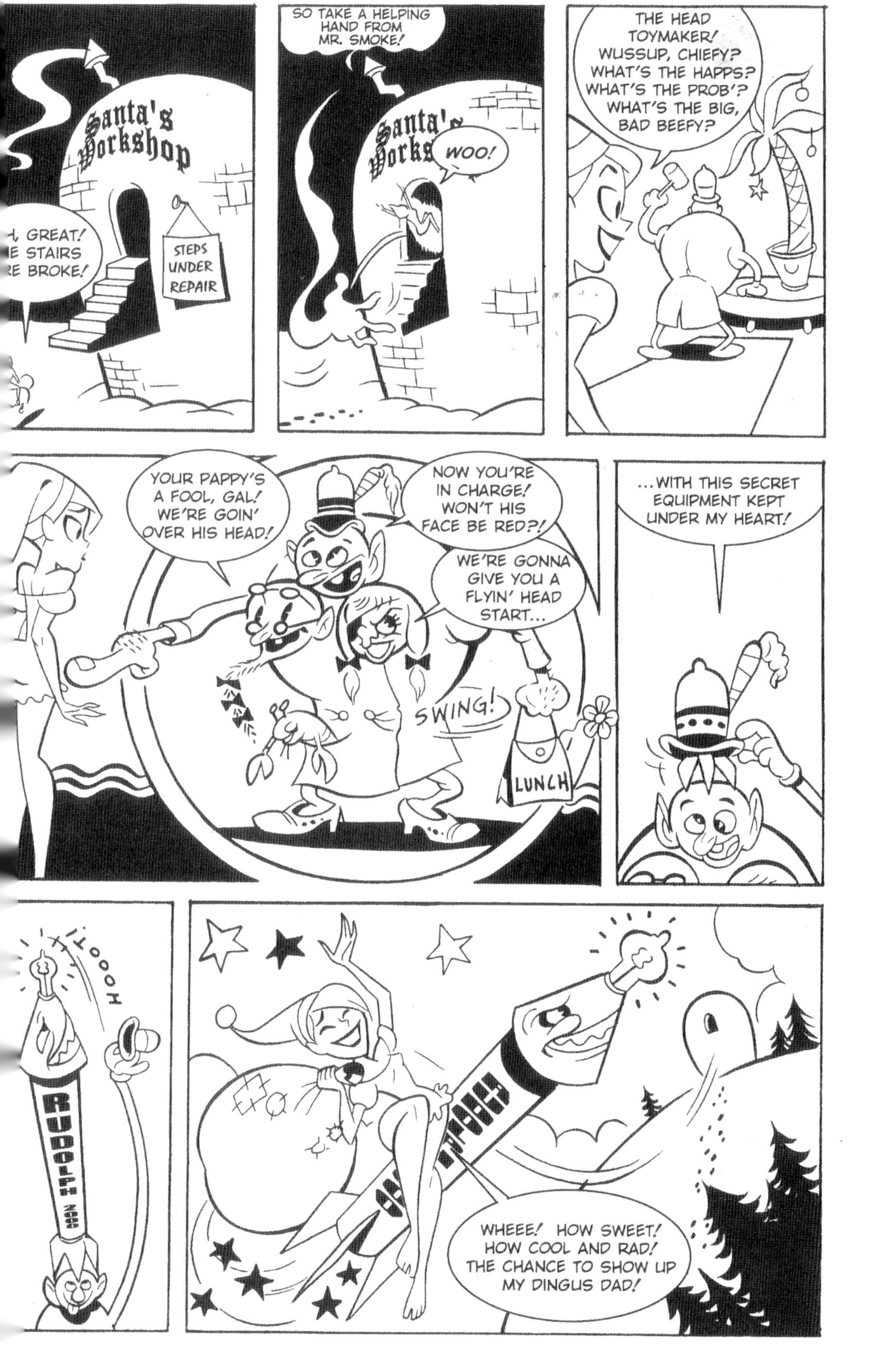
Santa's Workshop
-H, GREAT! -E STAIRS -RE BROKE!
STEPS UNDER REPAIR
SO TAKE A HELPING HAND FROM MR. SMOKE!
WOO!
THE HEAD TOYMAKER! WUSSUP, CHIEFY? WHAT'S THE HAPPS? WHAT'S THE PROB'? WHAT'S THE BIG, BAD BEEFY?
YOUR PAPPY'S A FOOL, GAL! WE'RE GOIN' OVER HIS HEAD!
NOW YOU'RE IN CHARGE! WON'T HIS FACE BE RED?!
WE'RE GONNA GIVE YOU A FLYIN' HEAD START...
SWING!
LUNCH
...WITH THIS SECRET EQUIPMENT KEPT UNDER MY HEART!
HOOOT!
RUDOLPH 2000
WHEEE! HOW SWEET! HOW COOL AND RAD! THE CHANCE TO SHOW UP MY DINGUS DAD!

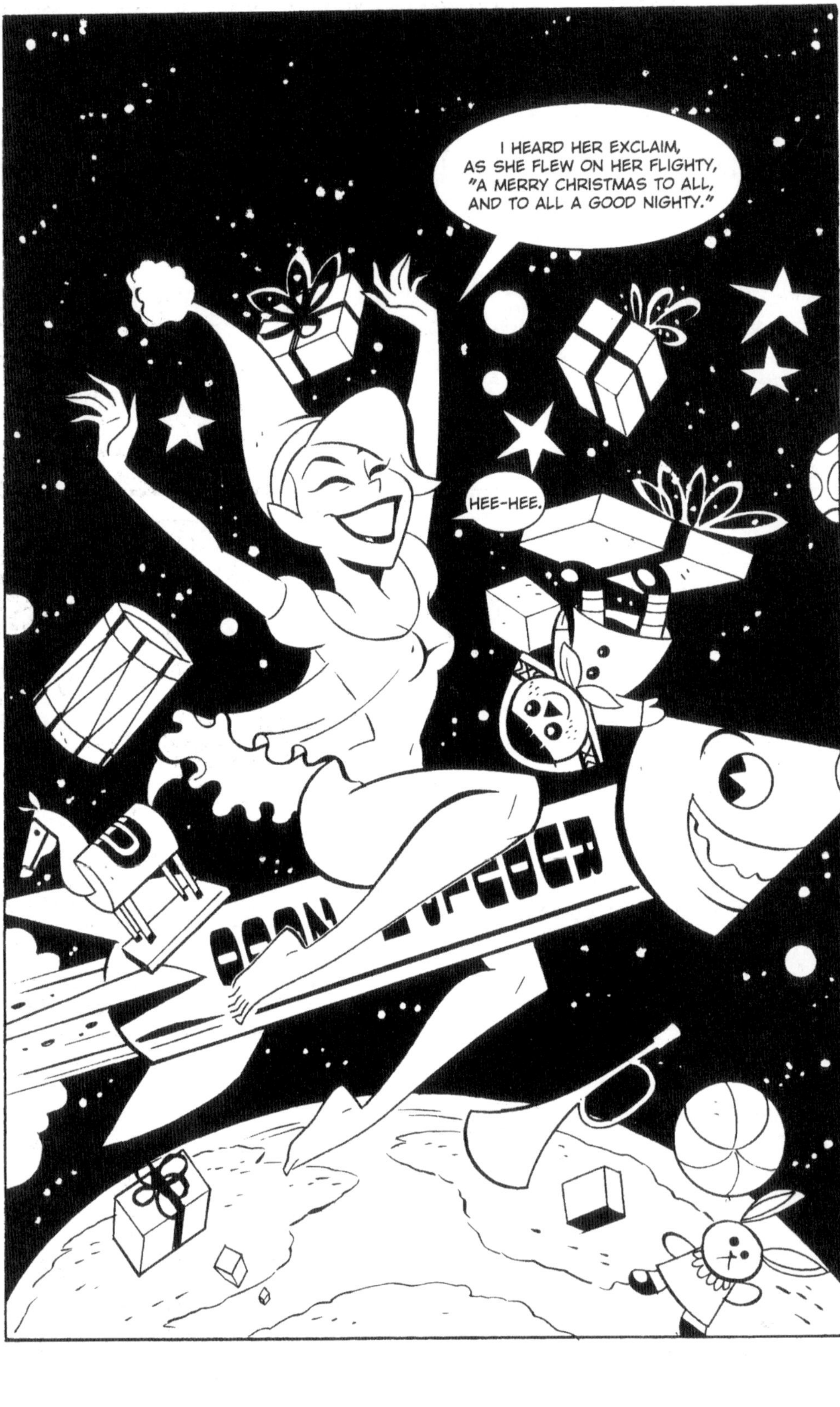
I HEARD HER EXCLAIM, AS SHE FLEW ON HER FLIGHTY, "A MERRY CHRISTMAS TO ALL, AND TO ALL A GOOD NIGHTY."
HEE-HEE.

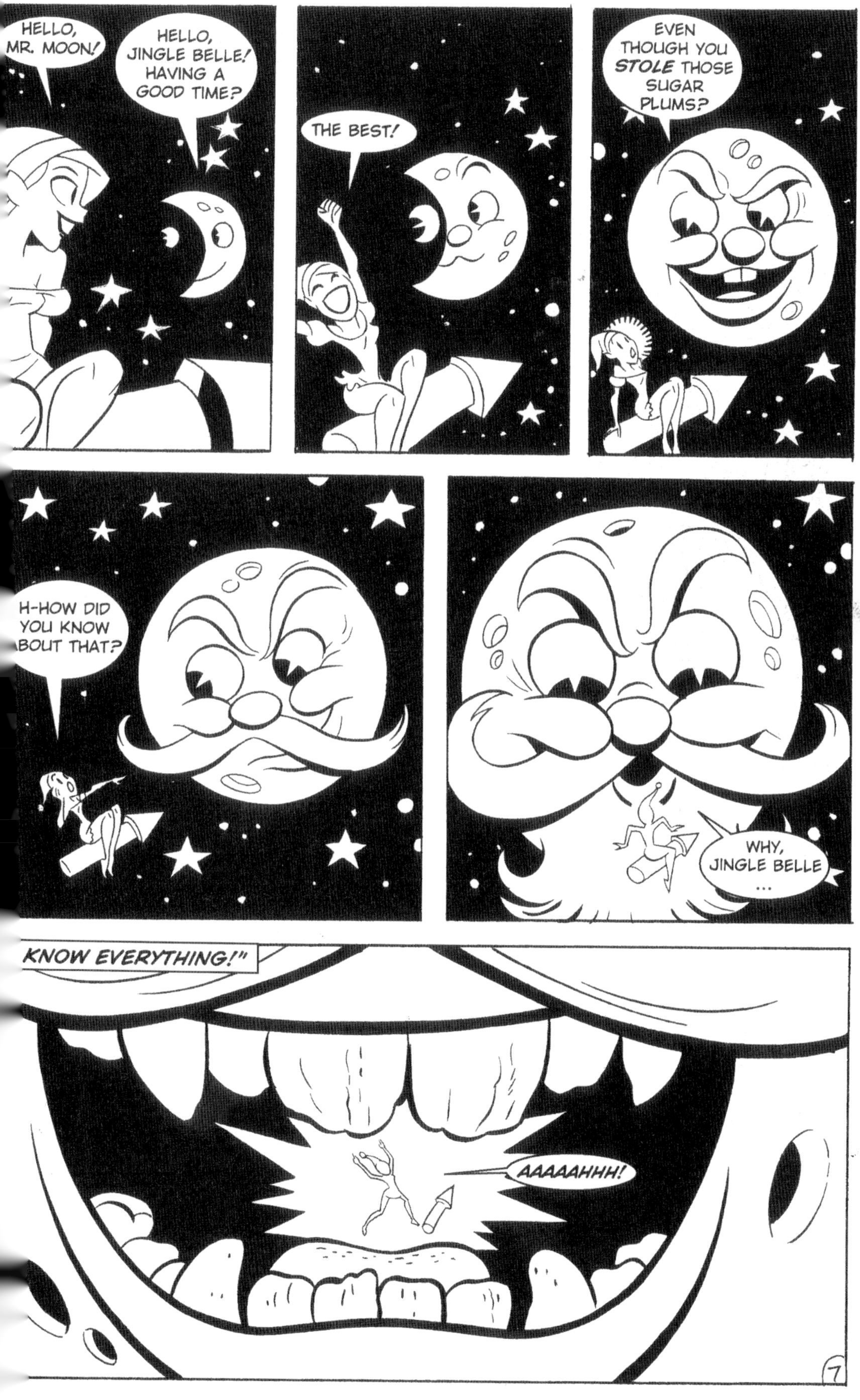
HELLO, MR. MOON!
HELLO, JINGLE BELLE! HAVING A GOOD TIME?
THE BEST!
EVEN THOUGH YOU STOLE THOSE SUGAR PLUMS?
H-HOW DID YOU KNOW BOUT THAT?
WHY, JINGLE BELLE ...
KNOW EVERYTHING!"
AAAAAHHH!
7

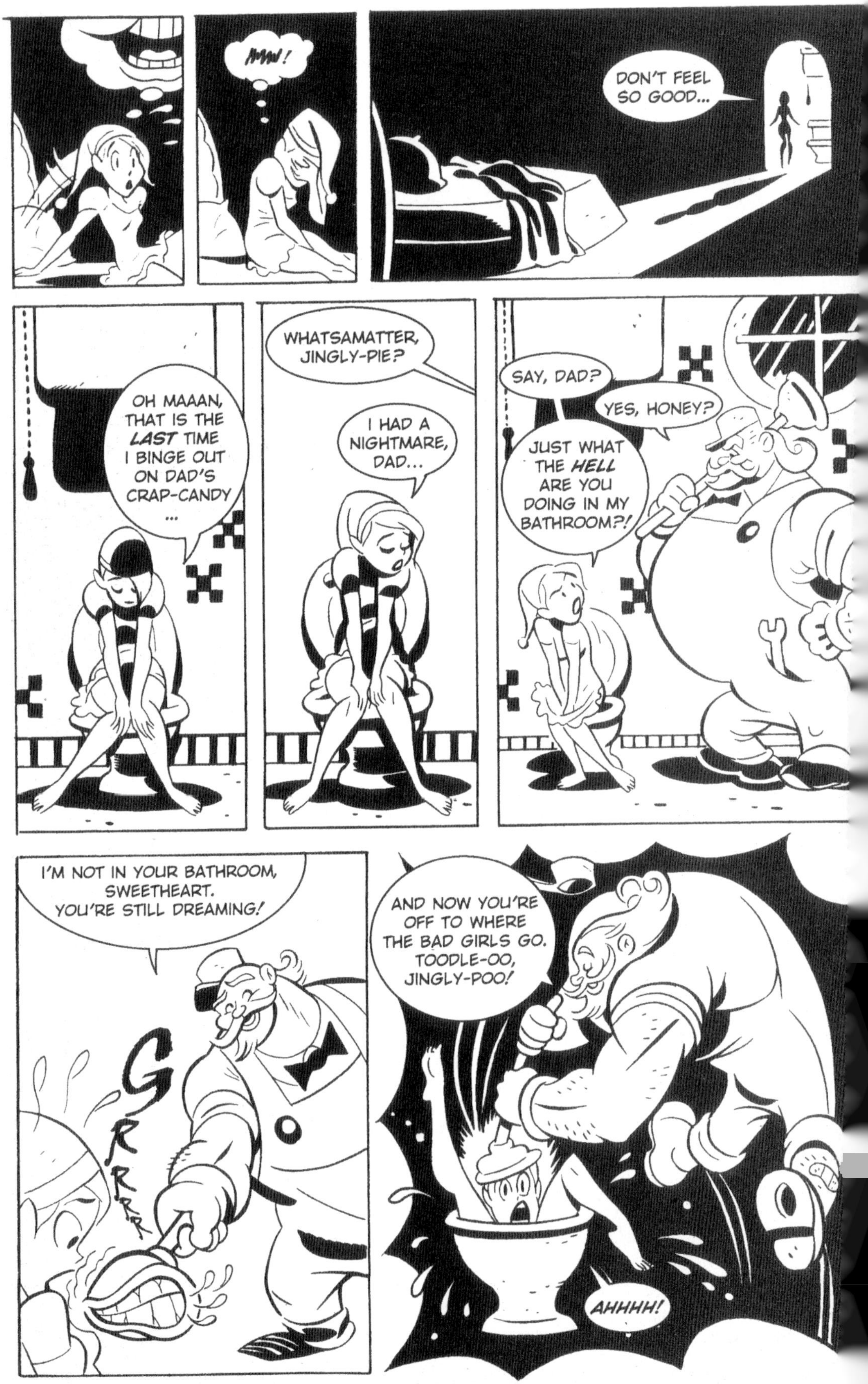
MMM!
DON'T FEEL SO GOOD...
OH MAAAN, THAT IS THE LAST TIME I BINGE OUT ON DAD'S CRAP-CANDY ...
WHATSAMATTER, JINGLY-PIE?
I HAD A NIGHTMARE, DAD...
SAY, DAD?
YES, HONEY?
JUST WHAT THE HELL ARE YOU DOING IN MY BATHROOM?!
I'M NOT IN YOUR BATHROOM, SWEETHEART. YOU'RE STILL DREAMING!
GRRRRR
AND NOW YOU'RE OFF TO WHERE THE BAD GIRLS GO. TOODLE-OO, JINGLY-POO!
AHHHH!

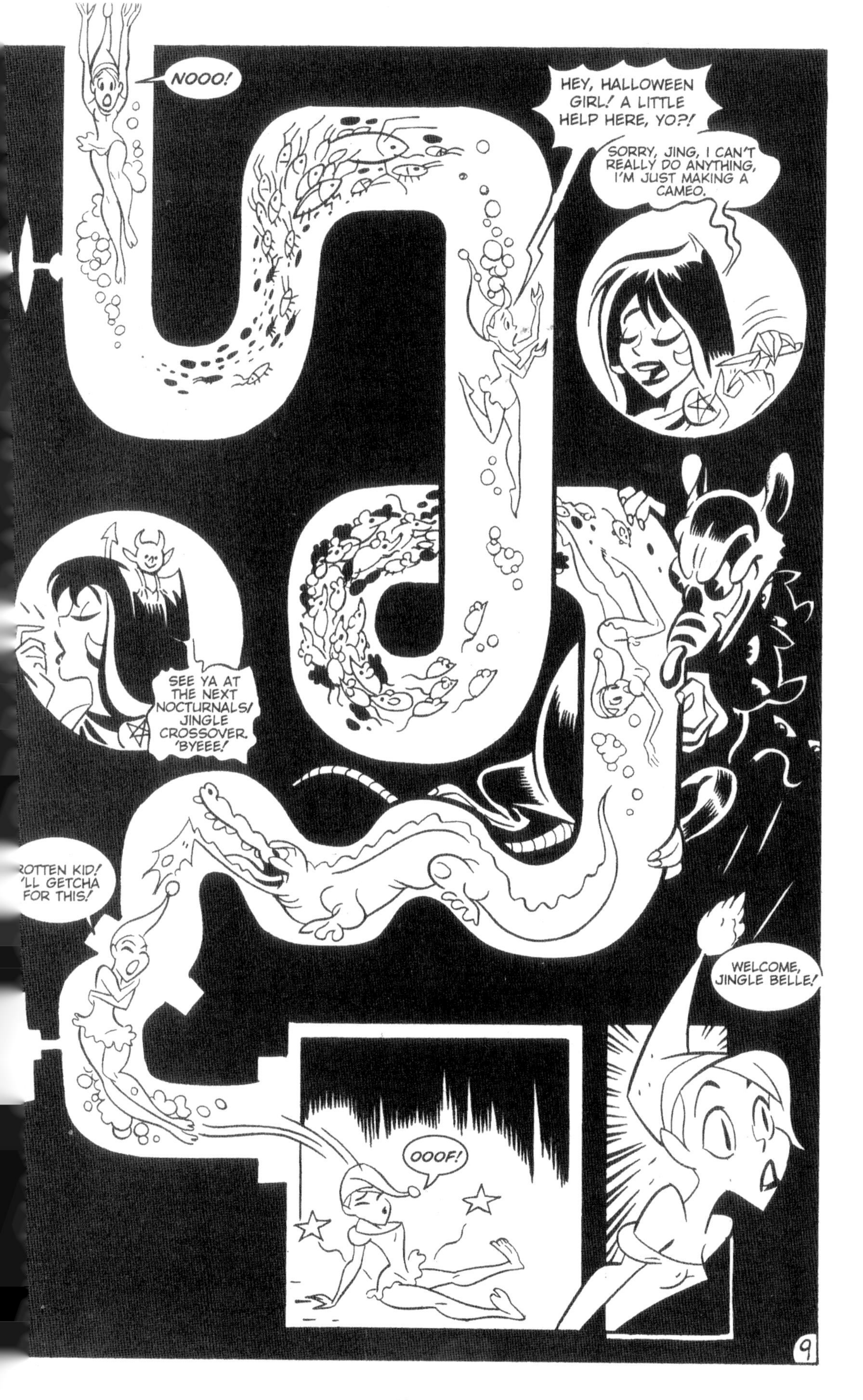
NOOO!
HEY, HALLOWEEN GIRL! A LITTLE HELP HERE, YO?!
SORRY, JING, I CAN'T REALLY DO ANYTHING, I'M JUST MAKING A CAMEO.
SEE YA AT THE NEXT NOCTURNALS/ JINGLE CROSSOVER. 'BYEEE!
ROTTEN KID! I'LL GETCHA FOR THIS!
WELCOME, JINGLE BELLE!
OOOF!
9

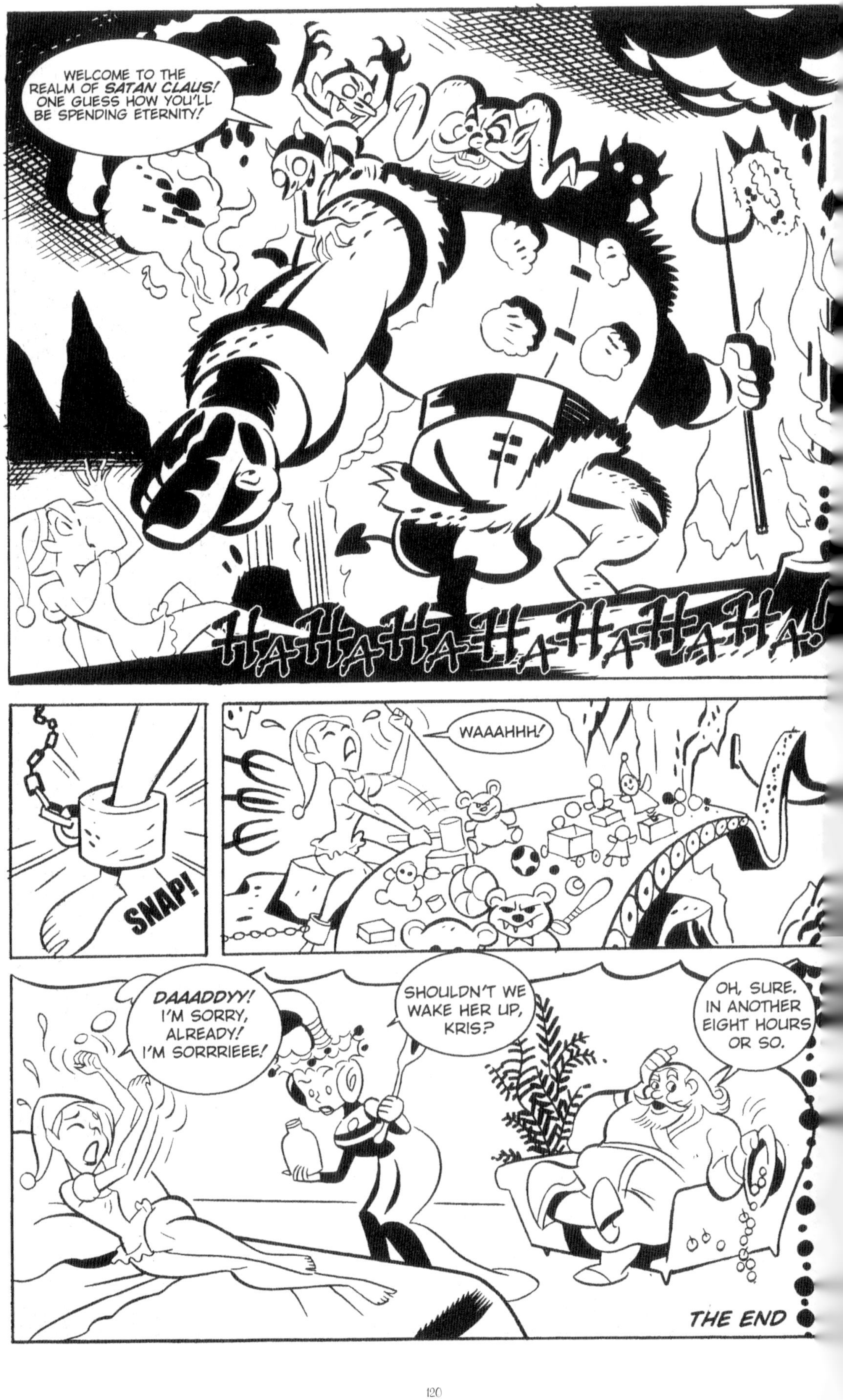
WELCOME TO THE REALM OF SATAN CLAUS! ONE GUESS HOW YOU'LL BE SPENDING ETERNITY!
HAHAHAHAHAHAHAHAHA!
SNAP!
WAAAHHH!
DAAADDYY! I'M SORRY, ALREADY! I'M SORRRIEEE!
SHOULDN'T WE WAKE HER UP, KRIS?
OH, SURE. IN ANOTHER EIGHT HOURS OR SO.
THE END

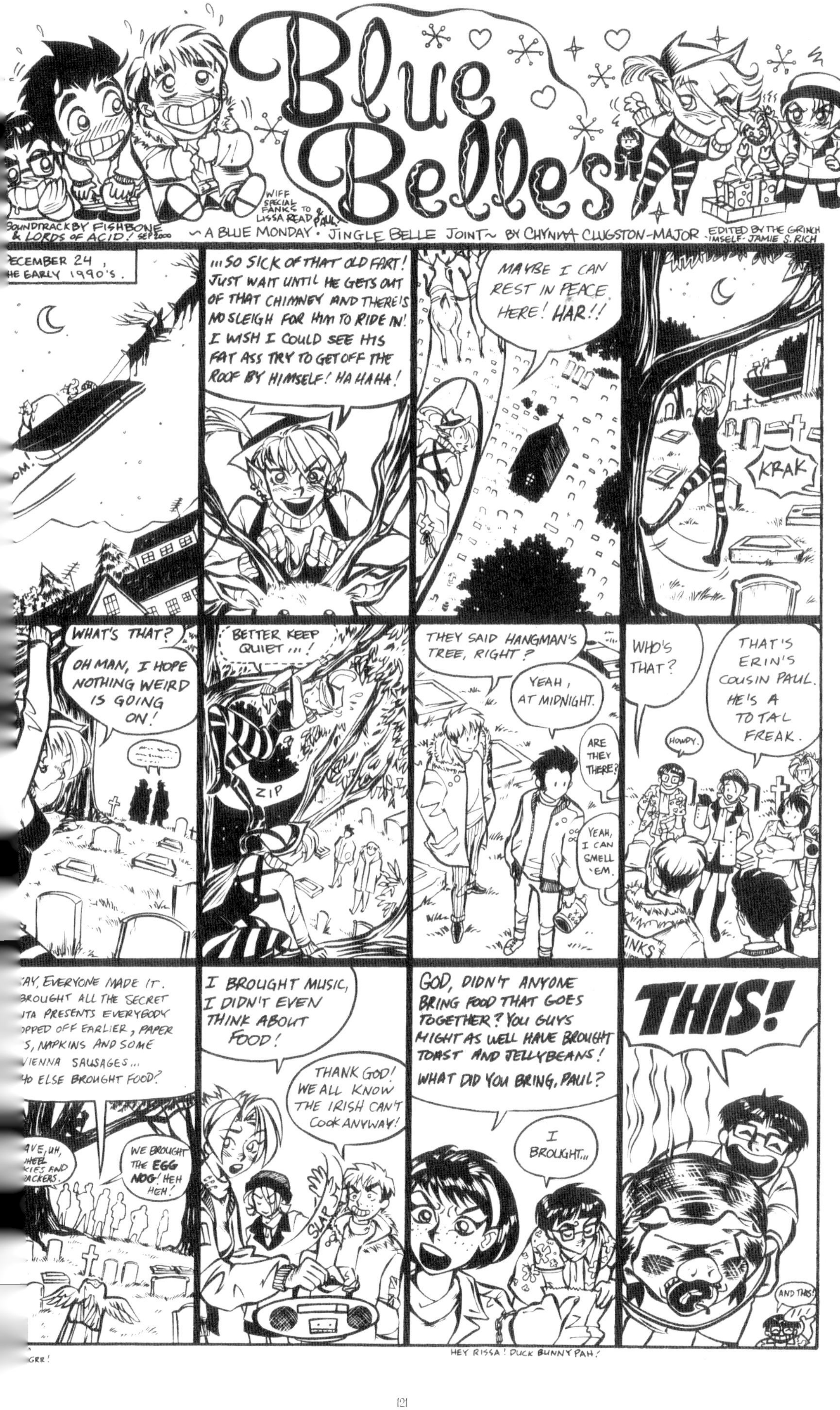
Blue Belle's
WIFF SPECIAL FANKS TO LISSA READ & PAUL!
SOUNDTRACK BY FISHBONE & LORDS OF ACID! SEP 2000
~A BLUE MONDAY • JINGLE BELLE JOINT~ BY CHYNNA CLUGSTON-MAJOR
EDITED BY THE GRINCH IMSELF- JAMIE S. RICH
ECEMBER 24, HE EARLY 1990'S.
OOM!
...SO SICK OF THAT OLD FART! JUST WAIT UNTIL HE GETS OUT OF THAT CHIMNEY AND THERE'S NO SLEIGH FOR HIM TO RIDE IN! I WISH I COULD SEE HIS FAT ASS TRY TO GET OFF THE ROOF BY HIMSELF! HA HAHA!
MAYBE I CAN REST IN PEACE HERE! HAR!!
KRAK
WHAT'S THAT?
OH MAN, I HOPE NOTHING WEIRD IS GOING ON!
BETTER KEEP QUIET...!
ZIP
THEY SAID HANGMAN'S TREE, RIGHT?
YEAH, AT MIDNIGHT.
ARE THEY THERE?
YEAH, I CAN SMELL 'EM.
WHO'S THAT?
THAT'S ERIN'S COUSIN PAUL. HE'S A TOTAL FREAK.
HOWDY.
INKS
AY, EVERYONE MADE IT. BROUGHT ALL THE SECRET NTA PRESENTS EVERYBODY OPPED OFF EARLIER, PAPER S, NAPKINS AND SOME VIENNA SAUSAGES... HO ELSE BROUGHT FOOD?
AVE, UH, HEEL KIES AND ACKERS.
WE BROUGHT THE EGG NOG! HEH HEH!
GRR!
I BROUGHT MUSIC, I DIDN'T EVEN THINK ABOUT FOOD!
THANK GOD! WE ALL KNOW THE IRISH CAN'T COOK ANYWAY!
SLAP
GOD, DIDN'T ANYONE BRING FOOD THAT GOES TOGETHER? YOU GUYS MIGHT AS WELL HAVE BROUGHT TOAST AND JELLYBEANS! WHAT DID YOU BRING, PAUL?
I BROUGHT...
HEY RISSA! DUCK BUNNY PAH!
THIS!
AND THIS!

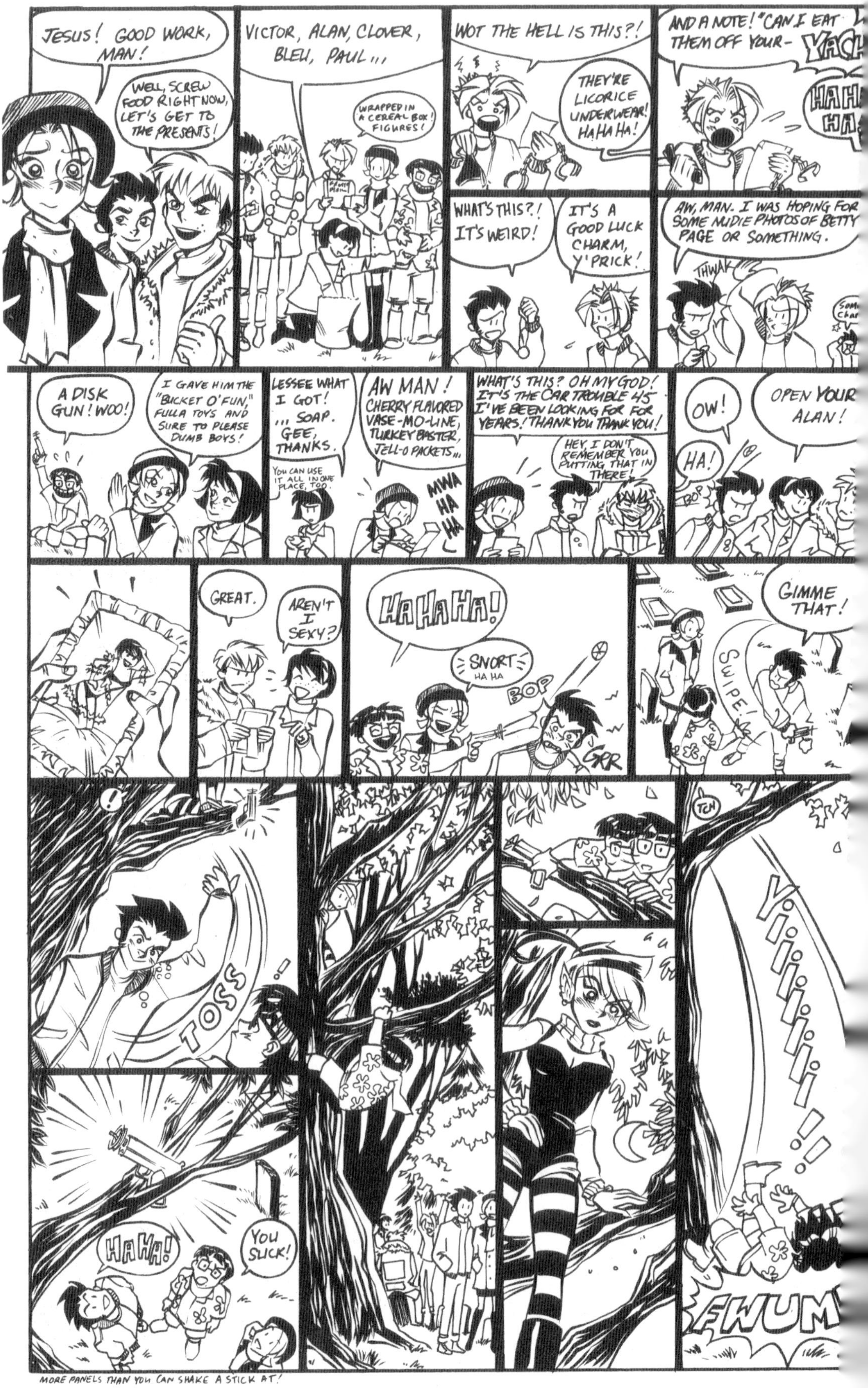
JESUS! GOOD WORK, MAN!
WELL, SCREW FOOD RIGHT NOW, LET'S GET TO THE PRESENTS!
VICTOR, ALAN, CLOVER, BLEU, PAUL...
WRAPPED IN A CEREAL BOX! FIGURES!
WOT THE HELL IS THIS?!
THEY'RE LICORICE UNDERWEAR! HAHAHA!
AND A NOTE! "CAN I EAT THEM OFF YOUR-
YACH
HAHA HA
WHAT'S THIS?! IT'S WEIRD!
IT'S A GOOD LUCK CHARM, Y'PRICK!
AW, MAN. I WAS HOPING FOR SOME NUDIE PHOTOS OF BETTY PAGE OR SOMETHING.
THWAK
A DISK GUN! WOO!
I GAVE HIM THE "BUCKET O'FUN," FULLA TOYS AND SURE TO PLEASE DUMB BOYS!
LESSEE WHAT I GOT! ... SOAP. GEE, THANKS.
You can use it all in one place, too.
AW MAN! CHERRY FLAVORED VASE-MO-LINE, TURKEY BASTER, JELL-O PACKETS...
MWA HA HA
WHAT'S THIS? OH MY GOD! IT'S THE CAR TROUBLE 45 I'VE BEEN LOOKING FOR FOR YEARS! THANK YOU THANK YOU!
HEY, I DON'T REMEMBER YOU PUTTING THAT IN THERE!
OW!
HA!
BOP
OPEN YOUR ALAN!
GREAT.
AREN'T I SEXY?
HAHAHA!
SNORT HA HA
BOP
GRR
GIMME THAT!
SWIPE!
TOSS
TCH
YIIIIIIII!!
HAHA!
YOU SUCK!
FWUM

MORE PANELS THAN YOU CAN SHAKE A STICK AT!

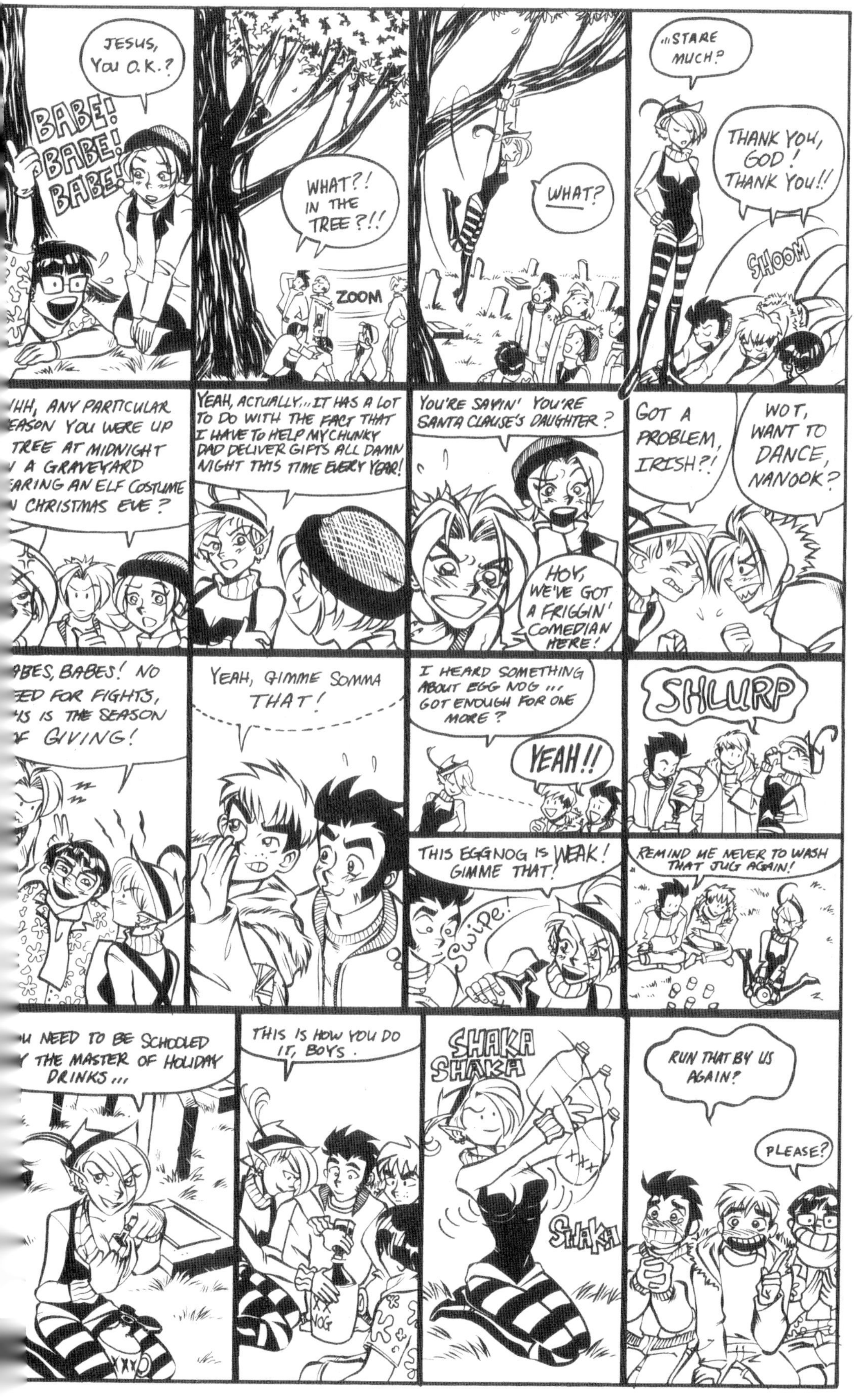
JESUS, YOU O.K.?
BABE! BABE! BABE!
WHAT?! IN THE TREE?!!
ZOOM
WHAT?
...STARE MUCH?
THANK YOU, GOD! THANK YOU!!
SHOOM
HH, ANY PARTICULAR
EASON YOU WERE UP
TREE AT MIDNIGHT
N A GRAVEYARD
EARING AN ELF COSTUME
N CHRISTMAS EVE?
YEAH, ACTUALLY... IT HAS A LOT TO DO WITH THE FACT THAT I HAVE TO HELP MY CHUNKY DAD DELIVER GIFTS ALL DAMN NIGHT THIS TIME EVERY YEAR!
YOU'RE SAYIN' YOU'RE SANTA CLAUSE'S DAUGHTER?
HOY, WE'VE GOT A FRIGGIN' COMEDIAN HERE!
GOT A PROBLEM, IRISH?!
WOT, WANT TO DANCE, NANOOK?
ABES, BABES! NO
EED FOR FIGHTS,
IS IS THE SEASON
F GIVING!
YEAH, GIMME SOMMA THAT!
I HEARD SOMETHING ABOUT EGG NOG... GOT ENOUGH FOR ONE MORE?
YEAH!!
SHLURP
THIS EGGNOG IS WEAK! GIMME THAT!
SWIPE!
REMIND ME NEVER TO WASH THAT JUG AGAIN!
U NEED TO BE SCHOOLED
Y THE MASTER OF HOLIDAY
DRINKS...
THIS IS HOW YOU DO IT, BOYS.
NOG
SHAKA SHAKA
SHAKA
RUN THAT BY US AGAIN?
PLEASE?

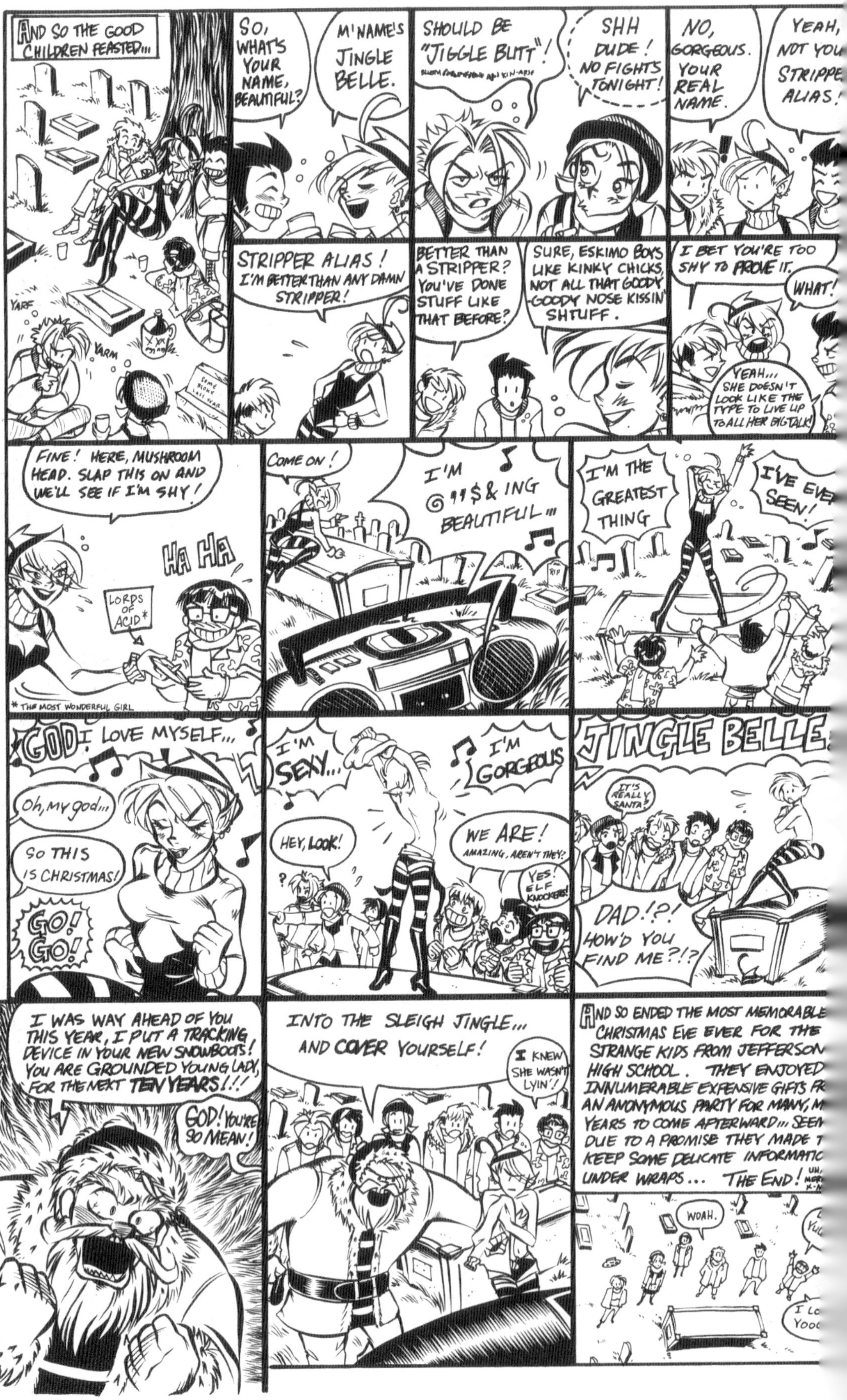
AND SO THE GOOD CHILDREN FEASTED...
YARF
YARM
SOME BLOKE LAST YEAR
SO, WHAT'S YOUR NAME, BEAUTIFUL?
M'NAME'S JINGLE BELLE.
SHOULD BE "JIGGLE BUTT"!
SHH DUDE! NO FIGHTS TONIGHT!
NO, GORGEOUS. YOUR REAL NAME.
YEAH, NOT YOU STRIPPE ALIAS!
STRIPPER ALIAS! I'M BETTER THAN ANY DAMN STRIPPER!
BETTER THAN A STRIPPER? YOU'VE DONE STUFF LIKE THAT BEFORE?
SURE, ESKIMO BOYS LIKE KINKY CHICKS, NOT ALL THAT GOODY GOODY NOSE KISSIN' SHTUFF.
I BET YOU'RE TOO SHY TO PROVE IT.
WHAT!
YEAH... SHE DOESN'T LOOK LIKE THE TYPE TO LIVE UP TO ALL HER BIG TALK!
FINE! HERE, MUSHROOM HEAD. SLAP THIS ON AND WE'LL SEE IF I'M SHY!
HA HA
LORDS OF ACID*
* THE MOST WONDERFUL GIRL
COME ON!
I'M @#$& ING BEAUTIFUL...
RIP
I'M THE GREATEST THING
I'VE EVE SEEN!
GOD! I LOVE MYSELF...
Oh, my god...
SO THIS IS CHRISTMAS!
GO! GO!
I'M SEXY...
I'M GORGEOUS
HEY, LOOK!
WE ARE! AMAZING, AREN'T THEY?
YES! ELF KNOCKERS!
JINGLE BELLE!
IT'S REALLY SANTA?
DAD!?! HOW'D YOU FIND ME?!?
I WAS WAY AHEAD OF YOU THIS YEAR, I PUT A TRACKING DEVICE IN YOUR NEW SNOWBOOTS! YOU ARE GROUNDED YOUNG LADY, FOR THE NEXT TEN YEARS!!!
GOD! YOU'RE SO MEAN!
INTO THE SLEIGH JINGLE... AND COVER YOURSELF!
I KNEW SHE WASN'T LYIN'!
AND SO ENDED THE MOST MEMORABLE CHRISTMAS EVE EVER FOR THE STRANGE KIDS FROM JEFFERSON HIGH SCHOOL. THEY ENJOYED INNUMERABLE EXPENSIVE GIFTS FR AN ANONYMOUS PARTY FOR MANY, M YEARS TO COME AFTERWARD... SEEM DUE TO A PROMISE THEY MADE T KEEP SOME DELICATE INFORMATIO UNDER WRAPS... THE END!
WOAH.
I LO YOOO

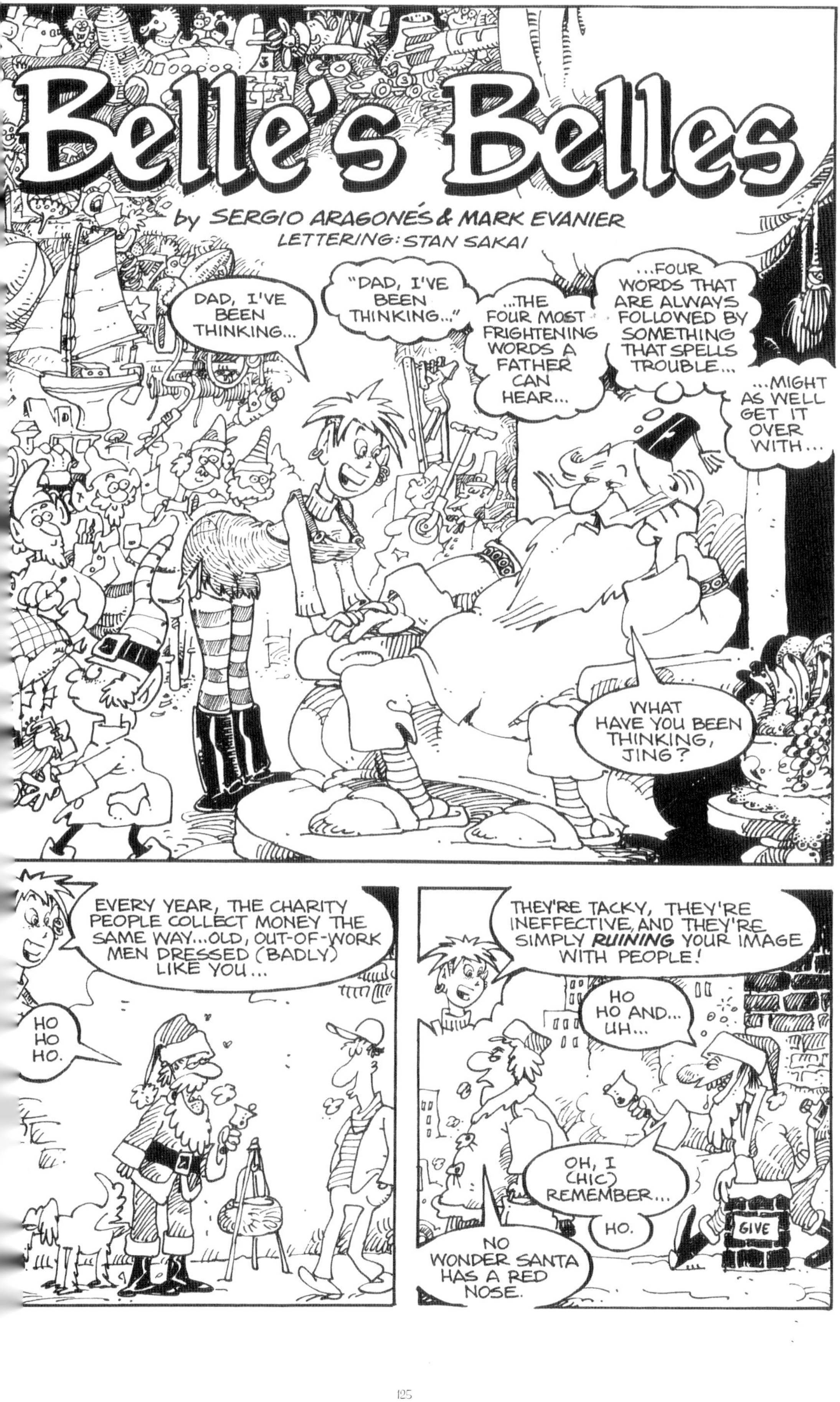
Belle's Belles
by SERGIO ARAGONÉS & MARK EVANIER
LETTERING: STAN SAKAI
DAD, I'VE BEEN THINKING...
"DAD, I'VE BEEN THINKING..."
...THE FOUR MOST FRIGHTENING WORDS A FATHER CAN HEAR...
...FOUR WORDS THAT ARE ALWAYS FOLLOWED BY SOMETHING THAT SPELLS TROUBLE...
...MIGHT AS WELL GET IT OVER WITH...
WHAT HAVE YOU BEEN THINKING, JING?
EVERY YEAR, THE CHARITY PEOPLE COLLECT MONEY THE SAME WAY...OLD, OUT-OF-WORK MEN DRESSED (BADLY) LIKE YOU...
HO HO HO.
THEY'RE TACKY, THEY'RE INEFFECTIVE, AND THEY'RE SIMPLY *RUINING* YOUR IMAGE WITH PEOPLE!
HO HO AND... UH...
OH, I (HIC) REMEMBER...
HO.
GIVE
NO WONDER SANTA HAS A RED NOSE.

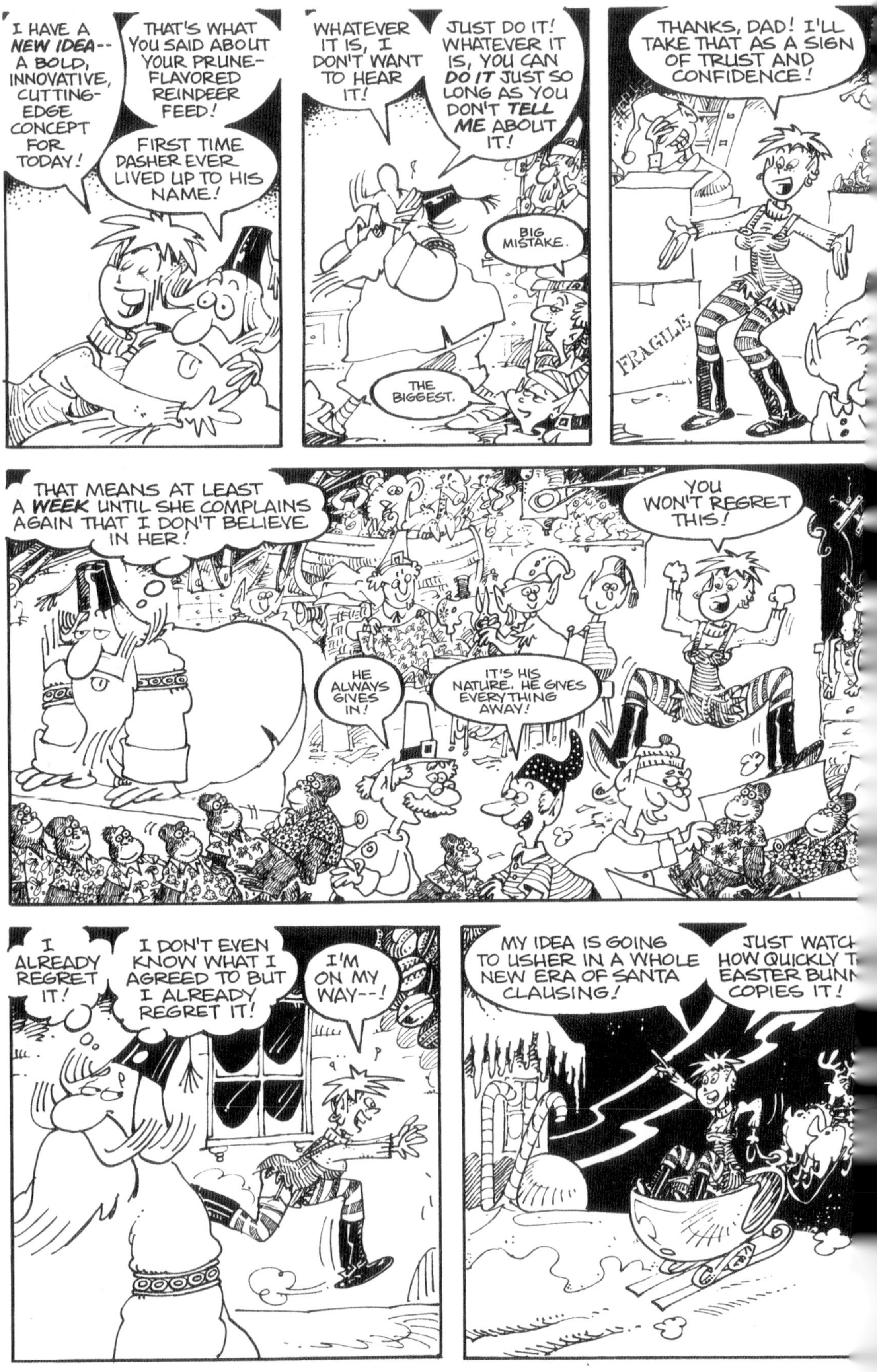
I HAVE A **NEW IDEA**-- A BOLD, INNOVATIVE, CUTTING-EDGE CONCEPT FOR TODAY!
THAT'S WHAT YOU SAID ABOUT YOUR PRUNE-FLAVORED REINDEER FEED!
FIRST TIME DASHER EVER LIVED UP TO HIS NAME!
WHATEVER IT IS, I DON'T WANT TO HEAR IT!
JUST DO IT! WHATEVER IT IS, YOU CAN **DO IT** JUST SO LONG AS YOU DON'T **TELL ME** ABOUT IT!
BIG MISTAKE.
THE BIGGEST.
THANKS, DAD! I'LL TAKE THAT AS A SIGN OF TRUST AND CONFIDENCE!
FRAGILE
THAT MEANS AT LEAST A **WEEK** UNTIL SHE COMPLAINS AGAIN THAT I DON'T BELIEVE IN HER!
YOU WON'T REGRET THIS!
HE ALWAYS GIVES IN!
IT'S HIS NATURE. HE GIVES EVERYTHING AWAY!
I ALREADY REGRET IT!
I DON'T EVEN KNOW WHAT I AGREED TO BUT I ALREADY REGRET IT!
I'M ON MY WAY--!
MY IDEA IS GOING TO USHER IN A WHOLE NEW ERA OF SANTA CLAUSING!

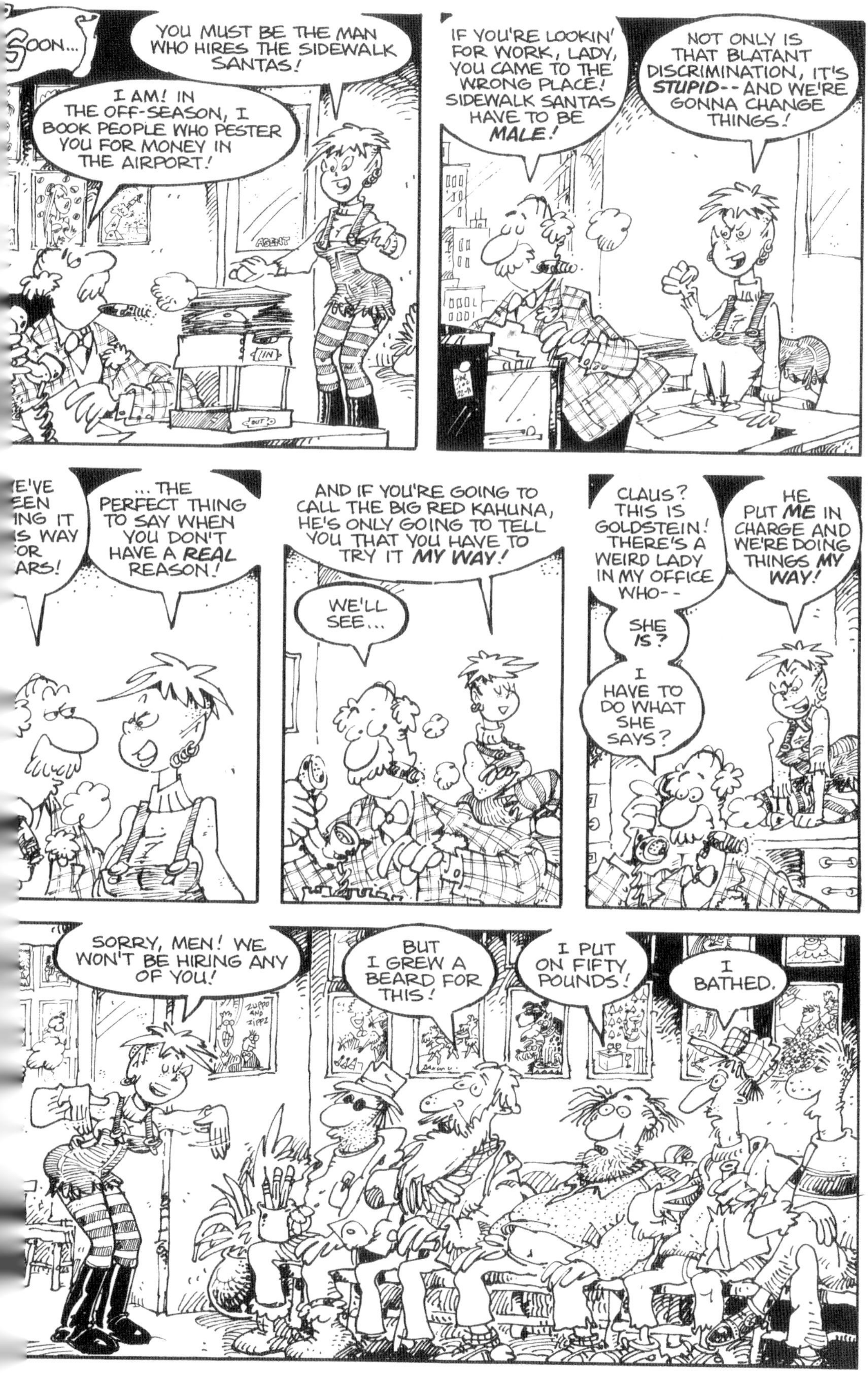
SOON...
YOU MUST BE THE MAN WHO HIRES THE SIDEWALK SANTAS!
I AM! IN THE OFF-SEASON, I BOOK PEOPLE WHO PESTER YOU FOR MONEY IN THE AIRPORT!
AGENT
IN
OUT
IF YOU'RE LOOKIN' FOR WORK, LADY, YOU CAME TO THE WRONG PLACE! SIDEWALK SANTAS HAVE TO BE MALE!
NOT ONLY IS THAT BLATANT DISCRIMINATION, IT'S STUPID-- AND WE'RE GONNA CHANGE THINGS!
E'VE EEN ING IT S WAY OR ARS!
... THE PERFECT THING TO SAY WHEN YOU DON'T HAVE A REAL REASON!
AND IF YOU'RE GOING TO CALL THE BIG RED KAHUNA, HE'S ONLY GOING TO TELL YOU THAT YOU HAVE TO TRY IT MY WAY!
WE'LL SEE...
CLAUS? THIS IS GOLDSTEIN! THERE'S A WEIRD LADY IN MY OFFICE WHO--
SHE IS?
I HAVE TO DO WHAT SHE SAYS?
HE PUT ME IN CHARGE AND WE'RE DOING THINGS MY WAY!
SORRY, MEN! WE WON'T BE HIRING ANY OF YOU!
ZUPPO AND ZIPPI
BUT I GREW A BEARD FOR THIS!
I PUT ON FIFTY POUNDS!
I BATHED.

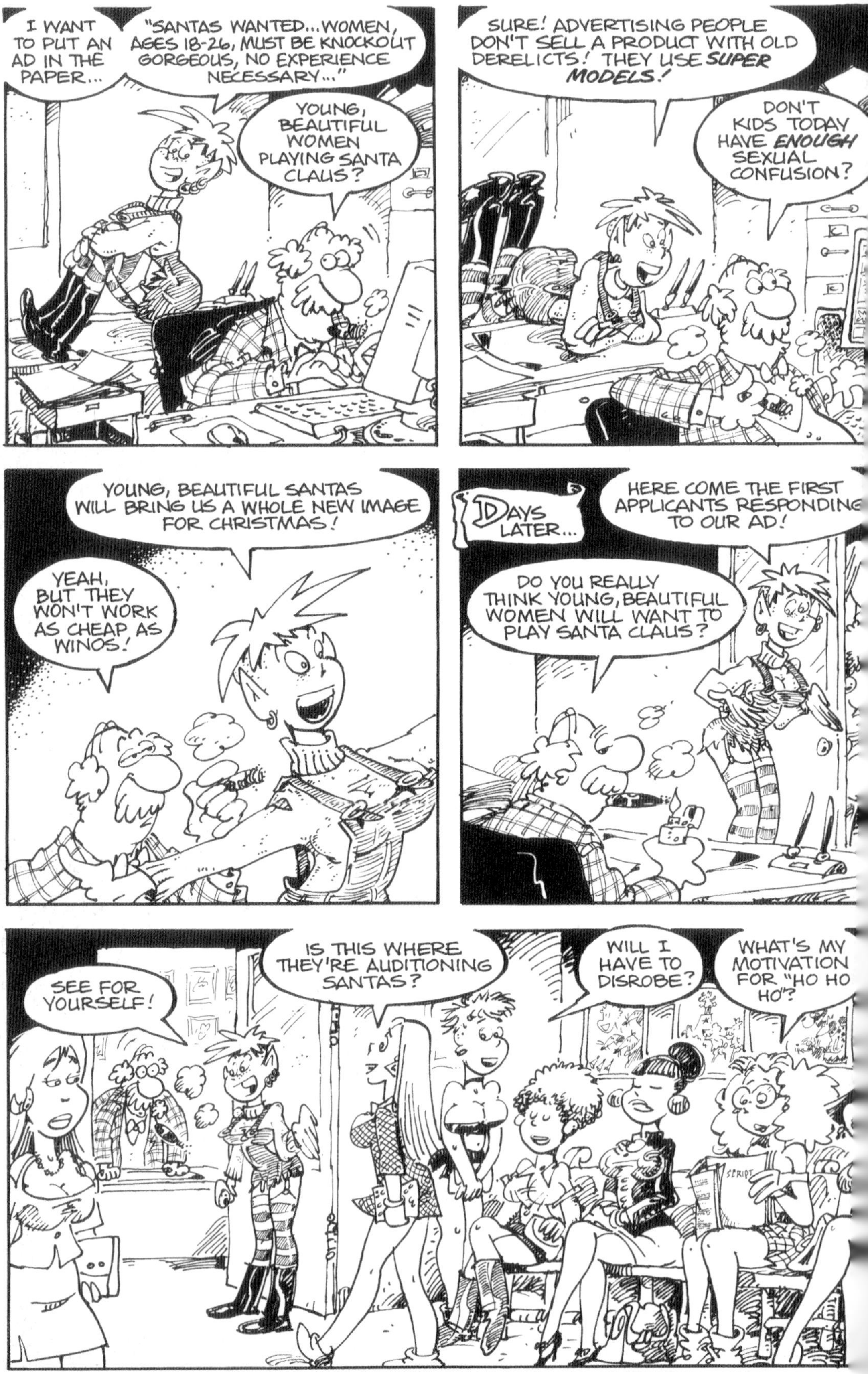
I WANT TO PUT AN AD IN THE PAPER...
"SANTAS WANTED...WOMEN, AGES 18-26, MUST BE KNOCKOUT GORGEOUS, NO EXPERIENCE NECESSARY..."
YOUNG, BEAUTIFUL WOMEN PLAYING SANTA CLAUS?
SURE! ADVERTISING PEOPLE DON'T SELL A PRODUCT WITH OLD DERELICTS! THEY USE SUPER MODELS!
DON'T KIDS TODAY HAVE ENOUGH SEXUAL CONFUSION?
YOUNG, BEAUTIFUL SANTAS WILL BRING US A WHOLE NEW IMAGE FOR CHRISTMAS!
YEAH, BUT THEY WON'T WORK AS CHEAP AS WINOS!
DAYS LATER...
HERE COME THE FIRST APPLICANTS RESPONDING TO OUR AD!
DO YOU REALLY THINK YOUNG, BEAUTIFUL WOMEN WILL WANT TO PLAY SANTA CLAUS?
SEE FOR YOURSELF!
IS THIS WHERE THEY'RE AUDITIONING SANTAS?
WILL I HAVE TO DISROBE?
WHAT'S MY MOTIVATION FOR "HO HO HO"?
SCRIPT

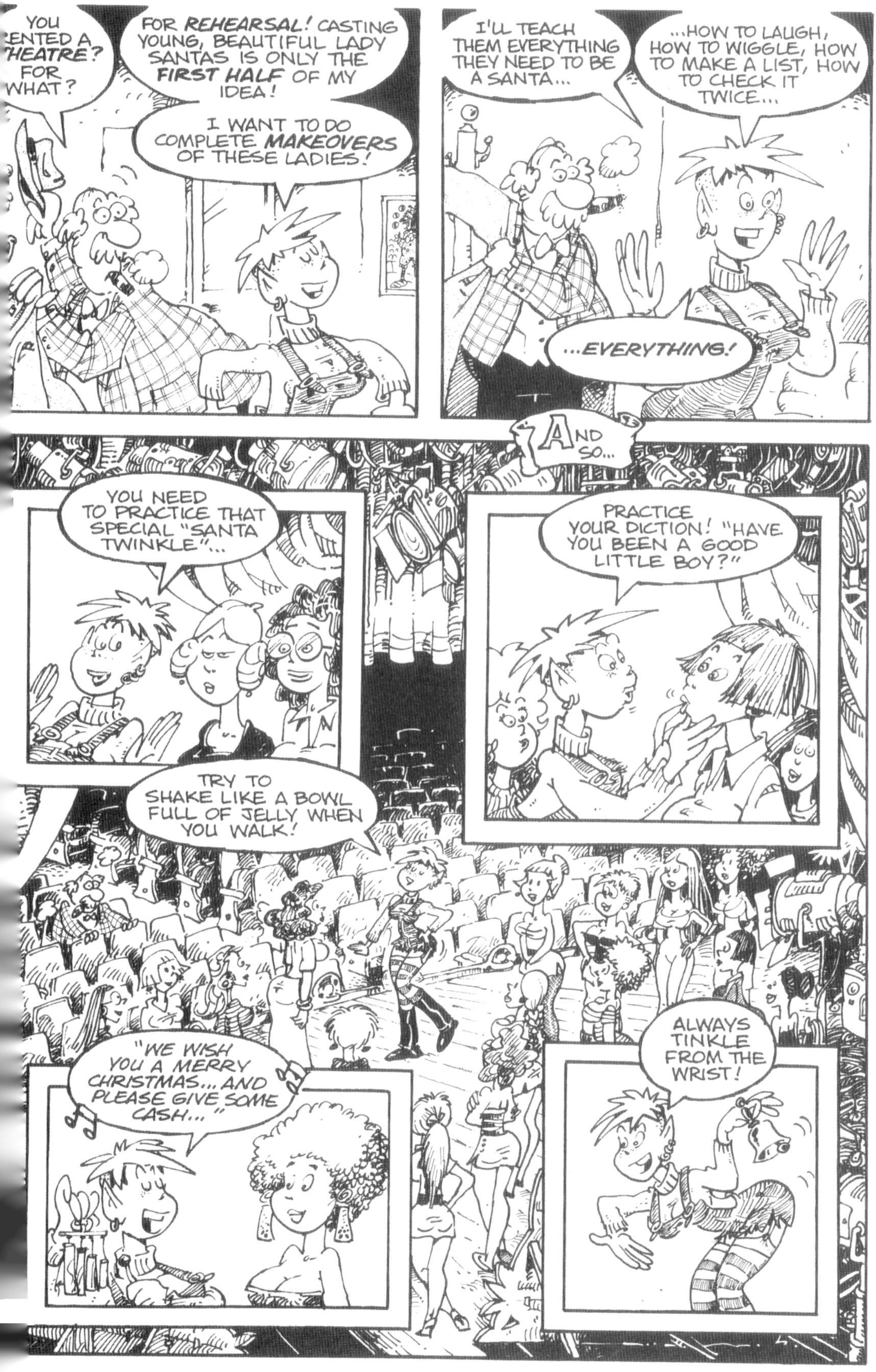
YOU RENTED A THEATRE? FOR WHAT?
FOR REHEARSAL! CASTING YOUNG, BEAUTIFUL LADY SANTAS IS ONLY THE FIRST HALF OF MY IDEA!
I WANT TO DO COMPLETE MAKEOVERS OF THESE LADIES!
I'LL TEACH THEM EVERYTHING THEY NEED TO BE A SANTA...
...HOW TO LAUGH, HOW TO WIGGLE, HOW TO MAKE A LIST, HOW TO CHECK IT TWICE...
...EVERYTHING!
AND SO...
YOU NEED TO PRACTICE THAT SPECIAL "SANTA TWINKLE"...
PRACTICE YOUR DICTION! "HAVE YOU BEEN A GOOD LITTLE BOY?"
TRY TO SHAKE LIKE A BOWL FULL OF JELLY WHEN YOU WALK!
"WE WISH YOU A MERRY CHRISTMAS... AND PLEASE GIVE SOME CASH..."
ALWAYS TINKLE FROM THE WRIST!

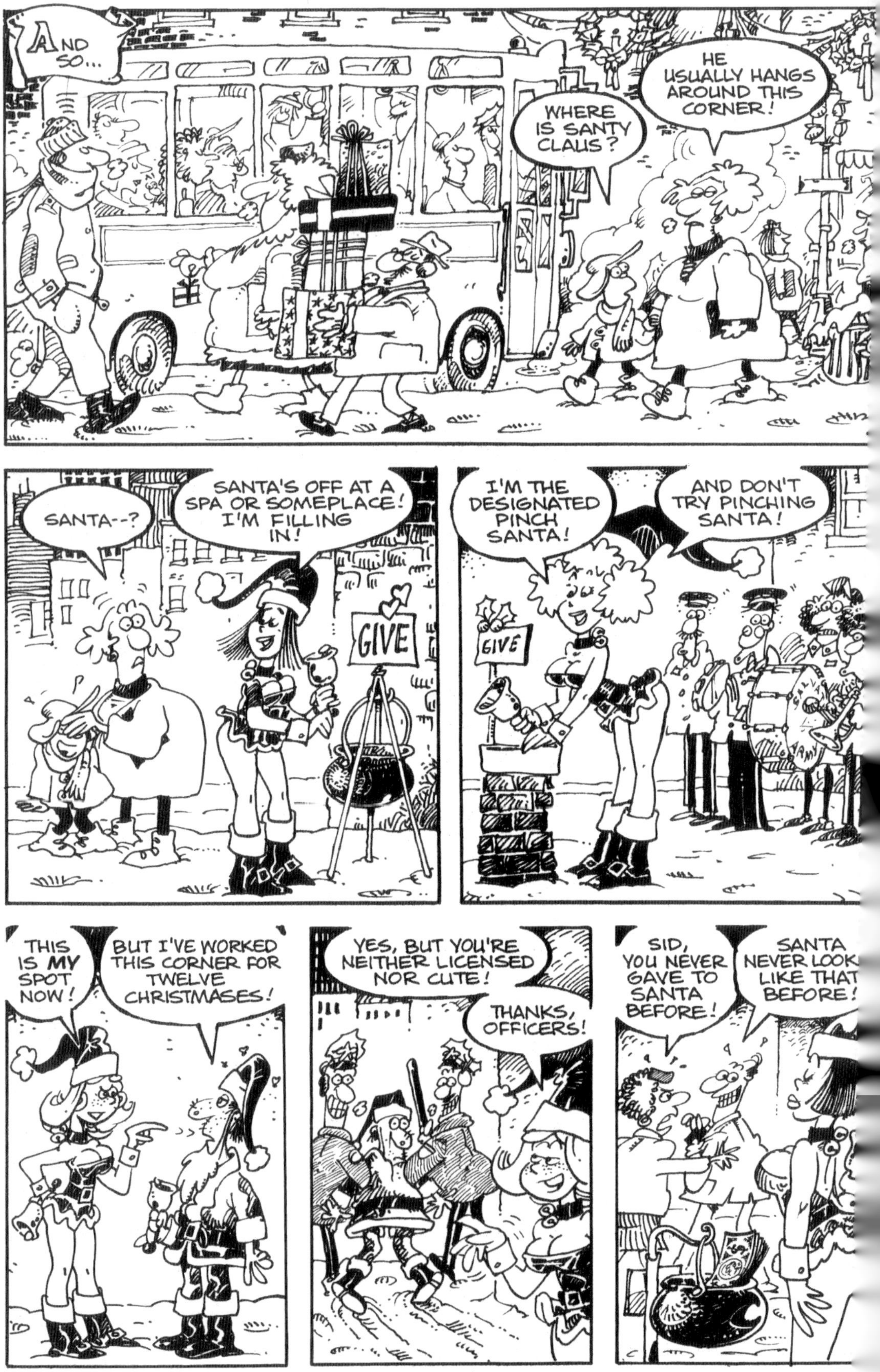

AND SO...
WHERE IS SANTY CLAUS?
HE USUALLY HANGS AROUND THIS CORNER!
SANTA--?
SANTA'S OFF AT A SPA OR SOMEPLACE! I'M FILLING IN!
GIVE
I'M THE DESIGNATED PINCH SANTA!
AND DON'T TRY PINCHING SANTA!
GIVE
THIS IS MY SPOT NOW!
BUT I'VE WORKED THIS CORNER FOR TWELVE CHRISTMASES!
YES, BUT YOU'RE NEITHER LICENSED NOR CUTE!
THANKS, OFFICERS!
SID, YOU NEVER GAVE TO SANTA BEFORE!
SANTA NEVER LOOK LIKE THAT BEFORE!

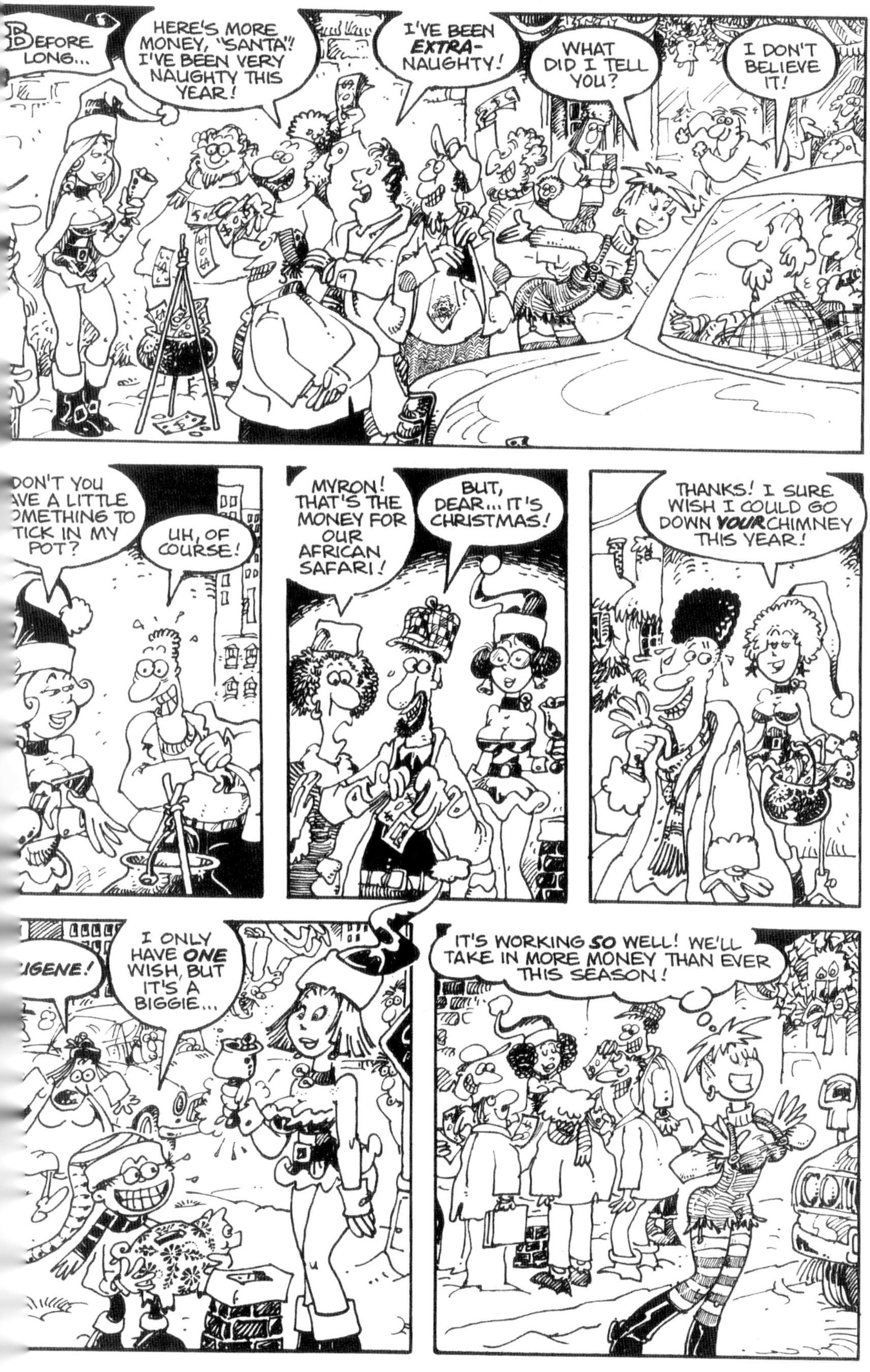
BEFORE LONG...
HERE'S MORE MONEY, "SANTA"! I'VE BEEN VERY NAUGHTY THIS YEAR!
I'VE BEEN EXTRA-NAUGHTY!
WHAT DID I TELL YOU?
I DON'T BELIEVE IT!
DON'T YOU AVE A LITTLE OMETHING TO TICK IN MY POT?
UH, OF COURSE!
MYRON! THAT'S THE MONEY FOR OUR AFRICAN SAFARI!
BUT, DEAR... IT'S CHRISTMAS!
THANKS! I SURE WISH I COULD GO DOWN YOUR CHIMNEY THIS YEAR!
IGENE!
I ONLY HAVE ONE WISH, BUT IT'S A BIGGIE...
IT'S WORKING SO WELL! WE'LL TAKE IN MORE MONEY THAN EVER THIS SEASON!

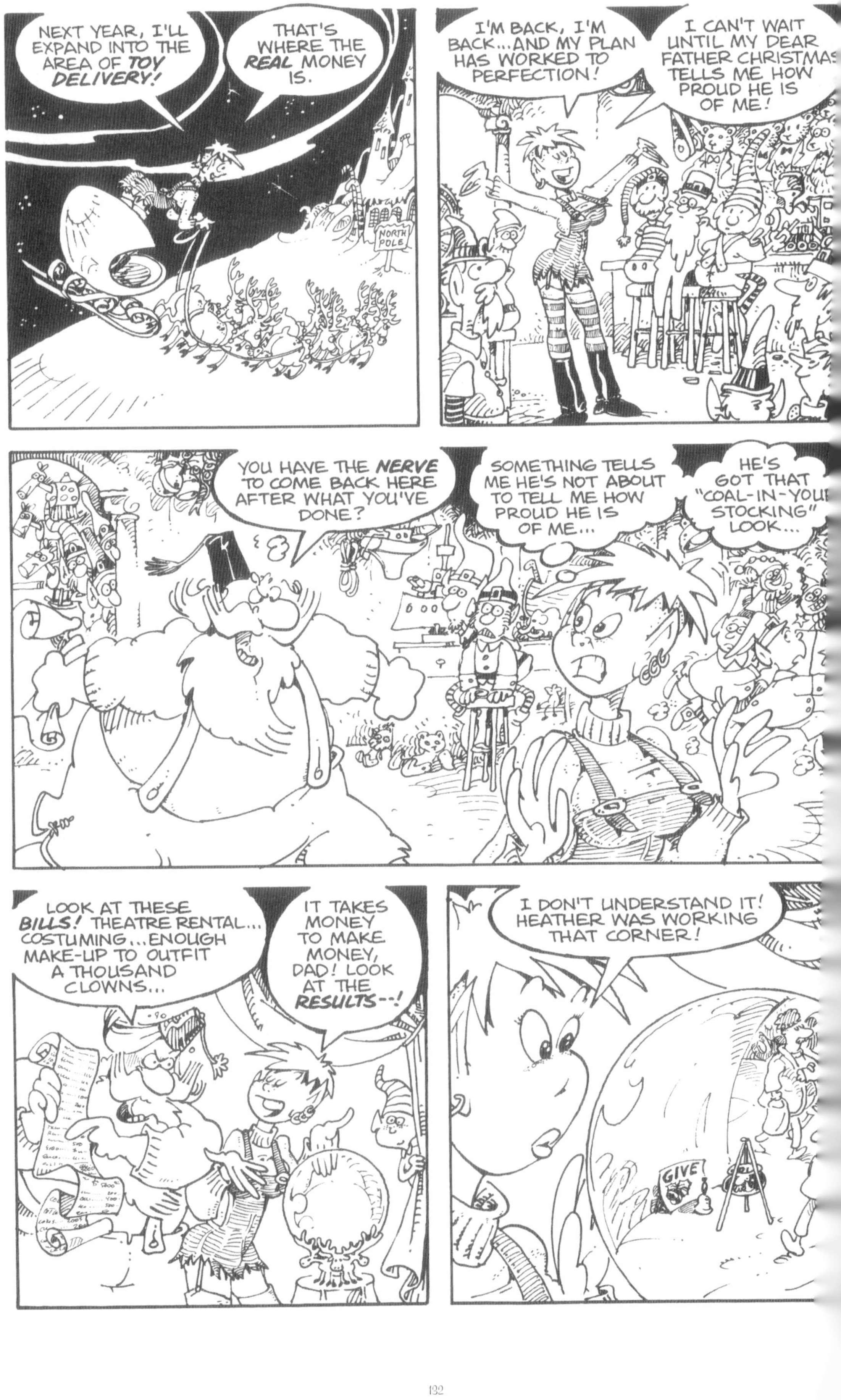
NEXT YEAR, I'LL EXPAND INTO THE AREA OF **TOY DELIVERY!**
THAT'S WHERE THE **REAL** MONEY IS.
NORTH POLE
I'M BACK, I'M BACK...AND MY PLAN HAS WORKED TO PERFECTION!
I CAN'T WAIT UNTIL MY DEAR FATHER CHRISTMAS TELLS ME HOW PROUD HE IS OF ME!
YOU HAVE THE **NERVE** TO COME BACK HERE AFTER WHAT YOU'VE DONE?
SOMETHING TELLS ME HE'S NOT ABOUT TO TELL ME HOW PROUD HE IS OF ME...
HE'S GOT THAT "COAL-IN-YOUR STOCKING" LOOK...
LOOK AT THESE **BILLS!** THEATRE RENTAL... COSTUMING...ENOUGH MAKE-UP TO OUTFIT A THOUSAND CLOWNS...
IT TAKES MONEY TO MAKE MONEY, DAD! LOOK AT THE **RESULTS**--!
I DON'T UNDERSTAND IT! HEATHER WAS WORKING THAT CORNER!
GIVE

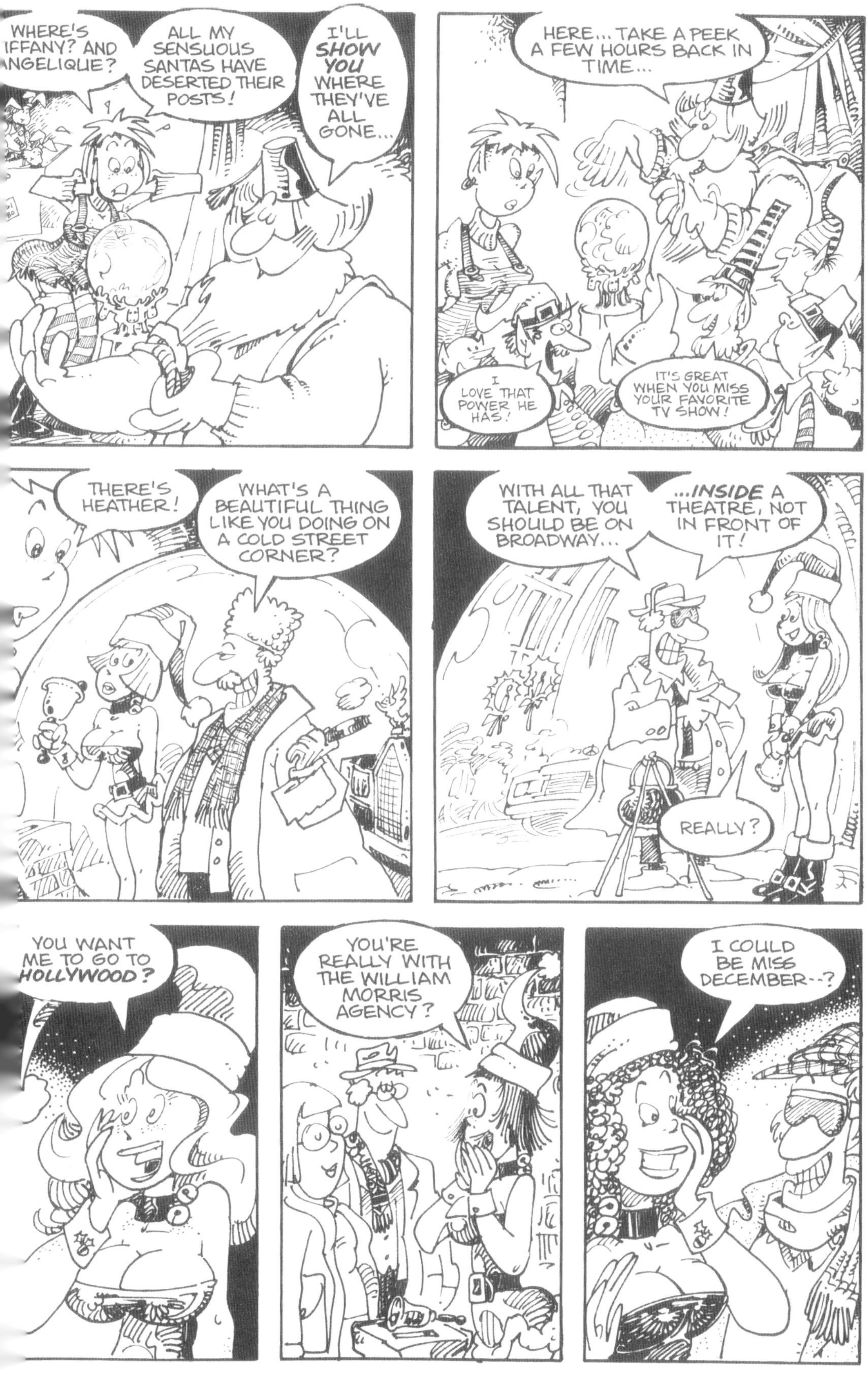
WHERE'S IFFANY? AND NGELIQUE?
ALL MY SENSUOUS SANTAS HAVE DESERTED THEIR POSTS!
I'LL **SHOW YOU** WHERE THEY'VE ALL GONE...
HERE... TAKE A PEEK A FEW HOURS BACK IN TIME...
I LOVE THAT POWER HE HAS!
IT'S GREAT WHEN YOU MISS YOUR FAVORITE TV SHOW!
THERE'S HEATHER!
WHAT'S A BEAUTIFUL THING LIKE YOU DOING ON A COLD STREET CORNER?
WITH ALL THAT TALENT, YOU SHOULD BE ON BROADWAY...
...**INSIDE** A THEATRE, NOT IN FRONT OF IT!
REALLY?
YOU WANT ME TO GO TO **HOLLYWOOD**?
YOU'RE REALLY WITH THE WILLIAM MORRIS AGENCY?
I COULD BE MISS DECEMBER--?

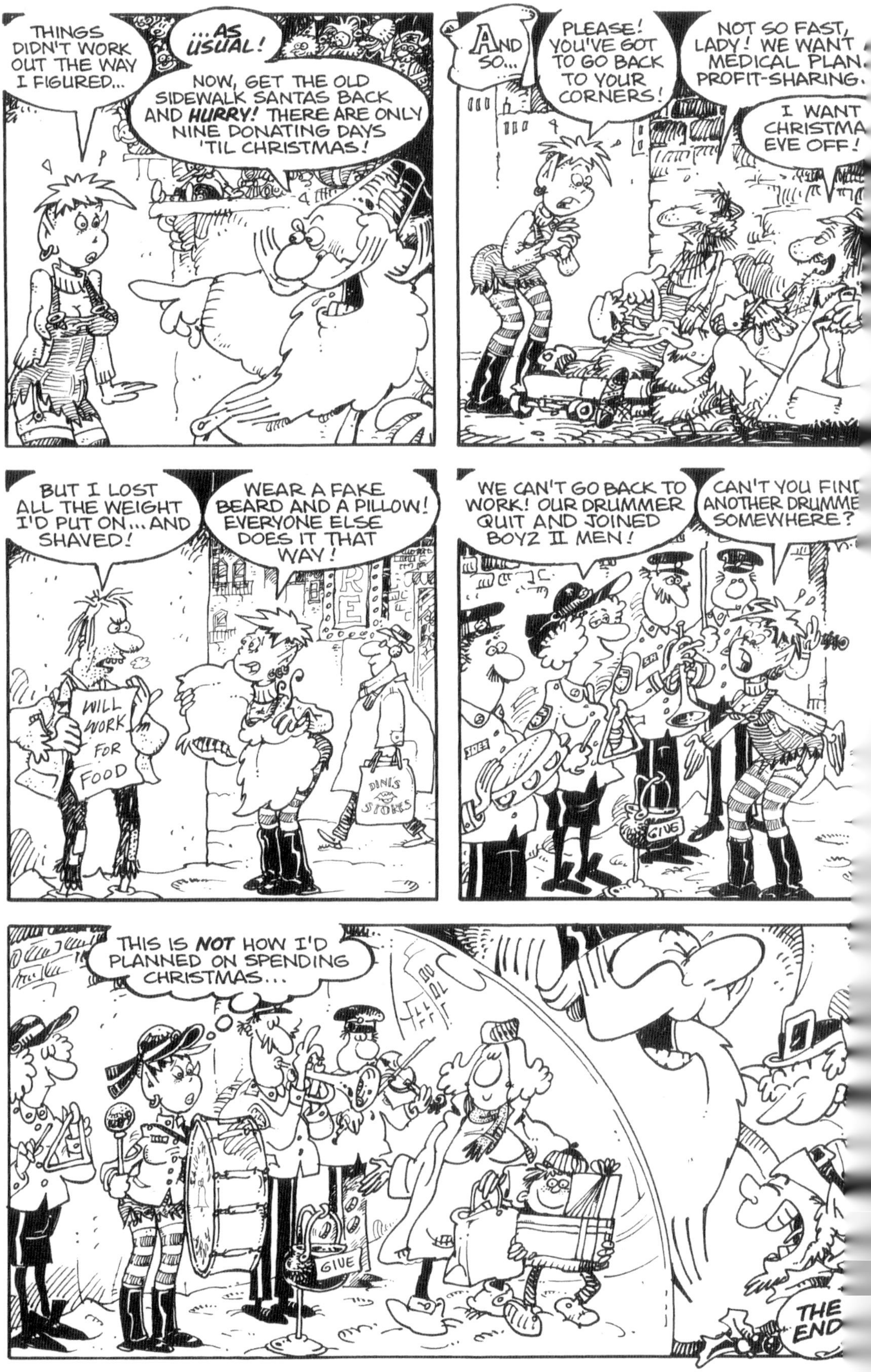
THINGS DIDN'T WORK OUT THE WAY I FIGURED...
...AS USUAL!
NOW, GET THE OLD SIDEWALK SANTAS BACK AND HURRY! THERE ARE ONLY NINE DONATING DAYS 'TIL CHRISTMAS!
AND SO...
PLEASE! YOU'VE GOT TO GO BACK TO YOUR CORNERS!
NOT SO FAST, LADY! WE WANT MEDICAL PLAN PROFIT-SHARING
I WANT CHRISTMA EVE OFF!
BUT I LOST ALL THE WEIGHT I'D PUT ON...AND SHAVED!
WEAR A FAKE BEARD AND A PILLOW! EVERYONE ELSE DOES IT THAT WAY!
WILL WORK FOR FOOD
DINI'S STORES
WE CAN'T GO BACK TO WORK! OUR DRUMMER QUIT AND JOINED BOYZ II MEN!
CAN'T YOU FIND ANOTHER DRUMME SOMEWHERE?
GIVE
THIS IS NOT HOW I'D PLANNED ON SPENDING CHRISTMAS...
GIVE
THE END

Coal Comfort

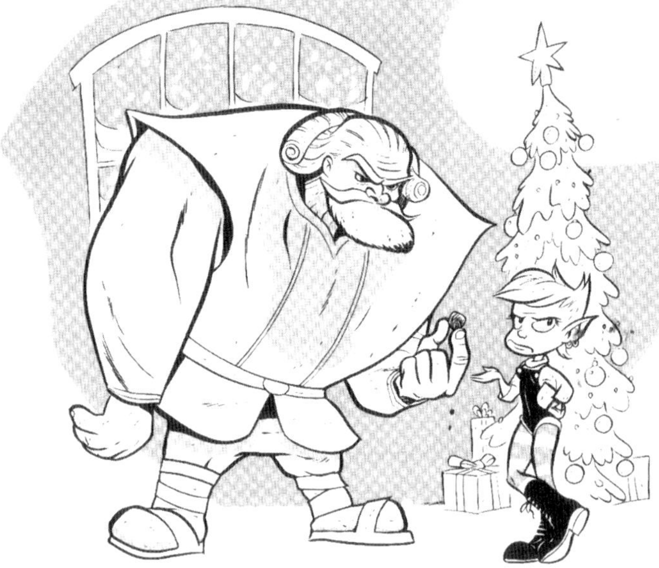

A question has been posed by some tots we hold dear
About the coal Jingle Belle gets from Santa each year.
What becomes of our naughty teen's holiday lumps?
Does she stack them in piles or just toss them in clumps?
Does she roll them 'neath her bed, all grimy and dusty
Or bounce them off the head of her dumb cousin, Rusty?

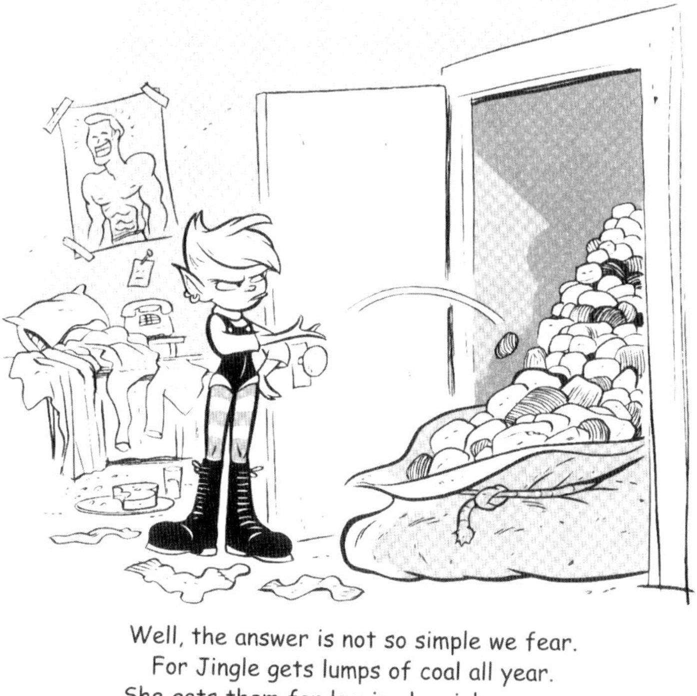

Well, the answer is not so simple we fear.
For Jingle gets lumps of coal all year.
She gets them for leaving her igloo a mess
And dripping eggnog on her mom's royal dress.
For partying in the workshop with the Eskimo boys,
And for selling Mattel Santa's new plans for toys.

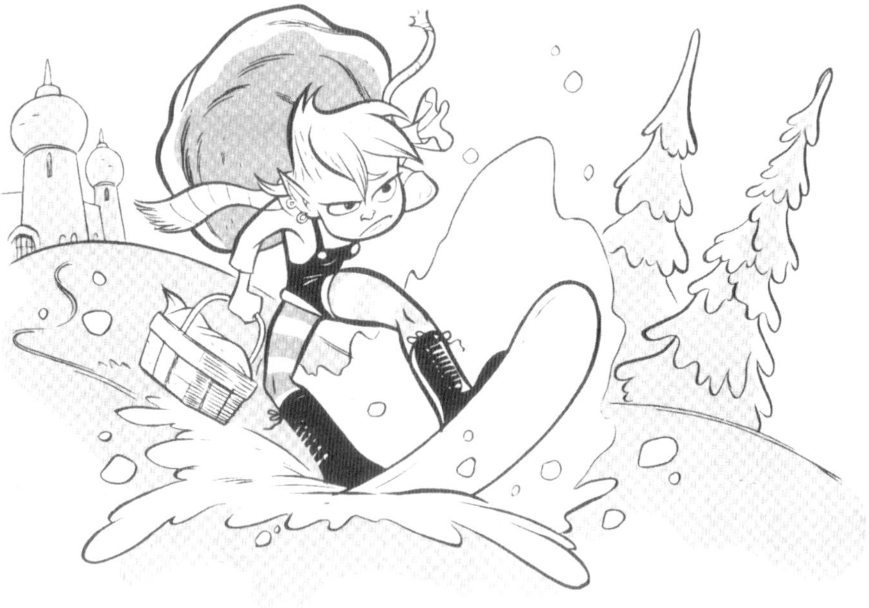

So it's hundreds of lumps, many more than just one.
Naughty Jingle collects before the year's done.
While Santa and crew toast another Christmas Eve,
Visits to good children and the toys they receive,
No one sees our young elfling has fast away flown,
Snowboarding, coal in hand, on a quest of her own.

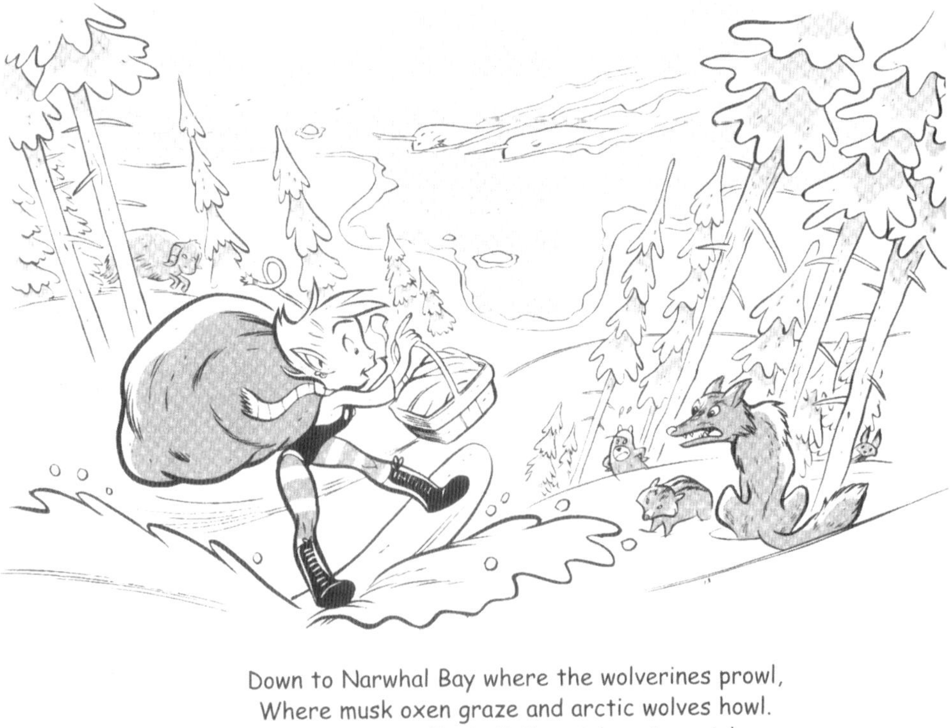

Down to Narwhal Bay where the wolverines prowl,
Where musk oxen graze and arctic wolves howl.
Hither comes Jingle Belle quick as two winks,
Unfazed by this gathering of lemming and lynx.
Wild creatures that few people call sweet or good,
Not bad, but like Jingle, somewhat misunderstood.

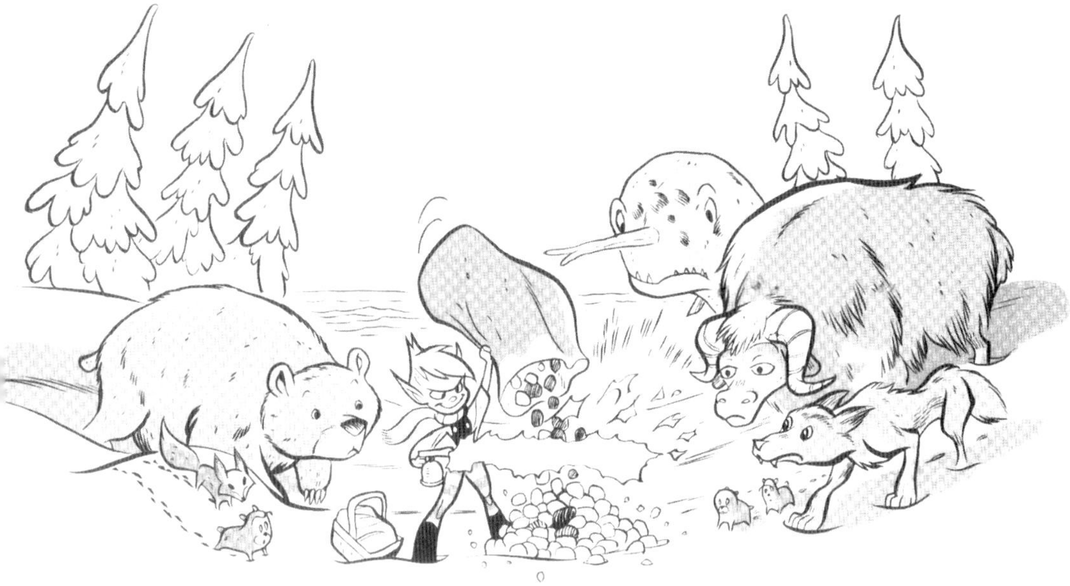

And now with her year's worth of coal piled high,
Jing pulls out her blowtorch and lets the flames fly.
The critters draw close to its warm, friendly glow,
As around them cold polar winds bitterly blow.

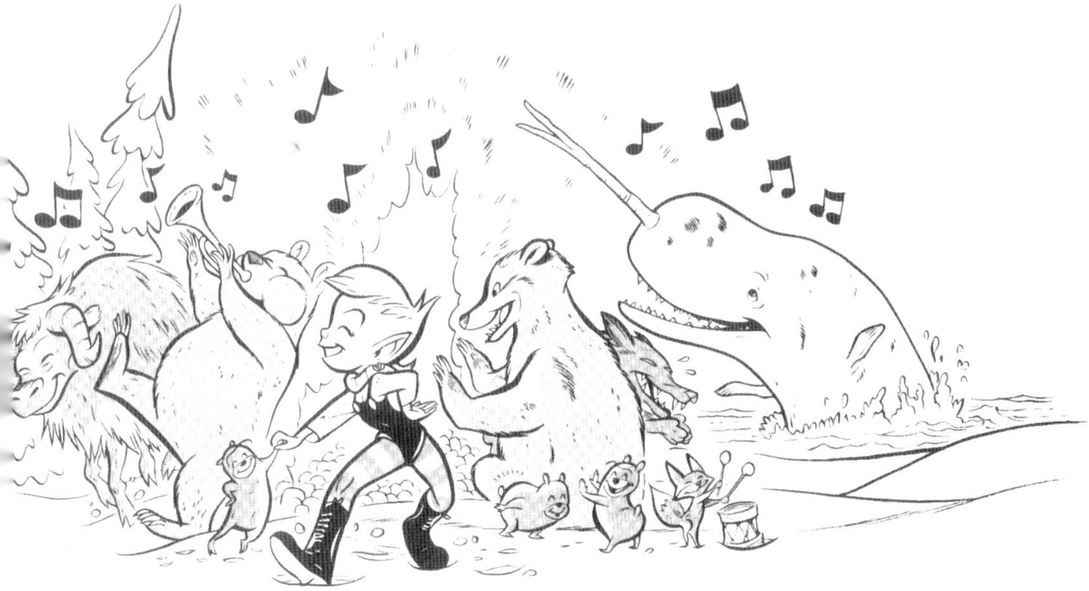

For Christmas is Christmas, and it shouldn't be missed.
Even though you're no longer on Santa's gift list.
So you've been a bit naughty, there's always next year!
The true sin would be letting one pass without cheer.
So gather your friends; build the fire up bright
And do the Jing thing, namely party all night!

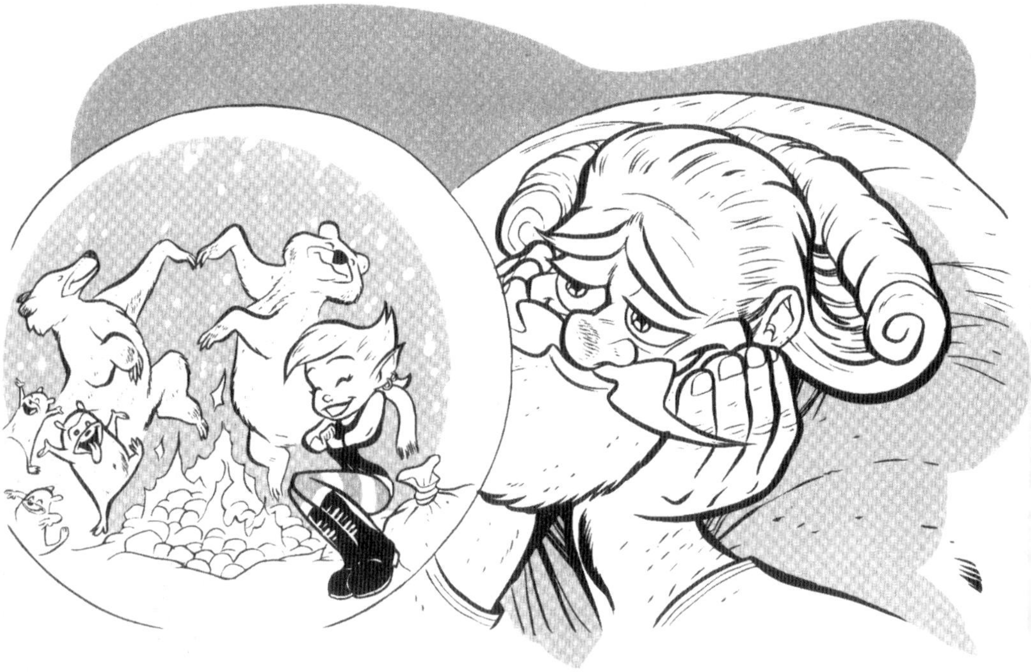

And what does St. Nick think of his little girl's ways
As he looks down on her with his magical gaze?
Well, truth to be told, old Santa's quite proud.
Sure, Jingle is known to be rude, wild and loud.
But any girl who'd throw her friends a holiday fete,
Can't be all bad. Perhaps there's hope for her yet.

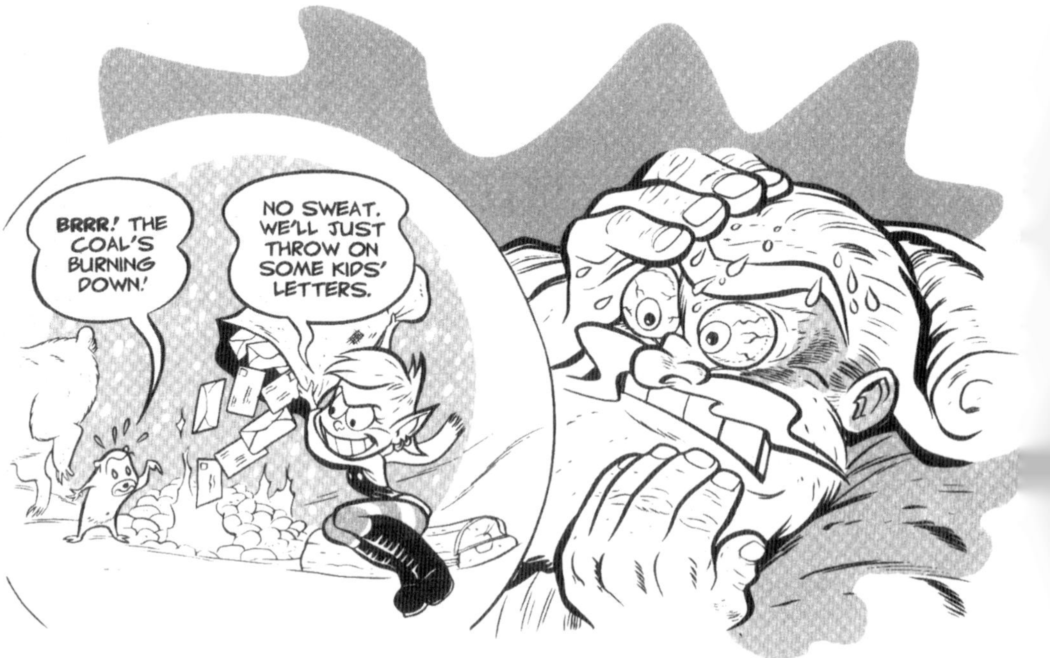

BRRR! THE COAL'S BURNING DOWN!
NO SWEAT. WE'LL JUST THROW ON SOME KIDS' LETTERS.

Don't bet.

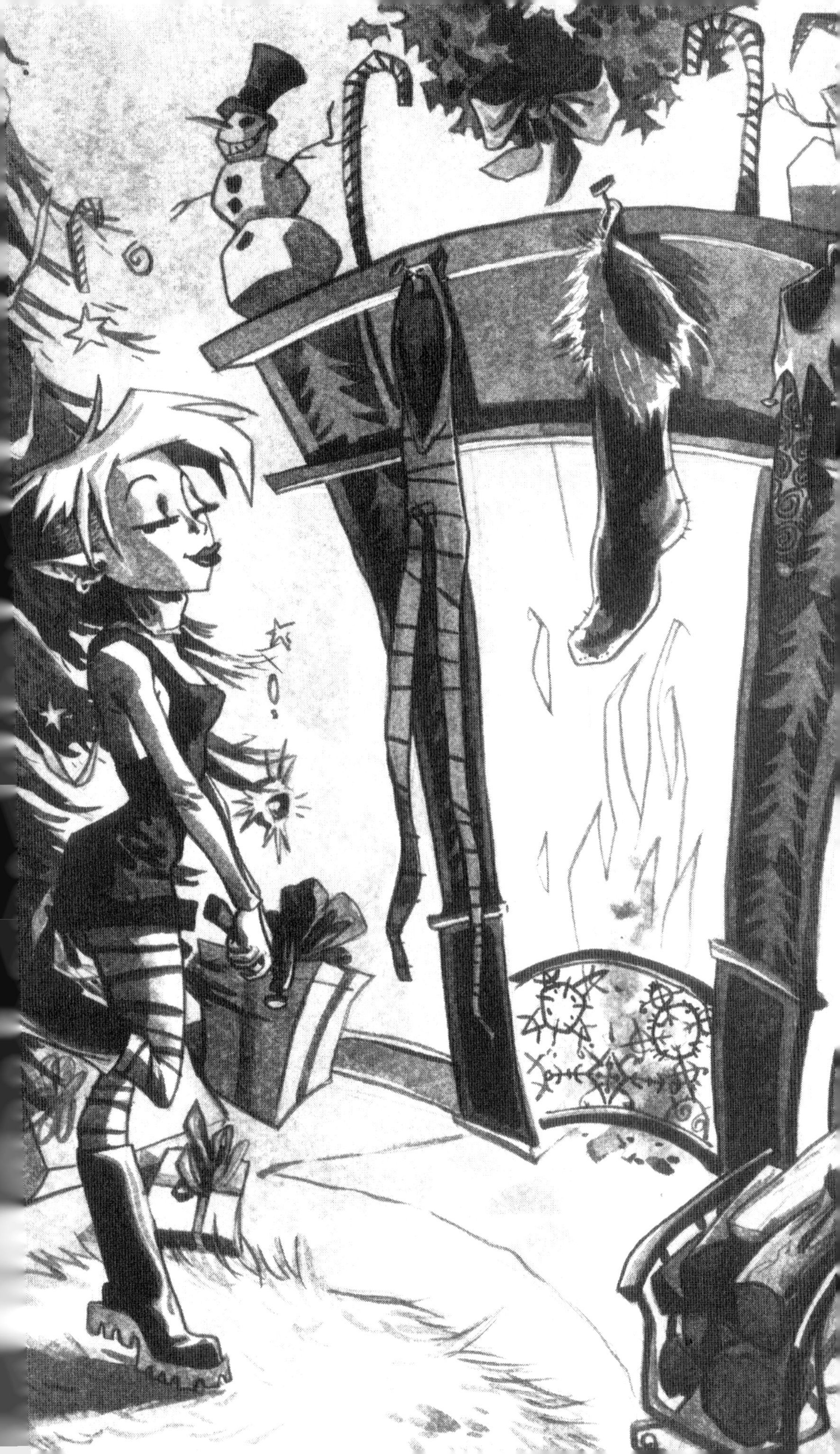

The Mighty Elves

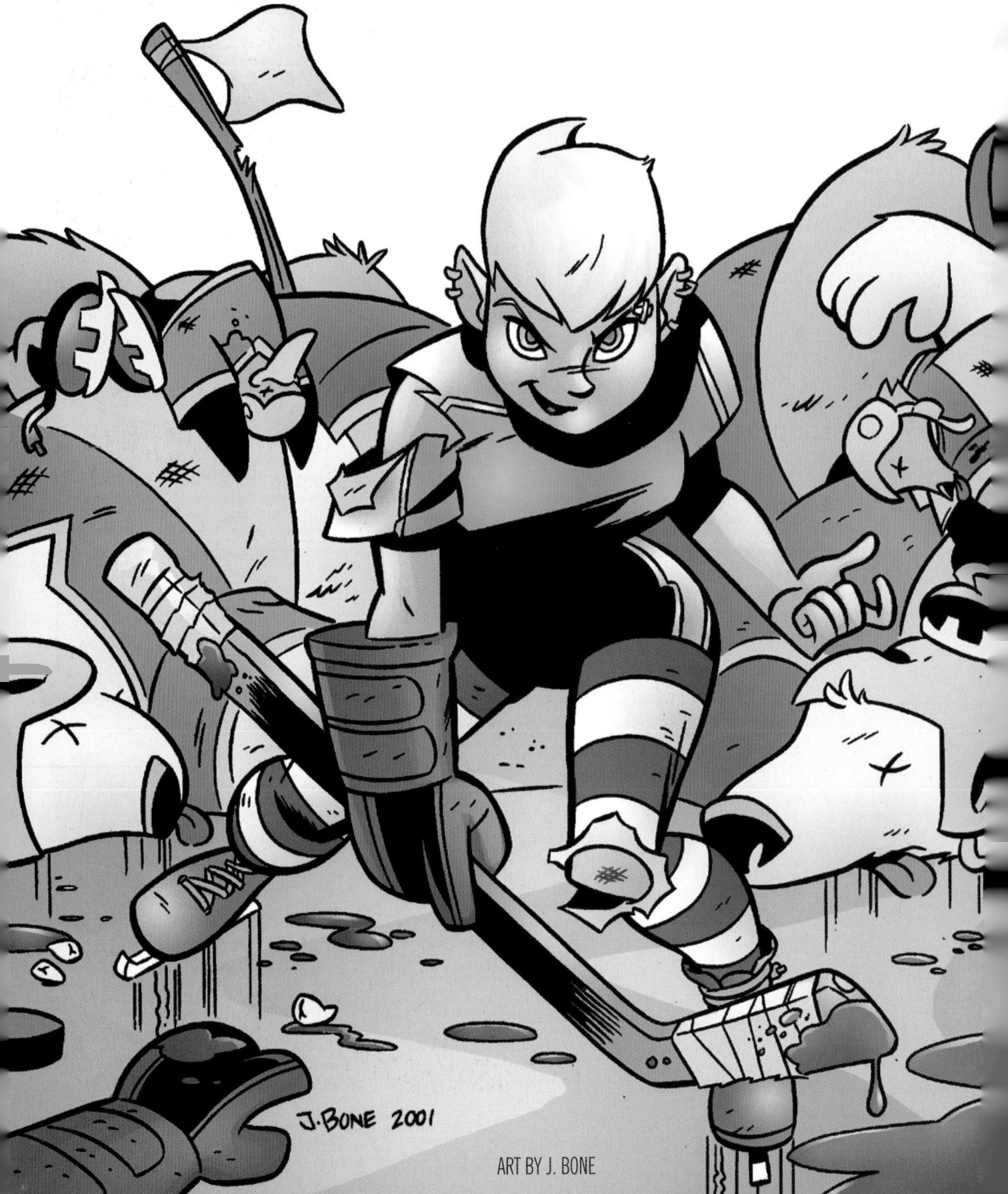
J.BONE 2001

ART BY J. BONE

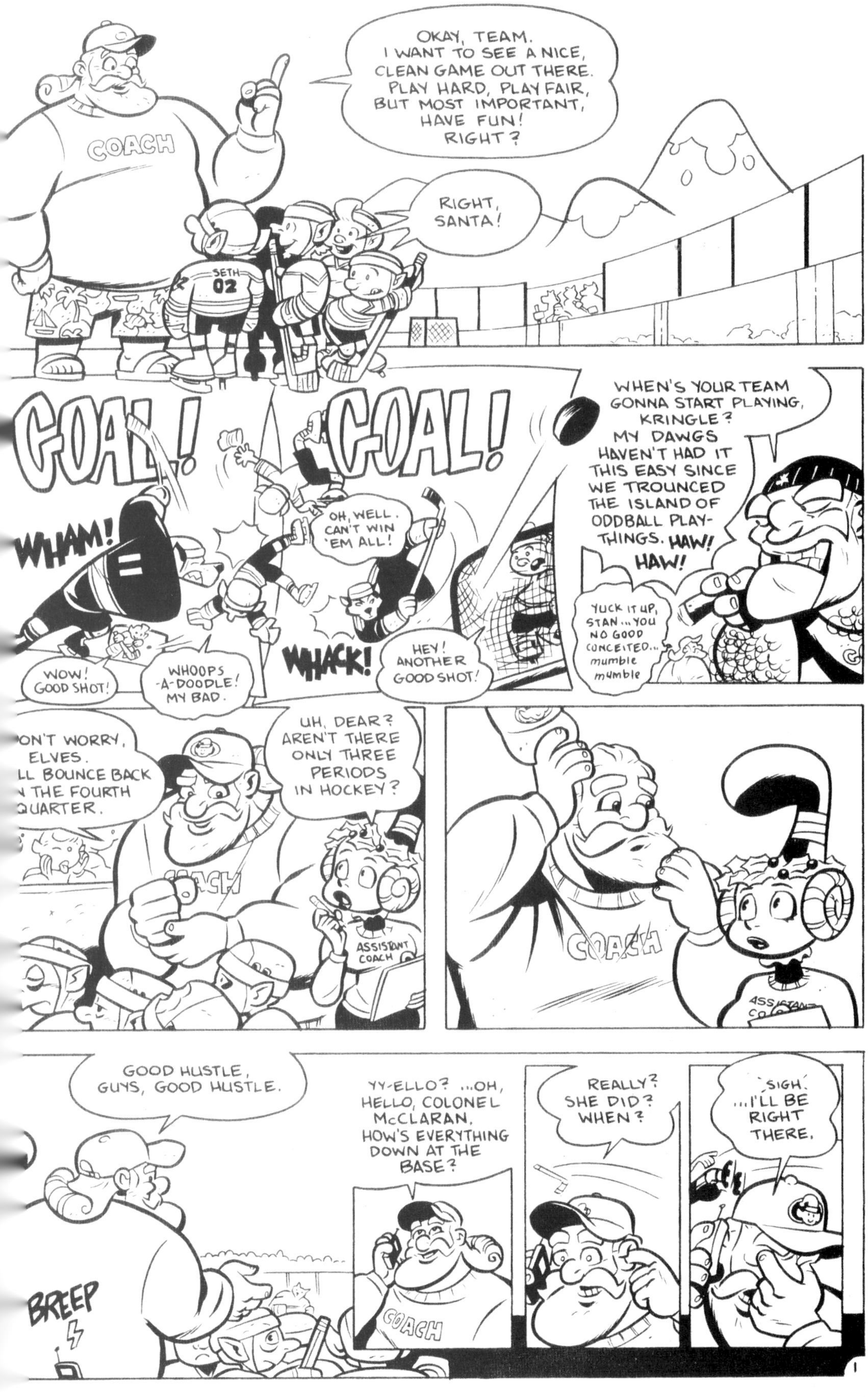
OKAY, TEAM. I WANT TO SEE A NICE, CLEAN GAME OUT THERE. PLAY HARD, PLAY FAIR, BUT MOST IMPORTANT, HAVE FUN! RIGHT?
RIGHT, SANTA!
SETH 02
GOAL!
GOAL!
WHAM!
OH, WELL. CAN'T WIN 'EM ALL!
WHEN'S YOUR TEAM GONNA START PLAYING, KRINGLE? MY DAWGS HAVEN'T HAD IT THIS EASY SINCE WE TROUNCED THE ISLAND OF ODDBALL PLAYTHINGS. HAW! HAW!
YUCK IT UP, STAN... YOU NO GOOD CONCEITED... mumble mumble
WHACK!
WOW! GOOD SHOT!
WHOOPS-A-DOODLE! MY BAD.
HEY! ANOTHER GOOD SHOT!
ON'T WORRY, ELVES. LL BOUNCE BACK N THE FOURTH QUARTER.
UH, DEAR? AREN'T THERE ONLY THREE PERIODS IN HOCKEY?
COACH
ASSISTANT COACH
COACH
GOOD HUSTLE, GUYS, GOOD HUSTLE.
BREEP
YY-ELLO? ...OH, HELLO, COLONEL McCLARAN. HOW'S EVERYTHING DOWN AT THE BASE?
COACH
REALLY? SHE DID? WHEN?
SIGH ...I'LL BE RIGHT THERE.

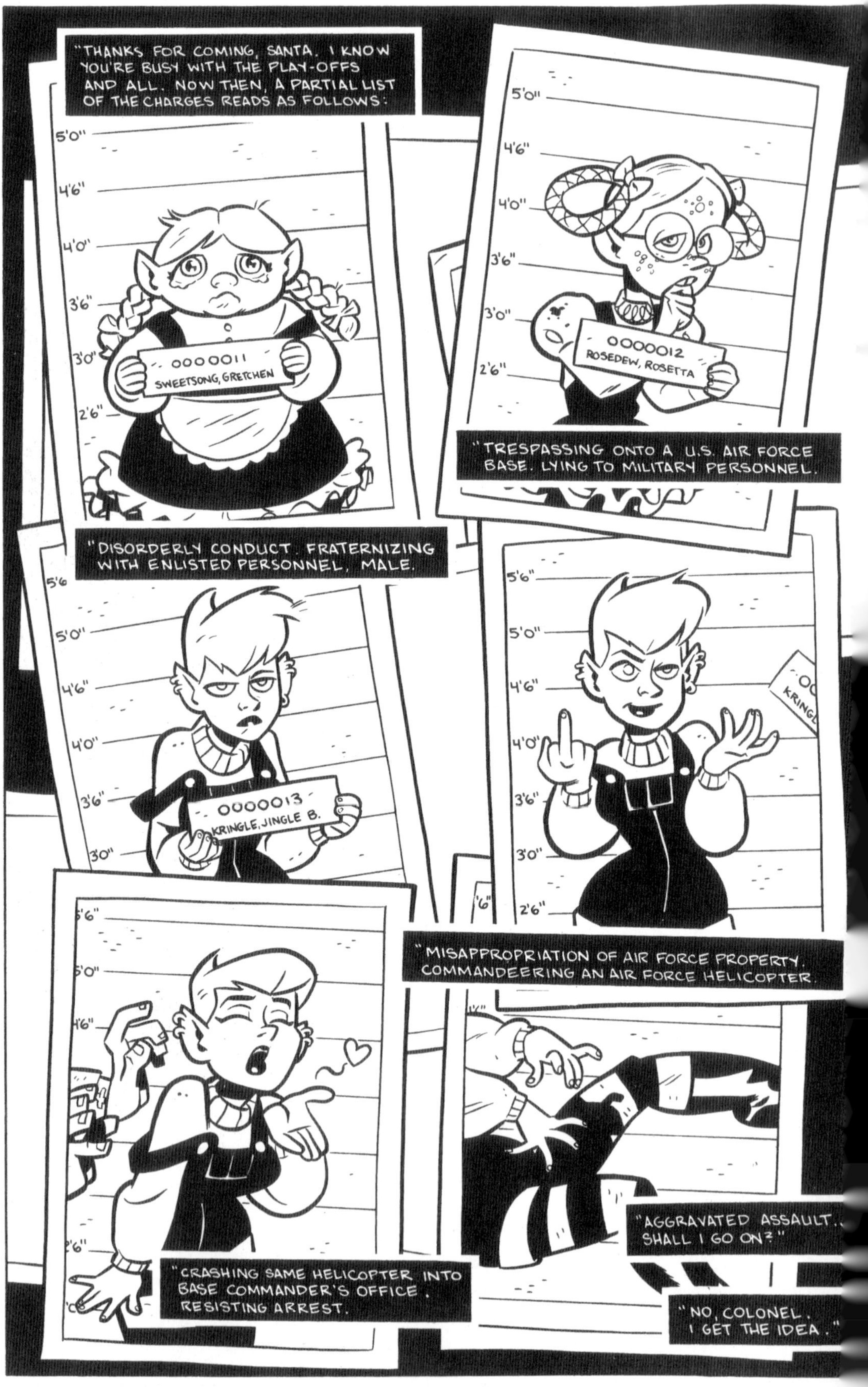
"THANKS FOR COMING, SANTA. I KNOW YOU'RE BUSY WITH THE PLAY-OFFS AND ALL. NOW THEN, A PARTIAL LIST OF THE CHARGES READS AS FOLLOWS:
0000011
SWEETSONG, GRETCHEN
0000012
ROSEDEW, ROSETTA
"TRESPASSING ONTO A U.S. AIR FORCE BASE. LYING TO MILITARY PERSONNEL.
"DISORDERLY CONDUCT. FRATERNIZING WITH ENLISTED PERSONNEL, MALE.
0000013
KRINGLE, JINGLE B.
"MISAPPROPRIATION OF AIR FORCE PROPERTY. COMMANDEERING AN AIR FORCE HELICOPTER.
"CRASHING SAME HELICOPTER INTO BASE COMMANDER'S OFFICE. RESISTING ARREST.
"AGGRAVATED ASSAULT... SHALL I GO ON?"
"NO, COLONEL. I GET THE IDEA."

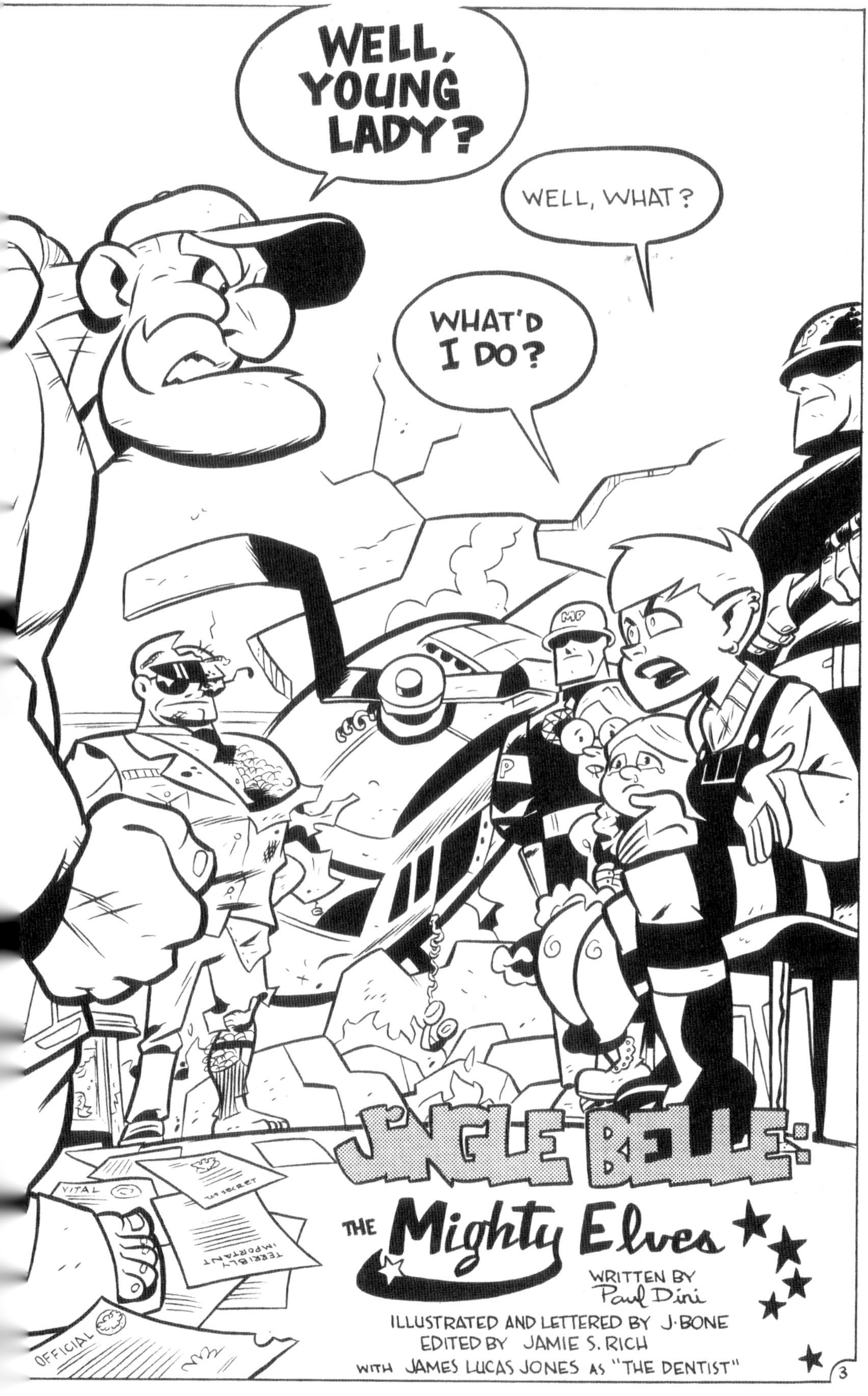
WELL, YOUNG LADY?
WELL, WHAT?
WHAT'D I DO?
VITAL
TOP SECRET
TERRIBLY IMPORTANT
OFFICIAL
JINGLE BELLE:
THE Mighty Elves
WRITTEN BY
Paul Dini
ILLUSTRATED AND LETTERED BY J·BONE
EDITED BY JAMIE S. RICH
WITH JAMES LUCAS JONES AS "THE DENTIST"
3

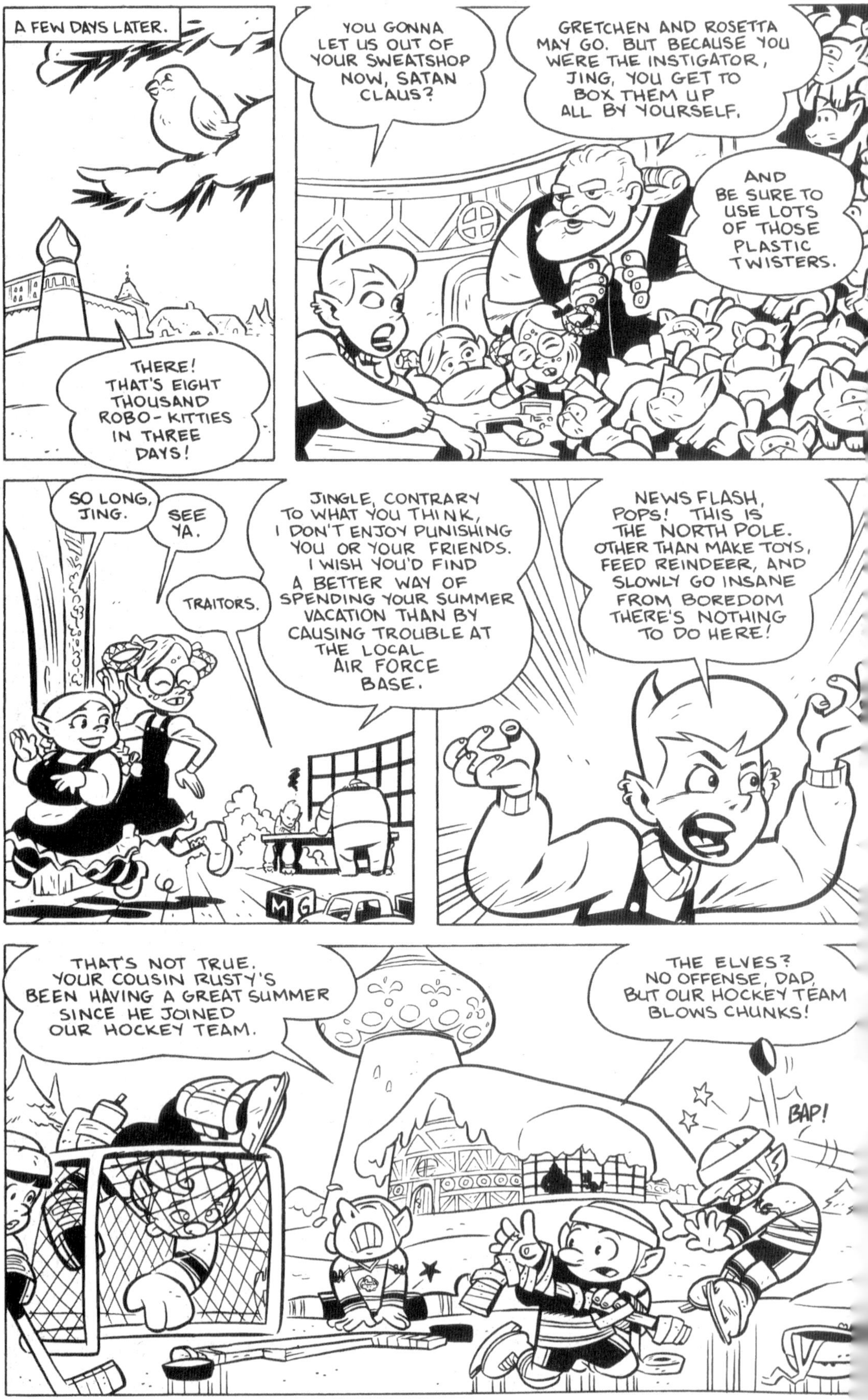
A FEW DAYS LATER.
THERE! THAT'S EIGHT THOUSAND ROBO-KITTIES IN THREE DAYS!
YOU GONNA LET US OUT OF YOUR SWEATSHOP NOW, SATAN CLAUS?
GRETCHEN AND ROSETTA MAY GO. BUT BECAUSE YOU WERE THE INSTIGATOR, JING, YOU GET TO BOX THEM UP ALL BY YOURSELF.
AND BE SURE TO USE LOTS OF THOSE PLASTIC TWISTERS.
SO LONG, JING.
SEE YA.
TRAITORS.
JINGLE, CONTRARY TO WHAT YOU THINK, I DON'T ENJOY PUNISHING YOU OR YOUR FRIENDS. I WISH YOU'D FIND A BETTER WAY OF SPENDING YOUR SUMMER VACATION THAN BY CAUSING TROUBLE AT THE LOCAL AIR FORCE BASE.
NEWS FLASH, POPS! THIS IS THE NORTH POLE. OTHER THAN MAKE TOYS, FEED REINDEER, AND SLOWLY GO INSANE FROM BOREDOM THERE'S NOTHING TO DO HERE!
THAT'S NOT TRUE. YOUR COUSIN RUSTY'S BEEN HAVING A GREAT SUMMER SINCE HE JOINED OUR HOCKEY TEAM.
THE ELVES? NO OFFENSE, DAD, BUT OUR HOCKEY TEAM BLOWS CHUNKS!
BAP!

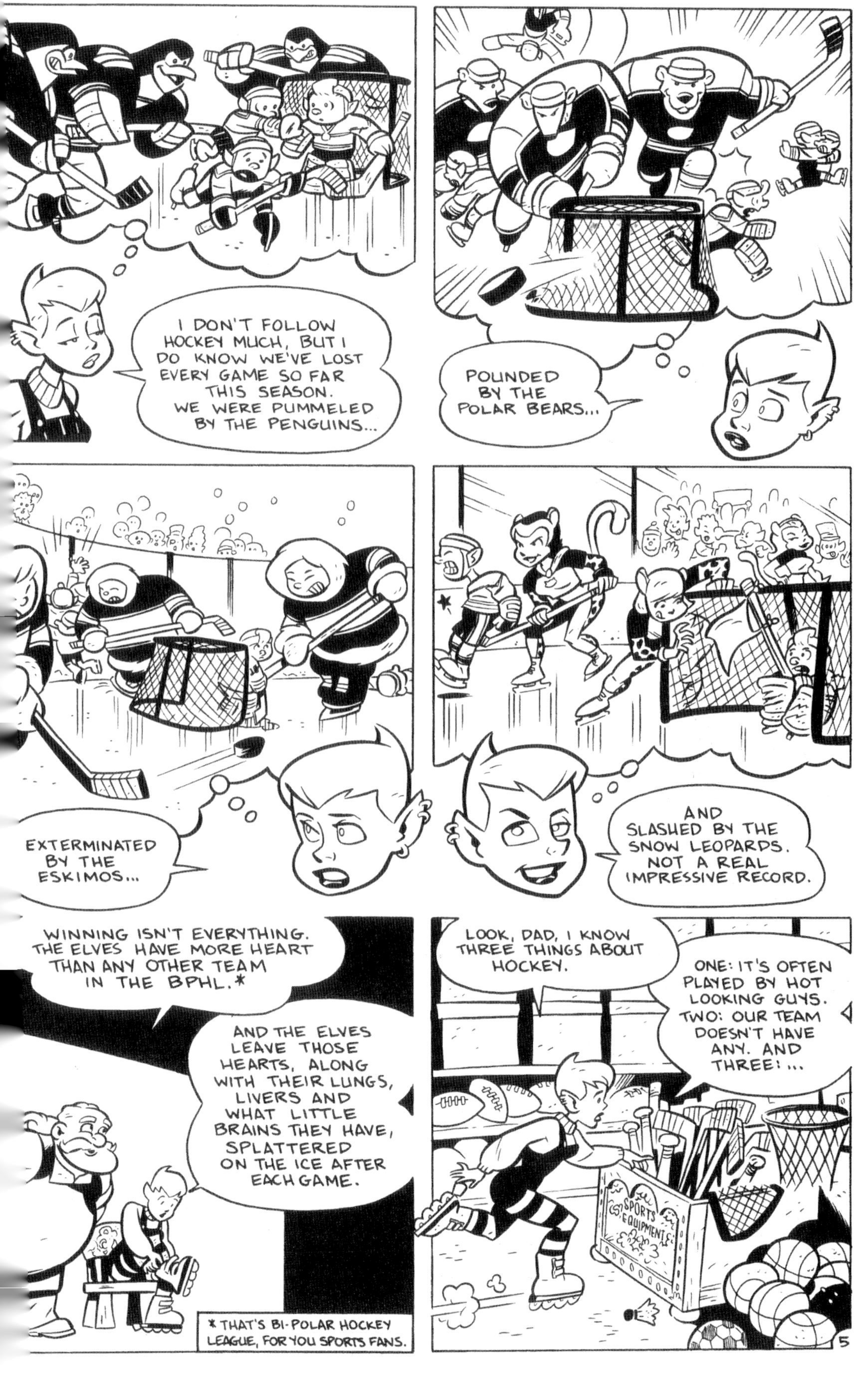
I DON'T FOLLOW HOCKEY MUCH, BUT I DO KNOW WE'VE LOST EVERY GAME SO FAR THIS SEASON. WE WERE PUMMELED BY THE PENGUINS...
POUNDED BY THE POLAR BEARS...
EXTERMINATED BY THE ESKIMOS...
AND SLASHED BY THE SNOW LEOPARDS. NOT A REAL IMPRESSIVE RECORD.
WINNING ISN'T EVERYTHING. THE ELVES HAVE MORE HEART THAN ANY OTHER TEAM IN THE BPHL.*
AND THE ELVES LEAVE THOSE HEARTS, ALONG WITH THEIR LUNGS, LIVERS AND WHAT LITTLE BRAINS THEY HAVE, SPLATTERED ON THE ICE AFTER EACH GAME.
* THAT'S BI-POLAR HOCKEY LEAGUE, FOR YOU SPORTS FANS.
LOOK, DAD, I KNOW THREE THINGS ABOUT HOCKEY.
ONE: IT'S OFTEN PLAYED BY HOT LOOKING GUYS. TWO: OUR TEAM DOESN'T HAVE ANY. AND THREE: ...
SPORTS EQUIPMENT
5

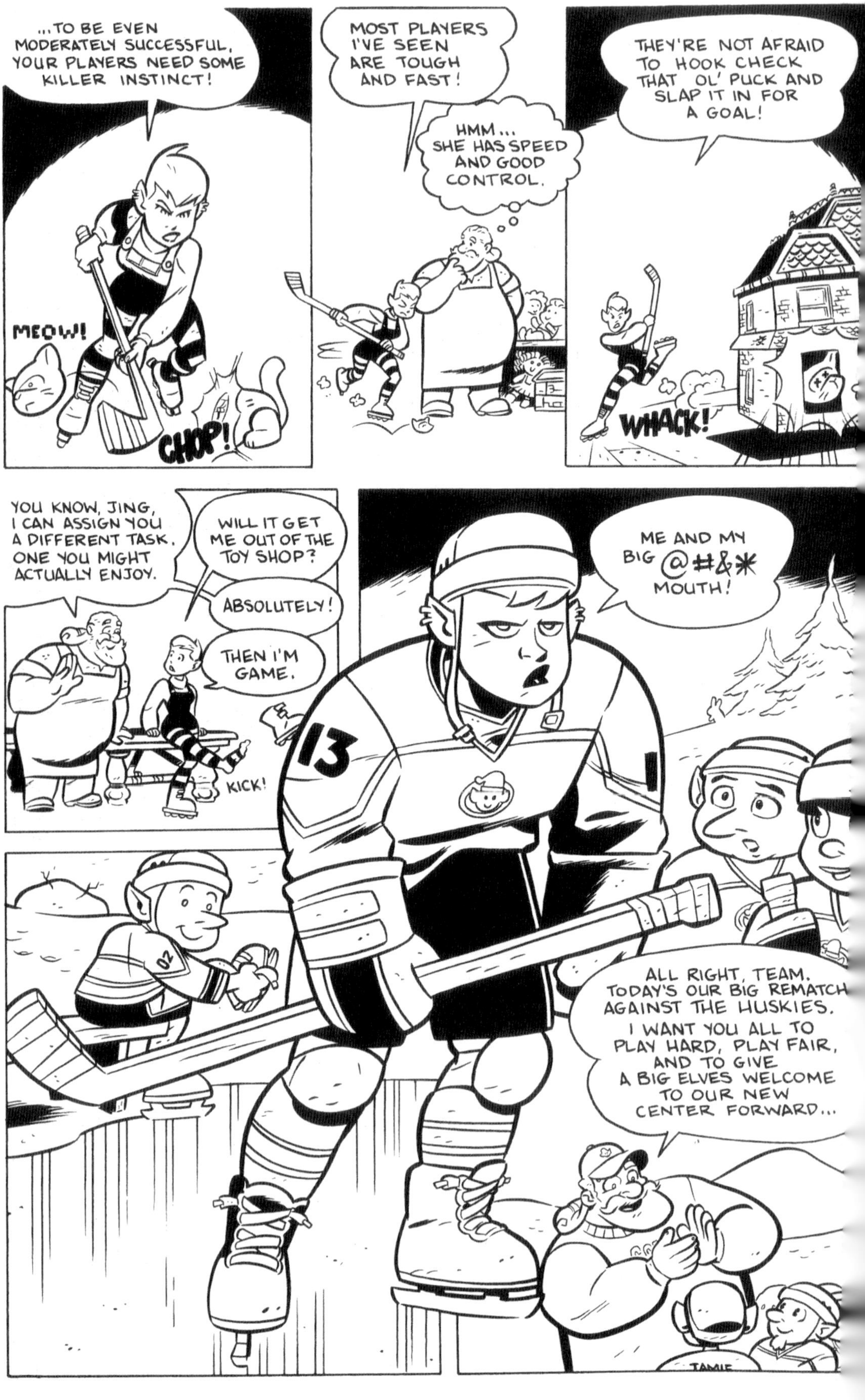
...TO BE EVEN MODERATELY SUCCESSFUL, YOUR PLAYERS NEED SOME KILLER INSTINCT!
MEOW!
CHOP!
MOST PLAYERS I'VE SEEN ARE TOUGH AND FAST!
HMM... SHE HAS SPEED AND GOOD CONTROL.
THEY'RE NOT AFRAID TO HOOK CHECK THAT OL' PUCK AND SLAP IT IN FOR A GOAL!
WHACK!
YOU KNOW, JING, I CAN ASSIGN YOU A DIFFERENT TASK. ONE YOU MIGHT ACTUALLY ENJOY.
WILL IT GET ME OUT OF THE TOY SHOP?
ABSOLUTELY!
THEN I'M GAME.
KICK!
ME AND MY BIG @#&* MOUTH!
13
ALL RIGHT, TEAM. TODAY'S OUR BIG REMATCH AGAINST THE HUSKIES. I WANT YOU ALL TO PLAY HARD, PLAY FAIR, AND TO GIVE A BIG ELVES WELCOME TO OUR NEW CENTER FORWARD...

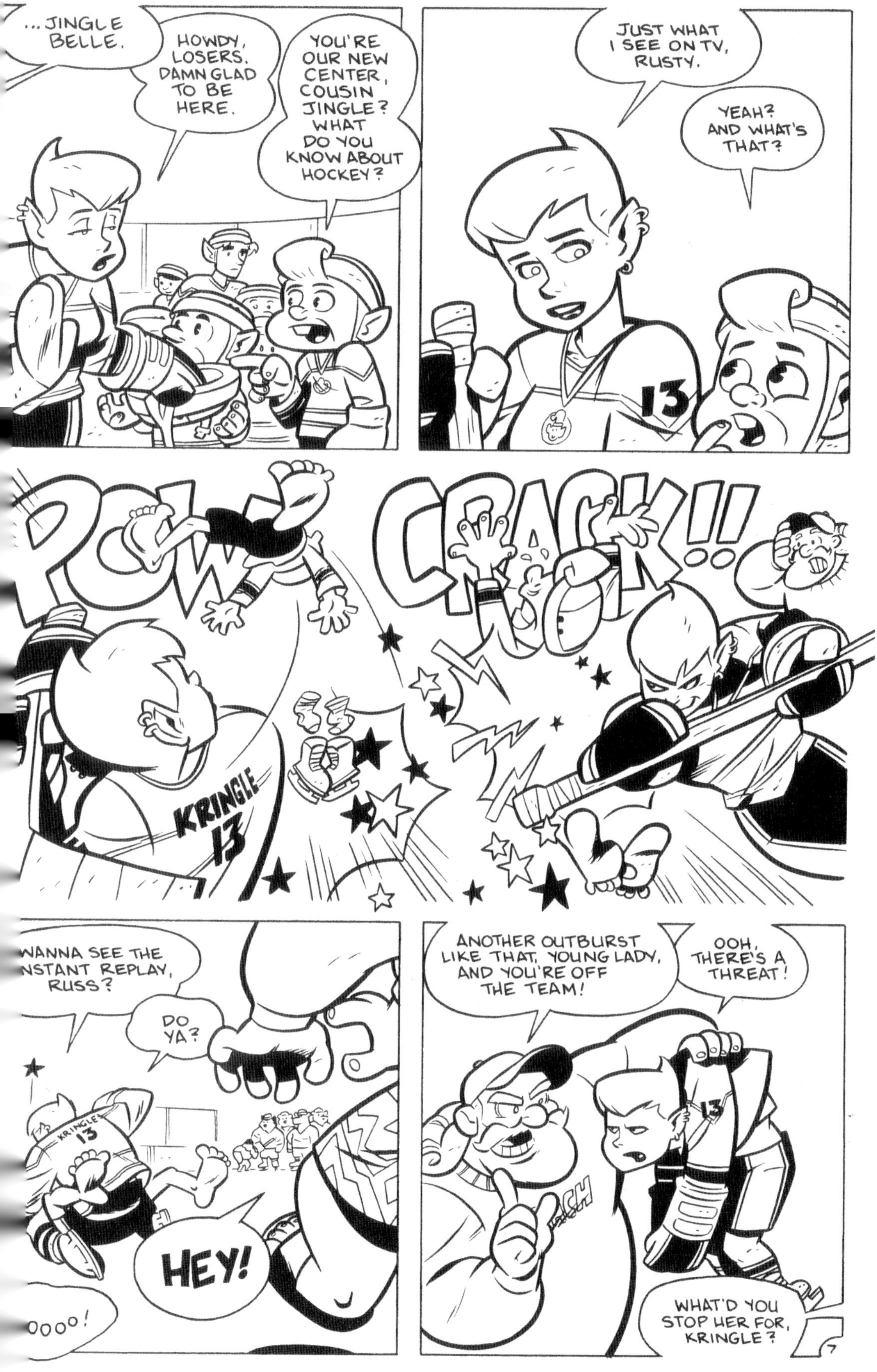
...JINGLE BELLE.
HOWDY, LOSERS. DAMN GLAD TO BE HERE.
YOU'RE OUR NEW CENTER, COUSIN JINGLE? WHAT DO YOU KNOW ABOUT HOCKEY?
JUST WHAT I SEE ON TV, RUSTY.
YEAH? AND WHAT'S THAT?
13
POW
CRACK!!
KRINGLE 13
WANNA SEE THE INSTANT REPLAY, RUSS?
DO YA?
KRINGLE 13
HEY!
OOOO!
ANOTHER OUTBURST LIKE THAT, YOUNG LADY, AND YOU'RE OFF THE TEAM!
OOH, THERE'S A THREAT!
13
COACH
WHAT'D YOU STOP HER FOR, KRINGLE?
7

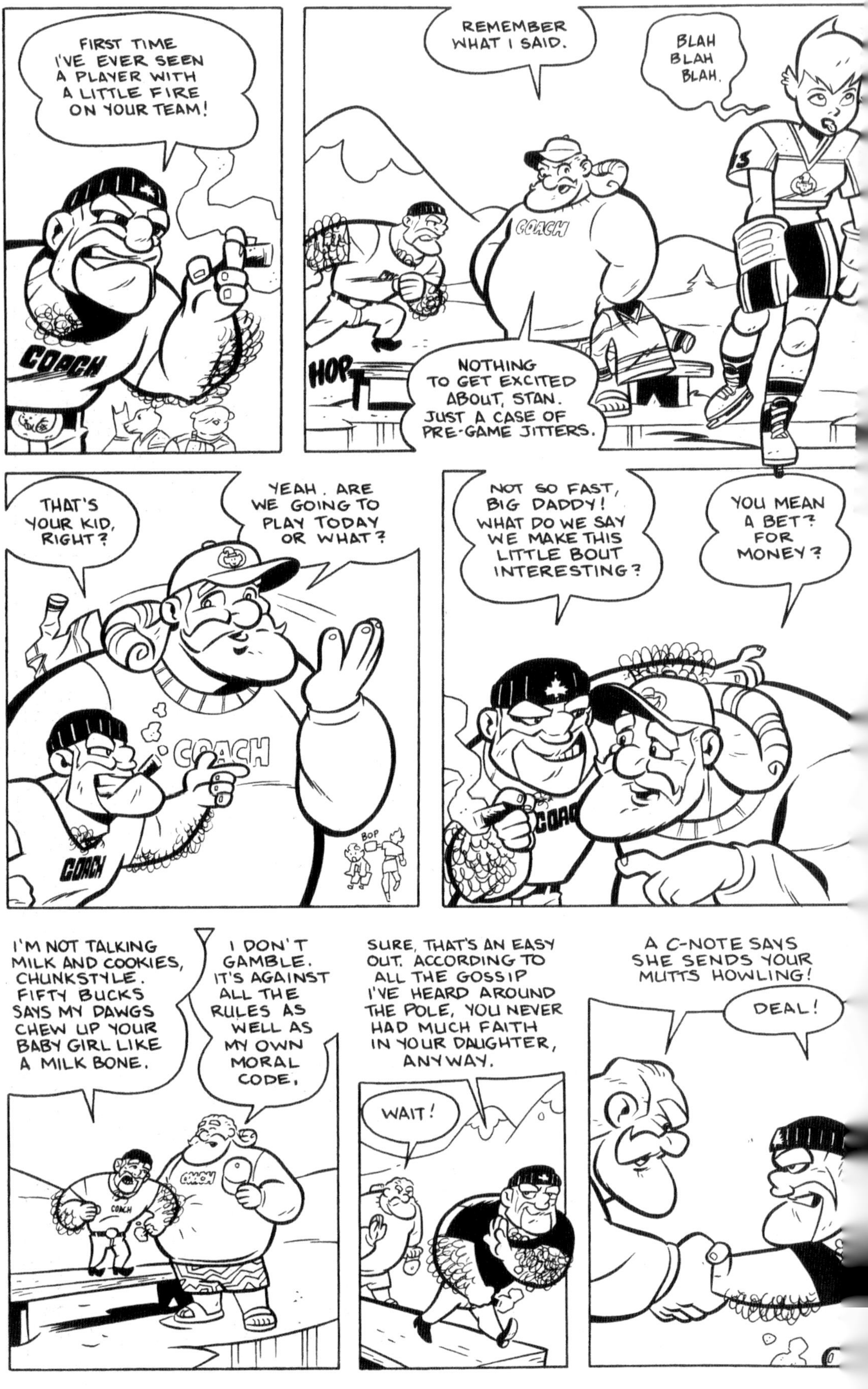
FIRST TIME I'VE EVER SEEN A PLAYER WITH A LITTLE FIRE ON YOUR TEAM!
COACH
REMEMBER WHAT I SAID.
BLAH BLAH BLAH.
COACH
HOP
NOTHING TO GET EXCITED ABOUT, STAN. JUST A CASE OF PRE-GAME JITTERS.
THAT'S YOUR KID, RIGHT?
YEAH. ARE WE GOING TO PLAY TODAY OR WHAT?
COACH
COACH
BOP
NOT SO FAST, BIG DADDY! WHAT DO WE SAY WE MAKE THIS LITTLE BOUT INTERESTING?
YOU MEAN A BET? FOR MONEY?
I'M NOT TALKING MILK AND COOKIES, CHUNKSTYLE. FIFTY BUCKS SAYS MY DAWGS CHEW UP YOUR BABY GIRL LIKE A MILK BONE.
I DON'T GAMBLE. IT'S AGAINST ALL THE RULES AS WELL AS MY OWN MORAL CODE.
COACH
COACH
SURE, THAT'S AN EASY OUT. ACCORDING TO ALL THE GOSSIP I'VE HEARD AROUND THE POLE, YOU NEVER HAD MUCH FAITH IN YOUR DAUGHTER, ANYWAY.
WAIT!
A C-NOTE SAYS SHE SENDS YOUR MUTTS HOWLING!
DEAL!

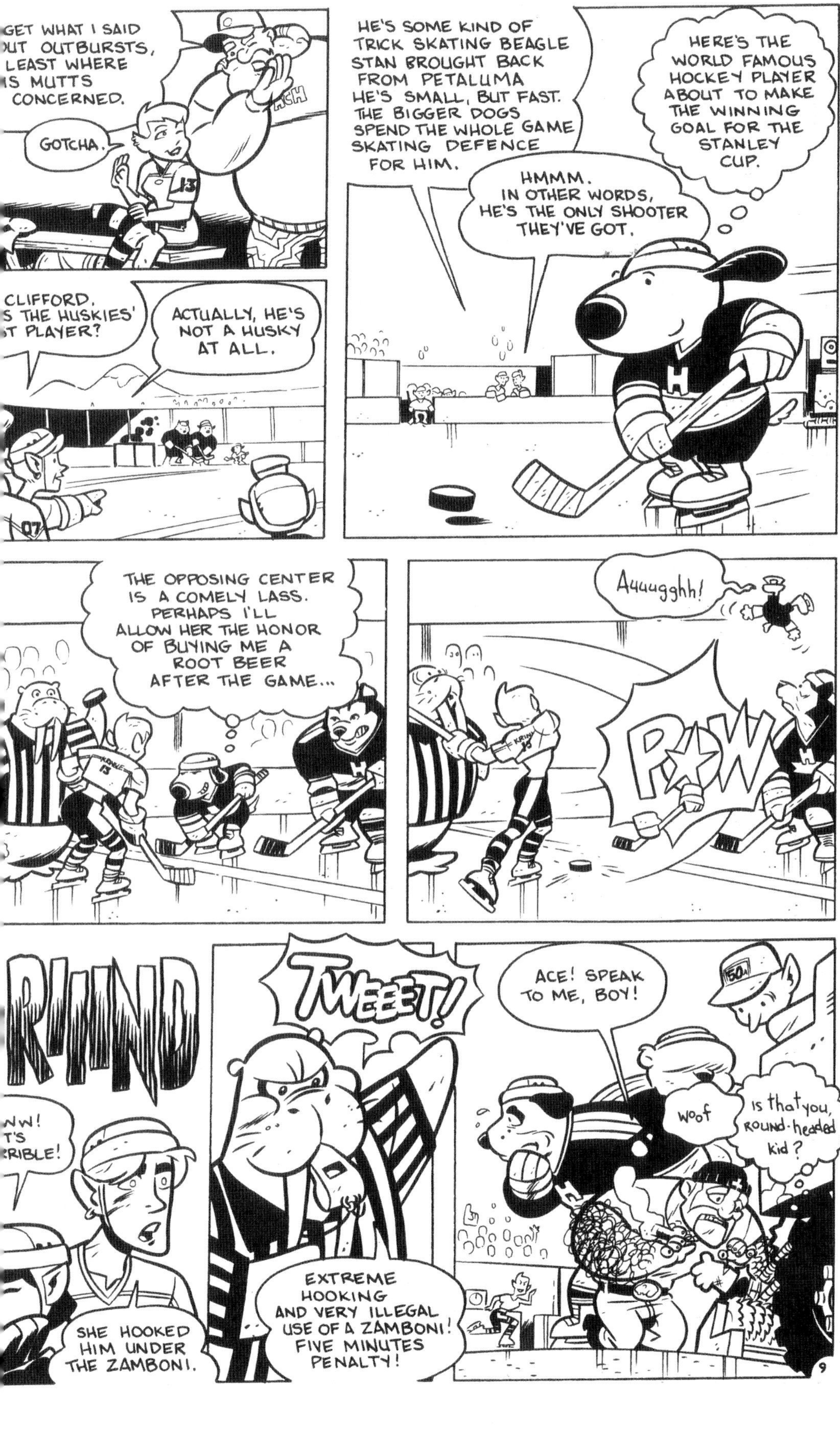
GET WHAT I SAID
UT OUTBURSTS,
LEAST WHERE
S MUTTS
CONCERNED.
GOTCHA.
HE'S SOME KIND OF TRICK SKATING BEAGLE STAN BROUGHT BACK FROM PETALUMA HE'S SMALL, BUT FAST. THE BIGGER DOGS SPEND THE WHOLE GAME SKATING DEFENCE FOR HIM.
HMMM. IN OTHER WORDS, HE'S THE ONLY SHOOTER THEY'VE GOT.
HERE'S THE WORLD FAMOUS HOCKEY PLAYER ABOUT TO MAKE THE WINNING GOAL FOR THE STANLEY CUP.
CLIFFORD.
S THE HUSKIES'
T PLAYER?
ACTUALLY, HE'S NOT A HUSKY AT ALL.
THE OPPOSING CENTER IS A COMELY LASS. PERHAPS I'LL ALLOW HER THE HONOR OF BUYING ME A ROOT BEER AFTER THE GAME...
Auuugghh!
POW
RIIIND
WW!
T'S
RIBLE!
SHE HOOKED HIM UNDER THE ZAMBONI.
TWEEET!
EXTREME HOOKING AND VERY ILLEGAL USE OF A ZAMBONI! FIVE MINUTES PENALTY!
ACE! SPEAK TO ME, BOY!
Woof
Is that you, Round-headed kid?
9

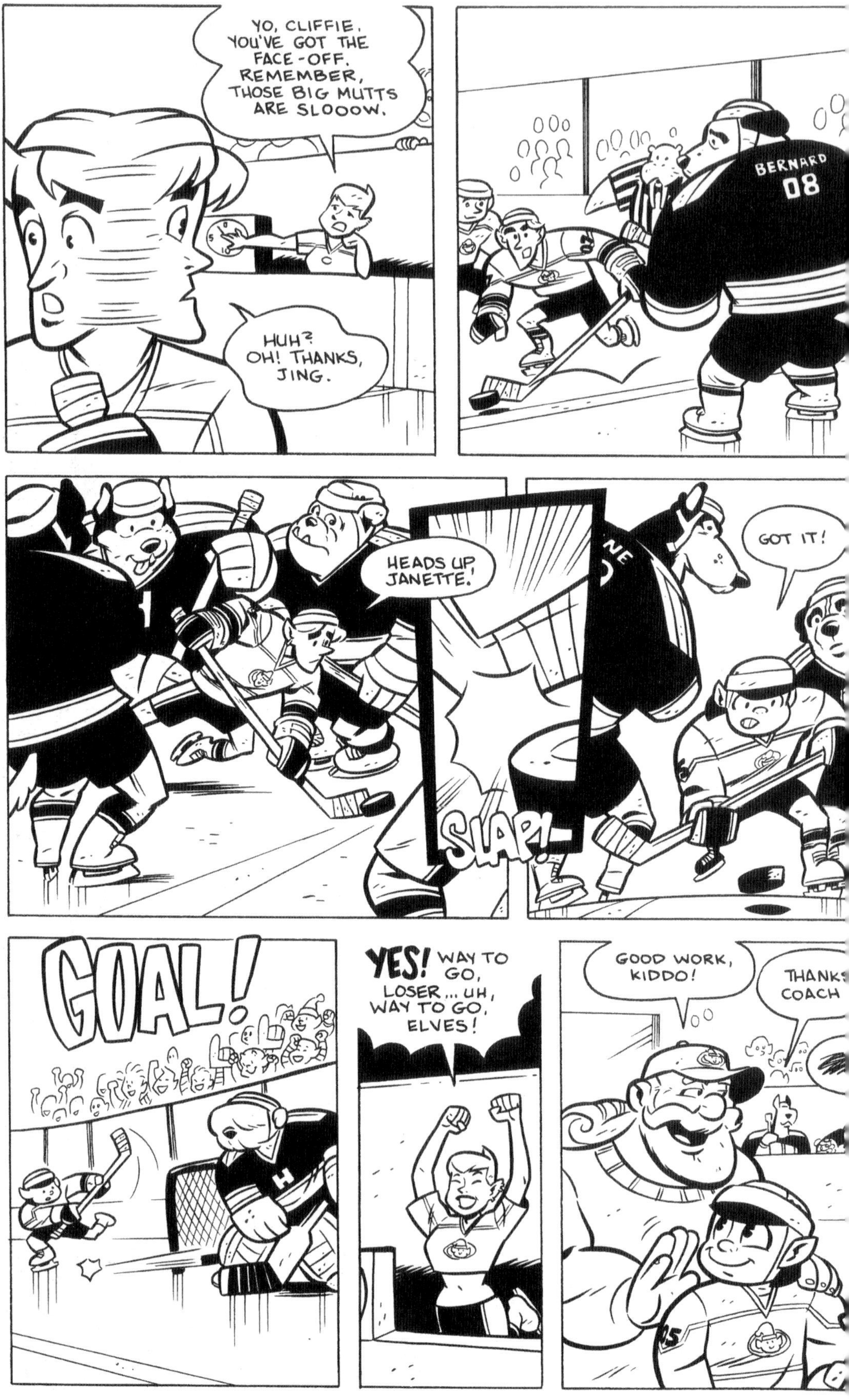
YO, CLIFFIE. YOU'VE GOT THE FACE-OFF. REMEMBER, THOSE BIG MUTTS ARE SLOOOW.
HUH? OH! THANKS, JING.
BERNARD 08
HEADS UP JANETTE!
SLAP!
GOT IT!
GOAL!
YES! WAY TO GO, LOSER... UH, WAY TO GO, ELVES!
GOOD WORK, KIDDO!
THANKS COACH

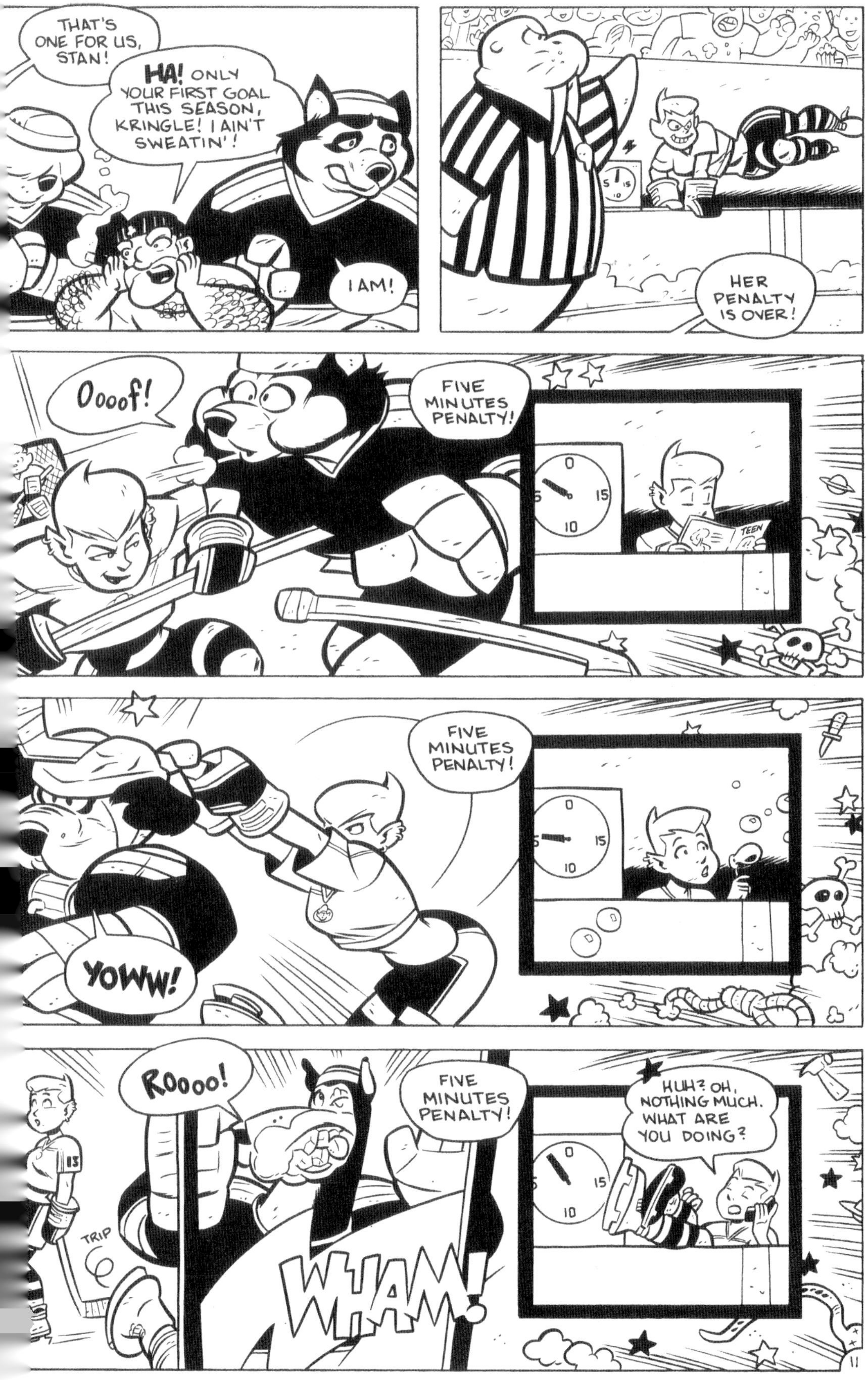
THAT'S ONE FOR US, STAN!
HA! ONLY YOUR FIRST GOAL THIS SEASON, KRINGLE! I AIN'T SWEATIN'!
I AM!
HER PENALTY IS OVER!
Oooof!
FIVE MINUTES PENALTY!
TEEN
FIVE MINUTES PENALTY!
YOWW!
ROOOO!
FIVE MINUTES PENALTY!
HUH? OH, NOTHING MUCH. WHAT ARE YOU DOING?
TRIP
WHAM!
11

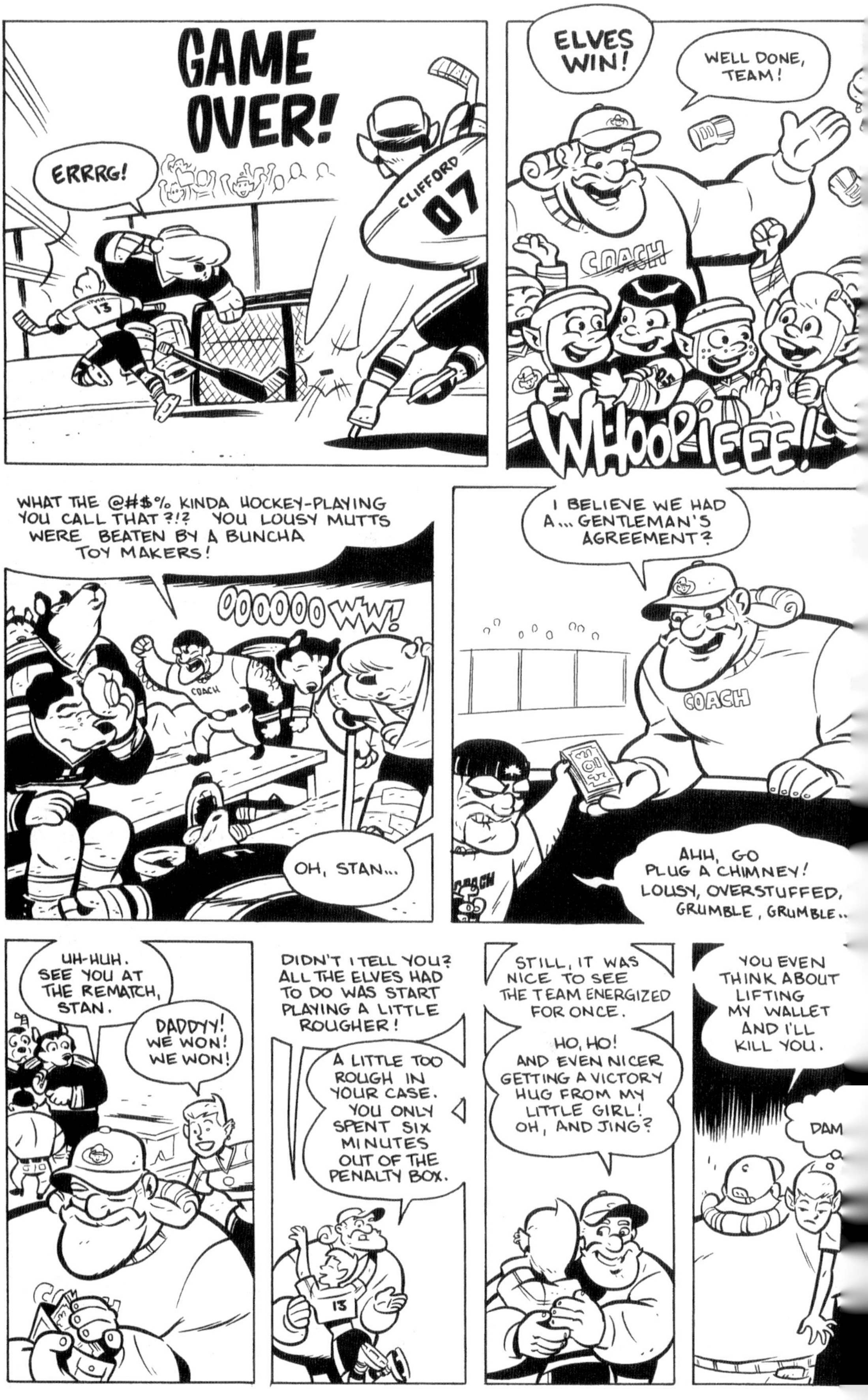
GAME OVER!
ERRRG!
CLIFFORD 07
ELVES WIN!
WELL DONE, TEAM!
COACH
WHOOPIEEE!
WHAT THE @#$% KINDA HOCKEY-PLAYING YOU CALL THAT?!? YOU LOUSY MUTTS WERE BEATEN BY A BUNCHA TOY MAKERS!
OOOOOOWW!
COACH
OH, STAN...
I BELIEVE WE HAD A... GENTLEMAN'S AGREEMENT?
COACH
AHH, GO PLUG A CHIMNEY! LOUSY, OVERSTUFFED, GRUMBLE, GRUMBLE...
UH-HUH. SEE YOU AT THE REMATCH, STAN.
DADDYY! WE WON! WE WON!
DIDN'T I TELL YOU? ALL THE ELVES HAD TO DO WAS START PLAYING A LITTLE ROUGHER!
A LITTLE TOO ROUGH IN YOUR CASE. YOU ONLY SPENT SIX MINUTES OUT OF THE PENALTY BOX.
13
STILL, IT WAS NICE TO SEE THE TEAM ENERGIZED FOR ONCE.
HO, HO! AND EVEN NICER GETTING A VICTORY HUG FROM MY LITTLE GIRL! OH, AND JING?
YOU EVEN THINK ABOUT LIFTING MY WALLET AND I'LL KILL YOU.
DAM

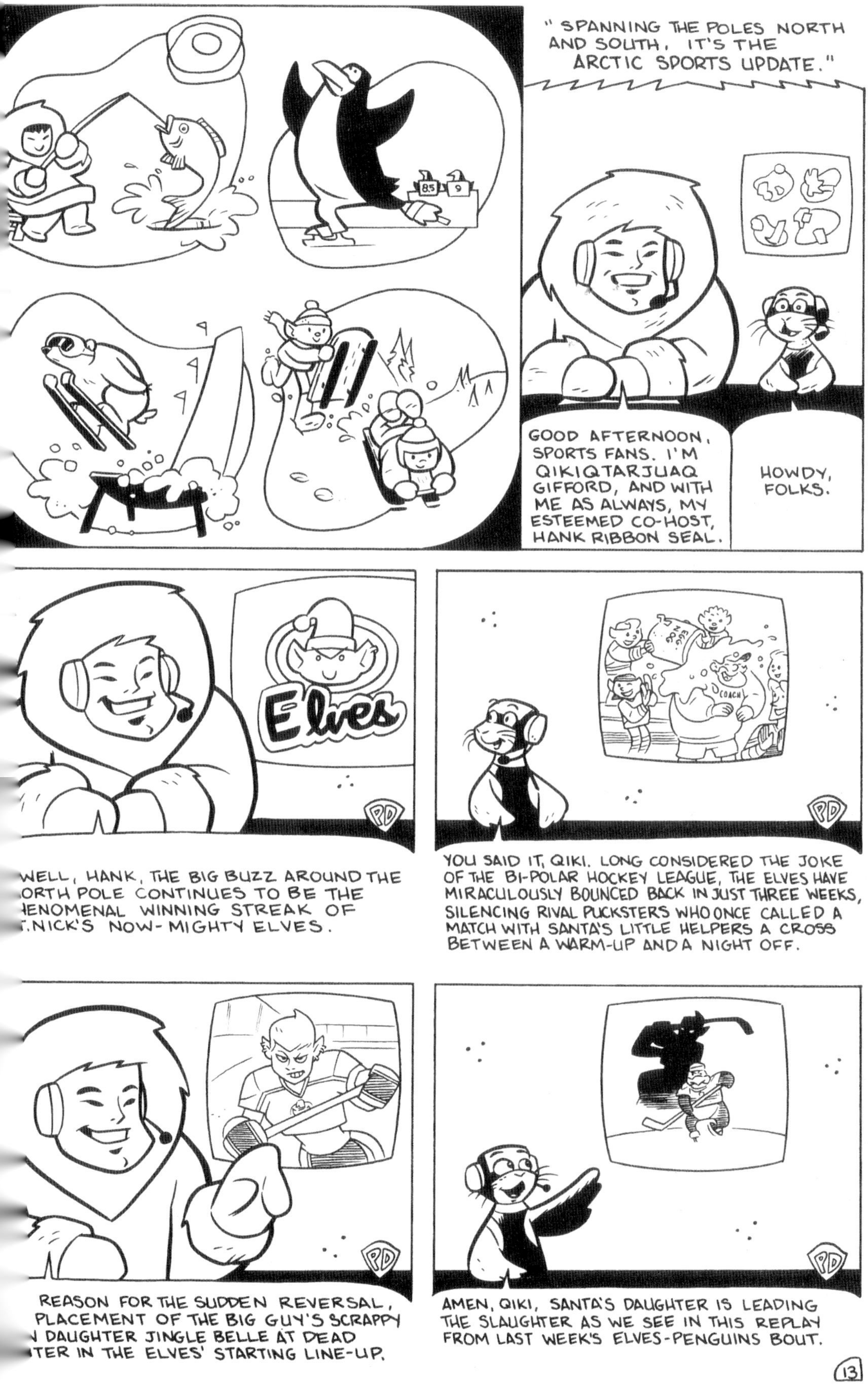
"SPANNING THE POLES NORTH AND SOUTH, IT'S THE ARCTIC SPORTS UPDATE."
8.5
9
GOOD AFTERNOON, SPORTS FANS. I'M QIKIQTARJUAQ GIFFORD, AND WITH ME AS ALWAYS, MY ESTEEMED CO-HOST, HANK RIBBON SEAL.
HOWDY, FOLKS.
Elves
WELL, HANK, THE BIG BUZZ AROUND THE ORTH POLE CONTINUES TO BE THE HENOMENAL WINNING STREAK OF T.NICK'S NOW-MIGHTY ELVES.
COACH
YOU SAID IT, QIKI. LONG CONSIDERED THE JOKE OF THE BI-POLAR HOCKEY LEAGUE, THE ELVES HAVE MIRACULOUSLY BOUNCED BACK IN JUST THREE WEEKS, SILENCING RIVAL PUCKSTERS WHO ONCE CALLED A MATCH WITH SANTA'S LITTLE HELPERS A CROSS BETWEEN A WARM-UP AND A NIGHT OFF.
REASON FOR THE SUDDEN REVERSAL, PLACEMENT OF THE BIG GUY'S SCRAPPY N DAUGHTER JINGLE BELLE AT DEAD TER IN THE ELVES' STARTING LINE-UP.
AMEN, QIKI, SANTA'S DAUGHTER IS LEADING THE SLAUGHTER AS WE SEE IN THIS REPLAY FROM LAST WEEK'S ELVES-PENGUINS BOUT.
13

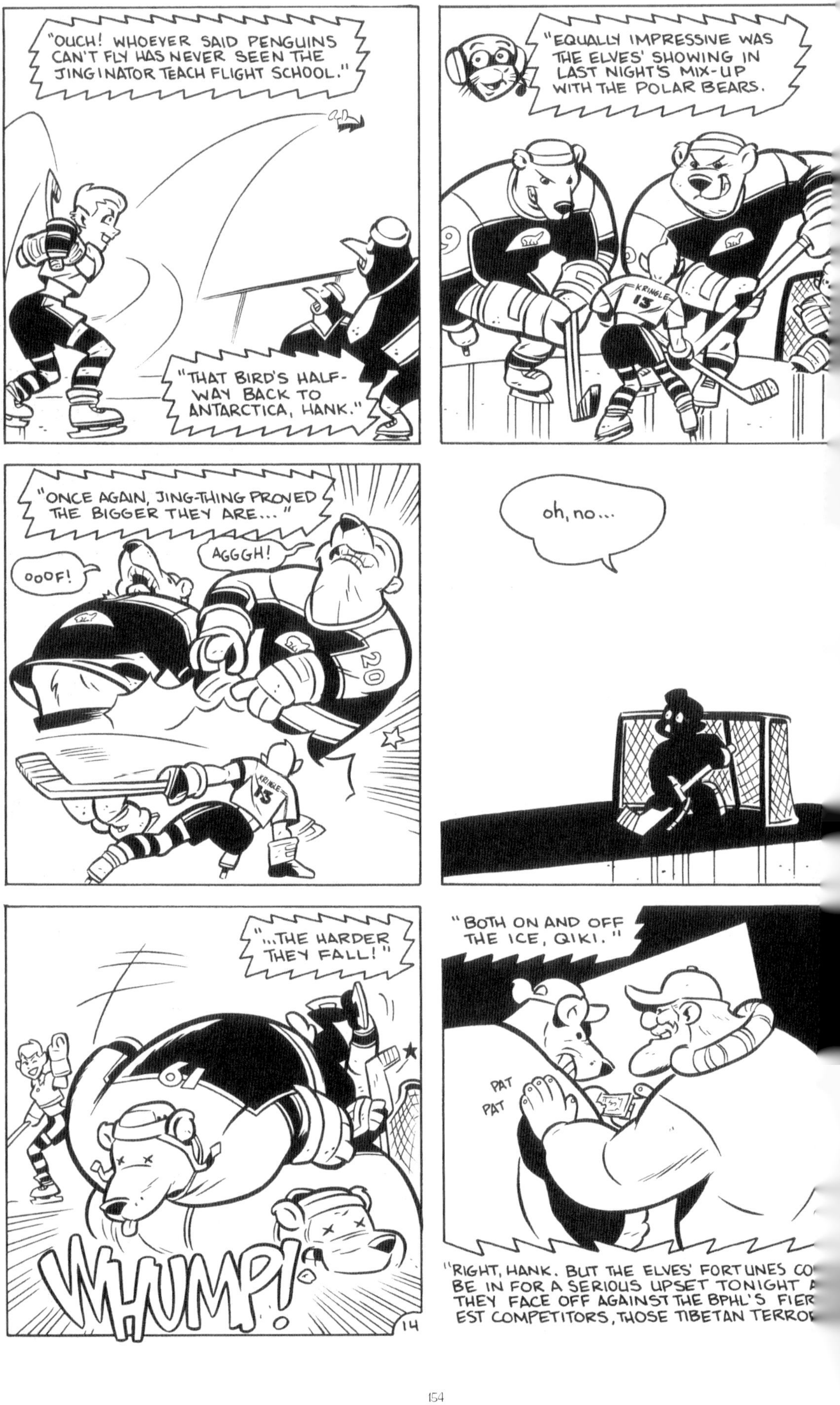
"OUCH! WHOEVER SAID PENGUINS CAN'T FLY HAS NEVER SEEN THE JINGINATOR TEACH FLIGHT SCHOOL."
"THAT BIRD'S HALF-WAY BACK TO ANTARCTICA, HANK."
"EQUALLY IMPRESSIVE WAS THE ELVES' SHOWING IN LAST NIGHT'S MIX-UP WITH THE POLAR BEARS.
KRINGLE 13
"ONCE AGAIN, JING-THING PROVED THE BIGGER THEY ARE..."
OOOF!
AGGGH!
20
KRINGLE 13
oh, no...
"...THE HARDER THEY FALL!"
WHUMP!
14
"BOTH ON AND OFF THE ICE, QIKI."
PAT
PAT
"RIGHT, HANK. BUT THE ELVES' FORTUNES CO
BE IN FOR A SERIOUS UPSET TONIGHT A
THEY FACE OFF AGAINST THE BPHL'S FIER
EST COMPETITORS, THOSE TIBETAN TERRO

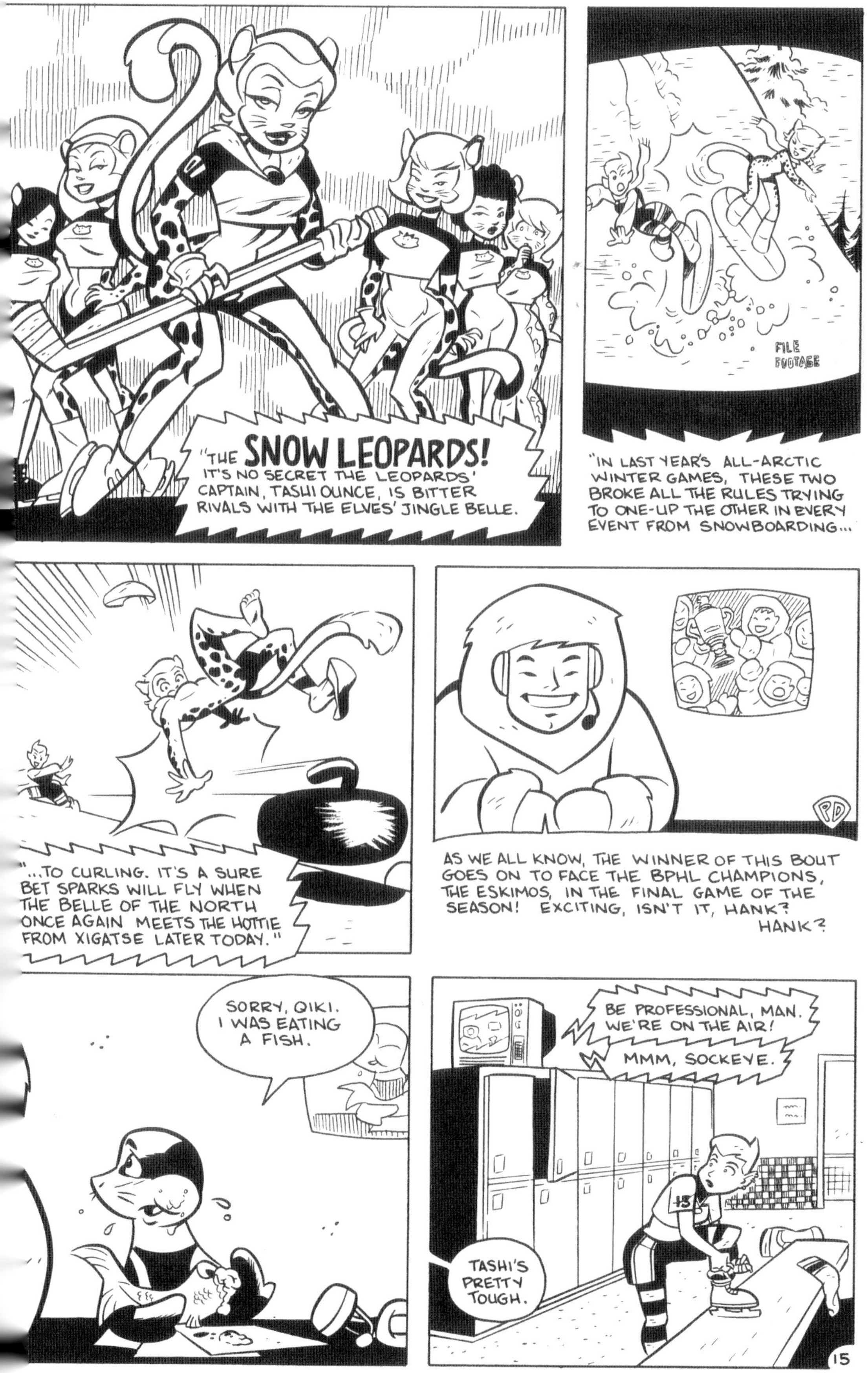
"THE SNOW LEOPARDS! IT'S NO SECRET THE LEOPARDS' CAPTAIN, TASHI OUNCE, IS BITTER RIVALS WITH THE ELVES' JINGLE BELLE.
FILE FOOTAGE
"IN LAST YEAR'S ALL-ARCTIC WINTER GAMES, THESE TWO BROKE ALL THE RULES TRYING TO ONE-UP THE OTHER IN EVERY EVENT FROM SNOWBOARDING...
"...TO CURLING. IT'S A SURE BET SPARKS WILL FLY WHEN THE BELLE OF THE NORTH ONCE AGAIN MEETS THE HOTTIE FROM XIGATSE LATER TODAY."
AS WE ALL KNOW, THE WINNER OF THIS BOUT GOES ON TO FACE THE BPHL CHAMPIONS, THE ESKIMOS, IN THE FINAL GAME OF THE SEASON! EXCITING, ISN'T IT, HANK?
HANK?
SORRY, QIKI. I WAS EATING A FISH.
BE PROFESSIONAL, MAN. WE'RE ON THE AIR!
MMM, SOCKEYE.
TASHI'S PRETTY TOUGH.
15

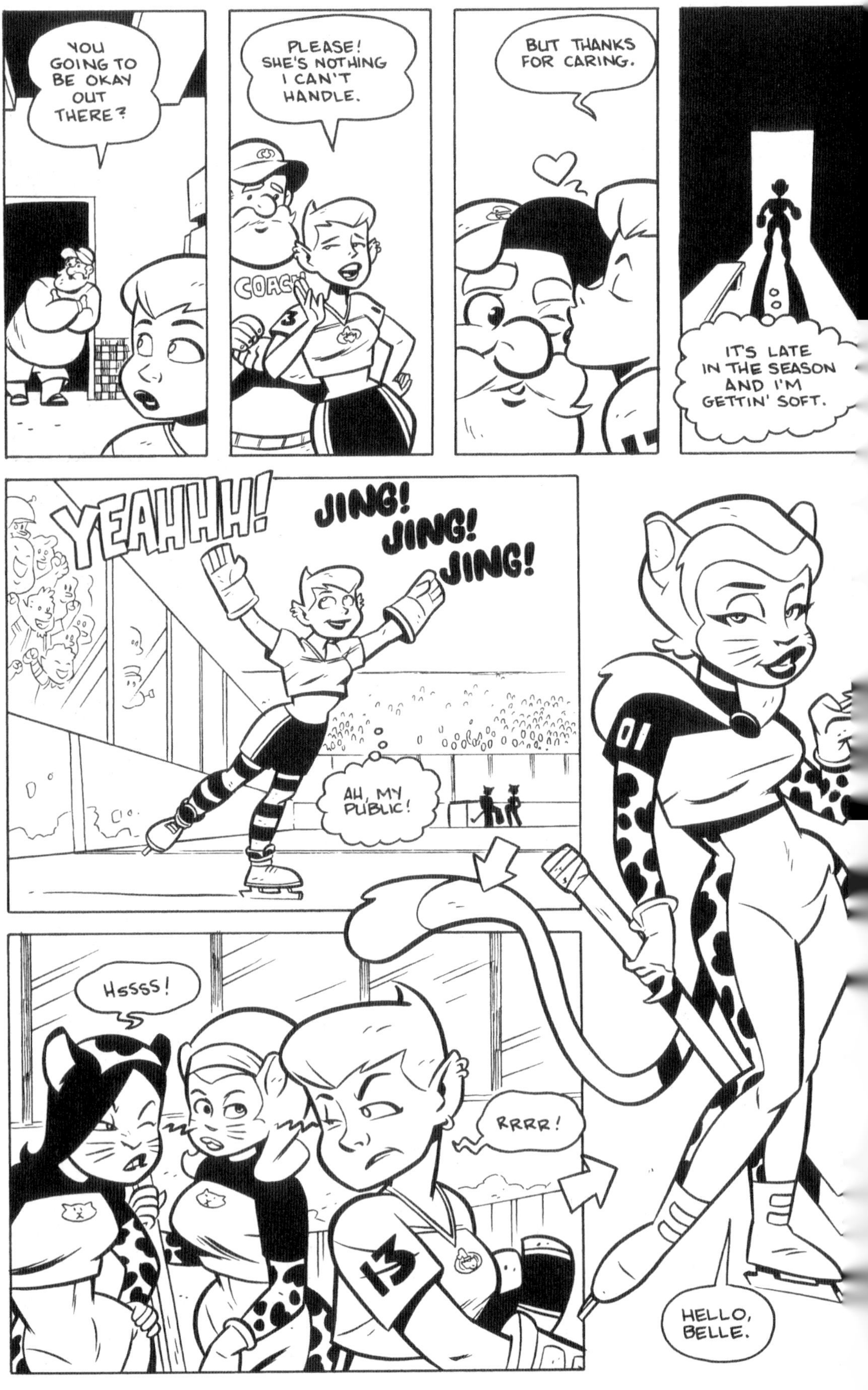

YOU GOING TO BE OKAY OUT THERE?
PLEASE! SHE'S NOTHING I CAN'T HANDLE.
BUT THANKS FOR CARING.
IT'S LATE IN THE SEASON AND I'M GETTIN' SOFT.
YEAHHH!
JING! JING! JING!
AH, MY PUBLIC!
HSSSS!
RRRR!
HELLO, BELLE.

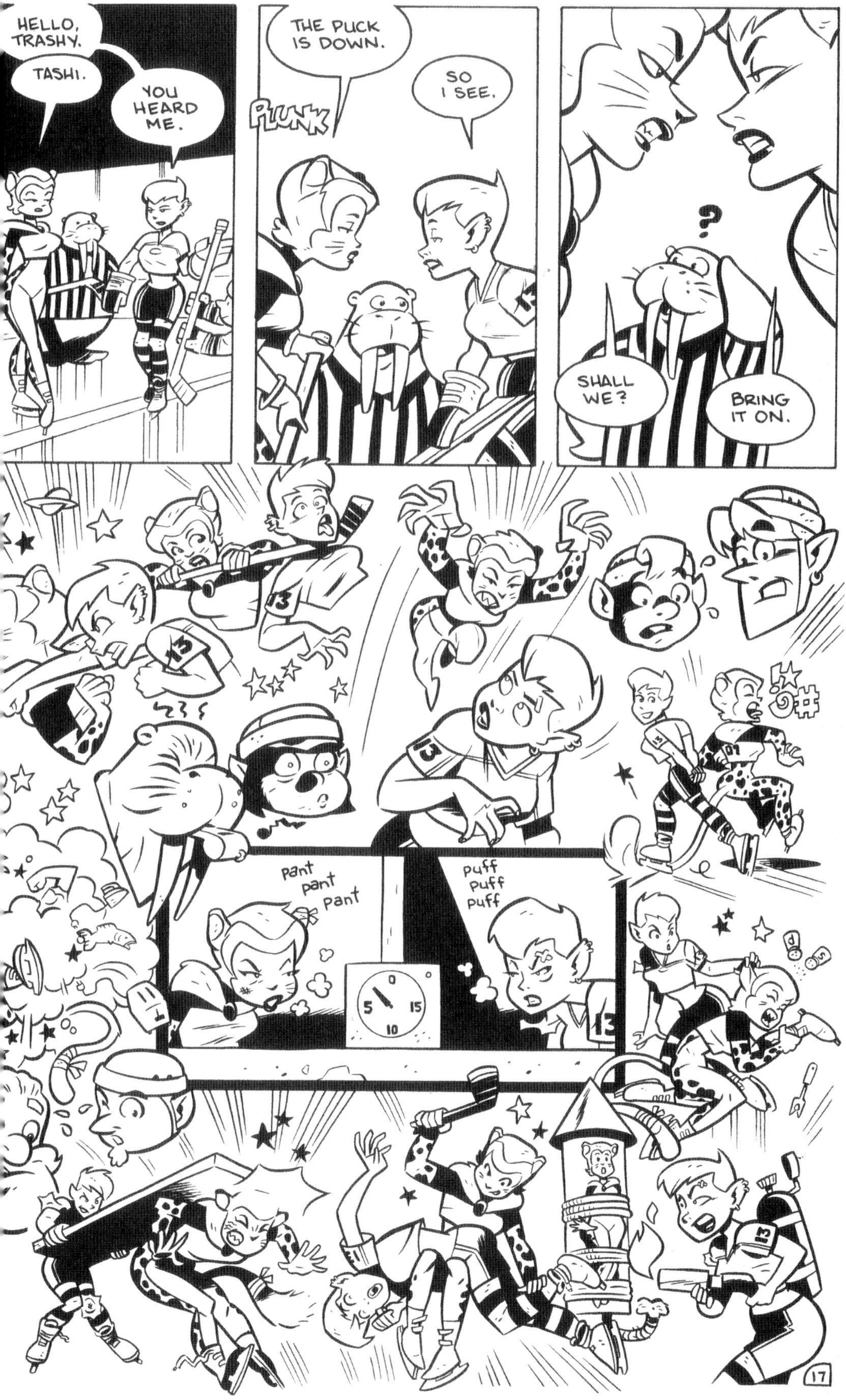
HELLO, TRASHY.
TASHI.
YOU HEARD ME.
THE PUCK IS DOWN.
PLUNK
SO I SEE.
?
SHALL WE?
BRING IT ON.
pant pant pant
puff puff puff
17

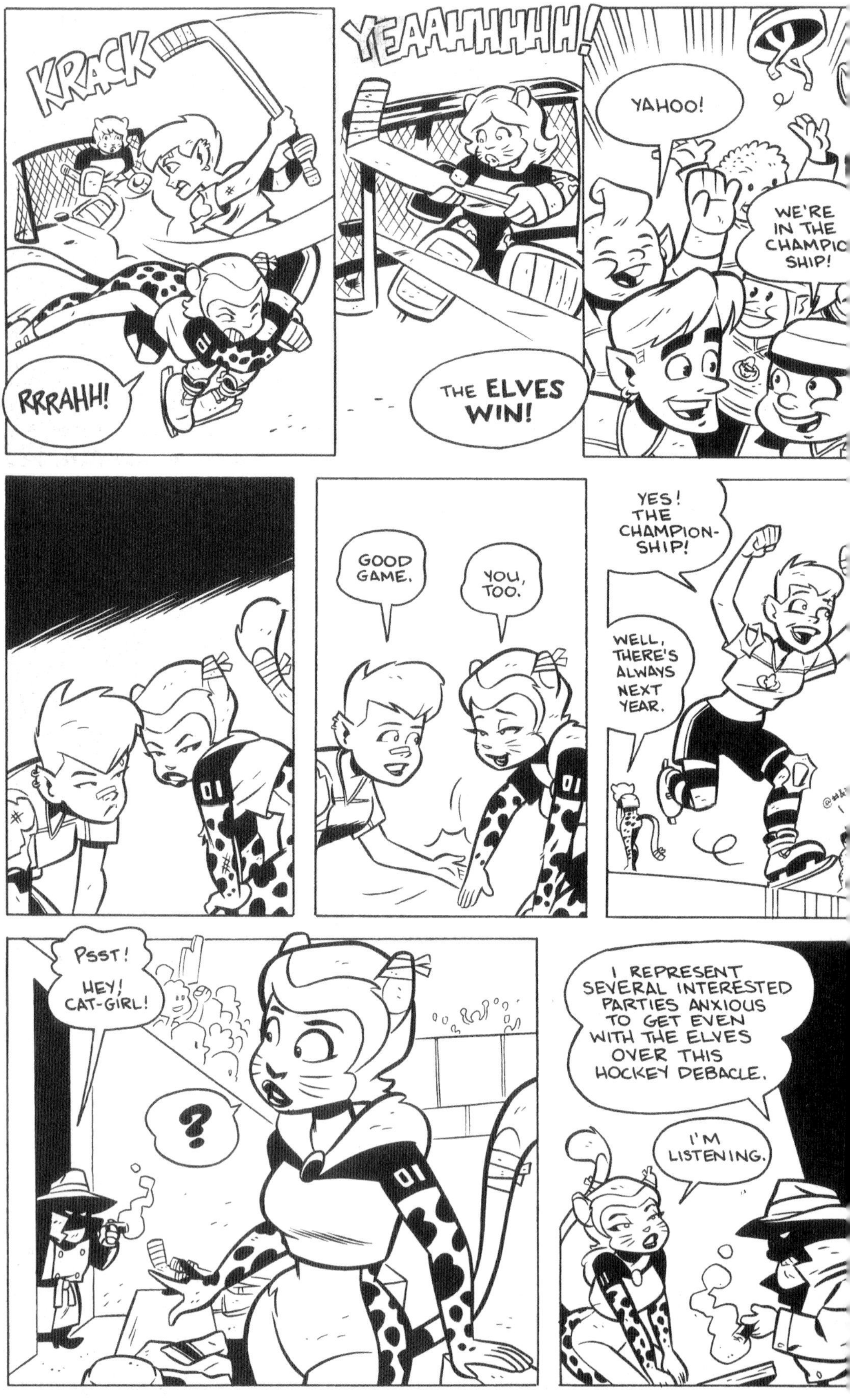
KRACK
RRRAHH!
YEAAHHHHH!
THE ELVES WIN!
YAHOO!
WE'RE IN THE CHAMPIONSHIP!
GOOD GAME.
YOU, TOO.
YES! THE CHAMPIONSHIP!
WELL, THERE'S ALWAYS NEXT YEAR.
PSST!
HEY! CAT-GIRL!
?
I REPRESENT SEVERAL INTERESTED PARTIES ANXIOUS TO GET EVEN WITH THE ELVES OVER THIS HOCKEY DEBACLE.
I'M LISTENING.

GOOD.

HAW!

This is RICH!

Santa's rinky-tink little elves have always been the joke of the local hockey league. But now that they have a shot at the championship, it's driving you Nuts!

Such fine Sportsmen!

YEAH SO, YOU GONNA HELP US, EH?

ABSOLUTELY! No one wants to see Kringle go down in defeat more than the ol' Bliz Wiz!

Of course I'm going to cost you.

MONEY'S NO OBJECT.

COACH

Keep it. I want the Championship Cup.

NO! NOT THE DAD-BLASTED CUP!

WHY THAT?

19

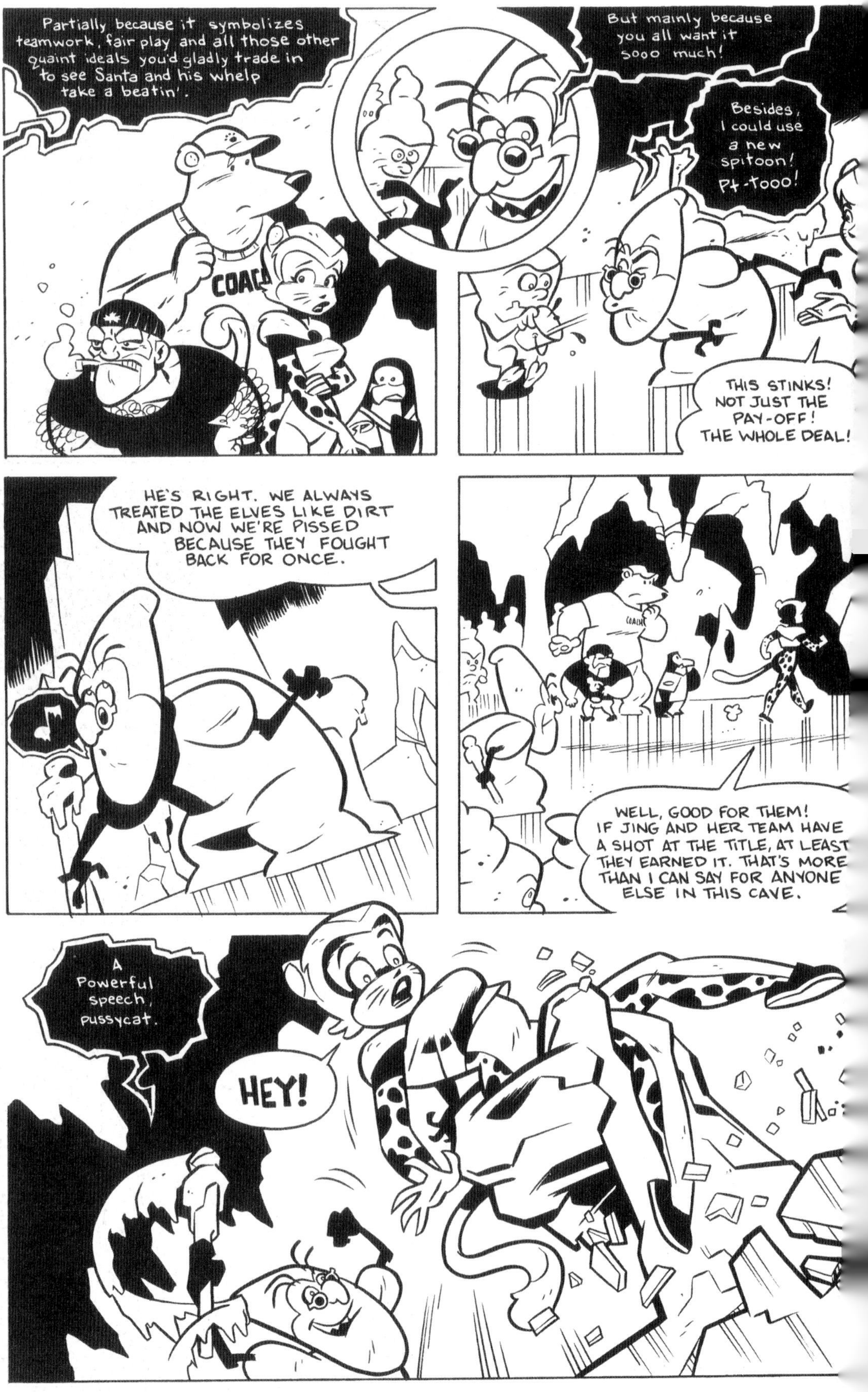
Partially because it symbolizes teamwork, fair play and all those other quaint ideals you'd gladly trade in to see Santa and his whelp take a beatin'.
But mainly because you all want it sooo much!
Besides, I could use a new spitoon! Pt-tooo!
THIS STINKS! NOT JUST THE PAY-OFF! THE WHOLE DEAL!
HE'S RIGHT. WE ALWAYS TREATED THE ELVES LIKE DIRT AND NOW WE'RE PISSED BECAUSE THEY FOUGHT BACK FOR ONCE.
WELL, GOOD FOR THEM! IF JING AND HER TEAM HAVE A SHOT AT THE TITLE, AT LEAST THEY EARNED IT. THAT'S MORE THAN I CAN SAY FOR ANYONE ELSE IN THIS CAVE.
A Powerful speech, pussycat.
HEY!

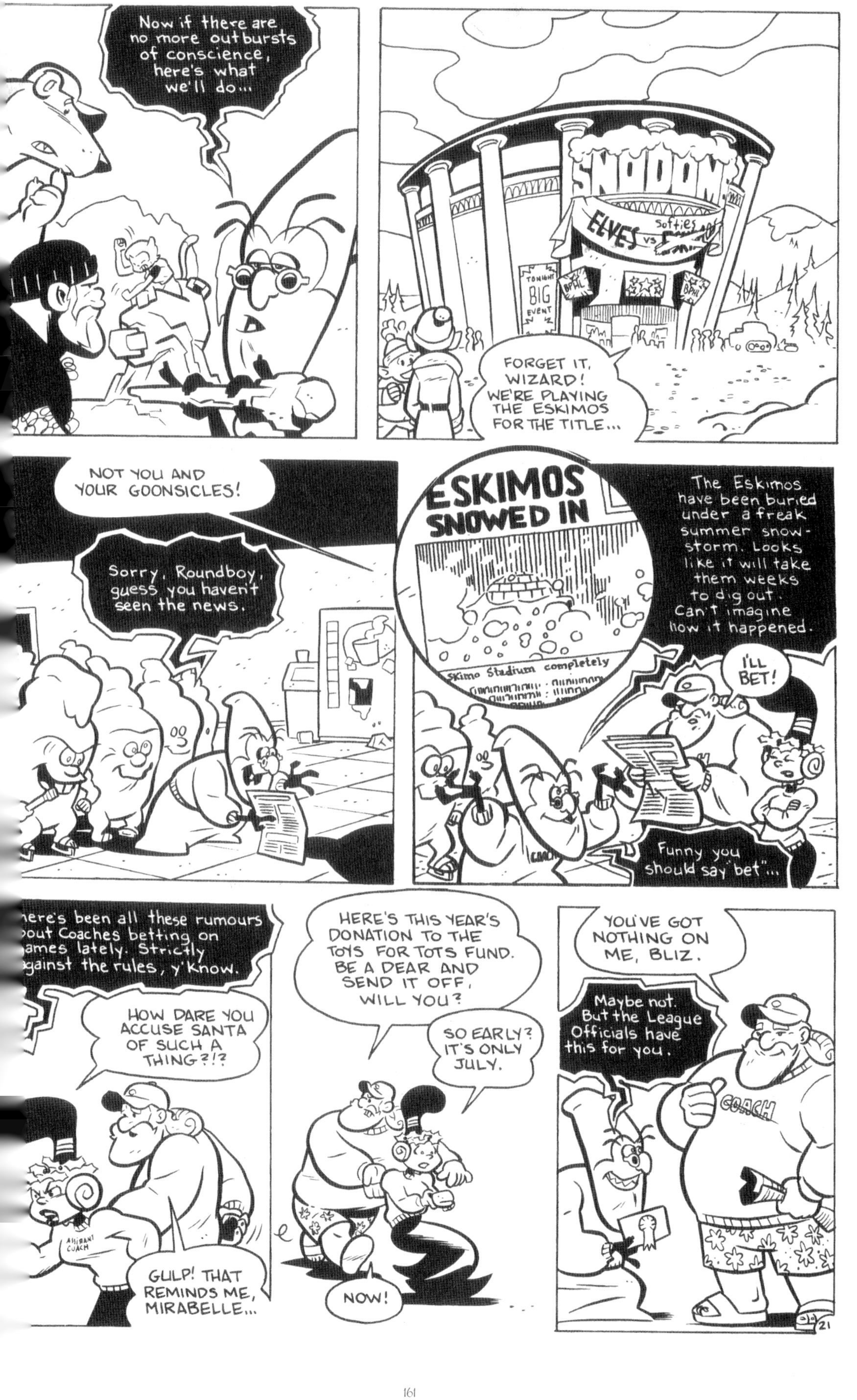
Now if there are no more outbursts of conscience, here's what we'll do...
SNOODOME
ELVES vs Softies
TONIGHT BIG EVENT
BPHL
FORGET IT, WIZARD! WE'RE PLAYING THE ESKIMOS FOR THE TITLE...
NOT YOU AND YOUR GOONSICLES!
Sorry, Roundboy, guess you haven't seen the news.
ESKIMOS SNOWED IN
Skimo Stadium completely
The Eskimos have been buried under a freak summer snow-storm. Looks like it will take them weeks to dig out. Can't imagine how it happened.
I'LL BET!
COACH
Funny you should say "bet"...
here's been all these rumours bout Coaches betting on ames lately. Strictly gainst the rules, y'know.
HOW DARE YOU ACCUSE SANTA OF SUCH A THING?!?
ASSISTANT COACH
GULP! THAT REMINDS ME, MIRABELLE...
HERE'S THIS YEAR'S DONATION TO THE TOYS FOR TOTS FUND. BE A DEAR AND SEND IT OFF, WILL YOU?
SO EARLY? IT'S ONLY JULY.
NOW!
YOU'VE GOT NOTHING ON ME, BLIZ.
Maybe not. But the League Officials have this for you.
COACH
21

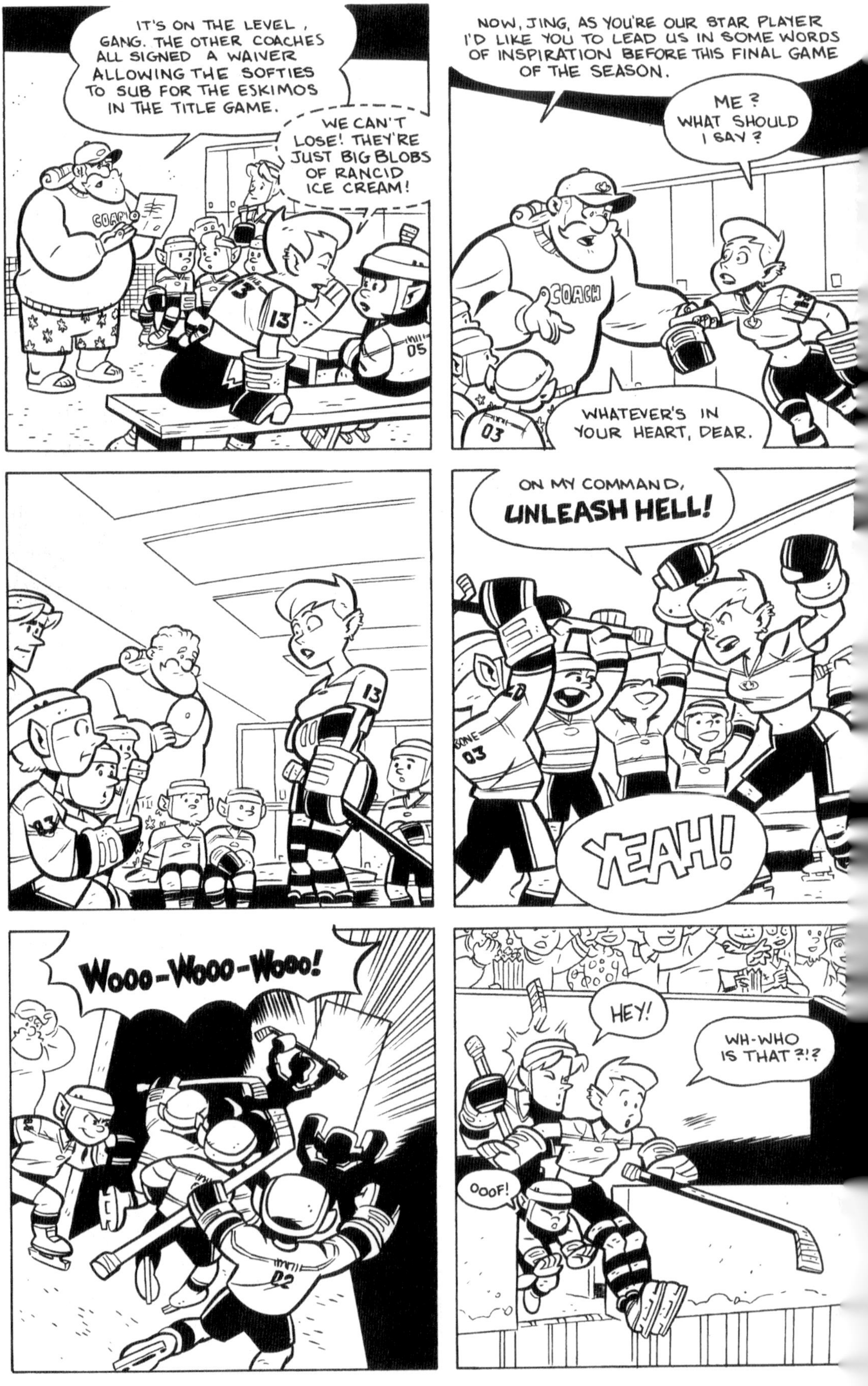
IT'S ON THE LEVEL, GANG. THE OTHER COACHES ALL SIGNED A WAIVER ALLOWING THE SOFTIES TO SUB FOR THE ESKIMOS IN THE TITLE GAME.
WE CAN'T LOSE! THEY'RE JUST BIG BLOBS OF RANCID ICE CREAM!
COACH
13
05
NOW, JING, AS YOU'RE OUR STAR PLAYER I'D LIKE YOU TO LEAD US IN SOME WORDS OF INSPIRATION BEFORE THIS FINAL GAME OF THE SEASON.
ME? WHAT SHOULD I SAY?
COACH
WHATEVER'S IN YOUR HEART, DEAR.
03
13
03
ON MY COMMAND, UNLEASH HELL!
BONE 03
YEAH!
Wooo-Wooo-Wooo!
02
HEY!
WH-WHO IS THAT?!?
OOOF!

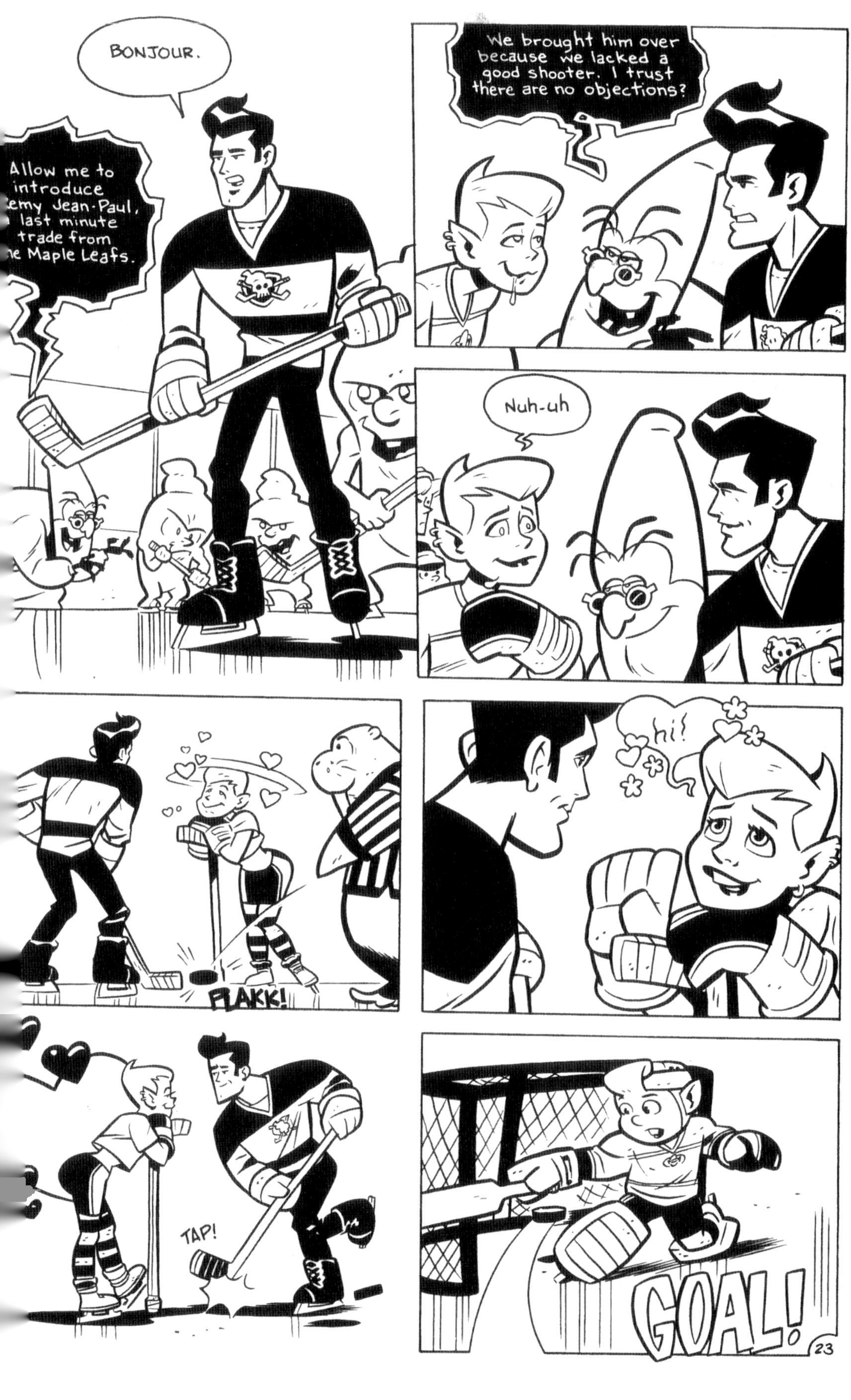
BONJOUR.
Allow me to introduce emy Jean-Paul, last minute trade from e Maple Leafs.
We brought him over because we lacked a good shooter. I trust there are no objections?
Nuh-uh
FLAKK!
hi!
TAP!
GOAL!
23

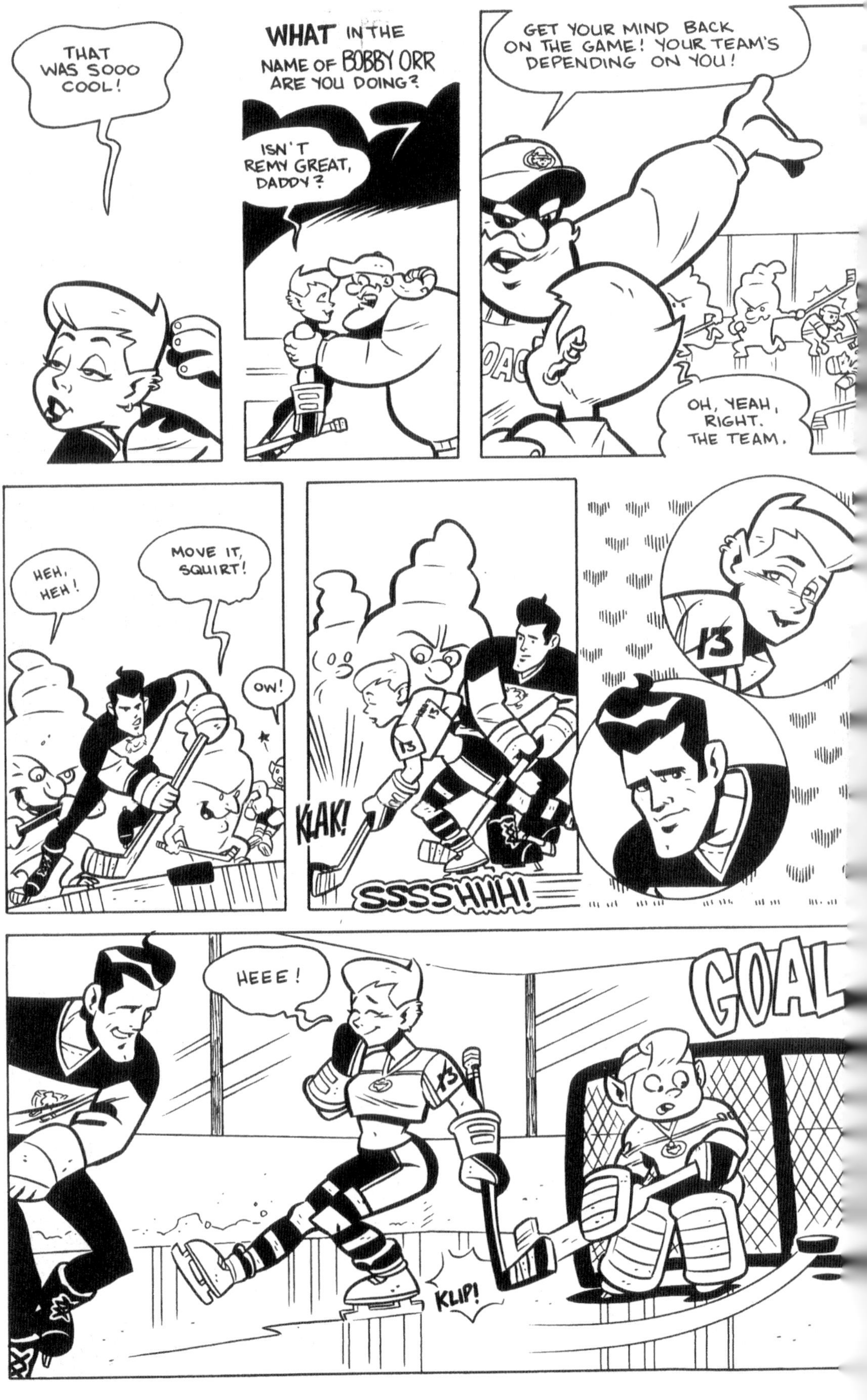
THAT WAS SOOO COOL!
WHAT IN THE NAME OF BOBBY ORR ARE YOU DOING?
ISN'T REMY GREAT, DADDY?
GET YOUR MIND BACK ON THE GAME! YOUR TEAM'S DEPENDING ON YOU!
OH, YEAH, RIGHT. THE TEAM.
HEH, HEH!
MOVE IT, SQUIRT!
OW!
KLAK!
SSSSHHH!
HEEE!
GOAL
KLIP!

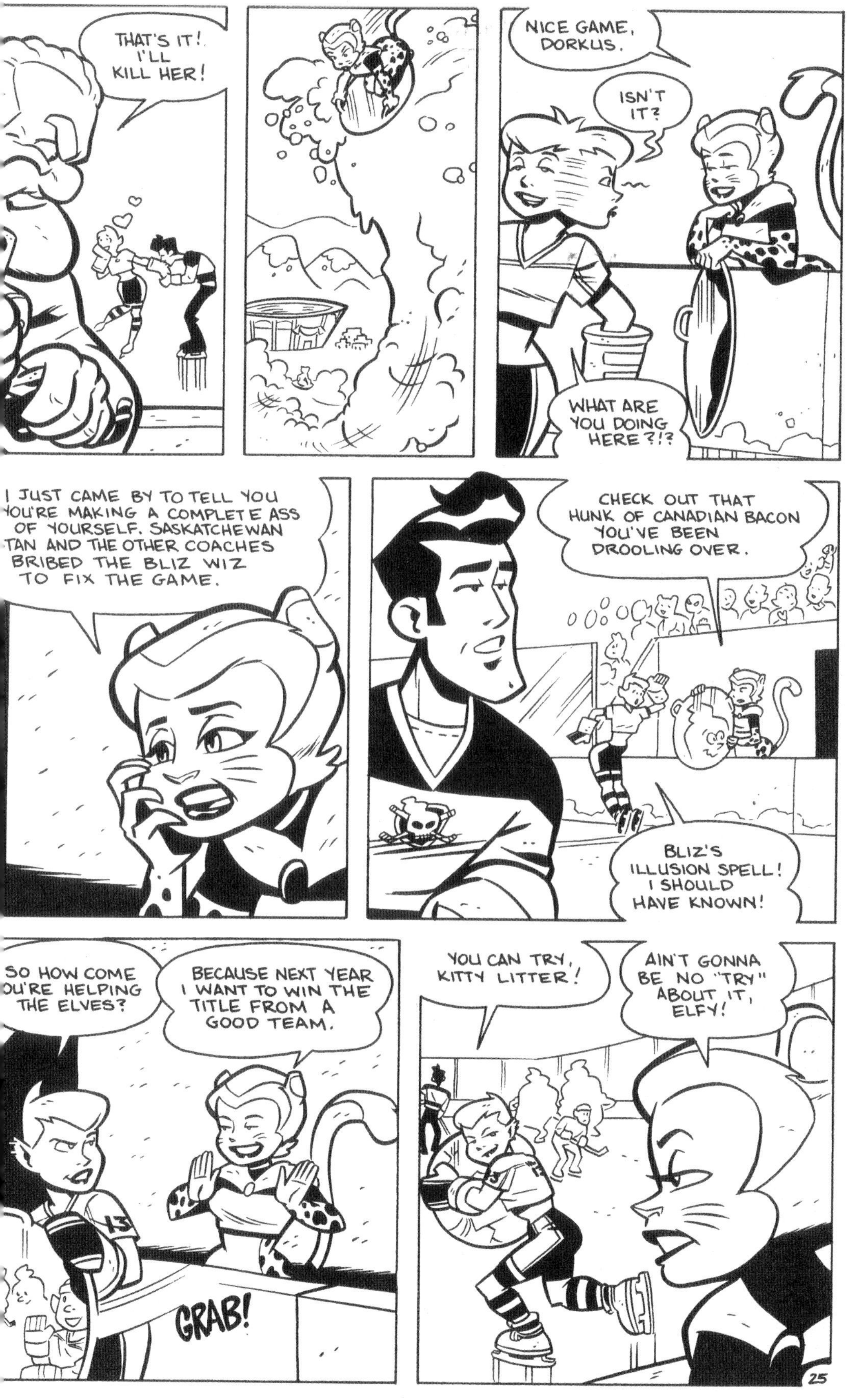
THAT'S IT! I'LL KILL HER!
NICE GAME, DORKUS.
ISN'T IT?
WHAT ARE YOU DOING HERE?!?
I JUST CAME BY TO TELL YOU YOU'RE MAKING A COMPLETE ASS OF YOURSELF. SASKATCHEWAN TAN AND THE OTHER COACHES BRIBED THE BLIZ WIZ TO FIX THE GAME.
CHECK OUT THAT HUNK OF CANADIAN BACON YOU'VE BEEN DROOLING OVER.
BLIZ'S ILLUSION SPELL! I SHOULD HAVE KNOWN!
SO HOW COME YOU'RE HELPING THE ELVES?
BECAUSE NEXT YEAR I WANT TO WIN THE TITLE FROM A GOOD TEAM.
GRAB!
YOU CAN TRY, KITTY LITTER!
AIN'T GONNA BE NO "TRY" ABOUT IT, ELFY!
25

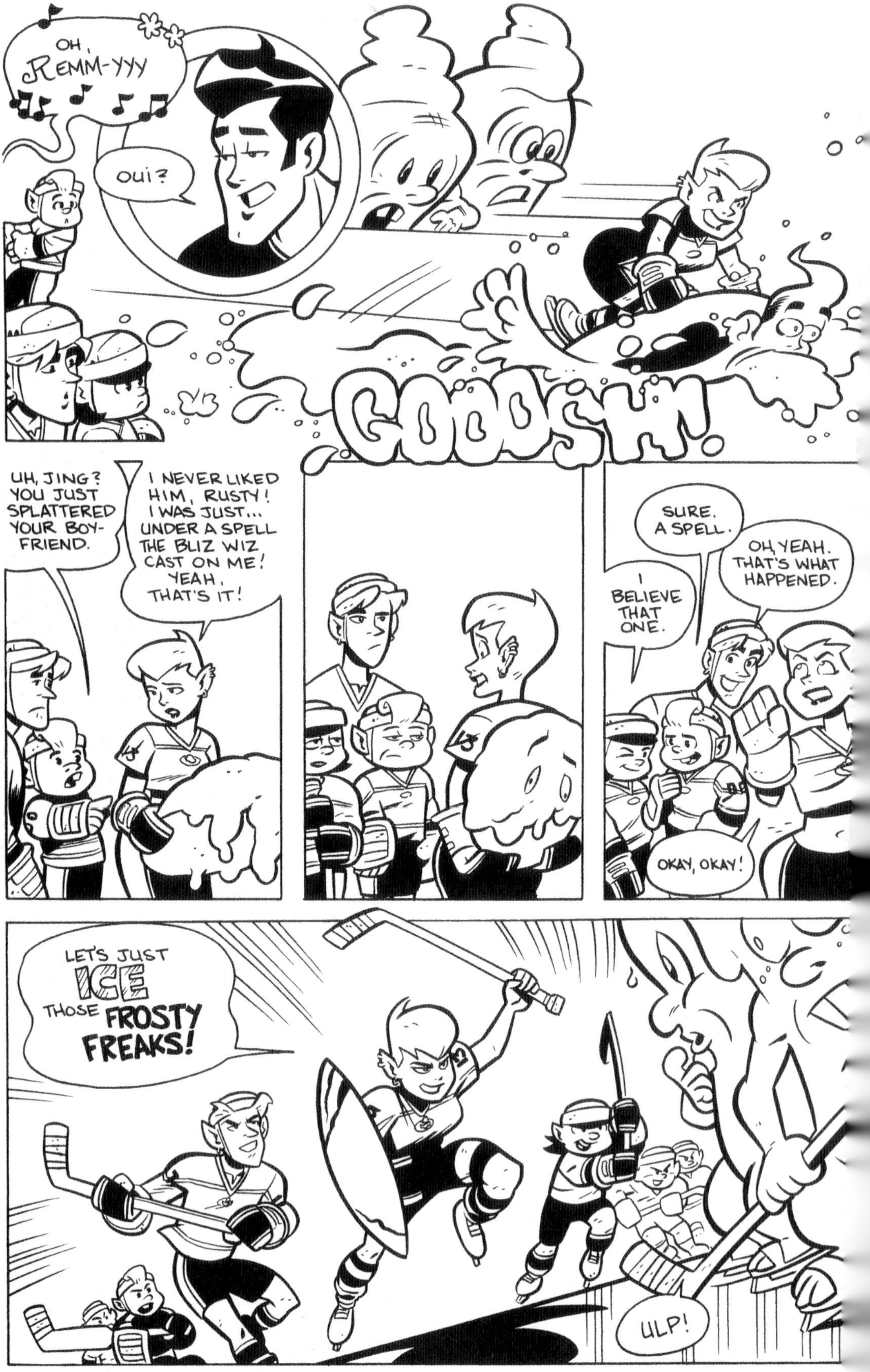

OH, REMM-YYY
OUI?
GOOOSH!
UH, JING? YOU JUST SPLATTERED YOUR BOY-FRIEND.
I NEVER LIKED HIM, RUSTY! I WAS JUST... UNDER A SPELL THE BLIZ WIZ CAST ON ME! YEAH, THAT'S IT!
SURE. A SPELL.
I BELIEVE THAT ONE.
OH, YEAH. THAT'S WHAT HAPPENED.
OKAY, OKAY!
LET'S JUST ICE THOSE FROSTY FREAKS!
ULP!

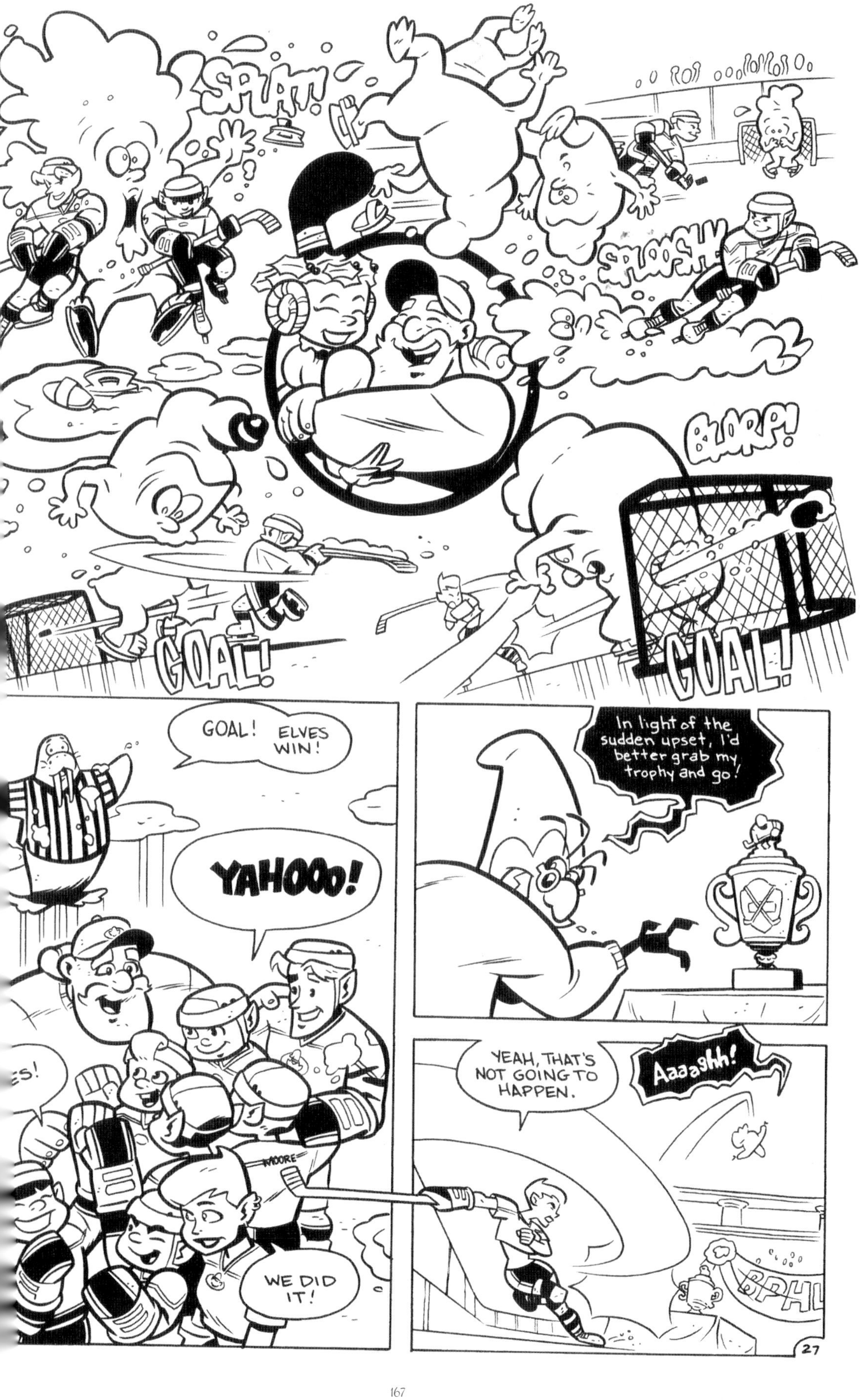
SPLAT!
SPLOOSH!
BLORP!
GOAL!
GOAL!
GOAL! ELVES WIN!
YAHOOO!
ES!
MOORE
WE DID IT!
In light of the sudden upset, I'd better grab my trophy and go!
YEAH, THAT'S NOT GOING TO HAPPEN.
Aaaaghh!
BPHL
27

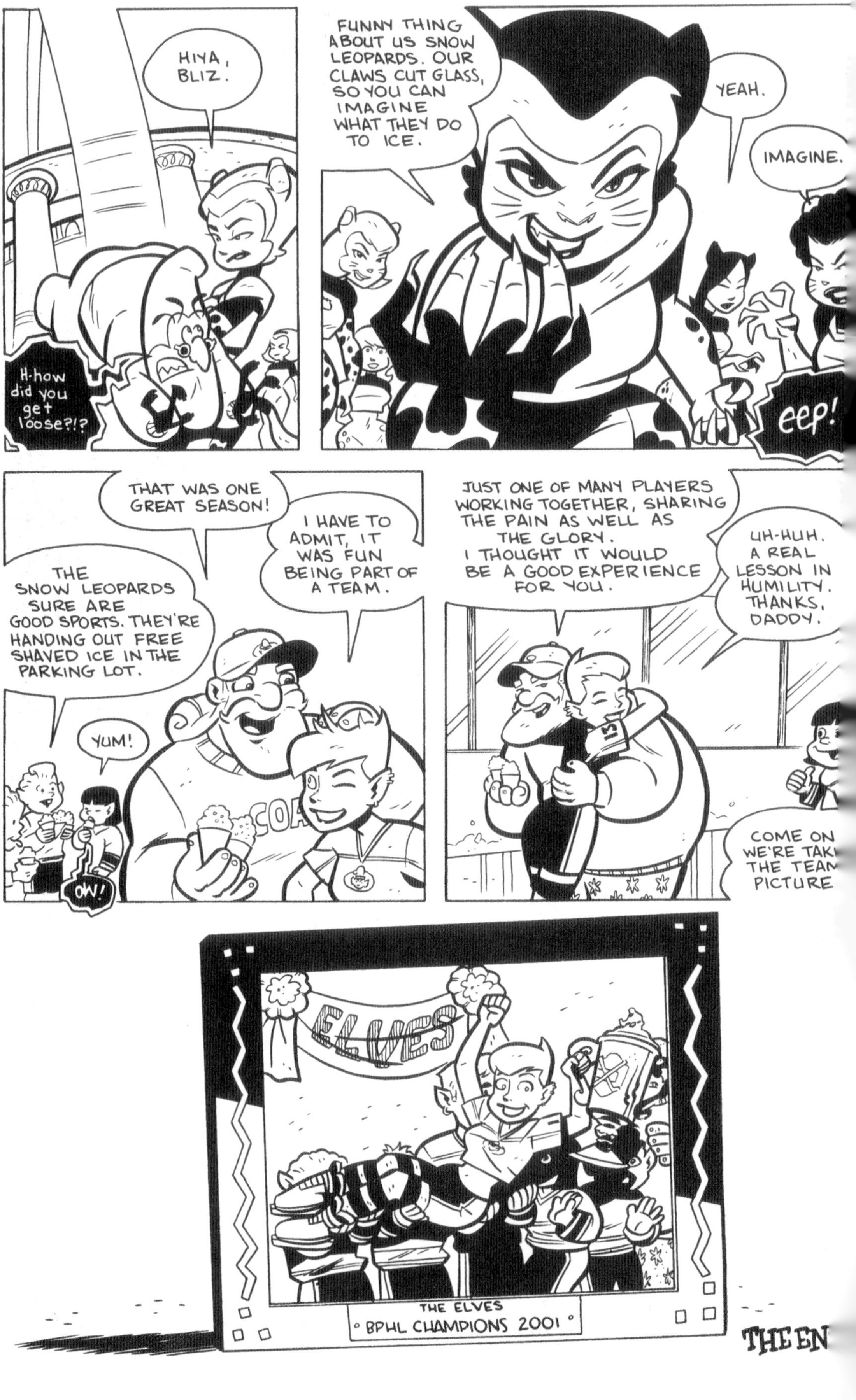
HIYA, BLIZ.
H-how did you get loose?!?
FUNNY THING ABOUT US SNOW LEOPARDS. OUR CLAWS CUT GLASS, SO YOU CAN IMAGINE WHAT THEY DO TO ICE.
YEAH.
IMAGINE.
eep!
THAT WAS ONE GREAT SEASON!
THE SNOW LEOPARDS SURE ARE GOOD SPORTS. THEY'RE HANDING OUT FREE SHAVED ICE IN THE PARKING LOT.
I HAVE TO ADMIT, IT WAS FUN BEING PART OF A TEAM.
YUM!
OW!
JUST ONE OF MANY PLAYERS WORKING TOGETHER, SHARING THE PAIN AS WELL AS THE GLORY. I THOUGHT IT WOULD BE A GOOD EXPERIENCE FOR YOU.
UH-HUH. A REAL LESSON IN HUMILITY. THANKS, DADDY.
COME ON WE'RE TAK THE TEAM PICTURE
ELVES
THE ELVES
BPHL CHAMPIONS 2001
THE EN

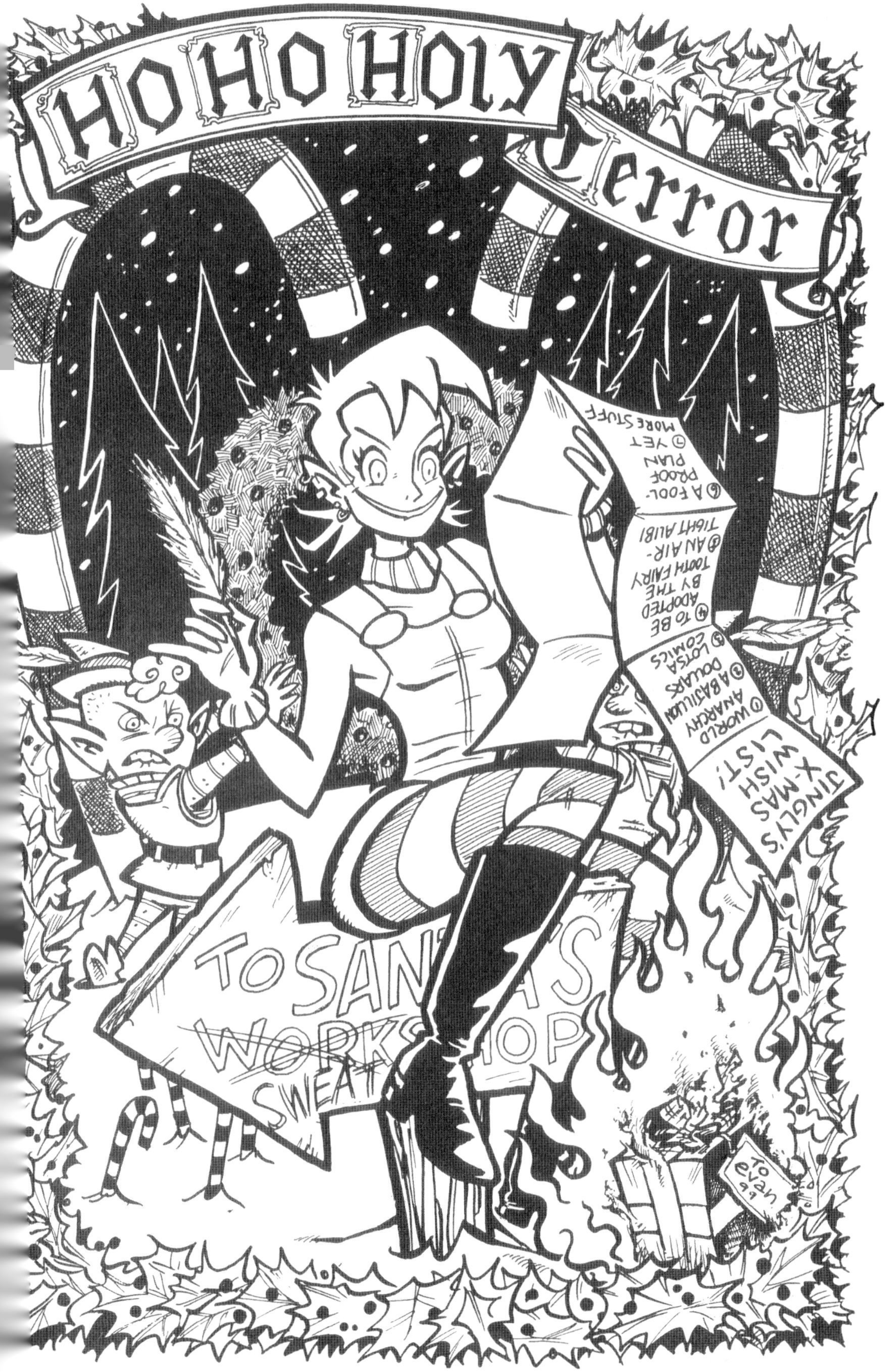
HO HO HOLY Terror
JINGLY'S X-MAS WISH LIST!
1 WORLD ANARCHY
2 A BAJILLION DOLLARS
3 LOTSA COMICS
4 TO BE ADOPTED BY THE TOOTH FAIRY
5 AN AIR-TIGHT ALIBI
6 A FOOL-PROOF PLAN
7 YET MORE STUFF
TO SAN S
WORKS HOP
SWEAT

Jubilee

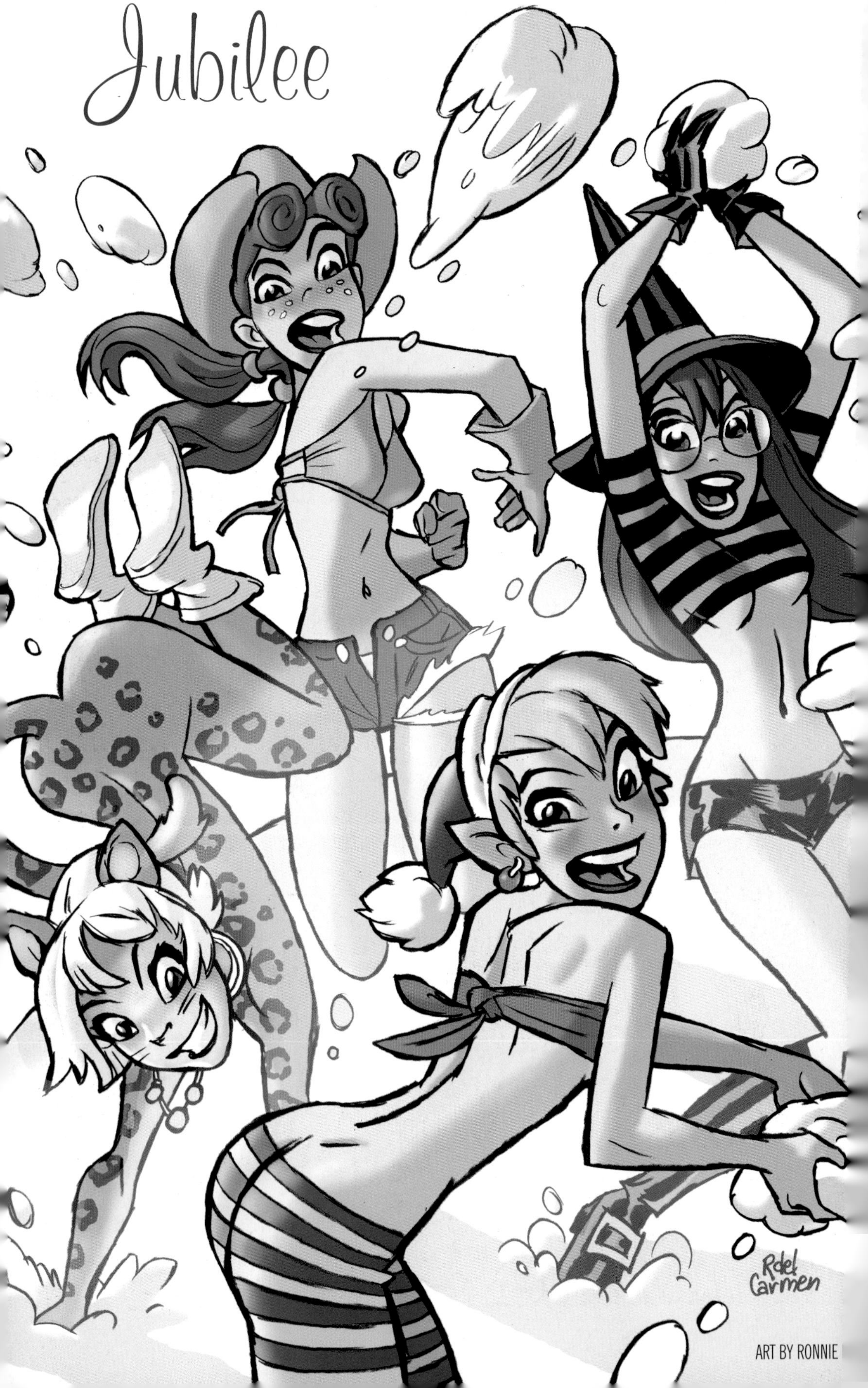
Rdel Carmen

ART BY RONNIE

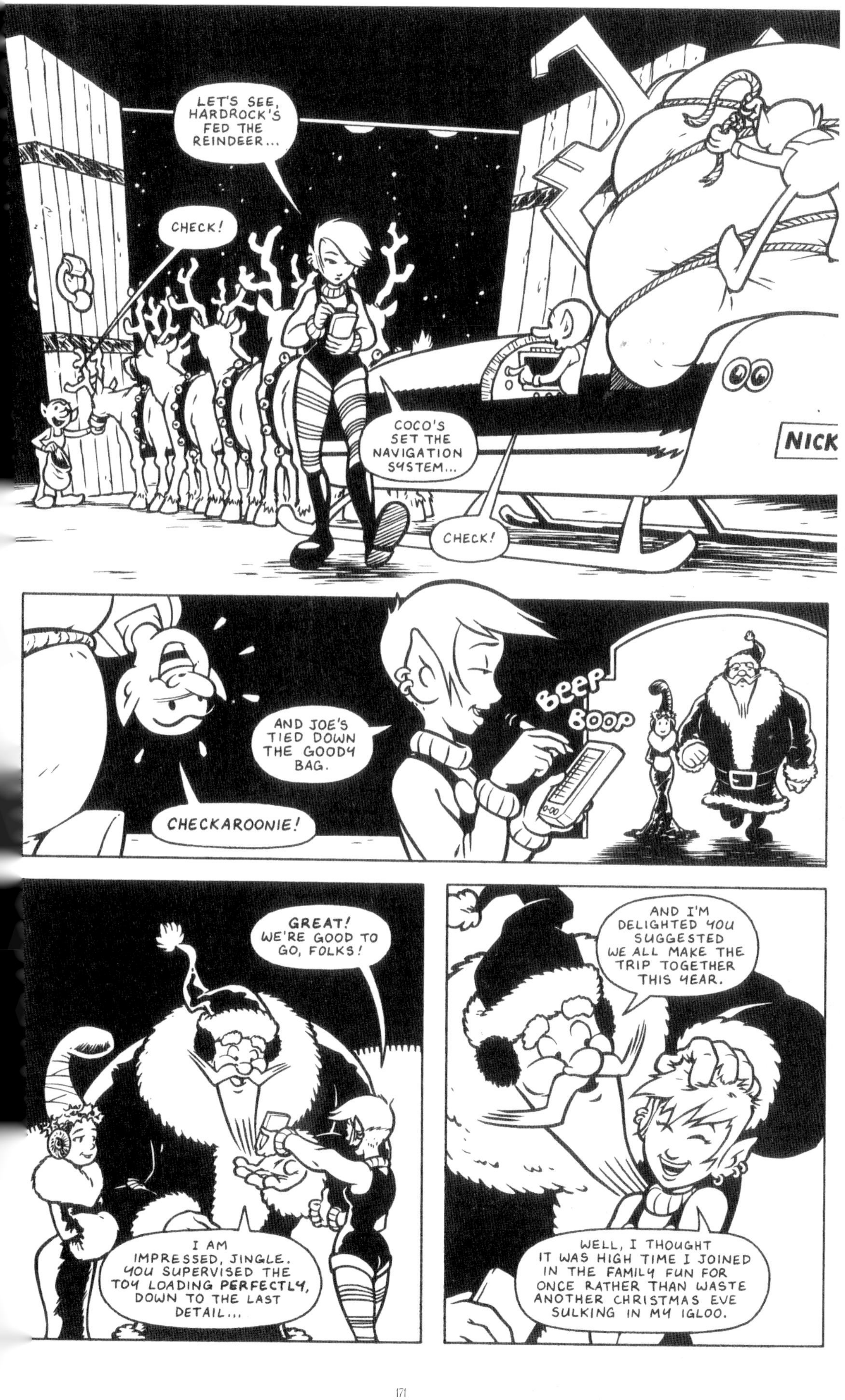
LET'S SEE, HARDROCK'S FED THE REINDEER...
CHECK!
COCO'S SET THE NAVIGATION SYSTEM...
CHECK!
NICK
AND JOE'S TIED DOWN THE GOODY BAG.
CHECKAROONIE!
BEEP BOOP
GREAT! WE'RE GOOD TO GO, FOLKS!
I AM IMPRESSED, JINGLE. YOU SUPERVISED THE TOY LOADING PERFECTLY, DOWN TO THE LAST DETAIL...
AND I'M DELIGHTED YOU SUGGESTED WE ALL MAKE THE TRIP TOGETHER THIS YEAR.
WELL, I THOUGHT IT WAS HIGH TIME I JOINED IN THE FAMILY FUN FOR ONCE RATHER THAN WASTE ANOTHER CHRISTMAS EVE SULKING IN MY IGLOO.

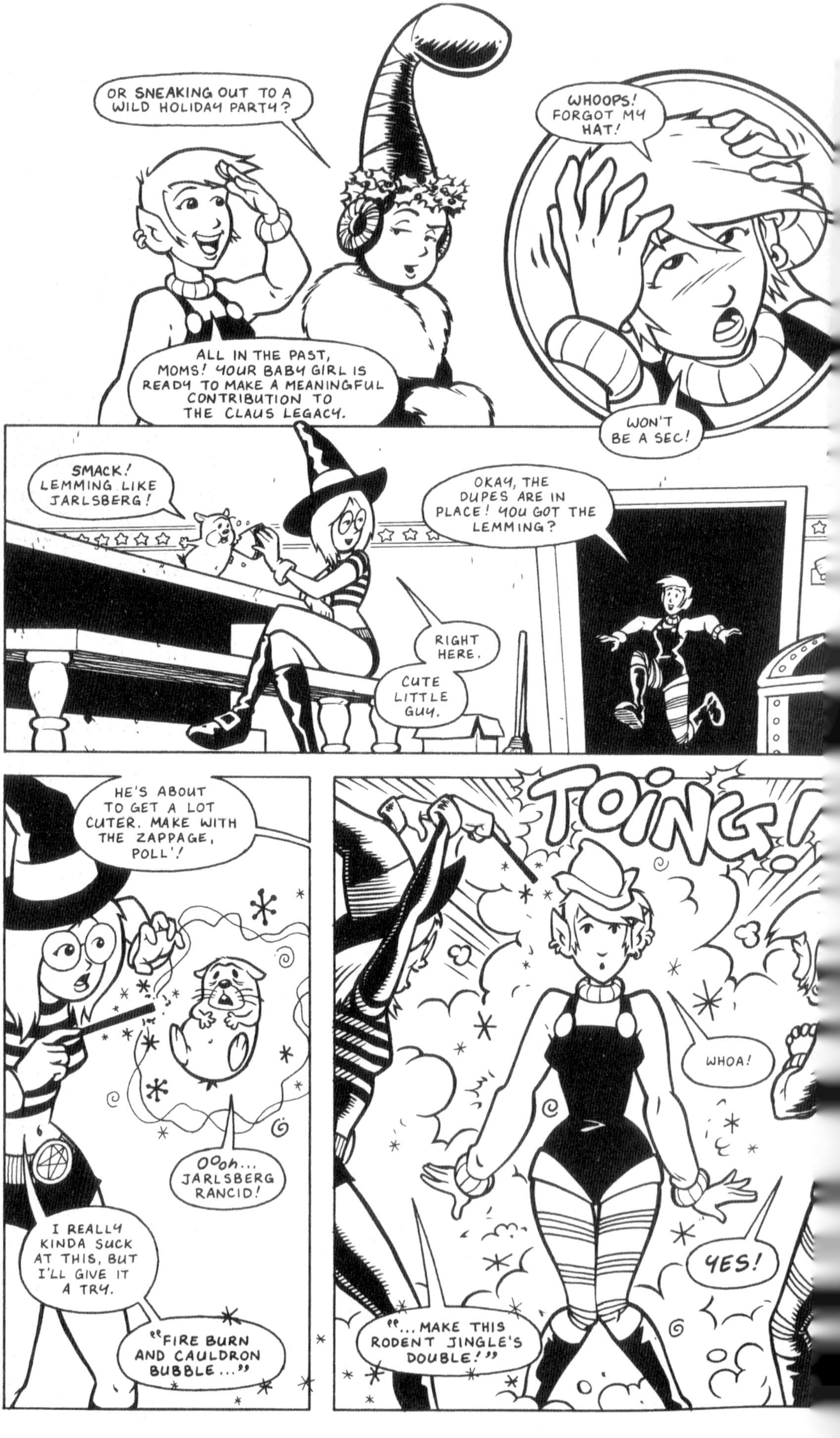
OR SNEAKING OUT TO A WILD HOLIDAY PARTY?
ALL IN THE PAST, MOMS! YOUR BABY GIRL IS READY TO MAKE A MEANINGFUL CONTRIBUTION TO THE CLAUS LEGACY.
WHOOPS! FORGOT MY HAT!
WON'T BE A SEC!
SMACK! LEMMING LIKE JARLSBERG!
OKAY, THE DUPES ARE IN PLACE! YOU GOT THE LEMMING?
RIGHT HERE.
CUTE LITTLE GUY.
HE'S ABOUT TO GET A LOT CUTER. MAKE WITH THE ZAPPAGE, POLL'!
OOoh... JARLSBERG RANCID!
I REALLY KINDA SUCK AT THIS, BUT I'LL GIVE IT A TRY.
"FIRE BURN AND CAULDRON BUBBLE..."
TOING!
WHOA!
YES!
"...MAKE THIS RODENT JINGLE'S DOUBLE!"

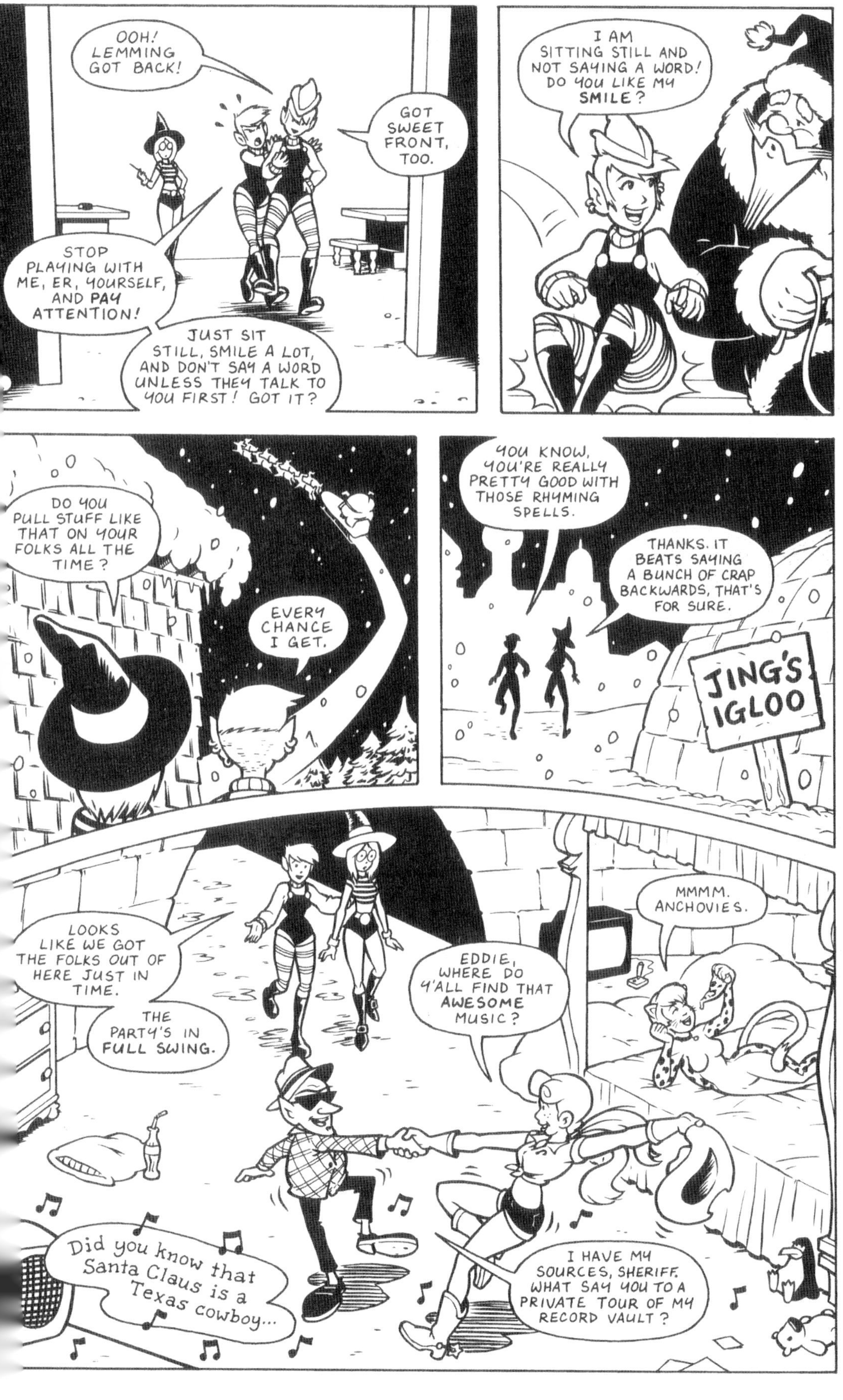
OOH! LEMMING GOT BACK!
GOT SWEET FRONT, TOO.
STOP PLAYING WITH ME, ER, YOURSELF, AND PAY ATTENTION!
JUST SIT STILL, SMILE A LOT, AND DON'T SAY A WORD UNLESS THEY TALK TO YOU FIRST! GOT IT?
I AM SITTING STILL AND NOT SAYING A WORD! DO YOU LIKE MY SMILE?
DO YOU PULL STUFF LIKE THAT ON YOUR FOLKS ALL THE TIME?
EVERY CHANCE I GET.
YOU KNOW, YOU'RE REALLY PRETTY GOOD WITH THOSE RHYMING SPELLS.
THANKS. IT BEATS SAYING A BUNCH OF CRAP BACKWARDS, THAT'S FOR SURE.
JING'S IGLOO
LOOKS LIKE WE GOT THE FOLKS OUT OF HERE JUST IN TIME.
THE PARTY'S IN FULL SWING.
EDDIE, WHERE DO Y'ALL FIND THAT AWESOME MUSIC?
MMMM. ANCHOVIES.
Did you know that Santa Claus is a Texas cowboy...
I HAVE MY SOURCES, SHERIFF. WHAT SAY YOU TO A PRIVATE TOUR OF MY RECORD VAULT?

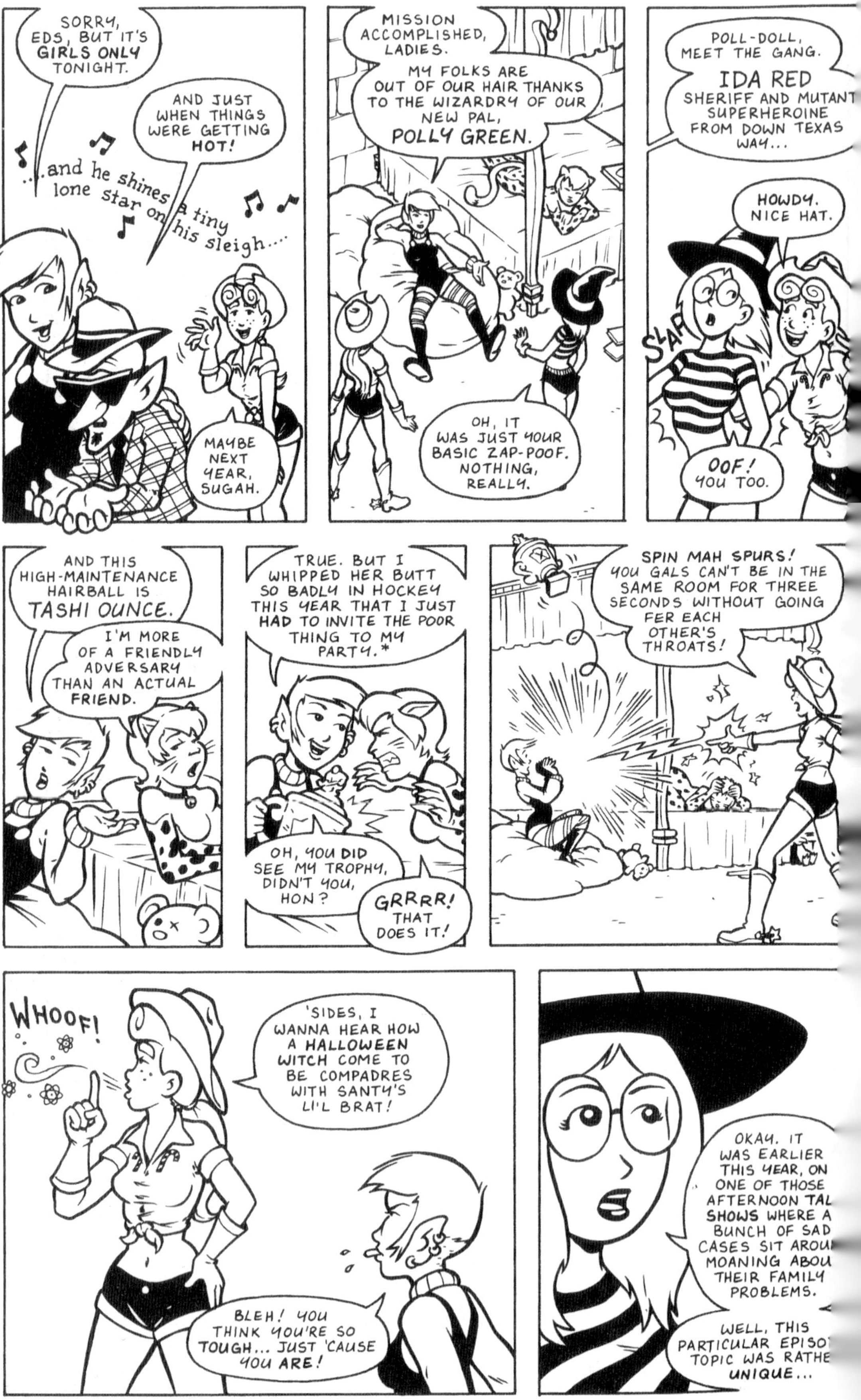
SORRY, EDS, BUT IT'S GIRLS ONLY TONIGHT.
AND JUST WHEN THINGS WERE GETTING HOT!
...and he shines a tiny lone star on his sleigh....
MAYBE NEXT YEAR, SUGAH.
MISSION ACCOMPLISHED, LADIES.
MY FOLKS ARE OUT OF OUR HAIR THANKS TO THE WIZARDRY OF OUR NEW PAL, POLLY GREEN.
OH, IT WAS JUST YOUR BASIC ZAP-POOF. NOTHING, REALLY.
POLL-DOLL, MEET THE GANG.
IDA RED
SHERIFF AND MUTANT SUPERHEROINE FROM DOWN TEXAS WAY...
HOWDY. NICE HAT.
SLAP
OOF! YOU TOO.
AND THIS HIGH-MAINTENANCE HAIRBALL IS TASHI OUNCE.
I'M MORE OF A FRIENDLY ADVERSARY THAN AN ACTUAL FRIEND.
TRUE. BUT I WHIPPED HER BUTT SO BADLY IN HOCKEY THIS YEAR THAT I JUST HAD TO INVITE THE POOR THING TO MY PARTY.*
OH, YOU DID SEE MY TROPHY, DIDN'T YOU, HON?
GRRRR! THAT DOES IT!
SPIN MAH SPURS! YOU GALS CAN'T BE IN THE SAME ROOM FOR THREE SECONDS WITHOUT GOING FER EACH OTHER'S THROATS!
WHOOF!
'SIDES, I WANNA HEAR HOW A HALLOWEEN WITCH COME TO BE COMPADRES WITH SANTY'S LI'L BRAT!
BLEH! YOU THINK YOU'RE SO TOUGH... JUST 'CAUSE YOU ARE!
OKAY. IT WAS EARLIER THIS YEAR, ON ONE OF THOSE AFTERNOON TAL SHOWS WHERE A BUNCH OF SAD CASES SIT AROU MOANING ABOU THEIR FAMILY PROBLEMS.
WELL, THIS PARTICULAR EPISO TOPIC WAS RATHE UNIQUE...

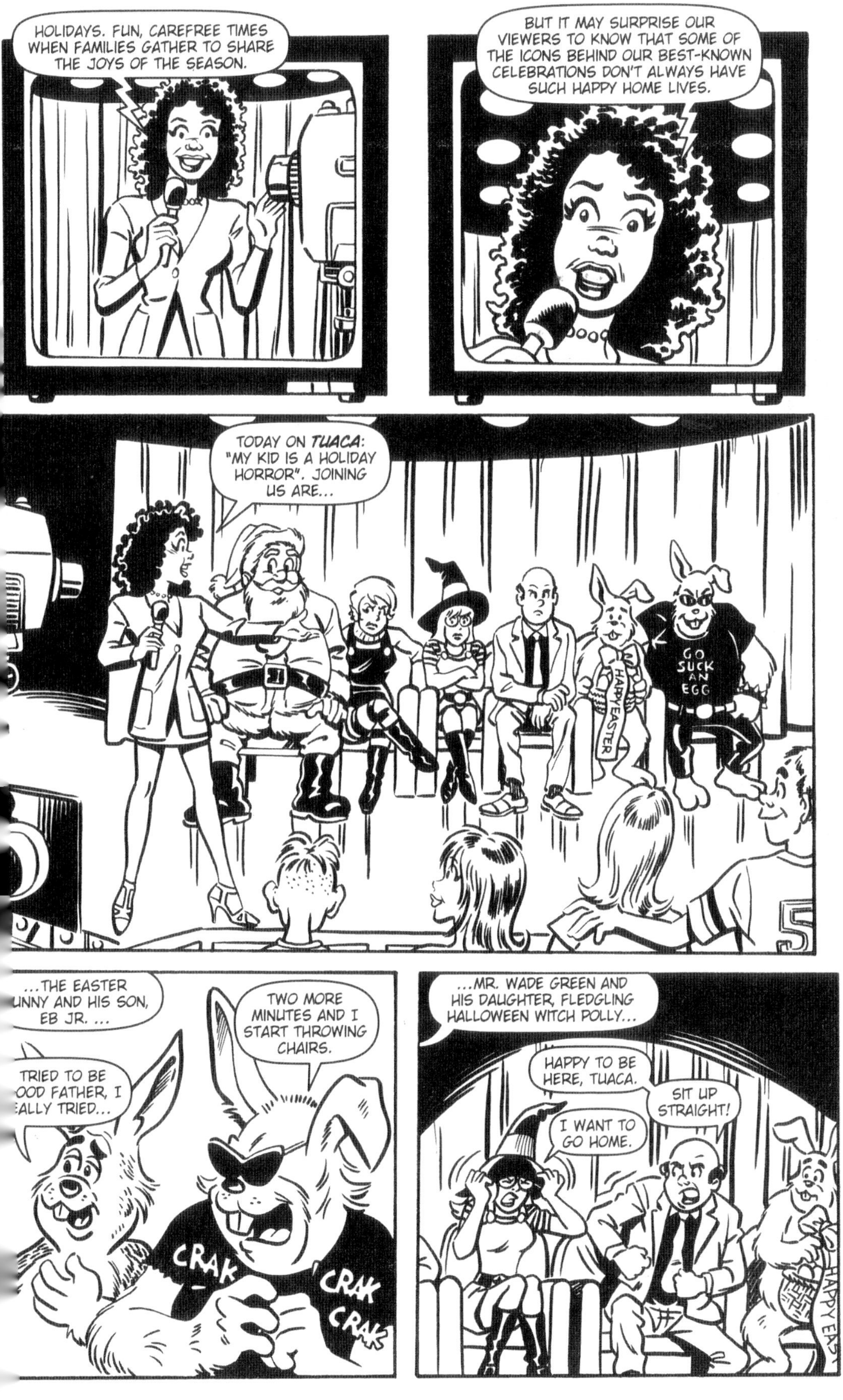
HOLIDAYS. FUN, CAREFREE TIMES WHEN FAMILIES GATHER TO SHARE THE JOYS OF THE SEASON.
BUT IT MAY SURPRISE OUR VIEWERS TO KNOW THAT SOME OF THE ICONS BEHIND OUR BEST-KNOWN CELEBRATIONS DON'T ALWAYS HAVE SUCH HAPPY HOME LIVES.
TODAY ON TUACA: "MY KID IS A HOLIDAY HORROR". JOINING US ARE...
HAPPY EASTER
GO SUCK AN EGG
...THE EASTER UNNY AND HIS SON, EB JR. ...
TWO MORE MINUTES AND I START THROWING CHAIRS.
TRIED TO BE OOD FATHER, I EALLY TRIED...
CRAK
CRAK
CRAK
...MR. WADE GREEN AND HIS DAUGHTER, FLEDGLING HALLOWEEN WITCH POLLY...
HAPPY TO BE HERE, TUACA.
SIT UP STRAIGHT!
I WANT TO GO HOME.
HAPPY EAS

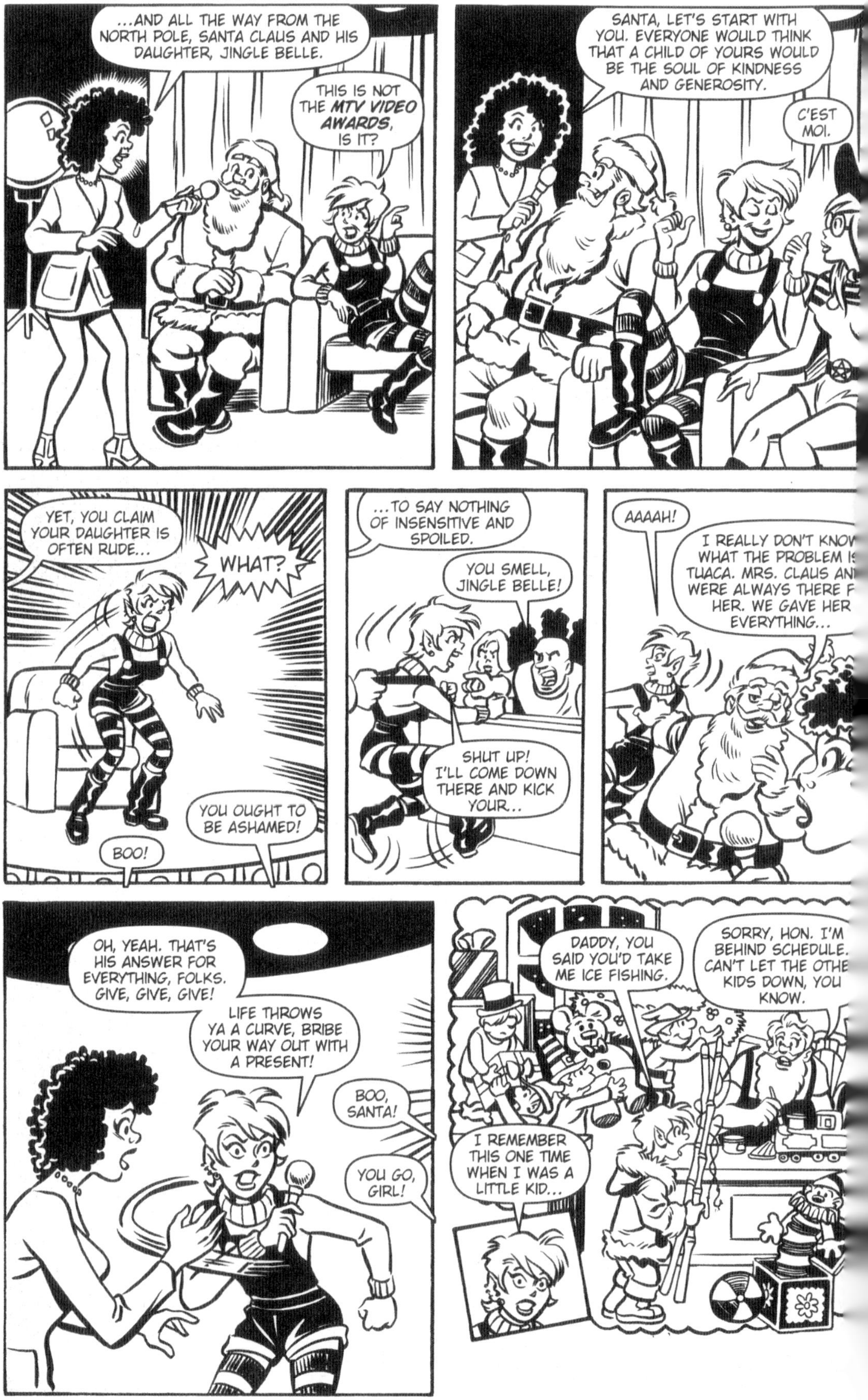
...AND ALL THE WAY FROM THE NORTH POLE, SANTA CLAUS AND HIS DAUGHTER, JINGLE BELLE.
THIS IS NOT THE MTV VIDEO AWARDS, IS IT?
SANTA, LET'S START WITH YOU. EVERYONE WOULD THINK THAT A CHILD OF YOURS WOULD BE THE SOUL OF KINDNESS AND GENEROSITY.
C'EST MOI.
YET, YOU CLAIM YOUR DAUGHTER IS OFTEN RUDE...
WHAT?
YOU OUGHT TO BE ASHAMED!
BOO!
...TO SAY NOTHING OF INSENSITIVE AND SPOILED.
YOU SMELL, JINGLE BELLE!
SHUT UP! I'LL COME DOWN THERE AND KICK YOUR...
AAAAH!
I REALLY DON'T KNOW WHAT THE PROBLEM IS TUACA. MRS. CLAUS AND I WERE ALWAYS THERE FOR HER. WE GAVE HER EVERYTHING...
OH, YEAH. THAT'S HIS ANSWER FOR EVERYTHING, FOLKS. GIVE, GIVE, GIVE!
LIFE THROWS YA A CURVE, BRIBE YOUR WAY OUT WITH A PRESENT!
BOO, SANTA!
YOU GO, GIRL!
I REMEMBER THIS ONE TIME WHEN I WAS A LITTLE KID...
DADDY, YOU SAID YOU'D TAKE ME ICE FISHING.
SORRY, HON. I'M BEHIND SCHEDULE. CAN'T LET THE OTHER KIDS DOWN, YOU KNOW.

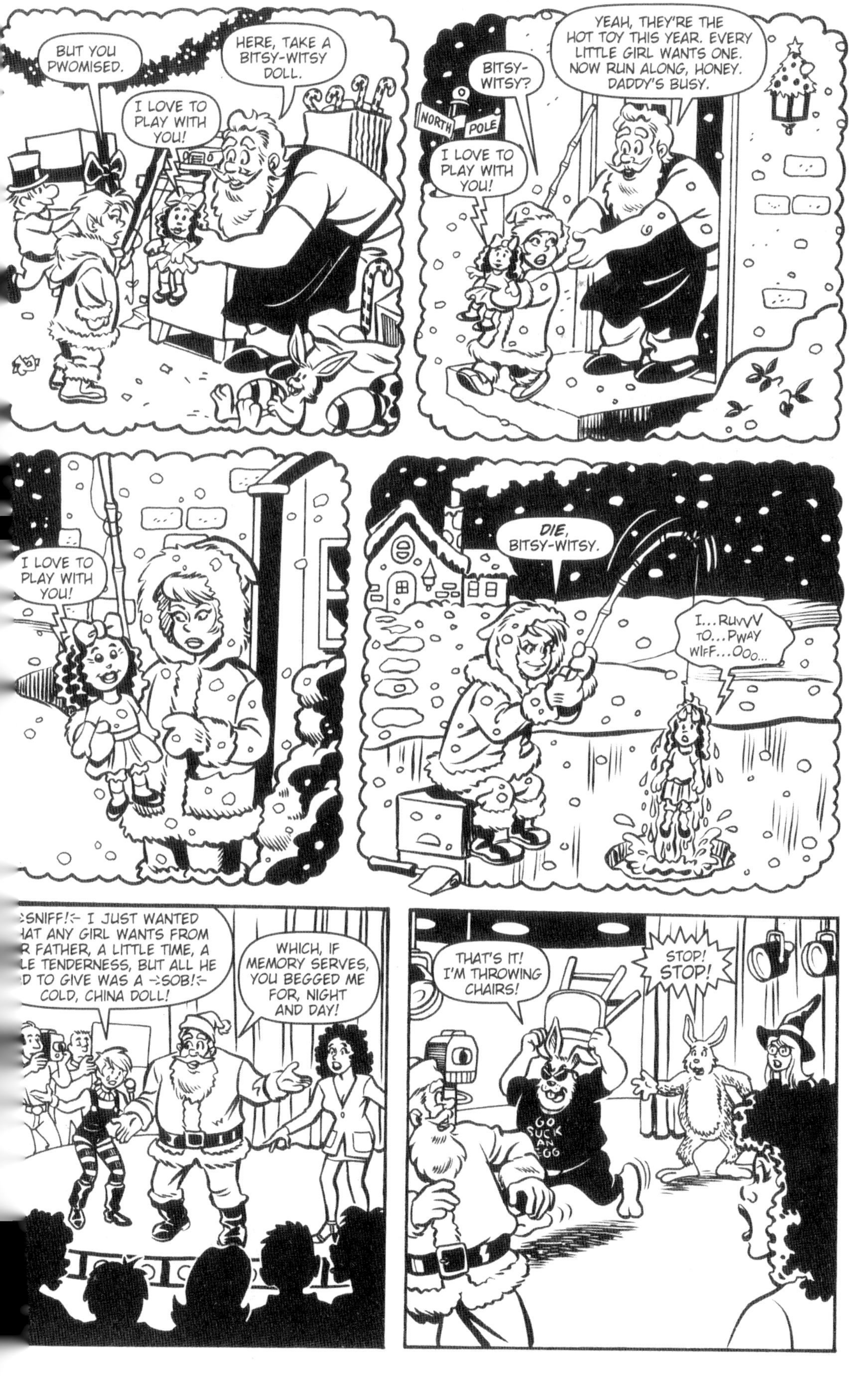
BUT YOU PWOMISED.
HERE, TAKE A BITSY-WITSY DOLL.
I LOVE TO PLAY WITH YOU!
BITSY-WITSY?
YEAH, THEY'RE THE HOT TOY THIS YEAR. EVERY LITTLE GIRL WANTS ONE. NOW RUN ALONG, HONEY. DADDY'S BUSY.
NORTH
POLE
I LOVE TO PLAY WITH YOU!
I LOVE TO PLAY WITH YOU!
DIE, BITSY-WITSY.
I...RUVVV TO...PWAY WIFF...OOO...
SNIFF! I JUST WANTED HAT ANY GIRL WANTS FROM R FATHER, A LITTLE TIME, A LE TENDERNESS, BUT ALL HE D TO GIVE WAS A SOB! COLD, CHINA DOLL!
WHICH, IF MEMORY SERVES, YOU BEGGED ME FOR, NIGHT AND DAY!
THAT'S IT! I'M THROWING CHAIRS!
STOP! STOP!
GO SUCK AN EGG

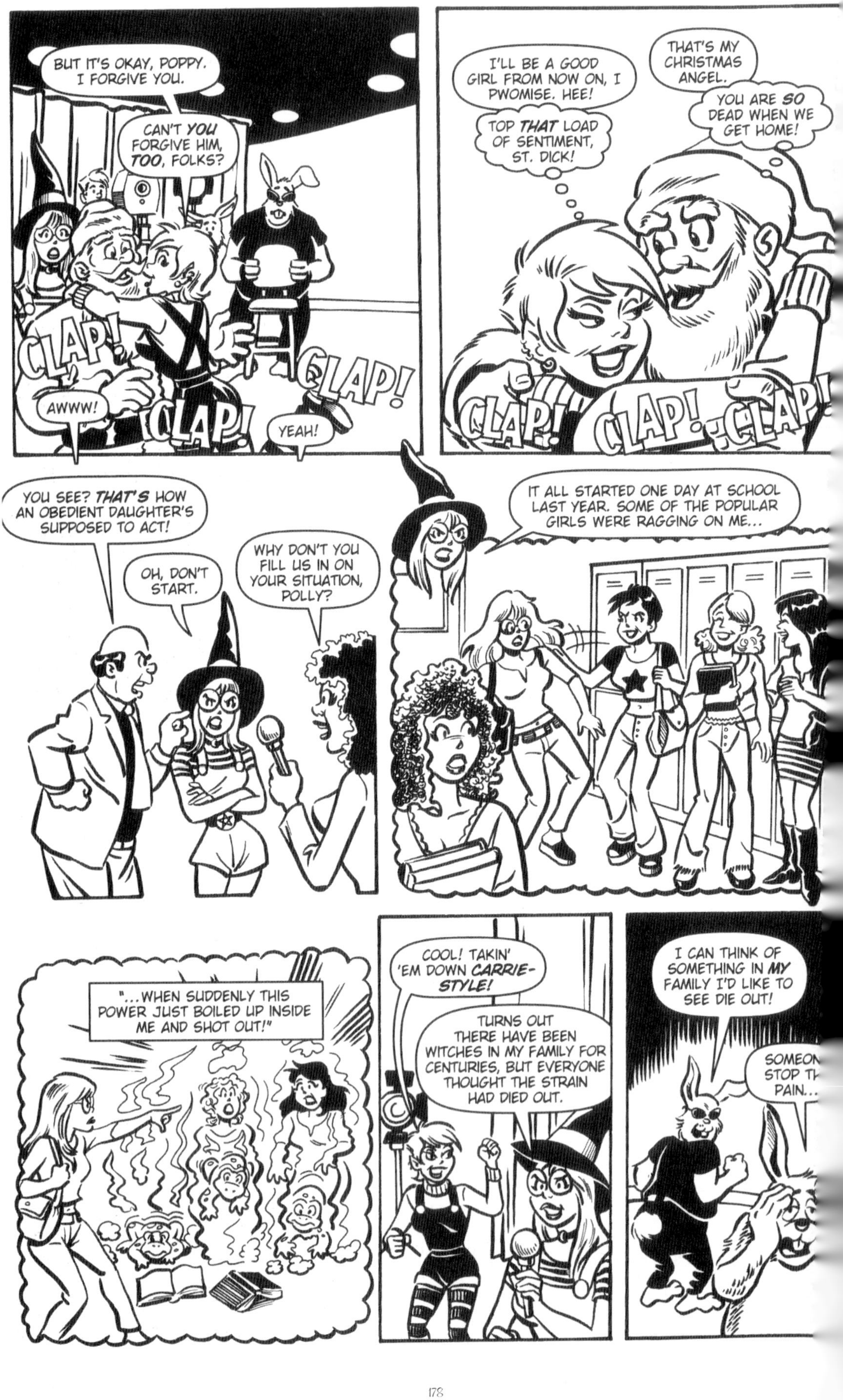
BUT IT'S OKAY, POPPY. I FORGIVE YOU.
CAN'T YOU FORGIVE HIM, TOO, FOLKS?
CLAP!
CLAP!
CLAP!
AWWW!
YEAH!
I'LL BE A GOOD GIRL FROM NOW ON, I PWOMISE. HEE!
TOP THAT LOAD OF SENTIMENT, ST. DICK!
THAT'S MY CHRISTMAS ANGEL.
YOU ARE SO DEAD WHEN WE GET HOME!
CLAP!
CLAP!
CLAP!
YOU SEE? THAT'S HOW AN OBEDIENT DAUGHTER'S SUPPOSED TO ACT!
OH, DON'T START.
WHY DON'T YOU FILL US IN ON YOUR SITUATION, POLLY?
IT ALL STARTED ONE DAY AT SCHOOL LAST YEAR. SOME OF THE POPULAR GIRLS WERE RAGGING ON ME...
"...WHEN SUDDENLY THIS POWER JUST BOILED UP INSIDE ME AND SHOT OUT!"
COOL! TAKIN' 'EM DOWN CARRIE-STYLE!
TURNS OUT THERE HAVE BEEN WITCHES IN MY FAMILY FOR CENTURIES, BUT EVERYONE THOUGHT THE STRAIN HAD DIED OUT.
I CAN THINK OF SOMETHING IN MY FAMILY I'D LIKE TO SEE DIE OUT!
SOMEON STOP TH PAIN...

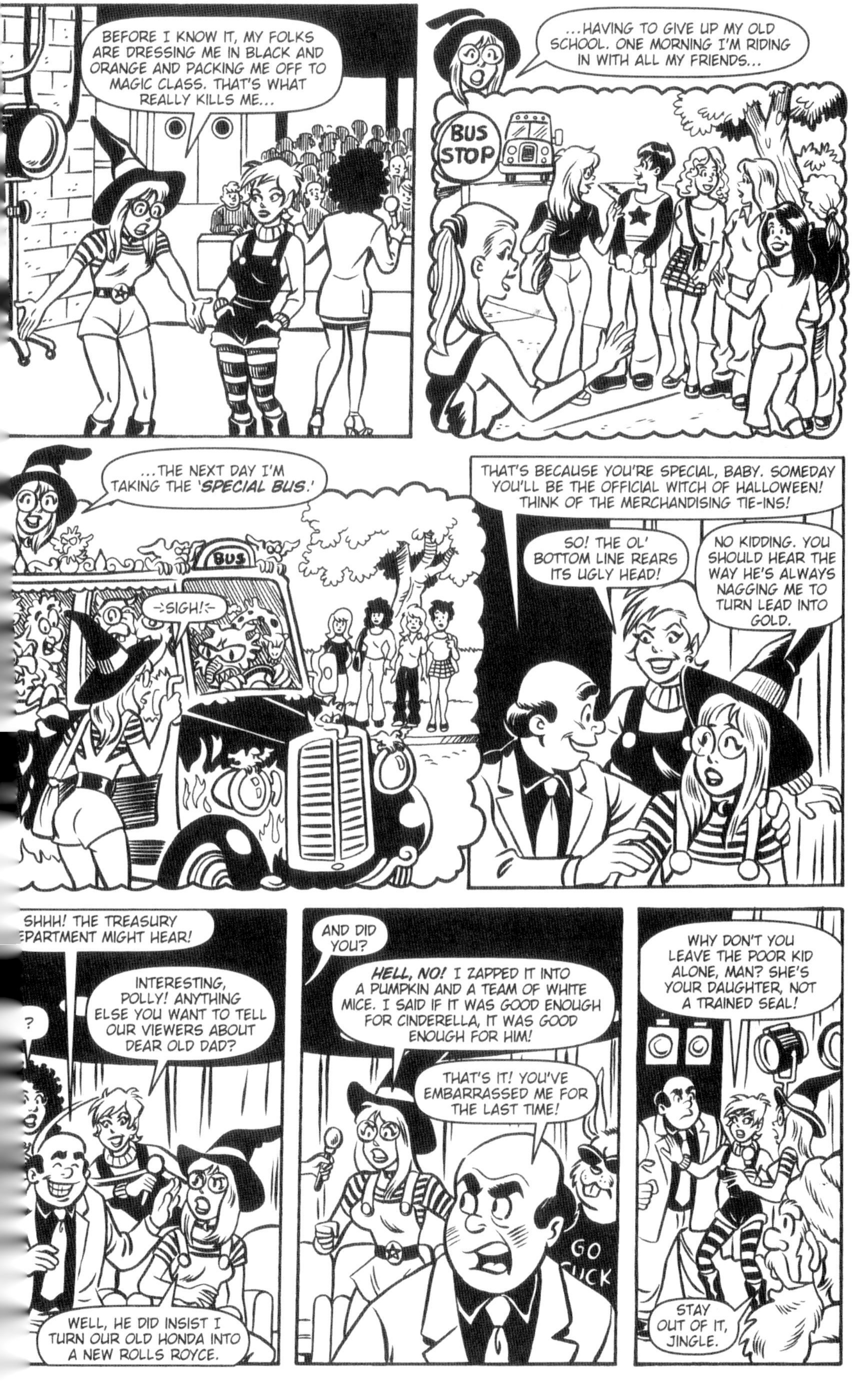
BEFORE I KNOW IT, MY FOLKS ARE DRESSING ME IN BLACK AND ORANGE AND PACKING ME OFF TO MAGIC CLASS. THAT'S WHAT REALLY KILLS ME...
...HAVING TO GIVE UP MY OLD SCHOOL. ONE MORNING I'M RIDING IN WITH ALL MY FRIENDS...
BUS STOP
...THE NEXT DAY I'M TAKING THE '*SPECIAL BUS*.'
BUS
-SIGH!-
THAT'S BECAUSE YOU'RE SPECIAL, BABY. SOMEDAY YOU'LL BE THE OFFICIAL WITCH OF HALLOWEEN! THINK OF THE MERCHANDISING TIE-INS!
SO! THE OL' BOTTOM LINE REARS ITS UGLY HEAD!
NO KIDDING. YOU SHOULD HEAR THE WAY HE'S ALWAYS NAGGING ME TO TURN LEAD INTO GOLD.
SHHH! THE TREASURY EPARTMENT MIGHT HEAR!
INTERESTING, POLLY! ANYTHING ELSE YOU WANT TO TELL OUR VIEWERS ABOUT DEAR OLD DAD?
?
WELL, HE DID INSIST I TURN OUR OLD HONDA INTO A NEW ROLLS ROYCE.
AND DID YOU?
HELL, NO! I ZAPPED IT INTO A PUMPKIN AND A TEAM OF WHITE MICE. I SAID IF IT WAS GOOD ENOUGH FOR CINDERELLA, IT WAS GOOD ENOUGH FOR HIM!
THAT'S IT! YOU'VE EMBARRASSED ME FOR THE LAST TIME!
GO
WHY DON'T YOU LEAVE THE POOR KID ALONE, MAN? SHE'S YOUR DAUGHTER, NOT A TRAINED SEAL!
STAY OUT OF IT, JINGLE.

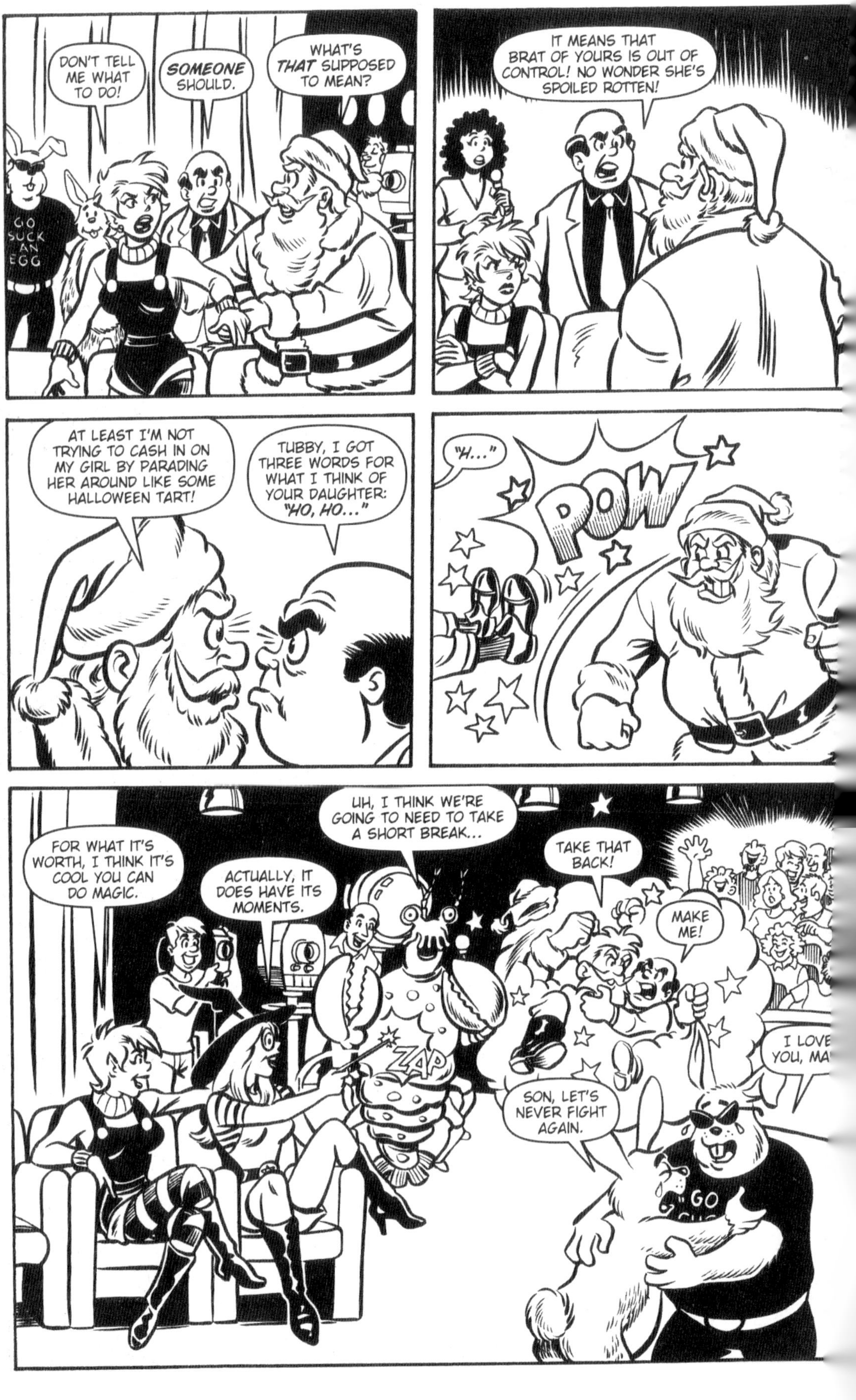
GO SUCK AN EGG
DON'T TELL ME WHAT TO DO!
SOMEONE SHOULD.
WHAT'S THAT SUPPOSED TO MEAN?
IT MEANS THAT BRAT OF YOURS IS OUT OF CONTROL! NO WONDER SHE'S SPOILED ROTTEN!
AT LEAST I'M NOT TRYING TO CASH IN ON MY GIRL BY PARADING HER AROUND LIKE SOME HALLOWEEN TART!
TUBBY, I GOT THREE WORDS FOR WHAT I THINK OF YOUR DAUGHTER: "HO, HO..."
"H..."
POW
FOR WHAT IT'S WORTH, I THINK IT'S COOL YOU CAN DO MAGIC.
ACTUALLY, IT DOES HAVE ITS MOMENTS.
UH, I THINK WE'RE GOING TO NEED TO TAKE A SHORT BREAK...
TAKE THAT BACK!
MAKE ME!
ZAP
I LOVE YOU, MA
SON, LET'S NEVER FIGHT AGAIN.
"GO

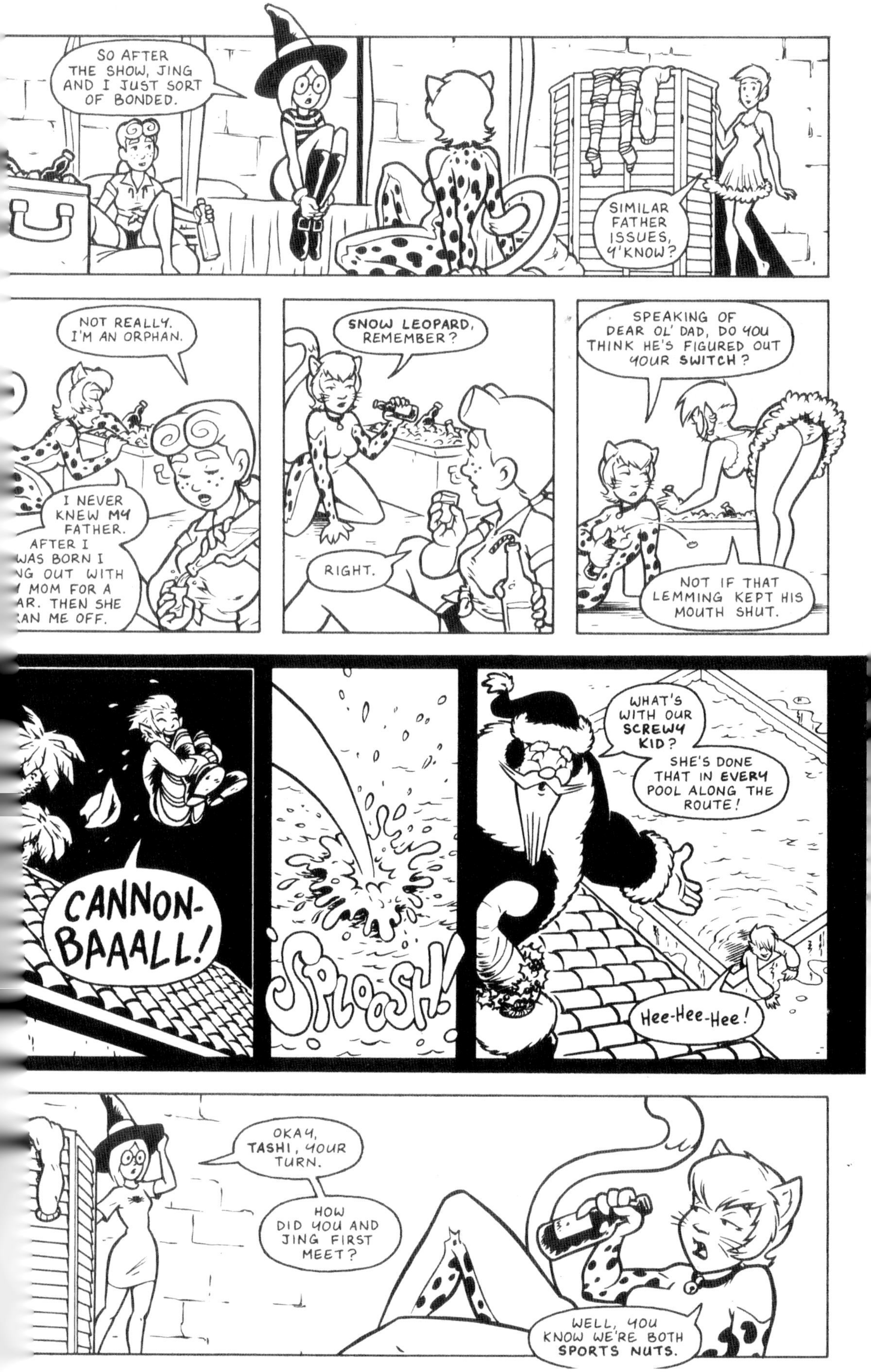

SO AFTER THE SHOW, JING AND I JUST SORT OF BONDED.
SIMILAR FATHER ISSUES, Y'KNOW?
NOT REALLY. I'M AN ORPHAN.
I NEVER KNEW MY FATHER.
AFTER I WAS BORN I NG OUT WITH MOM FOR A AR. THEN SHE AN ME OFF.
SNOW LEOPARD, REMEMBER?
RIGHT.
SPEAKING OF DEAR OL' DAD, DO YOU THINK HE'S FIGURED OUT YOUR SWITCH?
NOT IF THAT LEMMING KEPT HIS MOUTH SHUT.
CANNON-BAAALL!
SPLOOSH!
WHAT'S WITH OUR SCREWY KID?
SHE'S DONE THAT IN EVERY POOL ALONG THE ROUTE!
Hee-Hee-Hee!
OKAY, TASHI, YOUR TURN.
HOW DID YOU AND JING FIRST MEET?
WELL, YOU KNOW WE'RE BOTH SPORTS NUTS.

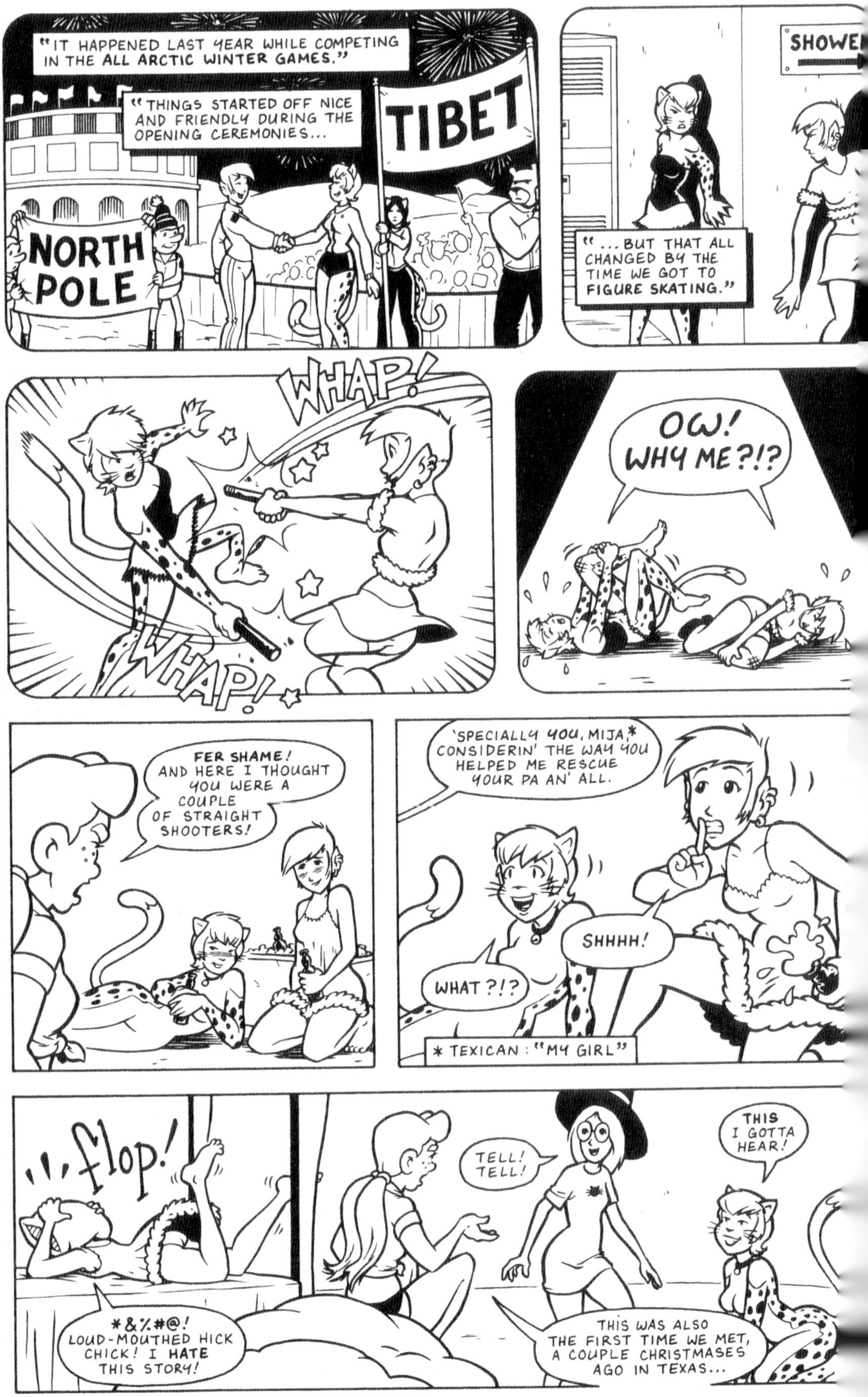
"IT HAPPENED LAST YEAR WHILE COMPETING IN THE ALL ARCTIC WINTER GAMES."
"THINGS STARTED OFF NICE AND FRIENDLY DURING THE OPENING CEREMONIES...
TIBET
NORTH POLE
SHOWE
"...BUT THAT ALL CHANGED BY THE TIME WE GOT TO FIGURE SKATING."
WHAP!
WHAP!
OW! WHY ME?!?
FER SHAME! AND HERE I THOUGHT YOU WERE A COUPLE OF STRAIGHT SHOOTERS!
'SPECIALLY YOU, MIJA,* CONSIDERIN' THE WAY YOU HELPED ME RESCUE YOUR PA AN' ALL.
SHHHH!
WHAT?!?
* TEXICAN: "MY GIRL"
flop!
TELL! TELL!
THIS I GOTTA HEAR!
*&%#@! LOUD-MOUTHED HICK CHICK! I HATE THIS STORY!
THIS WAS ALSO THE FIRST TIME WE MET, A COUPLE CHRISTMASES AGO IN TEXAS...

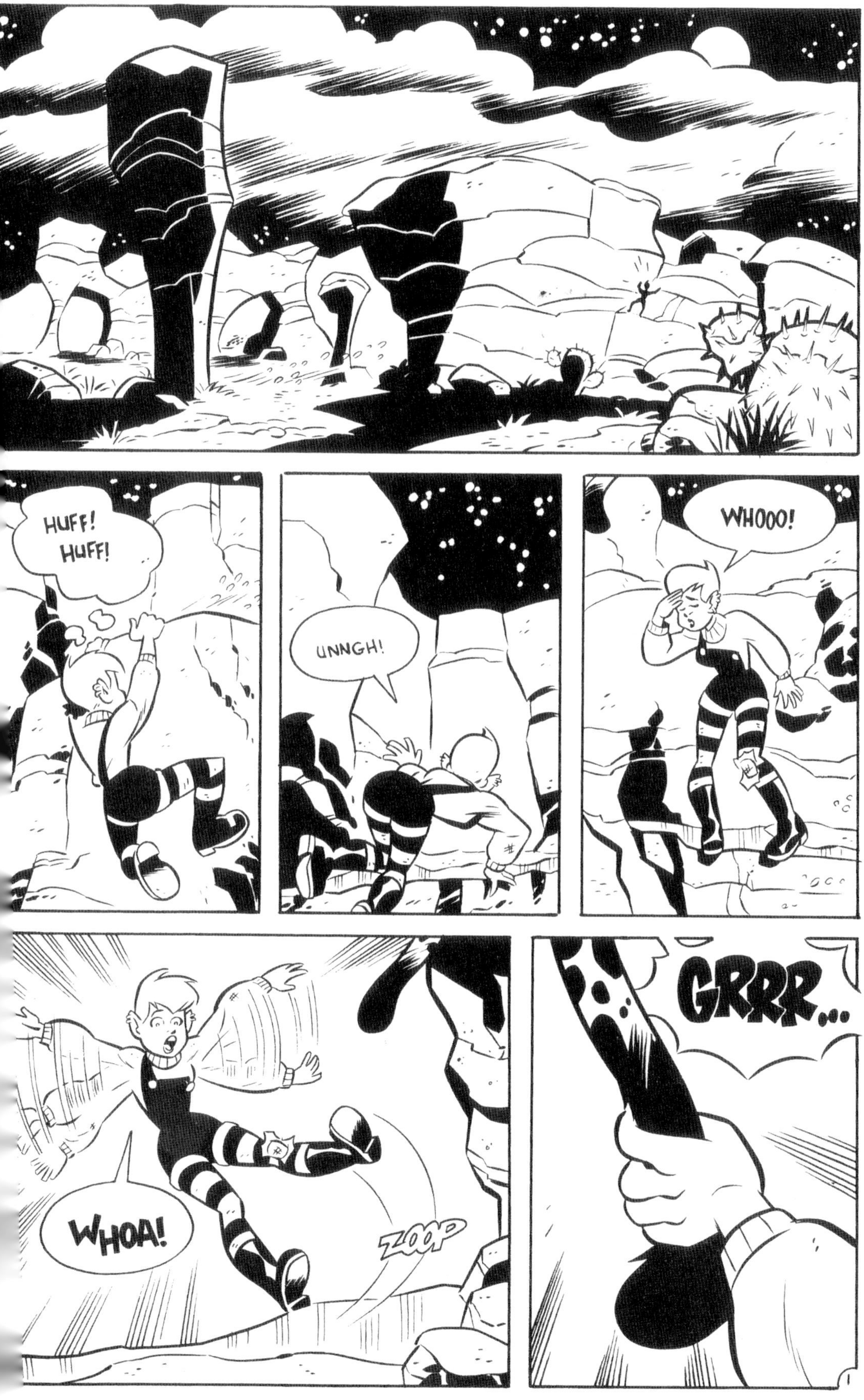
HUFF! HUFF!
UNNGH!
WHOOO!
WHOA!
ZOOP
GRRR...

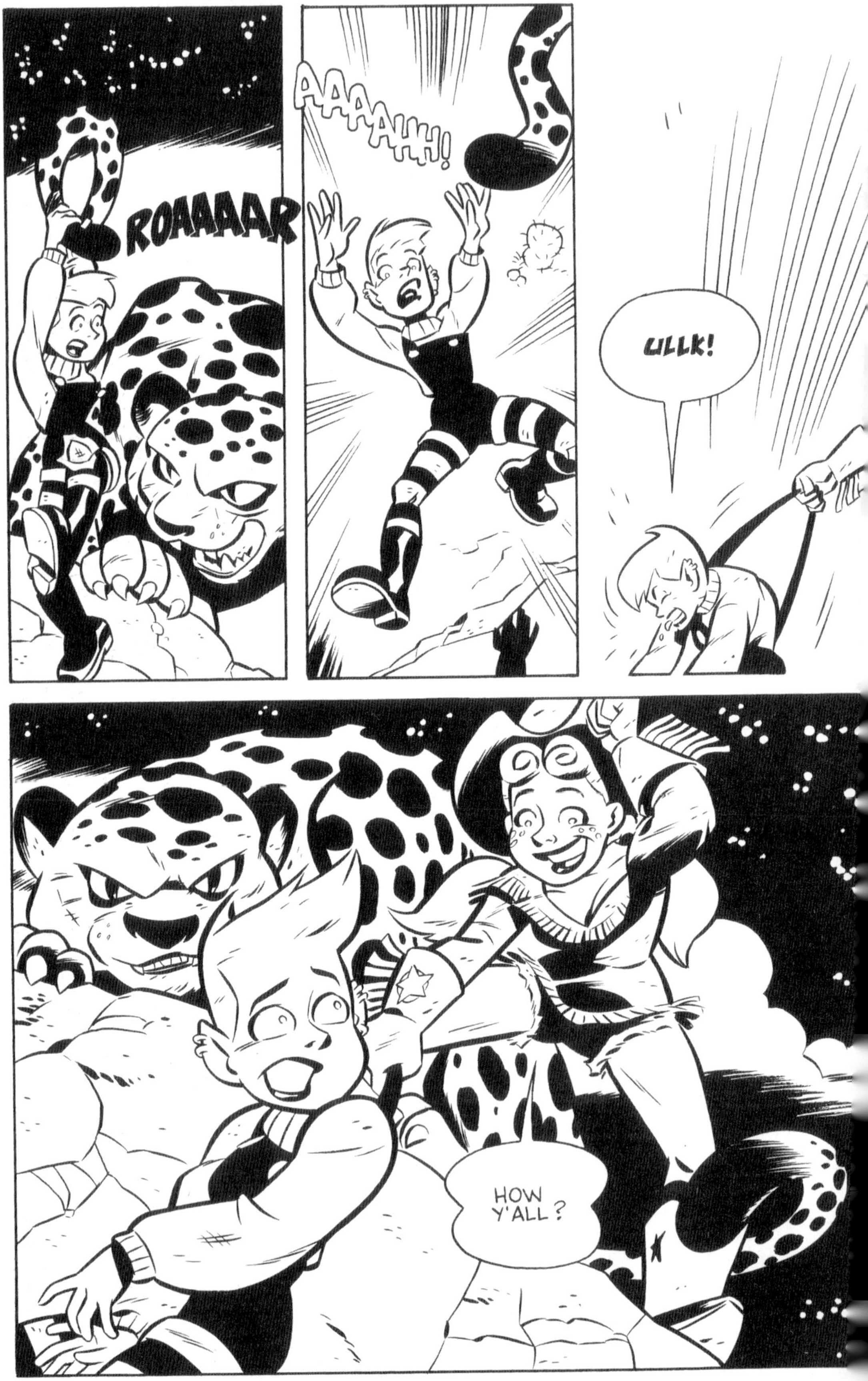
ROAAAAR
AAAAAHH!
ULLK!
HOW Y'ALL?

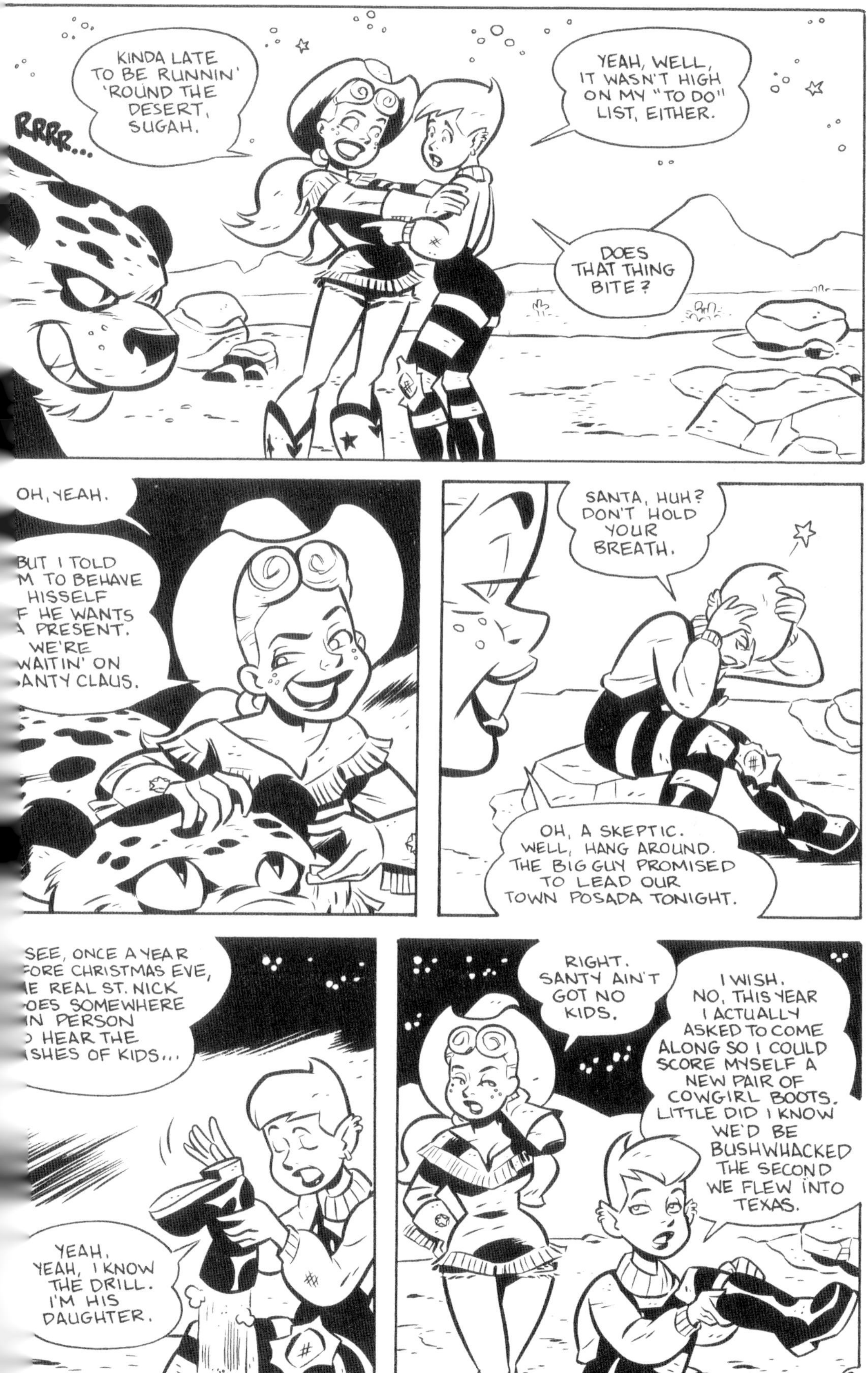
KINDA LATE TO BE RUNNIN' 'ROUND THE DESERT, SUGAH.
RRRR...
YEAH, WELL, IT WASN'T HIGH ON MY "TO DO" LIST, EITHER.
DOES THAT THING BITE?
OH, YEAH.
BUT I TOLD M TO BEHAVE HISSELF F HE WANTS A PRESENT. WE'RE WAITIN' ON ANTY CLAUS.
SANTA, HUH? DON'T HOLD YOUR BREATH.
OH, A SKEPTIC. WELL, HANG AROUND. THE BIG GUY PROMISED TO LEAD OUR TOWN POSADA TONIGHT.
SEE, ONCE A YEAR FORE CHRISTMAS EVE, E REAL ST. NICK OES SOMEWHERE IN PERSON O HEAR THE SHES OF KIDS...
YEAH, YEAH, I KNOW THE DRILL. I'M HIS DAUGHTER.
RIGHT. SANTY AIN'T GOT NO KIDS.
I WISH. NO, THIS YEAR I ACTUALLY ASKED TO COME ALONG SO I COULD SCORE MYSELF A NEW PAIR OF COWGIRL BOOTS. LITTLE DID I KNOW WE'D BE BUSHWHACKED THE SECOND WE FLEW INTO TEXAS.
3

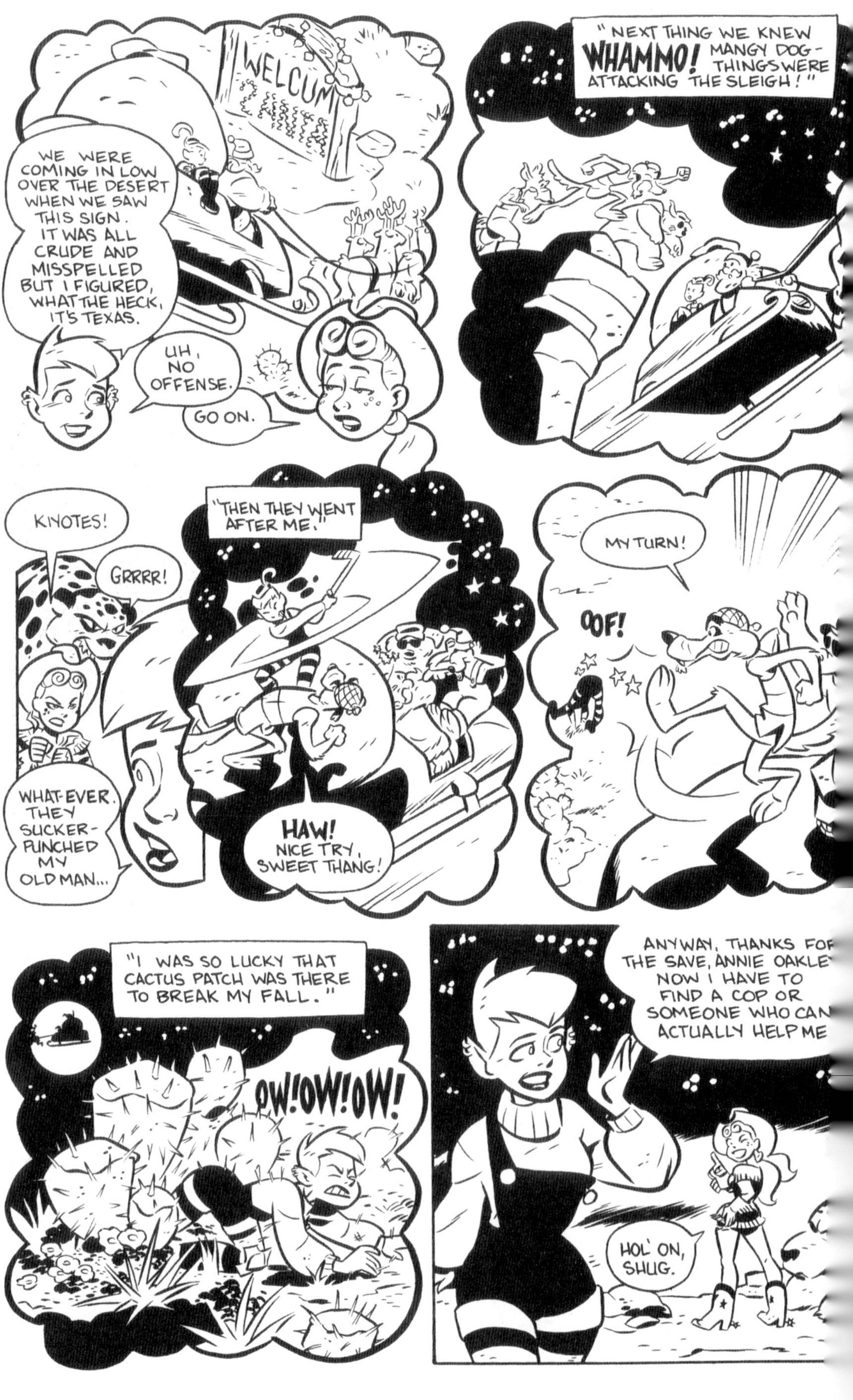
WE WERE COMING IN LOW OVER THE DESERT WHEN WE SAW THIS SIGN. IT WAS ALL CRUDE AND MISSPELLED BUT I FIGURED, WHAT THE HECK, IT'S TEXAS.
WELCUM
UH, NO OFFENSE.
GO ON.
"NEXT THING WE KNEW WHAMMO! MANGY DOG-THINGS WERE ATTACKING THE SLEIGH!"
KIYOTES!
GRRRR!
WHAT-EVER. THEY SUCKER-PUNCHED MY OLD MAN...
"THEN THEY WENT AFTER ME."
HAW! NICE TRY, SWEET THANG!
MY TURN!
OOF!
"I WAS SO LUCKY THAT CACTUS PATCH WAS THERE TO BREAK MY FALL."
OW!OW!OW!
ANYWAY, THANKS FO
THE SAVE, ANNIE OAKLE
NOW I HAVE TO
FIND A COP OR
SOMEONE WHO CAN
ACTUALLY HELP ME
HOL' ON, SHUG.

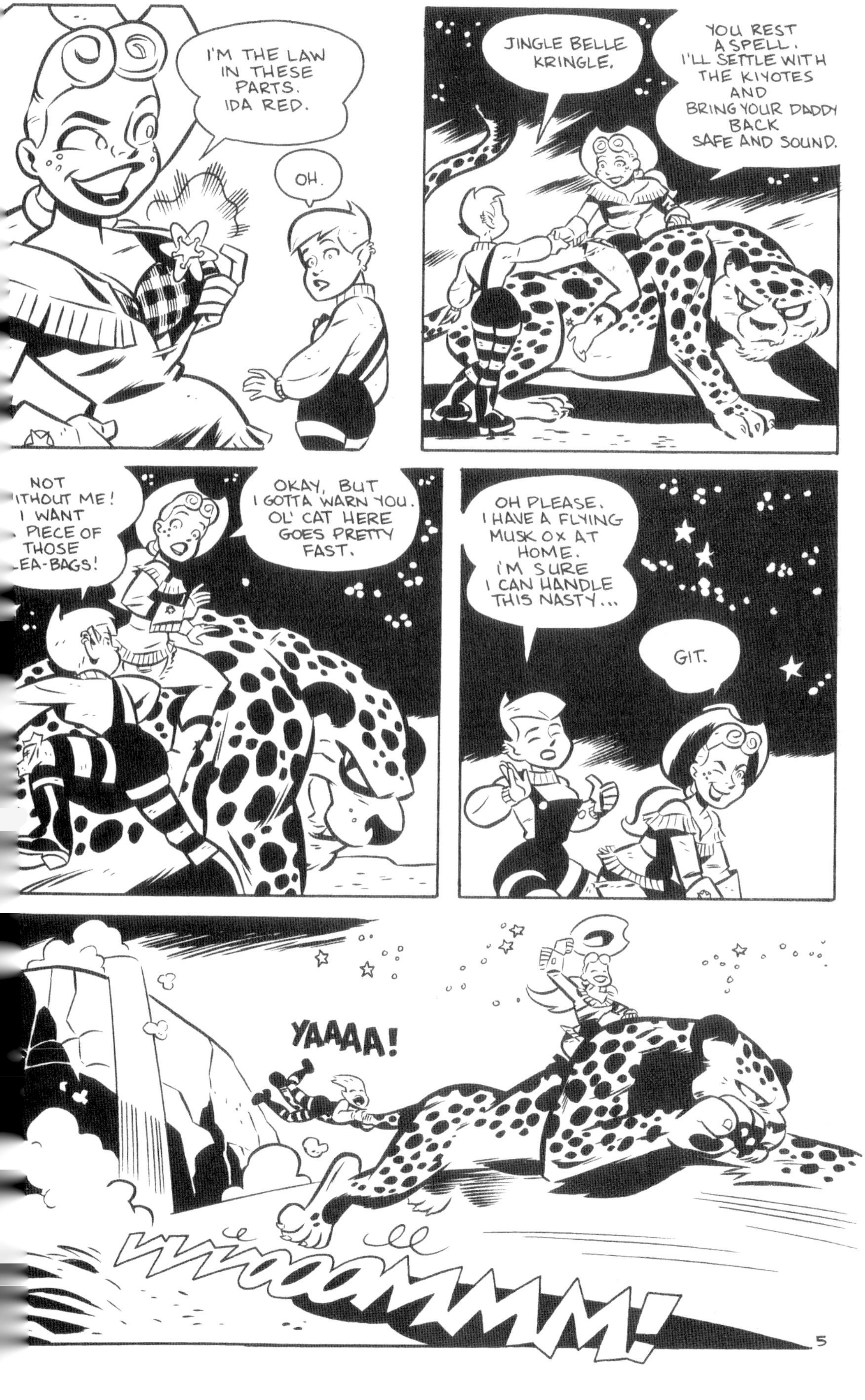
I'M THE LAW IN THESE PARTS. IDA RED.
OH.
JINGLE BELLE KRINGLE.
YOU REST A SPELL. I'LL SETTLE WITH THE KIYOTES AND BRING YOUR DADDY BACK SAFE AND SOUND.
NOT ITHOUT ME! I WANT PIECE OF THOSE LEA-BAGS!
OKAY, BUT I GOTTA WARN YOU. OL' CAT HERE GOES PRETTY FAST.
OH PLEASE. I HAVE A FLYING MUSK OX AT HOME. I'M SURE I CAN HANDLE THIS NASTY...
GIT.
YAAAA!
WHOOMMM!
5

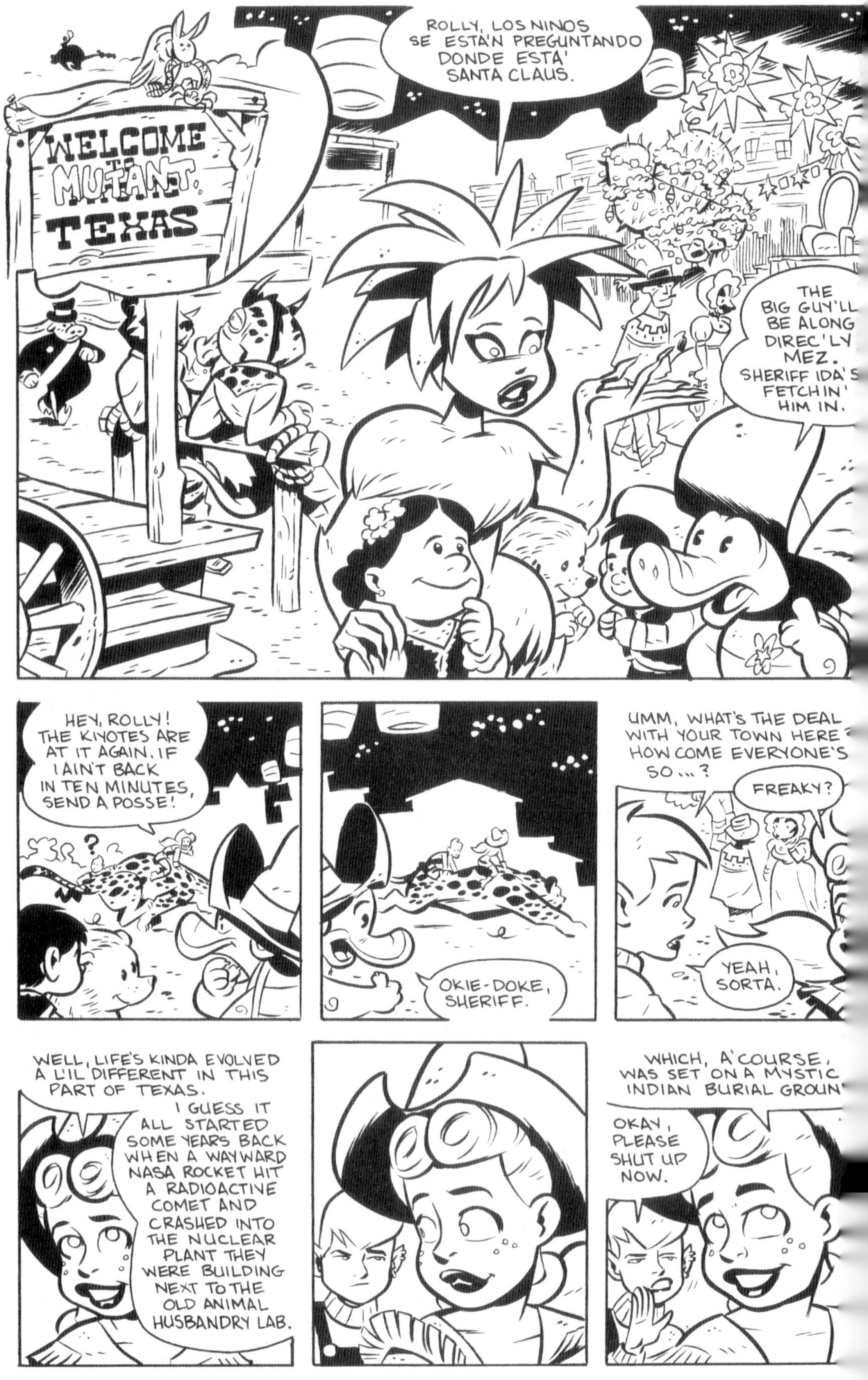
WELCOME TO MUTANT, TEXAS
ROLLY, LOS NINOS SE ESTA'N PREGUNTANDO DONDE ESTA' SANTA CLAUS.
THE BIG GUY'LL BE ALONG DIREC'LY MEZ. SHERIFF IDA'S FETCHIN' HIM IN.
HEY, ROLLY! THE KIYOTES ARE AT IT AGAIN. IF I AIN'T BACK IN TEN MINUTES, SEND A POSSE!
OKIE-DOKE, SHERIFF.
UMM, WHAT'S THE DEAL WITH YOUR TOWN HERE? HOW COME EVERYONE'S SO...?
FREAKY?
YEAH, SORTA.
WELL, LIFE'S KINDA EVOLVED A L'IL DIFFERENT IN THIS PART OF TEXAS.
I GUESS IT ALL STARTED SOME YEARS BACK WHEN A WAYWARD NASA ROCKET HIT A RADIOACTIVE COMET AND CRASHED INTO THE NUCLEAR PLANT THEY WERE BUILDING NEXT TO THE OLD ANIMAL HUSBANDRY LAB.
WHICH, A'COURSE, WAS SET ON A MYSTIC INDIAN BURIAL GROUN
OKAY, PLEASE SHUT UP NOW.

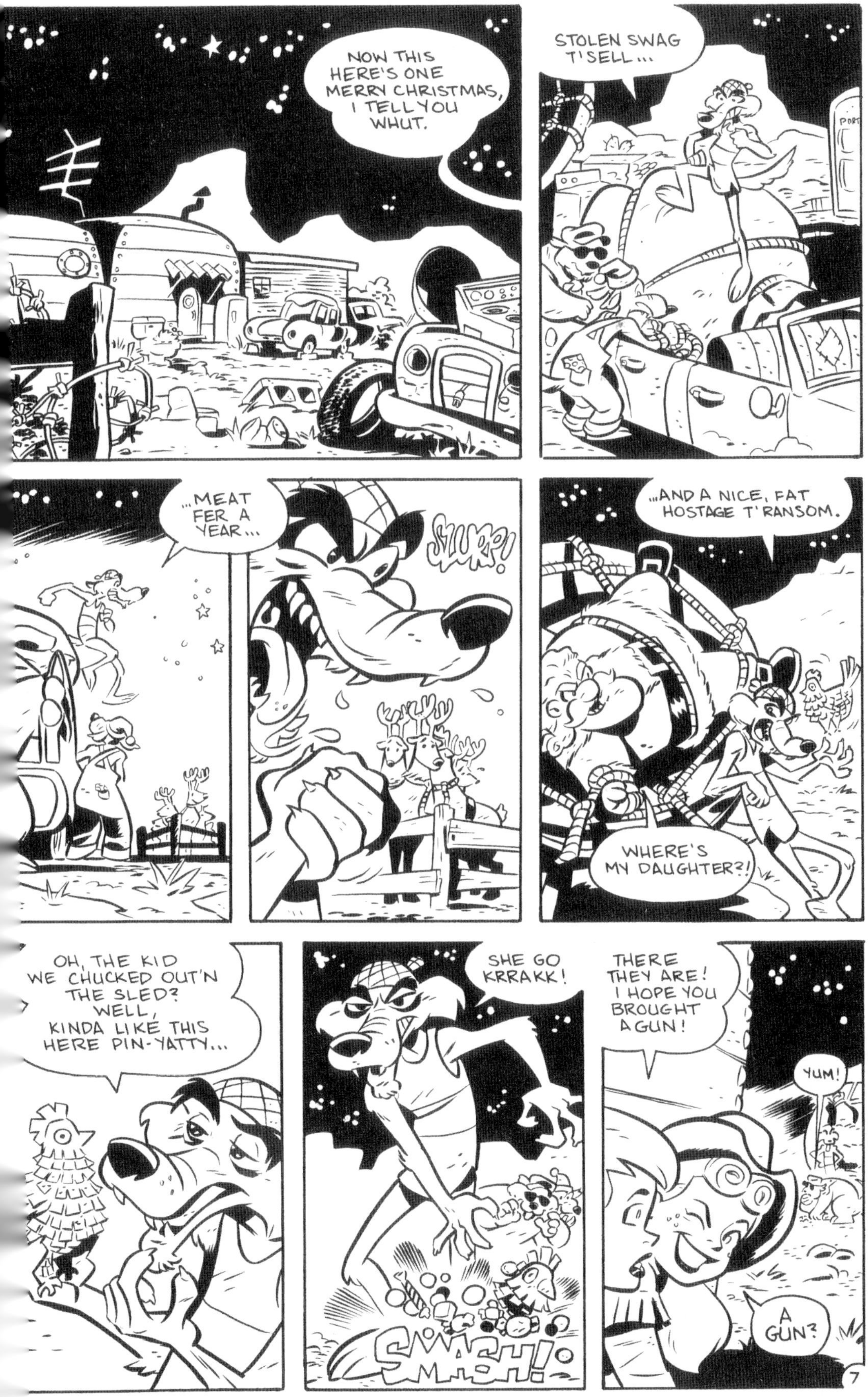
NOW THIS HERE'S ONE MERRY CHRISTMAS, I TELL YOU WHUT.
STOLEN SWAG T'SELL...
...MEAT FER A YEAR...
SLURP!
...AND A NICE, FAT HOSTAGE T'RANSOM.
WHERE'S MY DAUGHTER?!
OH, THE KID WE CHUCKED OUT'N THE SLED? WELL, KINDA LIKE THIS HERE PIN-YATTY...
SHE GO KRRAKK!
SMASH!
THERE THEY ARE! I HOPE YOU BROUGHT A GUN!
YUM!
A GUN?
7

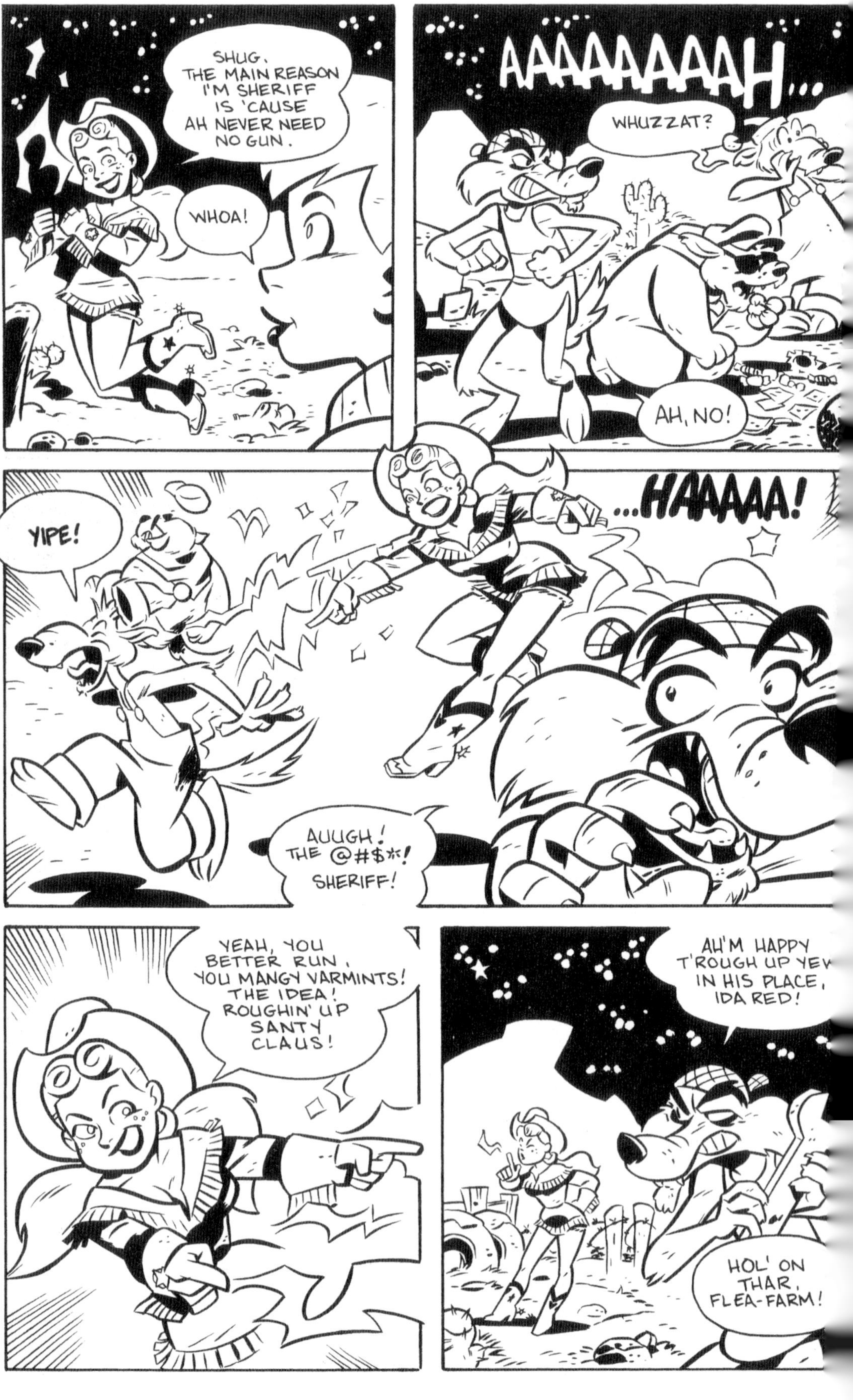
SHUG. THE MAIN REASON I'M SHERIFF IS 'CAUSE AH NEVER NEED NO GUN.
WHOA!
AAAAAAAAAH...
WHUZZAT?
AH, NO!
...HAAAAA!
YIPE!
AUUGH! THE @#$*! SHERIFF!
YEAH, YOU BETTER RUN, YOU MANGY VARMINTS! THE IDEA! ROUGHIN' UP SANTY CLAUS!
AH'M HAPPY T'ROUGH UP YEW IN HIS PLACE, IDA RED!
HOL' ON THAR, FLEA-FARM!

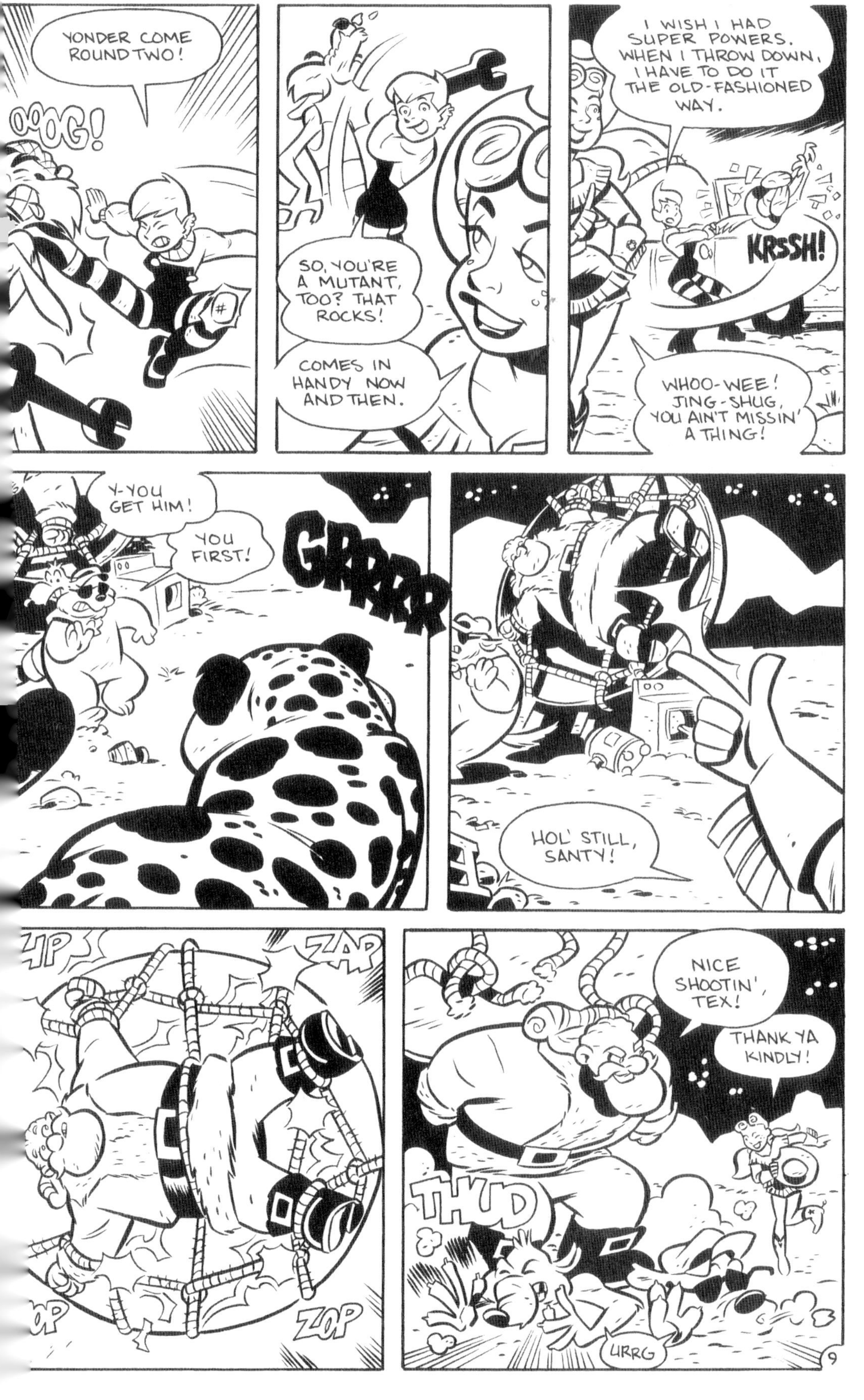
YONDER COME ROUND TWO!
OOOG!
SO, YOU'RE A MUTANT, TOO? THAT ROCKS!
COMES IN HANDY NOW AND THEN.
I WISH I HAD SUPER POWERS. WHEN I THROW DOWN, I HAVE TO DO IT THE OLD-FASHIONED WAY.
KRSSH!
WHOO-WEE! JING-SHUG, YOU AIN'T MISSIN' A THING!
Y-YOU GET HIM!
YOU FIRST!
GRRRRR
HOL' STILL, SANTY!
ZAP
ZOP
NICE SHOOTIN', TEX!
THANK YA KINDLY!
THUD
URRG
9

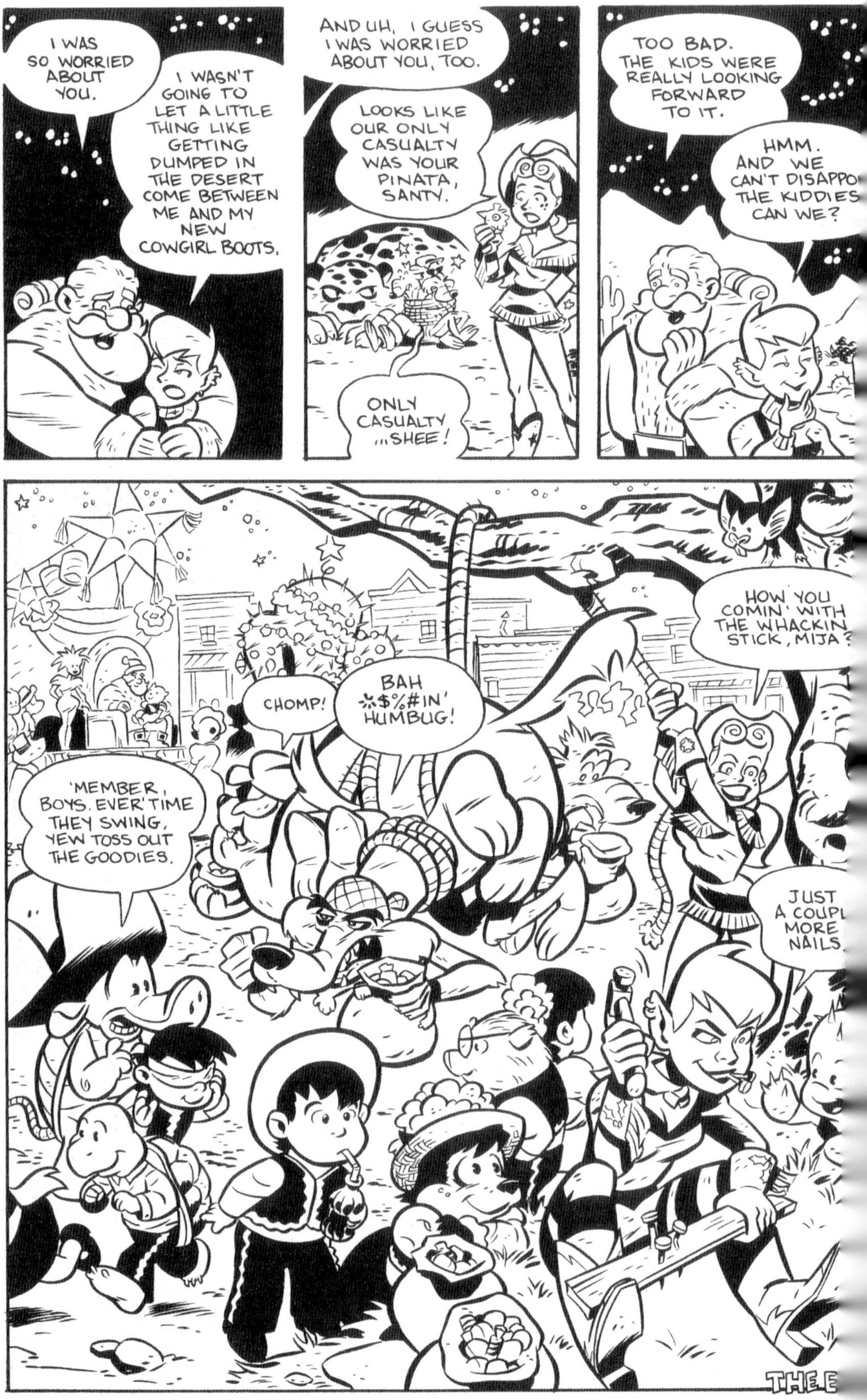
I WAS SO WORRIED ABOUT YOU.
I WASN'T GOING TO LET A LITTLE THING LIKE GETTING DUMPED IN THE DESERT COME BETWEEN ME AND MY NEW COWGIRL BOOTS.
AND UH, I GUESS I WAS WORRIED ABOUT YOU, TOO.
LOOKS LIKE OUR ONLY CASUALTY WAS YOUR PINATA, SANTY.
ONLY CASUALTY ...SHEE!
TOO BAD. THE KIDS WERE REALLY LOOKING FORWARD TO IT.
HMM. AND WE CAN'T DISAPPO THE KIDDIES CAN WE?
CHOMP!
BAH ※$%#IN' HUMBUG!
HOW YOU COMIN' WITH THE WHACKIN STICK, MIJA?
'MEMBER, BOYS. EVER'TIME THEY SWING, YEW TOSS OUT THE GOODIES.
JUST A COUPL MORE NAILS.
THE E

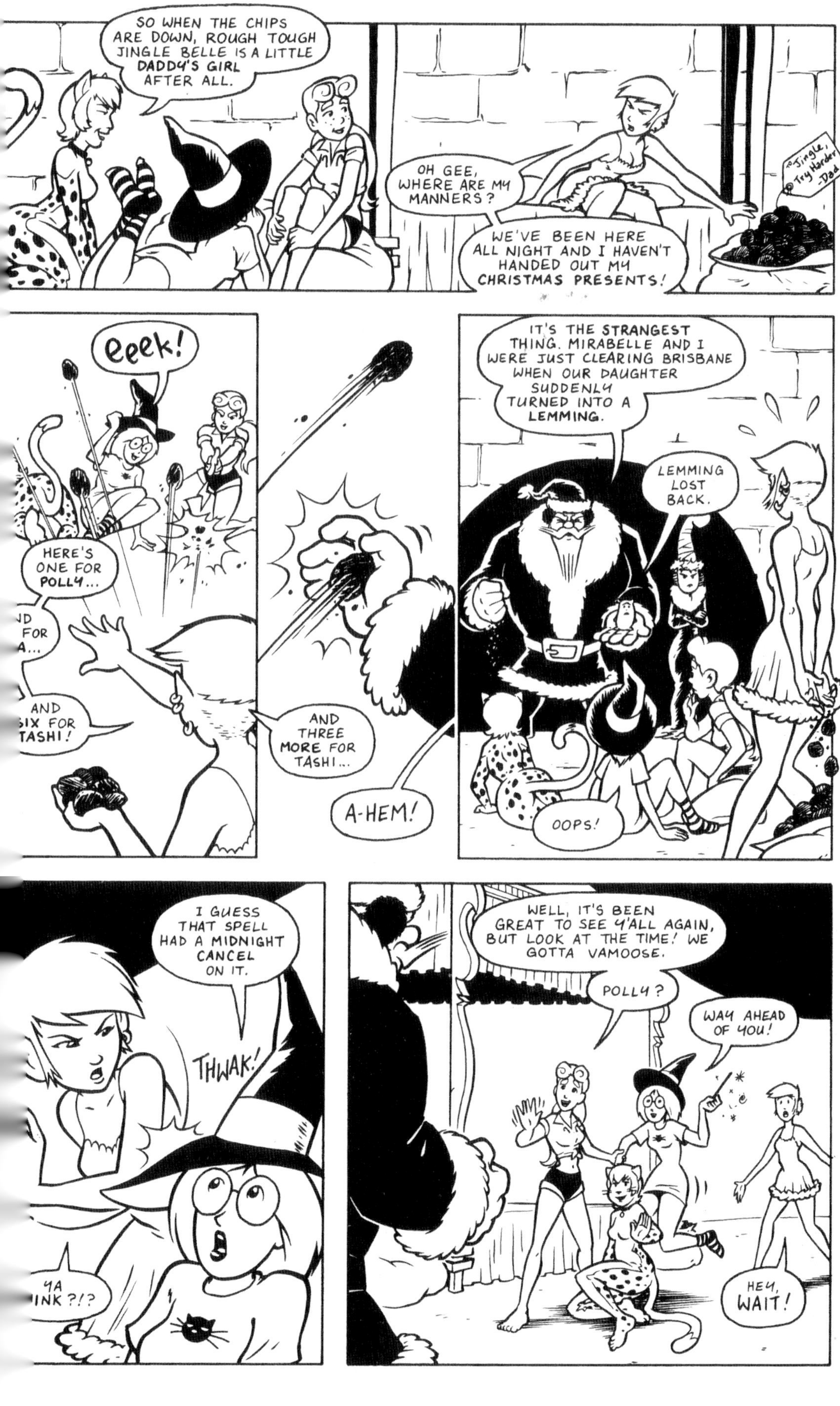
SO WHEN THE CHIPS ARE DOWN, ROUGH TOUGH JINGLE BELLE IS A LITTLE DADDY'S GIRL AFTER ALL.
OH GEE, WHERE ARE MY MANNERS?
WE'VE BEEN HERE ALL NIGHT AND I HAVEN'T HANDED OUT MY CHRISTMAS PRESENTS!
Jingle, Try Harder -Dad.
eeek!
HERE'S ONE FOR POLLY...
AND SIX FOR TASHI!
AND THREE MORE FOR TASHI...
A-HEM!
IT'S THE STRANGEST THING. MIRABELLE AND I WERE JUST CLEARING BRISBANE WHEN OUR DAUGHTER SUDDENLY TURNED INTO A LEMMING.
LEMMING LOST BACK.
OOPS!
I GUESS THAT SPELL HAD A MIDNIGHT CANCEL ON IT.
THWAK!
WELL, IT'S BEEN GREAT TO SEE Y'ALL AGAIN, BUT LOOK AT THE TIME! WE GOTTA VAMOOSE.
POLLY?
WAY AHEAD OF YOU!
HEY, WAIT!

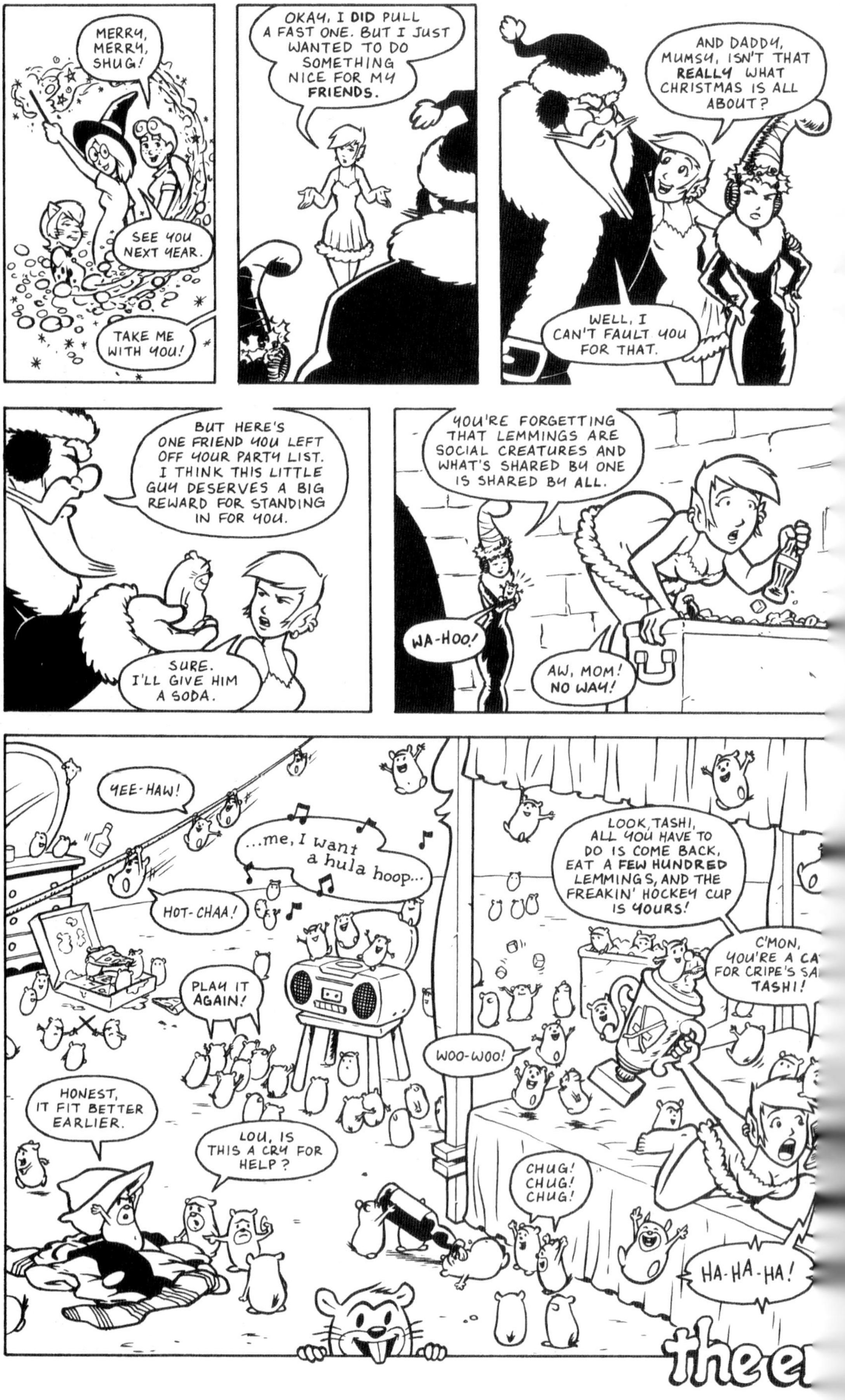
MERRY, MERRY, SHUG!
SEE YOU NEXT YEAR.
TAKE ME WITH YOU!
OKAY, I DID PULL A FAST ONE. BUT I JUST WANTED TO DO SOMETHING NICE FOR MY FRIENDS.
AND DADDY, MUMSY, ISN'T THAT REALLY WHAT CHRISTMAS IS ALL ABOUT?
WELL, I CAN'T FAULT YOU FOR THAT.
BUT HERE'S ONE FRIEND YOU LEFT OFF YOUR PARTY LIST. I THINK THIS LITTLE GUY DESERVES A BIG REWARD FOR STANDING IN FOR YOU.
SURE. I'LL GIVE HIM A SODA.
YOU'RE FORGETTING THAT LEMMINGS ARE SOCIAL CREATURES AND WHAT'S SHARED BY ONE IS SHARED BY ALL.
WA-HOO!
AW, MOM! NO WAY!
YEE-HAW!
...me, I want a hula hoop...
HOT-CHAA!
PLAY IT AGAIN!
LOOK, TASHI, ALL YOU HAVE TO DO IS COME BACK, EAT A FEW HUNDRED LEMMINGS, AND THE FREAKIN' HOCKEY CUP IS YOURS!
WOO-WOO!
HONEST, IT FIT BETTER EARLIER.
LOU, IS THIS A CRY FOR HELP?
CHUG! CHUG! CHUG!
HA-HA-HA!

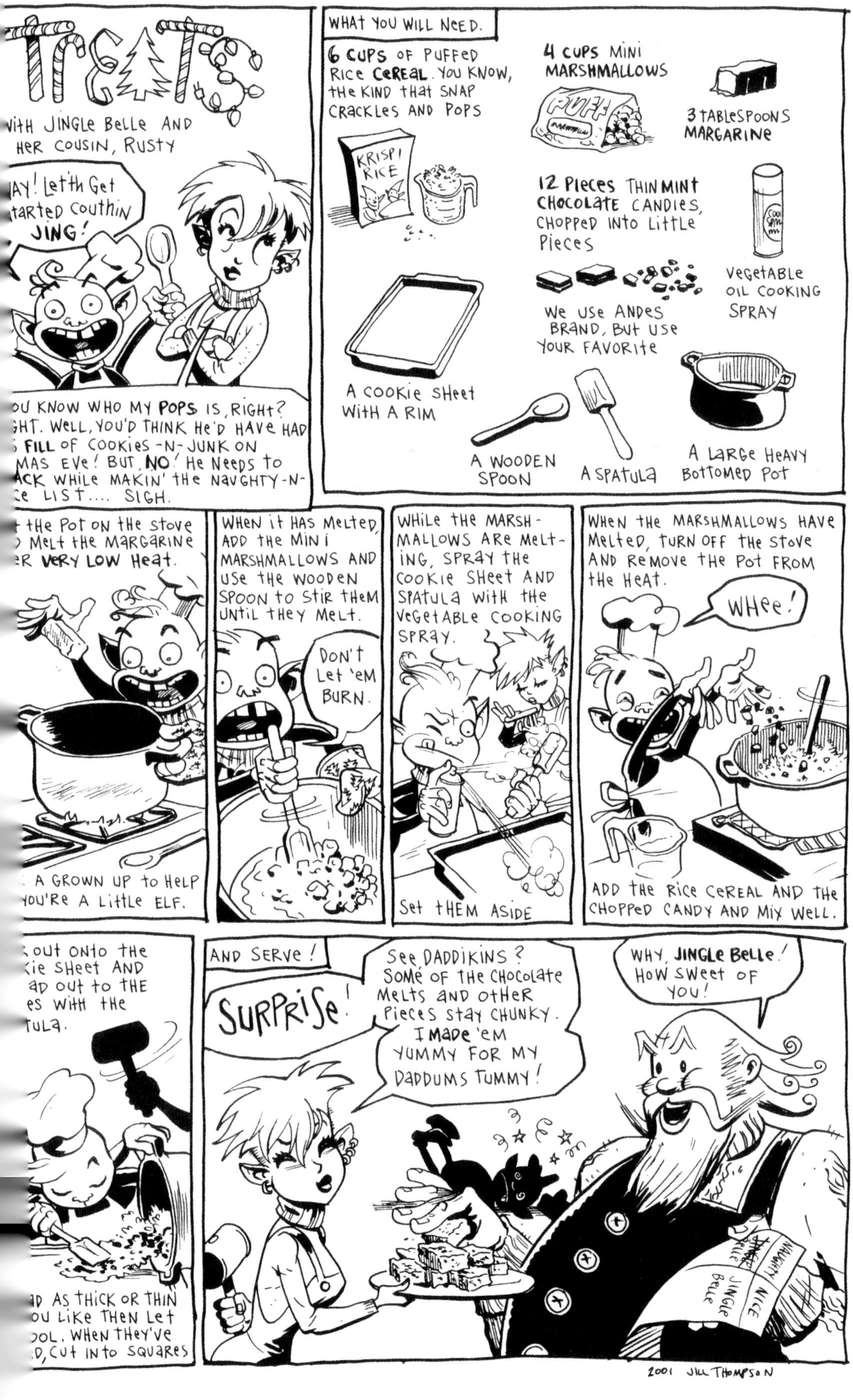

TREATS
with JINGLE BELLE AND HER COUSIN, RUSTY
AY! Let'th Get tarted Couthin JING!
OU KNOW WHO MY POPS IS, RIGHT? GHT. WELL, YOU'D THINK HE'D HAVE HAD FILL OF COOKIES-N-JUNK ON MAS EVE! BUT, NO! He Needs to ACK WHILE MAKIN' THE NAUGHTY-N-CE LIST.... SIGH.
WHAT YOU WILL NEED.
6 CUPS OF PUFFED RICE CEREAL. YOU KNOW, THE KIND THAT SNAP CRACKLES AND POPS
KRISPI RICE
4 CUPS MINI MARSHMALLOWS
PUFF
3 TABLESPOONS MARGARINE
12 PIECES THIN MINT CHOCOLATE CANDIES, CHOPPED INTO LITTLE PIECES
WE USE ANDES BRAND, BUT USE YOUR FAVORITE
VEGETABLE OIL COOKING SPRAY
A COOKIE SHEET WITH A RIM
A WOODEN SPOON
A SPATULA
A LARGE HEAVY BOTTOMED POT
t THE POT ON THE STOVE MELT THE MARGARINE ER VERY LOW HEAT.
A GROWN UP TO HELP YOU'RE A LITTLE ELF.
WHEN IT HAS MELTED, ADD THE MINI MARSHMALLOWS AND USE THE WOODEN SPOON TO STIR THEM UNTIL THEY MELT.
DON'T LET 'EM BURN.
WHILE THE MARSHMALLOWS ARE MELTING, SPRAY THE COOKIE SHEET AND SPATULA WITH THE VEGETABLE COOKING SPRAY.
SET THEM ASIDE
WHEN THE MARSHMALLOWS HAVE MELTED, TURN OFF THE STOVE AND REMOVE THE POT FROM THE HEAT.
WHEE!
ADD THE RICE CEREAL AND THE CHOPPED CANDY AND MIX WELL.
OUT ONTO THE KIE SHEET AND AD OUT TO THE ES WITH THE TULA.
D AS THICK OR THIN OU LIKE THEN LET OOL. WHEN THEY'VE D, CUT INTO SQUARES
AND SERVE!
SURPRISE!
SEE DADDIKINS? SOME OF THE CHOCOLATE MELTS AND OTHER PIECES STAY CHUNKY. I MADE 'EM YUMMY FOR MY DADDUMS TUMMY!
WHY, JINGLE BELLE! HOW SWEET OF YOU!
NAUGHTY NICE JINGLE BELLE
2001 JILL THOMPSON

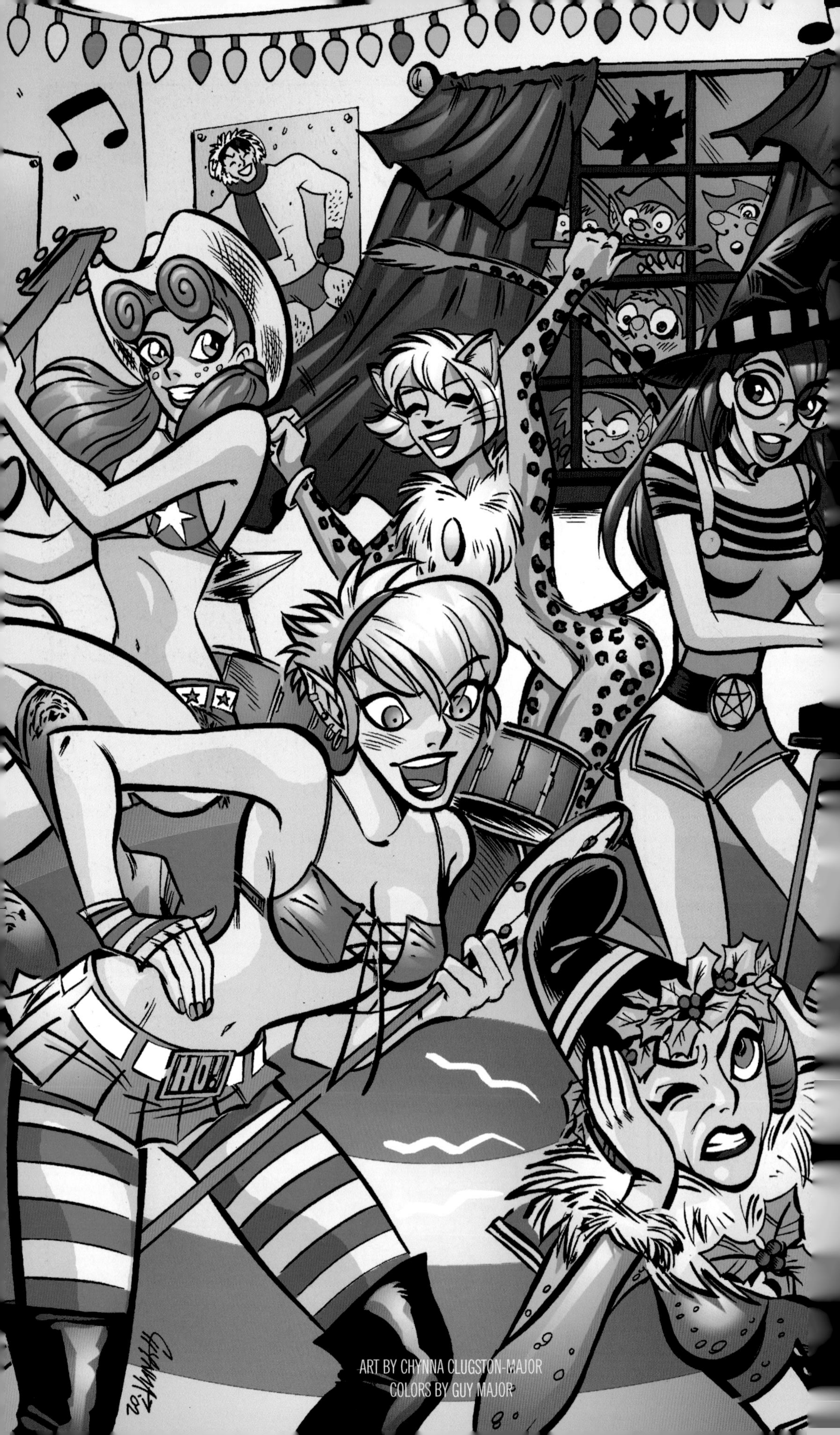
HO!

ART BY CHYNNA CLUGSTON-MAJOR
COLORS BY GUY MAJOR

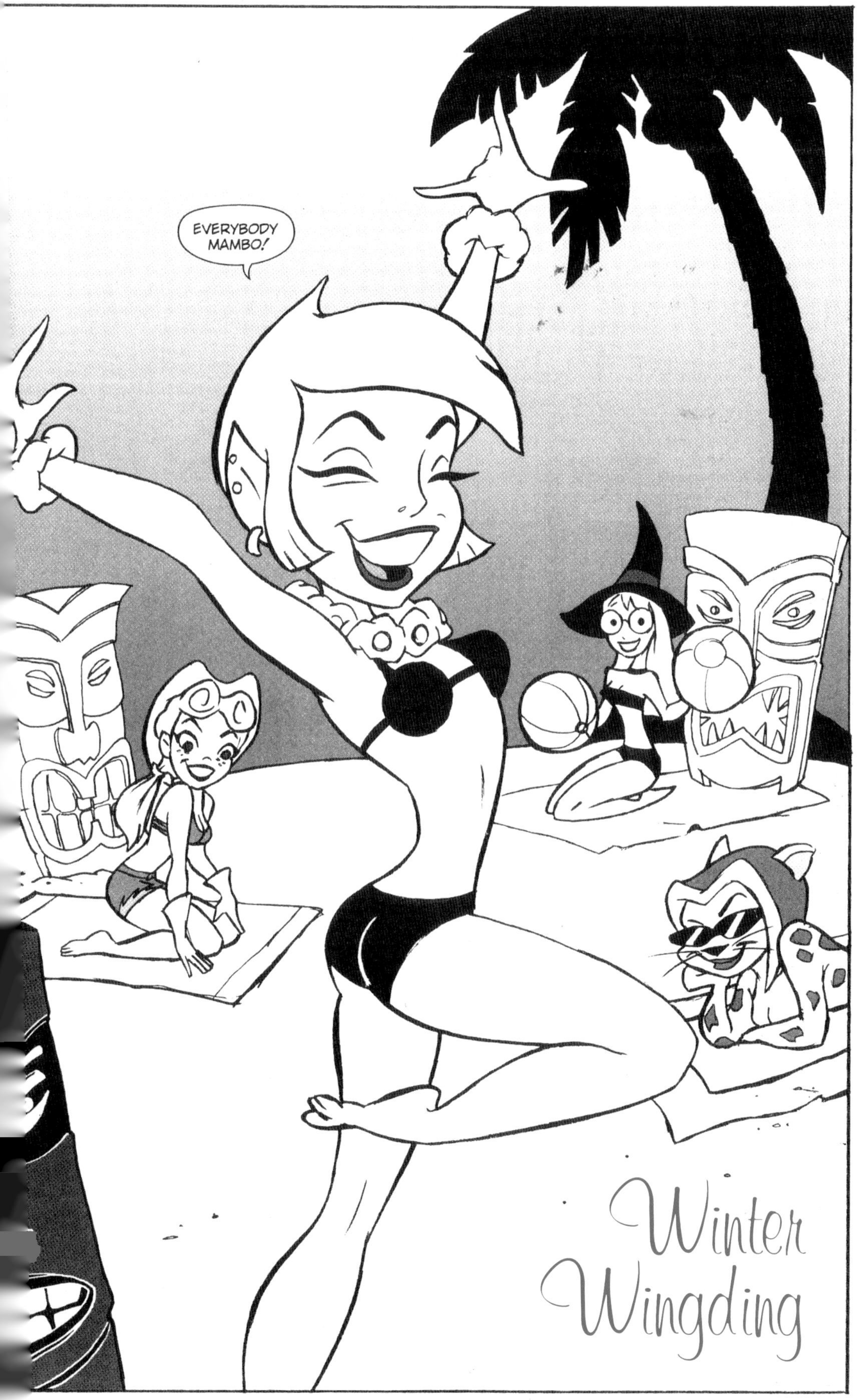
EVERYBODY MAMBO!
Winter Wingding

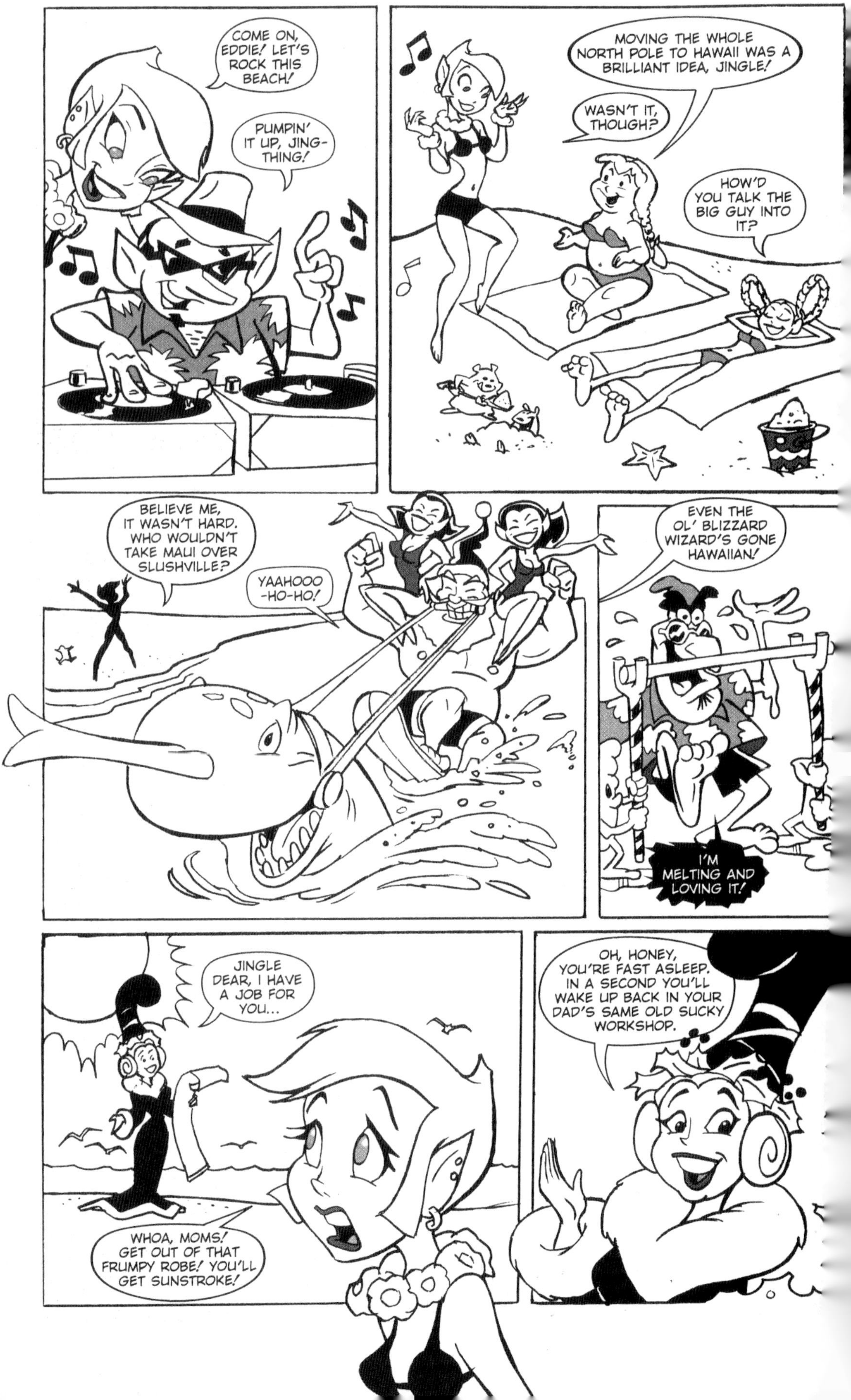
COME ON, EDDIE! LET'S ROCK THIS BEACH!
PUMPIN' IT UP, JING-THING!
MOVING THE WHOLE NORTH POLE TO HAWAII WAS A BRILLIANT IDEA, JINGLE!
WASN'T IT, THOUGH?
HOW'D YOU TALK THE BIG GUY INTO IT?
BELIEVE ME, IT WASN'T HARD. WHO WOULDN'T TAKE MAUI OVER SLUSHVILLE?
YAAHOOO -HO-HO!
EVEN THE OL' BLIZZARD WIZARD'S GONE HAWAIIAN!
I'M MELTING AND LOVING IT!
JINGLE DEAR, I HAVE A JOB FOR YOU...
WHOA, MOMS! GET OUT OF THAT FRUMPY ROBE! YOU'LL GET SUNSTROKE!
OH, HONEY, YOU'RE FAST ASLEEP. IN A SECOND YOU'LL WAKE UP BACK IN YOUR DAD'S SAME OLD SUCKY WORKSHOP.

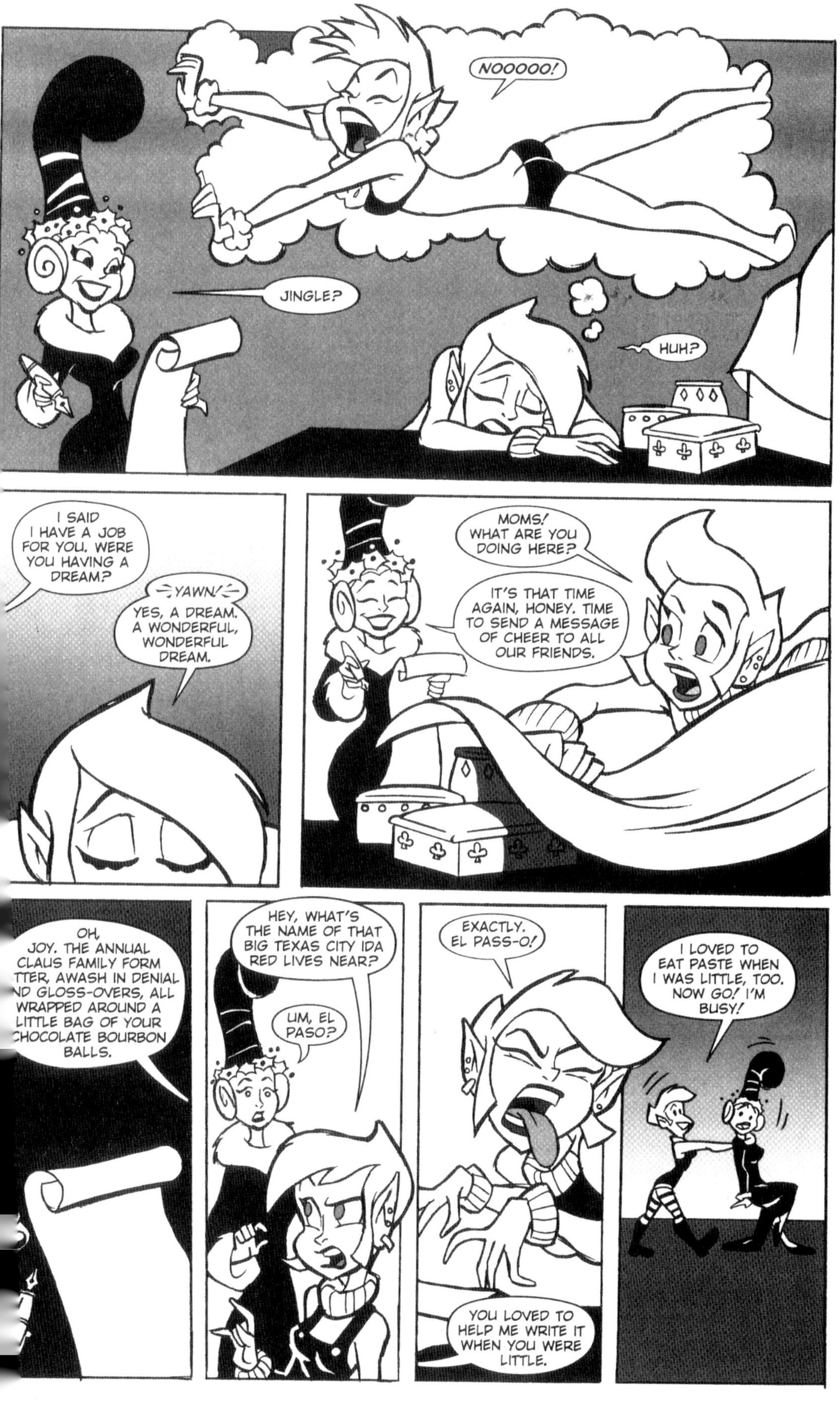
NOOOOO!
JINGLE?
HUH?
I SAID I HAVE A JOB FOR YOU. WERE YOU HAVING A DREAM?
YAWN!
YES, A DREAM. A WONDERFUL, WONDERFUL DREAM.
MOMS! WHAT ARE YOU DOING HERE?
IT'S THAT TIME AGAIN, HONEY. TIME TO SEND A MESSAGE OF CHEER TO ALL OUR FRIENDS.
OH, JOY. THE ANNUAL CLAUS FAMILY FORM TTER, AWASH IN DENIAL ND GLOSS-OVERS, ALL WRAPPED AROUND A LITTLE BAG OF YOUR CHOCOLATE BOURBON BALLS.
HEY, WHAT'S THE NAME OF THAT BIG TEXAS CITY IDA RED LIVES NEAR?
UM, EL PASO?
EXACTLY. EL PASS-O!
YOU LOVED TO HELP ME WRITE IT WHEN YOU WERE LITTLE.
I LOVED TO EAT PASTE WHEN I WAS LITTLE, TOO. NOW GO! I'M BUSY!

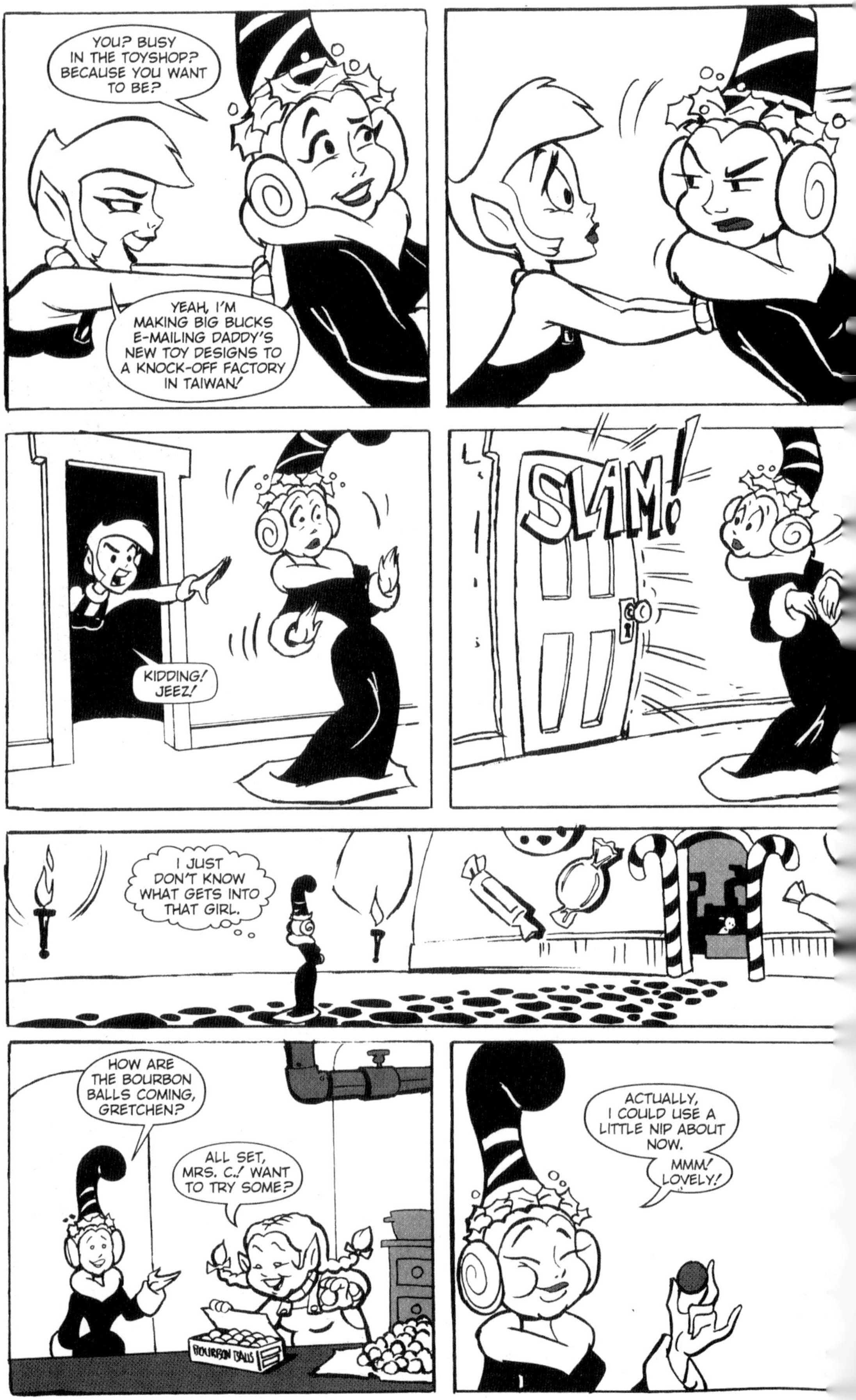
YOU? BUSY IN THE TOYSHOP? BECAUSE YOU WANT TO BE?
YEAH, I'M MAKING BIG BUCKS E-MAILING DADDY'S NEW TOY DESIGNS TO A KNOCK-OFF FACTORY IN TAIWAN!
KIDDING! JEEZ!
SLAM!
I JUST DON'T KNOW WHAT GETS INTO THAT GIRL.
HOW ARE THE BOURBON BALLS COMING, GRETCHEN?
ALL SET, MRS. C.! WANT TO TRY SOME?
BOURBON BALLS
ACTUALLY, I COULD USE A LITTLE NIP ABOUT NOW.
MMM! LOVELY!

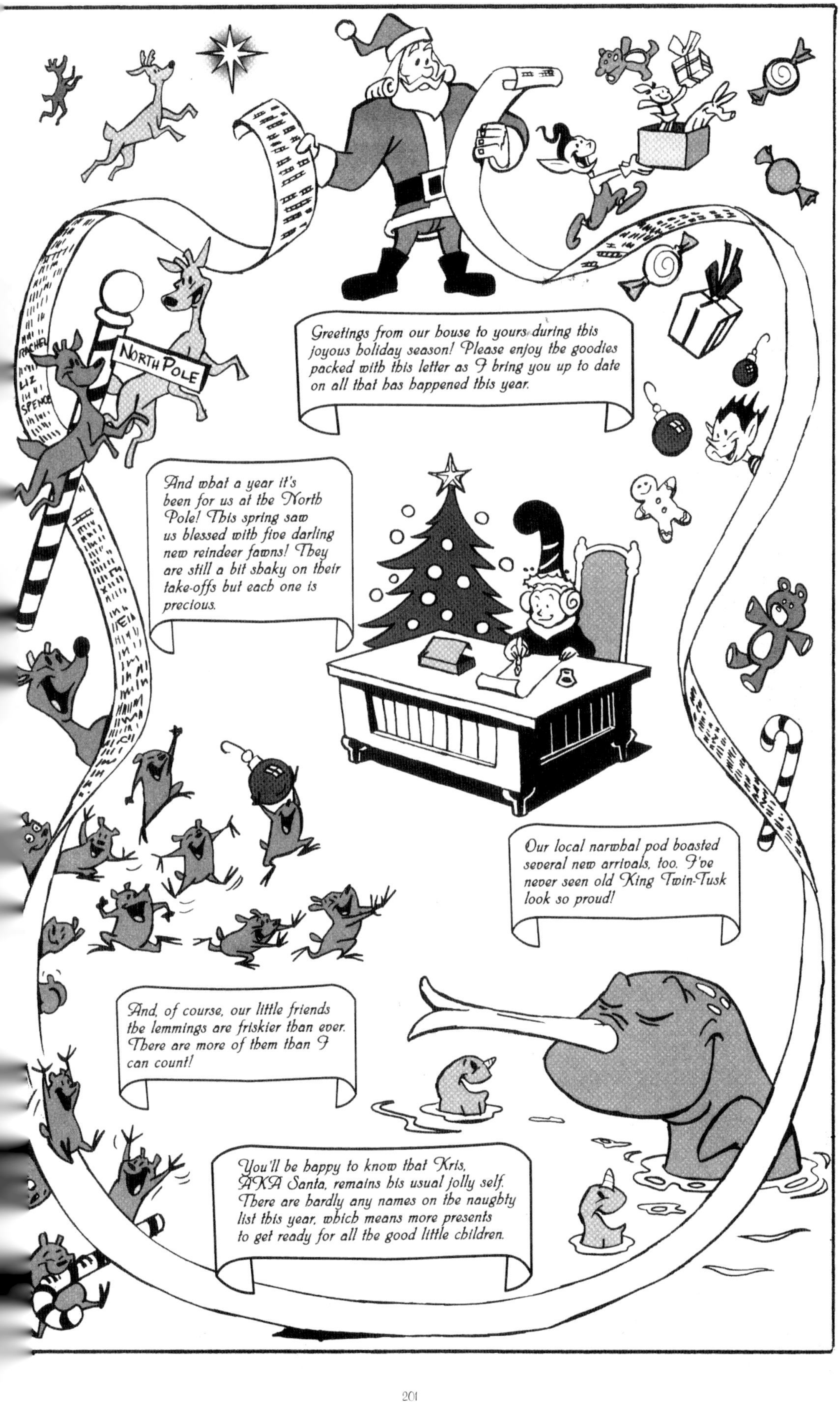
NORTH POLE
Greetings from our house to yours during this joyous holiday season! Please enjoy the goodies packed with this letter as I bring you up to date on all that has happened this year.
And what a year it's been for us at the North Pole! This spring saw us blessed with five darling new reindeer fawns! They are still a bit shaky on their take-offs but each one is precious.
Our local narwhal pod boasted several new arrivals, too. I've never seen old King Twin-Tusk look so proud!
And, of course, our little friends the lemmings are friskier than ever. There are more of them than I can count!
You'll be happy to know that Kris, AKA Santa, remains his usual jolly self. There are hardly any names on the naughty list this year, which means more presents to get ready for all the good little children.

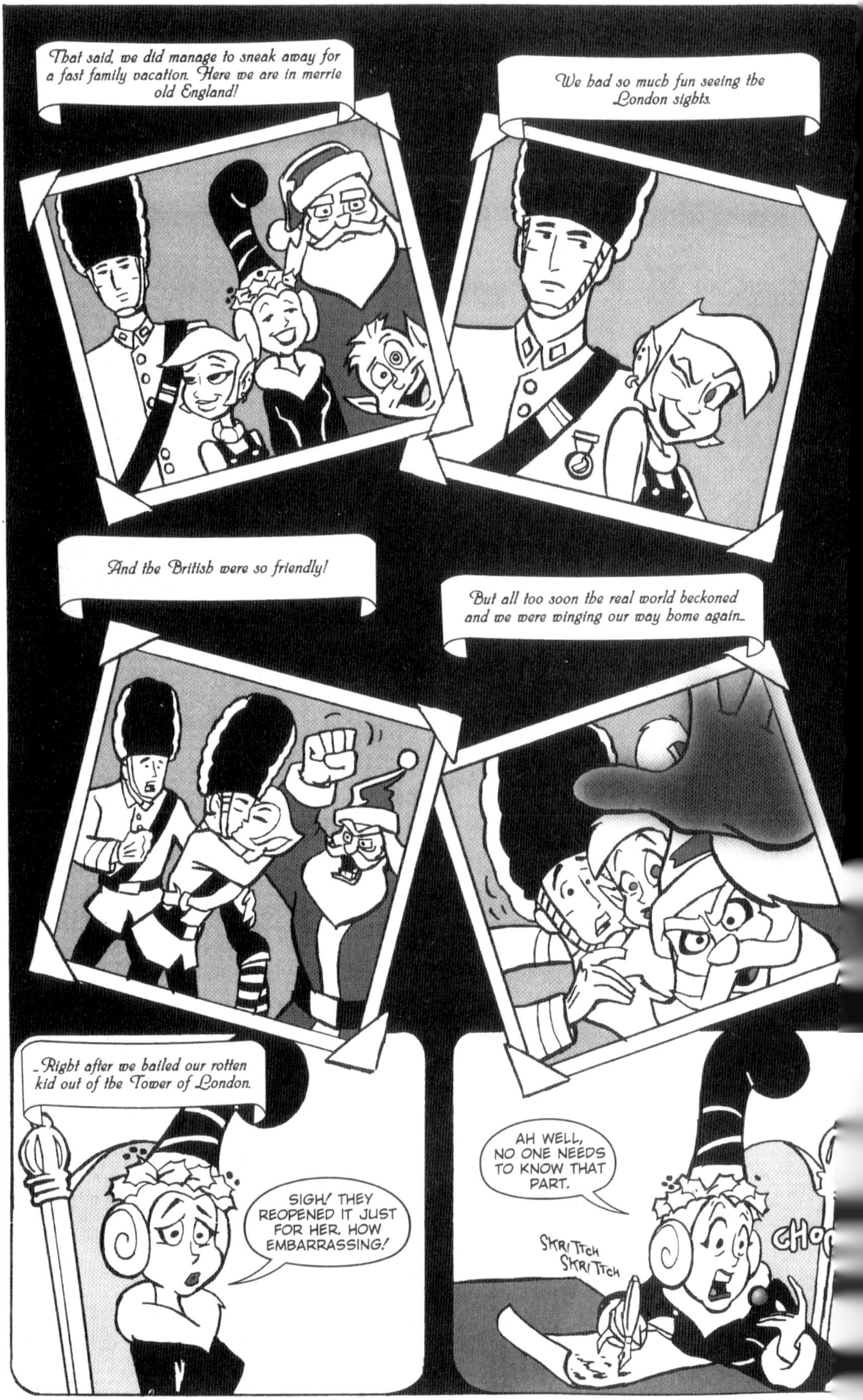

That said, we did manage to sneak away for a fast family vacation. Here we are in merrie old England!
We had so much fun seeing the London sights.
And the British were so friendly!
But all too soon the real world beckoned and we were winging our way home again...
...Right after we bailed our rotten kid out of the Tower of London.
SIGH! THEY REOPENED IT JUST FOR HER. HOW EMBARRASSING!
AH WELL, NO ONE NEEDS TO KNOW THAT PART.
SKRITTCH SKRITTCH

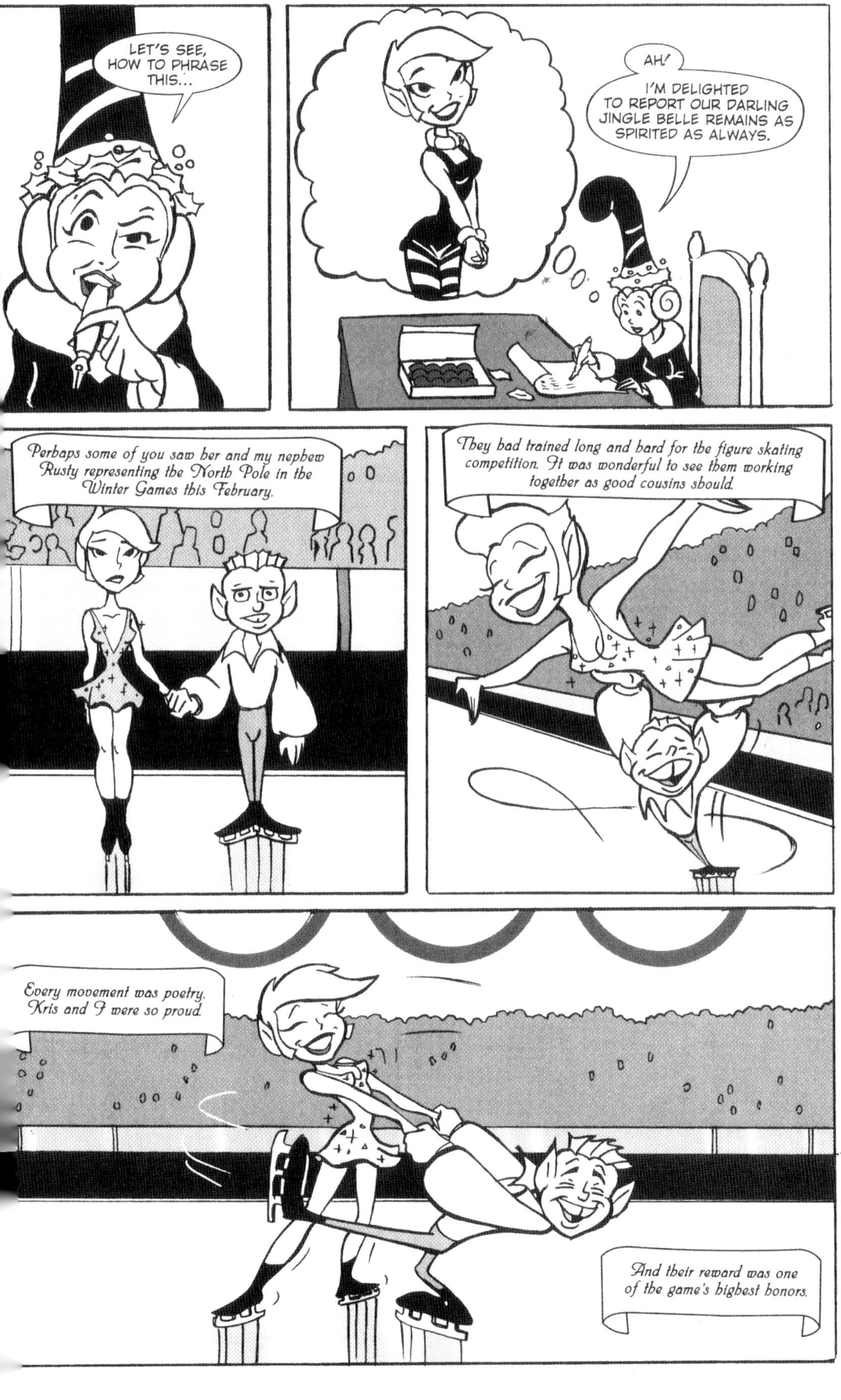
LET'S SEE, HOW TO PHRASE THIS...
AH!
I'M DELIGHTED TO REPORT OUR DARLING JINGLE BELLE REMAINS AS SPIRITED AS ALWAYS.
Perhaps some of you saw her and my nephew Rusty representing the North Pole in the Winter Games this February.
They had trained long and hard for the figure skating competition. It was wonderful to see them working together as good cousins should.
Every movement was poetry. Kris and I were so proud.
And their reward was one of the game's highest honors.

BRONZE?!? YOU LITTLE SCREW-UP! I OUGHT TO KILL YOU WHERE YOU STAND!

B-BUT YOU WERE THE ONE WHO SLIPPED! OWW!

Fortunately the cameras cut away before anyone saw Jingle give Rusty the concussion.

Once again, our pride and joy displayed the same foul temper and selfishness that has earned her a place on the naughty list for the last hundred and sixty...

SKRITCH SKRITCH

I'M NOT LEAVING THAT SENTENCE IN, THOUGH I REALLY SHOULD! TEACH THE LITTLE BRAT A LESSON...GRUMBLE... GRUMBLE...

THOUGH MAYBE JINGLE'S RIGHT. MAYBE I SHOULDN'T GLOSS OVER THE UNPLEASANT THINGS. AFTER ALL, SHE DOES CAUSE MOST OF THEM!

CHOMP CHOMP

YOU WANT HONESTY, LITTLE MISSY? FINE! HOW ABOUT THIS FIASCO?

Jingle's brief time in the spotlight only fueled her desire for more. Thus we we all surprised when our darling angel to us of her deep desire to produce...

A TV CHRISTMAS SPECIAL?

IT'LL ROCK, TRUST ME!

I LOVE SPECIALS

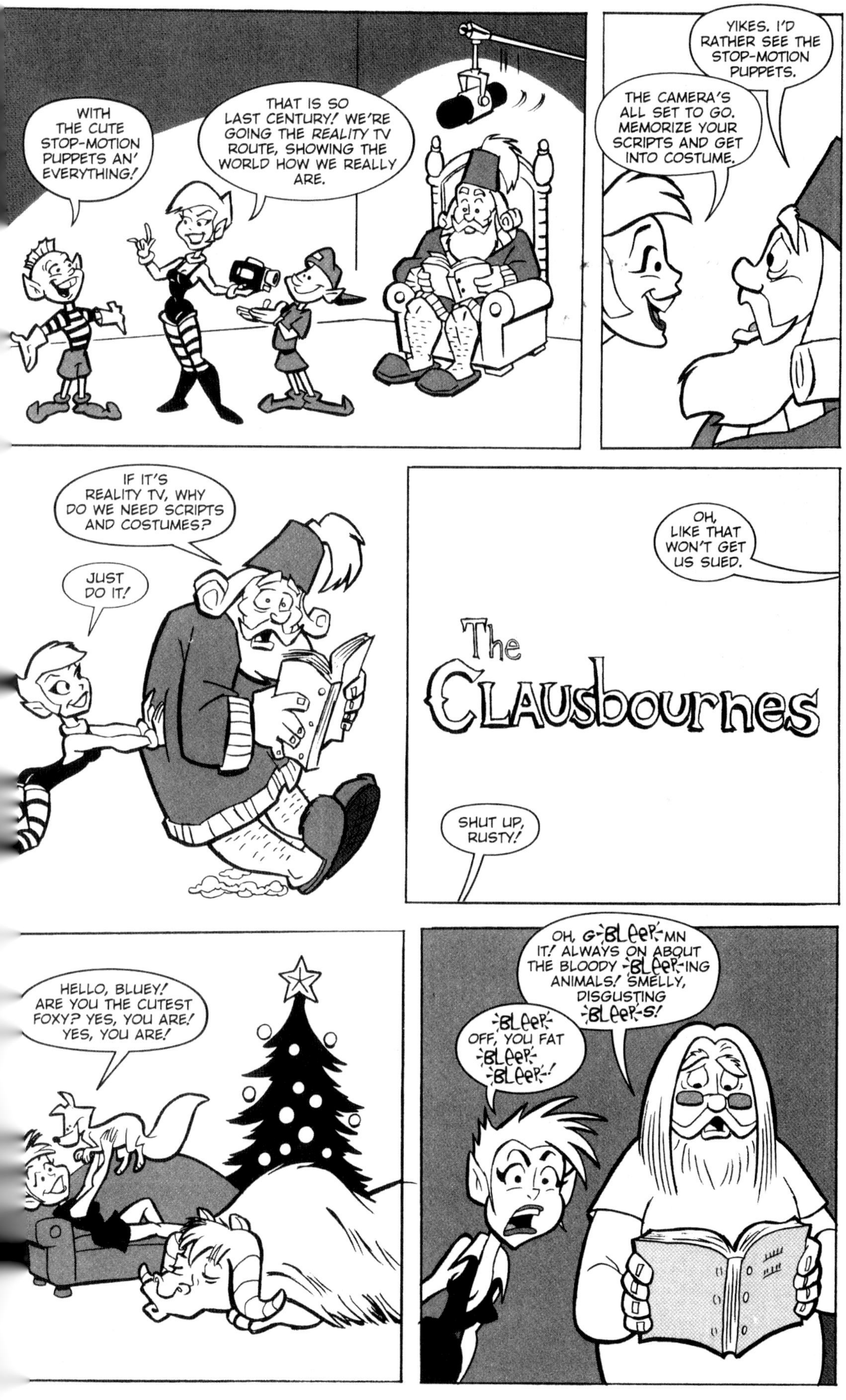
WITH THE CUTE STOP-MOTION PUPPETS AN' EVERYTHING!
THAT IS SO LAST CENTURY! WE'RE GOING THE REALITY TV ROUTE, SHOWING THE WORLD HOW WE REALLY ARE.
THE CAMERA'S ALL SET TO GO. MEMORIZE YOUR SCRIPTS AND GET INTO COSTUME.
YIKES. I'D RATHER SEE THE STOP-MOTION PUPPETS.
IF IT'S REALITY TV, WHY DO WE NEED SCRIPTS AND COSTUMES?
JUST DO IT!
OH, LIKE THAT WON'T GET US SUED.
The CLAUSBOURNES
SHUT UP, RUSTY!
HELLO, BLUEY! ARE YOU THE CUTEST FOXY? YES, YOU ARE! YES, YOU ARE!
OH, G-BLEEP-MN IT! ALWAYS ON ABOUT THE BLOODY -BLEEP-ING ANIMALS! SMELLY, DISGUSTING -BLEEP-S!
-BLEEP- OFF, YOU FAT -BLEEP- -BLEEP-!

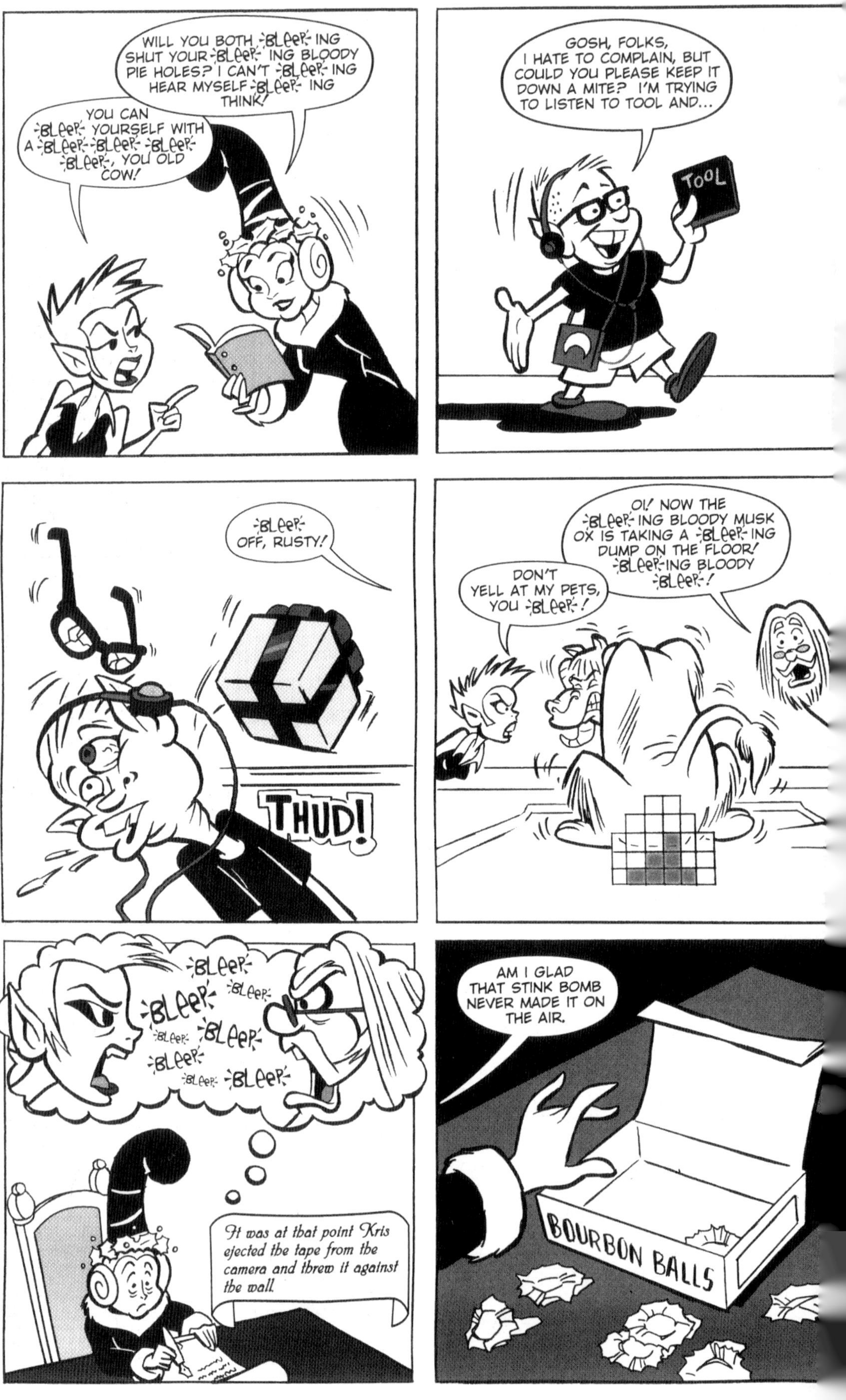
WILL YOU BOTH -BLEEP- ING SHUT YOUR -BLEEP- ING BLOODY PIE HOLES? I CAN'T -BLEEP- ING HEAR MYSELF -BLEEP- ING THINK!
YOU CAN -BLEEP- YOURSELF WITH A -BLEEP- -BLEEP- -BLEEP- -BLEEP-, YOU OLD COW!
GOSH, FOLKS, I HATE TO COMPLAIN, BUT COULD YOU PLEASE KEEP IT DOWN A MITE? I'M TRYING TO LISTEN TO TOOL AND...
TOOL
-BLEEP- OFF, RUSTY!
THUD!
OI! NOW THE -BLEEP- ING BLOODY MUSK OX IS TAKING A -BLEEP- ING DUMP ON THE FLOOR! -BLEEP- ING BLOODY -BLEEP- !
DON'T YELL AT MY PETS, YOU -BLEEP- !
-BLEEP- -BLEEP- -BLEEP- -BLEEP- -BLEEP- -BLEEP- -BLEEP- -BLEEP- -BLEEP-
It was at that point Kris ejected the tape from the camera and threw it against the wall.
AM I GLAD THAT STINK BOMB NEVER MADE IT ON THE AIR.
BOURBON BALLS

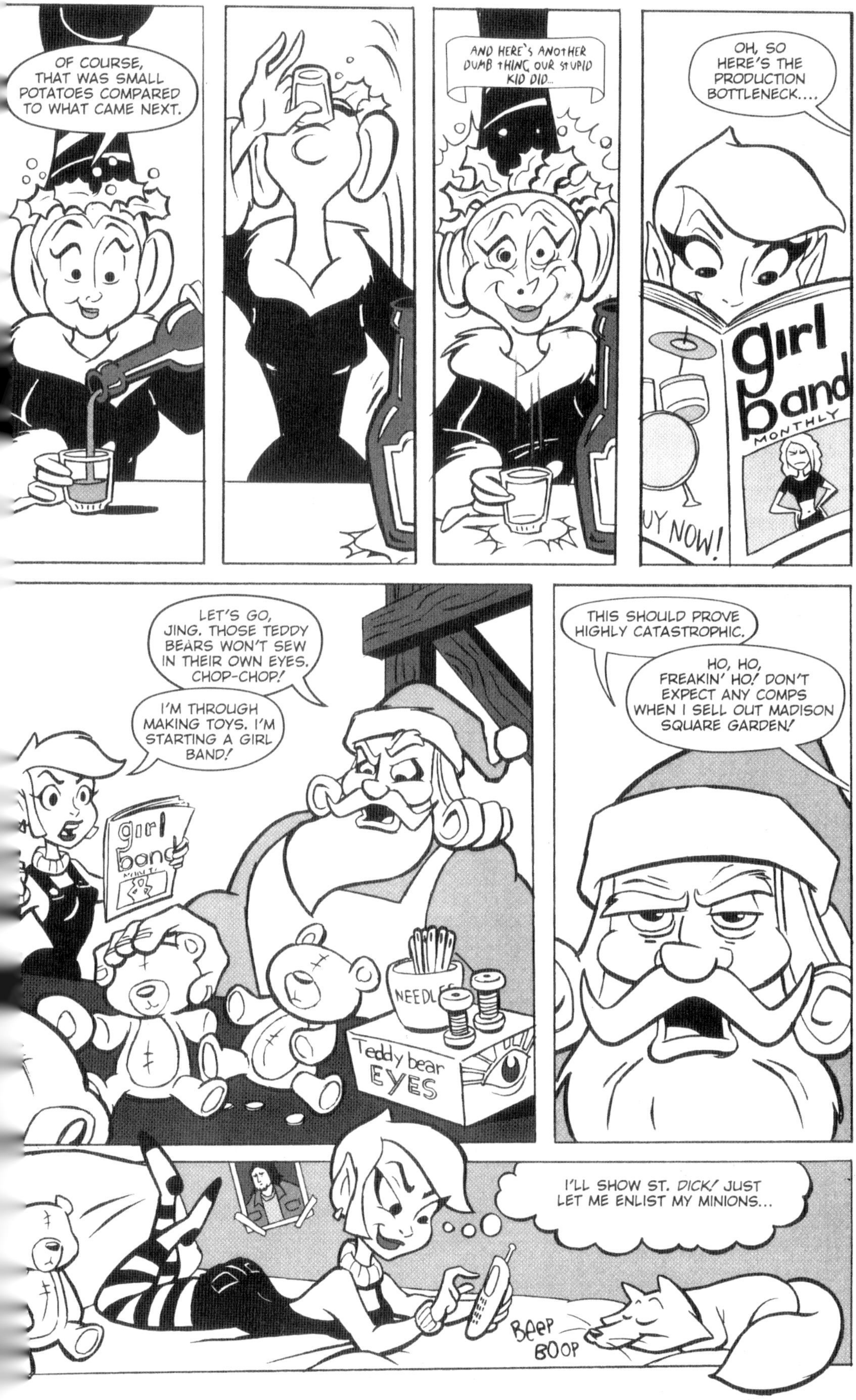
OF COURSE, THAT WAS SMALL POTATOES COMPARED TO WHAT CAME NEXT.
AND HERE'S ANOTHER DUMB THING OUR STUPID KID DID...
OH, SO HERE'S THE PRODUCTION BOTTLENECK....
girl band MONTHLY
UY NOW!
LET'S GO, JING. THOSE TEDDY BEARS WON'T SEW IN THEIR OWN EYES. CHOP-CHOP!
I'M THROUGH MAKING TOYS. I'M STARTING A GIRL BAND!
girl band
NEEDLES
Teddy bear EYES
THIS SHOULD PROVE HIGHLY CATASTROPHIC.
HO, HO, FREAKIN' HO! DON'T EXPECT ANY COMPS WHEN I SELL OUT MADISON SQUARE GARDEN!
I'LL SHOW ST. DICK! JUST LET ME ENLIST MY MINIONS...
BEEP BOOP

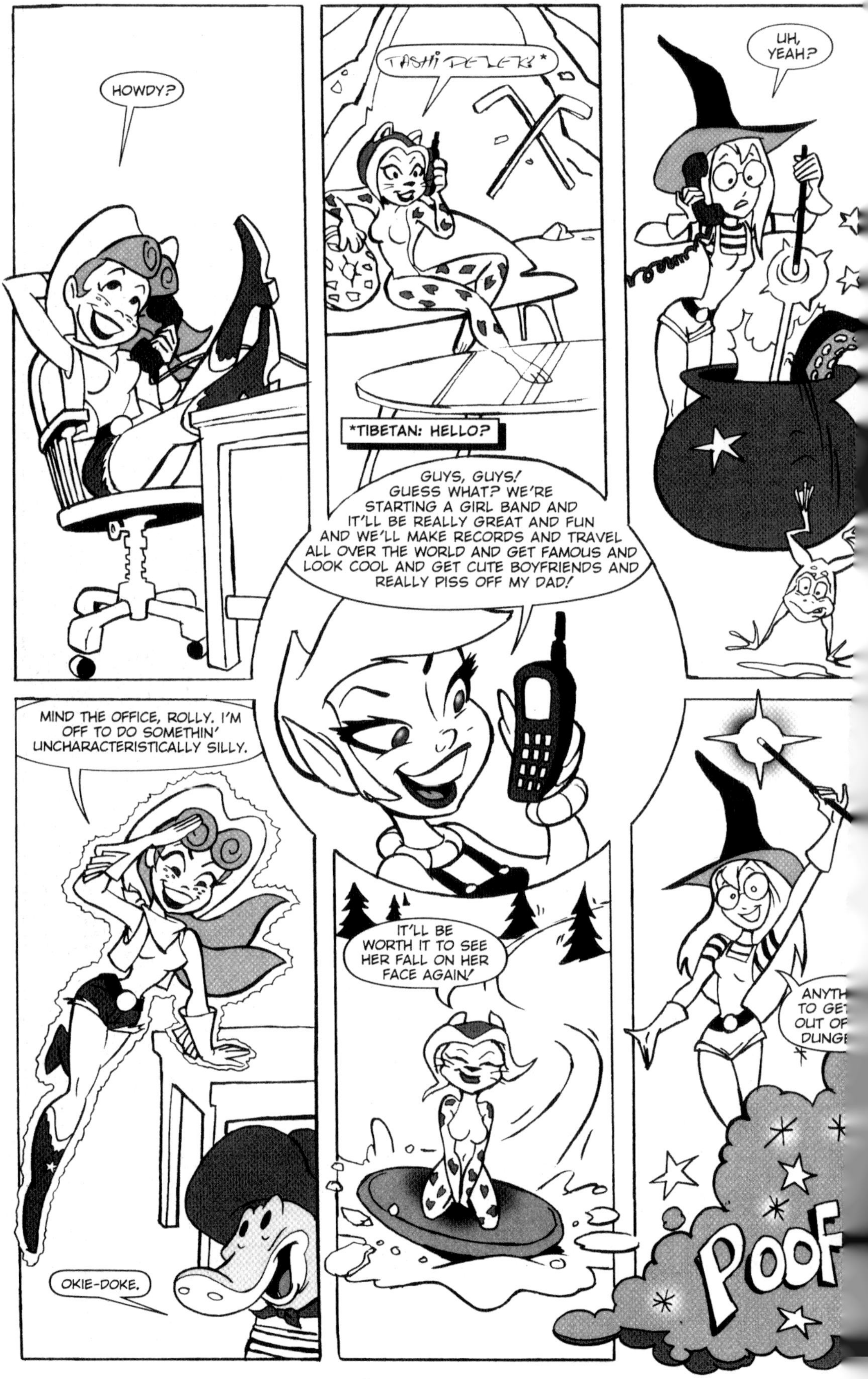
HOWDY?
TASHI DELEK!*
*TIBETAN: HELLO?
UH, YEAH?
GUYS, GUYS! GUESS WHAT? WE'RE STARTING A GIRL BAND AND IT'LL BE REALLY GREAT AND FUN AND WE'LL MAKE RECORDS AND TRAVEL ALL OVER THE WORLD AND GET FAMOUS AND LOOK COOL AND GET CUTE BOYFRIENDS AND REALLY PISS OFF MY DAD!
MIND THE OFFICE, ROLLY. I'M OFF TO DO SOMETHIN' UNCHARACTERISTICALLY SILLY.
OKIE-DOKE.
IT'LL BE WORTH IT TO SEE HER FALL ON HER FACE AGAIN!
ANYTH
TO GET
OUT OF
DUNGE
POOF

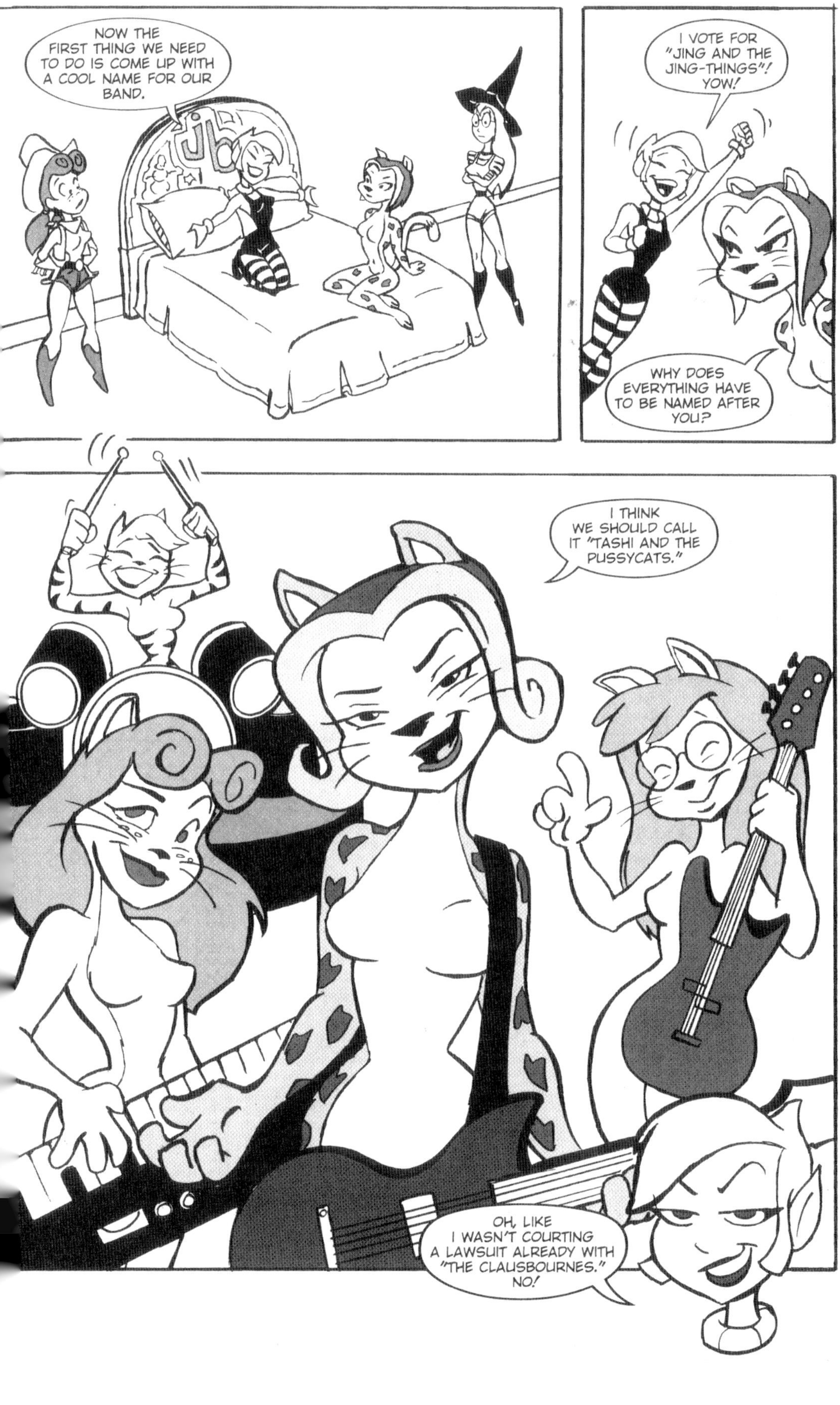
NOW THE FIRST THING WE NEED TO DO IS COME UP WITH A COOL NAME FOR OUR BAND.
I VOTE FOR "JING AND THE JING-THINGS"! YOW!
WHY DOES EVERYTHING HAVE TO BE NAMED AFTER YOU?
I THINK WE SHOULD CALL IT "TASHI AND THE PUSSYCATS."
OH, LIKE I WASN'T COURTING A LAWSUIT ALREADY WITH "THE CLAUSBOURNES." NO!

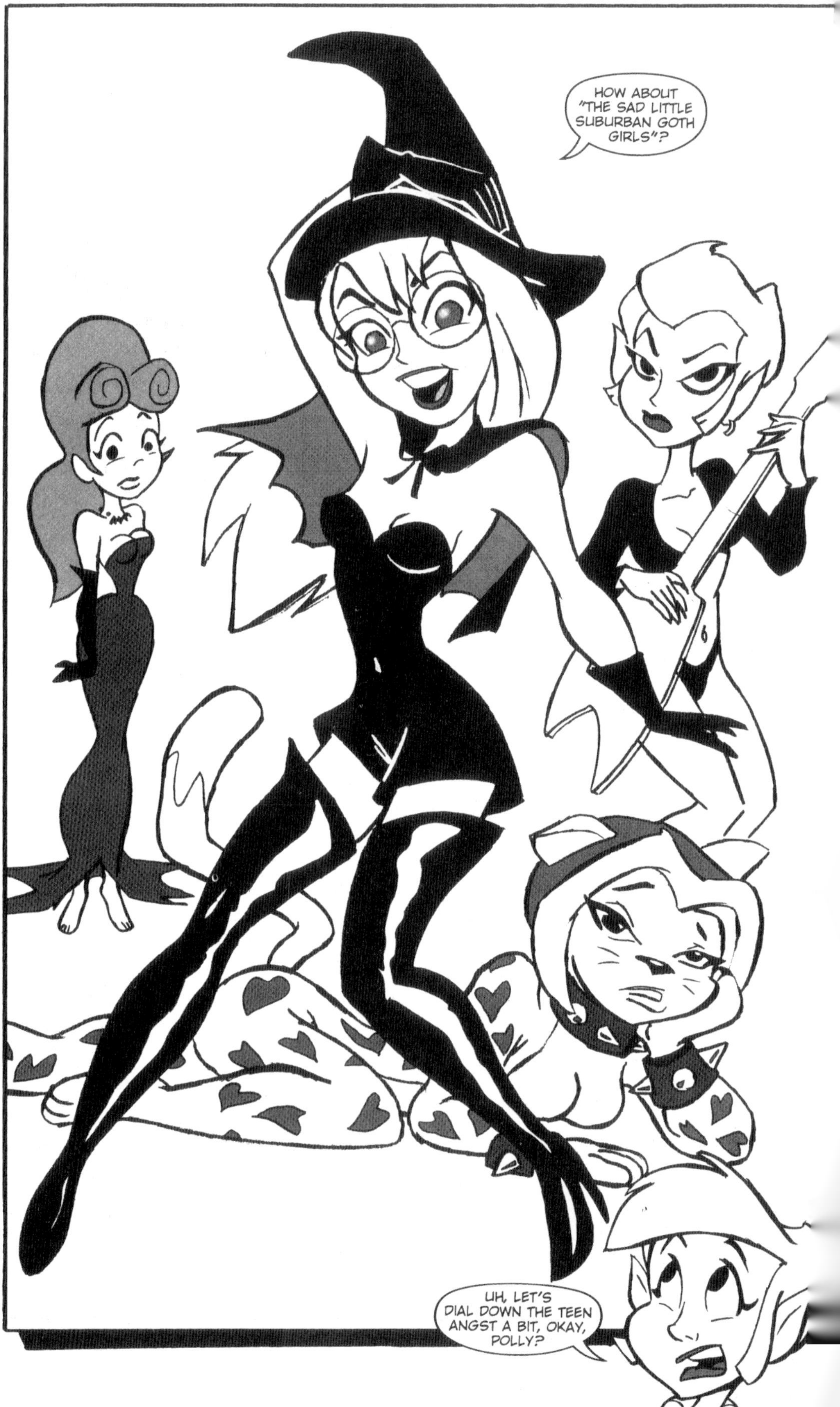
HOW ABOUT "THE SAD LITTLE SUBURBAN GOTH GIRLS"?
UH, LET'S DIAL DOWN THE TEEN ANGST A BIT, OKAY, POLLY?

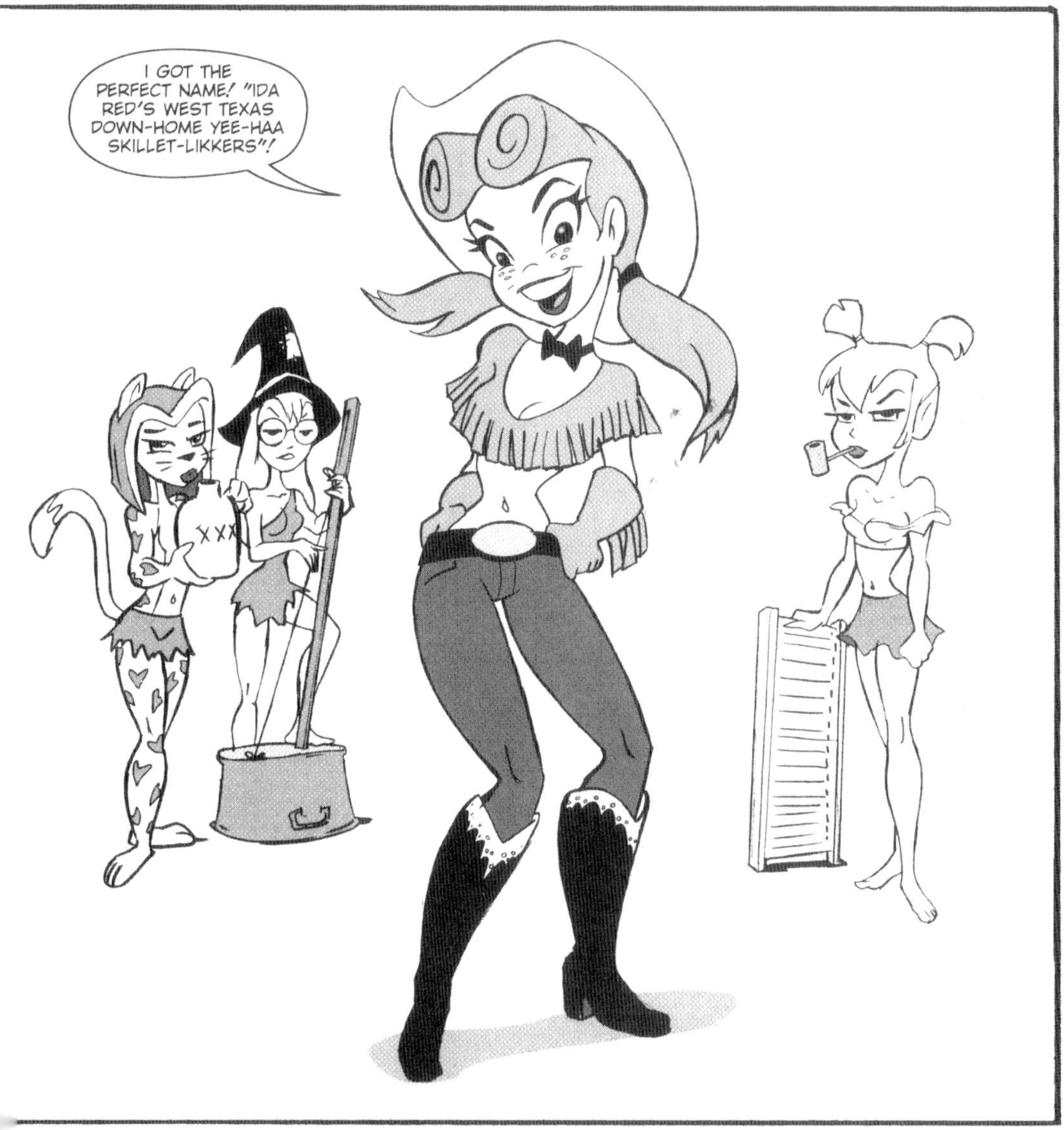
I GOT THE PERFECT NAME! "IDA RED'S WEST TEXAS DOWN-HOME YEE-HAA SKILLET-LIKKERS"!

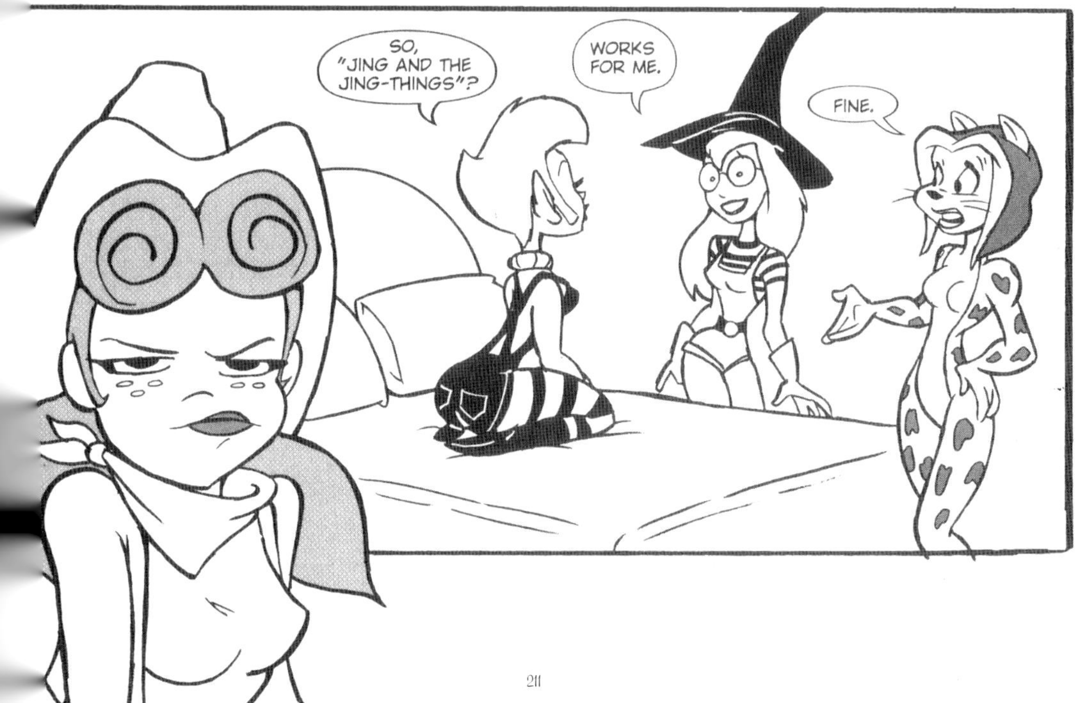
SO, "JING AND THE JING-THINGS"?
WORKS FOR ME.
FINE.

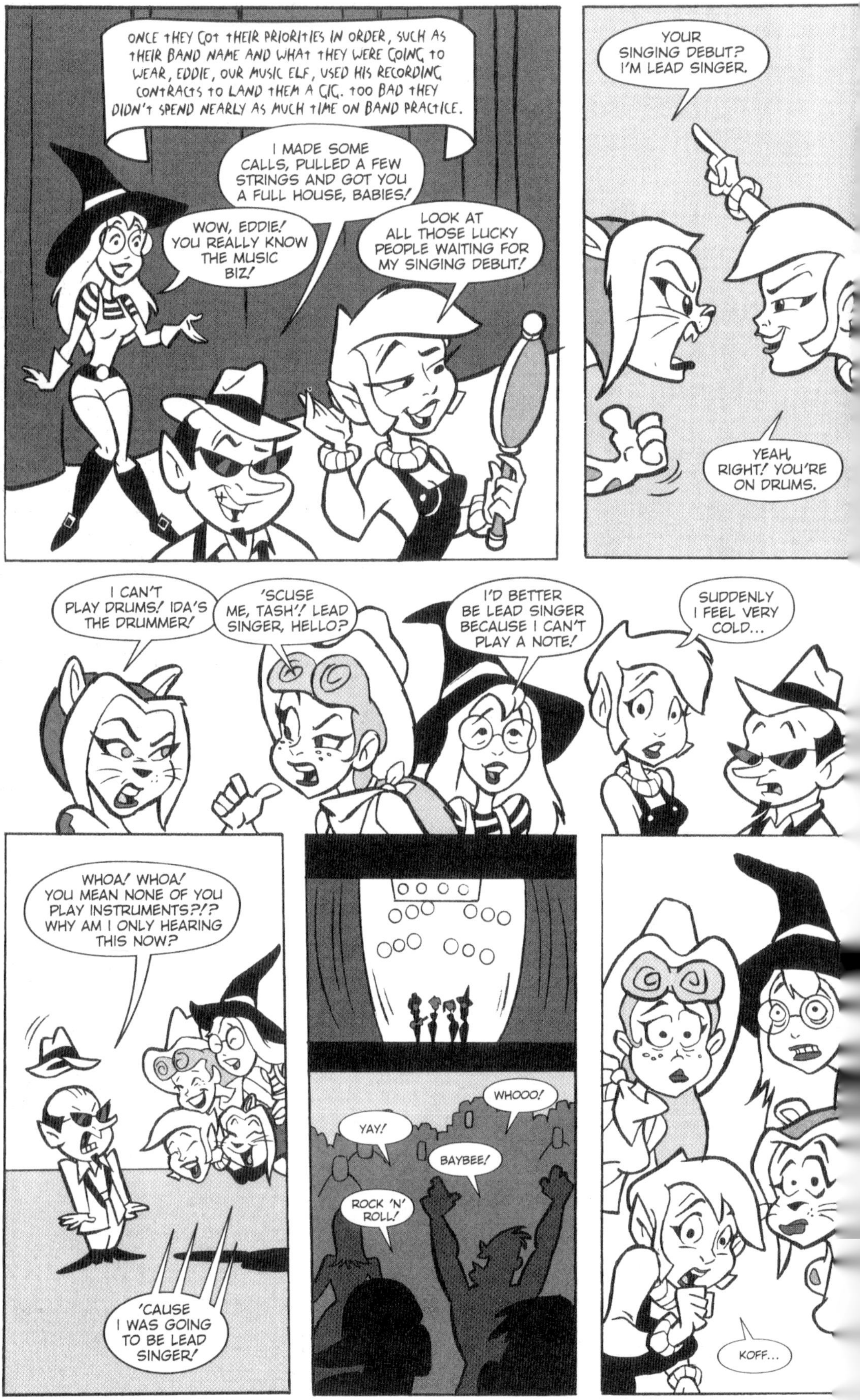
ONCE THEY GOT THEIR PRIORITIES IN ORDER, SUCH AS THEIR BAND NAME AND WHAT THEY WERE GOING TO WEAR, EDDIE, OUR MUSIC ELF, USED HIS RECORDING CONTRACTS TO LAND THEM A GIG. TOO BAD THEY DIDN'T SPEND NEARLY AS MUCH TIME ON BAND PRACTICE.
I MADE SOME CALLS, PULLED A FEW STRINGS AND GOT YOU A FULL HOUSE, BABIES!
WOW, EDDIE! YOU REALLY KNOW THE MUSIC BIZ!
LOOK AT ALL THOSE LUCKY PEOPLE WAITING FOR MY SINGING DEBUT!
YOUR SINGING DEBUT? I'M LEAD SINGER.
YEAH, RIGHT! YOU'RE ON DRUMS.
I CAN'T PLAY DRUMS! IDA'S THE DRUMMER!
'SCUSE ME, TASH'! LEAD SINGER, HELLO?
I'D BETTER BE LEAD SINGER BECAUSE I CAN'T PLAY A NOTE!
SUDDENLY I FEEL VERY COLD...
WHOA! WHOA! YOU MEAN NONE OF YOU PLAY INSTRUMENTS?!? WHY AM I ONLY HEARING THIS NOW?
'CAUSE I WAS GOING TO BE LEAD SINGER!
WHOOO!
YAY!
BAYBEE!
ROCK 'N' ROLL!
KOFF...

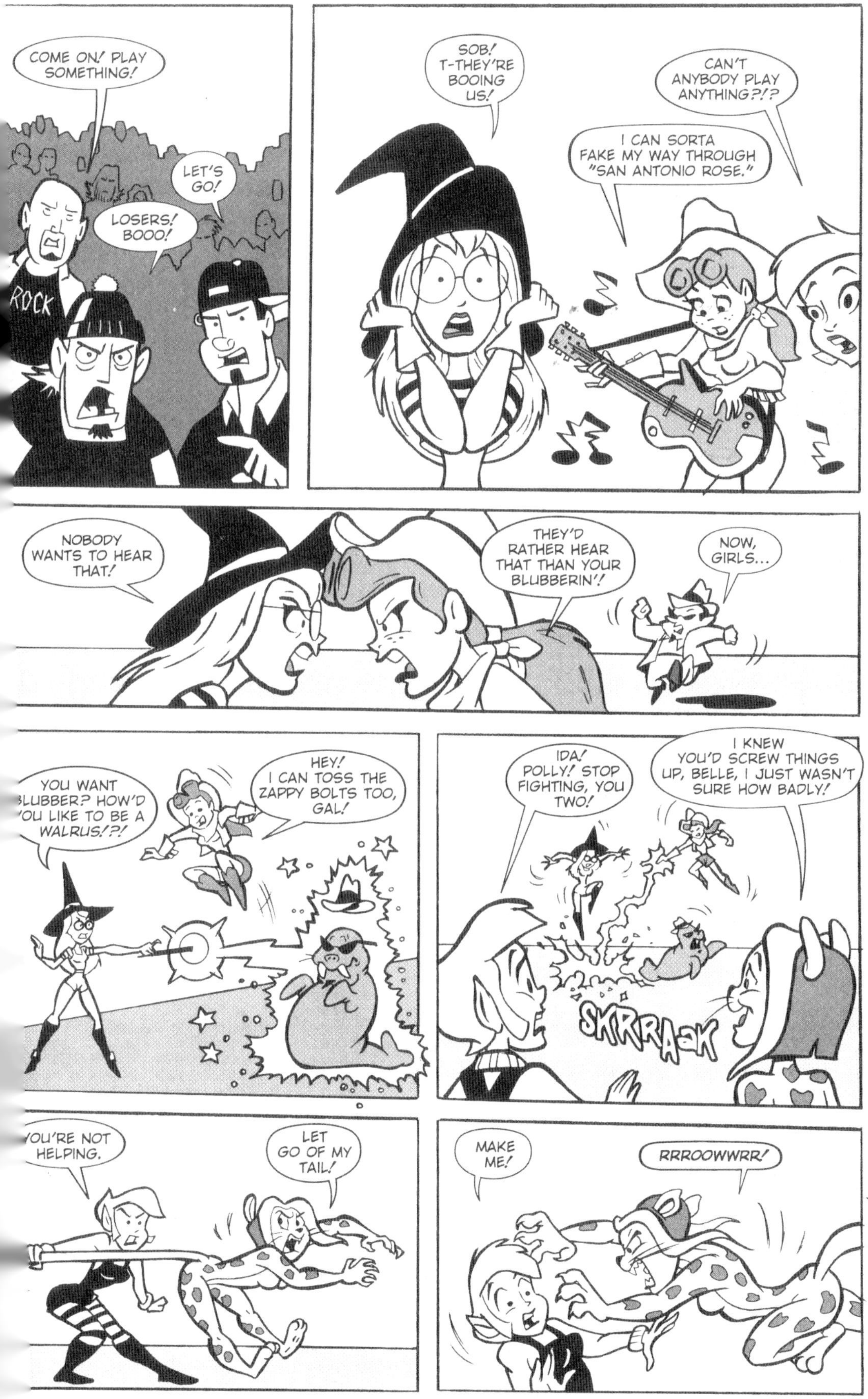

COME ON! PLAY SOMETHING!
LET'S GO!
LOSERS! BOOO!
ROCK
SOB! T-THEY'RE BOOING US!
CAN'T ANYBODY PLAY ANYTHING?!?
I CAN SORTA FAKE MY WAY THROUGH "SAN ANTONIO ROSE."
NOBODY WANTS TO HEAR THAT!
THEY'D RATHER HEAR THAT THAN YOUR BLUBBERIN'!
NOW, GIRLS...
YOU WANT BLUBBER? HOW'D YOU LIKE TO BE A WALRUS!?!
HEY! I CAN TOSS THE ZAPPY BOLTS TOO, GAL!
IDA! POLLY! STOP FIGHTING, YOU TWO!
I KNEW YOU'D SCREW THINGS UP, BELLE, I JUST WASN'T SURE HOW BADLY!
SKRRAAK
YOU'RE NOT HELPING.
LET GO OF MY TAIL!
MAKE ME!
RRROOWWRR!

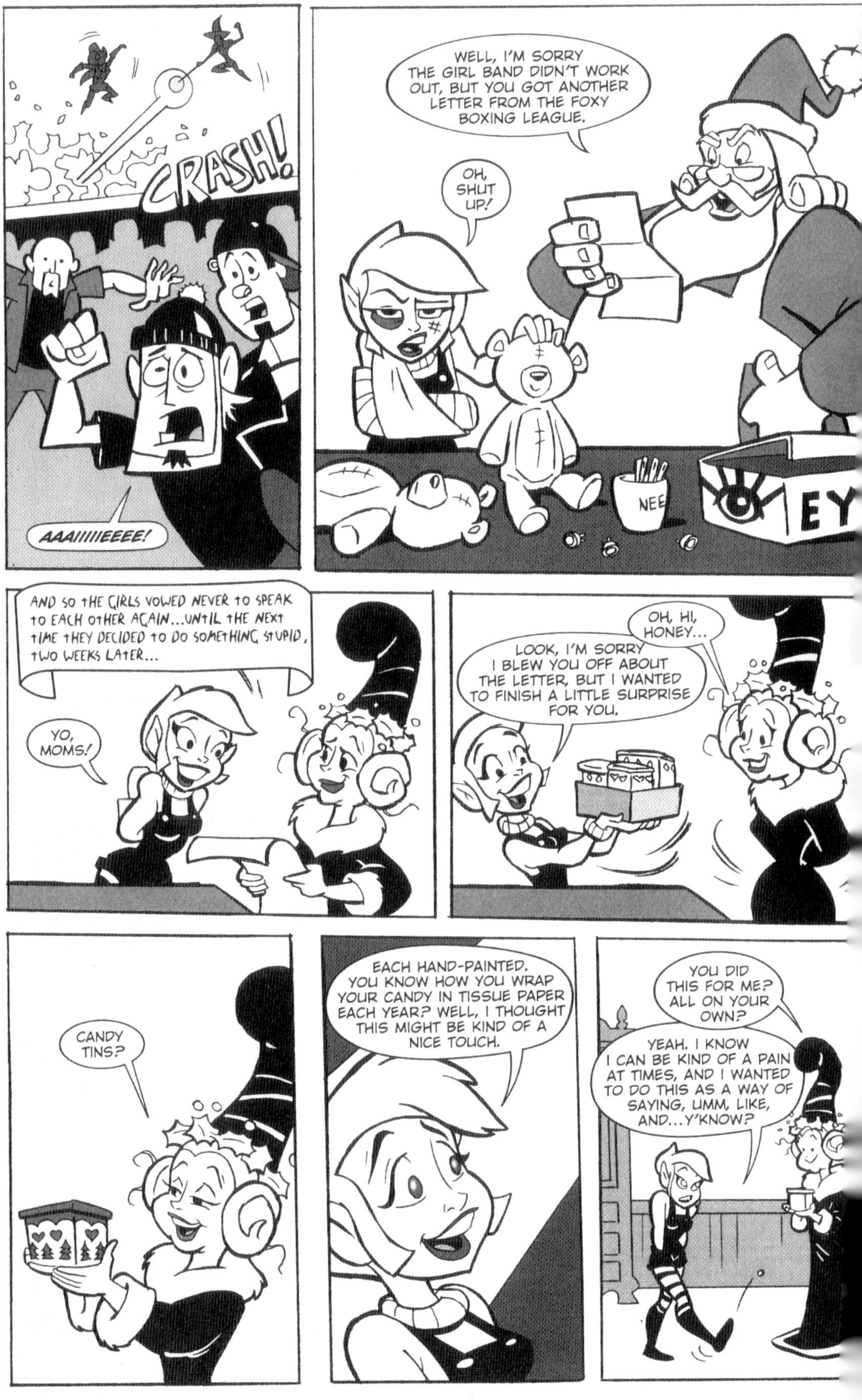
CRASH!
AAAIIIIIEEEE!
WELL, I'M SORRY THE GIRL BAND DIDN'T WORK OUT, BUT YOU GOT ANOTHER LETTER FROM THE FOXY BOXING LEAGUE.
OH, SHUT UP!
NEE
EY
AND SO THE GIRLS VOWED NEVER TO SPEAK TO EACH OTHER AGAIN...UNTIL THE NEXT TIME THEY DECIDED TO DO SOMETHING STUPID, TWO WEEKS LATER...
YO, MOMS!
OH, HI, HONEY...
LOOK, I'M SORRY I BLEW YOU OFF ABOUT THE LETTER, BUT I WANTED TO FINISH A LITTLE SURPRISE FOR YOU.
CANDY TINS?
EACH HAND-PAINTED. YOU KNOW HOW YOU WRAP YOUR CANDY IN TISSUE PAPER EACH YEAR? WELL, I THOUGHT THIS MIGHT BE KIND OF A NICE TOUCH.
YOU DID THIS FOR ME? ALL ON YOUR OWN?
YEAH. I KNOW I CAN BE KIND OF A PAIN AT TIMES, AND I WANTED TO DO THIS AS A WAY OF SAYING, UMM, LIKE, AND...Y'KNOW?

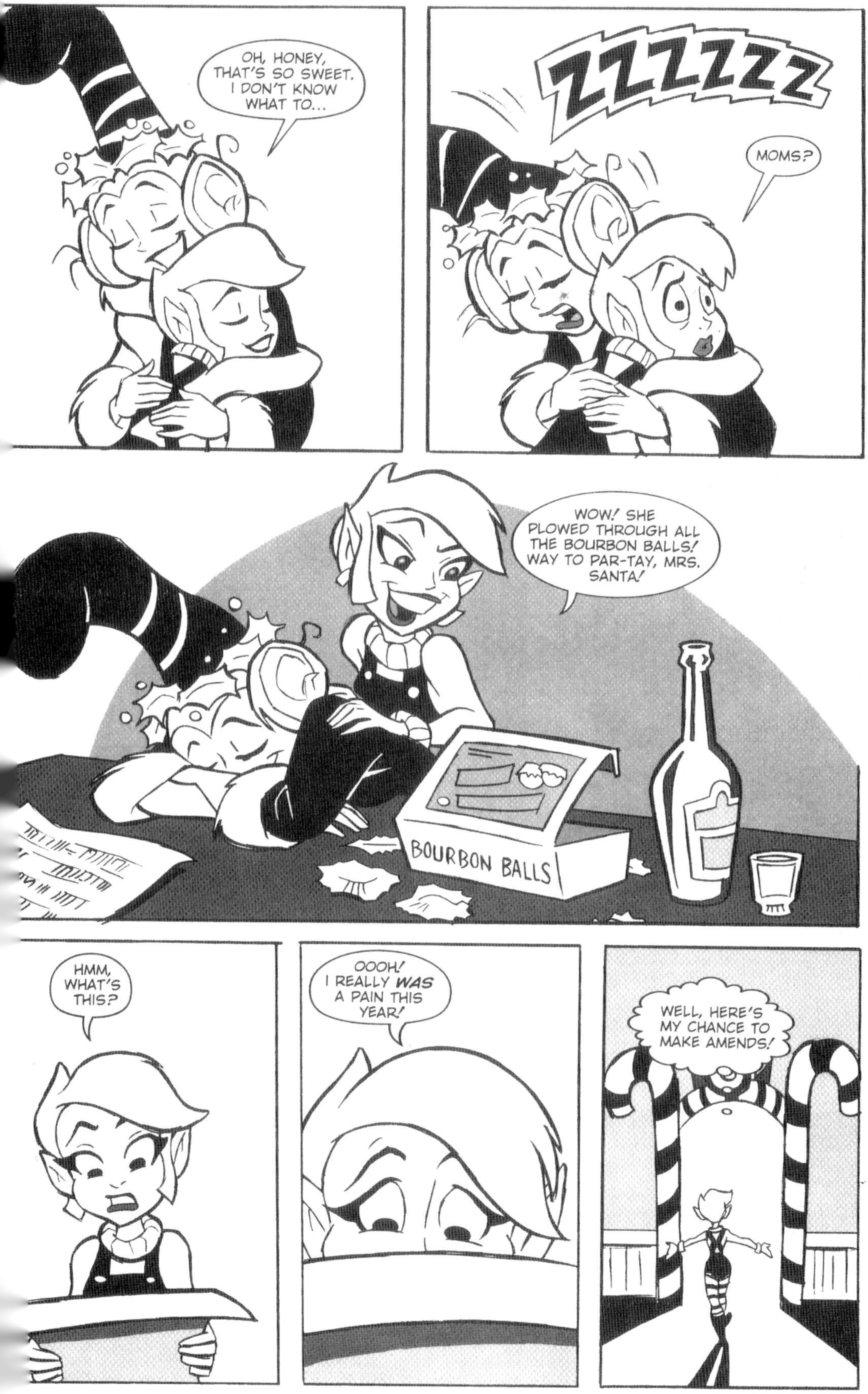
OH, HONEY, THAT'S SO SWEET. I DON'T KNOW WHAT TO...
ZZZZZZ
MOMS?
WOW! SHE PLOWED THROUGH ALL THE BOURBON BALLS! WAY TO PAR-TAY, MRS. SANTA!
BOURBON BALLS
HMM, WHAT'S THIS?
OOOH! I REALLY **WAS** A PAIN THIS YEAR!
WELL, HERE'S MY CHANCE TO MAKE AMENDS!

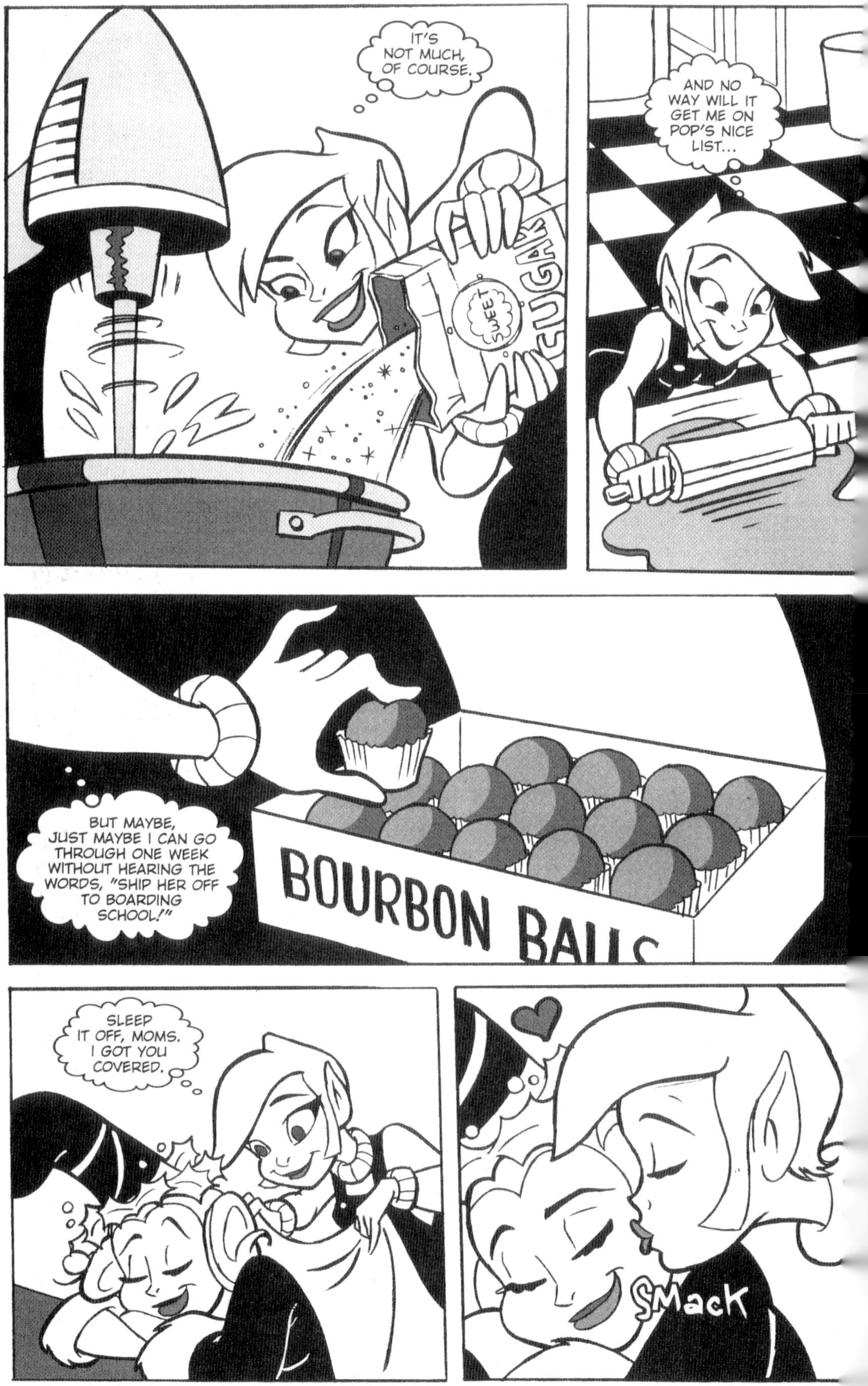
IT'S NOT MUCH, OF COURSE.
SWEET SUGAR
AND NO WAY WILL IT GET ME ON POP'S NICE LIST...
BUT MAYBE, JUST MAYBE I CAN GO THROUGH ONE WEEK WITHOUT HEARING THE WORDS, "SHIP HER OFF TO BOARDING SCHOOL!"
BOURBON BALLS
SLEEP IT OFF, MOMS. I GOT YOU COVERED.
SMack

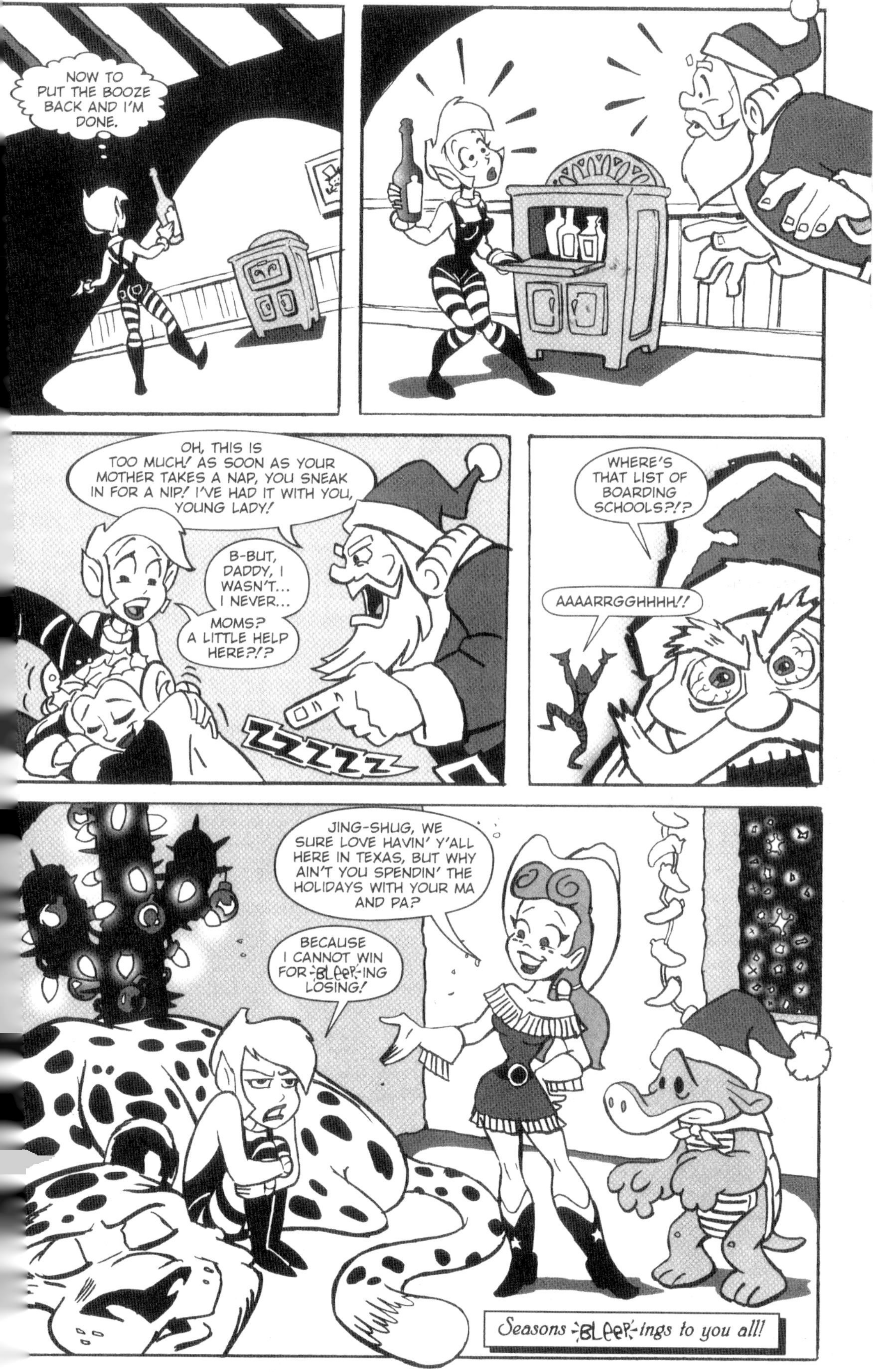
NOW TO PUT THE BOOZE BACK AND I'M DONE.
OH, THIS IS TOO MUCH! AS SOON AS YOUR MOTHER TAKES A NAP, YOU SNEAK IN FOR A NIP! I'VE HAD IT WITH YOU, YOUNG LADY!
B-BUT, DADDY, I WASN'T... I NEVER...
MOMS? A LITTLE HELP HERE?!?
ZZZZZ
WHERE'S THAT LIST OF BOARDING SCHOOLS?!?
AAAARRGHHHH!!
JING-SHUG, WE SURE LOVE HAVIN' Y'ALL HERE IN TEXAS, BUT WHY AIN'T YOU SPENDIN' THE HOLIDAYS WITH YOUR MA AND PA?
BECAUSE I CANNOT WIN FOR -BLEEP-ING LOSING!
Seasons -BLEEP-ings to you all!

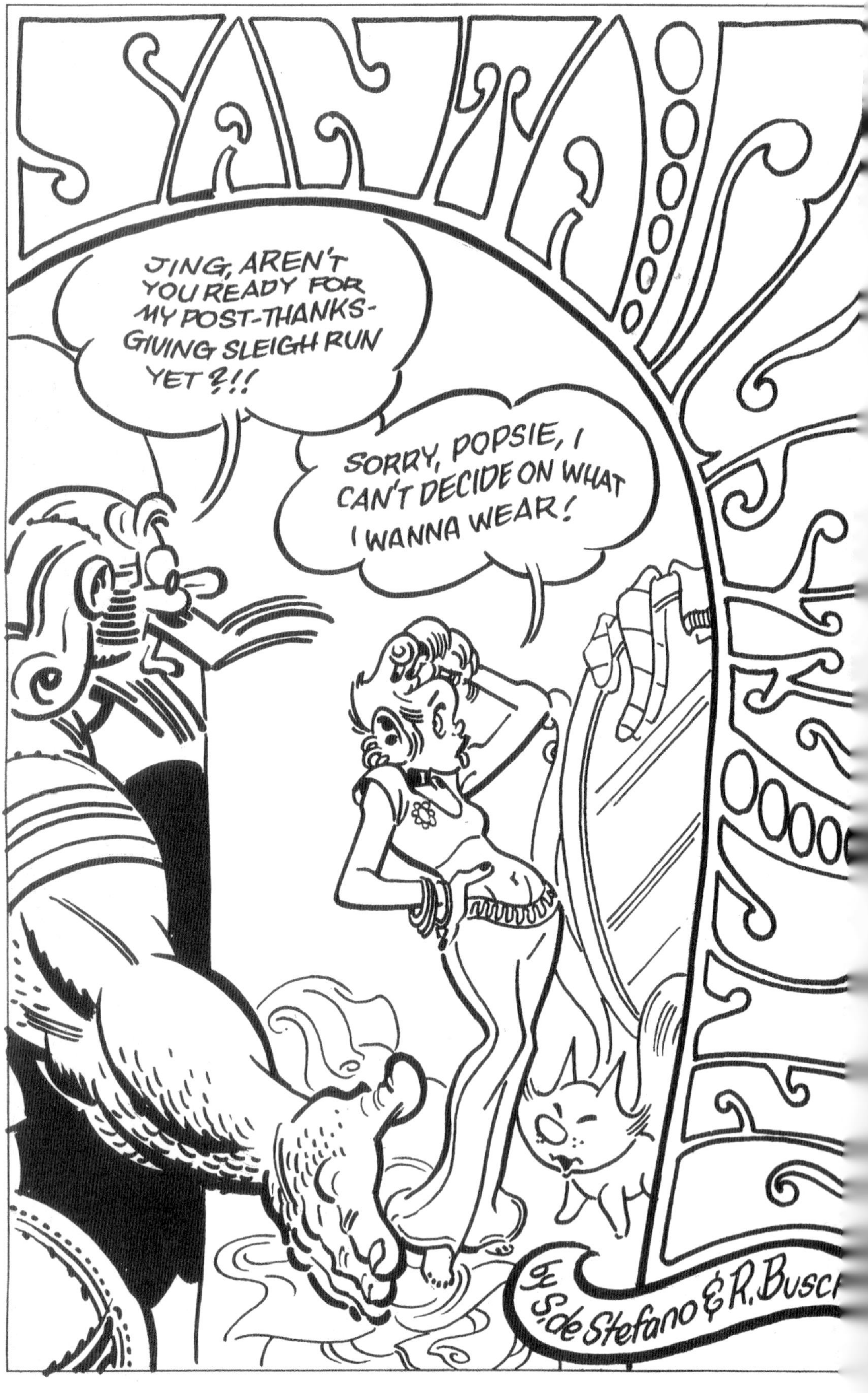
JING, AREN'T YOU READY FOR MY POST-THANKS-GIVING SLEIGH RUN YET ?!!
SORRY, POPSIE, I CAN'T DECIDE ON WHAT I WANNA WEAR!
by S. de Stefano & R. Busc

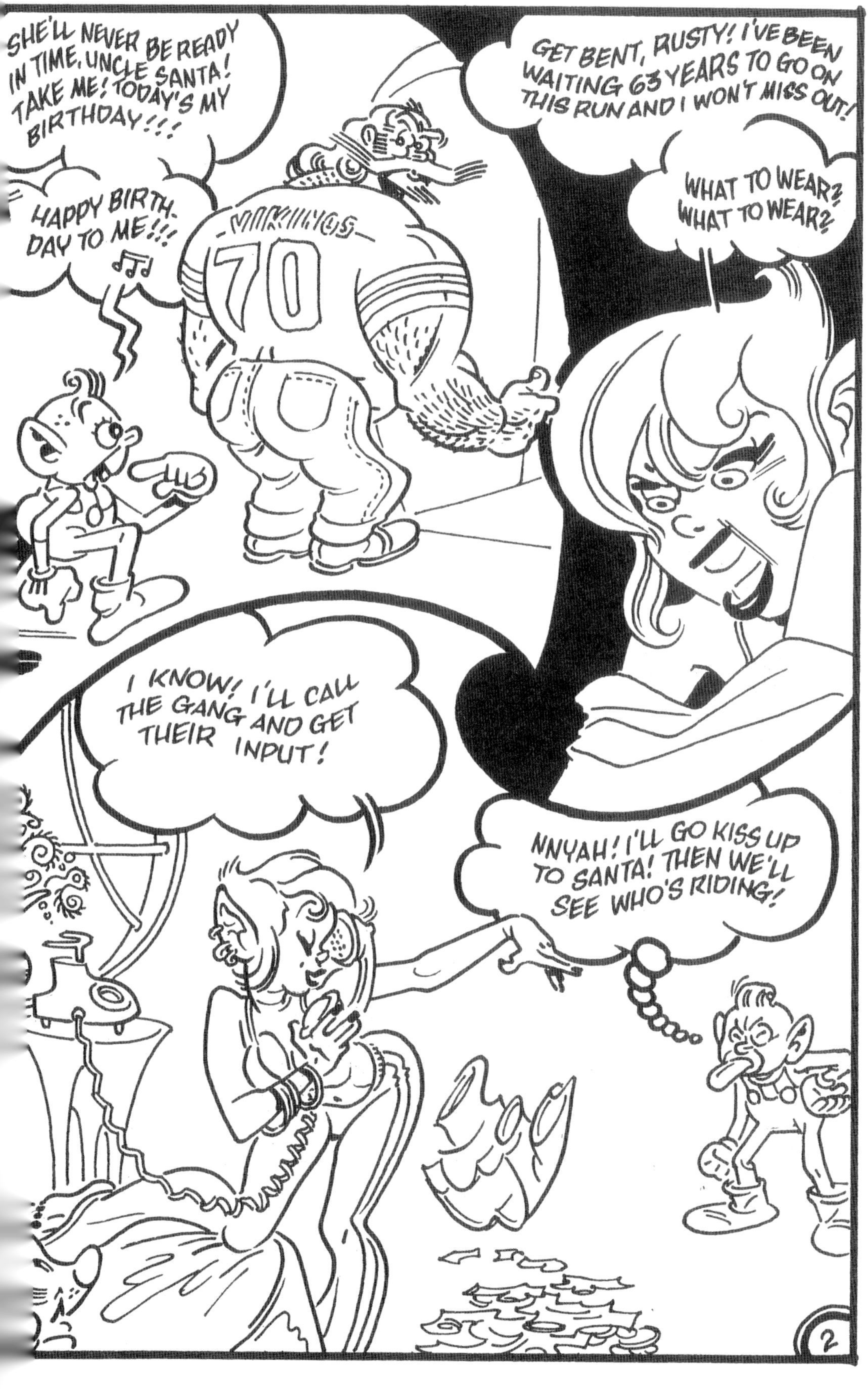
SHE'LL NEVER BE READY IN TIME, UNCLE SANTA! TAKE ME! TODAY'S MY BIRTHDAY!!!
GET BENT, RUSTY! I'VE BEEN WAITING 63 YEARS TO GO ON THIS RUN AND I WON'T MISS OUT!
HAPPY BIRTH-DAY TO ME!!!
VIKINGS
70
WHAT TO WEAR? WHAT TO WEAR?
I KNOW! I'LL CALL THE GANG AND GET THEIR INPUT!
NNYAH! I'LL GO KISS UP TO SANTA! THEN WE'LL SEE WHO'S RIDING!
2

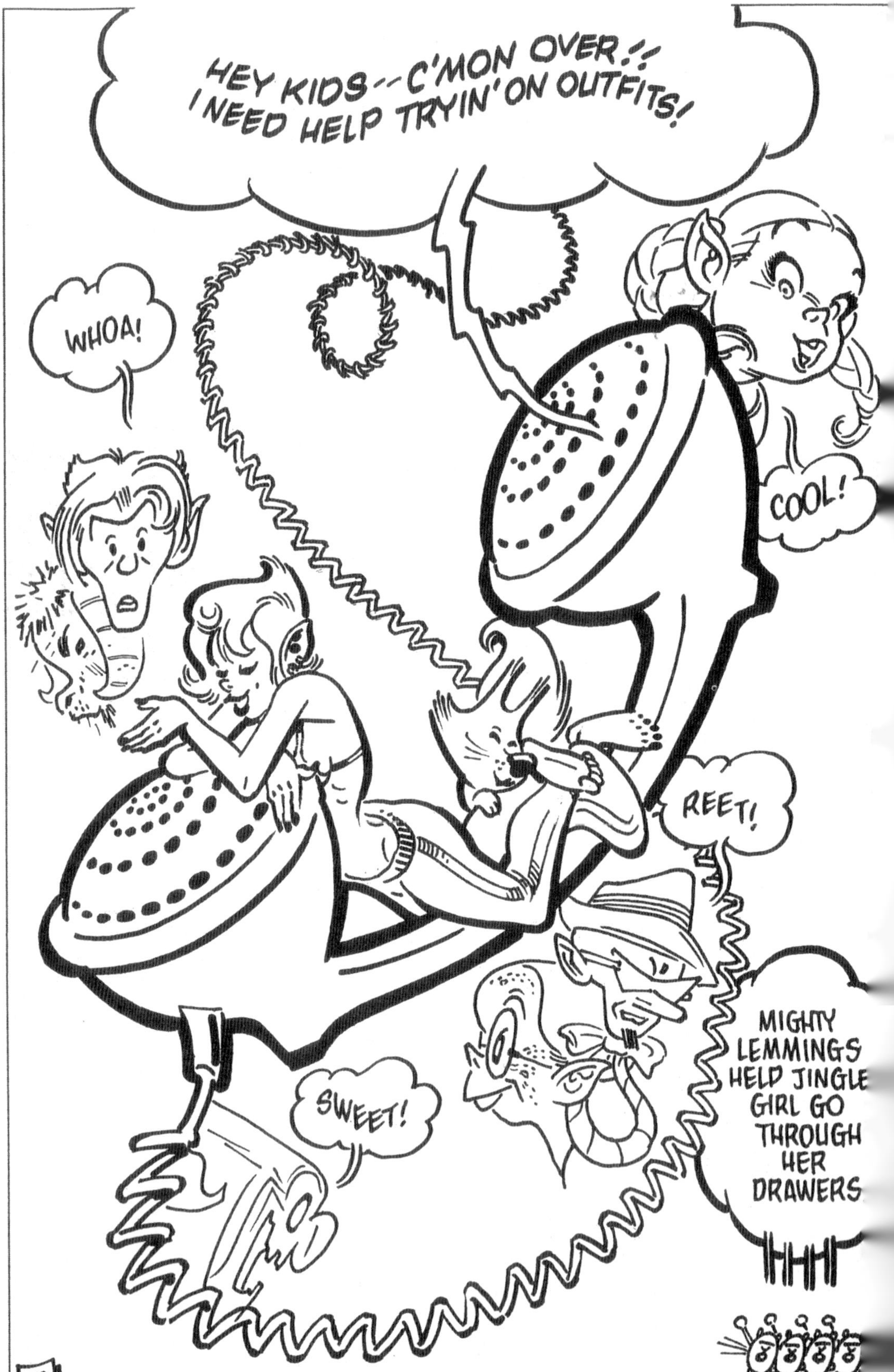
HEY KIDS--C'MON OVER!!
I NEED HELP TRYIN' ON OUTFITS!
WHOA!
COOL!
REET!
SWEET!
MIGHTY LEMMINGS HELP JINGLE GIRL GO THROUGH HER DRAWERS
3

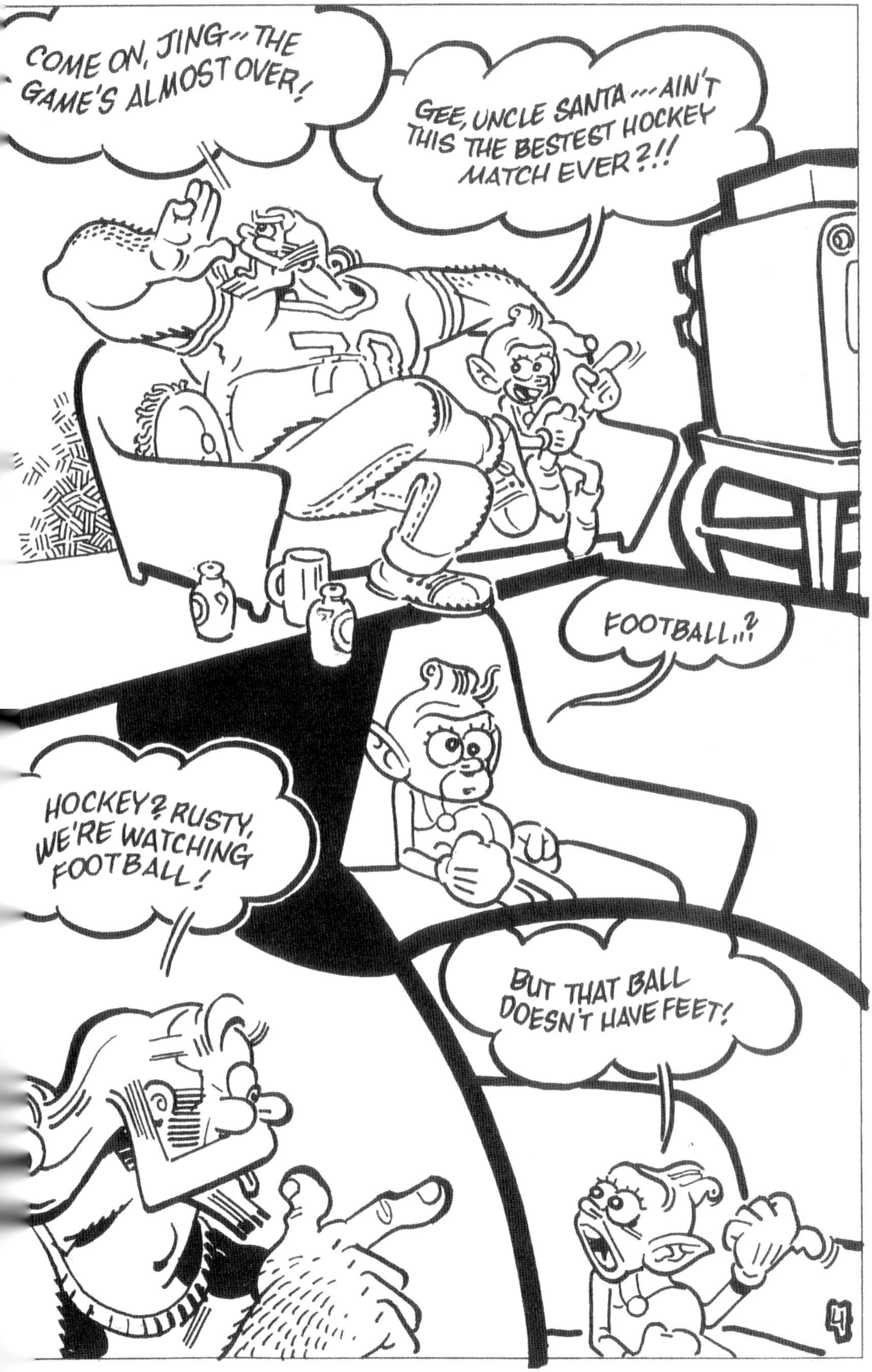
COME ON, JING-- THE GAME'S ALMOST OVER!
GEE, UNCLE SANTA--- AIN'T THIS THE BESTEST HOCKEY MATCH EVER?!!
FOOTBALL...?
HOCKEY? RUSTY, WE'RE WATCHING FOOTBALL!
BUT THAT BALL DOESN'T HAVE FEET!
4

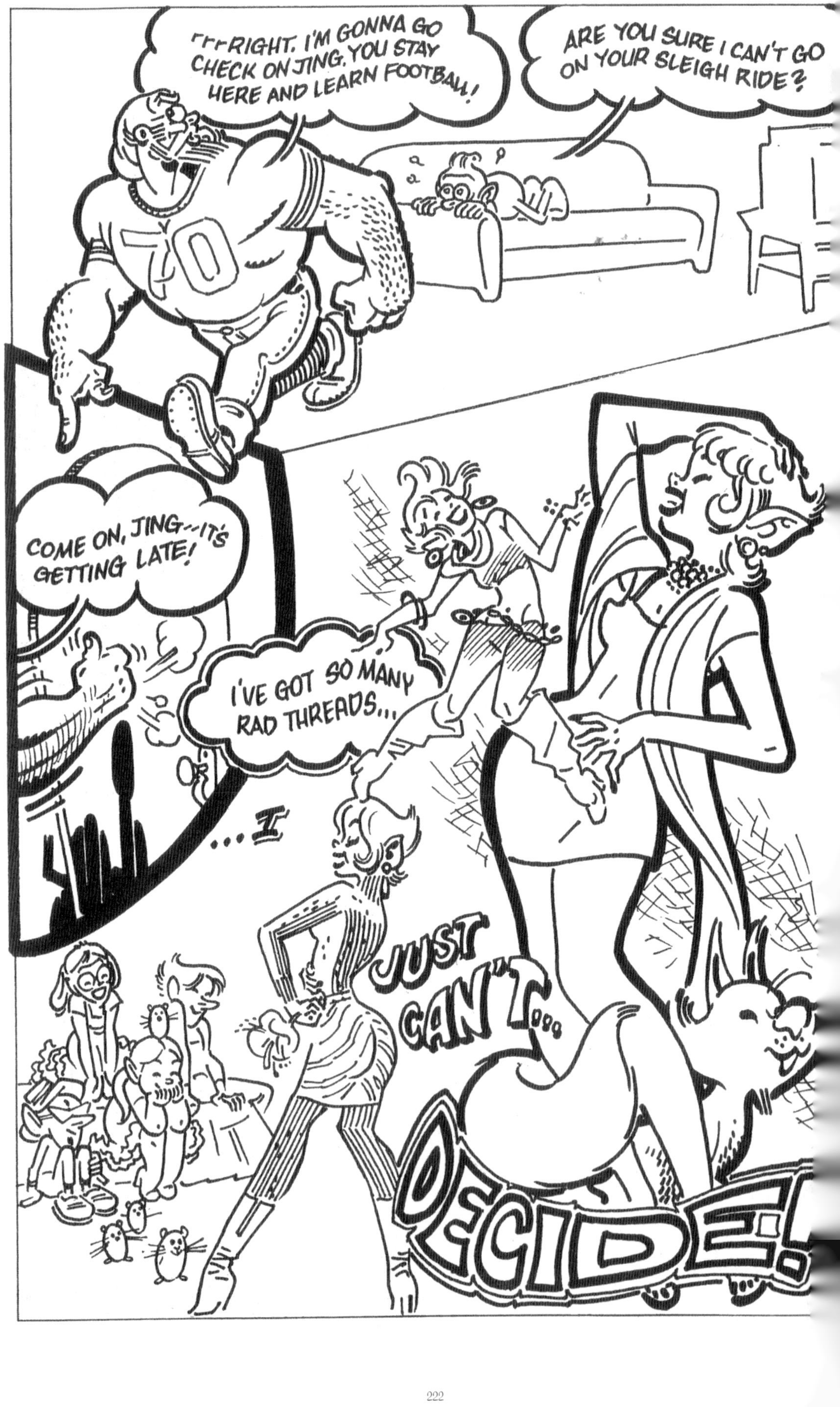

…RIGHT. I'M GONNA GO CHECK ON JING. YOU STAY HERE AND LEARN FOOTBALL!
ARE YOU SURE I CAN'T GO ON YOUR SLEIGH RIDE?
COME ON, JING--IT'S GETTING LATE!
I'VE GOT SO MANY RAD THREADS...
...I
JUST CAN'T...
DECIDE!

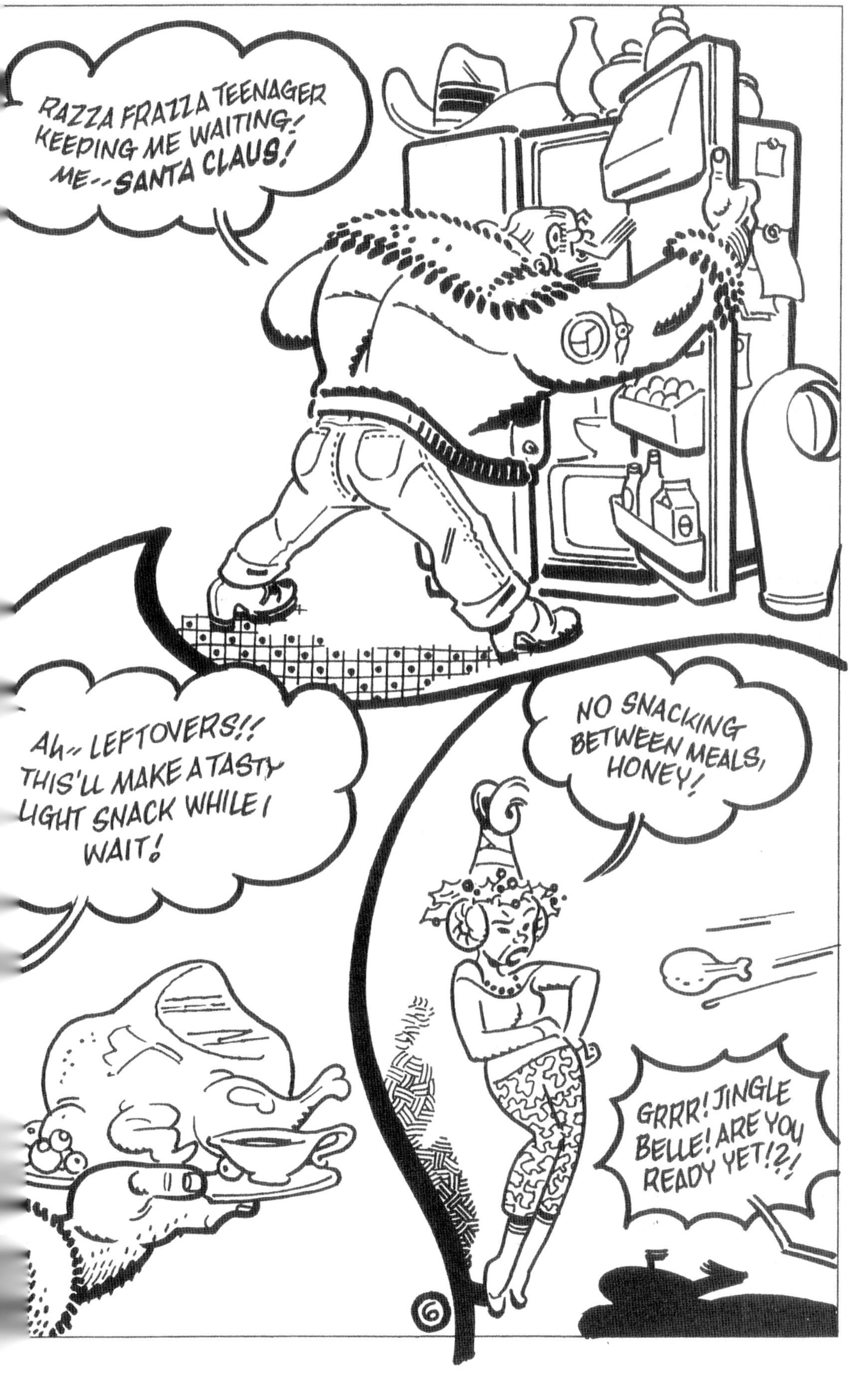
RAZZA FRAZZA TEENAGER KEEPING ME WAITING! ME--SANTA CLAUS!
AH-- LEFTOVERS!! THIS'LL MAKE A TASTY LIGHT SNACK WHILE I WAIT!
NO SNACKING BETWEEN MEALS, HONEY!
GRRR! JINGLE BELLE! ARE YOU READY YET!?!

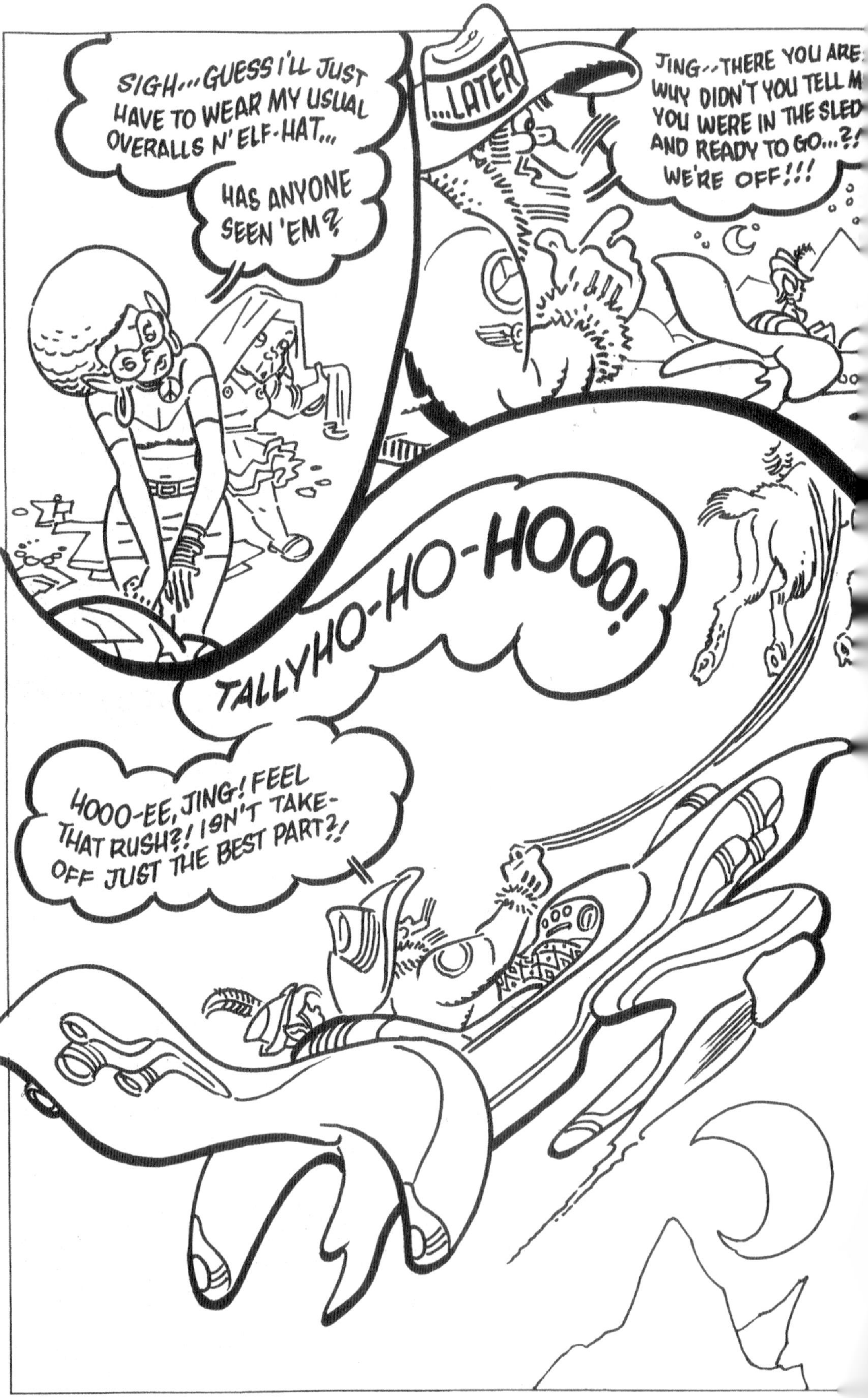
SIGH...GUESS I'LL JUST HAVE TO WEAR MY USUAL OVERALLS N' ELF-HAT...
HAS ANYONE SEEN 'EM?
...LATER
JING--THERE YOU ARE! WHY DIDN'T YOU TELL ME YOU WERE IN THE SLED AND READY TO GO...?! WE'RE OFF!!!
TALLYHO-HO-HOOO!!
HOOO-EE, JING! FEEL THAT RUSH?! ISN'T TAKE-OFF JUST THE BEST PART?!

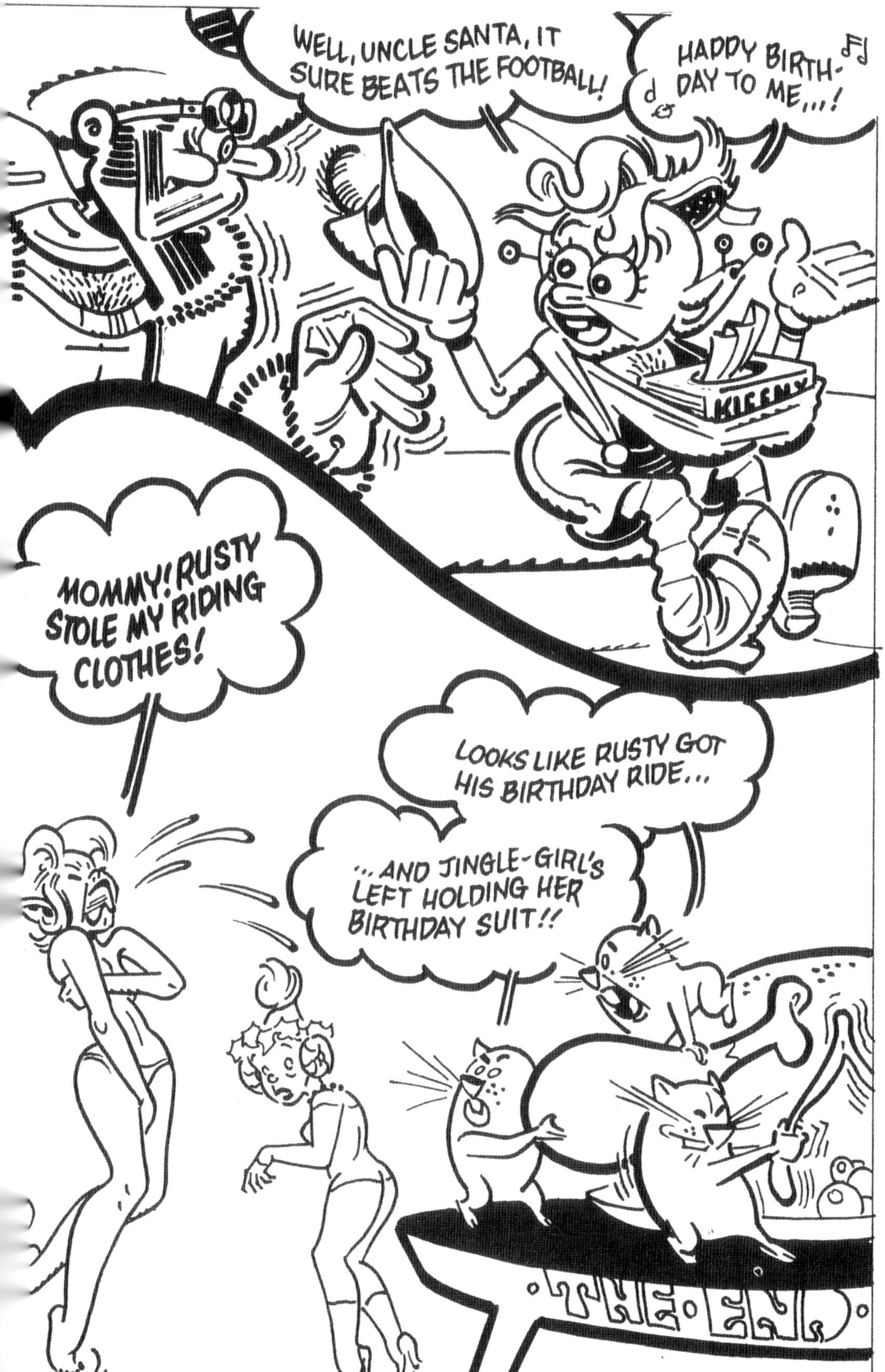
WELL, UNCLE SANTA, IT SURE BEATS THE FOOTBALL!
HAPPY BIRTH-DAY TO ME,..!
MOMMY! RUSTY STOLE MY RIDING CLOTHES!
LOOKS LIKE RUSTY GOT HIS BIRTHDAY RIDE...
...AND JINGLE-GIRL'S LEFT HOLDING HER BIRTHDAY SUIT!!
THE END

A Very Special Jingle Belle Special

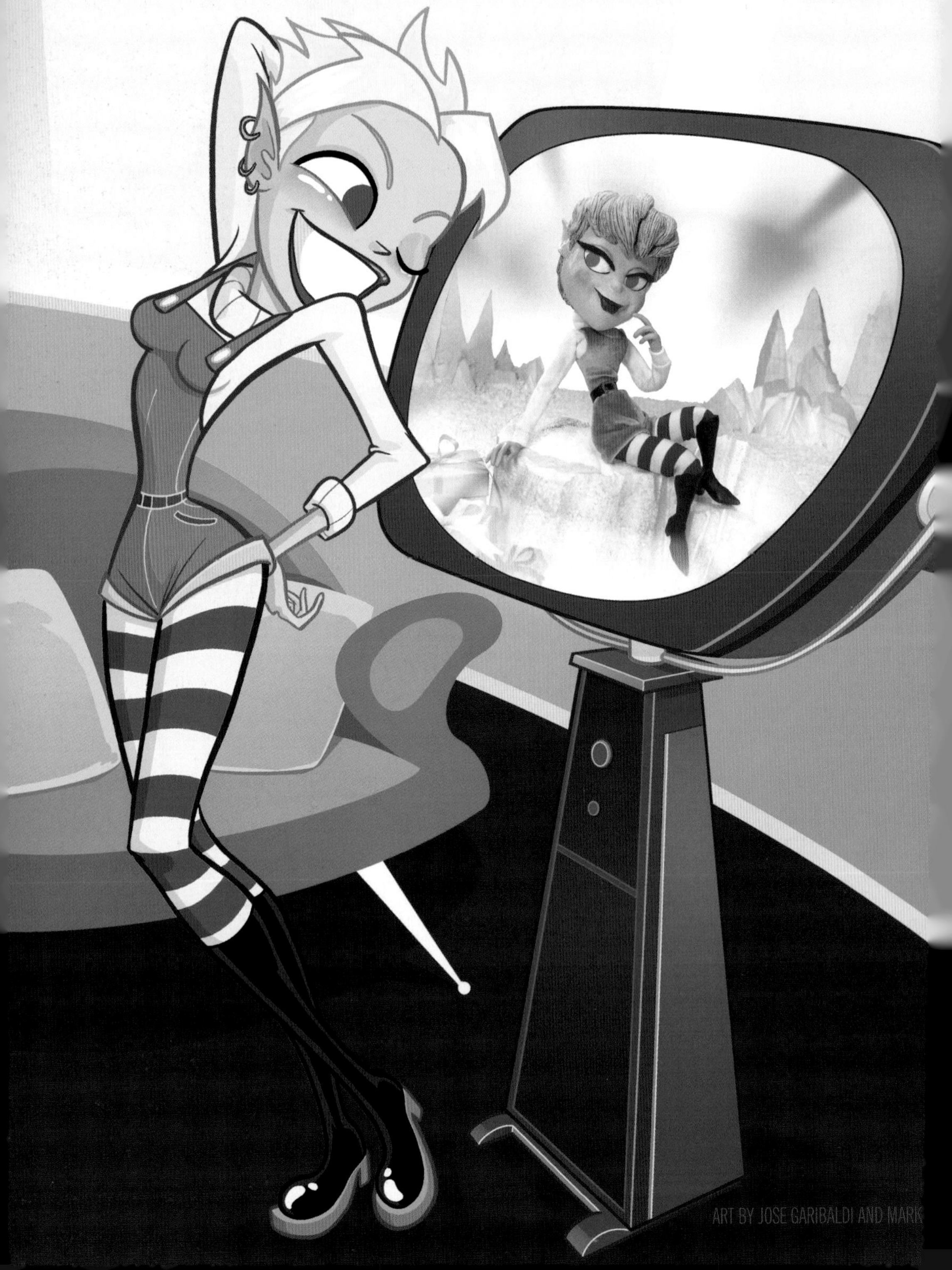

ART BY JOSE GARIBALDI AND MARK

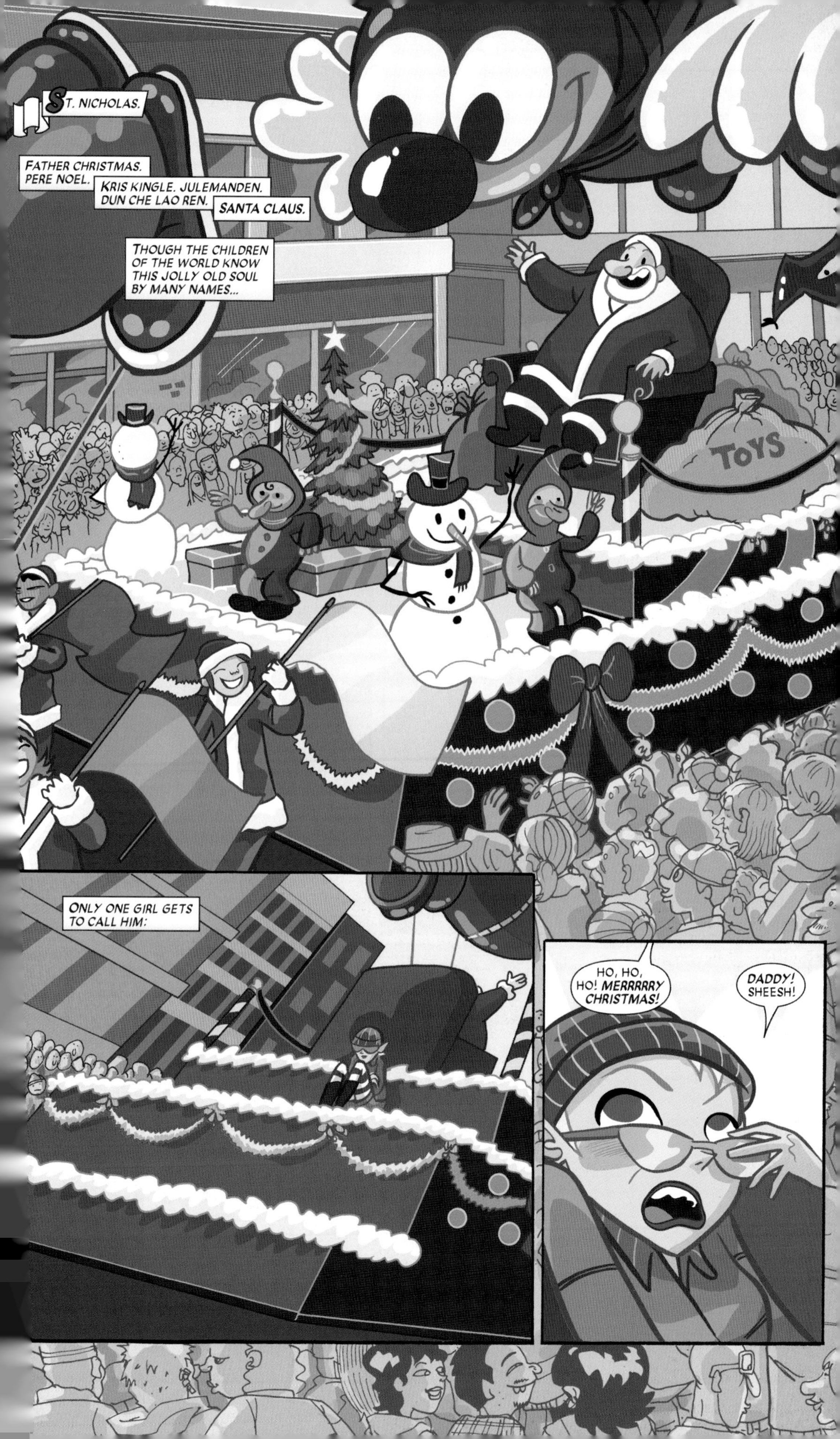

ST. NICHOLAS.
FATHER CHRISTMAS. PERE NOEL.
KRIS KINGLE. JULEMANDEN. DUN CHE LAO REN.
SANTA CLAUS.
THOUGH THE CHILDREN OF THE WORLD KNOW THIS JOLLY OLD SOUL BY MANY NAMES...
TOYS
ONLY ONE GIRL GETS TO CALL HIM:
HO, HO, HO! MERRRRRY CHRISTMAS!
DADDY! SHEESH!

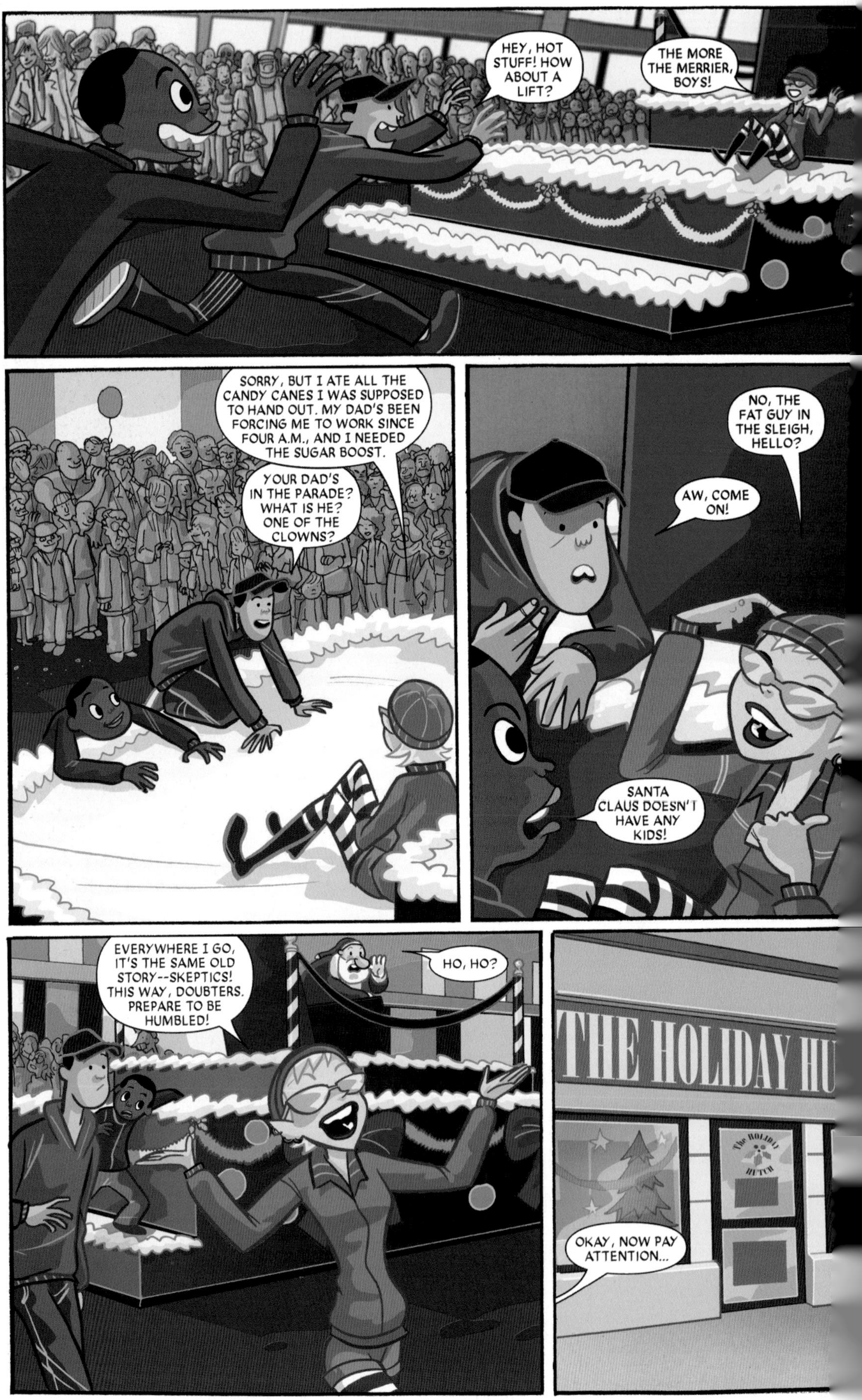
HEY, HOT STUFF! HOW ABOUT A LIFT?
THE MORE THE MERRIER, BOYS!
SORRY, BUT I ATE ALL THE CANDY CANES I WAS SUPPOSED TO HAND OUT. MY DAD'S BEEN FORCING ME TO WORK SINCE FOUR A.M., AND I NEEDED THE SUGAR BOOST.
YOUR DAD'S IN THE PARADE? WHAT IS HE? ONE OF THE CLOWNS?
NO, THE FAT GUY IN THE SLEIGH, HELLO?
AW, COME ON!
SANTA CLAUS DOESN'T HAVE ANY KIDS!
EVERYWHERE I GO, IT'S THE SAME OLD STORY--SKEPTICS! THIS WAY, DOUBTERS. PREPARE TO BE HUMBLED!
HO, HO?
THE HOLIDAY HU
OKAY, NOW PAY ATTENTION...

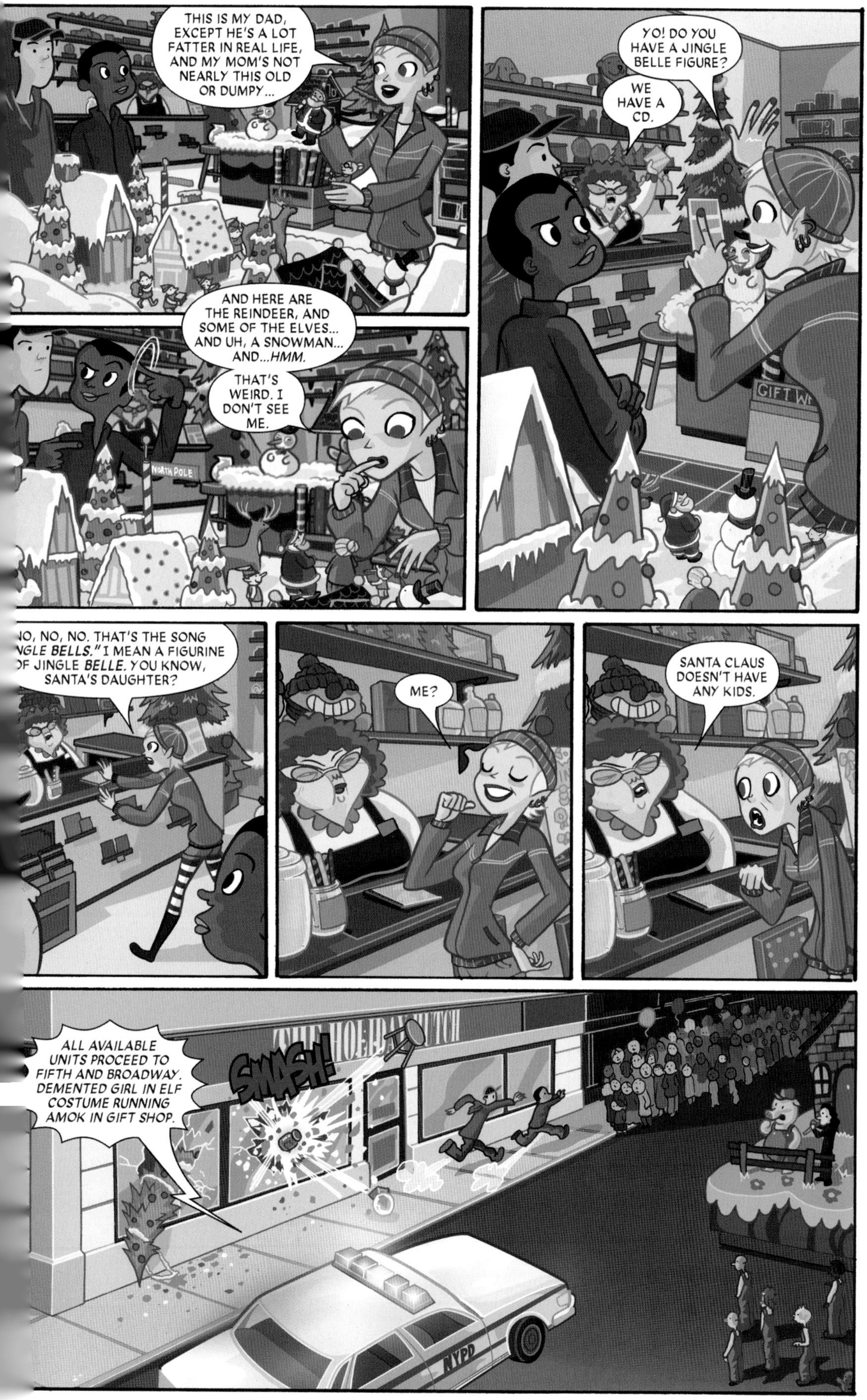
THIS IS MY DAD, EXCEPT HE'S A LOT FATTER IN REAL LIFE, AND MY MOM'S NOT NEARLY THIS OLD OR DUMPY...
YO! DO YOU HAVE A JINGLE BELLE FIGURE?
WE HAVE A CD.
AND HERE ARE THE REINDEER, AND SOME OF THE ELVES... AND UH, A SNOWMAN... AND...HMM.
THAT'S WEIRD. I DON'T SEE ME.
NORTH POLE
GIFT W
NO, NO, NO. THAT'S THE SONG "JINGLE BELLS." I MEAN A FIGURINE OF JINGLE BELLE. YOU KNOW, SANTA'S DAUGHTER?
ME?
SANTA CLAUS DOESN'T HAVE ANY KIDS.
ALL AVAILABLE UNITS PROCEED TO FIFTH AND BROADWAY. DEMENTED GIRL IN ELF COSTUME RUNNING AMOK IN GIFT SHOP.
SMASH!
NYPD

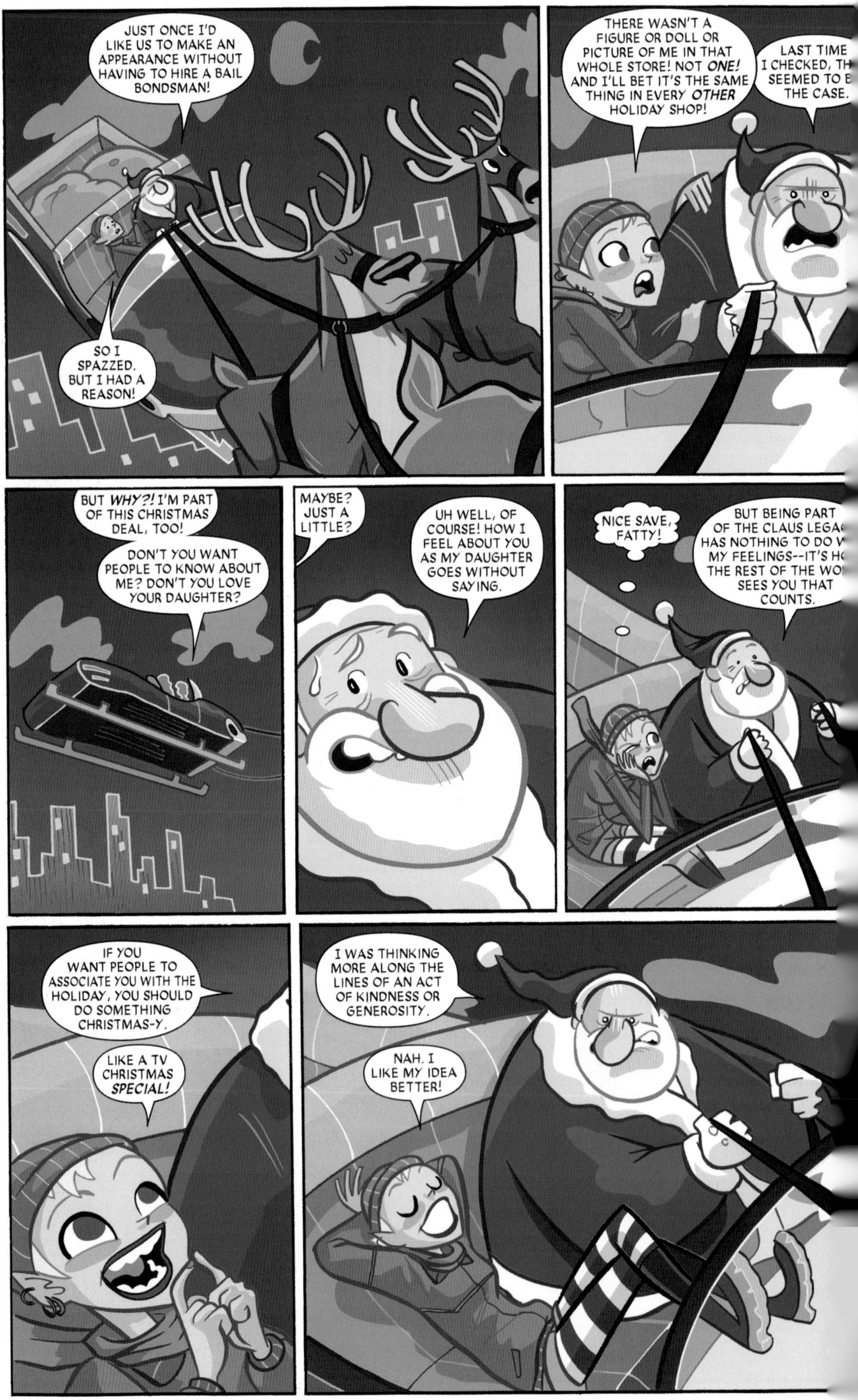
JUST ONCE I'D LIKE US TO MAKE AN APPEARANCE WITHOUT HAVING TO HIRE A BAIL BONDSMAN!
SO I SPAZZED. BUT I HAD A REASON!
THERE WASN'T A FIGURE OR DOLL OR PICTURE OF ME IN THAT WHOLE STORE! NOT *ONE!* AND I'LL BET IT'S THE SAME THING IN EVERY *OTHER* HOLIDAY SHOP!
LAST TIME I CHECKED, TH SEEMED TO B THE CASE.
BUT *WHY?!* I'M PART OF THIS CHRISTMAS DEAL, TOO!
DON'T YOU WANT PEOPLE TO KNOW ABOUT ME? DON'T YOU LOVE YOUR DAUGHTER?
MAYBE? JUST A LITTLE?
UH WELL, OF COURSE! HOW I FEEL ABOUT YOU AS MY DAUGHTER GOES WITHOUT SAYING.
NICE SAVE, FATTY!
BUT BEING PART OF THE CLAUS LEGA HAS NOTHING TO DO W MY FEELINGS--IT'S H THE REST OF THE WO SEES YOU THAT COUNTS.
IF YOU WANT PEOPLE TO ASSOCIATE YOU WITH THE HOLIDAY, YOU SHOULD DO SOMETHING CHRISTMAS-Y.
LIKE A TV CHRISTMAS *SPECIAL!*
I WAS THINKING MORE ALONG THE LINES OF AN ACT OF KINDNESS OR GENEROSITY.
NAH. I LIKE MY IDEA BETTER!

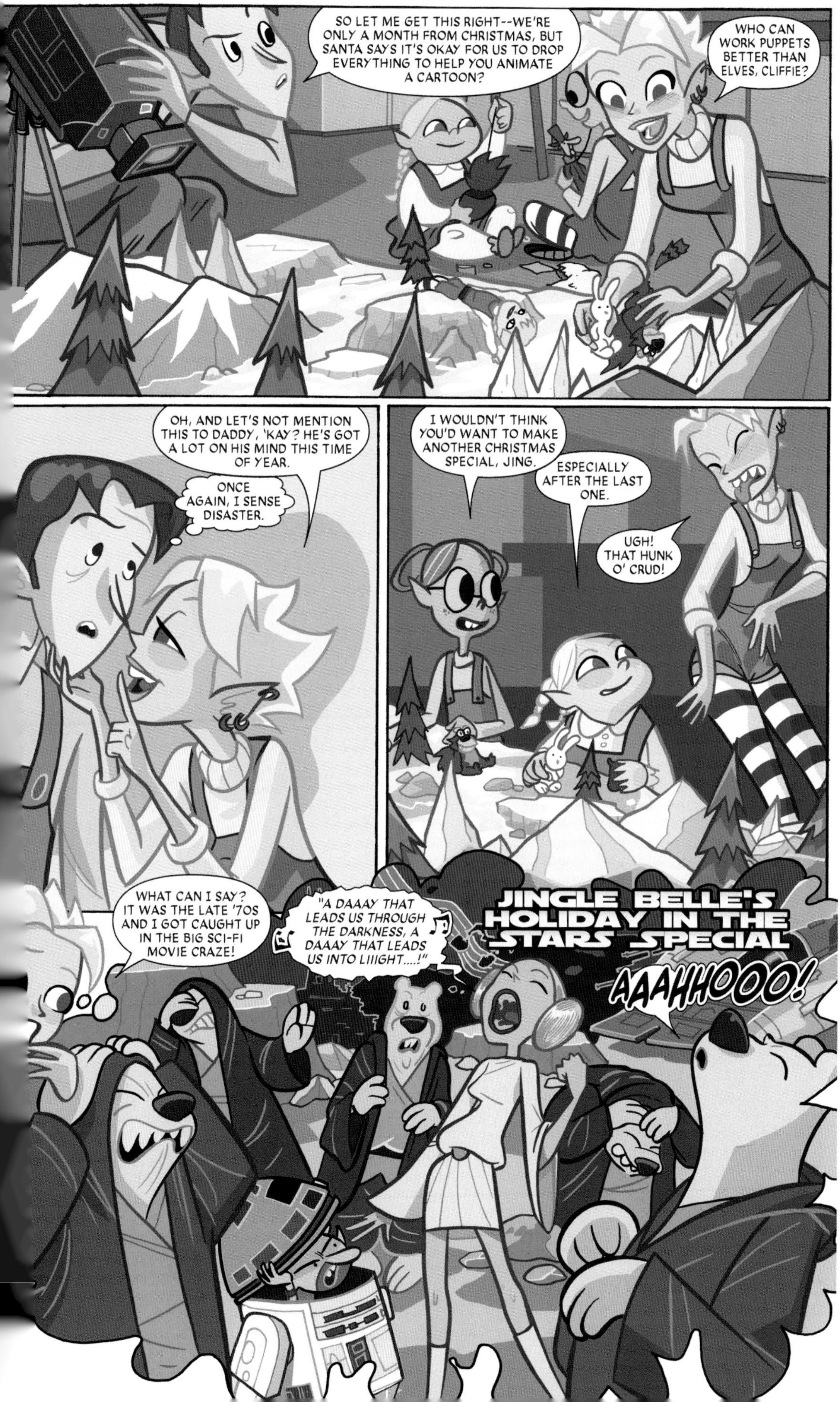
SO LET ME GET THIS RIGHT--WE'RE ONLY A MONTH FROM CHRISTMAS, BUT SANTA SAYS IT'S OKAY FOR US TO DROP EVERYTHING TO HELP YOU ANIMATE A CARTOON?
WHO CAN WORK PUPPETS BETTER THAN ELVES, CLIFFIE?
OH, AND LET'S NOT MENTION THIS TO DADDY, 'KAY? HE'S GOT A LOT ON HIS MIND THIS TIME OF YEAR.
ONCE AGAIN, I SENSE DISASTER.
I WOULDN'T THINK YOU'D WANT TO MAKE ANOTHER CHRISTMAS SPECIAL, JING.
ESPECIALLY AFTER THE LAST ONE.
UGH! THAT HUNK O' CRUD!
WHAT CAN I SAY? IT WAS THE LATE '70S AND I GOT CAUGHT UP IN THE BIG SCI-FI MOVIE CRAZE!
"A DAAAY THAT LEADS US THROUGH THE DARKNESS, A DAAAY THAT LEADS US INTO LIIIGHT....!"
JINGLE BELLE'S HOLIDAY IN THE STARS SPECIAL
AAAHHOOOO!

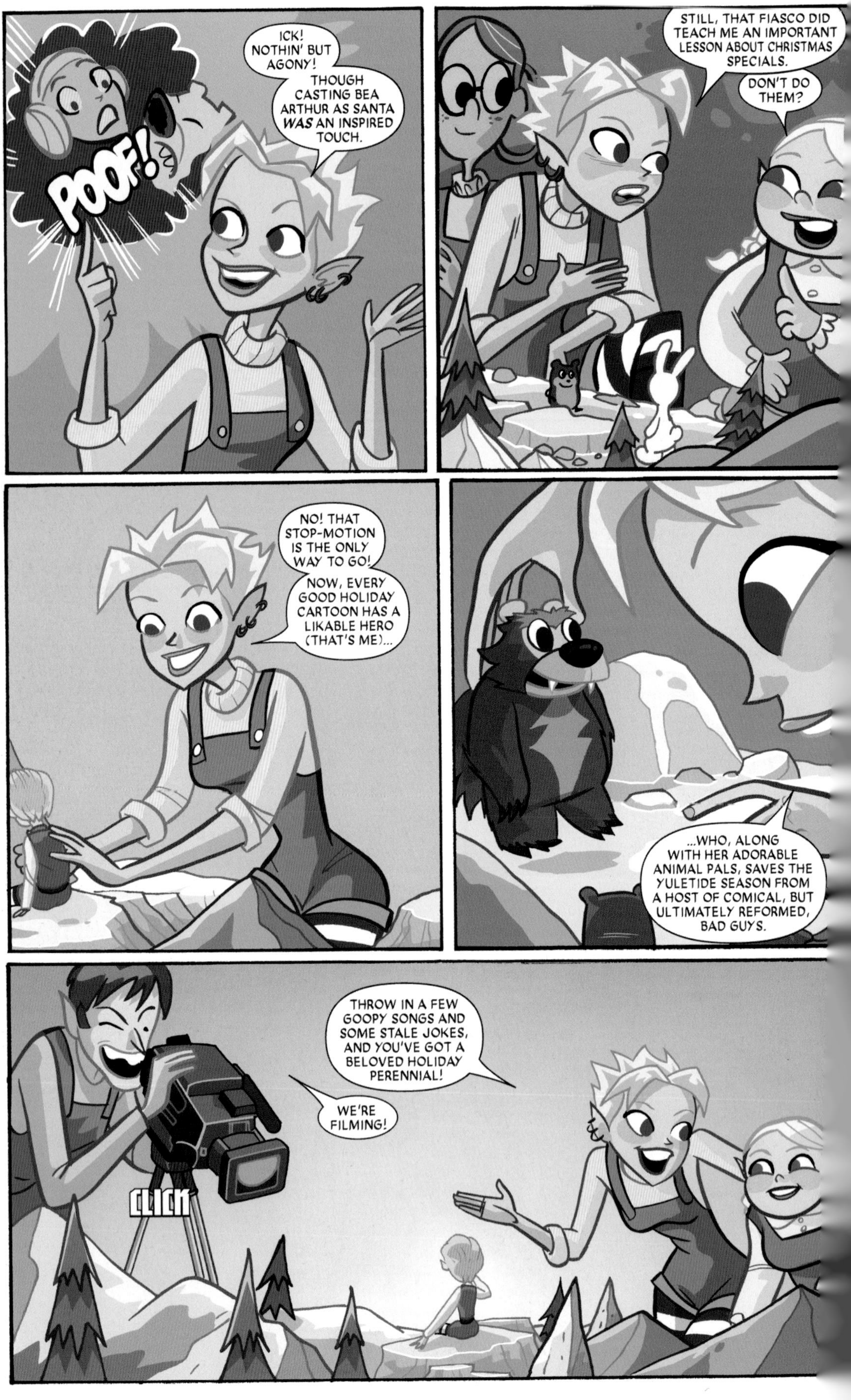
ICK! NOTHIN' BUT AGONY!
THOUGH CASTING BEA ARTHUR AS SANTA *WAS* AN INSPIRED TOUCH.
POOF!!
STILL, THAT FIASCO DID TEACH ME AN IMPORTANT LESSON ABOUT CHRISTMAS SPECIALS.
DON'T DO THEM?
NO! THAT STOP-MOTION IS THE ONLY WAY TO GO!
NOW, EVERY GOOD HOLIDAY CARTOON HAS A LIKABLE HERO (THAT'S ME)...
...WHO, ALONG WITH HER ADORABLE ANIMAL PALS, SAVES THE YULETIDE SEASON FROM A HOST OF COMICAL, BUT ULTIMATELY REFORMED, BAD GUYS.
THROW IN A FEW GOOPY SONGS AND SOME STALE JOKES, AND YOU'VE GOT A BELOVED HOLIDAY PERENNIAL!
WE'RE FILMING!
CLICK

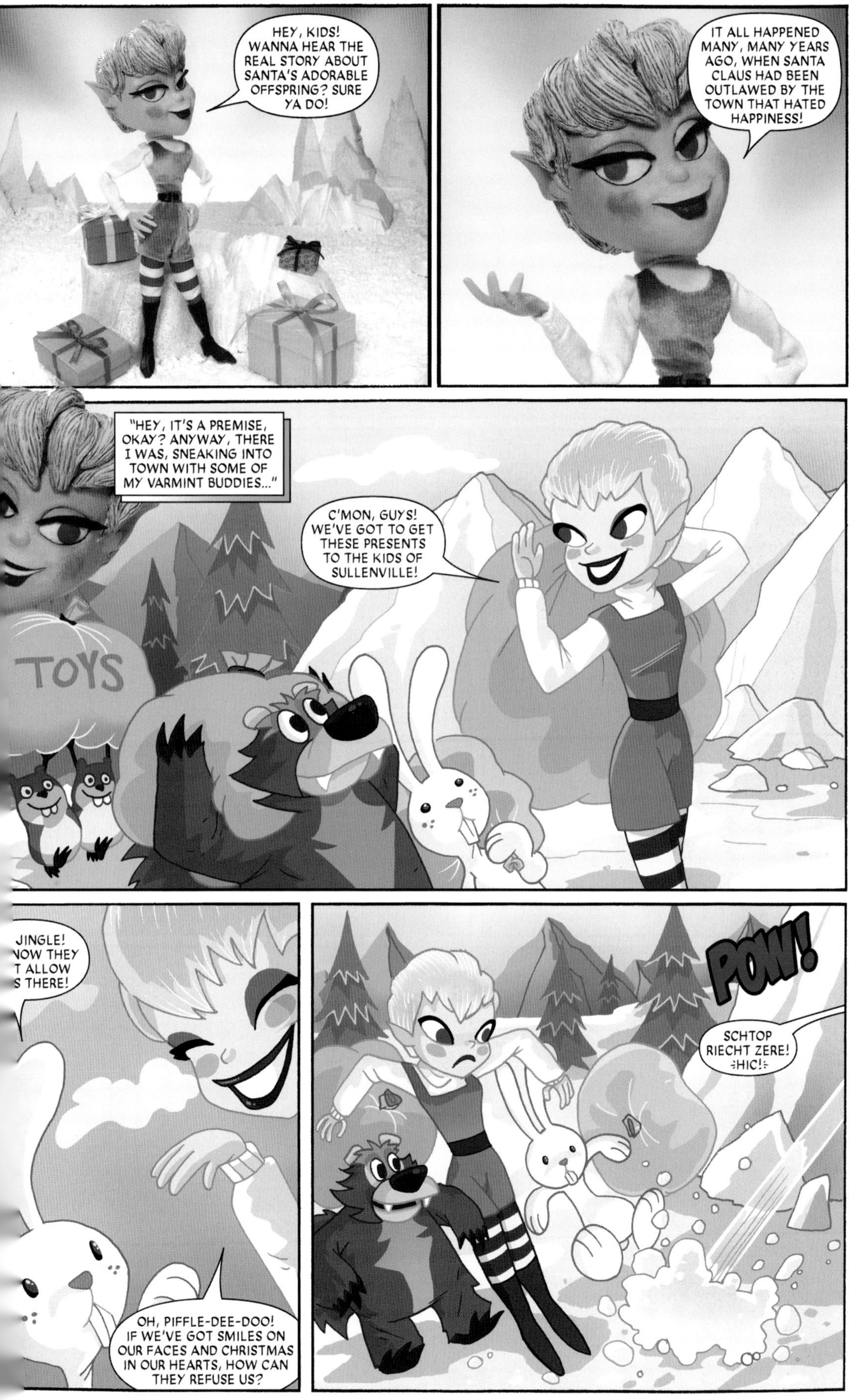
HEY, KIDS! WANNA HEAR THE REAL STORY ABOUT SANTA'S ADORABLE OFFSPRING? SURE YA DO!
IT ALL HAPPENED MANY, MANY YEARS AGO, WHEN SANTA CLAUS HAD BEEN OUTLAWED BY THE TOWN THAT HATED HAPPINESS!
"HEY, IT'S A PREMISE, OKAY? ANYWAY, THERE I WAS, SNEAKING INTO TOWN WITH SOME OF MY VARMINT BUDDIES..."
C'MON, GUYS! WE'VE GOT TO GET THESE PRESENTS TO THE KIDS OF SULLENVILLE!
TOYS
JINGLE! NOW THEY T ALLOW S THERE!
OH, PIFFLE-DEE-DOO! IF WE'VE GOT SMILES ON OUR FACES AND CHRISTMAS IN OUR HEARTS, HOW CAN THEY REFUSE US?
POW!
SCHTOP RIECHT ZERE! HIC!

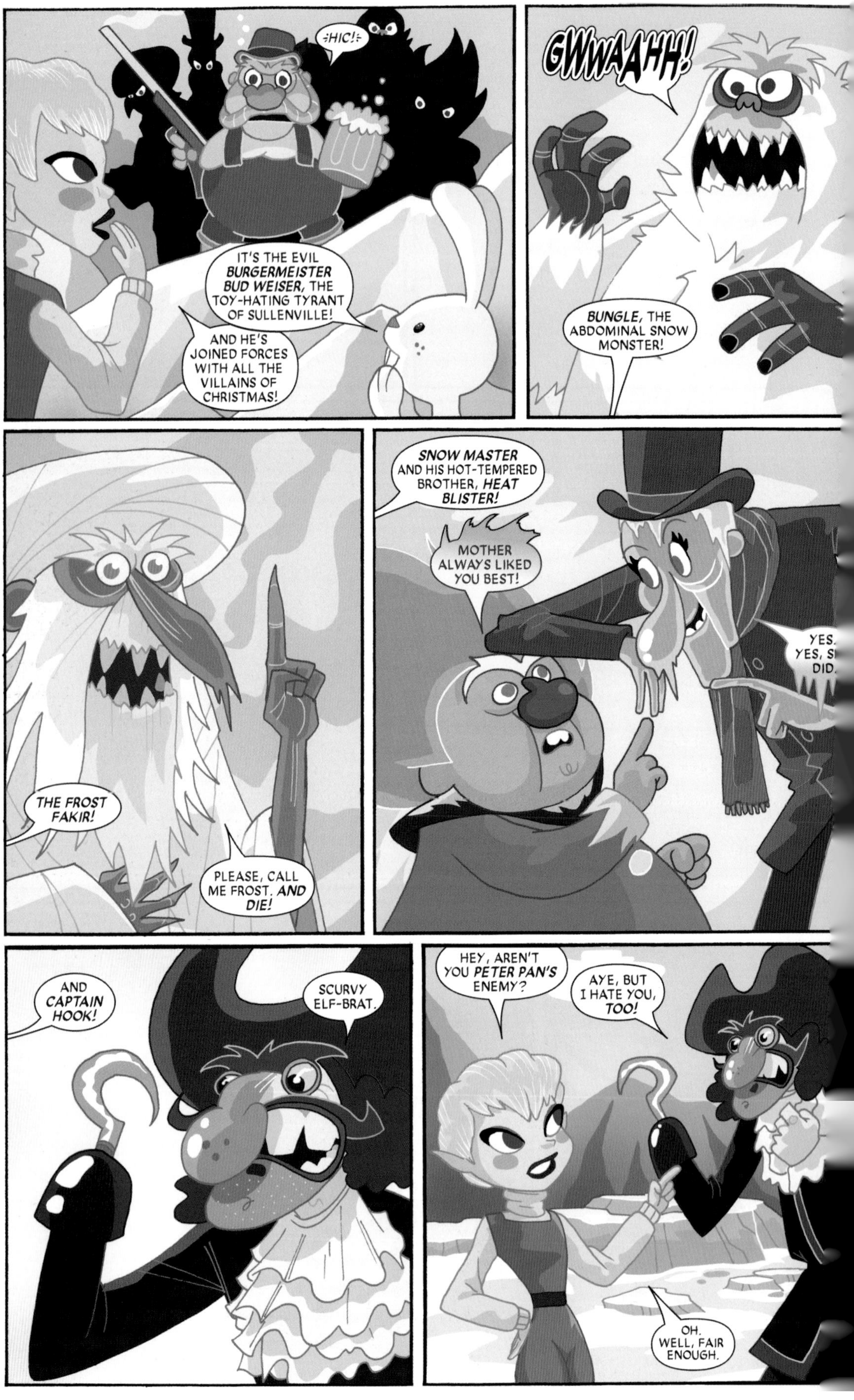
:HIC!:
IT'S THE EVIL BURGERMEISTER BUD WEISER, THE TOY-HATING TYRANT OF SULLENVILLE!
AND HE'S JOINED FORCES WITH ALL THE VILLAINS OF CHRISTMAS!
GWWAAHH!
BUNGLE, THE ABDOMINAL SNOW MONSTER!
THE FROST FAKIR!
PLEASE, CALL ME FROST. AND DIE!
SNOW MASTER AND HIS HOT-TEMPERED BROTHER, HEAT BLISTER!
MOTHER ALWAYS LIKED YOU BEST!
AND CAPTAIN HOOK!
SCURVY ELF-BRAT.
HEY, AREN'T YOU PETER PAN'S ENEMY?
AYE, BUT I HATE YOU, TOO!
OH. WELL, FAIR ENOUGH.

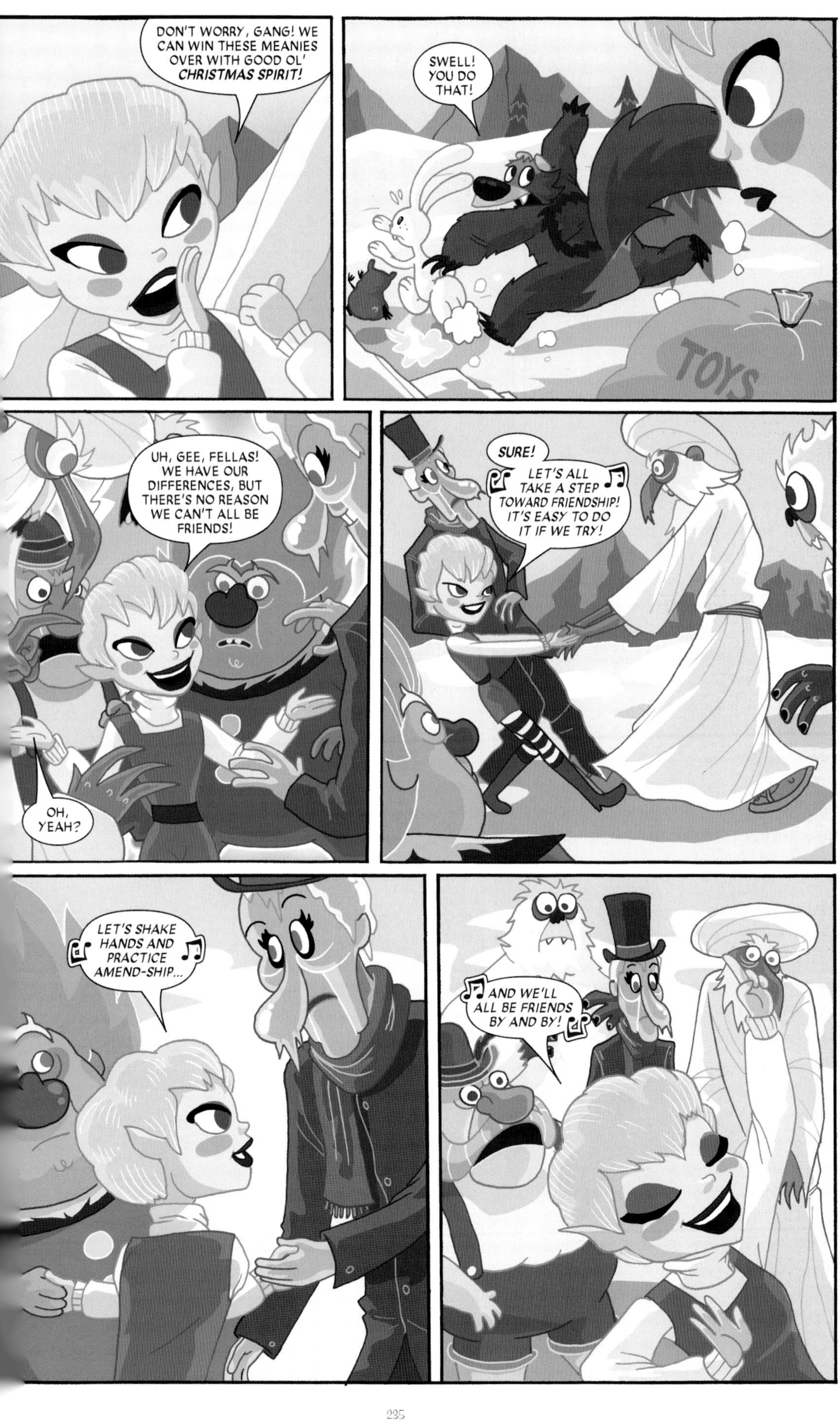
DON'T WORRY, GANG! WE CAN WIN THESE MEANIES OVER WITH GOOD OL' CHRISTMAS SPIRIT!
SWELL! YOU DO THAT!
TOYS
UH, GEE, FELLAS! WE HAVE OUR DIFFERENCES, BUT THERE'S NO REASON WE CAN'T ALL BE FRIENDS!
OH, YEAH?
SURE!
LET'S ALL TAKE A STEP TOWARD FRIENDSHIP! IT'S EASY TO DO IT IF WE TRY!
LET'S SHAKE HANDS AND PRACTICE AMEND-SHIP...
AND WE'LL ALL BE FRIENDS BY AND BY!

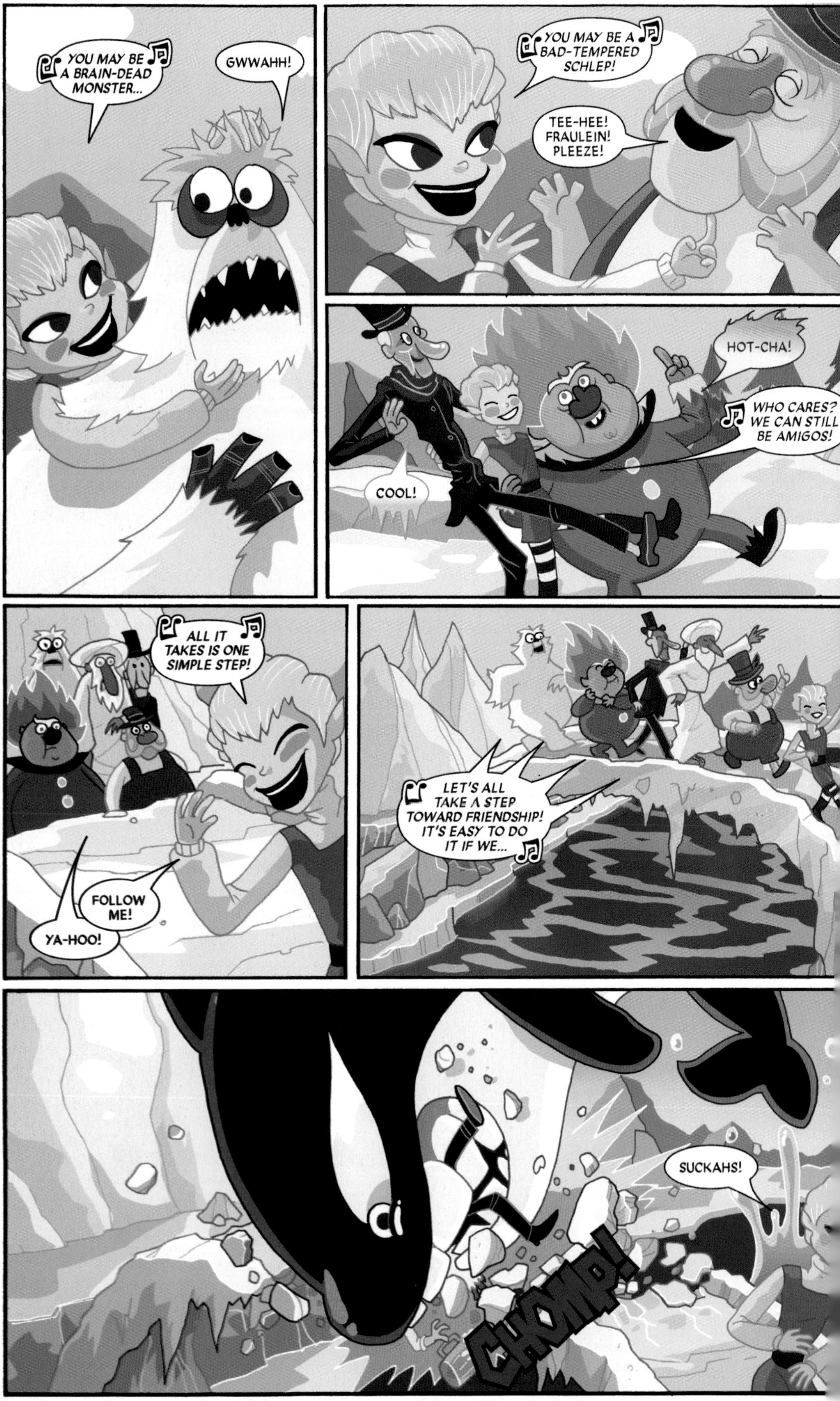
YOU MAY BE A BRAIN-DEAD MONSTER...
GWWAHH!
YOU MAY BE A BAD-TEMPERED SCHLEP!
TEE-HEE! FRAULEIN! PLEEZE!
HOT-CHA!
WHO CARES? WE CAN STILL BE AMIGOS!
COOL!
ALL IT TAKES IS ONE SIMPLE STEP!
FOLLOW ME!
YA-HOO!
LET'S ALL TAKE A STEP TOWARD FRIENDSHIP! IT'S EASY TO DO IT IF WE...
SUCKAHS!
CHOMP!

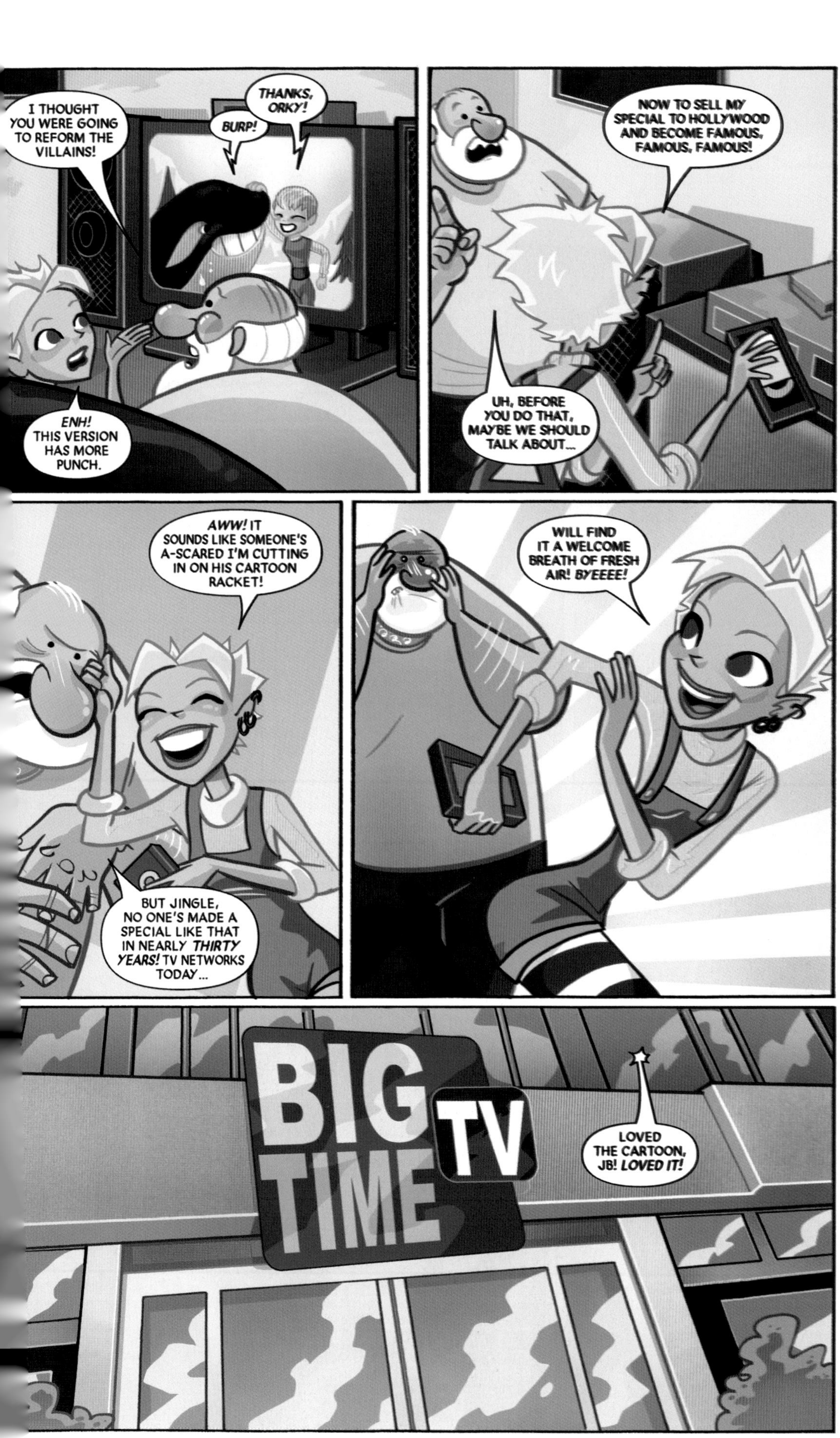
I THOUGHT YOU WERE GOING TO REFORM THE VILLAINS!
BURP!
THANKS, ORKY!
ENH! THIS VERSION HAS MORE PUNCH.
NOW TO SELL MY SPECIAL TO HOLLYWOOD AND BECOME FAMOUS, FAMOUS, FAMOUS!
UH, BEFORE YOU DO THAT, MAYBE WE SHOULD TALK ABOUT...
AWW! IT SOUNDS LIKE SOMEONE'S A-SCARED I'M CUTTING IN ON HIS CARTOON RACKET!
BUT JINGLE, NO ONE'S MADE A SPECIAL LIKE THAT IN NEARLY THIRTY YEARS! TV NETWORKS TODAY...
WILL FIND IT A WELCOME BREATH OF FRESH AIR! BYEEEE!
BIG TIME TV
LOVED THE CARTOON, JB! LOVED IT!

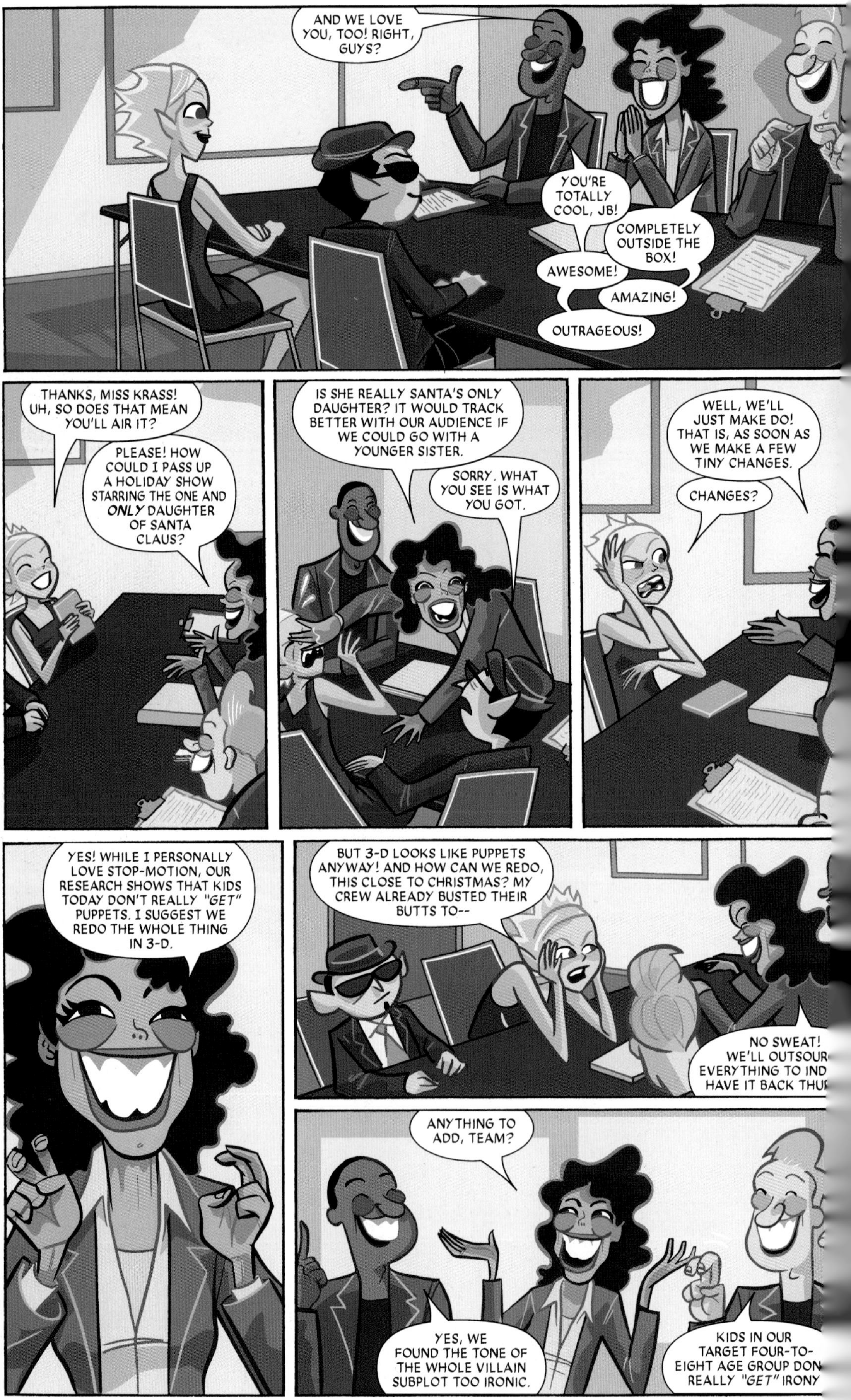
AND WE LOVE YOU, TOO! RIGHT, GUYS?
YOU'RE TOTALLY COOL, JB!
COMPLETELY OUTSIDE THE BOX!
AWESOME!
AMAZING!
OUTRAGEOUS!
THANKS, MISS KRASS! UH, SO DOES THAT MEAN YOU'LL AIR IT?
PLEASE! HOW COULD I PASS UP A HOLIDAY SHOW STARRING THE ONE AND ONLY DAUGHTER OF SANTA CLAUS?
IS SHE REALLY SANTA'S ONLY DAUGHTER? IT WOULD TRACK BETTER WITH OUR AUDIENCE IF WE COULD GO WITH A YOUNGER SISTER.
SORRY. WHAT YOU SEE IS WHAT YOU GOT.
WELL, WE'LL JUST MAKE DO! THAT IS, AS SOON AS WE MAKE A FEW TINY CHANGES.
CHANGES?
YES! WHILE I PERSONALLY LOVE STOP-MOTION, OUR RESEARCH SHOWS THAT KIDS TODAY DON'T REALLY "GET" PUPPETS. I SUGGEST WE REDO THE WHOLE THING IN 3-D.
BUT 3-D LOOKS LIKE PUPPETS ANYWAY! AND HOW CAN WE REDO, THIS CLOSE TO CHRISTMAS? MY CREW ALREADY BUSTED THEIR BUTTS TO--
NO SWEAT! WE'LL OUTSOUR EVERYTHING TO IND HAVE IT BACK THU
ANYTHING TO ADD, TEAM?
YES, WE FOUND THE TONE OF THE WHOLE VILLAIN SUBPLOT TOO IRONIC.
KIDS IN OUR TARGET FOUR-TO-EIGHT AGE GROUP DON REALLY "GET" IRONY

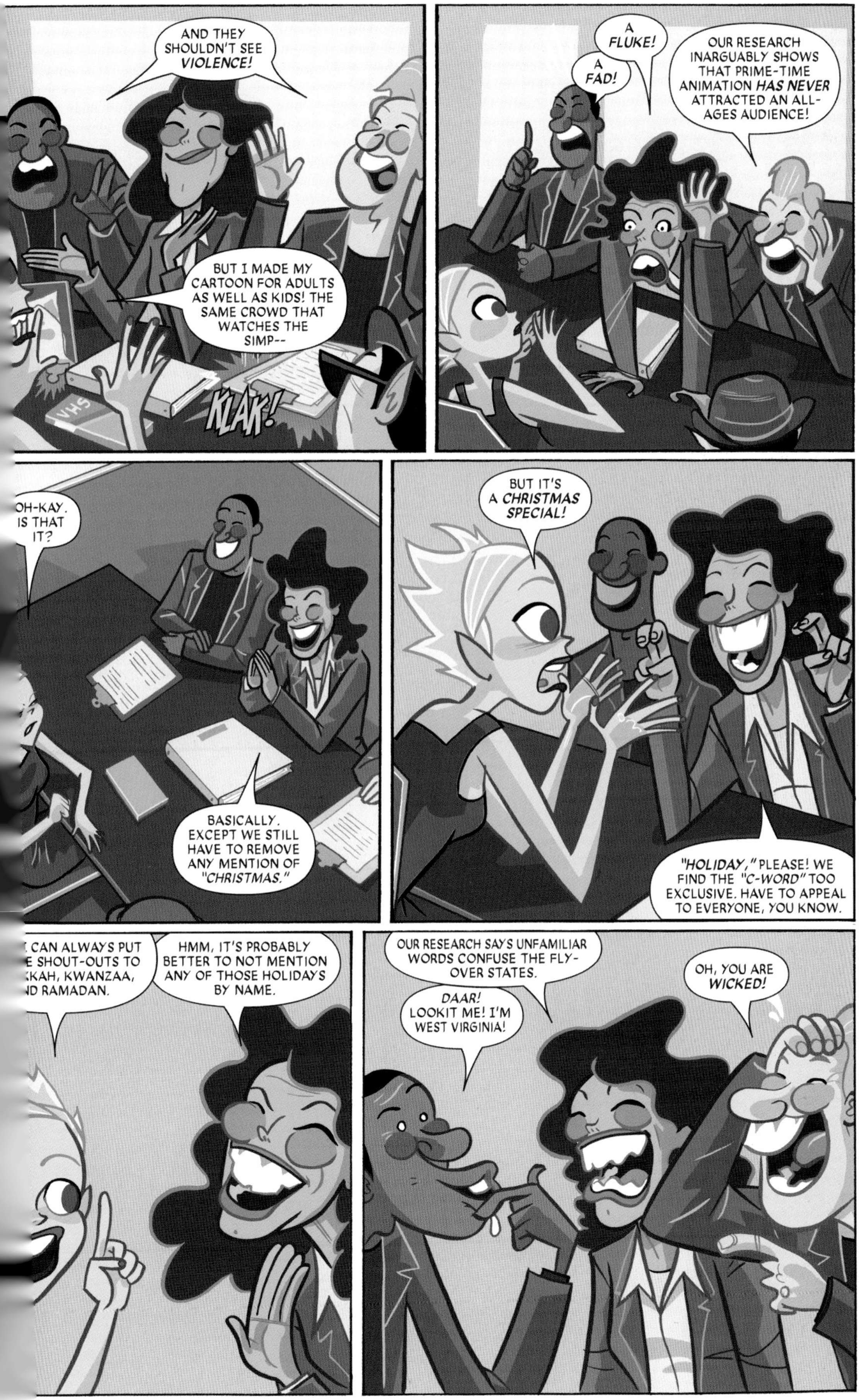
AND THEY SHOULDN'T SEE *VIOLENCE!*
BUT I MADE MY CARTOON FOR ADULTS AS WELL AS KIDS! THE SAME CROWD THAT WATCHES THE SIMP--
KLAK!
A *FLUKE!*
A *FAD!*
OUR RESEARCH INARGUABLY SHOWS THAT PRIME-TIME ANIMATION *HAS NEVER* ATTRACTED AN ALL-AGES AUDIENCE!
OH-KAY. IS THAT IT?
BASICALLY. EXCEPT WE STILL HAVE TO REMOVE ANY MENTION OF "*CHRISTMAS.*"
BUT IT'S A *CHRISTMAS SPECIAL!*
"*HOLIDAY,*" PLEASE! WE FIND THE "*C-WORD*" TOO EXCLUSIVE. HAVE TO APPEAL TO EVERYONE, YOU KNOW.
CAN ALWAYS PUT SHOUT-OUTS TO KKAH, KWANZAA, ND RAMADAN.
HMM, IT'S PROBABLY BETTER TO NOT MENTION ANY OF THOSE HOLIDAYS BY NAME.
OUR RESEARCH SAYS UNFAMILIAR WORDS CONFUSE THE FLY-OVER STATES.
DAAR! LOOKIT ME! I'M WEST VIRGINIA!
OH, YOU ARE *WICKED!*

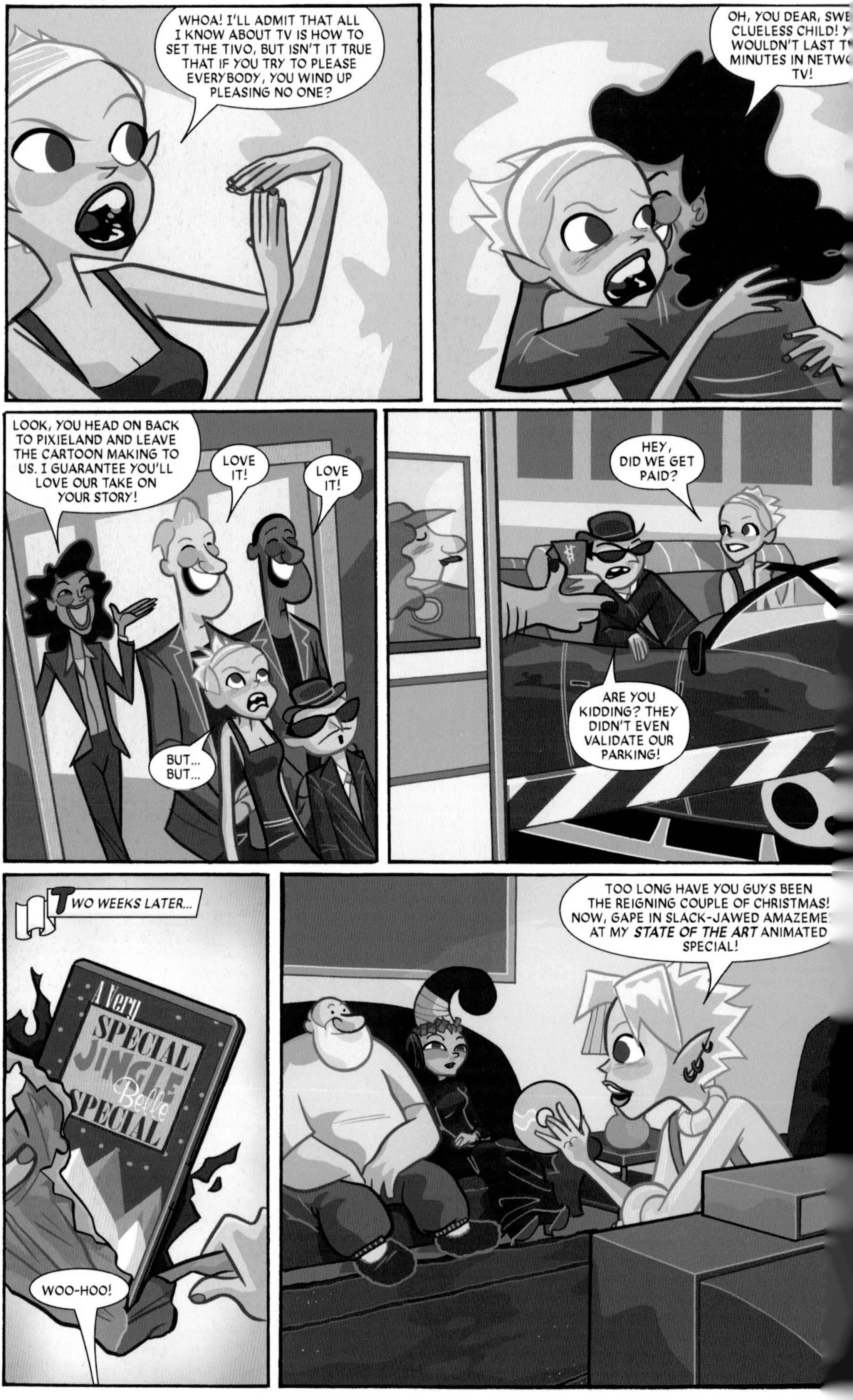

WHOA! I'LL ADMIT THAT ALL I KNOW ABOUT TV IS HOW TO SET THE TIVO, BUT ISN'T IT TRUE THAT IF YOU TRY TO PLEASE EVERYBODY, YOU WIND UP PLEASING NO ONE?
OH, YOU DEAR, SWE CLUELESS CHILD! Y WOULDN'T LAST T MINUTES IN NETW TV!
LOOK, YOU HEAD ON BACK TO PIXIELAND AND LEAVE THE CARTOON MAKING TO US. I GUARANTEE YOU'LL LOVE OUR TAKE ON YOUR STORY!
LOVE IT!
LOVE IT!
BUT... BUT...
HEY, DID WE GET PAID?
ARE YOU KIDDING? THEY DIDN'T EVEN VALIDATE OUR PARKING!
TWO WEEKS LATER...
A Very SPECIAL JINGLE Belle SPECIAL
WOO-HOO!
TOO LONG HAVE YOU GUYS BEEN THE REIGNING COUPLE OF CHRISTMAS! NOW, GAPE IN SLACK-JAWED AMAZEME AT MY STATE OF THE ART ANIMATED SPECIAL!

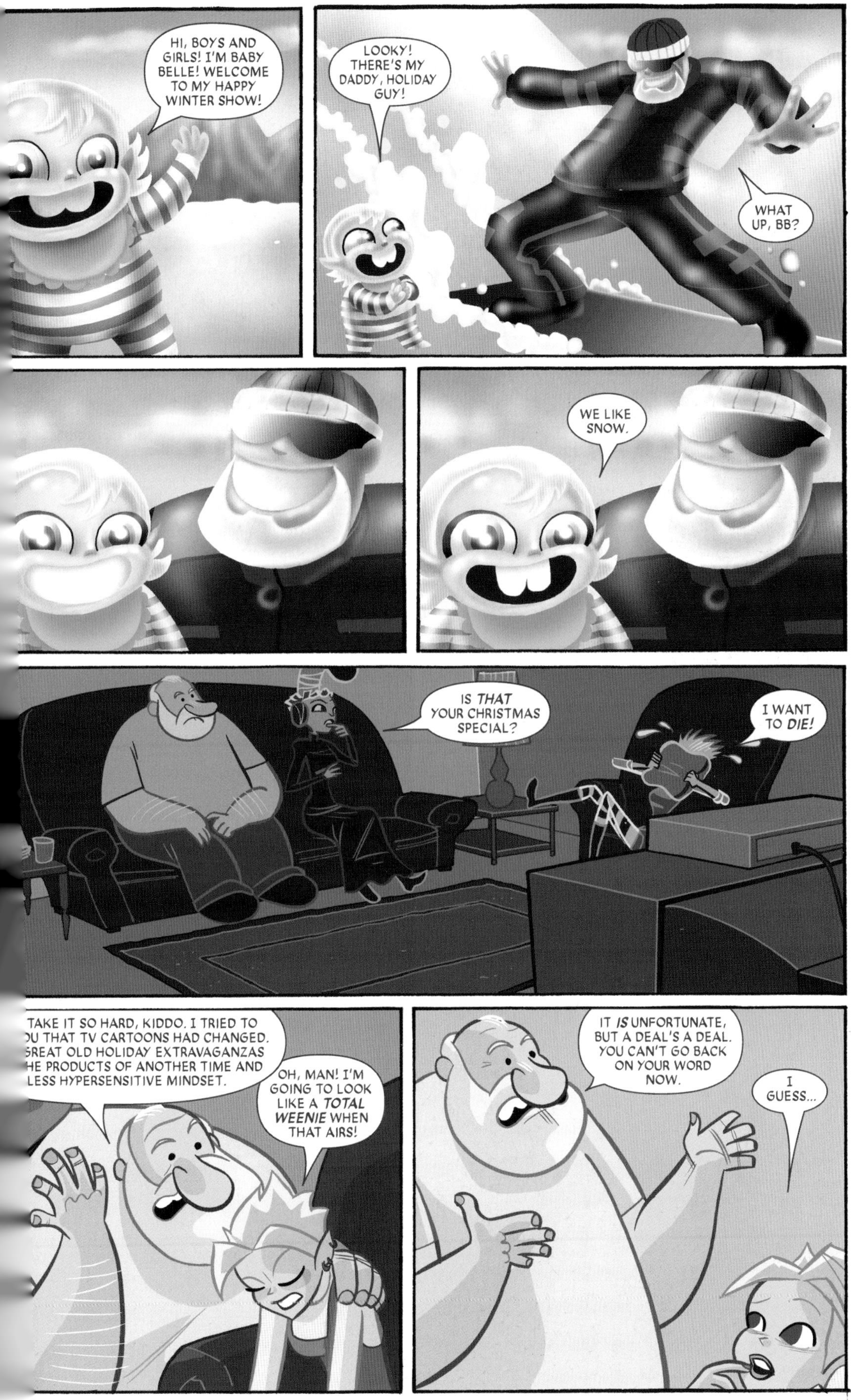
HI, BOYS AND GIRLS! I'M BABY BELLE! WELCOME TO MY HAPPY WINTER SHOW!
LOOKY! THERE'S MY DADDY, HOLIDAY GUY!
WHAT UP, BB?
WE LIKE SNOW.
IS *THAT* YOUR CHRISTMAS SPECIAL?
I WANT TO *DIE!*
TAKE IT SO HARD, KIDDO. I TRIED TO OU THAT TV CARTOONS HAD CHANGED. GREAT OLD HOLIDAY EXTRAVAGANZAS HE PRODUCTS OF ANOTHER TIME AND LESS HYPERSENSITIVE MINDSET.
OH, MAN! I'M GOING TO LOOK LIKE A *TOTAL WEENIE* WHEN THAT AIRS!
IT *IS* UNFORTUNATE, BUT A DEAL'S A DEAL. YOU CAN'T GO BACK ON YOUR WORD NOW.
I GUESS...

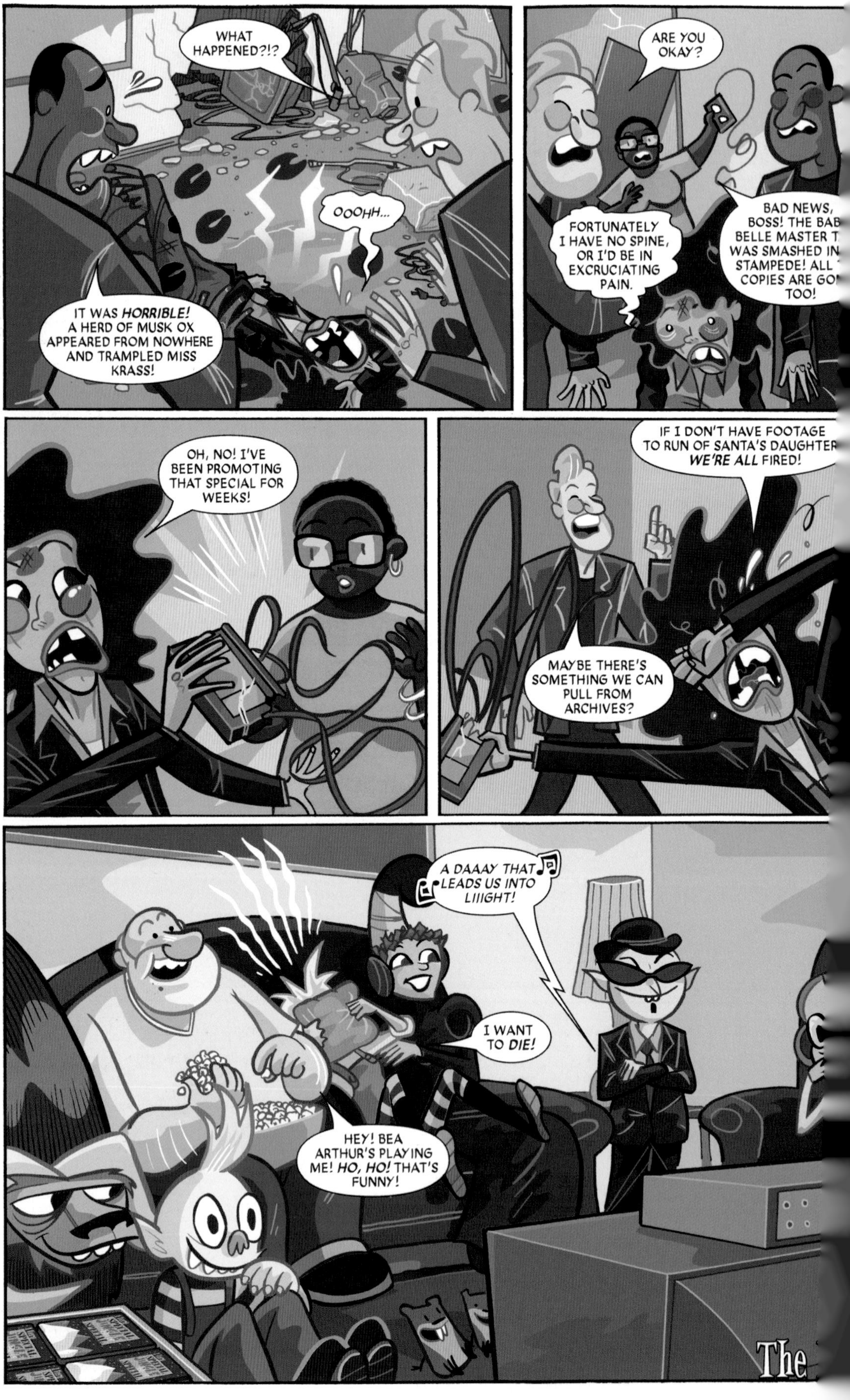
WHAT HAPPENED?!?
OOOHH...
IT WAS HORRIBLE! A HERD OF MUSK OX APPEARED FROM NOWHERE AND TRAMPLED MISS KRASS!
ARE YOU OKAY?
FORTUNATELY I HAVE NO SPINE, OR I'D BE IN EXCRUCIATING PAIN.
BAD NEWS, BOSS! THE BAB BELLE MASTER T WAS SMASHED IN STAMPEDE! ALL COPIES ARE GO TOO!
OH, NO! I'VE BEEN PROMOTING THAT SPECIAL FOR WEEKS!
IF I DON'T HAVE FOOTAGE TO RUN OF SANTA'S DAUGHTER WE'RE ALL FIRED!
MAYBE THERE'S SOMETHING WE CAN PULL FROM ARCHIVES?
A DAAAY THAT LEADS US INTO LIIIGHT!
I WANT TO DIE!
HEY! BEA ARTHUR'S PLAYING ME! HO, HO! THAT'S FUNNY!
The

POLLY GREEN IN "NIBBLE, NIBBLE"

ONCE UPON A TIME THERE WAS A CUTE LITTLE HALLOWEEN WITCH NAMED POLLY GREEN.

HI.

SHE LIVED IN A SPOOKY OLD MAGICAL TOWER...

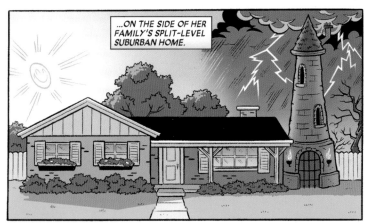

...ON THE SIDE OF HER FAMILY'S SPLIT-LEVEL SUBURBAN HOME.

POLLY WORKED HER SPELLS, HER ENCHANTMENTS, AND HEXES ON THOSE WHO SERVED THEM.

YOU'D THINK THAT THE GREENS MIGHT BE SCARED TO HAVE A WITCH IN THEIR FAMILY.

TRESPASSERS WILL BE TOAD!

ZAPPING ZONE!

KEEP OUT!

BUT THEY WEREN'T.

I WANT A NEW CAR!

AN ADDITION TO THE HOUSE!

SWIMMING POOL!

BEAUTY POTIONS!

ONCE THEY REALIZED POLLY COULD WORK MAGIC, THE GREENS BEGAN TO TREAT HER AS THEIR OWN PERSONAL GENIE, PESTERING HER TO CONJURE UP ONE MIRACLE AFTER ANOTHER.

I WANT IT!

NOW! NOW! NOW!

GIMMIE! GIMMIE!

I NEED IT!

AND IT ONLY GOT WORSE AT CHRISTMAS.

I REALLY WANT THAT NEW HUMMER, POLLY! OR AT LEAST AN SUV! SOLID GOLD, THIS TIME!

NO, NO, NO, NO!

HEY, AN SUV FOR ME, TOO!

I'D LIKE A YACHT...

YOU *HAVE* TO!

ANY *REAL* WITCH WOULD BE HAPPY TO ZAP UP PRESENTS FOR HER LOVING FAMILY!

IF I EVER GET A *"LOVING FAMILY,"* I'LL KEEP THAT IN MIND!

WHEW! SAFE AT LAST!

OH, NO! DON'T THEY EVER QUIT?!

HIYA, KIDDO! MERRY, MERRY, AND ALL THAT!

OH, JINGL THANK GOOD IT'S YOU

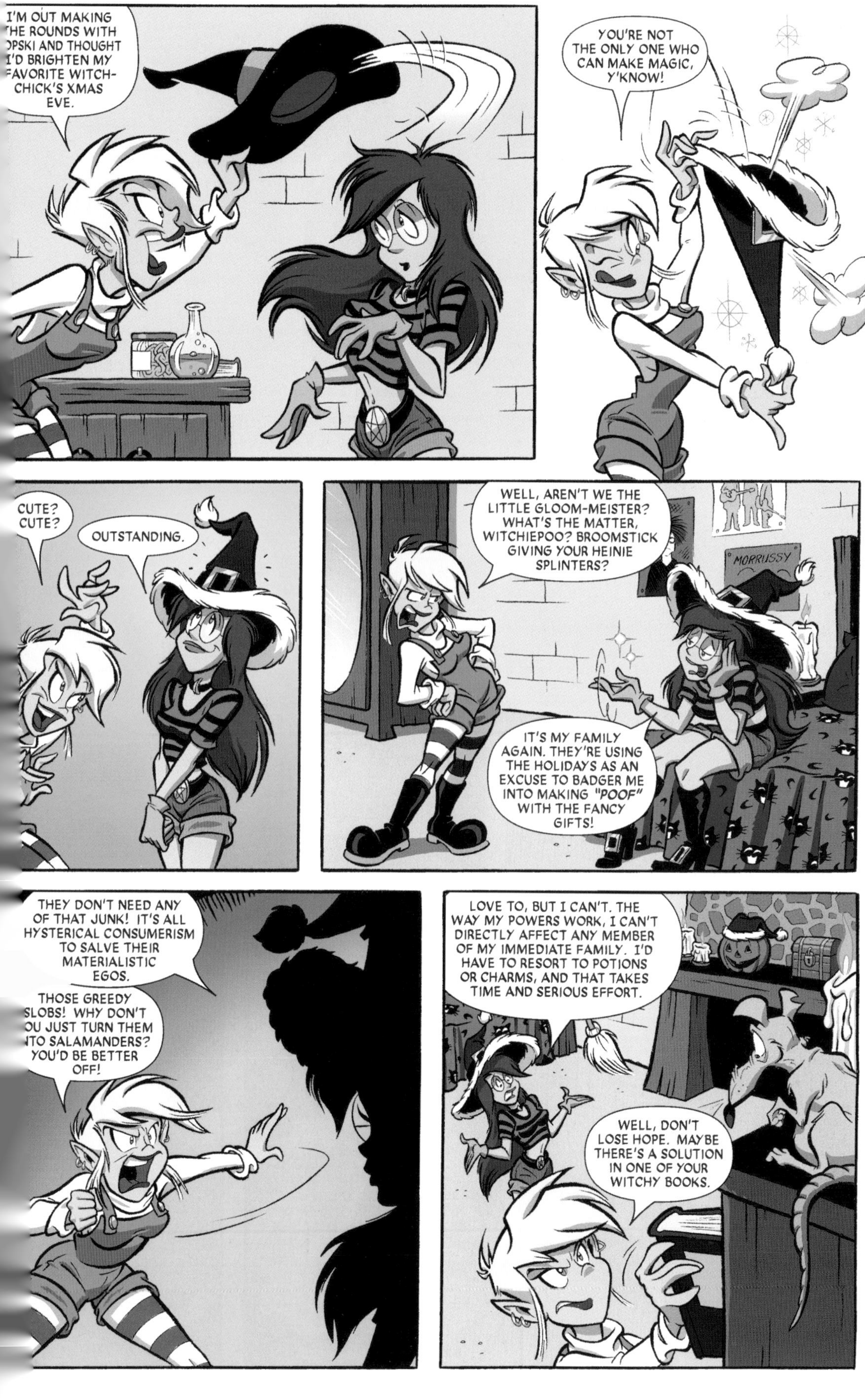
I'M OUT MAKING THE ROUNDS WITH OPSKI AND THOUGHT I'D BRIGHTEN MY FAVORITE WITCH-CHICK'S XMAS EVE.
YOU'RE NOT THE ONLY ONE WHO CAN MAKE MAGIC, Y'KNOW!
CUTE? CUTE?
OUTSTANDING.
WELL, AREN'T WE THE LITTLE GLOOM-MEISTER? WHAT'S THE MATTER, WITCHIEPOO? BROOMSTICK GIVING YOUR HEINIE SPLINTERS?
MORRISSY
IT'S MY FAMILY AGAIN. THEY'RE USING THE HOLIDAYS AS AN EXCUSE TO BADGER ME INTO MAKING "POOF" WITH THE FANCY GIFTS!
THEY DON'T NEED ANY OF THAT JUNK! IT'S ALL HYSTERICAL CONSUMERISM TO SALVE THEIR MATERIALISTIC EGOS.
THOSE GREEDY SLOBS! WHY DON'T YOU JUST TURN THEM INTO SALAMANDERS? YOU'D BE BETTER OFF!
LOVE TO, BUT I CAN'T. THE WAY MY POWERS WORK, I CAN'T DIRECTLY AFFECT ANY MEMBER OF MY IMMEDIATE FAMILY. I'D HAVE TO RESORT TO POTIONS OR CHARMS, AND THAT TAKES TIME AND SERIOUS EFFORT.
WELL, DON'T LOSE HOPE. MAYBE THERE'S A SOLUTION IN ONE OF YOUR WITCHY BOOKS.

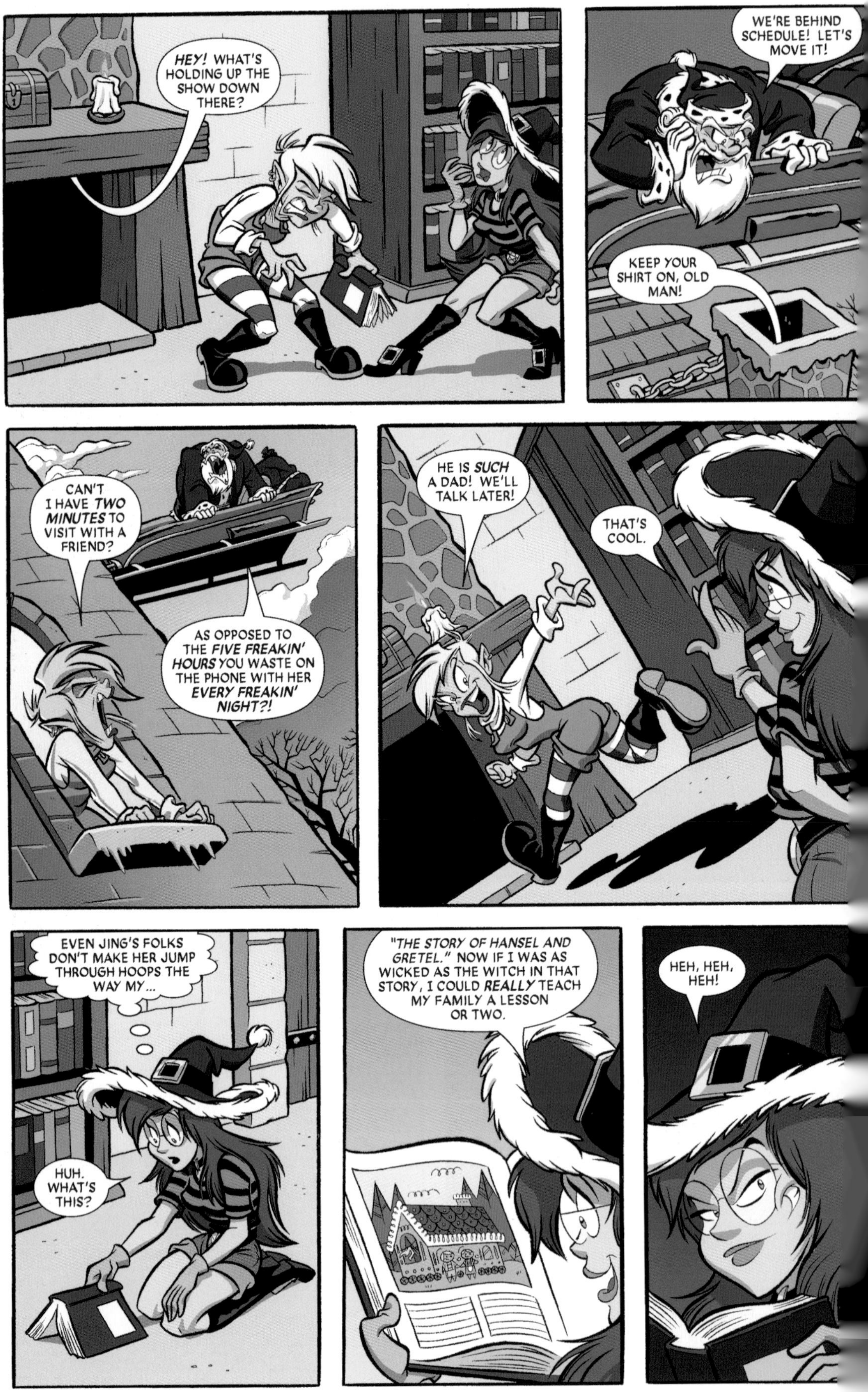
HEY! WHAT'S HOLDING UP THE SHOW DOWN THERE?
WE'RE BEHIND SCHEDULE! LET'S MOVE IT!
KEEP YOUR SHIRT ON, OLD MAN!
CAN'T I HAVE TWO MINUTES TO VISIT WITH A FRIEND?
AS OPPOSED TO THE FIVE FREAKIN' HOURS YOU WASTE ON THE PHONE WITH HER EVERY FREAKIN' NIGHT?!
HE IS SUCH A DAD! WE'LL TALK LATER!
THAT'S COOL.
EVEN JING'S FOLKS DON'T MAKE HER JUMP THROUGH HOOPS THE WAY MY...
HUH. WHAT'S THIS?
"THE STORY OF HANSEL AND GRETEL." NOW IF I WAS AS WICKED AS THE WITCH IN THAT STORY, I COULD REALLY TEACH MY FAMILY A LESSON OR TWO.
HEH, HEH, HEH!

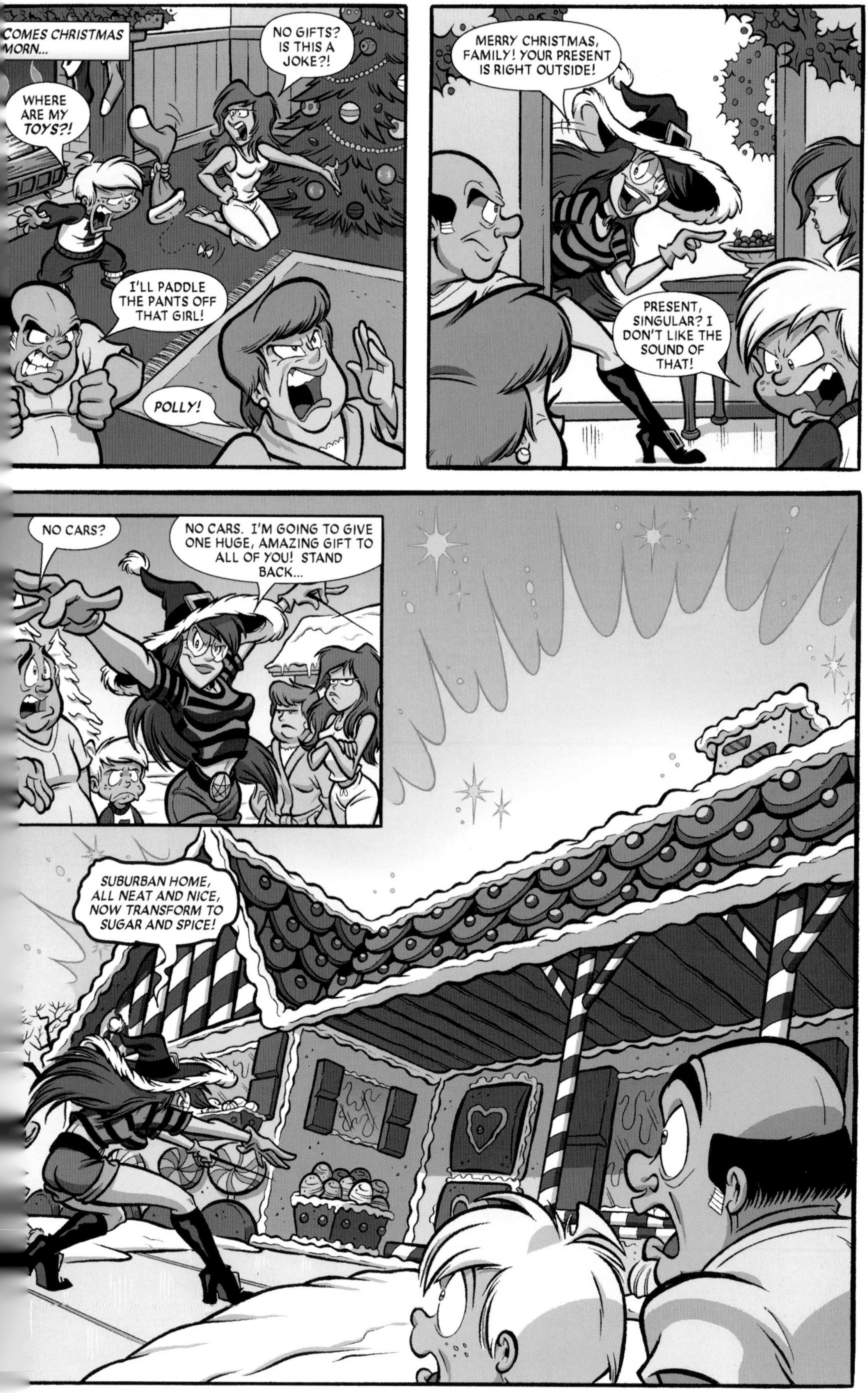
COMES CHRISTMAS MORN...
NO GIFTS? IS THIS A JOKE?!
WHERE ARE MY TOYS?!
I'LL PADDLE THE PANTS OFF THAT GIRL!
POLLY!
MERRY CHRISTMAS, FAMILY! YOUR PRESENT IS RIGHT OUTSIDE!
PRESENT, SINGULAR? I DON'T LIKE THE SOUND OF THAT!
NO CARS?
NO CARS. I'M GOING TO GIVE ONE HUGE, AMAZING GIFT TO ALL OF YOU! STAND BACK...
SUBURBAN HOME, ALL NEAT AND NICE, NOW TRANSFORM TO SUGAR AND SPICE!

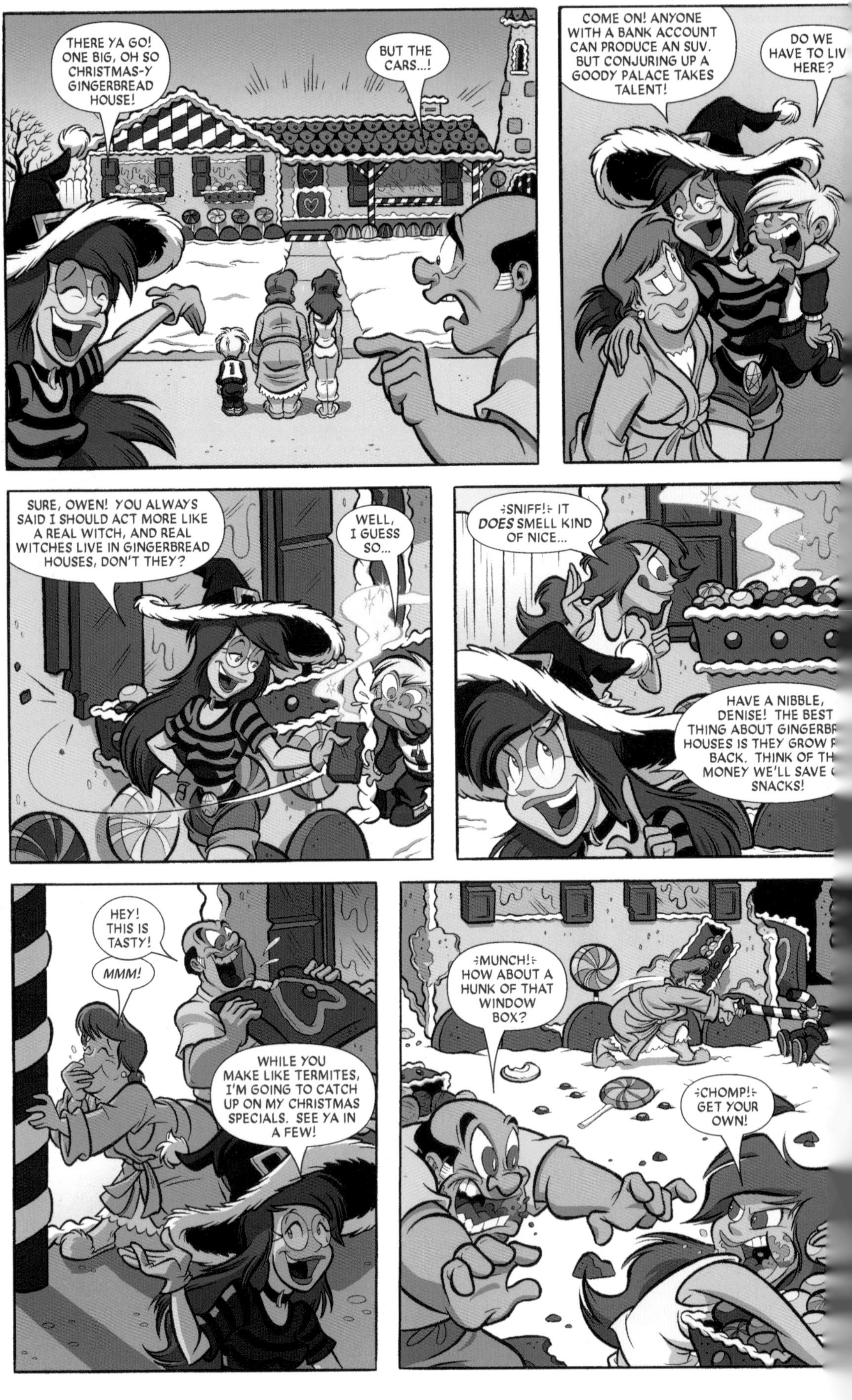
THERE YA GO! ONE BIG, OH SO CHRISTMAS-Y GINGERBREAD HOUSE!
BUT THE CARS...!
COME ON! ANYONE WITH A BANK ACCOUNT CAN PRODUCE AN SUV. BUT CONJURING UP A GOODY PALACE TAKES TALENT!
DO WE HAVE TO LIV HERE?
SURE, OWEN! YOU ALWAYS SAID I SHOULD ACT MORE LIKE A REAL WITCH, AND REAL WITCHES LIVE IN GINGERBREAD HOUSES, DON'T THEY?
WELL, I GUESS SO...
SNIFF! IT *DOES* SMELL KIND OF NICE...
HAVE A NIBBLE, DENISE! THE BEST THING ABOUT GINGERBR HOUSES IS THEY GROW R BACK. THINK OF TH MONEY WE'LL SAVE SNACKS!
HEY! THIS IS TASTY!
MMM!
WHILE YOU MAKE LIKE TERMITES, I'M GOING TO CATCH UP ON MY CHRISTMAS SPECIALS. SEE YA IN A FEW!
MUNCH! HOW ABOUT A HUNK OF THAT WINDOW BOX?
CHOMP! GET YOUR OWN!

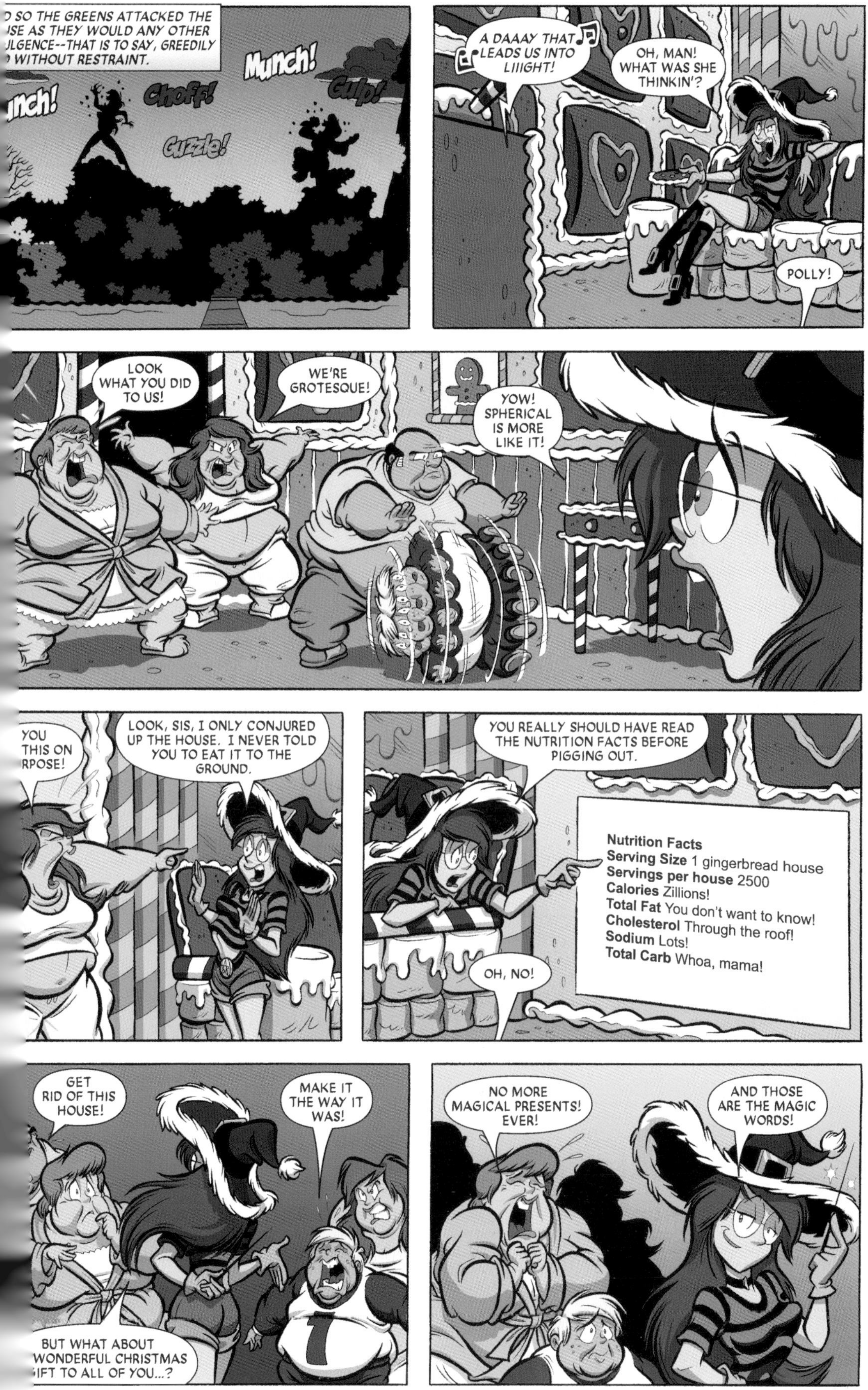

SO THE GREENS ATTACKED THE
SE AS THEY WOULD ANY OTHER
ULGENCE--THAT IS TO SAY, GREEDILY
WITHOUT RESTRAINT.
Munch!
Choff!
Gulp!
Guzzle!
A DAAAY THAT LEADS US INTO LIIIGHT!
OH, MAN! WHAT WAS SHE THINKIN'?
POLLY!
LOOK WHAT YOU DID TO US!
WE'RE GROTESQUE!
YOW! SPHERICAL IS MORE LIKE IT!
YOU THIS ON RPOSE!
LOOK, SIS, I ONLY CONJURED UP THE HOUSE. I NEVER TOLD YOU TO EAT IT TO THE GROUND.
YOU REALLY SHOULD HAVE READ THE NUTRITION FACTS BEFORE PIGGING OUT.
Nutrition Facts
Serving Size 1 gingerbread house
Servings per house 2500
Calories Zillions!
Total Fat You don't want to know!
Cholesterol Through the roof!
Sodium Lots!
Total Carb Whoa, mama!
OH, NO!
GET RID OF THIS HOUSE!
MAKE IT THE WAY IT WAS!
BUT WHAT ABOUT WONDERFUL CHRISTMAS IFT TO ALL OF YOU...?
NO MORE MAGICAL PRESENTS! EVER!
AND THOSE ARE THE MAGIC WORDS!

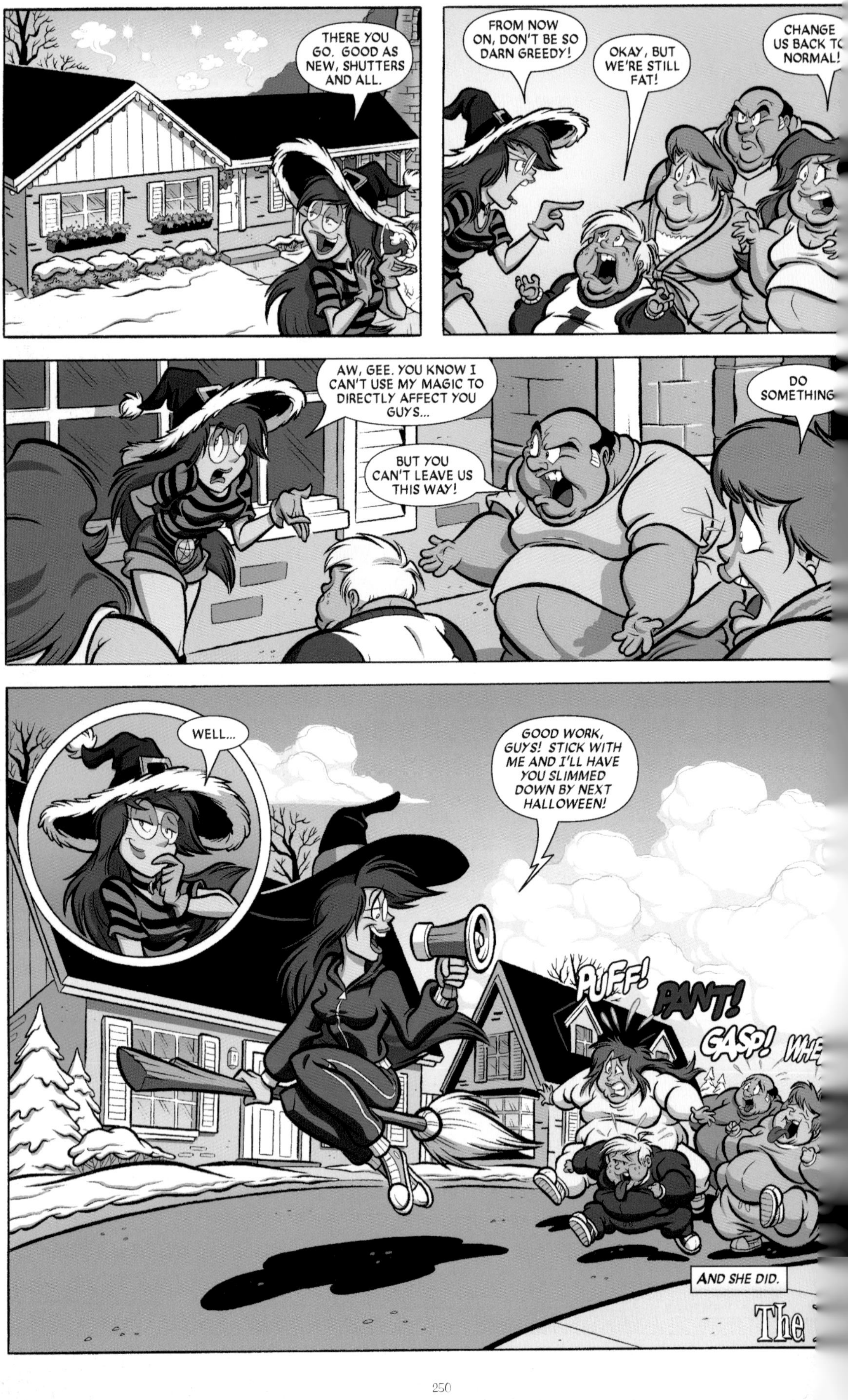
THERE YOU GO. GOOD AS NEW, SHUTTERS AND ALL.
FROM NOW ON, DON'T BE SO DARN GREEDY!
OKAY, BUT WE'RE STILL FAT!
CHANGE US BACK TO NORMAL!
AW, GEE. YOU KNOW I CAN'T USE MY MAGIC TO DIRECTLY AFFECT YOU GUYS...
BUT YOU CAN'T LEAVE US THIS WAY!
DO SOMETHING
WELL...
GOOD WORK, GUYS! STICK WITH ME AND I'LL HAVE YOU SLIMMED DOWN BY NEXT HALLOWEEN!
PUFF!
PANT!
GASP!
AND SHE DID.
The

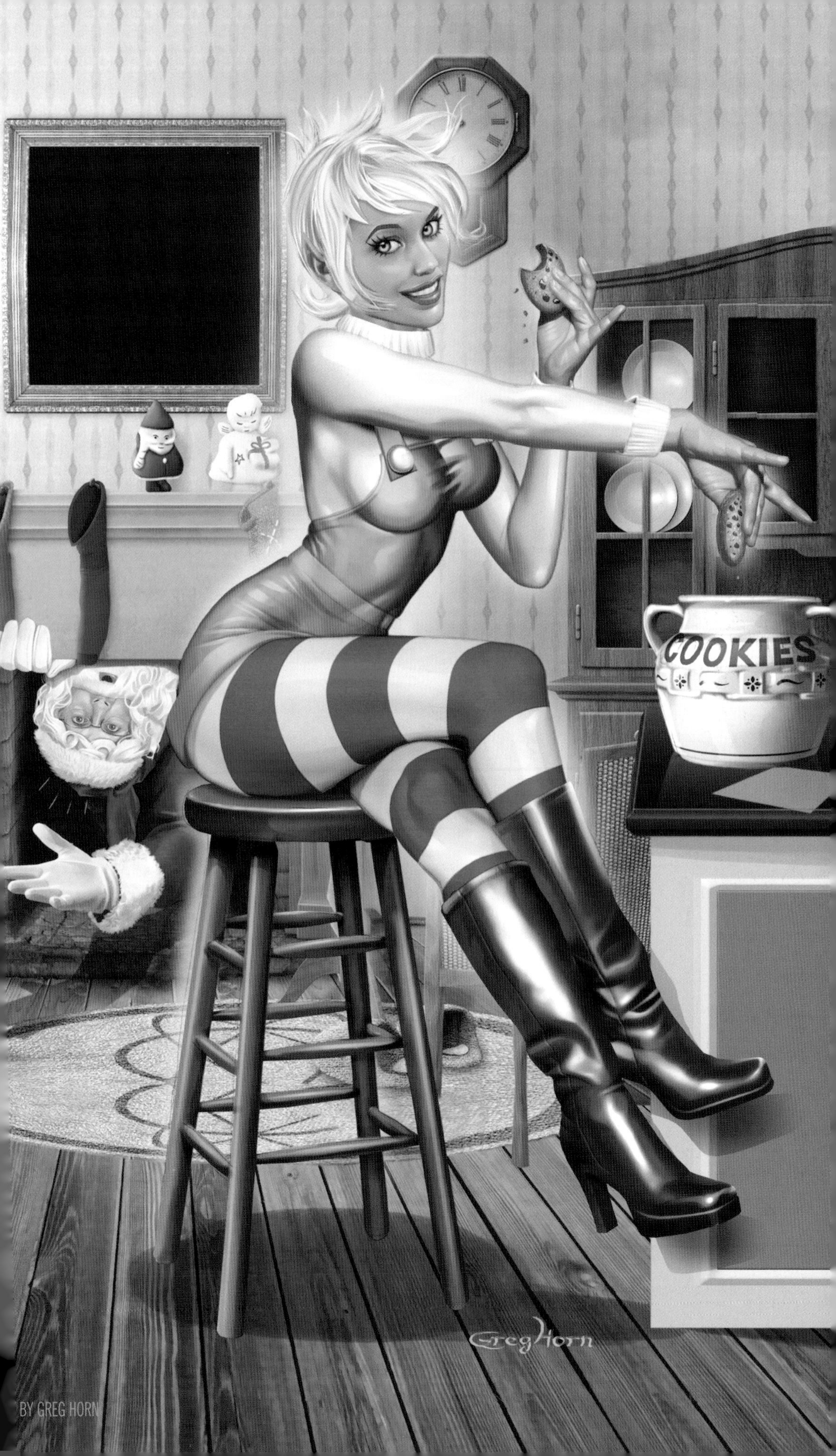
COOKIES
Greg Horn

BY GREG HORN

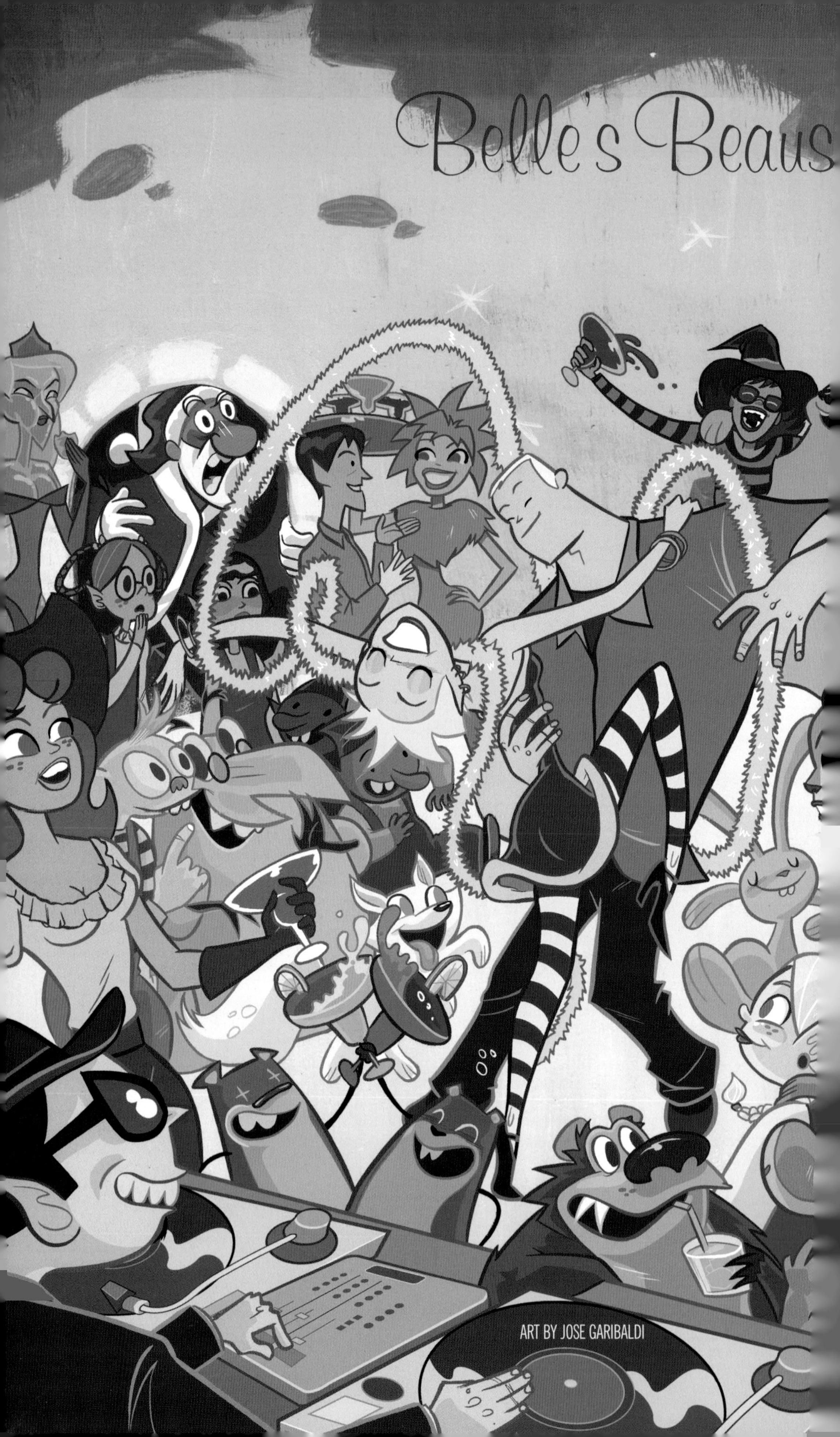
Belle's Beaus
ART BY JOSE GARIBALDI

In Russia, Santa Claus has been transformed into the story of Ded Moroz, or Grandfather Frost. A tall, elegant figure in royal robes, he appears at Christmas to give presents to good children.

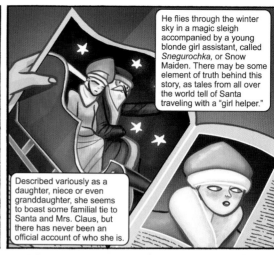

He flies through the winter sky in a magic sleigh accompanied by a young blonde girl assistant, called *Snegurochka*, or Snow Maiden. There may be some element of truth behind this story, as tales from all over the world tell of Santa traveling with a "girl helper."

Described variously as a daughter, niece or even granddaughter, she seems to boast some familial tie to Santa and Mrs. Claus, but there has never been an official account of who she is.

Visual reports place her age at about teen, though given the many times she has been seen over the years, she'd have to be at least three hundred.

Not hard to believe, as Santa Claus himself is said to be nearly two thousand years old.

The good Saint Nick is known for being notoriously secretive, routinely turning down all requests for interviews. He has rarely said much about his family life, and even less about this mystery girl.

SANTA CLAUS IN PERSON!
He's the real deal, kids!

Reports of her continue to this day. Perhaps she is actually kin to the great man, or simply a delusional teen trying to associate herself with the Santa Claus legend. After months of research, the only thing I know for certain is her name:

Belle's Beaus

Jingle Belle.

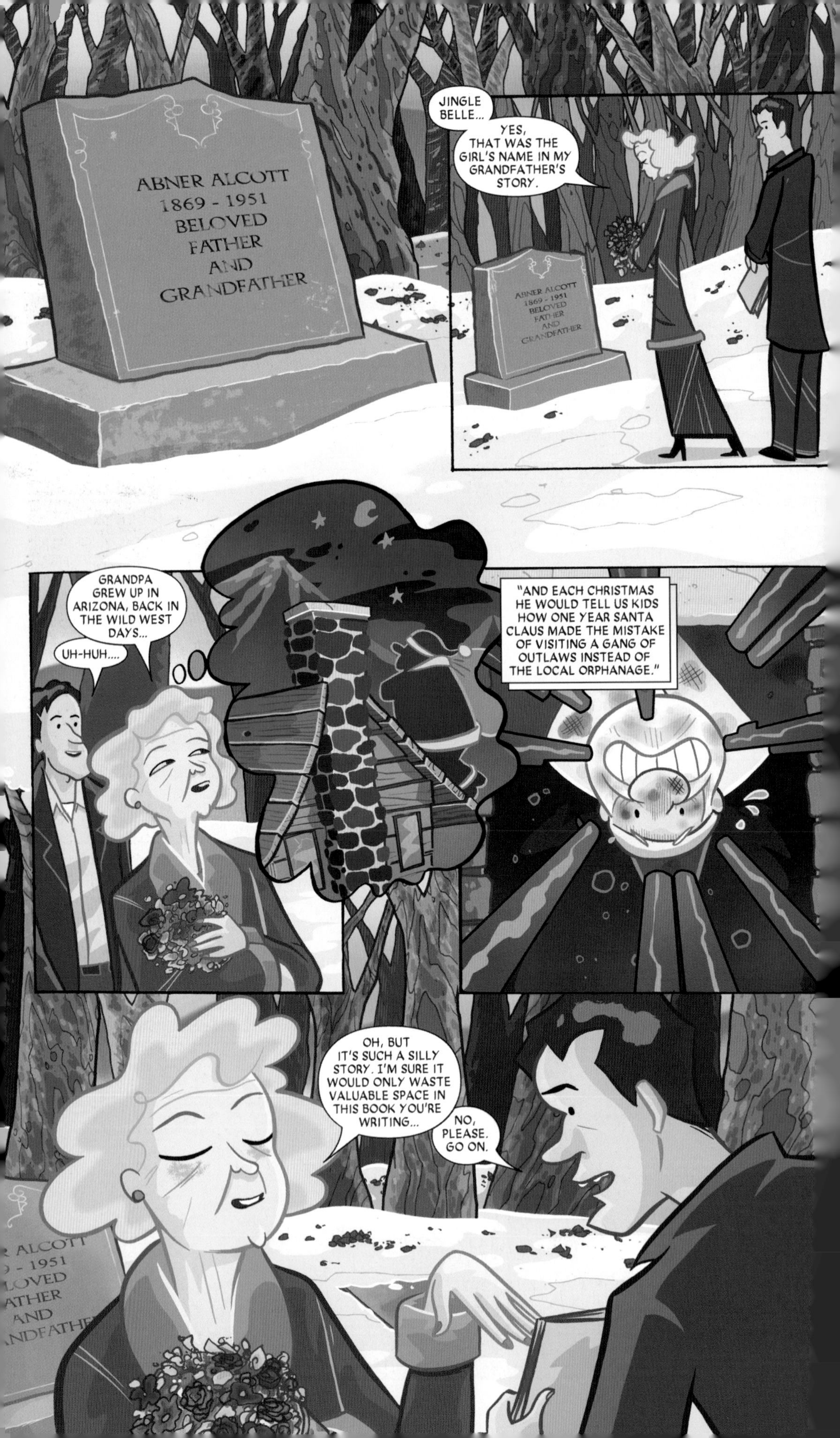
ABNER ALCOTT
1869 - 1951
BELOVED
FATHER
AND
GRANDFATHER
JINGLE BELLE...
YES, THAT WAS THE GIRL'S NAME IN MY GRANDFATHER'S STORY.
GRANDPA GREW UP IN ARIZONA, BACK IN THE WILD WEST DAYS...
UH-HUH....
"AND EACH CHRISTMAS HE WOULD TELL US KIDS HOW ONE YEAR SANTA CLAUS MADE THE MISTAKE OF VISITING A GANG OF OUTLAWS INSTEAD OF THE LOCAL ORPHANAGE."
OH, BUT IT'S SUCH A SILLY STORY. I'M SURE IT WOULD ONLY WASTE VALUABLE SPACE IN THIS BOOK YOU'RE WRITING...
NO, PLEASE. GO ON.

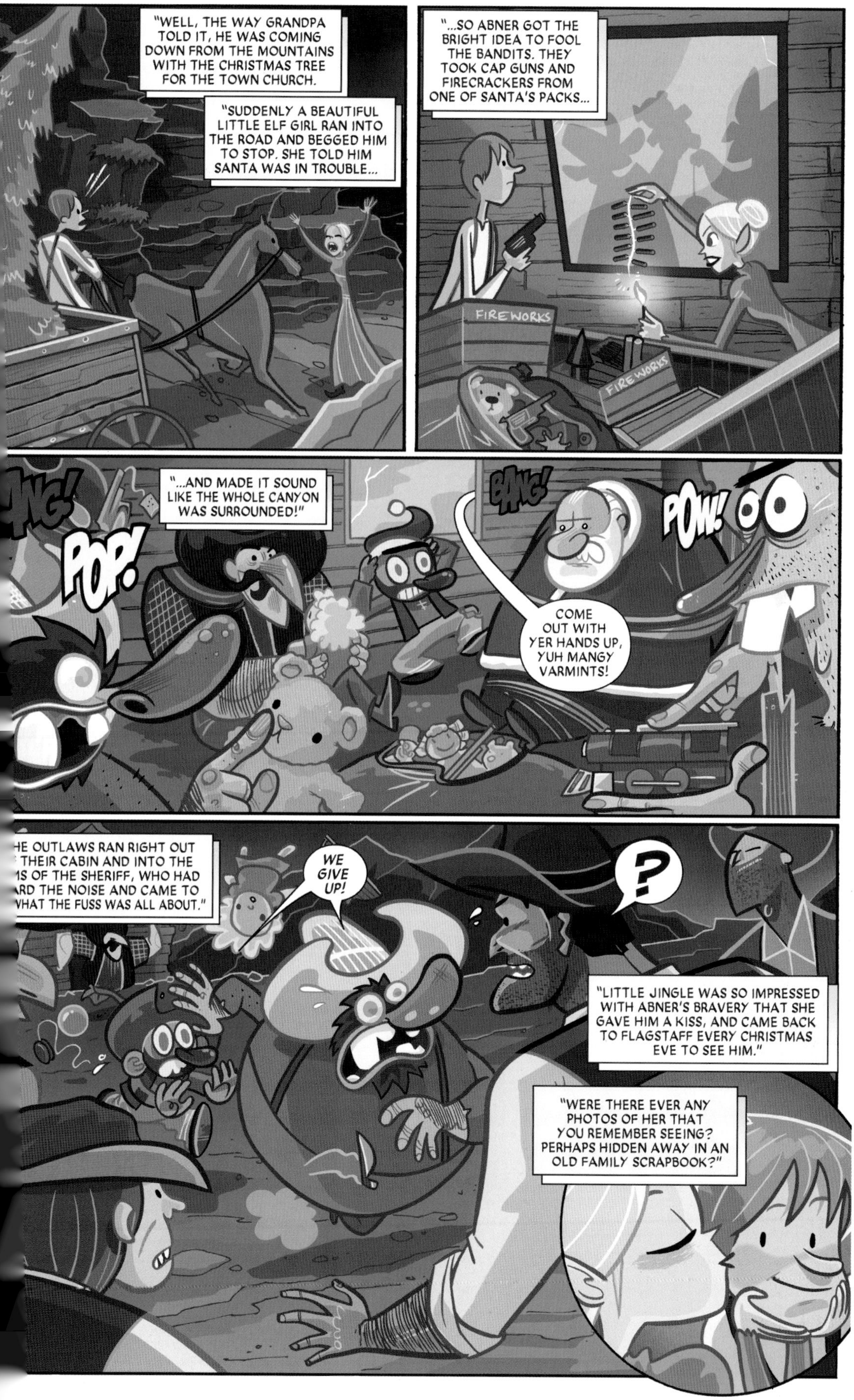
"WELL, THE WAY GRANDPA TOLD IT, HE WAS COMING DOWN FROM THE MOUNTAINS WITH THE CHRISTMAS TREE FOR THE TOWN CHURCH.
"SUDDENLY A BEAUTIFUL LITTLE ELF GIRL RAN INTO THE ROAD AND BEGGED HIM TO STOP. SHE TOLD HIM SANTA WAS IN TROUBLE...
"...SO ABNER GOT THE BRIGHT IDEA TO FOOL THE BANDITS. THEY TOOK CAP GUNS AND FIRECRACKERS FROM ONE OF SANTA'S PACKS...
FIRE WORKS
FIRE WORKS
ANG!
POP!
"...AND MADE IT SOUND LIKE THE WHOLE CANYON WAS SURROUNDED!"
BANG!
POW!
COME OUT WITH YER HANDS UP, YUH MANGY VARMINTS!
HE OUTLAWS RAN RIGHT OUT THEIR CABIN AND INTO THE MS OF THE SHERIFF, WHO HAD ARD THE NOISE AND CAME TO WHAT THE FUSS WAS ALL ABOUT."
WE GIVE UP!
?
"LITTLE JINGLE WAS SO IMPRESSED WITH ABNER'S BRAVERY THAT SHE GAVE HIM A KISS, AND CAME BACK TO FLAGSTAFF EVERY CHRISTMAS EVE TO SEE HIM."
"WERE THERE EVER ANY PHOTOS OF HER THAT YOU REMEMBER SEEING? PERHAPS HIDDEN AWAY IN AN OLD FAMILY SCRAPBOOK?"

OH, HEAVENS NO! IT WAS JUST A STORY! A BIT OF NONSENSE GRANDPA USED TO KEEP MY SISTERS AND ME QUIET WHILE MOTHER FIXED CHRISTMAS DINNER.

OVER THE YEARS THERE HAVE BEEN OTHER ACCOUNTS OF AN ELF GIRL WITH THE SAME NAME MATCHING THE SAME DESCRIPTION...

TRUST ME, MR. SMITH. MY GRANDFATHER, BLESS HIM, HAD A VERY VIVID IMAGINATION. AS FOND AS I AM OF THAT OLD STORY, THERE ISN'T A WORD OF TRUTH IN IT.

IF YOU SAY SO, MRS. NEWELL.

THE FLAGSTAFF GAZETTE
December 25th 1884
CHRISTMAS EVE MIRACLE!
BANDIT GANG FOILED!

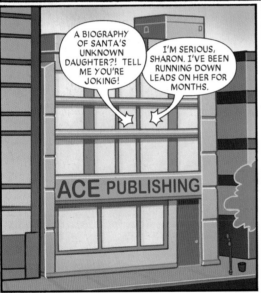

A BIOGRAPHY OF SANTA'S UNKNOWN DAUGHTER?! TELL ME YOU'RE JOKING!

I'M SERIOUS, SHARON. I'VE BEEN RUNNING DOWN LEADS ON HER FOR MONTHS.

ACE PUBLISHING

PETE, THE MODERN WORLD BARELY ACCEPTS THE EXISTENCE OF *SANTA CLAUS* ANY MORE, MUCH LESS HIS ALLEGED TEENY BOPPER *OFF SPRING!*

THAT'S WHY MY BOOK IS SUCH A NATURAL! IT'S UNRAVELING A REAL-LIFE MYSTERY, BIGGER THAN BIGFOOT, UFOS, THE LOCH NESS MONSTER...

I'D *RATHER* YOU WERE WRITING ABOUT NESSIE. NESSIE SELLS!

YOU'RE THE HOTTEST DETECTIVE WRITER ON THE MARKET. YOU KNOW I'D SUPPORT YOU ON ANYTHING YOU HAVE YOUR HEART SET ON, BUT THIS? WHY A KID'S BOOK?

IT'S MORE THAN THAT, SHARON. IT'S...WELL, I DON'T KNOW, REALLY. MAYBE IT'S A WAY FOR ME TO CONNECT WITH PART OF *MY* CHILDHOOD...

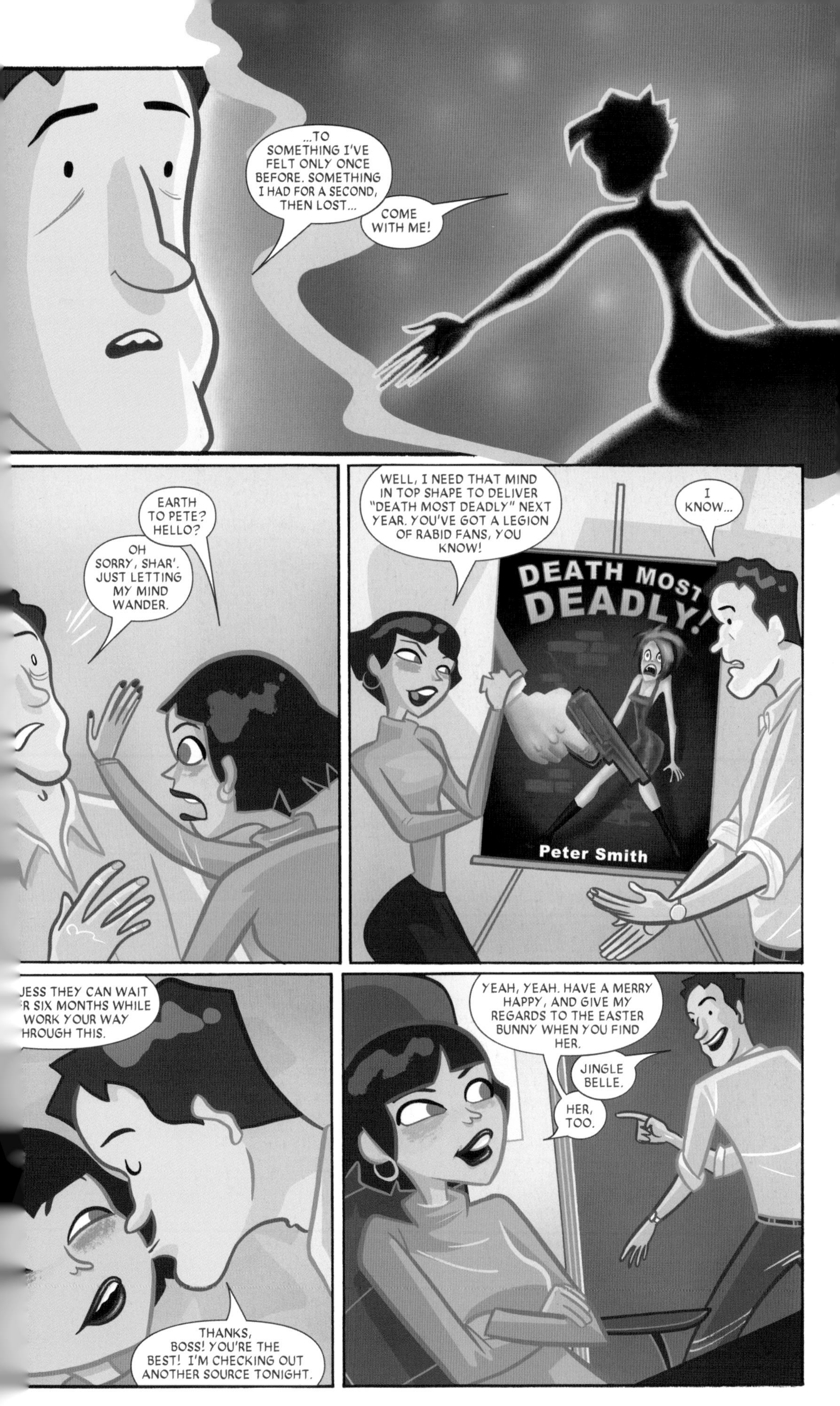
...TO SOMETHING I'VE FELT ONLY ONCE BEFORE. SOMETHING I HAD FOR A SECOND, THEN LOST...
COME WITH ME!
EARTH TO PETE? HELLO?
OH SORRY, SHAR'. JUST LETTING MY MIND WANDER.
WELL, I NEED THAT MIND IN TOP SHAPE TO DELIVER "DEATH MOST DEADLY" NEXT YEAR. YOU'VE GOT A LEGION OF RABID FANS, YOU KNOW!
I KNOW...
DEATH MOST DEADLY!
Peter Smith
JESS THEY CAN WAIT R SIX MONTHS WHILE WORK YOUR WAY HROUGH THIS.
THANKS, BOSS! YOU'RE THE BEST! I'M CHECKING OUT ANOTHER SOURCE TONIGHT.
YEAH, YEAH. HAVE A MERRY HAPPY, AND GIVE MY REGARDS TO THE EASTER BUNNY WHEN YOU FIND HER.
JINGLE BELLE.
HER, TOO.

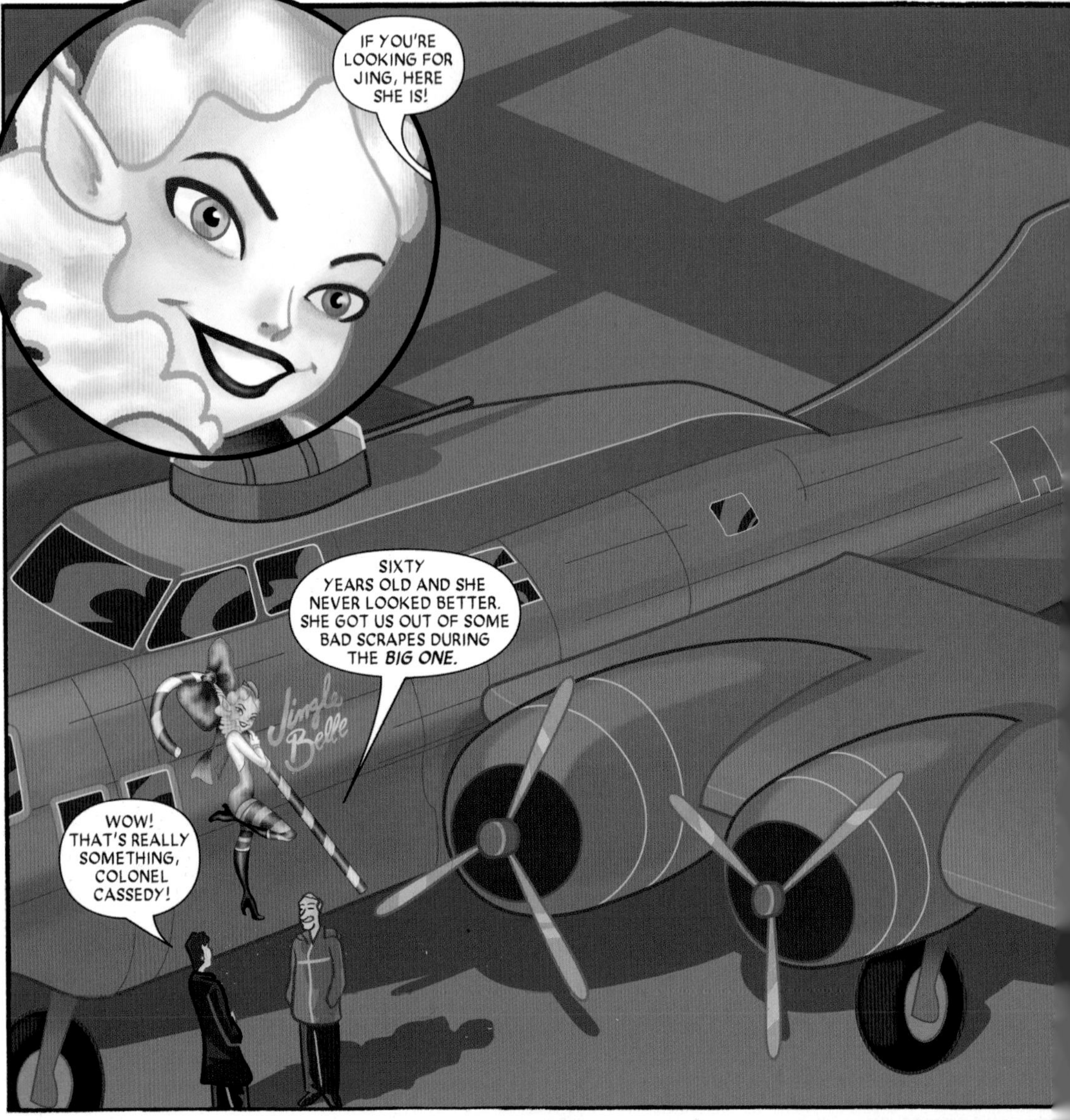
IF YOU'RE LOOKING FOR JING, HERE SHE IS!
SIXTY YEARS OLD AND SHE NEVER LOOKED BETTER. SHE GOT US OUT OF SOME BAD SCRAPES DURING THE *BIG ONE.*
Jingle Belle
WOW! THAT'S REALLY SOMETHING, COLONEL CASSEDY!

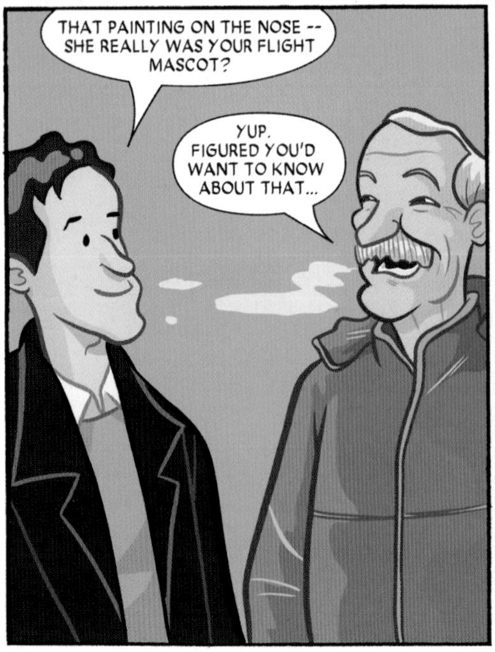
THAT PAINTING ON THE NOSE -- SHE REALLY WAS YOUR FLIGHT MASCOT?
YUP. FIGURED YOU'D WANT TO KNOW ABOUT THAT...

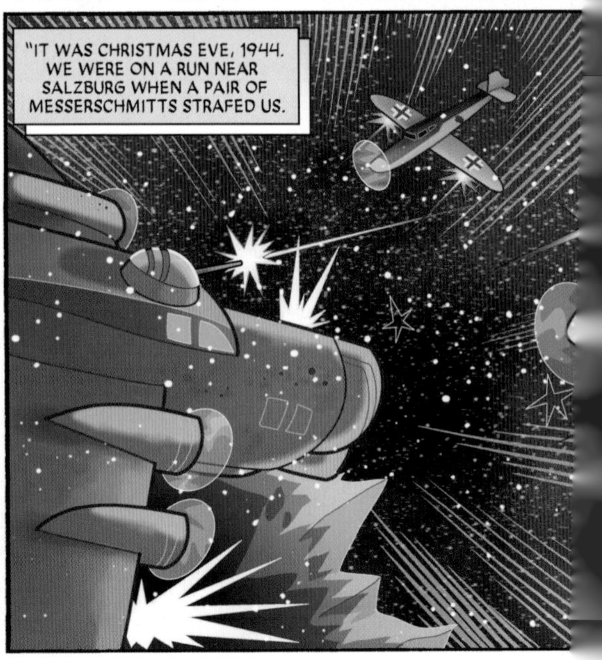
"IT WAS CHRISTMAS EVE, 1944. WE WERE ON A RUN NEAR SALZBURG WHEN A PAIR OF MESSERSCHMITTS STRAFED US.

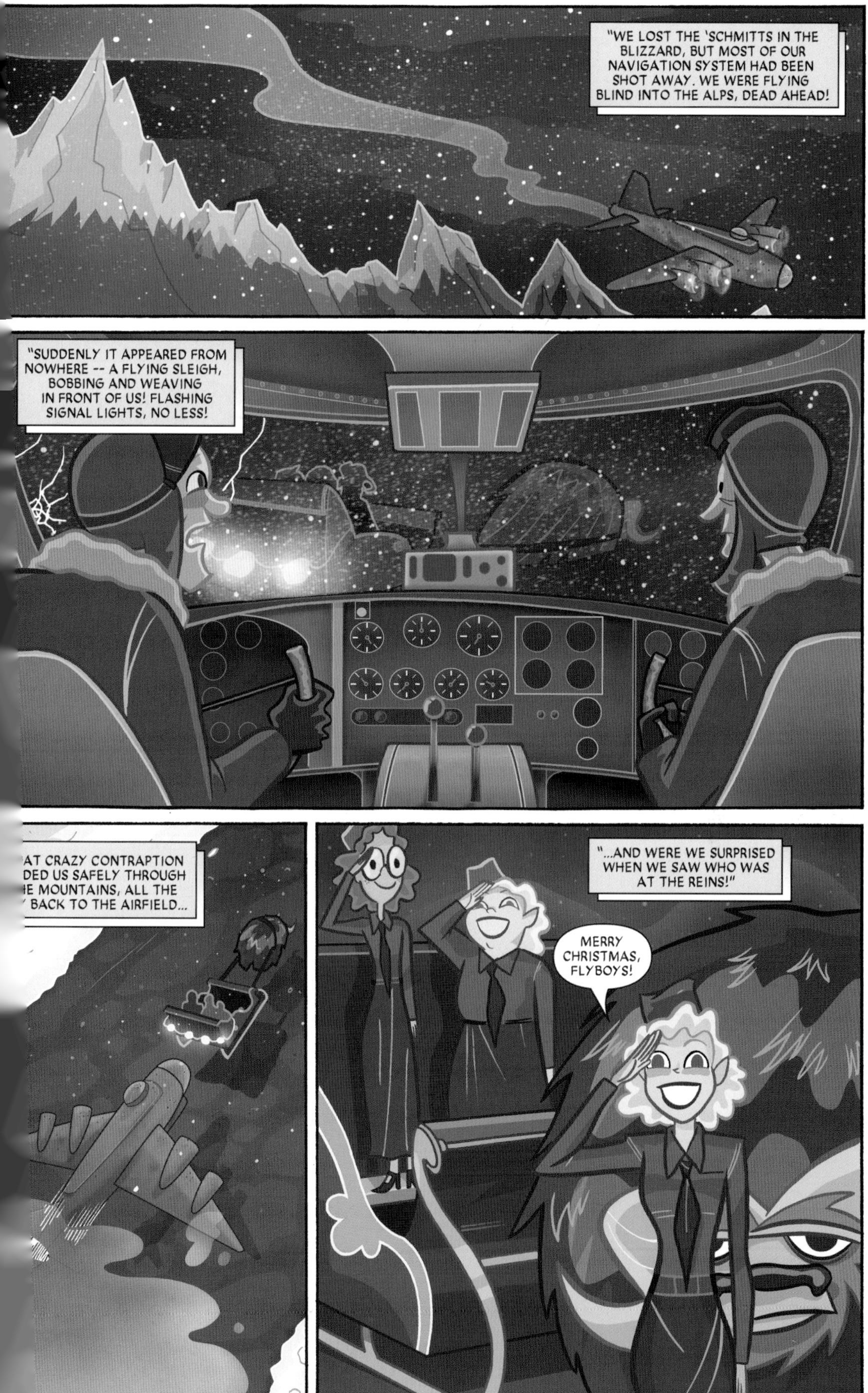
"WE LOST THE 'SCHMITTS IN THE BLIZZARD, BUT MOST OF OUR NAVIGATION SYSTEM HAD BEEN SHOT AWAY. WE WERE FLYING BLIND INTO THE ALPS, DEAD AHEAD!
"SUDDENLY IT APPEARED FROM NOWHERE -- A FLYING SLEIGH, BOBBING AND WEAVING IN FRONT OF US! FLASHING SIGNAL LIGHTS, NO LESS!
AT CRAZY CONTRAPTION DED US SAFELY THROUGH E MOUNTAINS, ALL THE BACK TO THE AIRFIELD...
"...AND WERE WE SURPRISED WHEN WE SAW WHO WAS AT THE REINS!"
MERRY CHRISTMAS, FLYBOYS!

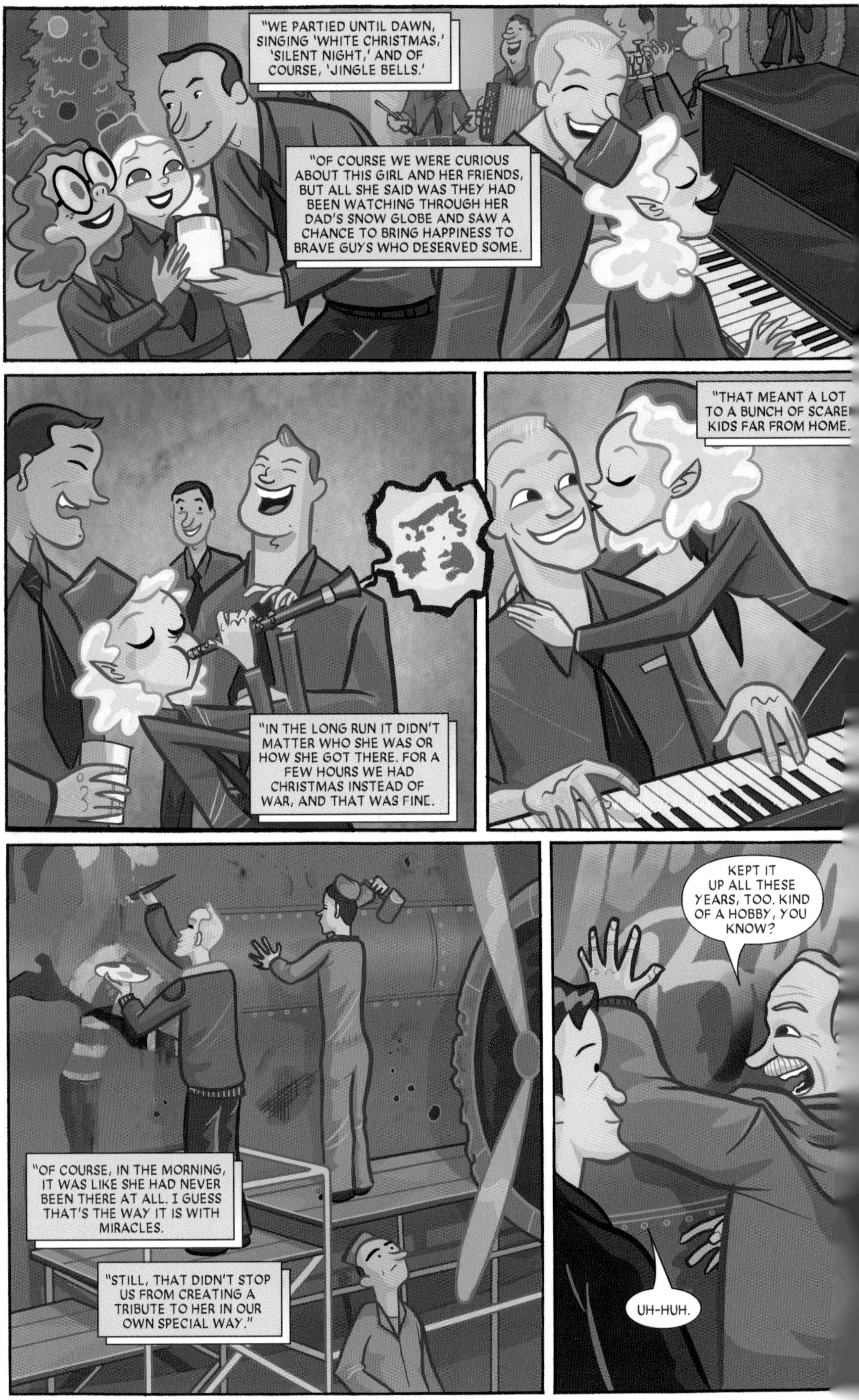
"WE PARTIED UNTIL DAWN, SINGING 'WHITE CHRISTMAS,' 'SILENT NIGHT,' AND OF COURSE, 'JINGLE BELLS.'
"OF COURSE WE WERE CURIOUS ABOUT THIS GIRL AND HER FRIENDS, BUT ALL SHE SAID WAS THEY HAD BEEN WATCHING THROUGH HER DAD'S SNOW GLOBE AND SAW A CHANCE TO BRING HAPPINESS TO BRAVE GUYS WHO DESERVED SOME.
"IN THE LONG RUN IT DIDN'T MATTER WHO SHE WAS OR HOW SHE GOT THERE. FOR A FEW HOURS WE HAD CHRISTMAS INSTEAD OF WAR, AND THAT WAS FINE.
"THAT MEANT A LOT TO A BUNCH OF SCARE KIDS FAR FROM HOME.
"OF COURSE, IN THE MORNING, IT WAS LIKE SHE HAD NEVER BEEN THERE AT ALL. I GUESS THAT'S THE WAY IT IS WITH MIRACLES.
"STILL, THAT DIDN'T STOP US FROM CREATING A TRIBUTE TO HER IN OUR OWN SPECIAL WAY."
KEPT IT UP ALL THESE YEARS, TOO. KIND OF A HOBBY, YOU KNOW?
UH-HUH.

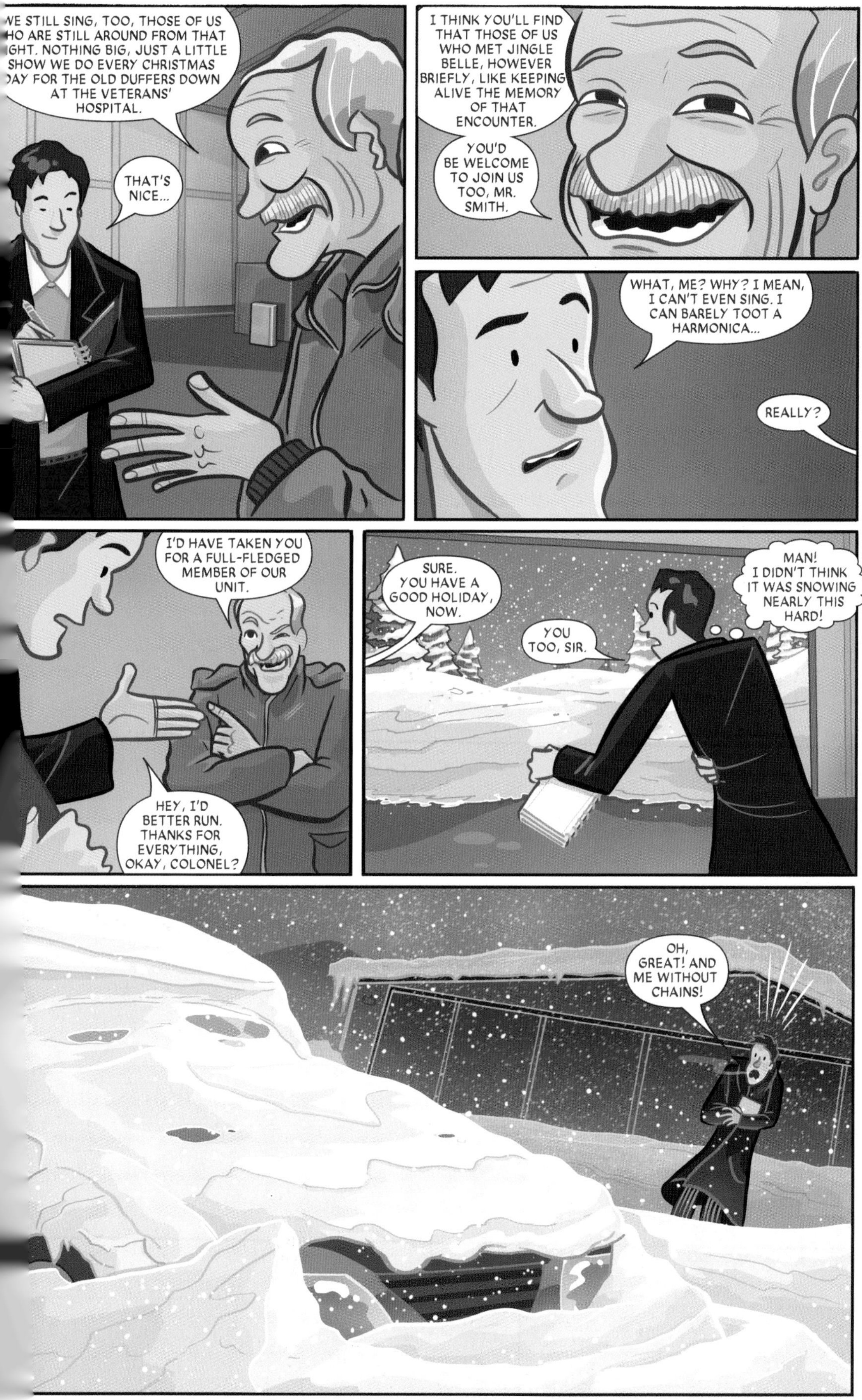
VE STILL SING, TOO, THOSE OF US HO ARE STILL AROUND FROM THAT IGHT. NOTHING BIG, JUST A LITTLE SHOW WE DO EVERY CHRISTMAS AY FOR THE OLD DUFFERS DOWN AT THE VETERANS' HOSPITAL.
THAT'S NICE...
I THINK YOU'LL FIND THAT THOSE OF US WHO MET JINGLE BELLE, HOWEVER BRIEFLY, LIKE KEEPING ALIVE THE MEMORY OF THAT ENCOUNTER.
YOU'D BE WELCOME TO JOIN US TOO, MR. SMITH.
WHAT, ME? WHY? I MEAN, I CAN'T EVEN SING. I CAN BARELY TOOT A HARMONICA...
REALLY?
I'D HAVE TAKEN YOU FOR A FULL-FLEDGED MEMBER OF OUR UNIT.
HEY, I'D BETTER RUN. THANKS FOR EVERYTHING, OKAY, COLONEL?
SURE. YOU HAVE A GOOD HOLIDAY, NOW.
YOU TOO, SIR.
MAN! I DIDN'T THINK IT WAS SNOWING NEARLY THIS HARD!
OH, GREAT! AND ME WITHOUT CHAINS!

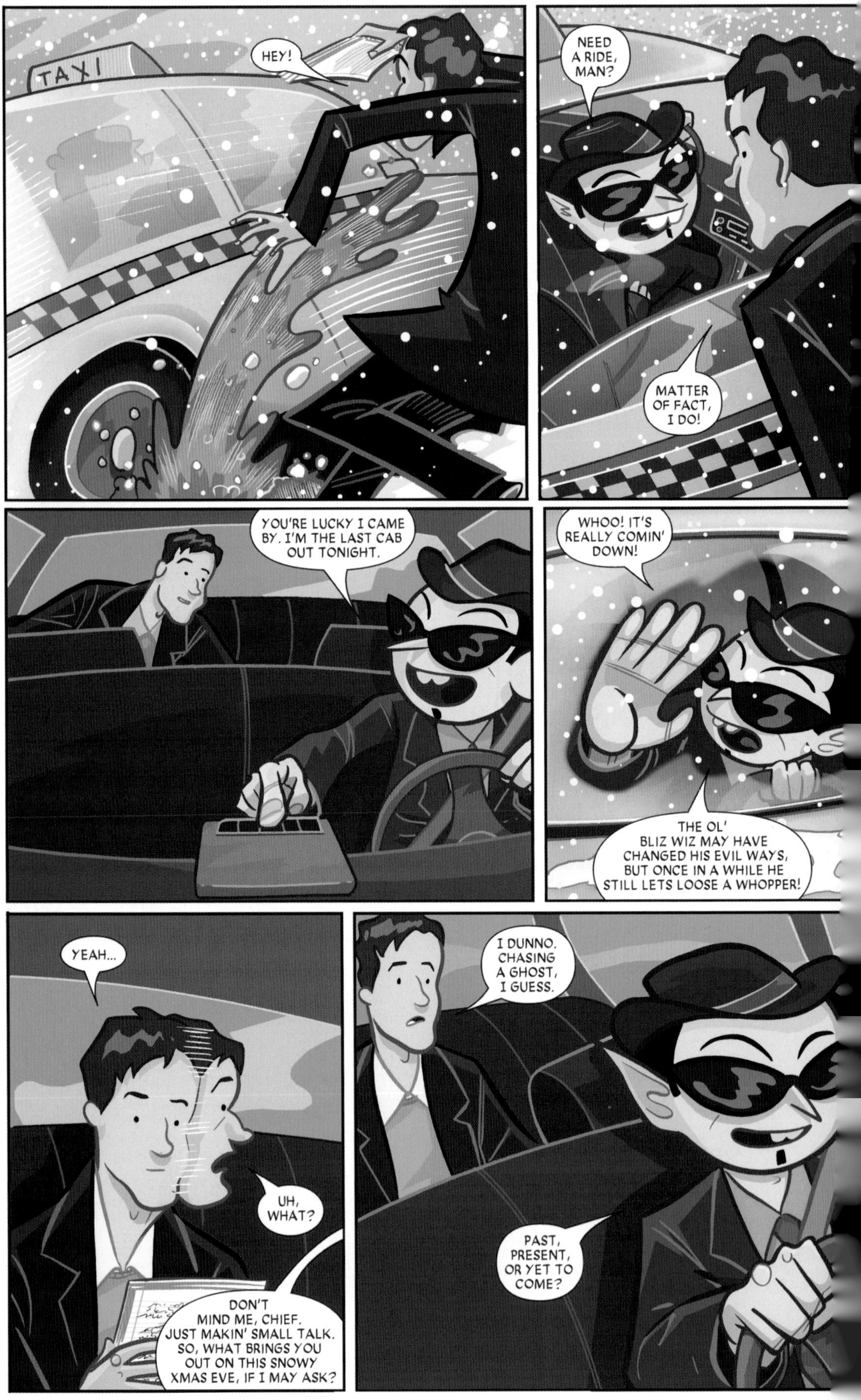
HEY!
NEED A RIDE, MAN?
MATTER OF FACT, I DO!
YOU'RE LUCKY I CAME BY. I'M THE LAST CAB OUT TONIGHT.
WHOO! IT'S REALLY COMIN' DOWN!
THE OL' BLIZ WIZ MAY HAVE CHANGED HIS EVIL WAYS, BUT ONCE IN A WHILE HE STILL LETS LOOSE A WHOPPER!
YEAH...
UH, WHAT?
DON'T MIND ME, CHIEF. JUST MAKIN' SMALL TALK. SO, WHAT BRINGS YOU OUT ON THIS SNOWY XMAS EVE, IF I MAY ASK?
I DUNNO. CHASING A GHOST, I GUESS.
PAST, PRESENT, OR YET TO COME?

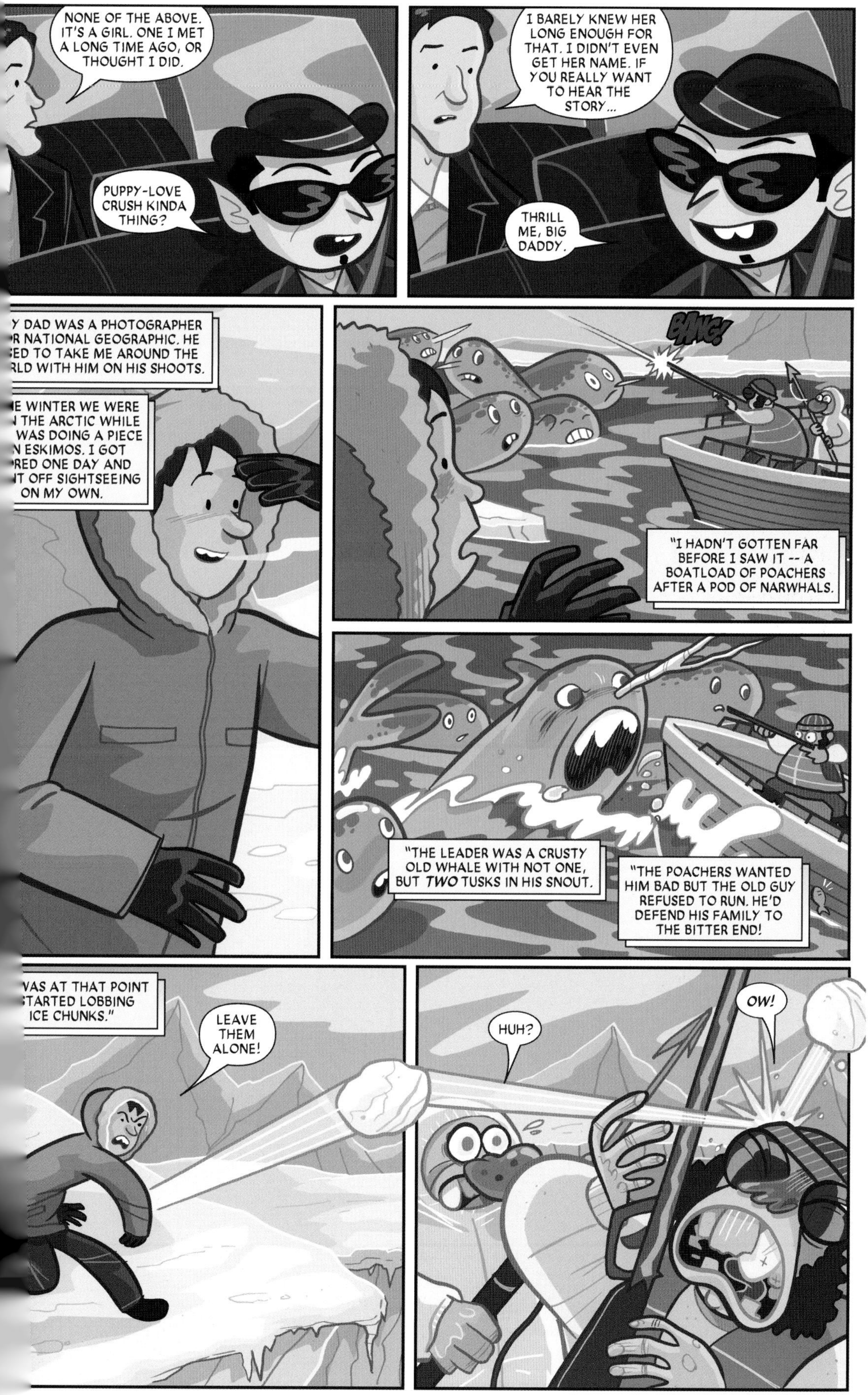
NONE OF THE ABOVE. IT'S A GIRL. ONE I MET A LONG TIME AGO, OR THOUGHT I DID.
PUPPY-LOVE CRUSH KINDA THING?
I BARELY KNEW HER LONG ENOUGH FOR THAT. I DIDN'T EVEN GET HER NAME. IF YOU REALLY WANT TO HEAR THE STORY...
THRILL ME, BIG DADDY.
Y DAD WAS A PHOTOGRAPHER R NATIONAL GEOGRAPHIC. HE SED TO TAKE ME AROUND THE RLD WITH HIM ON HIS SHOOTS.
E WINTER WE WERE N THE ARCTIC WHILE WAS DOING A PIECE N ESKIMOS. I GOT RED ONE DAY AND T OFF SIGHTSEEING ON MY OWN.
BANG!
"I HADN'T GOTTEN FAR BEFORE I SAW IT -- A BOATLOAD OF POACHERS AFTER A POD OF NARWHALS.
"THE LEADER WAS A CRUSTY OLD WHALE WITH NOT ONE, BUT *TWO* TUSKS IN HIS SNOUT.
"THE POACHERS WANTED HIM BAD BUT THE OLD GUY REFUSED TO RUN. HE'D DEFEND HIS FAMILY TO THE BITTER END!
VAS AT THAT POINT STARTED LOBBING ICE CHUNKS."
LEAVE THEM ALONE!
HUH?
OW!

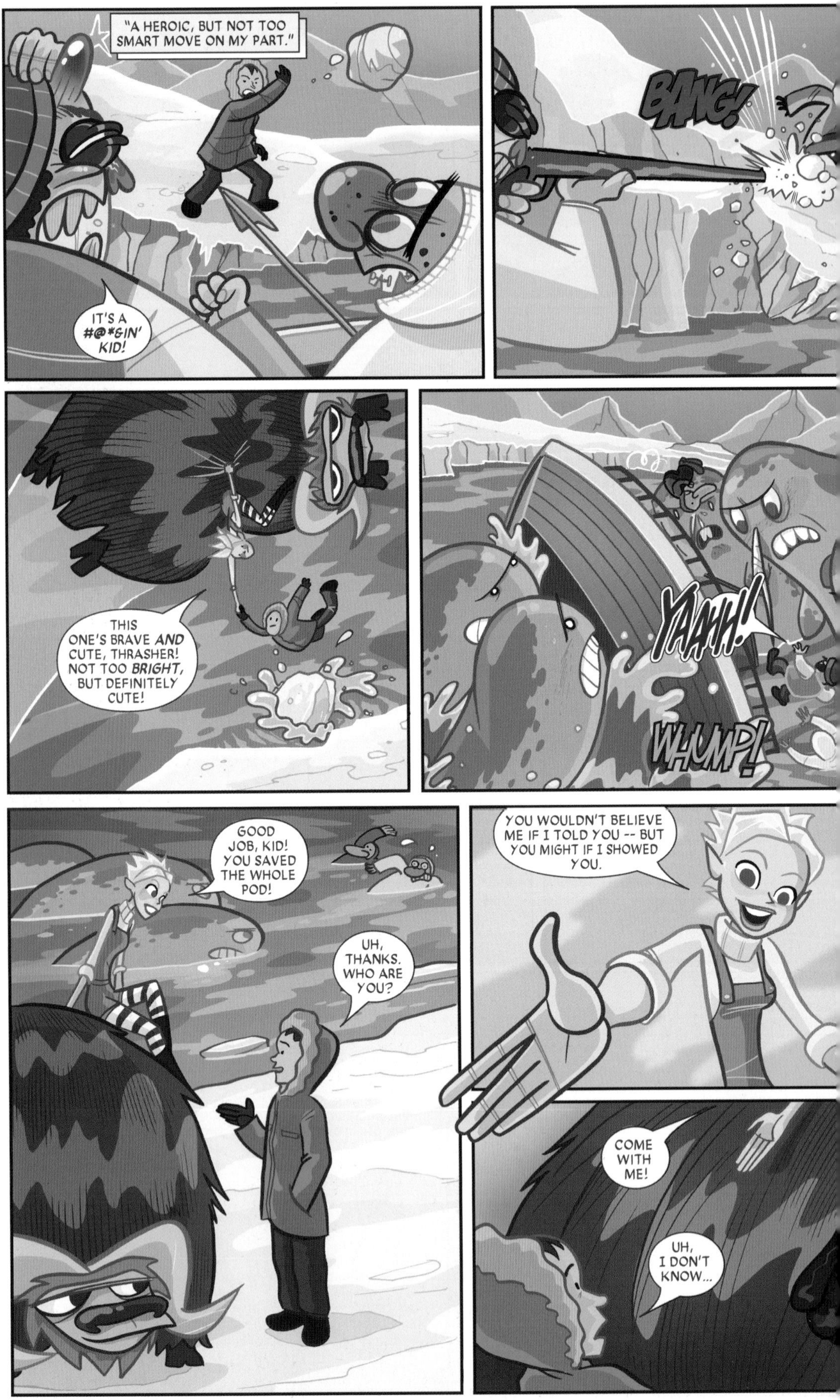
"A HEROIC, BUT NOT TOO SMART MOVE ON MY PART."
IT'S A #@*&IN' KID!
BANG!
THIS ONE'S BRAVE AND CUTE, THRASHER! NOT TOO BRIGHT, BUT DEFINITELY CUTE!
YAAHH!
WHUMP!
GOOD JOB, KID! YOU SAVED THE WHOLE POD!
UH, THANKS. WHO ARE YOU?
YOU WOULDN'T BELIEVE ME IF I TOLD YOU -- BUT YOU MIGHT IF I SHOWED YOU.
COME WITH ME!
UH, I DON'T KNOW...

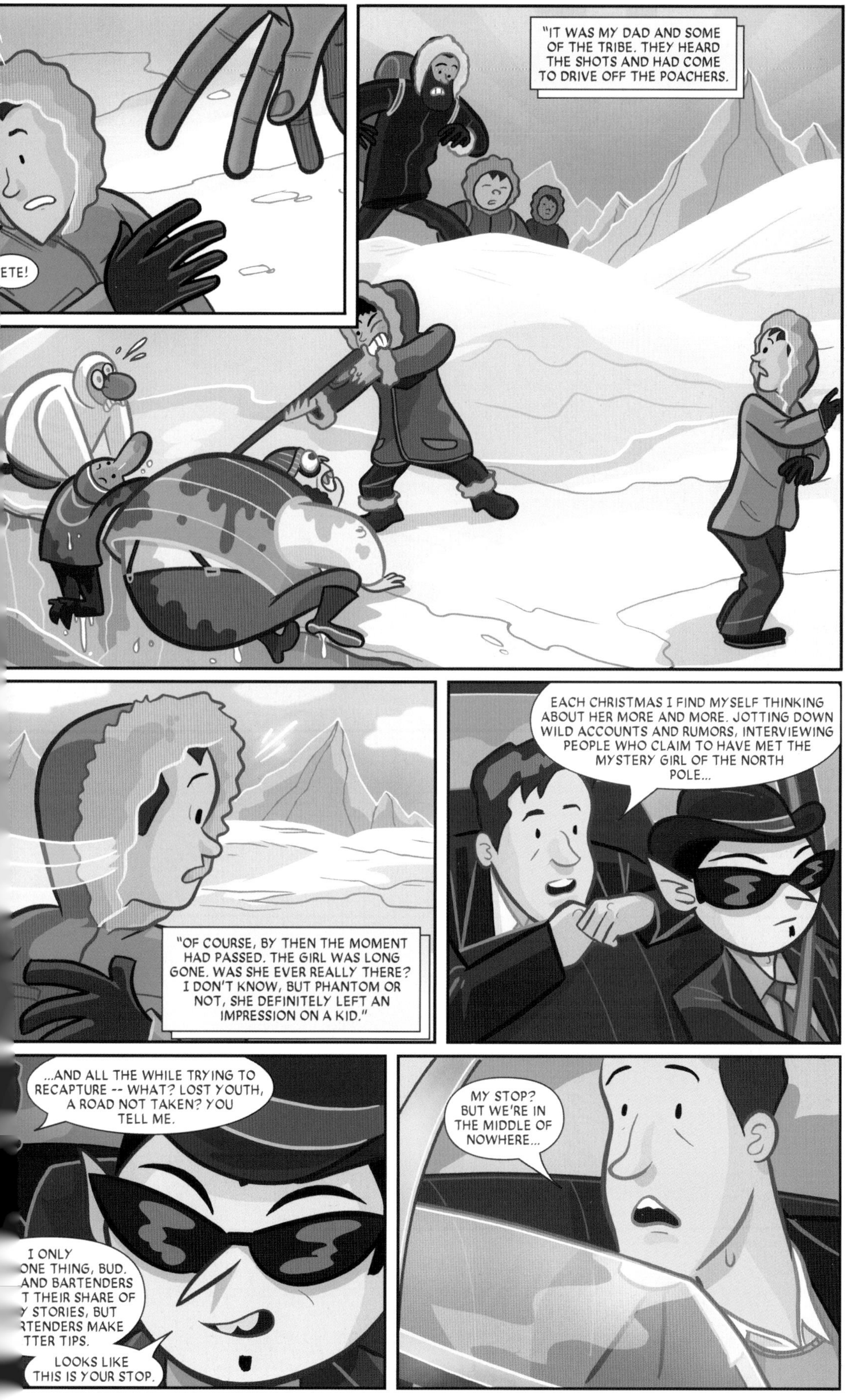
ETE!
"IT WAS MY DAD AND SOME OF THE TRIBE. THEY HEARD THE SHOTS AND HAD COME TO DRIVE OFF THE POACHERS.
"OF COURSE, BY THEN THE MOMENT HAD PASSED. THE GIRL WAS LONG GONE. WAS SHE EVER REALLY THERE? I DON'T KNOW, BUT PHANTOM OR NOT, SHE DEFINITELY LEFT AN IMPRESSION ON A KID."
EACH CHRISTMAS I FIND MYSELF THINKING ABOUT HER MORE AND MORE. JOTTING DOWN WILD ACCOUNTS AND RUMORS, INTERVIEWING PEOPLE WHO CLAIM TO HAVE MET THE MYSTERY GIRL OF THE NORTH POLE...
...AND ALL THE WHILE TRYING TO RECAPTURE -- WHAT? LOST YOUTH, A ROAD NOT TAKEN? YOU TELL ME.
I ONLY ONE THING, BUD. AND BARTENDERS T THEIR SHARE OF Y STORIES, BUT RTENDERS MAKE TTER TIPS.
LOOKS LIKE THIS IS YOUR STOP.
MY STOP? BUT WE'RE IN THE MIDDLE OF NOWHERE...

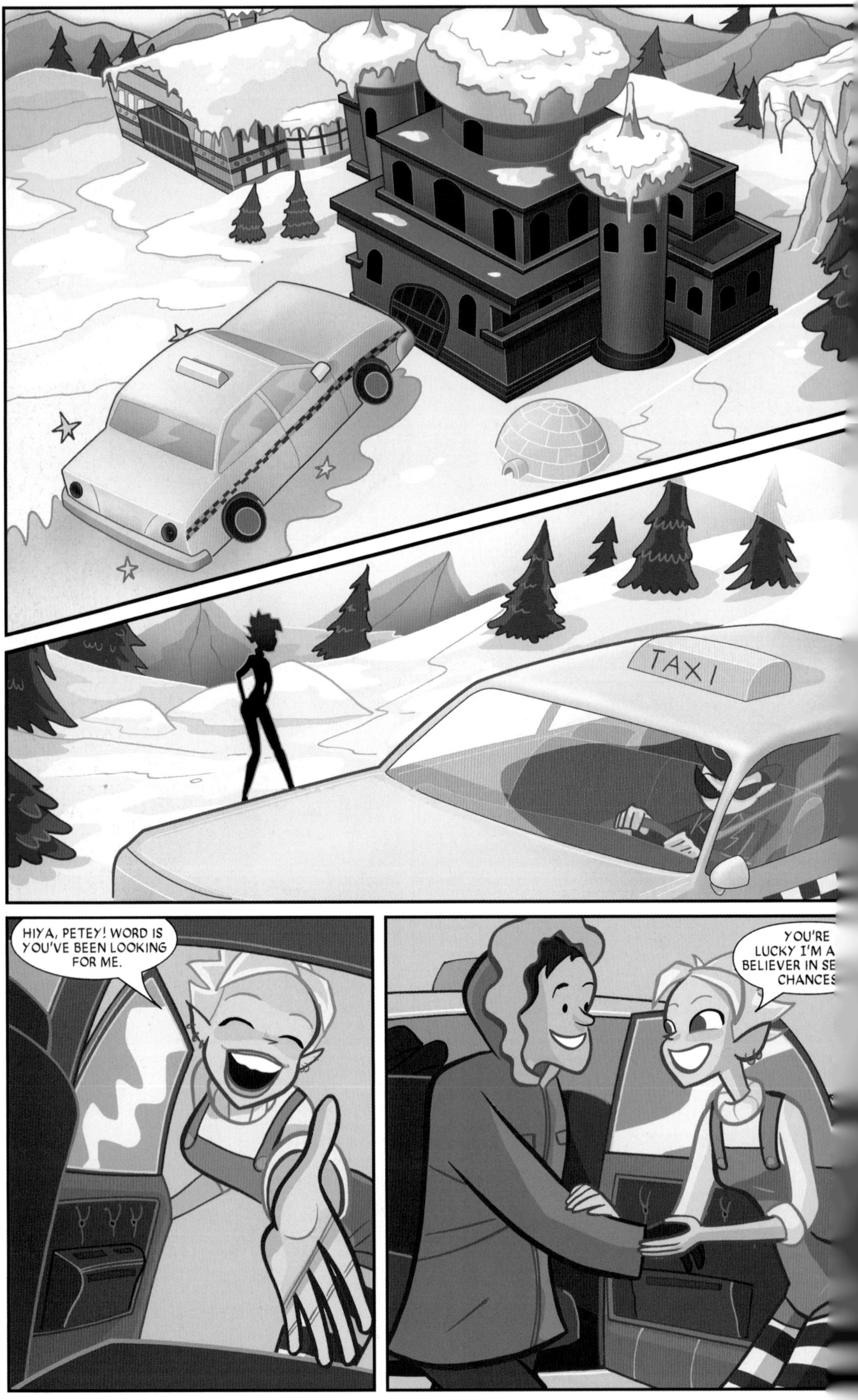
TAXI
HIYA, PETEY! WORD IS YOU'VE BEEN LOOKING FOR ME.
YOU'RE LUCKY I'M A BELIEVER IN SE CHANCES

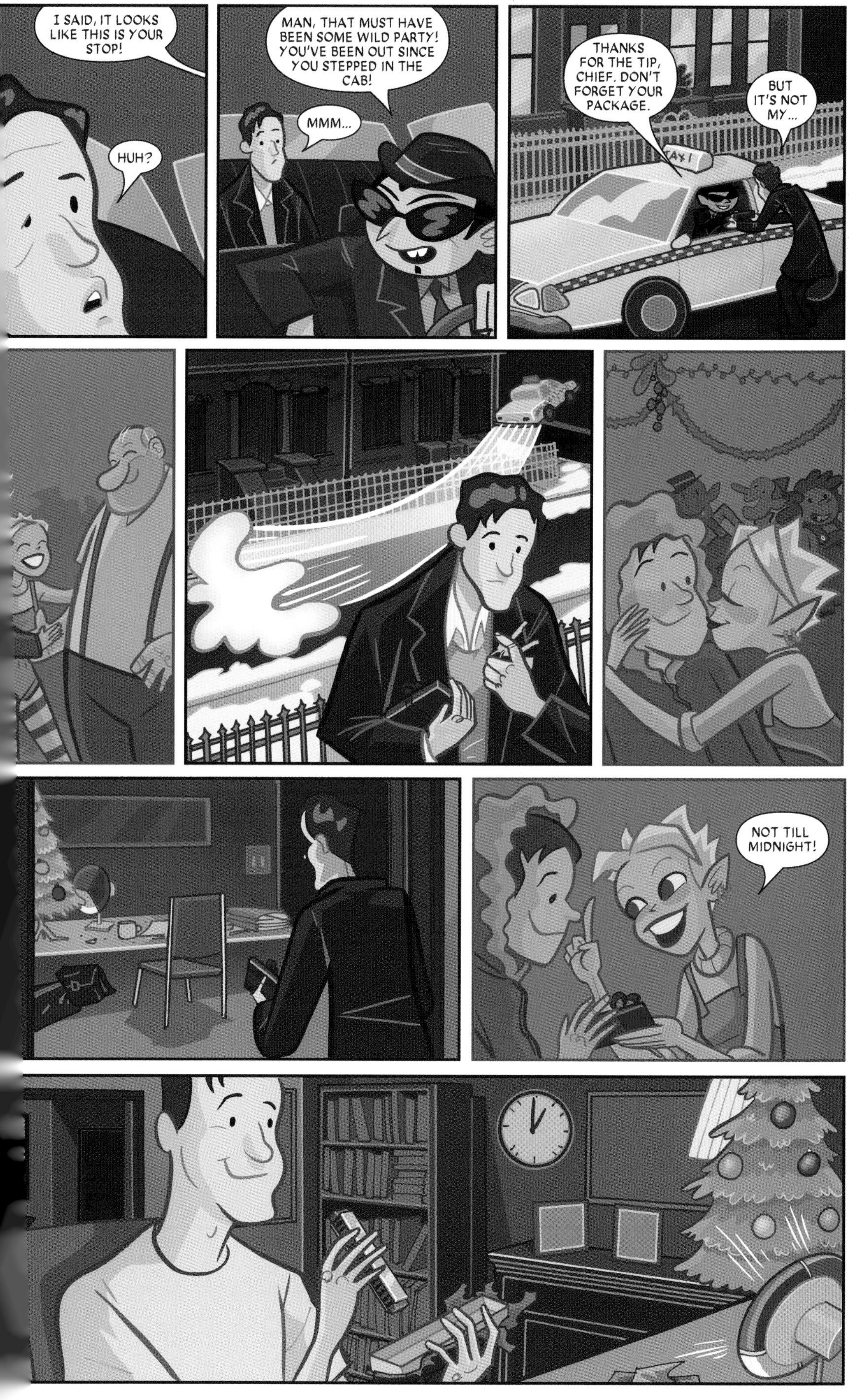
I SAID, IT LOOKS LIKE THIS IS YOUR STOP!
HUH?
MAN, THAT MUST HAVE BEEN SOME WILD PARTY! YOU'VE BEEN OUT SINCE YOU STEPPED IN THE CAB!
MMM...
THANKS FOR THE TIP, CHIEF. DON'T FORGET YOUR PACKAGE.
BUT IT'S NOT MY...
TAXI
NOT TILL MIDNIGHT!

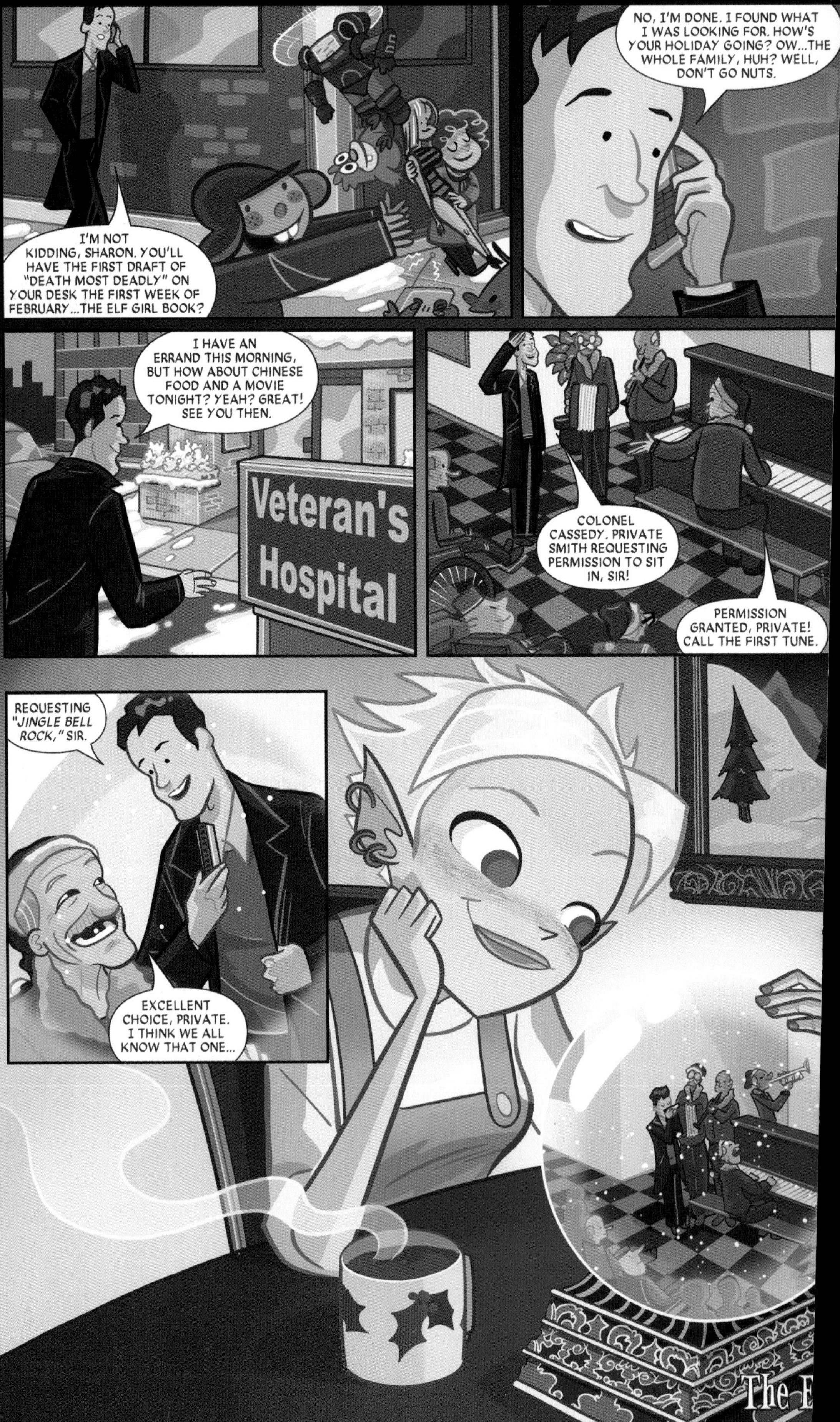
I'M NOT KIDDING, SHARON. YOU'LL HAVE THE FIRST DRAFT OF "DEATH MOST DEADLY" ON YOUR DESK THE FIRST WEEK OF FEBRUARY...THE ELF GIRL BOOK?
NO, I'M DONE. I FOUND WHAT I WAS LOOKING FOR. HOW'S YOUR HOLIDAY GOING? OW...THE WHOLE FAMILY, HUH? WELL, DON'T GO NUTS.
I HAVE AN ERRAND THIS MORNING, BUT HOW ABOUT CHINESE FOOD AND A MOVIE TONIGHT? YEAH? GREAT! SEE YOU THEN.
Veteran's Hospital
COLONEL CASSEDY. PRIVATE SMITH REQUESTING PERMISSION TO SIT IN, SIR!
PERMISSION GRANTED, PRIVATE! CALL THE FIRST TUNE.
REQUESTING "JINGLE BELL ROCK," SIR.
EXCELLENT CHOICE, PRIVATE. I THINK WE ALL KNOW THAT ONE...
The E

Kiyotes' Christmas Party

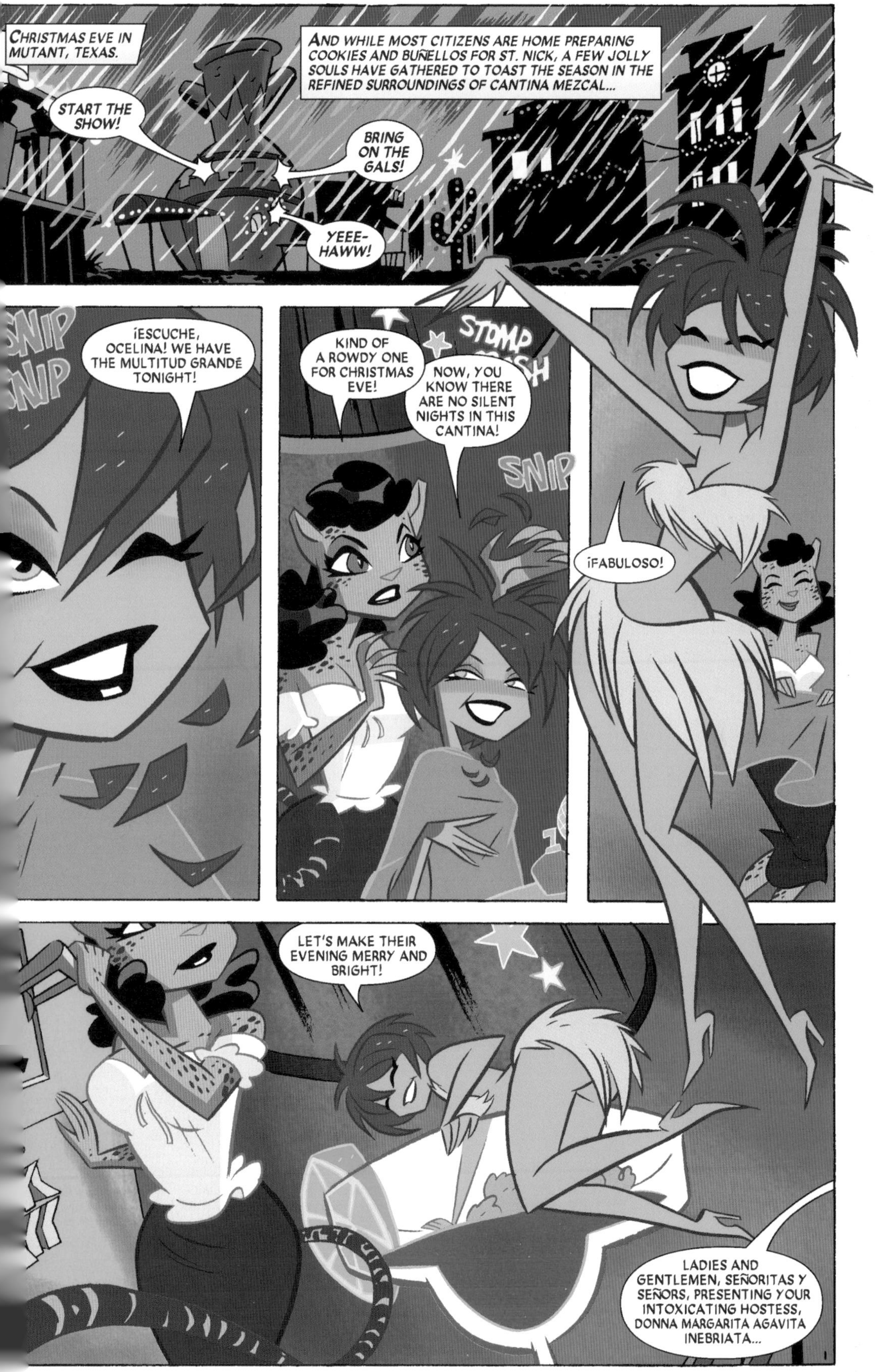

CHRISTMAS EVE IN MUTANT, TEXAS.
AND WHILE MOST CITIZENS ARE HOME PREPARING COOKIES AND BUÑELLOS FOR ST. NICK, A FEW JOLLY SOULS HAVE GATHERED TO TOAST THE SEASON IN THE REFINED SURROUNDINGS OF CANTINA MEZCAL...
START THE SHOW!
BRING ON THE GALS!
YEEE-HAWW!
SNIP
SNIP
¡ESCUCHE, OCELINA! WE HAVE THE MULTITUD GRANDÉ TONIGHT!
STOMP
KIND OF A ROWDY ONE FOR CHRISTMAS EVE!
NOW, YOU KNOW THERE ARE NO SILENT NIGHTS IN THIS CANTINA!
SNIP
¡FABULOSO!
LET'S MAKE THEIR EVENING MERRY AND BRIGHT!
LADIES AND GENTLEMEN, SEÑORITAS Y SEÑORS, PRESENTING YOUR INTOXICATING HOSTESS, DONNA MARGARITA AGAVITA INEBRIATA...

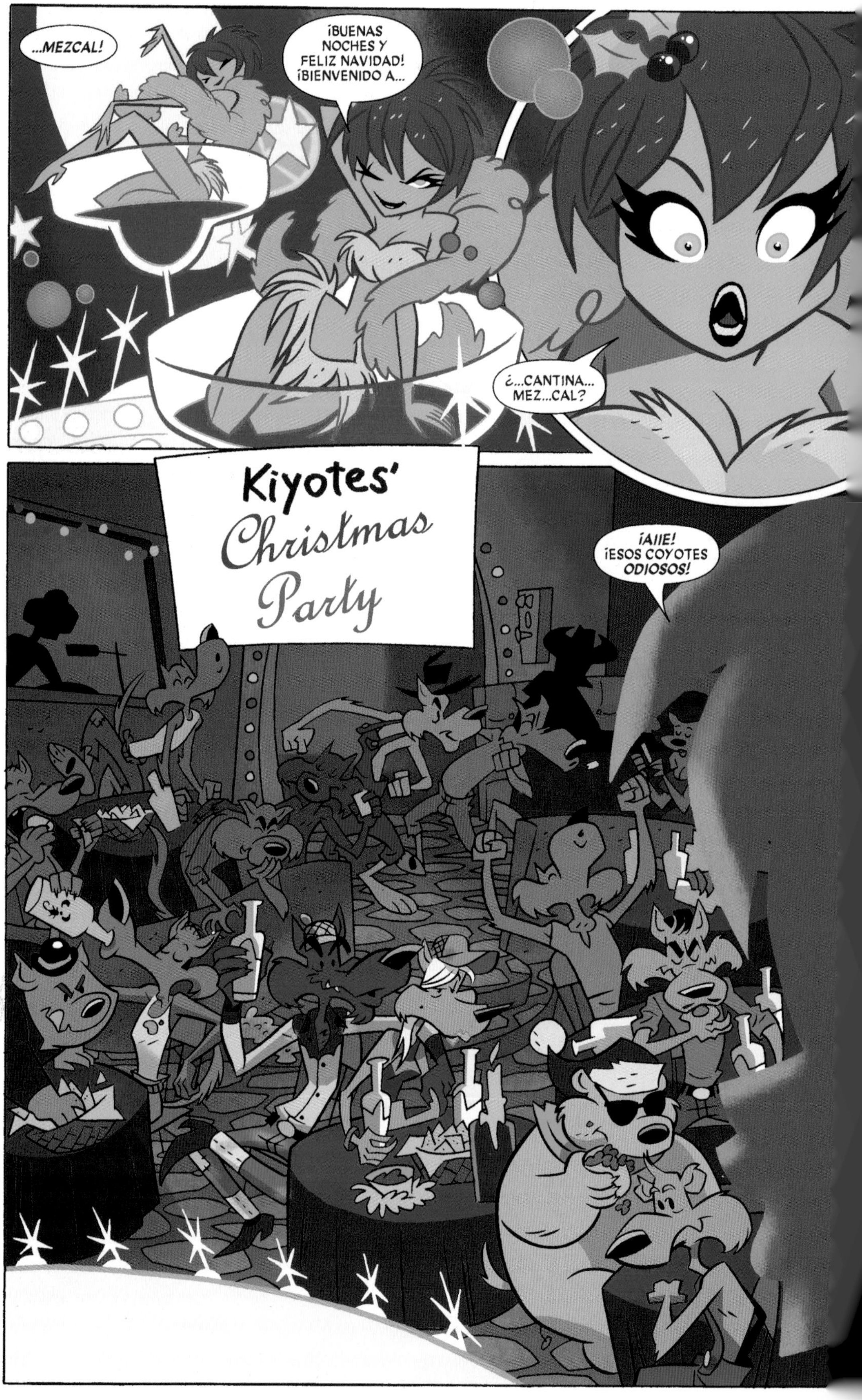
...MEZCAL!
¡BUENAS NOCHES Y FELIZ NAVIDAD! ¡BIENVENIDO A...
¿...CANTINA... MEZ...CAL?
Kiyotes' Christmas Party
¡AIIE! ¡ESOS COYOTES ODIOSOS!

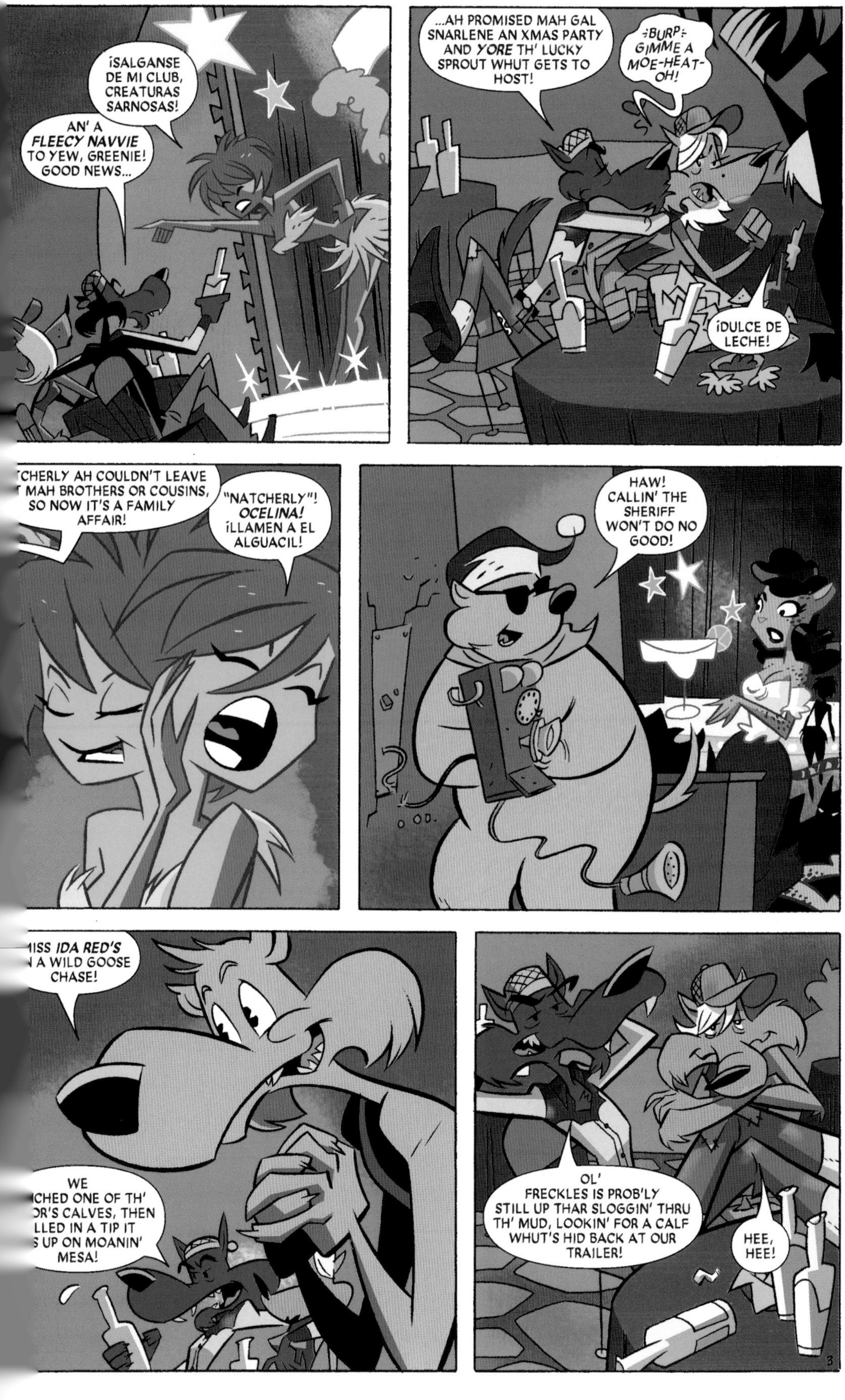
¡SALGANSE DE MI CLUB, CREATURAS SARNOSAS!
AN' A FLEECY NAVVIE TO YEW, GREENIE! GOOD NEWS...
...AH PROMISED MAH GAL SNARLENE AN XMAS PARTY AND YORE TH' LUCKY SPROUT WHUT GETS TO HOST!
÷BURP÷ GIMME A MOE-HEAT-OH!
¡DULCE DE LECHE!
TCHERLY AH COULDN'T LEAVE
T MAH BROTHERS OR COUSINS, SO NOW IT'S A FAMILY AFFAIR!
"NATCHERLY"! OCELINA! ¡LLAMEN A EL ALGUACIL!
HAW! CALLIN' THE SHERIFF WON'T DO NO GOOD!
IISS IDA RED'S
N A WILD GOOSE CHASE!
WE
ICHED ONE OF TH'
OR'S CALVES, THEN
LLED IN A TIP IT
S UP ON MOANIN' MESA!
OL' FRECKLES IS PROB'LY STILL UP THAR SLOGGIN' THRU TH' MUD, LOOKIN' FOR A CALF WHUT'S HID BACK AT OUR TRAILER!
HEE, HEE!
3

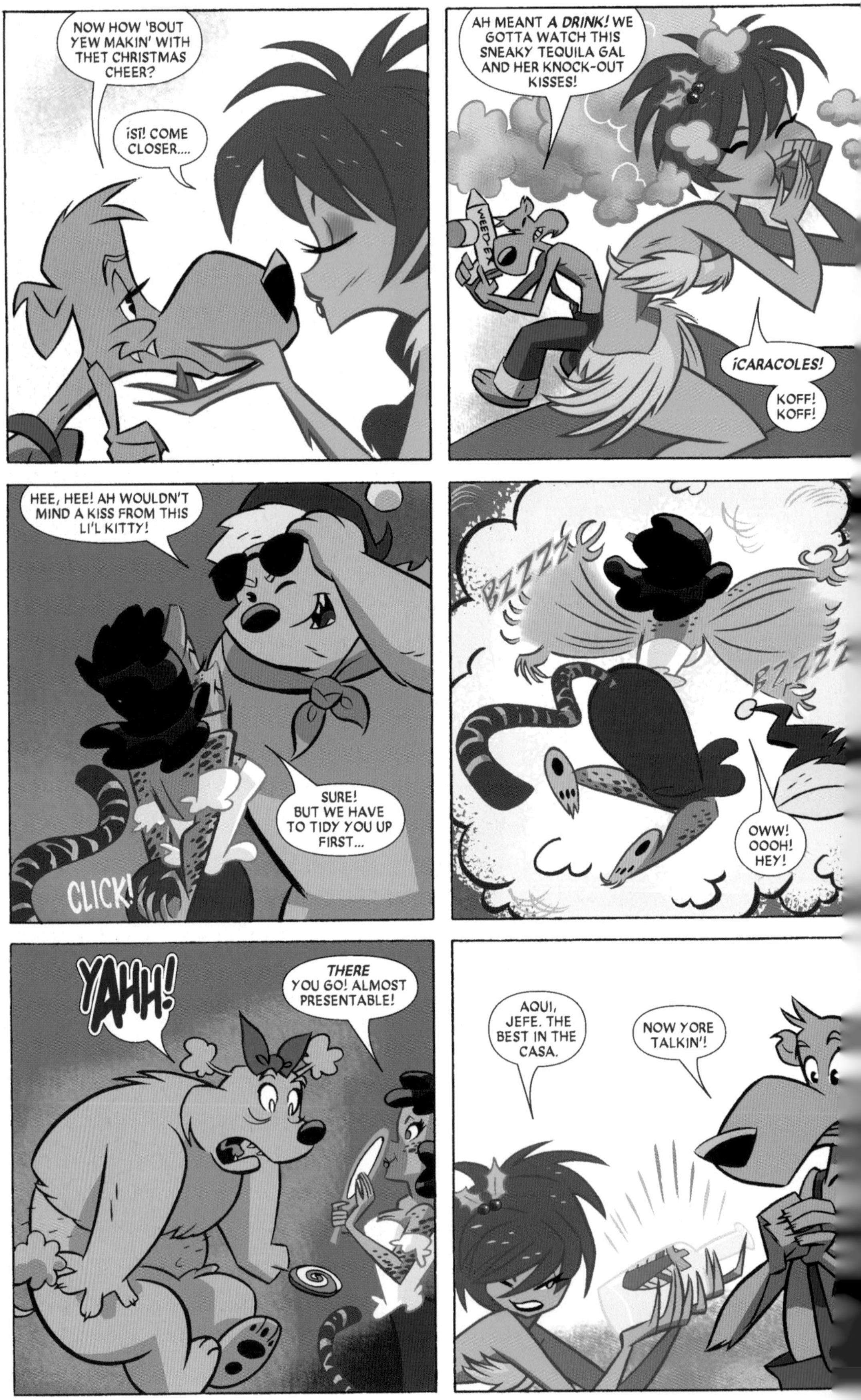
NOW HOW 'BOUT YEW MAKIN' WITH THET CHRISTMAS CHEER?
¡SI! COME CLOSER....
AH MEANT A DRINK! WE GOTTA WATCH THIS SNEAKY TEQUILA GAL AND HER KNOCK-OUT KISSES!
WEED-EX
¡CARACOLES!
KOFF! KOFF!
HEE, HEE! AH WOULDN'T MIND A KISS FROM THIS LI'L KITTY!
SURE! BUT WE HAVE TO TIDY YOU UP FIRST...
CLICK!
BZZZZ
BZZZZ
OWW! OOOH! HEY!
YAHH!
THERE YOU GO! ALMOST PRESENTABLE!
AQUI, JEFE. THE BEST IN THE CASA.
NOW YORE TALKIN'!

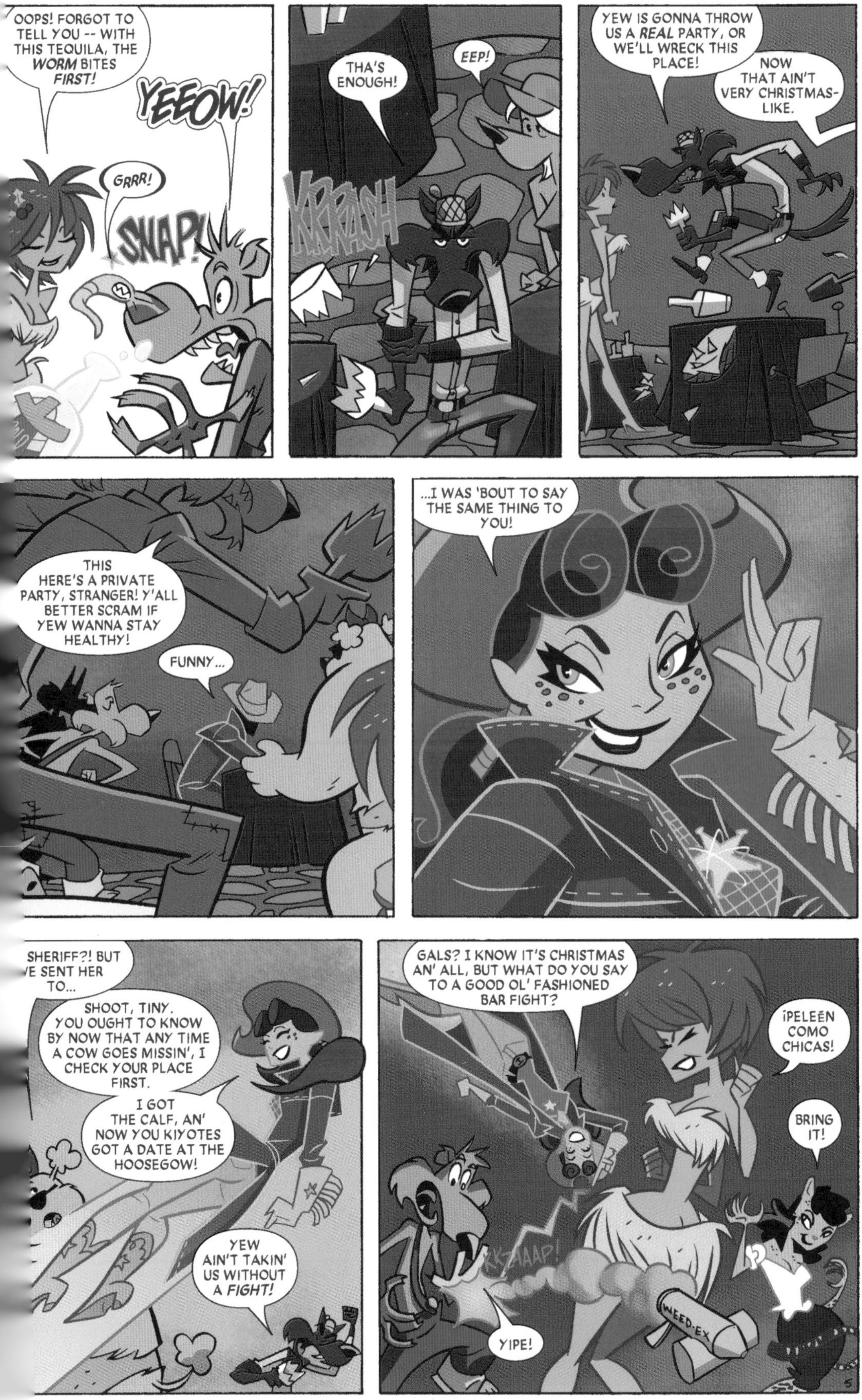
OOPS! FORGOT TO TELL YOU -- WITH THIS TEQUILA, THE WORM BITES FIRST!
YEEOW!
GRRR!
SNAP!
THA'S ENOUGH!
EEP!
KRRASH
YEW IS GONNA THROW US A REAL PARTY, OR WE'LL WRECK THIS PLACE!
NOW THAT AIN'T VERY CHRISTMAS-LIKE.
THIS HERE'S A PRIVATE PARTY, STRANGER! Y'ALL BETTER SCRAM IF YEW WANNA STAY HEALTHY!
FUNNY...
...I WAS 'BOUT TO SAY THE SAME THING TO YOU!
SHERIFF?! BUT WE SENT HER TO...
SHOOT, TINY. YOU OUGHT TO KNOW BY NOW THAT ANY TIME A COW GOES MISSIN', I CHECK YOUR PLACE FIRST.
I GOT THE CALF, AN' NOW YOU KIYOTES GOT A DATE AT THE HOOSEGOW!
YEW AIN'T TAKIN' US WITHOUT A FIGHT!
GALS? I KNOW IT'S CHRISTMAS AN' ALL, BUT WHAT DO YOU SAY TO A GOOD OL' FASHIONED BAR FIGHT?
¡PELEÉN COMO CHICAS!
BRING IT!
KKZHAAP!
WEED-EX
YIPE!
5

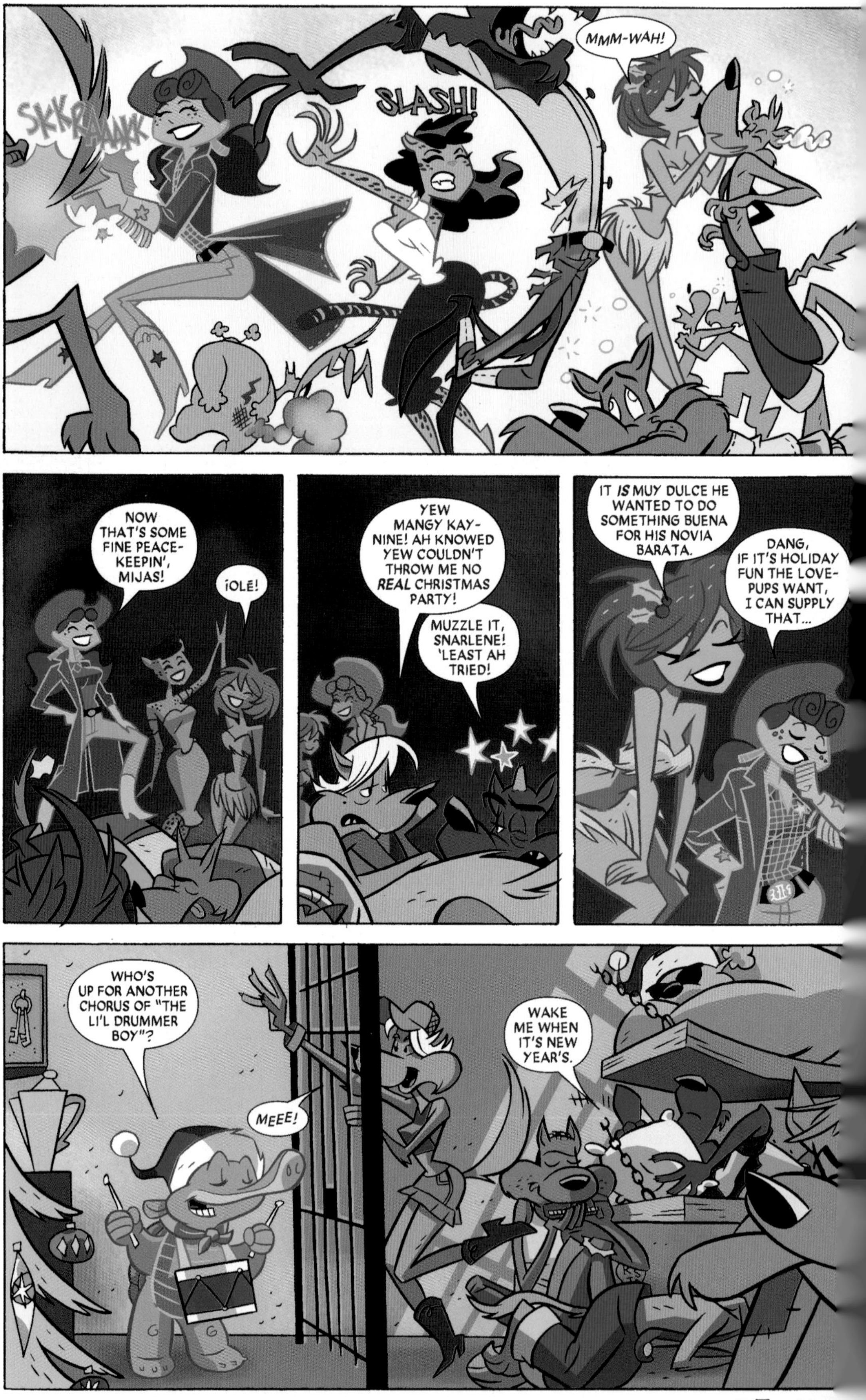
SKKRAAAKK
SLASH!
MMM-WAH!
NOW THAT'S SOME FINE PEACE-KEEPIN', MIJAS!
¡OLÉ!
YEW MANGY KAY-NINE! AH KNOWED YEW COULDN'T THROW ME NO REAL CHRISTMAS PARTY!
MUZZLE IT, SNARLENE! 'LEAST AH TRIED!
IT IS MUY DULCE HE WANTED TO DO SOMETHING BUENA FOR HIS NOVIA BARATA.
DANG, IF IT'S HOLIDAY FUN THE LOVE-PUPS WANT, I CAN SUPPLY THAT...
WHO'S UP FOR ANOTHER CHORUS OF "THE LI'L DRUMMER BOY"?
MEEE!
WAKE ME WHEN IT'S NEW YEAR'S.

The En

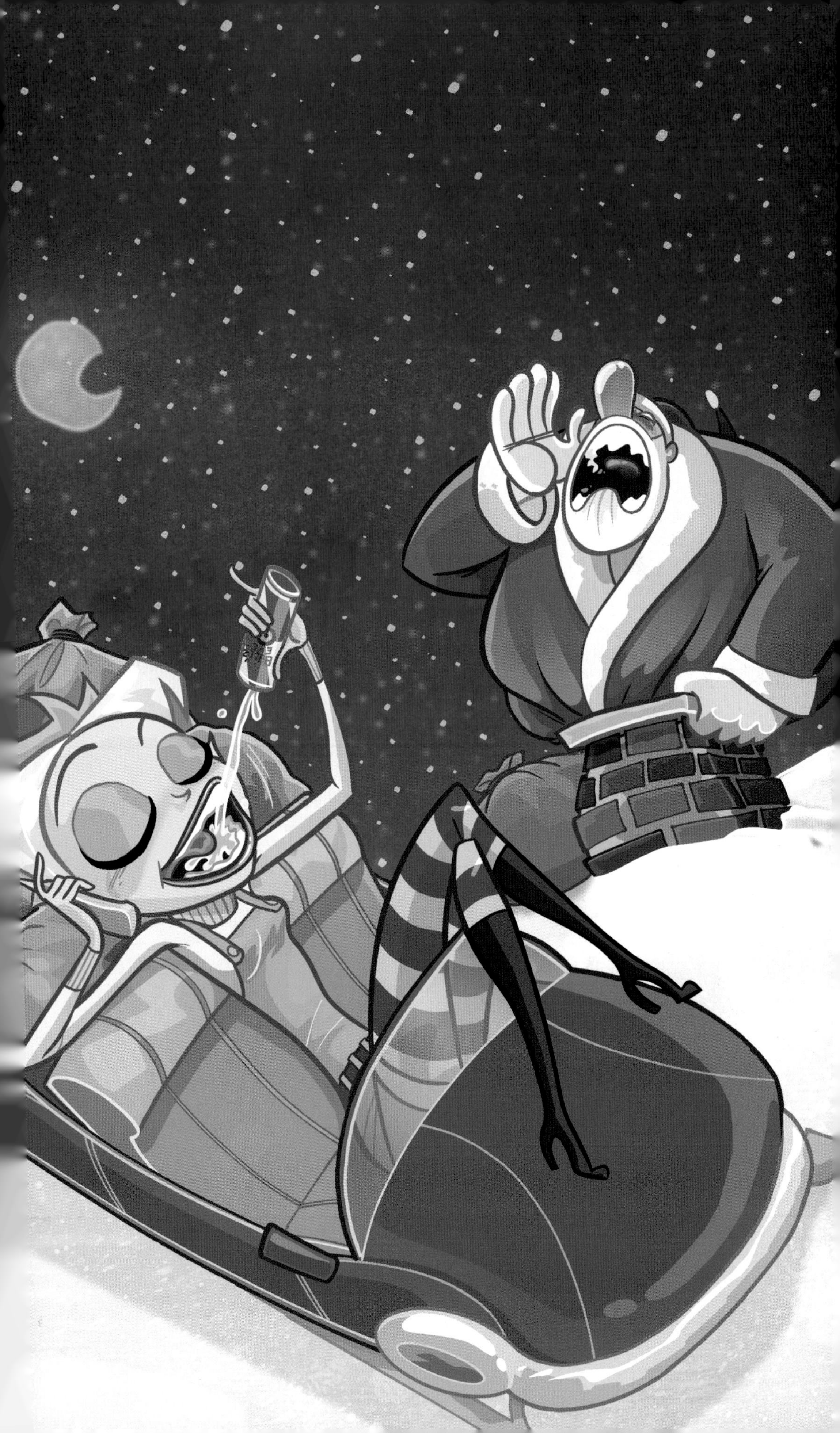

Ring-a-Ding Jing

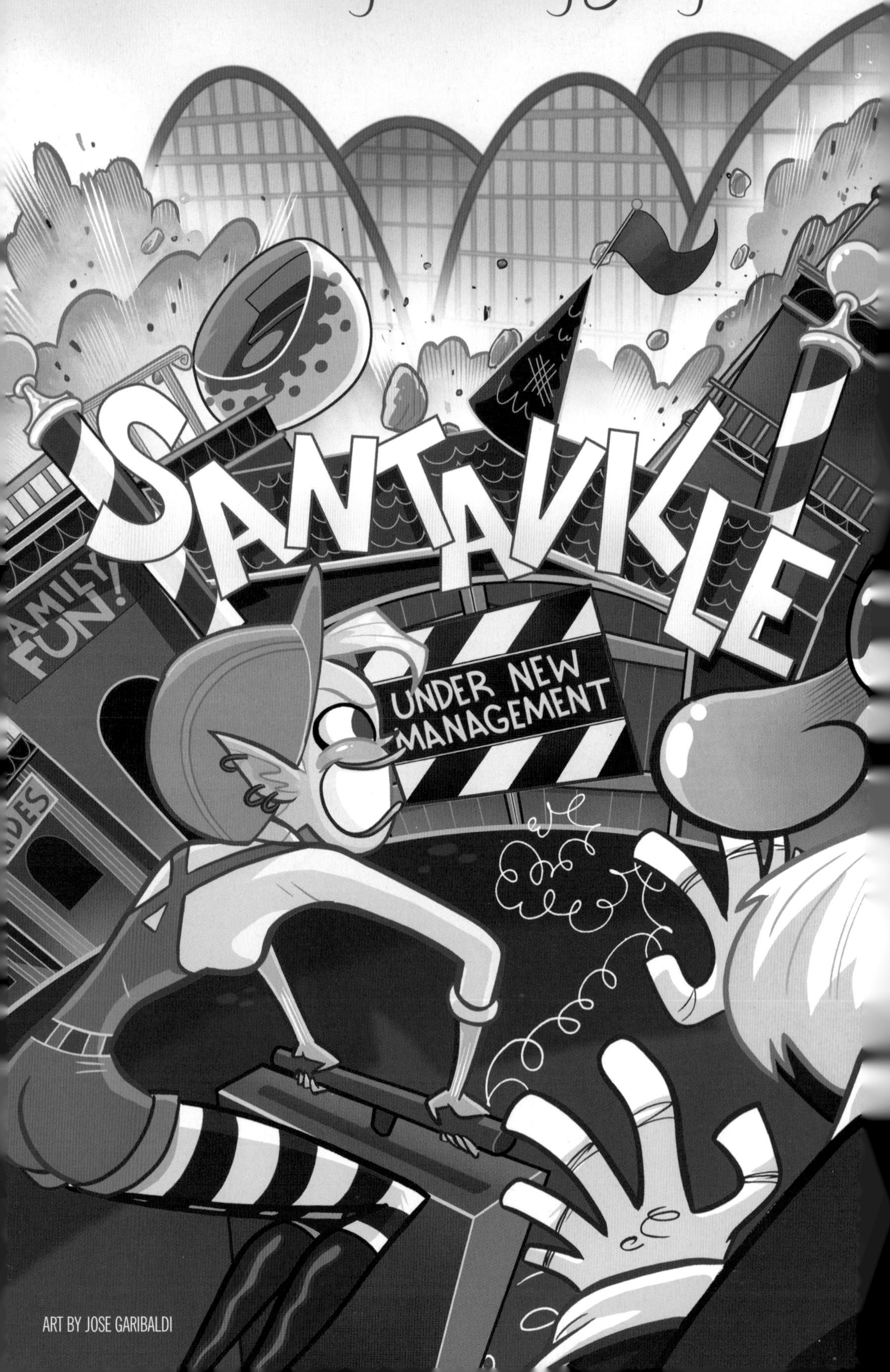
SANTAVILLE
AMILY FUN!
UNDER NEW MANAGEMENT

ART BY JOSE GARIBALDI

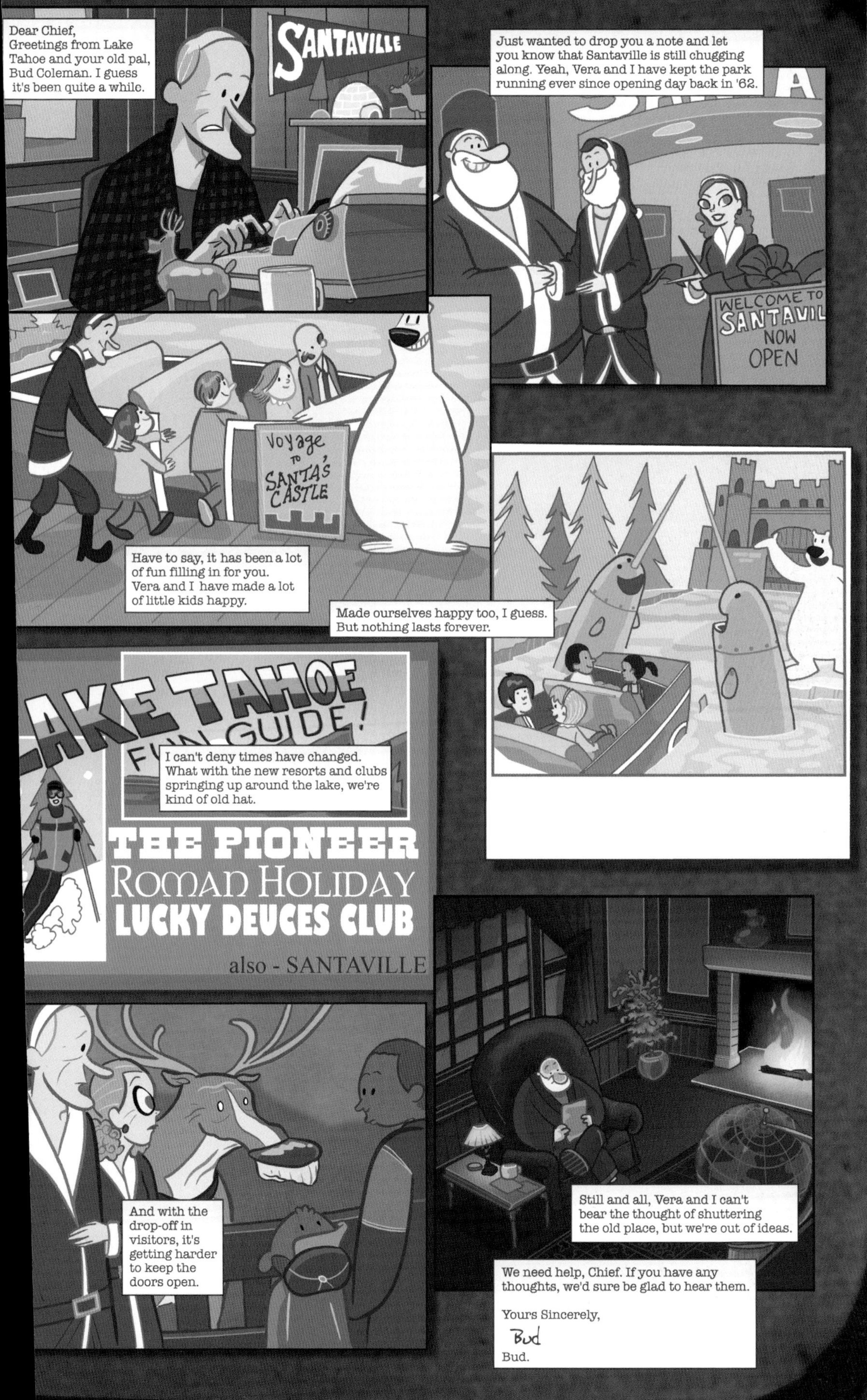

Dear Chief,
Greetings from Lake Tahoe and your old pal, Bud Coleman. I guess it's been quite a while.
SANTAVILLE
Just wanted to drop you a note and let you know that Santaville is still chugging along. Yeah, Vera and I have kept the park running ever since opening day back in '62.
WELCOME TO SANTAVIL NOW OPEN
VOYAGE TO SANTA'S CASTLE
Have to say, it has been a lot of fun filling in for you. Vera and I have made a lot of little kids happy.
Made ourselves happy too, I guess. But nothing lasts forever.
LAKE TAHOE FUN GUIDE!
I can't deny times have changed. What with the new resorts and clubs springing up around the lake, we're kind of old hat.
THE PIONEER
ROMAN HOLIDAY
LUCKY DEUCES CLUB
also - SANTAVILLE
And with the drop-off in visitors, it's getting harder to keep the doors open.
Still and all, Vera and I can't bear the thought of shuttering the old place, but we're out of ideas.
We need help, Chief. If you have any thoughts, we'd sure be glad to hear them.
Yours Sincerely,
Bud
Bud.

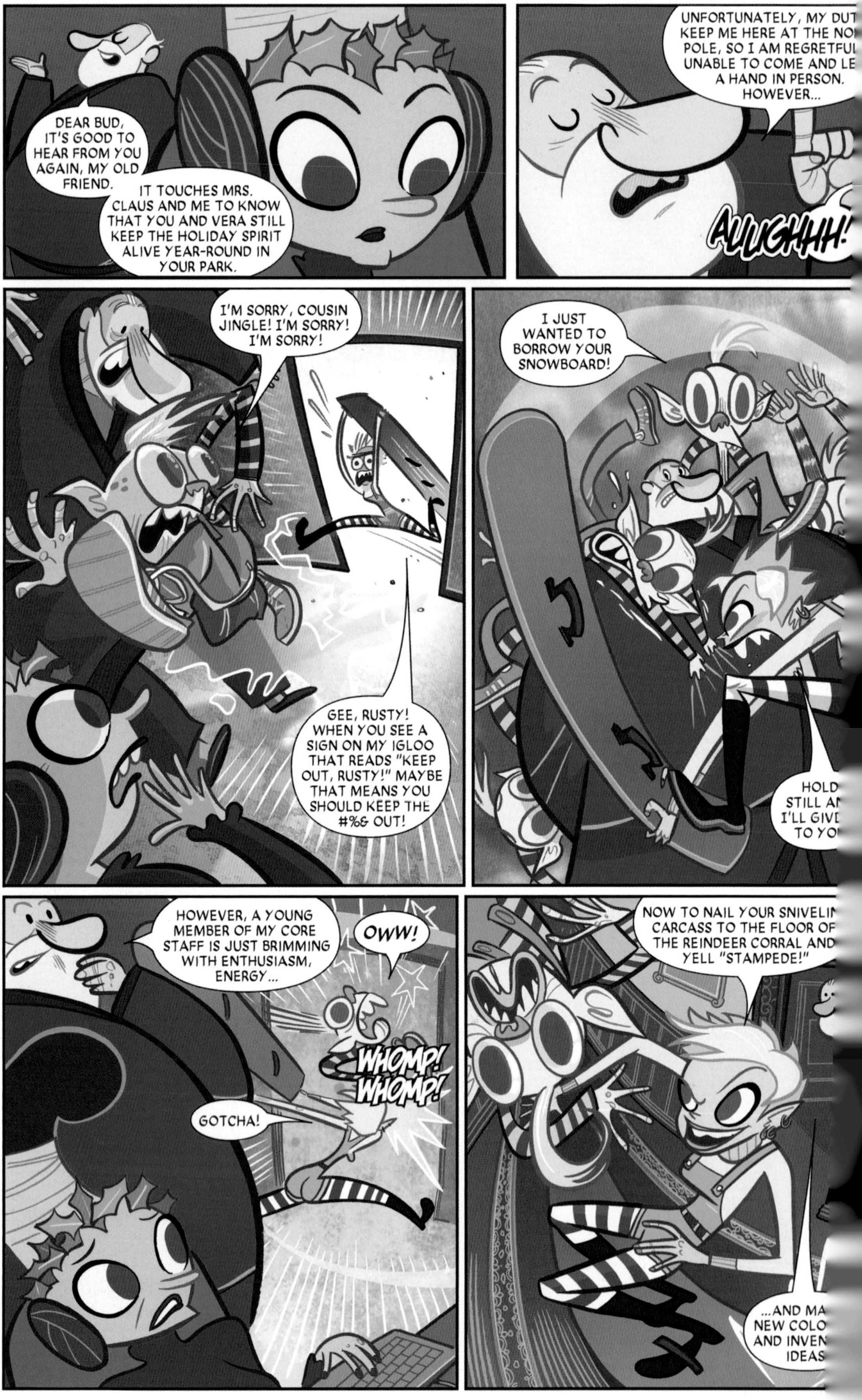
DEAR BUD, IT'S GOOD TO HEAR FROM YOU AGAIN, MY OLD FRIEND.
IT TOUCHES MRS. CLAUS AND ME TO KNOW THAT YOU AND VERA STILL KEEP THE HOLIDAY SPIRIT ALIVE YEAR-ROUND IN YOUR PARK.
UNFORTUNATELY, MY DUT KEEP ME HERE AT THE NO POLE, SO I AM REGRETFU UNABLE TO COME AND LE A HAND IN PERSON. HOWEVER...
AUUGHHH!
I'M SORRY, COUSIN JINGLE! I'M SORRY! I'M SORRY!
GEE, RUSTY! WHEN YOU SEE A SIGN ON MY IGLOO THAT READS "KEEP OUT, RUSTY!" MAYBE THAT MEANS YOU SHOULD KEEP THE #%& OUT!
I JUST WANTED TO BORROW YOUR SNOWBOARD!
HOLD STILL AN I'LL GIVE TO YO
HOWEVER, A YOUNG MEMBER OF MY CORE STAFF IS JUST BRIMMING WITH ENTHUSIASM, ENERGY...
OWW!
WHOMP! WHOMP!
GOTCHA!
NOW TO NAIL YOUR SNIVELIN CARCASS TO THE FLOOR OF THE REINDEER CORRAL AND YELL "STAMPEDE!"
...AND MA NEW COLO AND INVEN IDEAS

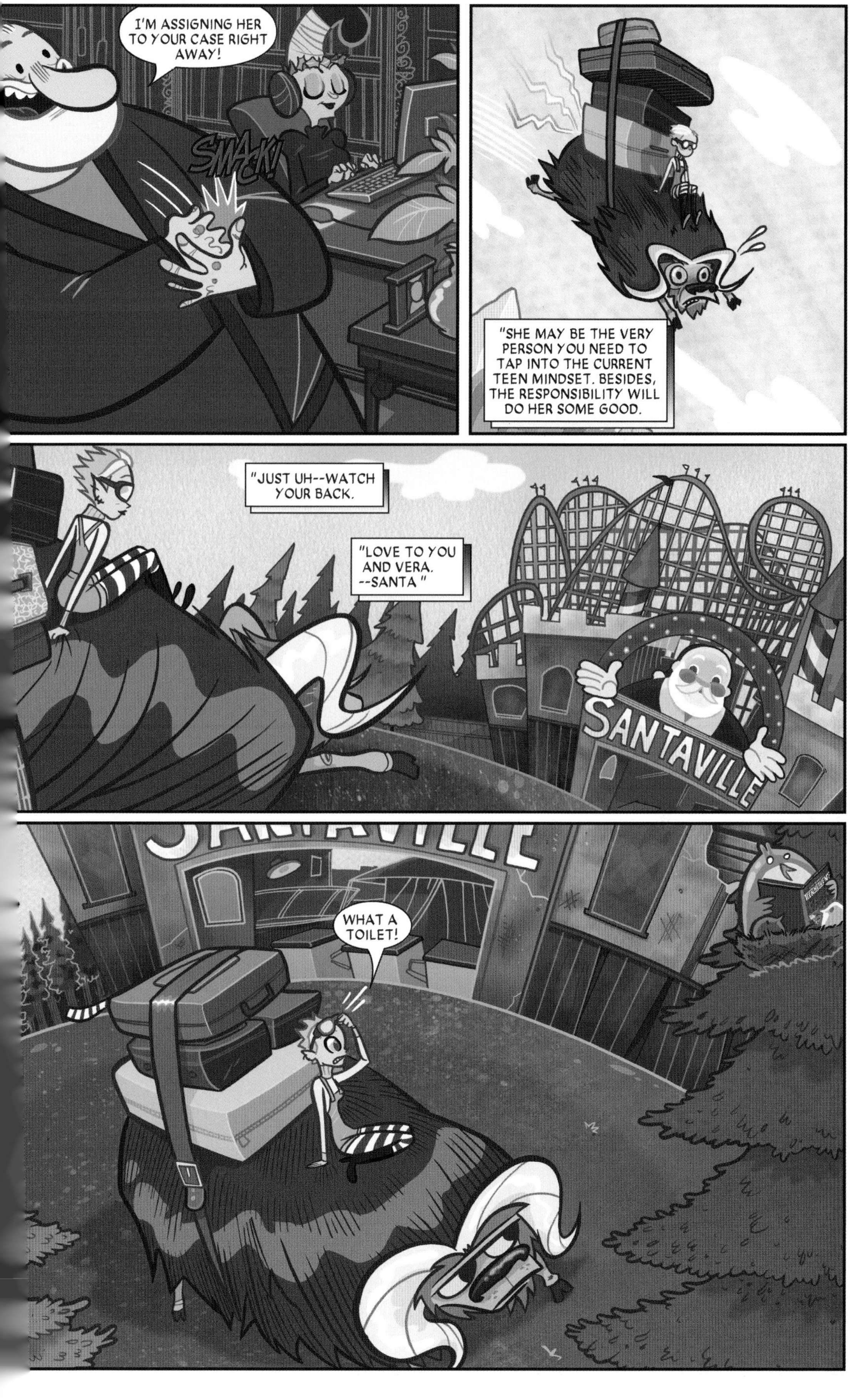
I'M ASSIGNING HER TO YOUR CASE RIGHT AWAY!
SMACK!
"SHE MAY BE THE VERY PERSON YOU NEED TO TAP INTO THE CURRENT TEEN MINDSET. BESIDES, THE RESPONSIBILITY WILL DO HER SOME GOOD.
"JUST UH--WATCH YOUR BACK.
"LOVE TO YOU AND VERA. --SANTA"
SANTAVILLE
WHAT A TOILET!

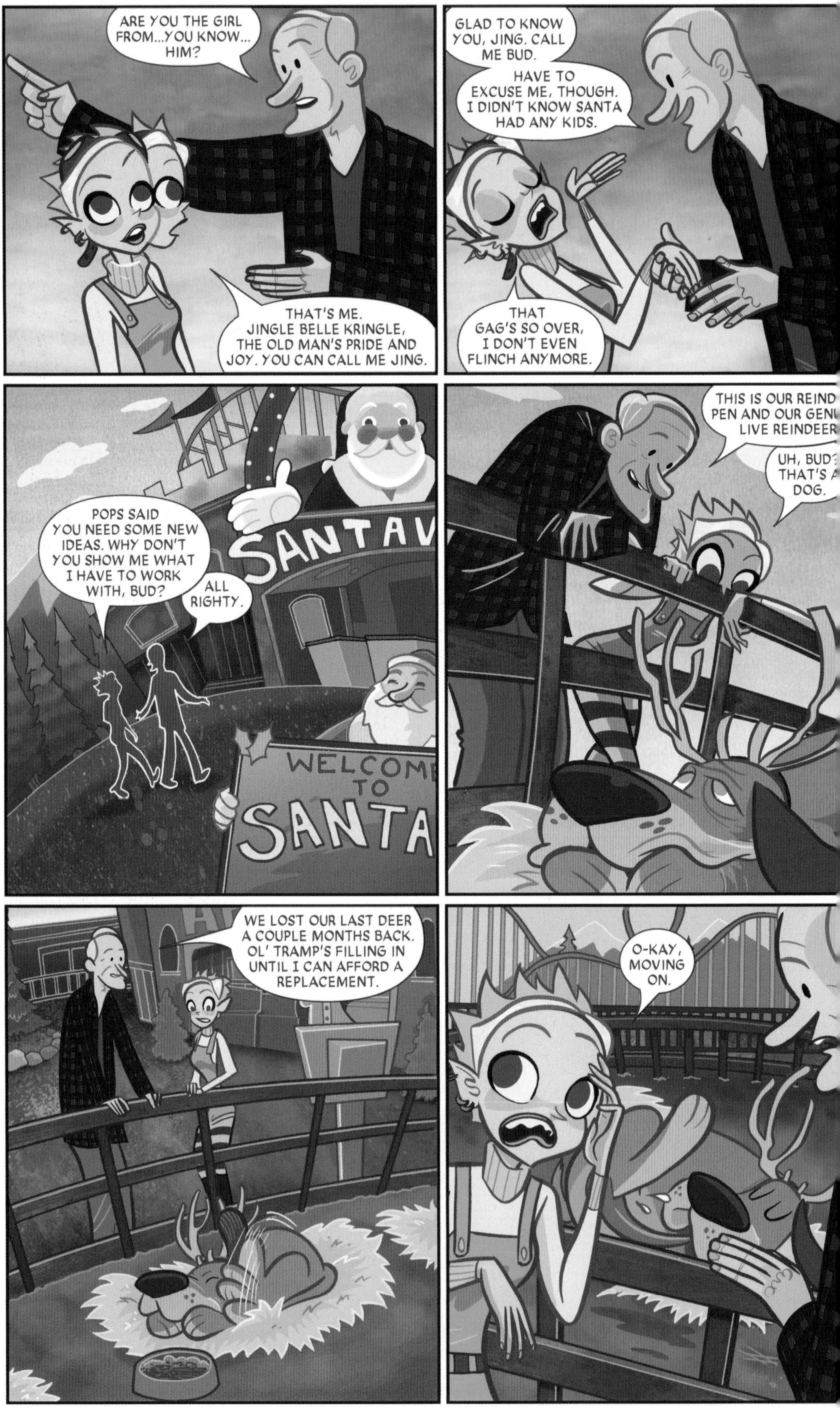

ARE YOU THE GIRL FROM...YOU KNOW... HIM?
THAT'S ME. JINGLE BELLE KRINGLE, THE OLD MAN'S PRIDE AND JOY. YOU CAN CALL ME JING.
GLAD TO KNOW YOU, JING. CALL ME BUD.
HAVE TO EXCUSE ME, THOUGH. I DIDN'T KNOW SANTA HAD ANY KIDS.
THAT GAG'S SO OVER, I DON'T EVEN FLINCH ANYMORE.
SANTAV
POPS SAID YOU NEED SOME NEW IDEAS. WHY DON'T YOU SHOW ME WHAT I HAVE TO WORK WITH, BUD?
ALL RIGHTY.
WELCOME TO SANTA
THIS IS OUR REIND PEN AND OUR GENU LIVE REINDEER
UH, BUD? THAT'S A DOG.
WE LOST OUR LAST DEER A COUPLE MONTHS BACK. OL' TRAMP'S FILLING IN UNTIL I CAN AFFORD A REPLACEMENT.
O-KAY, MOVING ON.

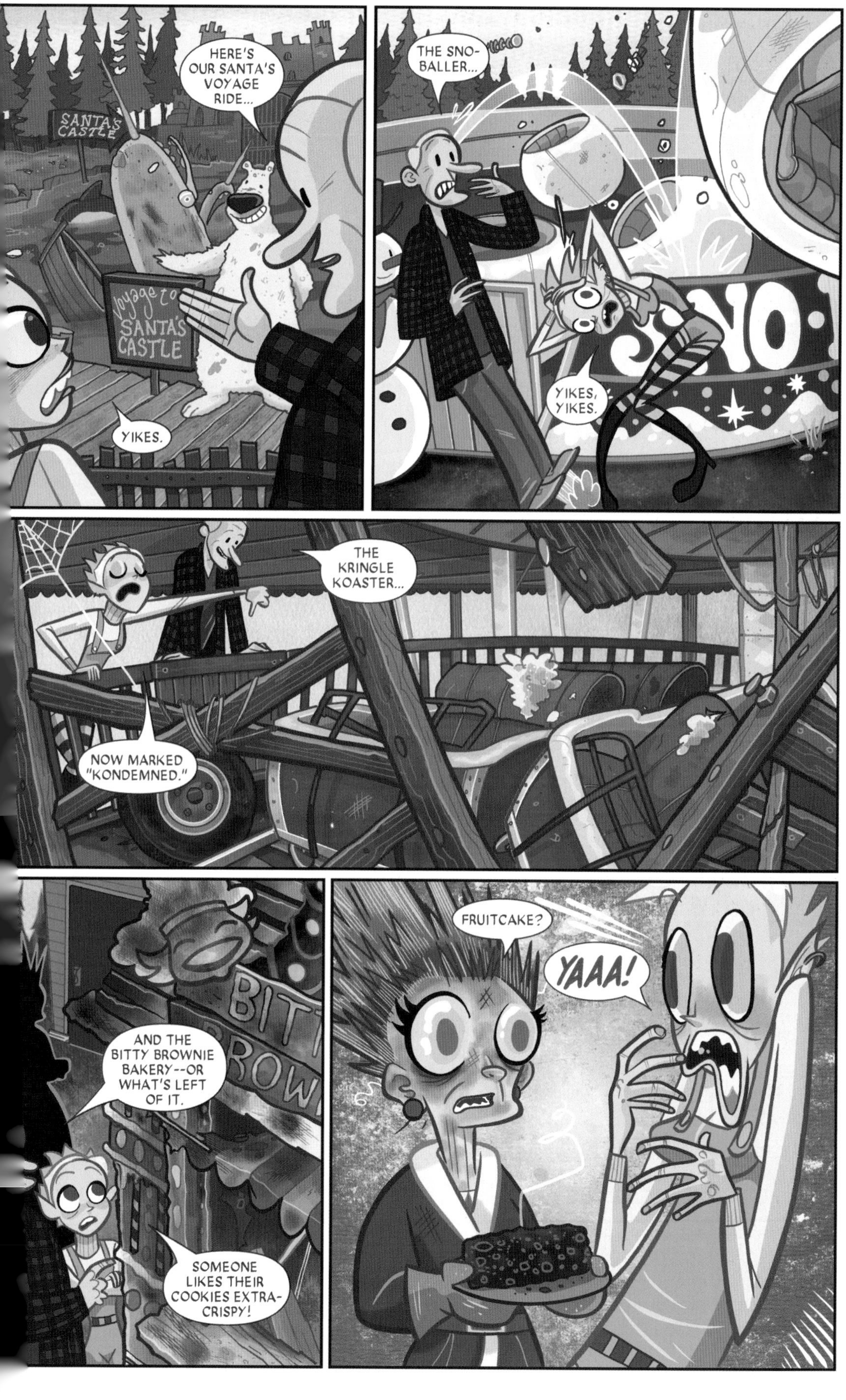
SANTA'S CASTLE
HERE'S OUR SANTA'S VOYAGE RIDE...
VOYAGE TO SANTA'S CASTLE
YIKES.
THE SNO-BALLER...
YIKES, YIKES.
THE KRINGLE KOASTER...
NOW MARKED "KONDEMNED."
AND THE BITTY BROWNIE BAKERY--OR WHAT'S LEFT OF IT.
SOMEONE LIKES THEIR COOKIES EXTRA-CRISPY!
FRUITCAKE?
YAAA!

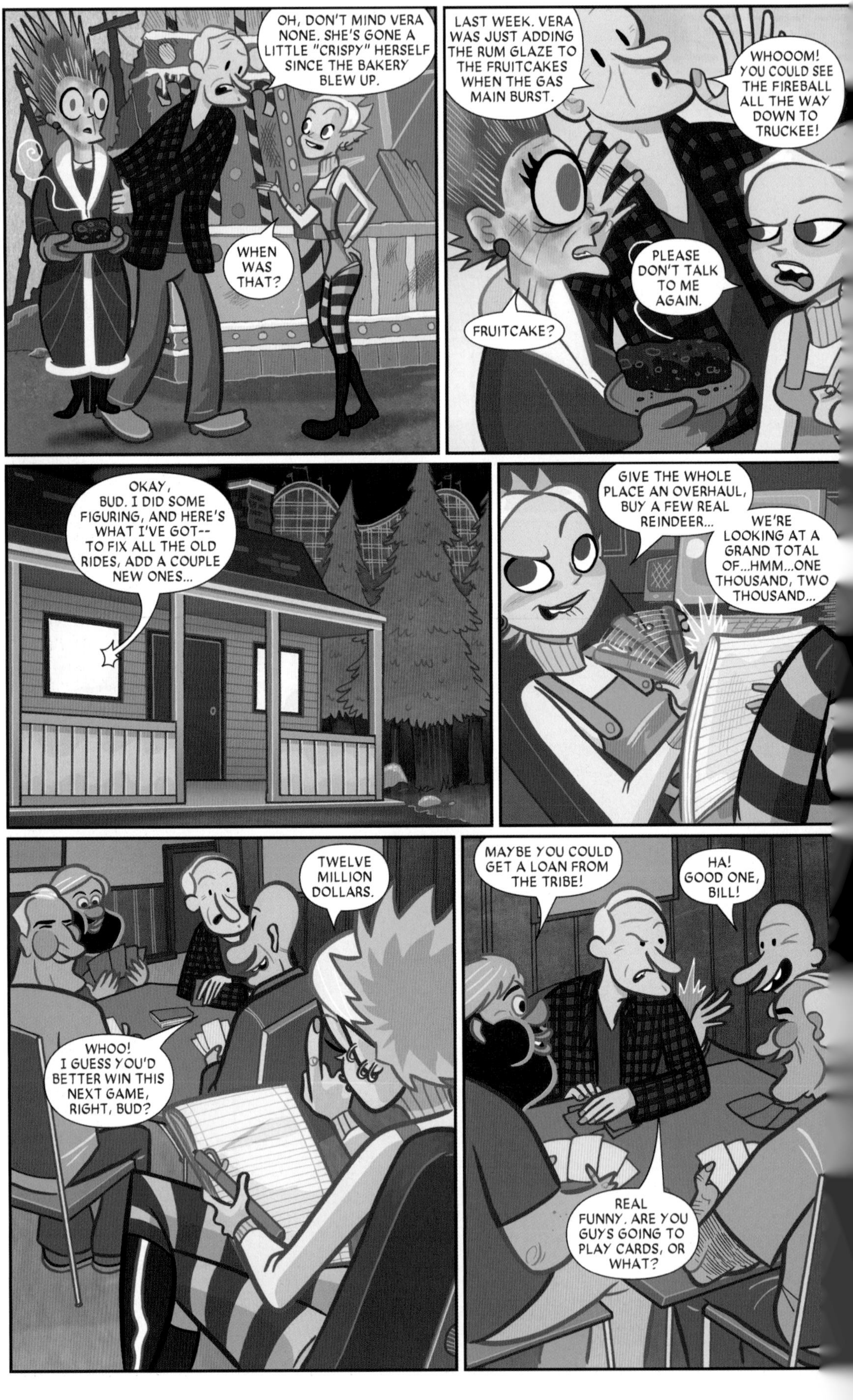

OH, DON'T MIND VERA NONE. SHE'S GONE A LITTLE "CRISPY" HERSELF SINCE THE BAKERY BLEW UP.
WHEN WAS THAT?
LAST WEEK. VERA WAS JUST ADDING THE RUM GLAZE TO THE FRUITCAKES WHEN THE GAS MAIN BURST.
WHOOOM! YOU COULD SEE THE FIREBALL ALL THE WAY DOWN TO TRUCKEE!
FRUITCAKE?
PLEASE DON'T TALK TO ME AGAIN.
OKAY, BUD. I DID SOME FIGURING, AND HERE'S WHAT I'VE GOT-- TO FIX ALL THE OLD RIDES, ADD A COUPLE NEW ONES...
GIVE THE WHOLE PLACE AN OVERHAUL, BUY A FEW REAL REINDEER...
WE'RE LOOKING AT A GRAND TOTAL OF...HMM...ONE THOUSAND, TWO THOUSAND...
TWELVE MILLION DOLLARS.
WHOO! I GUESS YOU'D BETTER WIN THIS NEXT GAME, RIGHT, BUD?
MAYBE YOU COULD GET A LOAN FROM THE TRIBE!
HA! GOOD ONE, BILL!
REAL FUNNY. ARE YOU GUYS GOING TO PLAY CARDS, OR WHAT?

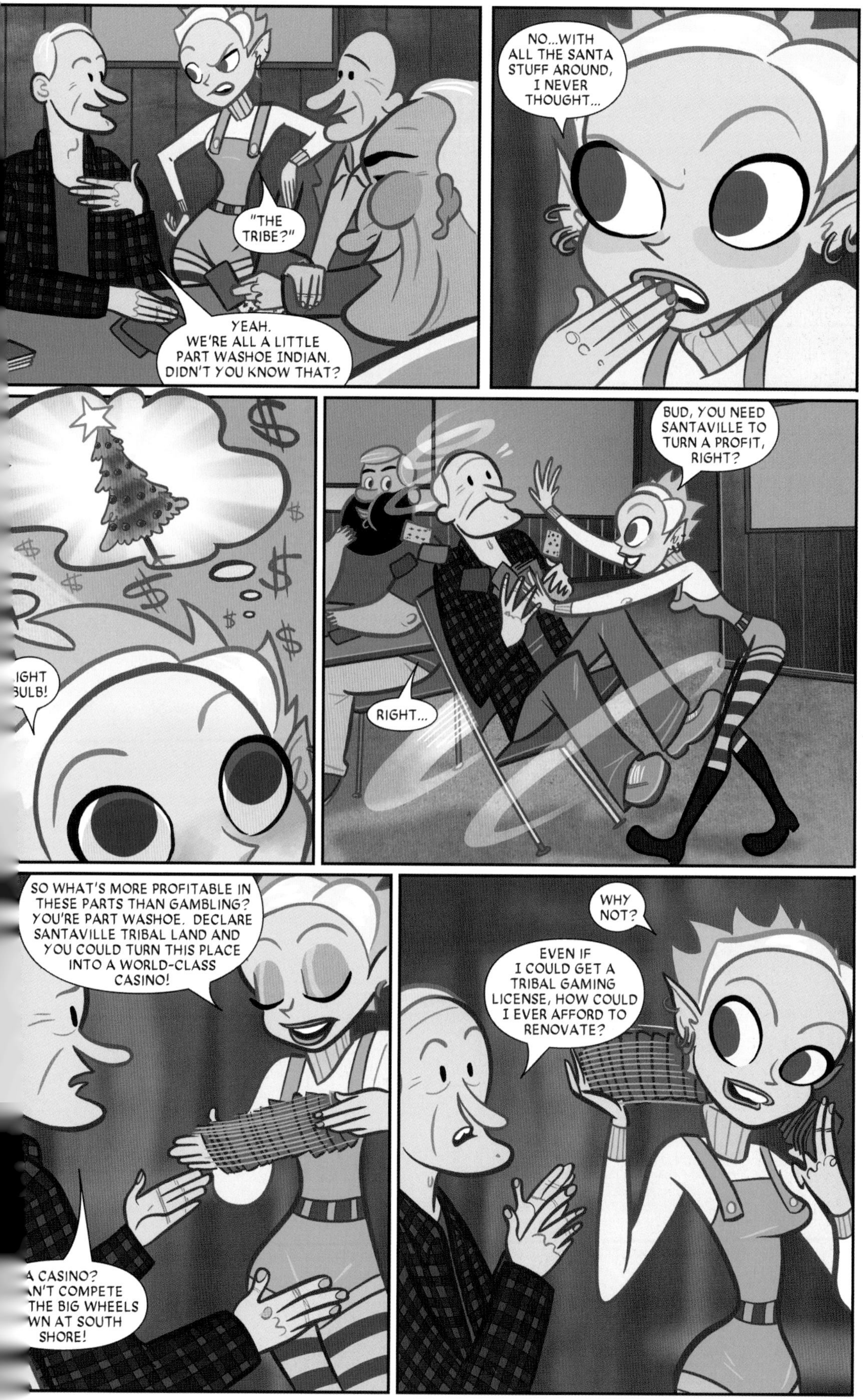
"THE TRIBE?"
YEAH. WE'RE ALL A LITTLE PART WASHOE INDIAN. DIDN'T YOU KNOW THAT?
NO...WITH ALL THE SANTA STUFF AROUND, I NEVER THOUGHT...
IGHT BULB!
BUD, YOU NEED SANTAVILLE TO TURN A PROFIT, RIGHT?
RIGHT...
SO WHAT'S MORE PROFITABLE IN THESE PARTS THAN GAMBLING? YOU'RE PART WASHOE. DECLARE SANTAVILLE TRIBAL LAND AND YOU COULD TURN THIS PLACE INTO A WORLD-CLASS CASINO!
A CASINO? AN'T COMPETE THE BIG WHEELS WN AT SOUTH SHORE!
WHY NOT?
EVEN IF I COULD GET A TRIBAL GAMING LICENSE, HOW COULD I EVER AFFORD TO RENOVATE?

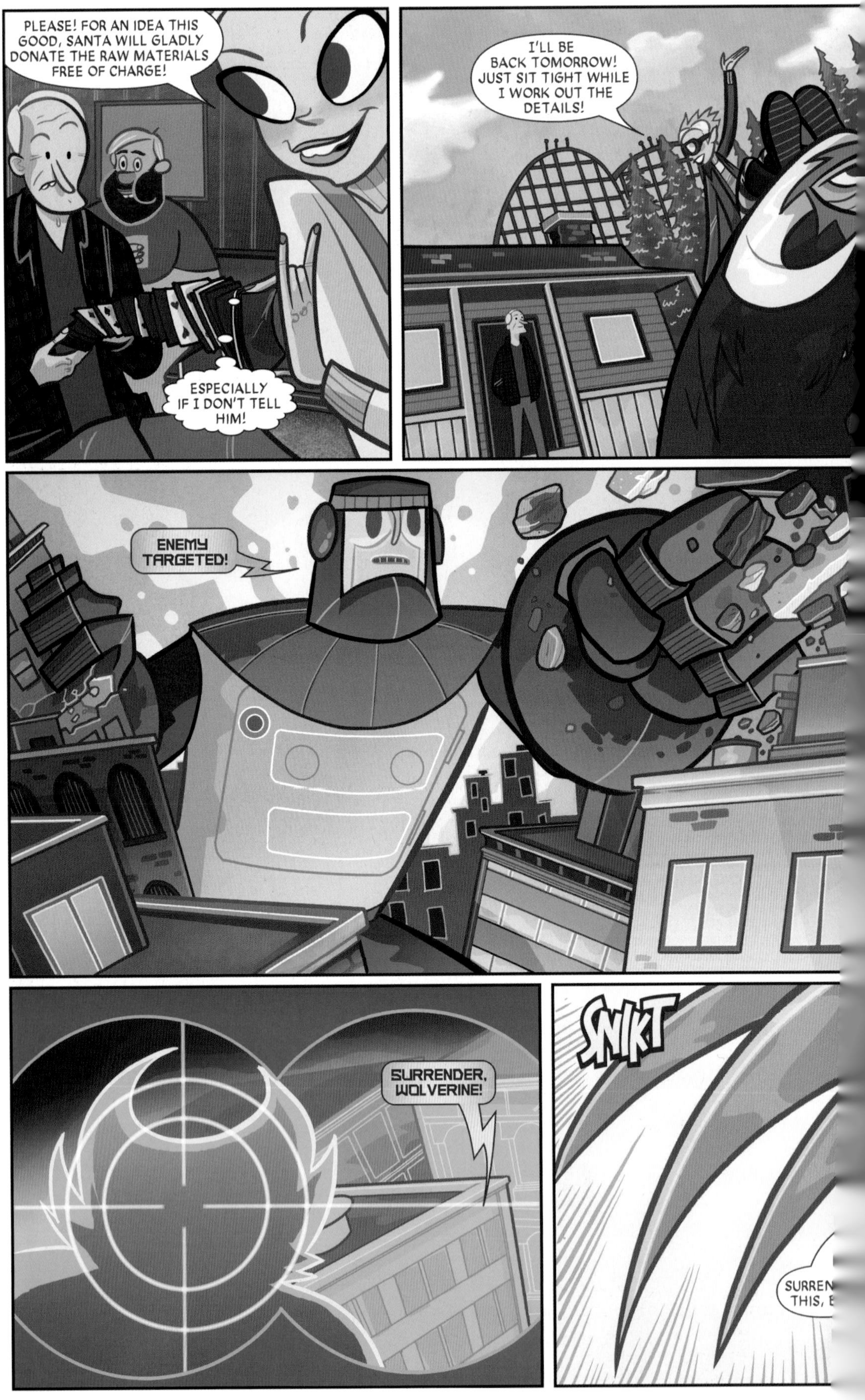
PLEASE! FOR AN IDEA THIS GOOD, SANTA WILL GLADLY DONATE THE RAW MATERIALS FREE OF CHARGE!
ESPECIALLY IF I DON'T TELL HIM!
I'LL BE BACK TOMORROW! JUST SIT TIGHT WHILE I WORK OUT THE DETAILS!
ENEMY TARGETED!
SURRENDER, WOLVERINE!
SNIKT

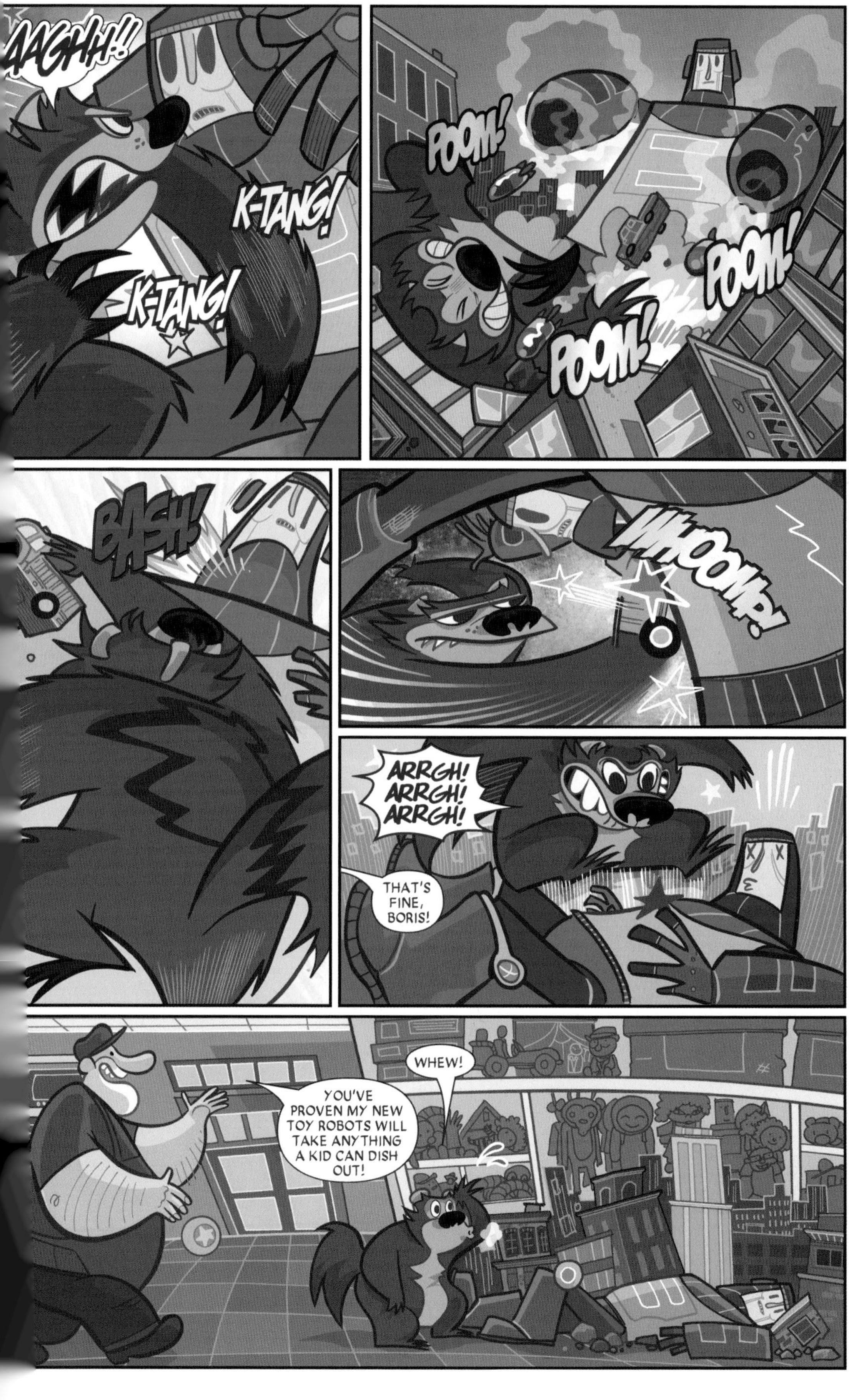
AAGHH!!
K-TANG!
K-TANG!
POOM!
POOM!
POOM!
BASH!
WHOOMP!
ARRGH! ARRGH! ARRGH!
THAT'S FINE, BORIS!
YOU'VE PROVEN MY NEW TOY ROBOTS WILL TAKE ANYTHING A KID CAN DISH OUT!
WHEW!

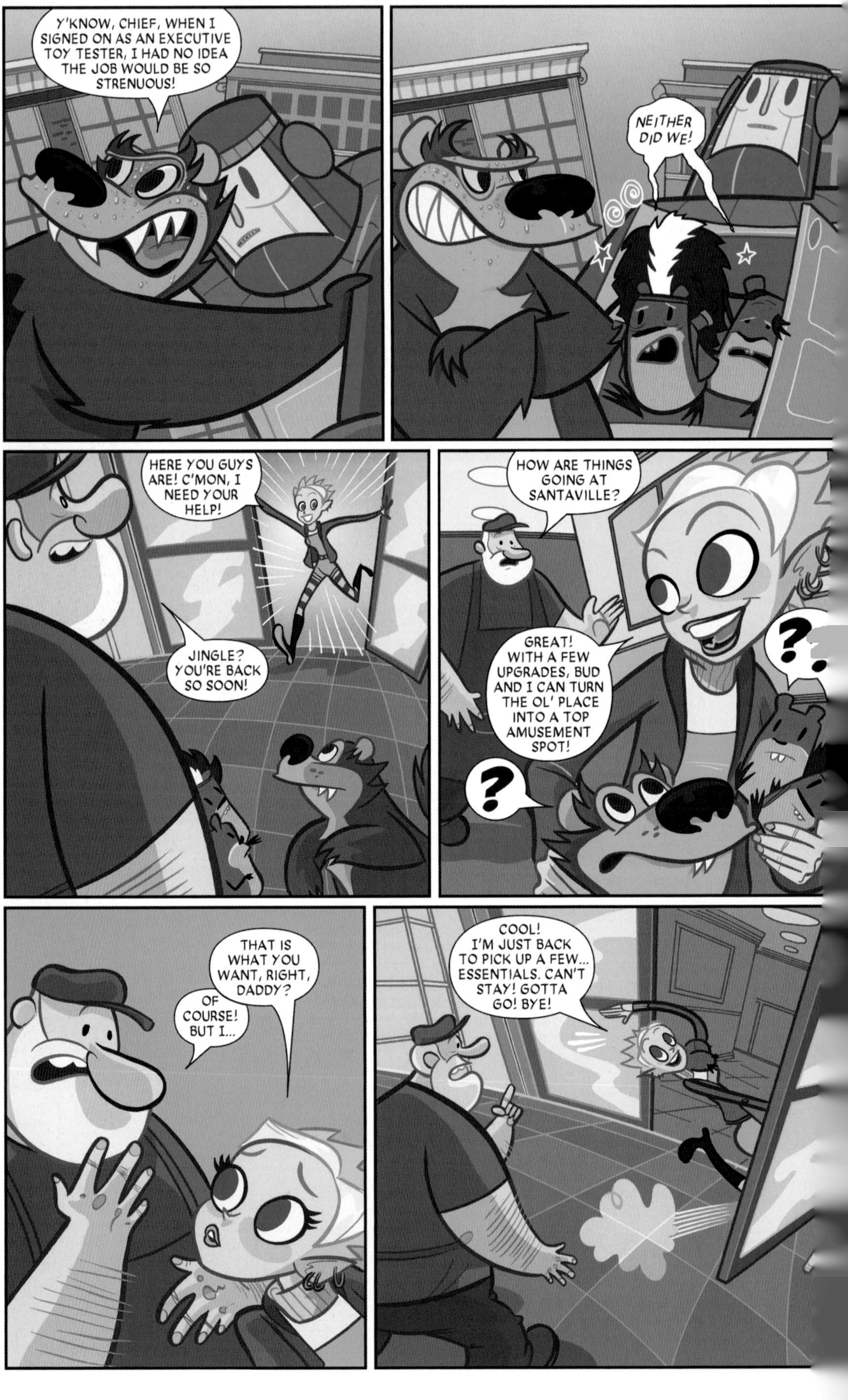
Y'KNOW, CHIEF, WHEN I SIGNED ON AS AN EXECUTIVE TOY TESTER, I HAD NO IDEA THE JOB WOULD BE SO STRENUOUS!
NEITHER DID WE!
HERE YOU GUYS ARE! C'MON, I NEED YOUR HELP!
JINGLE? YOU'RE BACK SO SOON!
HOW ARE THINGS GOING AT SANTAVILLE?
GREAT! WITH A FEW UPGRADES, BUD AND I CAN TURN THE OL' PLACE INTO A TOP AMUSEMENT SPOT!
?
?
THAT IS WHAT YOU WANT, RIGHT, DADDY?
OF COURSE! BUT I...
COOL! I'M JUST BACK TO PICK UP A FEW... ESSENTIALS. CAN'T STAY! GOTTA GO! BYE!

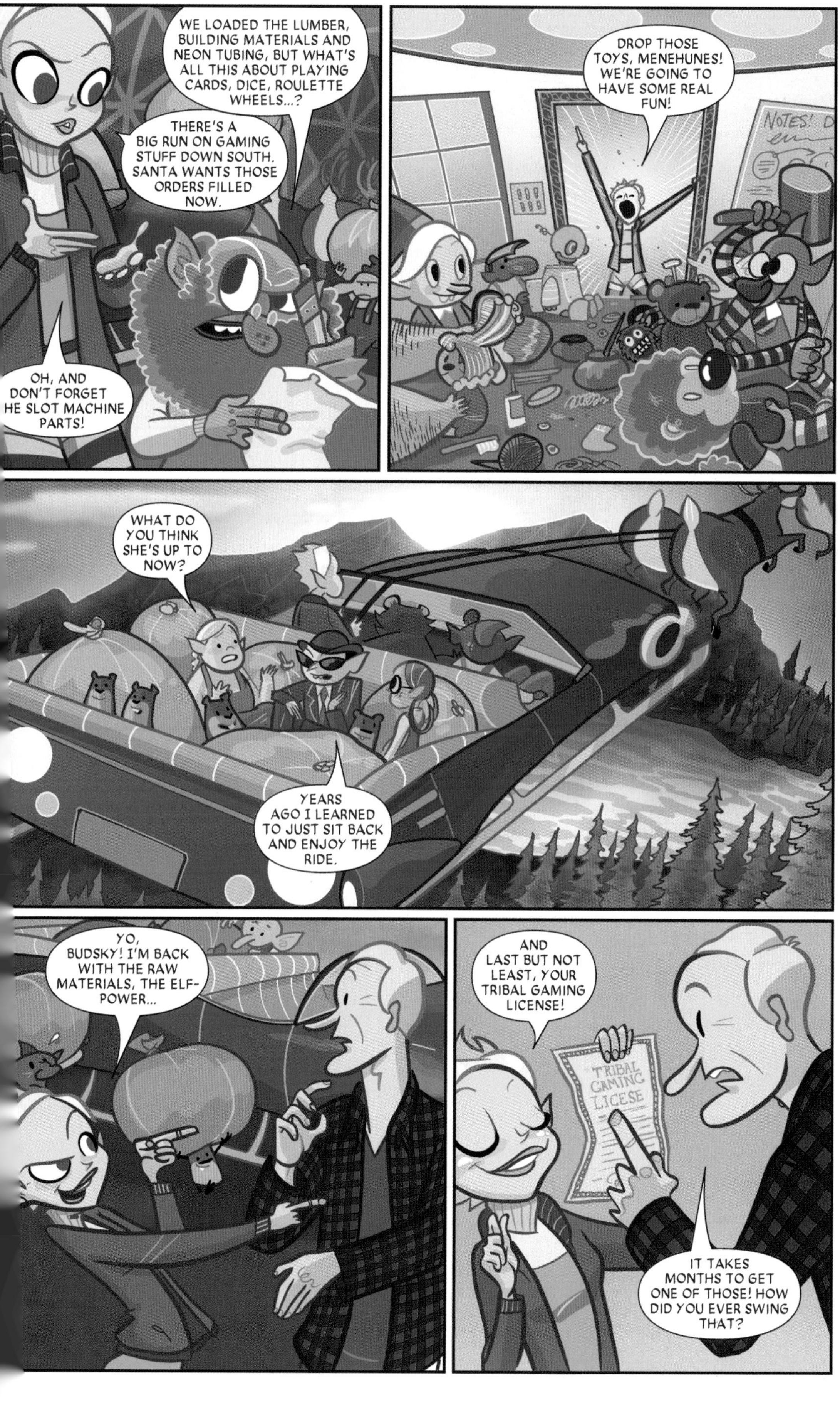
WE LOADED THE LUMBER, BUILDING MATERIALS AND NEON TUBING, BUT WHAT'S ALL THIS ABOUT PLAYING CARDS, DICE, ROULETTE WHEELS...?
THERE'S A BIG RUN ON GAMING STUFF DOWN SOUTH. SANTA WANTS THOSE ORDERS FILLED NOW.
OH, AND DON'T FORGET HE SLOT MACHINE PARTS!
DROP THOSE TOYS, MENEHUNES! WE'RE GOING TO HAVE SOME REAL FUN!
NOTES!
WHAT DO YOU THINK SHE'S UP TO NOW?
YEARS AGO I LEARNED TO JUST SIT BACK AND ENJOY THE RIDE.
YO, BUDSKY! I'M BACK WITH THE RAW MATERIALS, THE ELF-POWER...
AND LAST BUT NOT LEAST, YOUR TRIBAL GAMING LICENSE!
TRIBAL GAMING LICESE
IT TAKES MONTHS TO GET ONE OF THOSE! HOW DID YOU EVER SWING THAT?

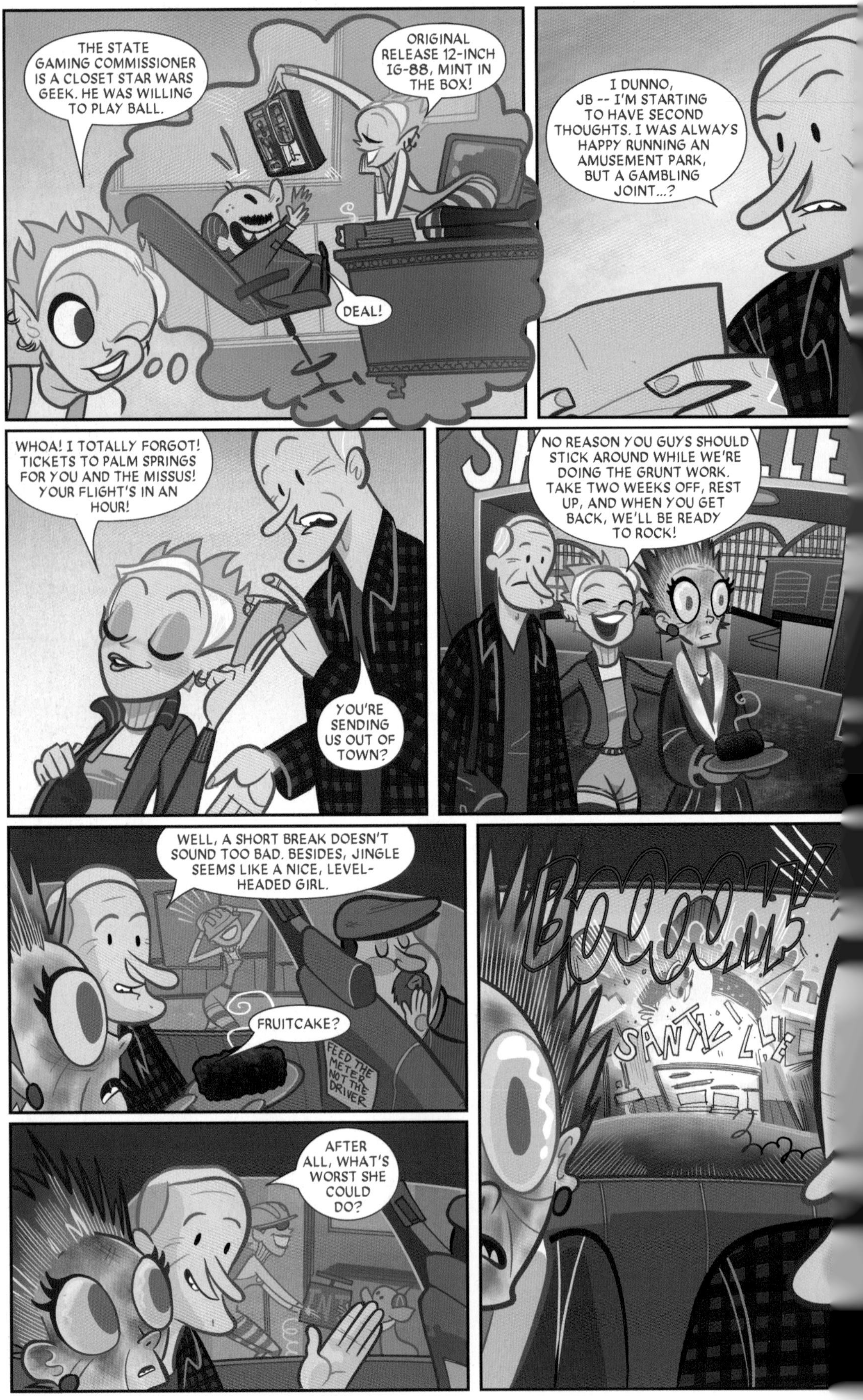
THE STATE GAMING COMMISSIONER IS A CLOSET STAR WARS GEEK. HE WAS WILLING TO PLAY BALL.
ORIGINAL RELEASE 12-INCH IG-88, MINT IN THE BOX!
DEAL!
I DUNNO, JB -- I'M STARTING TO HAVE SECOND THOUGHTS. I WAS ALWAYS HAPPY RUNNING AN AMUSEMENT PARK, BUT A GAMBLING JOINT...?
WHOA! I TOTALLY FORGOT! TICKETS TO PALM SPRINGS FOR YOU AND THE MISSUS! YOUR FLIGHT'S IN AN HOUR!
YOU'RE SENDING US OUT OF TOWN?
NO REASON YOU GUYS SHOULD STICK AROUND WHILE WE'RE DOING THE GRUNT WORK. TAKE TWO WEEKS OFF, REST UP, AND WHEN YOU GET BACK, WE'LL BE READY TO ROCK!
WELL, A SHORT BREAK DOESN'T SOUND TOO BAD. BESIDES, JINGLE SEEMS LIKE A NICE, LEVEL-HEADED GIRL.
FRUITCAKE?
FEED THE METER NOT THE DRIVER
AFTER ALL, WHAT'S WORST SHE COULD DO?
TNT
BOOOOOOM!
SANTAVILLE

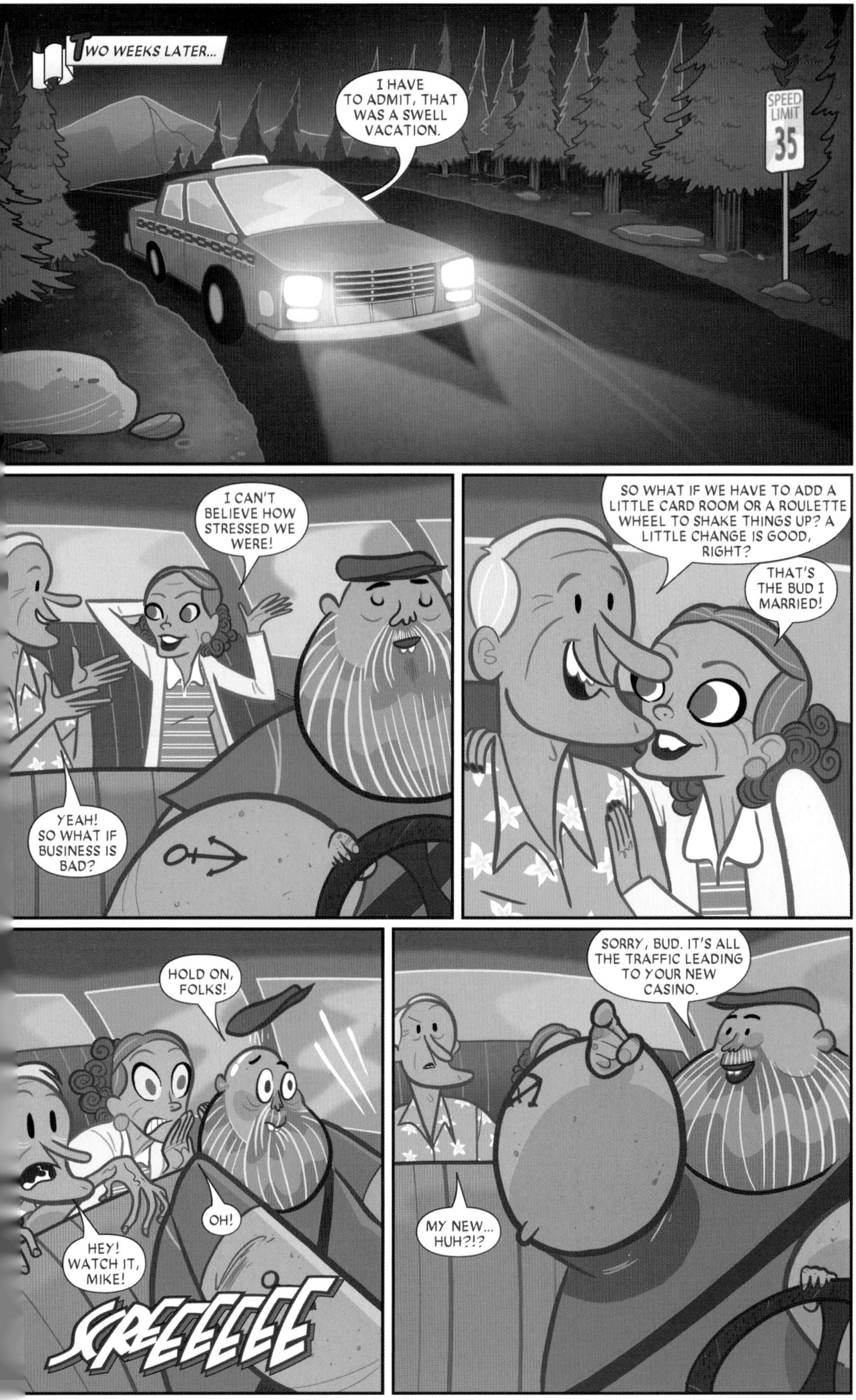
TWO WEEKS LATER...
I HAVE TO ADMIT, THAT WAS A SWELL VACATION.
SPEED LIMIT 35
I CAN'T BELIEVE HOW STRESSED WE WERE!
YEAH! SO WHAT IF BUSINESS IS BAD?
SO WHAT IF WE HAVE TO ADD A LITTLE CARD ROOM OR A ROULETTE WHEEL TO SHAKE THINGS UP? A LITTLE CHANGE IS GOOD, RIGHT?
THAT'S THE BUD I MARRIED!
HOLD ON, FOLKS!
OH!
HEY! WATCH IT, MIKE!
SCREEEEEE
SORRY, BUD. IT'S ALL THE TRAFFIC LEADING TO YOUR NEW CASINO.
MY NEW... HUH?!?

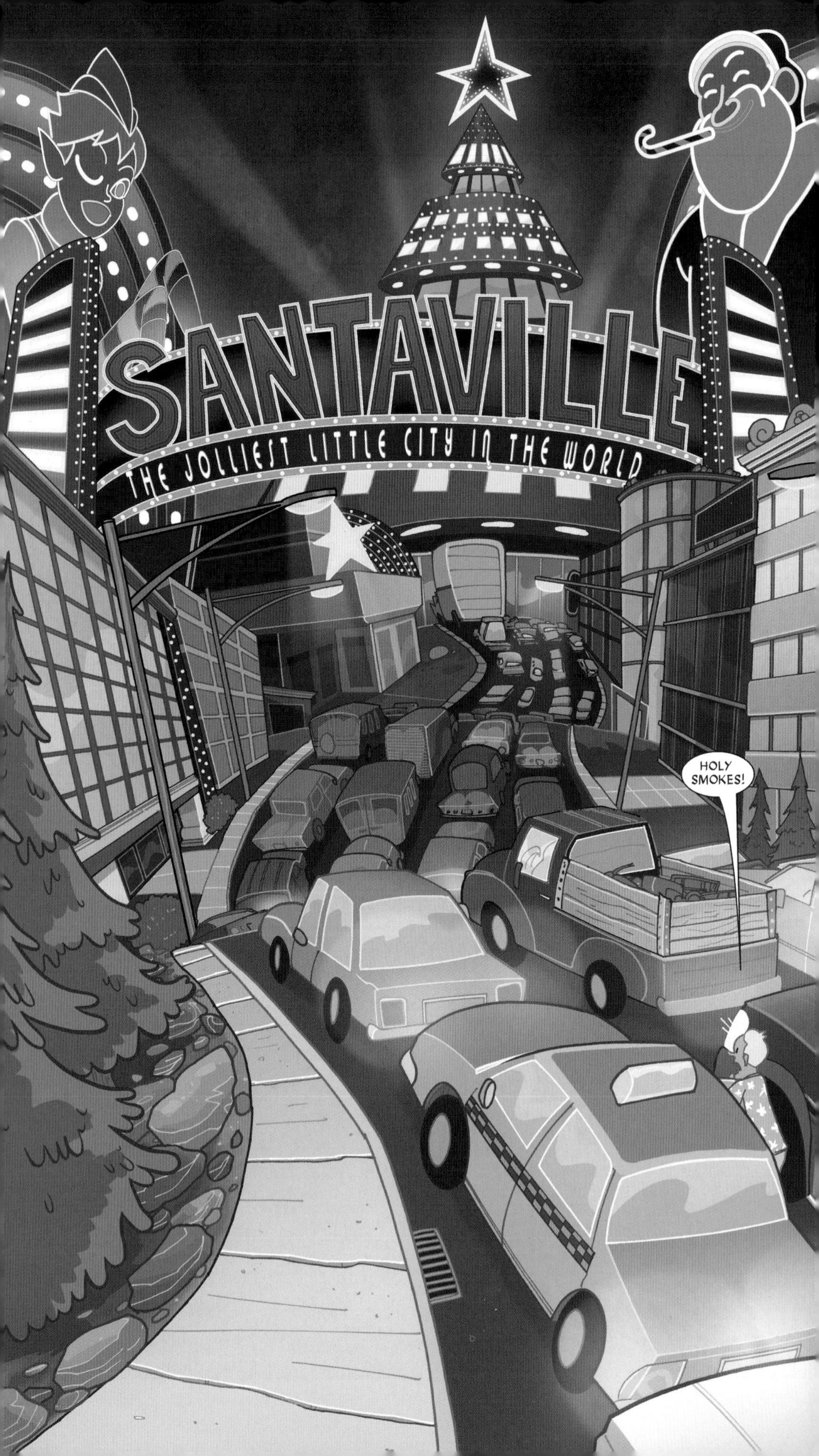
SANTAVILLE
THE JOLLIEST LITTLE CITY IN THE WORLD
HOLY SMOKES!

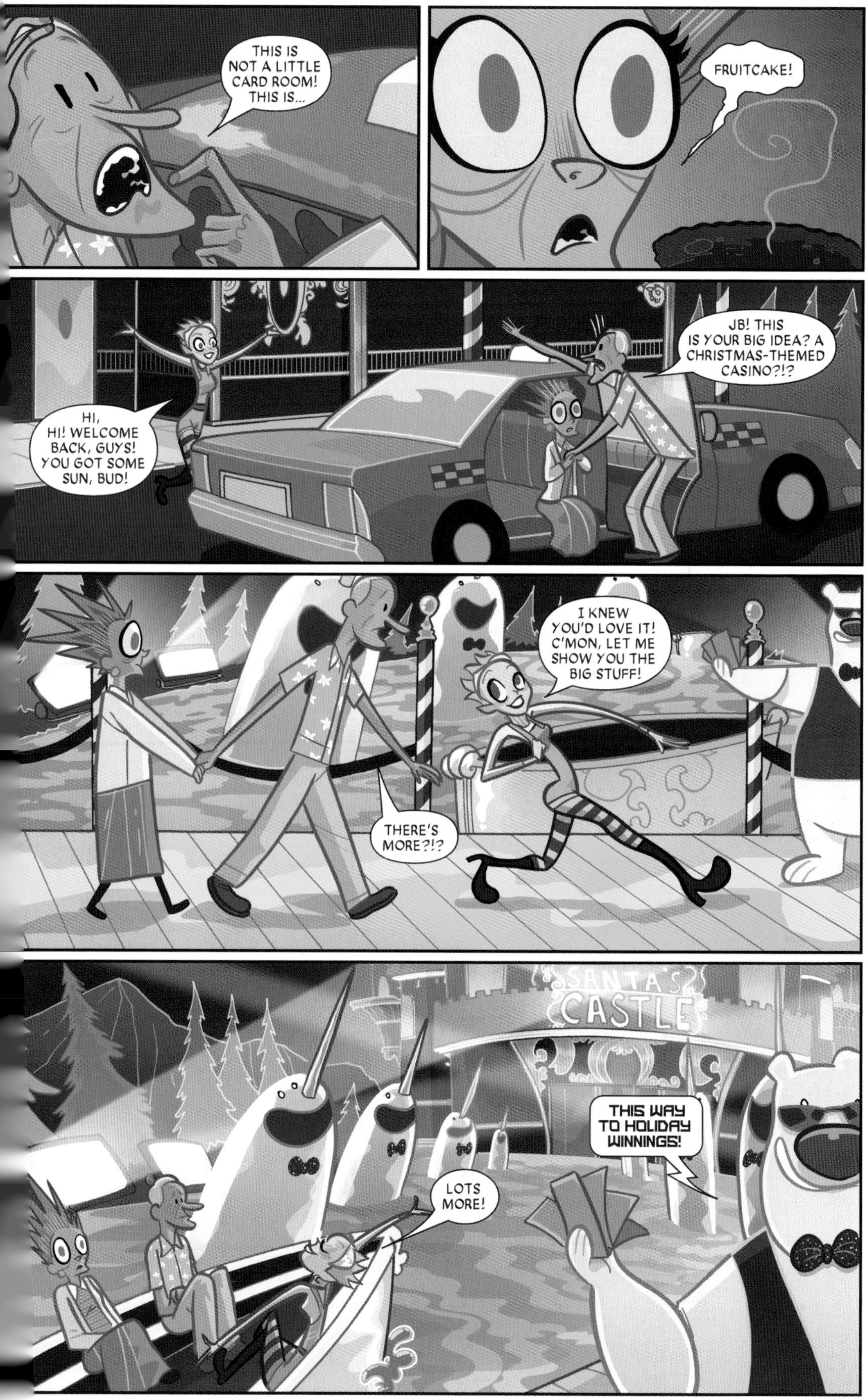
THIS IS NOT A LITTLE CARD ROOM! THIS IS...
FRUITCAKE!
JB! THIS IS YOUR BIG IDEA? A CHRISTMAS-THEMED CASINO?!?
HI, HI! WELCOME BACK, GUYS! YOU GOT SOME SUN, BUD!
I KNEW YOU'D LOVE IT! C'MON, LET ME SHOW YOU THE BIG STUFF!
THERE'S MORE?!?
SANTA'S CASTLE
THIS WAY TO HOLIDAY WINNINGS!
LOTS MORE!

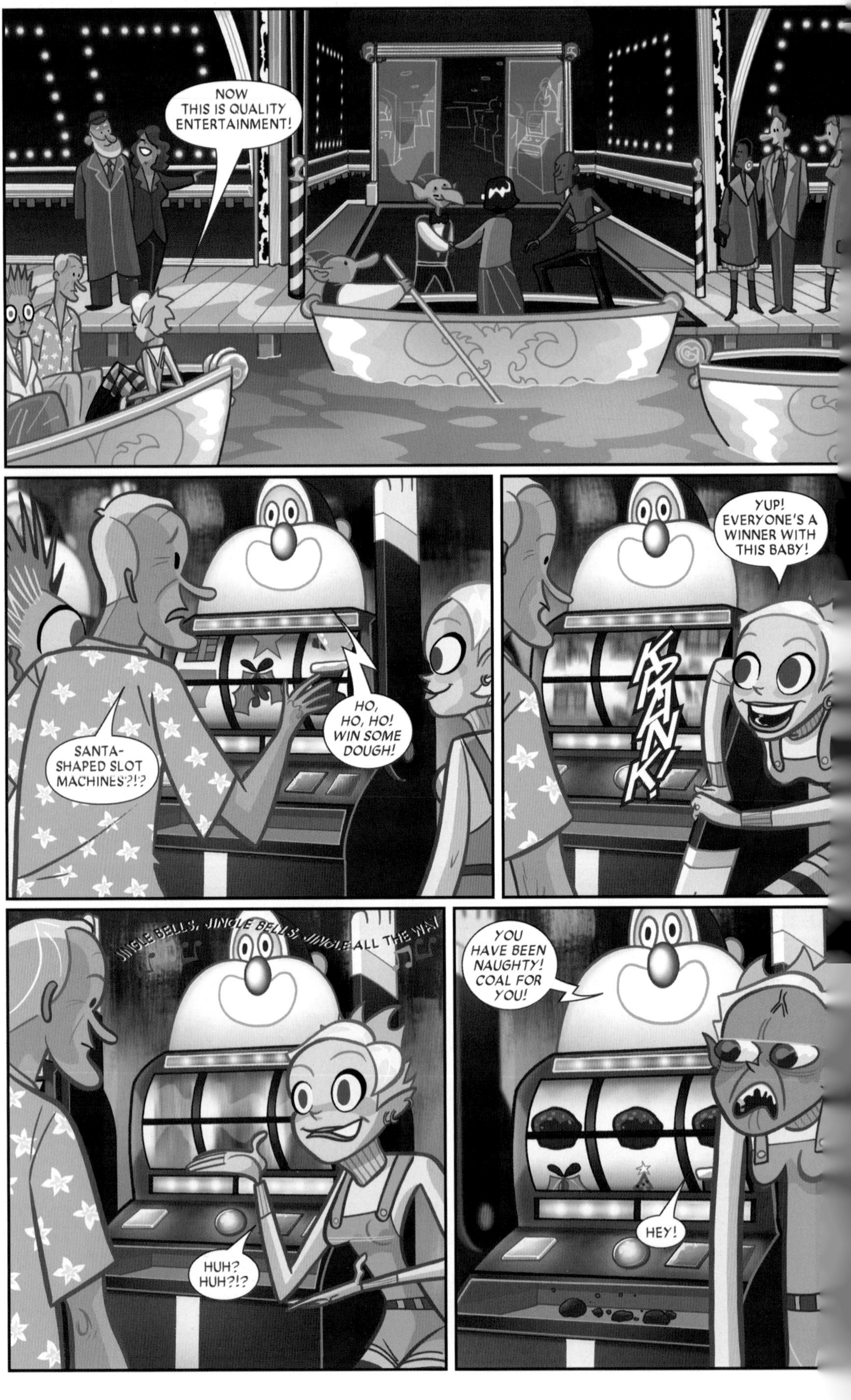
NOW THIS IS QUALITY ENTERTAINMENT!
SANTA-SHAPED SLOT MACHINES?!?
HO, HO, HO! WIN SOME DOUGH!
YUP! EVERYONE'S A WINNER WITH THIS BABY!
KRANK!
JINGLE BELLS, JINGLE BELLS, JINGLE ALL THE WAY
HUH? HUH?!?
YOU HAVE BEEN NAUGHTY! COAL FOR YOU!
HEY!

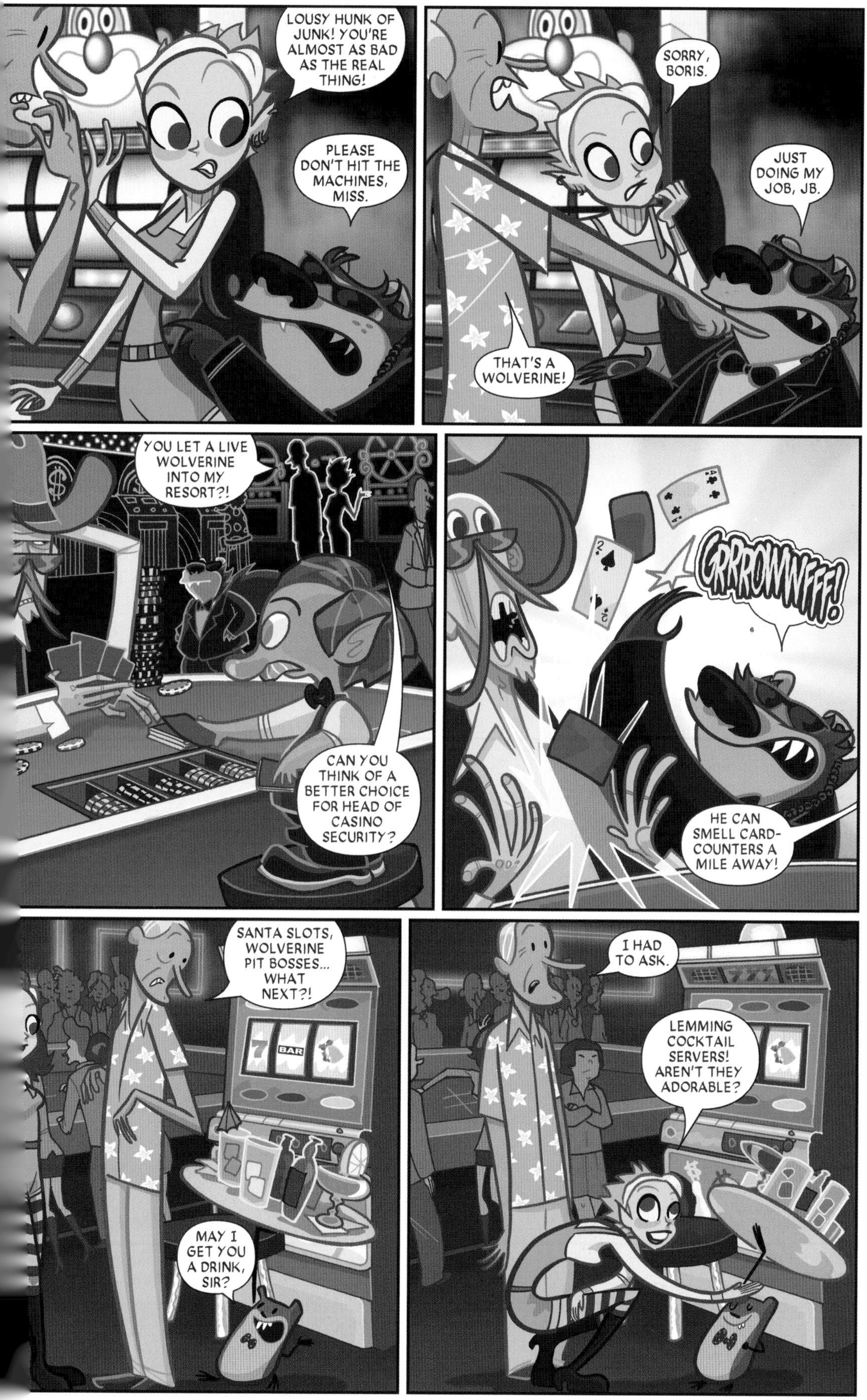
LOUSY HUNK OF JUNK! YOU'RE ALMOST AS BAD AS THE REAL THING!
PLEASE DON'T HIT THE MACHINES, MISS.
SORRY, BORIS.
JUST DOING MY JOB, JB.
THAT'S A WOLVERINE!
YOU LET A LIVE WOLVERINE INTO MY RESORT?!
CAN YOU THINK OF A BETTER CHOICE FOR HEAD OF CASINO SECURITY?
GRRROWWFFF!
HE CAN SMELL CARD-COUNTERS A MILE AWAY!
SANTA SLOTS, WOLVERINE PIT BOSSES... WHAT NEXT?!
MAY I GET YOU A DRINK, SIR?
I HAD TO ASK.
LEMMING COCKTAIL SERVERS! AREN'T THEY ADORABLE?

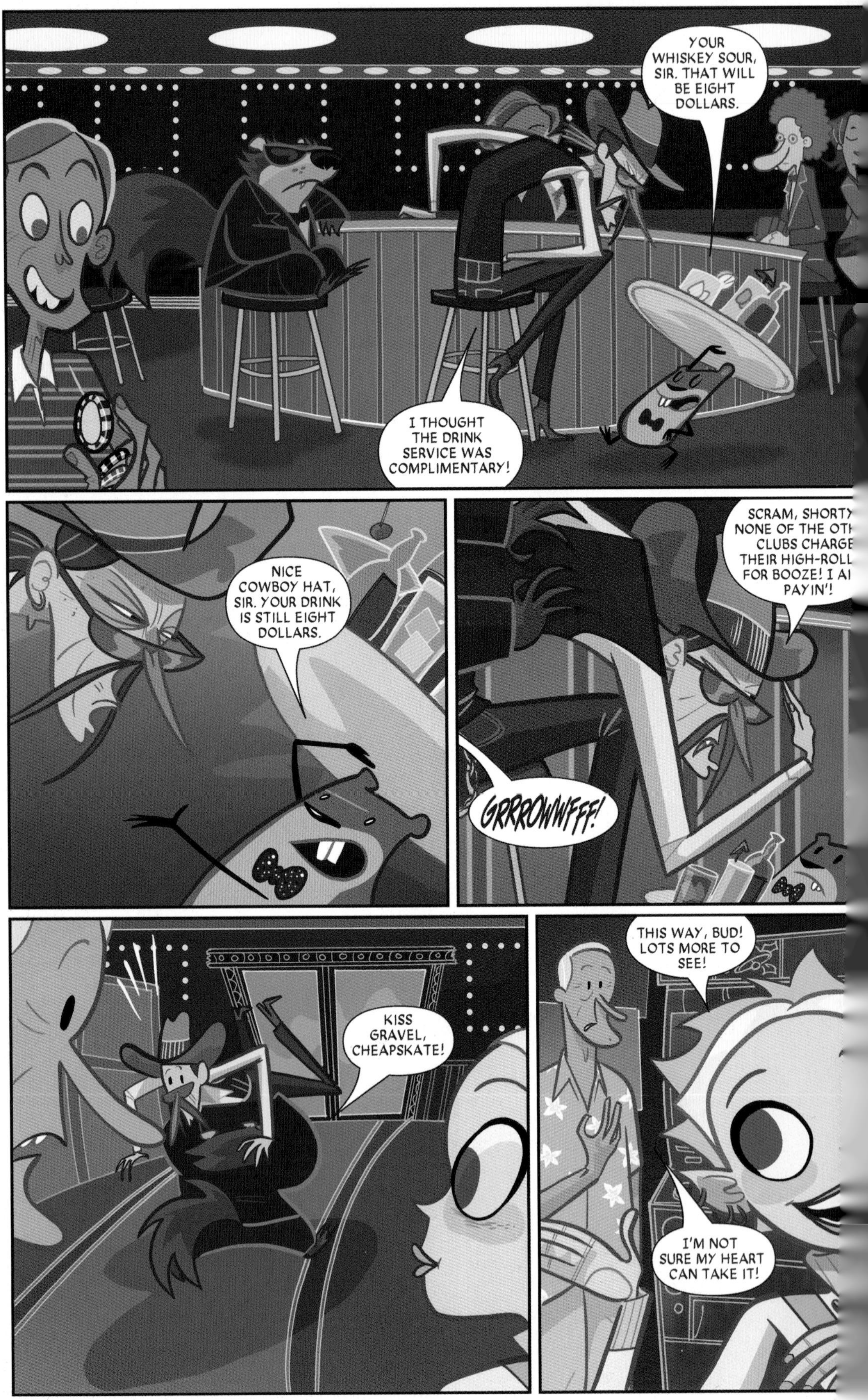
YOUR WHISKEY SOUR, SIR. THAT WILL BE EIGHT DOLLARS.
I THOUGHT THE DRINK SERVICE WAS COMPLIMENTARY!
NICE COWBOY HAT, SIR. YOUR DRINK IS STILL EIGHT DOLLARS.
SCRAM, SHORTY NONE OF THE OTH CLUBS CHARGE THEIR HIGH-ROLL FOR BOOZE! I AI PAYIN'!
GRRROWWFFF!
KISS GRAVEL, CHEAPSKATE!
THIS WAY, BUD! LOTS MORE TO SEE!
I'M NOT SURE MY HEART CAN TAKE IT!

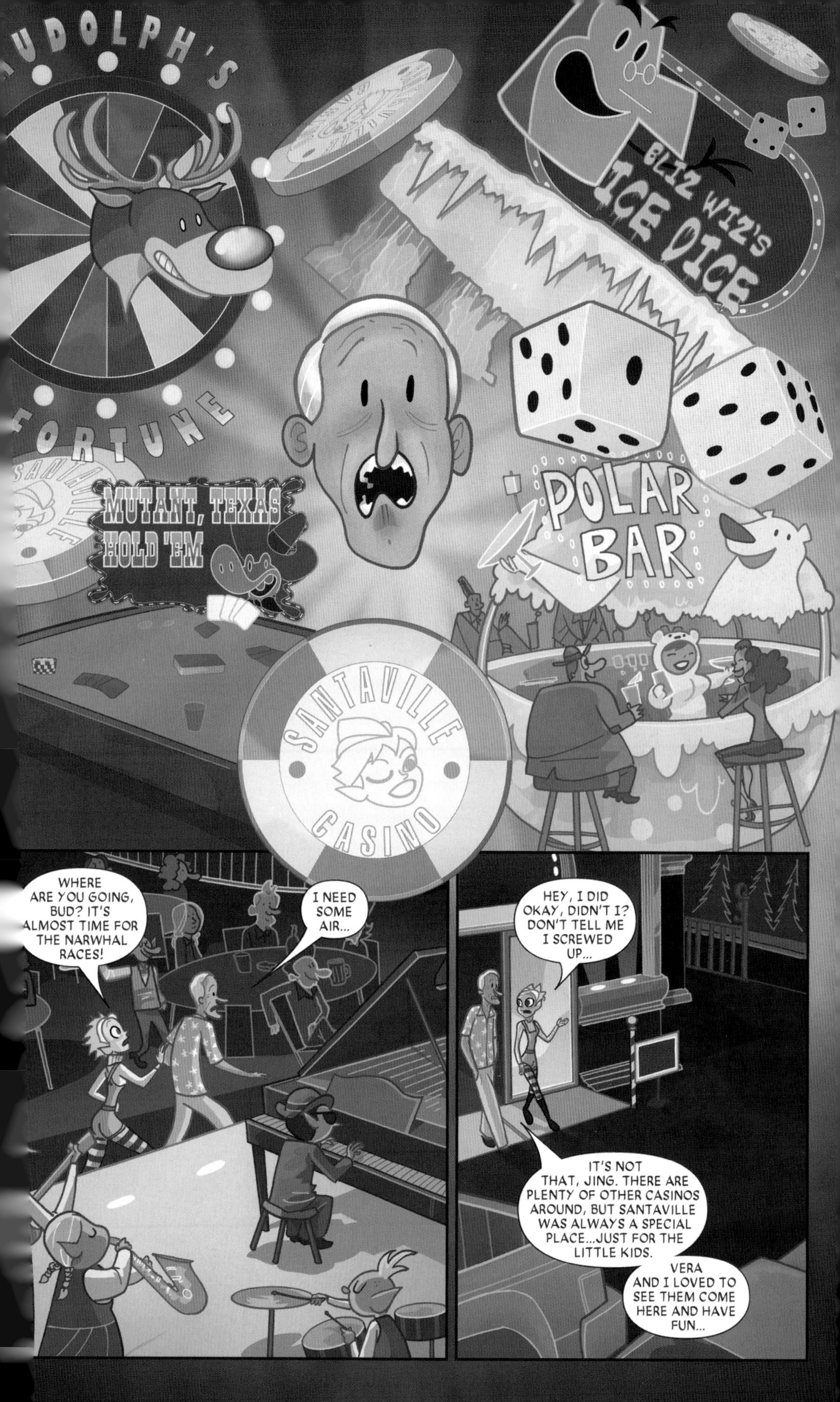
RUDOLPH'S
FORTUNE
BLIZ WIZ'S
ICE DICE
MUTANT, TEXAS
HOLD 'EM
POLAR
BAR
SANTAVILLE
CASINO
WHERE ARE YOU GOING, BUD? IT'S ALMOST TIME FOR THE NARWHAL RACES!
I NEED SOME AIR...
HEY, I DID OKAY, DIDN'T I? DON'T TELL ME I SCREWED UP...
IT'S NOT THAT, JING. THERE ARE PLENTY OF OTHER CASINOS AROUND, BUT SANTAVILLE WAS ALWAYS A SPECIAL PLACE...JUST FOR THE LITTLE KIDS.
VERA AND I LOVED TO SEE THEM COME HERE AND HAVE FUN...

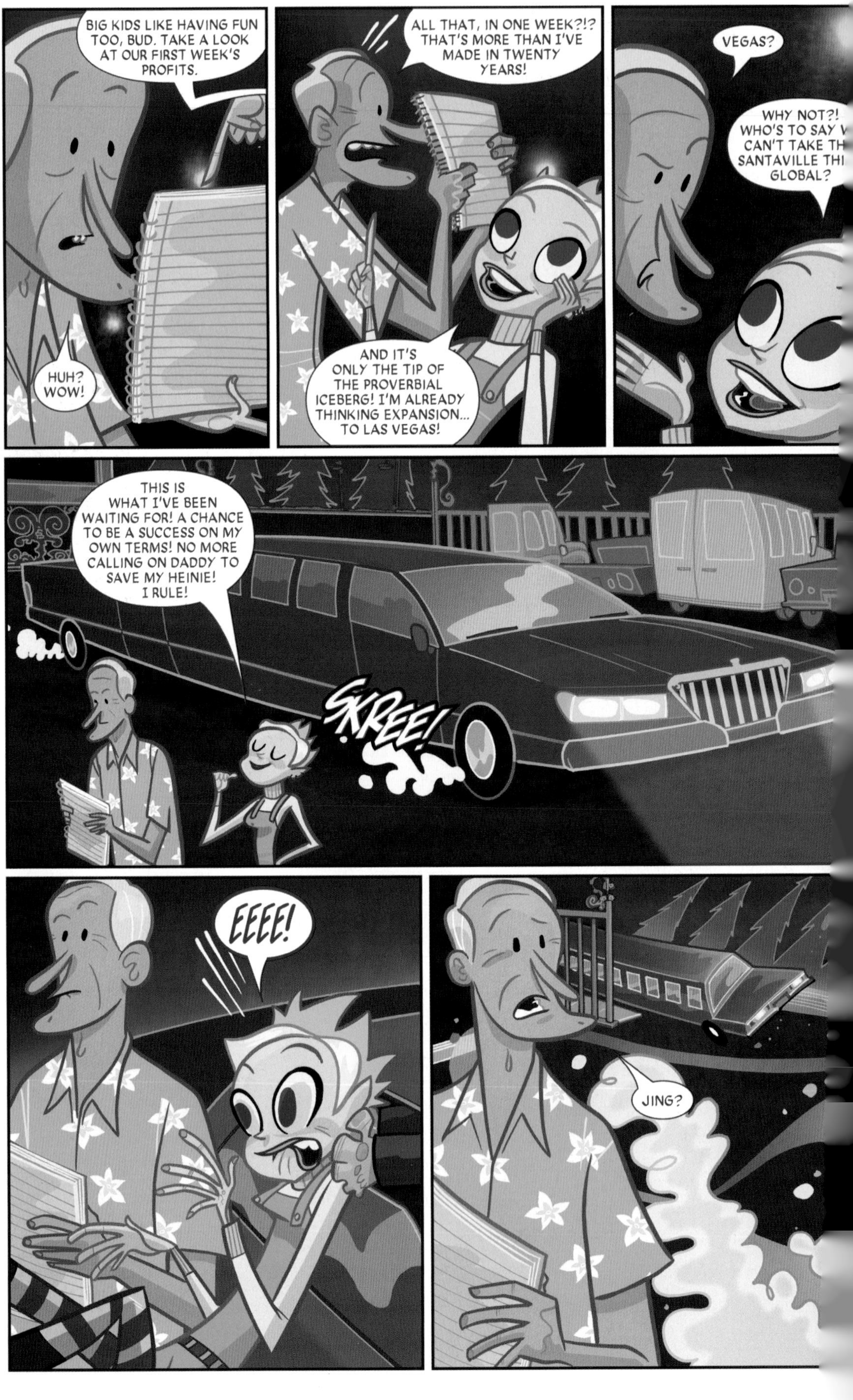
BIG KIDS LIKE HAVING FUN TOO, BUD. TAKE A LOOK AT OUR FIRST WEEK'S PROFITS.
HUH? WOW!
ALL THAT, IN ONE WEEK?!? THAT'S MORE THAN I'VE MADE IN TWENTY YEARS!
AND IT'S ONLY THE TIP OF THE PROVERBIAL ICEBERG! I'M ALREADY THINKING EXPANSION... TO LAS VEGAS!
VEGAS?
WHY NOT?! WHO'S TO SAY W CAN'T TAKE TH SANTAVILLE THI GLOBAL?
THIS IS WHAT I'VE BEEN WAITING FOR! A CHANCE TO BE A SUCCESS ON MY OWN TERMS! NO MORE CALLING ON DADDY TO SAVE MY HEINIE! I RULE!
SKREE!
EEEE!
JING?

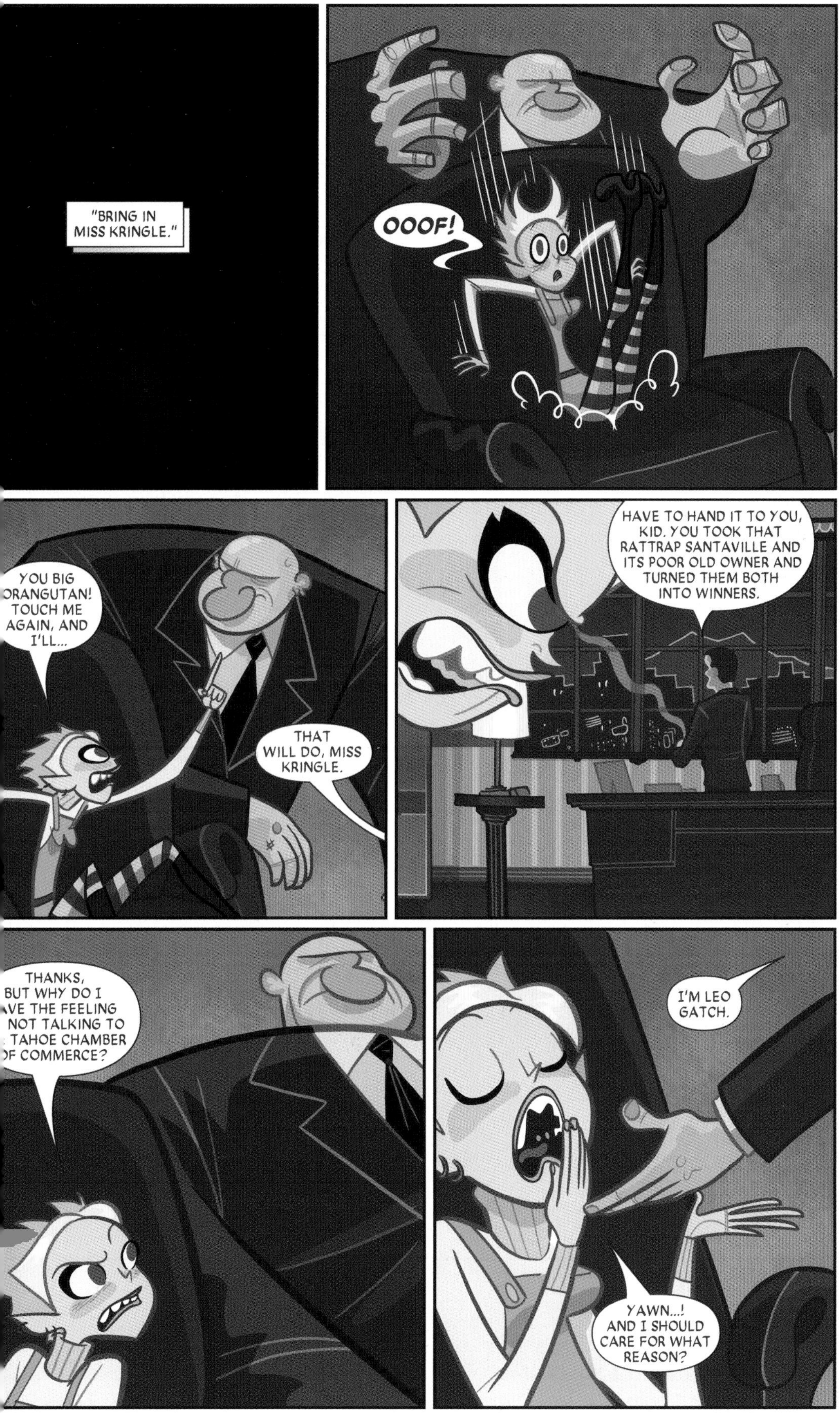
"BRING IN MISS KRINGLE."
OOOF!
YOU BIG ORANGUTAN! TOUCH ME AGAIN, AND I'LL...
THAT WILL DO, MISS KRINGLE.
HAVE TO HAND IT TO YOU, KID. YOU TOOK THAT RATTRAP SANTAVILLE AND ITS POOR OLD OWNER AND TURNED THEM BOTH INTO WINNERS.
THANKS, BUT WHY DO I VE THE FEELING NOT TALKING TO TAHOE CHAMBER OF COMMERCE?
I'M LEO GATCH.
YAWN...! AND I SHOULD CARE FOR WHAT REASON?

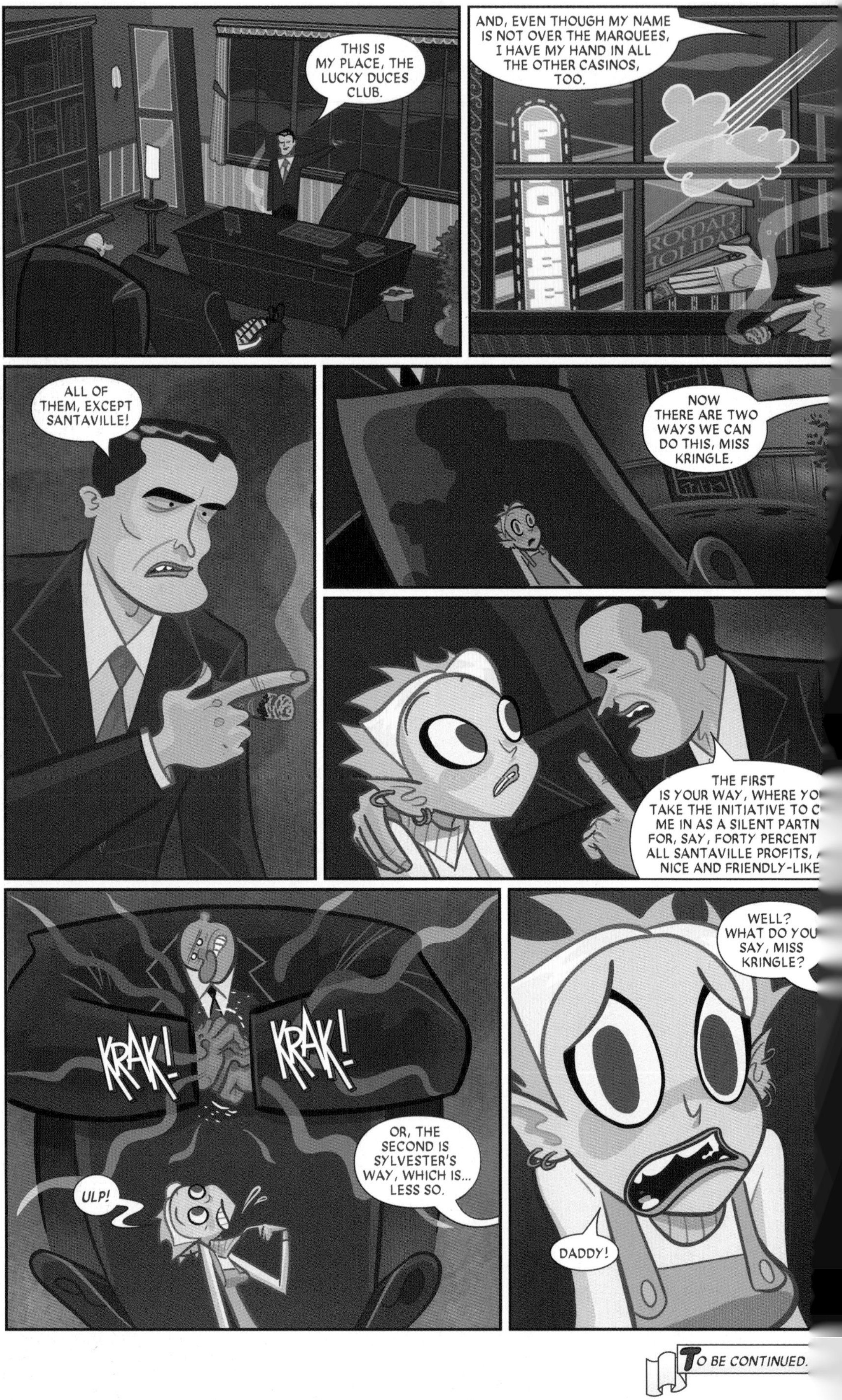
THIS IS MY PLACE, THE LUCKY DUCES CLUB.
AND, EVEN THOUGH MY NAME IS NOT OVER THE MARQUEES, I HAVE MY HAND IN ALL THE OTHER CASINOS, TOO.
ROMAN HOLIDAY
ALL OF THEM, EXCEPT SANTAVILLE!
NOW THERE ARE TWO WAYS WE CAN DO THIS, MISS KRINGLE.
THE FIRST IS YOUR WAY, WHERE YO TAKE THE INITIATIVE TO C ME IN AS A SILENT PARTN FOR, SAY, FORTY PERCENT ALL SANTAVILLE PROFITS, NICE AND FRIENDLY-LIKE
KRAK! KRAK!
OR, THE SECOND IS SYLVESTER'S WAY, WHICH IS... LESS SO.
ULP!
WELL? WHAT DO YOU SAY, MISS KRINGLE?
DADDY!
TO BE CONTINUED.

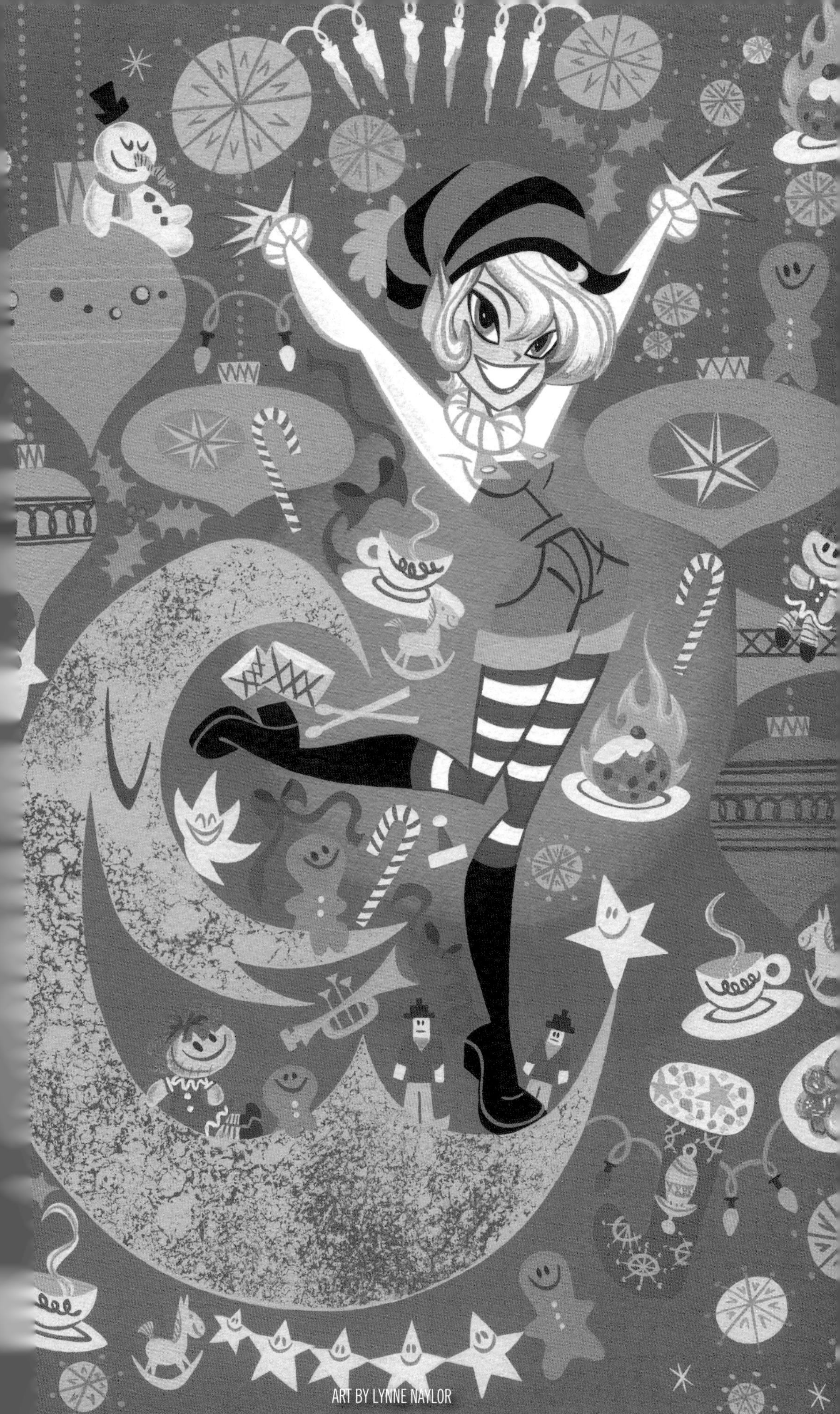

ART BY LYNNE NAYLOR

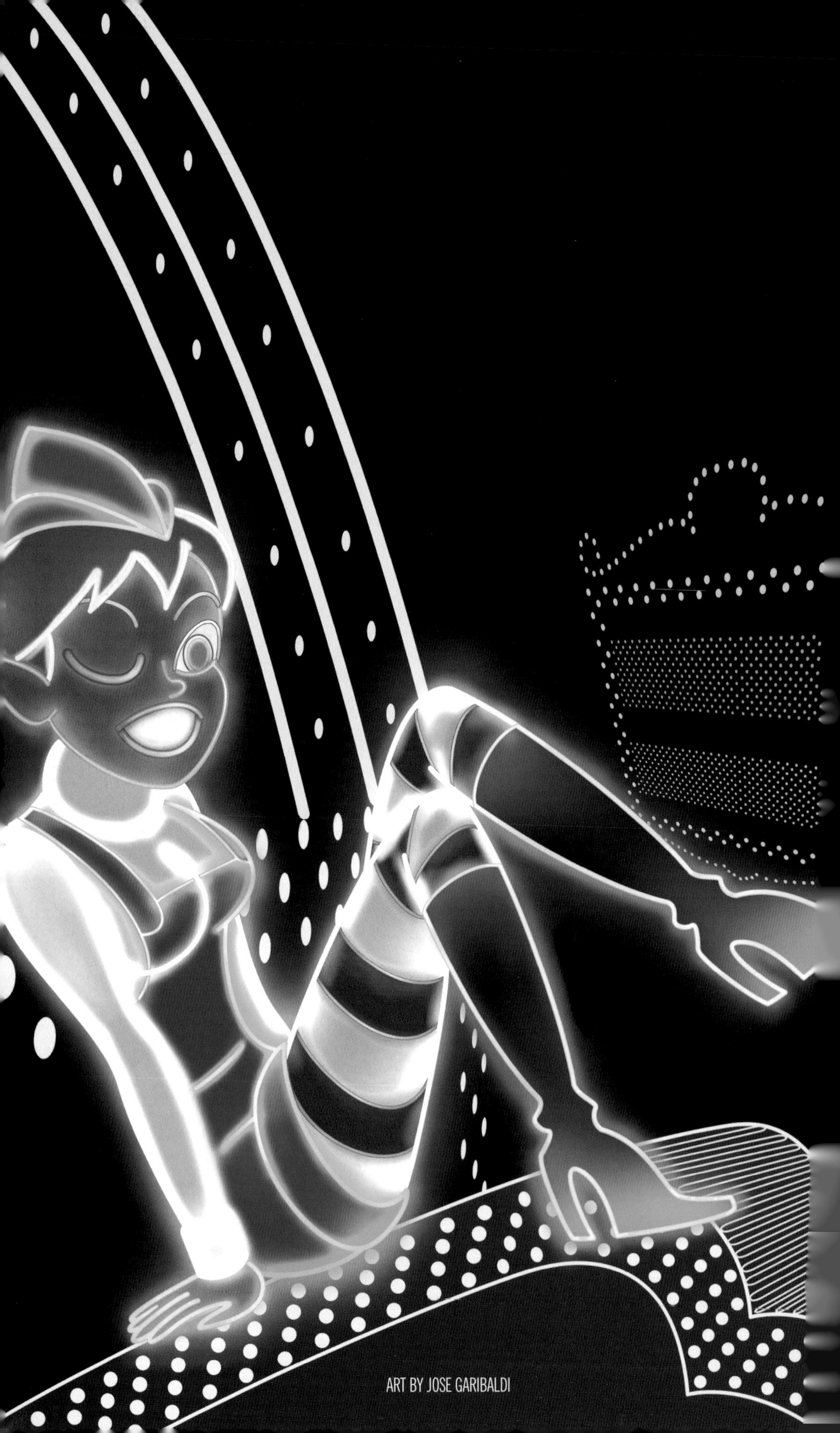

ART BY JOSE GARIBALDI

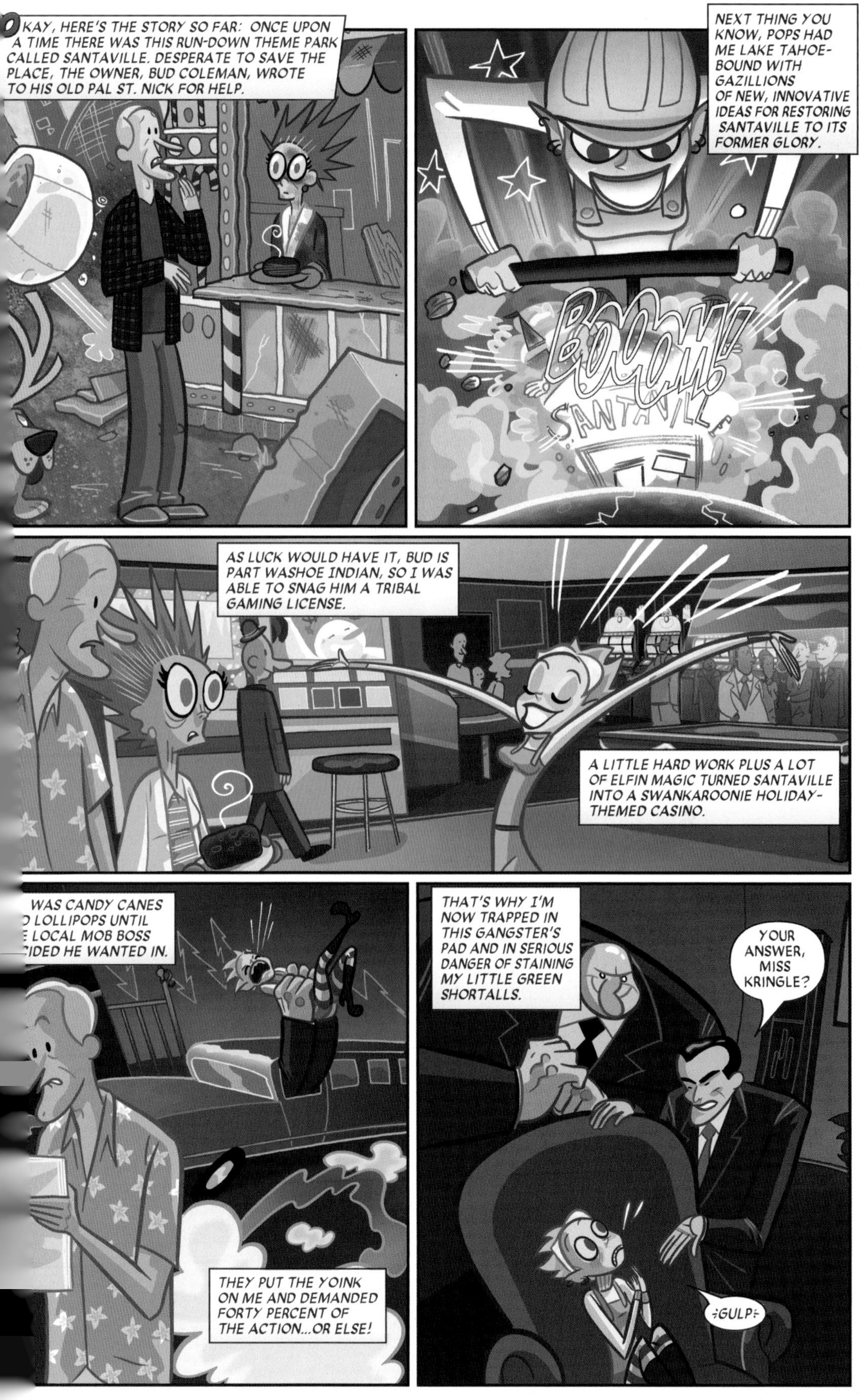
OKAY, HERE'S THE STORY SO FAR: ONCE UPON A TIME THERE WAS THIS RUN-DOWN THEME PARK CALLED SANTAVILLE. DESPERATE TO SAVE THE PLACE, THE OWNER, BUD COLEMAN, WROTE TO HIS OLD PAL ST. NICK FOR HELP.
NEXT THING YOU KNOW, POPS HAD ME LAKE TAHOE-BOUND WITH GAZILLIONS OF NEW, INNOVATIVE IDEAS FOR RESTORING SANTAVILLE TO ITS FORMER GLORY.
BOOOM!
SANTAVILLE
AS LUCK WOULD HAVE IT, BUD IS PART WASHOE INDIAN, SO I WAS ABLE TO SNAG HIM A TRIBAL GAMING LICENSE.
A LITTLE HARD WORK PLUS A LOT OF ELFIN MAGIC TURNED SANTAVILLE INTO A SWANKAROONIE HOLIDAY-THEMED CASINO.
WAS CANDY CANES
D LOLLIPOPS UNTIL
E LOCAL MOB BOSS
CIDED HE WANTED IN.
THEY PUT THE YOINK ON ME AND DEMANDED FORTY PERCENT OF THE ACTION...OR ELSE!
THAT'S WHY I'M NOW TRAPPED IN THIS GANGSTER'S PAD AND IN SERIOUS DANGER OF STAINING MY LITTLE GREEN SHORTALLS.
YOUR ANSWER, MISS KRINGLE?
GULP

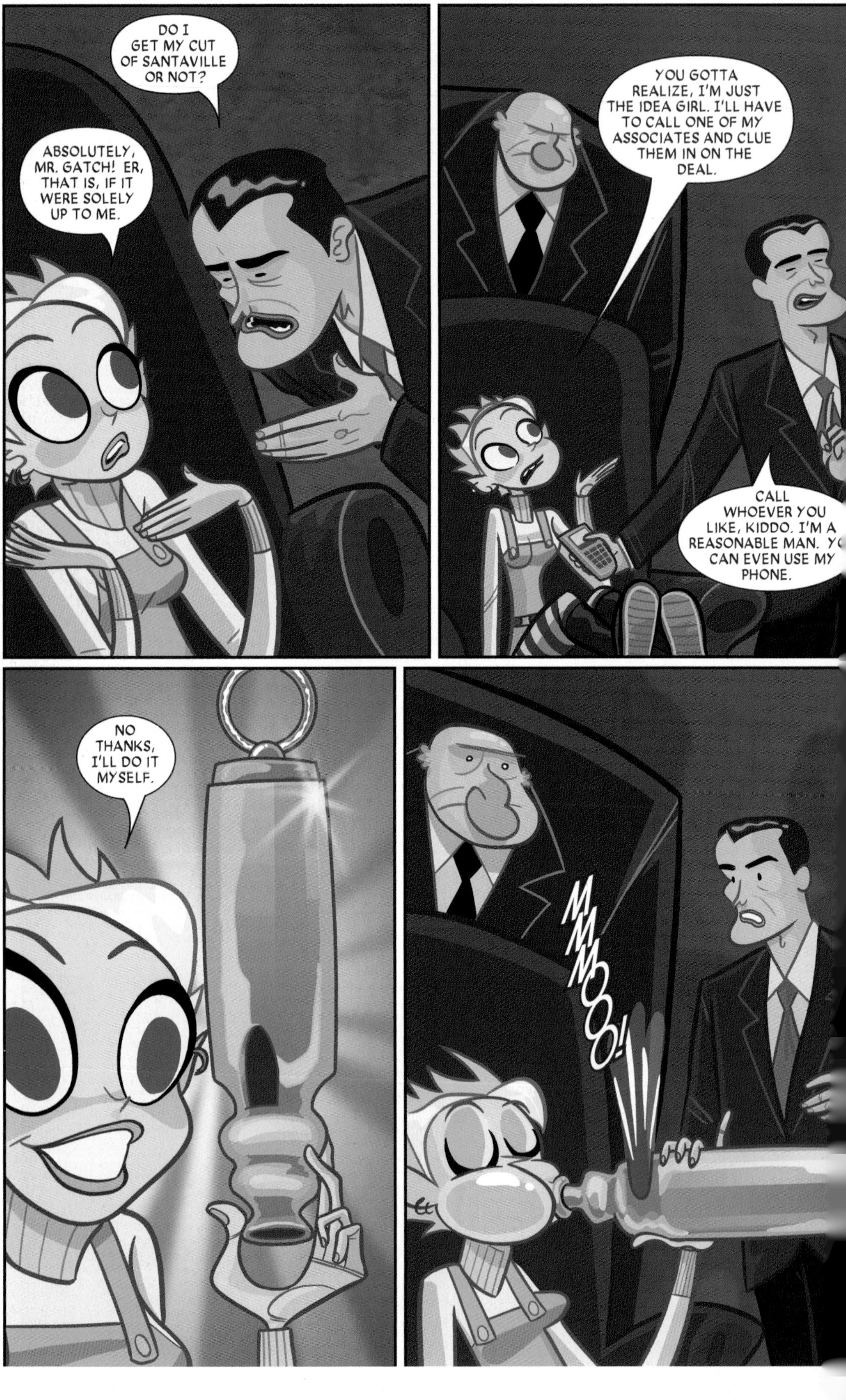
DO I GET MY CUT OF SANTAVILLE OR NOT?
ABSOLUTELY, MR. GATCH! ER, THAT IS, IF IT WERE SOLELY UP TO ME.
YOU GOTTA REALIZE, I'M JUST THE IDEA GIRL. I'LL HAVE TO CALL ONE OF MY ASSOCIATES AND CLUE THEM IN ON THE DEAL.
CALL WHOEVER YOU LIKE, KIDDO. I'M A REASONABLE MAN. YO CAN EVEN USE MY PHONE.
NO THANKS, I'LL DO IT MYSELF.
MMMOOO!

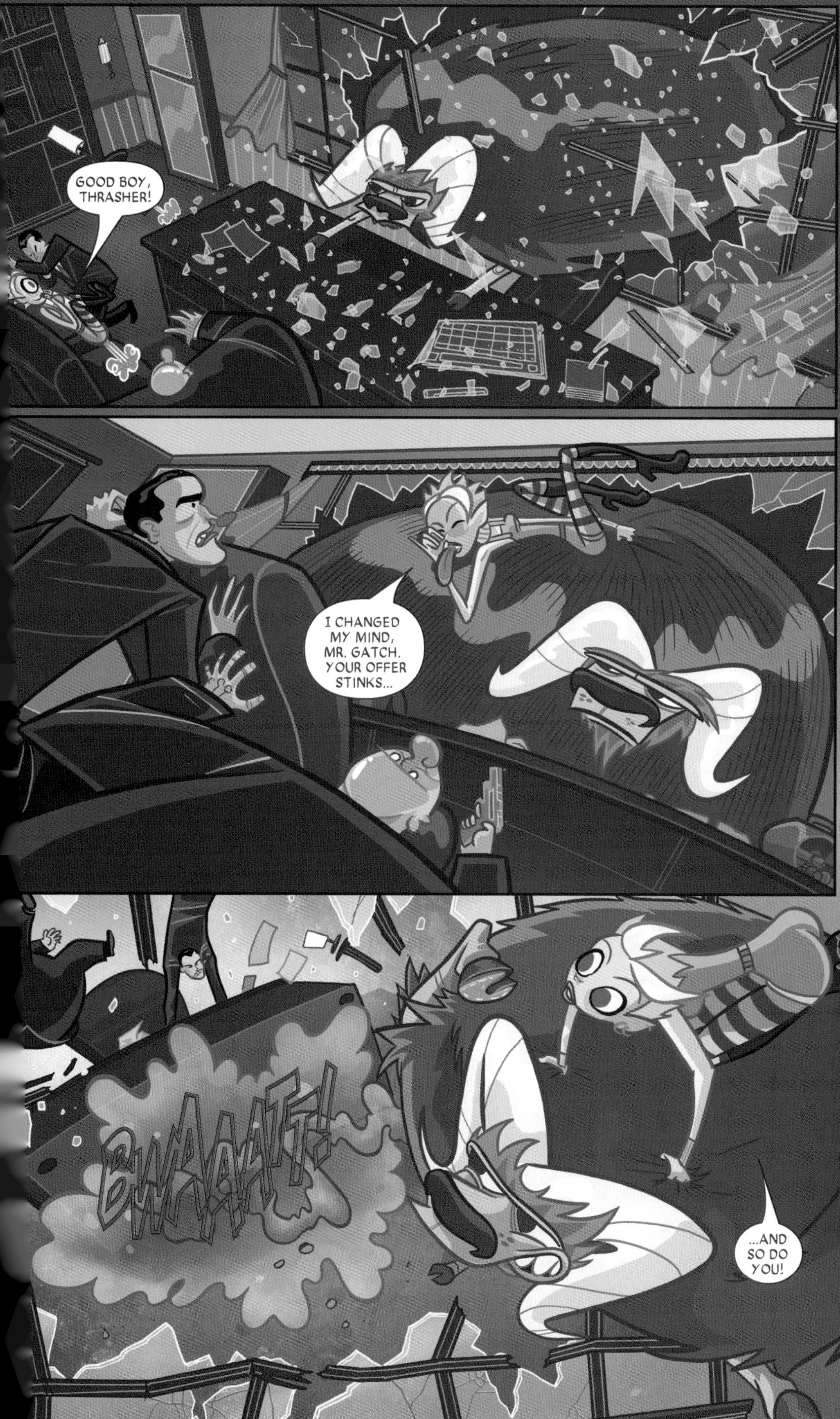
GOOD BOY, THRASHER!
I CHANGED MY MIND, MR. GATCH. YOUR OFFER STINKS...
BWAAAT!
...AND SO DO YOU!

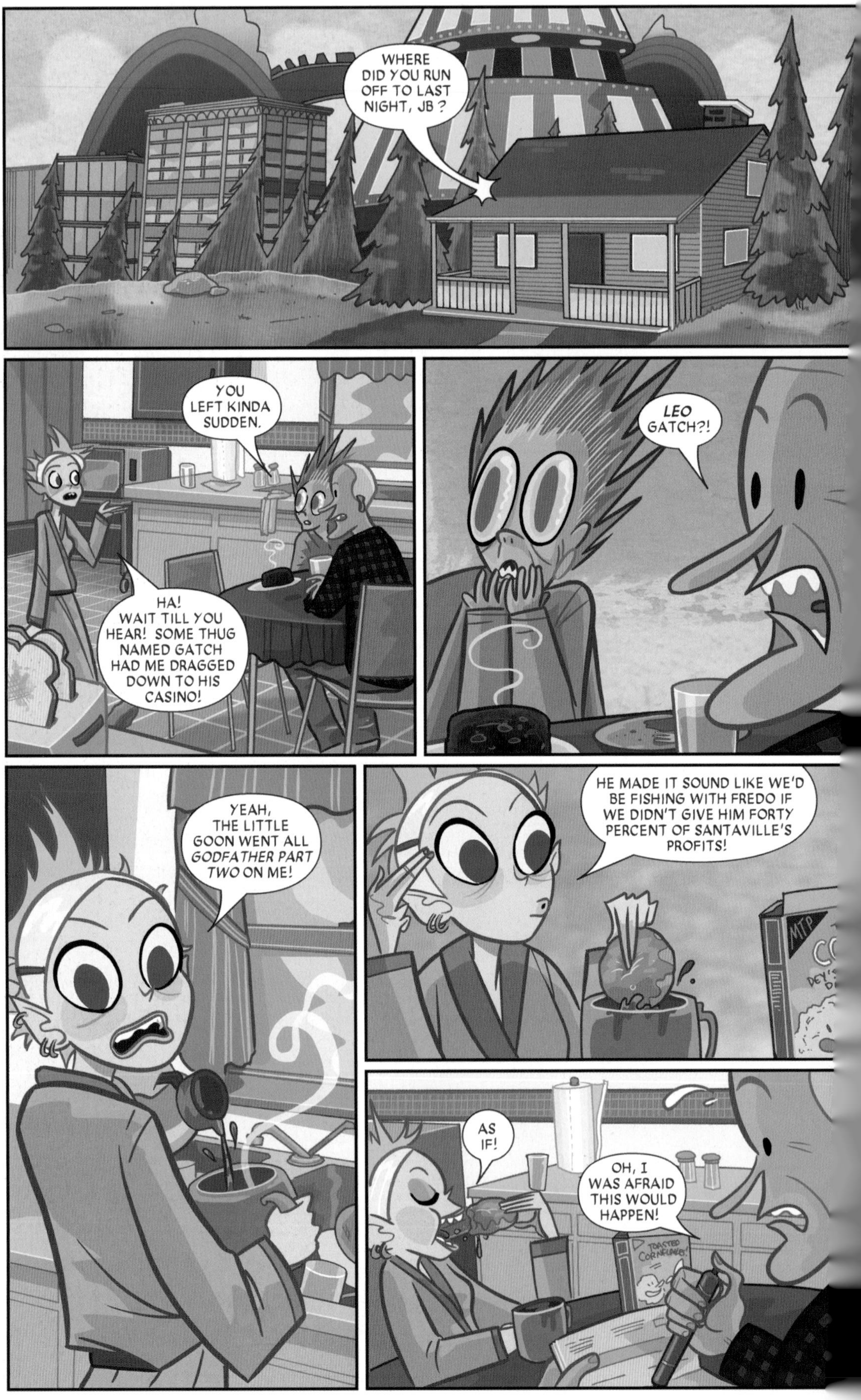
WHERE DID YOU RUN OFF TO LAST NIGHT, JB?
YOU LEFT KINDA SUDDEN.
HA! WAIT TILL YOU HEAR! SOME THUG NAMED GATCH HAD ME DRAGGED DOWN TO HIS CASINO!
LEO GATCH?!
YEAH, THE LITTLE GOON WENT ALL *GODFATHER PART TWO* ON ME!
HE MADE IT SOUND LIKE WE'D BE FISHING WITH FREDO IF WE DIDN'T GIVE HIM FORTY PERCENT OF SANTAVILLE'S PROFITS!
MTP
AS IF!
OH, I WAS AFRAID THIS WOULD HAPPEN!
TOASTED CORNFLAKES!

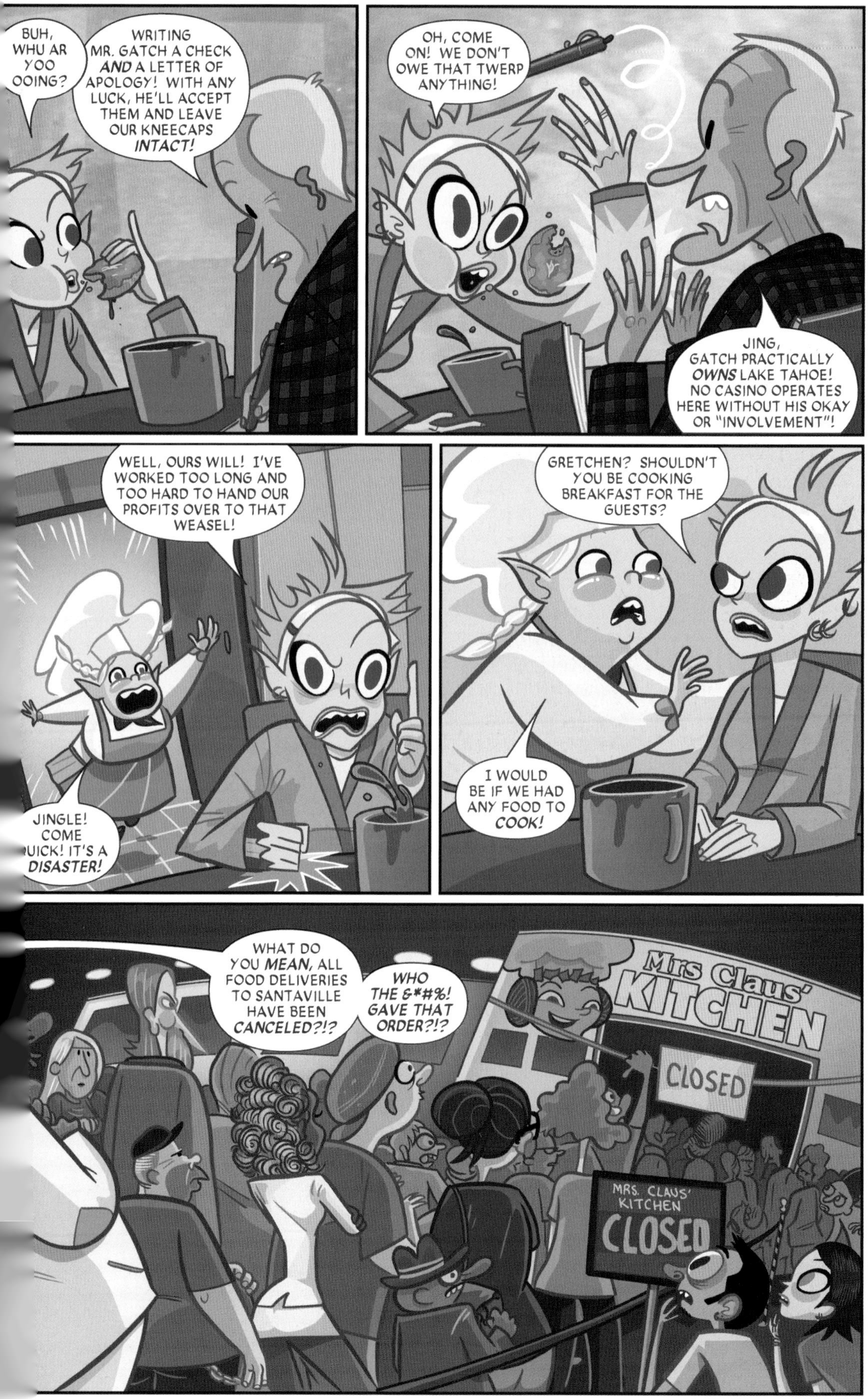
BUH, WHU AR YOO OOING?
WRITING MR. GATCH A CHECK AND A LETTER OF APOLOGY! WITH ANY LUCK, HE'LL ACCEPT THEM AND LEAVE OUR KNEECAPS INTACT!
OH, COME ON! WE DON'T OWE THAT TWERP ANYTHING!
JING, GATCH PRACTICALLY OWNS LAKE TAHOE! NO CASINO OPERATES HERE WITHOUT HIS OKAY OR "INVOLVEMENT"!
WELL, OURS WILL! I'VE WORKED TOO LONG AND TOO HARD TO HAND OUR PROFITS OVER TO THAT WEASEL!
JINGLE! COME UICK! IT'S A DISASTER!
GRETCHEN? SHOULDN'T YOU BE COOKING BREAKFAST FOR THE GUESTS?
I WOULD BE IF WE HAD ANY FOOD TO COOK!
WHAT DO YOU MEAN, ALL FOOD DELIVERIES TO SANTAVILLE HAVE BEEN CANCELED?!?
WHO THE &*#%! GAVE THAT ORDER?!?
Mrs Claus' KITCHEN
CLOSED
MRS. CLAUS' KITCHEN
CLOSED

LEO *GATCH?!?* SINCE WHEN IS *HE* IN CHARGE OF LOCAL FOOD DISTRIB--

WHAT?

REALLY? THAT LONG, HUH? AND THE BOOZE AND SODA TOO-- FIGURES.

I TOLD YOU HE WAS TOUGH.

READY FOR MORE BAD NEWS, KID?

OH, GOOD! JUST WHAT I NEED!

I'LL GIVE IT TO YA STRAIGHT, SWEETS. WE GOT NO HEADLINERS FOR OUR SHOW ROOM.

EDDIE, YOU'RE THE ELF WHO'S CONNECTED TO THE ENTERTAINMENT BIZ! WHAT ABOUT ALL THE A-LIST TALENT YOU WERE GOING TO LINE UP?!?

I'M OUTGUNNED, JB!

EVERY SINGER, COMIC, OR NOVELTY ACT I CALLED SAID GATCH WOULD BLACKBALL THEM IF THEY EVER SET FOOT IN SANTAVILLE!

THAT'S IT! I'M CALLING THE C

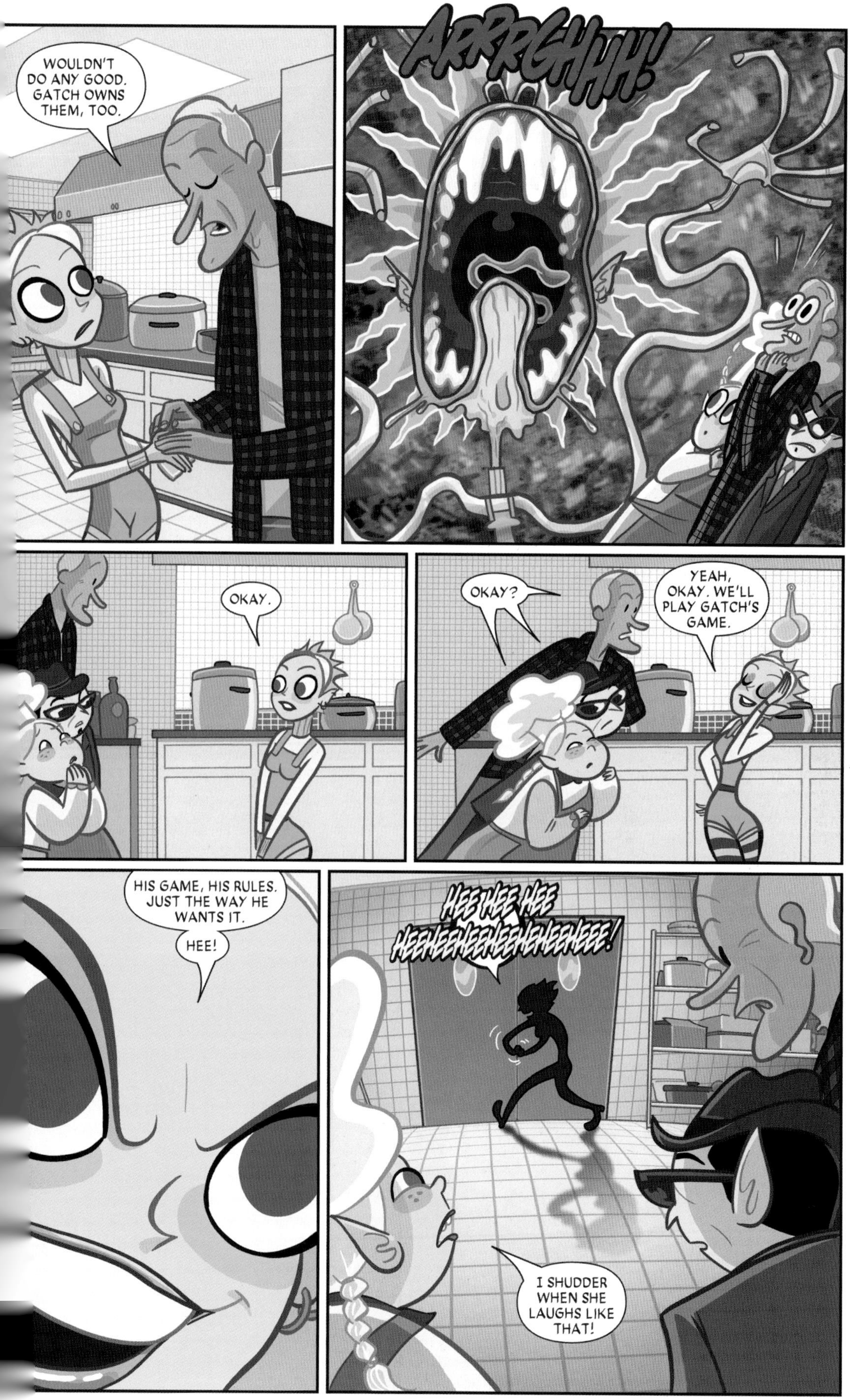
WOULDN'T DO ANY GOOD. GATCH OWNS THEM, TOO.
ARRRGHHH!
OKAY.
OKAY?
YEAH, OKAY. WE'LL PLAY GATCH'S GAME.
HIS GAME, HIS RULES. JUST THE WAY HE WANTS IT.
HEE!
HEE HEE HEE HEEHEEHEEHEEHEHEEHEEE!
I SHUDDER WHEN SHE LAUGHS LIKE THAT!

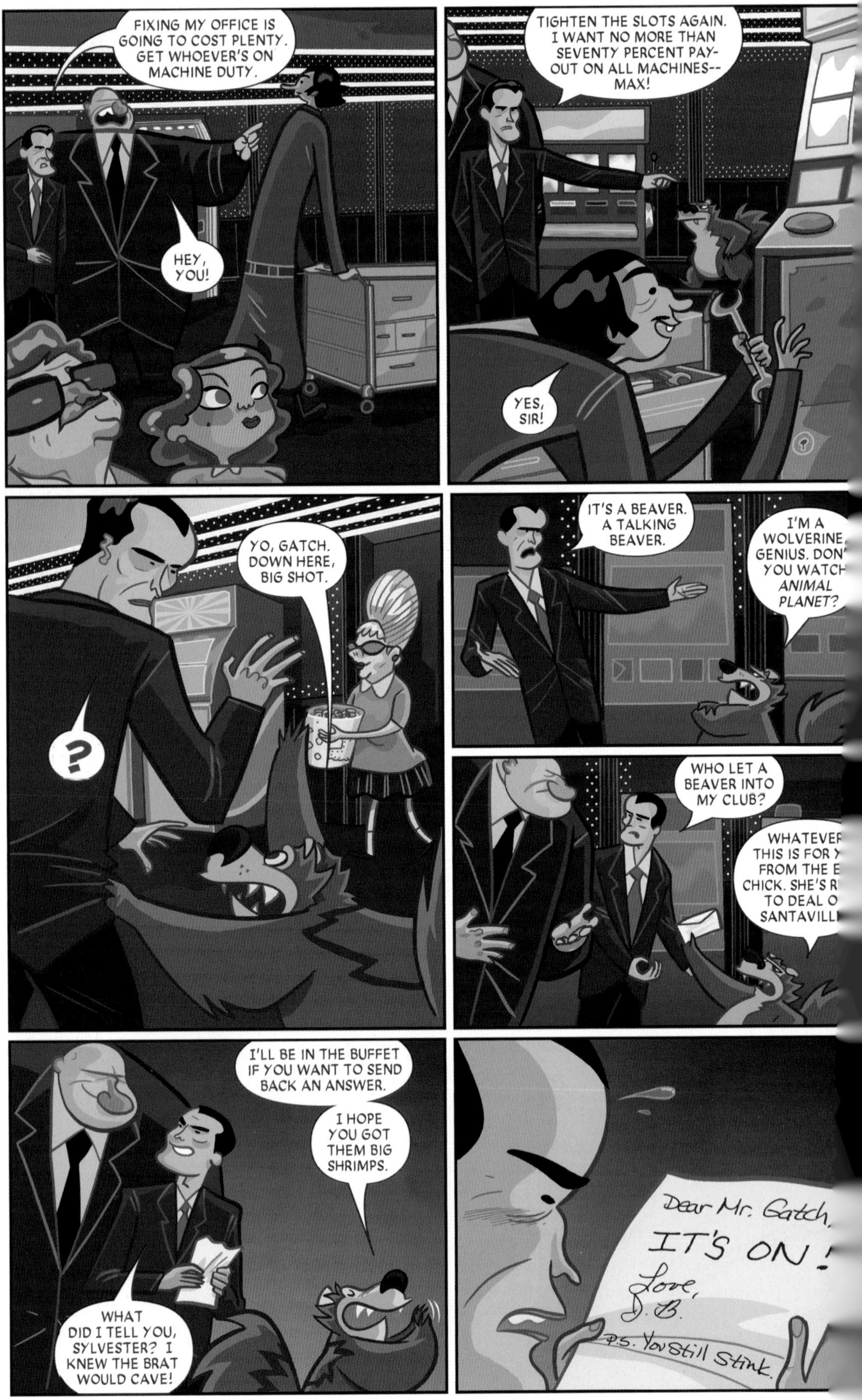
FIXING MY OFFICE IS GOING TO COST PLENTY. GET WHOEVER'S ON MACHINE DUTY.
HEY, YOU!
TIGHTEN THE SLOTS AGAIN. I WANT NO MORE THAN SEVENTY PERCENT PAY-OUT ON ALL MACHINES-- MAX!
YES, SIR!
YO, GATCH. DOWN HERE, BIG SHOT.
?
IT'S A BEAVER. A TALKING BEAVER.
I'M A WOLVERINE GENIUS. DON YOU WATCH ANIMAL PLANET?
WHO LET A BEAVER INTO MY CLUB?
WHATEVER THIS IS FOR FROM THE CHICK. SHE'S TO DEAL SANTAVILL
I'LL BE IN THE BUFFET IF YOU WANT TO SEND BACK AN ANSWER.
I HOPE YOU GOT THEM BIG SHRIMPS.
WHAT DID I TELL YOU, SYLVESTER? I KNEW THE BRAT WOULD CAVE!
Dear Mr. Gatch,
IT'S ON!
Love,
D. B.
P.S. You Still Stink.

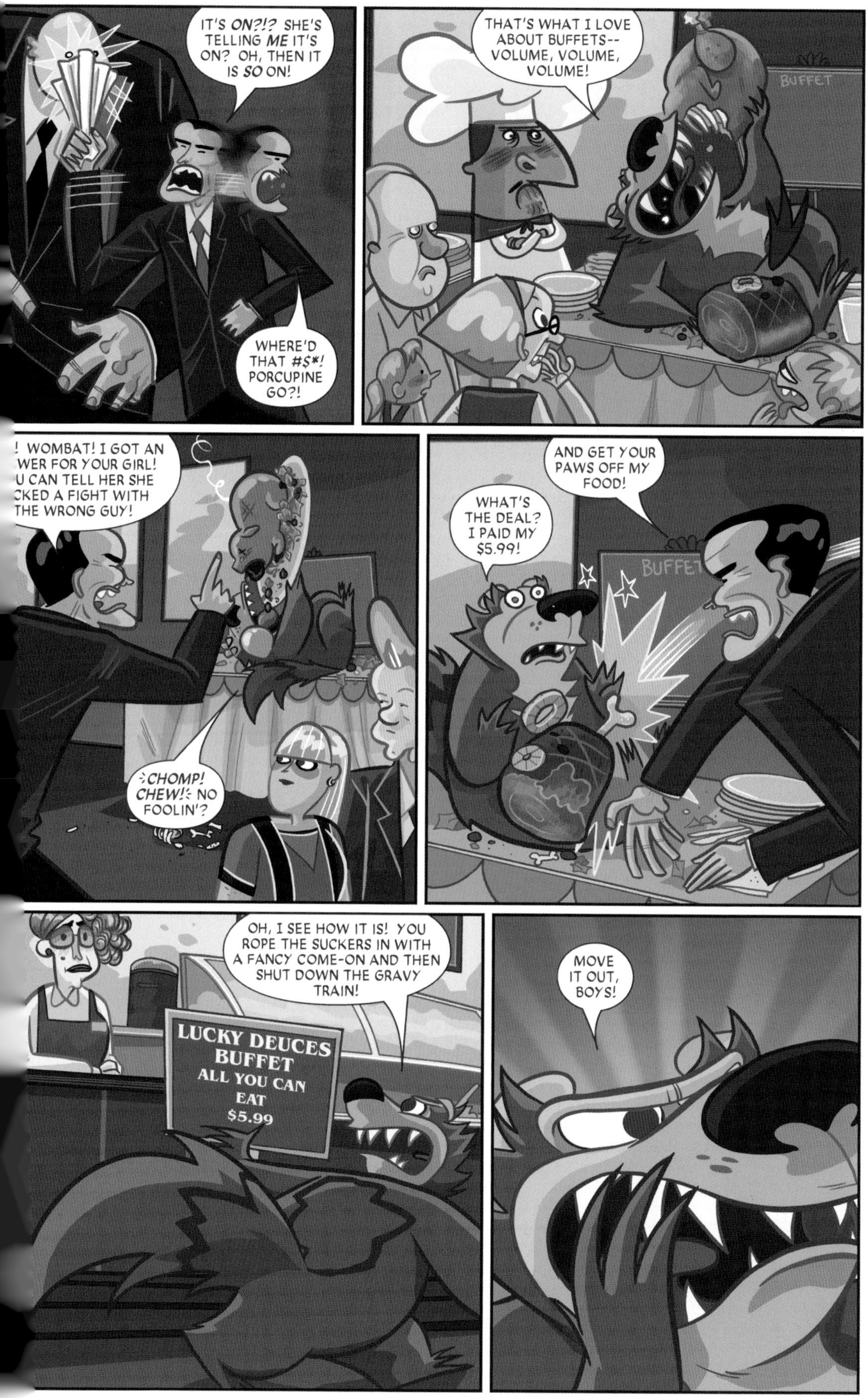
IT'S ON?!? SHE'S TELLING ME IT'S ON? OH, THEN IT IS SO ON!
WHERE'D THAT #$*! PORCUPINE GO?!
THAT'S WHAT I LOVE ABOUT BUFFETS-- VOLUME, VOLUME, VOLUME!
BUFFET
! WOMBAT! I GOT AN WER FOR YOUR GIRL! U CAN TELL HER SHE CKED A FIGHT WITH THE WRONG GUY!
CHOMP! CHEW! NO FOOLIN'?
AND GET YOUR PAWS OFF MY FOOD!
WHAT'S THE DEAL? I PAID MY $5.99!
BUFFET
OH, I SEE HOW IT IS! YOU ROPE THE SUCKERS IN WITH A FANCY COME-ON AND THEN SHUT DOWN THE GRAVY TRAIN!
LUCKY DEUCES BUFFET ALL YOU CAN EAT $5.99
MOVE IT OUT, BOYS!

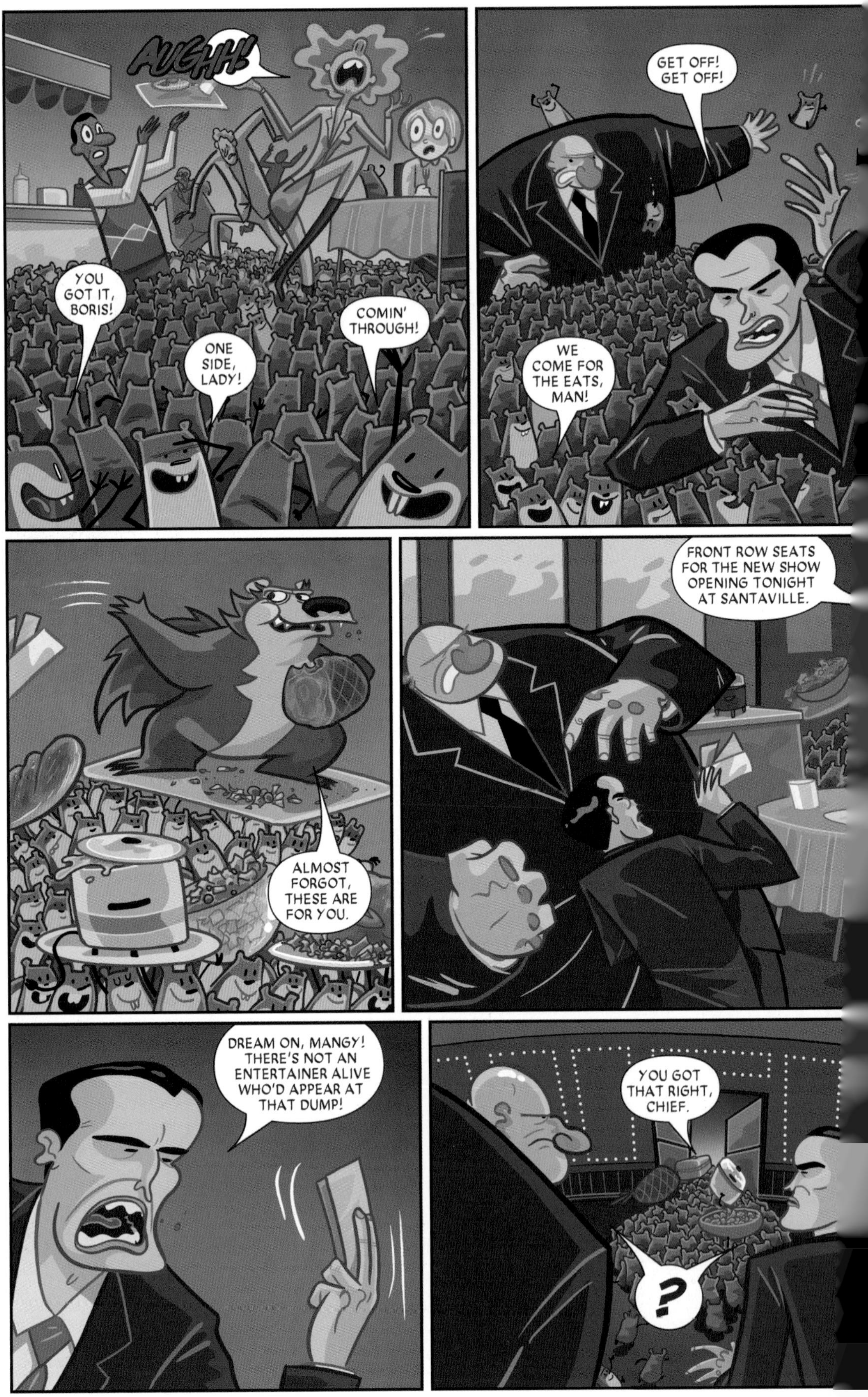
AUGHH!
YOU GOT IT, BORIS!
ONE SIDE, LADY!
COMIN' THROUGH!
GET OFF! GET OFF!
WE COME FOR THE EATS, MAN!
ALMOST FORGOT, THESE ARE FOR YOU.
FRONT ROW SEATS FOR THE NEW SHOW OPENING TONIGHT AT SANTAVILLE.
DREAM ON, MANGY! THERE'S NOT AN ENTERTAINER ALIVE WHO'D APPEAR AT THAT DUMP!
YOU GOT THAT RIGHT, CHIEF.
?

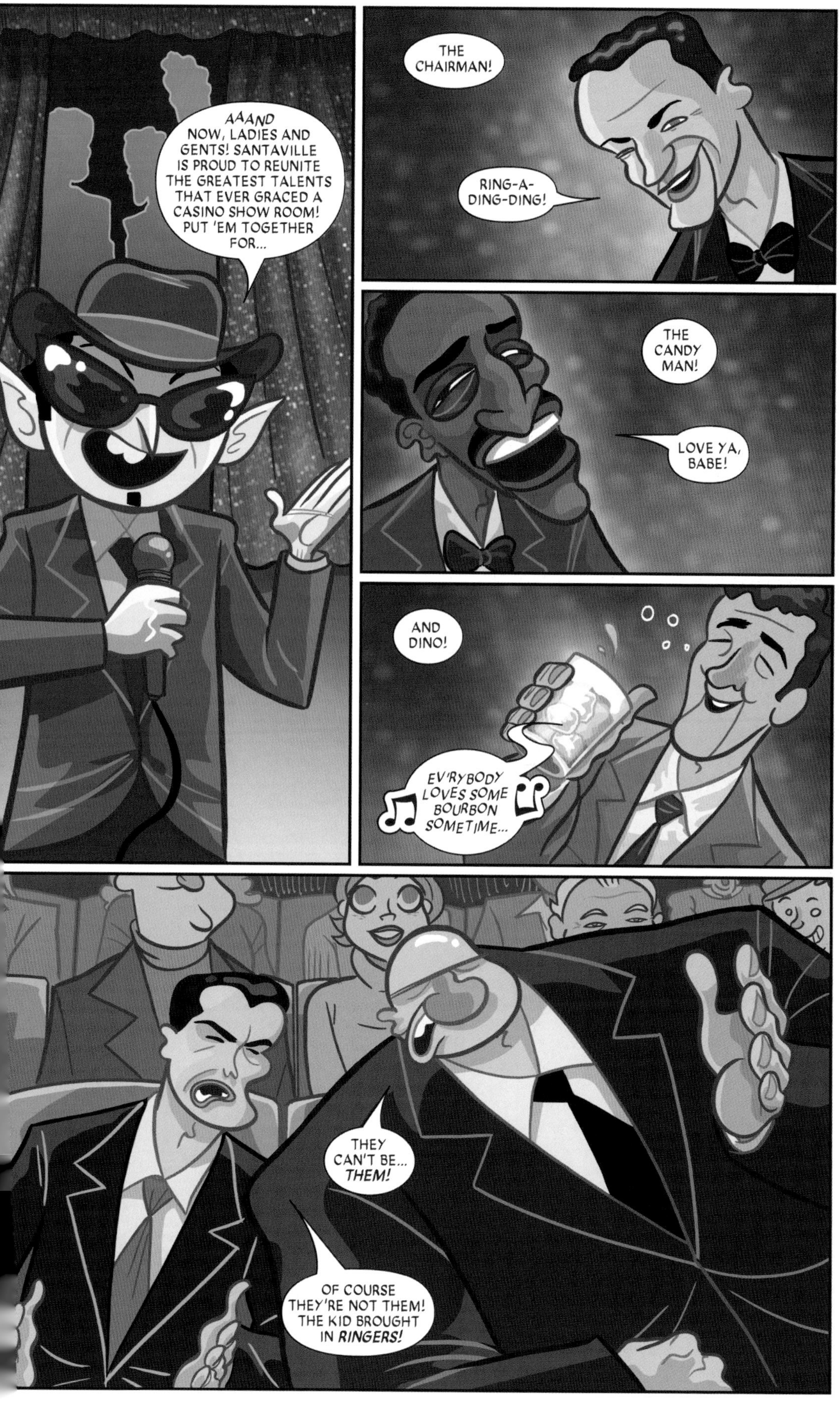
AAAND NOW, LADIES AND GENTS! SANTAVILLE IS PROUD TO REUNITE THE GREATEST TALENTS THAT EVER GRACED A CASINO SHOW ROOM! PUT 'EM TOGETHER FOR...
THE CHAIRMAN!
RING-A-DING-DING!
THE CANDY MAN!
LOVE YA, BABE!
AND DINO!
EV'RYBODY LOVES SOME BOURBON SOMETIME...
THEY CAN'T BE... *THEM!*
OF COURSE THEY'RE NOT THEM! THE KID BROUGHT IN *RINGERS!*

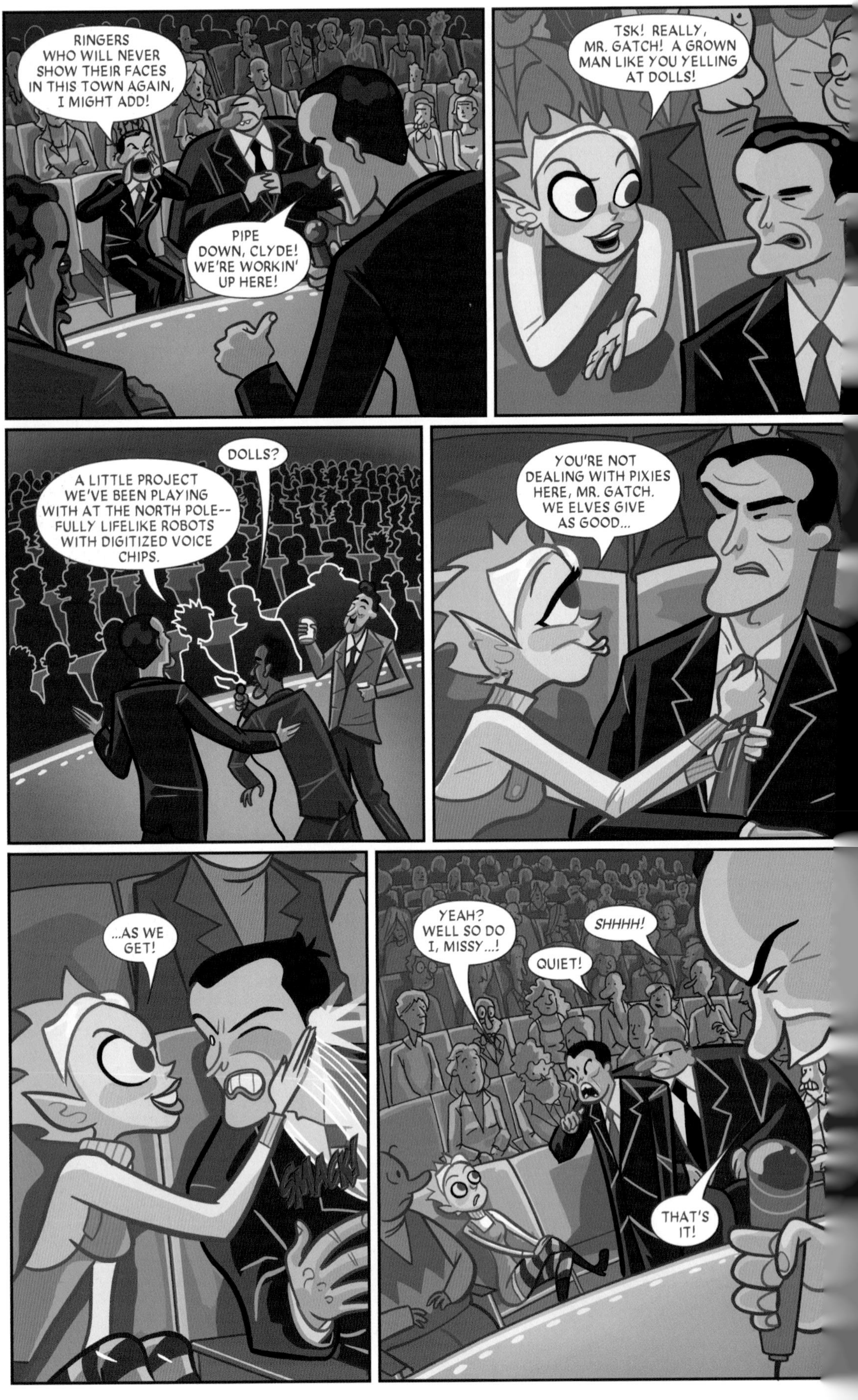
RINGERS WHO WILL NEVER SHOW THEIR FACES IN THIS TOWN AGAIN, I MIGHT ADD!
PIPE DOWN, CLYDE! WE'RE WORKIN' UP HERE!
TSK! REALLY, MR. GATCH! A GROWN MAN LIKE YOU YELLING AT DOLLS!
A LITTLE PROJECT WE'VE BEEN PLAYING WITH AT THE NORTH POLE-- FULLY LIFELIKE ROBOTS WITH DIGITIZED VOICE CHIPS.
DOLLS?
YOU'RE NOT DEALING WITH PIXIES HERE, MR. GATCH. WE ELVES GIVE AS GOOD...
...AS WE GET!
YEAH? WELL SO DO I, MISSY...!
SHHHH!
QUIET!
THAT'S IT!

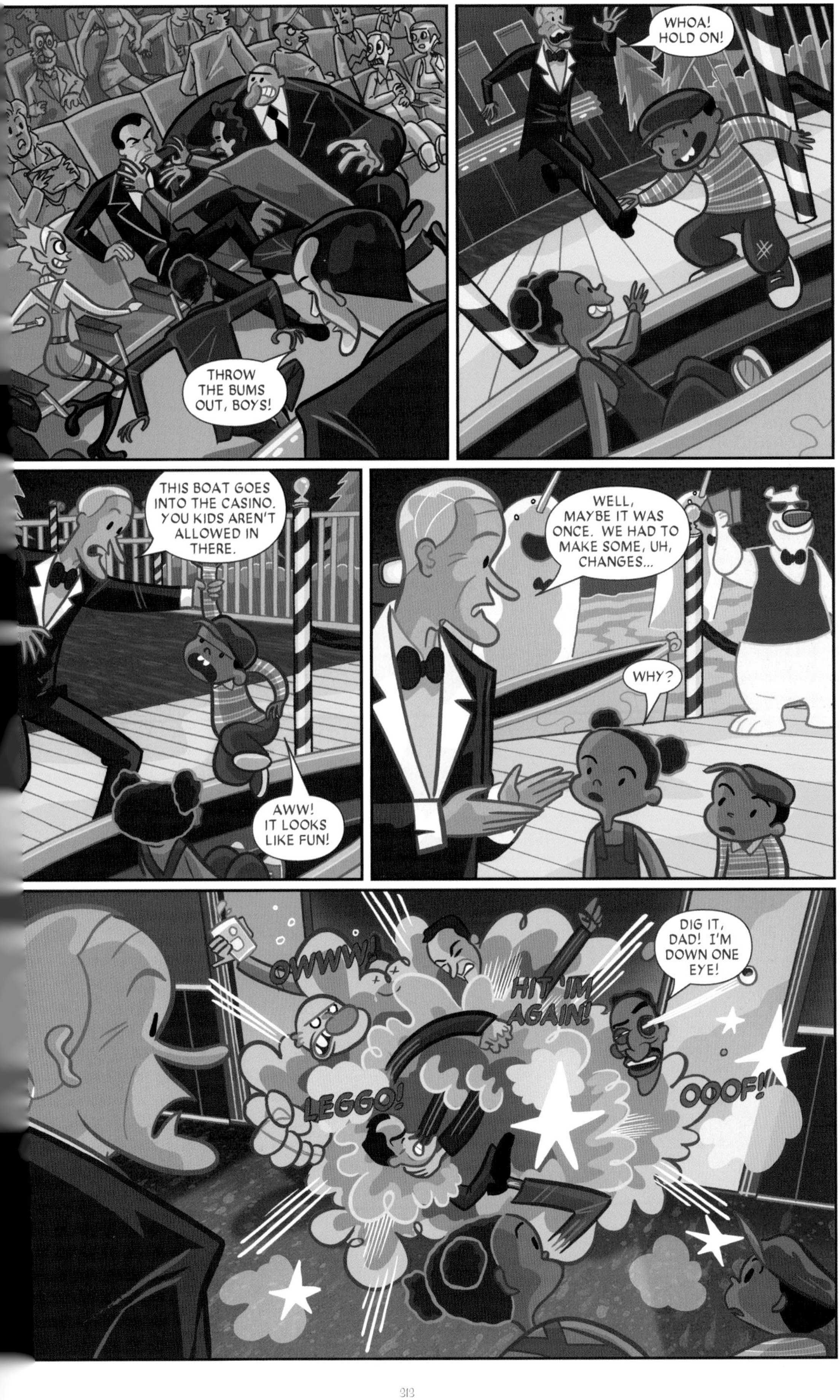
THROW THE BUMS OUT, BOYS!
WHOA! HOLD ON!
THIS BOAT GOES INTO THE CASINO. YOU KIDS AREN'T ALLOWED IN THERE.
AWW! IT LOOKS LIKE FUN!
WELL, MAYBE IT WAS ONCE. WE HAD TO MAKE SOME, UH, CHANGES...
WHY?
OWWW!
DIG IT, DAD! I'M DOWN ONE EYE!
HIT 'IM AGAIN!
LEGGO!
OOOF!

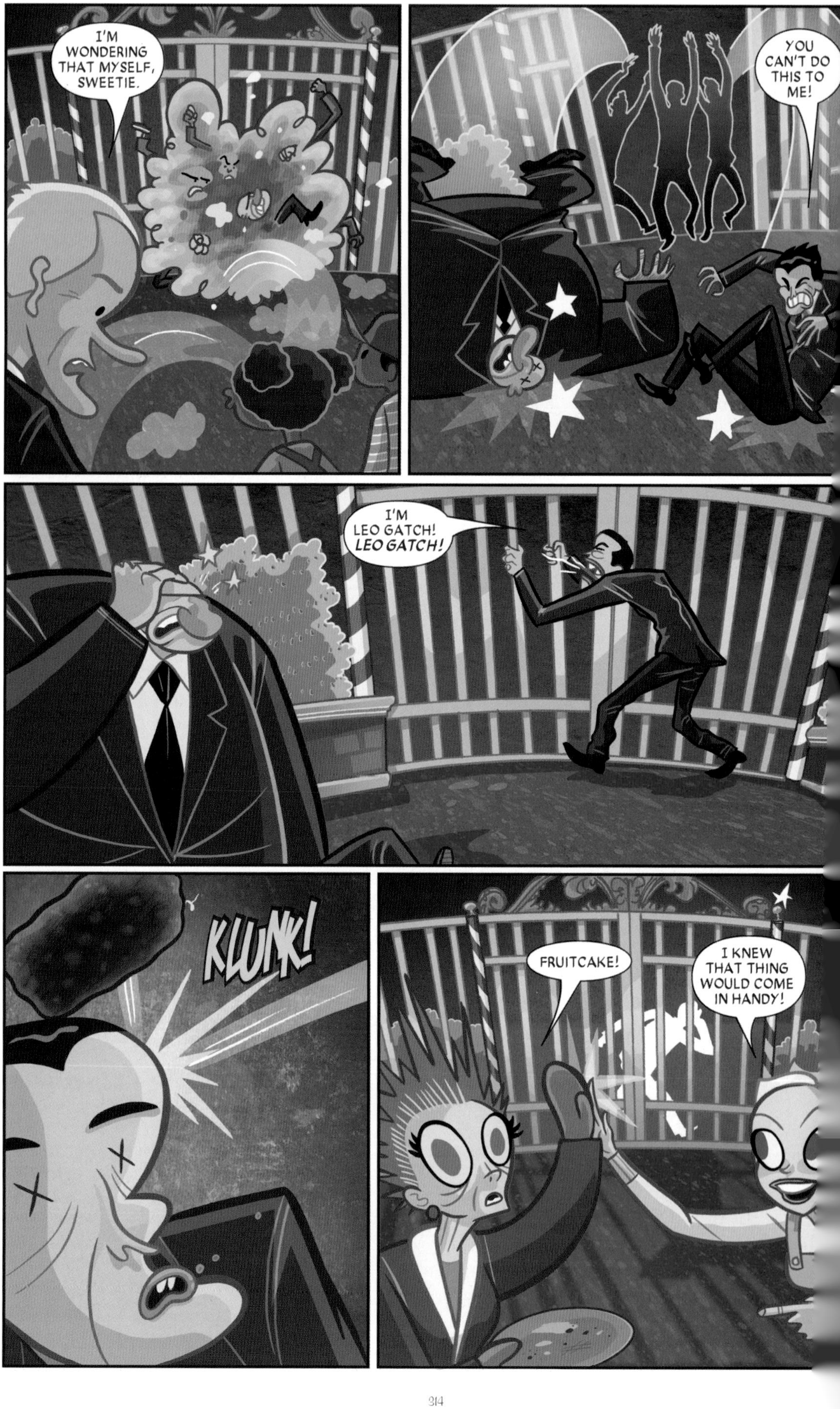
I'M WONDERING THAT MYSELF, SWEETIE.
YOU CAN'T DO THIS TO ME!
I'M LEO GATCH! *LEO GATCH!*
KLUNK!
FRUITCAKE!
I KNEW THAT THING WOULD COME IN HANDY!

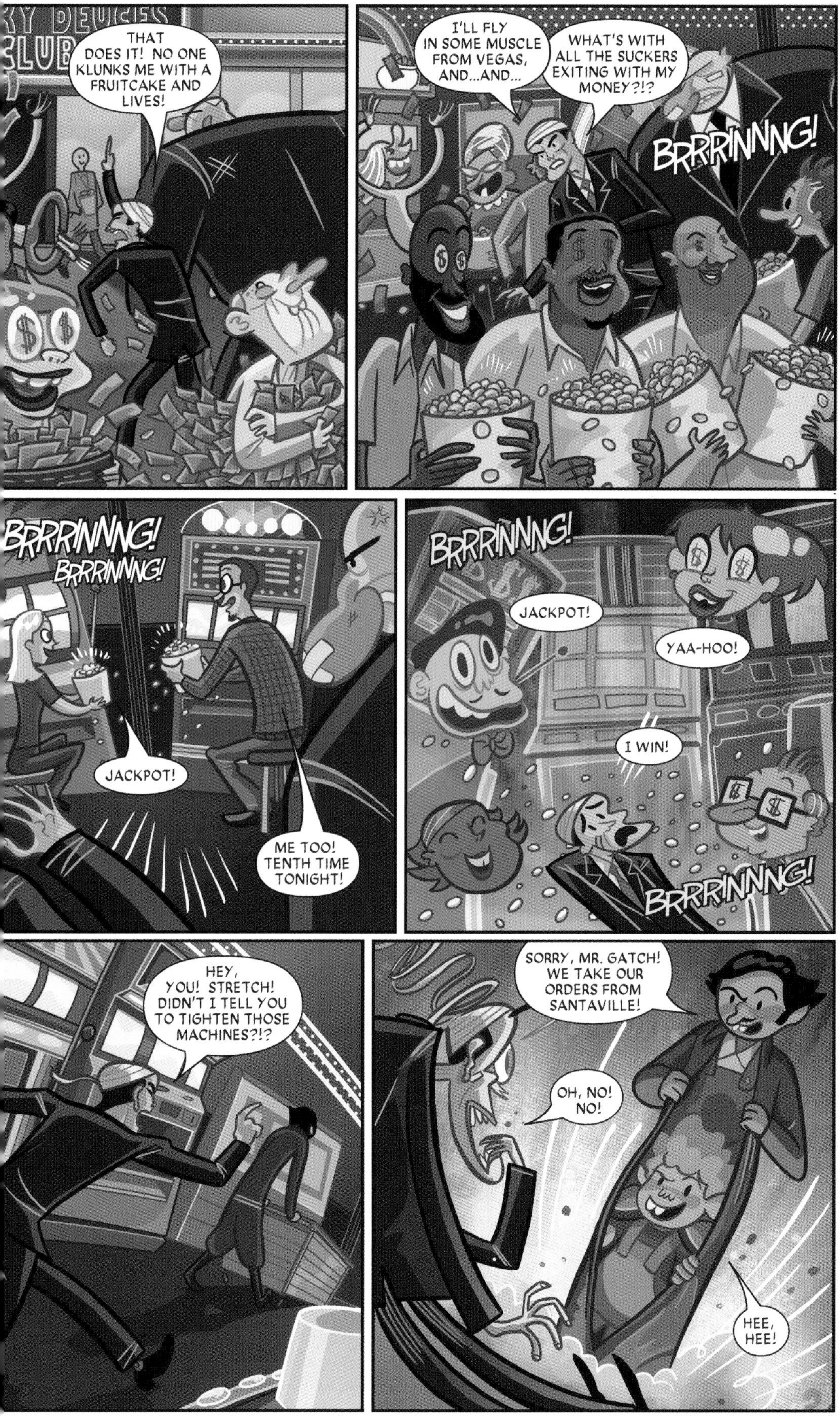
THAT DOES IT! NO ONE KLUNKS ME WITH A FRUITCAKE AND LIVES!
I'LL FLY IN SOME MUSCLE FROM VEGAS, AND...AND...
WHAT'S WITH ALL THE SUCKERS EXITING WITH MY MONEY?!?
BRRRINNNG!
BRRRINNNG!
BRRRINNNG!
JACKPOT!
ME TOO! TENTH TIME TONIGHT!
BRRRINNNG!
JACKPOT!
YAA-HOO!
I WIN!
BRRRINNNG!
HEY, YOU! STRETCH! DIDN'T I TELL YOU TO TIGHTEN THOSE MACHINES?!?
SORRY, MR. GATCH! WE TAKE OUR ORDERS FROM SANTAVILLE!
OH, NO! NO!
HEE, HEE!

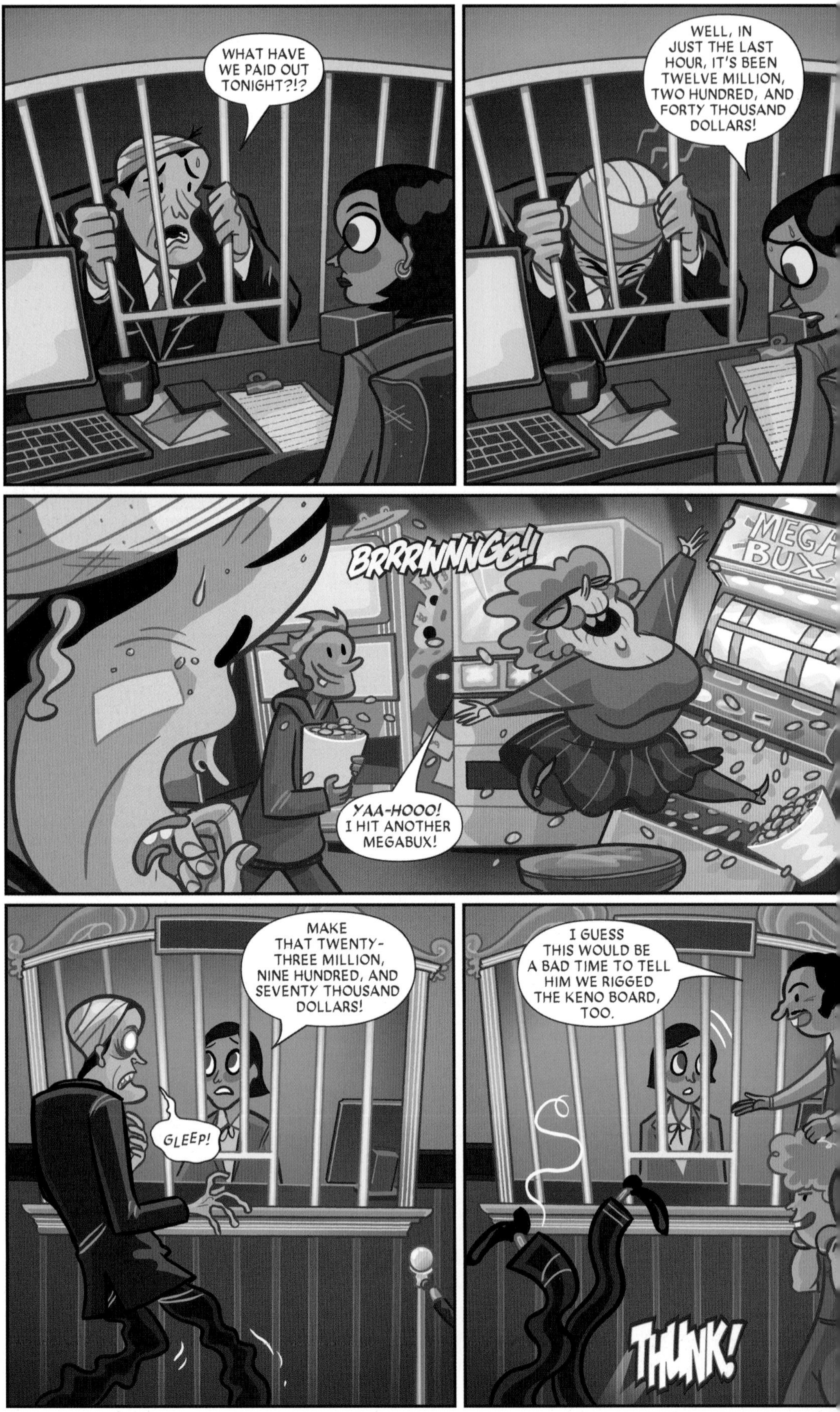
WHAT HAVE WE PAID OUT TONIGHT?!?
WELL, IN JUST THE LAST HOUR, IT'S BEEN TWELVE MILLION, TWO HUNDRED, AND FORTY THOUSAND DOLLARS!
BRRRINNNGG!!
MEGA BUX
YAA-HOOO! I HIT ANOTHER MEGABUX!
MAKE THAT TWENTY-THREE MILLION, NINE HUNDRED, AND SEVENTY THOUSAND DOLLARS!
GLEEP!
I GUESS THIS WOULD BE A BAD TIME TO TELL HIM WE RIGGED THE KENO BOARD, TOO.
THUNK!

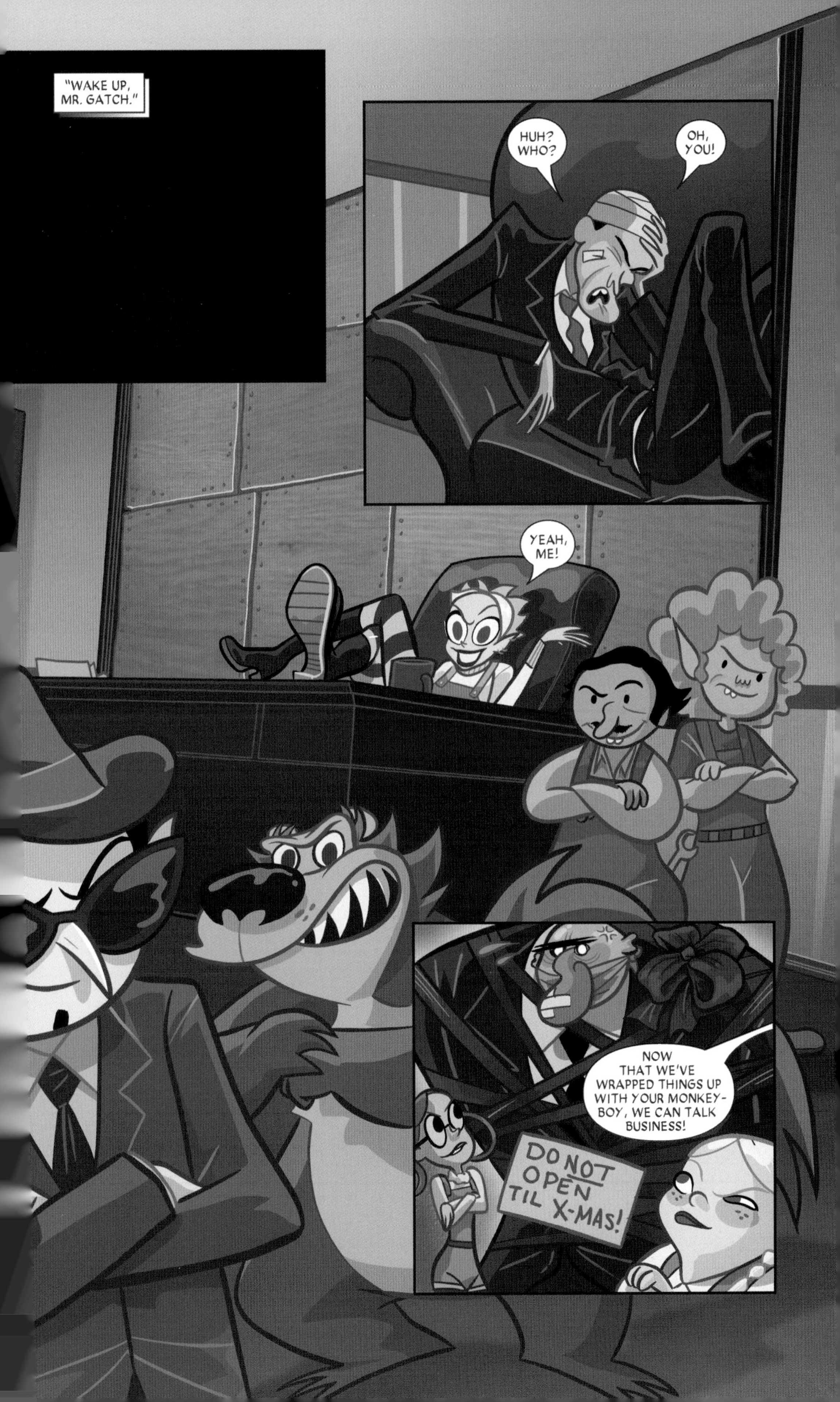
"WAKE UP, MR. GATCH."
HUH? WHO?
OH, YOU!
YEAH, ME!
NOW THAT WE'VE WRAPPED THINGS UP WITH YOUR MONKEY-BOY, WE CAN TALK BUSINESS!
DO NOT OPEN TIL X-MAS!

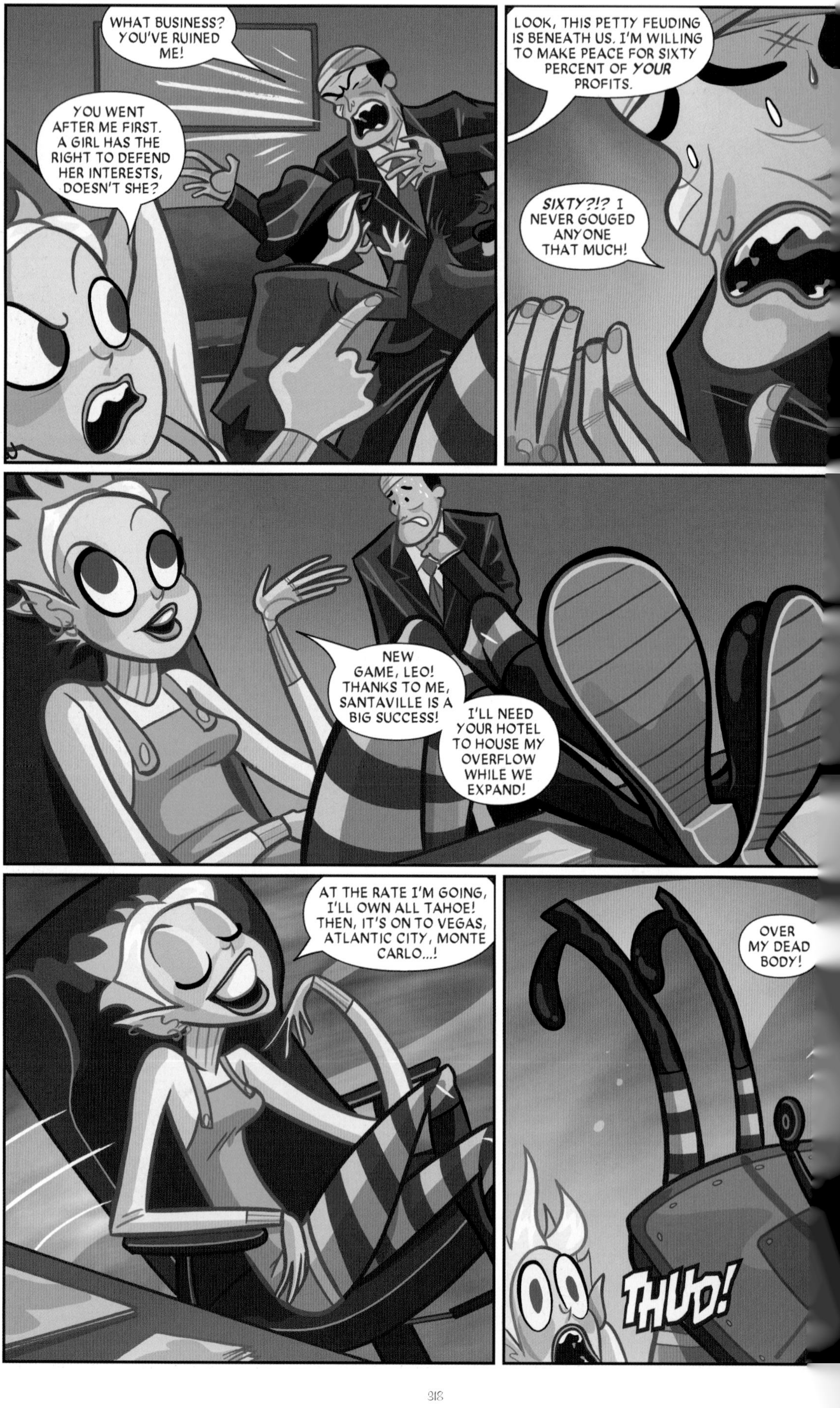
WHAT BUSINESS? YOU'VE RUINED ME!
YOU WENT AFTER ME FIRST. A GIRL HAS THE RIGHT TO DEFEND HER INTERESTS, DOESN'T SHE?
LOOK, THIS PETTY FEUDING IS BENEATH US. I'M WILLING TO MAKE PEACE FOR SIXTY PERCENT OF *YOUR* PROFITS.
SIXTY?!? I NEVER GOUGED ANYONE THAT MUCH!
NEW GAME, LEO! THANKS TO ME, SANTAVILLE IS A BIG SUCCESS!
I'LL NEED YOUR HOTEL TO HOUSE MY OVERFLOW WHILE WE EXPAND!
AT THE RATE I'M GOING, I'LL OWN ALL TAHOE! THEN, IT'S ON TO VEGAS, ATLANTIC CITY, MONTE CARLO...!
OVER MY DEAD BODY!
THUD!

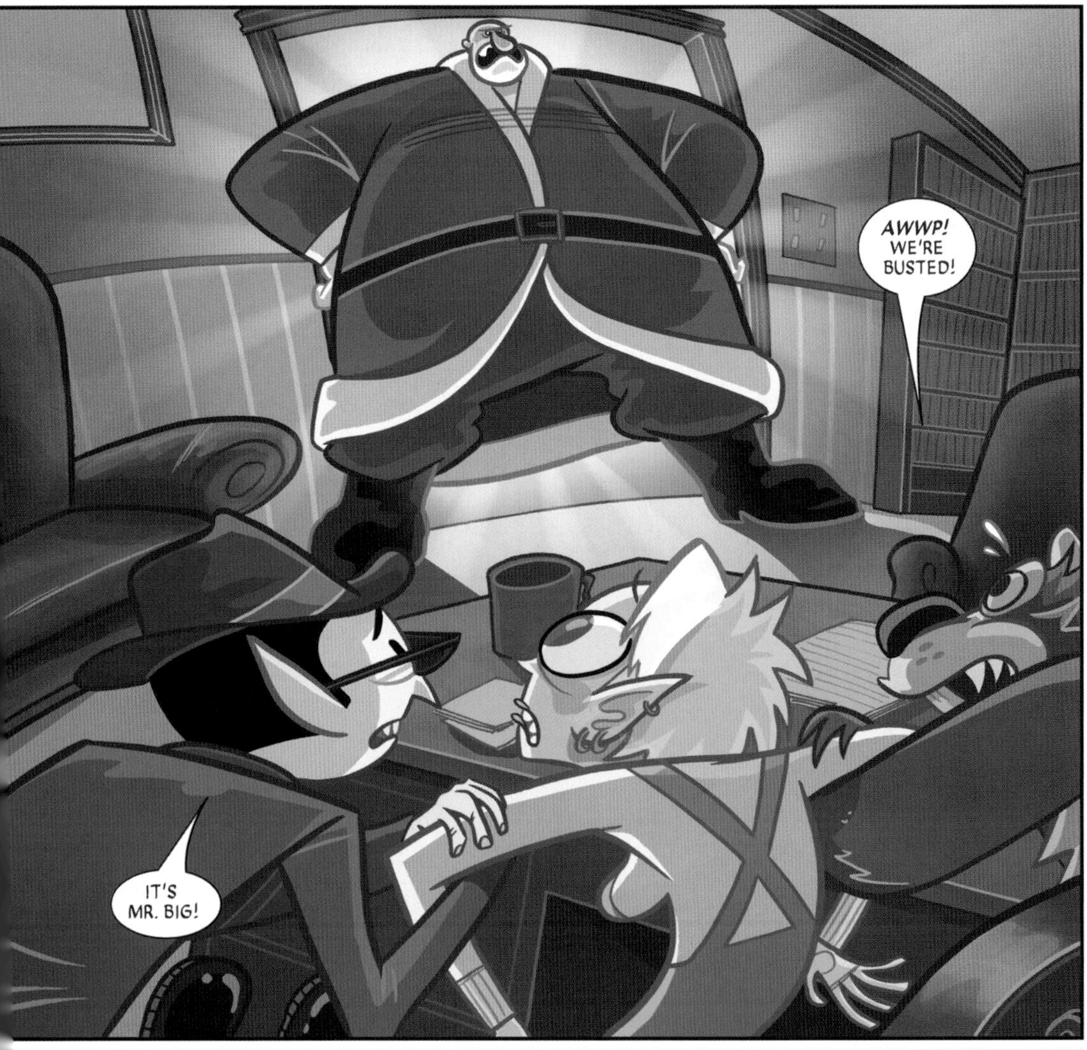
AWWP! WE'RE BUSTED!
IT'S MR. BIG!

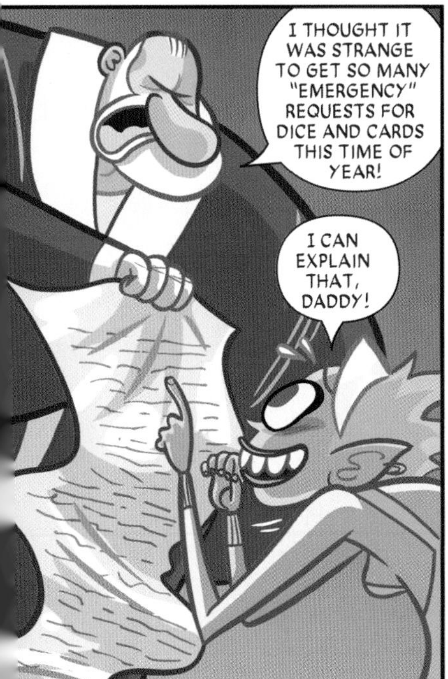
I THOUGHT IT WAS STRANGE TO GET SO MANY "EMERGENCY" REQUESTS FOR DICE AND CARDS THIS TIME OF YEAR!
I CAN EXPLAIN THAT, DADDY!

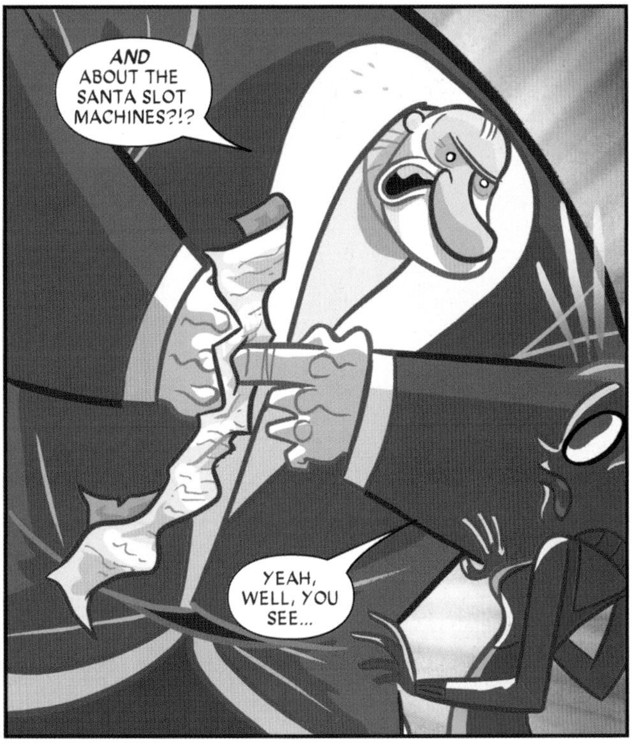
AND ABOUT THE SANTA SLOT MACHINES?!?
YEAH, WELL, YOU SEE...

HOW DARE YOU USE *MY IMAGE* TO PROMOTE A GAMBLING JOINT?!?

THAT'S IT! SOMEONE SQUEALED!

WHICH ONE OF YOU SMURFS RATTED ME OUT?!?

NOT ME!

I DID IT, JINGLE.

BUD?!? I THOUGHT WE WERE PARTNERS!

WE WERE--AT FIRST.

THEN I REALIZED HOW MUCH SANTAVILLE HAD CHANGED. IT WASN'T A PLACE KIDS WERE WELCOME ANYMORE, AND I DIDN'T WANT THAT.

SO YOU'RE SHUTTING DOWN?

AS A CASINO, YES WE'VE MADE M THAN ENOUGH M TO TURN SANTA BACK INTO A STA THE-ART AMUSEME

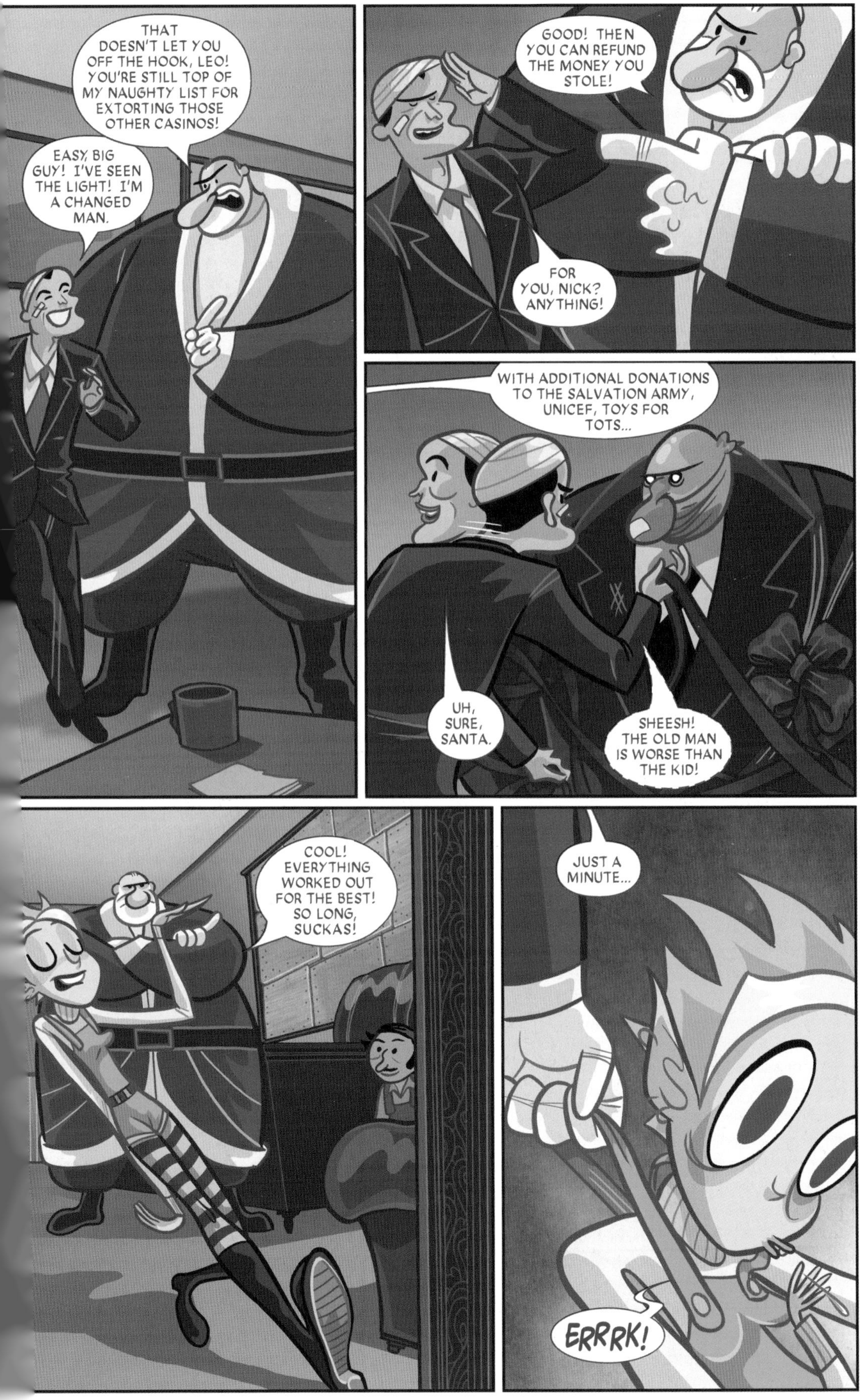

THAT DOESN'T LET YOU OFF THE HOOK, LEO! YOU'RE STILL TOP OF MY NAUGHTY LIST FOR EXTORTING THOSE OTHER CASINOS!
EASY, BIG GUY! I'VE SEEN THE LIGHT! I'M A CHANGED MAN.
GOOD! THEN YOU CAN REFUND THE MONEY YOU STOLE!
FOR YOU, NICK? ANYTHING!
WITH ADDITIONAL DONATIONS TO THE SALVATION ARMY, UNICEF, TOYS FOR TOTS...
UH, SURE, SANTA.
SHEESH! THE OLD MAN IS WORSE THAN THE KID!
COOL! EVERYTHING WORKED OUT FOR THE BEST! SO LONG, SUCKAS!
JUST A MINUTE...
ERRRK!

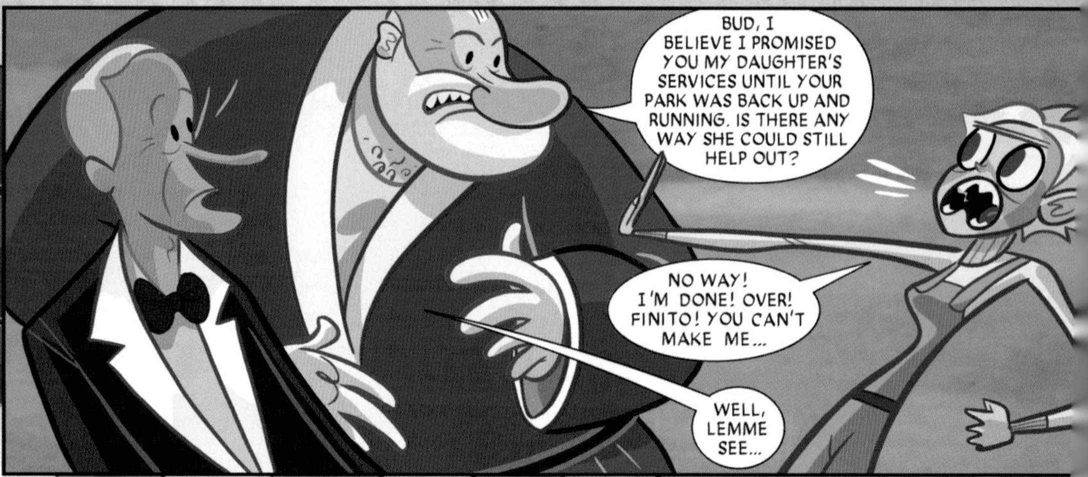
BUD, I BELIEVE I PROMISED YOU MY DAUGHTER'S SERVICES UNTIL YOUR PARK WAS BACK UP AND RUNNING. IS THERE ANY WAY SHE COULD STILL HELP OUT?
NO WAY! I'M DONE! OVER! FINITO! YOU CAN'T MAKE ME...
WELL, LEMME SEE...

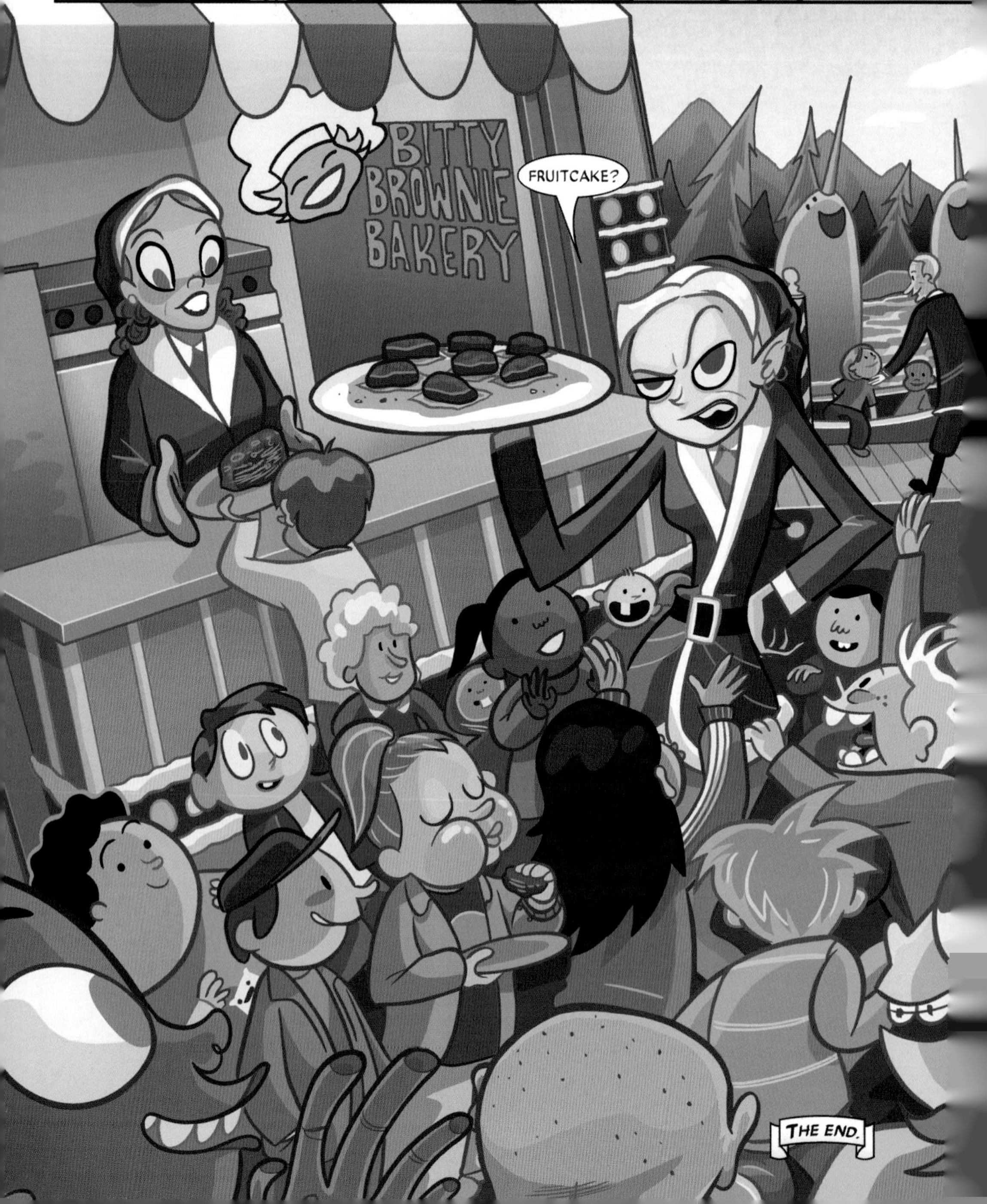
BITTY BROWNIE BAKERY
FRUITCAKE?
THE END.

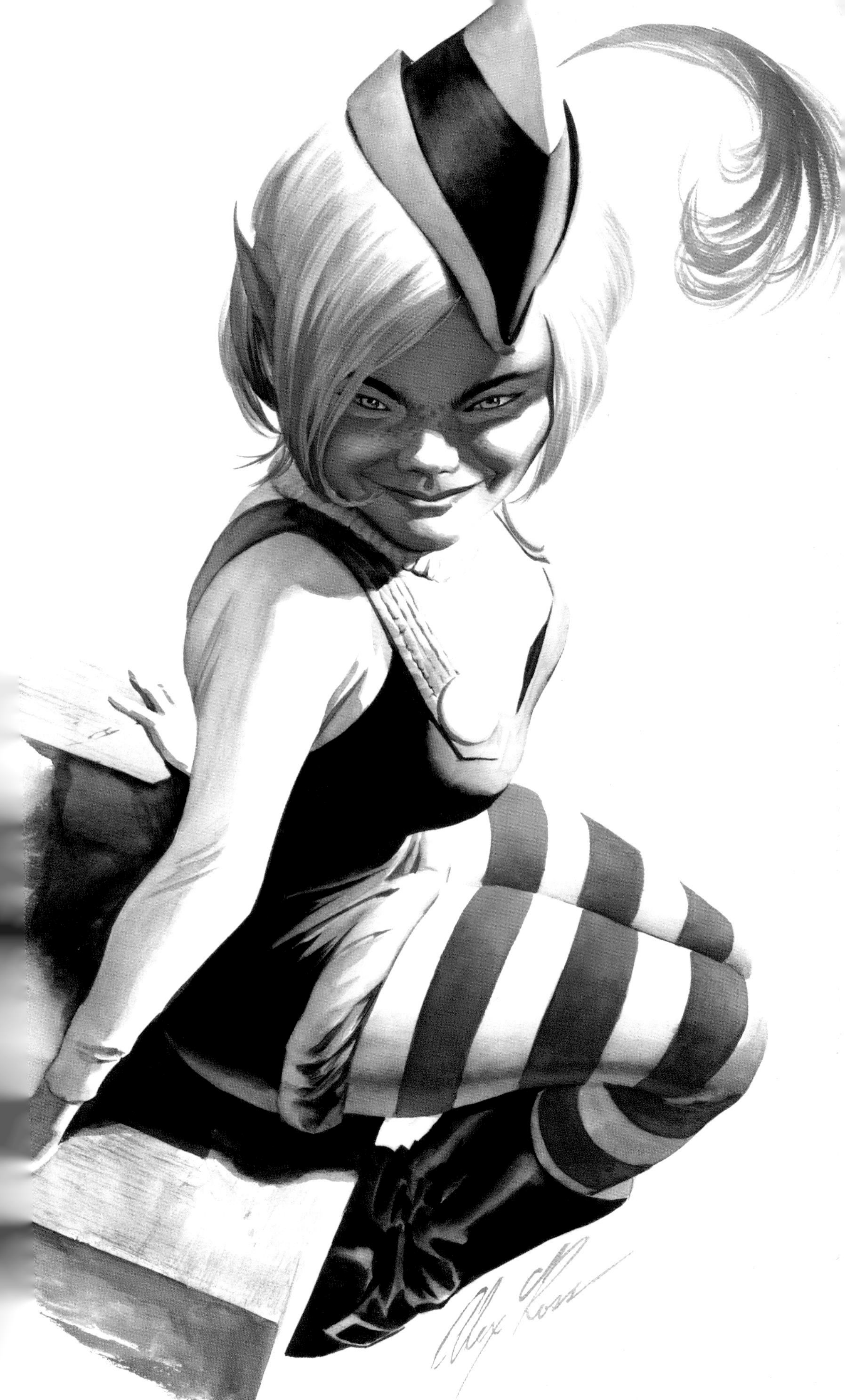
Alex Ross

ART BY ALEX ROSS

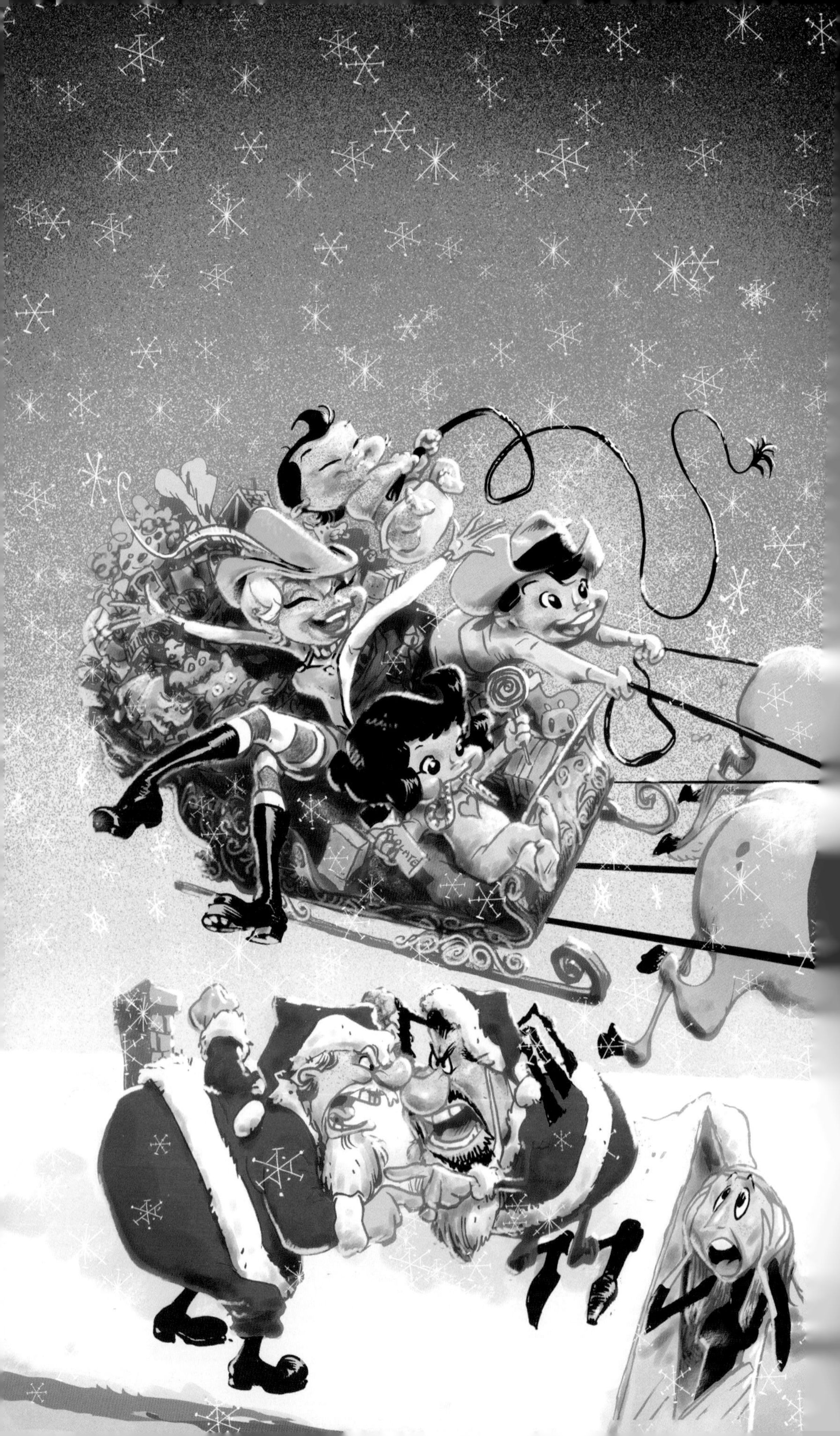

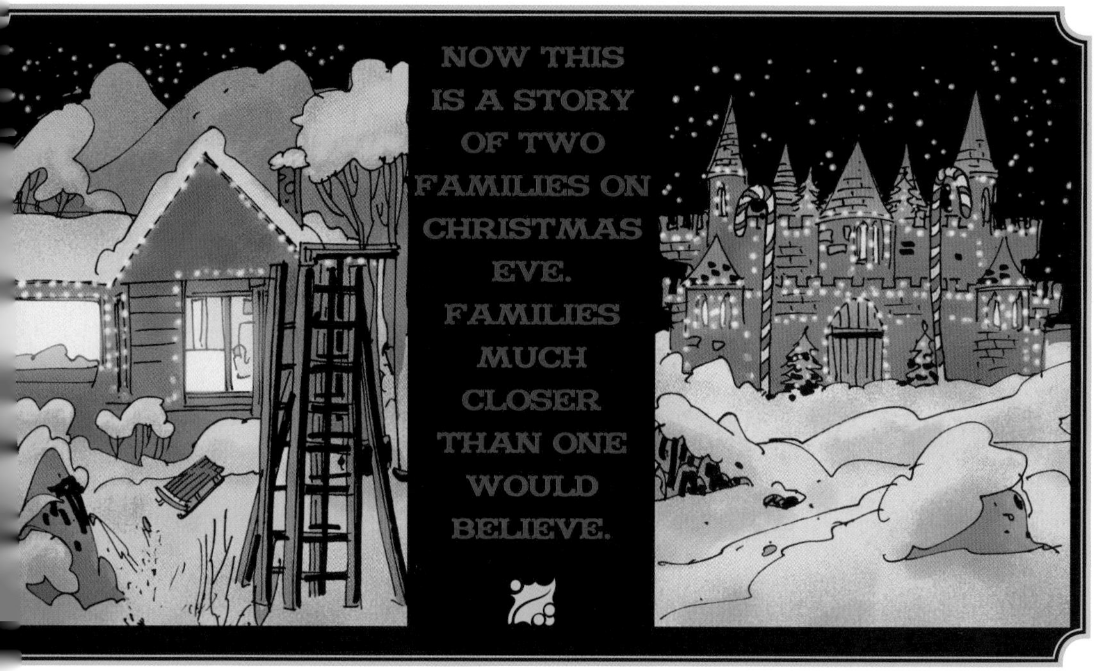
NOW THIS IS A STORY OF TWO FAMILIES ON CHRISTMAS EVE. FAMILIES MUCH CLOSER THAN ONE WOULD BELIEVE.

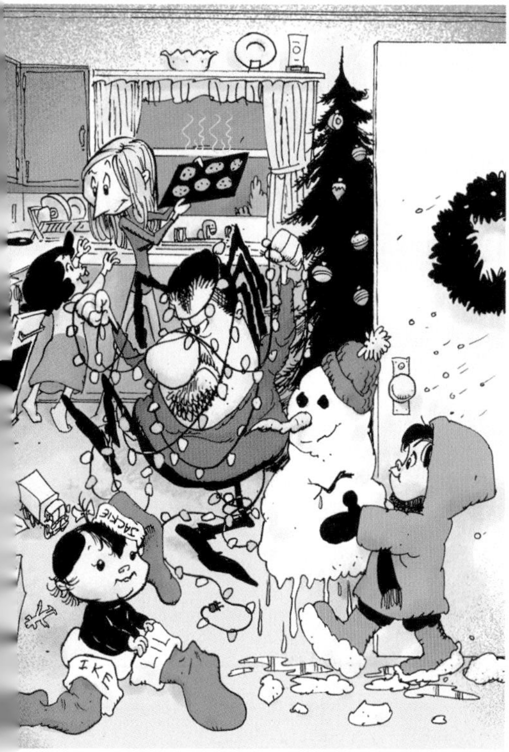
JACKIE
IKE

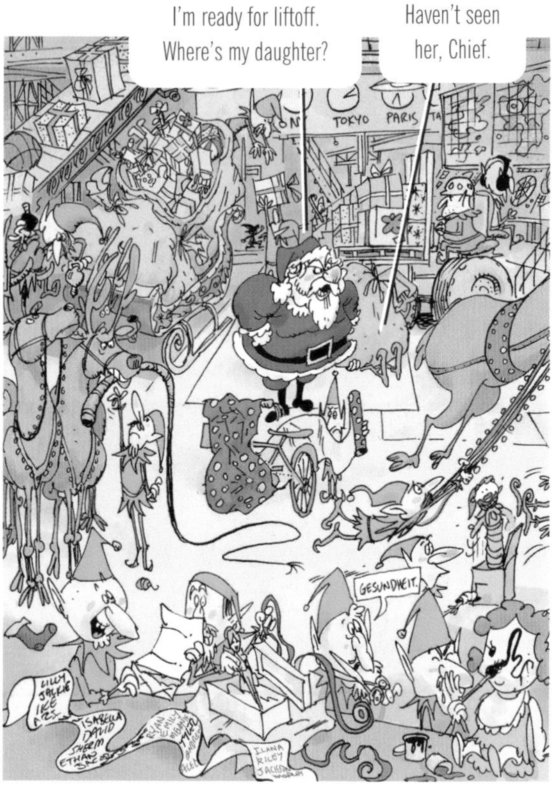
I'm ready for liftoff. Where's my daughter?
Haven't seen her, Chief.
TOKYO
PARIS
GESUNDHEIT.

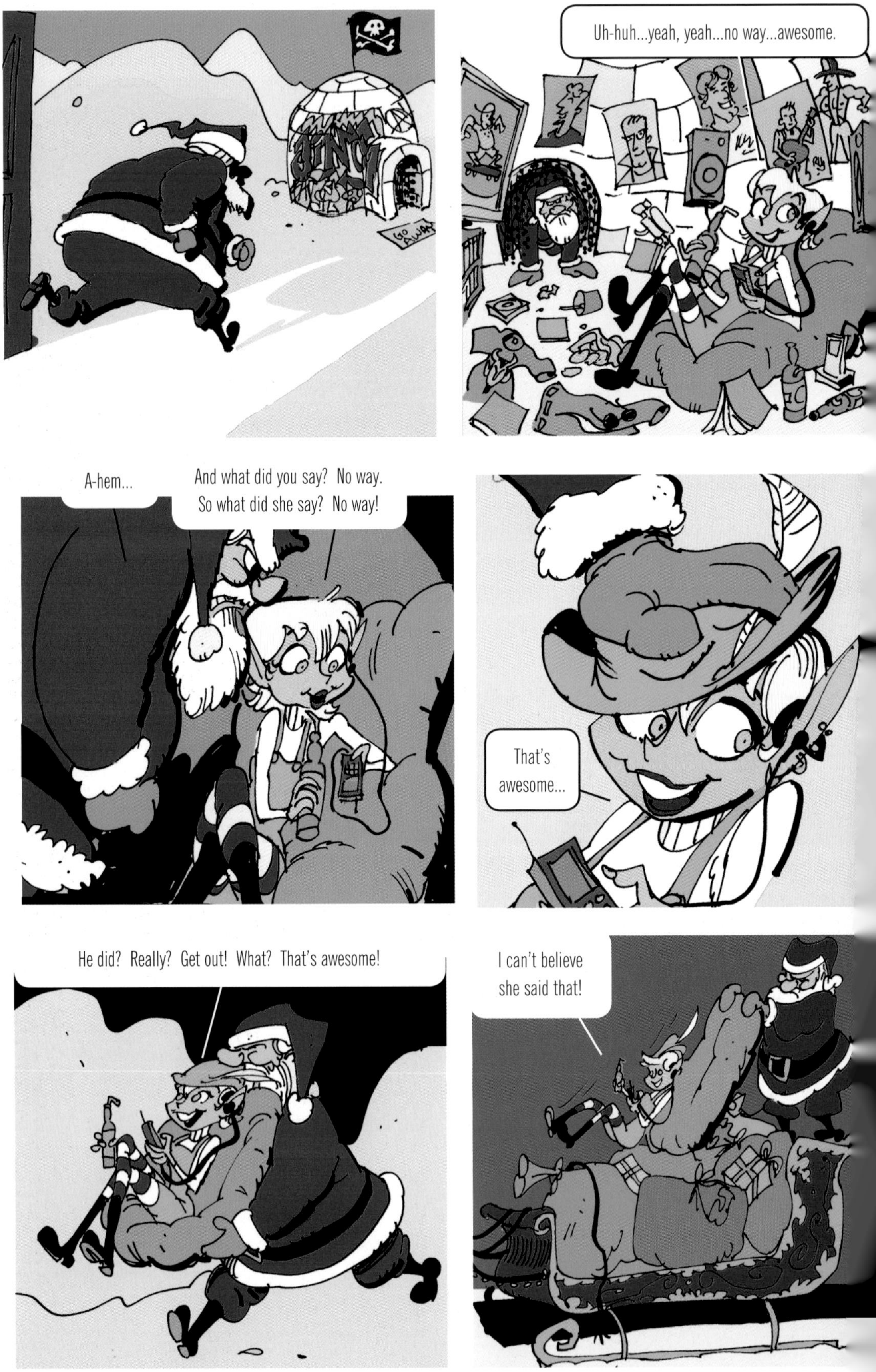
GO AWAY
Uh-huh...yeah, yeah...no way...awesome.
A-hem...
And what did you say? No way.
So what did she say? No way!
That's
awesome...
He did? Really? Get out! What? That's awesome!
I can't believe
she said that!

Hey!

Got a little holiday going on here called "Christmas." You may have heard of it.

Unfortunately.

I love help t, but sick, I ave ework, ave a te...

Heard it before. Didn't buy it then. Buckle up.

SNAP!

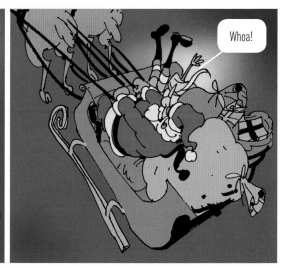

Whoa!

Okay!

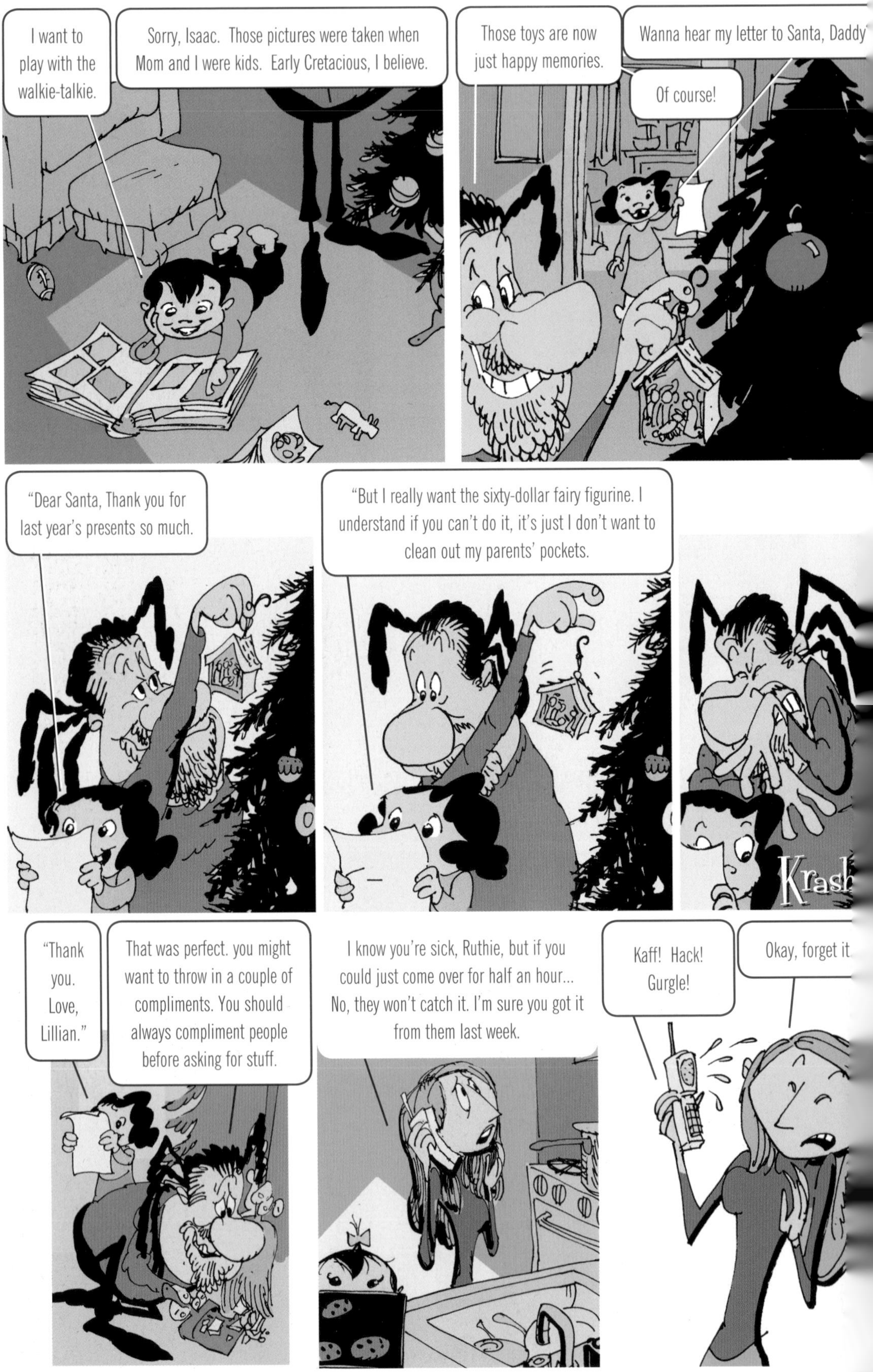
I want to play with the walkie-talkie.
Sorry, Isaac. Those pictures were taken when Mom and I were kids. Early Cretacious, I believe.
Those toys are now just happy memories.
Wanna hear my letter to Santa, Daddy
Of course!
"Dear Santa, Thank you for last year's presents so much.
"But I really want the sixty-dollar fairy figurine. I understand if you can't do it, it's just I don't want to clean out my parents' pockets.
Krash
"Thank you. Love, Lillian."
That was perfect. you might want to throw in a couple of compliments. You should always compliment people before asking for stuff.
I know you're sick, Ruthie, but if you could just come over for half an hour... No, they won't catch it. I'm sure you got it from them last week.
Kaff! Hack! Gurgle!
Okay, forget it

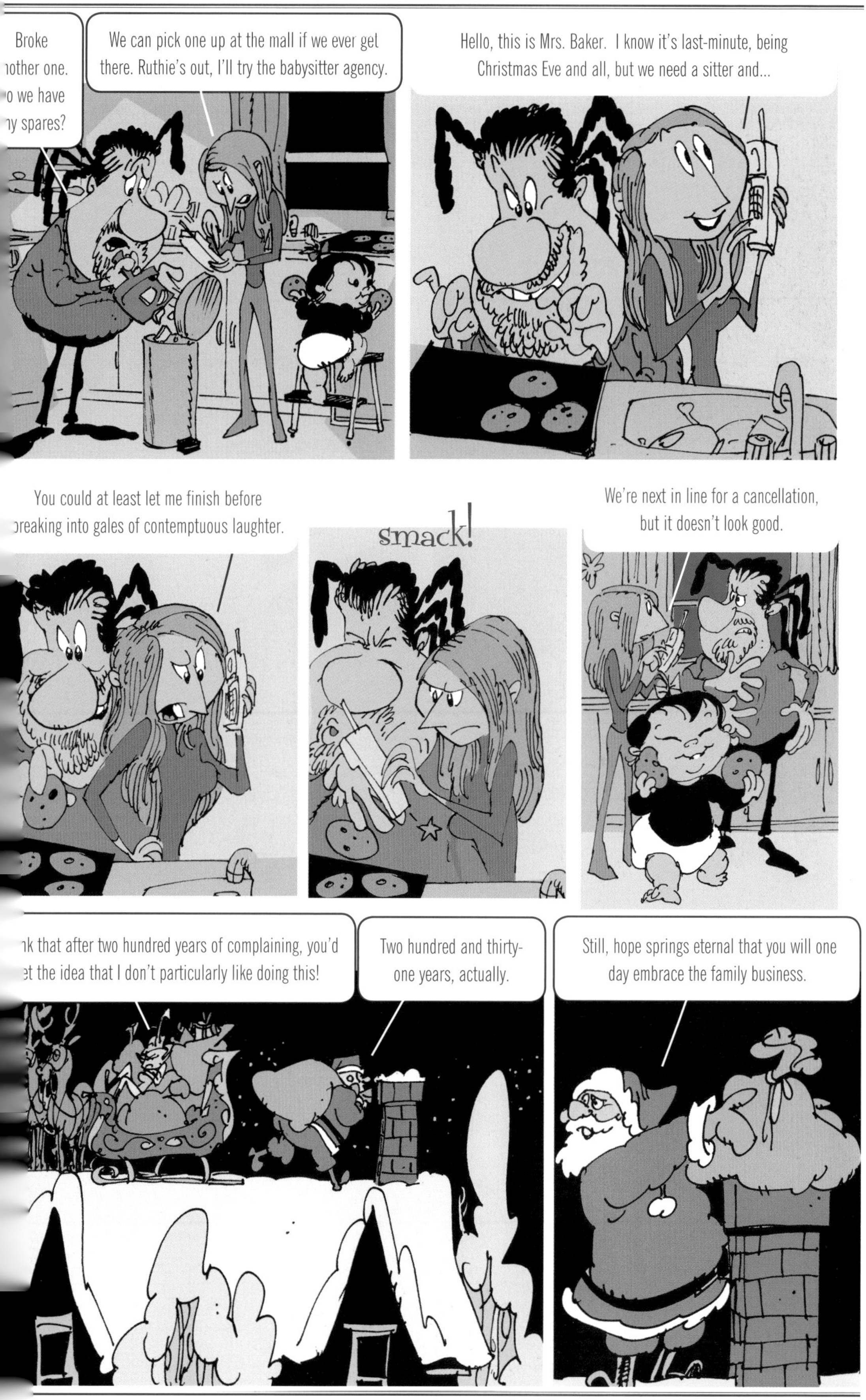
Broke
nother one.
o we have
ny spares?
We can pick one up at the mall if we ever get there. Ruthie's out, I'll try the babysitter agency.
Hello, this is Mrs. Baker. I know it's last-minute, being Christmas Eve and all, but we need a sitter and...
You could at least let me finish before
reaking into gales of contemptuous laughter.
smack!
We're next in line for a cancellation, but it doesn't look good.
nk that after two hundred years of complaining, you'd
et the idea that I don't particularly like doing this!
Two hundred and thirty-one years, actually.
Still, hope springs eternal that you will one day embrace the family business.

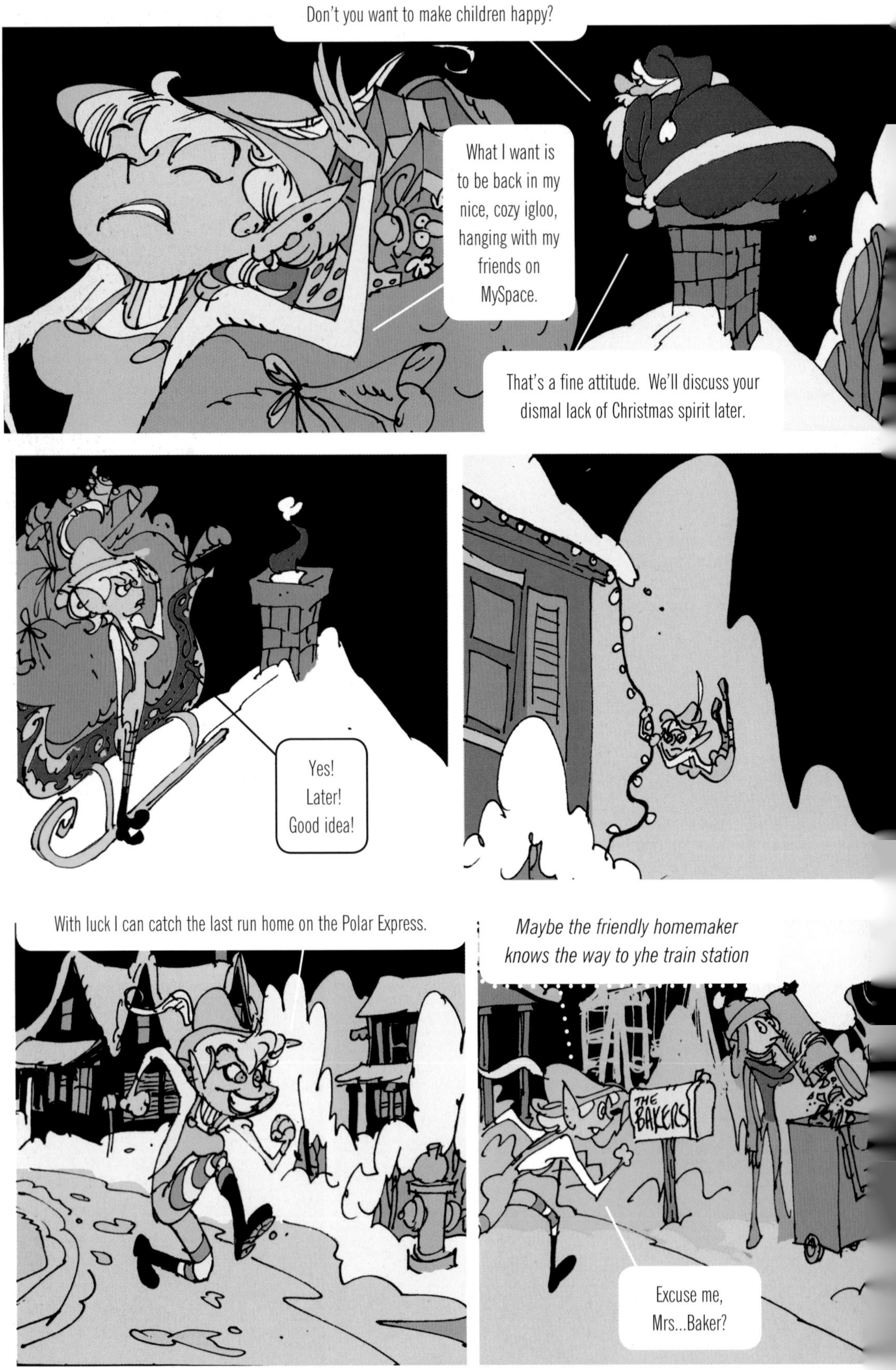
Don't you want to make children happy?
What I want is to be back in my nice, cozy igloo, hanging with my friends on MySpace.
That's a fine attitude. We'll discuss your dismal lack of Christmas spirit later.
Yes! Later! Good idea!
With luck I can catch the last run home on the Polar Express.
Maybe the friendly homemaker knows the way to yhe train station
THE BAKERS
Excuse me, Mrs...Baker?

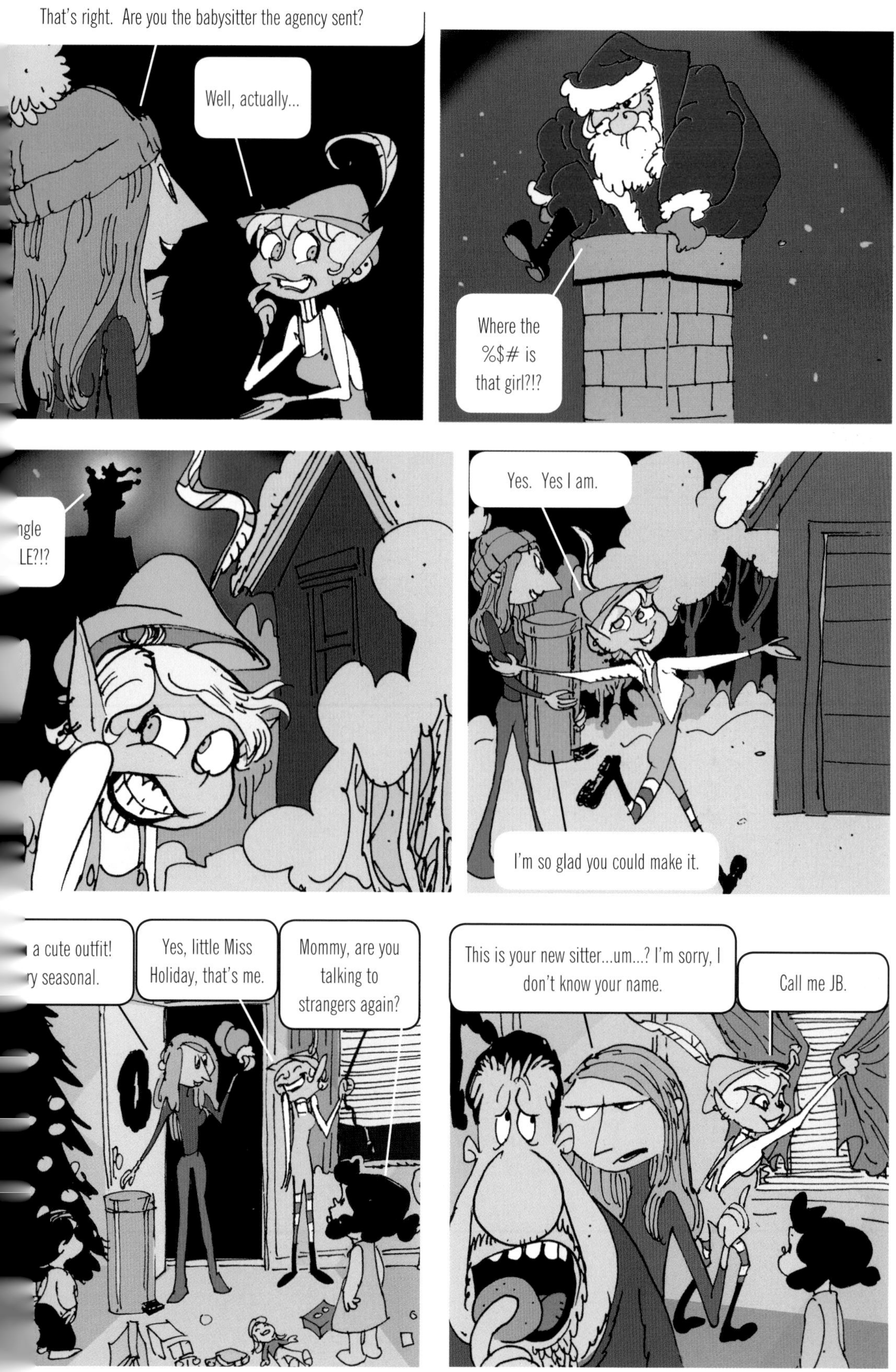
That's right. Are you the babysitter the agency sent?
Well, actually...
Where the %$# is that girl?!?
ngle
LE?!?
Yes. Yes I am.
I'm so glad you could make it.
a cute outfit!
ry seasonal.
Yes, little Miss Holiday, that's me.
Mommy, are you talking to strangers again?
This is your new sitter...um...? I'm sorry, I don't know your name.
Call me JB.

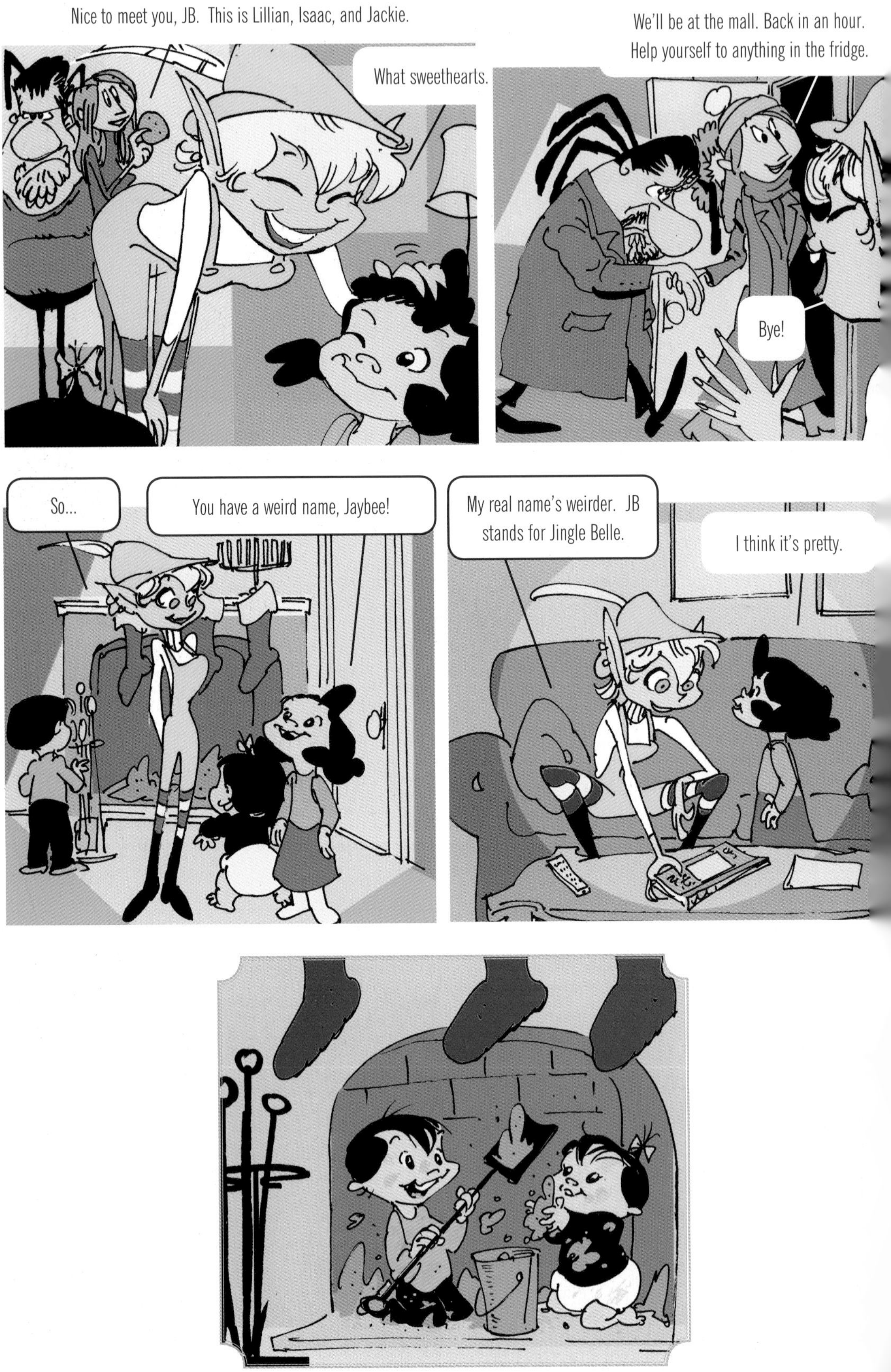

Nice to meet you, JB. This is Lillian, Isaac, and Jackie.
What sweethearts.
We'll be at the mall. Back in an hour. Help yourself to anything in the fridge.
Bye!
So...
You have a weird name, Jaybee!
My real name's weirder. JB stands for Jingle Belle.
I think it's pretty.

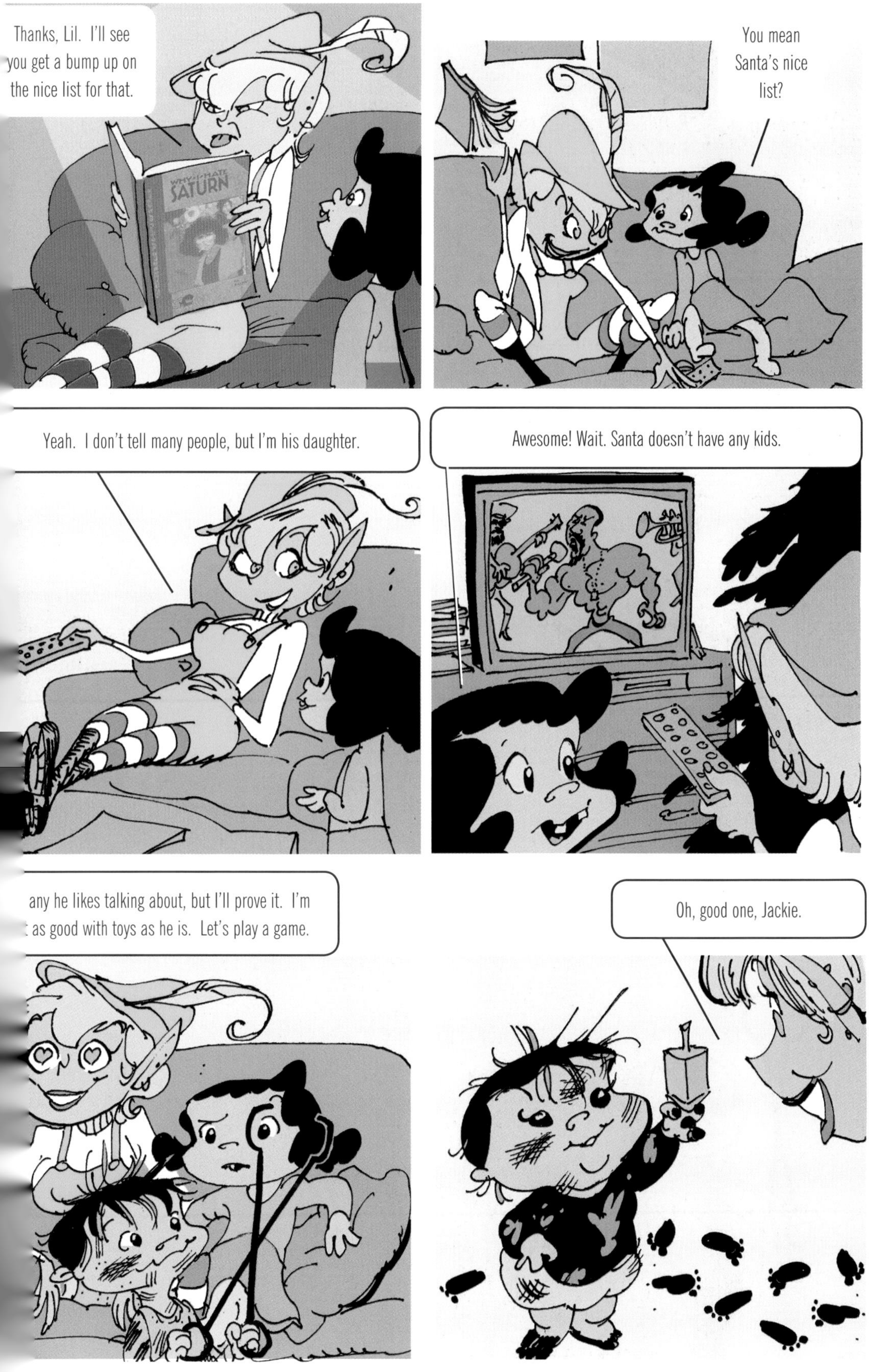
Thanks, Lil. I'll see you get a bump up on the nice list for that.
SATURN
You mean Santa's nice list?
Yeah. I don't tell many people, but I'm his daughter.
Awesome! Wait. Santa doesn't have any kids.
any he likes talking about, but I'll prove it. I'm
as good with toys as he is. Let's play a game.
Oh, good one, Jackie.

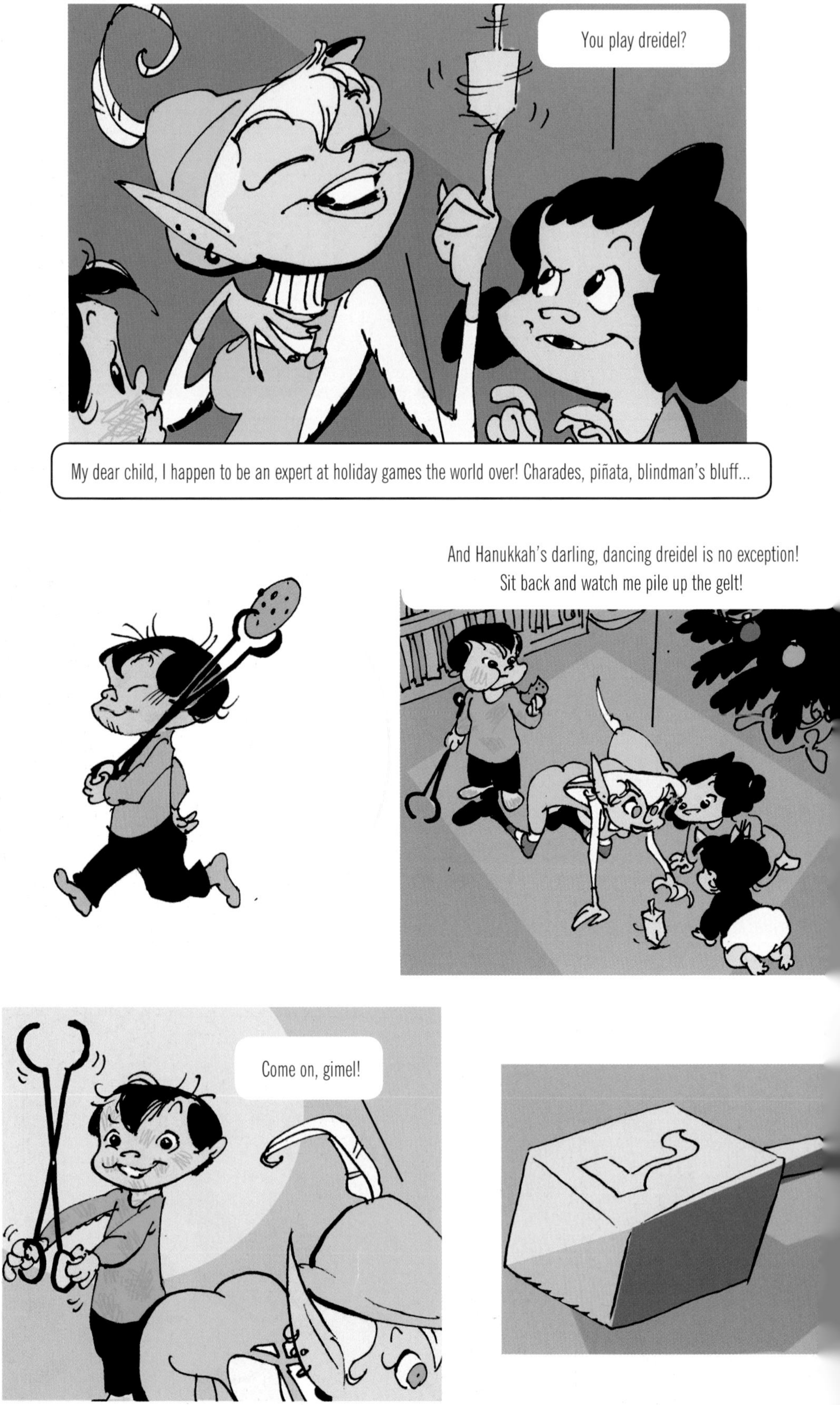
You play dreidel?
My dear child, I happen to be an expert at holiday games the world over! Charades, piñata, blindman's bluff...
And Hanukkah's darling, dancing dreidel is no exception! Sit back and watch me pile up the gelt!
Come on, gimel!

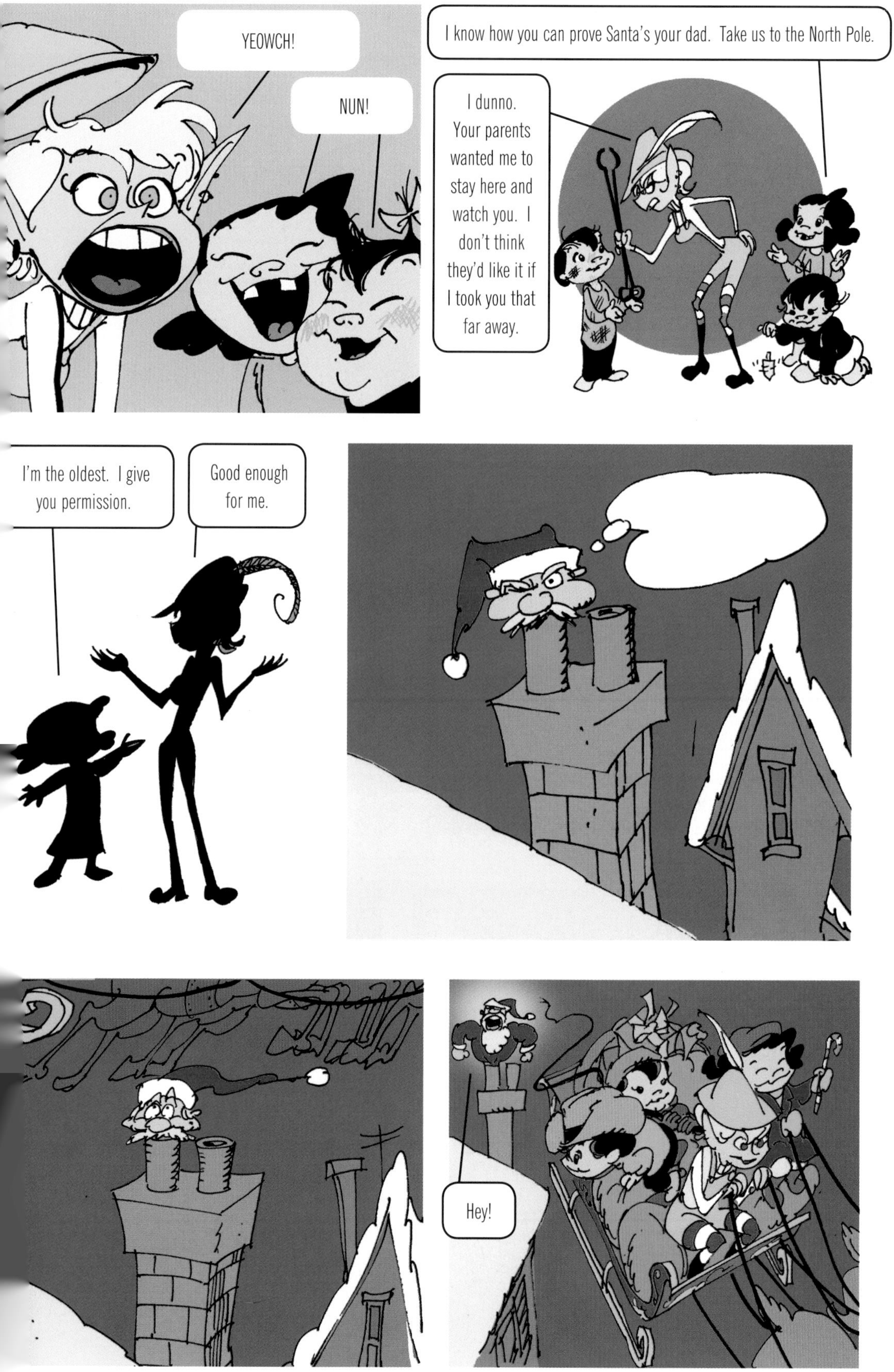
YEOWCH!
NUN!
I know how you can prove Santa's your dad. Take us to the North Pole.
I dunno. Your parents wanted me to stay here and watch you. I don't think they'd like it if I took you that far away.
I'm the oldest. I give you permission.
Good enough for me.
Hey!

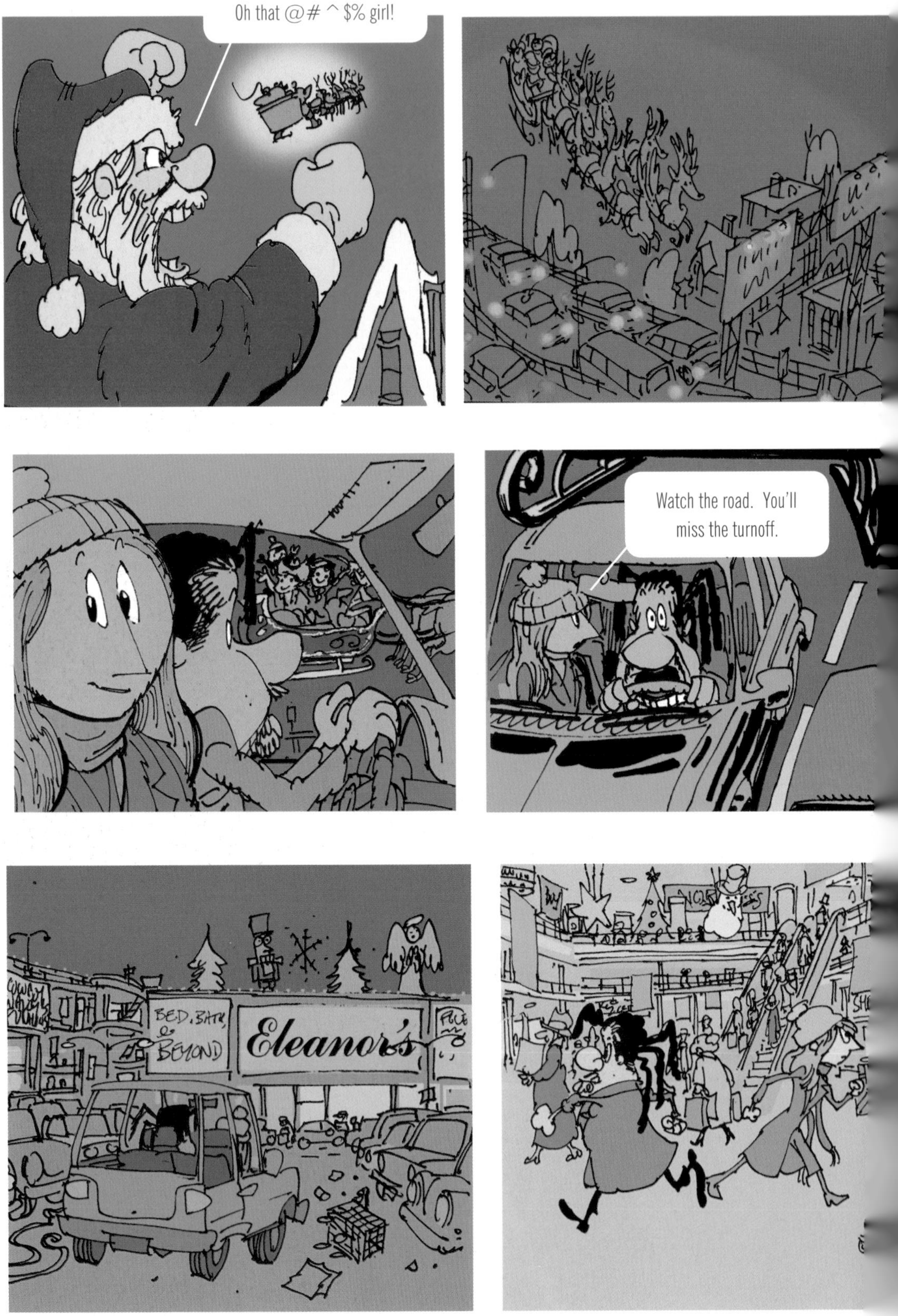
Oh that @# ^ $% girl!
Watch the road. You'll miss the turnoff.
BED, BATH, & BEYOND
Eleanor's

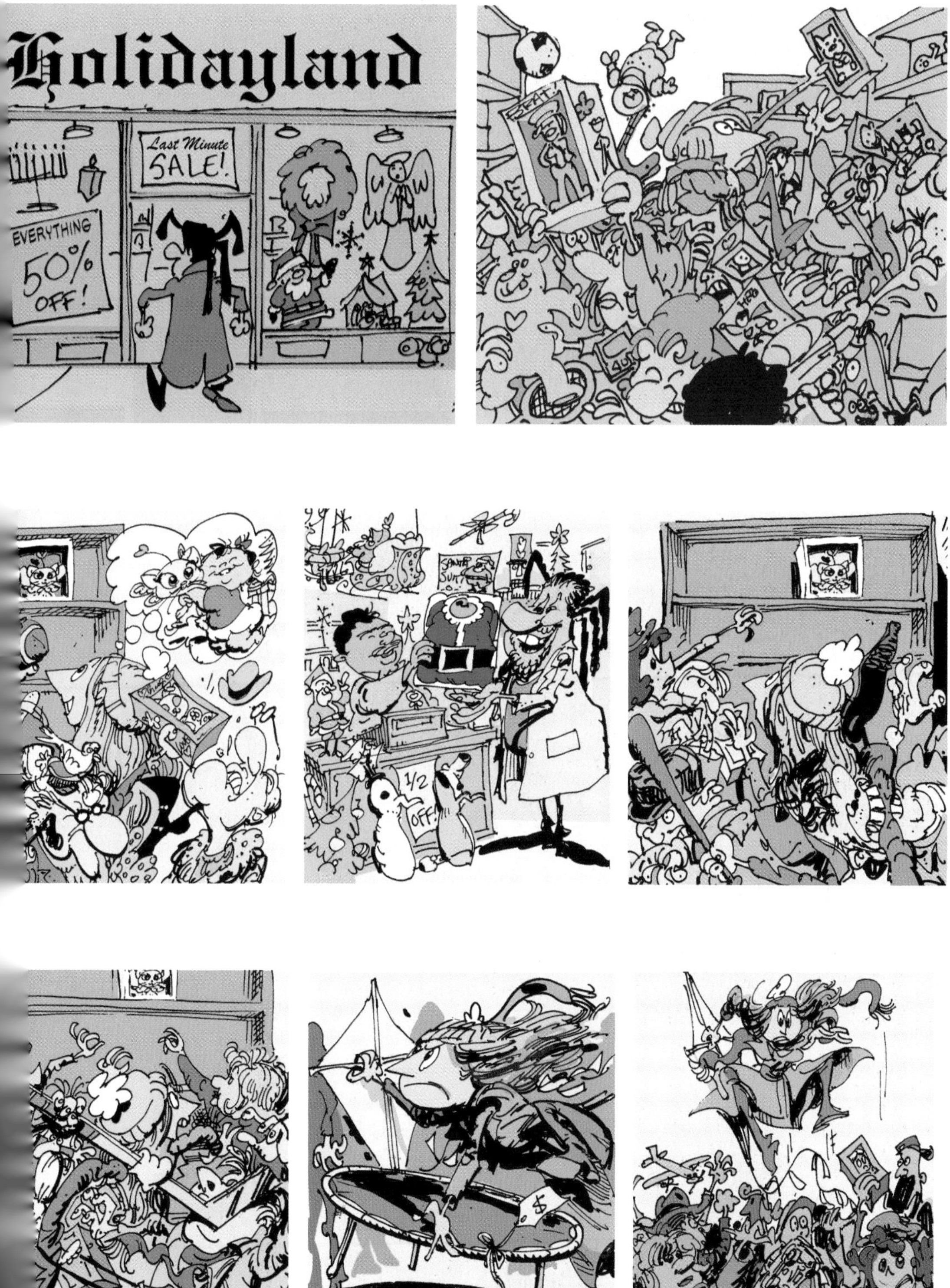
Holidayland
Last Minute SALE!
EVERYTHING 50% OFF!
1/2 OFF

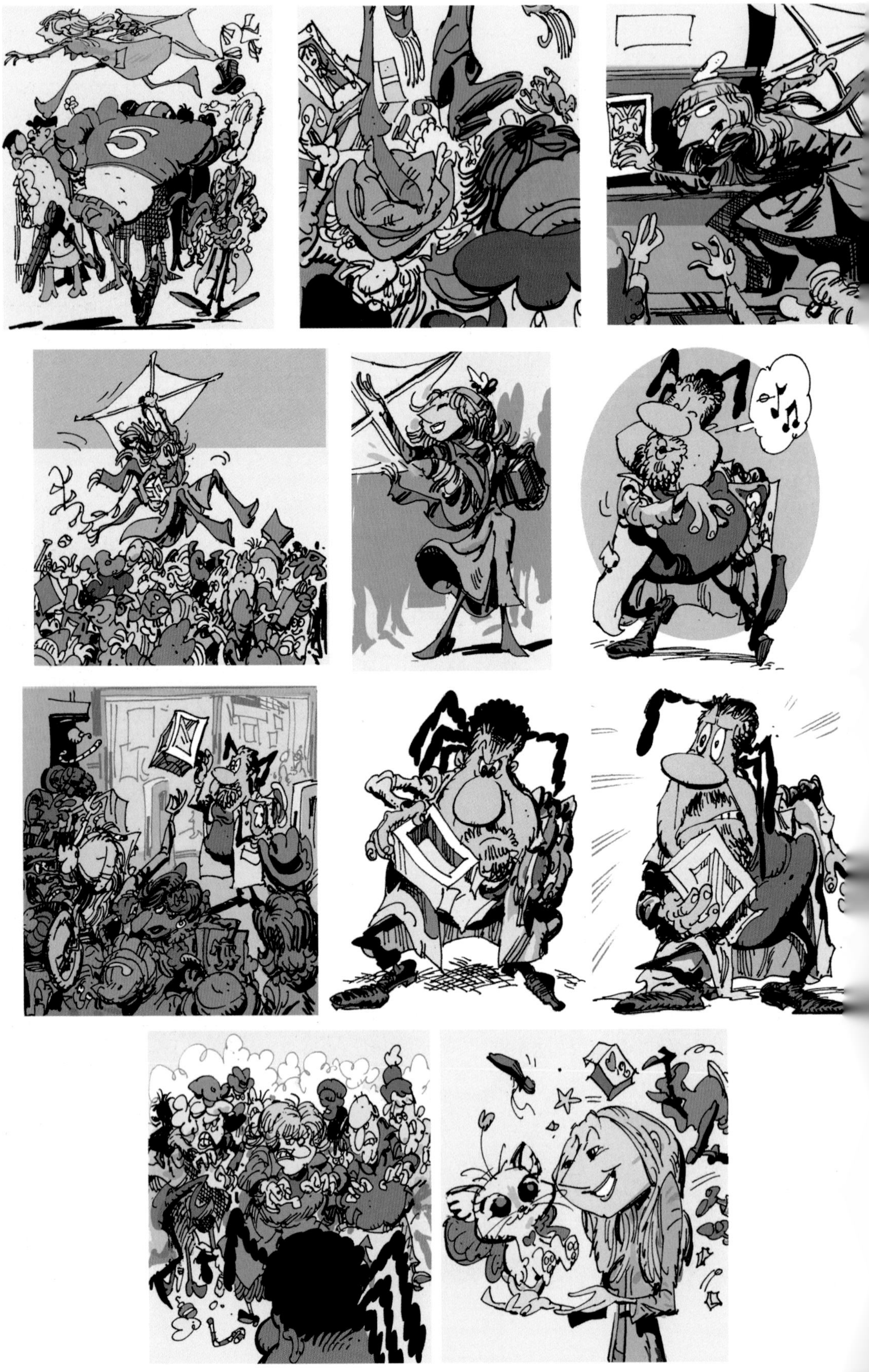

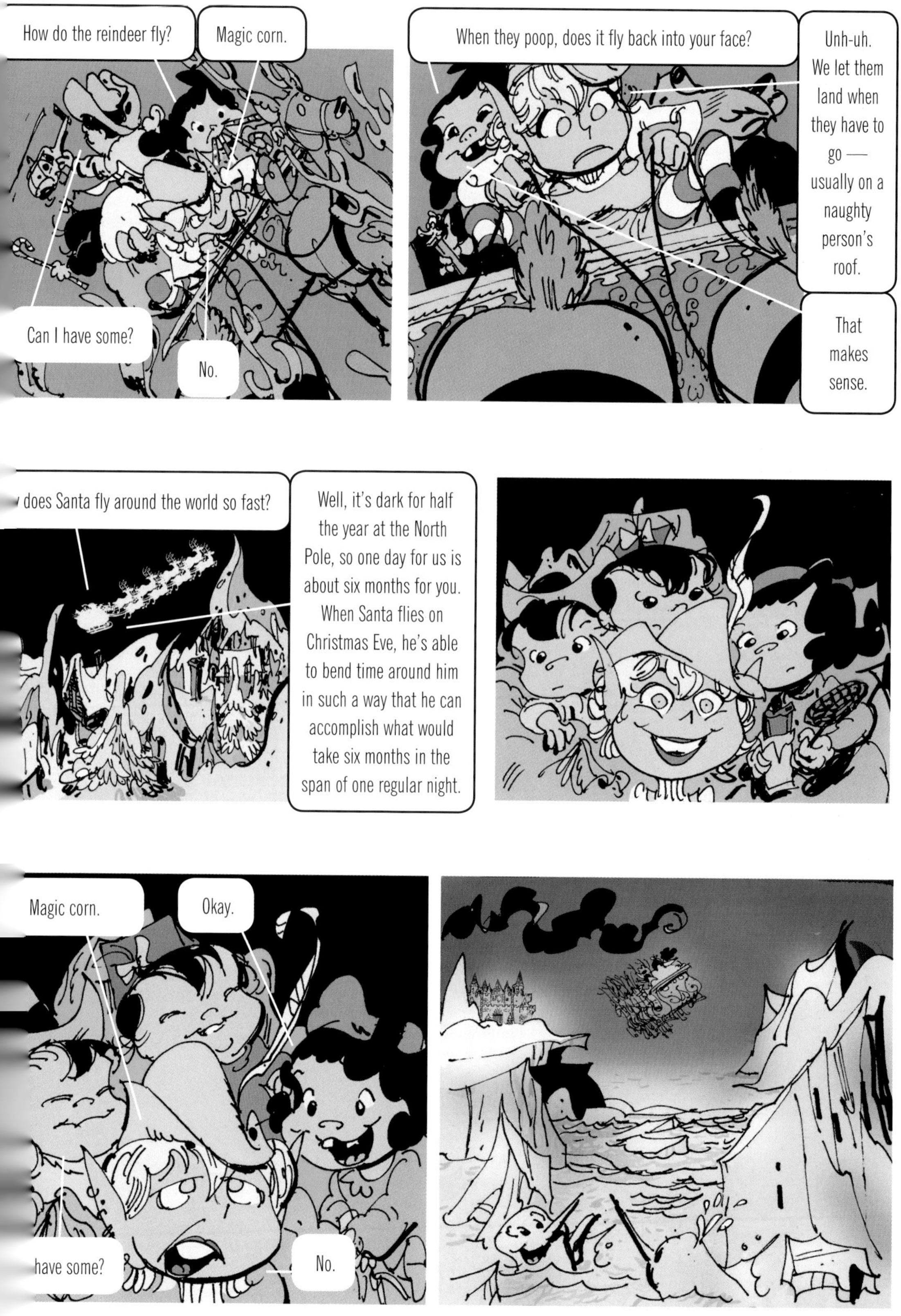
How do the reindeer fly?
Magic corn.
Can I have some?
No.
When they poop, does it fly back into your face?
Unh-uh. We let them land when they have to go — usually on a naughty person's roof.
That makes sense.
does Santa fly around the world so fast?
Well, it's dark for half the year at the North Pole, so one day for us is about six months for you. When Santa flies on Christmas Eve, he's able to bend time around him in such a way that he can accomplish what would take six months in the span of one regular night.
Magic corn.
Okay.
have some?
No.

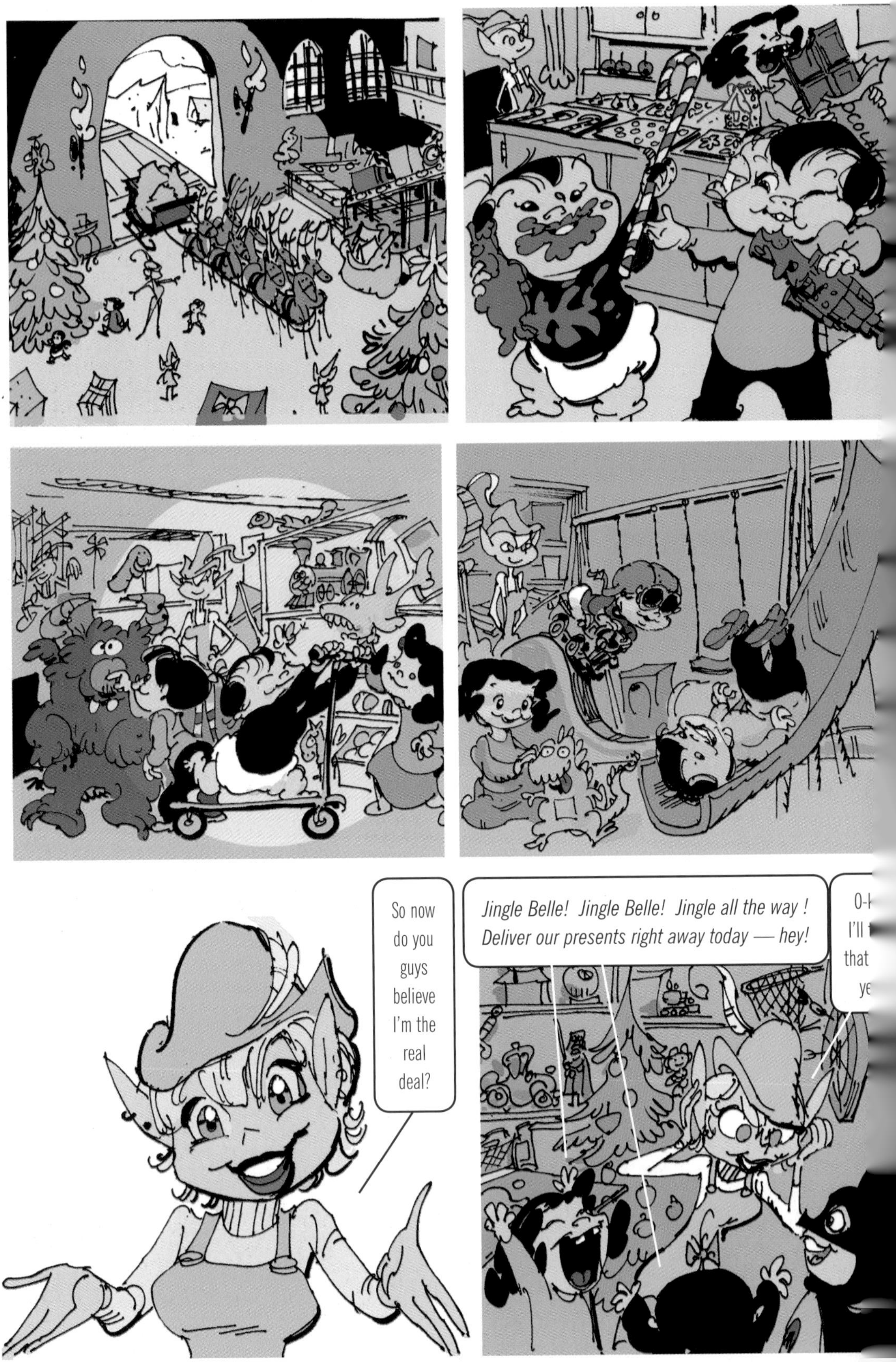
So now do you guys believe I'm the real deal?
Jingle Belle! Jingle Belle! Jingle all the way! Deliver our presents right away today — hey!

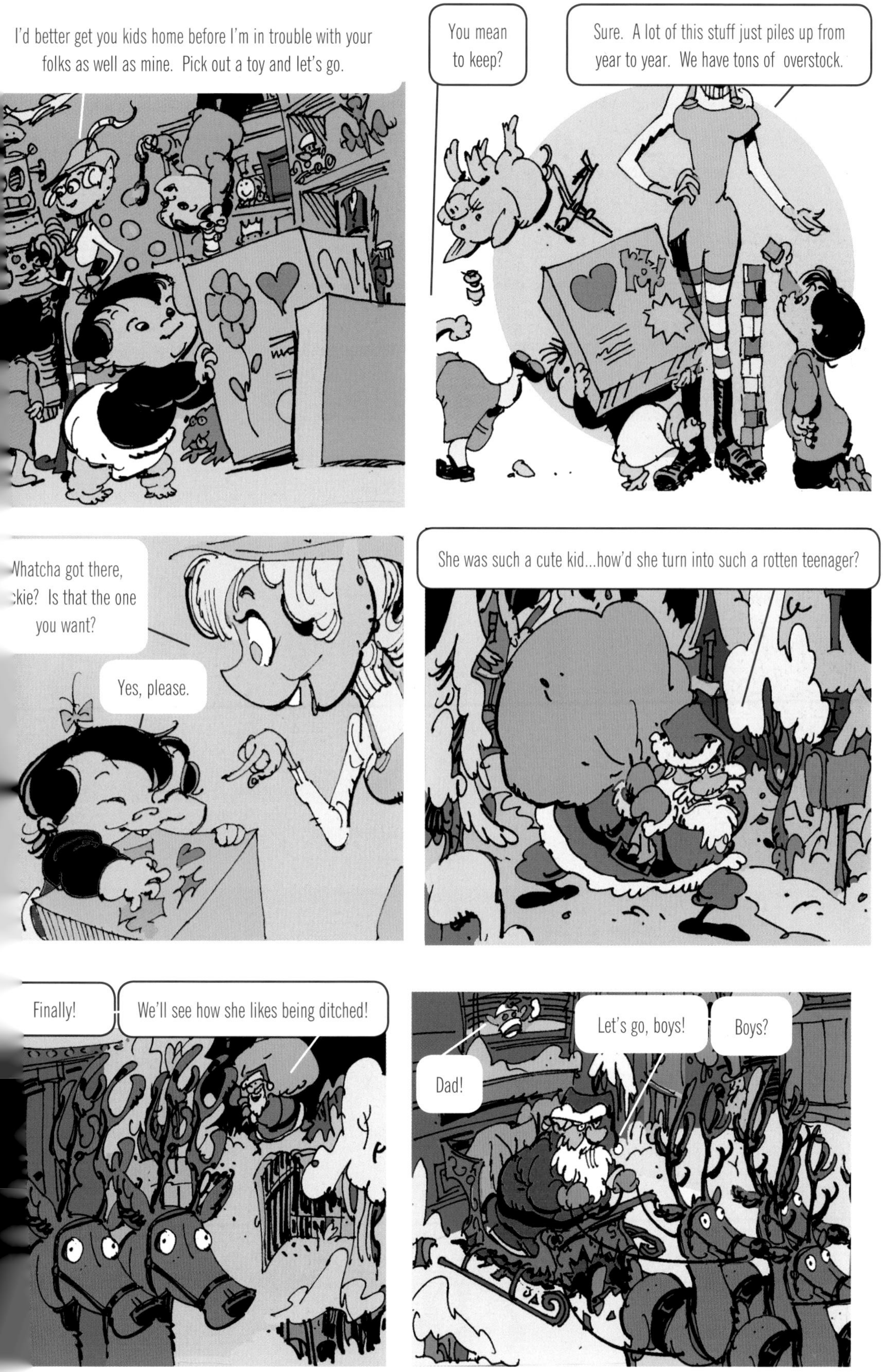
I'd better get you kids home before I'm in trouble with your folks as well as mine. Pick out a toy and let's go.
You mean to keep?
Sure. A lot of this stuff just piles up from year to year. We have tons of overstock.
Whatcha got there, ckie? Is that the one you want?
Yes, please.
She was such a cute kid...how'd she turn into such a rotten teenager?
Finally!
We'll see how she likes being ditched!
Let's go, boys!
Boys?
Dad!

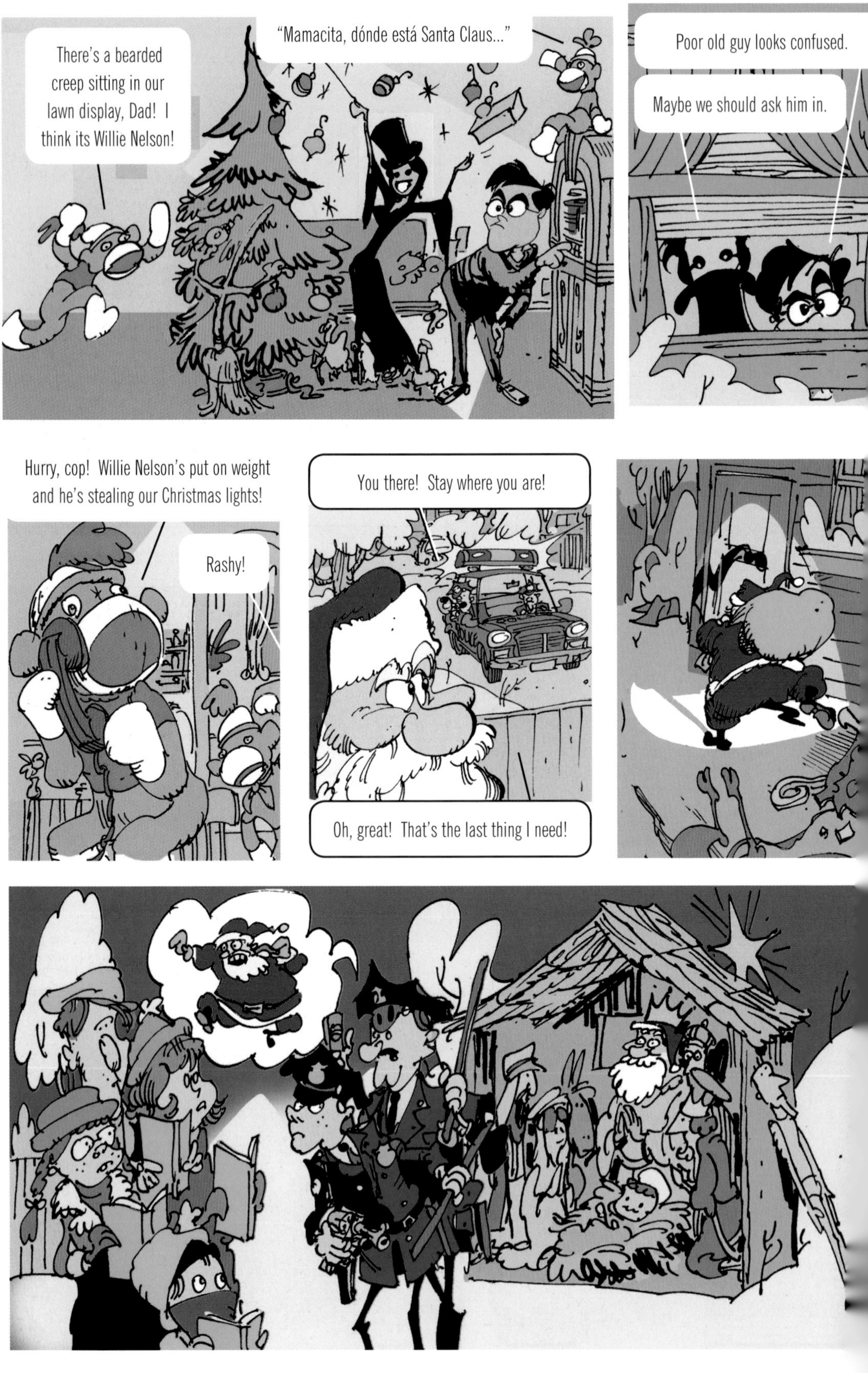
There's a bearded creep sitting in our lawn display, Dad! I think its Willie Nelson!
"Mamacita, dónde está Santa Claus..."
Poor old guy looks confused.
Maybe we should ask him in.
Hurry, cop! Willie Nelson's put on weight and he's stealing our Christmas lights!
Rashy!
You there! Stay where you are!
Oh, great! That's the last thing I need!

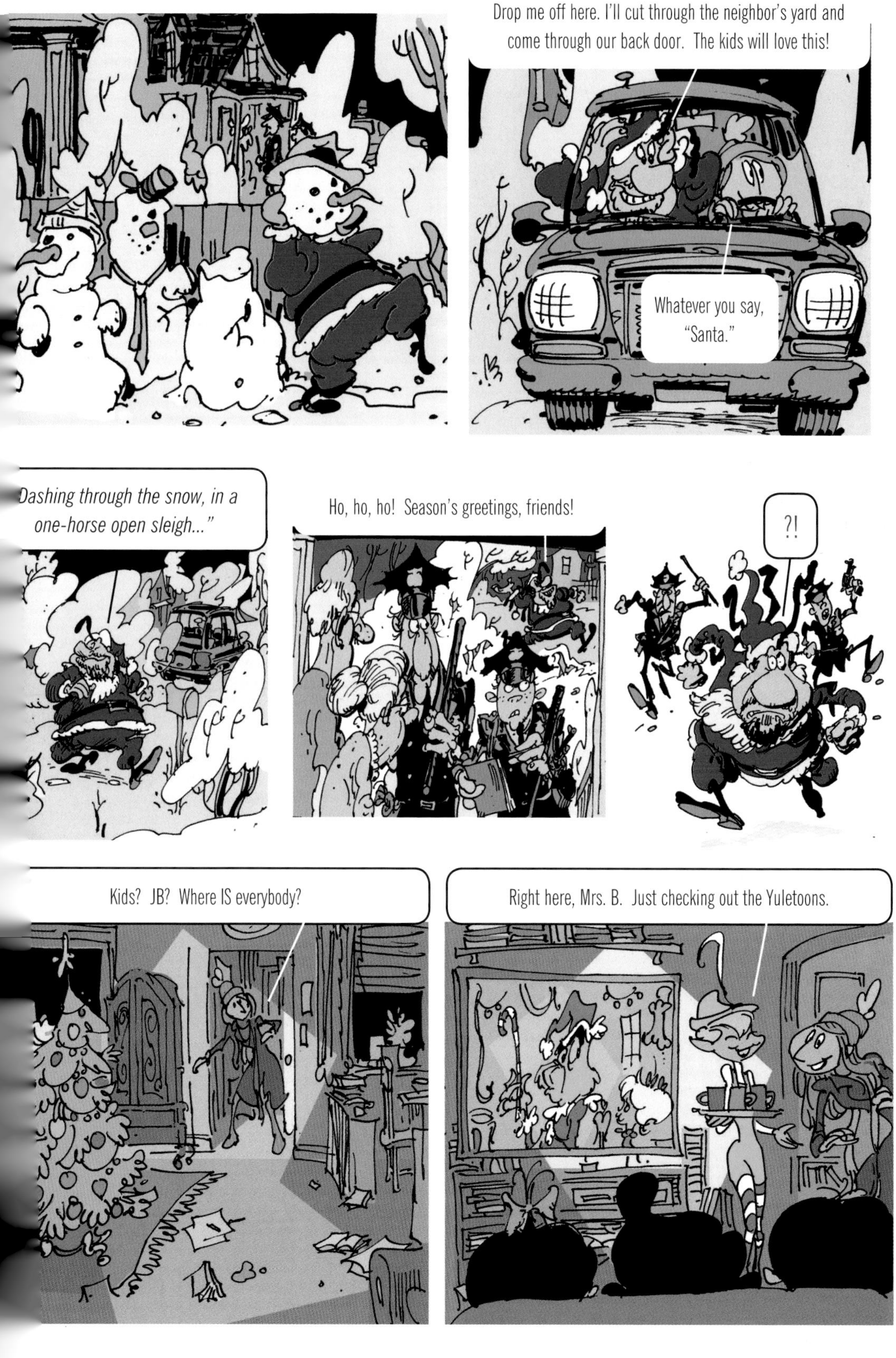
Drop me off here. I'll cut through the neighbor's yard and come through our back door. The kids will love this!
Whatever you say, "Santa."
"Dashing through the snow, in a one-horse open sleigh..."
Ho, ho, ho! Season's greetings, friends!
?!
Kids? JB? Where IS everybody?
Right here, Mrs. B. Just checking out the Yuletoons.

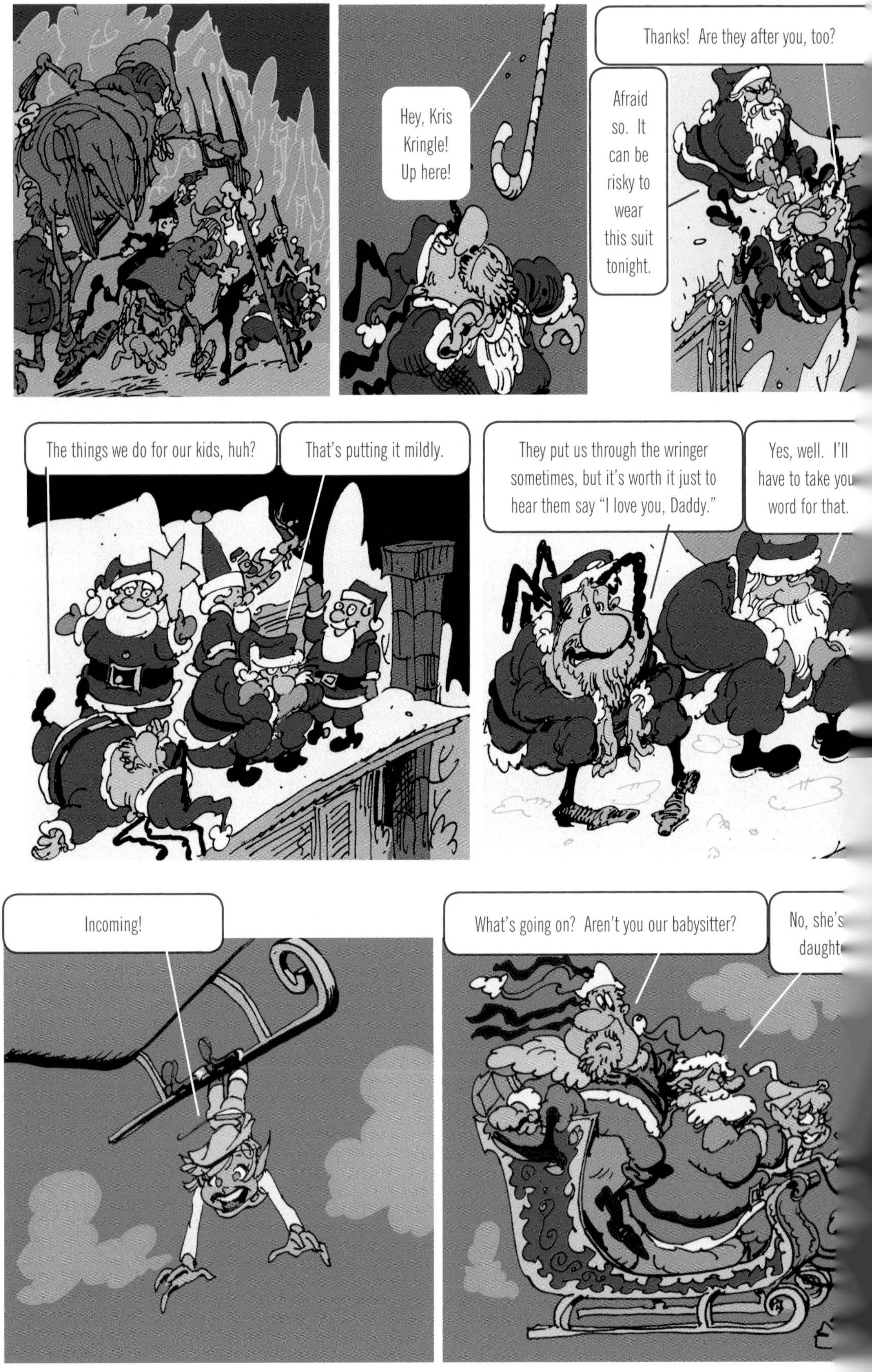
Hey, Kris Kringle! Up here!
Thanks! Are they after you, too?
Afraid so. It can be risky to wear this suit tonight.
The things we do for our kids, huh?
That's putting it mildly.
They put us through the wringer sometimes, but it's worth it just to hear them say "I love you, Daddy."
Yes, well. I'll have to take you
word for that.
Incoming!
What's going on? Aren't you our babysitter?
No, she's
daught

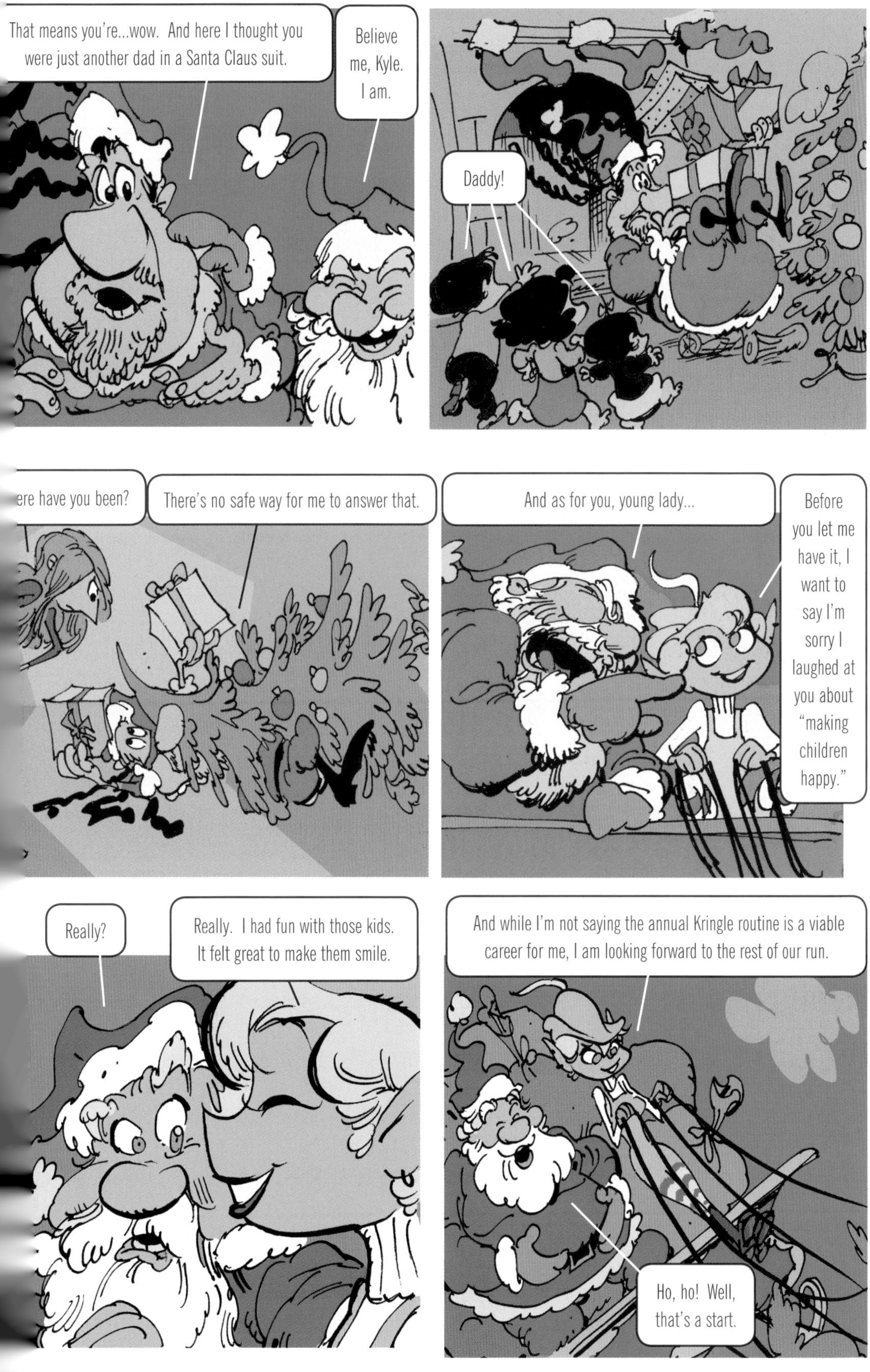
That means you're...wow. And here I thought you were just another dad in a Santa Claus suit.
Believe me, Kyle. I am.
Daddy!
ere have you been?
There's no safe way for me to answer that.
And as for you, young lady...
Before you let me have it, I want to say I'm sorry I laughed at you about "making children happy."
Really?
Really. I had fun with those kids. It felt great to make them smile.
And while I'm not saying the annual Kringle routine is a viable career for me, I am looking forward to the rest of our run.
Ho, ho! Well, that's a start.

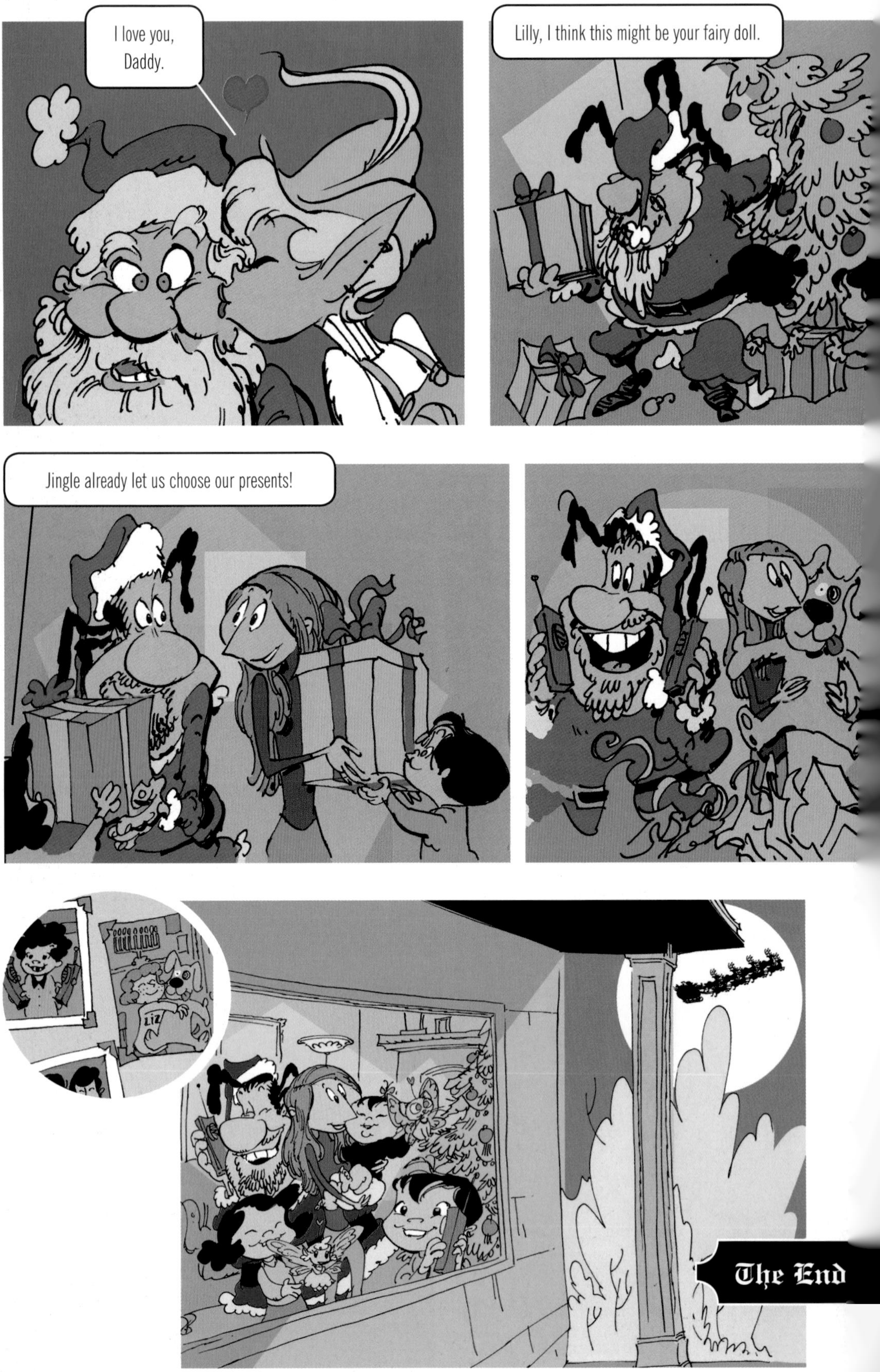
I love you, Daddy.
Lilly, I think this might be your fairy doll.
Jingle already let us choose our presents!
The End

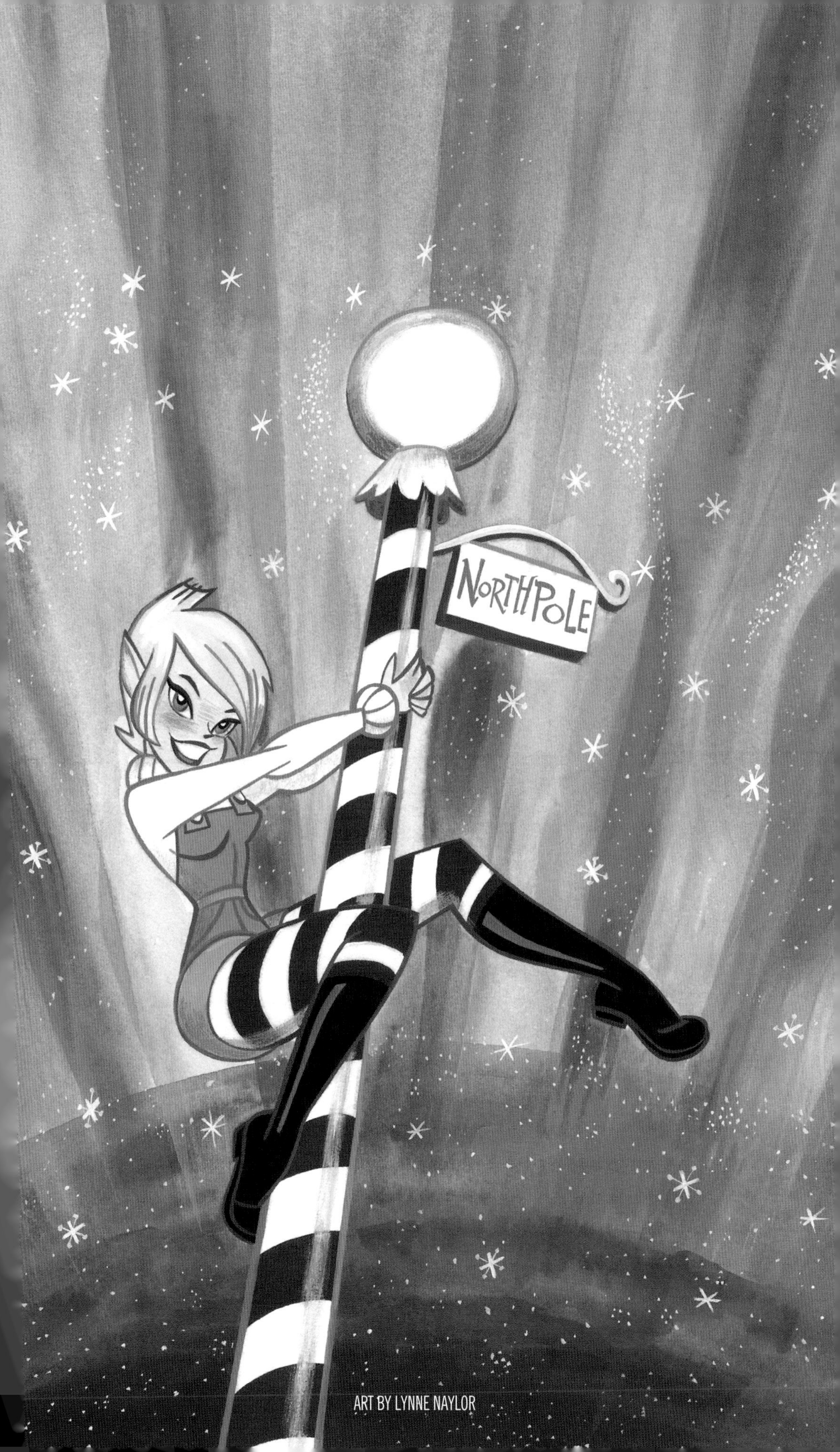
NORTH POLE

ART BY LYNNE NAYLOR

The Fight Before Christmas

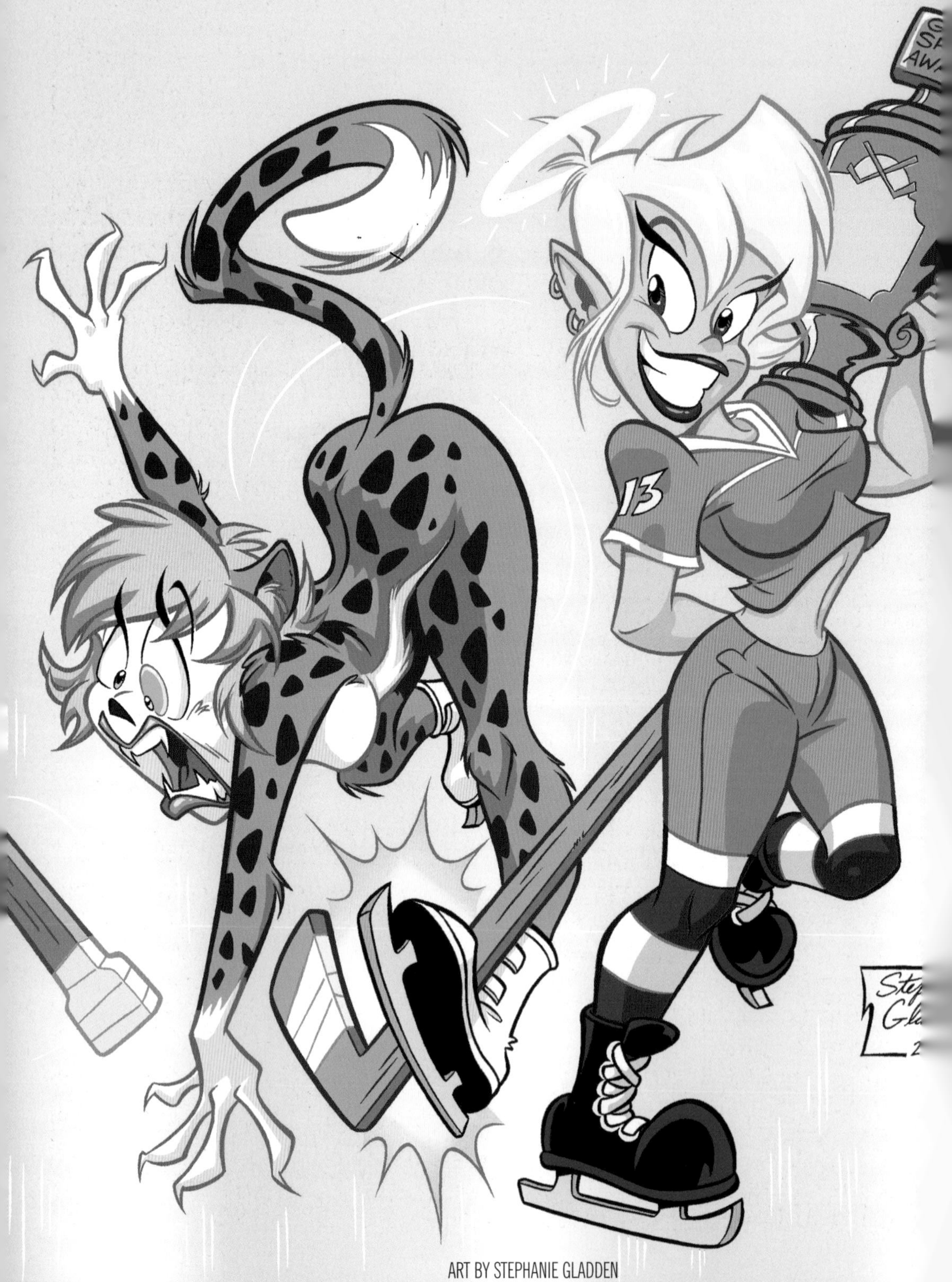
13

ART BY STEPHANIE GLADDEN

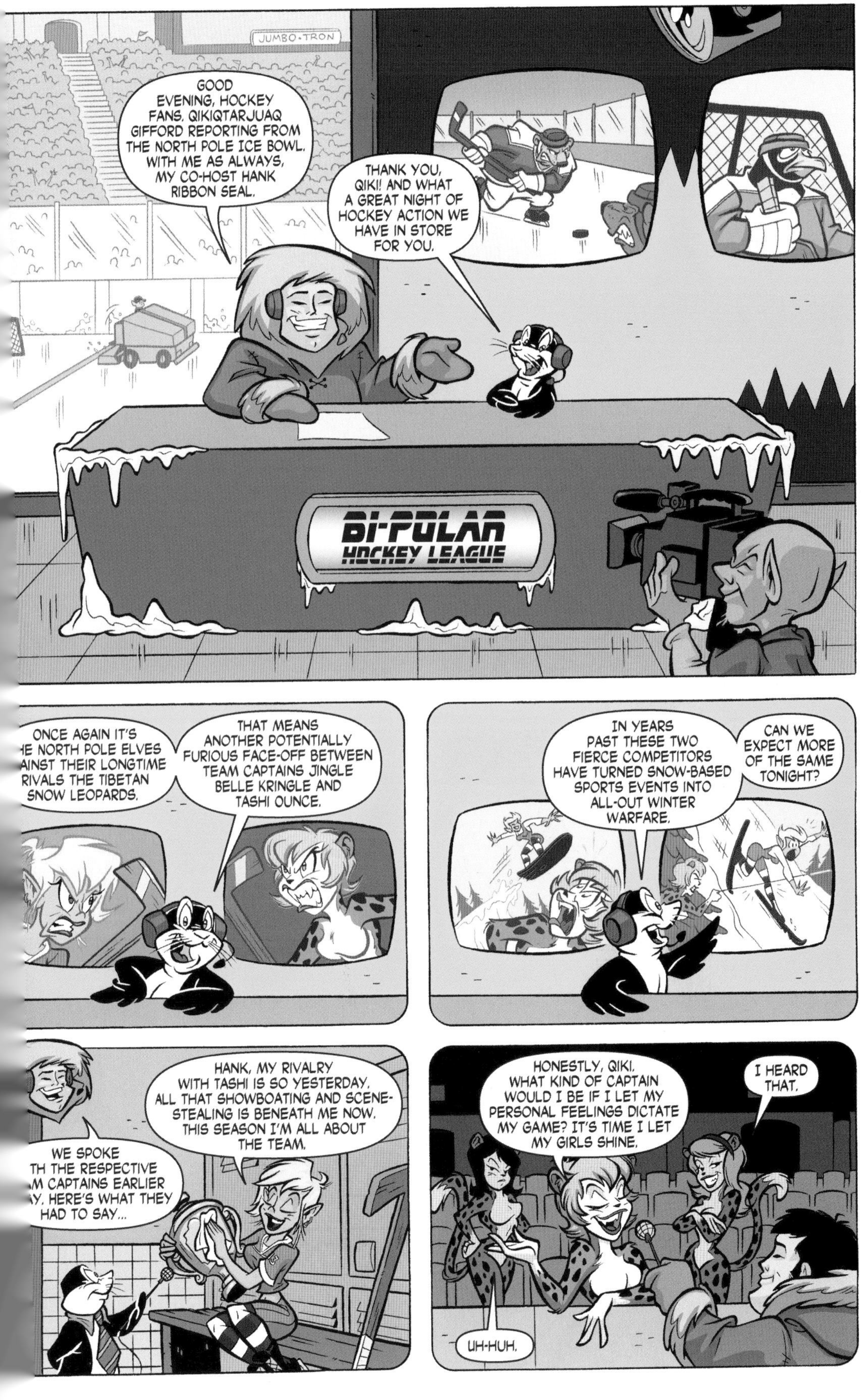
JUMBO-TRON
GOOD EVENING, HOCKEY FANS, QIKIQTARJUAQ GIFFORD REPORTING FROM THE NORTH POLE ICE BOWL. WITH ME AS ALWAYS, MY CO-HOST HANK RIBBON SEAL.
THANK YOU, QIKI! AND WHAT A GREAT NIGHT OF HOCKEY ACTION WE HAVE IN STORE FOR YOU.
BI-POLAR HOCKEY LEAGUE
ONCE AGAIN IT'S HE NORTH POLE ELVES AINST THEIR LONGTIME RIVALS THE TIBETAN SNOW LEOPARDS.
THAT MEANS ANOTHER POTENTIALLY FURIOUS FACE-OFF BETWEEN TEAM CAPTAINS JINGLE BELLE KRINGLE AND TASHI OUNCE.
IN YEARS PAST THESE TWO FIERCE COMPETITORS HAVE TURNED SNOW-BASED SPORTS EVENTS INTO ALL-OUT WINTER WARFARE.
CAN WE EXPECT MORE OF THE SAME TONIGHT?
WE SPOKE TH THE RESPECTIVE M CAPTAINS EARLIER Y. HERE'S WHAT THEY HAD TO SAY...
HANK, MY RIVALRY WITH TASHI IS SO YESTERDAY. ALL THAT SHOWBOATING AND SCENE-STEALING IS BENEATH ME NOW. THIS SEASON I'M ALL ABOUT THE TEAM.
HONESTLY, QIKI, WHAT KIND OF CAPTAIN WOULD I BE IF I LET MY PERSONAL FEELINGS DICTATE MY GAME? IT'S TIME I LET MY GIRLS SHINE.
I HEARD THAT.
UH-HUH.

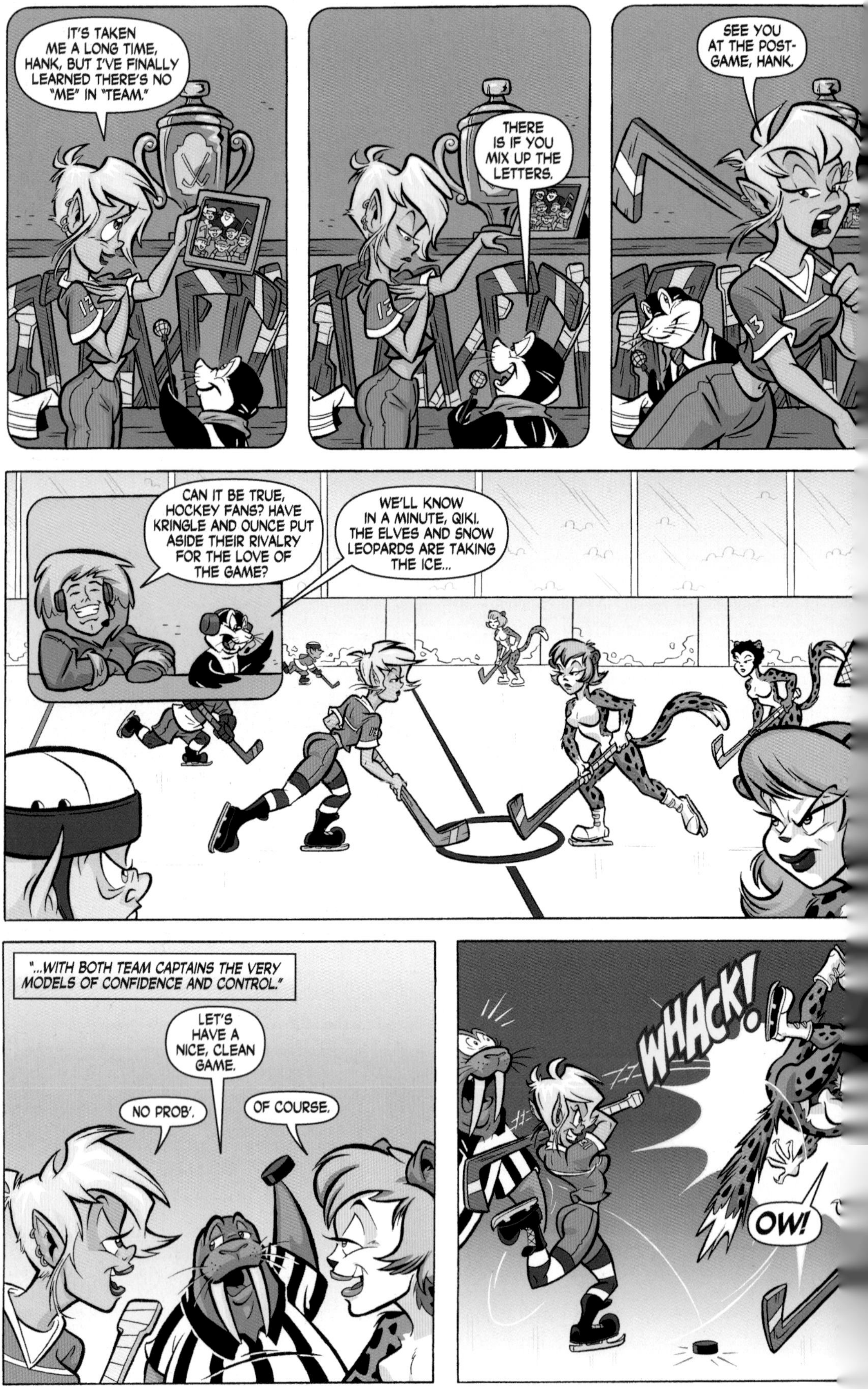
IT'S TAKEN ME A LONG TIME, HANK, BUT I'VE FINALLY LEARNED THERE'S NO "ME" IN "TEAM."
THERE IS IF YOU MIX UP THE LETTERS.
SEE YOU AT THE POST-GAME, HANK.
CAN IT BE TRUE, HOCKEY FANS? HAVE KRINGLE AND OUNCE PUT ASIDE THEIR RIVALRY FOR THE LOVE OF THE GAME?
WE'LL KNOW IN A MINUTE, QIKI. THE ELVES AND SNOW LEOPARDS ARE TAKING THE ICE...
"...WITH BOTH TEAM CAPTAINS THE VERY MODELS OF CONFIDENCE AND CONTROL."
LET'S HAVE A NICE, CLEAN GAME.
NO PROB'.
OF COURSE.
WHACK!
OW!

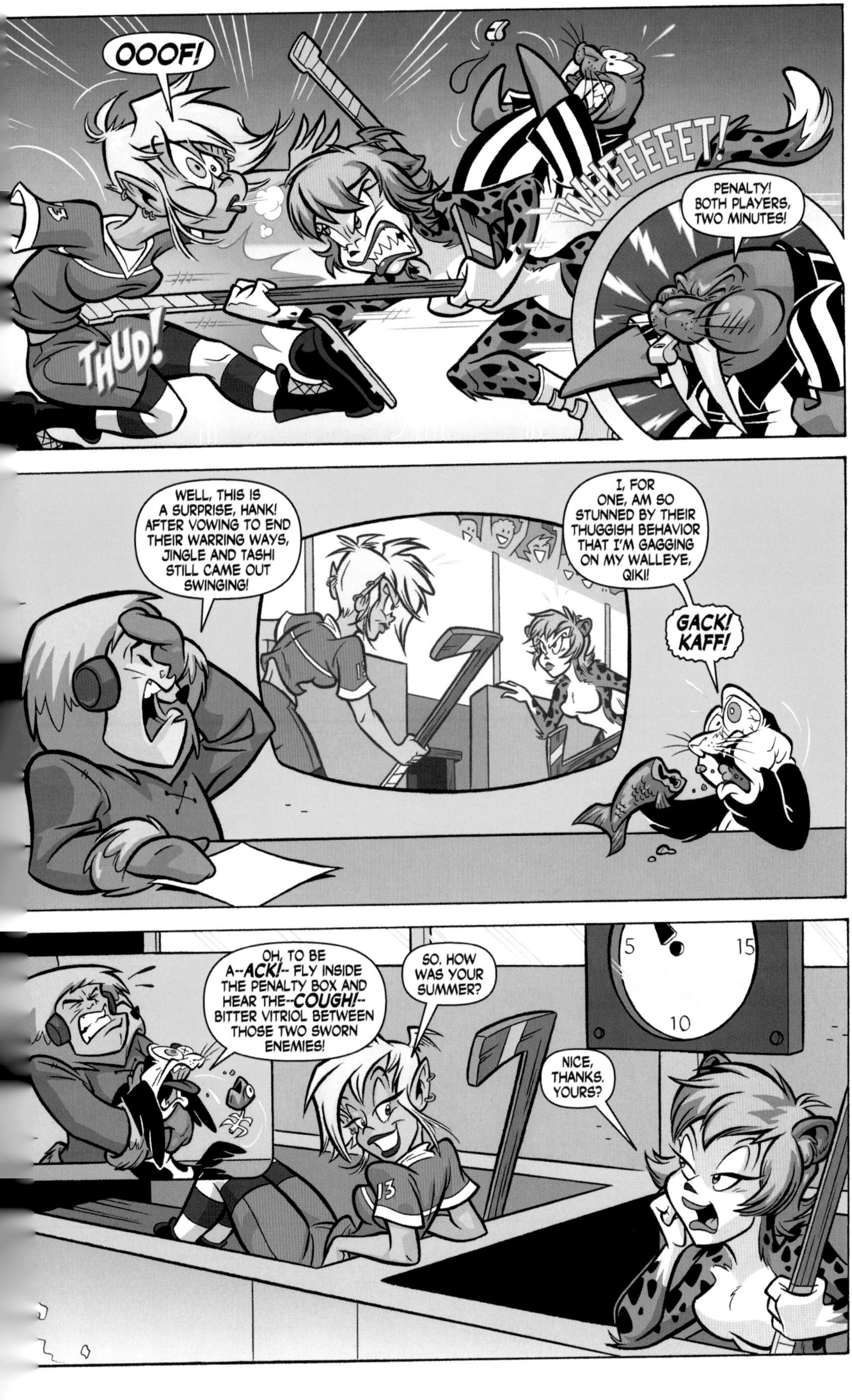

OOOF!
THUD!
WHEEEEEET!
PENALTY! BOTH PLAYERS, TWO MINUTES!
WELL, THIS IS A SURPRISE, HANK! AFTER VOWING TO END THEIR WARRING WAYS, JINGLE AND TASHI STILL CAME OUT SWINGING!
I, FOR ONE, AM SO STUNNED BY THEIR THUGGISH BEHAVIOR THAT I'M GAGGING ON MY WALLEYE, QIKI!
GACK! KAFF!
OH, TO BE A--ACK!-- FLY INSIDE THE PENALTY BOX AND HEAR THE--COUGH!-- BITTER VITRIOL BETWEEN THOSE TWO SWORN ENEMIES!
SO, HOW WAS YOUR SUMMER?
NICE, THANKS. YOURS?

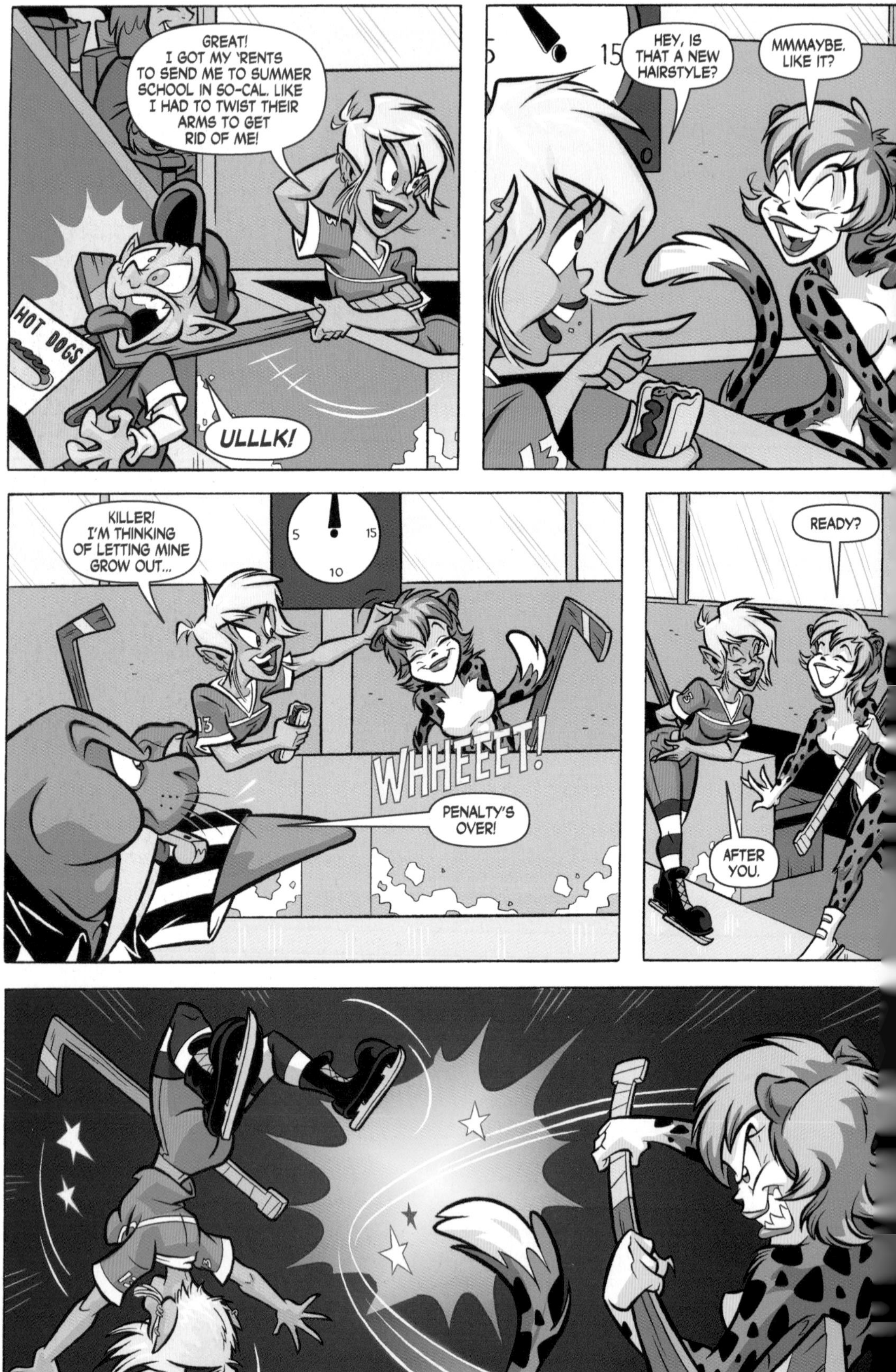
GREAT! I GOT MY 'RENTS TO SEND ME TO SUMMER SCHOOL IN SO-CAL. LIKE I HAD TO TWIST THEIR ARMS TO GET RID OF ME!
HOT DOGS
ULLLK!
HEY, IS THAT A NEW HAIRSTYLE?
MMMAYBE. LIKE IT?
KILLER! I'M THINKING OF LETTING MINE GROW OUT...
WHHEEET!
PENALTY'S OVER!
READY?
AFTER YOU.

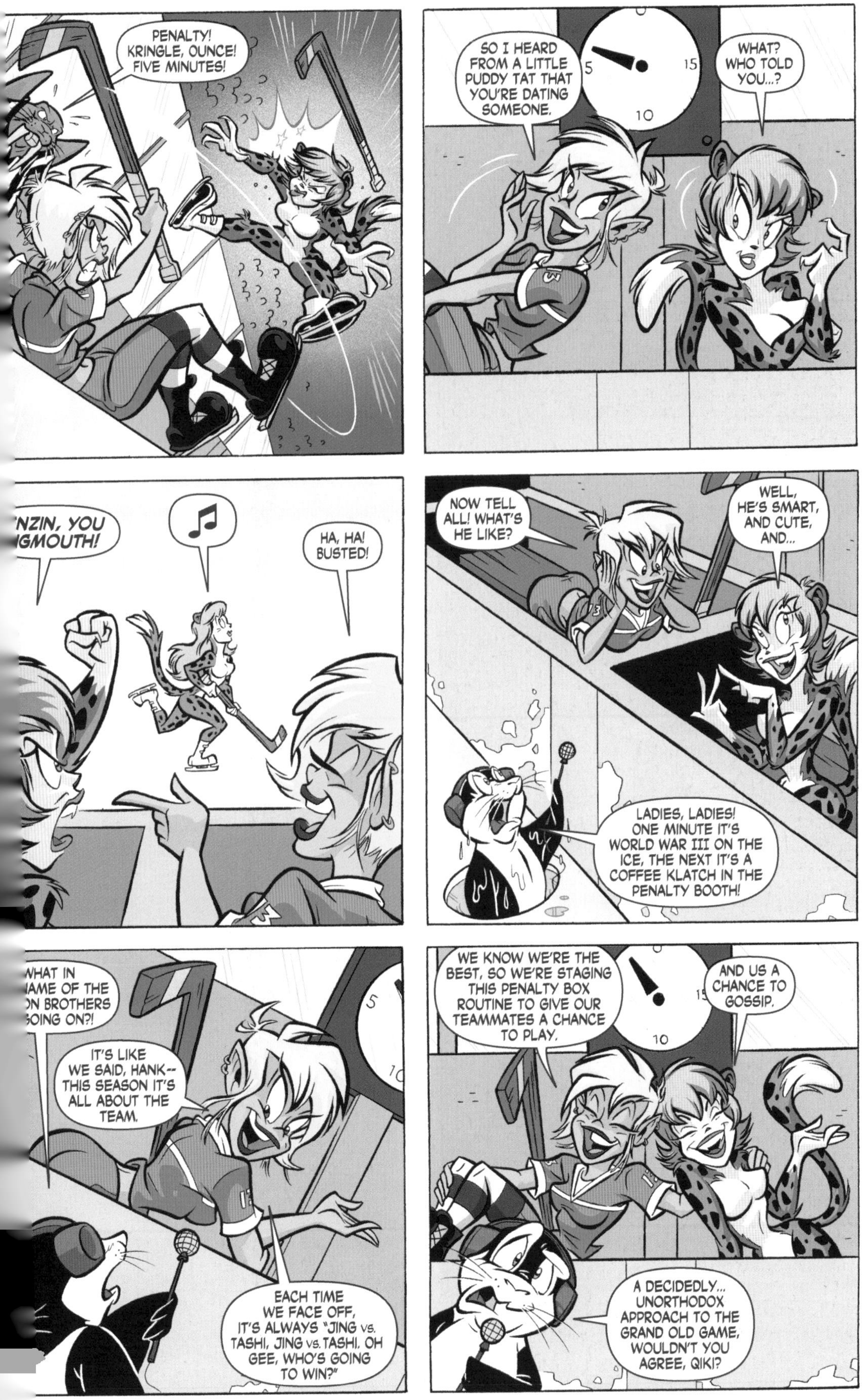
PENALTY! KRINGLE, OUNCE! FIVE MINUTES!
SO I HEARD FROM A LITTLE PUDDY TAT THAT YOU'RE DATING SOMEONE.
5
15
10
WHAT? WHO TOLD YOU...?
NZIN, YOU GMOUTH!
♫
HA, HA! BUSTED!
NOW TELL ALL! WHAT'S HE LIKE?
WELL, HE'S SMART, AND CUTE, AND...
LADIES, LADIES! ONE MINUTE IT'S WORLD WAR III ON THE ICE, THE NEXT IT'S A COFFEE KLATCH IN THE PENALTY BOOTH!
WHAT IN AME OF THE ON BROTHERS GOING ON?!
IT'S LIKE WE SAID, HANK-- THIS SEASON IT'S ALL ABOUT THE TEAM.
EACH TIME WE FACE OFF, IT'S ALWAYS "JING vs. TASHI, JING vs. TASHI, OH GEE, WHO'S GOING TO WIN?"
WE KNOW WE'RE THE BEST, SO WE'RE STAGING THIS PENALTY BOX ROUTINE TO GIVE OUR TEAMMATES A CHANCE TO PLAY.
AND US A CHANCE TO GOSSIP.
A DECIDEDLY... UNORTHODOX APPROACH TO THE GRAND OLD GAME, WOULDN'T YOU AGREE, QIKI?

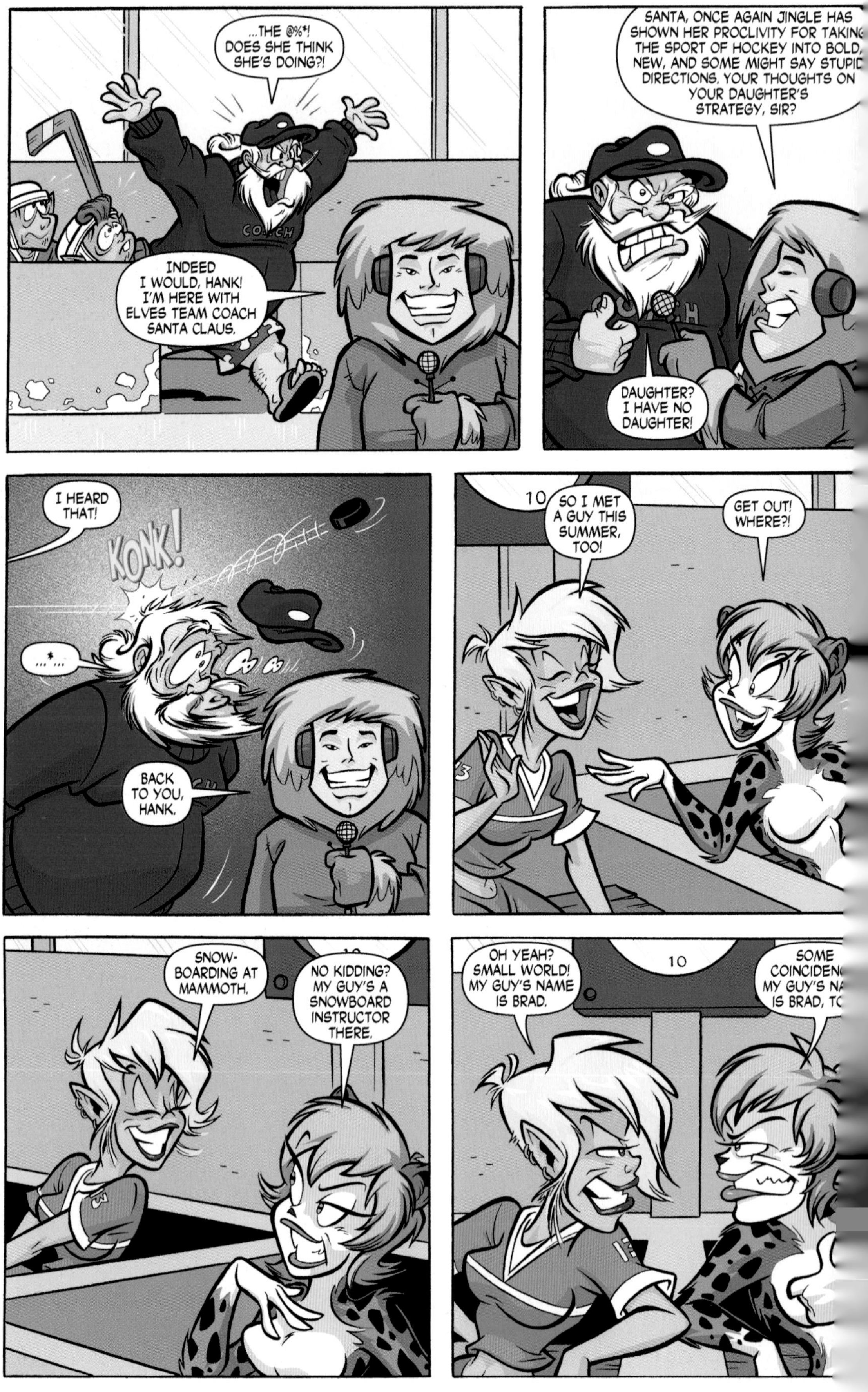
...THE @%*! DOES SHE THINK SHE'S DOING?!
INDEED I WOULD, HANK! I'M HERE WITH ELVES TEAM COACH SANTA CLAUS.
SANTA, ONCE AGAIN JINGLE HAS SHOWN HER PROCLIVITY FOR TAKIN THE SPORT OF HOCKEY INTO BOLD, NEW, AND SOME MIGHT SAY STUPID DIRECTIONS. YOUR THOUGHTS ON YOUR DAUGHTER'S STRATEGY, SIR?
DAUGHTER? I HAVE NO DAUGHTER!
I HEARD THAT!
KONK!
...*...
BACK TO YOU, HANK.
10
SO I MET A GUY THIS SUMMER, TOO!
GET OUT! WHERE?!
SNOW-BOARDING AT MAMMOTH.
NO KIDDING? MY GUY'S A SNOWBOARD INSTRUCTOR THERE.
OH YEAH? SMALL WORLD! MY GUY'S NAME IS BRAD.
10
SOME COINCIDEN MY GUY'S NA IS BRAD, T

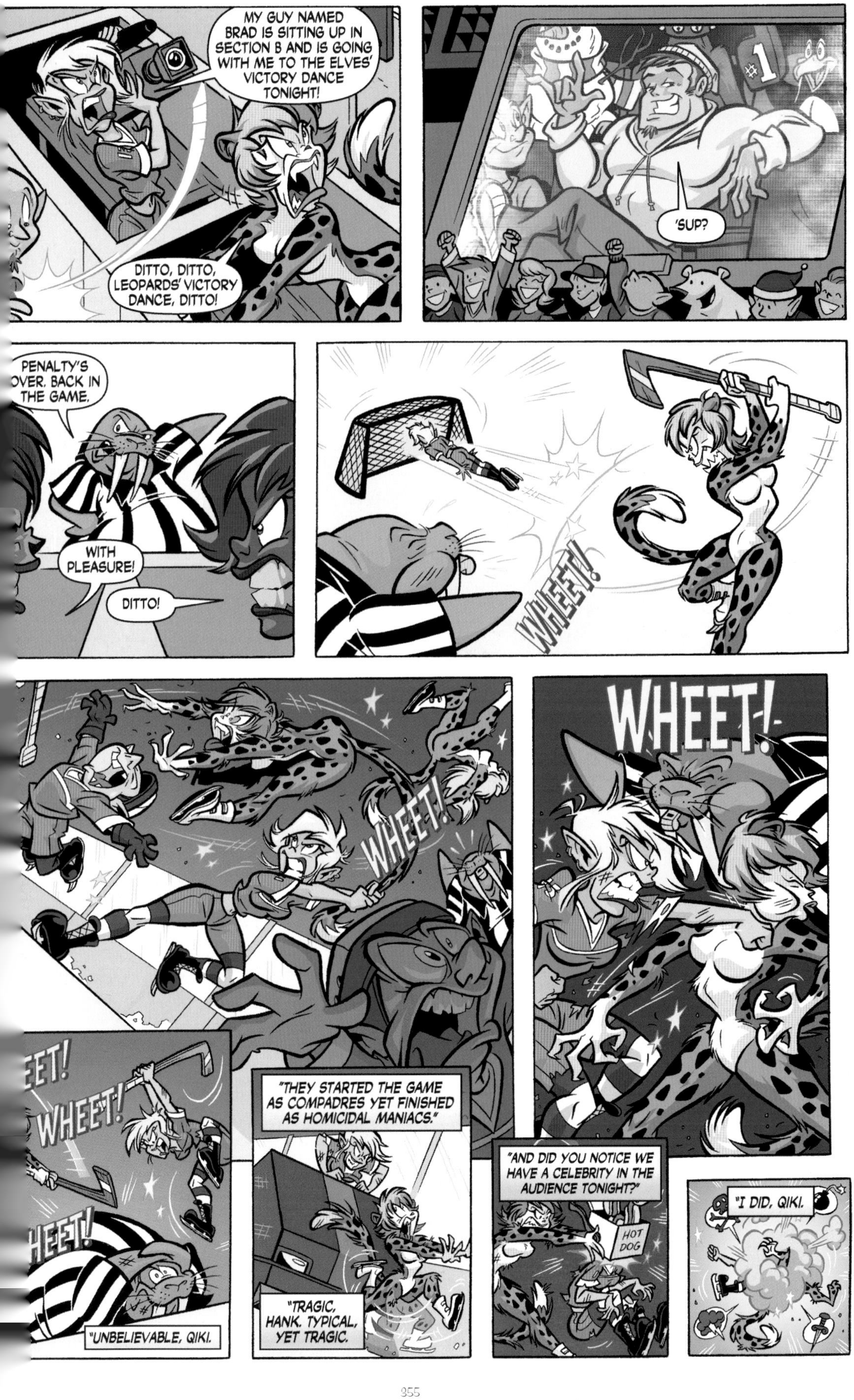

MY GUY NAMED BRAD IS SITTING UP IN SECTION B AND IS GOING WITH ME TO THE ELVES' VICTORY DANCE TONIGHT!
DITTO, DITTO, LEOPARDS' VICTORY DANCE, DITTO!
#1
'SUP?
PENALTY'S OVER. BACK IN THE GAME.
WITH PLEASURE!
DITTO!
WHEET!
WHEET!
WHEET!
EET!
WHEET!
HEET!
"UNBELIEVABLE, QIKI.
"THEY STARTED THE GAME AS COMPADRES YET FINISHED AS HOMICIDAL MANIACS."
"TRAGIC, HANK. TYPICAL, YET TRAGIC.
"AND DID YOU NOTICE WE HAVE A CELEBRITY IN THE AUDIENCE TONIGHT?"
HOT DOG
"I DID, QIKI.

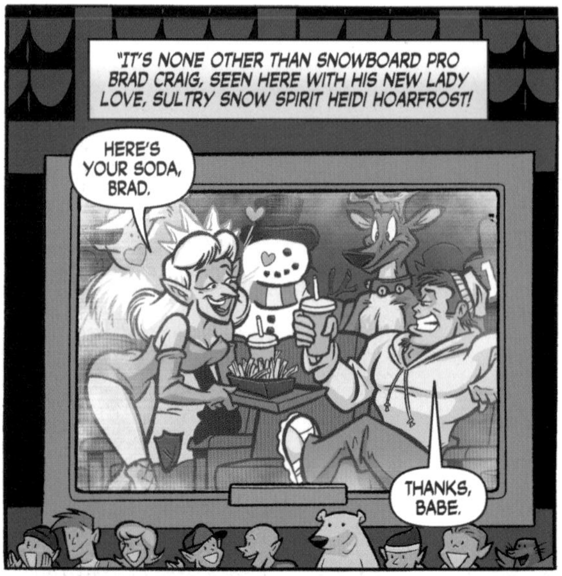
"IT'S NONE OTHER THAN SNOWBOARD PRO BRAD CRAIG, SEEN HERE WITH HIS NEW LADY LOVE, SULTRY SNOW SPIRIT HEIDI HOARFROST!
HERE'S YOUR SODA, BRAD.
THANKS, BABE.

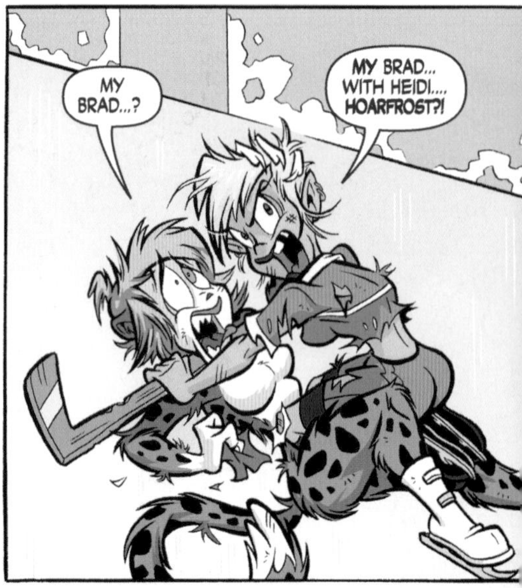
MY BRAD...?
MY BRAD... WITH HEIDI.... HOARFROST?!

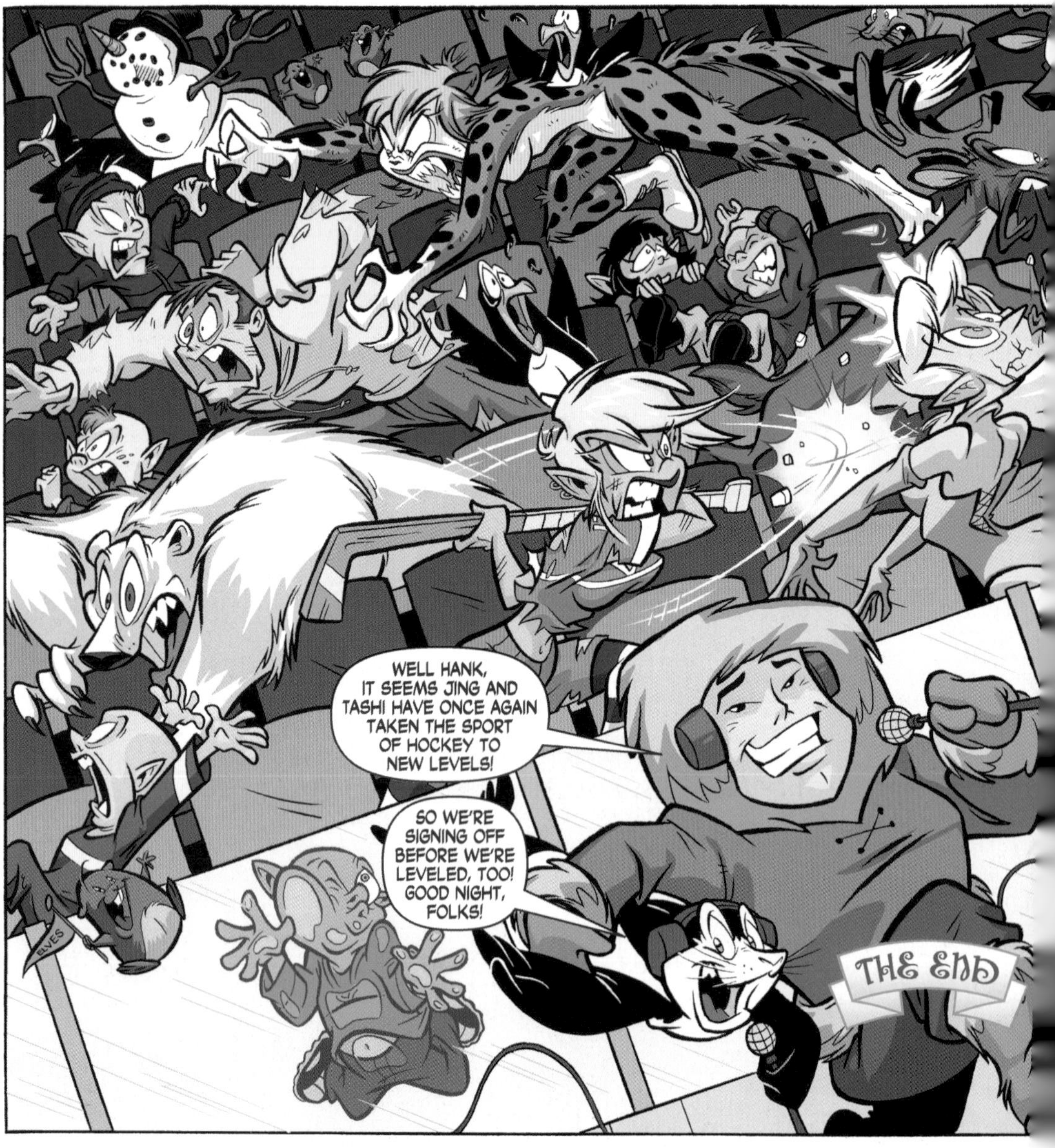
WELL HANK, IT SEEMS JING AND TASHI HAVE ONCE AGAIN TAKEN THE SPORT OF HOCKEY TO NEW LEVELS!
SO WE'RE SIGNING OFF BEFORE WE'RE LEVELED, TOO! GOOD NIGHT, FOLKS!
ELVES
THE END

Hot Rod Lemming

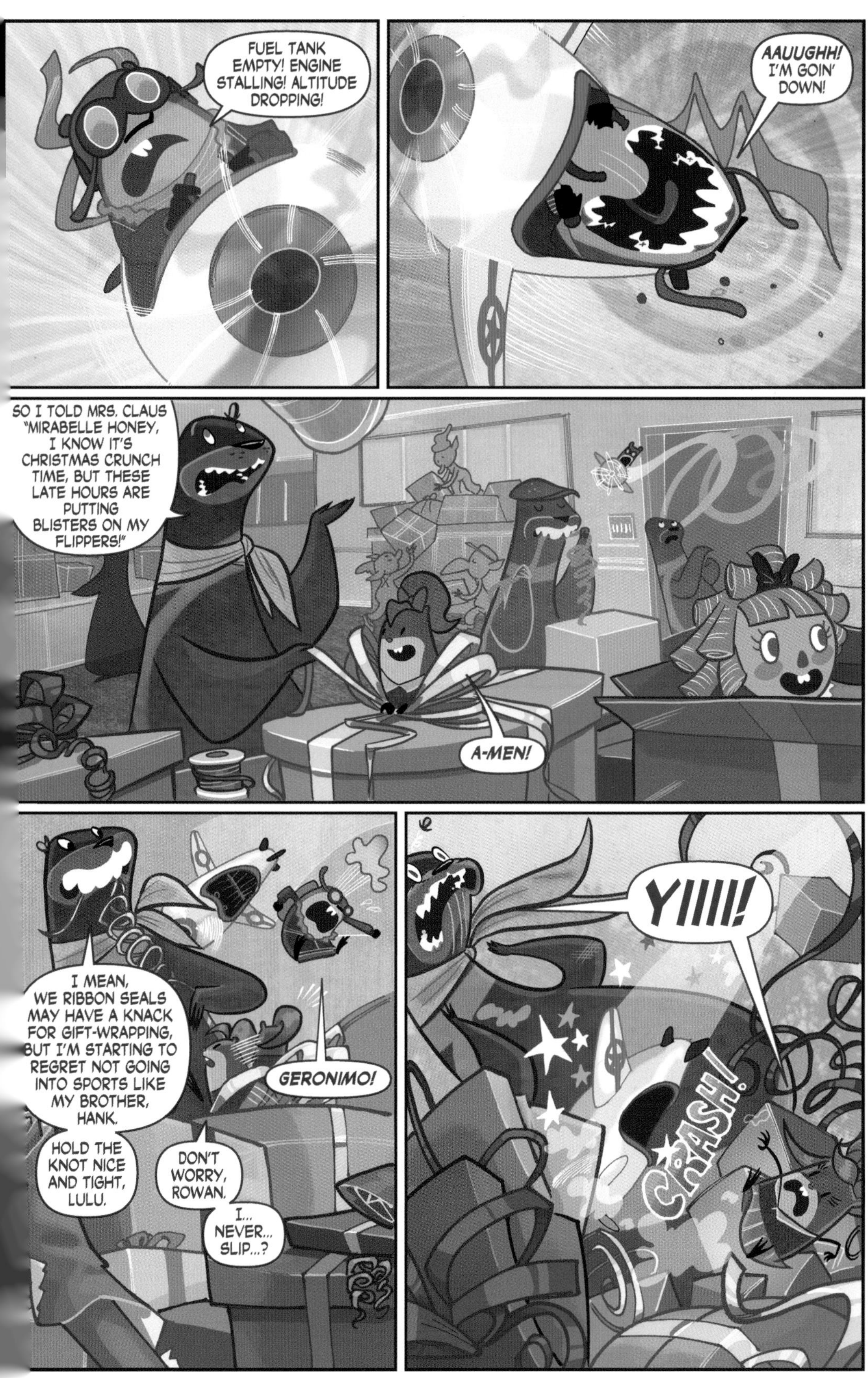
FUEL TANK EMPTY! ENGINE STALLING! ALTITUDE DROPPING!
AAUUGHH! I'M GOIN' DOWN!
SO I TOLD MRS. CLAUS "MIRABELLE HONEY, I KNOW IT'S CHRISTMAS CRUNCH TIME, BUT THESE LATE HOURS ARE PUTTING BLISTERS ON MY FLIPPERS!"
A-MEN!
I MEAN, WE RIBBON SEALS MAY HAVE A KNACK FOR GIFT-WRAPPING, BUT I'M STARTING TO REGRET NOT GOING INTO SPORTS LIKE MY BROTHER, HANK.
GERONIMO!
HOLD THE KNOT NICE AND TIGHT, LULU.
DON'T WORRY, ROWAN.
I... NEVER... SLIP...?
YIIII!
CRASH!

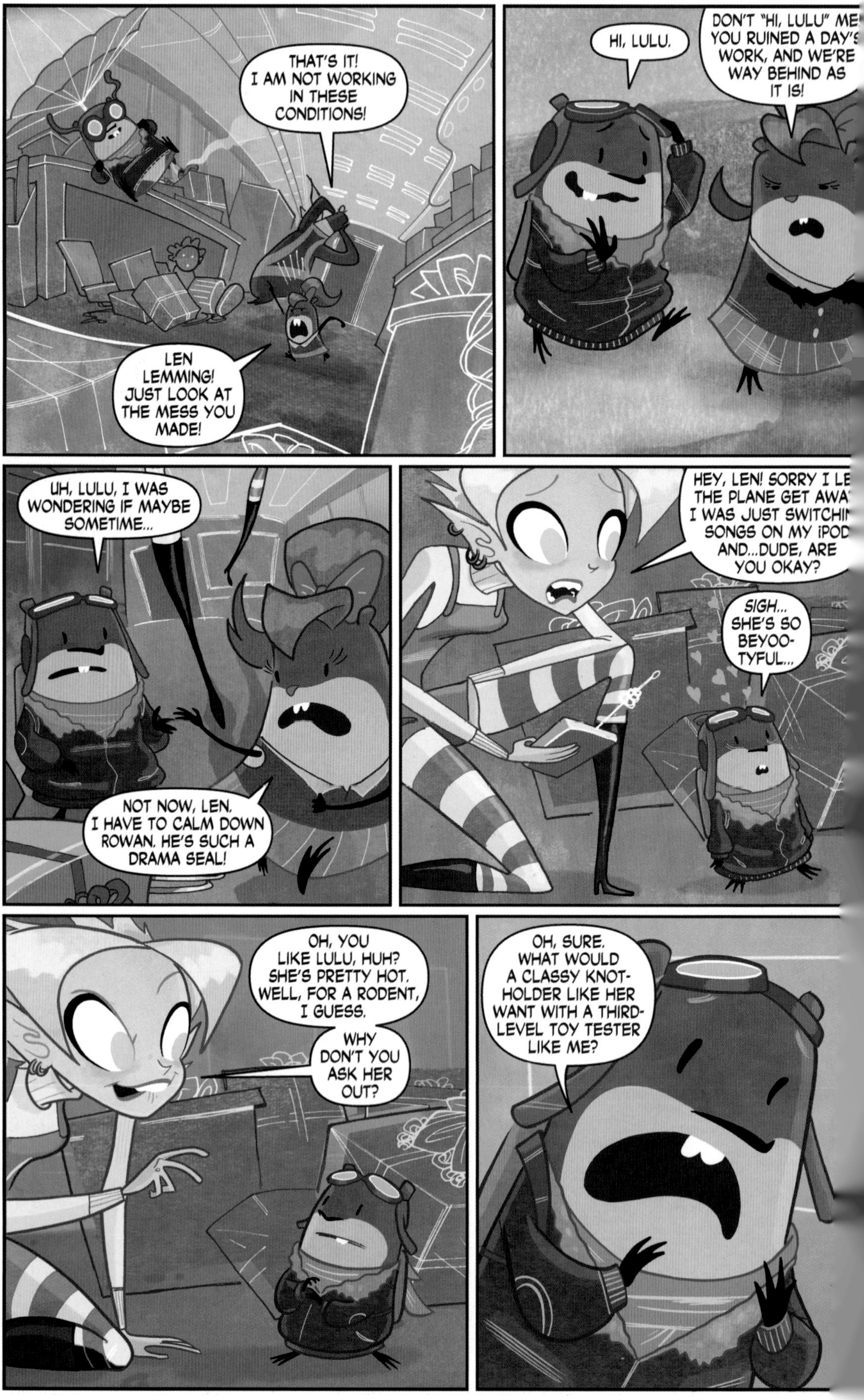
THAT'S IT! I AM NOT WORKING IN THESE CONDITIONS!
LEN LEMMING! JUST LOOK AT THE MESS YOU MADE!
HI, LULU.
DON'T "HI, LULU" ME
YOU RUINED A DAY'
WORK, AND WE'RE WAY BEHIND AS IT IS!
UH, LULU, I WAS WONDERING IF MAYBE SOMETIME...
NOT NOW, LEN. I HAVE TO CALM DOWN ROWAN. HE'S SUCH A DRAMA SEAL!
HEY, LEN! SORRY I LE
THE PLANE GET AWA
I WAS JUST SWITCHIN
SONGS ON MY iPOD
AND...DUDE, ARE YOU OKAY?
SIGH... SHE'S SO BEYOO-TYFUL...
OH, YOU LIKE LULU, HUH? SHE'S PRETTY HOT. WELL, FOR A RODENT, I GUESS.
WHY DON'T YOU ASK HER OUT?
OH, SURE. WHAT WOULD A CLASSY KNOT-HOLDER LIKE HER WANT WITH A THIRD-LEVEL TOY TESTER LIKE ME?

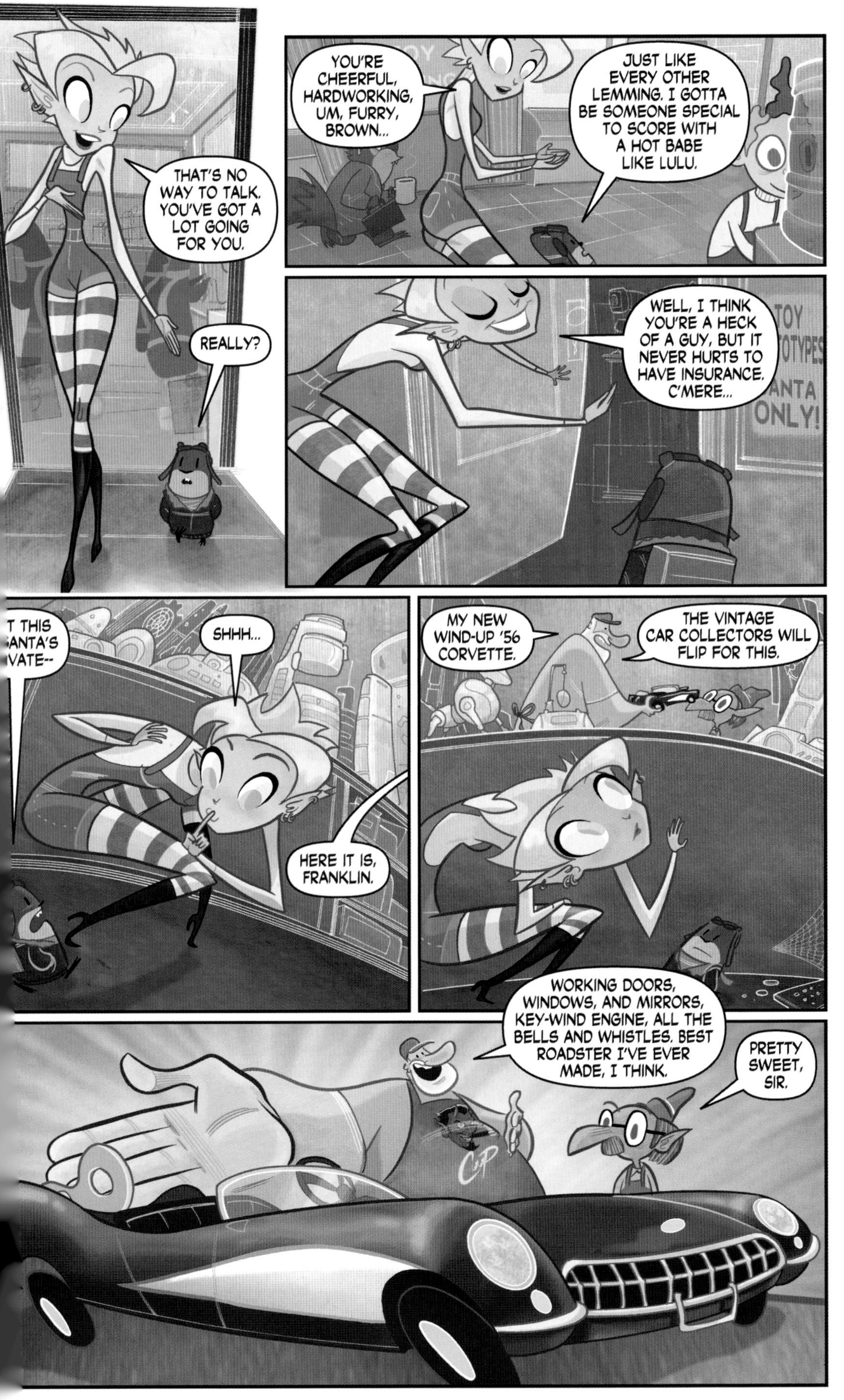
THAT'S NO WAY TO TALK. YOU'VE GOT A LOT GOING FOR YOU.
REALLY?
YOU'RE CHEERFUL, HARDWORKING, UM, FURRY, BROWN...
JUST LIKE EVERY OTHER LEMMING. I GOTTA BE SOMEONE SPECIAL TO SCORE WITH A HOT BABE LIKE LULU.
WELL, I THINK YOU'RE A HECK OF A GUY, BUT IT NEVER HURTS TO HAVE INSURANCE. C'MERE...
TOY
ONLY!
T THIS
ANTA'S
VATE--
SHHH...
HERE IT IS, FRANKLIN.
MY NEW WIND-UP '56 CORVETTE.
THE VINTAGE CAR COLLECTORS WILL FLIP FOR THIS.
WORKING DOORS, WINDOWS, AND MIRRORS, KEY-WIND ENGINE, ALL THE BELLS AND WHISTLES. BEST ROADSTER I'VE EVER MADE, I THINK.
PRETTY SWEET, SIR.

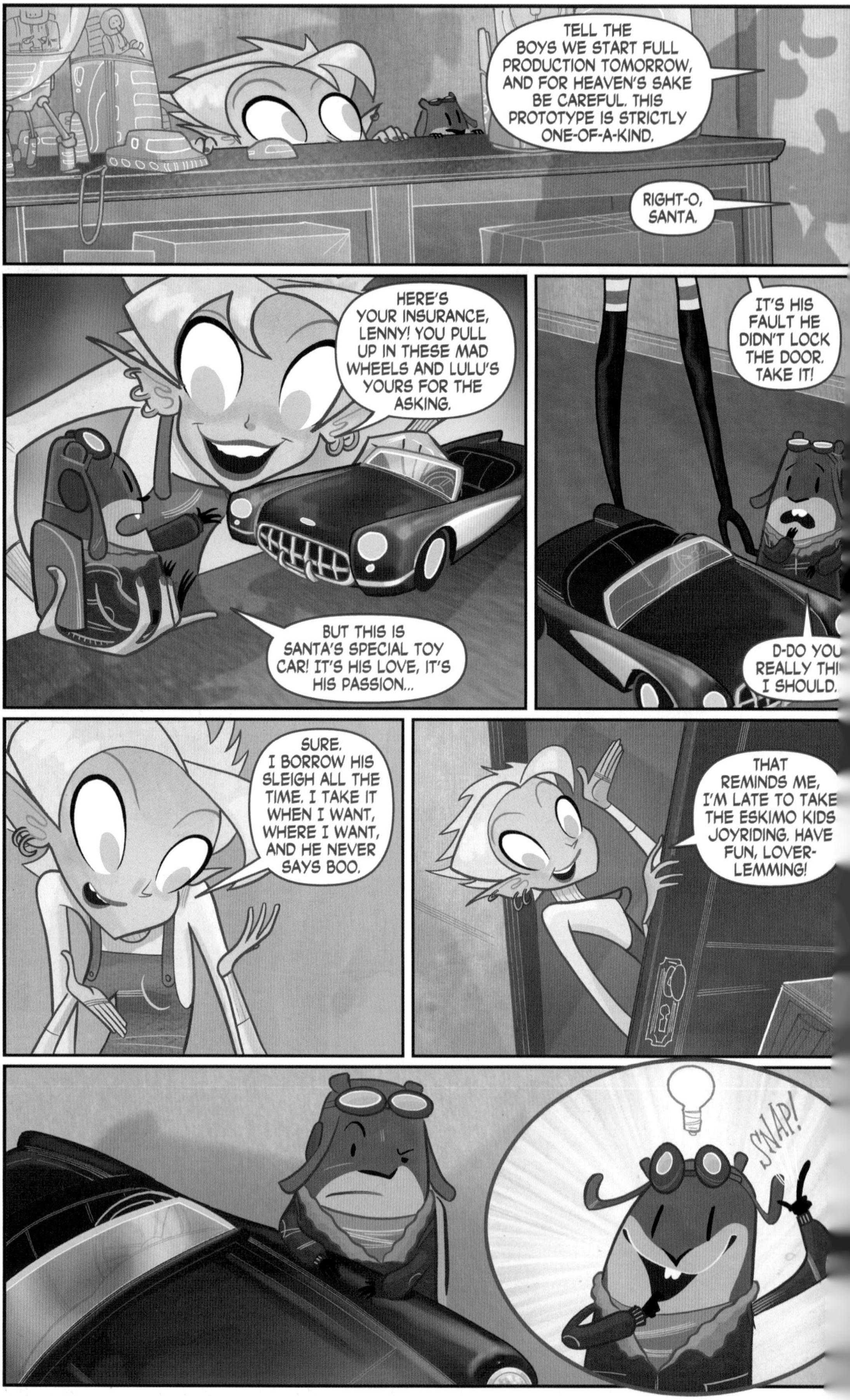
TELL THE BOYS WE START FULL PRODUCTION TOMORROW, AND FOR HEAVEN'S SAKE BE CAREFUL. THIS PROTOTYPE IS STRICTLY ONE-OF-A-KIND.
RIGHT-O, SANTA.
HERE'S YOUR INSURANCE, LENNY! YOU PULL UP IN THESE MAD WHEELS AND LULU'S YOURS FOR THE ASKING.
BUT THIS IS SANTA'S SPECIAL TOY CAR! IT'S HIS LOVE, IT'S HIS PASSION...
IT'S HIS FAULT HE DIDN'T LOCK THE DOOR. TAKE IT!
D-DO YOU REALLY THI I SHOULD.
SURE. I BORROW HIS SLEIGH ALL THE TIME. I TAKE IT WHEN I WANT, WHERE I WANT, AND HE NEVER SAYS BOO.
THAT REMINDS ME, I'M LATE TO TAKE THE ESKIMO KIDS JOYRIDING. HAVE FUN, LOVER-LEMMING!
SNAP!

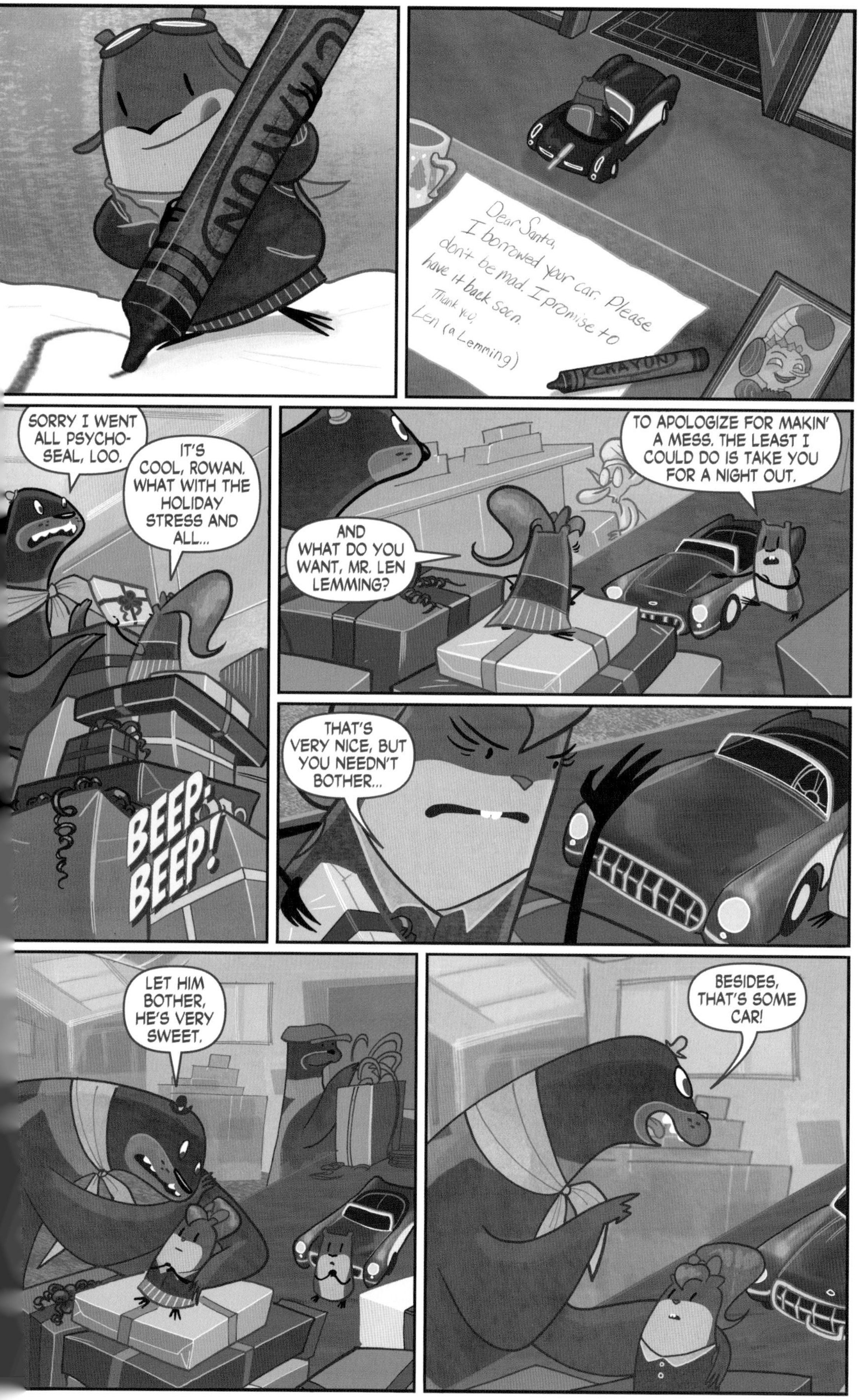
Dear Santa,
I borrowed your car. Please don't be mad. I promise to have it back soon.
Thank you,
Len (a Lemming)
CRAYON
SORRY I WENT ALL PSYCHO-SEAL, LOO.
IT'S COOL, ROWAN. WHAT WITH THE HOLIDAY STRESS AND ALL...
BEEP-BEEP!
TO APOLOGIZE FOR MAKIN' A MESS. THE LEAST I COULD DO IS TAKE YOU FOR A NIGHT OUT.
AND WHAT DO YOU WANT, MR. LEN LEMMING?
THAT'S VERY NICE, BUT YOU NEEDN'T BOTHER...
LET HIM BOTHER, HE'S VERY SWEET.
BESIDES, THAT'S SOME CAR!

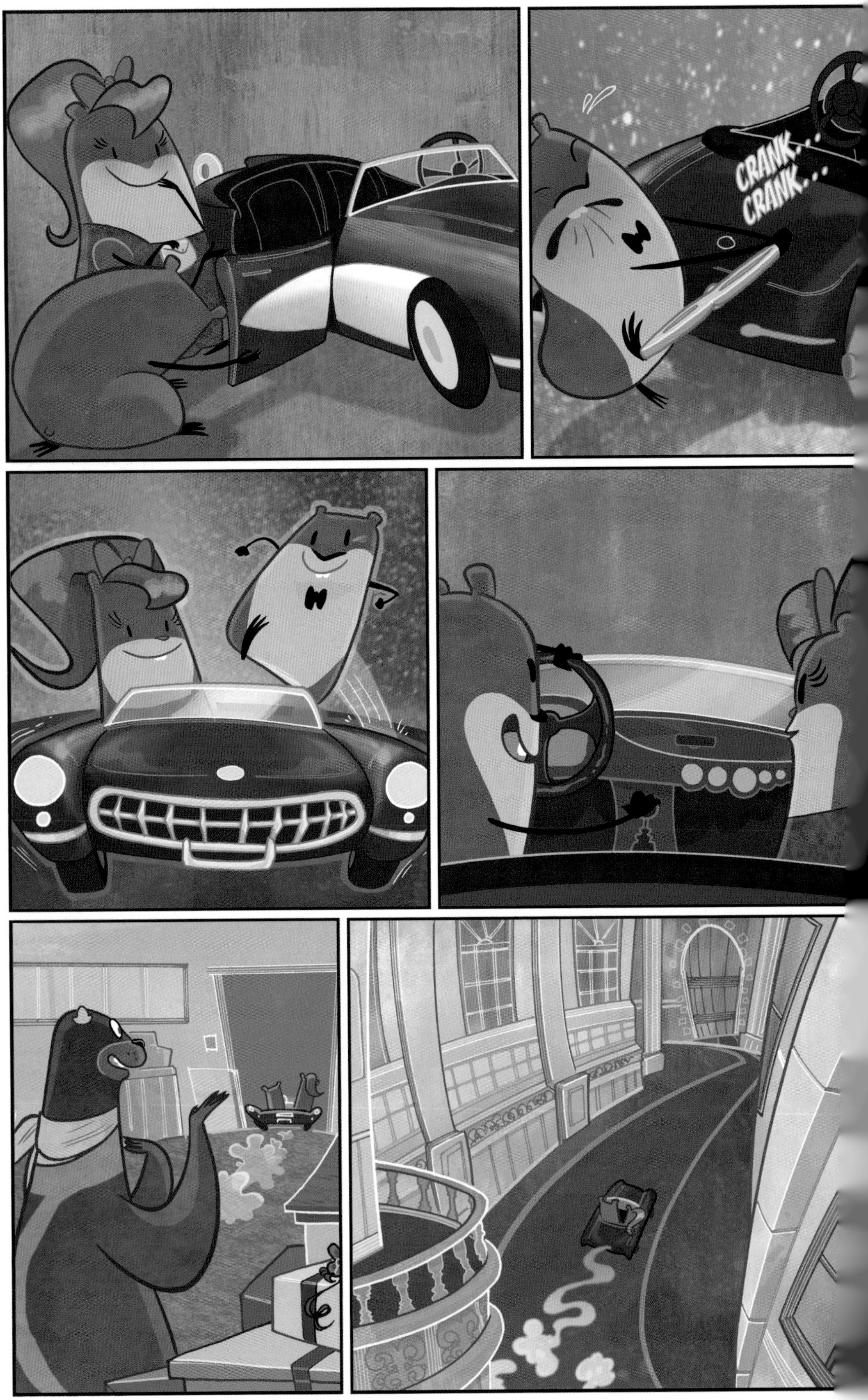
CRANK...
CRANK...

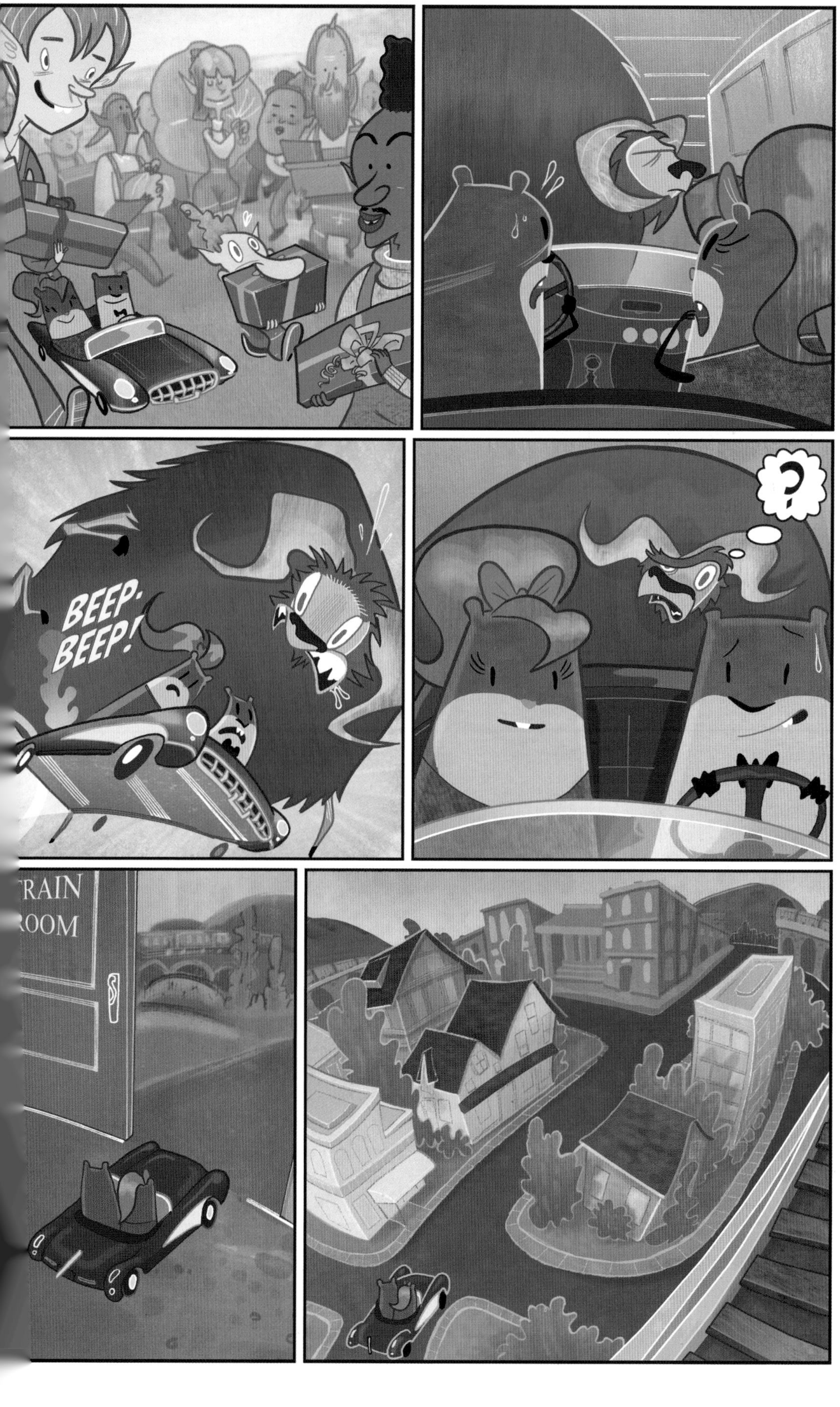
BEEP. BEEP!
?
TRAIN
ROOM

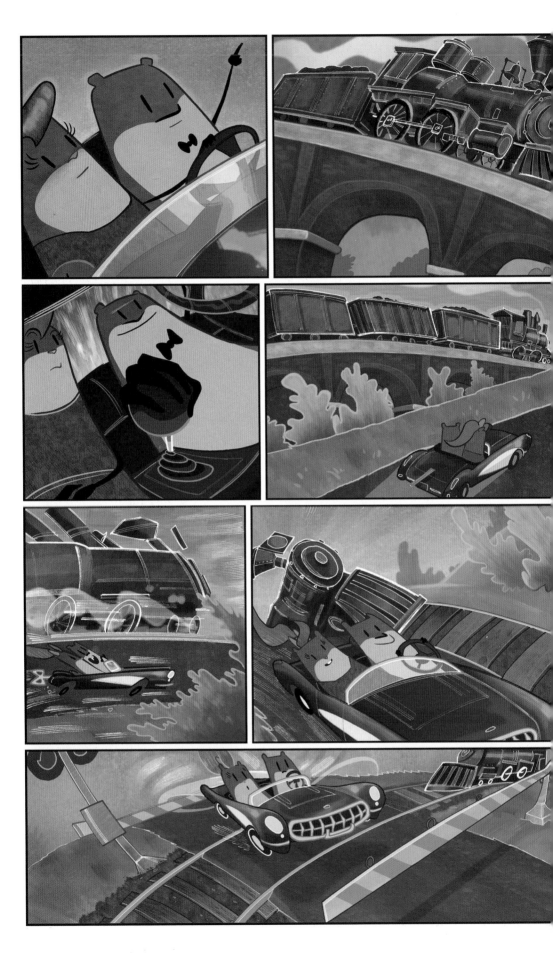

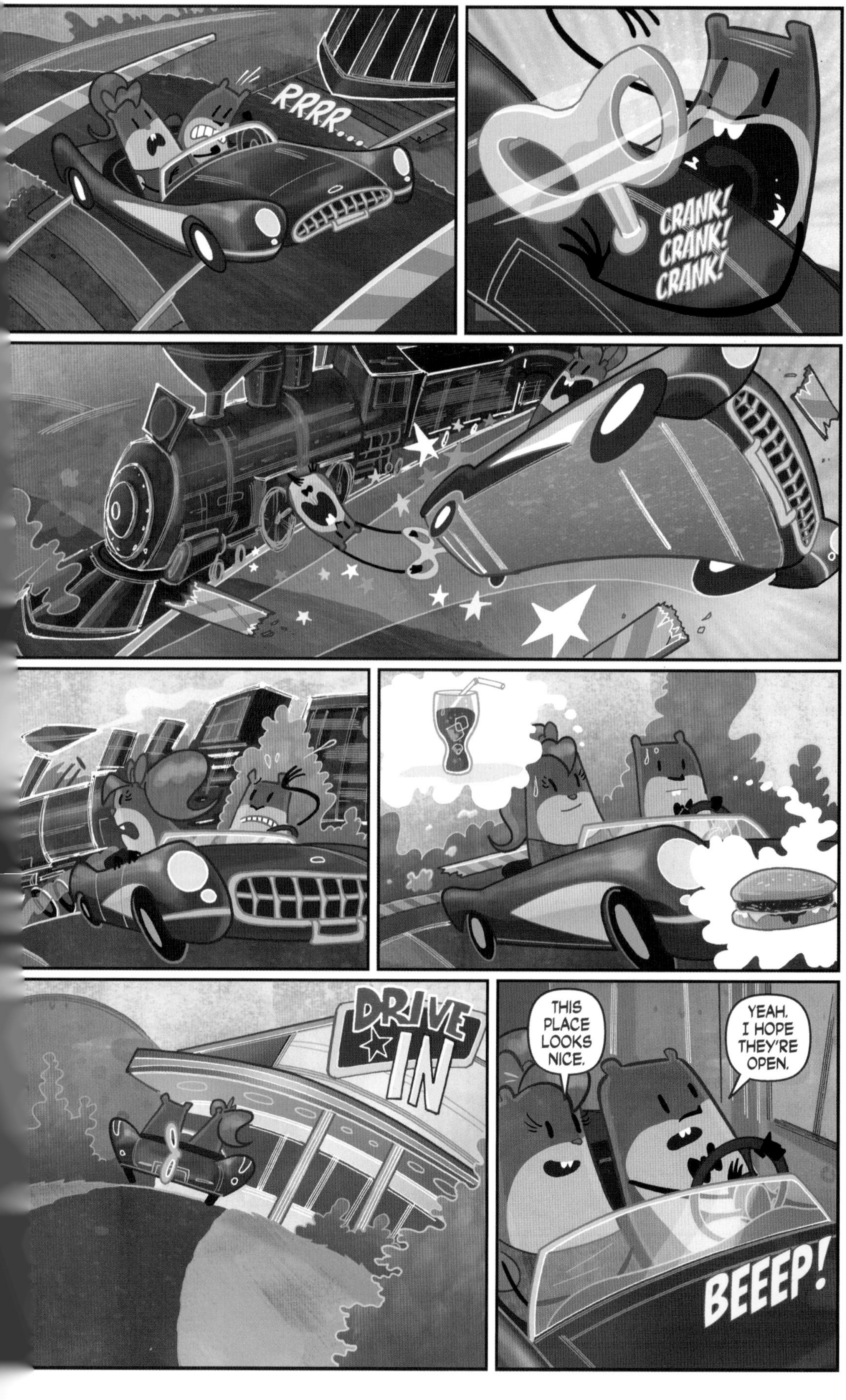
RRRR....
CRANK! CRANK! CRANK!
DRIVE IN
THIS PLACE LOOKS NICE.
YEAH. I HOPE THEY'RE OPEN.
BEEEP!

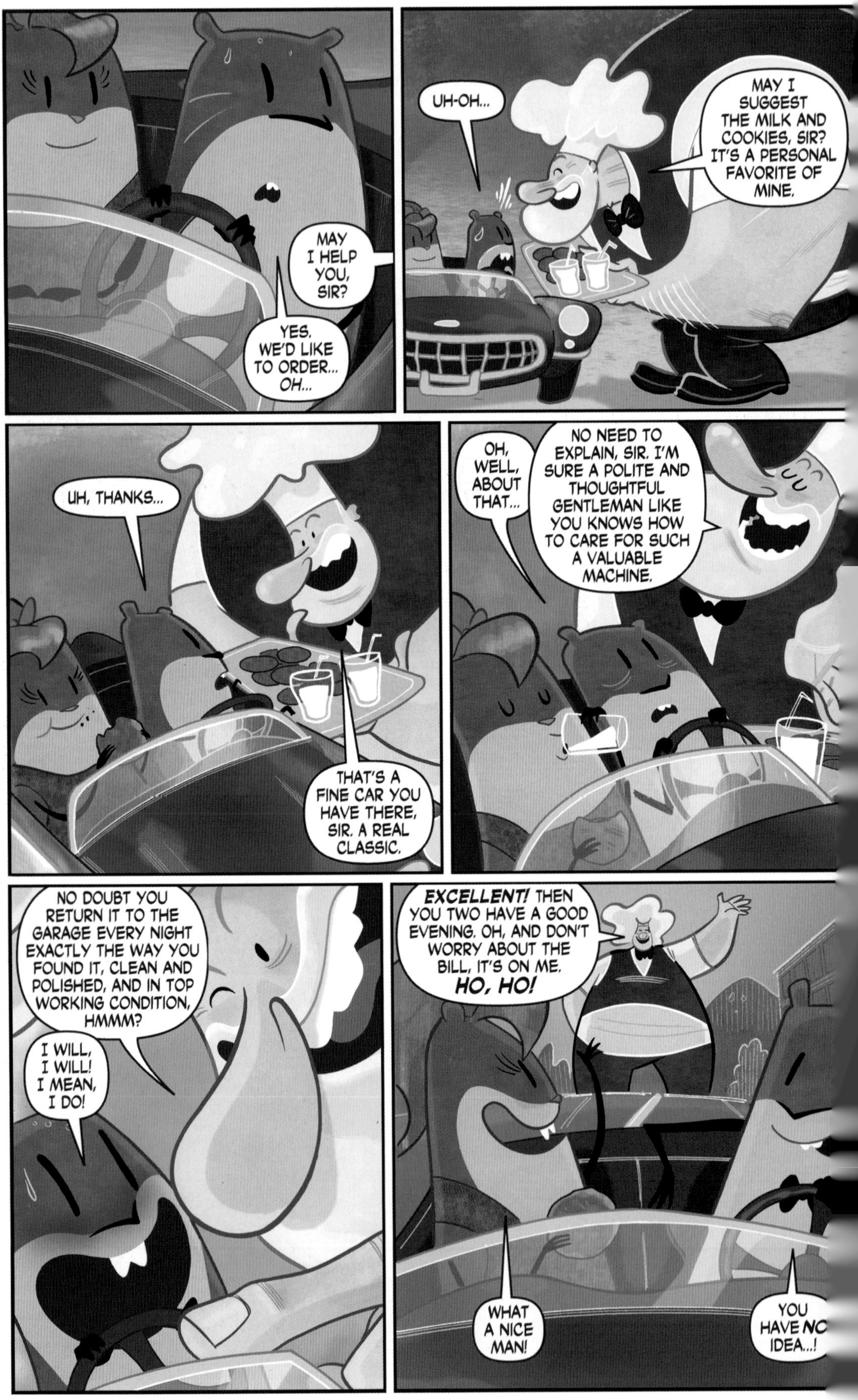
MAY I HELP YOU, SIR?
YES. WE'D LIKE TO ORDER... OH...
UH-OH...
MAY I SUGGEST THE MILK AND COOKIES, SIR? IT'S A PERSONAL FAVORITE OF MINE.
UH, THANKS...
THAT'S A FINE CAR YOU HAVE THERE, SIR. A REAL CLASSIC.
OH, WELL, ABOUT THAT...
NO NEED TO EXPLAIN, SIR. I'M SURE A POLITE AND THOUGHTFUL GENTLEMAN LIKE YOU KNOWS HOW TO CARE FOR SUCH A VALUABLE MACHINE.
NO DOUBT YOU RETURN IT TO THE GARAGE EVERY NIGHT EXACTLY THE WAY YOU FOUND IT, CLEAN AND POLISHED, AND IN TOP WORKING CONDITION, HMMM?
I WILL, I WILL! I MEAN, I DO!
EXCELLENT! THEN YOU TWO HAVE A GOOD EVENING. OH, AND DON'T WORRY ABOUT THE BILL, IT'S ON ME. HO, HO!
WHAT A NICE MAN!
YOU HAVE NO IDEA...!

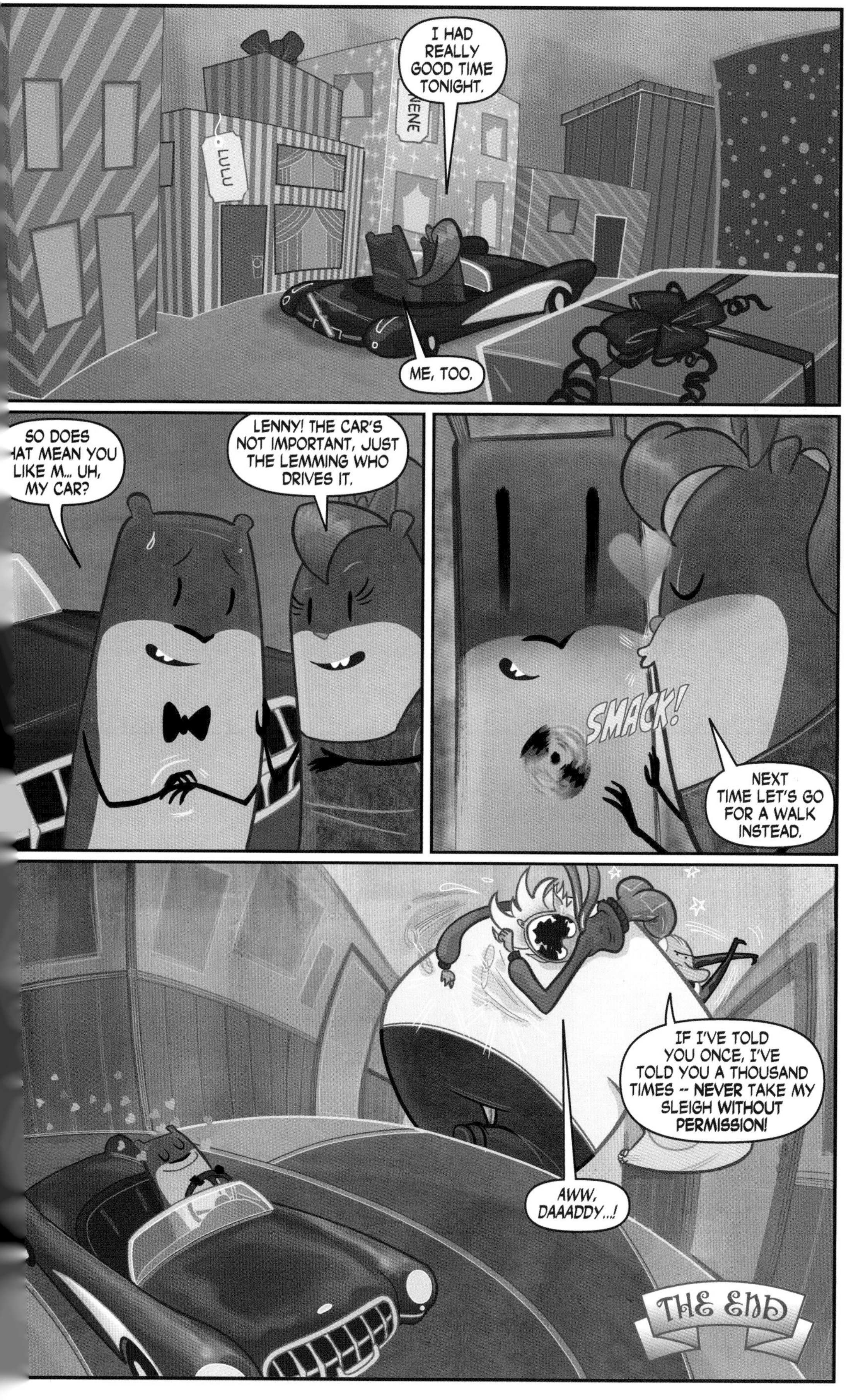
LULU
VENE
I HAD REALLY GOOD TIME TONIGHT.
ME, TOO.
SO DOES HAT MEAN YOU LIKE M... UH, MY CAR?
LENNY! THE CAR'S NOT IMPORTANT, JUST THE LEMMING WHO DRIVES IT.
SMACK!
NEXT TIME LET'S GO FOR A WALK INSTEAD.
IF I'VE TOLD YOU ONCE, I'VE TOLD YOU A THOUSAND TIMES -- NEVER TAKE MY SLEIGH WITHOUT PERMISSION!
AWW, DAAADDY...!
THE END

Oh, Christmas Tree

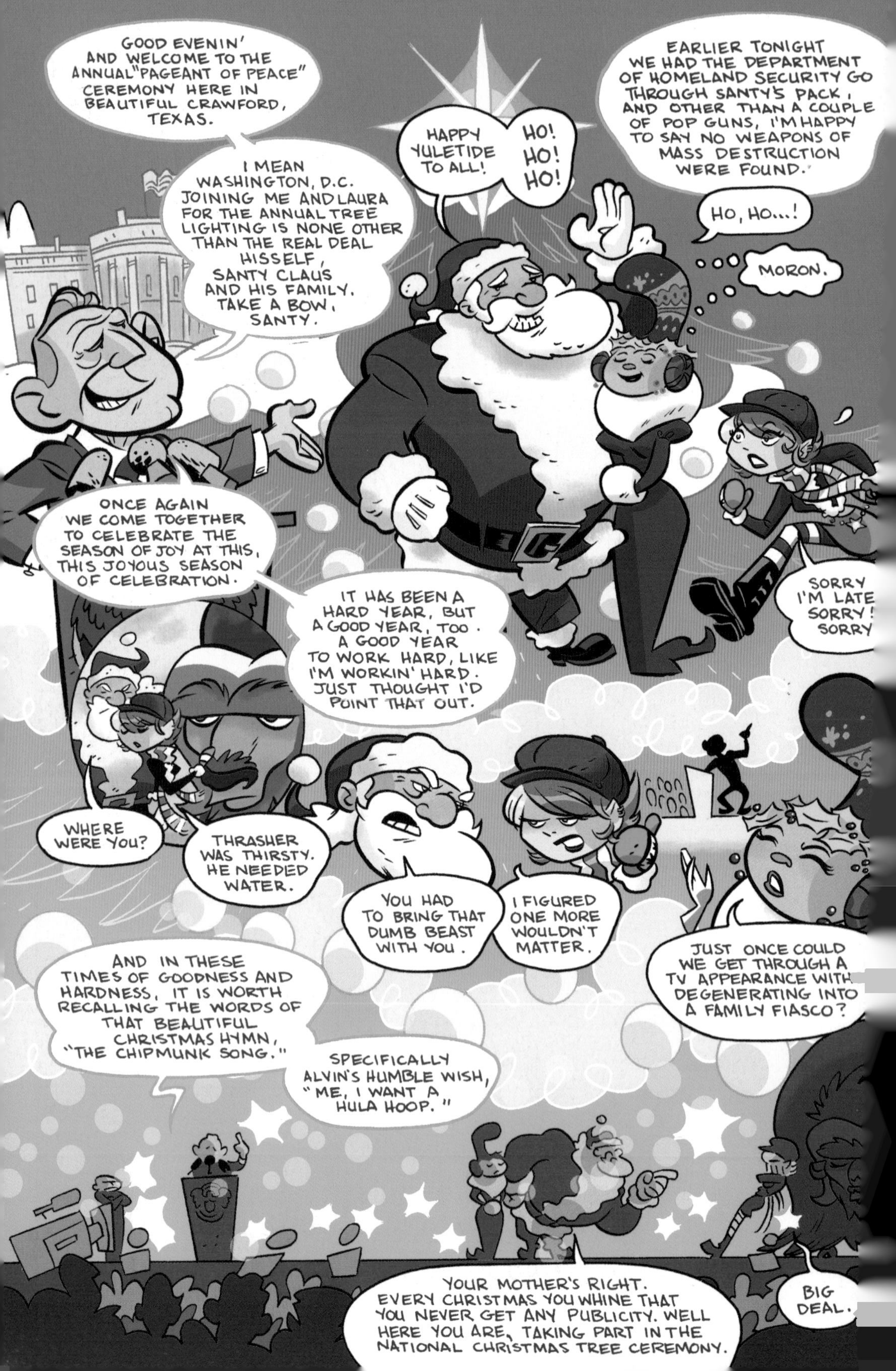
GOOD EVENIN' AND WELCOME TO THE ANNUAL "PAGEANT OF PEACE" CEREMONY HERE IN BEAUTIFUL CRAWFORD, TEXAS.
I MEAN WASHINGTON, D.C. JOINING ME AND LAURA FOR THE ANNUAL TREE LIGHTING IS NONE OTHER THAN THE REAL DEAL HISSELF, SANTY CLAUS AND HIS FAMILY. TAKE A BOW, SANTY.
HAPPY YULETIDE TO ALL!
HO! HO! HO!
EARLIER TONIGHT WE HAD THE DEPARTMENT OF HOMELAND SECURITY GO THROUGH SANTY'S PACK, AND OTHER THAN A COUPLE OF POP GUNS, I'M HAPPY TO SAY NO WEAPONS OF MASS DESTRUCTION WERE FOUND.
HO, HO...!
MORON.
ONCE AGAIN WE COME TOGETHER TO CELEBRATE THE SEASON OF JOY AT THIS, THIS JOYOUS SEASON OF CELEBRATION.
IT HAS BEEN A HARD YEAR, BUT A GOOD YEAR, TOO. A GOOD YEAR TO WORK HARD, LIKE I'M WORKIN' HARD. JUST THOUGHT I'D POINT THAT OUT.
SORRY I'M LATE SORRY! SORRY
WHERE WERE YOU?
THRASHER WAS THIRSTY. HE NEEDED WATER.
YOU HAD TO BRING THAT DUMB BEAST WITH YOU.
I FIGURED ONE MORE WOULDN'T MATTER.
JUST ONCE COULD WE GET THROUGH A TV APPEARANCE WITH DEGENERATING INTO A FAMILY FIASCO?
AND IN THESE TIMES OF GOODNESS AND HARDNESS, IT IS WORTH RECALLING THE WORDS OF THAT BEAUTIFUL CHRISTMAS HYMN, "THE CHIPMUNK SONG."
SPECIFICALLY ALVIN'S HUMBLE WISH, "ME, I WANT A HULA HOOP."
YOUR MOTHER'S RIGHT. EVERY CHRISTMAS YOU WHINE THAT YOU NEVER GET ANY PUBLICITY. WELL HERE YOU ARE, TAKING PART IN THE NATIONAL CHRISTMAS TREE CEREMONY.
BIG DEAL.

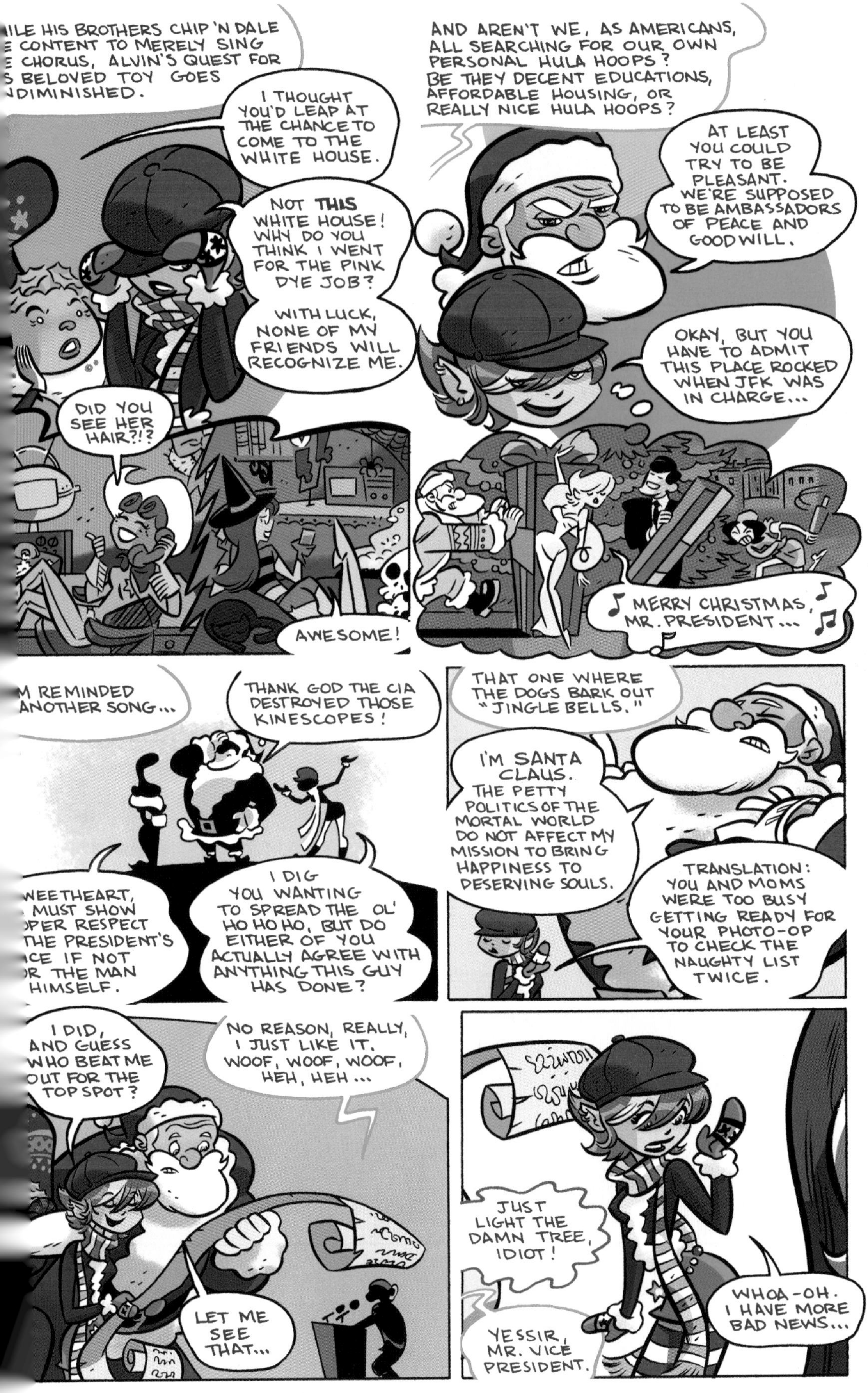

HILE HIS BROTHERS CHIP 'N DALE E CONTENT TO MERELY SING E CHORUS, ALVIN'S QUEST FOR S BELOVED TOY GOES NDIMINISHED.
I THOUGHT YOU'D LEAP AT THE CHANCE TO COME TO THE WHITE HOUSE.
NOT THIS WHITE HOUSE! WHY DO YOU THINK I WENT FOR THE PINK DYE JOB?
WITH LUCK, NONE OF MY FRIENDS WILL RECOGNIZE ME.
DID YOU SEE HER HAIR?!?
AWESOME!
AND AREN'T WE, AS AMERICANS, ALL SEARCHING FOR OUR OWN PERSONAL HULA HOOPS? BE THEY DECENT EDUCATIONS, AFFORDABLE HOUSING, OR REALLY NICE HULA HOOPS?
AT LEAST YOU COULD TRY TO BE PLEASANT. WE'RE SUPPOSED TO BE AMBASSADORS OF PEACE AND GOODWILL.
OKAY, BUT YOU HAVE TO ADMIT THIS PLACE ROCKED WHEN JFK WAS IN CHARGE...
MERRY CHRISTMAS, MR. PRESIDENT...
M REMINDED ANOTHER SONG...
THANK GOD THE CIA DESTROYED THOSE KINESCOPES!
WEETHEART, MUST SHOW OPER RESPECT THE PRESIDENT'S ICE IF NOT R THE MAN HIMSELF.
I DIG YOU WANTING TO SPREAD THE OL' HO HO HO, BUT DO EITHER OF YOU ACTUALLY AGREE WITH ANYTHING THIS GUY HAS DONE?
THAT ONE WHERE THE DOGS BARK OUT "JINGLE BELLS."
I'M SANTA CLAUS. THE PETTY POLITICS OF THE MORTAL WORLD DO NOT AFFECT MY MISSION TO BRING HAPPINESS TO DESERVING SOULS.
TRANSLATION: YOU AND MOMS WERE TOO BUSY GETTING READY FOR YOUR PHOTO-OP TO CHECK THE NAUGHTY LIST TWICE.
I DID, AND GUESS WHO BEAT ME OUT FOR THE TOP SPOT?
NO REASON, REALLY, I JUST LIKE IT. WOOF, WOOF, WOOF, HEH, HEH...
LET ME SEE THAT...
JUST LIGHT THE DAMN TREE, IDIOT!
YESSIR, MR. VICE PRESIDENT.
WHOA-OH. I HAVE MORE BAD NEWS...

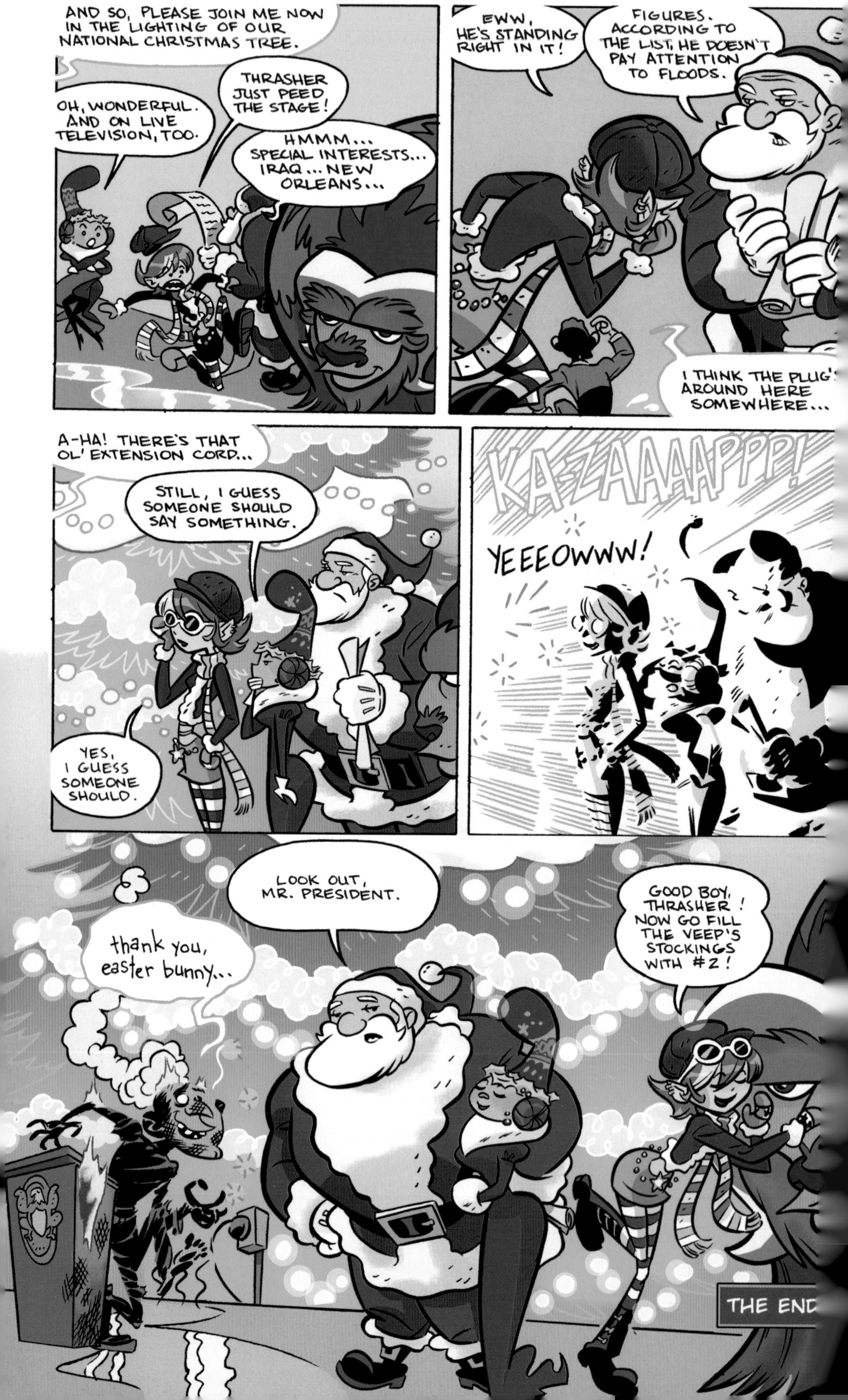
AND SO, PLEASE JOIN ME NOW IN THE LIGHTING OF OUR NATIONAL CHRISTMAS TREE.
OH, WONDERFUL. AND ON LIVE TELEVISION, TOO.
THRASHER JUST PEED THE STAGE!
HMMM... SPECIAL INTERESTS... IRAQ... NEW ORLEANS...
EWW, HE'S STANDING RIGHT IN IT!
FIGURES. ACCORDING TO THE LIST, HE DOESN'T PAY ATTENTION TO FLOODS.
I THINK THE PLUG'S AROUND HERE SOMEWHERE...
A-HA! THERE'S THAT OL' EXTENSION CORD...
STILL, I GUESS SOMEONE SHOULD SAY SOMETHING.
YES, I GUESS SOMEONE SHOULD.
KA-ZAAAAAPPP!
YEEEOWWW!
LOOK OUT, MR. PRESIDENT.
thank you, easter bunny...
GOOD BOY, THRASHER! NOW GO FILL THE VEEP'S STOCKINGS WITH #2!
THE END

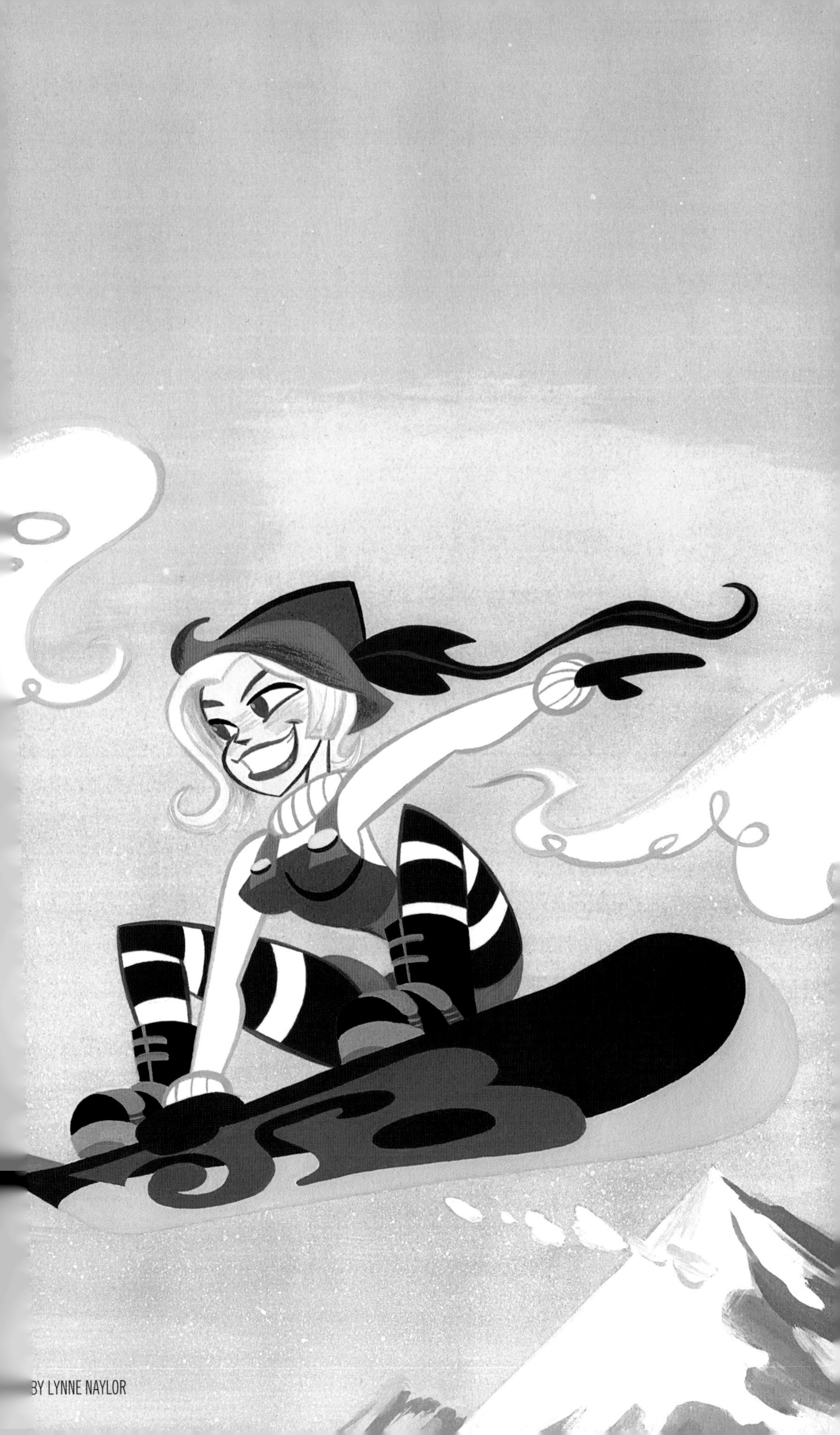

BY LYNNE NAYLOR

Santa Claus vs. Frankenstein

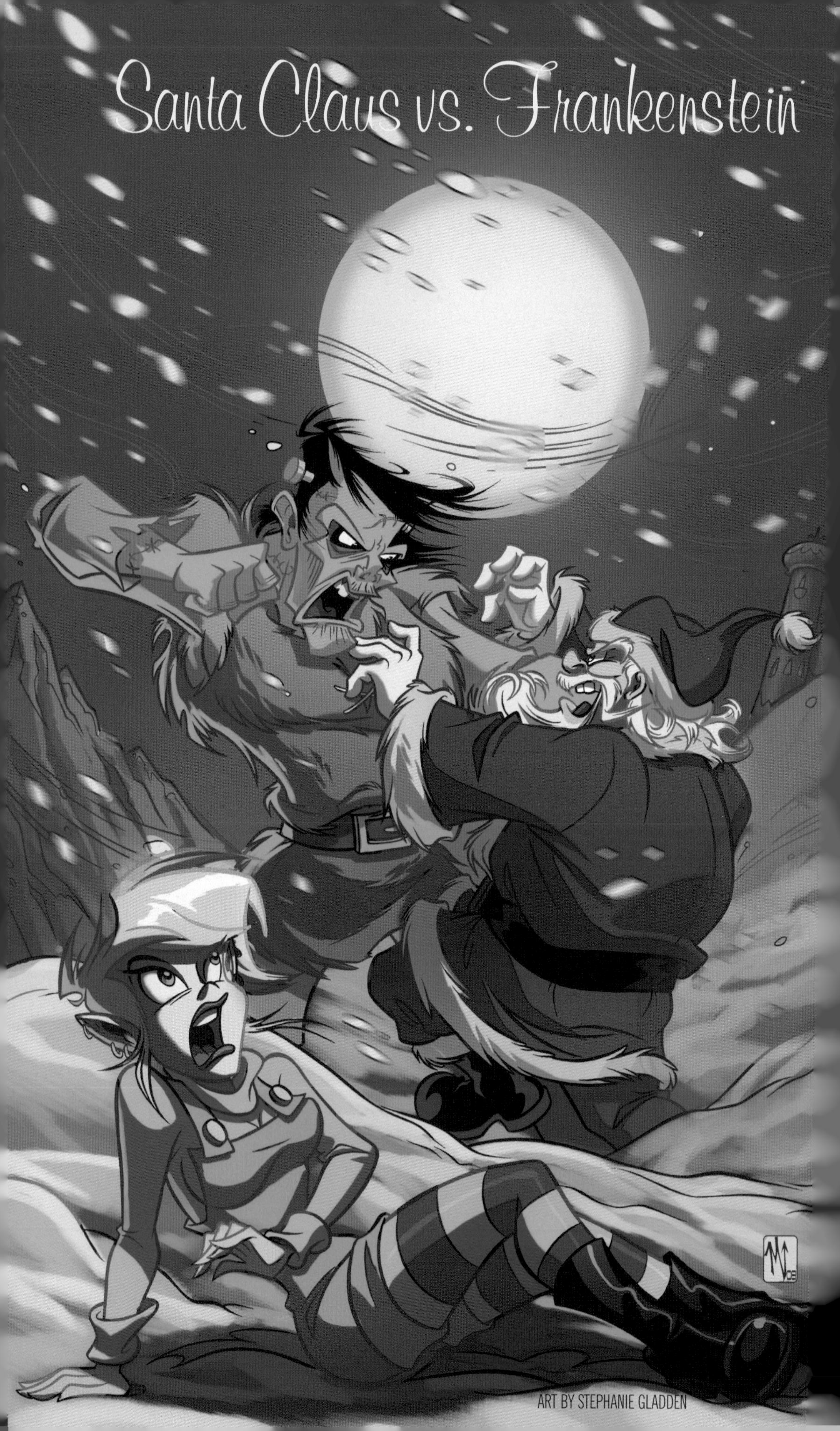

ART BY STEPHANIE GLADDEN

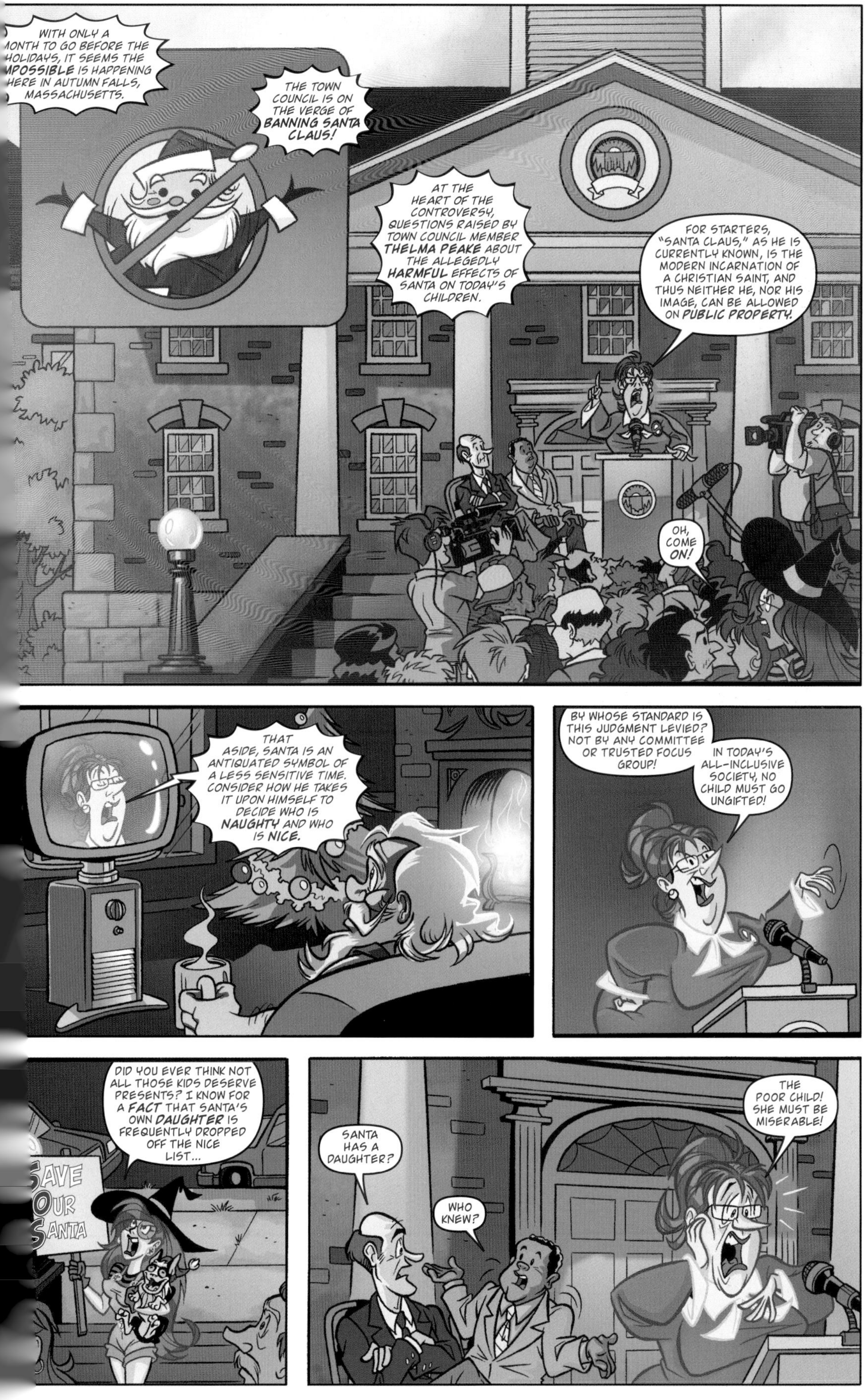

WITH ONLY A MONTH TO GO BEFORE THE HOLIDAYS, IT SEEMS THE IMPOSSIBLE IS HAPPENING HERE IN AUTUMN FALLS, MASSACHUSETTS.
THE TOWN COUNCIL IS ON THE VERGE OF BANNING SANTA CLAUS!
AT THE HEART OF THE CONTROVERSY, QUESTIONS RAISED BY TOWN COUNCIL MEMBER THELMA PEAKE ABOUT THE ALLEGEDLY HARMFUL EFFECTS OF SANTA ON TODAY'S CHILDREN.
FOR STARTERS, "SANTA CLAUS," AS HE IS CURRENTLY KNOWN, IS THE MODERN INCARNATION OF A CHRISTIAN SAINT, AND THUS NEITHER HE, NOR HIS IMAGE, CAN BE ALLOWED ON PUBLIC PROPERTY.
OH, COME ON!
THAT ASIDE, SANTA IS AN ANTIQUATED SYMBOL OF A LESS SENSITIVE TIME. CONSIDER HOW HE TAKES IT UPON HIMSELF TO DECIDE WHO IS NAUGHTY AND WHO IS NICE.
BY WHOSE STANDARD IS THIS JUDGMENT LEVIED? NOT BY ANY COMMITTEE OR TRUSTED FOCUS GROUP!
IN TODAY'S ALL-INCLUSIVE SOCIETY, NO CHILD MUST GO UNGIFTED!
DID YOU EVER THINK NOT ALL THOSE KIDS DESERVE PRESENTS? I KNOW FOR A FACT THAT SANTA'S OWN DAUGHTER IS FREQUENTLY DROPPED OFF THE NICE LIST...
SAVE OUR SANTA
SANTA HAS A DAUGHTER?
WHO KNEW?
THE POOR CHILD! SHE MUST BE MISERABLE!

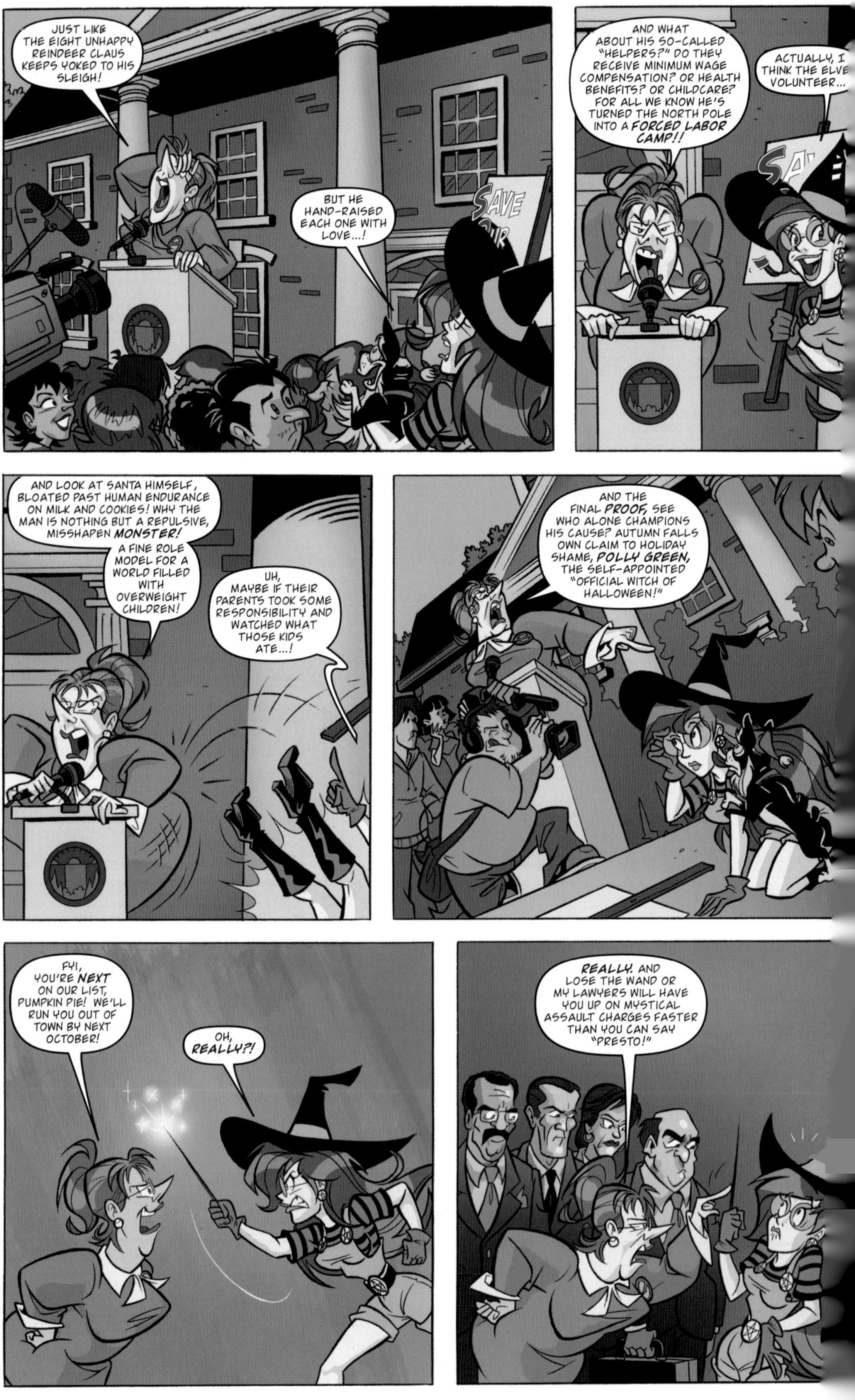
JUST LIKE THE EIGHT UNHAPPY REINDEER CLAUS KEEPS YOKED TO HIS SLEIGH!
BUT HE HAND-RAISED EACH ONE WITH LOVE...!
SAVE
AND WHAT ABOUT HIS SO-CALLED "HELPERS?" DO THEY RECEIVE MINIMUM WAGE COMPENSATION? OR HEALTH BENEFITS? OR CHILDCARE? FOR ALL WE KNOW HE'S TURNED THE NORTH POLE INTO A FORCED LABOR CAMP!!
ACTUALLY, I THINK THE ELVE VOLUNTEER...
AND LOOK AT SANTA HIMSELF, BLOATED PAST HUMAN ENDURANCE ON MILK AND COOKIES! WHY THE MAN IS NOTHING BUT A REPULSIVE, MISSHAPEN MONSTER!
A FINE ROLE MODEL FOR A WORLD FILLED WITH OVERWEIGHT CHILDREN!
UH, MAYBE IF THEIR PARENTS TOOK SOME RESPONSIBILITY AND WATCHED WHAT THOSE KIDS ATE...!
AND THE FINAL PROOF, SEE WHO ALONE CHAMPIONS HIS CAUSE? AUTUMN FALLS OWN CLAIM TO HOLIDAY SHAME, POLLY GREEN, THE SELF-APPOINTED "OFFICIAL WITCH OF HALLOWEEN!"
FYI, YOU'RE NEXT ON OUR LIST, PUMPKIN PIE! WE'LL RUN YOU OUT OF TOWN BY NEXT OCTOBER!
OH, REALLY?!
REALLY. AND LOSE THE WAND OR MY LAWYERS WILL HAVE YOU UP ON MYSTICAL ASSAULT CHARGES FASTER THAN YOU CAN SAY "PRESTO!"

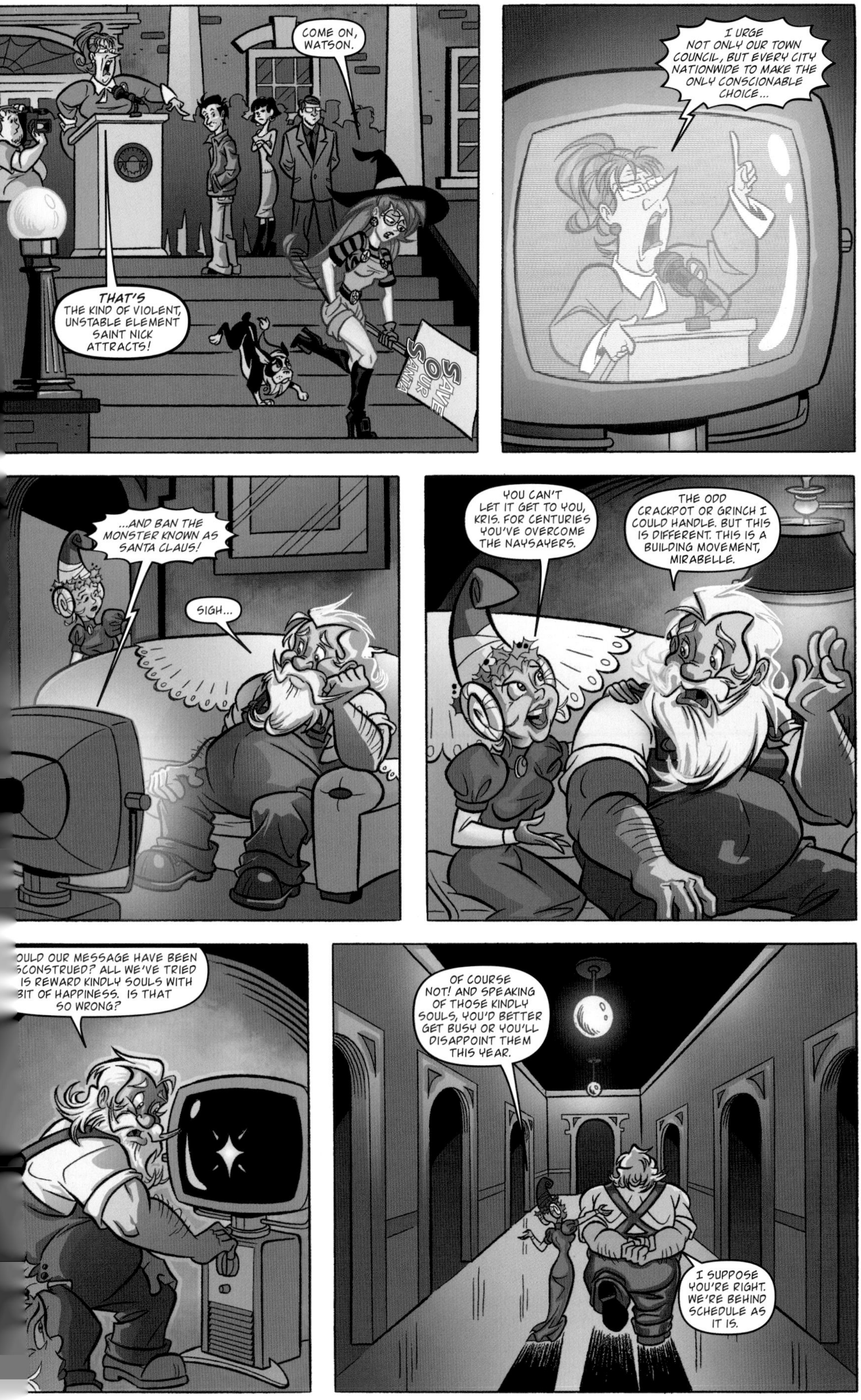
COME ON, WATSON.
THAT'S THE KIND OF VIOLENT, UNSTABLE ELEMENT SAINT NICK ATTRACTS!
SAVE OUR SANTA
I URGE NOT ONLY OUR TOWN COUNCIL, BUT EVERY CITY NATIONWIDE TO MAKE THE ONLY CONSCIONABLE CHOICE...
...AND BAN THE MONSTER KNOWN AS SANTA CLAUS!
SIGH...
YOU CAN'T LET IT GET TO YOU, KRIS. FOR CENTURIES YOU'VE OVERCOME THE NAYSAYERS.
THE ODD CRACKPOT OR GRINCH I COULD HANDLE. BUT THIS IS DIFFERENT. THIS IS A BUILDING MOVEMENT, MIRABELLE.
OULD OUR MESSAGE HAVE BEEN SCONSTRUED? ALL WE'VE TRIED IS REWARD KINDLY SOULS WITH BIT OF HAPPINESS. IS THAT SO WRONG?
OF COURSE NOT! AND SPEAKING OF THOSE KINDLY SOULS, YOU'D BETTER GET BUSY OR YOU'LL DISAPPOINT THEM THIS YEAR.
I SUPPOSE YOU'RE RIGHT. WE'RE BEHIND SCHEDULE AS IT IS.

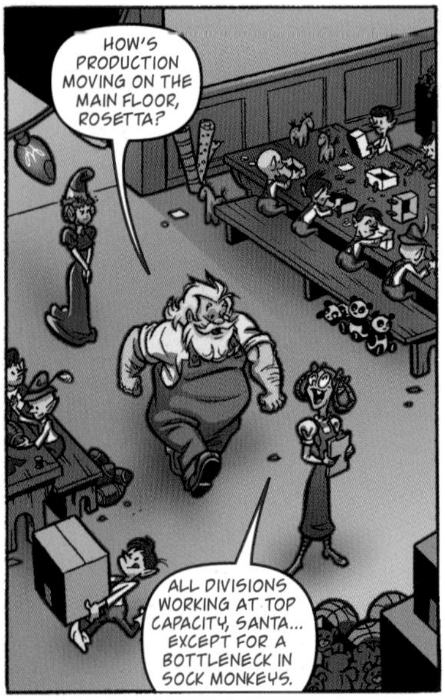
HOW'S PRODUCTION MOVING ON THE MAIN FLOOR, ROSETTA?
ALL DIVISIONS WORKING AT TOP CAPACITY, SANTA... EXCEPT FOR A BOTTLENECK IN SOCK MONKEYS.

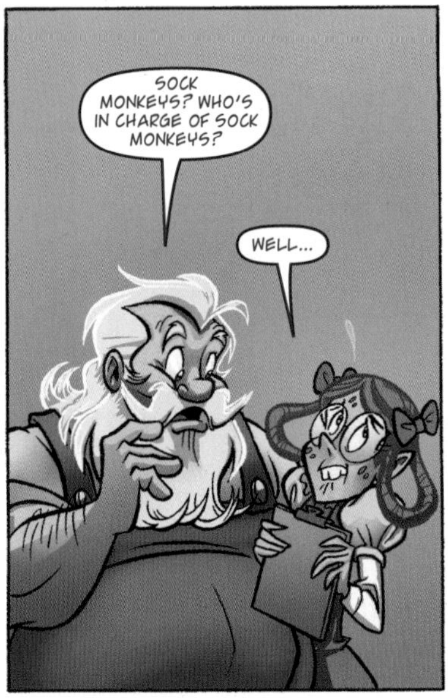
SOCK MONKEYS? WHO'S IN CHARGE OF SOCK MONKEYS?
WELL...

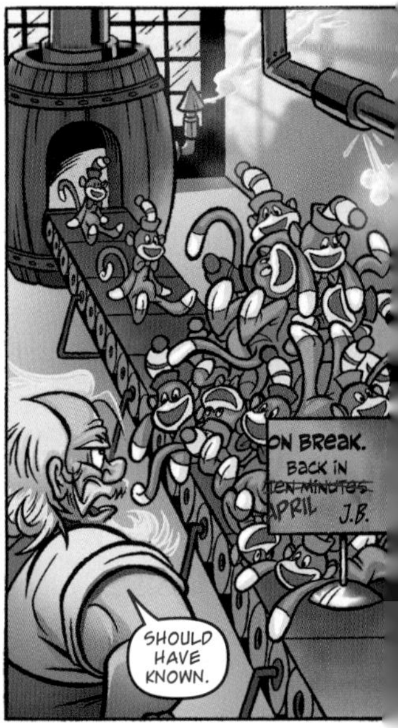
ON BREAK.
BACK IN
TEN MINUTES
APRIL
J.B.
SHOULD HAVE KNOWN.

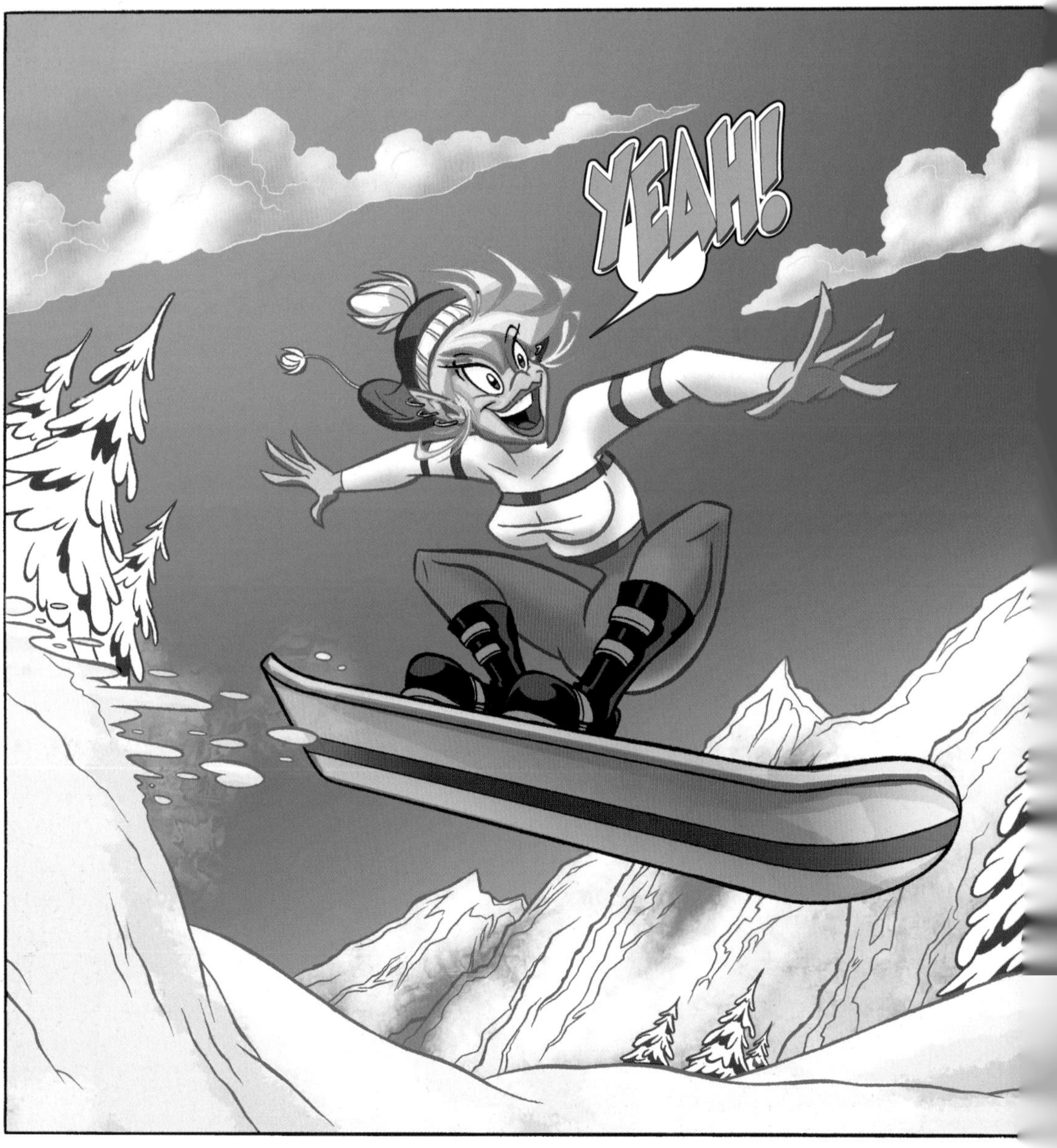
YEAH!

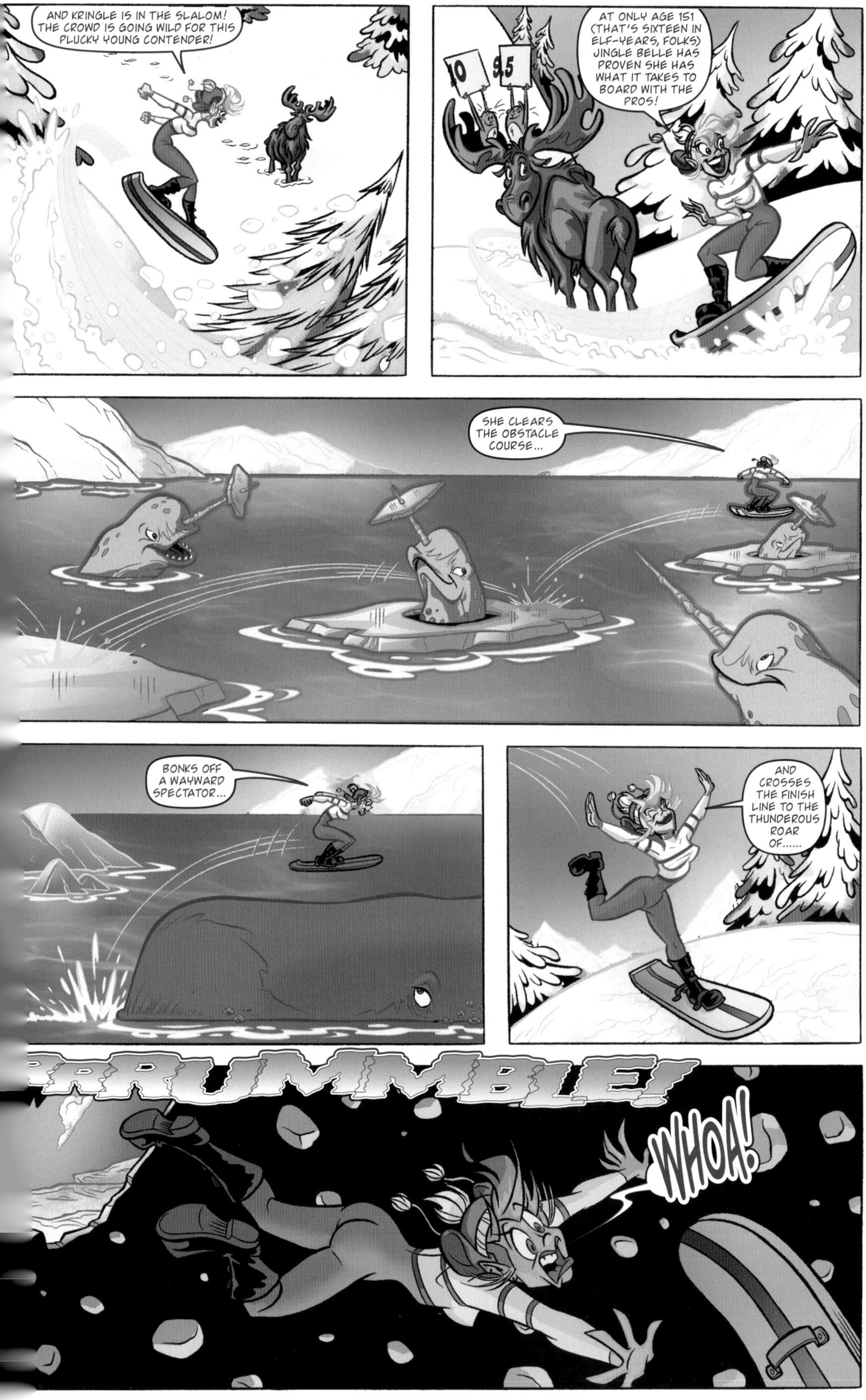
AND KRINGLE IS IN THE SLALOM! THE CROWD IS GOING WILD FOR THIS PLUCKY YOUNG CONTENDER!
10
9.5
AT ONLY AGE 151 (THAT'S SIXTEEN IN ELF-YEARS, FOLKS) JINGLE BELLE HAS PROVEN SHE HAS WHAT IT TAKES TO BOARD WITH THE PROS!
SHE CLEARS THE OBSTACLE COURSE...
BONKS OFF A WAYWARD SPECTATOR...
AND CROSSES THE FINISH LINE TO THE THUNDEROUS ROAR OF......
RRUMMBLE!
WHOA!

OW! ANOTHER GOOD SLOPE GONE TO SLUSH! THANKS, GLOBAL WARMING!
I BETTER SPLIT THIS PIT BEFORE ANYTHING ELSE...
YEO

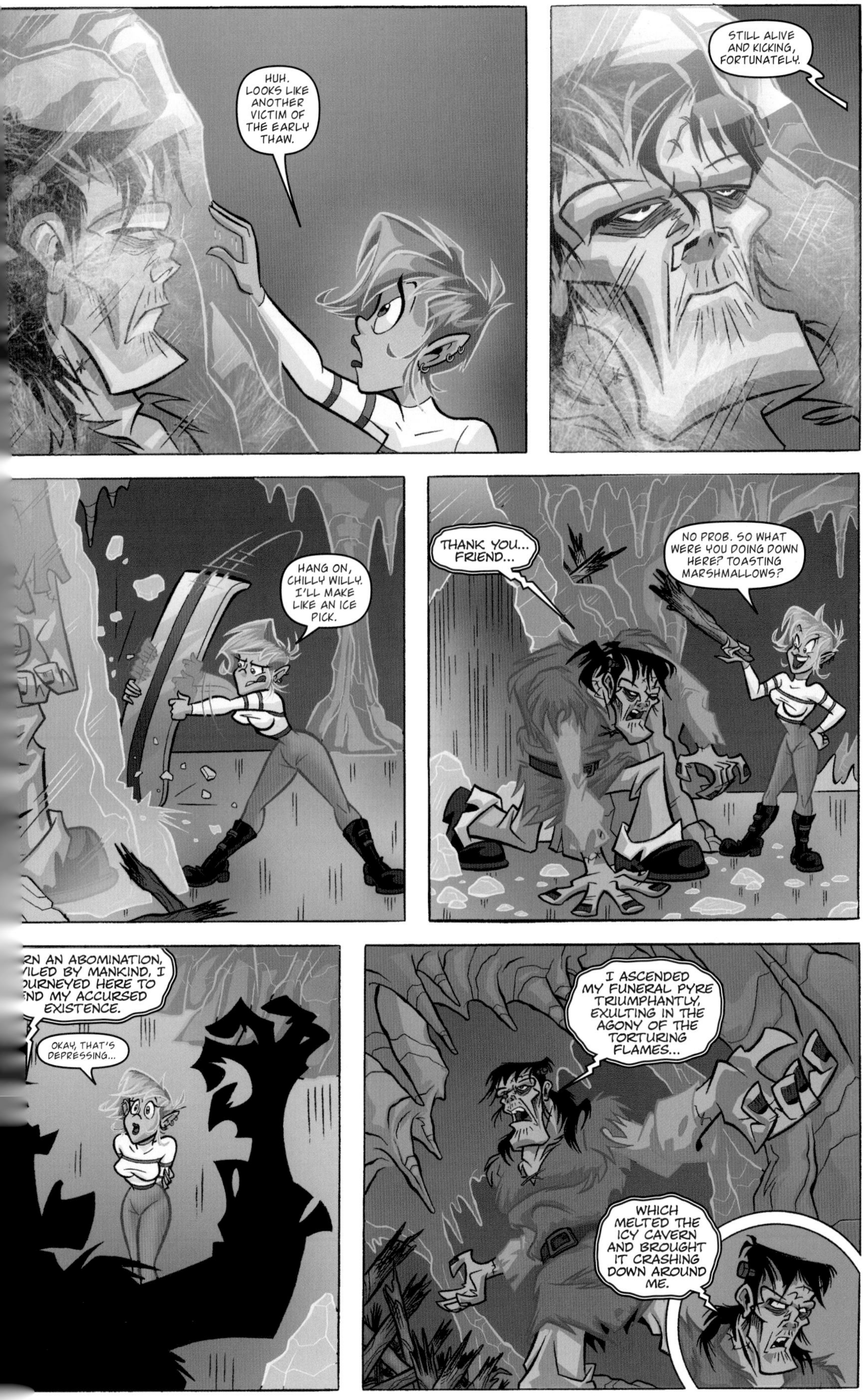
HUH. LOOKS LIKE ANOTHER VICTIM OF THE EARLY THAW.
STILL ALIVE AND KICKING, FORTUNATELY.
HANG ON, CHILLY WILLY. I'LL MAKE LIKE AN ICE PICK.
THANK YOU... FRIEND...
NO PROB. SO WHAT WERE YOU DOING DOWN HERE? TOASTING MARSHMALLOWS?
RN AN ABOMINATION, VILED BY MANKIND, I OURNEYED HERE TO END MY ACCURSED EXISTENCE.
OKAY, THAT'S DEPRESSING...
I ASCENDED MY FUNERAL PYRE TRIUMPHANTLY, EXULTING IN THE AGONY OF THE TORTURING FLAMES...
WHICH MELTED THE ICY CAVERN AND BROUGHT IT CRASHING DOWN AROUND ME.

OVER TWO HUNDRED YEARS I WAITED FOR A RESCUER. I DIDN'T KNOW SHE'D BE SO PRETTY.

YOU'RE SORT OF CUTE YOURSELF, IN A GOTH-EMO-DEATH METAL KINDA WAY.

LET'S GET OUT OF HERE. GIVE ME A...

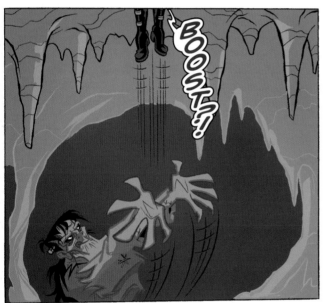

BOOST!

WHOO! BIG BOY'S STRONGER THAN HE LOOKS!

THERE'S SOMETHING FAMILIAR ABOUT HIM, TOO...

I'M SURE I'VE SEEN YOUR FACE SOMEPLACE BEFORE...

A POLICE NOTICE, NO DOUBT. I AM KNOWN AS DEMON, OGRE, CREATURE...

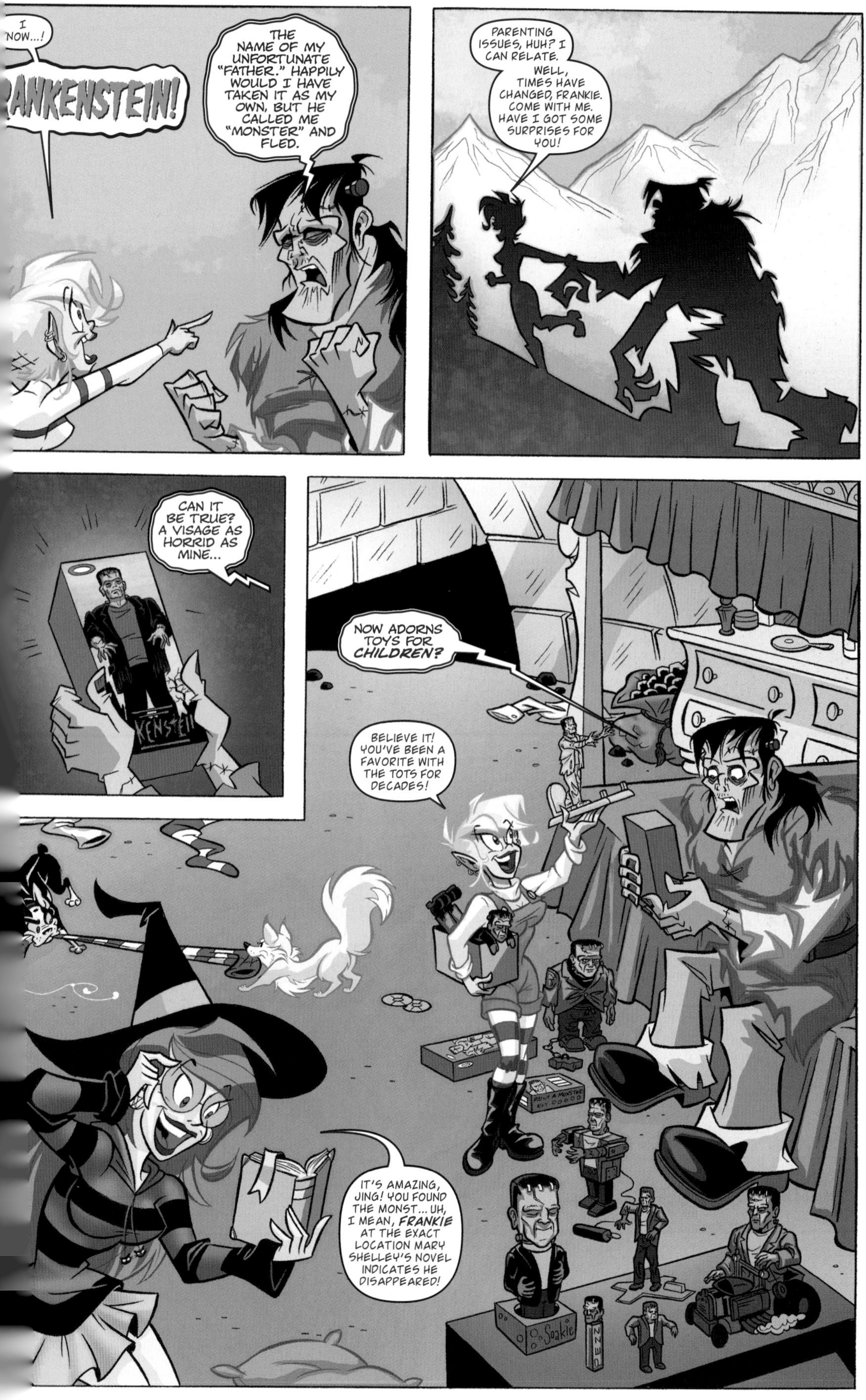

I NOW...!
RANKENSTEIN!
THE NAME OF MY UNFORTUNATE "FATHER." HAPPILY WOULD I HAVE TAKEN IT AS MY OWN, BUT HE CALLED ME "MONSTER" AND FLED.
PARENTING ISSUES, HUH? I CAN RELATE.
WELL, TIMES HAVE CHANGED, FRANKIE. COME WITH ME. HAVE I GOT SOME SURPRISES FOR YOU!
CAN IT BE TRUE? A VISAGE AS HORRID AS MINE...
NOW ADORNS TOYS FOR CHILDREN?
BELIEVE IT! YOU'VE BEEN A FAVORITE WITH THE TOTS FOR DECADES!
IT'S AMAZING, JING! YOU FOUND THE MONST... UH, I MEAN, FRANKIE AT THE EXACT LOCATION MARY SHELLEY'S NOVEL INDICATES HE DISAPPEARED!

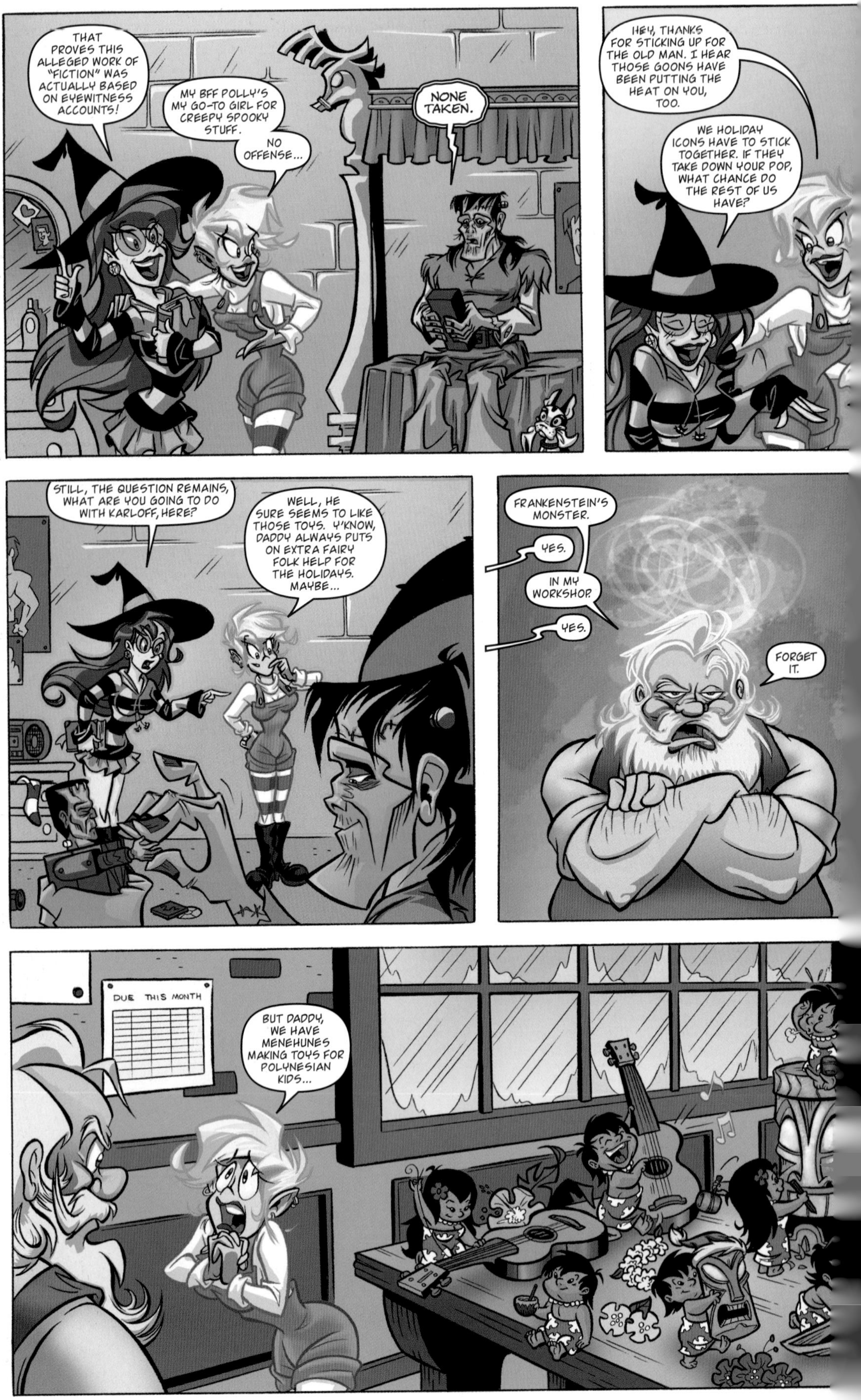
THAT PROVES THIS ALLEGED WORK OF "FICTION" WAS ACTUALLY BASED ON EYEWITNESS ACCOUNTS!
MY BFF POLLY'S MY GO-TO GIRL FOR CREEPY SPOOKY STUFF.
NO OFFENSE...
NONE TAKEN.
HEY, THANKS FOR STICKING UP FOR THE OLD MAN. I HEAR THOSE GOONS HAVE BEEN PUTTING THE HEAT ON YOU, TOO.
WE HOLIDAY ICONS HAVE TO STICK TOGETHER. IF THEY TAKE DOWN YOUR POP, WHAT CHANCE DO THE REST OF US HAVE?
STILL, THE QUESTION REMAINS, WHAT ARE YOU GOING TO DO WITH KARLOFF, HERE?
WELL, HE SURE SEEMS TO LIKE THOSE TOYS. Y'KNOW, DADDY ALWAYS PUTS ON EXTRA FAIRY FOLK HELP FOR THE HOLIDAYS. MAYBE...
FRANKENSTEIN'S MONSTER.
YES.
IN MY WORKSHOP.
YES.
FORGET IT.
DUE THIS MONTH
BUT DADDY, WE HAVE MENEHUNES MAKING TOYS FOR POLYNESIAN KIDS...

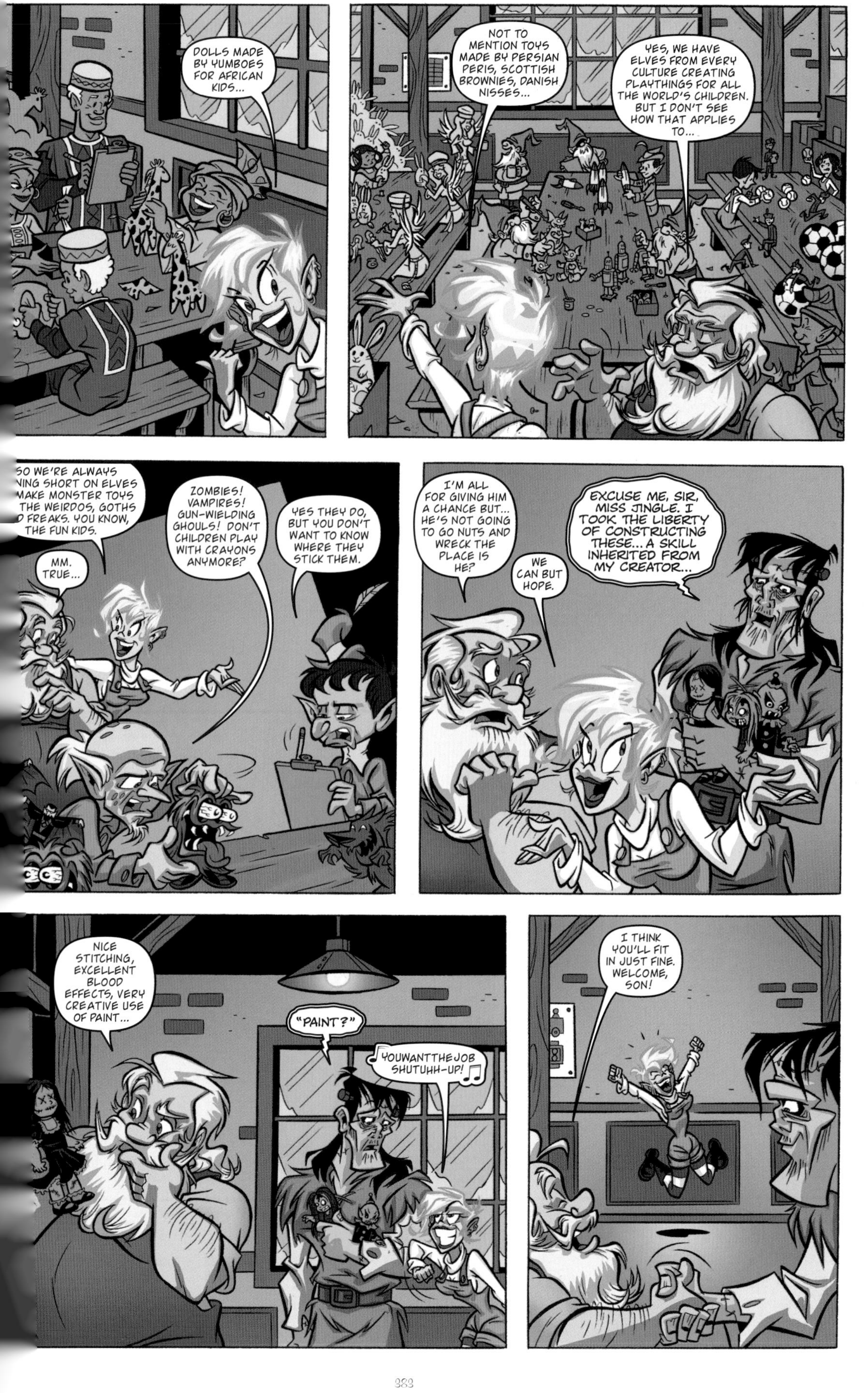
DOLLS MADE BY YUMBOES FOR AFRICAN KIDS...
NOT TO MENTION TOYS MADE BY PERSIAN PERIS, SCOTTISH BROWNIES, DANISH NISSES...
YES, WE HAVE ELVES FROM EVERY CULTURE CREATING PLAYTHINGS FOR ALL THE WORLD'S CHILDREN. BUT I DON'T SEE HOW THAT APPLIES TO...
SO WE'RE ALWAYS NING SHORT ON ELVES MAKE MONSTER TOYS THE WEIRDOS, GOTHS D FREAKS. YOU KNOW, THE FUN KIDS.
MM. TRUE...
ZOMBIES! VAMPIRES! GUN-WIELDING GHOULS! DON'T CHILDREN PLAY WITH CRAYONS ANYMORE?
YES THEY DO, BUT YOU DON'T WANT TO KNOW WHERE THEY STICK THEM.
I'M ALL FOR GIVING HIM A CHANCE BUT... HE'S NOT GOING TO GO NUTS AND WRECK THE PLACE IS HE?
WE CAN BUT HOPE.
EXCUSE ME, SIR, MISS JINGLE. I TOOK THE LIBERTY OF CONSTRUCTING THESE... A SKILL INHERITED FROM MY CREATOR...
NICE STITCHING, EXCELLENT BLOOD EFFECTS, VERY CREATIVE USE OF PAINT...
"PAINT?"
YOUWANTTHEJOB SHUTUHH-UP!
I THINK YOU'LL FIT IN JUST FINE. WELCOME, SON!

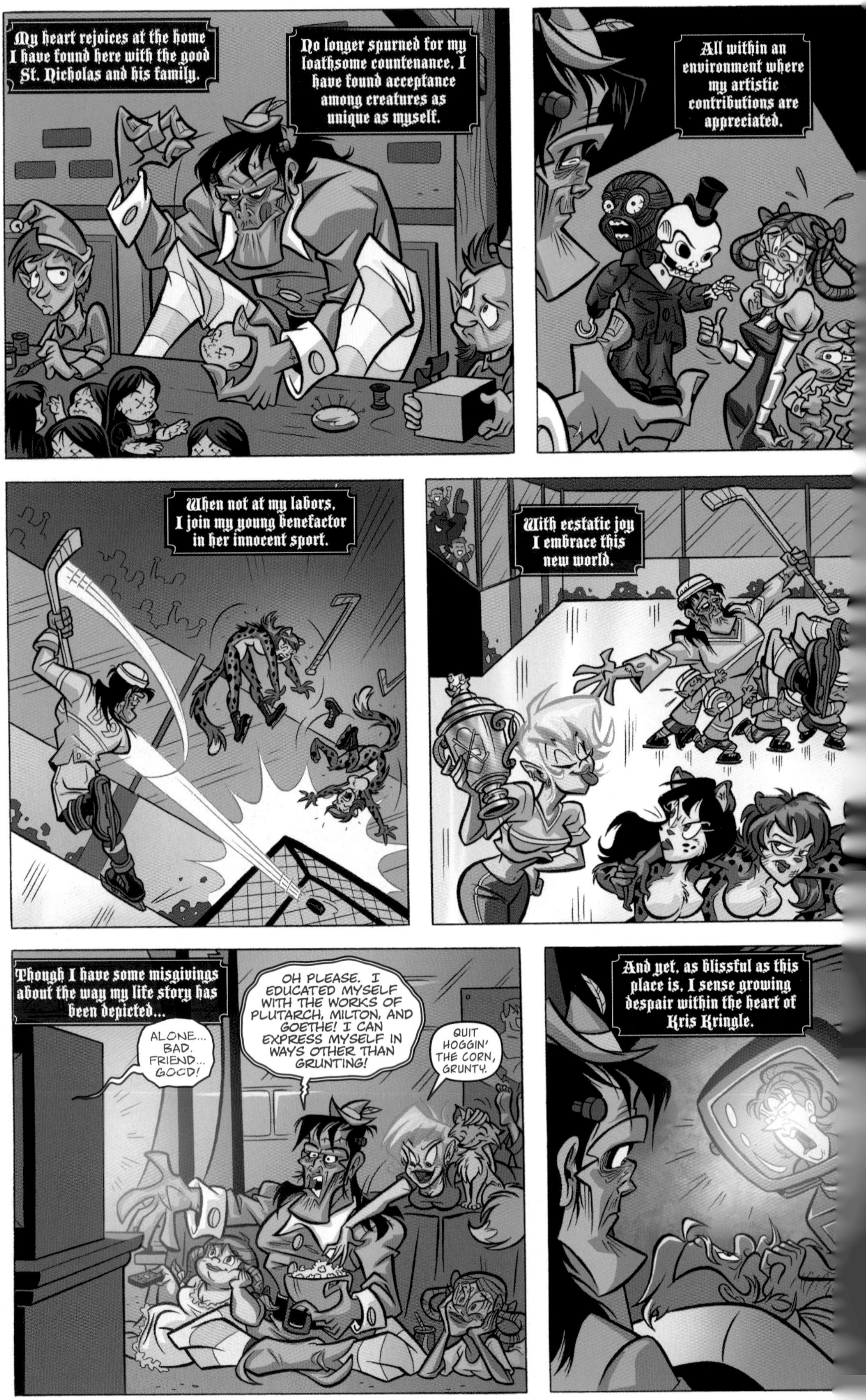
My heart rejoices at the home I have found here with the good St. Nicholas and his family.
No longer spurned for my loathsome countenance, I have found acceptance among creatures as unique as myself.
All within an environment where my artistic contributions are appreciated.
When not at my labors, I join my young benefactor in her innocent sport.
With ecstatic joy I embrace this new world.
Though I have some misgivings about the way my life story has been depicted...
ALONE... BAD. FRIEND... GOOD!
OH PLEASE. I EDUCATED MYSELF WITH THE WORKS OF PLUTARCH, MILTON, AND GOETHE! I CAN EXPRESS MYSELF IN WAYS OTHER THAN GRUNTING!
QUIT HOGGIN' THE CORN, GRUNTY.
And yet, as blissful as this place is, I sense growing despair within the heart of Kris Kringle.

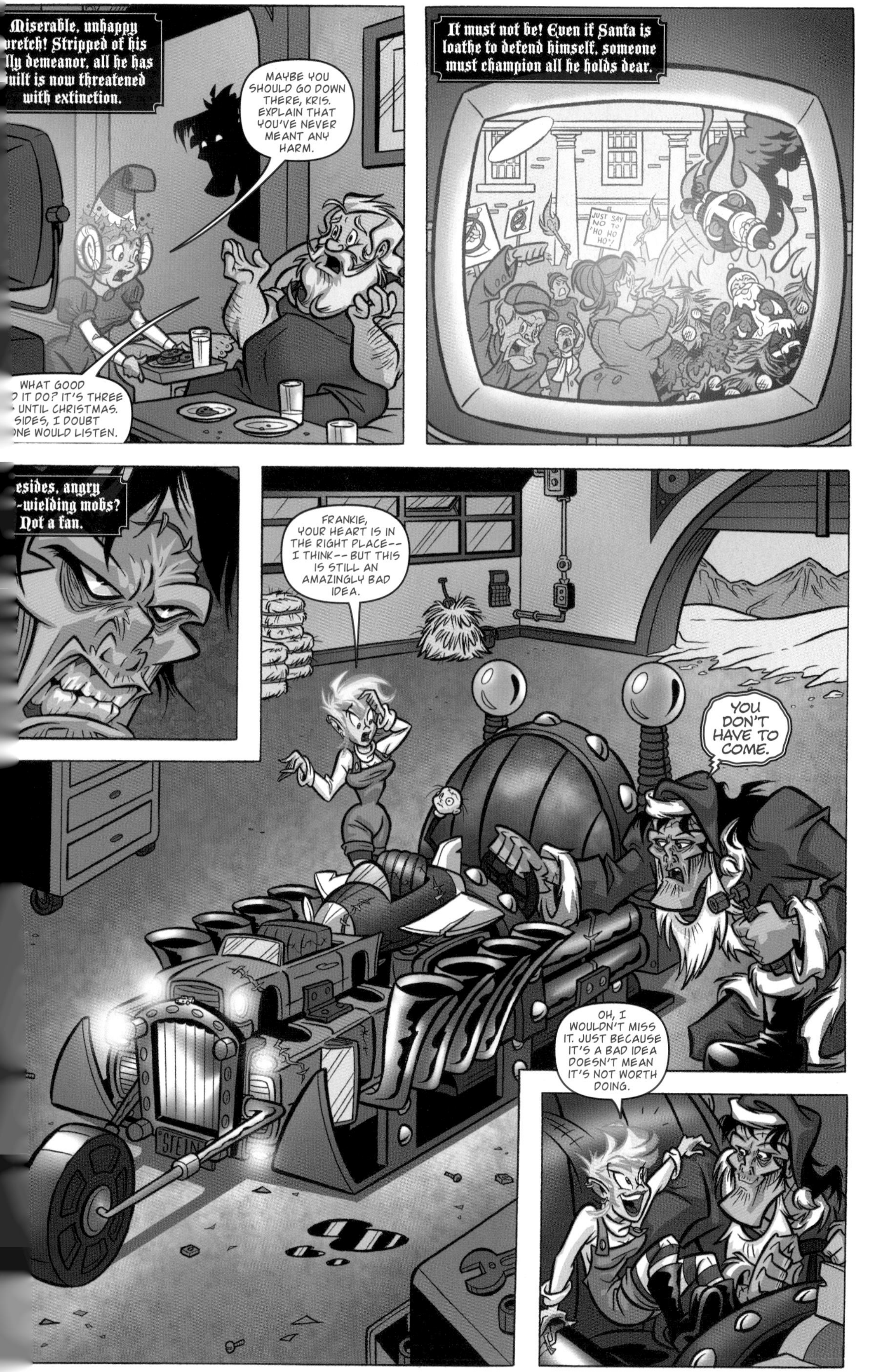
Miserable, unhappy
wretch! Stripped of his
lly demeanor, all he has
uilt is now threatened
with extinction.
MAYBE YOU SHOULD GO DOWN THERE, KRIS. EXPLAIN THAT YOU'VE NEVER MEANT ANY HARM.
WHAT GOOD
O IT DO? IT'S THREE
UNTIL CHRISTMAS.
SIDES, I DOUBT
ONE WOULD LISTEN.
It must not be! Even if Santa is loathe to defend himself, someone must champion all he holds dear.
JUST SAY NO TO 'HO HO HO'!
esides, angry
-wielding mobs?
Not a fan.
FRANKIE, YOUR HEART IS IN THE RIGHT PLACE-- I THINK-- BUT THIS IS STILL AN AMAZINGLY BAD IDEA.
YOU DON'T HAVE TO COME.
OH, I WOULDN'T MISS IT. JUST BECAUSE IT'S A BAD IDEA DOESN'T MEAN IT'S NOT WORTH DOING.
STEIN

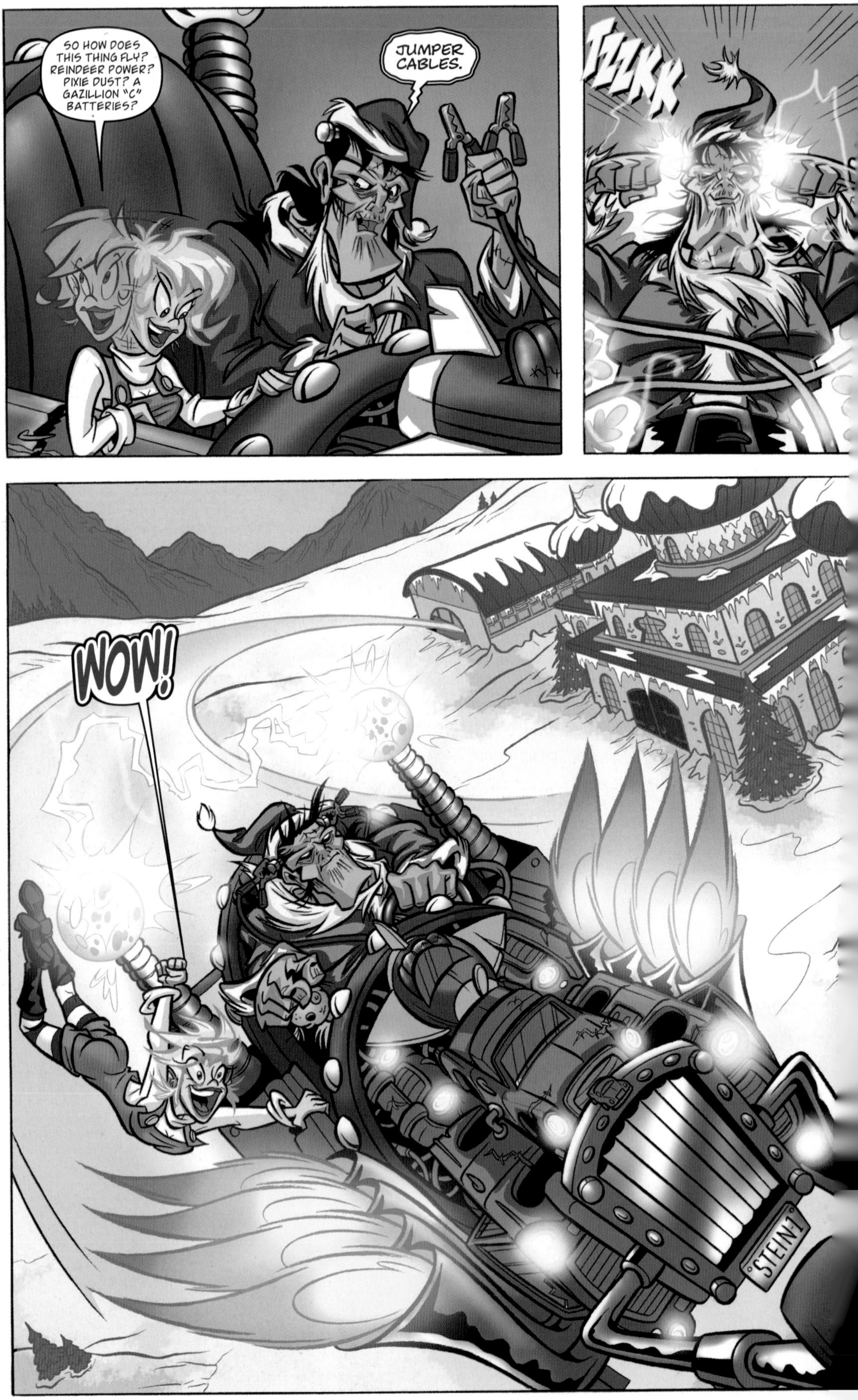
SO HOW DOES THIS THING FLY? REINDEER POWER? PIXIE DUST? A GAZILLION "C" BATTERIES?
JUMPER CABLES.
TZZKK
WOW!
STEIN 1

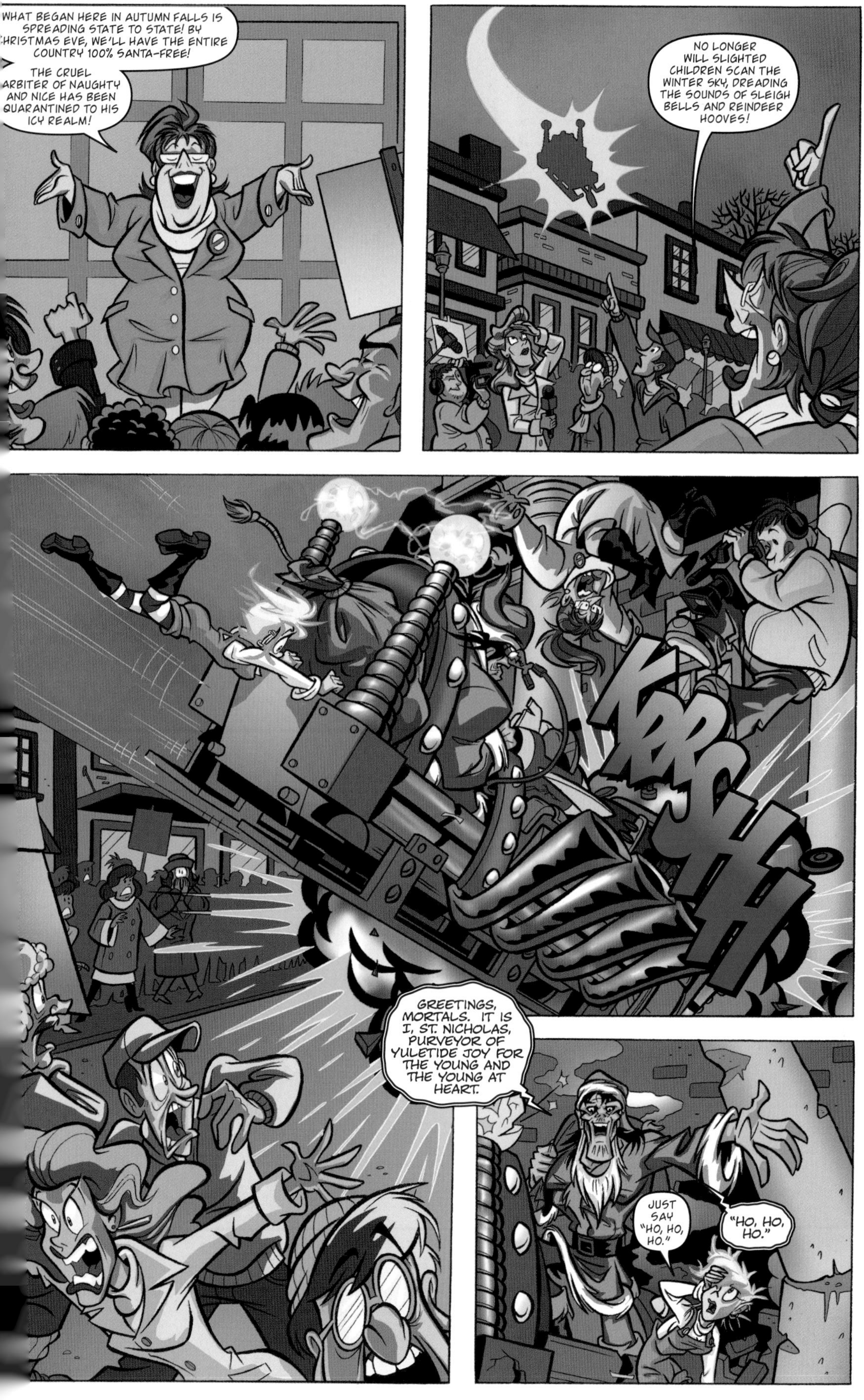
WHAT BEGAN HERE IN AUTUMN FALLS IS SPREADING STATE TO STATE! BY CHRISTMAS EVE, WE'LL HAVE THE ENTIRE COUNTRY 100% SANTA-FREE!
THE CRUEL ARBITER OF NAUGHTY AND NICE HAS BEEN QUARANTINED TO HIS ICY REALM!
NO LONGER WILL SLIGHTED CHILDREN SCAN THE WINTER SKY, DREADING THE SOUNDS OF SLEIGH BELLS AND REINDEER HOOVES!
KRRSSH
GREETINGS, MORTALS. IT IS I, ST. NICHOLAS, PURVEYOR OF YULETIDE JOY FOR THE YOUNG AND THE YOUNG AT HEART.
JUST SAY "HO, HO, HO."
"HO, HO, HO."

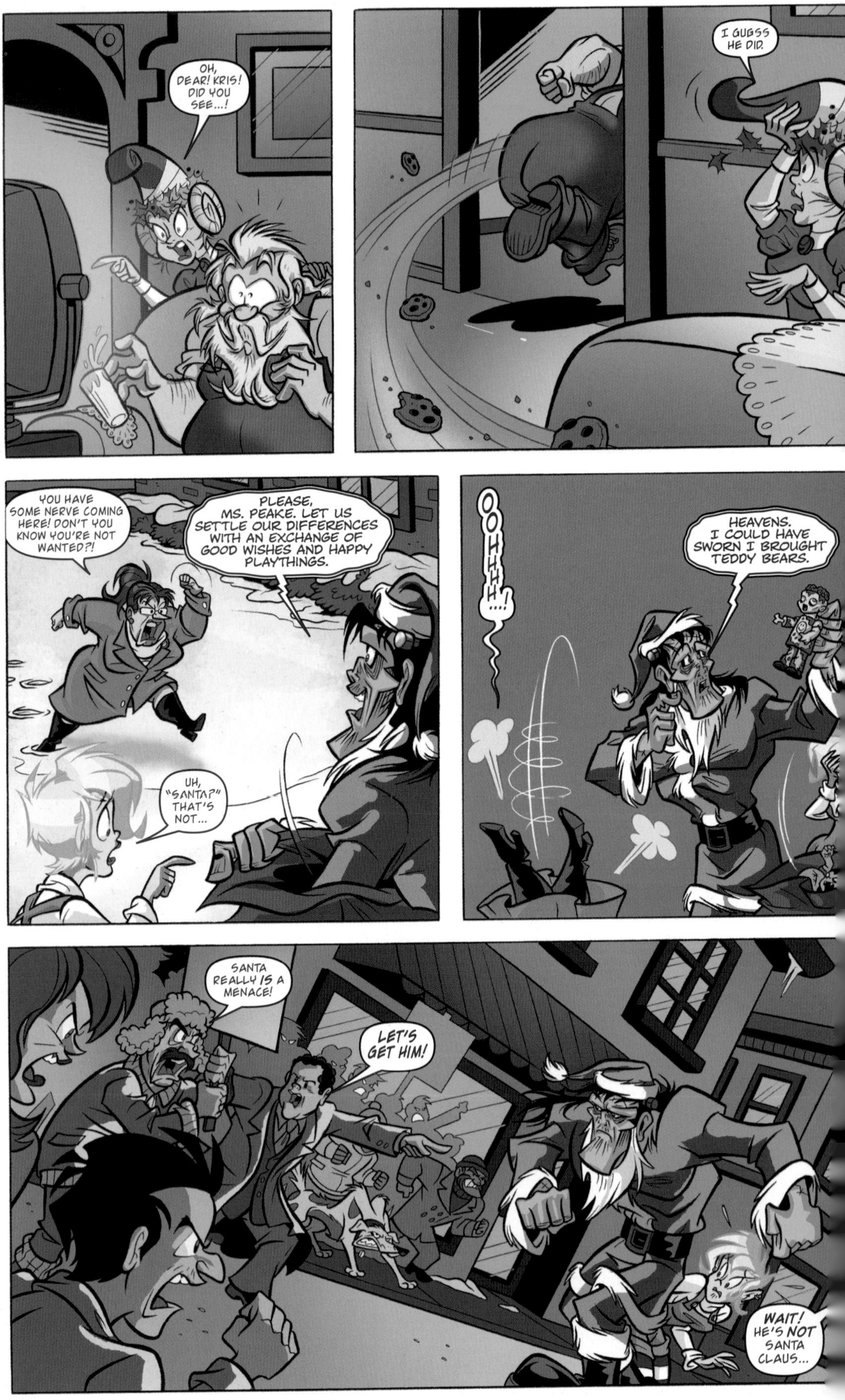
OH, DEAR! KRIS! DID YOU SEE...!
I GUESS HE DID.
YOU HAVE SOME NERVE COMING HERE! DON'T YOU KNOW YOU'RE NOT WANTED?!
PLEASE, MS. PEAKE. LET US SETTLE OUR DIFFERENCES WITH AN EXCHANGE OF GOOD WISHES AND HAPPY PLAYTHINGS.
UH, "SANTA?" THAT'S NOT...
OOHHHH...!
HEAVENS. I COULD HAVE SWORN I BROUGHT TEDDY BEARS.
SANTA REALLY IS A MENACE!
LET'S GET HIM!
WAIT! HE'S NOT SANTA CLAUS...

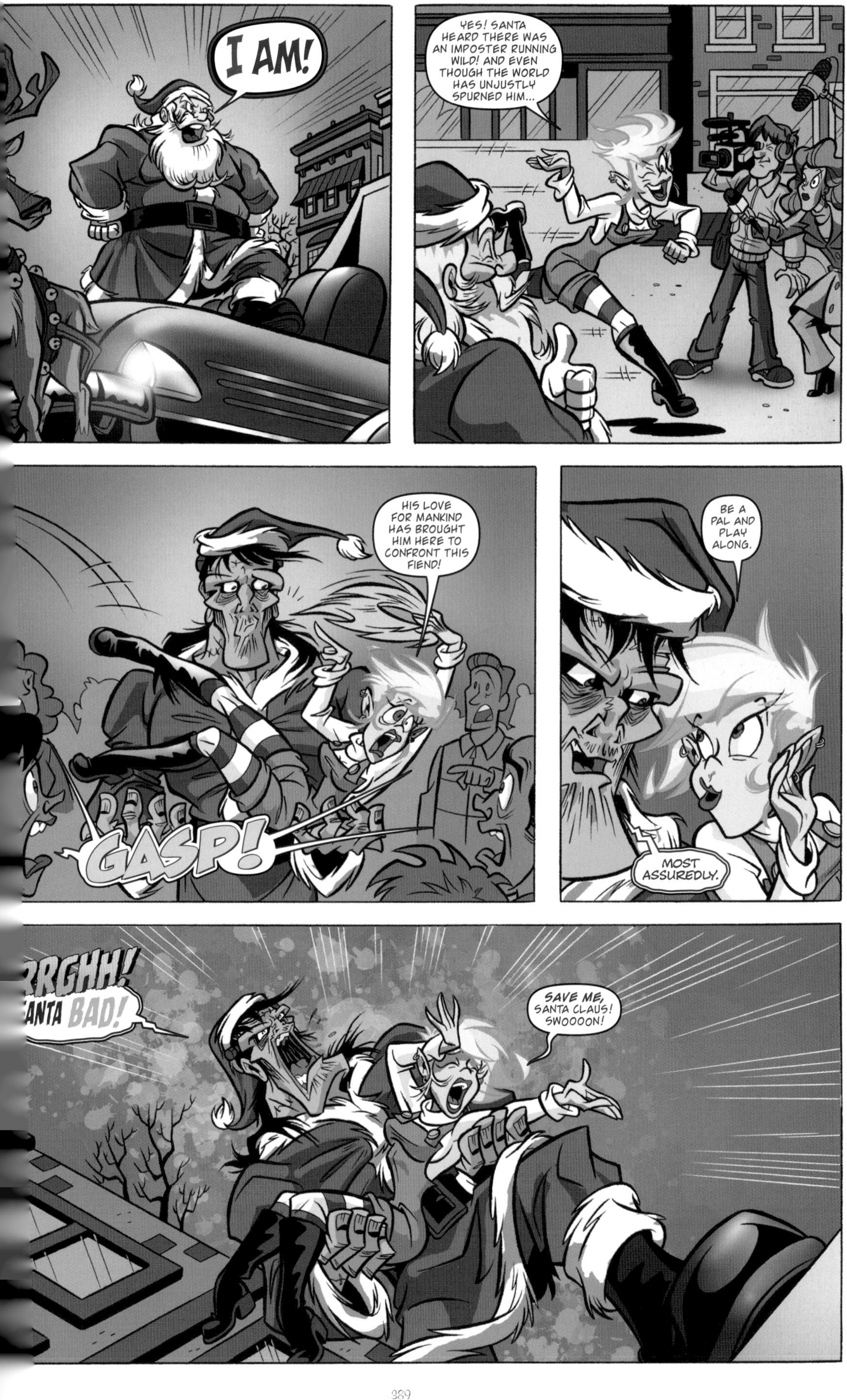
I AM!
YES! SANTA HEARD THERE WAS AN IMPOSTER RUNNING WILD! AND EVEN THOUGH THE WORLD HAS UNJUSTLY SPURNED HIM...
HIS LOVE FOR MANKIND HAS BROUGHT HIM HERE TO CONFRONT THIS FIEND!
GASP!
BE A PAL AND PLAY ALONG.
MOST ASSUREDLY.
RRGHH! ANTA BAD!
SAVE ME, SANTA CLAUS! SWOOOON!

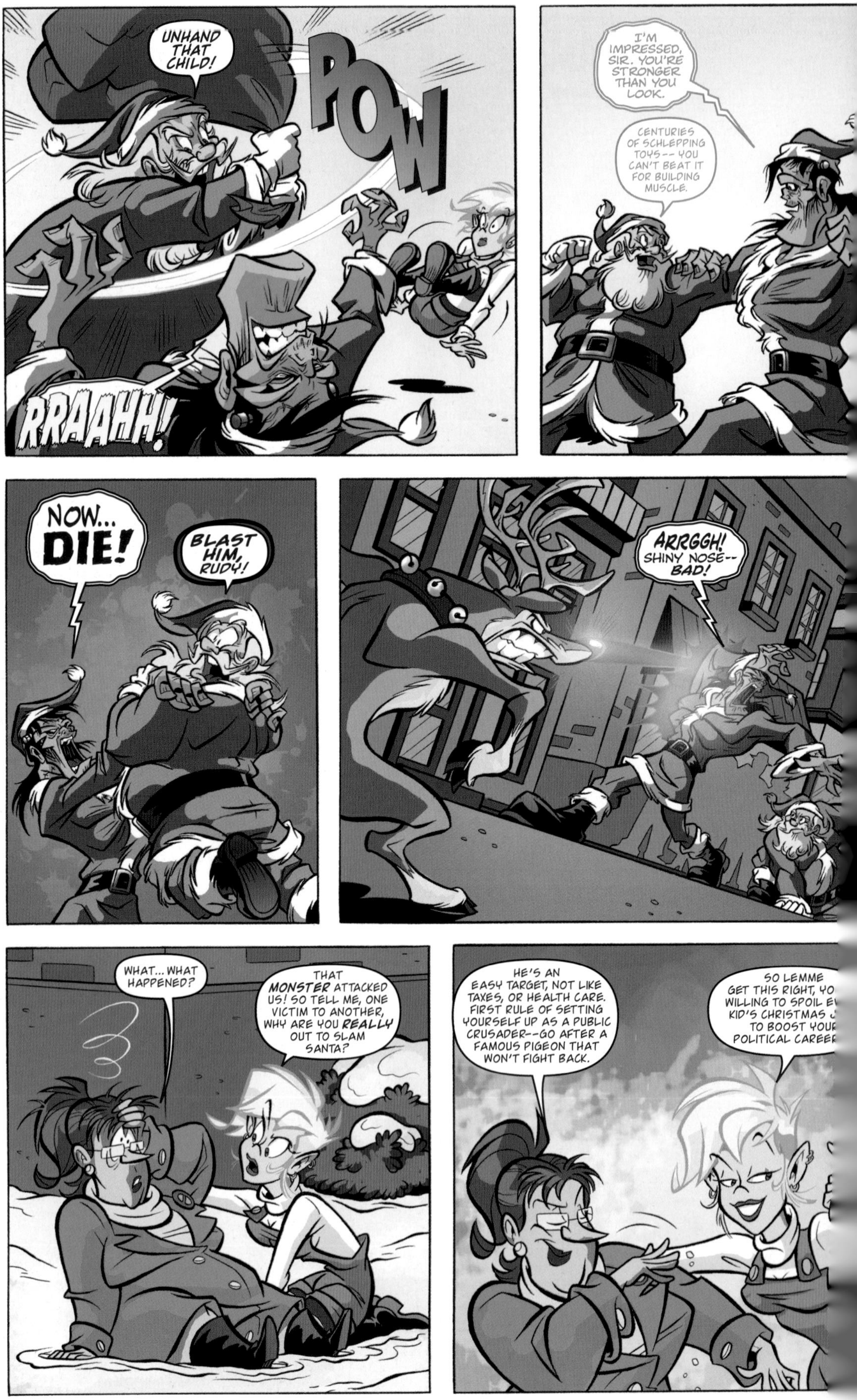
UNHAND THAT CHILD!
POW
RRAAHH!
I'M IMPRESSED, SIR. YOU'RE STRONGER THAN YOU LOOK.
CENTURIES OF SCHLEPPING TOYS-- YOU CAN'T BEAT IT FOR BUILDING MUSCLE.
NOW... DIE!
BLAST HIM, RUDY!
ARRGGH! SHINY NOSE-- BAD!
WHAT... WHAT HAPPENED?
THAT MONSTER ATTACKED US! SO TELL ME, ONE VICTIM TO ANOTHER, WHY ARE YOU REALLY OUT TO SLAM SANTA?
HE'S AN EASY TARGET, NOT LIKE TAXES, OR HEALTH CARE. FIRST RULE OF SETTING YOURSELF UP AS A PUBLIC CRUSADER--GO AFTER A FAMOUS PIGEON THAT WON'T FIGHT BACK.
SO LEMME GET THIS RIGHT, YO WILLING TO SPOIL EV KID'S CHRISTMAS J TO BOOST YOUR POLITICAL CAREER

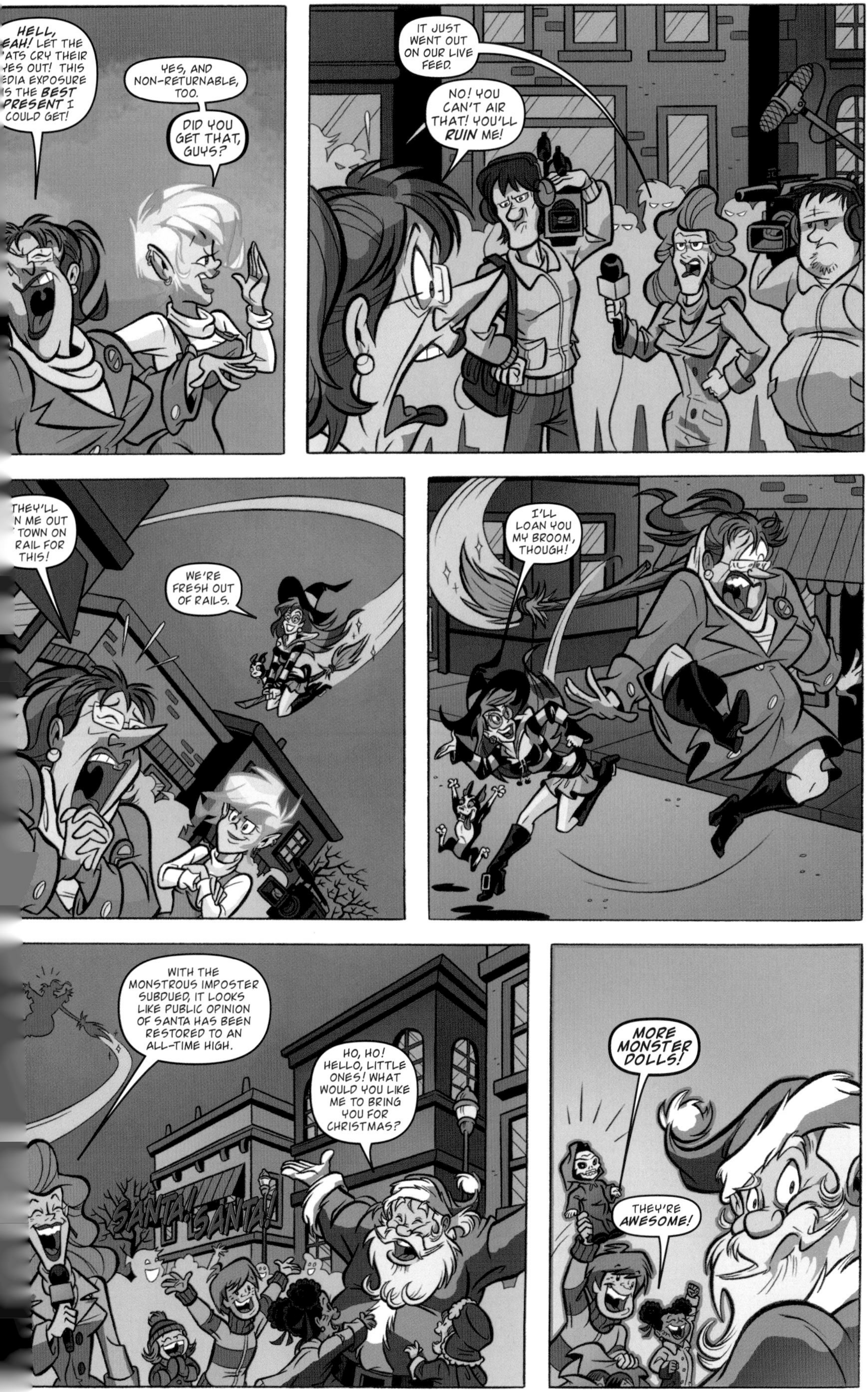
HELL, EAH! LET THE ATS CRY THEIR YES OUT! THIS EDIA EXPOSURE S THE BEST PRESENT I COULD GET!
YES, AND NON-RETURNABLE, TOO.
DID YOU GET THAT, GUYS?
IT JUST WENT OUT ON OUR LIVE FEED.
NO! YOU CAN'T AIR THAT! YOU'LL RUIN ME!
THEY'LL N ME OUT TOWN ON RAIL FOR THIS!
WE'RE FRESH OUT OF RAILS.
I'LL LOAN YOU MY BROOM, THOUGH!
WITH THE MONSTROUS IMPOSTER SUBDUED, IT LOOKS LIKE PUBLIC OPINION OF SANTA HAS BEEN RESTORED TO AN ALL-TIME HIGH.
HO, HO! HELLO, LITTLE ONES! WHAT WOULD YOU LIKE ME TO BRING YOU FOR CHRISTMAS?
SANTA! SANTA!
MORE MONSTER DOLLS!
THEY'RE AWESOME!

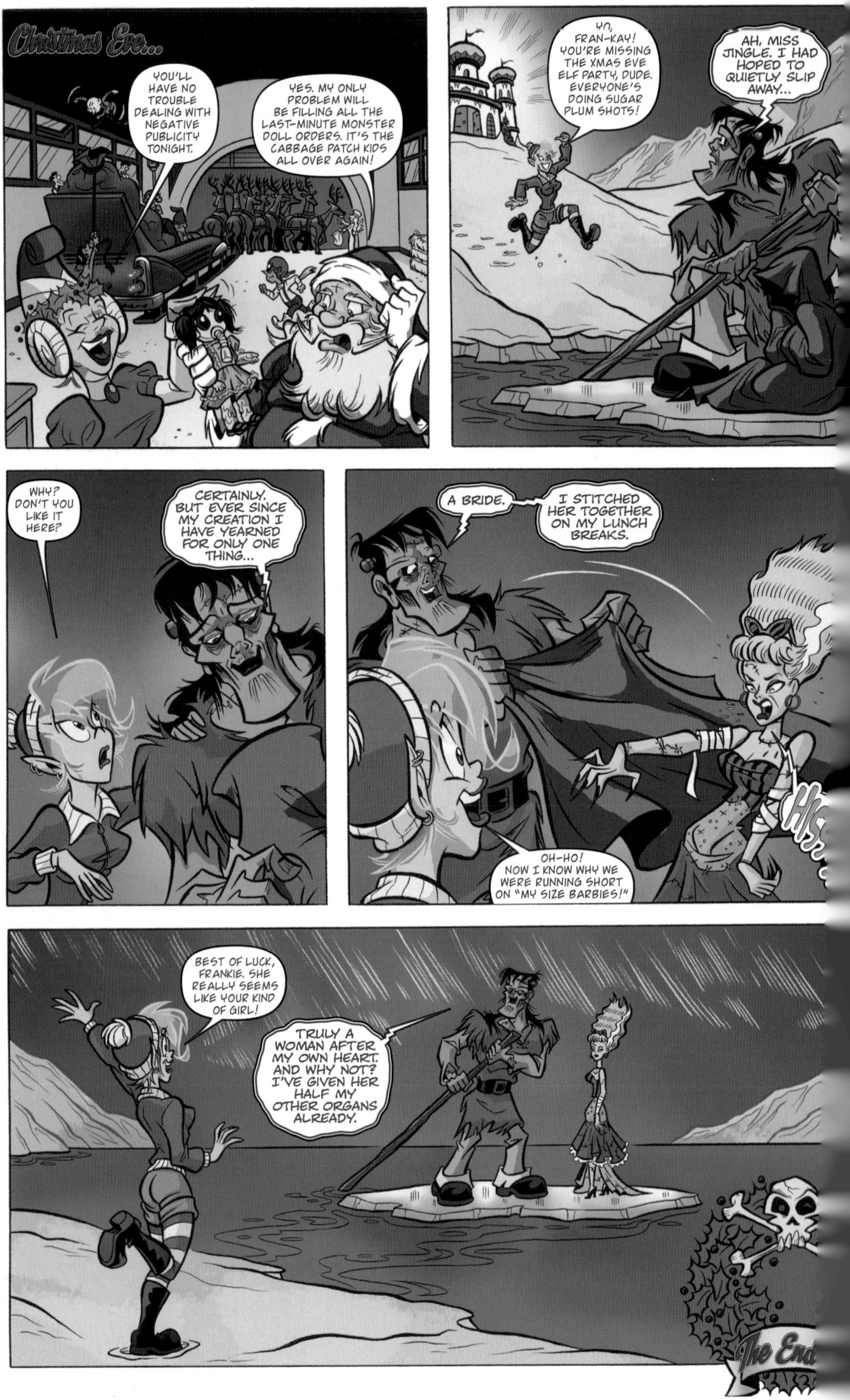
Christmas Eve...
YOU'LL HAVE NO TROUBLE DEALING WITH NEGATIVE PUBLICITY TONIGHT.
YES. MY ONLY PROBLEM WILL BE FILLING ALL THE LAST-MINUTE MONSTER DOLL ORDERS. IT'S THE CABBAGE PATCH KIDS ALL OVER AGAIN!
YO, FRAN-KAY! YOU'RE MISSING THE XMAS EVE ELF PARTY, DUDE. EVERYONE'S DOING SUGAR PLUM SHOTS!
AH, MISS JINGLE. I HAD HOPED TO QUIETLY SLIP AWAY...
WHY? DON'T YOU LIKE IT HERE?
CERTAINLY. BUT EVER SINCE MY CREATION I HAVE YEARNED FOR ONLY ONE THING...
A BRIDE.
I STITCHED HER TOGETHER ON MY LUNCH BREAKS.
OH-HO! NOW I KNOW WHY WE WERE RUNNING SHORT ON "MY SIZE BARBIES!"
BEST OF LUCK, FRANKIE. SHE REALLY SEEMS LIKE YOUR KIND OF GIRL!
TRULY A WOMAN AFTER MY OWN HEART. AND WHY NOT? I'VE GIVEN HER HALF MY OTHER ORGANS ALREADY.

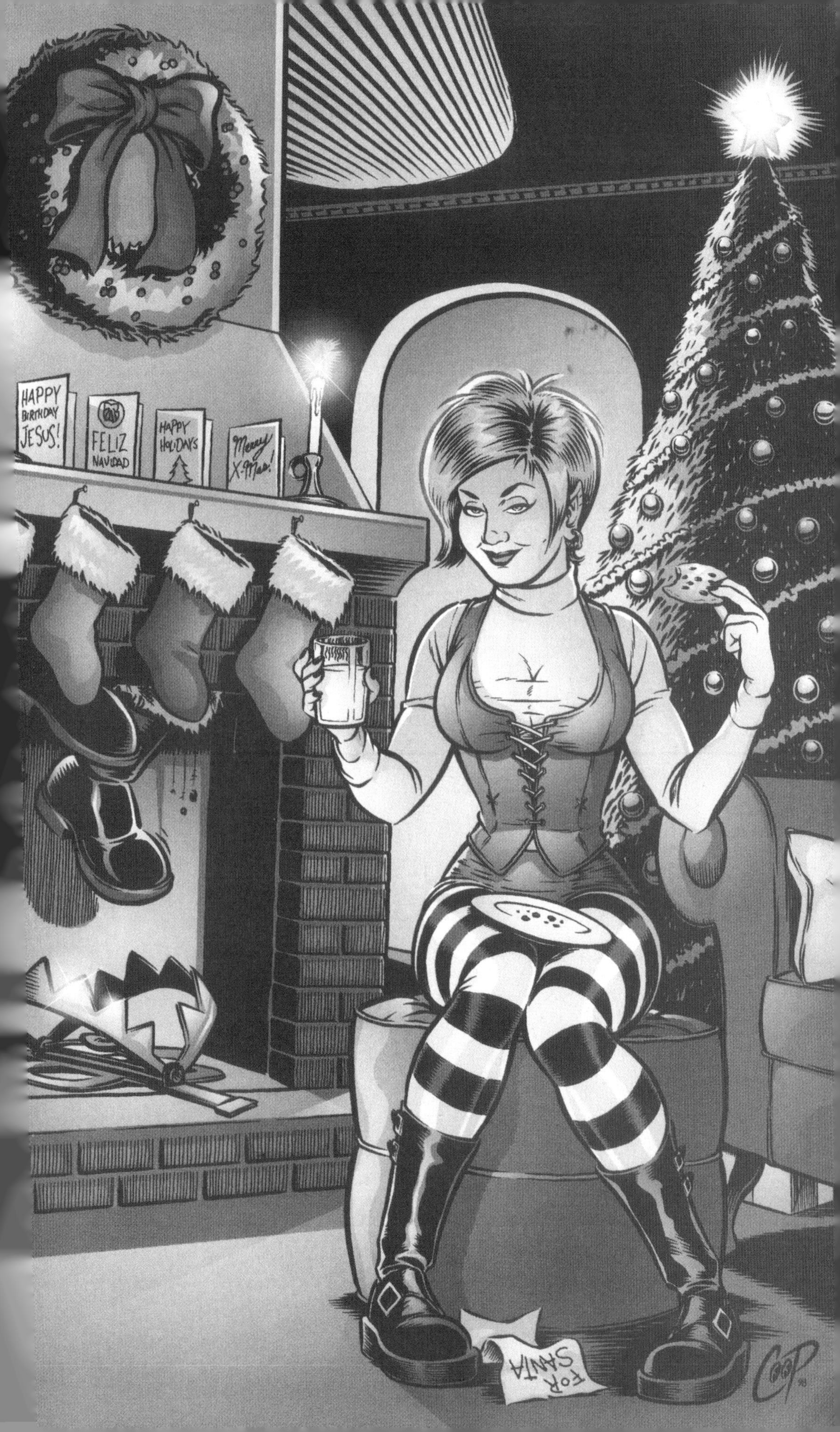
HAPPY BIRTHDAY JESUS!
FELIZ NAVIDAD
HAPPY HOLIDAYS
Merry X-Mas!
FOR SANTA
Coop

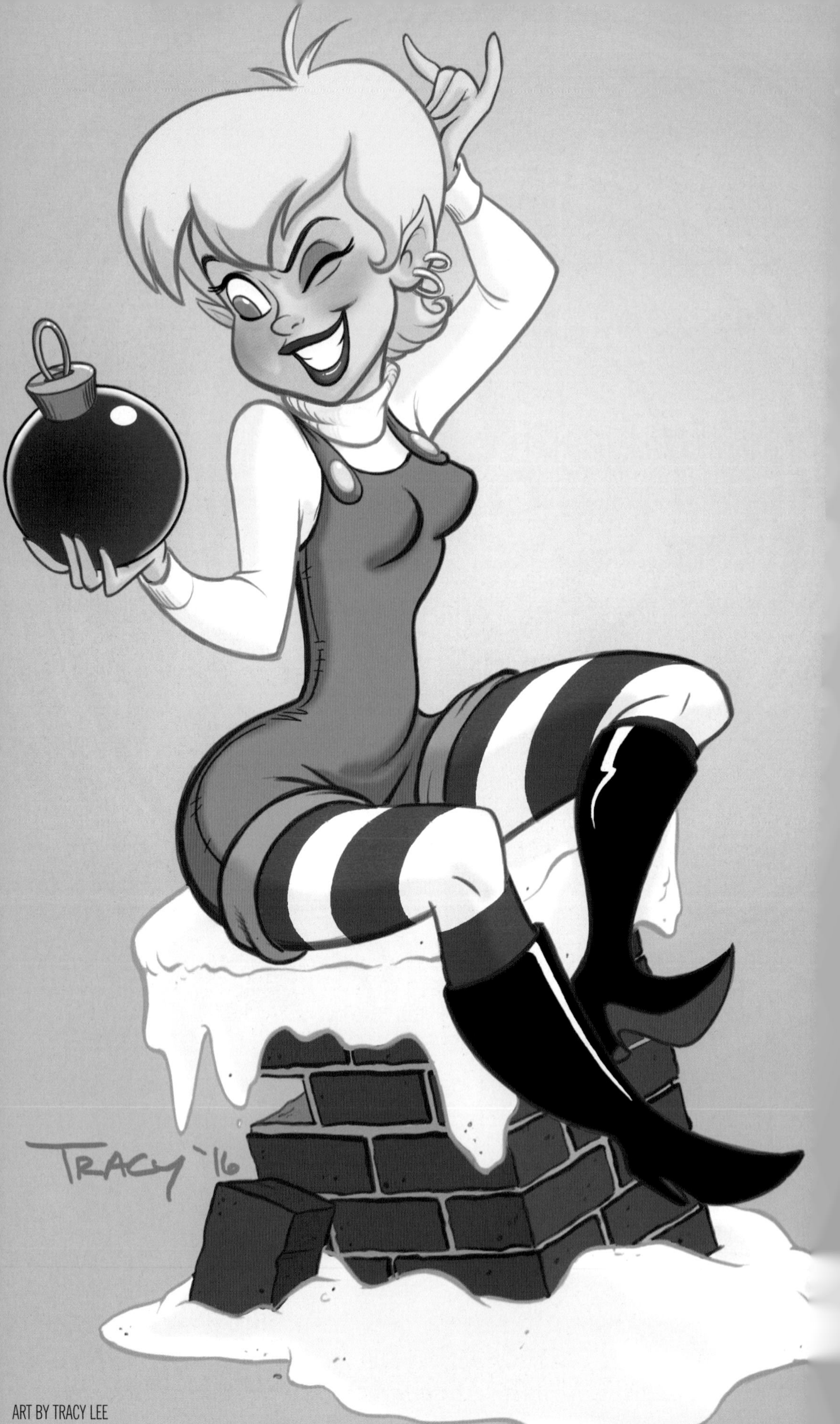
TRACY '16
ART BY TRACY LEE

Grounded

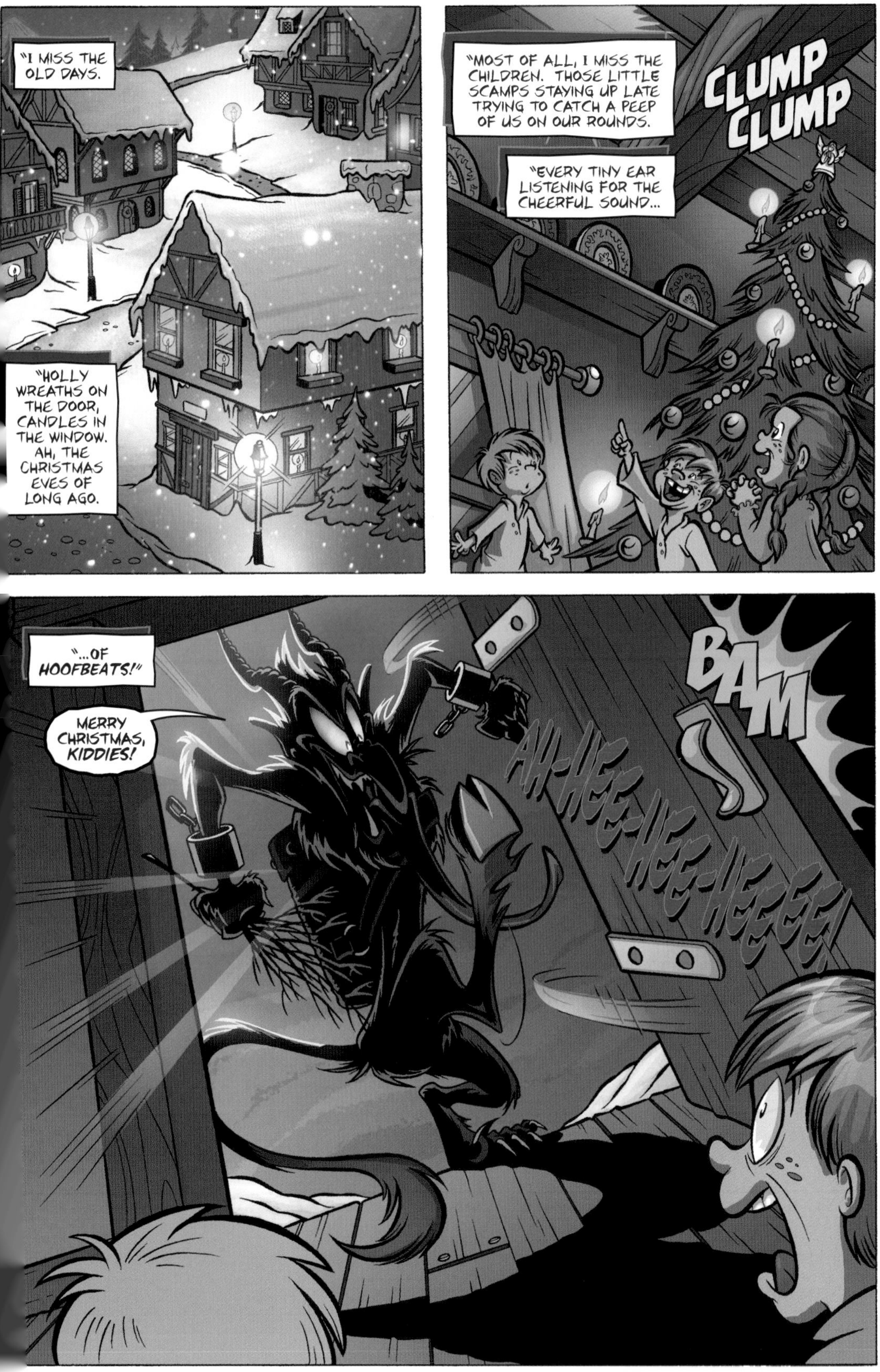
"I MISS THE OLD DAYS.
"HOLLY WREATHS ON THE DOOR, CANDLES IN THE WINDOW. AH, THE CHRISTMAS EVES OF LONG AGO.
"MOST OF ALL, I MISS THE CHILDREN. THOSE LITTLE SCAMPS STAYING UP LATE TRYING TO CATCH A PEEP OF US ON OUR ROUNDS.
CLUMP CLUMP
"EVERY TINY EAR LISTENING FOR THE CHEERFUL SOUND...
"...OF HOOFBEATS!"
MERRY CHRISTMAS, KIDDIES!
BAM
AH-HEE-HEE-HEE-HEEEE!

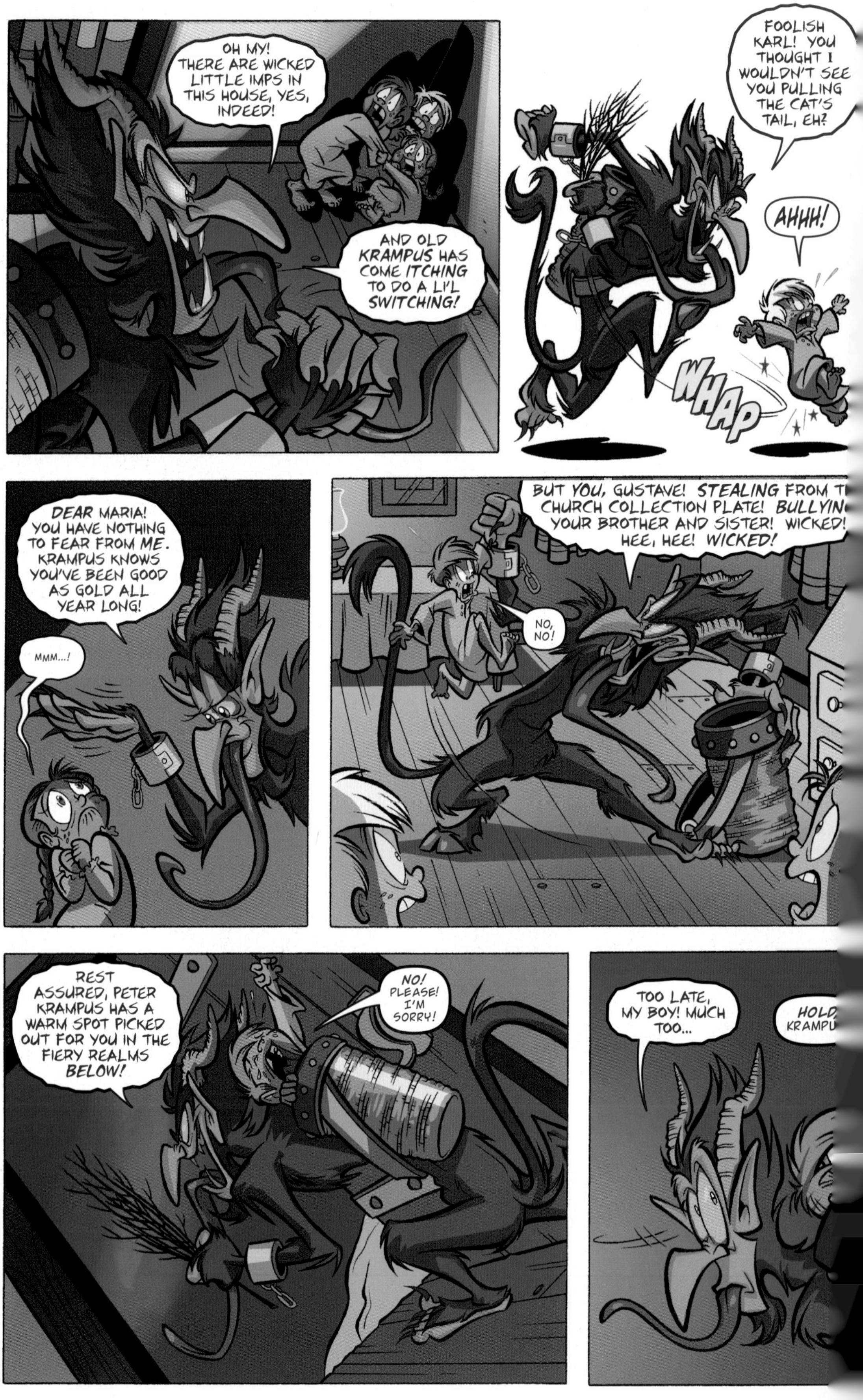
OH MY! THERE ARE WICKED LITTLE IMPS IN THIS HOUSE, YES, INDEED!
AND OLD KRAMPUS HAS COME ITCHING TO DO A LI'L SWITCHING!
FOOLISH KARL! YOU THOUGHT I WOULDN'T SEE YOU PULLING THE CAT'S TAIL, EH?
AHHH!
WHAP
DEAR MARIA! YOU HAVE NOTHING TO FEAR FROM ME. KRAMPUS KNOWS YOU'VE BEEN GOOD AS GOLD ALL YEAR LONG!
MMM...!
BUT YOU, GUSTAVE! STEALING FROM T CHURCH COLLECTION PLATE! BULLYIN YOUR BROTHER AND SISTER! WICKED! HEE, HEE! WICKED!
NO, NO!
REST ASSURED, PETER KRAMPUS HAS A WARM SPOT PICKED OUT FOR YOU IN THE FIERY REALMS BELOW!
NO! PLEASE! I'M SORRY!
TOO LATE, MY BOY! MUCH TOO...
HOLD KRAMPU

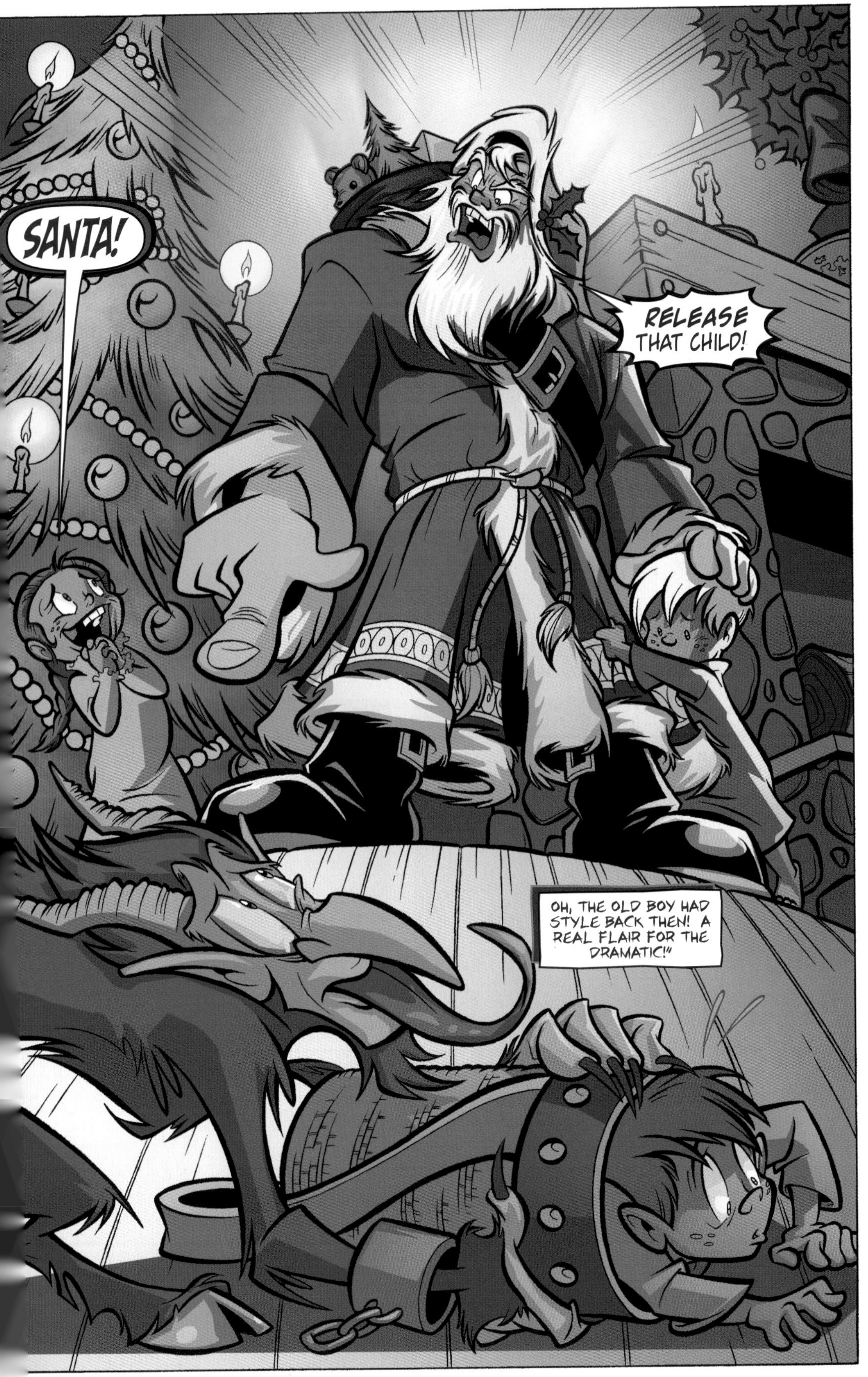
SANTA!
RELEASE THAT CHILD!
OH, THE OLD BOY HAD STYLE BACK THEN! A REAL FLAIR FOR THE DRAMATIC!"

HO, HO! I THINK THEY'VE LEARNED THEIR LESSON! THEY'LL BE GOOD CHILDREN FROM NOW ON!

AS YOU SAY, SANTA.

IN THOSE DAYS WE REALLY KNEW HOW TO SCARE THE 'NAUGHTY' OUT OF THE TOTS. AND DON'T THINK THEIR FOLKS WEREN'T GRATEFUL!

IT'S NOT LIKE NOW WHEN *EVERY* CHILD GOES UNPUNISHED! NOW IT'S SUGARPLUMS AND CELL PHONES FOR ALL!

CANDY CANES AND FLAT SCREEN TVS! ANYTHING THE BRATS WANT IS THEIRS FOR THE ASKING!

DISCIPLINE! *FEAR!* ALL THE TRICKS WE USED TO KEEP THE WHELPS IN LINE HAVE BEEN TOSSED OUT THE WINDOW!

TSK, TSK...

IT'S *SANTA'S* FAULT! THE OLD FOOL'S GONE SOFTER THAN HIS BELLY! PROBABLY DOESN'T EVEN HAND OUT *COAL* ANYMORE!

UM, YE... NOW AB... THIS URG... MESSA...

GIVE IT HERE!

HM. A *WITCH.* YOU'RE NO KIN TO CLAUS.

NOPE, BUT I'M BFF WITH HIS DAUGHTER.

BESIDES, ALL OF THE ELVES WERE TOO SCARED TO COME. ME, I'M INTO THE HORROR STUFF

THE TWIRPS ARE RIGHT TO... SCARED. FOR OVER TWO... HUNDRED YEARS, NONE HA... *DARED* BRAVE THE LAIR OF KRAMPUS!

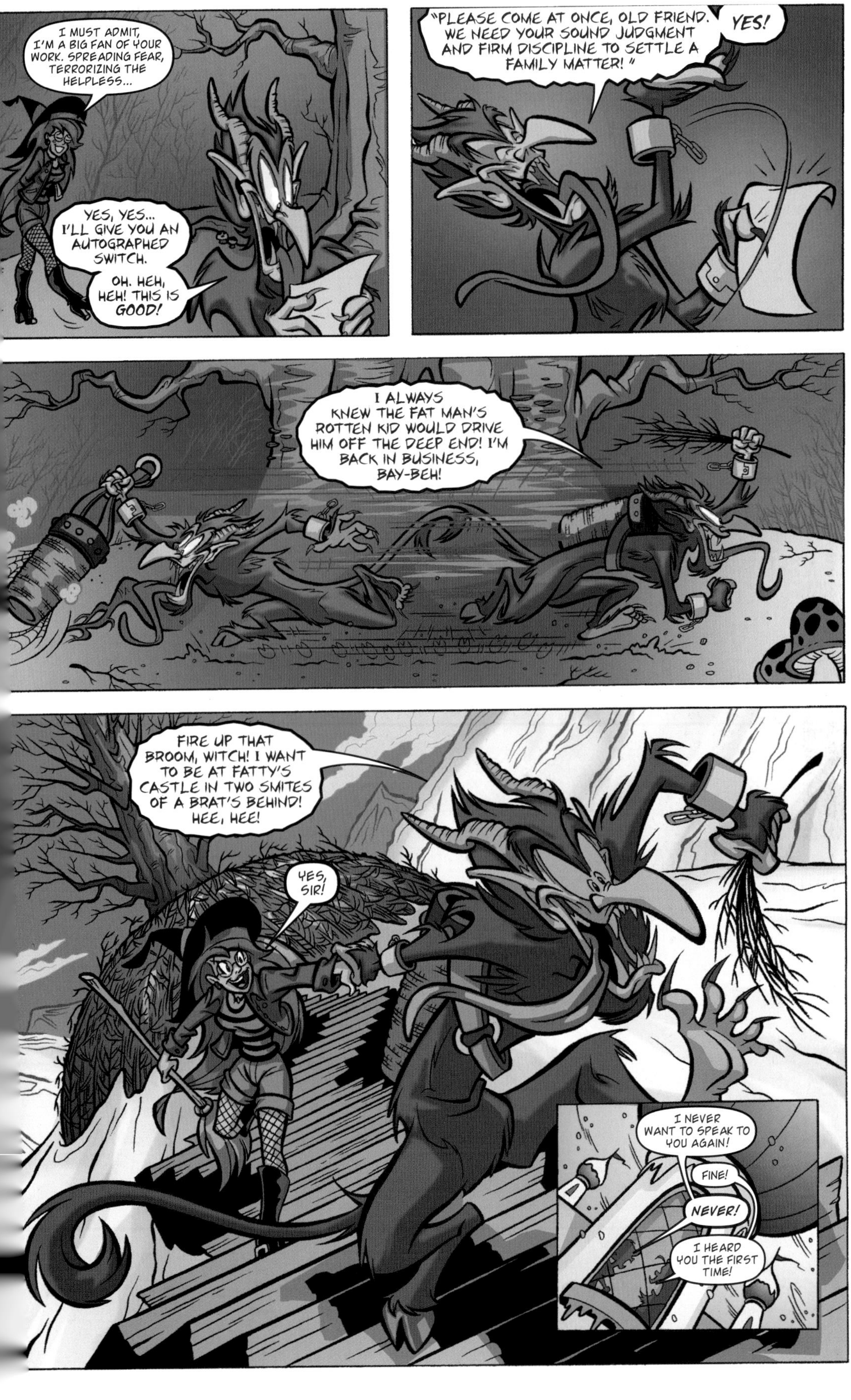
I MUST ADMIT, I'M A BIG FAN OF YOUR WORK. SPREADING FEAR, TERRORIZING THE HELPLESS...
YES, YES... I'LL GIVE YOU AN AUTOGRAPHED SWITCH.
OH. HEH, HEH! THIS IS GOOD!
"PLEASE COME AT ONCE, OLD FRIEND. WE NEED YOUR SOUND JUDGMENT AND FIRM DISCIPLINE TO SETTLE A FAMILY MATTER!"
YES!
I ALWAYS KNEW THE FAT MAN'S ROTTEN KID WOULD DRIVE HIM OFF THE DEEP END! I'M BACK IN BUSINESS, BAY-BEH!
FIRE UP THAT BROOM, WITCH! I WANT TO BE AT FATTY'S CASTLE IN TWO SMITES OF A BRAT'S BEHIND! HEE, HEE!
YES, SIR!
I NEVER WANT TO SPEAK TO YOU AGAIN!
FINE!
NEVER!
I HEARD YOU THE FIRST TIME!

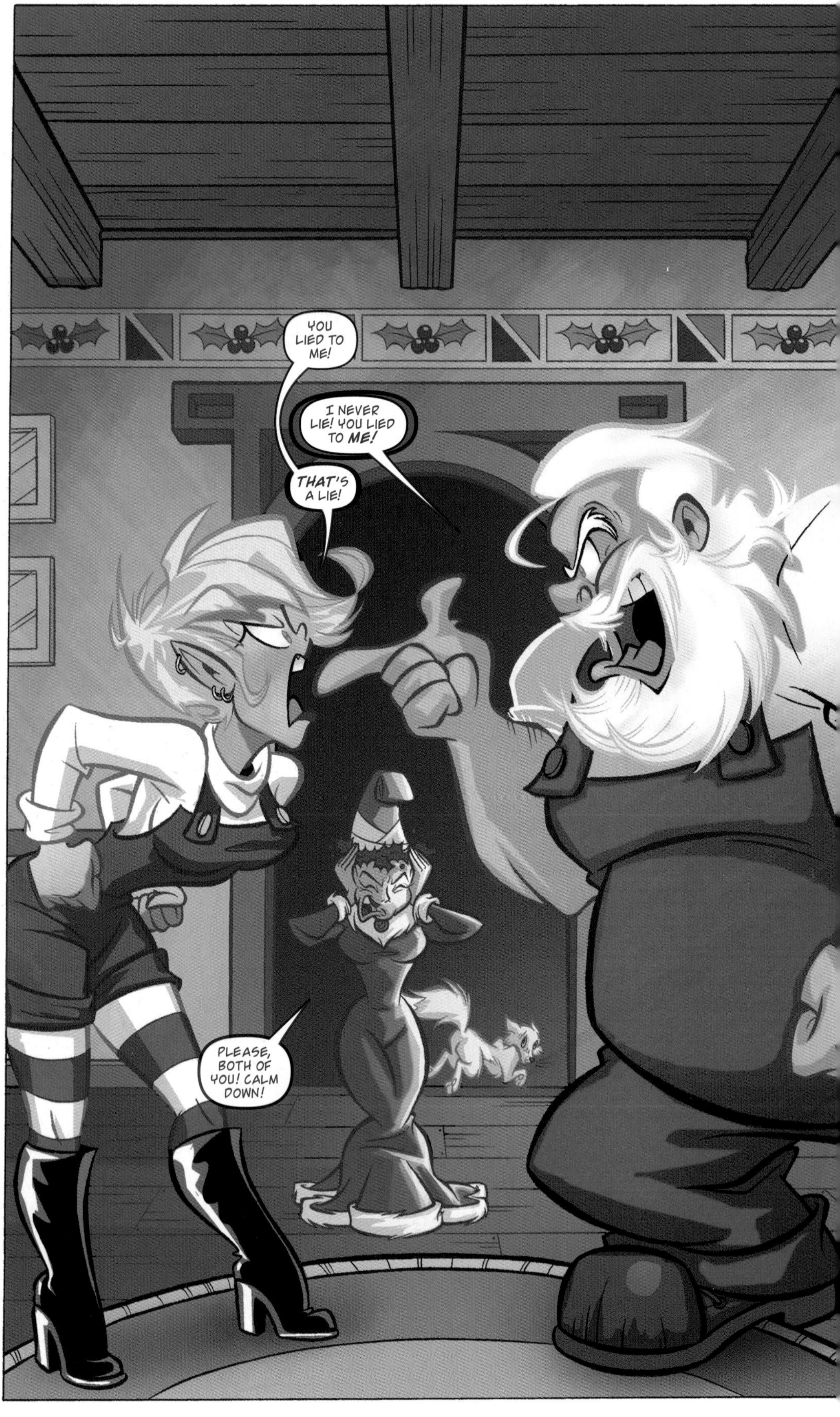

YOU LIED TO ME!
I NEVER LIE! YOU LIED TO ME!
THAT'S A LIE!
PLEASE, BOTH OF YOU! CALM DOWN!

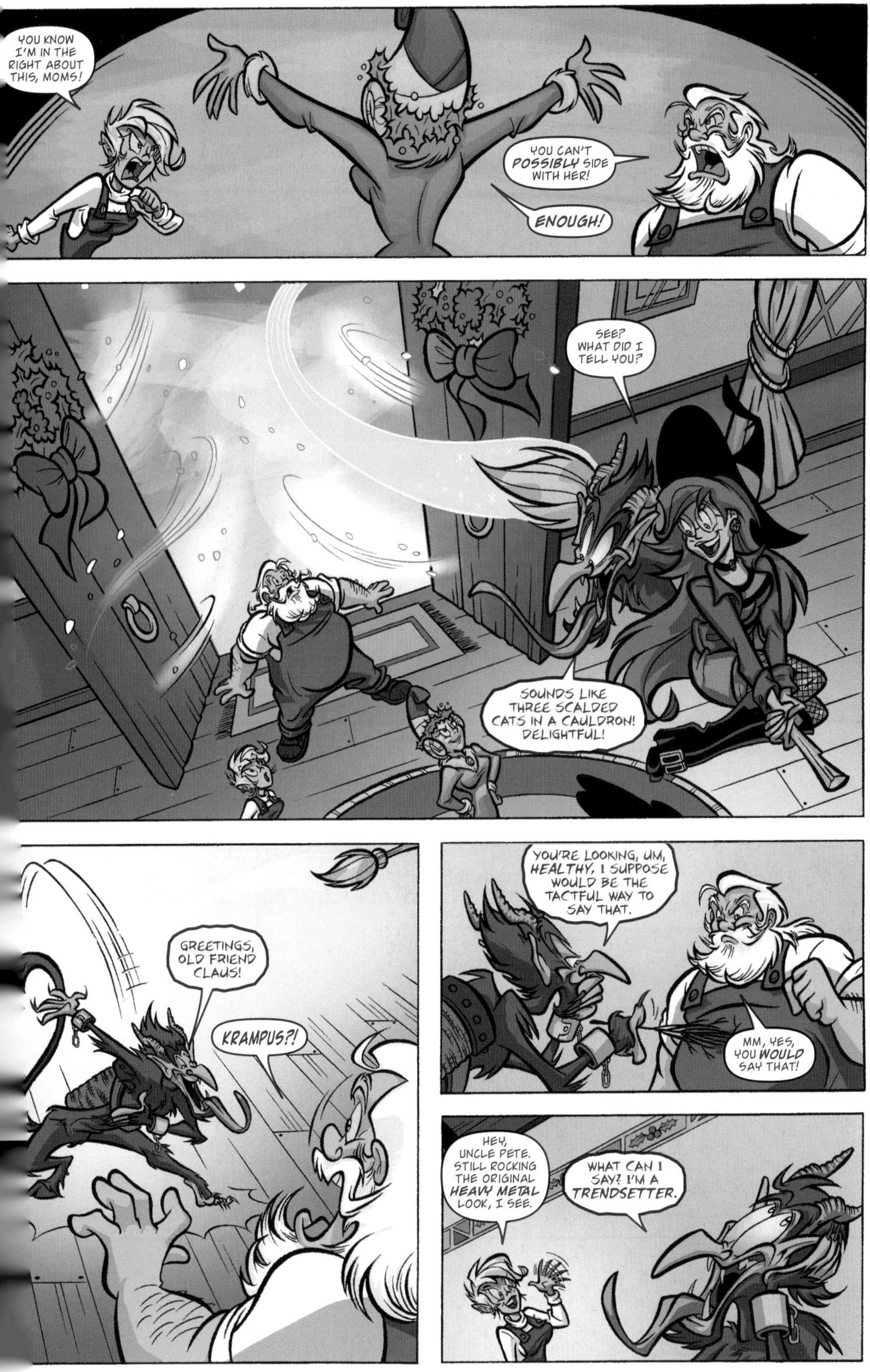
YOU KNOW I'M IN THE RIGHT ABOUT THIS, MOMS!
YOU CAN'T POSSIBLY SIDE WITH HER!
ENOUGH!
SEE? WHAT DID I TELL YOU?
SOUNDS LIKE THREE SCALDED CATS IN A CAULDRON! DELIGHTFUL!
GREETINGS, OLD FRIEND CLAUS!
KRAMPUS?!
YOU'RE LOOKING, UM, HEALTHY, I SUPPOSE WOULD BE THE TACTFUL WAY TO SAY THAT.
MM, YES, YOU WOULD SAY THAT!
HEY, UNCLE PETE. STILL ROCKING THE ORIGINAL HEAVY METAL LOOK, I SEE.
WHAT CAN I SAY? I'M A TRENDSETTER.

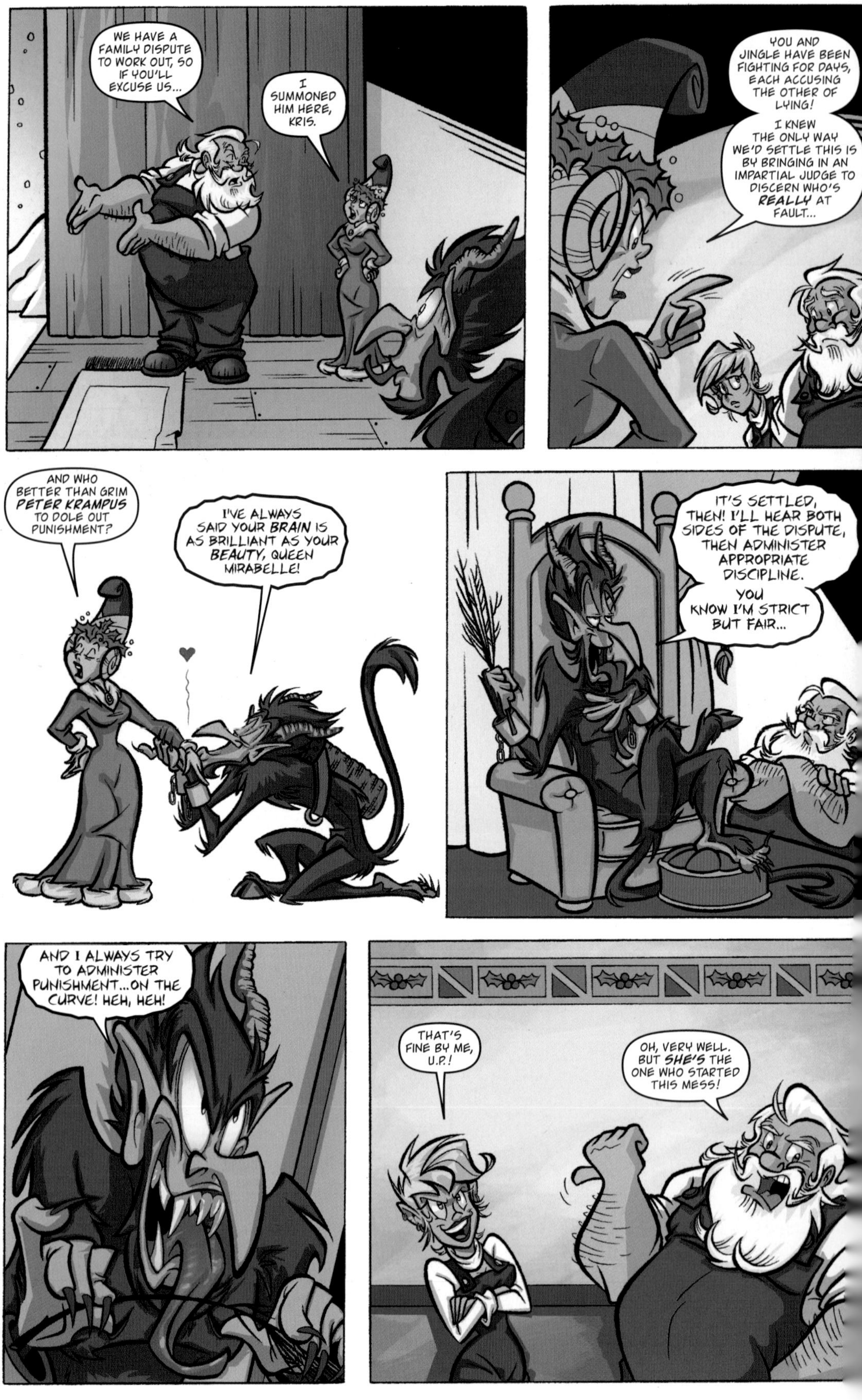
WE HAVE A FAMILY DISPUTE TO WORK OUT, SO IF YOU'LL EXCUSE US...
I SUMMONED HIM HERE, KRIS.
YOU AND JINGLE HAVE BEEN FIGHTING FOR DAYS, EACH ACCUSING THE OTHER OF LYING!
I KNEW THE ONLY WAY WE'D SETTLE THIS IS BY BRINGING IN AN IMPARTIAL JUDGE TO DISCERN WHO'S REALLY AT FAULT...
AND WHO BETTER THAN GRIM PETER KRAMPUS TO DOLE OUT PUNISHMENT?
I'VE ALWAYS SAID YOUR BRAIN IS AS BRILLIANT AS YOUR BEAUTY, QUEEN MIRABELLE!
IT'S SETTLED, THEN! I'LL HEAR BOTH SIDES OF THE DISPUTE, THEN ADMINISTER APPROPRIATE DISCIPLINE.
YOU KNOW I'M STRICT BUT FAIR...
AND I ALWAYS TRY TO ADMINISTER PUNISHMENT...ON THE CURVE! HEH, HEH!
THAT'S FINE BY ME, U.P.!
OH, VERY WELL. BUT SHE'S THE ONE WHO STARTED THIS MESS!

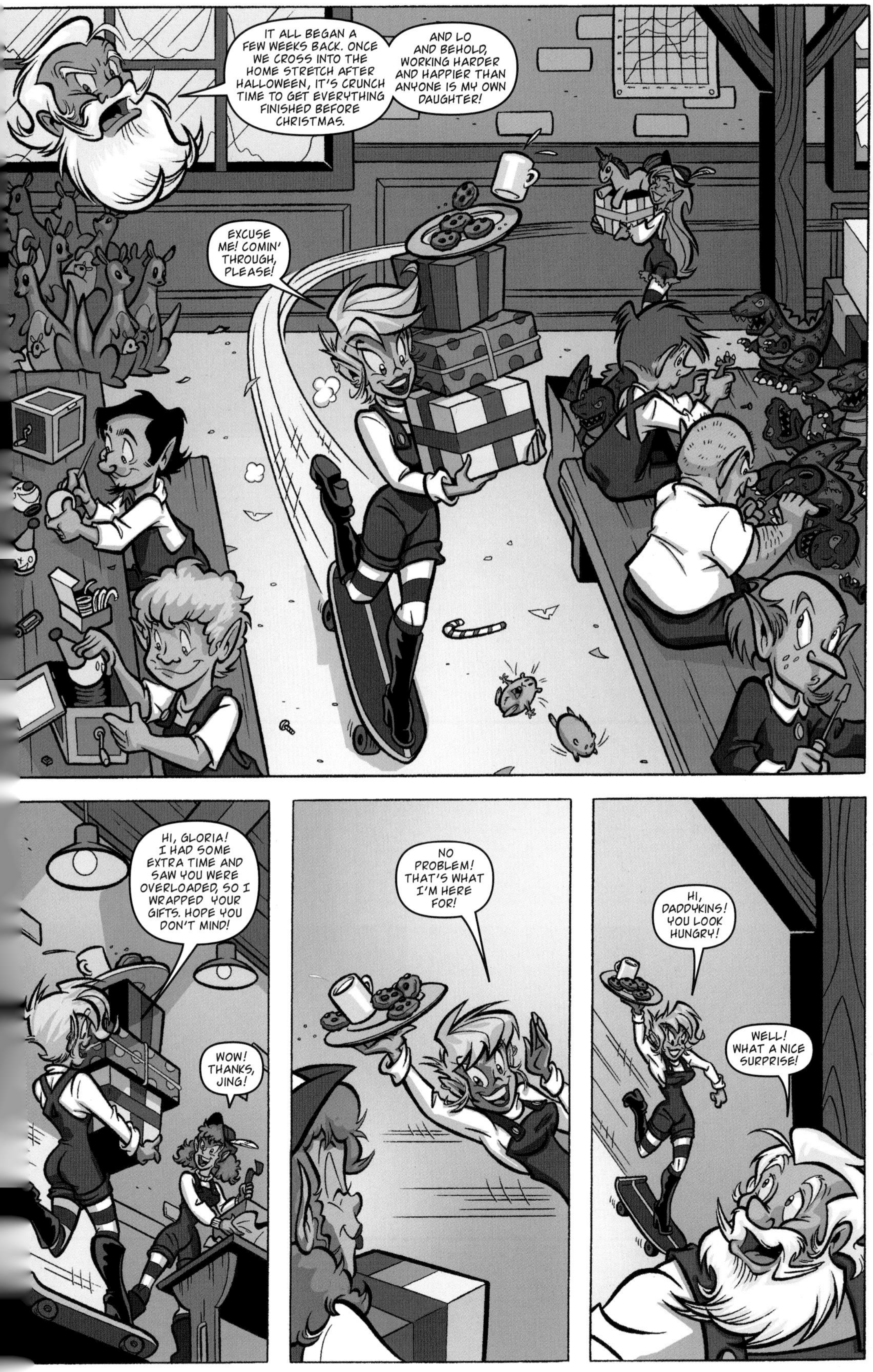
IT ALL BEGAN A FEW WEEKS BACK. ONCE WE CROSS INTO THE HOME STRETCH AFTER HALLOWEEN, IT'S CRUNCH TIME TO GET EVERYTHING FINISHED BEFORE CHRISTMAS.
AND LO AND BEHOLD, WORKING HARDER AND HAPPIER THAN ANYONE IS MY OWN DAUGHTER!
EXCUSE ME! COMIN' THROUGH, PLEASE!
HI, GLORIA! I HAD SOME EXTRA TIME AND SAW YOU WERE OVERLOADED, SO I WRAPPED YOUR GIFTS. HOPE YOU DON'T MIND!
WOW! THANKS, JING!
NO PROBLEM! THAT'S WHAT I'M HERE FOR!
HI, DADDYKINS! YOU LOOK HUNGRY!
WELL! WHAT A NICE SURPRISE!

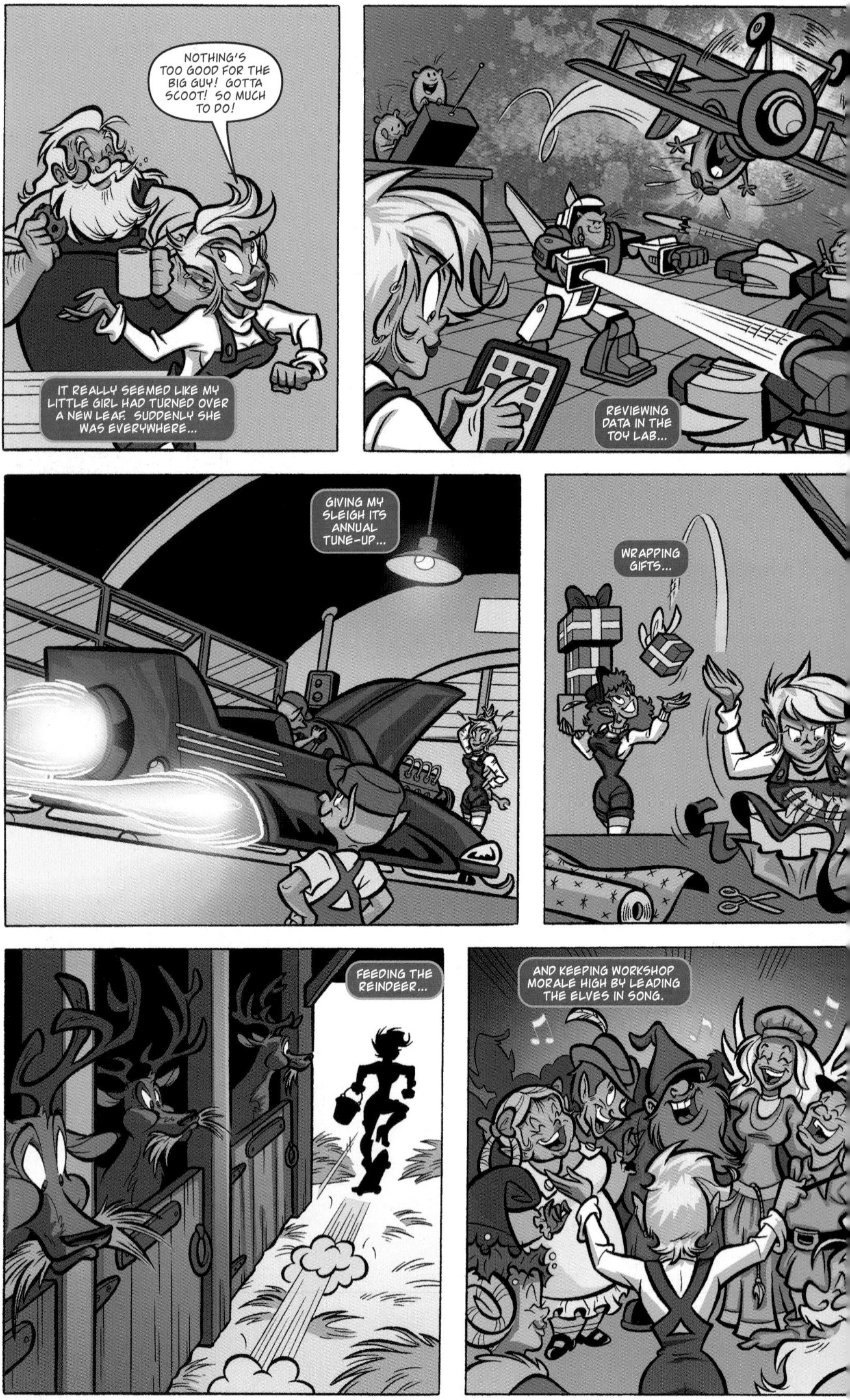
NOTHING'S TOO GOOD FOR THE BIG GUY! GOTTA SCOOT! SO MUCH TO DO!
IT REALLY SEEMED LIKE MY LITTLE GIRL HAD TURNED OVER A NEW LEAF. SUDDENLY SHE WAS EVERYWHERE...
REVIEWING DATA IN THE TOY LAB...
GIVING MY SLEIGH ITS ANNUAL TUNE-UP...
WRAPPING GIFTS...
FEEDING THE REINDEER...
AND KEEPING WORKSHOP MORALE HIGH BY LEADING THE ELVES IN SONG.

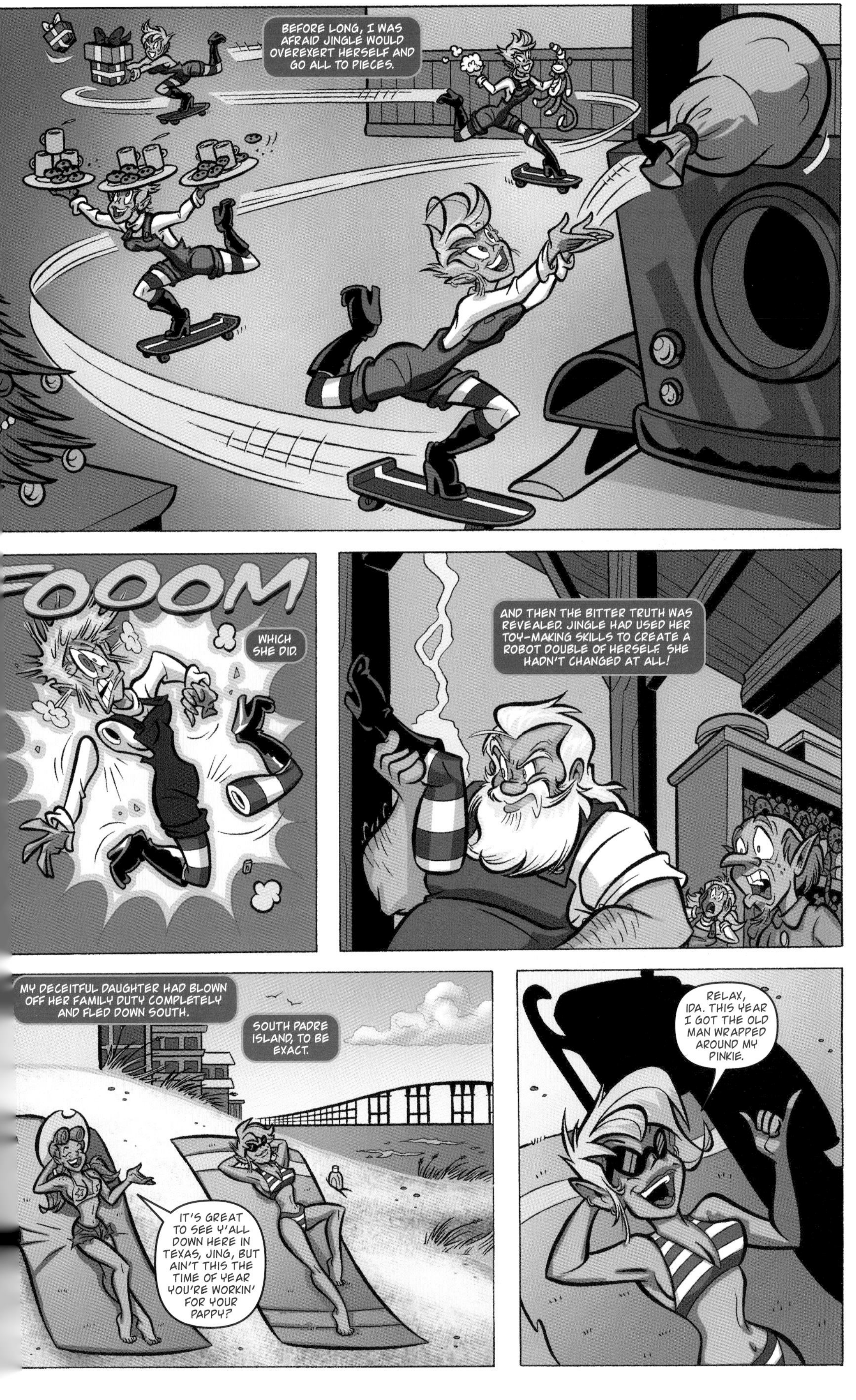
BEFORE LONG, I WAS AFRAID JINGLE WOULD OVEREXERT HERSELF AND GO ALL TO PIECES.
FOOOM
WHICH SHE DID.
AND THEN THE BITTER TRUTH WAS REVEALED. JINGLE HAD USED HER TOY-MAKING SKILLS TO CREATE A ROBOT DOUBLE OF HERSELF. SHE HADN'T CHANGED AT ALL!
MY DECEITFUL DAUGHTER HAD BLOWN OFF HER FAMILY DUTY COMPLETELY AND FLED DOWN SOUTH.
SOUTH PADRE ISLAND, TO BE EXACT.
IT'S GREAT TO SEE Y'ALL DOWN HERE IN TEXAS, JING, BUT AIN'T THIS THE TIME OF YEAR YOU'RE WORKIN' FOR YOUR PAPPY?
RELAX, IDA. THIS YEAR I GOT THE OLD MAN WRAPPED AROUND MY PINKIE.

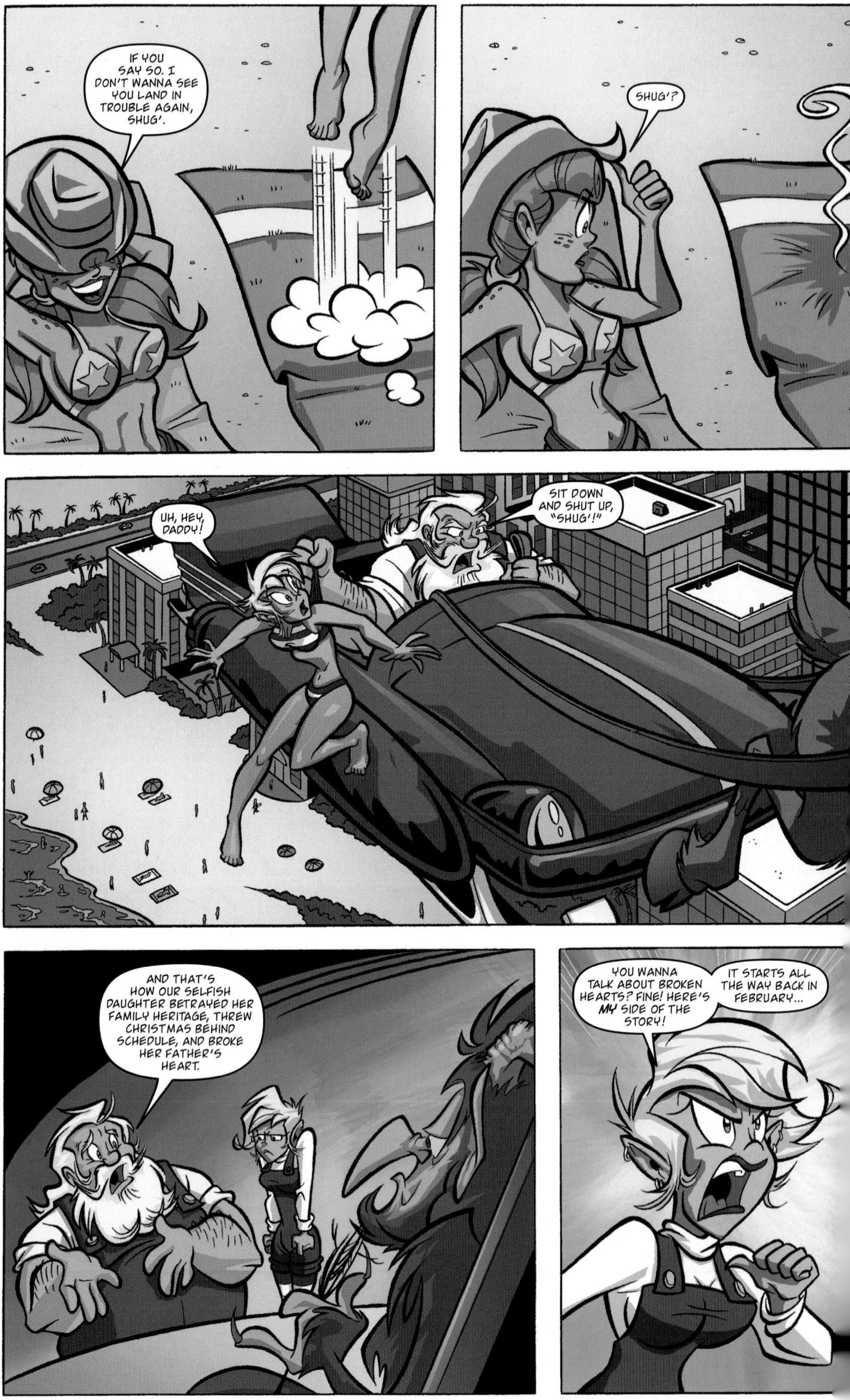
IF YOU SAY SO. I DON'T WANNA SEE YOU LAND IN TROUBLE AGAIN, SHUG'.
SHUG'?
UH, HEY, DADDY!
SIT DOWN AND SHUT UP, "SHUG'!"
AND THAT'S HOW OUR SELFISH DAUGHTER BETRAYED HER FAMILY HERITAGE, THREW CHRISTMAS BEHIND SCHEDULE, AND BROKE HER FATHER'S HEART.
YOU WANNA TALK ABOUT BROKEN HEARTS? FINE! HERE'S MY SIDE OF THE STORY!
IT STARTS ALL THE WAY BACK IN FEBRUARY...

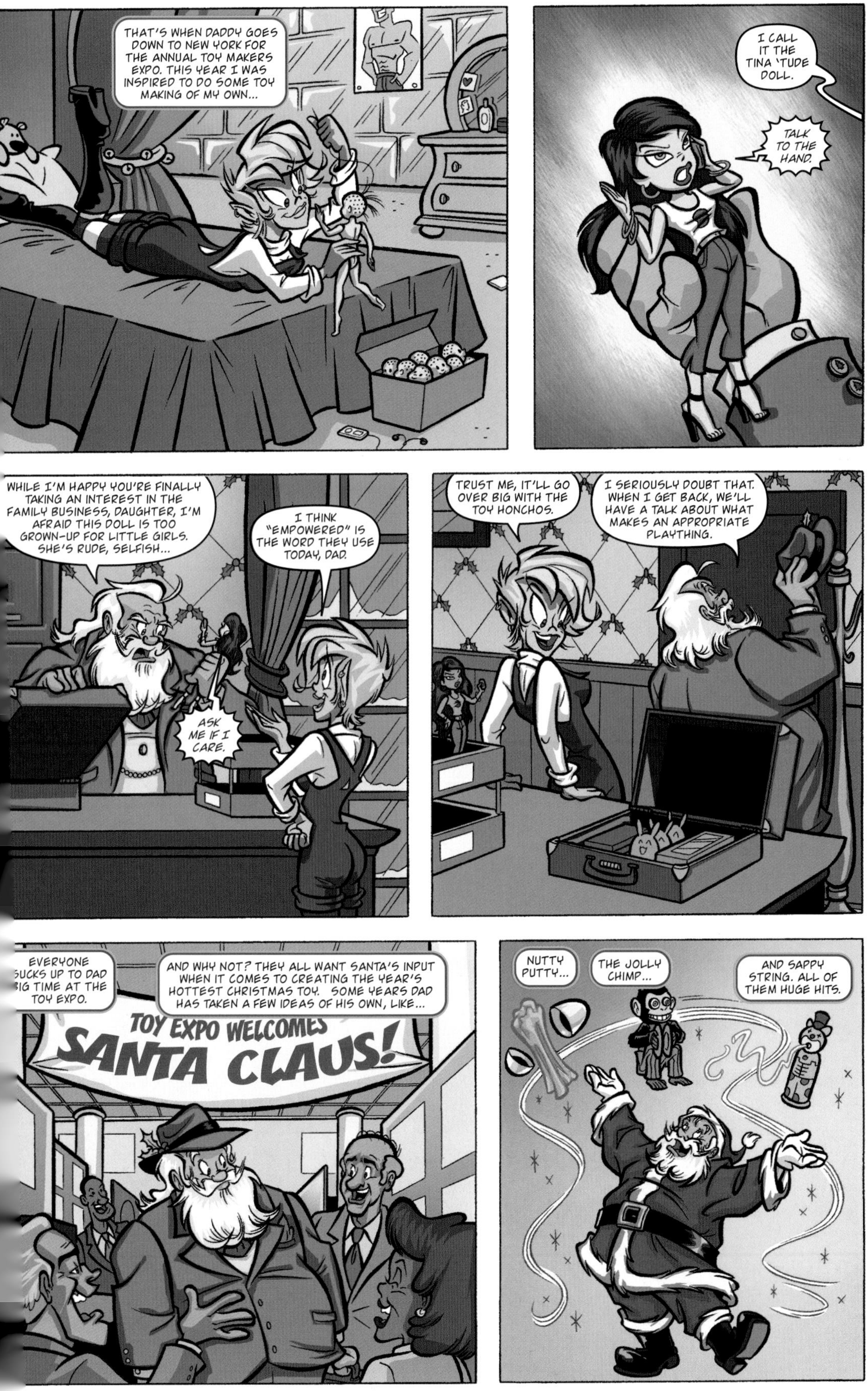
THAT'S WHEN DADDY GOES DOWN TO NEW YORK FOR THE ANNUAL TOY MAKERS EXPO. THIS YEAR I WAS INSPIRED TO DO SOME TOY MAKING OF MY OWN...
I CALL IT THE TINA 'TUDE DOLL.
TALK TO THE HAND.
WHILE I'M HAPPY YOU'RE FINALLY TAKING AN INTEREST IN THE FAMILY BUSINESS, DAUGHTER, I'M AFRAID THIS DOLL IS TOO GROWN-UP FOR LITTLE GIRLS. SHE'S RUDE, SELFISH...
ASK ME IF I CARE.
I THINK "EMPOWERED" IS THE WORD THEY USE TODAY, DAD.
TRUST ME, IT'LL GO OVER BIG WITH THE TOY HONCHOS.
I SERIOUSLY DOUBT THAT. WHEN I GET BACK, WE'LL HAVE A TALK ABOUT WHAT MAKES AN APPROPRIATE PLAYTHING.
EVERYONE SUCKS UP TO DAD BIG TIME AT THE TOY EXPO.
AND WHY NOT? THEY ALL WANT SANTA'S INPUT WHEN IT COMES TO CREATING THE YEAR'S HOTTEST CHRISTMAS TOY. SOME YEARS DAD HAS TAKEN A FEW IDEAS OF HIS OWN, LIKE...
TOY EXPO WELCOMES SANTA CLAUS!
NUTTY PUTTY...
THE JOLLY CHIMP...
AND SAPPY STRING. ALL OF THEM HUGE HITS.

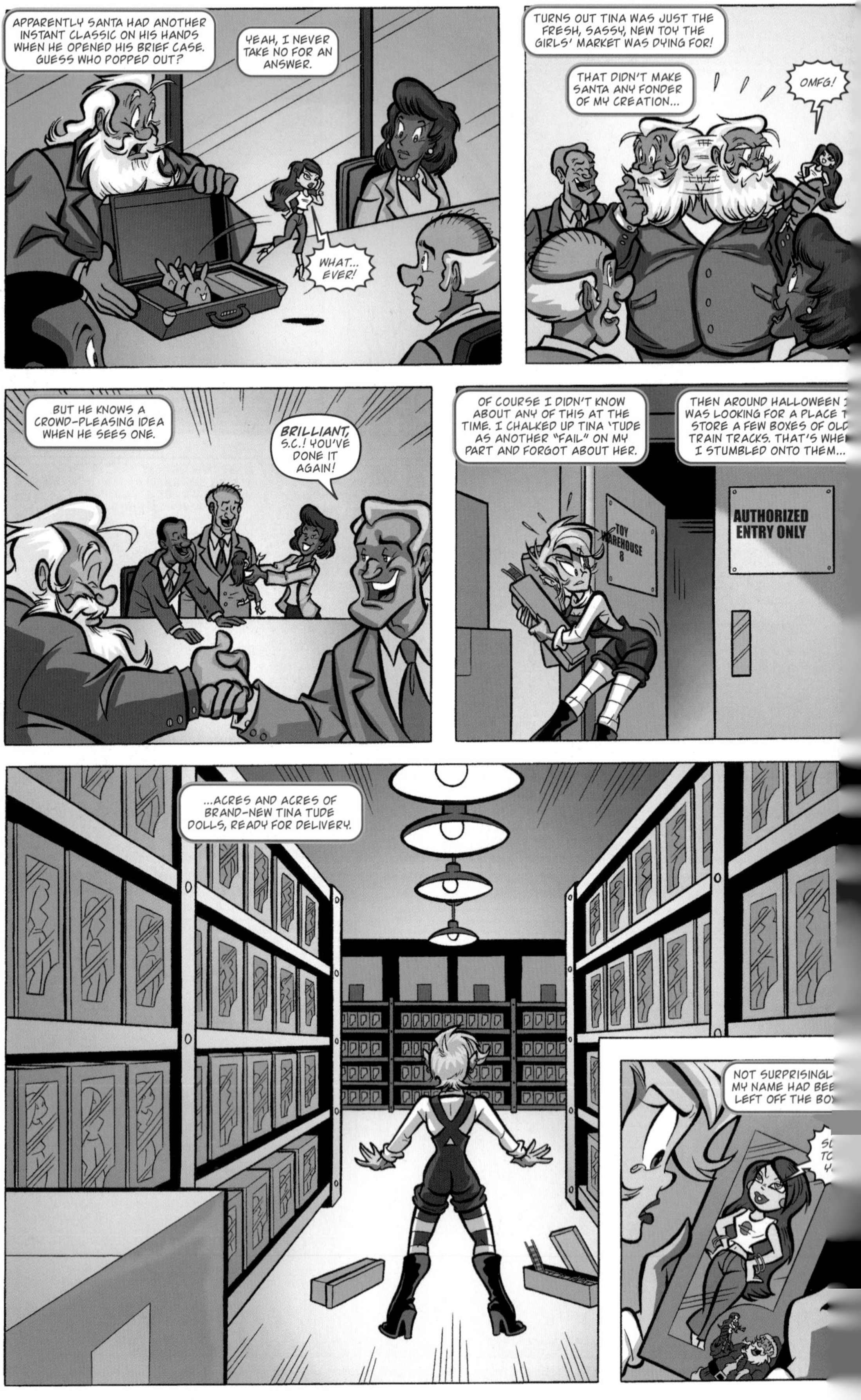
APPARENTLY SANTA HAD ANOTHER INSTANT CLASSIC ON HIS HANDS WHEN HE OPENED HIS BRIEF CASE. GUESS WHO POPPED OUT?
YEAH, I NEVER TAKE NO FOR AN ANSWER.
WHAT... EVER!
TURNS OUT TINA WAS JUST THE FRESH, SASSY, NEW TOY THE GIRLS' MARKET WAS DYING FOR!
THAT DIDN'T MAKE SANTA ANY FONDER OF MY CREATION...
OMFG!
BUT HE KNOWS A CROWD-PLEASING IDEA WHEN HE SEES ONE.
BRILLIANT, S.C.! YOU'VE DONE IT AGAIN!
OF COURSE I DIDN'T KNOW ABOUT ANY OF THIS AT THE TIME. I CHALKED UP TINA 'TUDE AS ANOTHER "FAIL" ON MY PART AND FORGOT ABOUT HER.
THEN AROUND HALLOWEEN
WAS LOOKING FOR A PLACE
STORE A FEW BOXES OF OL
TRAIN TRACKS. THAT'S WHE
I STUMBLED ONTO THEM...
TOY WAREHOUSE 8
AUTHORIZED ENTRY ONLY
...ACRES AND ACRES OF BRAND-NEW TINA TUDE DOLLS, READY FOR DELIVERY.
NOT SURPRISINGL
MY NAME HAD BEE
LEFT OFF THE BO

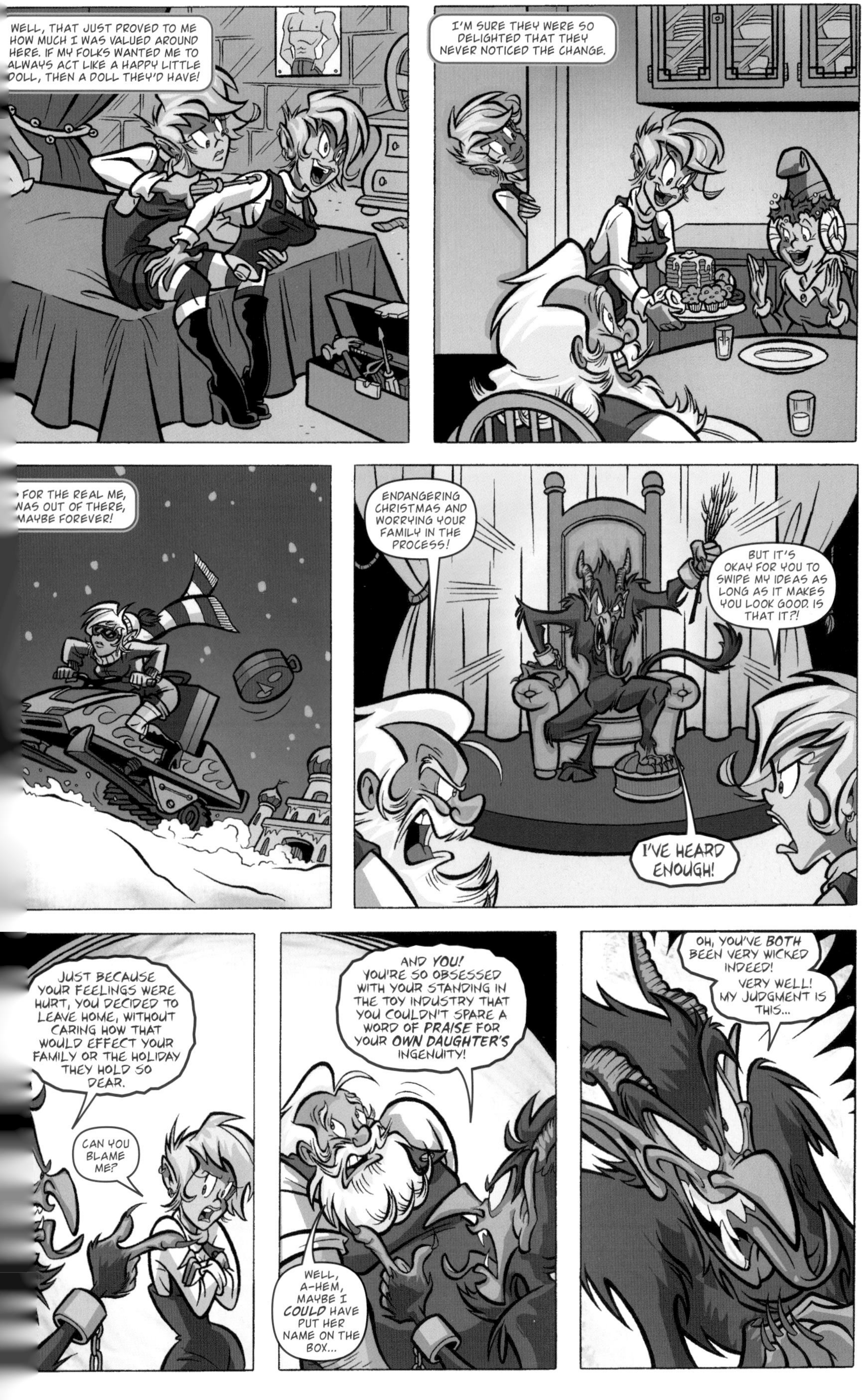
WELL, THAT JUST PROVED TO ME HOW MUCH I WAS VALUED AROUND HERE. IF MY FOLKS WANTED ME TO ALWAYS ACT LIKE A HAPPY LITTLE DOLL, THEN A DOLL THEY'D HAVE!
I'M SURE THEY WERE SO DELIGHTED THAT THEY NEVER NOTICED THE CHANGE.
FOR THE REAL ME, WAS OUT OF THERE, MAYBE FOREVER!
ENDANGERING CHRISTMAS AND WORRYING YOUR FAMILY IN THE PROCESS!
BUT IT'S OKAY FOR YOU TO SWIPE MY IDEAS AS LONG AS IT MAKES YOU LOOK GOOD. IS THAT IT?!
I'VE HEARD ENOUGH!
JUST BECAUSE YOUR FEELINGS WERE HURT, YOU DECIDED TO LEAVE HOME, WITHOUT CARING HOW THAT WOULD EFFECT YOUR FAMILY OR THE HOLIDAY THEY HOLD SO DEAR.
CAN YOU BLAME ME?
AND YOU! YOU'RE SO OBSESSED WITH YOUR STANDING IN THE TOY INDUSTRY THAT YOU COULDN'T SPARE A WORD OF PRAISE FOR YOUR OWN DAUGHTER'S INGENUITY!
WELL, A-HEM, MAYBE I COULD HAVE PUT HER NAME ON THE BOX...
OH, YOU'VE BOTH BEEN VERY WICKED INDEED!
VERY WELL! MY JUDGMENT IS THIS...

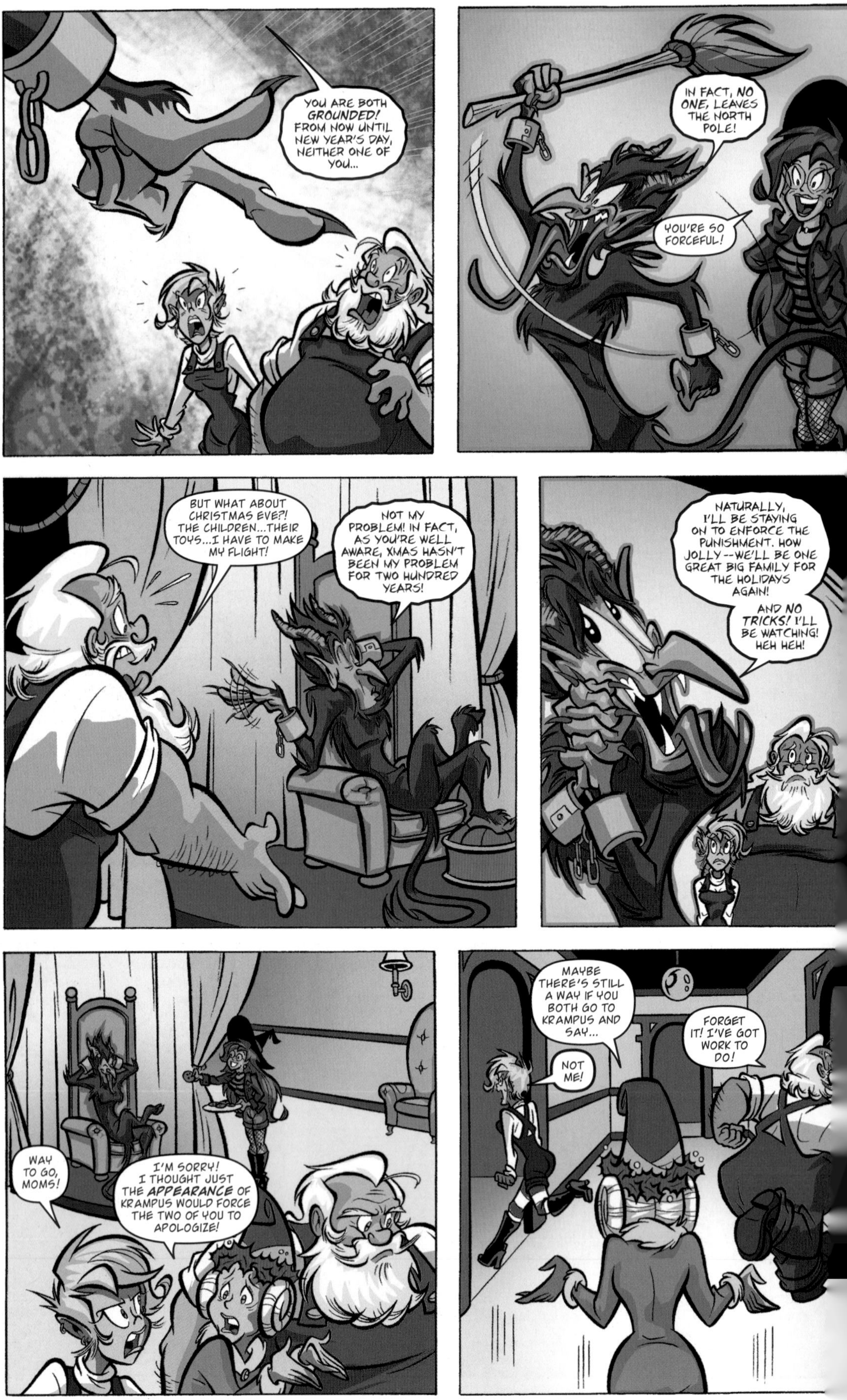
YOU ARE BOTH GROUNDED! FROM NOW UNTIL NEW YEAR'S DAY, NEITHER ONE OF YOU...
IN FACT, NO ONE, LEAVES THE NORTH POLE!
YOU'RE SO FORCEFUL!
BUT WHAT ABOUT CHRISTMAS EVE?! THE CHILDREN...THEIR TOYS...I HAVE TO MAKE MY FLIGHT!
NOT MY PROBLEM! IN FACT, AS YOU'RE WELL AWARE, XMAS HASN'T BEEN MY PROBLEM FOR TWO HUNDRED YEARS!
NATURALLY, I'LL BE STAYING ON TO ENFORCE THE PUNISHMENT. HOW JOLLY--WE'LL BE ONE GREAT BIG FAMILY FOR THE HOLIDAYS AGAIN!
AND NO TRICKS! I'LL BE WATCHING! HEH HEH!
WAY TO GO, MOMS!
I'M SORRY! I THOUGHT JUST THE APPEARANCE OF KRAMPUS WOULD FORCE THE TWO OF YOU TO APOLOGIZE!
MAYBE THERE'S STILL A WAY IF YOU BOTH GO TO KRAMPUS AND SAY...
NOT ME!
FORGET IT! I'VE GOT WORK TO DO!

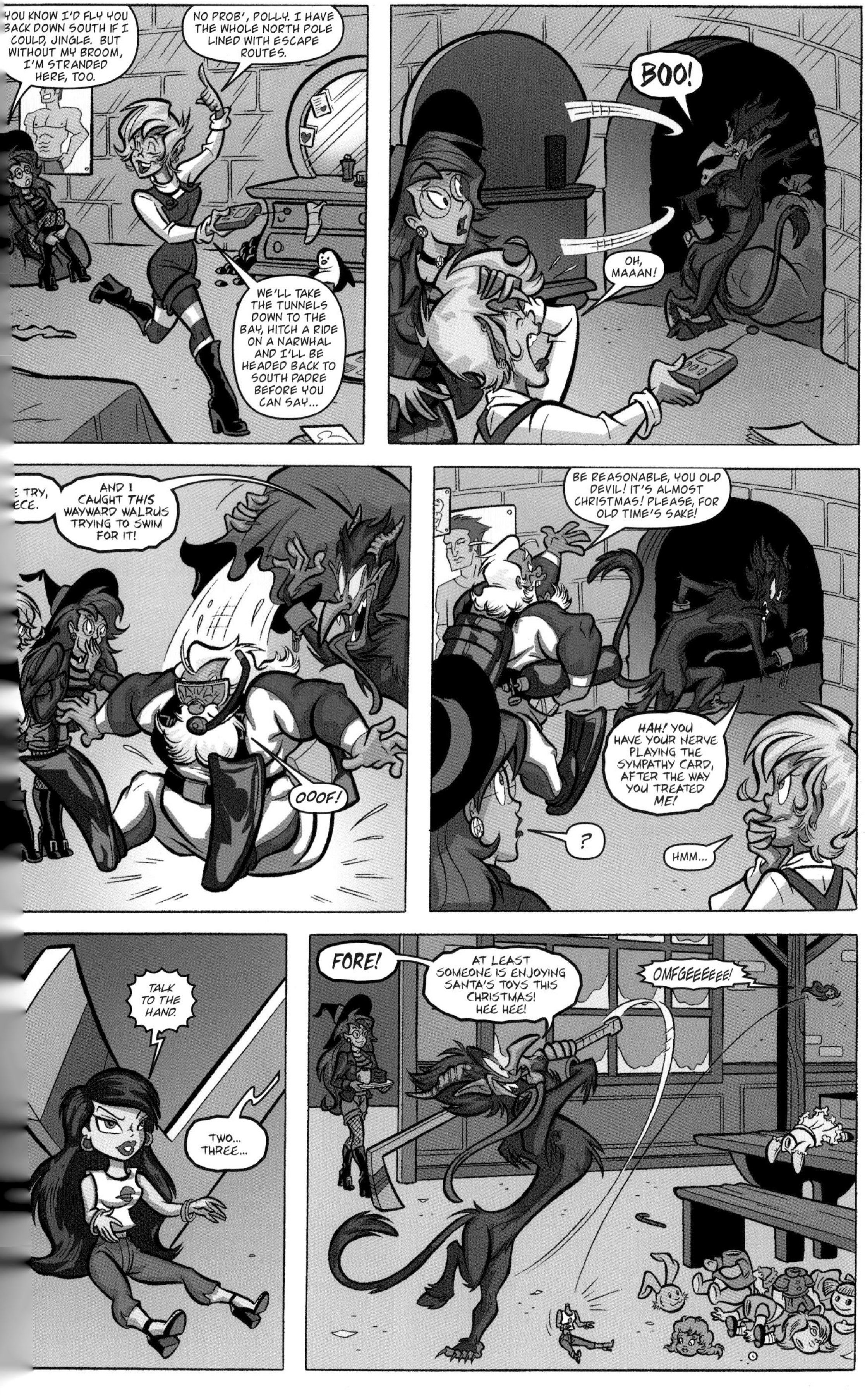

YOU KNOW I'D FLY YOU BACK DOWN SOUTH IF I COULD, JINGLE. BUT WITHOUT MY BROOM, I'M STRANDED HERE, TOO.
NO PROB', POLLY. I HAVE THE WHOLE NORTH POLE LINED WITH ESCAPE ROUTES.
WE'LL TAKE THE TUNNELS DOWN TO THE BAY, HITCH A RIDE ON A NARWHAL AND I'LL BE HEADED BACK TO SOUTH PADRE BEFORE YOU CAN SAY...
BOO!
OH, MAAAN!
AND I CAUGHT THIS WAYWARD WALRUS TRYING TO SWIM FOR IT!
OOOF!
BE REASONABLE, YOU OLD DEVIL! IT'S ALMOST CHRISTMAS! PLEASE, FOR OLD TIME'S SAKE!
HAH! YOU HAVE YOUR NERVE PLAYING THE SYMPATHY CARD, AFTER THE WAY YOU TREATED ME!
?
HMM...
TALK TO THE HAND.
TWO... THREE...
FORE!
AT LEAST SOMEONE IS ENJOYING SANTA'S TOYS THIS CHRISTMAS! HEE HEE!
OMFGEEEEeee!

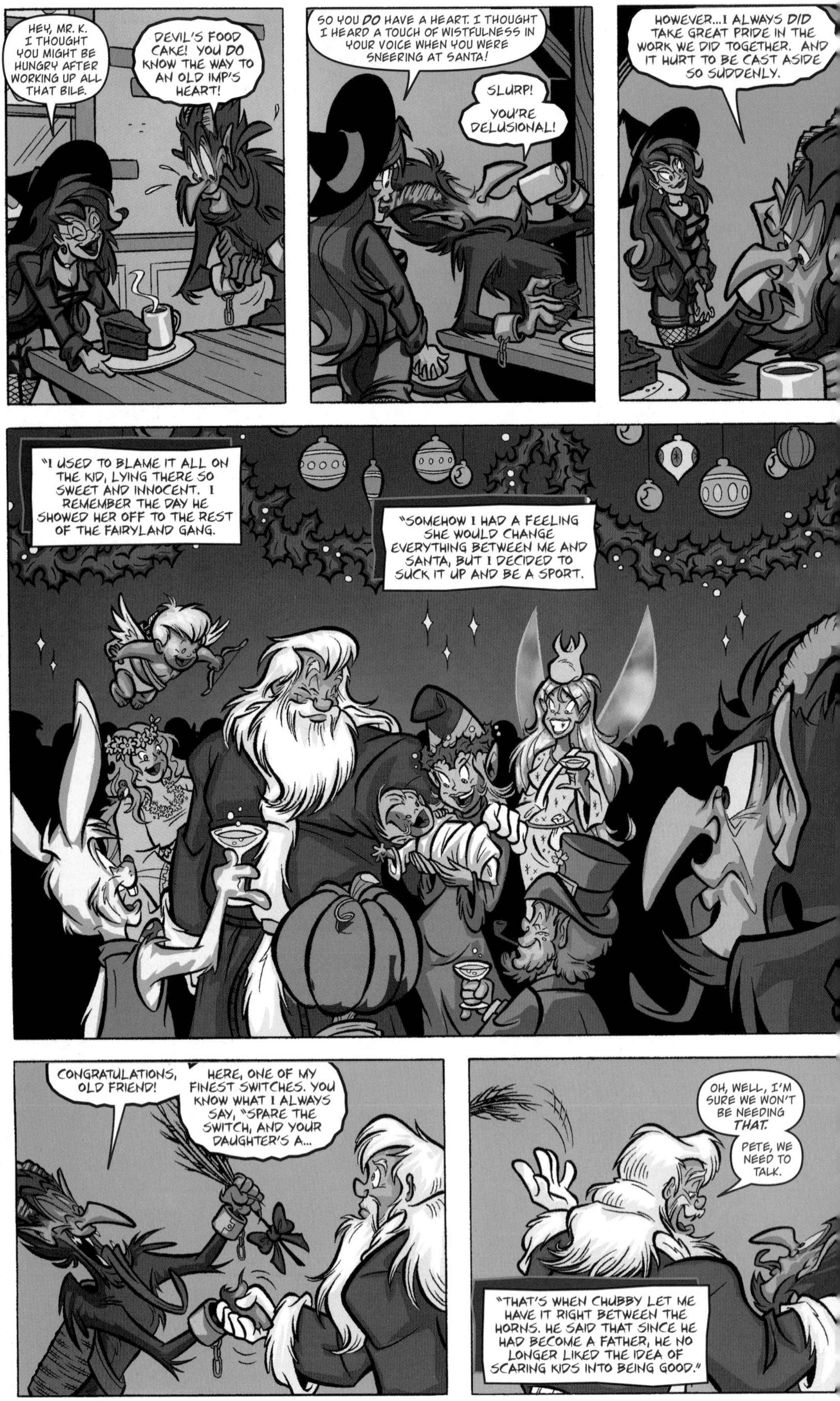
HEY, MR. K. I THOUGHT YOU MIGHT BE HUNGRY AFTER WORKING UP ALL THAT BILE.
DEVIL'S FOOD CAKE! YOU DO KNOW THE WAY TO AN OLD IMP'S HEART!
SO YOU DO HAVE A HEART. I THOUGHT I HEARD A TOUCH OF WISTFULNESS IN YOUR VOICE WHEN YOU WERE SNEERING AT SANTA!
SLURP!
YOU'RE DELUSIONAL!
HOWEVER...I ALWAYS DID TAKE GREAT PRIDE IN THE WORK WE DID TOGETHER. AND IT HURT TO BE CAST ASIDE SO SUDDENLY.
"I USED TO BLAME IT ALL ON THE KID, LYING THERE SO SWEET AND INNOCENT. I REMEMBER THE DAY HE SHOWED HER OFF TO THE REST OF THE FAIRYLAND GANG.
"SOMEHOW I HAD A FEELING SHE WOULD CHANGE EVERYTHING BETWEEN ME AND SANTA, BUT I DECIDED TO SUCK IT UP AND BE A SPORT.
CONGRATULATIONS, OLD FRIEND!
HERE, ONE OF MY FINEST SWITCHES. YOU KNOW WHAT I ALWAYS SAY, "SPARE THE SWITCH, AND YOUR DAUGHTER'S A...
OH, WELL, I'M SURE WE WON'T BE NEEDING THAT.
PETE, WE NEED TO TALK.
"THAT'S WHEN CHUBBY LET ME HAVE IT RIGHT BETWEEN THE HORNS. HE SAID THAT SINCE HE HAD BECOME A FATHER, HE NO LONGER LIKED THE IDEA OF SCARING KIDS INTO BEING GOOD."

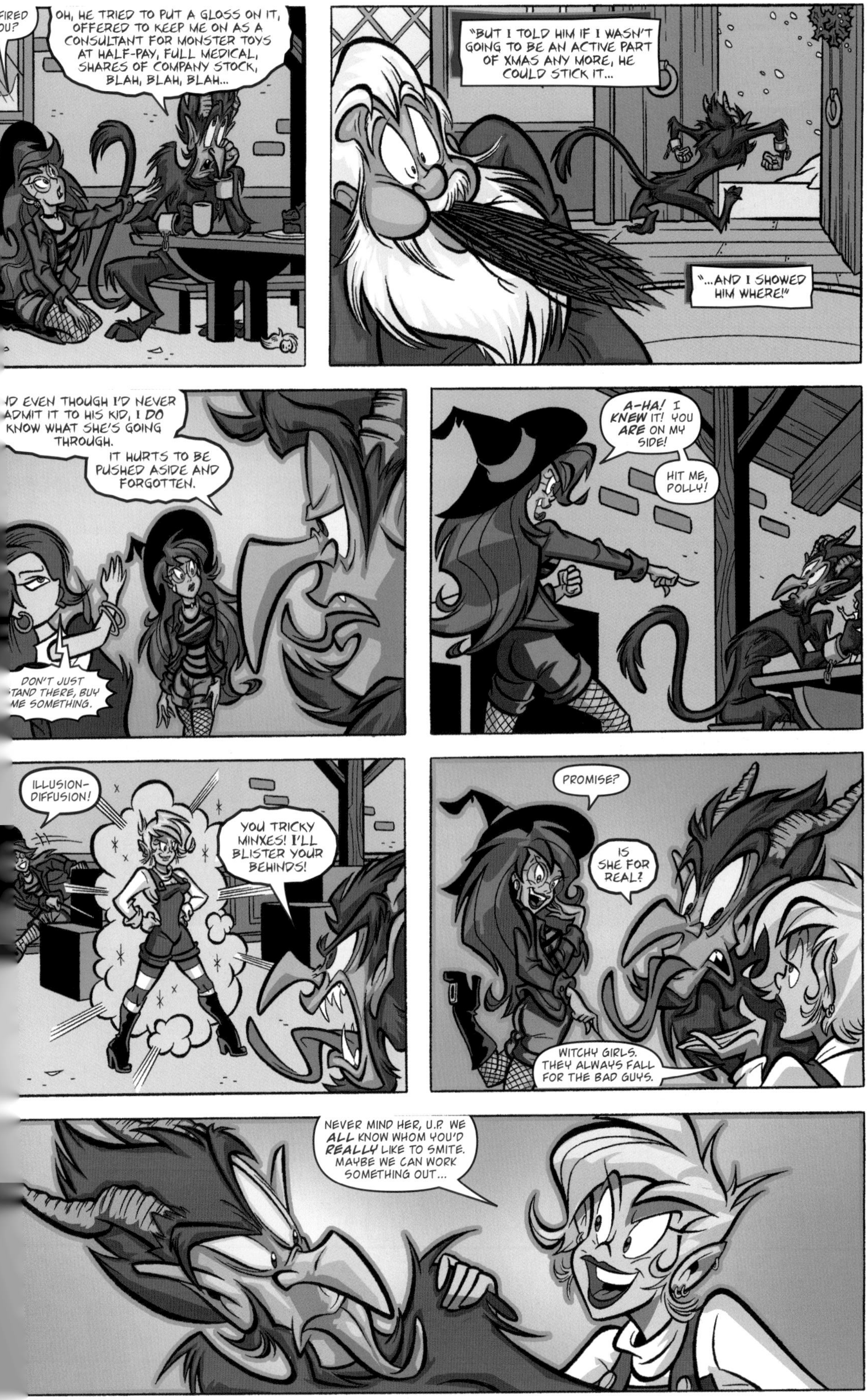
FIRED
OU?
OH, HE TRIED TO PUT A GLOSS ON IT, OFFERED TO KEEP ME ON AS A CONSULTANT FOR MONSTER TOYS AT HALF-PAY, FULL MEDICAL, SHARES OF COMPANY STOCK, BLAH, BLAH, BLAH...
"BUT I TOLD HIM IF I WASN'T GOING TO BE AN ACTIVE PART OF XMAS ANY MORE, HE COULD STICK IT...
"...AND I SHOWED HIM WHERE!"
ND EVEN THOUGH I'D NEVER ADMIT IT TO HIS KID, I DO KNOW WHAT SHE'S GOING THROUGH.
IT HURTS TO BE PUSHED ASIDE AND FORGOTTEN.
DON'T JUST STAND THERE, BUY ME SOMETHING.
A-HA! I KNEW IT! YOU ARE ON MY SIDE!
HIT ME, POLLY!
ILLUSION-DIFFUSION!
YOU TRICKY MINXES! I'LL BLISTER YOUR BEHINDS!
PROMISE?
IS SHE FOR REAL?
WITCHY GIRLS. THEY ALWAYS FALL FOR THE BAD GUYS.
NEVER MIND HER, U.P. WE ALL KNOW WHOM YOU'D REALLY LIKE TO SMITE. MAYBE WE CAN WORK SOMETHING OUT...

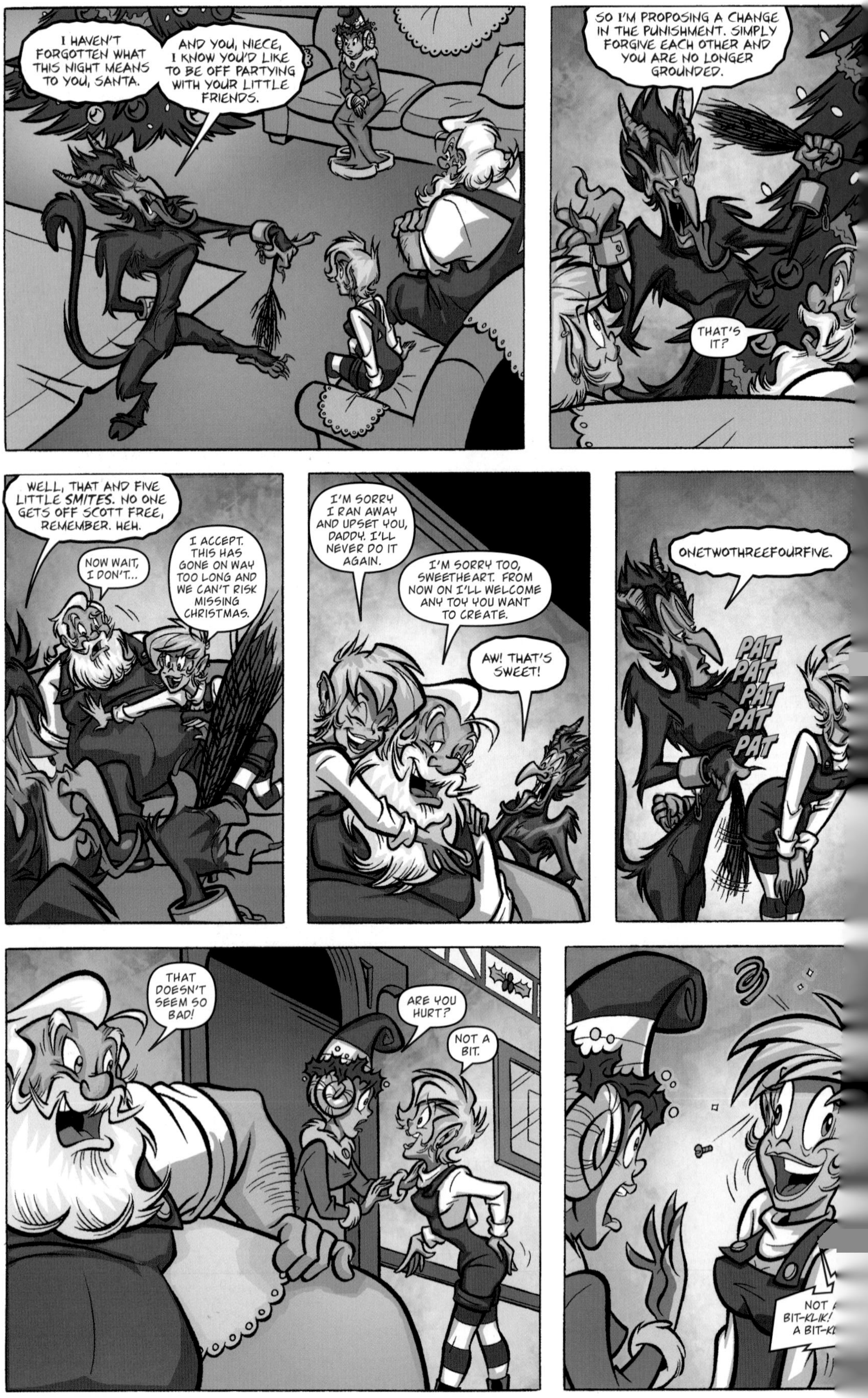
I HAVEN'T FORGOTTEN WHAT THIS NIGHT MEANS TO YOU, SANTA.
AND YOU, NIECE, I KNOW YOU'D LIKE TO BE OFF PARTYING WITH YOUR LITTLE FRIENDS.
SO I'M PROPOSING A CHANGE IN THE PUNISHMENT. SIMPLY FORGIVE EACH OTHER AND YOU ARE NO LONGER GROUNDED.
THAT'S IT?
WELL, THAT AND FIVE LITTLE SMITES. NO ONE GETS OFF SCOTT FREE, REMEMBER. HEH.
NOW WAIT, I DON'T...
I ACCEPT. THIS HAS GONE ON WAY TOO LONG AND WE CAN'T RISK MISSING CHRISTMAS.
I'M SORRY I RAN AWAY AND UPSET YOU, DADDY. I'LL NEVER DO IT AGAIN.
I'M SORRY TOO, SWEETHEART. FROM NOW ON I'LL WELCOME ANY TOY YOU WANT TO CREATE.
AW! THAT'S SWEET!
ONETWOTHREEFOURFIVE.
PAT PAT PAT PAT PAT
THAT DOESN'T SEEM SO BAD!
ARE YOU HURT?
NOT A BIT.
BIT-KLIK!

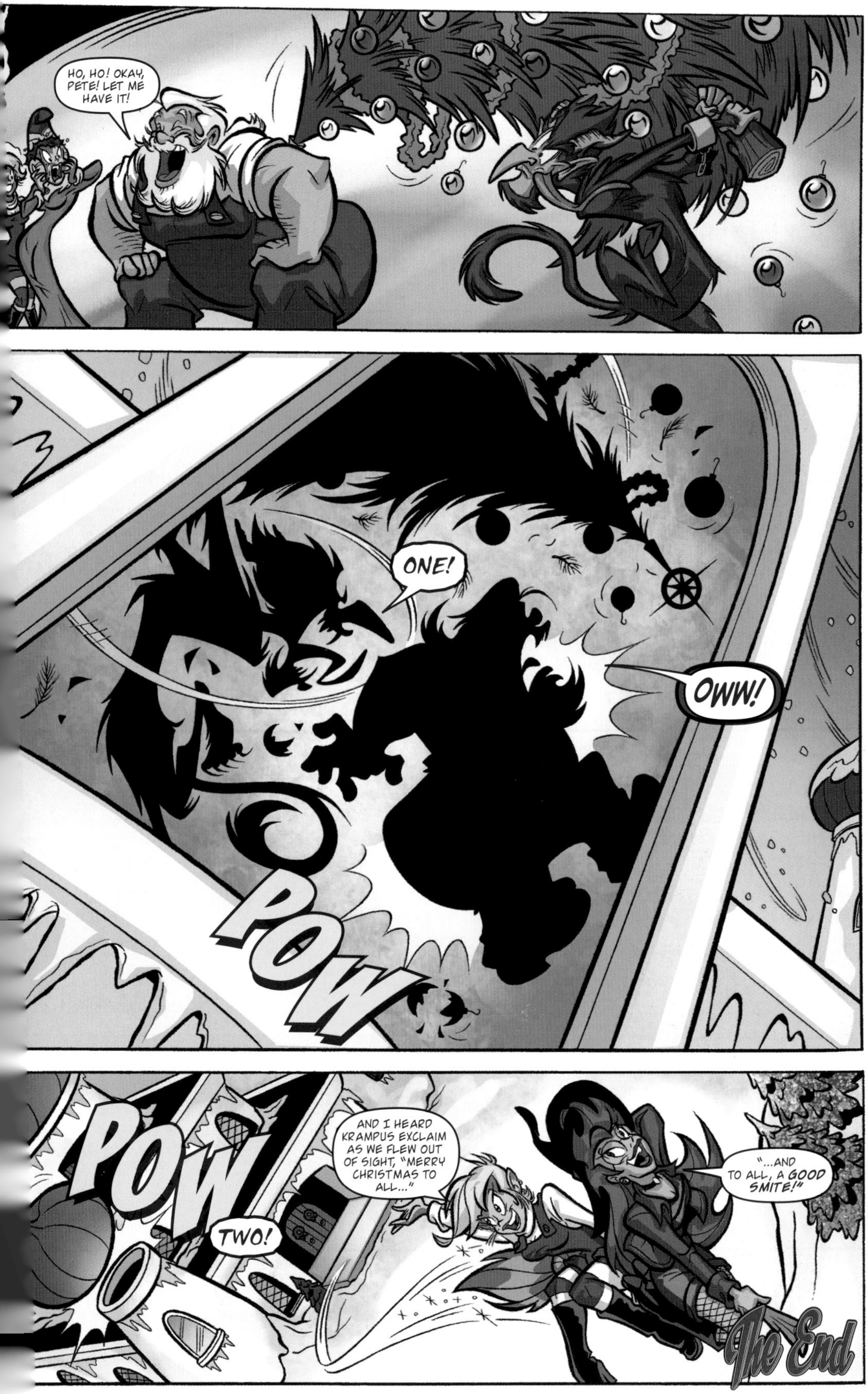
HO, HO! OKAY, PETE! LET ME HAVE IT!
ONE!
OWW!
POW
POW
TWO!
AND I HEARD KRAMPUS EXCLAIM AS WE FLEW OUT OF SIGHT, "MERRY CHRISTMAS TO ALL..."
"...AND TO ALL, A GOOD SMITE!"
The End

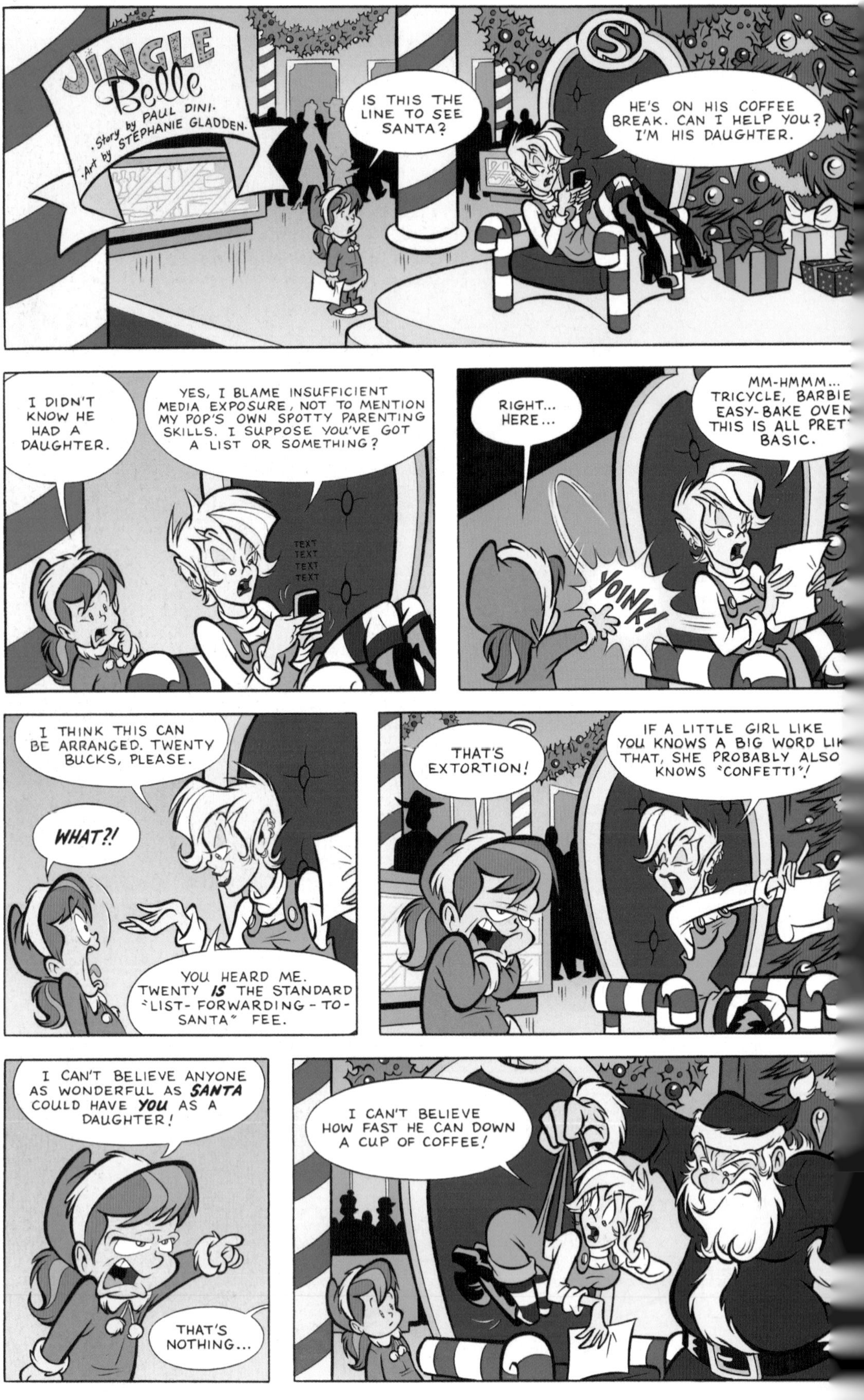
JINGLE Belle
Story by PAUL DINI
Art by STEPHANIE GLADDEN.
IS THIS THE LINE TO SEE SANTA?
HE'S ON HIS COFFEE BREAK. CAN I HELP YOU? I'M HIS DAUGHTER.
I DIDN'T KNOW HE HAD A DAUGHTER.
YES, I BLAME INSUFFICIENT MEDIA EXPOSURE, NOT TO MENTION MY POP'S OWN SPOTTY PARENTING SKILLS. I SUPPOSE YOU'VE GOT A LIST OR SOMETHING?
TEXT TEXT TEXT TEXT
RIGHT... HERE...
YOINK!
MM-HMMM... TRICYCLE, BARBIE EASY-BAKE OVEN THIS IS ALL PRETT BASIC.
I THINK THIS CAN BE ARRANGED. TWENTY BUCKS, PLEASE.
WHAT?!
YOU HEARD ME. TWENTY IS THE STANDARD "LIST-FORWARDING-TO-SANTA" FEE.
THAT'S EXTORTION!
IF A LITTLE GIRL LIKE YOU KNOWS A BIG WORD LIK THAT, SHE PROBABLY ALSO KNOWS "CONFETTI"!
I CAN'T BELIEVE ANYONE AS WONDERFUL AS SANTA COULD HAVE YOU AS A DAUGHTER!
THAT'S NOTHING...
I CAN'T BELIEVE HOW FAST HE CAN DOWN A CUP OF COFFEE!

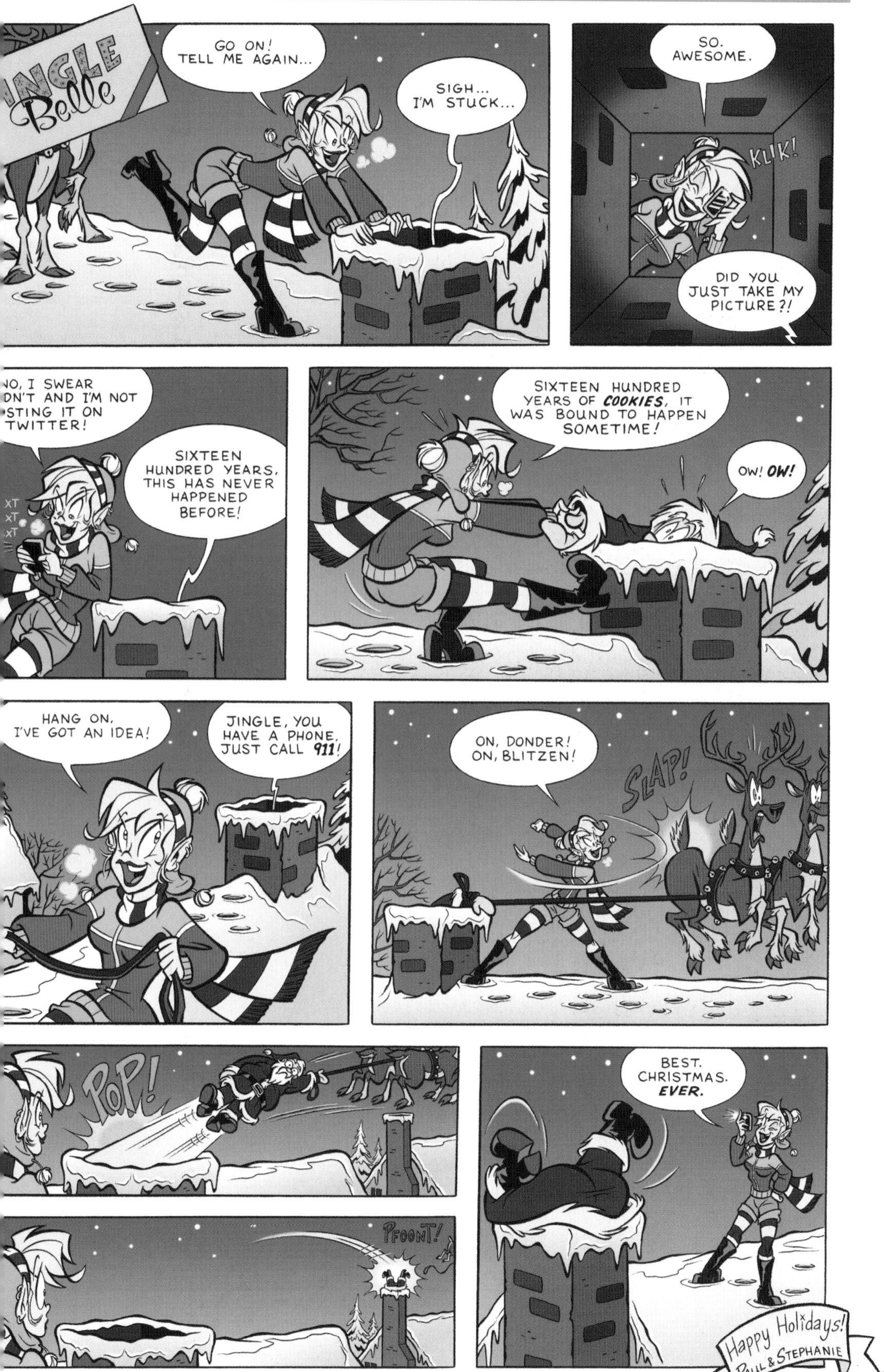
NGLE Belle
GO ON! TELL ME AGAIN...
SIGH... I'M STUCK...
SO. AWESOME.
KLIK!
DID YOU JUST TAKE MY PICTURE?!
NO, I SWEAR
DN'T AND I'M NOT
STING IT ON
TWITTER!
SIXTEEN HUNDRED YEARS, THIS HAS NEVER HAPPENED BEFORE!
SIXTEEN HUNDRED YEARS OF COOKIES, IT WAS BOUND TO HAPPEN SOMETIME!
OW! OW!
HANG ON, I'VE GOT AN IDEA!
JINGLE, YOU HAVE A PHONE, JUST CALL 911!
ON, DONDER! ON, BLITZEN!
SLAP!
POP!
PFOONT!
BEST. CHRISTMAS. EVER.
Happy Holidays! Paul & Stephanie

GREETINGS, FOLKS. HANK RIBBON SEAL HERE WITH A STUNNING UPSET AT THE 2010 WINTER GAMES.

EMERGING AS THE SURPRISE FRONT-RUNNER IN WOMEN'S CURLING IS NONE OTHER THAN THE NORTH POLE TEAM LEAD BY *JINGLE BELLE KRINGLE*.

JINGLE Belle
Story by Paul Dini · Art by Stephanie Gladden

"KRINGLE - SEEN HERE IN FILE FOOTAGE HUMILIATING HER FAMOUS FATHER - HAS APPARENTLY CLEANED UP HER ACT IN HER QUEST FOR OLYMPIC GOLD."

PLEASE HELP

I AM A POOR ORPHAN

WHAT'S YOUR SECRET, JING?

TEAMWORK, HANK.

I'M NOTHING WITHOUT MY SWEEPER, *POLLY GREEN*.

I'D LIKE TO SAY HI TO MY FAMILY BACK IN AUTUMN FALLS, AND TO ALERT POTENTIAL *SPONSERS* THAT I WELCOME ANY AND *ALL* ENDORSEMENT OPPORTUNITIES...

THAT'S GREAT, POL'. GET BACK OF THE HOG LINE, SWEETIE.

NIKE! CALL ME!

SHOVE!

SEEMS A TAD UNCONVENTIONAL A *WITCH* ON YOU CURLING TEAM

NOT THE WAY *SHE* HANDLES HER BROOM. CHECK OUT THE KID IN ACTION...

WICKY WACKY *WOO!*

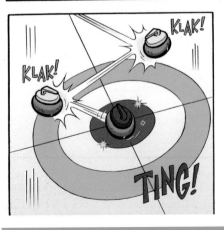

KLAK!

KLAK!

TING!

JUST LIKE *MAGIC*, EH, JING?

WE PREFER TO THINK OF IT AS THE WINNER'S EDGE, HANK.

DISQUALIFIE

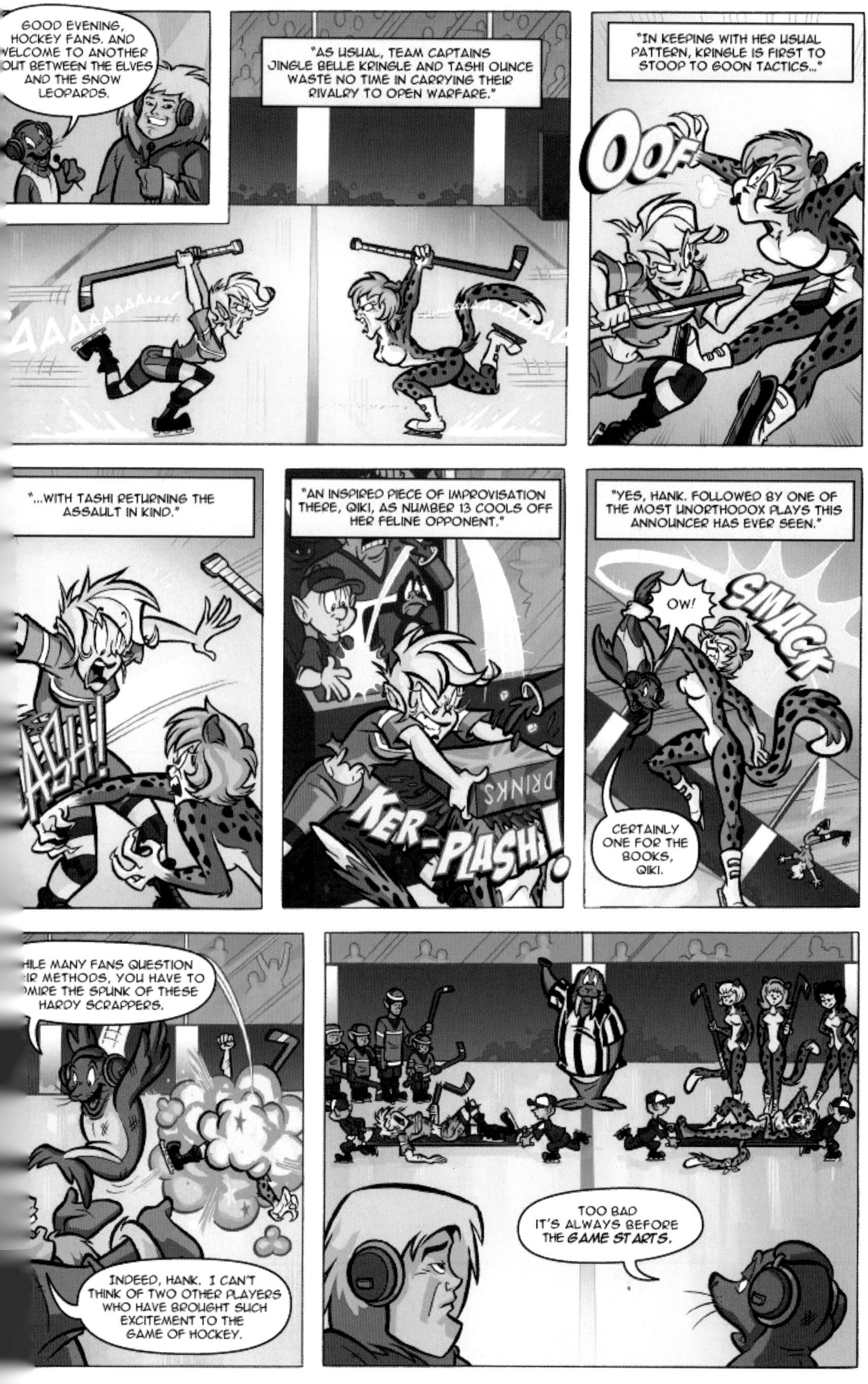
GOOD EVENING, HOCKEY FANS. AND WELCOME TO ANOTHER OUT BETWEEN THE ELVES AND THE SNOW LEOPARDS.
"AS USUAL, TEAM CAPTAINS JINGLE BELLE KRINGLE AND TASHI OUNCE WASTE NO TIME IN CARRYING THEIR RIVALRY TO OPEN WARFARE."
"IN KEEPING WITH HER USUAL PATTERN, KRINGLE IS FIRST TO STOOP TO GOON TACTICS..."
OOF
"...WITH TASHI RETURNING THE ASSAULT IN KIND."
"AN INSPIRED PIECE OF IMPROVISATION THERE, QIKI, AS NUMBER 13 COOLS OFF HER FELINE OPPONENT."
DRINKS
KER-PLASH!
"YES, HANK. FOLLOWED BY ONE OF THE MOST UNORTHODOX PLAYS THIS ANNOUNCER HAS EVER SEEN."
OW!
SMACK
CERTAINLY ONE FOR THE BOOKS, QIKI.
HILE MANY FANS QUESTION EIR METHODS, YOU HAVE TO MIRE THE SPUNK OF THESE HARDY SCRAPPERS.
INDEED, HANK. I CAN'T THINK OF TWO OTHER PLAYERS WHO HAVE BROUGHT SUCH EXCITEMENT TO THE GAME OF HOCKEY.
TOO BAD IT'S ALWAYS BEFORE THE GAME STARTS.

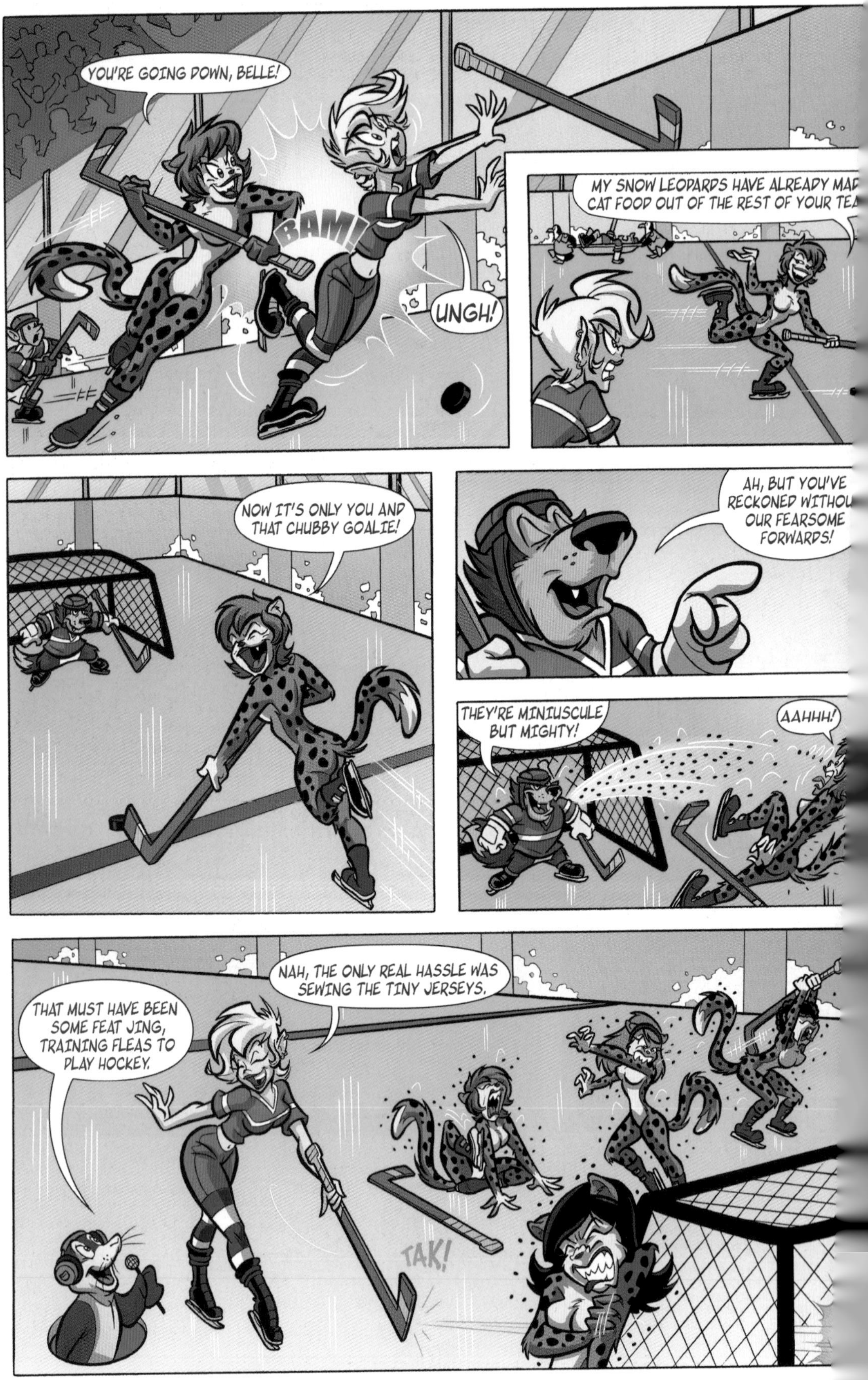
YOU'RE GOING DOWN, BELLE!
BAM!
UNGH!
MY SNOW LEOPARDS HAVE ALREADY MA
CAT FOOD OUT OF THE REST OF YOUR TE
NOW IT'S ONLY YOU AND THAT CHUBBY GOALIE!
AH, BUT YOU'VE RECKONED WITHOU OUR FEARSOME FORWARDS!
THEY'RE MINIUSCULE BUT MIGHTY!
AAHHH!
NAH, THE ONLY REAL HASSLE WAS SEWING THE TINY JERSEYS.
THAT MUST HAVE BEEN SOME FEAT JING, TRAINING FLEAS TO PLAY HOCKEY.
TAK!

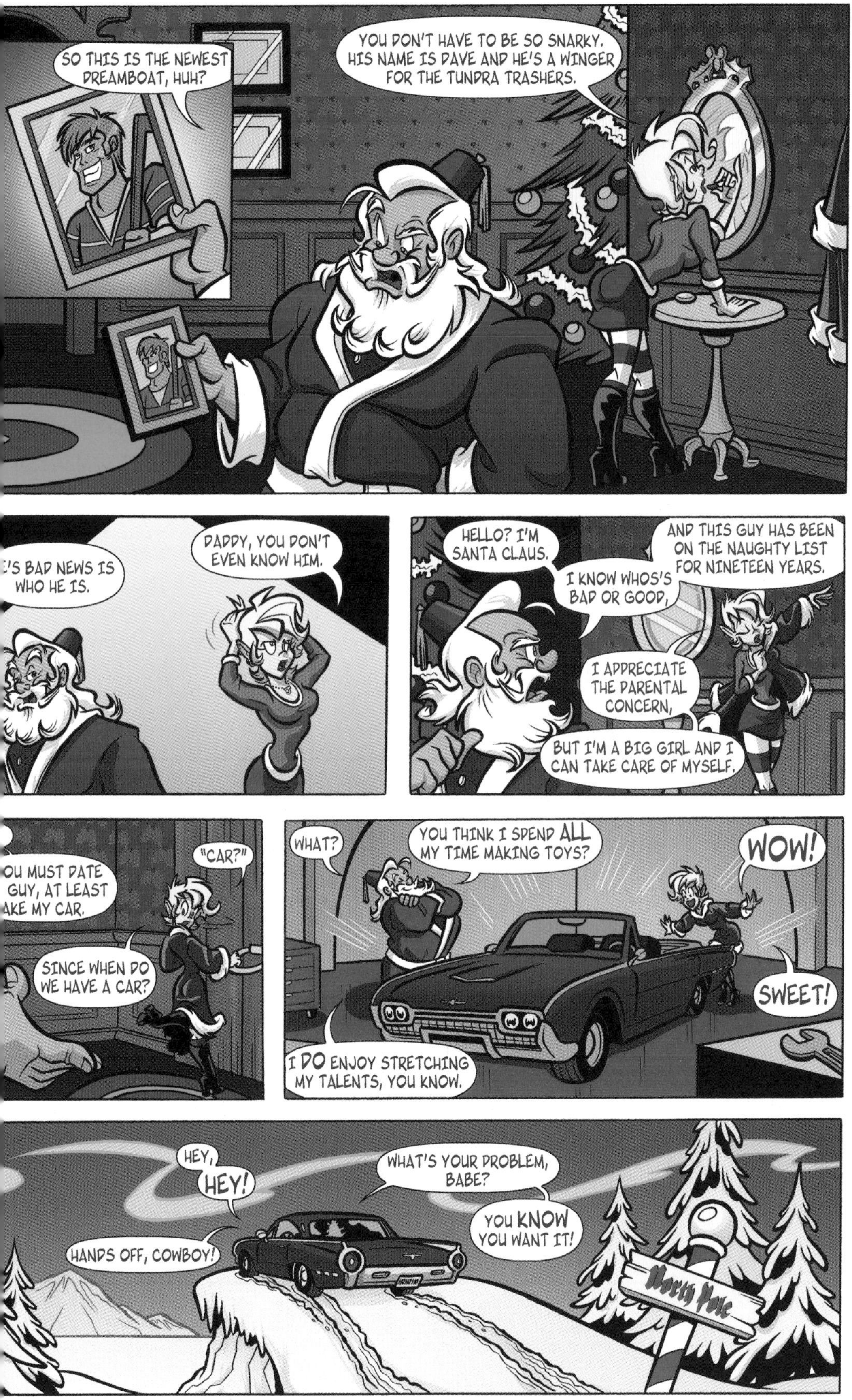
SO THIS IS THE NEWEST DREAMBOAT, HUH?
YOU DON'T HAVE TO BE SO SNARKY. HIS NAME IS DAVE AND HE'S A WINGER FOR THE TUNDRA TRASHERS.
'S BAD NEWS IS WHO HE IS.
DADDY, YOU DON'T EVEN KNOW HIM.
HELLO? I'M SANTA CLAUS.
I KNOW WHOS'S BAD OR GOOD,
AND THIS GUY HAS BEEN ON THE NAUGHTY LIST FOR NINETEEN YEARS.
I APPRECIATE THE PARENTAL CONCERN,
BUT I'M A BIG GIRL AND I CAN TAKE CARE OF MYSELF.
OU MUST DATE GUY, AT LEAST AKE MY CAR.
"CAR?"
SINCE WHEN DO WE HAVE A CAR?
WHAT?
YOU THINK I SPEND ALL MY TIME MAKING TOYS?
WOW!
SWEET!
I DO ENJOY STRETCHING MY TALENTS, YOU KNOW.
HEY, HEY!
WHAT'S YOUR PROBLEM, BABE?
YOU KNOW YOU WANT IT!
HANDS OFF, COWBOY!
North Pole

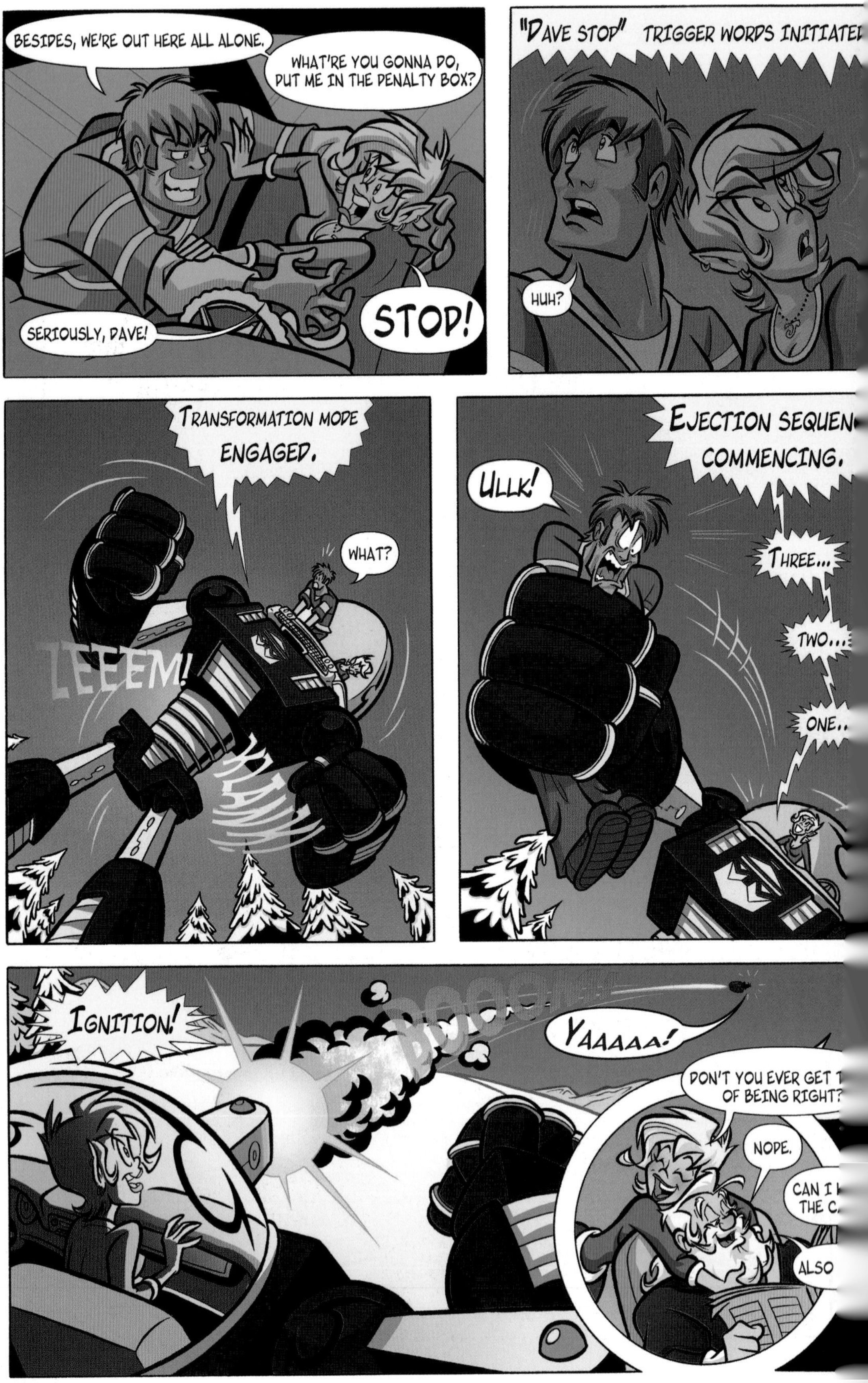

BESIDES, WE'RE OUT HERE ALL ALONE.
WHAT'RE YOU GONNA DO, PUT ME IN THE PENALTY BOX?
SERIOUSLY, DAVE!
STOP!
"DAVE STOP" TRIGGER WORDS INITIATE
HUH?
TRANSFORMATION MODE ENGAGED.
WHAT?
ZEEEM!
KLANK
EJECTION SEQUEN
COMMENCING.
ULLK!
THREE...
TWO...
ONE..
IGNITION!
YAAAAA!
DON'T YOU EVER GET T
OF BEING RIGHT?
NOPE.
CAN I
THE C
ALSO

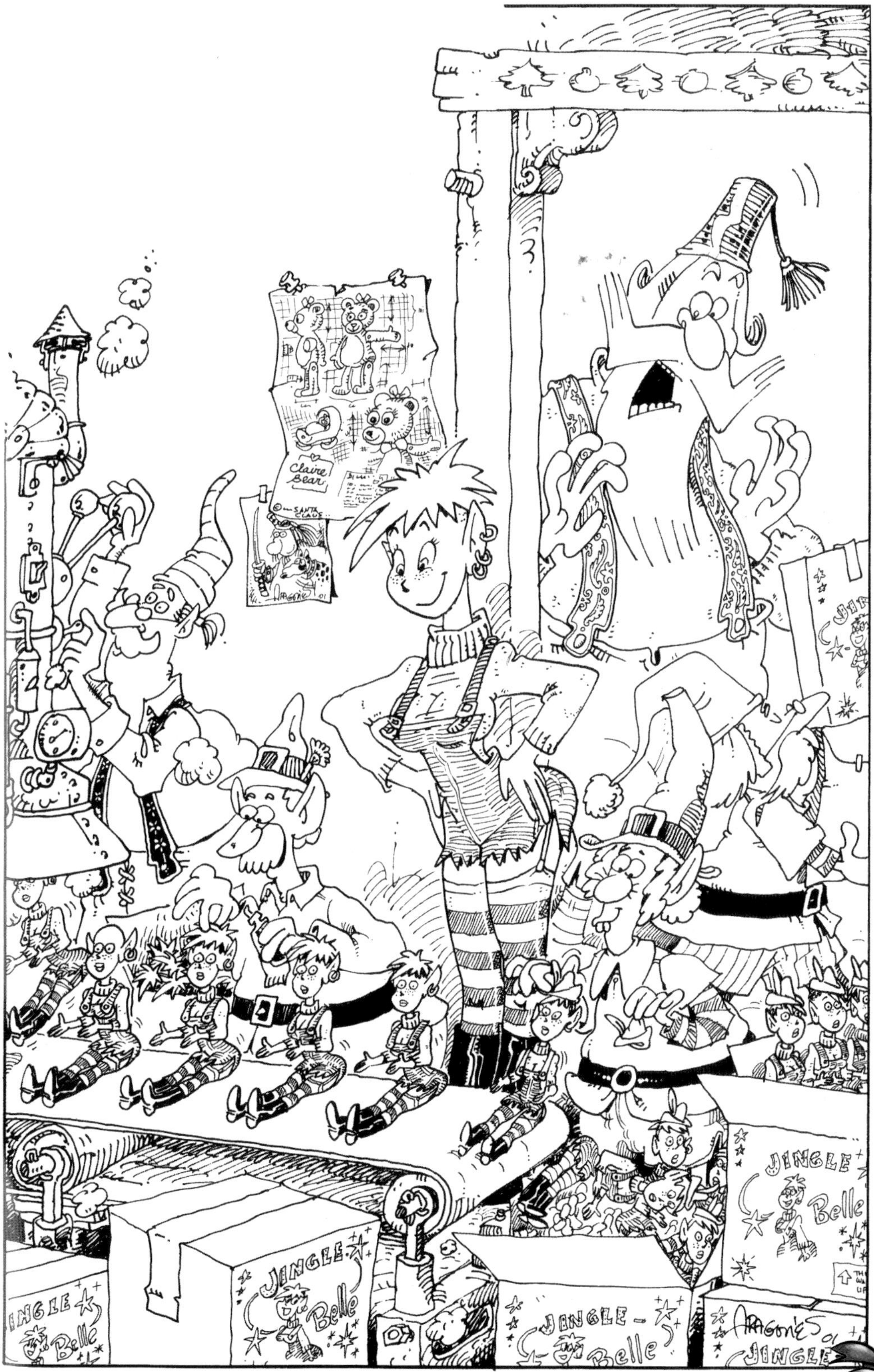
Claire Bear
JINGLE Belle
JINGLE Belle
JINGLE Belle
JINGLE Belle
ARAGONÉS '01
JINGLE

ART BY SERGIO ARAGONES

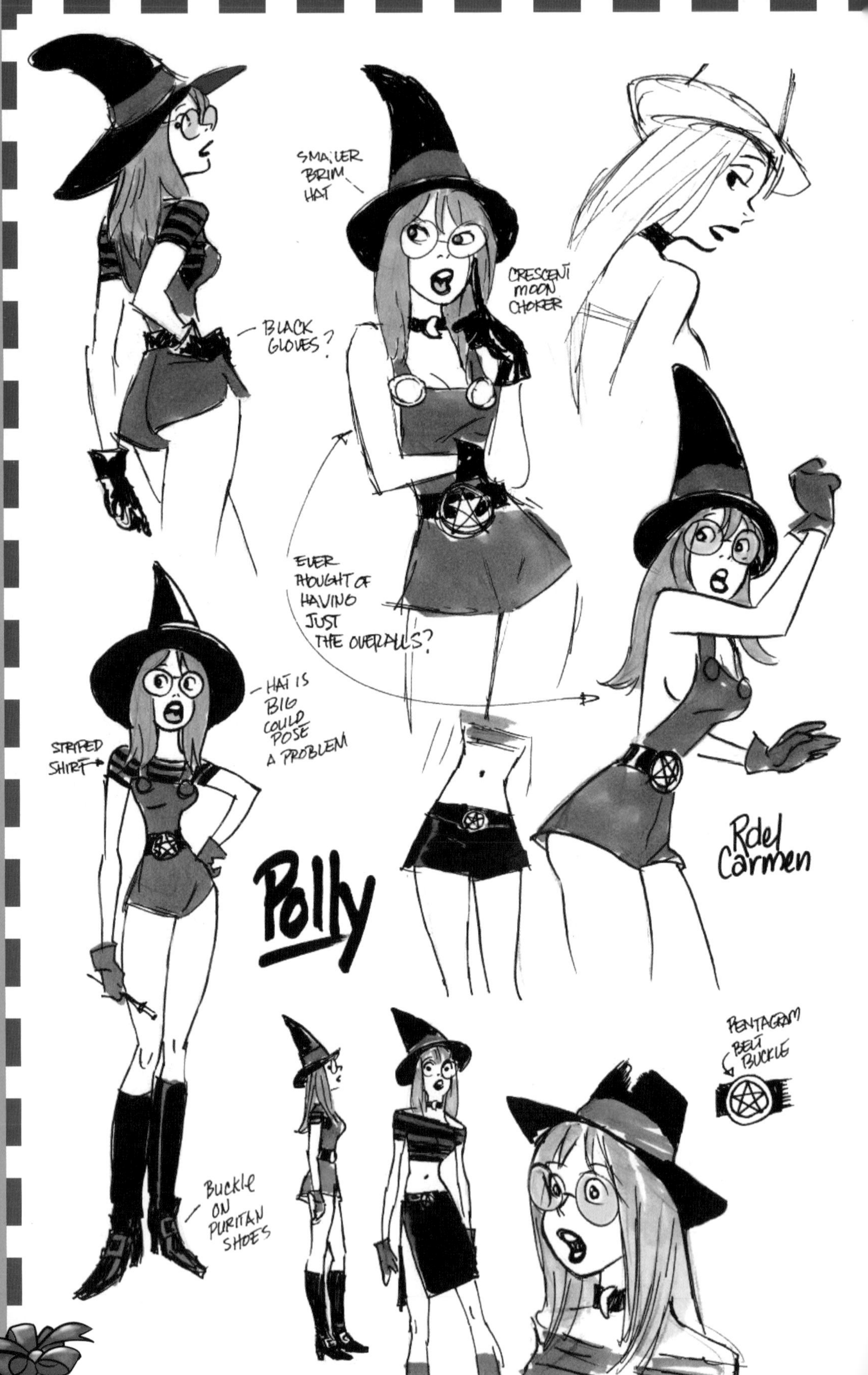
SMALLER BRIM HAT
BLACK GLOVES?
CRESCENT MOON CHOKER
EVER THOUGHT OF HAVING JUST THE OVERALLS?
HAT IS BIG COULD POSE A PROBLEM
STRIPED SHIRT
Polly
Rdel Carmen
PENTAGRAM BELT BUCKLE
Buckle ON PURITAN SHOES

ART BY RONNIE DEL CARMEN

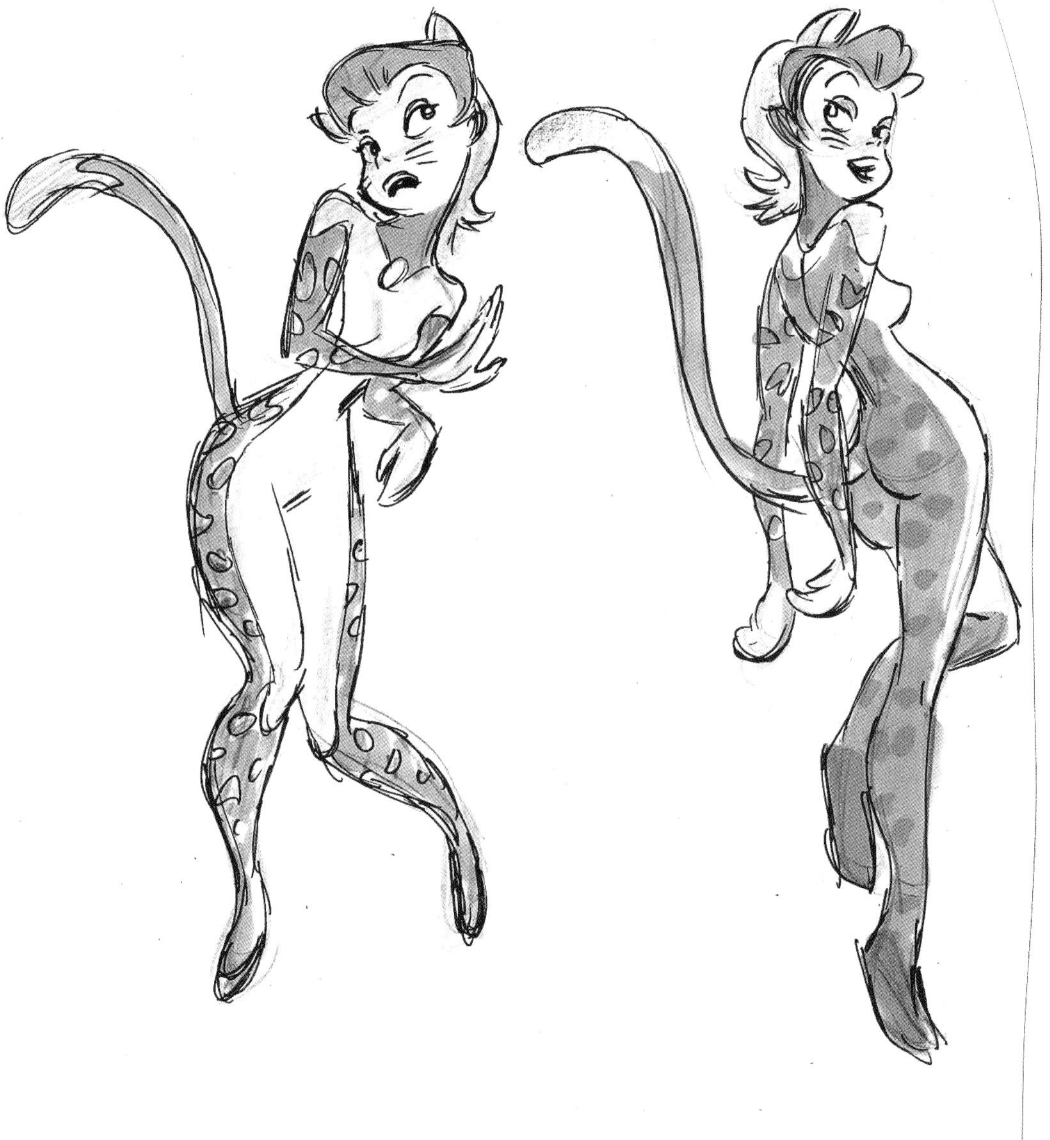

ART BY RONNIE DEL CARMEN

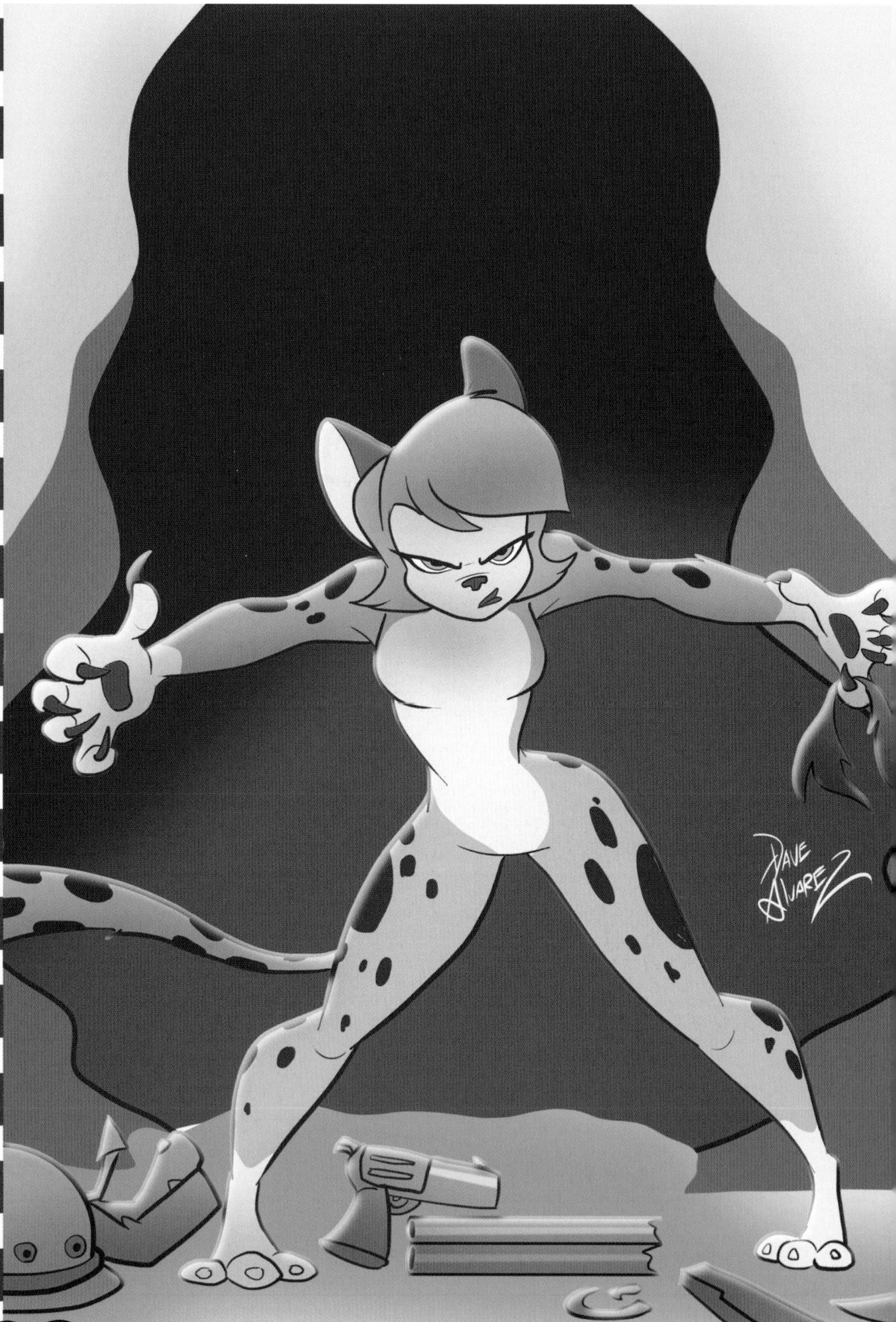
DAVE ALVAREZ

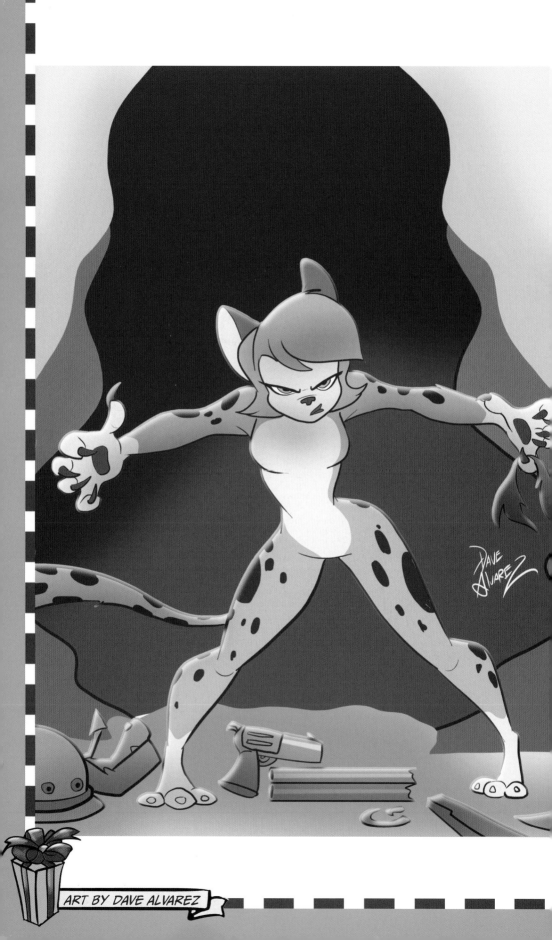

ART BY DAVE ALVAREZ

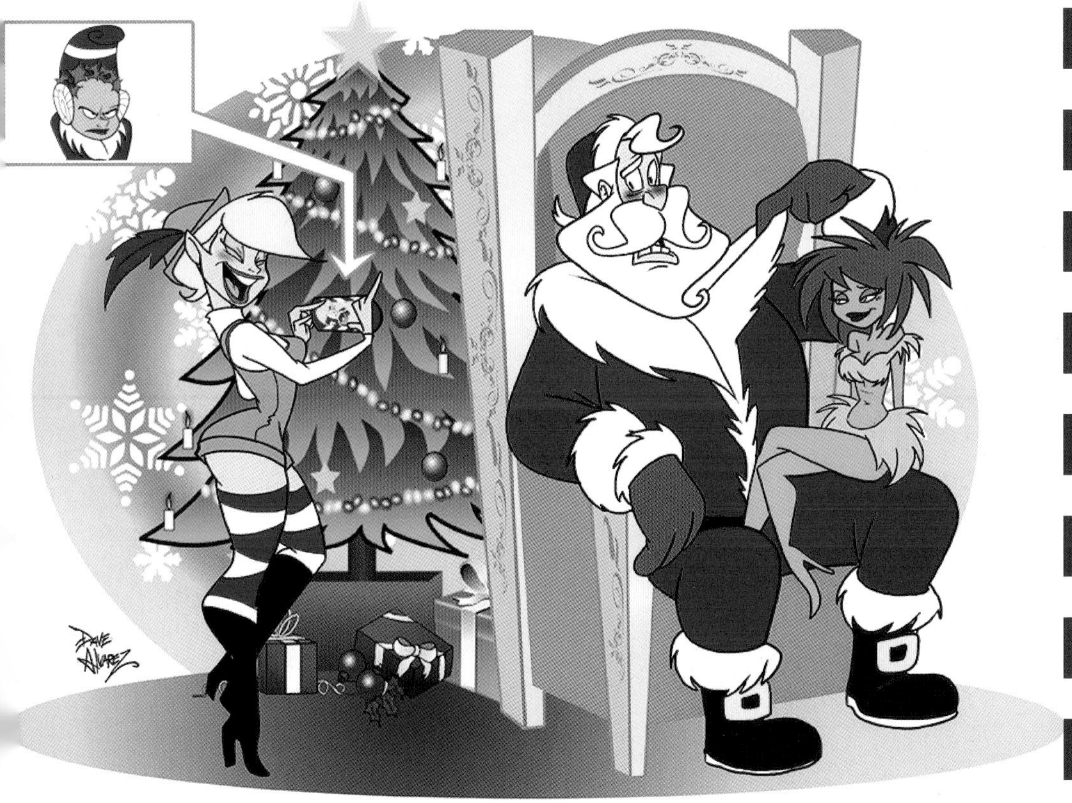
DAVE ALVAREZ

ART BY DAVE ALVAREZ

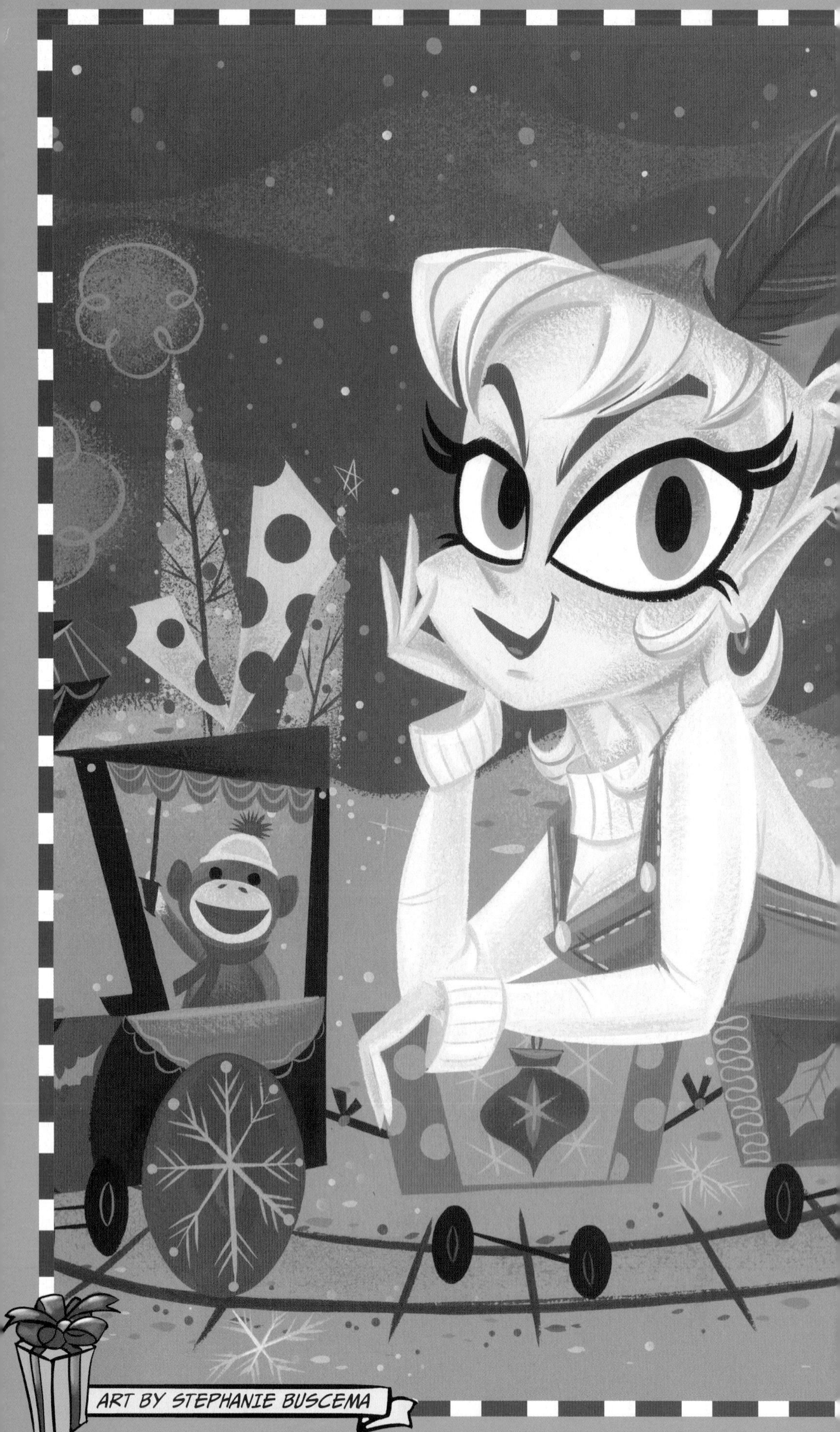
ART BY STEPHANIE BUSCEMA

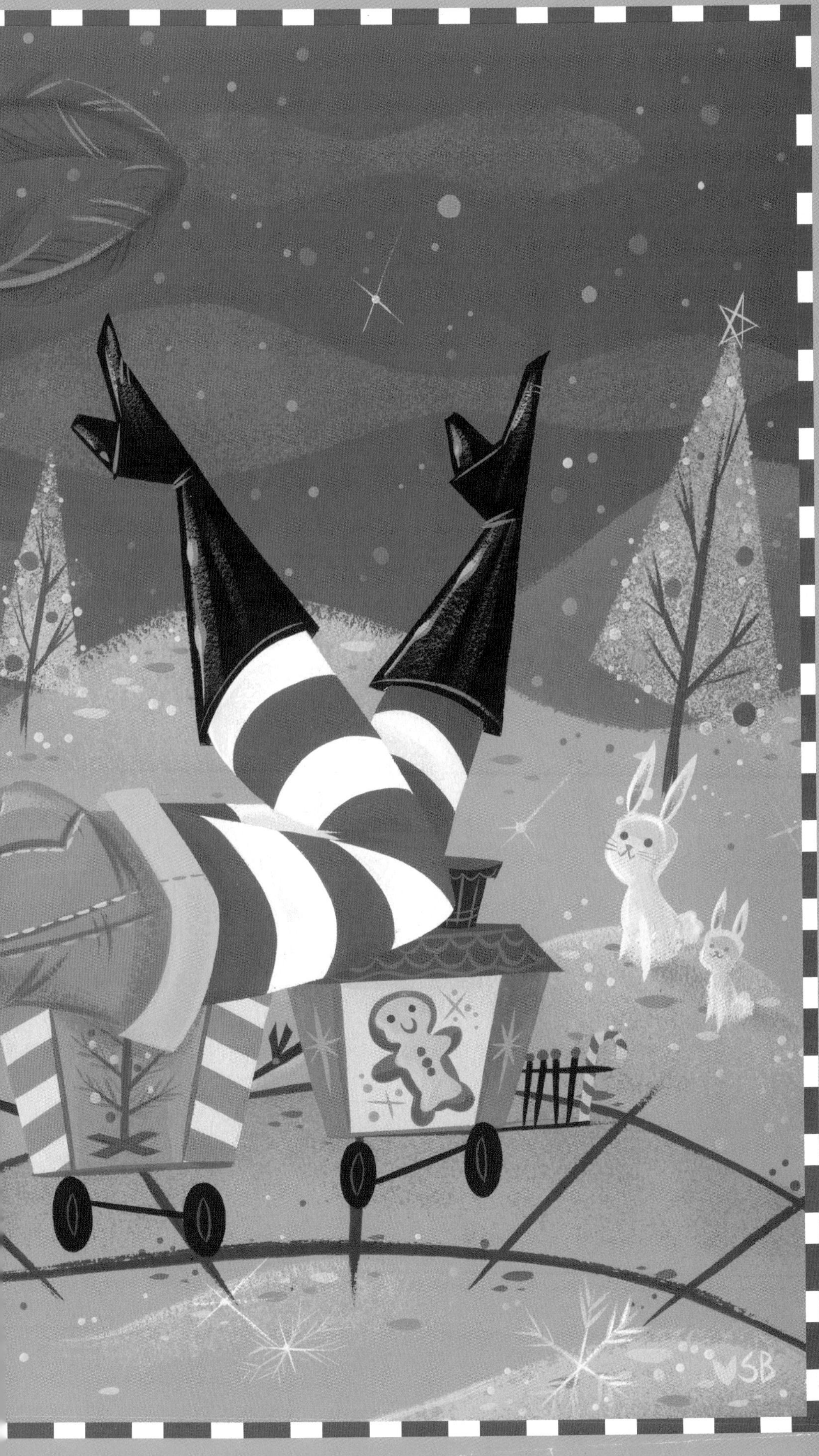
SB

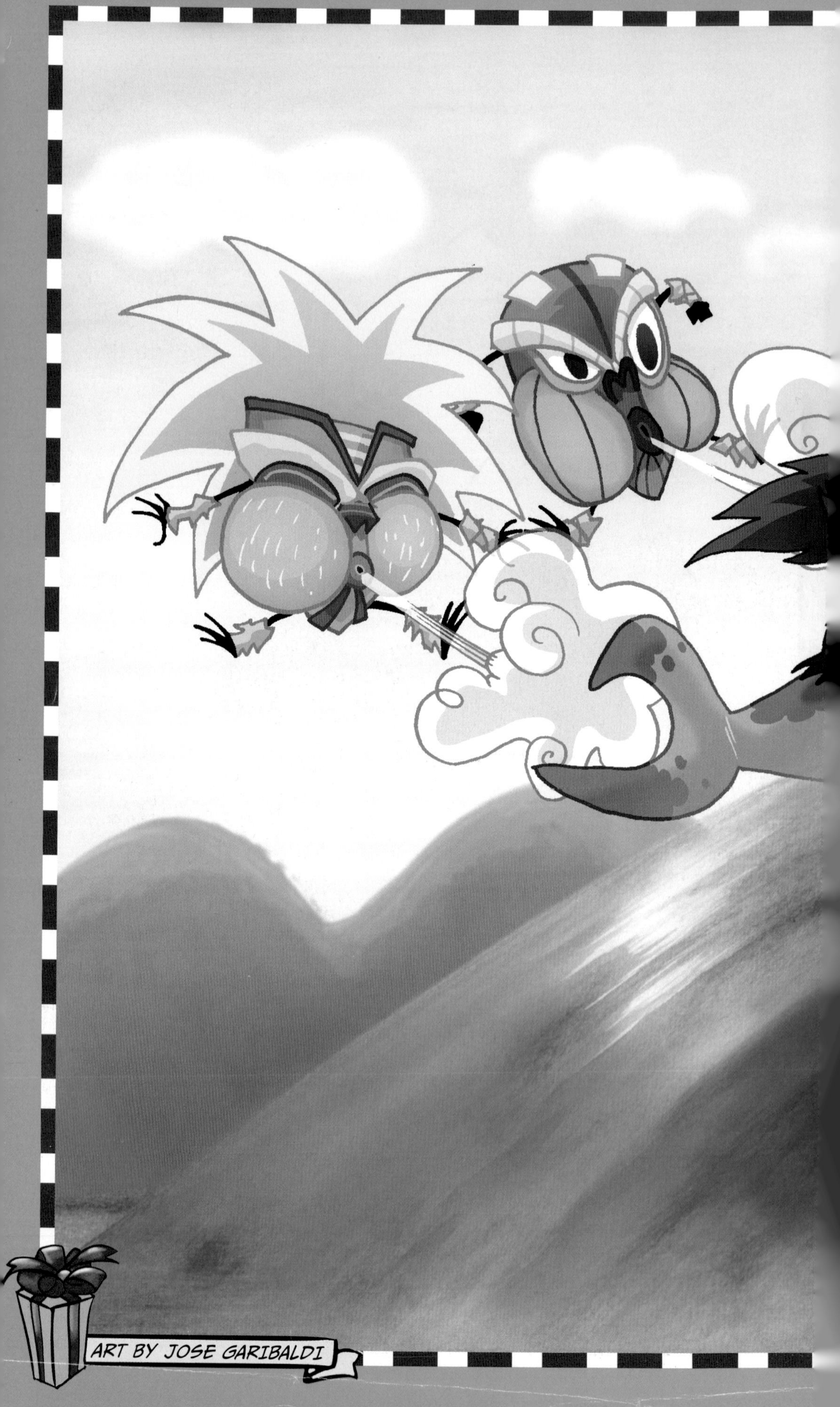
ART BY JOSE GARIBALDI

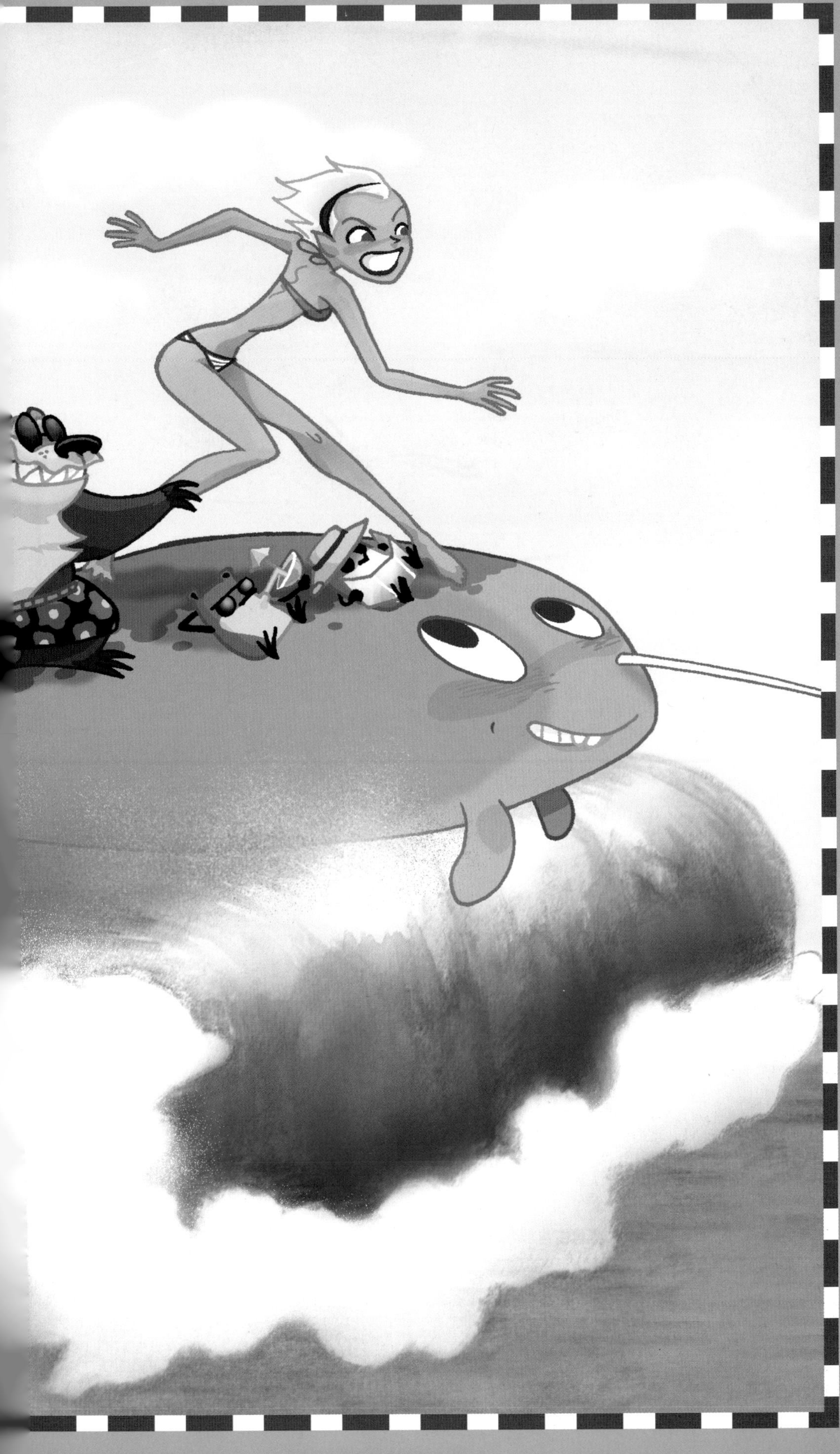

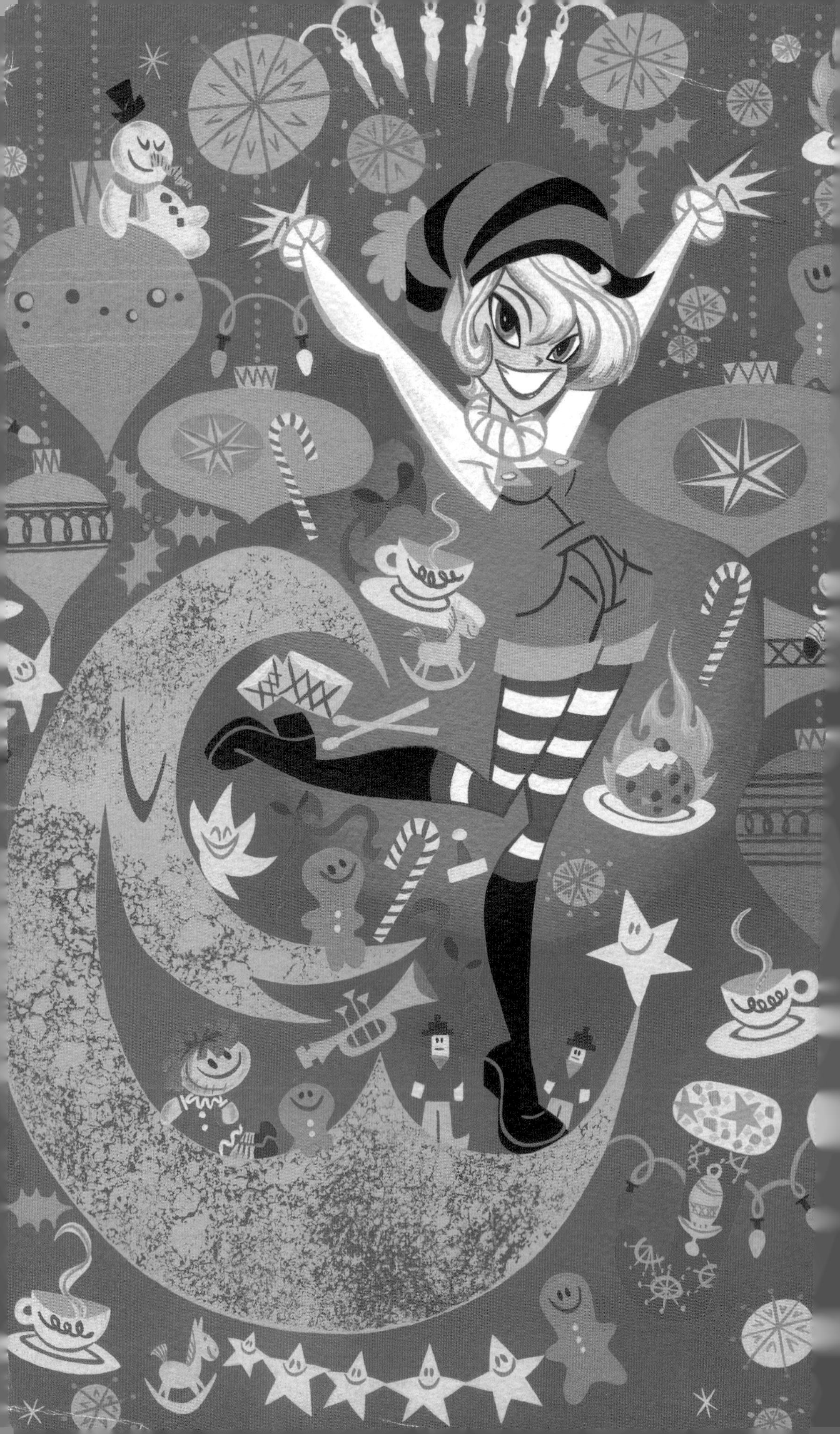